1988 Supplement to

The Link Family, Antecedents and Descendants of John Jacob Link 1417–1951

Compiled by
The Descendants of John Jacob Link

HERITAGE BOOKS
2019

HERITAGE BOOKS

AN IMPRINT OF HERITAGE BOOKS, INC.

Books, CDs, and more—Worldwide

For our listing of thousands of titles see our website
at
www.HeritageBooks.com

Published 2019 by
HERITAGE BOOKS, INC.
Publishing Division
5810 Ruatan Street
Berwyn Heights, Md. 20740

Heritage Books by the author:

1988 Supplement to The Link Family, Antecedents and Descendants of John Jacob Link, 1417–1951
Compiled by the Descendants of John Jacob Link

The Link Family, Antecedents and Descendants of John Jacob Link, 1417–1951
Paxson Link

CD-ROM: *The Link Family, Antecedents and Descendants of John Jacob Link, 1417–1951 by Paxson Link (1951)*
and the *1988 Supplement to* The Link Family, Antecedents and Descendants of John Jacob Link, 1417–1951

International Standard Book Number
Paperbound: 978-0-7884-1817-4

CONTENTS

This book is dedicated to those family members who worked so hard to collect and preserve the story of our family for the generations yet to come.

IN MEMORY OF
JOHN JACOB LINK
(HANS JACOB LINCKH)
B. 10-20-1682 D. 4- -1738
WHO IMMIGRATED TO AMERICA IN 1733
FROM GROSSGARTACH, GERMANY;
THIS PAVILION IS DEDICATED
BY HIS DESCENDANTS, AUGUST 28, 1977.

Photograph courtesy of Vanda White

Memorial erected by The Descendants of John Jacob Link to commemorate the dedication of the Link pavilion on the grounds of Saint James Lutheran Church, Uvilla, West Virginia.

FOREWORD

The Link Family, Antecedents and Descendants of John Jacob Link (1417-1951), was published by Paxson Link at Paris, Illinois, in 1951. The book contains a well-researched and well-documented history of John Jacob Link and his family, who immigrated to America in 1733, and of their antecedents in Germany. The book also contains a genealogy of all the descendants of John Jacob Link in America who were known at the time the book was published. Information on the later generations was compiled largely from the contributions of persons who were contacted during the late 1940s, as their names became identified as descendants during the researching of the book. This collection of information resulted in a large and relatively complete genealogy; entries for more than five thousand of the descendants of John Jacob Link were given in the genealogy, eighteen hundred and eighty-six of them in the Eighth Generation alone. Each descendant down to and including the Eighth Generation in the book was assigned an identifying serial number.

In the early 1980s, numerous persons expressed the desire that the book should be updated to reflect changes in the biographies of the descendants, as well as to add the new descendants in the Ninth and subsequent generations. A group known as the "Descendants of John Jacob Link" who meet annually in August at Uvilla, Jefferson County, West Virginia, undertook in 1980-1983 to send inquiries to as many of the original contributors as could be contacted. Several hundred persons replied with information on the Ninth, Tenth, and even Eleventh Generations of the Link genealogy, and also with additions or corrections to the earlier generations. When the compilation of the newly collected material began, the family planned to publish a second edition of *The Link Family*; however, the second edition did not materialize. Instead, the information submitted by the respondents was used as the source of material for a supplement to the Link genealogy, which was prepared in 1986.

Further corrections and additions were invited when the 1986 supplement was printed, and again, many responses were received. The information obtained between 1986 and 1988 was incorporated into the 1988 revision of the supplement (hereinafter called the "1988 Supplement").

The 1988 Supplement was originally printed as four separate volumes in loose-leaf format. Volume I (Additions and Corrections to the Third Through Seventh Generations) was designed to promulgate instructions for making pen-and-ink changes to *The Link Family* and to provide copy for making cut-and-paste additions. Volume II (Revised Eighth Generation) was intended to completely replace the Eighth Generation in the genealogy, and Volumes III and IV (Ninth, Tenth, and Eleventh Generations) were intended to be appendices; consequently, the page format of these volumes emulated the font and page size of *The Link Family* as closely as possible. This edition of the 1988 Supplement consolidates the four volumes into one book for the reader's convenience; however, the page format of the former volumes (two panels per page for the Eighth through the Eleventh Generations) has remained the same in order to preclude the expense of new typesetting.

Much care was taken to ensure the accuracy of the 1988 Supplement. Although time will certainly reveal new family facts, as well as omissions, the book committee hopes that what does appear may be useful to future generations of the Link family.

No further expansion of the genealogy is planned, as descendants of John Jacob Link now number well into the thousands. Family members are encouraged to collect and preserve genealogical data pertaining to their respective family branches, and to share this data through the many means now available, such as genealogical and family web sites and software.

The Link Family Book Committee
January 2001

ACKNOWLEDGMENTS

Many persons contributed information for this Supplement. Much of the credit is due to the Reverend James Lester Link, who served many years as historian for the Descendants of John Jacob Link. Mrs. Amy Tibbs researched the revised biographies of John George and Martha Link (Supplement Nos. 16 and 51) and submitted entries for the many descendants of those early ancestors. Mrs. Bonnie Cullison listed the numerous descendants of Daniel Link Demory (1866-1940) for the 1986 Supplement and organized responses containing the information on this branch for the 1988 Supplement. Mrs. Thelma Hulvey Meyer submitted much new information on the Hulvey branch of the family. Mrs. Florence Hendricks Moore contributed information that she had compiled for her book, *Descendants of Albert(us) Henricks(on), 1673-1984* (Beidel Printing House, Inc., Shippensburg, Pennsylvania, 1985).

The acknowledgments would not be complete without mentioning the significant contributions of Mr. Robert L. Hess, who painstakingly compiled the submitted information into the Supplement. Mr. Hess devoted many hours to verifying, organizing, indexing, typing, and proofreading the information contained in chapters 1 through 5. The book committee thanks Mr. Hess for his efforts, for without them, this book would not exist.

HOW TO USE THIS BOOK

Organization

The 1988 Supplement contains five chapters. Chapter 1 lists the additions and corrections to the Third through the Seventh Generations of *The Link Family* genealogy. These corrections and additions have been provided in the form of a supplement to the original book, rather than as a new edition of the book, in order to minimize the cost of providing the information.

Chapter 2 is a revised genealogy of the Eighth Generation of the descendants. The information in the revised Eighth Generation consists of: 1) updated information on members of the Eighth Generation whose names appeared in the original Link book (including the names of children born after the book was published); 2) new entries for members of certain branches of the descendants who for one reason or another were not included in the original book; and 3) for the convenience of those readers who do not have a copy of the book, reproductions of entries from the original book even for all those members of the Eighth Generation for whom the information is unchanged. All the children of the Eighth Generation have been assigned serial identification numbers in the Supplement to facilitate identifying their relationships with previous and subsequent generations. (In the original book, identification numbers were not given for members of the Ninth and subsequent generations.) The revised Eighth Generation replaces in its entirety the genealogy of the Eighth Generation (pages 620-774) in *The Link History*.

Chapter 3 is a genealogy listing members of the Ninth Generation who were known at the time of the compilation in 1988. These entries were based on the information submitted by the respondents to inquiries in 1980-1984 and in 1986-1988. This chapter also includes entries for each of the descendants whose names did appear in the original book, even in those cases where no additional information was received, in order that serial identification numbers could be assigned to them.

Chapters 4 and 5 are a genealogy of the Tenth and Eleventh Generations who were known at the time of the compilation. These latter generations are not complete, since the individuals listed therein include only those for whom information was submitted for the Supplement. Even so, there are more than a thousand descendants listed in the Tenth Generation and over a hundred in the Eleventh Generation.

The Appendix presents some photographs of "Link landmarks" in Jefferson County, West Virginia, as well as images of other documents judged to be of interest to users of the Supplement.

Lastly, the Index lists the names of all descendants of John Jacob Link who appear in Chapters 1 through 5. The names are listed in alphabetical order with their respective Supplement identification numbers. Unlike the index of the original genealogy, the names of spouses of the descendants and other relatives by marriage are not included in this index.

Numbering System

For those persons whose names appear in both *The Link Family* and this Supplement, the serial identification number is the same as that assigned in *The Link Family*. New numbers were assigned to persons whose biographies had not appeared in the original book, or for whom numbers had never been assigned. In each case where an addition was made and the next serial number for that generation was already in use, the previous serial number was assigned with a letter of the alphabet appended to the number. For example, entry No. 51 in *The Link Family*, Martha Link, lists no children for Martha. The names of her seven children were added in the 1988 Supplement and assigned numbers 179A through 179G, since 179 was the last serial number used for the children's generation immediately preceding Martha's entry in *The Link Family*.

The notation "(Sup)" before any number indicates that either the entry for the person is new, or that the information is revised from that published in *The Link Family*.

Chapter 1

Additions and Corrections to the
Third Through Seventh Generations

This chapter contains additions and corrections to pages 203-620
of the original book.

Generation	Entry Number(s)	Page Number(s) in The Link Family
Third	16	207
Fourth	51	215
Fifth	179A-298	249-280
Sixth	557A-1187	323-420
Seventh	1392A-2592	442-606

ADDITIONS AND CORRECTIONS TO THE THIRD GENERATION

The Link Family, pages 203-214

- -

On page 207 of the book, write alongside entry No. 16 [JOHN GEORGE LINK] the notation: "See (Sup) 16", to call attention to the following revised entry:

(Sup) 16 JOHN GEORGE LINK (John Adam[2], John Jacob[1]) was born October 23, 1768, near Woodsborough in Frederick County, Maryland. He was the son of John Adam and Mary Elizabeth Miller Link [see The Link Family, pages 201-202, No. 2]. During the 1796 presidential election, George Link voted in Frederick County. In 1805 he inherited land from his father, John Adam Link I, located in Frederick, Maryland, and he also purchased land in Washington County, Maryland. About 1807 George disposed of these properties and joined his brothers in Jefferson County, (West) Virginia, where on April 1, 1808, he purchased a tract of land of the Darke grant by Lord Fairfax from Jacob Manning and wife Mary Darke Manning. George married Martha ("Patsy") Link, his niece, on January 3, 1809, in Washington County, Maryland. Nineteen years younger than George, she was the daughter of John Adam and Jane Ogle Link [The Link Family, page 205, No. 12]. The marriage was an elopement and performed against the will of Martha Link's parents and family. Their first son, Daniel was born November 19, 1809, and baptized in nearby Shepherdstown, (West) Virginia. In 1810 George moved his family to Bourbon County, Kentucky, to be near his brother Jacob and his wife Elizabeth, who had left Virginia to live in Kentucky in 1799. On February 7, 1811, George purchased 111-1/2 acres of land in Fayette County, Kentucky. There the second child, John, was born to George and Martha on August 22, 1812. George and his family then left Kentucky, after he had sold his land in Fayette County, and moved to Montgomery County, Ohio. Upon arrival in Ohio, George Link purchased land on April 1, 1815, 3-1/2 miles south of Kettering, Ohio, from William and Sarah Patterson (Land Book D, page 214) and on April 7, 1816, 64 acres from James and Phebe Steel and Joseph and Hennatta Pierce (Book E, page 44). George and Martha became members there of David's Reformed Church (now known as "David's United Church of Christ"), Kettering, Ohio. Five more children were born there. The family lived in Van Buren Township (now Kettering) just outside Dayton. George died there on February 2, 1840. His will, which mentioned his wife Martha and the seven children, was dated July 12, 1836, and filed March 7, 1840. Martha remained on the farm with three sons, John, Adam, and Thomas, until her death July 10, 1854. Their children will be carried down in the Fifth Generation, under Martha's name [see Supplement No. 51].

- -

On page 215 of the book, write alongside entry No. 51 [MARTHA LINK] the notation: "See (Sup) 51", to call attention to the following revised entry:

(Sup) 51   MARTHA LINK (John Adam II[3], John Adam I[2], John Jacob[1]) was born October 23, 1787, in Jefferson County, West Virginia. She was the daughter of John Adam and Jane Ogle Link, Jr [see <u>The Link Family</u>, pages 205-206, No. 12]. Martha was raised with her four sisters and two brothers on her parents' farm, located three miles south of Shepherdstown in Berkeley County, Virginia (now Jefferson County, West Virginia). On January 3, 1809, in Hagerstown, Maryland, she married John George Link, her uncle [<u>TLF</u> page, 205, No. 16; and Supplement No. 16]. He was nineteen years older than Martha, and had moved the previous year to the Shepherdstown area from Maryland, to be closer to his brother Adam (Martha's father). The marriage, an elopement, was performed against the will of Martha's parents and family. At first George and Martha lived in Jefferson County, (West) Virginia, where their first son was born. In 1810 the family moved to Fayette County, Kentucky, where their second son was born. In 1815 the family moved again, this time to Montgomery County, Ohio, where five more children were born to George and Martha. George died on February 2, 1840 (having named Martha and all seven of the children in his will). In the 1850 census of Montgomery County, Martha then age 64 is listed as residing on their farm with sons John, then 37 years old; Adam, 24 years; and Thomas, 20 years. Martha died July 10, 1854, and is buried with her husband George and three sons Daniel, Adam, and George, Jr., in Beaverton Cemetery, Kettering (formerly Van Buren Township), Ohio.

(Sup) 179A	i	Daniel Link, born November 19, 1809.
(Sup) 179B	ii	John Link, born August 22, 1812.
(Sup) 179C	iii	Elizabeth Link, born November 3, 1815.
(Sup) 179D	iv	Susan Link, born about 1818.
(Sup) 179E	v	George Link, Jr., born about 1821.
(Sup) 179F	vi	Adam Link, born 1826.
(Sup) 179G	vii	Thomas Link, born May 14, 1829.

On page 222 of the book, alongside No. 82 [DANIEL LINK], write the notation: "See (Sup) 179A."

On page 223 of the book, alongside No. 83 [ADAM LINK], write the notation: "See (Sup) 179F."

ADDITIONS & CORRECTIONS TO THE FIFTH GENERATION

The Link Family, pages 245-315

- -

Add Nos. 179A through 179G. On page 249 of the book [between No. 179 ALEXANDER NATHANIEL REMSBERG, and No. 180 ADAM LINK] write the notation: "Add (Sup) 179A - 179G", to call attention to the following seven new entries:

(Sup) 179A DANIEL LINK (Martha[4], John Adam II[3], John Adam I[2], John Jacob[1]) was born November 19, 1809, in Jefferson County (West) Virginia. [He was the son of John George and Martha Link; see The Link Family, page 207, No. 16; and Supplement Nos. 16 and 51]. His birth date is from St. Peter's Lutheran Church records, Shepherdstown, West Virginia. Daniel accompanied his parents when they moved soon after his birth to Fayette County, Kentucky, and again when they moved from there to Montgomery County, Ohio, in 1815. He married Clementine McGrew in Montgomery County, Ohio, about 1830. She was of Irish descent, born November 7, 1809. They had four children. (Approximate dates of their births are from Montgomery, Ohio, census records.) Daniel died May 1, 1836, at the age of twenty-six. Clementine died March 8, 1872. They are buried alongside his parents George and Martha Link in Beavertown Cemetery, Kettering, Ohio.

  (Sup) 557A i Jacob Link, born about 1830.
  (Sup) 557B ii Adaline Link, born about 1832.
  (Sup) 557C iii Sarah Link, born about 1834.
  (Sup) 557D iv John Link, born about 1836.

(Sup) 179B JOHN LINK (Martha[4], John Adam II[3], John Adam I[2], John Jacob[1]) was born August 22, 1812 in Fayette County, Kentucky. He was the son of John George and Martha Link [Supplement Nos. 16 and 51]. His parents moved to Montgomery County, Ohio, shortly after his birth. In 1850, ten years after his father's death, John resided with his mother and two brothers on their farm in Kettering (now Van Buren Township), Montgomery County, Ohio. John did not marry. In later years he lived with the John Gebhart family, where he was at the time of the 1870 census.

(Sup) 179C ELIZABETH LINK (Martha[4], John Adam II[3], John Adam I[2], John Jacob[1]) was born November 3, 1815, in Van Buren Township, Montgomery County, Ohio. She was the daughter of John George and Martha Link [Supplement Nos. 16 and 51]. On June 26, 1839, Elizabeth married Joseph Jacobs at the Reformed Church in Kettering, Ohio. They had one child, born in Shelby County, Ohio, after which they moved to Indiana. For reasons of health Elizabeth returned to Ohio, but her husband was unwilling to leave Indiana, and they were divorced. Elizabeth returned to Montgomery County, Ohio, with her small son. There on February 8, 1849, she married Kennedy Morton. He was from Cincinnati, Ohio, and as a youth had been a post carrier between Piqua, Ohio, and Fort Defiance. Elizabeth and Kennedy Morton had four children. They lived in Montgomery County until 1861, when they moved to Turtle Creek Township, Shelby County, Ohio, and then in 1886 to Sidney, Ohio. Elizabeth died April 20, 1896, and Kennedy died December 5, 1906; they are buried in Graceland Cemetery, Sidney, Ohio.

     CHILD OF ELIZABETH AND JOSEPH JACOBS
  (Sup) 557E i Martin Van Buren Jacobs, born October 13, 1840.

     CHILDREN OF ELIZABETH AND KENNEDY MORTON
  (Sup) 557F ii Mary Elizabeth Morton.
  (Sup) 557G iii Rebecca Jane Morton.
  (Sup) 557H iv John Morton.
  (Sup) 557I v George W. Morton.

(Sup) 179D   SUSAN LINK (Martha[4], John Adam II[3], John Adam I[2], John Jacob[1]) was born about 1818, Van Buren Township, Montgomery County, Ohio. She was the daughter of John George and Martha Link [Supplement Nos. 16 and 51]. She was living there, unmarried at 22 years of age, at the time her father's will was probated in 1840.

(Sup) 179E   GEORGE LINK, JR. (Martha[4], John Adam II[3], John Adam I[2], John Jacob[1]) was the son of John George and Martha Link [Supplement Nos. 16 and 51]. George, Jr., was born about 1821 in Van Buren Township, Montgomery County, Ohio. He died there at the age of 25, on July 28, 1846, and is buried at Beavertown Cemetery, Kettering, Ohio.

(Sup) 179F   ADAM LINK (Martha[4], John Adam II[3], John Adam I[2], John Jacob[1]) was born in 1826, Van Buren Township, Montgomery County, Ohio. He was the son of John George and Martha Link [see The Link Family, page 207, No. 16; and Supplement Nos. 16 and 51.] Adam did not marry. In 1850, at the age of 24, he was living with his widowed mother and two brothers on the family farm three miles south of Dayton, in Montgomery County, Ohio. He died at the age of forty-eight on February 15, 1874, and is buried alongside his parents in Beaverton Cemetery, Kettering, Ohio. [Note: the entry for Adam Link in The Link Family, No. 83 on page 223, describes another Adam Link who was not the son of John George Link (No. 16) and Martha Link (No. 51). Both of these Adam Links were listed in the 1850 census: the former, the one reported here, was age 24, born in Ohio, unmarried, and living with his widowed mother Martha Link; the latter was age 27 years, birthplace Kentucky, married with a family, and a resident of Highland County. The relationship between the two, if any, is not known.]

(Sup) 179G   THOMAS LINK (Martha[4], John Adam II[3], John Adam I[2], John Jacob[1]) was born May 14, 1829, near Dayton, in Van Buren Township, Montgomery County, Ohio. Thomas was the son of John George and Martha Link [Supplement Nos. 16 and 51]. His father died when he was eleven years old. In 1850, at the age of 20, he resided with his widowed mother and two brothers on the family farm. About 1860 he married Anne Welsh. They moved to Montgomery County, near Dayton, Indiana (a community apparently named after, and probably settled from, his community of Dayton, Montgomery County, Ohio). He died December 7, 1869, and is buried at Riverside Cemetery, Andrews, Indiana.

    (Sup) 557J   i Ollie Link, born about 1861.
    (Sup) 557K   ii John Link, born 1863.

No. 197A.   On page 255 of the book, write alongside No. 197A [ADAM LINK DEMORY] the notation: "See (Sup)", to call attention to the following revised entry:

(Sup) 197A   ADAM LINK DEMORY (Rebecca[4], John Adam II[3], John Adam I[2], John Jacob[1]) was born April, 1833, in Loudoun County, Virginia. He married Sarah Christine Dailey, who was born at Harpers Ferry, (West) Virginia. Adam and Sarah made their home in Jefferson County, West Virginia. Adam died at the age of thirty-six in August, 1869, and is buried in the Lutheran Cemetery at Uvilla, West Virginia. Sarah married, second, Thomas J. Ingram March 24, 1875, at Bolivar, Jefferson County, West Virginia; they had at least two children, born in 1876 and 1879. It is believed Sarah is buried at Harper's Cemetery, Harpers Ferry, Virginia.

         641   i Molly Demory.
         642   ii Fountain Alexander Demory, born November 20, 1860.
         643   iii Minnie Elizabeth Demory, born December 24, 1861.
         644   iv Martha Ellen Demory, born November 2, 1863.
         645   v Adam Link Demory, Jr.
    (Sup) 645A   vi Daniel Link Demory, born August 13, 1866.

No. 248 DANIEL LINK [married Sophia Wachter; page 266]. Correct the name of their second child, to read "Adam Daniel Garrell Link."

No. 298 MARY MAGDALENE LINK [married John William Augustus Smith; page 280]. Ninth line; correct his birth date, to: "April 10, 1822 (or according to his funeral booklet, February 20, 1825)."

ADDITIONS & CORRECTIONS TO THE <u>SIXTH</u> GENERATION

The <u>Link</u> Family, pages 315-436

- -

Add Nos. 557A through 557K. Write in the book, on page 323 [between No. 557 LAURA REMSBERG, and No. 558 THOMAS JEFFERSON LINK] the notation: "(Sup) 557A - 557K", to indicate the following eleven new entries:

(Sup) 557A   JACOB LINK (Daniel[5], Martha[4], John Adam II[3], John Adam I[2], John Jacob[1]) was the son of Daniel and Clementine McGrew Link [Supplement No. 179A]. Jacob was born about 1830 in Van Buren Township, Montgomery County, Ohio.

(Sup) 557B   ADALINE LINK (Daniel[5], Martha[4], John Adam II[3], John Adam I[2], John Jacob[1]) was the daughter of Daniel and Clementine McGrew Link [Supplement No. 179A]. Adaline was born about 1832 in Van Buren Township, Montgomery County, Ohio.

(Sup) 557C   SARAH LINK (Daniel[5], Martha[4], John Adam II[3], John Adam I[2], John Jacob[1]) was the daughter of Daniel and Clementine McGrew Link Supplement No. 179A]. Sarah was born about 1834 in Van Buren Township, Montgomery County, Ohio.

(Sup) 557D   JOHN LINK (Daniel[5], Martha[4], John Adam II[3], John Adam I[2], John Jacob[1]) was the son of Daniel and Clementine McGrew Link [Supplement No. 179A]. John was born about 1836 in Van Buren Township, Montgomery County, Ohio.

(Sup) 557E   MARTIN VAN BUREN JACOBS (Elizabeth[5], Martha[4], John Adam II[3], John Adam I[2], John Jacob[1]) was the son of Joseph and Elizabeth Link Jacobs [see Supplement No. 179C]. Martin was born October 13, 1840, in Shelby County, Ohio. After his birth, his parents moved to Indiana, where they were divorced. Martin's mother remarried, and he was raised with two half-brothers and two half-sisters in the home of his stepfather Kennedy Morton in Van Buren Township, Shelby County, Ohio. There he married Charlotte Anne Baker March 14, 1861. She was the daughter of Joseph and Barbara Monty Baker. Martin and Charlotte lived in Sidney, Ohio, until about 1868 when they moved to Andrews, Indiana. A year later they moved to Huntington, Indiana. Charlotte died July 26, 1898, and is buried at Mt. Hope Cemetery, Huntington. In 1899 Martin Jacobs married Lydia Bridges. He died August 25, 1903, and is buried in Mt. Hope Cemetery.

    (Sup) 1392A   i   John Adam Jacobs, born about 1862.
    (Sup) 1392B   ii   Elizabeth B. Jacobs, born about 1864.
    (Sup) 1392C   iii   Franklin F. Jacobs, born about 1866.
    (Sup) 1392D   iv   Martin A. Jacobs, born about 1867.
    (Sup) 1392E   v   George Lowell Jacobs, born May 4, 1869.
    (Sup) 1392F   vi   Minnie Jacobs, born about 1871.
    (Sup) 1392G   vii   William A. Jacobs, born about 1874.

(Sup) 557F   MARY ELIZABETH MORTON (Elizabeth[5], Martha[4], John Adam II[3], John Adam I[2], John Jacob[1]) was the daughter of Kennedy and Elizabeth Link Jacobs Morton [Supplement No. 179C]. She was born about 1854 in Montgomery County, Ohio. She married Peter Martin.

    (Sup) 1392H   i Grace Martin

(Sup) 557G   REBECCA JANE MORTON (Elizabeth[5], Martha[4], John Adam II[3], John Adam I[2], John Jacob[1]) was the daughter of Kennedy and Elizabeth Link Jacobs Morton [see Supplement No. 179C]. She was born about 1852 in Montgomery County, Ohio. She married Taylor Hipple.

(Sup) 557H   JOHN MORTON (Elizabeth[5], Martha[4], John Adam II[3], John Adam I[2], John Jacob[1]) was the son of Kennedy and Elizabeth Link Jacobs Morton [Supplement No. 179C]. John was born about 1854 in Montgomery County, Ohio.

(Sup) 557I   GEORGE W. MORTON (Elizabeth[5], Martha[4], John Adam II[3], John Adam I[2], John Jacob[1]) was the son of Kennedy and Elizabeth Link Jacobs Morton [see Supplement No. 179C]. George was born about 1856 in Montgomery County, Ohio. He married Nellie Elliott.

(Sup) 557J   OLLIE LINK (Thomas[5], Martha[4], John Adam II[3], John Adam I[2], John Jacob[1]) was the daughter of Thomas and Anne Welsh Link [Supplement No. 179G]. Ollie was born about 1861, in Montgomery County, Ohio. She married William Dean.

(Sup) 557K   JOHN LINK (Thomas[5], Martha[4], John Adam II[3], John Adam I[2], John Jacob[1]) was the son of Thomas and Anne Welsh Link [Supplement No. 179G]. John was born in 1863 in Montgomery County, Ohio. He died unmarried December 9, 1930, and is buried in Beaverton Cemetery, Kettering, Montgomery County, Ohio.

No. 571 ROBERT CAMPBELL HESS [married Nannie Vogelways; page 326]. Add: "Nannie died December 27, 1956, and is buried in Prospect Hill Cemetery, Washington, D.C."

No. 582 JOHN ALEXANDER LINK [page 329]. Correct last line of text to read: "He is buried in the Snyder-Hendricks Cemetery on Ridge Road near Shepherdstown, West Virginia."

No. 585 JACOB ALBERT LINK [married Sarah Narcissa Blew; page 329]. Add to text: "She died August 8, 1857, and is buried in the Elmwood Cemetery at Shepherdstown, West Virginia."

No. 593 NANCY HARMAN [page 332]. Add to text: "Nancy died February 18, 1955, and is buried in Edge Hill Cemetery at Charles Town."

No. 596   JAMES LAWRENCE HARMAN [page 332]. Add to text: "He died March 10, 1965, and is buried in Elmwood Cemetery at Shepherdstown."

No. 625   IDA HORTENSE THRAVES [married George E. Sommer; page 338]. Correct the surname of her husband and their children, to "Sommer."

No. 642   FOUNTAIN ALEXANDER DEMORY [page 341]. Delete last sentence of text and add: ". . .and is buried in Harper Cemetery at Harper's Ferry, West Virginia."

Add No. 645A. Write in the book on page 341 [between No. 645 ADAM LINK DEMORY, JR., and No. 646 GEORGE ALEXANDER DEMORY]: "(Sup) 645A", to indicate the following new entry:

(Sup) 645A   DANIEL LINK DEMORY (Adam[5], Rebecca[4], John Adam II[3], John Adam I[2], John Jacob[1]) was the son of Adam Link and Sarah Christina Dailey Demory [see The Link Family, No. 197A, pages 255-256; and Supplement No. 197A]. Daniel was born August 13, 1866, at Charles Town, West Virginia. He left home after his father died and his mother remarried, and he never returned to West Virginia or kept in touch with any of his family. He went to Kansas where he married. Daniel married Hattie Edith Rapp February 19, 1891, at Newton, Kansas. She was the daughter of Adam and Minerva Hall Rapp and was born March 6, 1869, at West Brooklyn, Illinois. They later moved to Missouri, next to Oklahoma, and then to south Texas where he died 20 January, 1940.

(Sup) 1616B	i	Ralph Earl Demory, born January 12, 1892.
(Sup) 1616C	ii	Glen Robert Demory, born November 18, 1893.
(Sup) 1616D	iii	Alma Lizzie Demory, born January 23, 1895.
(Sup) 1616E	iv	Sarah Minerva Demory, born August 16, 1896.
(Sup) 1616F	v	Hattie Edith Demory, born February 22, 1898.
(Sup) 1616G	vi	John Daniel Link Demory, born November 28, 1899.
(Sup) 1616H	vii	Floyd Albert Demory, born December 6, 1901.
(Sup) 1616I	viii	Pearl Ella Demory, born June 7, 1903.
(Sup) 1616J	ix	Raymond Frank Demory, born July 7, 1905.
(Sup) 1616K	x	Grace May Demory, born February 8, 1908.
(Sup) 1616L	xi	Bethel Jane Demory, born December 7, 1910.

No. 651   WALTER MILTON DEMORY [married Irene Mable Mohler; page 342]. Add to text: "Irene died April 25, 1969 and is buried in Elmwood Cemetery at Shepherdstown, West Virginia."

No. 670   GEORGE CONRAD LINK [married Kate Lee Hendricks; page 345]. Correct and amplify her birthdate: "Kate was born June 13, 1861, the daughter of John and Sarah Bane Hendricks . . ."

No. 671   WILLIAM CRUZEN LINK [married Emma Kate Keesecker; page 345]. Add to text: "She died August 12, 1953, and is buried in Elmwood Cemetery, Shepherdstown."

No. 676   ADAM CRUZEN LINK [married Margaret Elizabeth Jones; page 346]. Add to text: "She died July 28, 1952, and is buried in Elmwood Cemetery at Shepherdstown."

No. 679   JOHN ALLEN LINK [married Lula Clegett Moore; page 346]. Add to text: "Lula died May 31, 1951, and is buried in Edge Hill Cemetery at Charles Town."

No. 682   ELBERT VAUGHEN LINK [married Jessie Harwood Mohler; page 347]. Add to text: "She died September 27, 1966, and is buried in Elmwood Cemetery, Shepherdstown."

No. 688   JAMES ALLEN HENDRICKS [married Sarah Louise Lemen; page 348]. Add to text: "James died November 21, 1953. They are buried in Elmwood Cemetery at Shepherdstown, West Virginia."

No. 689   ESTHER HENDRICKS [married Jessie Alexander Engle; page 348]. Add to text: "She died in 1957. They are buried in Edge Hill Cemetery at Charles Town, West Virgiia."

No. 690   LEROY HENDRICKS [married Maud Virginia Moler; page 348]. Add to text: "She was the daughter of Adam and Cora Daniels Moler. LeRoy died September 29, 1971, and Maud died January 22, 1962; they are buried in Elmwood Cemetery at Shepherdstown, West Virginia."

No. 691   DANIEL WEBSTER HENDRICKS, JR. [married Sarah Virginia Link; page 348]. Add to text: "Sarah's father was Daniel's second cousin, William Harman Link [The Link Family, page 324, No. 563; and page 445, No.1410]. Daniel died December 17, 1956, and Sarah died February 7, 1960; they are buried in Elmwood Cemetery at Shepherdstown, West Virginia."

No. 693   ALLEN MILLER LINK [page 348]. Add: "He died in 1966, and she died August 6, 1987; they are buried in Elmwood Cemetery at Shepherdstown, West Virginia."

No. 695   EDITH MAE LINK [married James Henry Myers; page 349]. Add to test: "He died August 17, 1964, and she died August 27, 1981; they are buried in Edge Hill Cemetery at Charles Town, West Virginia."

No. 696   ALLEDA RUTH LINK [page 349]. Add: "She died June 11, 1976, and is buried in Elmwood Cemetery, Shepherdstown, West Virginia."

No. 697   CHARLES ROCKEY LINK [married Effa Robinson; page 439]. Add: "He died November 12, 1969, and she died June 26, 1981; they are buried in Mount Hebron Cemetery, Winchester, Virginia."

No. 698   GRACE LEE LINK [page 349]. Add: "She resided at Shepherdstown, West Virginia. In her later years she was at the National Lutheran home for the Aged at Washington, D. C. Grace died February 2, 1978, and is buried in Elmwood Cemetery at Shepherdstown."

No. 702   LELIA LARUE REINHART [page 349]. Add: "She died July 13, 1970, and is buried in Elmwood Cemetery at Shepherdstown, West Virginia."

No. 704   CHARLES HUGH REINHART [married Irma Idella Snyder; page 349]. Add to text: "Charles died December 18, 1957, and Irma died January 29, 1977; they are buried in Elmwood Cemetery at Shepherdstown, West Virginia."

No. 705   MARY VIRGINIA REINHART [married Marvin Knott; page 350]. Add: "She died April 15, 1954, and he died October 25, 1957. They are buried in Elmwood Cemetery at Shepherdstown, West Virginia."

No. 706   AGNES GIBSON REINHART [married William Boyd Link; page 350]. Add: "William died March 11, 1952, and Agnes died June 13, 1972; they are buried in Elmwood Cemetery at Shepherdstown, West Virginia."

No. 783. Write in the book on page 360, alongside No. 783 [ADAM DANIEL GARL LINK], the notation "See Sup", to call attention to the following revised entry:

(Sup) 783   ADAM DANIEL GARRELL LINK (Daniel[5], Adam[4], Daniel[3], John Adam I[2], John Jacob[1]) was born December 24, 1866, in Frederick County, Maryland. "Garl" married Grace Ellen Bowers, September 25, 1890, at Westminster, Maryland. She was the daughter of John Henry and Mary Jane (Orndorff) Bowers and was born May 29, 1868. Garl and Grace Ellen resided at Baltimore, Maryland. He possessed a hall clock made by his third-great-grandfather John Adam Link I; it is inlaid in the upper part with the inscription "Adam Linck - 1773." (In 1988 the clock was owned by his daughter Marie Elizabeth (Link) Zumstein and granddaughter Grace Marie (Zumstein) Hofstetter at St. Michael's, Maryland.) Grace Ellen died January 21, 1944, and Garl died February 6, 1957.

(Sup) 1862	i	Lewis Wilberforce Link, born July 19, 1891.
(Sup) 1863	ii	Eugene Bowers Link, born October 28, 1892.
(Sup) 1864	iii	Marie Elizabeth Link, born October 16, 1894.
(Sup) 1865	iv	Ralph Aubrey Link, born January 9, 1899.

No. 830 FRANK LINK [married Elsie Frances Barton; page 367]. Add to text: "Elsie died October 24, 1954, and Frank died December 24, 1957; they are buried in Greenmound Cemetery at Kilbourne, Ohio."

No. 923 NETHANIAH LINK [pages 384-385]. Correct the name of the third child, to read "iii Wendell Athey Link."

No. 927 FRANCIS MARION LINK [married Pearl Hillis; pages 385-386]. Add to text: "Pearl died December 7, 1960, and Francis died June 1, 1961; they are buried in Edgar Cemetery at Paris, Illinois."

No. 951 FRANK LAFOE LINK [married Minnie Bell Johnston; page 389]. Add to text: "Minnie died August 10, 1970, and is buried in Edgar Cemetery at Paris, Illinois."

No. 1187 ELIZABETH HANNAH LINK [married Dr. Elmer Longpré; page 420]. Add to text: "Elmer died March 31, 1955; and Elizabeth died January 19, 1973, at St. Petersburg, Florida."

CORRECTIONS AND ADDITIONS TO THE SEVENTH GENERATION

The Link Family, pages 436-620.

- -

Add Nos. 1392A through 1392H. Write in the book on page 442 [between No. 1392 ELIZABETH GAVER, and 1393 TELSIE JEFFERSON LINK] the notation: "(Sup) 1392A - 1392H", to call attention to the following eight new entries:

(Sup) 1392A   JOHN ADAM JACOBS (Martin[6], Elizabeth[5], Martha[4], John Adam II[3], John Adam I[2], John Jacob[1]) was the son of Martin Van Buren and Charlotte Anne Baker Jacobs [Supplement No. 557E]. John was born about 1862, at Sidney, Ohio. He married Anne Pumphrey.

        (Sup) 4265   i   Clarence Jacobs.
        (Sup) 4266   ii   Donna Jacobs.
        (Sup) 4267 iii   Lehman Jacobs.

(Sup) 1392B   ELIZABETH B. JACOBS (Martin[6], Elizabeth[5], Martha[4], John Adam II[3], John Adam I[2], John Jacob[1]) was the daughter of Martin Van Buren and Charlotte Anne Baker Jacobs [Supplement No. 557E]. Elizabeth was born about 1864 at Sidney, Ohio. She married Martin Hildebrand.

        (Sup) 4268   i   Ethel Hildebrand.
        (Sup) 4269   ii   John Hildebrand.
        (Sup) 4270 iii   Paul Hildebrand.

(Sup) 1392C   FRANKLIN FONROSE JACOBS (Martin[6], Elizabeth[5], Martha[4], John Adam II[3], John Adam I[2], John Jacob[1]) was the son of Martin Van Buren and Charlotte Anne Baker Jacobs [Supplement No. 557E]. Franklin was born in 1865 at Sidney, Ohio. He married Minnie Schwicho. She was born in 1874. Franklin died in 1936, and Minnie died in 1971 at Indianapolis, Indiana.

        (Sup) 4271   i   Alma Jacobs, born in 1895.
        (Sup) 4272   ii   Charlotte Jacobs, born in 1896.
        (Sup) 4273 iii   Marietta Jacobs, born in 1898.
        (Sup) 4274   iv   Edna Jacobs, born in 1900.
        (Sup) 4275   v   Frank Lowell Jacobs, born in 1902.
        (Sup) 4276   vi   Irvin Jacobs, born in 1904.
        (Sup) 4277 vii   Robert Jacobs, born in 1906.
        (Sup) 4278 viii   Lillian Jacobs, born in 1907.
        (Sup) 4279   ix   Ralph Reed Jacobs, born September 15, 1909.
        (Sup) 4280   x   Clarabell Jacobs, born in 1911.

(Sup) 1392D   MARTIN A. JACOBS (Martin[6], Elizabeth[5], Martha[4], John Adam II[3], John Adam I[2], John Jacob[1]) was the son of Martin Van Buren and Charlotte Anne Baker Jacobs [Supplement No. 557E]. Martin was born about 1867 in Indiana. He married Merle Reed. Martin died December, 1936, and is buried in Memorial Park at Indianapolis, Indiana.

        (Sup) 4281   i   Norwell Jacobs.

(Sup) 1392E   GEORGE LOWELL JACOBS (Martin[6], Elizabeth[5], Martha[4], John Adam II[3], John Adam I[2], John Jacob[1]) was the son of Martin Van Buren and Charlotte Anne Baker Jacobs [Supplement No. 557E]. George was born May 4, 1869, at Huntington, Indiana. He studied architecture in Chicago, and his work was exhibited at the Chicago World's Fair. He worked as a naval architect in the Navy Yard at Norfolk, Virginia. George married Virgie Ricketts, on November 16, 1896, at Georgetown, Washington. She was born January 15, 1870, the daughter of Richard E. and Christie Anne Ricketts of Rockville, Maryland. George and Virgie lived in Portsmouth, Virginia, for about five years. They then moved to Mariners Harbor, Staten Island, New York, where he worked in the shipyards and at the St. George Station of the Lighthouse Department for many years. He then worked for five years in construction for Shell Oil Company at Aruba, Dutch West Indies. After retiring at the age of 70 years, he returned to work during World War II in the McWilliams Shipyard as a ships' foreman. George died February 26, 1952, and Virgie died December 20, 1954. They are buried at Ocean View Cemetery, Staten Island, New York.

(Sup) 4282	i	Amy Lee Jacobs, born September 21, 1898.
(Sup) 4283	ii	Richard Van Buren Jacobs, born in 1899.
(Sup) 4284	iii	Virgie Louise Jacobs, born February 19, 1901.
(Sup) 4285	iv	Esther DeEtta Jacobs, born about 1903.
(Sup) 4286	v	George Lowell Jacobs, Jr., born March 22, 1906.

(Sup) 1392F   MINNIE JACOBS (Martin[6], Elizabeth[5], Martha[4], John Adam II[3], John Adam I[2], John Jacob[1]) was the daughter of Martin Van Buren and Charlotte Anne Baker Jacobs [Supplement No. 557E]. Minnie was born about 1871 at Huntington, Indiana. She married George Yopst.

(Sup) 4287	i	Mable Yopst.
(Sup) 4288	ii	Willis Yopst.
(Sup) 4289	iii	Walter Yopst.
(Sup) 4290	iv	Marguerite Yopst.
(Sup) 4291	v	Jay Yopst.
(Sup) 4292	vi	Mildred Yopst.

(Sup) 1392G   WILLIAM A. JACOBS (Martin[6], Elizabeth[5], Martha[4], John Adam II[3], John Adam I[2], John Jacob[1]) was the son of Martin Van Buren and Charlotte Anne Baker Jacobs [Supplement No. 557E]. William was born about 1874 at Huntington, Indiana; he died young.

(Sup) 1392H   GRACE MARTIN (Mary Elizabeth[6], Elizabeth[5], Martha[4], John Adam II[3], John Adam I[2], John Jacob[1]) was the daughter of Peter and Mary Elizabeth Morton Martin [Supplement No. 557F].

No. 1394 WILLIAM BOYD LINK [married Agnes Gibson Reinhart; page 442]. Add: "William died March 11, 1952, and Agnes died June 13, 1972; they are buried in Elmwood Cemetery at Shepherdstown, West Virginia."

No. 1395 MAMIE ESTHER LINK [married Harry Manning Lemen; page 443]. Add to text: "Harry died January 1, 1953, and is buried at Uvilla."

No. 1399 ADAM FRANCIS JONES [married Alice Rebecca Lemen; page 443]. Correct the last two sentences to read: "Alice died December 17, 1934, at Bakerton, and Adam died March 18, 1945, at Halltown in Jefferson County, West Virginia. They are both buried in Elmwood Cemetery at Shepherdstown, West Virginia."

No. 1400 ROBERT LUTHER JONES [page 444]. Add to text: "Robert died October 4, 1956, and is buried in Elmwood Cemetery at Shepherdstown."

No. 1401. Write in the book on page 444, alongside No. 1401 [ERNEST DRAWBAUGH JONES], the notation: "See Sup", to call attention to the following revised entry:

(Sup) 1401 ERNEST DRAWBAUGH JONES (Mary[6], Adam[5], Alexander[4], John Adam II[3], John Adam I[2], John Jacob[1]) was born April 23, 1880, in Jefferson County, West Virginia. He married his cousin, John Elsie Link [The Link Family, page 450, No. 1424] on September 16, 1908. Elsie was the daughter of John Luther and Estelle Snader Link [The Link Family, page 324, No. 564] and was born December 4, 1890, at Irvington, New Jersey. Ernest and Elsie made their home at Uvilla, Jefferson County, West Virginia, where he died January 4, 1949. She died January 30, 1968, at Charles Town, West Virginia. They are buried in St. James Lutheran Church Cemetery at Uvilla.

(Sup) 2790   i   Elsie Catherine Jones, born February 25, 1910.
(Sup) 2790A   ii   Edgar Carlton Jones, born July 7, 1921.
(Sup) 2791   iii   Ernest Mercer Jones, born June 4, 1922.
(Sup) 2792   iv   Patricia Ann Jones, born September 24, 1927.
(Sup) 2793   v   John Link Jones, born June 23, 1930.

No. 1406 WILLIAM MORGAN JONES [married Elsie May Gore; page 444]. Add to text: "She died August 11, 1964, and William died January 14, 1969; they are buried in Edge Hill Cemetery at Charles Town, West Virginia."

No. 1407 LAURA LINK [page 445]. Add to text: "Laura died January 16, 1955, and is buried in Elmwood Cemetery at Shepherdstown."

No. 1409 ANN REBECCA LINK [page 445]. Add to text: "She died December 15, 1971, and is buried in the St. James Church Cemetery at Uvilla, Jefferson County, West Virginia."

No. 1410 SARAH VIRGINIA LINK [pages 445-456]. Add before the final sentence: "Sarah died February 7, 1960, at Charles Town, West Virginia."

No. 1411   JOHN WILLIAM LINK [married Helen Elizabeth Link; page 446]. Add to text: "The Reverend John William Link died January 10, 1975, at the age of 92 years. Helen died November 26, 1983. Their bodies are interred at Elmwood Cemetery, Shepherdstown, West Virginia."

No. 1413   MARTHA SMITH LINK [page 447]. Add to text: "Martha died July 30, 1976, and is buried at Uvilla."

No. 1415   ADAM BAKER LINK [married Ethel Ruth Landis; page 448]. Add to text: "He died January 14, 1966, and she died October 20, 1983: they are buried in Edge Hill Cemetery at Charles Town, West Virginia."

No. 1416   SAMUEL WESLEY LINK [page 448]. Add to text: "Wesley died November 10, 1982, and is buried in Edge Hill Cemetery at Charles Town, West Virginia."

No. 1418   DENNIS DANIELS LINK [married Mildred Etta Bradley: pages 448-449]. Add: "Mildred died October 1, 1973, and Dennis died December 18, 1975; they are buried in Edge Hill Cemetery at Charles Town, West Virginia."

No. 1421   JAMES LESTER LINK [married Martha Constance Coiner; page 449]. Next-to-last sentence, correct her father's name to read "Homer Briley Coiner". Add to text: "She died May 4, 1962. Lester retired to Jefferson County, West Virginia, where he continued to perform extensive historical and genealogical researches. He served as chaplain and historian of the Link Family Reunion Committee and was an extensive contributor to this Supplement. He then moved to Richfield, North Carolina. He died March 9, 1987, at Salisbury, North Carolina. Lester and Martha are buried in Zion Lutheran Cemetery near Waynesboro, Augusta County, Virginia."

No. 1422   LILLIE ESTELLE LINK [page 449]. Add: "She died July 26, 1961, and is buried in Elmwood Cemetery at Shepherdstown."

No. 1423   ERNEST ALBERT LINK [married Anne Winston Jones; page 450]. His full name was: "Ernest Albert Link". Add to text: "Albert died February 14, 1965, and Anne died June 24, 1973; they are buried in Elmwood Cemetery at Shepherdstown, West Virginia."

No. 1425   LESTER WAITE LINK [married Barbara Elizabeth Shott; page 451].
Add to text: "Barbara died June 4, 1967, and Lester died May 13, 1973. They
are buried in Moravian Cemetery, Lebanon, Pennsylvania."

No. 1432   IRVING CHENEY HESS [page 452]. Next to last sentence: marriage
place is "Oroville, California". Also, add to text: "Catherine died June 9,
1969, at San Diego."

No. 1435   GUY LINK HESS [page 453]. Add to text: "Thana died October 10,
1969, and is buried at Palestine, Texas. Guy died August 9, 1973, and is buried
at Houston."

No. 1436   Write in the book on page 453, alongside No. 1436 [HARRY LEE HESS],
the notation: "See Sup", to call attention to the following entry:

> (Sup) 1436   HARRY LEE HESS (John[6], Elizabeth[5], Alexander[4], John
> Adam II[3], John Adam I[2], John Jacob[1]) was born November 29, 1888, at
> Baltimore, Maryland. He attended Baltimore Polytechnic and in 1910 received
> his degree in mechanical engineering from Stanford University, California.
> Harry was employed as an engineer in the California gold fields from 1911 to
> 1918. During World War I he was in the U.S. Army and was commissioned an
> officer of the Coast Artillery while in France. At the conclusion of the
> war he returned to Cailifornia and became Harbor Engineer for the City of
> Oakland until 1930. He then worked on the design of ships and gold dredges,
> until his retirement in 1956. Harry married Else Freda Jaeggi December 20,
> 1924, at Berkeley, California. She was the daughter of Leopold and Bertha
> Meyer Jaeggi and was born December 1, 1880, at Columbus, Nebraska. Else
> received a B.A. degree from the Univerity of California, Berkeley, and was a
> teacher in the Oakland public schools. She died May 30, 1980, and Harry
> died April 26, 1986. They are buried in Mountain View Cemetery at Oakland.
>
> (Sup) 2880   i Robert Lee Hess, born November 4, 1926.

No. 1437   FLORENCE WOODSIDE HESS [page 454]. Add to text: "Florence died
October 25, 1976, in Falls Church, Virginia, and is buried in Edge Hill Cemetery
at Charles Town, West Virginia."

No. 1445   ELLA BUTLER HESS [pages 455-456]. Add: "Ella died March 3, 1953,
and Edgar died about 1955. They are buried in Davis Ridge Cemetery, Baltimore,
Maryland."

No. 1446   SUE VIRGINIA HESS [page 456]. Add: "Sue died January 2, 1980, and
is buried in Elmwood Cemetery, Shepherdstown, West Virginia."

No. 1448. Write in the book on page 456, alongside No. 1448 [ROBERT CAMPBELL HESS, JR.], the notation: "See Sup", to call attention to the following revised entry:

> (Sup) 1448   ROBERT CAMPBELL HESS, JR. (Robert[6], Mary[5], Alexander[4], John Adam II[3], John Adam I[2], John Jacob[1]) was born August 23, 1912, at Washington, D.C. He married Helene Thomas Webster, November 24, 1939. She was the daughter of Arthur B. and Annie T. Thomas Webster and was born May 5, 1913, at Deals Island, Maryland. Robert became a market specialist, and he and Helene lived in Washington. Robert and Helene had no children. Helene died January 11, 1947, and is buried in Prospect Hill Cemetery at Washington, D.C.   Robert married, second, Harriet Cull July 14, 1951. Harriet was the daughter of Lincoln and Christine Cull and was born in Oakland, Nebraska. Robert and Harriet both worked for the U.S. Department of Agriculture. They were transferred to New Brunswick, New Jersey, in 1952 and established a residence in East Brunswick in July 1955. Harriet died in April 1984 and is buried at Washington, D.C.

No. 1451   JEANETTE LUCA McKEE [page 457]. Add to text: "She died in 1971 at Charles Town, West Virginia."

No. 1456   HARRIET ROUSH McKEE [married John Marvin Hawk; page 458]. Add to text: "He died May 27, 1974, and she died June 15,1986. They are buried in Rosedale Cemetery at Martinsburg."

No. 1466   BETTIE NEIL OSBOURN [page 459]. Add to text: "Bettie died May 3, 1952, and is buried in Elmwood Cemetery at Shepherdstown."

No. 1467   ROGER MILLER OSBOURN [married Catherine Virginia Moler; page 459]. Add to text: "Catherine died November 27, 1961, and Roger died July 25, 1971; they are buried in Elmwood Cemetery at Shepherdstown, West Virginia."

No. 1474   SAMUEL EDMUND OSBOURN [married Mary Day Poore; page 460]. Add to text: "Samuel died April 5, 1968, and Mary died March 25, 1977. They are buried in Elmwood Cemetery at Shepherdstown, West Virginia."

No. 1475   JOHN MELVIN OSBOURN [married Virginia Allnot Osbourn; page 461]. Add to text: "Virginia died in 1960 and is buried in Edge Hill Cemetery at Charles Town, West Virginia."

No. 1476 ANN ELIZABETH OSBOURN [page 461]. Add to text: "She died October 13, 1964, and is buried in Elmwood Cemetery at Shepherdstown, West Virginia."

No. 1478 WALTER ALLEN OSBOURN [married Laura Matthews; page 461]. Add to text: "He died July 4, 1955, and is buried in Elmwood Cemetery, Shepherdstown, West Virginia. She died January 2, 1980, and is buried at Washington, D.C."

No. 1479 CLEON SCOTT OSBOURN [married Beth Loring Neal; pages 461-462]. Add to text: "She died in 1957, and he died July 23, 1972; they are buried in Elmwood Cemetery at Shepherdstown, West Virginia."

No. 1480 ALICE LINK OSBOURN [page 462]. Add: "Alice died March 7, 1960, and is buried in Elmwood Cemetery at Shepherdstown, West Virginia."

No. 1482 JAMES THOMAS LINK [page 462]. Add: "He died November 29, 1955, and is buried in Mount Olivet Cemetery at Parkersburg." .

No. 1483 HELEN MARIA LINK [page 462]. Add: "She died September 21, 1960, and is buried in Elmwood Cemetery at Shepherdstown, West Virginia.

No. 1484   ANNA MOORE LINK [page 462]. Add: "She taught in the Charles Town schools from 1922 to 1929. In July 1929 she accepted a Civil Service position with the Smithsonian Institution Library in Washington, D.C., and received the A.B. degree in library science in June, 1933. In October 1952 she transferred to the National Gallery of Art Library, where she became head librarian from 1966 to 1972. On retirement, she traveled abroad extensively and continued to enjoy the urbane benefits of her residence in Washington."

No. 1485 ALBERT BLEW LINK [pages 462-463]. Add to text: "The Rev. Albert B. Link died December 21, 1986."

No. 1486 MARGARET WYATT LINK [married Herbert O'Keef; page 463]. Add their daughter:

"(Sup) 2936A   i Sallie Corbett O'Keef, born July 17, 1948."

No. 1487 WALLACE GIBSON LINK [married Frances Dudley Smith; page 463]. Add their third child:

"(Sup) 2938A   iii Harriett Link, born November 29, 1949."

Nos. 1489 to 1491. Write in the book on page 464, alongside No. 1489 [NANCY ALICE LINK, No. 1490 [JOHN CARSWELL LINK], and No. 1491]CHARLES ROBERT LINK], the notation; "See Sup", to call attention to the following three revised entries:

(Sup) 1489 NANCY ALICE LINK (Adam[6], Thomas[5], Alexander[4], John Adam II[3], John Adam I[2], John Jacob[1]) was born December 8, 1912, at Campbellsville, Kentucky. She married Forrest Wayne Powars November 28, 1942, at Washington, D.C. Forrest was born April 15, 1913, at Powars Siding, Colorado. His parents were Forrest Leslie and Anna Bess Mason Powars. Nancy was a graduate of Peace Junior College at Raleigh, North Carolina. Before her marriage she was an editor for the Bureau of American Ethnology of the Smithsonian Institution at Washington, D.C. Forrest graduated with an A.B. degree from Colorado State college of Education at Greeley, Colorado. He earned an M.A. degree there in postgraduate work and became a teacher and athletic coach in Washington, D.C. During World War II he served as an officer in the U.S. Navy for four years. He worked for twenty-five years as an insurance agent and then became an insurance broker. Nancy and Forrest founded a publishing company, Link Press, Inc., in 1983.

(Sup) 2939   i Grace Wallace Powars, born December 17, 1943.
(Sup) 2939A   ii Forrest Mason Powars, born November 1, 1947.
(Sup) 2939B iii Wayne Link Powars, born August 25, 1950.
(Sup) 2939C   iv David Scott Powars, born January 26, 1953.

(Sup) 1490 JOHN CARSWELL LINK (Adam[6], Thomas[5], Alexander[4], John Adam II[3], John Adam I[2], John Jacob[1]) was born February 10, 1914, at Campbellsville, Kentucky. On completion of public schools at Raleigh, North Carolina, he entered Davidson College. John was employed by General Motors Acceptance Corporation at Raleigh, North Carolina. This employment was interrupted by four years' service during World War II in the U.S. Army Air Corps. After his discharge he returned to General Motors Acceptance Corporation in Raleigh. He was transferred to Washington, D.C., and then as Branch Manager to Uniontown, Pennsylvania. After thirty-six years with the company he retired in May 1977. John married Clara George November 21, 1953, at Washington, D.C. She was the daughter of Chester Sayler and Nellie Hockensmith George and was born May 30, 1931, (near St. John) in Stafford County, Kansas. Clara attended public schools in Stafford and Edwards Counties and graduated from the Wichita Business College, Wichita, Kansas. She was employed by General Motors Acceptance Corporation at Wichita and at Washington, DC.

(Sup) 2939D   i George Wallace Link, born April 29, 1955.
(Sup) 2939E   ii John Gibson Link, born March 8, 1957.
(Sup) 2939F iii Joan Clara Link, born April 15, 1963.

(Sup) 1491   CHARLES ROBERT LINK (Adam[6], Thomas[5], Alexander[4], John Adam II[3], John Adam I[2], John Jacob[1]) was born December 31, 1918, at Campbellsville, Kentucky. He graduated from Oak Ridge Military Academy and Hampden-Sydney College. During World War II he was commissioned a captain in the Air Transport Corps and served as a pilot for four years overseas and in the United States. Upon his discharge he entered the insurance adjustment business and lived at Seattle, Washington. He married Jeanette Kathryn Whims, January 21, 1944, at Seattle. Kathryn was born February 9, 1919, at Vancouver, British Columbia. Her parents were Charles A. and Ruth May O'Neal Whims.

    (Sup) 2940   i   Judith Kathryn Link, born October 26, 1944.
    (Sup) 2940A ii Robert Gibson Link, born August 10, 1948.
    (Sup) 2940B iii David Charles Link, born November 10, 1955.

No. 1495   WALTER ALLEN HARMAN [married Mary Elizabeth Ballenger; page 465]. Add to text: "She died July 27, 1967."

No. 1496   CHARLES HENRY HARMAN [married (2) Dorothy Charlotte Steedman; page 465]. Add to text: "He died July 31, 1976, at Baltimore, and Dorothy died December 31, 1987."

Nos. 1581 to 1586. Correct the surname of No. 1581 WILBUR SOMMERS [page 479], through No. 1586 JAMES SOMMERS [page 480], to: "SOMMER."

No. 1586   JAMES SOMMER [married Gertude Baumann; page 480]. Correct the name of their daughter, to:

    "(Sup) 3120   i Jeanne Sommer, born September 27, 1921."

No. 1590   MARILLA HUBER [married (2) Marshall H. Bixler; page 481]. Add to text: "Marilla attended Bowling Green State University, Ohio. Marshall died in 1962. Marilla moved to Tucson, Arizona. She was active in the Daughters of American Colonists, of which she was vice president in 1984."

Add Nos. 1616B through 1616L. Write in the book on page 484 [between No. 1616A CARROL DONNAHUE WHITE, and No. 1617 LEONARD LEE DEMORY] the notation: "(Sup) 1616B-1616L", to call attention to the following eleven new entries:

(Sup) 1616B   RALPH EARL DEMORY (Daniel[6], Adam[5], Rebecca[4], John Adam II[3], John Adam I[2], John Jacob[1]) was the son of Daniel Link and Hattie Edith Rapp Demory [see Supplement No. 645A]. Ralph was born January 12, 1892, at Heston, Kansas. He married Esse Ratcliff December 1, 1927. She was born June 24, 1909, at Okeene, Oklahoma. Ralph died November 23, 1970, at Rockport, Texas.

          (Sup) 3150.1A   i   Ross Earl Demory, born November 5, 1928.
          (Sup) 3150.1B   ii   Ina Zoe Demory, born December 22, 1932.
          (Sup) 3150.1C iii   Gena Beth Demory, born January 24, 1935.

(Sup) 1616C   GLEN ROBERT DEMORY (Daniel[6], Adam[5], Rebecca[4], John Adam[3], John Adam I[2], John Jacob[1]) was the son of Daniel Link and Hattie Edith Rapp Demory [see Supplement No. 645A]. Glen Robert was born November 18, 1893, at Heston, Kansas. He married Cora (maiden name not known) in January, 1946; they had no children. He died February 23, 1968, in Bee County, Texas.

(Sup) 1616D   ALMA LIZZIE DEMORY (Daniel[6], Adam[5], Rebecca[4], John Adam II[3], John Adam I[2], John Jacob[1]) was the daughter of Daniel Link and Hattie Edith Rapp Demory [see Supplement No. 645A]. She was born January 23, 1895, at Heston, Kansas. She married Thomas G. Jakeway October 12, 1920. He was born January 1, 1893, and he died in 1980 at Tulsa, Oklahoma.

          (Sup) 3150.2A   i   Margie Fay Jakeway, born September 1, 1921.
          (Sup) 3150.2B   ii   Earl Thomas Jakeway, born November 10, 1923.
          (Sup) 3150.2C iii   Marilyn Maxine Jakeway, born Dec 13, 1924.
          (Sup) 3150.2D   iv   Luetta L. Jakeway, born October 27, 1926.
          (Sup) 3150.2E   v   Richard Eugene Jakeway, born October 4, 1928.

(Sup) 1616E   SARAH MINERVA DEMORY (Daniel[6], Adam[5], Rebecca[4], John Adam II[3], John Adam I[2], John Jacob[1]) was the daughter of Daniel Link and Hattie Edith Rapp Demory [see Supplement No. 645A]. Sarah was born August 16, 1896, in Douglas County, Missouri. She married Arthur L. Hackler August 12, 1921. Arthur was born December 20, 1897. He died March 3, 1935, at Cloud Chief, Oklahoma.

          (Sup) 3150.3A   i   Olive Lee Hackler, born September 18, 1922.
          (Sup) 3150.3B   ii   Daniel Lawrence Hackler, born Nov 4, 1923.
          (Sup) 3150.3C iii   Glen Elwood Hackler, born December 12, 1924.
          (Sup) 3150.3D   iv   Lloyd Junior Hackler, born March 23, 1925.
          (Sup) 3150.3E   v   Raymond Frank Hackler, born October 12, 1927.
          (Sup) 3150.3F   vi   Arthur Leroy Hackler, Jr., born June 18, 1929.
          (Sup) 3150.3G vii   Edith Golden Hackler, born August 31, 1931.
          (Sup) 3150.3H viii   Lillian Maxine Hackler, born August 17, 1933.

(Sup) 1616F   HATTIE EDITH DEMORY (Daniel[6], Adam[5], Rebecca[4], John Adam II[3], John Adam I[2], John Jacob[1]) was the daughter of Daniel Link and Hattie Edith Rapp Demory [see Supplement No. 645A].   Hattie was born February 22, 1898, at Heston, Kansas.   She married Alfred Lee Putnam September 12, 1917. He was the son of David Meek and Minerva Carolina Mason Putnam and was born July 27, 1896, in Douglas County, Missouri. Alfred died May 8, 1980, at Tulsa, Oklahoma.

     (Sup) 3150.4A   i   Alta May Putnam, born August 1, 1918.
     (Sup) 3150.4B   ii   Lee Alvin Putnam, born May 18, 1920.
     (Sup) 3150.4C iii   Daisy Pearl Putnam, born February 18, 1922.
     (Sup) 3150.4D   iv   Roy Frank Putnam, born May 10, 1924.
     (Sup) 3150.4E   v   Beverly Ruth Putnam, born July 7, 1935.

(Sup) 1616G   JOHN DANIEL LINK DEMORY (Daniel[6], Adam[5], Rebecca[4], John Adam II[3], John Adam I[2], John Jacob[1]) was the son of Daniel Link and Hattie Edith Rapp Demory [see Supplement No. 645A].   John was born November 28, 1899, in Douglas County, Missouri. He married Alla Grey December 25, 1923. She was born June 4, 1905 in Douglas County.

     (Sup) 3150.5A   i   Lloyd Hubert Demory, born November 29, 1924.
     (Sup) 3150.5B   ii   Rosalie Faye Demory, born December 10, 1927.
     (Sup) 3150.5C iii   Vivian Edith Demory, born June 7, 1933.

(Sup) 1616H   FLOYD ALBERT DEMORY (Daniel[6], Adam[5], Rebecca[4], John Adam II[3], John Adam I[2], John Jacob[1]) was the son of Daniel Link and Hattie Edith Rapp Demory [see Supplement No. 645A]. He was born December 6, 1901, in Douglas County, Missouri. He married Lorene Harris June 24, 1928. She was born February 9, 1909. Floyd died August 11, 1960, at Aransas Pass, Texas.

     (Sup) 3150.6A   i   Nettie May Demory, born May 25, 1929.
     (Sup) 3150.6B   ii   Jessie Pearl Demory, born December 14, 1930.
     (Sup) 3150.6C iii   Georgia Fay Demory, born October 3, 1932.
     (Sup) 3150.6D   iv   Betty Jane Demory, born July 25, 1936.
     (Sup) 3150.6E   v   Margie Ray Demory, born December 3, 1940.
     (Sup) 3150.6F   vi   John Albert Demory, born December 2, 1943.
     (Sup) 3150.6G vii   Raymond Frank Demory, born November 27, 1945.

(Sup) 1616I   PEARL ELLA DEMORY (Daniel[6], Adam[5], Rebecca[4], John Adam II[3], John Adam I[2], John Jacob[1]) was the daughter of Daniel Link and Hattie Edith Rapp Demory [see Supplement No. 645A]. She was born June 7, 1903, in Douglas County, Missouri. She married Jesse George Putnam April 26, 1923, at Beeville, Texas. He was the son of David Meek and Minerva Caroline Mason Putnam and was born January 7, 1900, in Douglas County, Missouri. Jesse and Pearl resided in Oklahoma. She died September 13, 1976, at Madill, Oklahoma, and is buried in the Woodberry-Forest Cemetery in Madill.

     (Sup) 3150.7A   i   Velma Blanche Putnam, born November 8, 1923.
     (Sup) 3150.7B   ii   Bonnie Ella Putnam, born April 12, 1926.
     (Sup) 3150.7C iii   Jesse Robert Putnam, born December 31, 1927.
     (Sup) 3150.7D   iv   Georgia May Putnam, born February 7, 1929.

(Sup) 1616J   RAYMOND FRANK DEMORY (Daniel[6], Adam[5], Rebecca[4], John Adam II[3], John Adam I[2], John Jacob[1]) was the son of Daniel Link and Hattie Edith Rapp Demory [see Supplement No. 645A]. He was born July 7, 1905, in Douglas County, Missouri. He died July 4, 1933, in Bee County, Texas.

(Sup) 1616K   GRACE MAY DEMORY (Daniel[6], Adam[5], Rebecca[4], John Adam II[3], John Adam I[2], John Jacob[1]) was the daughter of Daniel Link and Hattie Edith Rapp Demory [see Supplement No. 645A]. Grace was born February 8, 1908, in Douglas County, Missouri. She married Luby Harrell October 11, 1930. He was born August 8, 1904, and died November 8, 1942, in Bee County, Texas.

> (Sup) 3150.8A   i   Luby Allan Harrell, born November 29, 1931.
> (Sup) 3150.8B   ii   James Edward Harrell, born February 4, 1934.
> (Sup) 3150.8C   iii Barbara Jane Harrell, born January 28, 1939.
> (Sup) 3150.8D   iv   Robert Martin Harrell, born November 11, 1940.

(Sup) 1616L   BETHEL JANE DEMORY (Daniel[6], Adam[5], Rebecca[4], John Adam II[3], John Adam I[2], John Jacob[1]) was the daughter of Daniel Link and Hattie Edith Rapp Demory [see Supplement No. 645A]. She was born December 7, 1910, in Douglas County, Missouri. She married Walter Willoughby Hill June 1, 1946. Walter was born October 31, 1898. He had a son by a former marriage.

> Stepson   i   Walter Willoughby Hill, Jr., born Aug 8, 1923.

No. 1629.   Write in the book on page 485, alongside No.1629 [CHARLES WILLIAM DEMORY, the notation: "See Sup", to call attention to the following revised entry:

(Sup) 1629   CHARLES WILLIAM DEMORY (Henry[6], John[5], Rebecca[4], John Adam I[3], John Adam I[2], John Jacob[1]) was born November 12, 1912, at Taylorstown, Virginia. Charles was a contractor with Demory Brothers Construction and president of Demory Enterprises, Inc., at Gaithersburg, Maryland. He married Erma Elizabeth Carnes August 24, 1935. She was the daughter of Edgar Franklin and Sarah Frances Myers Carnes of Taylorstown, Virginia. After retirement Charles managed real estate. He was a trustee and lay leader of Grace Methodist Church at Gaithersburg.

> (Sup) 3173   i   Priscilla Diane Demory, born December 12, 1938.
> (Sup) 3174   ii   Charles William Demory, Jr., born Nov 17, 1939.
> (Sup) 3175   iii Larry Sidney Demory, born January 7, 1942.
> (Sup) 3176   iv   Edwin Franklin Demory, born March 3, 1945.
> (Sup) 3176A   v   Linda Carol Demory, born December 28, 1948.
> (Sup) 3176B   vi   Stephen Eric Demory, born July 15, 1951.

Nos. 1639 through 1645. Write in the book on page 486, alongside No. 1639 [IRIS ANNA BELL DEMORY], No. 1640 [HOWARD GRIFFITH DEMORY], No. 1641 [NAOMI ARBUTIS DEMORY], No. 1642 [MILTON DALE DEMORY], No. 1643 [JUANITA MOLER DEMORY], No. 1644 [VELMA LOUISE DEMORY], and No. 1645 [REBECCA JANE DEMORY], the notation: "See Sup", to call attention to the following seven revised entries:

(Sup) 1639   IRIS ANNABEL DEMORY (Walter[6], John[5], Rebecca[4], John Adam I[3], John Adam I[2], John Jacob[1]) was born August 15, 1923. She married Charles William Osbourn, Jr., September 18, 1942. Charles, son of Charles William and Leoath McKee Osbourn, was born March 10, 1922. He received the A.B. degree in education and a Masters degree in physical education from Shepherd College, and he taught school in Jefferson County, West Virginia, for twenty-six years.

    (Sup) 3185   i   Larry William Osbourn, born September 25, 1943.
    (Sup) 3186   ii   Nancy Carolina Osbourn, born February 27, 1945.
    (Sup) 3186A iii Mark Eugene Osbourn, born October 18, 1951.

(Sup) 1640   HOWARD GRIFFITH DEMORY (Walter[6], John[5], Rebecca[4], John Adam II[3], John Adam I[2], John Jacob[1]) was born November 5, 1924. He married Marguerite Staubs October 31, 1946. Marguerite was the daughter of Charles Edward and Estella Pauline McAtee Staubs and was born September 19, 1928. Marguerite died March 23, 1967. Howard married, second, her sister Charlotte P. Staubs November 18, 1967. Charlotte was born November 5, 1924. She was a career employee of the U.S. government in Washington, D.C.

    (Sup) 3187   i   Pamela Jean Demory, born September 14, 1947.
    (Sup) 3188   ii   Sharon Dian Demory, born December 13, 1948.
    (Sup) 3188A iii Cheryl Lynn Demory.

(Sup) 1641   NAOMI ARBUTIS DEMORY (Walter[6], John[5], Rebecca[4], John Adam II[3], John Adam I[2], John Jacob[1]) was born August 1, 1926. She married William Bernard Keesecker July 4, 1944. William was the son of William Ross and Rebecca Jane Keesecker and was born December 13, 1926. Naomi and William were divorced in November 1951. She married, second, Harvey Allen Miller, son of Enoch George and Mida Virginia Drake Miller on July 23, 1955. Harvey was born October 19, 1918.

CHILDREN OF NAOMI AND WILLIAM
    (Sup) 3189   i Rebecca Jane Keesecker, born June 5, 1945.
    (Sup) 3190   ii Mary Louise Keesecker, born February 23, 1947.

CHILDREN OF NAOMI AND HARVEY
    (Sup) 3190A iii George Allen Miller, born March 21, 1956.
    (Sup) 3190B iv Mida Virginia Miller, born February 12, 1969.

(Sup) 1642   MILTON DALE DEMORY (Walter[6], John[5], Rebecca[4], John Adam II[3], John Adam I[2], John Jacob[1]) was born January 14, 1928. He married Ann Custer April 26, 1951. She was the daughter of Charles Henry and Ann Gregory Custer and was born February 16, 1926.

    (Sup) 3190C i Frank Nick Demory, born January 2, 1948.
    (Sup) 3190D ii Walter Dale Demory, born September 24, 1953.

(Sup) 1643   JUANITA MOLER DEMORY (Walter[6], John[5], Rebecca[4], John Adam II[3], John Adam I[2], John Jacob[1]) was born March 15, 1929. Juanita married Charles Griffin Moler June 7, 1949, at Hagerstown, Maryland. He was the son of John Griffin and Madge Elizabeth Grove Moler. Charles received a B.S. degree in physics from Shepherd College, Shepherdstown, West Virginia, May 30, 1952. He was employed by IBM as a field engineer in the General Systems Division.

(Sup) 3190E   i   John Jeffery Charles Moler, born August 9, 1954.
(Sup) 3190F   ii   Charmayne Danita Moler, born March 14, 1957.
(Sup) 3190G   iii Lisa Denise Moler, born October 20, 1959.
(Sup) 3190H   iv   Tina Marie Moler, born October 18, 1965.

(Sup) 1644   VELMA LOUISE DEMORY (Walter[6], John[5], Rebecca[4], John Adam II[3], John Adam I[2], John Jacob[1]) was born November 1, 1930. She married Raleigh William Moler October 18, 1948. He was born November 26, 1924.

(Sup) 1645   REBECCA JANE DEMORY (Walter[6], John[5], Rebecca[4], John Adam II[3], John Adam I[2], John Jacob[1]) was born October 20, 1932. She married James Arthur Prather, III, June 18, 1950. He was the son of James Arthur and Cora Belle Malatt Prather, Jr., and was born December 24, 1930.

(Sup) 3190I   i   James Arthur Prather, IV, born October 31, 1951.
(Sup) 3190J   ii   Deborah Jane Prather, born October 18, 1953.
(Sup) 3190K   iii Corrinne Rebecca Prather, born October 18, 1956.
(Sup) 3190L   iv   Melissa Beth Prather, born April 22, 1964.

No. 1664   CLARA DOUGLAS HENDRICKS [married Wilbur Alonza Morris; page 489]. Add to text: "Clara died March 10, 1952, and is buried in Elmwood Cemetery in Shepherdstown."

No. 1666   EDITH IOLA HENDRICKS [pages 489-490]. Add to text: "Edith died May 12, 1948, and is buried in Elmwood Cemetery at Shepherdstown."

No. 1668   LELIA PEARL MOLER [married Norvel Bryant Jenkins; page 490]. Add to text: "Norvel died January 1, 1968, and is buried in Edge Hill Cemetery at Charles Town, West Virginia."

No. 1671   EDNA TANNER LINK [married Jacob Henry Bender; page 490]. Add: "He died November 5, 1959, and she died July 16, 1972; they are buried in Elmwood Cemetery at Shepherdstown, West Virginia."

No. 1672 HELEN ELIZABETH LINK [pages 490-491]. Add: "Helen died November 26, 1983, in Jefferson County, West Virginia."

No. 1678 DANIEL RUSSELL NICHOLS [married Mildred Virginia Maddox; page 491]. Add to text: "Mildred died January 10, 1979, and is buried in Pleasant View Cemetery near Martinsburg, West Virginia."

No. 1679 WILLIAM PRESTON LINK [married Ruth Agnes Boyer; page 491]. Add to text: "William died October 28, 1955, and Ruth died November 18, 1964; they are buried in Elmwood Cemetery at Shepherdstown, West Virginia."

No. 1680 KATHRYN CLYMER LINK [married Henry James Seibert; page 491]. Add: "They resided at Martinsburg, West Virginia. He died in 1983."

Nos. 1681 through 1686. Write in the book on page 492, alongside Nos. 1681 [DANIEL CRUZEN LINK], through 1686 [FLORENCE EVELYN LINK], the notation: "See Sup", to call attention to the following six revised entries:

(Sup) 1681   DANIEL CRUZEN LINK (Adam[6], Daniel[5], John Adam III[4], John Adam II[3], John Adam I[2], John Jacob was born September 23, 1906. He married Helen Meade Ellis, December 22, 1937. Helen was born September 24, 1906. Daniel graduated from Western Maryland College and received the M.S. degree in education from the University of Maryland in 1942. He became a teacher and then an administrator and principal, serving twenty-four years in the schools of Prince William County, Virginia, before retiring in 1974. Helen died November 2, 1973, and Daniel died August 18,1984. They are buried in Stonewall Memory Gardens at Manassas, Virginia.

    (Sup) 3264   i Daniel Cruzen Link, Jr., born March 30, 1940.
    (Sup) 3265   ii Margaret Ellis Link, born November 14, 1942.

(Sup) 1682   CHARLES ALBERT RONEMOUS (Annie[6], Daniel[5], John Adam III[4], John Adam II[3], John Adam I[2], John Jacob[1]) was born December 31, 1914. He died January 13, 1915, and is buried in Elmwood Cemetery at Shepherdstown, West Virginia.

(Sup) 1683   BOTELER MOORE LINK (John[6], Daniel[5], John Adam III[4], John Adam II[3], John Adam I[2], John Jacob[1]) was born October 30, 1910. He married Eva Lee Nichols, January 18, 1932. She was the daughter of William David and Hattie Matilda Buracker Nichols, and was born September 29, 1915. Boteler died July 25, 1968, and is buried in Pleasant View Cemetery at Baker Heights, near Martinsburg, West Virginia. Eva Lee married, second, Clifford Cecil Starliper July 14, 1974, in Jefferson County, West Virginia. Clifford died December 22, 1977. She married, third, Robert Luther Jones [see Supplement No. 2788] October 20, 1983.

    (Sup) 3266   i   David Allen Link, born October 22, 1932.
    (Sup) 3267   ii Howard Snyder Link, born February 10, 1935.
    (Sup) 3268   iii Boteler Moore Link, Jr., born July 24, 1940.
    (Sup) 3268A   iv John William Link, born September 28, 1950.

(Sup) 1684   CECIL MILLER LINK (John[6], Daniel[5], John Adam III[4], John Adam II[3], John Adam I[2], John Jacob[1]) was born August 12, 1912 near Halltown, Jefferson County, West Virginia. He died November 18, 1976, and is buried at Charles Town, West Virginia.

(Sup) 1685   MADALINE OSBOURN LINK (John[6], Daniel[5], John Adam III[4], John Adam II[3], John Adam I[2], John Jacob[1]) was born December 15, 1916. She married Walter Eldridge Woodson October 19, 1940, at Duffields, Jefferson County, West Virginia. He was the son of Walter Eldridge and Margaret Krouse Woodson and was born July 24, 1919, at Springfield, Hampshire County, West Virginia. They were divorced. Madeline married, second, John Herbert Jackson November 19, 1947, at Easton, Maryland. John, originally surnamed Issakson, was the son of August Issakson and was born in 1902.

CHILD OF MADELINE AND WALTER
(Sup) 3269   i John Walter Woodson, born September 2, 1941.

CHILD OF MADELINE AND JOHN
(Sup) 3269A   ii Allen Link Jackson, born March 3, 1952.

(Sup) 1686   FLORENCE EVELYN LINK (John[6], Daniel[5], John Adam III[4], John Adam II[3], John Adam I[2], John Jacob[1]) was born May 10, 1920. She married John Paul Lally May 31, 1941, at Hagerstown, Maryland. He was the son of William T. and Sarah Sullivan Lally, and was born August 16, 1918, at Youngstown, Ohio.

(Sup) 3270   i Madlyn Van Moore Lally, born October 8, 1942.
(Sup) 3270A   ii John Paul Lally, born September 19, 1951.

No. 1687   VAUGHEN HARWOOD LINK [married Helen Louise Snively; pages 492-493]. Add their third child:

"(Sup) 3272A   iii James Andrew Link, born January 17, 1952."

No. 1688   MABEL NEWTON HENDRICKS [married Leslie Daniels Duke; page 493]. Add to text: "He died December 15, 1973, and Mabel died November 17, 1971; they are buried in Edge Hill Cemetery at Charles Town, West Virginia."

No. 1690   LEON ARNOLD HENDRICKS [page 493]. Add: "He died December 25, 1968, and is buried in Elmwood Cemetery at Sheperdstown, West Virginia."

No. 1691   LESTER MOHLER HENDRICKS [MARRIED Dorothy Angela Footen; page 493]. Add to text: "He died January 7, 1959, and she died February 25, 1969. They are buried at Cumberland, Maryland."

Nos. 1696 through 1720. Write in the book on pages 494-497, alongside No. 1696 [FREDERICK WEBSTER DECK] through No. 1720 [GENEVIEVE LUCILLE HENDRICKS], the notation "See Sup", to call attention to the following twenty-four revised entries:

(Sup) 1696   FREDERICK WEBSTER DECK (Annie[6], Sarah[5], John Adam III[4], John Adam II[3], John Adam I[2], John Jacob[1]) was born March 28, 1896, at Washington, D.C. He entered George Washington University in 1914 and left in 1917 for World War I service with the U.S. Army in France as a second lieutenant. On returning home he married Mary Evelyn Jolls, February 3, 1921. She was born December 4, 1896, in Delaware. Shortly thereafter Fred was appointed a captain and assigned with the First Engineers in the Army of Occupation at Coblentz, Germany. He was thrown from a horse, seriously injuring his spine which required his retirement from the Army. He became a design and supervising engineer for the Philadelphia Electric Company. Captain Deck continued his studies. In 1924 he received a B.A. degree from George Washington University, later the postgraduate degree of Civil Engineer from the University of Colorado, and studied for a doctor's degree in mathematics at the University of Pennsylvania. Captain Deck died September 26, 1938.

    (Sup) 3278   i   Frederick Webster Deck, Jr., born Dec 14, 1925.
    (Sup) 3279   ii   William Meade Deck, born July 22, 1928.
    (Sup) 3280 iii   John Wheaton Deck, born March 28, 1932.

(Sup) 1697   GARLAND WILSON HENDRICKS (Harvey[6], Sarah[5], John Adam III[4], John Adam II[3], John Adam I[2], John Jacob[1]) was born July 7, 1891. He married Gertrude Cournelia Willis June 7, 1930. She was born October 20, 1894.

    (Sup) 3281   i   William Hampton Hendricks, born Sept 16, 1934.

(Sup) 1698   MARGERY ETHELDA HENDRICKS (Harvey[6], Sarah[5], John Adam III[4], John Adam II[3], John Adam I[2], John Jacob[1]) was born September 14, 1892. She married David Charles Ryder, May 1, 1922. He was the son of John Francis and Mary Ellen Ryder and was born February 22, 1900. They resided at Washington, D.C., where they both worked for the U.S. Government, and he was later employed by the Whelan Drug Company. She died April 1, 1978, at Washington.

    (Sup) 3282   i   Elizabeth Margery Ryder, born March 11, 1924.
    (Sup) 3283   ii   Patricia Ann Ryder, born June 22, 1930.

(Sup) 1699   ELIZABETH JANE HENDRICKS (Harvey[6], Sarah[5], John Adam III[4], John Adam II[3], John Adam I[2], John Jacob[1]) was born August 2, 1894. She married Benjamin Franklin Hartzell June 5, 1922. He was the son of Benjamin and Lutie Baldwin Hartzell and was born March 1, 1880. Benjamin died March 14, 1957, and Elizabeth died August 20, 1971; they are buried in Elmwood Cemetery at Shepherdstown, West Virginia.

(Sup) 1700   JOHN WILLIAM HENDRICKS (Harvey[6], Sarah[5], John Adam III[4], John Adam II[3], John Adam I[2], John Jacob[1]) was born March 19, 1897. He married Bessie Hamilton Osbourn December 24, 1934. She was the daughter of John Melvin and Bessie Hamilton Poston Osbourn and was born April 8, 1911 [see The Link Family, page 645, No. 2928]. Both John and Bessie Hendricks attended Shepherd College, West Virginia. John became a farmer. He died January 14, 1972, and is buried in Elmwood Cemetery at Shepherdstown, West Virginia.

    (Sup) 3284   i   John William Hendricks, Jr., born Feb 11, 1938.
    (Sup) 3285   ii   Ruth Marie Hendricks, born January 17, 1941.
    (Sup) 3285A iii   Mary Catherine Hendricks, born December 5, 1950.

(Sup) 1701   MINNIE HAMPTON HENDRICKS (Harvey^6, Sarah^5, John Adam III^4, John Adam II^3, John Adam I^2, John Jacob^1) was born January 22, 1902. She married William Howard Albin May 6, 1933. He was the son of William and Emma Dubbee Albin and was born June 30, 1903. Minnie died December 29, 1965, and Howard died March 27, 1971. They are buried at Charles Town, West Virginia.

(Sup) 1702   ALLEN LEMEN HENDRICKS (James^6, Sarah^5, John Adam III^4, John Adam II^3, John Adam I^2, John Jacob^1) was born July 19, 1900, at the family's "Woodside" farm in Jefferson County, West Virginia. Allen attended West Virginia University and graduated from Bliss Electrical School at Washington, D.C. He received a Life Teaching Certificate from Marshall University. Allen was employed by Westinghouse at Pittsburgh, Pennsylvania before moving to Martinsburg, West Virginia, where he taught machine shop. Allen married Caroline Newton Branham June 20, 1928. She was the daughter of William Ewell and Margaret Lemen Branham of Berkeley County, West Virginia, and was born July 20, 1903. Caroline graduated in 1921 from Shepherd College, West Virginia, and taught school for several years. Allen and Caroline lived at Martinsburg.

    (Sup) 3286   i Margaret Louise Hendricks, born Oct 15, 1929.

(Sup) 1703   KENNETH HENDRICKS ENGLE (Esther^6, Sarah^5, John Adam III^4, John Adam II^3, John Adam I^2, John Jacob^1) was born October 15, 1899, at Bakerton, Jefferson County, West Virginia. He attended Shepherd College, West Virginia, which he left to serve in World War I. Kenneth married Vera Mae Young March 17, 1926. He died July 25, 1947, and is buried in Edge Hill Cemetery at Charles Town, West Virginia.

    (Sup) 3287   i Janice Marie Engle, born November 1, 1928.
    (Sup) 3288   ii Ann Considine Engle, born May 6, 1931.

(Sup) 1704   JESSIE RUTHVEN ENGLE (Esther^6, Sarah^5, John Adam III^4, John Adam II^3, John Adam I^2, John Jacob^1) was born November 25, 1900. He married Dorothy Frances Phillips June 6, 1942. She was born May 23, 1907.

(Sup) 1705   DANIEL EVANS ENGLE (Esther^6, Sarah^5, John Adam III^4, John Adam II^3, John Adam I^2, John Jacob^1) was born February 19, 1903, at Bakerton, Jefferson County, West Virginia. He graduated from Shepherd College, West Virginia, and taught school before entering West Virginia University where he received a B.S degree in mechanical engineering. He was employed by United Engineers of New York City and Philadelphia before joining the Firestone Tire and Rubber Company at Akron, Ohio. Daniel helped establish plants in Europe, Asia, South America, Cuba, Canada, and the United States. He retired as assistant chief engineer February, 1968, after thirty-three years. Daniel married, first, Jean Frances Linton of Akron, Ohio. She was the daughter of Frank Linton and was born August 10, 1910. Jean died December 31, 1965. Daniel married, second, Grace Jeffries Fissel May 12, 1967. Grace was the widow of John Edwin Fissel of Baltimore, Maryland. She was the daughter of Edgar and Nora Jeffries and was born at Kingwood, West Virginia. She attended West Virginia University and became a school teacher.

CHILD OF DANIEL AND JEAN
    (Sup) 3289   i Barbara Jean Engle, born January 29, 1939.

(Sup) 1706 JAMES PRESTON MURRAY ENGLE (Esther[6], Sarah[5], John Adam III[4], John Adam II[3], John Adam I[2], John Jacob[1]) was born November 14, 1909, in Jefferson County, West Virginia. Preston graduated from West Virgina University with a B.S. degree in chemistry and worked on development of ferro-alloys for ship construction. He was employed by the Atomic Energy Commission and became involved with development of USS Nautilus, the first nuclear-powered submarine. He was also engaged in steam power generation. Preston had thirty technical publications and was granted five U.S. patents. He married, first, Ann Smith McMillan April 12, 1934, of Scottsdale, New York. Ann died December 6, 1976, and is buried at Tulsa, Oklahoma. Preston married, second, Mina Coombes of Stafford, Oklhoma May 19 1977, at London, England.

    (Sup) 3290   i Preston Murray Engle, born April 12, 1939.
    (Sup) 3291   ii Jean Catherine Engle, born August 5, 1943.

(Sup) 1707 JAMES ALLEN MADISON ENGLE (Esther[6], Sarah[5], John Adam III[4], John Adam II[3], John Adam I[2], John Jacob[1]) was born August 12, 1913, in Jefferson County, West Virginia. He attended West Virginia University. Madison married, first, Betty Jo Knapp October 21, 1939. She was born June 10, 1921. He married, second, Maude Enoch of Kentucky. Madison died December 25, 1967, and is buried at St. Petersburg, Florida.

CHILD OF MADISON AND BETTY JO
(Sup) 3292 Bruce Allen Engle, born November 14, 1941.

(Sup) 1708 CORA VIRGINIA HENDRICKS (LeRoy[6], Sarah[5], John Adam III[4], John Adam II[3], John Adam I[2], John Jacob[1]) was born January 17, 1901. She died March 10, 1910.

(Sup) 1709 REBECCA LEE HENDRICKS (LeRoy[6], Sarah[5], John Adam III[4], John Adam II[3], John Adam I[2], John Jacob[1]) was born July 2, 1903, in Jefferson County, West Virginia. She married Kenneth Brooks Moler October 20, 1924. He was born April 13, 1897. They were divorced, and he married, second, Edna Mason December 23, 1933. Kenneth died August, 1958 and is buried at Clarksburg, West Virginia. Rebecca died June 8, 1982, and is buried in Elmwood Cemetery at Shepherdstown, West Virginia.

    (Sup) 3293   i Rebecca Lee Moler, born October 24, 1926.

(Sup) 1710 MARGUARITE HENDRICKS (LeRoy[6], Sarah[5], John Adam III[4], John Adam II[3], John Adam I[2], John Jacob[1]) was born June 1, 1916.

(Sup) 1711 GILBERT LEO HENDRICKS (Daniel[6], Sarah[5], John Adam III[4], John Adam II[3], John Adam I[2], John Jacob[1]) was born November 25, 1899, at Bakerton, Jefferson County, West Virginia. He married Evelyn Elizabeth Maddox June 5, 1924. She was the daughter of Benjamin Ewell and Clarissa Virginia Derr Maddox and was born July 21, 1901, at Uvilla, Jefferson County. Gilbert and Evelyn both graduated from Shepherd College, West Virginia, and became teachers. He opened a general merchandise store at Duffields, Jefferson County, and served as the postmaster there. He retired to his "Clear Land" farm nearby. Daniel died September 19, 1970, and is buried in Elmwood Cemetery at Shepherdstown, West Virginia.

    (Sup) 3294   i Evelyn Maddox Hendricks, born May 19, 1929.
    (Sup) 3295   ii Gilbert Leo Hendricks, Jr., born July 10, 1931.
    (Sup) 3296 iii Daniel Ewell Hendricks, born April 23, 1934.
    (Sup) 3297   iv Sarah Virginia Ann Hendricks, born July 27, 1936.

(Sup) 1712   MARY VIRGINIA HENDRICKS (Daniel[6], Sarah[5], John Adam III[4], John Adam II[3], John Adam I[2], John Jacob[1]) was born May 7, 1902, at Bakerton, Jefferson County, West Virginia. She attended Shepherd College, West Virginia, then became a nurse to tend the wounded who came home from World War I. Mary married Alvin Meredith Ennis, June 18, 1920. He was the son of Thomas Covington and Ella May Darlington Ennis and was born August 17, 1900, at Charles Town, West Virginia. Alvin was a barber. He died June 15, 1969, and Mary died April 26, 1980, both at Charles Town.

    (Sup) 3298   i   Pearl Hendricks Ennis, born March 30, 1921.
    (Sup) 3299   ii Alvin Meredith Ennis, Jr., born March 21, 1924.

    (Sup) 1713   ANNA LOUISE HENDRICKS (Daniel[6], Sarah[5], John Adam III[4], John Adam II[3], John Adam I[2], John Jacob[1]) was born February 1, 1905. She attended Shepherd College, West Virginia, before entering nurses' training. Anna married, first, Edward Crawford McAmis June 5, 1924. He was the son of James and Ida Crawford McAmis and was born April, 1984, in Kentucky. Edward died January 21, 1927, at Washington, D.C. Anna married, second, a Mr. Davis at Washington. They were divorced. She married, third, Romley Harvill in June, 1929; he was from Georgia. Anna married, fourth, James Edgar Edwards. James was the son of Edgar Massey and Eda May Bolling Edwards and was born June 10, 1903, at Culpepper, Virginia.

                    CHILD OF ANNA AND EDWARD
    (Sup) 3300   i   Edward Crawford McAmis, Jr., born Aug 10, 1926.

                    CHILD OF ANNA AND JAMES
    (Sup) 3301   ii James Edgar Edwards, Jr., born April 20, 1943.

    (Sup) 1714   ESTHER LINK HENDRICKS (Daniel[6], Sarah[5], John Adam III[4], John Adam II[3], John Adam I[2], John Jacob[1]) was born November 15, 1907, at Uvilla, Jefferson County, West Virginia. She graduated from Shepherd College, West Virginia, and taught school. Esther married Glenn Elmo Crane March 4, 1927. He was the son of Charles Jacob and Sarah Harper Crane and was born February 21, 1904, at Georgetown, West Virginia. Glenn and Esther resided at Hagerstown, Maryland. He died January 13, 1957, at Hagerstown.

    (Sup) 3302   i   Bruce Melvin Crane, born January 4, 1928.
    (Sup) 3303   ii   Reva Jean Crane, born August 24, 1929.
    (Sup) 3304   iii Hilda Joyce Crane, born October 26, 1931.
    (Sup) 3305   iv   Richard Lee Crane, born October 8, 1935.
    (Sup) 3306   v   Robert Curtis Crane, born November 6, 1945.

    (Sup) 1715   FLORENCE GERTRUDE HENDRICKS (Daniel[6], Sarah[5], John Adam III[4], John Adam II[3], John Adam I[2], John Jacob[1]) was born June 9, 1910, at Uvilla, Jefferson County, West Virginia. She graduated from Martinsburg Business College with a degree in business administration and worked as a secretary. She married Charles William Moore June 9, 1936, at Harrisonburg, Virginia. He was the son of Charles Henry and Alice Gardner Moore and was born October 15, 1897. Charles was a farmer and auction sale clerk. In 1950 Florence and Charles bought the old hospital buliding at Charles Town, Virginia, and opened the first of the three nursing homes now at at Charles Town. Later Florence worked in the trust department of the Bank of Charles Town. She was active in the Daughters of the American Revolution, serving as State Treasurer, Vice Regent, Regent, and Vice President General. Charles died February 3, 1979, and is buried in Edge Hill Cemetery at Charles Town.

    (Sup) 3307   i   Sara Lee Moore, born October 1, 1937.
    (Sup) 3308   ii   Lou Ellen Moore, born September 1, 1941.
    (Sup) 3309   iii Mary Alice Moore, born July 1, 1944.
    (Sup) 3310   iv   Lucy Hendricks Moore, born January 11, 1949.

(Sup) 1716   DANIEL WEBSTER HENDRICKS, III (Daniel[6], Sarah[5], John Adam III[4], John Adam II[3], John Adam I[2], John Jacob[1]) was born October 11, 1912, at Uvilla, Jefferson County, West Virginia. He married Margaret Ellen Polhamus June 6, 1934. She was the daughter of Clinton Maynard and Sarah Ethel Dutterer Polhamus and was born March 8, 1914, at Berryville, Virginia. Daniel was a merchant at Shenandoah Junction, Jefferson County. He drowned in a motor boat accident on the Potomac River July 29, 1947, and is buried in Elmwood Cemetery at Shepherdstown, West Virginia. Margaret married, second, John C. (Happy) Myers. John was born in 1898. He died in 1981.

    (Sup) 3311   i   Daniel Webster Hendricks, IV, born May 30, 1935.
    (Sup) 3312   ii   Sarah Magaret Hendricks, born January 3, 1938.
    (Sup) 3313 iii   Mary Ellen Hendricks, born October 11, 1945.

(Sup) 1717   SARAH EVELYN HENDRICKS (Daniel[6], Sarah[5], John Adam III[4], John Adam II[3], John Adam I[2], John Jacob[1]) was born October 20, 1915, at Uvilla, Jefferson County, West Virginia. She married Woodrow Wilson Sims July 26, 1934. He was the son of John William and Minnie Watkins Sims and was born December 12, 1912, at Charles City, Virginia. Evelyn and Woodrow were divorced. She worked for the telephone company at Washington, D.C.; after retirement she resided at Silver Spring, Maryland.

    (Sup) 3314   i   John Robert Sims, born October 9, 1936.

(Sup) 1718   WILLIAM KNOX HENDRICKS (Daniel[6], Sarah[5], John Adam III[4], John Adam II[3], John Adam I[2], John Jacob[1]) was born September 17, 1917, at Uvilla, Jefferson County, West Virginia. He married Dorothy Beele Foxworth September 1, 1941. She was the daughter of Benjamin Franklin and Tula Mabel Collins Foxworth and was born January 1, 1921, at Florence, South Carolina. William and Dorothy lived at Hopewell, Virginia, where he was a Government .purchasing agent.

    (Sup) 3315   i   Rebecca Ann Hendricks, born August 10, 1942.
    (Sup) 3316   ii   William Knox Hendricks, Jr., born Mar 17, 1944.
    (Sup) 3317 iii   John Wayne Hendricks, born May 31, 1946.
    (Sup) 3317A iv   Kenneth Lee Hendricks, born January 26, 1950.

(Sup) 1719   REBECCA DANIELS HENDRICKS (Daniel[6], Sarah[5], John Adam III[4], John Adam II[3], John Adam I[2], John Jacob[1]) was born November 11, 1919, at Uvilla, Jefferson County, West Virginia. She attended Shepherd College, West Virginia, and then taught school at Winchester, Virgina. Rebecca married Walter Merlin Bly November 11, 1939. He was the son of Jesse Franklin and Vernie May Keller Bly and was born September 5, 1917, in Frederick County, Virginia. Walter was employed by the Veterans Administration at Winchester. Rebecca died August 3, 1966, at Charlottesville, Virginia, and is buried in Elmwood Cemetery at Shepherdstown, West Virgina. Merlin married, second, Margaret Coyle Marshall, widow of Paxson Marshall of Jefferson County.

    (Sup) 3318   i   Martha Ann Bly, born April 10, 1941.

(Sup) 1720   GENEVIEVE LUCILLE HENDRICKS (Daniel[6], Sarah[5], John Adam III[4], John Adam II[3], John Adam I[2], John Jacob[1]) was born June 16, 1923, at Uvilla, Jefferson County, West Virginia. She attended Shepherd College, West Virginia, and taught school in the area of Winchester, Virginia. Lucille married Donald Maxwell Walter, Jr., March 23, 1946. He was the son of Donald Maxwell and Eleanor Wilkins Walter and was born July 24, 1924, at Washington, D.C. Donald was in the real estate business at Winchester. Later he and Lucille operated a private ambulance service.

    (Sup) 3319   i   Donald Maxwell Walter, III, born June 7, 1947.
    (Sup) 3320   ii   Julia Ann Walter, born July 24, 1949.

No. 1724 DOROTHY THELMA LINK MYERS [married Stanley Earl Eye; pages 497-498]. Add to text: "He died September 30, 1977, and is buried in Edge Hill Cemetery at Charles Town, West Virginia."

No. 1726 VIRGINIA LEE MYERS [page 493]. Add: "She married Ralph Bush".

No. 1862 LEWIS WILBERFORCE LINK [page 511]. Add to text: "Lewis died May 2, 1987, at Doylestown, Pennsylvania."

No. 1863 EUGENE BOWERS LINK [married Amanda Maccubbin; page 511]. Add to text: "Eugene died May 28, 1973, and Amanda died January 18, 1977, Baltimore County, Maryland."

Nos. 1864 and 1865. Write in the book on pages 511-512, alongside No. 1864 [MARIE ELIZABETH LINK] and No. 1865 [RALPH AUBREY LINK], the notation "See Sup" to call attention to the following two revised entries:

(Sup) 1864   MARIE ELIZABETH LINK (Adam[6], Daniel[5], Adam[4], Daniel[3], John Adam I[2], John Jacob[1]) was born October 16, 1894, at Westminster, Maryland. She married, first, Frederick Allen Zumstein June 12, 1915. He was the son of Franklin and Sarah Jane (White) Zumstein and was born January 15, 1891. Marie and Frederick resided at Baltimore. He died October 24, 1918. She married, second, Theodore Hahn Ascherfeld January 25, 1944. Theodore was the son of Frederick and Letatia (Cousins) Asherfeld and was born October 9, 1888. Theodore died July 14, 1961, at Baltimore.

(Sup) 3443   i Grace Marie Zumstein, born April 9, 1916.
(Sup) 3444   ii Jane White Zumstein, born December 25, 1917.

(Sup) 1865   RALPH AUBREY LINK (Adam[6], Daniel[5], Adam[4], Daniel[3], John Adam I[2], John Jacob[1]) was born January 9, 1899, at Baltimore, Maryland. He married Mabel Louise Thalheimer, January 7, 1922. They were divorced in 1937. Ralph married, second, Frances Lydia Perry on May 14, 1951. She was born October 20, 1931. Ralph died May 28, 1969.

CHILDREN OF RALPH AND FRANCES
(Sup) 3444A   i Grace Ruth Link, born October 8, 1953.
(Sup) 3444B   ii Rebekah Elizabeth Link, born December 23, 1969.

Nos. 1956 to 1959. Write in the book on page 524, alongside No. 1956 [JOHN CHRISTIAN HULVEY, JR.], No. 1958 [BENJAMIN FRANKLIN HULVEY], and No. 1959 [CHARLES NEWTON HULVEY], the notation: "See Sup", to call attention to the following three revised entries:

(Sup) 1956   JOHN CHRISTIAN HULVEY, JR. (Elizabeth[6], Susan[5], John[4], Peter[3], Matthias[2], John Jacob[1]) was born September 2, 1879, in Augusta County, Virginia. He married Effie Greiner October 16, 1901, in Augusta County, Virginia. Effie was the daughter of Edward Granville and Martha Mowry Greiner and was born November 1, 1878, in Augusta County, Virginia. She died November 10, 1908, shortly after the birth of their twins, and she is buried at Pleasant View Lutheran Cemetery in Augusta County.   John married, second, Jane Fifer.

CHILDREN OF JOHN AND EFFIE
(Sup) 3636A   i   Virginia Hulvey, born September 13, 1902.
(Sup) 3636B   ii   Effie Thelma Hulvey, born Nov 9, 1908 (twin).
(Sup) 3636C   iii Tululu Hulvey, born November 9, 1908 (twin).

CHILDREN OF JOHN AND JANE
(Sup) 3636D   iv   John William Hulvey, born October 21, 1914.
(Sup) 3636E   v   Margaret Hulvey, born October 21, 1915.
(Sup) 3636F   vi   Helen Hulvey, born January 28, 1925.
(Sup) 3636G   vii Grace Hulvey, born December 27, 1928.

(Sup) 1958   BENJAMIN FRANKLIN HULVEY (Elizabeth[6], Susan[5], John[4], Peter[3], Matthias[2], John Jacob[1]) was born February 10, 1884, in Augusta County, Virginia. He married Lucy Sutton February 15, 1906, at Staunton, Virginia. She was born November 18, 1889, and died July 14, 1915. Benjamin died April 10, 1951, at Staunton.

(Sup) 3636H   i   Benjamin Franklin Hulvey Jr., born July 6, 1907.
(Sup) 3636I   ii   Mary Elizabeth Hulvey, born July 28, 1909.
(Sup) 3636J   iii Gladys Maude Hulvey, born December 18, 1910.
(Sup) 3636K   iv   Margaret Christine Hulvey, born July 1, 1913.
(Sup) 3636L   v   Howard M. Hulvey, born June 21, 1915.

(Sup) 1959   CHARLES NEWTON HULVEY (Elizabeth[6], Susan[5], John[4], Peter[3], Matthias[2], John Jacob[1]) was born April 2, 1887, in Augusta County, Virginia. He married Pearl Pickel in June, 1909, at Sweetwater, Tennessee. She was the daughter of William Wilkerson and Nancy Ann Cook Pickel. Charles was in the regular U.S. Army, retiring as a major with a medical disability in 1920. He then attended the University of Virginia, from which he attained a Master's Degree and LL.B. He became a professor in the School of Commerce at the University. He died May 18, 1937, and Pearl died in 1977. They are buried in the University of Virginia Cemetery at Charlottesville.

(Sup) 3636M   i   Charles Newton Hulvey, Jr., born May 13, 1913.
(Sup) 3636N   ii   Margaret Ann Hulvey, born November 6, 1915.
(Sup) 3636P   iii John William Hulvey, born April 5, 1921.

No. 1984 SIDNEY CHESTER LINK [pages 526-527]. Add to text: "Sidney died October 13, 1963, at Rockford, Illinois, and is buried at La Harpe, Illinois."

Nos. 1994 through 2003. Write in the book on pages 528-529, alongside No. 1994 [PEARL ELIZABETH LINK] through No. 2003 [WILLIAM LLOYD LINK], the following notation: "See Sup", to call attention to the following ten revised entries:

(Sup) 1994   PEARL ELIZABETH LINK (Frank[6], John[5], John[4], Peter[3], Matthias[2], John Jacob[1]) was born June 3, 1900, in Delaware County, Ohio. She married Theodore Baker January 1, 1921. He was born in 1896 and died April 15, 1977. Pearl died March 31, 1984.

    (Sup) 3693A   i   James Edwin Baker, born December 27, 1921.
    (Sup) 3693B   ii   David Theodore Baker, born August 28, 1924.
    (Sup) 3693C   iii   Carl Wilfred Baker, born September 24, 1925.
    (Sup) 3693D   iv   Alfred Wallace Baker, born February 19, 1929.
    (Sup) 3693E   v   Thomas Quentin Baker, born March 23, 1931.
    (Sup) 3693F   vi   Marilyn Jean Baker, born May 29, 1933.
    (Sup) 3693G   vii   Rita Carolyn Baker, born January 25, 1936.
    (Sup) 3693H   viii Sharon Elizabeth Baker, born August 31, 1942.

(Sup) 1995   ZELLA IRENE LINK (Frank[6], John[5], John[4], Peter[3], Matthias[2], John Jacob[1]) was born November 29, 1902, in Delaware County, Ohio. She married Shirley Arnold Terry, August 30, 1922, at Columbus, Ohio. Arnold was the son of Isaac Lee Terry and was born March 23, 1903, in Mason County, West Virginia. He died June 30, 1979.

    (Sup) 3693I   i   Ivor Floyd Terry, born April 13, 1923.
    (Sup) 3693J   ii   Harold Henry Terry, born June 2, 1924.
    (Sup) 3693K   iii   Frank Lee Terry, born August 13, 1926.
    (Sup) 3693L   iv   Elsie Elizabeth Terry, born August 24, 1928.
    (Sup) 3693M   v   Paul Earl Terry, born April 26, 1932.
    (Sup) 3693N   vi   Kenneth Eldon Terry, born April 2, 1933.
    (Sup) 3693P   vii   Dale Arnold Terry, born September 5, 1935.
    (Sup) 3693Q   viii Esther June Terry, born March 21, 1938.
    (Sup) 3693R   ix   Vinal Ray Terry, born October 1, 1940.
    (Sup) 3693S   x   Donald Alvin Terry, born October 31, 1941.
    (Sup) 3693T   xi   Sandra Lee Terry, born Jnuary 3, 1944.

(Sup) 1996   CARRIE LUCILLE LINK (Frank[6], John[5], John[4], Peter[3], Matthias[2], John Jacob[1]) was born December 16, 1904, in Delaware County, Ohio. She married Carroll Clyde Welch, July 3, 1926. He was the son of Clyde Welch and was born in Delaware County, February 23, 1904. Carrie and Carroll lived at Wildwood, Florida.

    (Sup) 3694   i   John Carroll Welch, born August 18, 1930.
    (Sup) 3695   ii   Jerry Link Welch, born October 27, 1935.

(Sup) 1997   JOHN RAYMOND LINK (Frank[6], John[5], John[4], Peter[3], Matthias[2], John Jacob[1]) was born October 19, 1907, in Delaware County, Ohio. He married Anna Lucille Mooney, August 20, 1929. She was born March 5, 1914. Raymond died March 5, 1966. Lucille married, second, John Emerson Riggin June 22, 1968. She died June 25, 1977.

    (Sup) 3695A   i   John Raymond Link, Jr., born June 10, 1933.
    (Sup) 3695B   ii   Robert Eugene Link, born December 27, 1936.
    (Sup) 3695C   iii   Nancy Muriel Link, born June 22, 1939.
    (Sup) 3695D   iv   Philip Allen Link, born September 24, 1941.
    (Sup) 3695E   v   Nita Louise Link, born July 8, 1945.

(Sup) 1998   ANNA MARIE LINK (Frank[6], John[5], John[4], Peter[3], Matthias[2], John Jacob[1]) was born February 28, 1911, at Sunbury, Delaware County, Ohio. She married Harry Max Daugherty, December 24, 1943, at Petaluma, California. He was born August 17, 1916, at London, Ohio. Anna Marie and Harry resided at Columbus, Ohio. She collected the extensive information on the descendents of Frank and Elsie Barton Link [Supplement Nos. 1994-1998].

    (Sup) 3695F   i   Philip Lee Daugherty, born February 3, 1947.
    (Sup) 3695G   ii   Susan Jane Daugherty, born July 8, 1948.

(Sup) 1999   KENNETH IVAN LINK (Frank[6], John[5], John[4], Peter[3], Matthias[2], John Jacob[1]) was born May 29, 1913, at Sunbury, Delaware County, Ohio. He married Maxine Claire Perfect, January 1, 1936, at Cardington, Ohio. She was the daughter of Clyde Perfect and was born September 15, 1914.

    (Sup) 3696   i   Suzanne Jane Link, born September 5, 1937.
    (Sup) 3697   ii Sherry Lynne Link, born August 5, 1939.
    (Sup) 3698   iii Stephan Kenneth Link, born August 24, 1943.
    (Sup) 3699   iv Linda Claire Link, born December 9, 1945.

(Sup) 2000   VINAL THURSTON LINK (Frank[6], John[5], John[4], Peter[3], Matthias[2], John Jacob[1]) was born October 8, 1914, in Delaware County, Ohio. He married Edna Krieger, June 15, 1940, at Columbus, Ohio. She was the daughter of Carl Krieger and was born November 19, 1909, at Columbus. Vinal and Edna lived at Sunbury, Ohio.

    (Sup) 3700   i Richard Louis Link, born June 1, 1941.
    (Sup) 3701   ii Donna Kay Link, born October 4, 1944.

(Sup) 2001   CHARLOTTE JUNE LINK (Frank[6], John[5], John[4], Peter[3], Matthias[2], John Jacob[1]) was born June 1, 1917, in Delaware County, Ohio. She married Harold Pittman, November 13, 1937, at Covington, Kentucky. He was born November 10, 1917, in Delaware County, Ohio. Charlotte and Harold lived at Delaware, Ohio, where he was a farmer.

    (Sup) 3702   i Carolyn June Pittman, born May 9, 1939.
    (Sup) 3703   ii Harold Edgar pittman, born July 21, 1941.

(Sup) 2002   JAMES FRANKLIN LINK (Frank[6], John[5], John[4], Peter[3], Matthias[2], John Jacob[1]) was born August 5, 1920, at Sunbury, Delaware County, Ohio. He married Betty Postle, June 15, 1942, at Centerburg, Ohio. She was born November 15, 1920, at Columbus, Ohio. James and Betty lived at Kilbourne, Ohio.

    (Sup) 3704   i Pamela Jo Link, born November 6, 1944.
    (Sup) 3704A   ii Wendy Sue Link, born April 9, 1949.

(Sup) 2003   WILLIAM LLOYD LINK (Frank[6], John[5], John[4], Peter[3], Matthias[2], John Jacob[1]) was born August 23, 1923, in Delaware County, Ohio. He married Sarah Jean Arthur, October 23, 1943, at Mount Gilead, Ohio. She was born March 3, 1923, in Delaware County.

    (Sup) 3705   i Victoria Ann Link, born March 3, 1947.
    (Sup) 3705A   ii William Lloyd Link, Jr., born January 9, 1952.

No. 2018. Write in the book on page 530, alongside No. 2018 [EMERY DALE LEFLER], the notation: "See Sup", to call attention to the following revised entry:

(Sup) 2018   EMERY DALE LEFLER (Ethel[6], John[5], John[4], Peter[3], Matthias[2], John Jacob[1]) was born March 14, 1926, at La Harpe, Illinois. He married Jo Ann Penn, June 14, 1952, at Dayton, Ohio. She was the daughter of Chester and Marie Penn and was born November 3, 1927.

    (Sup) 3705B   i Kenneth Alan Lefler, born June 12, 1953.
    (Sup) 3705C   ii Randall Eugene Lefler, born April 9, 1956.

No. 2153   HORACE LINK [married Martha Maud Rude; pages 459-550]. Add to text: "Maud died October 10, 1953, and Horace died February 11, 1960; they are buried in Edgar Cemetery at Paris, Illinois."

No. 2154   JOANNA CHRISTIE LINK [married James Edwin Vance; page 550]. Add: "Edwin died March, 1960, and is buried in Edgar Cemetery."

No. 2155   TATT LINK [married Arthur Jones; page 550]. Correct the seventh sentence to read: "... Madame Rachel Edgar chapter of D.A.R." Add after last sentence: "Tatt died February 26, 1966, and is buried in Edgar Cemetery."

No. 2162   LINDER LINK [page 552]. Add: "Linder died March, 1961, and is buried in Maple Park Cemetery at Springfield."

No. 2163   HUSTON CHRISTOPHER LINK [page 552]. Add: "He died February, 1958, and is buried in Oak Grove Cemetery at St. Louis."

No. 2164   KATHRYN LINK [married Frank Patterson Chambers; page 552]. Add to text: "Kathryn died September 3, 1967, and Frank died August 30, 1985; they are buried in Maple Park Cemetery at Springfield."

No. 2167   BESS LINK married Karl Barr; page 553]. Add to text: "She died August, 1959, and is buried in Edgar Cemetery at Paris, Illinois."

No. 2171   MARY MAGDALENE SMITH married Robert Nevins Parrish; page 553]. Correct her birth date, to read "September 30, 1980." Robert was the son of "James Edward and Hallie (Shepherd) Parrish ..." Replace the last sentence of the text, with: "Robert died December 6, 1940, at Kankakee, Illinois, and Mary died November 16, 1970, at Ashland, Kentucky; they are buried in Edgar Cemetery at Paris, Illinois."

No. 2183   FRED PARRISH [page 555]. Add to text: "Fred died July, 1958, and is buried in Edgar Cemetery."

No. 2185 MARY PARRISH [married John Crandall; page 556]. Add: "She died in 1968, and he died in 1975; they are buried in Edgar Cemetery at Paris, Illinois."

No. 2186 EDGAR PARRISH [married Ruth Curtis; page 556]. Add to text: "Edgar died June, 1962, and Ruth died November, 1976; they are buried in Edgar Cemetery at Paris, Illinois."

No. 2187 NILA LINK [married Homer Winn; page 556]. Add to text: "Homer died May, 1956, and Nila died February 2, 1970; they are buried in Edgar Cemetery at Paris, Illinois."

No. 2188 MARION HENRY LINK [married (2) Alma Wilhelmina Mills; page 556]. Add to text: "He died August 22, 1962, and Alma died November 27, 1970; they are buried in Edgar Cemetery at Paris, Illinois."

No. 2189. Write in the book on page 557, alongside No. 2189 [WENDELL A. LINK], the notation "See Sup", to call attention to the following revised entry:

(Sup) 2189 WENDELL ATHEY LINK (Nethaniah[6], Francis Marion[5], Peter[4], Peter[3], Matthias[2], John Jacob[1]) was born September 5, 1893, at Paris, Illinois. After his schooling he associated with his father in the manufacture of pharmaceuticals until World War II, when he went into camp recreation work for the benefit of enlisted men. He served in the armed forces. After World War II Wendall entered the real estate business. He married, first, Alline Hubbard, November 18, 1921. She was the daughter of John Hubbard. In 1942 he married, second, Elizabeth Parsons, daughter of John Parsons. Elizabeth was a teacher. After Wendall retired from the U.S. Government in 1958, they moved to Port St. Lucie, Florida. He died August 5, 1961, and Elizabeth died July 3, 1982, at Port St. Lucie.

CHILDREN OF WENDALL AND ALLINE
(Sup) 3892   i Wendall Hubbard Link, born September 27, 1922.
(Sup) 3893   ii Patricia Alline Link, born August 12, 1928.

No. 2190 EUGENE P. LINK [married Beulah Meyer; pages 557-558]. Add to text: "Eugene and Beulah resided at Plattsburgh, New York. She was noted for her lectures on Eleanor Roosevelt. Eugene retired form the State University of New York in 1977. He authored Labor-Religion Prophet, published in 1984, and The Social Ideas of American Physicians, 1988. A state scholarship to aid needy and able students was named for him, and an award for students in literature at Midland College, Nebraska, was named in honor of Beulah Meyer Link." Add their third child:

"(Sup) 3895A iii Bruce George Link, born September 5, 1949."

No. 2191 LIDA BELLE LINK [married George Schwegler; page 558]. Correct the spelling of her name, to "Lida Belle Link." Add their third child:

"(Sup) 3897A   iii Thomas Link Schwegler."

No. 2193 ANTON HULMAN LINK [page 559]. Add: "He died November 26, 1970, and is buried in Edgar Cemetery at Paris, Illinois."

No. 2194 BLANCHE LINK [married William Franklin Foley; page 559]. Add to text: "William died March 18, 1957, and Blanche died August 7, 1973; they are buried in Edgar Cemetery at Paris, Illinois."

No. 2196 WILLIAM FRANCIS LINK [page 559]. Add: "He died June 14, 1979, and is buried in Edgar Cemetery at Paris, Illinois."

No. 2239 JOSEPHINE OWEN LINK [pages 563-564]. Add to text: "In 1970 she married, third, Martin L. Luther, in Florida. Josephine died March 2, 1979, at Gulf Stream, Florida; her ashes are buried at Lakewood Cemetery, Minneapolis, Minnesota."

Nos. 2247 through 2249. Write in the book on pages 565-566, alongside No. 2247 [GEORGE THERON LINK], through No. 2249 [MARILYN CALMES LINK], the notation "See Sup", to call attention to the following three revised entries:

(Sup) 2247   GEORGE THERON LINK (Edwin[6], George[5], Matthias[4], Peter[3], Matthias[2], John Jacob[1]) was born January 28, 1897, at Chicago, Illinois. He attended Hamilton College, New York, where he was elected to Phi Beta Kappa in his junior year and received his B.A degree in 1918. After discharge from Army service as a 2nd lieutenant in World War I, he was employed by the Traveler's Insurance Company 1919-1922 and then managed the Link Piano Company for his father. In January, 1935, George joined his brother, Edwin, in founding Link Aviation Devices, Inc., at Binghamton, New York, to manufacture the famous Link Trainer and other aeronautical devices. George became vice president and treasurer of the company, which grew from a modest beginning to annual sales in excess of $12,000,000. George married Virginia Ellington January 25, 1922. She was the daughter of Bayard H. Ellington and was born May 7, 1899, at Richmond, Virginia. George and Virginia resided at Binghamton, New York, where he was director of the Marine Midland Bank, Vice Chairman of the Board of the Salvation Army, and a member of many service and social organizations. They later retired to Florida. George died July 19, 1977, at Fort Lauderdale, Florida, and Virginia died November 28, 1979, at her daughter's home at Wellesley, Massachusetts; they are buried in Vestal Hills Memorial Park at Binghamton, New York.

(Sup) 3933   i Virginia Ellington Link, born January 28, 1924.

(Sup) 2248   EDWIN ALBERT LINK, JR. (Edwin[6], George[5], Matthias[4], Peter[3], Matthias[2], John Jacob[1]) was born July 26, 1904, at Huntington, Indiana. At the age of six he moved with his parents to Binghamton, New York, where his father was part owner and manager of the Link Piano Company. Edwin, Jr., attended Bellefonte Academy, Pennsylvania; Lindsley Institute at Wheeling, West Virginia; and Los Angeles Polytechnic High School. He then returned to Binghamton, where he was employed in his father's factory producing pianos and theatre organs.

At the age of 23 Edwin learned to fly and began to search for a more efficient means of flight training. He spent the winter of 1927-28 experimenting in the organ factory with wind vents and other devices, and he and his brother George invented a training machine that simulated an airplane in flight. He founded a flying school, which by 1931 had 150 students; however, the depression in 1932 resulted in diminished classes.

Meanwhile, the trainers had come become popular in amusement parks. A few had been sold to air transport lines in the U.S. and Europe; in 1930 the Navy bought one, and in 1932 the Army ordered six. In 1934 the Army Air Corps was suddenly called upon to carry U.S. mail, and nearly a dozen Army pilots were killed in one week. The aviation world was stunned into the need for instrument training. Link Aviation, Inc., founded by Edwin and his brother George, were swamped with inquiries. From the end of 1934 their factory was on a production schedule which grew to huge proportions during World War II. The Link flight simulator was used eventually to train more than two million aviators, including 500,000 pilots during World War II.

Edwin was a co-author with Captain P. V. H. Weems of "Simplified Celestial Navigation", which was published in 1940, and which became a standard text for the armed services flying schools. Deep-sea exploration was one of his avocations. He invented deep-submergence equipment and was a co-founder of the Harbor Branch Foundation for oceanographic research. In 1958 Edwin Link established the Link Foundation, which awarded research grants in aeronautics and oceanography to more than 120 universities and other non-profit institutions.

Mr. Link was president and board chairman of Link Aviation until its merger with the General Precision Corporation in 1954. He was president and a director of General Precision until its merger with the Singer Company of Stamford, Connecticut, in 1968. Thereafter, he was a consultant to Singer.

Edwin married Marion Elizabeth Clayton June 6, 1931, at Ilion, New York. She was the daughter of Floyd A. and Elma Gray Clayton and was born November 15, 1907, at Ilion. She was secretary of Link Aviation Devices, Inc. Edwin and Marion resided at Binghamton, New York, and later also at Fort Pierce, Florida.

Edwin Link was honored with the Charles Lindbergh Award for contributions in science and technology, and by the Franklin Institute, the Smithsonian Institute, the Royal Society of Aeronautics of London, and the State University of New York at Binghamton which awarded him an honorary degree in science. Edwin died September 7, 1981, at his home at Binghamton.

(Sup) 3934   i William Martin Link, born January 1, 1938.
(Sup) 3935   ii Edwin Clayton Link, born November 30, 1941.

(Sup) 2249   MARILYN CALMES LINK (Edwin[6], George[5], Matthias[4], Peter[3], Matthias[2], John Jacob[1]) was born February 20, 1924, at Glendale, California. After her schooling she studied navigation and flying and became a registered commercial pilot. In 1949 she received a master's degree from the University of Illinois. She made her home at Binghamton, New York, and later at Vero Beach, Florida.

No. 2508 FRANK OVERTON HARRIS [page 596]. Add to text: "Frank died December 8, 1961, and is buried in Sunset Memorial Park, South Charleston, West Virginia."

No. 2509 DAISY SHEPPARD HARRIS [pages 596-597]. Add: "Daisy (who was called Margaret) died March 18, 1939, and is buried in Sunset Memorial Park, South Charleston, West Virginia."

No. 2510 ROBERT WILLIAMSON HARRIS [married Lyda Chambers; page 597]. Add to text: "Robert died August 16, 1971, and Lyda died may 5, 1962. They are buried in Riverview Cemetery at Middlepost, Ohio."

No. 2511. Write in the book on page 597, alongside No. 2511 [WALTER FRAZER HARRIS], the notation: "See Sup", to call attention to the following revised entry:

(Sup) 2511 WALTER FRAZER HARRIS (Ida[6], Franklin[5], Adam[4], Adam[3], Matthias[2], John Jacob[1]) was born February 20, 1883, at Manchester, Virginia. He married Mayme Burns of Glouster, Ohio, November 11, 1908. She was the daughter of Patrick and Catherine Burns and was born March 31, 1885. Walter died August 4, 1955, and Mayme died February 11, 1962. They are buried in Sacred Heart Cemetery, Pomeroy, Ohio.

(Sup) 4111A   i Walter Burns Harris, born June 16, 1910.

No. 2513 PAUL DAVIS LINK [page 597]. Add to text: "He was employed as a firemen by the Chesapeake & Ohio Railroad for forty-three years, until his retirement in 1961. Paul died July 23, 1963, and Cora died January 10, 1980. They are buried in Riverview Cemetery at Ronceverte, West Virgina."

No. 2514 CARRIE VIRGINIA LINK [page 597]. Add: "She was employed by the U.S. Census Bureau, from which she retired in April 1964. She died May 6, 1978, at Washington, D.C., and is buried in Riverview Cemetery at Ronceverte, West Virginia."

NO. 2515 GORDON LEE LINK [married Mary Frances Littlepage; page 597]. Add to text: "Lee died September 12, 1981. Mary resided at Winter Park, Florida."

No. 2516 MAX STUART LINK [page 598]. Add, before the final sentence: "He married Helen Adeline Arthur. She was the daughter of James Henry and Laura Byrd Arthur." Add at end of text: "After his death she resided at Wewahitchka, Florida."

No. 2532 MARY MARGARET WHITACRE [married Denzil Morton Ferguson; page 600]. Add to text: "Mary died May, 1955, at St. Petersburg, Florida."

No. 2542 JEROME LONGPRE' [page 601]. Correct his date of death, to read "January 27, 1909."

No. 2543 FRANCES EUGENIA LONGPRE' [married James Emmett, Jr.; page 601]. Add their third child:

    "(Sup) 4148A iii Mary Shaun Emmett, born November 9, 1950."

No. 2544 JANE ELIZABETH LONGPRE' [page 601]. Add: "She died June 30, 1923."

No. 2546. Write in the book on page 601, alongside No. 2546 [MARY PREVOST LONGPRE'], the notation "See Sup", to call attention to the following revised entry:

(Sup) 2546 MARY PREVOST LONGPRE' (Elizabeth[6], Samuel[5], Lewis[4], Christian[2], Matthias[2], John Jacob[1]) was born April 18, 1915. She married, first, Thomas David Gunning, January 26, 1952. He was born September 5, 1918; Thomas died May 9, 1959. Mary married, second, John Richard Scott, June 1, 1963. John was born February 5, 1918.

CHILDREN OF MARY AND THOMAS
(Sup) 4148B   i Jeanne Longpré Gunning, born October 27, 1952.
(Sup) 4148C ii David Lavery Gunning, born October 27, 1952.
(Sup) 4148D iii Patrick James Gunning, born August 4, 1955.

No. 2589 KATHERINE EVANS WYATT [married Harold E. Perkins; page 605]. Add: "He died at Minneapolis, Minnesota, and she died at Sun City, California; they are buried at Rushville, Indiana."

No. 2590 MARY LOUISE WYATT [married Ivan L. Wiles; page 605]. Correct
his birth date, to "June 13, 1898." Add to text: "In 1956 Ivan became
executive vice president of General Motors for dealer relations. He retired
in 1957. He received an honorary LL.D. degree in 1955 and was president of
the Board of Trustees of Wabash College, 1958-65. Mary and Ivan retired at
Scottsdale, Arizona. She died there July 27, 1978, and he died there
November 10, 1986; they are buried in Memorial Gardens of Valley
Presbyterian Church at Scottsdale."

No. 2591 JOHN BURT WYATT [page 605]. Add to text: "John attended
Wabash College, where he was a member of Beta Theta Pi. He became an agent
for Northwestern Mutual Life Insurance Company. He served as an elder of
the Presbyterian Church."

No. 2592 MARTHA WYATT [married John H, Davis; page 606]. Add: "She
lived at Sun City, California."

Chapter 2

Revised Eighth Generation

This material completely replaces the Eighth Generation in *The
Link Family*, pages 620-774. It contains new entries and revised
entries, together with reproductions of the Eighth Generation
entries that remain unchanged from the original book.

Generation	*Entry Numbers*
Eighth	2739-4292

The biographies on the following pages replace the genealogy of the Eighth Generation in The Link Family, pages 620-774.

The notation "(Sup)" before any biography indicates either that the entry for the individual is new, or that the information is revised from that appearing in the book.

2739 MARY CLEONE PITTMAN (Mary[7], Ann Sophia[6], George[5], John[4], Elizabeth[3], John Adam I[2], John Jacob[1]) was born May 23, 1873.

2740 GEORGE BRIGHT PITTMAN (Mary[7], Ann Sophia[6], George[5], John[4], Elizabeth[3], John Adam I[2], John Jacob[1]) was born January 5, 1876. He died August 1, 1882.

2741 AGNES THEO PITTMAN (Mary[7], Ann Sophia[6], George[5], John[4], Elizabeth[3], John Adam I[2], John Jacob[1]) was born February 28, 1879. She died July 25, 1882.

2742 SAMUEL WISHARD PITTMAN (Mary[7], Ann Sophia[6], George[5], John[4], Elizabeth[3], John Adam I[2], John Jacob[1]) was born July 1, 1881. He died July 31, 1882.

2743 THOMAS LAWRENCE PITTMAN (Mary[7], Ann Sophia[6], George[5], John[4], Elizabeth[3], John Adam I[2], John Jacob[1]) was born March 4, 1883.

2744 MARTHA SOPHIA PITTMAN (Mary[7], Ann Sophia[6], George[5], John[4], Elizabeth[3], John Adam I[2], John Jacob[1]) was born November 9, 1885.

2745 JOHN WINFIELD SCOTT SOUDER (William[7], Elizabeth[6], George[5], John[4], Elizabeth[3], John Adam I[2], John Jacob[1]) was born October 25, 1888, and died June 26, 1892.

2746 HOWARD DOUGLAS HAMILTON (Cora[7], Milton[6], George[5], John[4], Elizabeth[3], John Adam I[2], John Jacob[1]) was born December 12, 1880. He died October 2, 1881.

2747 EVELYN STUART HAMILTON (Cora[7], Milton[6], George[5], John[4], Elizabeth[3], John Adam I[2], John Jacob[1]) was born March 10, 1884.

2748 ARTHUR MILTON HAMILTON (Cora[7], Milton[6], George[5], John[4], Elizabeth[3], John Adam I[2], John Jacob[1]) was born November 1, 1888.

2749 DAVID G. HAMILTON (Cora[7], Milton[6], George[5], John[4], Elizabeth[3], John Adam I[2], John Jacob[1]) was born August 17, 1891.

2750 CORA CAMPBELL HAMILTON (Cora[7], Milton[6], George[5], John[4], Elizabeth[3], John Adam I[2], John Jacob[1]) was born July 19, 1895. She died July 20, 1895.

2751 JASON E. McBRIDE (Mary[7], George[6], John[5], John[4], Elizabeth[3], John Adam I[2], John Jacob[1]) was born September 18, 1870. He married Flora Keehn in November, 1891, and they had one child.

2752 ORIEN W. McBRIDE (Mary[7], George[6], John[5], John[4], Elizabeth[3], John Adam I[2], John Jacob[1]) was born April 15, 1875. He married Emma Walker in November, 1895.

2753 EFFIE McBRIDE (Mary[7], George[6], John[5], John[4], Elizabeth[3], John Adam I[2], John Jacob[1]) was born January 19, 1882.

2754 MAUDE McBRIDE (Mary[7], George[6], John[5], John[4], Elizabeth[3], John Adam I[2], John Jacob[1]) was born March 31, 1889.

2755 RUSHTON D. NILES (Anna[7], Charles[6], Christian[5], John[4], Elizabeth[3], John Adam I[2], John Jacob[1]) was born August 30, 1879, at Tiffin, Ohio. He married Grace Markley, and they had a daughter, named Mariam.

2756 JO ANN PATES (Claire[7], Joseph[6] Christian[5], John[4], Elizabeth[3], John Adam I[2], John Jacob[1]) was born January 12, 1932.

2757 MARY LOU PATES (Claire[7], Joseph[6], Christian[5], John[4], Elizabeth[3], John Adam I[2], John Jacob[1]) was born December 24, 1934. She and Nancy were twins.

2758 NANCY CLAIRE PATES (Claire[7], Joseph[6], Christian[5], John[4], Elizabeth[3], John Adam I[2], John Jacob[1]) was born December 24, 1934. She and Mary were twins.

2758A SCOTT STONER CHANDLER (Sarah[7], Joseph[6], Christian[5], John[4], Elizabeth[3], John Adam I[2], John Jacob[1]) was born December 6, 1933.

2759 LLOYD GORDON STONER (Raleigh[7], John[6], Dennis[5], John[4], Elizabeth[3], John Adam I[2], John Jacob[1]) was born August 9, 1899, at Larned, Kansas. He married Edith Dauer, November 24, 1920, at Salina, Kansas. Edith was born at Salina, October 15, 1896.

(Sup) 5001   † Marjorie Louise Stoner, born April 25, 1928.

2760 MARJORIE M. STONER (Raleigh[7], John[6], Dennis[5], John[4], Elizabeth[3], John Adam I[2], John Jacob[1]) was born November 29, 1902, at Larned, Kansas.

2761 FRANK NORRIS STONER (Jesse[7], John[6], Dennis[5], John[4], Elizabeth[3], John Adam I[2], John Jacob[1]) was born November 4, 1890, at Larned, Kansas. He married Florence H. Low, September 30, 1937, at La Porte, Indiana. Florence was the daughter of Nathan and Jennie Kramer Low and was born March 25, 1900, at La Porte. They had no children.

2762 RUTH STONER (Jesse[7], John[6], Dennis[5], John[4], Elizabeth[3], John Adam I[2], John Jacob[1]) was born July 4, 1895, at Larned, Kansas. She married Elmer H. Slaybaugh in 1924. They had no children.

2763 JESSE LEE STONER (Jesse[7], John[6], Dennis[5], John[4], Elizabeth[3], John Adam I[2], John Jacob[1]) was born November 21, 1906, at Lincoln, Nebraska. He died June 6, 1923.

2764 LEE ROWLAND STONER, JR. (Lee[7], Thomas[6], Dennis[5], John[4], Elizabeth[3], John Adam I[2], John Jacob[1]) was born November 27, 1917, at Troy, Ohio. He married Ruth Hafley, October 7, 1944, at Delmar, New York. During World War II he was commissioned a Lieutenant j.g. in the U. S. Navy and saw action in the South Pacific. He was a graduate M. D. and after the war specialized in Eye, Ear, Nose and Throat at Syracuse, New York.

(Sup) 5002   i Donna Lee Stoner, born September 30, 1945.
(Sup) 5003   ii Patricia Gale Stoner, born December 11, 1947.

2765 CHARLES THOMAS STONER (Lee[7], Thomas[6], Dennis[5], John[4], Elizabeth[3], John Adam I[2], John Jacob[1]) was born December 17, 1919, at Troy, Ohio. He married Ruth Boggs, June 4, 1949, at Dayton, Ohio. During World War II he was a Sergeant in the 9th U. S. Air Group and served in the European Theater of Operations.

2766 MARJORY ELLEN STONER (Lee[7], Thomas[6], Dennis[5], John[4], Elizabeth[3], John Adam I[2], John Jacob[1]) was born January 10, 1923, at Woodcliff, New Jersey. She married John Farnum Dye, August 12, 1949, at Detroit, Michigan.

2767 EDWARD RAYMOND STONER (Lee[7], Thomas[6], Dennis[5], John[4], Elizabeth[3], John Adam I[2], John Jacob[1]) was born September 8, 1926, at East Orange, New Jersey. He was a Sergeant in the 100th U. S. Infantry in the European Theater of Operations during World War II.

2768 JOHN RESLEY STONER (Lee[7], Thomas[6], Dennis[5], John[4], Elizabeth[3], John Adam I[2], John Jacob[1]) was born May 21, 1928, at East Orange, New Jersey. He served in the U. S. Army of Occupation in Europe in World War II.

2769 DONALD MOORHEAD (Helen[7], Thomas[6], Dennis[5], John[4], Elizabeth[3], John Adam I[2], John Jacob[1]) was born May 27, 1922, at Tiffin, Ohio. He married Pearl Cooper, June 13, 1944, at Bryn Athyn, Pennsylvania.

2770 CLARENCE M. SPECK (Ruth[7], Thomas[6], Dennis[5], John[4], Elizabeth[3], John Adam I[2], John Jacob[1]) was born at Tiffin, Ohio.

2771 FRANK A. SPECK (Ruth[7], Thomas[6], Dennis[5], John[4], Elizabeth[3], John Adam I[2], John Jacob[1]) was born at Tiffin, Ohio. He married Loretta Rorbach.

2772 JOHN LAWRENCE STONER (John[7], Thomas[6], Dennis[5], John[4], Elizabeth[3], John Adam I[2], John Jacob[1]) was born August 22, 1934, at Pittsburgh, Pennsylvania, where he died January 22, 1945.

2773 DANIEL THOMAS STONER (John[7], Thomas[6], Dennis[5], John[4], Elizabeth[3], John Adam I[2], John Jacob[1]) was born July 24, 1936, at Pittsburgh, Pennsylvania.

2774 JAMES ALLAN STONER (John[7], Thomas[6], Dennis[5], John[4], Elizabeth[3], John Adam I[2], John Jacob[1]) was born September 4, 1938, at Washington, D. C.

2775 ROBERT LEE STONER (John[7], Thomas[6], Dennis[5], John[4], Elizabeth[3], John Adam I[2], John Jacob[1]) was born October 29, 1940, at Washington, D. C.

2776 WILLIAM JOSEPH STONER (John[7], Thomas[6], Dennis[5], John[4], Elizabeth[3], John Adam I[2], John Jacob[1]) was born December 4, 1943, at Riverdale, Maryland.

2777 MARY ANN STONER (John[7], Thomas[6], Dennis[5], John[4], Elizabeth[3], John Adam I[2], John Jacob[1]) was born February 13, 1947, at Riverdale, Maryland.

2778 MARY VIRGINIA GAVER (Clayton[7], Theodore[6], Margaret[5], Catherine[4], John Adam II[3], John Adam I[2], John Jacob[1]) was born December 10, 1906, at Washington, D. C. She became Librarian at the State Teachers College at Trenton, New Jersey.

2779 PERCY CLENDENING GAVER (Clayton[7], Theodore[6], Margaret[5], Catherine[4], John Adam II[3], John Adam I[2], John Jacob[1]) was born January 10, 1912, at Washington, D. C. He died at Blacksburg, Virginia, February 10, 1933, while a student at Virginia Polytechnic Institute.

2780 LYDIA SHAW GAVER (Clayton[7], Theodore[6], Margaret[5], Catherine[4], John Adam II[3] John Adam I[2], John Jacob[1]) was born September 3, 1918, at Danville, Virginia. She married Ruben Comer Harvey, June 28, 1941, at Danville.

(Sup) 5004   i Daniel Gaver Harvey, born December 3, 1945.

2781 THOMAS HENRY LEMEN (Mamie[7], Thomas[6], Adam[5], Alexander[4], John Adam II[3], John Adam I[2], John Jacob[1]) was the son of Harry Manning and Mamie Esther Link Lemen [The Link Family, page 443, No. 1395]. Thomas was born July 20, 1908, at Duffields, Jefferson County, West Virginia. He was a merchant. He married Nancy Elizabeth Osbourn, June 7, 1938. She was the daughter of John Melvin and Bessie Hamilton Poston Osbourn and was born February 15, 1905, at Shenandoah Junction, Jefferson County [The Link Family, page 645, No. 2927]. Nancy graduated from Shepherd College, West Virginia. Thomas and Nancy resided at Summit Point, West Virginia. He died July 27, 1950, and she died February 8, 1984. They are buried in Elmwood Cemetery at Shepherdstown, West Virginia.

(Sup) 5005   i Joanne Stuart Lemen, born February 6, 1942.
(Sup) 5006   ii James Henry Lemen, born February 4, 1944.

2782 FRANKLIN HAGER JONES (Adam[7], Mary[6], Adam[5], Alexander[4], John Adam II[3], John Adam I[2], John Jacob[1]) was the son of Adam Francis and Alice Lemen Jones [The Link Family, page 443, No. 1399]. He was born December 11, 1904, at Shepherdstown, West Virginia. Franklin married Agnes E. Trussell April 2, 1930, and they lived at Bakerton, Jefferson County, West Virginia. Agnes was the daughter of Harry Gilbert and Lena Virginia Engle Trussell and was born February 12, 1908, at Uvilla, Jefferson County. Franklin died January 15, 1979, and is buried in Fairview Cemetery at Bolivar (near Harper's Ferry), West Virginia.

(Sup) 5007   i Barbara Ellen Jones, born January 21, 1931.
(Sup) 5008   ii Charlotte Rae Jones, born March 31, 1939.

(Sup) 2783 MARY MARGARET JONES (Adam[7], Mary[6], Adam[5], Alexander[4], John Adam II[3], John Adam I[2], John Jacob[1]) was the daughter of Adam Francis and Alice Lemen Jones [The Link Family, page 443, No. 1399]. She was born August 21, 1906, at Engles, Jefferson County, West Virginia. She married Frank William Trussell February 10, 1930. He was the son of Harry Gilbert and Lena Virginia Engle Trussell and was born May 5, 1906, at Uvilla, Jefferson County, West Virginia. Frank was an engineer. He and Mary lived at Cumberland, Maryland, where during World War II he was a member of the Minutemen of Maryland. She died August 12, 1978, and is buried at Cumberland.

(Sup) 5009   i   Mary Norma Trussell, born August 11, 1931.
(Sup) 5010   ii Joyce Lee Trussell, born March 25, 1936.

(Sup) 2784 DAVID MARTIN JONES (Adam[7], Mary[6], Adam[5], Alexander[4], John Adam II[3], John Adam I[2], John Jacob[1]) was the son of Adam Francis and Alice Lemen Jones [The Link Family, page 443, No. 1399]. David was born August 21, 1911, at Uvilla, Jefferson County, West Virginia. He married Minno V. Staubs September 30, 1933. She was the daughter of Charles W. and Lula May Snyder Staubs and was born May 27, 1913, at Harpers Ferry, West Virginia. They lived at Bolivar, Jefferson County.

(Sup) 5011   i   Larry William Jones, born September 29, 1936.
(Sup) 5012   ii   Martin David Jones, born May 13, 1939.
(Sup) 5013   iii Virginia Mae Jones, born December 29, 1941.
(Sup) 5014   iv   Mary Louise Jones, born Septemebr 5, 1945.

(Sup) 2785 RALPH BANKS JONES (Adam[7], Mary[6], Adam[5], Alexander[4], John Adam II[3], John Adam I[2], John Jacob[1]) was the son of Adam Francis and Alice Lemen Jones [The Link Family, page 443, No. 1399]. Ralph was born September 29, 1915, at Uvilla, Jefferson County, West Virginia. He married Blanche Elizabeth James July 2, 1935. She was the daughter of Benjamin Franklin and Molly May Dennison James and was born May 26, 1921, in Jefferson County. Ralph and Blanche lived at Halltown, Jefferson County.

(Sup) 5015   i   Ralph Jerry Jones, born August 19, 1936.
(Sup) 5016   ii   Gary Eugene Jones, born December 14, 1940.
(Sup) 5017   iii Benjamin Roger Jones, born January 19, 1943.

(Sup) 2786 SARAH ELIZABETH JONES (Adam[7], Mary[6], Adam[5], Alexander[4], John Adam II[3], John Adam I[2], John Jacob[1]) was the daughter of Adam Francis and Alice Lemen Jones [The Link Family, page 443, No. 1399]. She was born February 25, 1926, at Bakerton, Jefferson County, West Virginia. She married Roy William Runion April 20, 1945. Roy was the son of John Clarence and Nina Virginia Miller Runion and was born April 26, 1926, at Charles Town, West Virginia.

(Sup) 5018   i   Nancy Lee Runion, born April 20, 1946.
(Sup) 5019   ii   Donald William Runion, born August 7, 1947.
(Sup) 5020   iii John Clarence Runion, born April 8, 1950.
(Sup) 5021   iv   Charles Robert Runion, born October 17, 1951.

(Sup) 2787 OSCAR BLACKFORD JONES (Robert[7], Mary[6], Adam[5], Alexander[4], John Adam II[3], John Adam I[2], John Jacob[1]) was the son of Robert Luther and Helen Blackford Jones [The Link Family, page 444, No. 1400]. Oscar was born January 5, 1907, at Shenandoah Junction, Jefferson County, West Virginia. He graduated from Shepherd College, West Virginia, and became a teacher. He died December 23, 1978, and is buried in Elmwood Cemetery at Shepherdstown.

(Sup) 2788 ROBERT LUTHER JONES, JR. (Robert[7], Mary[6], Adam[5], Alexander[4], John Adam II[3], John Adam I[2], John Jacob[1]) was the son of Robert Luther and Helen Blackford Jones [The Link Family, page 444, No. 1400]. Robert, Jr. was born March 28, 1911, at Shenandoah Junction, Jefferson County, West Virginia. He married, first, Virginia Lee Smallwood on September 29, 1931. She was the daughter of Daniel Cleveland and Mary Catherine Jackson Smallwood and was born February 20, 1907, at Charles Town, West Virginia. Virginia died September 20, 1976, and is buried in Pleasantview Cemetery near Martinsburg, West Virginia. Robert married, second, Eva Lee Nichols Link Starliper, October 20, 1983, at Hagerstown, Maryland. She was the daughter of William David and Hattie Matilda Buracker Nichols and was born September 29, 1915, at Stanley, Virginia. Eva had been married, first, to Boteler Moore Link [Supplement No. 1683], and, second, to Clifford Cecil Starliper.

CHILD OF ROBERT AND VIRGINIA

(Sup) 5022   i   Marshall Ronemous Jones, born July 16, 1932.

(Sup) 2789 MARY JANE JACKSON JONES (Robert[7], Mary[6], Adam[5], Alexander[4], John Adam II[3], John Adam I[2], John Jacob[1]) was the daughter of Robert Luther and Helen Blackford Jones [The Link Family, page 444, No. 1400]. Mary Jane was born September 24, 1914, at Shenandoah Junction, Jefferson County, West Virginia. She died November 11, 1986, and is buried in Elmwood Cemetery at Shepherdstown, West Virginia.

(Sup) 2790 ELSIE CATHERINE JONES (Ernest[7], Mary[6], Adam[5], Alexander[4], John Adam II[3], John Adam I[2], John Jacob[1]) was the daughter of Ernest Drawbaugh and John Elsie (Link) Jones [The Link Family, pages 444 and 450, Nos. 1401 and 1424; and Supplement No. 1401]. She was born February 25, 1910, at Uvilla, Jefferson County, West Virginia. Elsie received an A.B. degree from Shepherd College, West Virginia, with highest scholastic honors, and an M.A. degree from the University of Maryland. She married Jennings Linton Hanson March 3, 1939. He was the son of Alvin Lee and Sarah Louise Linton Hanson and was born November 29, 1917, at La Plata, Maryland. He served in the U.S. Army during World War II. Elsie taught in the public school systems of Charles and Washington Counties, Maryland; Jefferson County, West Virginia; and Sarasota County, Florida. After retirement, Elsie made fashion-dressed porcelain dolls. She died June 23, 1987, at Venice, Florida, and is buried in Gulf Pines Estates at Englewood, Florida.

(Sup) 5023   i   Catherine Louise Hanson, born February 11, 1940.
(Sup) 5024   ii Jennings Linton Hanson, Jr., born April 9, 1941.

(Sup) 2790A EDGAR CARLTON JONES (Ernest[7], Mary[6], Adam[5], Alexander[4], John Adam II[3], John Adam I[2], John Jacob[1]) was the son of Ernest Drawbaugh and John Elsie Link Jones [The Link Family, pages 444 and 450, Nos. 1401 and 1424; and Supplement No. 1401]. He was born and died July 7, 1921, at Uvilla, Jefferson County, West Virginia, and is buried in St. James Lutheran Church Cemetery at Uvilla.

(Sup) 2791 ERNEST MERCER JONES (Ernest[7], Mary[6], Adam[5], Alexander[4], John Adam II[3], John Adam I[2], John Jacob[1]) was the son of Ernest Drawbaugh and John Elsie Link Jones [The Link Family, pages 441 and 450, Nos. 1401 and 1424; and Supplement No. 1401]. Mercer was born June 4, 1922, at Uvilla, Jefferson County, West Virginia. He graduated from the Newport News (Virginia) Shipyard Drydock School and served in the U.S. Navy through the end of World War II, seeing duty in the Pacific. On discharge he returned to Jefferson County and took over operation of the family farm. Mercer married Mary Louise Young October 12, 1944. She was born June 17, 1929, at Mount Airy, North Carolina. He died in a motorcycle accident at La Plata, Maryland, June 15, 1952, and is buried in St. James Lutheran Church cemetery at Uvilla, Jefferson County, West Virginia.

(Sup) 5025   i   Ernest Mercer Jones, Jr., born January 11, 1946.
(Sup) 5026   ii William Michael Jones, born January 2, 1953.

(Sup) 2792 PATRICIA ANN JONES (Ernest[7], Mary[6], Adam[5], Alexander[4], John Adam II[3], John Adam I[2], John Jacob[1]) was the daughter of Ernest Drawbaugh and John Elsie Link Jones [The Link Family, pages 444 and 450, Nos. 1401 and 1424; and Supplement No. 1401]. Patsy was born September 24, 1927, at Uvilla, Jefferson County, West Virginia. She was valedictorian of the 1945 class at Shepherdstown High School and attended Shepherd College, West Virginia. She married Douglas Lee Currier May 16, 1946. He was the son of Burton Dale and Arlene Blake Currier and was born April 14, 1926, at Town of Lyndon, Vermont. Douglas served in World War II with the 17th Airborne Parachute Infantry and saw action spearheading the Rhine crossing in Germany; he then served with the 82nd Airborne. He was later an engineer on the Baltimore and Ohio Railroad. Patsy and Douglas resided in Jefferson County. She was a member of the Magna Charta Dames, Daughters of American Colonists, and Daughters of the American Revolution.

(Sup) 5027   i   Douglas Lee Currier, Jr., born August 6, 1947.
(Sup) 5028   ii Peggy Ann Currier, born November 23, 1948.

(Sup) 2793 JOHN LINK JONES (Ernest[7], Mary[6], Adam[5], Alexander[4], John Adam II[3], John Adam I[2], John Jacob[1]) was the son of Ernest Drawbaugh and John Elsie Link Jones [The Link Family, pages 444 and 450, Nos. 1401 and 1424; and Supplement No. 1401]. Jack was born June 23, 1930, at Uvilla, Jefferson County, West Virginia. He was handicapped by the loss of a leg in a 1942 farming accident. He attended George Washington University 1948-1949, Shepherd College 1949-1951, and graduated from West Virginia University in 1953 with a B.S. degree in agriculture. He then received a B.A. degree in secondary education from Shepherd College in 1955. He taught at Warren County High School, Front Royal, Virginia. Jack married Mary Jane McLaney March 26, 1959, at Shepherdstown, West Virginia. She was the daughter of John M. and Vesta Winn McLaney of Arlington, Virginia, and was born September 18, 1936, at Washington, D.C. Jack and Mary Jane moved to Savage, Maryland, and he taught in Arundel Junior High at Odenton, Maryland. In 1963 Jack completed his M.A. degree in science education, and in 1966 received a Doctorate of Education from the University of Maryland. He was a science teacher in the Ann Arundel public school system and coached the track and field team at Ann Arundel High School. Mary Jane received a B.S. degree in home economics from Lynwood College, Virginia, and taught in Howard County, Maryland, public schools.

(Sup) 5029   i   Cynthia Karen Jones, born May 20, 1963.
(Sup) 5030   ii John Link Jones II, born August 9, 1966.

(Sup) 2794 WILLIAM MORGAN JONES, JR. (William[7], Mary[6], Adam[5], Alexander[4], John Adam II[3], John Adam I[2], John Jacob[1]) was the son of William Morgan and Elsie Gore Jones [The Link Family, page 444. No. 1406; and Supplement No. 1406]. William, Jr., was born October 9, 1923, at Charles Town, West Virginia, where he died April 18, 1931.

(Sup) 2795 ALLEN GORE JONES (William[7], Mary[6], Adam[5], Alexander[4], John Adam II[3], John Adam I[2], John Jacob[1]) was the son of William Morgan and Elsie Gore Jones [The Link Family, page 444, No. 1406; and Supplement No. 1406]. Allen was born August 27, 1926, at Charles Town, West Virginia, where he died August 2, 1929.

(Sup) 2796 MARY LINK HARTZELL (Laura[7], Adam[6], Adam[5], Alexander[4], John Adam II[3], John Adam I[2], John Jacob[1]) was the daughter of Herbert Harold and Laura Link Hartzell [The Link Family, page 445, No. 1407; and Supplement No. 1407]. Mary was born October 16, 1903, at Duffields, West Virginia. She died February 26, 1905.

(Sup) 2797 GLADYS LINK HARTZELL (Laura[7], Adam[6], Adam[5], Alexander[4], John Adam II[3], John Adam I[2], John Jacob[1]) was the daughter of Herbert Harold and Laura Link Hartzell [The Link Family, page 445, No. 1407; and Supplement No. 1407]. Gladys was born September 19, 1905, at Duffields, West Virginia. After completing public school education, Gladys entered the University of West Virginia, where she received her A.B. degree. She did postgraduate work at Columbia University and received her M.A. degree there. She became a teacher in the high school at Shepherdstown, West Virginia. She was a member of the D.A.R. with lineage to several qualifying ancestors. Gladys and her mother owned some valuable and interesting relics once used by John Adam Link II, which are pictured in this history. Gladys died December 9, 1980, and is buried in Elmwood Cemetery at Shepherdstown, West Virginia.

(Sup) 2798 KATHERINE LINK (Henry[7], Adam[6], Adam[5], Alexander[4], John Adam II[3], John Adam I[2], John Jacob[1]) was the daughter of Henry Clay and Margaret Foster Link [The Link Family, page 445, No. 1408]. Katherine was born November 7, 1908, at Flatonia, Texas. She married, first, Rudolph Louis Weyel, September 1, 1929. He was the son of Ferdinand Albert and Mary Gastring Weyel and was born June 28, 1907. Rudolph and Katherine lived at Houston, Texas. He died September 1, 1974, and is buried in Memorial Oaks Cemetery at Houston. Katherine married, second, Balfour J. Augst January 3, 1976, at Houston. Balfour was born March 1, 1912, in Michigan. A graduate of the University of Michigan, he was a chemist and engineer, and in 1966 moved to Houston where he was an engineering consultant.

(Sup) 5031   i   Rudolph Louis Weyel, Jr., born October 6, 1931.
(Sup) 5032   ii   Frances Louise Weyel, born June 17, 1936 (twin).
(Sup) 5033   iii   Foster Link Weyel, born June 17, 1936 (twin).

2799 HARRY CLEM LINK (Henry[7], Adam[6], Adam[5], Alexander[4], John Adam II[3], John Adam I[2], John Jacob[1]) was born April 14, 1910, at Flatonia, Texas.

2800 HARRISON FOSTER LINK (Henry[7], Adam[6], Adam[5], Alexander[4], John Adam II[3], John Adam I[2], John Jacob[1]) was born October 9, 1915, at Flatonia, Texas.

2801 LEONARD LINK HOUGH (Ann[7], William[6], Adam[5], Alexander[4], John Adam II[3], John Adam I[2], John Jacob[1]) was born February 2, 1896, at Bakerton, West Virginia. He married Esther Bellias, March 27, 1921. Esther was born August 23, 1900, at Kansas City, Missouri. Both Leonard and Esther were accidentally killed, August 23, 1924.

2802 SALLIE VIRGINIA HOUGH (Ann[7], William[6], Adam[5], Alexander[4], John Adam II[3], John Adam I[2], John Jacob[1]) was born August 19, 1898, at Bakerton, West Virginia. She married Dennis Joseph Norton, son of Patrick Joseph and Mary Daily Norton, December 19, 1925. Dennis was born October 15, 1890. He died March 3, 1944, and is buried at Rosedale Cemetery, Martinsburg, West Virginia. Sallie became a graduate nurse. She and Dennis had no children.

2803 LILLY REBECCA HOUGH (Ann[7], William[6], Adam[5], Alexander[4], John Adam II[3], John Adam I[2], John Jacob[1]) was born October 8, 1900, at Bakerton, West Virginia. She died September 24, 1902, at Bakerton and is buried in St. James Cemetery, Uvilla, West Virginia.

(Sup) 2804 MARTHA MAE HOUGH (Ann[7], William[6], Adam[5], Alexander[4], John Adam II[3], John Adam I[2], John Jacob[1]) was the daughter of Charles Joseph and Ann Rebecca (Link) Hough [The Link Family, page 445, No. 1409]. Martha was born September 22, 1902, at Bakerton, Jefferson County, West Virginia. She married Arthur Raymond Glaser, January 4, 1926. He was the son of George W. and Lillie Louise (Omer) Glaser and was born July 6, 1895, at Chambersburg, Pennsylvania. Arthur died August 4, 1944, and is buried in Worland Cemetery at Chambersburg. Martha died May 5, 1987.

(Sup) 5034   i   Gloria Lee Glaser, born March 9, 1928.

(Sup) 2805 MARY ELIZABETH HOUGH (Ann[7], William[6], Adam[5], Alexander[4], John Adam II[3], John Adam I[2], John Jacob[1]) was the daughter of Charles Joseph and Ann Rebecca Link Hough [The Link Family, page 445, No. 1409; and Supplement No. 1409]. Mary was born October 1, 1904, at Bakerton, Jefferson County, West Virginia. She married Joseph Abraham Brunk, January 12, 1924. He was the son of John Henry and Viola Frances Funk Brunk and was born November 17, 1897. Joseph was in the 13th Cavalry, U. S. Army, in World War I. Mary died November 17, 1970, and is buried in Rosedale Cemetery at Martinsburg, West Virginia.

(Sup) 5035   i   Joseph Burton Brunk, born January 6, 1925.
(Sup) 5036   ii   Betty June Brunk, born March 8, 1926.
(Sup) 5037   iii   John Henry Brunk, born November 28, 1928.
(Sup) 5038   iv   Barbara Jean Brunk, born April 17, 1932.
(Sup) 5039   v   Virginia Ann Brunk, born September 6, 1933.
(Sup) 5040   vi   Robert Kenneth Brunk, born November 23, 1938.

(Sup) 2806 CHARLES JOSEPH HOUGH, JR. (Ann[7], William[6], Adam[5], Alexander[4], John Adam II[3], John Adam I[2], John Jacob[1]) was the son of Charles Joseph and Ann Rebecca Link Hough [The Link Family, page 445, No. 1409; and Supplement No. 1409]. Charles was born October 17, 1906, at Martinsburg, West Virginia. He married, first, Ella Monroe Brown, July 13, 1926. Ella was the daughter of Orin and Elizabeth Devears Brown and was born November 11, 1906, at Middleway, West Virginia. Charles married, second, on May 23, 1936, Letha Myrtle Whitacre; she was the daughter of Harry Y. and Bertha Cornelia Peacemaker Whitacre. Charles married, third, Elo Elizabeth Myrick, August 23, 1948. Elo was the daughter of William Henry and Margaret Elizabeth Leslel Myrick and was born October 10, 1911, at Dry Branch, Georgia. She attended Middle College, Georgia.

CHILD OF CHARLES AND ELLA
(Sup) 5041   i   Charles Joseph Hough III, born Feb 17, 1927.

CHILD OF CHARLES AND ELO
(Sup) 5042   ii   Paula Rosemary Hough, born July 18, 1949.
(Sup) 5042A   iii   Charles Richard Hough, born April 16, 1951.
(Sup) 5042B   iv   William Joseph Hough, born December 17, 1952.

(Sup) 2807 GRACE CORNELIA HOUGH. (Ann[7], William[6], Adam[5], Alexander[4], John Adam II[3], John Adam I[2], John Jacob[1]) was the daughter of Charles Joseph and Ann Rebecca Link Hough [The Link Family, page 445, No. 1409; and Supp. No. 1409]. Grace was born April 30, 1909, at Martinsburg, West Virginia. She married, first, Wilbur Herbert Amos, March 28, 1930. He was born April 4, 1899. Grace married, second, Frank Louis Saville, February 24, 1940. Frank was the son of Frank Taylor and Bertie Lee Pearrell Saville and was born November 21, 1914, at Hedgesville, West Virginia.

(Sup) 5043   i   Frank Louis Saville, Jr., born January 2, 1941.
(Sup) 5044   ii   Victor Leslie Glover Saville, born Jan 3, 1942.
(Sup) 5045   iii   Sallye Ann Saville, born February 3, 1945.
(Sup) 5046   iv   Henry Paul Saville, born August 21, 1949.

(Sup) 2808 JOHN HUGO HOUGH (Ann[7], William[6], Adam[5], Alexander[4], John Adam II[3], John Adam I[2], John Jacob[1]) was the son of Charles Joseph and Ann (Rebecca) Link Hough [The Link Family, page 445, No. 1409]. John was born June 10, 1911, at Martinsburg, West Virginia. He married, first, Virginia Irene Fisher, January 6, 1933. She was the daughter of Charles Cass and Viola Blanche (Edmonds) Fisher and was born October 6, 1909, at Charles Town, West Virginia. Virginia died October 20, 1946, and was buried at Mt. Olivet Cemetery, Baltimore, Maryland. John married, second, Addie Blanche (March) Bennett, August 6, 1947. Addie was born July 27, 1902, at Lillian, Northumberland County, Virginia, the daughter of Addison Hall and Malvina Tolson (Butler) March.

(Sup) 5047   i   Joan Sandra Hough, born September 11, 1933.
(Sup) 5048   ii John Hugo Hough, Jr., born June 2, 1937.

(Sup) 2809 WOODROW WILSON HOUGH (Ann[7], William[6], Adam[5], Alexander[4], John Adam II[3], John Adam I[2], John Jacob[1]) was the son of Charles Joseph and Ann Rebecca (Link) Hough [The Link Family, page 445, No. 1409]. Woodrow was born October 30, 1913, at Martinsburg, West Virginia. He was a coxswain in the U.S. Navy during World War II and served aboard an LST at the invasion of the Normandy Beach Head in France. He also was in the North African campaign. Woodrow married, first, Genevieve Ruby Downs May 17, 1933. She was the daughter of Ruby and Eva Yvonne (Gyeates) Downs. Woodrow married, second, Thelma Irene Turner April 24, 1937. Thelma was the daughter of Samuel and Cora Lee (Cubbage) Turner and was born December 28, 1914, at Harrisonburg, Virginia. Woodrow died May 6, 1971, and Thelma died November 27, 1986.

CHILD OF WOODROW AND RUBY

(Sup) 5049   i   Joyce Ann Hough, born November 20, 1936.

CHILD OF WOODROW AND THELMA

(Sup) 5050   ii Woodrow Wilson Hough, Jr., born April 14, 1946.
(Sup) 5050A   iii Debra Kay Hough, born August 2, 1952.

(Sup) 2810 FRANCES IRENE HOUGH (Ann[7], William[6], Adam[5], Alexandery[4], John Adam II[3], John Adam I[2], John Jacob[1]) was the daughter of Charles Joseph and Ann Rebecca (Link) Hough [The Link Family, page 445, No. 1409]. Frances was born May 5, 1916, at Martinsburg, West Virginia. She married Woodrow Pearrell Saville, March 23, 1935. Woodrow was the son of Frank Taylor and Bertie Lee (Pearrell) Saville, and was born January 28, 1913, at Hedgesville, West Virginia. Frances died May 30, 1984, and is buried in Pleasant View Memory Gardens at Martinsburg, West Virginia.

(Sup) 5051   i   Patricia Ann Saville, born November 9, 1935.
(Sup) 5052   ii Jo Ann Saville, born May 24, 1939.
(Sup) 5053   iii Woodrow Pearell Saville, born March 5, 1942.
(Sup) 5054   iv Richard Taylor Saville, born March 9, 1945.
(Sup) 5055   v   Frances Irene Saville, born March 29, 1947.

(Sup) 2811 DANIELLS PERSHING BAKER HOUGH (Ann[7], William[6], Adam[5], Alexander[4], John Adam II[3], John Adam I[2], John Jacob[1]) was the son of Charles Joseph and Ann Rebecca Link Hough [The Link Family, page 445, No. 1409]. Daniells was born September 12, 1918, at Martinsburg, West Virginia. He served in the U.S. Navy for two years in the Pacific Theater. He was awarded the Pacific Theater ribbon with one star, American Theater ribbon, Victory Medal and Philippine Theater ribbon. Daniells married Gladiola Marie Clark, December 23, 1939. Gladys was born April 18, 1921, at Martinsburg, the daughter of Cecil Harrison and Nora Edith Wright Clark. Daniells died April 6, 1970, and is buried in Pleasant View Memory Gardens at Martinsburg. Gladys married, second, Eric Carl Lowner October 20, 1973, at Parkville, Maryland.

(Sup) 5056   i   Daniells Pershing Baker Hough, Jr., born
                  December 10, 1940.

(Sup) 5057   ii Rebecca Ann Hough, born August 20, 1947.
(Sup) 5058   iii Sally Virginia Hough, born November 12, 1949.
(Sup) 5058A   iv Cornelia Juanita Hough, born June 16, 1950.
(Sup) 5058B   v   Robert Jerome Hough, born November 6, 1952.
(Sup) 5058C   vi John William Hough, born July 13, 1956.

(Sup) 2812 PAUL VINCENT HOUGH (Ann[7], William[6], Adam[5], Alexander[4], John Adam II[3], John Adam I[2], John Jacob[1]) was the son of Charles Joseph and Ann Rebecca Link Hough [The Link Family, page 445, No. 1409]. Paul was born February 11, 1921, at Martinsburg, West Virginia. During World War II he served three years as a U.S. Navy gunner's mate in the European, African, and Middle East theaters. Paul married Pauline Shiver, January 5, 1945. She was born July 25, 1920, at Cherry Run, West Virginia. Paul died September 27, 1983, at Martinsburg.

(Sup) 5059   i   Phillip Van Hough, born October 22, 1945.
(Sup) 5060   ii Mary Colleen Hough, born January 13, 1948.
(Sup) 5060A   iii Paulette Jeanette Hough, born January 16, 1951.
(Sup) 5060B   iv Karen Elaine Hough, born March 21, 1957.

(Sup) 2813 JOHN WILLIAM LINK, JR. (John[7], William[6], Adam[5], Alexander[4], John Adam II[3], John Adam I[2], John Jacob[1]) was the son of John William and Helen Elizabeth Link [The Link Family, pages 446 and 490; Nos. 1411 and 1672]. John William, Jr., was born February 25, 1914, at Strasburg, Virginia. He receive an A.B. degree from Wittenburg College in 1934 and did postgraduate work at the Union Theological Seminary, New York. He became an organist—a minister of music. John William married Verna Mae Hahn, daughter of Atlas Eugene and Elizabeth (Hurtsell) Hahn. John William and Verna Mae lived at Mt. Pleasant, North Carolina. They were divorced in 1959. He later resided at Grants, New Mexico. In 1976 he returned to Shepherdstown, West Virginia, where he was active in music and served as president of the Descendents of John Jacob Link. He retired to Florida in 1981, first at Fort Walton Beach with his son's family, and then at Niceville. John William died March 17, 1986, at Biloxi, Mississippi, and is buried in Elmwood Cemetery at Shepherdstown, West Virginia.

(Sup) 5061   i   John William Link, III, born September 12, 1953.

(Sup) 2814 ELIZABETH MELVIN LINK (John[7], William[6], Adam[5], Alexander[4], John Adam II[3], John Adam I[2], John Jacob[1]) was the daughter of John William and Helen Elizabeth Link [The Link Family, pages 446 and 490; Nos. 1411 and 1672]. Elizabeth was born May 25, 1917, at Strasburg, Virginia. She received her A.B. degree from the Women's College of the University of North Carolina (Greensboro) in 1938 and became a teacher. Elizabeth married Charles Richard Russell, Jr., October 2, 1938. He was the son of Dr. Charles Richard and Maude Edith Allred Russell and was born at Forest City, North Carolina, January 23, 1911. Charles was a merchant at Granite Falls, North Carolina. Elizabeth and Charles were divorced. He died October 25, 1964, at Mountain Home, Tennessee, and is buried in the Methodist Cemetery, Granite Falls, North Carolina. Elizabeth died January 5, 1972, at Hillsdale, Michigan, and is buried in Elmwood Cemetery at Shepherdstown, West Virginia.

(Sup) 5062   i   Elizabeth June Russell, born April 29, 1942.
(Sup) 5063   ii Martha Link Russell, born January 13, 1947.
(Sup) 5064   iii Charles Richard Russell, III, born Sept 9, 1948.

(Sup) 2815 ARTHUR STANLEY LINK (John[7], William[6], Adam[5], Alexander[4], John Adam II[3], John Adam I[2], John Jacob[1]) was the son of John William and Helen Elizabeth Link [The Link Family, pages 446 and 490; Nos. 1411 and 1672]. Arthur was born August 8, 1920, at New Market, Virginia. He attended the University of North Carolina, where he was a member of Phi Beta Kappa and Alpha Kappa Delta and graduated with highest honors in 1941. He took his M.A. degree at the University of North Carolina in 1942. He taught in the Air Force and ASTP programs at North Carolina State College in 1943-1944 and for the V-12 program at the University of North Carolina in the summer of 1944. In 1945 Arthur was awarded his Ph.D. degree from the University of North Carolina. He was assistant professor of history at Princeton University and then associate professor of history at Northwestern University. His volumes on the "Life of Woodrow Wilson" were published beginning in 1947. Arthur was a member of the American Historical Association, the Mississippi Valley Historical Association, and the Southern Historical association. He married Margaret McDowell Douglas June 2, 1945. She was the daughter of James McDowell and Anniebell Munroe Douglas and was born July 22, 1918, at Davidson, North Carolina. In 1938 Margaret graduated from Agnes Scott College with an A.B. degree. She received an M.A. degree in sociology at the University of North Carolina in 1943; was assistant professor at Queens College, Charlotte, North Carolina, 1943-1945; and became a research associate in the Office of Population Research at Princeton.

(Sup) 5065   i   Arthur Stanley Link, Jr., born November 2, 1946.
(Sup) 5066   ii James Douglas Link, born April 20, 1950.
(Sup) 5066A iii Margaret McDowell Link, born August 30, 1951.
(Sup) 5066B iv William Allen Link.

(Sup) 2816 ELINOR LOUISE LINK (John[7], William[6], Adam[5], Alexander[4], John Adam II[3], John Adam I[2], John Jacob[1]) was the daughter of John William and Helen Elizabeth Link [The Link Family, pages 446 and 490; Nos. 1411 and 1672]. Elinor was born February 23, 1923, at Danville, Virginia. She received her A.B. degree from Lenoir-Rhyne College in 1943. After a year at the University of North Carolina she studied at the Manhattan School of Music, where she was awarded the degree of Bachelor of Music in 1944. Elinor married, first, Anthony Paul Costa, June 12, 1947. Anthony was born March 25, 1920, at New York, New York. He was the son of Antonio and Franchesca Paola Brusca Costa. During World War II, Anthony was a Staff Sergeant in the North African campaign and received the Good Conduct Medal, Defense Ribbon, E.T.O. and A.F.M.E. He received his education at New York University and Manhattan School of Music, where he attained the degree of Bachelor of Music in 1948. Elinor married, second, Joseph R. Cagan in 1968. Joseph was an artist and Chairman of Art in the New York City high schools.

(Sup) 5066C   i Douglas Link Costa, born March 8, 1948.

(Sup) 2817 HOLLAND ROCKEY COFFINBERGER (Margaret[7], William[6], Adam[5], Alexander[4], John Adam II[3], John Adam I[2], John Jacob[1]) was the son of William Elmer and Margaret Link Coffinberger [The Link Family, page 446, No. 1412]. Holland was born April 23, 1903, at Shepherdstown, West Virginia. He married Hester Virginia Braithwaite, March 10, 1923. She was the daughter of Benjamin F. and Adelia Kisner Braithwaite and was born June 19, 1905, at Martinsburg, West Virginia. Hester died in 1972, and Holland died in 1980. They are buried in Rosedale Cemetery at Martinsburg, West Virginia.

(Sup) 5067   i Paul Edward Coffinberger, born October 30, 1923.
(Sup) 5068   ii Mary Hester Coffinberger, born June 4, 1926.

(Sup) 2818 GRACE OLEO COFFINBERGER (Margaret[7], William[6], Adam[5], Alexander[4], John Adam II[3], John Adam I[2], John Jacob[1]) was the daughter of William Elmer and Margaret Link Coffinberger [The Link Family, page 446, No. 1412]. Grace was born March 24, 1904, at Shepherdstown, West Virginia. She married, first, John William Patterson, Jr., June 2, 1919, at Clear Springs, Maryland. He was the son of John William and Elmyra Abigail Franks Patterson and was born January 25, 1893, at Martinsburg, West Virginia. She married, second, Robert Sylvester Whittington December 24, 1939. Robert was the son of Joseph and Mamie Ring Whittington, and was born November 10, 1904, at Vanclevesville, West Virginia. Grace died April 13, 1971, and is buried in Rosedale Cemetery at Martinsburg, West Virginia.

CHILDREN OF GRACE AND JOHN

(Sup) 5069   i   Lucy Mae Patterson, born January 9, 1921.
(Sup) 5070   ii Virginia Lee Patterson, born September 28, 1923.
(Sup) 5071   iii Rose Elaine Patterson, born August 24, 1927.

(Sup) 2819 WALTER WELLINGTON SPEROW COFFINBERGER (Margaret[7], William[6], Adam[5], Alexander[4], John Adam II[3], John Adam I[2], John Jacob[1]) was the son of William Elmer and Margaret Link Coffinberger [The Link Family, page 446, No. 1412]. Walter was born March 30, 1907, at Shepherdstown, West Virginia. He married, first, Reba Cathaleen Rush. They were divorced. Walter married, second, Mildred Elnora Fogle. Mildred was the daughter of Frederick Martin and Mary Elizabeth (Peel) Fogle and was born in Adams County, Indiana. Mildred died in 1986, and Walter died March 30, 1987.

CHILDREN OF WALTER AND MILDRED

(Sup) 5072 i James Walter Coffinberger, born June 28, 1945.
(Sup) 5073 ii Rose Elaine Coffinberger, born Dec 28, 1946.
(Sup) 5074 iii William Frederick Coffinberger, born Aug 20, 1949.

(Sup) 2820 ELMER MAE COFFINBERGER (Margaret[7], William[6], Adam[5], Alexander[4], John Adam II[3], John Adam I[2], John Jacob[1]) was the daughter of William Elmer and Margaret Link Coffinberger [The Link Family, page 446, No. 1412]. She was born June 1, 1911, in Jefferson County, West Virginia. She married James Franklin Cloud, son of Charles B. and Lula M. Crouse Cloud. October 7, 1933. James was born January 19, 1908, at Martinsburg, West Virginia. She died August 30, 1974, and is buried in Rosedale Cemetery at Martinsburg.

(Sup) 5075 i Doris Link Cloud, born February 24, 1936.
(Sup) 5076 ii Nancy Lou Cloud, born February 28, 1939.
(Sup) 5077 iii James Douglas Cloud, born November 23, 1941.
(Sup) 5078 iv William Calvin Cloud, born September 4, 1943.
(Sup) 5079 v David Martin Cloud, born October 4, 1944.
(Sup) 5080 vi Cornelia Dianne Cloud, born March 21, 1948.

(Sup) 2821 LEDA CORNELIA COFFINBERGER (Margaret[7], William[6], Adam[5], Alexander[4], John Adam II[3], John Adam I[2], John Jacob[1]) was the daughter of William Elmer and Margaret Link Coffinberger [The Link Family, page 446, No. 1412]. Cornelia was born November 19, 1912, in Jefferson County, West Virginia. She married, first, Scott Alvy Neibert, December 25, 1931. He was the son of Christian Phillip and Bessie Virginia Kershner Neibert and was born October 24, 1910, at Broadfording, Maryland. They were divorced. Cornelia married, second, Kenneth J. Deardorff April 29, 1955. Kenneth was born December 14, 1921, at Ortanna, Pennsylvania. They were divorced in 1979.

(Sup) 5081 i Betty Jeanene Neibert, born May 26, 1933.
(Sup) 5082 ii Richard Duane Neibert, born October 20, 1934.
(Sup) 5083 iii Fay Rene Neibert, born April 29, 1938.

(Sup) 2822 BERTHA LINK COFFINBERGER (Margaret[7], William[6], Adam[5], Alexander[4], John Adam II[3], John Adam I[2], John Jacob[1]) was the daughter of William Elmer and Margaret Link Coffinberger [The Link Family, page 446, No. 1412]. Bertha was born October 9, 1914, at Shepherdstown, West Virginia. She married, first, Bernard Nelson Whittington December 3, 1932, at Hagerstown, Maryland. He was the son of Joseph Sylvester and Mamie Ring Whittington and was born December 31, 1911, in Frederick County, Virginia. Bernard died in 1972 and is buried in Rosedale Cemetery at Martinsburg, West Virginia. Bertha married, second, Robert William Whittington, January 4, 1974. He was the son of George W. and Mary Agnes Hough Whittington. Robert died May 22, 1975, and is buried in Edge Hill Cemetery at Charles Town, West Virginia.

CHILDREN OF BERTHA AND BERNARD

(Sup) 5084 i Jo Ann Whittington, born September 7, 1933.
(Sup) 5085 ii Wilma Arlene Whittington, born October 9, 1935.
(Sup) 5086 iii Bernard Nelson Whittington, Jr., born July 1, 1944.

(Sup) 2823 WILLIAM CALVIN COFFINBERGER (Margaret[7], William[6], Adam[5], Alexander[4], John Adam II[3], John Adam I[2], John Jacob[1]) was the son of William Elmer and Margaret Link Coffinberger [The Link Family, page 446, No. 1412]. William was born July 11, 1923, at Martinsburg, West Virginia. He married Kathleen Mae Cooper, November 19, 1943, at Hagerstown, Maryland. Kathleen was the daughter of Theodore William and Ada Mae Easterday Cooper and was born December 23, 1923, at Hagerstown. William served in the U.S. Forces in World War II. He died January 24, 1948, and is buried at Martinsburg, West Virginia.

(Sup) 5087 i Cheryl Ann Coffinberger, born April 8, 1945.

(Sup) 2824 JAMES LINK COFFINBERGER (Martha[7], William[6], Adam[5], Alexander[4], John Adam II[3], John Adam I[2], John Jacob[1]) was the son of James Clifton and Martha Link Coffinberger [The Link Family, page 447, No. 1413]. James was born February 21, 1905, at Duffields, Jefferson County, West Virginia. He married Ida Mae Gageby December 20, 1924, Ida was the daughter of David and Nora Agnes Van Horn Gageby and was born July 8, 1904, at Bunker Hill, Berkeley County, West Virginia. James died December 4, 1982, and is buried in Bunker Hill Cemetery. Ida Mae died in 1983.

(Sup) 5088 i David Clifton Coffinberger, born Nov 15, 1927.
(Sup) 5089 ii Anne Virginia Coffinberger, born August 29, 1931.

(Sup) 2825 MARTHA PAULINE COFFINBERGER (Martha[7], William[6], Adam[5], Alexander[4], John Adam II[3], John Adam I[2], John Jacob[1]) was the daughter of James Clifton and Martha Link Coffinberger [The Link Family, page 447, No. 1413]. She was born June 6, 1907, at Shepherdstown, West Virginia, where she died February 7, 1912.

(Sup) 2826   MARGARET VIOLET COFFINBERGER (Martha^7, William^6, Adam^5, Alexander^4, John Adam II^3, John Adam I^2, John Jacob^1) was the daughter of James Clifton and Martha Link Coffinberger [The Link Family, page 447, No. 1413]. Margaret was born August 19, 1909, at Shepherdstown, West Virginia. She married Hugh S. Robinette November 16, 1927. He was born in 1908. They were divorced. Margaret died February 10, 1972, and is buried in the Lutheran Churchyard at Uvilla, Jefferson County, West Virginia.

(Sup) 2827   WILLIAM BANKS COFFINBERGER (Martha^7, William^6, Adam^5, Alexander^4, John Adam II^3, John Adam I^2, John Jacob^1) was the son of James Clifton and Martha Link Coffinberger [The Link Family, page 447, No. 1413]. William was born August 19, 1912, at Bardane, Jefferson County, West Virginia. He was a manager for J. C. Penney Company stores. William married Amanda Elizabeth Huff November 28, 1934. She was the daughter of James H. and Mary Elizabeth (Anderson) Huff and was born August 11, 1917, at Wheeling, West Virginia.

(Sup) 5090   i   James William Coffinberger, born Aug 31, 1935.
(Sup) 5091   ii   Joan Elizabeth Coffinberger, born Oct 15, 1937.
(Sup) 5092   iii Richard Lee Coffinberger, born March 27, 1948.

(Sup) 2828   DANIEL HENRY COFFINBERGER (Martha^7, William^6, Adam^5, Alexander^4, John Adam II^3, John Adam I^2, John Jacob^1) was the son of James Clifton and Martha Link Coffinberger [The Link Family, page 447, No. 1413]. Daniel was born August 26, 1914, at Bardane, West Virginia. He married Marguerite Johnston in May 1934. She was the daughter of Benjamin Franklin and Nellie Vernon (Custer) Johnston and was born May 20, 1912, at Winchester, Virginia.

(Sup) 5093   i   Sandra Lou Coffinberger, born July 15, 1936.
(Sup) 5094   ii   Deane Lee Coffinberger, born October 24, 1942.

(Sup) 2829   EUNICE ENGLE COFFINBERGER (Martha^7, William^6, Adam^5, Alexander^4, John Adam II^3, John Adam I^2, John Jacob^1) was the daughter of James Clifton and Martha Link Coffinberger [The Link Family, page 447, No. 1413]. Eunice was born November 17, 1916, at Bardane, Jefferson County, West Virginia. She married Lee French Evans August 13, 1937. Lee was born June 26, 1915, at Cumberland, Maryland. He was the son of Samuel and Nannie Elizabeth (Joy) Evans. Lee was killed in a motor vehicle accident August 24, 1943, at Cumberland, Maryland. Eunice died March 9, 1987.

(Sup) 5095   i   Ronald Lee Evans, born June 16, 1938.
(Sup) 5096   ii   Samuel Wayne Evans, born March 19, 1940.
(Sup) 5097   iii Eunice Diane Evans, born March 27, 1942.

(Sup) 2830   LEE MATTHIAS COFFINBERGER (Martha^7, William^6, Adam^5, Alexander^4, John Adam II^3, John Adam I^2, John Jacob^1) was the son of James Clifton and Martha Link Coffinberger [The Link Family, page 447, No. 1413]. Lee was born January 24, 1919, at Bardane, Jefferson County, West Virginia. He entered military service with the U.S. Army in World War II. September 17, 1942. He served overseas in Scotland, England, France, Belgium, Luxembourg, Holland, and Germany with the 503rd QM Company attached to First Army Headquarters and was discharged October 17, 1945. Lee married Helen M. Russler July 2, 1946. She was the daughter of Homer E. and Lillian Dodson Russler and was born December 17, 1925, at Martinsburg, West Virginia. Lee was a chemical analyst with Martin Marietta Corporation at Martinsburg from March, 1942, until his retirement in 1981.

(Sup) 5098   i   David Lee Coffinberger, born September 9, 1949.
(Sup) 5099   ii   Sherlyn Kay Coffinberger.

(Sup) 2831   JOHN HARMAN COFFINBERGER (Martha^7, William^6, Adam^5, Alexander^4, John Adam II^3, John Adam I^2, John Jacob^1) was the son of James Clifton and Martha Link Coffinberger [The Link Family, page 447, No. 1413]. John was born March 27, 1921, at Martinsburg, West Virginia. He married Evelyn Lee Cammer, August 30, 1946. She was the daughter of Leroy Marion and Julia Ann Barthlow Cammer and was born July 23, 1928, at Martinsburg, West Virginia. John entered military service for World War II, September 10, 1942. He was sent overseas in August 1943 and saw service in the 3437th Ordnance Detachment of the Second Army in Scotland, England, France, Belgium, and Germany. He was in the famous Battle of the Bulge. He was discharged from service November 26, 1945.

(Sup) 5100   i   Susan Marie Coffinberger, born March 12, 1949.
(Sup) 5101   ii   John Bradley Coffinberger, born Oct 29, 1957.

(Sup) 2832   NANNIE WISE COFFINBERGER (Martha^7, William^6, Adam^5, Alexander^4, John Adam II^3, John Adam I^2, John Jacob^1) was the daughter of James Clifton and Martha Link Coffinberger [The Link Family, page 447, No. 1413]. Nannie was born November 27, 1922, at Martinsburg, West Virginia. Nannie married Howard Philiphert Leber, Jr., December 6, 1940. Howard was the son of Howard Philiphert and Carrie Katie Houser Leber and was born October 30, 1924, at Hanover, Pennsylvania. Nannie and Howard were divorced. She married, second, Samuel Kipe.

CHILD OF NANNIE AND HOWARD
(Sup) 5102   i   Babeth Lorraine Leber Kipe, born Oct 25, 1946.

CHILDREN OF NANNIE AND SAMUEL
(Sup) 5103   ii   Mary Elizabeth Kipe, born March 11, 1949.
(Sup) 5104   iii John Kenneth Kipe, born April 17, 1954.

(Sup) 2833   MARY EDNA COFFINBERGER (Martha[7], William[6], Adam[5], Alexander[4], John Adam II[3], John Adam I[2], John Jacob[1]) was the daughter of James Clifton and Martha Link Coffinberger [The Link Family, page 447, No. 1413]. Mary was born January 31, 1926, at Martinsburg, West Virginia. She married Calvin McKown Caldwell May 15, 1949. Calvin was the son of Gilbert Spurrier and Louise Paige Linton Caldwell and was born July 5, 1927, at Martinsburg. Calvin studied watchmaking and engraving at Horological Institute of Pittsburgh, Pennsylvania. He owned the Roberts Jewelry store at Martinsburg.

(Sup) 5105   i   Mark Steven Caldwell, born March 17, 1951.
(Sup) 5106   ii   Elizabeth Paige Caldwell, born June 3, 1952.
(Sup) 5107   iii Mary Martha Caldwell, born January 16, 1954.
(Sup) 5108   iv   Calvin William Caldwell, born February 28, 1957.

(Sup) 2834   DENNIS CLIFTON COFFINBERGER (Martha[7], William[6], Adam[5], Alexander[4], John Adam II[3], John Adam I[2], John Jacob[1]) was the son of James Clifton and Martha Link Coffinberger [The Link Family, page 447, No. 1413]. Dennis was born July 27, 1928, at Martinsburg, West Virginia. He served in World War II in the Fourth Replacement Division of the U.S. Army, and was overseas from October 15, 1946, to March, 1948. Dennis married Frances Louise Sine October 28, 1948. She was the daughter of William Roscoe and Mary Edith Lawrence Sine and was born February 21, 1930, at Martinsburg, West Virginia. Dennis was a postal clerk with the Shepherdstown Post Office.

(Sup) 5109   i   Beverly Jean Coffinberger, born Sept 5, 1949.
(Sup) 5110   ii   Dennis Clifton Coffinberger.
(Sup) 5111   iii Drew Steven Coffinberger.
(Sup) 5112   iv   Timothy Daniels Coffinberger.
(Sup) 5113   v   Mildred Frances Coffinberger.

(Sup) 2835   HOWARD BAYRLE LINK (Adam[7], William[6], Adam[5], Alexander[4], John Adam II[3], John Adam I[2], John Jacob[1]) was the son of Adam Baker and Ethel Landis Link [The Link Family, page 447, No. 1415]. Bayrle was born September 5, 1918, at Charles Town, West Virginia. He married Alice Cary Polhamus, January 30, 1943. She was the daughter of Clinton Maynard and Mary Joseph Fenton Polhamus and was born August 25, 1921, at Summit Point, West Virginia. Bayrle studied at Roanoke College and served in the 355th Regiment of the Engineers Corps of the U.S. Army in World War II as a sergeant. He entered service October 20, 1942, was sent overseas October 20, 1943, was in the Normandy beachhead, and saw service in France and Germany being one of the group which threw the first bridge across the Rhine for the invasion. He was awarded ribbons and stars for the Normandy Campaign, Battle of Northern France, Battle of the Rhineland, Battle of the Ardennes, and the Central European Campaign. He was discharged October 20, 1945, after which he became associated with his father in the mercantile business in Charles Town, West Virginia, which he managed.

(Sup) 5114   i   Howard Bayrle Link, Jr., born September 3, 1943.
(Sup) 5115   ii   Kitty Karyl Link born May 2, 1947.
(Sup) 5116   iii Linda Louise Link, born October 26, 1948.

(Sup) 2836   ADAM BAKER LINK, JR. (Adam[7], William[6], Adam[5], Alexander[4], John Adam II[3], John Adam I[2], John Jacob[1]) was the son of Adam Baker and Ethel Landis Link [The Link Family, page 447, No. 1415]. Adam, Jr., was born June 14, 1920, at Charles Town, West Virginia. He served with the 2006th Ordnance Materiel Company of the Eighth Air Force overseas; he was in service three years and eight months. Adam married Margaret Isabel Marlow, January 15, 1943. She was the daughter of George Samuel and Ida Virginia Fleming Marlow and was born May 13, 1922, at Charles Town. Adam and Margaret both studied at Shepherd College. They had "Broadview Farm", near Shenandoah Junction, Jefferson County, West Virginia.

(Sup) 5117   i   Pamela Marlow Link, born September 28, 1946.
(Sup) 5118   ii   Adam Baker Link III, born April 5, 1951.

(Sup) 2837   MILDRED LOUISE LINK (Adam[7], William[6], Adam[5], Alexander[4], John Adam II[3], John Adam I[2], John Jacob[1]) was the daughter of Adam Baker and Ethel Landis Link [The Link Family, page 447, No. 1415]. Mildred was born May 23, 1925, at Charles Town, West Virginia, where she died September 23, 1931, and is buried in Edge Hill Cemetery.

(Sup) 2838   VIOLA ELOISE LINK (Samuel[7], William[6], Adam[5], Alexander[4], John Adam II[3], John Adam I[2], John Jacob[1]) was the daughter of Samuel Wesley and Grace Mills Link [The Link Family, page 448, No. 1416]. Eloise was born March 30, 1916, in Jefferson County, West Virginia. She studied at Shepherd College, West Virginia, and became a teacher. She married Marvin Edwards May 7, 1944. He was the son of Joseph and Sara Rockmaker Edwards and was born September 24, 1900, at Hoboken, New Jersey. Marvin was a chemist. Eloise died December 23, 1976, and Marvin died July 6, 1978. They are buried at Winchester, Virginia.

(Sup) 2839   CHARLOTTE MARION LINK (Samuel[7], William[6], Adam[5], Alexander[4], John Adam II[3], John Adam I[2], John Jacob[1]) was the daughter of Samuel Wesley and Grace Mills Link [The Link Family, page 448, No. 1416]. Marion was born January 14, 1919, at Bakerton, Jefferson County, West Virginia. She married Elihu Arthur Grabiner November 16, 1947. He was the son of Joseph Ralph and Jenny Fink Grabiner and was born February 26, 1918, at Chicago, Illinois. Marion and Arthur were divorced October, 1955. She was in the construction business in New York City and Washington, D.C., and then worked for an office machine company for fifteen years. In 1981 she retired and resided at Shenandoah Junction, Jefferson County.

(Sup) 2840 HILDRED LA HUE LINK (Samuel[7], William[6], Adam[5], Alexander[4], John Adam II[3], John Adam I[2], John Jacob[1]) was the daughter of Samuel Wesley and Grace Mills Link [The Link Family, page 448, No. 1416]. Hildred was born July 20, 1920, at Charles Town, West Virginia. She married George Gilbert Frocke January 10, 1939. He was the son of Abraham Jacob and Florence Alverene Stotler Frocke and was born December 19, 1916, at Brunswick, Maryland. George was employed at the Union Station, Washington, D.C. Hildred and George later resided at Charles Town.

(Sup) 5119   i   Glenda Gail Frocke, born March 6, 1940.
(Sup) 5120   ii   Patricia Lee Frocke, born May 15, 1942.
(Sup) 5121   iii George Gilbert Frocke, Jr., born Jan 17, 1944.

(Sup) 2841 FRANCES REBECCA LINK (Samuel[7], William[6], Adam[5], Alexander[4], John Adam II[3], John Adam I[2], John Jacob[1]) was the daughter of Samuel Wesley and Grace Mills Link [The Link Family, page 448, No. 1416]. Frances was born February 20, 1922, at Strasburg, Virginia. She married Richard Vern Owens November 1, 1944. He was the son of Fred Cecil and Lodema Dee McVickers Owens and was born November 1, 1922, at Fresno, California.

(Sup) 5122   i   Frances Dee Owens, born July 24, 1945.
(Sup) 5123   ii   Sandra Jean Owens, born October 29, 1946.
(Sup) 5123A   iii Deborah Ann Owens, born February 21, 1951.
(Sup) 5123B   iv   Richard Frederick Owens, born September 5, 1952.

(Sup) 2842 SAMUEL WESLEY LINK, JR. (Samuel[7], William[6], Adam[5], Alexander[4], John Adam II[3], John Adam I[2], John Jacob[1]) was the son of Samuel Wesley and Grace Mills Link [The Link Family, page 448, No. 1416]. Samuel, Jr., was born November 8, 1924, at Shenandoah Junction, Jefferson County, West Virginia, where he died November 30, 1924. He is buried in St. James Church cemetery at Uvilla, Jefferson County, West Virginia.

(Sup) 2843 JAMES DANIEL LINK (Samuel[7], William[6], Adam[5], Alexander[4], John Adam II[3], John Adam I[2], John Jacob[1]) was the son of Samuel Wesley and Grace Mills Link [The Link Family, page 448, No. 1416]. Jimmy was born May 7, 1926, at Duffields, Jefferson County, West Virginia. He served in the U.S. Navy and studied at Shepherd College and the University of West Virginia. He lived at at Charles Town, West Virginia, and at Washington, D.C., where he worked for the Heart Institute of the National Institutes of Health, and then for the Federal Food and Drug Administration.

(Sup) 2844 WILLIAM BYRON LINK (Samuel[7], William[6], Adam[5], Alexander[4], John Adam II[3], John Adam I[2], John Jacob[1]) was the son of Samuel Wesley and Grace Mills Link [The Link Family, page 448, No. 1416]. William was born March 25, 1928, at Duffields, Jefferson County, West Virginia. After enlisting in the U.S. Army Air Corps for three years from 1946 to 1949, he received a B.S. degree from Shepherd College in 1953 with a major in chemistry. He studied at West Virginia University 1953-54. William was employed by the Veterans Center in Martinsburg, West Virginia, and then by the Federal Food and Drug Administration, Washington, D.C. He married Ruby Jean Burton August 10, 1956, at Washington, D.C. The daughter of Benjamin Albert and Florence Myrtis (Gannaway) Burton, she was born September 6, 1935, at Lincoln, Alabama, and she attended Alverson-Draughn Business College 1953-54. William retired from Civil Service May 3, 1985, with thirty-four years of service.

(Sup) 5124   i   Wesley Brian Link born July 16, 1957.
(Sup) 5125   ii   Gregory Charles Link, born April 27, 1959.
(Sup) 5126   iii David Gordon Link, born April 6, 1961.

(Sup) 2845 BETTY GENEVA LINK (Samuel[7], William[6], Adam[5], Alexander[4], John Adam II[3], John Adam I[2], John Jacob[1]) was the daughter of Samuel Wesley and Grace Mills Link [The Link Family, page 448, No. 1416]. Betty was born September 2, 1930, at Duffields, Jefferson County, West Virginia. She married Harry Neil Waters on November 15, 1948, at Hyattsville, Maryland. He was the son of Napoleon and Mamie Walters and was born July 17, 1927, in Georgia. Betty and Harry were divorced in 1966.

(Sup) 5127   i   Ronald Neal Walters, born June 29, 1950.
(Sup) 5128   ii   Lucinda Starr Walters, born November 15, 1951.
(Sup) 5129   iii Harry Paul Walters, born June 3, 1954.
(Sup) 5130   iv   Joseph Thomas Walters, born April 29, 1956.

(Sup) 2846 SAMUEL WESLEY LINK, JR. (Samuel[7], William[6], Adam[5], Alexander[4], John Adam II[3], John Adam I[2], John Jacob[1]) was the son of Samuel Wesley and Grace Mills Link [The Link Family, page 448, No. 1416]. Samuel, Jr., was born January 22, 1936, at Charles Town, West Virginia. He graduated from Shepherd College, West Virginia, in 1957. He was an accountant for the U.S. Department of the Army and became the Chief of Finance and Accounting at the U.S. Army Materiel Command at Alexandria, Virginia. In 1973 he was named the outstanding Defense Department Accountant by the Association of Military Comptrollers. Sam married Donna Jean Collins June 21, 1958. She was the daughter of Chester Le Roy and Elsie Steward Collins of Martinsburg, West Virginia. In partnership with Sam's brother James, Donna and Sam owned and operated the B&L Childrens Shop at Sterling, Virginia, from 1971 to 1980. Sam and Donna moved to Leesburg, Virginia, in 1987.

(Sup) 5131   i   John Stewart Link, born April 17, 1959.
(Sup) 5132   ii   Rhonda Jean Link, born April 30, 1965.

(Sup) 2847 LAWRENCE VINCENT LINK (Samuel[7], William[6], Adam[5], Alexander[4], John Adam II[3], John Adam I[2], John Jacob[1]) was the son of Samuel Wesley and Grace Mills Link [The Link Family, page 448, No. 1416]. Larry was born March 15, 1941, at Charles Town, West Virginia.

(Sup) 2848   WILLIAM HOMER LINK (James[7], William[6], Adam[5], Alexander[4], John Adam II[3], John Adam I[2], John Jacob[1]) was the son of James Lester and Martha Coiner Link [The Link Family, page 449, No. 1421]. William was born October 25, 1935, at Daytona Beach, Florida. He married Kathryn Anne Cooper September 14, 1962, at Columbia, South Carolina. She was the daughter of Luther Grady and Miriam Roberta Greever Cooper and was born January 17, 1938, at Guntur, India. William and Kathryn resided at Richfield, North Carolina.

(Sup) 5133   i   Susan Christine Link, born September 12, 1963.
(Sup) 5134   ii Mary Virginia Link, born April 30, 1965.
(Sup) 5135   iii David Jonathan Link, born May 16, 1968.

(Sup) 2849   MARTHA SUSAN LINK (James[7], William[6], Adam[5], Alexander[4], John Adam II[3], John Adam I[2], John Jacob[1]) was the daughter of James Lester and Martha Coiner Link [The Link Family, page 449, No. 1421]. Sue was born March 8, 1937, at Daytona Beach, Florida. She graduated from Lenoir-Rhyne College with an A.B. degree in elementary education. She married Jimmy Lane Bruce August 7, 1960, at Hickory, North Carolina. Jimmy was the son of Armond Glenn and Lillian Jacobs Bruce and was born December 1, 1937, in Rowan County, North Carolina. He graduated from Lenoir-Rhyne College and the Lutheran Theological Southern Seminary. Sue and Jimmy resided at Laurinburg, North Carolina.

(Sup) 5136   i   Jonathan Mark Bruce, born September 16, 1961.
(Sup) 5137   ii Martha Constance Bruce, born March 20, 1964.

(Sup) 2850   SARAH CONSTANCE LINK (James[7], William[6], Adam[5], Alexander[4], John Adam II[3], John Adam I[2], John Jacob[1]) was the daughter of James Lester and Martha Coiner Link [The Link Family, page 449, No. 1421]. Sarah was born July 7, 1940, at Bristol, Washington County, Virginia. She married Paul Lawrence Moose March 25, 1962, near Middlebrook, Augusta County, Virginia. He was the son of Paul Edward and Eunice Aura Lee Bowman Moose and was born June 14, 1938, at Statesville, North Carolina.

(Sup) 5138   i   David Lawrence Moose, born December 3, 1963.
(Sup) 5139   ii John Edward Moose, born May 1, 1968 (twin).
(Sup) 5140   iii Phillip James Moose, born May 1, 1968 (twin).

(Sup) 2851   JANET CHRISTINE LINK (James[7], William[6], Adam[5], Alexander[4], John Adam II[3], John Adam I[2], John Jacob[1]) was the daughter of James Lester and Martha Coiner Link [The Link Family, page 449, No. 1421]. Janet was born June 5, 1943, at Bristol, Sullivan County, Tennessee. She married Robert Washington Davis, Jr., December 16, 1963, at Frederick, Maryland. He was the son of Robert Washington and Elizabeth Mae Smiley Davis and was born December 8, 1938, in Augusta County, Virginia. Janet and Robert lived in Staunton, Virginia.

(Sup) 5141   i   Cynthia Christine Davis, born October 21, 1964.
(Sup) 5142   ii Robert Timothy Davis, born November 16, 1967.
(Sup) 5143   iii Andrea Elaine Davis, born April 6, 1972.

(Sup) 2852   ELEANOR ANNE LINK (Albert[7], John[6], Adam[5], Alexander[4], John Adam II[3], John Adam I[2], John Jacob[1]) was the daughter of Ernest Albert and Anne Jones Link [The Link Family, page 449, No. 1423]. Eleanor was born October 26, 1912, at Brooklyn, New York. She graduated from Manual Training High School (Brooklyn) in 1930 and from Brooklyn College in 1932. She attained her law degree from Brooklyn Law School in 1935. Following this, she did postgraduate work at Brooklyn Law Graduate School, graduating in 1937 during which year she passed the New York Bar examination and was admitted to practice. She became an attorney and counsellor-at-law, specializing in admiralty and international law in New York City. Eleanor married LeRoy Stuart Zider, Jr., November 11, 1939.

(Sup) 5144   i   LeRoy Stuart Zider, III, born May 13, 1942.
(Sup) 5145   ii Robert Bruce Zider, born April 1, 1948.

(Sup) 2853   OGLE WINSTON LINK (Albert[7], John[6], Adam[5], Alexander[4], John Adam II[3], John Adam I[2], John Jacob[1]) was the son of Ernest Albert and Anne Jones Link [The Link Family, page 449, No. 1423]. Winston was born December 16, 1914, at Brooklyn, New York. He graduated from Manual Training High School, Brooklyn, in 1932; from Merchants and Bankers School, New York City, in 1933; and from Polytechnic Institute of Brooklyn in 1937 in civil engineering. He was a scholarship student and president of his class at Polytechnic for four years, a member of Pi Kappa Phi of which he was president, and Tau Beta Pi national honorary engineering fraternity. After college he went into commercial photography, organizing his own studio and specializing in fashion, microscopic, aeronautical, analytical, and other technical branches of commercial photography. He had outstanding success in the field of industrial photography. Six of his photographs of steam railroads were purchased by the Museum of Modern Art, and he became known internationally for his sound recordings of steam locomotives. Winston married Vonda Marteal Oglesby January 25, 1942. She was the daughter of Robert Carlton and Lily Stampley Oglesby.

(Sup) 5146   i   Winston Conway Link, born April 2, 1945.

(Sup) 2854   ESTELLE ATTALA LINK (Albert[7], John[6], Adam[5], Alexander[4], John Adam II[3], John Adam I[2], John Jacob[1]) was the daughter of Ernest Albert and Anne Jones Link [The Link Family, page 449, No. 1423]. Estelle was born March 22, 1919, at Albany, New York. She died November 12, 1919, at Brooklyn, New York, and is buried in Elmwood Cemetery, Shepherdstown, West Virginia.

(Sup) 2855 ALBERT LINK, JR. (Albert[7], John[6], Adam[5], Alexander[4], John Adam II[3], John Adam I[2], John Jacob[1]) was the son of Ernest Albert and Anne Jones Link [The Link Family, page 449, No. 1423]. Albert, Jr., was born August 5, 1922, at Brooklyn, New York. After graduating from Manual Training High School (Brooklyn) in 1939, where he won the Gold Medal Award for scholarship, he graduated from Merchants and Bankers School (New York City) in 1940 and New York University in 1944. He won a scholarship at New York University, where he received the degree of Mechanical Engineer. He became a Radio Technician in the U.S. Navy during World War II, serving until 1946. He was then employed by the New York Telephone Company, with which he remained many years and in 1977 held the position of Operations Supervisor for Outside Plant Engineering. As an avocation Albert developed and managed a dance orchestra. On April 11, 1953, Albert married Elizabeth Margaret Dennison. She was the daughter of Thomas Joseph and Mary Marian Dennison, of Brewster, New York.

(Sup) 5147   i Lucinda Anne Link, born July 19, 1955.
(Sup) 5148   ii Albert Dennis Link, born October 1, 1958.

(Sup) 2856 BARBARA ANNE LINK (Lester[7], John[6], Adam[5], Alexander[4], John Adam II[3], John Adam I[2], John Jacob[1]) was the daughter of Lester Waite and Barbara Shott Link [The Link Family, page 451, No. 1425]. She was born October 26, 1925, at Reading, Pennsylvania. Barbara studied and became a beautician. She married Robert Edward Gehret on November 25, 1948. He was the son of Edward Mitchel and Viola Mae English Gehret and was born April 24, 1923. Robert was in the U.S. Navy from 1943 until his retirement in 1973. He and Barbara then resided at Shoemakersville, Pennsylvania.

(Sup) 5149   i   Michael Robert Gehret, born June 18, 1953.
(Sup) 5150   ii Nancy Eileen Gehret, born March 3, 1955.
(Sup) 5151   iii Jo Anne Gehret, born March 27, 1956.
(Sup) 5152   iv Kathleen Kay Gehret, born Mary 28, 1960.

(Sup) 2857 ROBERT OGLE LINK (Lester[7], John[6], Adam[5], Alexander[4], John Adam II[3], John Adam I[2], John Jacob[1]) was the son of Lester Waite and Barbara Shott Link [The Link Family, page 451, No. 1425]. Robert was born September 11, 1927, at Reading, Pennsylvania. He joined the U.S. Navy during World War II, where he became an aviation flight mechanic. He received a B.S. degree in engineering from Johns Hopkins University. He was employed by the Martin Marietta Corporation and other engineering companies and as a contract engineer. Robert married Blanche Allene Clauser on September 2, 1950, at Reading. She was born January 9, 1928, at Norristown, Pennsylvania. Robert and Blanche resided at Reading, Pennsylvania.

(Sup) 5153   i Stephen Alan Link, born May 20, 1952.
(Sup) 5154   ii John Robert Link, born April 8, 1955.

2858 MARGARET NANNIE GARDNER (Samuel[7], Nancy[6], Mary[5], Alexander[4], John Adam II[3], John Adam I[2], John Jacob[1]) was born December 4, 1908, at Pitcairn, Pennsylvania. She married Oscar Oliver Rugh, July 28, 1936.

(Sup) 5155   i Russell Duane Rugh, born June 8, 1938.

2859 WILLIAM FONTAINE GARDNER (Samuel[7], Nancy[6], Mary[5], Alexander[4], John Adam II[3], John Adam I[2], John Jacob[1]) was born November 8, 1910, at Pitcairn, Pennsylvania. He married Verna Elizabeth Weston, September 26, 1941. Verna was born May 16, 1915, at North Braddock, Pennsylvania. Her parents were William Miller and Neomi Effie Miller Weston. William entered military service September 22, 1943, and was assigned to Company F, 338th Infantry in the 86th Division. He was in action in Italy, where he was wounded August 17, 1944, and awarded the Purple Heart, as well as campaign ribbons and medals. He was discharged December 30, 1946.

(Sup) 5156   i William Robert Gardner, born December 1, 1946.

2860 EDWIN HARPER GARDNER (Samuel[7], Nancy[6], Mary[5], Alexander[4], John Adam II[3], John Adam I[2], John Jacob[1]) was born June 22, 1913, at Pitcairn, Pennsylvania.

2861 JOHN WILLIAM GARDNER (Samuel[7], Nancy[6], Mary[5], Alexander[4], John Adam II[3], John Adam I[2], John Jacob[1]) was born July 12, 1915, at Pitcairn, Pennsylvania. He married Alma Cline, September 2, 1944.

(Sup) 5157   i Larry Wayne Gardner, born April 23, 1946.
(Sup) 5158   ii James Charles Gardner, born October 1, 1947.

2862 CHARLES FRANKLIN GARDNER (Samuel[7], Nancy[6], Mary[5], Alexander[4], John Adam II[3], John Adam I[2], John Jacob[1]) was born October 21, 1917, at Pitcairn, Pennsylvania. He entered the Army Air Force June 1, 1942, as an airplane mechanic and rose to the grade of sergeant. He was discharged December 3, 1945.

2863 THOMAS ROBERT GARDNER (Samuel[7], Nancy[6], Mary[5], Alexander[4], John Adam II[3], John Adam I[2], John Jacob[1]) was born November 1, 1919, at Pitcairn, Pennsylvania.

2864 MARY EDNA GARDNER (Samuel[7], Nancy[6], Mary[5], Alexander[4], John Adam II[3], John Adam I[2], John Jacob[1]) was born January 14, 1922, at Pitcairn, Pennsylvania. She married Norman Frederick Cole, August 16, 1941, at Murrysville, Pennsylvania. Norman was the son of Richard Sidney and Emily Bertha Roberts Cole and was born December 29, 1917, at Murrysville, Pennsylvania. Norman was a member of the 318th Infantry, 80th Division of the U. S. Army during World War II, serving from July 1, 1942, to November 12, 1945.

(Sup) 5159   i Mary Louise Cole, born June 16, 1947.

2865 WALTER HOWARD GARDNER (Samuel[7], Nancy[6], Mary[5], Alexander[4], John Adam II[3], John Adam I[2], John Jacob[1]) was born May 28, 1924, at Pitcairn, Pennsylvania. He entered the Army Medical Corps, April 1, 1943, and served until December 8, 1945, during which time he was given a warrant of T/5.

2866 BETTY JANE GARDNER (Samuel[7], Nancy[6], Mary[5], Alexander[4], John Adam II[3], John Adam I[2], John Jacob[1]) was born September 21, 1926, at Pitcairn, Pennsylvania.

2867 MARJORIE ANN GARDNER (Samuel[7], Nancy[6], Mary[5], Alexander[4], John Adam II[3], John Adam I[2], John Jacob[1]) was born May 26, 1929, at Pitcairn, Pennsylvania.

2868 CLARENCE CAULTON GARDNER (Frank[7], Nancy[6], Mary[5], Alexander[4], John Adam II[3], John Adam I[2], John Jacob[1]) was born in November, 1906. He died in August, 1907, at Philadelphia, Pennsylvania.

2869 LILLIAN FLORENCE GARDNER (Frank[7], Nancy[6], Mary[5], Alexander[4], John Adam II[3], John Adam I[2], John Jacob[1]) was born April 25, 1908, at Philadelphia, Pennsylvania. She died February 5, 1925, at Arlington, Virginia, where she is buried in Columbus Gardens Cemetery.

2870 ELSIE VIRGINIA GARDNER (Frank[7], Nancy[6], Mary[5], Alexander[4], John Adam II[3], John Adam I[2], John Jacob[1]) was born June 6, 1914, at Arlington, Virginia. She married Charles Emil Hoch, March 13, 1940. Charles was born April 5, 1913, at Oakland, California. His parents were Emil and Antoinette Smart Hoch. Charles, after public schooling, graduated from Webb Institute of Naval Architecture and Marine Engineering at New York City. He served in World War II as a Major. He was a practicing Naval Architect and Marine Engineer.

2871 CHESTER WILLIAM GARDNER (Frank[7], Nancy[6], Mary[5], Alexander[4], John Adam II[3], John Adam I[2], John Jacob[1]) was born in May, 1920. He married Mabel Cristine Alton, November 8, 1941. Chester graduated from college with an A. B. degree and became a Certified Public Accountant.

2872 LOUISE GARDNER WINFIELD (Mary[7], Nancy[6], Mary[5], Alexander[4], John Adam II[3], John Adam I[2], John Jacob[1]) was born June 23, 1923, at Takoma Park, Maryland. After her public schooling, she graduated from Wilson Teachers College at Washington, D. C., with an A. B. degree and became a high school teacher in Washington.

(Sup) 2873 JOHN DAWSON HESS (Irving[7], John[6], Elizabeth[5], Alexander[4], Adam II[3], John Adam I[2], John Jacob[1]) was the son of Irving Cheney and Catherine Dawson Hess [The Link Family, page 452, No. 1432]. John was born December 11, 1926, at San Diego, California. He graduated from Fresno State College, California, in 1949 with a major in geology and performed post-graduate studies at the University of Southern California, the University of Oregon, and the University of Nevada School of Mines. John married Cleo Mae Garra, December 1948, at San Diego. She was born January 12, 1931, at San Diego, the daughter of William Vincent and Evelyn Gunderson Garra. In 1950 John worked for the U.S. Bureau of Reclamation at Fresno, and in 1951 he was employed by the Imperial Irrigation District in the Imperial Valley of California, where he was chief engineer for research, involved primarily in litigation on the California-Arizona water dispute. In 1953 he established his own consulting and testing laboratory in agri-

culture, hydrology, soil mechanics, and materials engineering. He was the president of the John D. Hess Testing Corporation of El Centro, and of Structural Behavior Engineering Laboratories, Inc., of Phoenix, Arizona. He married, second, Ada Louise Ramsey, June 8, 1967. Ada was born July 7, 1927, at Buffalo Gap, Texas, and lived in Arizona prior to her marriage to John. By a previous marriage she had two children, Mary and Ralph Ramsey. John was a registered engineering geologist in California, Arizona, and Idaho, and he performed extensive travel in connection with his business. He died during a visit to China in March, 1986.

CHILDREN OF JOHN AND CLEO

(Sup) 5160 i   John Irving Hess, born October 11, 1949.
(Sup) 5161 ii   Catharine Anne Hess, born March 10, 1951.
(Sup) 5162 iii Mary Teresa Hess, born July 17, 1952.
(Sup) 5163 iv   Patricia Irene Hess, born Jan 28, 1954 (twin).
(Sup) 5164 v   Paula Evelyn Hess, born Jan 28, 1954 (twin).
(Sup) 5165 vi   Denise Ellen Hess, born June 26, 1955.
(Sup) 5166 vii Cleo Michele Hess, born August 28, 1958.

(Sup) 2874 JOSEPH IRVING HESS (Irving[7], John[6], Elizabeth[5], Alexander[4], John Adam II[3], John Adam I[2], John Jacob[1]) was the son of Irving Cheney and Catherine Dawson Hess [The Link Family, page 452, No. 1432]. Joe was born March 26, 1929, at San Diego, California. He served in the U.S. Army from November 1950 until July 31, 1953, and saw extensive action with the 23rd Infantry Regiment of the 2nd Infantry (Indianhead) Division. He was severely wounded July 31, 1952, in Korea. He was at Letterman Army Hospital for a year. He later married Rosemarie Cohen, who had been his nurse there. She was the daughter of Samuel and Mary Cohen of Medford, Massachusetts and was born at Boston. Joe became successful in the real estate business in San Francisco. He and Rosemarie resided at Tiburon, Marin County, California.

(Sup) 5167 i   Sandra Catharine Hess, born October 25, 1960.
(Sup) 5168 ii   Gregory Dawson Hess, born August 6, 1962.

(Sup) 2875 JOHN THOMAS HESS (Guy[7], John[6], Elizabeth[5], Alexander[4], John Adam II[3], John Adam I[2], John Jacob[1]) was the son of Guy Link and Catherine Barringer Hess [The Link Family, page 453, No. 1435]. John was born January 16, 1907, at Baltimore, Maryland. He married Katherine Lila Davis, June 4, 1946. She was the daughter of Archibald Benjamin and Florence Ethel Dutton Davis and was born January 14, 1910, at Denver, Colorado. After studying to be a marine engineer, John became recreation supervisor for the City of Monrovia, California. He died November 5, 1975, and is buried at Forest Lawn Cemetery, Los Angeles, California.

(Sup) 5169 i   Robert Barringer Hess, born April 15, 1948.

Guy, Jr., was born December 6, 1919, at Houston, Texas. He finished public and high schools, studied two years at Texas A&M and entered military service. His duty took him to England in the Air Corps during World War II from 1943 to 1945, and he was discharged with a staff sergeant rating. In 1946 he reentered the Armed Forces. On May 15, 1943, he married Margaret Ruth Johnson, daughter of Nicholas James and Pauline White Johnson. She was born May 13, 1922, at St. Louis, Missouri.

(Sup) 5178   i   Barry Thomas Hess, born January 20, 1947.
(Sup) 5179   ii   Daniel Stephen Hess, born February 13, 1949.
(Sup) 5180   iii   Pamela Ruth Hess, born March 11, 1953.
(Sup) 5181   iv   Guy Link Hess, III, born December 4, 1964.

(Sup) 2880   ROBERT LEE HESS (Harry[7], John[6], Elizabeth[5], Alexander[4], John Adam II[3], John Adam I[2], John Jacob[1]) was the son of Harry Lee and Elise Jaeggi Hess [The Link Family, page 453, No. 1436; and Supplement No. 1436]. Robert was born November 4, 1926, at Oakland, California. He entered the U.S. Navy in 1944, serving through World War II until 1946. He graduated from the University of California at Berkeley and was commissioned an ensign in the Naval Reserve in 1949. After receiving his M.S. degree in physics in 1953, Robert served on active duty as a lieutenant with U.S. Navy air forces in the Pacific from November 1954 to October 1956. Returning to graduate studies, he received a Ph.D. in microwave electronics from the University of California, Berkeley, in 1959. He served again on extended active duty during the Vietnam conflict, from 1960 until 1963, as a lieutenant-commander with cruiser-destroyer forces in the Pacific; later at a naval laboratory at San Francisco, 1963-65; on the staff of the Commander-in-Chief Atlantic Fleet in 1979; and in the Office of the Chief of Naval Operations in 1982. Captain Hess served in the Naval Reserve as instructor of naval tactics, commanded various Reserve units in the Washington D.C. area, and became Inspector General for the mid-Atlantic states Naval Reserve region, 1980-82. His civilian employment was as a consultant for companies providing services to the Navy Department in the Washington area. He married Rebecca Jane Yingling July 2, 1965, at Hanover, Pennsylvania. She was the daughter of Charles Thomas and Lena Sheaffer Yingling and was born November 9, 1936, at Hanover, Pennsylvania. Rebecca studied at the Baltimore City Hospitals and became an X-ray technician. Robert and Rebecca resided at Vienna, Virginia. He was principal editor of this Supplement to The Link Family.

(Sup) 5182   i   Catherine Ann Hess, born May 27, 1966.
(Sup) 5183   ii   Elizabeth Lee Hess, born April 1, 1968.
(Sup) 5184   iii   Martha Sue Hess, born June 21, 1970.

(Sup) 2876   HELEN MARIE HESS (Guy[7], John[6], Elizabeth[5], Alexander[4], John Adam II[3], John Adam I[2], John Jacob[1]) was the daughter of Guy Link and Catherine Barringer Hess [The Link Family, page 453, No. 1435]. Helen was born August 7, 1910, at Baltimore, Maryland. She married Clayton Valentine Jones, September 2, 1937. He was the son of John C. and Edna Sophronia Jones and was born November 1, 1915, at Blanco, Texas. Clayton was graduated from Texas A&M College in animal husbandry. They lived in Houston, Texas, where he was a purchasing agent for Todd Shipyards. Helen and Clayton were divorced.

(Sup) 5170   i   Kathryn Janeen Jones, born February 7, 1940.
(Sup) 5171   ii   Clayleen Marie Jones, born July 13, 1942.
(Sup) 5172   iii   Jack Alton Jones, born March 31, 1946.
(Sup) 5173   iv   Deborah Jill Jones, born January 18, 1950.

(Sup) 2877   LEWIS LEE HESS (Guy[7], John[6], Elizabeth[5], Alexander[4], John Adam II[3], John Adam I[2], John Jacob[1]) was the son of Guy link and Catherine Barringer Hess [The Link Family, page 453, No. 1435]. Lewis was born March 9, 1912, at Baltimore, Maryland. He was an engineer in production of synthetic rubber, then assistant manager for engineering for a petroleum company in Houston, Texas. He married Orlean Janice Fretwell July 3, 1931. She was the daughter of Lawrence Delmond and Ellen Katherine Juddleston Fretwell and was born May 11, 1908, at Mart, Texas. Orlean died March 30, 1975. Lewis married, second, Carmen Sellars September 2, 1976.

(Sup) 5174   i   Guy Lawrence Hess, born August 2, 1934.
(Sup) 5175   ii   Lewis Lee Hess, Jr., born January 6, 1938.

(Sup) 2878   KATHERINE BARRINGER HESS (Guy[7], John[6], Elizabeth[5], Alexander[4], John Adam II[3], John Adam I[2], John Jacob[1]) was the daughter of Guy Link and Catherine Barringer Hess [The Link Family, page 453, No. 1435]. Katherine was born September 6, 1915, at Baltimore, Maryland. She married Neil Edward Watson, May 20, 1939. He was the son of Charles Edward and Frances Peake Watson and was born April 1, 1917, at Houston, Texas.

(Sup) 5176   i   Neil Watson, born October 28, 1949.
(Sup) 5177   ii   Deborah Watson, born September 3, 1952.

(Sup) 2879   GUY LINK HESS, JR. (Guy[7], John[6], Elizabeth[5], Alexander[4], John Adam II[3], John Adam I[2], John Jacob[1]) was the son of Guy Link and Catherine Barringer Hess [The Link Family, page 453, No. 1435].

(Sup) 2881 DAVID WILSON GLASS, IV (Florence[7], John[6], Elizabeth[5], Alexander[4], John Adam II[3], John Adam I[2], John Jacob[1]) was the son of David Wilson and Florence Hess Glass, III [The Link Family, page 454, No. 1437]. David, IV, was born January 2, 1917, at Baltimore, Maryland. On completing public schools in Baltimore he attended Gordon Military College at Barnesville, Georgia, and Emory University in Atlanta. In 1939 he was employed by the Commercial Credit Company in Baltimore, and from 1940 to 1942 was a field investigator in the mid-Atlantic states for the Commercial Investment Trust Corporation of New York. He served as a special agent in the Counter-Intelligence Corps of the U.S. Army Military Intelligence Service, 1942-1946. From 1947 to 1951 David was engaged by the Union Trust Company of Maryland while attending courses at the American Institute of Banking, Baltimore. In 1949 he received the B.S. degree in social science from Loyola College. From 1951 until his retirement in 1974, David was an employee in the Office of Security of the U.S. Central Intelligence Agency. David married Martha Elizabeth Lewis October 23, 1943, at Philadelphia, Pennsylvania. She was the daughter of William Osgood and Lola Elizabeth (Hooper) Lewis and was born October 8, 1922, at Hoopersville, Dorchester County, Maryland. Martha worked for Army Intelligence during 1942-46 and for the CIA from 1952 to 1972. After retirement, David researched American automobile history and was a collector of automotive trademarks and nameplates. He was a member of the Society of Automotive Historians, Antique Automobile Club of America, the Horseless Carriage Club of America, Alexandria-Washington Lodge of the A. F. and A. M., Scottish Rite, Shriners, and Sons of the American Revolution.

(Sup) 2882 JOHN STRIDER GLASS (Florence[7], John[6], Elizabeth[5], Alexander[4], John Adam II[3], John Adam I[2], John Jacob[1]) was the son of David Wilson and Florence Hess Glass, III [The Link Family, page 454, No. 1437]. John was born September 29, 1924, at Baltimore, Maryland. On completion of public schools in Baltimore, he studied at Johns Hopkins University. His studies were interrupted by service in the U.S. Army from September 1945 to December 1946, and he graduated from Johns Hopkins University with a Bachelor of Engineering degree in 1949. He moved to Albuquerque, New Mexico, where he married Margaret Helen Ewing August 23, 1952. She was the daughter of Fred Clark and Hazel Blanche (Raber) Ewing and was born March 28, 1922, at Salem, Oregon. Margaret graduated in 1944 from Willamette University. She died August 22, 1956, at Albuquerque. John received the degree of Master of Hospital Administrator in 1959 from the University of Minnesota. He became assistant administrator of Presbyterian Hospital Center, 1955-1962; administrator of Carrie Tingley Hospital for Crippled Children, 1962-1968; director of the North Central New Mexico Comprehensive Health Planning Council 1968-1976; and thereafter remained active in the administration of medical and health services.

(Sup) 5185 i Nancy Lee Glass, born August 1, 1954.

2883 WALTER FRANKLIN RAV, JR. (Mary[7], Thomas[6], Mary[5], Alexander[4], John Adam II[3], John Adam I[2], John Jacob[1]) was born August 22, 1902, at Harpers Ferry, West Virginia. He married Louise Fuller, November 7, 1942. Louise was born September 20, 1909, at Pine, Arizona. She was the daughter of Addison Everett and Katherine Isabell Byers Fuller. Louise, before marriage, was a registered nurse. Walter became a hotel manager.

(Sup) 5186 i Mary Katherine Rav, born October 7, 1943.
(Sup) 5187 ii Mary Agnes Rav, born March 25, 1946.

2884 THOMAS RUDOLPH RAV (Mary[7], Thomas[6], Mary[5], Alexander[4], John Adam II[3], John Adam I[2], John Jacob[1]) was born June 29, 1903, at Clarksburg, West Virginia. He married Gretchen Watson, July 2, 1932. She was the daughter of Allen and Ida Bauer Watson. Thomas graduated with an A. B. degree from Leland Stanford University and entered the finance business, becoming director and officer in six intercompany corporations in California, Texas and Utah. He was a member of the University Club at Los Angeles, California.

(Sup) 5188 i Thomas Watson Rav, born September 29, 1933.
(Sup) 5189 ii Sally Rav, born July, 27, 1936.

2885 HARRY LEWIS ECHOLS, JR. (Lillian[7], Thomas[6], Mary[5], Alexander[4], John Adam II[3], John Adam I[2], John Jacob[1]) was born July 12, 1915, in Arlington County, Virginia. He married Maty Hawes Lloyd, daughter of Edgar Lee and Lucy Virginia Butler Hawes, December 6, 1943. Maty was born December 1, 1902, at Flint Hill, Virginia. Harry enlisted in the American Air Forces, December 10, 1942, and served until February 17, 1946, a part of the time in the Philippines, during World War II.

2886 WILLIAM PORTERFIELD ECHOLS (Lillian[7], Thomas[6], Mary[5], Alexander[4], John Adam II[3], John Adam I[2], John Jacob[1]) was born August 28, 1918, at Washington, D. C. During World War II he entered service with the 672 Engineers, Topography Company, and was in active duty from October 29, 1942, until February 3, 1946, in France, Belgium and Germany.

2887 JUANITA ELAINE CROWN (Maude[7], Robert[6], Mary[5], Alexander[4], John Adam II[3], John Adam I[2], John Jacob[1]) was born November 18, 1903, at Washington, D. C.

2888 STANLEY CAMPBELL CROWN (Maude[7], Robert[6], Mary[5], Alexander[4], John Adam II[3], John Adam I[2], John Jacob[1]) was born July 29, 1906, at Washington, D. C.

2889 FENTON WILLIAM CROWN, JR. (Maude[7], Robert[6], Mary[5], Alexander[4], John Adam II[3], John Adam I[2], John Jacob[1]) was born June 22, 1909, at Washington, D. C.

2890 EDWARD HESS CROWN (Maude[7], Robert[6], Mary[5], Alexander[4], John Adam II[3], John Adam I[2], John Jacob[1]) was born December 3, 1913, at Washington, D. C.

2891 EMMA VIRGINIA CROWN (Maude[7], Robert[4], Mary[5], Alexander[4], John Adam II[3], John Adam I[2], John Jacob[1]) was born December 22, 1916, at Cherrydale, Virginia.

2892 ARTHUR CROWN (Maude[7], Robert[4], Mary[5], Alexander[4], John Adam II[3], John Adam I[2], John Jacob[1]).

2893 BEATRICE VIRGINIA ASHFORD (Margaret[7], Robert[6], Mary[5], Alexander[4], John Adam II[3], John Adam I[2], John Jacob[1]) was born November 18, 1906, at Washington, D. C. She married J. E. Fritchley.

2894 GLADYS HESS ASHFORD (Margaret[7], Robert[6], Mary[5], Alexander[4], John Adam II[3], John Adam I[2], John Jacob[1]) was born October 30, 1908, at Washington, D. C.

2895 ROBERT LEE ASHFORD (Margaret[7], Robert[6], Mary[5], Alexander[4], John Adam II[3], John Adam I[2], John Jacob[1]) was born July 7, 1912, at Washington, D. C.

2896 ALICE ASHFORD (Margaret[7], Robert[6], Mary[5], Alexander[4], John Adam II[3], John Adam I[2], John Jacob[1]) was born at Washington, D. C.

2897 JACQUILINE ASHFORD (Margaret[7], Robert[6], Mary[5], Alexander[4], John Adam II[3], John Adam I[2], John Jacob[1]) was born March 7, 1923, at Canton, Ohio.

(Sup) 2898 MARY ELIZABETH HESS (Gordon[7], Frank[6], Elizabeth[5], Alexander[4], John Adam II[3], John Adam[2], John Adam I[2], John Jacob[1]) was the daughter of Gordon Cumming and Mary Frances Cumming Hess [The Link Family, page 456, No. 1449]. Mary Elizabeth (Honey) was born March 14, 1919, at Hampton, Virginia. She married Robert Roland Johnson March 12, 1944, at Burlingame, California. After serving in World War with the U.S. Army, Robert graduated from Stanford University and became a chemical engineer. The Johnsons resided in San Carlos and later in Burlingame, California.

(Sup) 5190 i Cheryl Frances Johnson, born in May, 1950.
(Sup) 5191 ii Robert Gordon Johnson, born in April, 1952.

(Sup) 2899 VIRGINIA DARLING HESS (Gordon[7], Frank[6], Elizabeth[5], Alexander[4], John Adam II[3], John Adam I[2], John Jacob[1]) was the daughter of Gordon Cumming and Mary Frances Cumming Hess [The Link Family, page 456, No. 1449]. Virginia was born August 23, 1920, at San Francisco, California. She married Bernard John Goldsmith, May 16, 1943, at Hampton, Virginia. John was the son of Bernard Seaman and Elsie Caroline Meyer Goldsmith and was born April 22, 1919, at Oakland, California. He and Virginia both graduated from the University of California, Berkeley, in 1943. After serving as an officer in the Marine Corps in World War II, John pursued a career in elementary school education, and he retired as principal of a middle school in June, 1984. The Goldsmiths lived in Hollister, California.

(Sup) 5192 i Scott Warren Goldsmith, born September 24, 1947.
(Sup) 5193 ii John Bernard Goldsmith, born March 3, 1950.
(Sup) 5194 iii Lynn Elizabeth Goldsmith, born December 7, 1956.

(Sup) 2900 GORDON FRANK MacGINITIE (Beatrice[7], Frank[6], Elizabeth[5], Alexander[4], John Adam II[3], John Adam I[2], John Jacob[1]) was the son of Harry Dunlap and Emma Beatrice Hess MacGinitie [The Link Family, page 457, No. 1450]. Gordon was born December 28, 1935, at Arcata, California. He graduated from Stanford University.

(Sup) 2901 BEATRICE ANN MacGINITIE (Beatrice[7], Frank[6], Elizabeth[5], Alexander[4], John Adam II[3], John Adam I[2], John Jacob[1]) was the daughter of Harry Dunlap and Emma Beatrice Hess MacGinitie [The Link Family, page 457, No. 1450]. Bea Ann was born July 28, 1939. She married William Sausman Minkler August 5, 1961. He was the son of William Annin and Alice Mary Gooden Minkler and was born March 29, 1935, at Pittsburgh, Pennsylvania. William studied mechanical engineering at Carnegie-Mellon University, where he received a Ph.D. degree and was a member of Beta Theta Pi social fraternity, Sigma Xi, and Tau Beta Pi.

(Sup) 5195 i William Thomas Minkler, born April 3, 1963.
(Sup) 5196 ii Donald Burton Minkler, born April 23, 1965.
(Sup) 5197 iii Marjorie Alice Minkler, born July 12, 1967.
(Sup) 5198 iv Sharon Andrea Minkler, born January 6, 1969.

(Sup) 2902 HARRIETT VIRGINIA LEACH (Jeanette[7], Mary[6], Elizabeth[5], Alexander[4], John Adam II[3], John Adam I[2], John Jacob[1]) was the daughter of Earl Lester and Jeanette McKee Leach [The Link Family, page 457, No. 1451]. Harriett was born December 10, 1923, at Martinsburg, West Virginia. She received an A.B. degree from Shepherd College, Shepherdstown, West Virginia, in 1949. Harriett married David C. Mudge November 3, 1951, at Martinsburg, West Virginia. He was the son of George E. and Lottie Entler Mudge and was born September 27, 1915, at Martinsburg. Harriet and David resided at Martinsburg.

(Sup) 5199 i Robert E. Mudge, born December 24, 1954.

2903 ROBERT LEE McKEE (John[7], Mary[6], Mary[5], Alexander[4], John Adam II[3], John Adam I[2], John Jacob[1]) was born March 29, 1918, at Martinsburg, West Virginia. He married Margaret Frances Wilson, March 27, 1947, at Hagerstown, Maryland. Margaret was born March 26, 1918, at Morefield, West Virginia. She was the daughter of Joseph Henry and Aline Blanche Scott Wilson.

2904 JOHN STROTHER McKEE, JR. (John[7], Mary[6], Mary[5], Alexander[4], John Adam II[3], John Adam I[2], John Jacob[1]) was born February 6, 1920, at Martinsburg, West Virginia. He studied medicine after securing his A. B. degree at West Virginia State University, receiving his M. D. there in 1943. He did postgraduate work at Northwestern University in 1944 and entered the Navy, with commission of Lieutenant j.g., where he served until the end of World War II. On May 3, 1943,

(Sup) 2911 JOHN MARVIN HAWK (Harriet[7], Mary[6], Elizabeth[5], Alexander[4], John Adam II[3] John Adam I[2], John Jacob[1]) was the son of John Marvin and Harriet McKee Hawk [The Link Family, page 458, No. 1456]. John, Jr., was born January 30, 1934, at Martinsburg, West Virginia. He married Katherine Lee Grant June 14, 1958, at Martinsburg. She was the daughter of Harry and Abbie Tabler Grant and was born September 27, 1937, at Martinsburg. John attended Virginia Polytechnic Institute 1951-1955 and was employed by the Potomac Light and Power Company. Katherine graduated from Shepherd College, West Virginia.

(Sup) 5202B   i Mary Katherine Hawk, born April 1, 1961.
(Sup) 5202C   ii Laura Jon Hawk, born June 29, 1963.

2912 FRANCES CLARK OSBOURN (Herbert[7], Alexander[6], Jane[5], Alexander[4], John Adam II[3], John Adam I[2], John Jacob[1]) was born March 13, 1906, at Hyattsville, Maryland. After her elementary schooling, Frances studied at Notre Dame Academy, Washington, D. C. She married Russell Harrison Duckson, January 21, 1924. Russell was the son of Norvel Delmont and Frances Carliel Duckson and was born March 1, 1900, at Dayton, Ohio. He died February 8, 1946, and is buried at Dayton. Frances married Arthur John Boehm, October 25, 1932. Arthur was born March 8, 1906, at Mars, Pennsylvania. He was the son of Vernando Lewis and Ida Belle Little Boehm.

CHILD OF FRANCES AND RUSSELL

(Sup) 5203   i Kenneth Vincent Duckson, born July 19, 1928.

CHILDREN OF FRANCES AND ARTHUR

(Sup) 5204   ii John Edward Boehm, born July 17, 1940.
(Sup) 5205 iii Arthur John Boehm, Jr., born October 19, 1944.
(Sup) 5206   iv William Joseph Boehm, born December 30, 1947.

2913 RUTH ELIZABETH OSBOURN (Herbert[7], Alexander[6], Jane[5], Alexander[4], John Adam II[3], John Adam I[2], John Jacob[1]) was born March 21, 1908, at Hyattsville, Maryland. She married James Clement Cawood II, August 20, 1935. James was born December 16, 1899, at Leonardstown, Maryland. He was the son of James Clement and Alice Raley Cawood. James became a physician and surgeon and practiced at Washington, D. C. Ruth was educated at Notre Dame Academy, at Washington.

(Sup) 5207   i James Clement Cawood III, born June 4, 1936.
(Sup) 5208   ii June Matie Cawood, born June 25, 1940.
(Sup) 5209 iii Valentine Mark Cawood, born December 30, 1943.

2914 RAYMOND ALLEN OSBOURN (Herbert[7], Alexander[6], Jane[5], Alexander[4], John Adam II[3], John Adam I[2], John Jacob[1]) was born September 6, 1911, at Hyattsville, Maryland. He was educated at St. John's College, Washington, D. C., and Georgetown University, where he graduated in 1933 with a B. S. degree. He studied medicine at Georgetown University School of Medicine and was awarded his M. D. in 1940. He did advanced study in Mycology at Duke University in 1947 and at the Graduate School of Medicine, University of Pennsylvania, in 1948-49. Raymond was a specialist certified by the American Board of Dermatology

he married Jean Lenre Chandler at Ashland, Kentucky. Jean was the daughter of Simon B. and Maude Estelle Greene Chandler and was born April 6, 1920, at Columbia, Missouri. Jean graduated from Northwestern University in 1946. John practiced medicine at Lyndhurst, Ohio.

(Sup) 5200   i Susan Ann McKee, born May 6, 1944.
(Sup) 5201   ii John Douglas McKee, born May 3, 1947.

2905 LORENA WAUNITA McKEE (John[7], Mary[6], Mary[5], Alexander[4], John Adam II[3], John Adam I[2], John Jacob[1]) was born May 7, 1923, at Martinsburg, West Virginia.

2906 DONALD EUGENE McKEE (John[7], Mary[6], Mary[5], Alexander[4], John Adam II[3], John Adam I[2], John Jacob[1]) was born November 9, 1938, at Martinsburg, West Virginia.

2907 DOUGLAS PARKER McKEE (Ernest[7], Mary[6], Mary[5], Alexander[4], John Adam II[3], John Adam I[2], John Jacob[1]) was born June 9, 1919, at Martinsburg, West Virginia. He married Frances Hayes Langford, May 29, 1939. Frances was born December 24, 1920, at Martinsburg, and was the daughter of Samuel Mervyn and Nannie Louise Dorn Langford. Douglas was in World War II, entering service May 11, 1942. He was a First Lieutenant, a Bombardier with the Eighth Air Force, and completed thirty-one missions. He had won the Distinguished Flying Cross and the Air Medal with four Oak Leaves when he was shot down over Kirchheim-Bolander, November 5, 1944. His body was recovered and buried in Avon Cemetery in France.

(Sup) 5202   i Sherry Ann McKee, born May 6, 1940.

2908 VIRGINIA CATHERINE McKEE (Ernest[7], Mary[6], Mary[5], Alexander[4], John Adam II[3], John Adam I[2], John Jacob[1]) was born March 13, 1923, at Martinsburg, West Virginia, where she died March 13, 1923, and is buried in the Old Northern Cemetery.

2909 ANN HESS McKEE (Ernest[7], Mary[6], Mary[5], Alexander[4], John Adam II[3], John Adam I[2], John Jacob[1]) was born January 15, 1930, at Martinsburg, West Virginia. She married Thom Richard Keller, March 25, 1949. Thom was the son of James Henry and Bertha Boyd Myers Keller and was born April 23, 1928, at Martinsburg, West Virginia.

(Sup) 2910 IRIS GRAY HAWK (Harriet[7], Mary[6], Elizabeth[5], Alexander[4], John Adam II[3] John Adam I[2], John Jacob[1]) was the daughter of John Marvin and Harriet McKee Hawk [The Link Family, page 458, No. 1456]. Iris was born November 16, 1931, at Martinsburg, West Virginia. She married John David Phillips January 29, 1955, at Shepherdstown, West Virginia. He was the son of John Reese and Sarah Lewis Phillips and was born July 31, 1929, at Peckville, Pennsylvania. Iris graduated from Randolph Macon Womens College in 1953. Jack received a B.S. degree from the College of William and Mary and a master's degree in hospital administration from the Medical College of Virginia in 1958. They resided at Livingston, New Jersey, where Jack was executive vice president of Saint Barnabas Medical Center.

(Sup) 5202A   i Victoria Lynn Phillips, born May 6, 1958.

(Sup) 2924 JAMES POORE OSBOURN (Samuel[7], Nancy[6], John[5], Alexander[4], John Adam II[3], John Adam I[2], John Jacob[1]) was the son of Samuel Edmund and Mary Poore Osbourne [The Link Family, page 461, No. 1474]. James was born December 26, 1913. He received an A.B. degree from Harvard. He entered the diplomatic service and served as vice consul at Bucharest, Rumania, after World War II. James married Ann Buchanan Clay, April 12, 1947. She was the daughter of Alfred Thomas and Gladys Young (Staley) Clay. James died October 14, 1986, and is buried in Elmwood Cemetery at Shepherdstown, West Virginia.

(Sup) 2925 SAMUEL EDMUND OSBOURN, JR. (Samuel[7], Nancy[6], John[5], Alexander[4], John Adam II[3], John Adam I[2], John Jacob[1]) was the son of Samuel Edmund and Mary Poore Osbourn [The Link Family, page 461, No. 1474]. Samuel, Jr., was born March 20, 1917. He received his B.S. degree at Harvard and entered the insurance business at Germantown, Pennsylvania. He married Doris Eveline Baker June 7, 1958, at Bryn Mawr, Pennsylvania. She was the daughter of Dean Earl and Eveline West (Oram) Baker and was born October 2, 1924. Samuel and Doris resided at Norristown, Pennsylvania. He was director of Corporate Systems Life Insurance Company of North American until 1970, then a consulting systems analyst for National Information Systems four years, and later a systems engineer for Electronic Data Systems Corporation. He was an elder and trustee of the Presbyterian Church, a Fellow of Life Management Institute, and a member of many professional and social societies including the Masons, Quarter Century Club, Association of Systems Management, Society of Certified Data Processors, the Betzwood Civic Association, Sigma Alpha Epsilon Fraternity, and Harvard Club of Philadelphia.

(Sup) 5212   i   Samuel Edmund Osbourn III, born Sept 23, 1961.
(Sup) 5213   ii   Dean Baker Osbourn, born August 18, 1965.

(Sup) 2926 ELIZABETH DAY OSBOURN (Samuel[7], Nancy[6], John[5], Alexander[4], John Adam II[3], John Adam I[2], John Jacob[1]) was the daughter of Samuel Edmund and Mary Poore Osbourne [The Link Family, page 461, No. 1474]. Elizabeth was born September 17, 1919. She studied at Sarah Lawrence College. On May 3, 1941, she married Robert S. McCoy, who was the son of Harold J. McCoy. Elizabeth and Robert lived at Larchment, New York.

(Sup) 2927 NANCY ELIZABETH OSBOURN (John[7], Nancy[6], John[5], Alexander[4], John Adam II[3], John Adam I[2], John Jacob[1]) was the daughter of John Melvin and Bessie Poston Osbourn [The Link Family, page 461, No. 1475]. Nancy was born February 15, 1905, at Shenandoah Junction, Jefferson County, West Virginia. She graduated from Shepherd College, West Virginia, and became a school teacher. Nancy married Thomas Henry Lemen and was born July 20, 1908, at Duffields, Jefferson County [The Link Family, page 1623, No. 2781; and Supplement No. 2781]. Their children are listed under Thomas Henry Lemen, No. 2821. Nancy died July 27, 1950, and Thomas died February 8, 1984.

and Syphilology. He practiced at Washington, D. C. From 1941 to 1945 he was in the U. S. Army Medical Corps, serving in Australia and New Guinea with the rank of Major. After the war he taught at Georgetown University in addition to his private practice. He was the author of Syllabus of Medical Mycology, 1947, and of several articles to various medical journals. He was a Fellow of the American Medical Association, member of the District of Columbia Medical Society, Baltimore-Washington Dermatologic and the Georgetown Clinical Societies. He married Dorothea Elizabeth Schumann, April 22, 1942. Dorothea was born October 25, 1917, at Chillicothe, Ohio. Her parents were Fred Nicholas and Dorothea Voll Schumann.

(Sup) 5210   i   Raymond Voll Osbourn, born September 10, 1945.
(Sup) 5211   ii   Dorothea Elise Osbourn, born February 4, 1948.

2915 GERALDINE HIRST TEMPLEMAN (Delvia[7], John[6], Jane[5], Alexander[4], John Adam II[3], John Adam I[2], John Jacob[1]) was born July 25, 1919, at Leetown, West Virginia. After her public schooling she graduated from Shepherd College with an A. B. degree and became a teacher at Shepherdstown, West Virginia.

2916 VIVIAN OSBOURN MYERS (Bettie[7], John[6], Jane[5], Alexander[4], John Adam II[3], John Adam I[2], John Jacob[1]) was born October 31, 1911, at Shepherdstown, West Virginia.

(Sup) 2917 NORMA LOUISE OSBOURN (Roger[7], John[6], Jane[5], Alexander[4], John Adam II[3], John Adam I[2], John Jacob[1]) was the daughter of Roger Miller and Catherine Moler Osbourn [The Link Family, page 459, No. 1467]. Norma Louise was born July 18, 1909, at Bardane, West Virginia. She married Lawrence Francis Obrist, October 21, 1936. He was born August 26, 1900, at Brownsville, Maryland. His parents were John Robert and Annie Rebecca (Hull) Obrist. Lawrence was in the furniture manufacturing business at Hagerstown, Maryland. He died in 1965, and she died July 10, 1977, they are buried in Rest Haven Cemetery at Hagerstown.

2918 DANIEL ALLEN OSBOURN (Roger[7], John[6], Jane[5], Alexander[4], John Adam II[3], John Adam I[2], John Jacob[1]) was born June 16, 1912, at Hagerstown, Maryland. He died December 5, 1917, and was buried at Elmwood Cemetery at Shepherdstown, West Virginia.

2920 RICHARD ALTON OSBOURN (Frederick[7], David[6], Jane[5], Alexander[4], John Adam II[3], John Adam I[2], John Jacob[1]) was born March 18, 1930. He studied at the University of Maryland to become a physician and surgeon.

2921 JANE ANN OSBOURN (Frederick[7], David[6], Jane[5], Alexander[4], John Adam II[3], John Adam I[2], John Jacob[1]) was born January 30, 1932, at Takoma Park, Maryland.

2922 JOSEPH ALLEN OSBOURN (Frederick[7], David[6], Jane[5], Alexander[4], John Adam II[3], John Adam I[2], John Jacob[1]) was born June 22, 1933, at Takoma Park, Maryland.

2923 FREDERICK LIONELL OSBOURN, JR. (Frederick[7], David[6], Jane[5], Alexander[4], John Adam II[3], John Adam I[2], John Jacob[1]) was born September 6, 1946, at Washington, D. C.

studied at George Washington University. Helen married James Lynch, Jr., September 6, 1947, at Washington, D.C. He was the son of James and Mary Flaherty Lynch and was born August 10, 1922, at Baltimore, Maryland. James was assistant vice president of Riggs National Bank. Helen and James resided at Rockville, Maryland.

(Sup) 5217   i   Frances Wyatt Lynch, born January 30, 1949.
(Sup) 5218   ii   Nancy Gayle Lynch, born May 27, 1962.

(Sup) 2934   JAMES BURR OSBOURN   (Cleon[7], Nancy[6], John[5], Alexander[4], John Adam II[3], John Adam I[2], John Jacob[1]) was the son of Cleon Scott and Beth Neal Osbourn [The Link Family, page 461, No. 1479]. James was born January 88, 1928, at New Haven, Connecticut. He was educated at Horace Mann School for Boys and at Yale University, graduating in 1950 with an A.B. degree. He was commissioned an ensign in the U.S. Navy and assigned to the aircraft carrier Leyte.

(Sup) 2935   MARGARET ANNE LINK   (Albert[7], Jacob[6], Thomas[5], Alexander[4], John Adam II[3], John Adam I[2], John Jacob[1]) was the daughter of Albert Blue and Sally Barnes Link [The Link Family, page 463, No. 1485]. Margaret was born July 2, 1947, at New Orleans, Louisiana.

(Sup) 2936   ROBERT BARNES LINK   (Albert[7], Jacob[6], Thomas[5], Alexander[4], John Adam II[3], John Adam I[2], John Jacob[1]) was the son of Albert Blue and Sally Barnes Link [The Link Family, page 463, No. 1485]. Robert was born February 13, 1950, at New Orleans, Louisiana.

(Sup) 2936A   SALLIE CORBETT O'KEEF   (Margaret[7], Jacob[6], Thomas[5], Alexander[4], John Adam II[3], John Adam I[2], John Jacob[1]) was born July 17, 1948, at Raleigh, North Carolina. [She was the daughter of Margaret Wyatt Link and Herbert Edward O'Keef; see The Link Family, page 463, No. 1486; and Supplement No. 1486.] Sallie graduated from the University of North Carolina, Chapel Hill, in June, 1970, with a B.S. degree in nursing and was president of her senior class. Sallie then attended the University of Durham in England during the summer of 1966. She married Dr. Eugene Simpson, Jr., on June 20, 1970, at Chapel Hill, North Carolina. He was the son of Eugene Myers and Annie Lois Ferebee Simpson. Dr. Simpson graduated from the University of North Carolina in chemistry in June 1969, and received his M.D. degree from the Bowman Gray School of Medicine, Winston-Salem, in May 1973.

(Sup) 5219   i   Jason Ferebee Simpson, born October 8, 1974.
(Sup) 5220   ii   Andrew Link Simpson, born October 16, 1978.

(Sup) 2928   BESSIE HAMILTON OSBOURN   (John[7], Nancy[6], John[5], Alexander[4], John Adam II[3], John Adam I[2], John Jacob[1]) was the daughter of John Melvin and Bessie Poston Osbourn [The Link Family, page 461, No. 1475]. Bessie was born April 8, 1911, at Shenandoah Junction, Jefferson County, West Virginia. She studied at Shepherd College, West Virginia. Bessie married John William Hendricks December 24, 1924. He was the son of Harvey Hampton and Minnie E. Brantner Hendricks and was born March 19, 1897, at Duffields, Jefferson County [The Link Family, page 494, No. 1700; and Supplement No. 1700]. John also studied at Shepherd College. He became a farmer. Their children are listed under John William Hendricks [The Link Family, No. 1700]. Bessie and John resided in Jefferson County, West Virginia. He died January 14, 1972, and is buried at Shepherdstown.

2929   ELEANOR CHRISTINE OSBOURN   (John[7], Nancy[6], John[5], Alexander[4], John Adam II[3], John Adam I[2], John Jacob[1]) was born November 28, 1919, at Shenandoah Junction, West Virginia. She studied at Shepherd College and became a registered nurse. Eleanor married Edward Porterfield Lloyd, March 9, 1943. Edward was born November 24, 1919, at Martinsburg, West Virginia.

2930   JANE WRIGHT HUNTER   (Ann[7], Nancy[6], John[5], Alexander[4], John Adam II[3], John Adam I[2], John Jacob[1]) was born October 6, 1911. Jane received her advanced education at Shepherd College, Shepherdstown, West Virginia, and became a librarian.

(Sup) 2931   JAMES OSBOURN HUNTER   (Ann[7], Nancy[6], John[5], Alexander[4], John Adam II[3], John Adam I[2], John Jacob[1]) was the son of Warren Hampton and Ann Elizabeth Osbourn Hunter [The Link Family, page 461, No. 1476]. James was born January 20, 1913, at Duffields, Jefferson County, West Virginia. He became a farmer. He married Betty Keplinger McKee March 27, 1948. Betty was the daughter of John Howard and Blanche Bitner McKee and was born November 9, 1915, at Kearneysville, West Virginia.

(Sup) 5214   i   James Osbourn Hunter, Jr., born March 14, 1949.
(Sup) 5215   ii   Ernest McKee Hunter, born August 16, 1950.
(Sup) 5216   iii   Ann Hampton Hunter, born September 4, 1952.

(Sup) 2932   MARY CHRISTINE HUNTER   (Ann[7], Nancy[6], John[5], Alexander[4], John Adam II[3], John Adam I[2], John Jacob[1]) was the daughter of Warren Hampton and Ann Elizabeth Osborn Hunter [The Link Family, page 461, No. 1476]. Mary Christine studied at Shepherd College, Shepherdstown, West Virginia, and went into secretarial work.

(Sup) 2933   HELEN WYATT OSBOURN   (Walter[7], Nancy[6], John[5], Alexander[4], John Adam II[3], John Adam I[2], John Jacob[1]) was the daughter of Walter Allen and Laura Matthews Osbourn [The Link Family, page 461, No. 1478]. Helen was born August 11, 1926, at Takoma Park, Maryland. She

(Sup) 2937 NANCY ANN LINK (Wallace[7], Adam[6], Thomas[5], Alexander[4], John Adam II[3], John Aam I[2], John Jacob[1]) was the daughter of Wallace Gibson and Frances Smith Link [The Link Family, page 463, No. 1487]. Nancy Ann was born September 6, 1935, at Raleigh, North Carolina. She graduated from the University of North Carolina in 1958. Nancy Ann taught school in BelAir, Maryland; Bisbee, Arizona; Sierra Vista, Arizona; and at Chung King University in Seoul, Korea. She married Charles Carlyle Davenport, Jr.. July 18, 1958, at Raleigh, North Carolina.

(Sup) 5221   i   Margaret Frances Davenport, born March 24, 1961.
(Sup) 5222   ii   Charles Carlyle Davenport III, born January 24, 1964.

(Sup) 2938 ELIZABETH IRENE LINK (Wallace[7], Adam[6], Thomas[5], Alexander[4], John Adam II[3], John Adam I[2], John Jacob[1]) was the daughter of Wallace Gibson and Frances Smith Link [The Link Family, page 463, No. 1487]. Irene was born February 18, 1940, at Raleigh, North Carolina. She graduated from East Carolina University June 1961 and then taught school. She married Willard Kent Baker July 1 1961 at Moody Air Force Base, Georgia. He was the son of Willard Franklin and Louise Elizabeth Baker and was born March 23, 1938, at Elizabeth City, North Carolina. Willard graduated from East Carolina University in 1960, served six years in the U.S. Air Force with tours in Vietnam and Alaska, and became a captain with Delta Airlines. Irene and Willard resided at Stone Mountain, Georgia.

(Sup) 5223   i   Willard Kent Baker, Jr., born November 26, 1963.
(Sup) 5224   ii   Wallace Link Baker, born May 15, 1967.
(Sup) 5225   iii William Scott Baker, born April 28, 1973.

(Sup) 2938A HARRIET LINK (Wallace[7], Adam[6], Thomas[5], Alexander[4], John Adam II[3], John Adam I[2], John Jacob[1]) was born November 29, 1949, at Raleigh, North Carolina. [She was the third daughter of Wallace Gibson and Frances Smith Link; see The Link Family, page 463, No. 1487; and Supplement No. 1487.] Harriet married Charles Ellis White, III, December 27, 1969, at Raleigh. He was the son of Charles Ellis and Kathryn Purdue White, Jr., and was born September 19, 1949, at Wilmington, North Carolina.

(Sup) 5226   i   Kathryn Elizabeth White, born March 8, 1971.
(Sup) 5227   ii   Christie Ellis White, born Feb 2, 1975 (twin).
(Sup) 5228   iii Ashley Ann White, February 2, 1975 (twin).

(Sup) 2939 GRACE WALLACE POWARS (Nancy[7], Adam[6], Thomas[5], Alexander[4], John Adam II[3], John Adam I[2], John Jacob[1]) was the daughter of Forrest Wayne and Nancy Link Powars [The Link Family, page 464, No. 1489; and Supplement No. 1489]. Grace was born December 17, 1943, at Chicago, Illinois. She attended the Moret School in Washington, D.C.; Sweet Briar College (Virginia); and received an A.B. degree in music from American University. She married Warren Lincoln Bouve' March 23, 1962. They were divorced in 1968. Grace married, second, William Ashton Banks August 9, 1969, at Washington, D.C. He was the son of William Smith and Mary Frances File Banks and was born April 24, 1943, at Beckley, West Virginia. Bill graduated from American University with a major in music and received a Master's degree in theology from the Washington Bible College. Grace and Bill taught music.

(Sup) 5229   i   Michele de Forest Bouve', born Dec 15, 1962.
(Sup) 5230   ii   Elizabeth Ashton Banks, born July 3, 1970.
(Sup) 5231   iii Nancy Link Banks, born March 14, 1972.
(Sup) 5232   iv   Kathryn Sturtevant Banks, born April 17, 1978.

(Sup) 2939A FORREST MASON POWARS (Nancy[7], Adam[6], Thomas[5], Alexander[4], John Adam II[3], John Adam I[2], John Jacob[1]) was born November 1, 1947, at Washington, D.C. [He was the second child of Forest Wayne and Nancy Link Powars; see The Link Family, page 464, No. 1489; and Supplement No. 1489.] Mason received a Bachelor's degree in communications from the University of Wyoming in 1972. He sang in shows given by the United States Services for U.S. Armed Forces overseas. He was employed in banking and then in the mortgage business. Mason married Linda Anne Krogmann, May 30, 1975, at Washington, D.C. She was the daughter of John Clement and Shirley Poston Krogmann and was born January 24, 1950, at Washington. Her maternal grandparents owned and lived on the Sully Plantation at Chantilly, Virginia. Linda graduated in the fine arts from Virginia Commonwealth University in 1973. Mason and Linda resided at Arlington, Virginia.

(Sup) 5233   i   Elizabeth Lindsey Powars, born June 26, 1977.
(Sup) 5234   ii   Mary Laura Powars, born July 8, 1981.
(Sup) 5234A   iii Catharine Virginia Powars, born April 14, 1987.

(Sup) 2939B WAYNE LINK POWARS (Nancy[7], Adam[6], Thomas[5], Alexander[4], John Adam II[3], John Adam I[2], John Jacob[1]) was born August 25, 1950, at Washington, D.C. [He was the third child of Forrest Wayne and Nancy Link Powers; see The Link Family, page 464, No. 1489; and Supplement No. 1489.] Link attended Admiral Farragut Academy at St. Petersburg and received a B.A. degree from Stetson University at De Land, Florida. He married Susan Lyles Behrens January 30, 1971, at De Land. She was the daughter of Herbert Edward and Peggy Jane Randol Behrens and was born March 24, 1951, at Coral Gables, Florida. Susan graduated from Stetson University. Link and Susan lived in Miami, Florida, where he had an investment company and she taught pre-school classes.

(Sup) 5235   i   Adam Link Powars, born March 30, 1974.
(Sup) 5236   ii   Virginia Lee Powars, born April 15, 1976.
(Sup) 5237   iii Mary Katherine Elizabeth Powars, born January 22, 1978.
(Sup) 5238   iv   Andrew Scott Powars, born November 1, 1980.
(Sup) 5239   v   Forrest Edward Powars, born July 6, 1983.
(Sup) 5239A   vi   William Wallace Powars, born September 3, 1985.

(Sup) 2939C DAVID SCOTT POWARS (Nancy[7], Adam[6], Thomas[5], Alexander[4], John Adam II[3], John Adam I[2], John Jacob[1]) was born January 26, 1953, at Washington, D.C. [He was the fourth child of Forrest Wayne and Nancy Link Powars; see The Link Family, page 464, No. 1489; and Supplement No. 1489.] David attended St. Stephens Episcopal School for Boys, Randolph-Macon College, and George Mason University. He attained a Master's Degree in geology from George Washington University and was employed as a geologist with the U.S. Geological Survey.

(Sup) 2939D GEORGE WALLACE LINK (John[7], Adam[6], Thomas[5], Alexander[4], John Adam II[3], John Adam I[2], John Jacob[1]) was the son of John Carswell and Clara George Link [see The Link Family, page 464, No. 1490; and Supplement No. 1490]. George was born April 29, 1955, at Washington, D.C. After attending public schools in Washington and Uniontown, Pennsylvania, George entered the University of Pittsburgh. He was a member of the university's national championship football team in 1976 and received the B.A. degree in 1977. He attained a Master of Counseling Education degree in 1982 and was employed as Chief Nuclear Medicine Technologist at Jefferson Center Hospital, Pittsburgh, Pennsylvania.

(Sup) 2939E JOHN GIBSON LINK (John[7], Adam[6], Thomas[5], Alexander[4], John Adam II[3], John Adam I[2], John Jacob[1]) was the son of John Carswell and Clara George Link [see The Link Family, page 464, No. 1490; and Supplement No. 1490]. John was born March 8, 1957, at Washington, D.C. He attended public schools in Washington, D.C., and Uniontown, Pennsylvania. He received a B.A. degree from Indiana University of Pennsylvania (at Indiana, Pennsylvania) in 1981; he was captain of the football team and received Honorable All American. John was employed as representative for the American Society of Composers, Authors, and Publishers at Pittsburg, Pennsylvania.

(Sup) 2939F JOAN CLARA LINK (John[7], Adam[6], Thomas[5], Alexander[4], John Adam II[3], John Adam I[2], John Jacob[1]) was the daughter of John Carswell and Clara Goerge Link [see The Link Family, page 464, No. 1490; and Supplement No. 1490]. She was born April 15, 1963, at Washington, D.C. On completing public schools at Uniontown, Pennsylvania, she attended Robert Morris College, Coraopolis, Pennsylvania, and was employed by a bank in Cincinnati, Ohio.

(Sup) 2940 JUDITH KATHRYN LINK (Charles[7], Adam[6], Thomas[5], Alexander[4], John Adam II[3], John Adam I[2], John Jacob[1]) was the daughter of Charles Robert and Jeanette Whims Link [The Link Family, page 464, No. 1491; and Supplement No. 1491]. Judith was born October 26, 1944, at Great Falls, Montana. She married Dennis Harlan Finney October 9, 1972, at Edmonds, Washington. Dennis was the son of Harold L. and Ethel Bowhall Finney and was born November 16, 1942, at Pearly, Minnesota. He served on a NOAH cartographic ship and captained a Washington State ferry.

(Sup) 5240   i   Jennifer Lee Finney, born September 1, 1973.
(Sup) 5241 ii Christopher Link Finney, born August 28, 1976.

(Sup) 2940A ROBERT GIBSON LINK (Charles[7], Adam[6], Thomas[5], Alexander[4], John Adam II[3], John Adam I[2], John Jacob[1]) was born August 10, 1948, at Seattle, Washington. [He was the second child of Charles Robert and Jeanette Whims Link; see The Link Family, page 464, No. 1491; and Supplement No. 1491.] Robert attended the University of Hawaii and then graduated from Washington State University. He was manager of the Seattle Trade Center and a food management expert. Robert married Jacklyn K. Burrier December 10, 1966, at Honolulu, Hawaii. She was the daughter of Thomas and Janet Cranis Burrier and was born August 20, 1948, at Orlando, Florida.

(Sup) 5242   i   Jeffrey Charles Link, born July 14, 1967.
(Sup) 5243 ii Gregory Thomas Link, born March 29, 1971.
(Sup) 5244 iii Bryan Gibson Link, born September 27, 1981.

(Sup) 2940B DAVID CHARLES LINK (Charles[7], Adam[6], Thomas[5], Alexander[4], John Adam II[3], John Adam I[2], John Jacob[1]) was born November 10, 1948, at Edmonds, Washington. [He was the third child of Charles Robert and Jeanette Whims Link; see The Link Family, page 464, No. 1491.] David graduated from the University of Washington and was an architectural designer at San Francisco, California.

2941 JOHN GILMAN STEWART (Winifred[7], Charles[6], Thomas[5], Alexander[4], John Adam II[3], John Adam I[2], John Jacob[1]) was born February 15, 1935.

2942 ANNE CAROL STEWART (Winifred[7], Charles[6], Thomas[5], Alexander[4], John Adam II[3], John Adam I[2], John Jacob[1]) was born April 18, 1939.

2943 BARBARA JANE STEWART (Winifred[7], Charles[6], Thomas[5], Alexander[4], John Adam II[3], John Adam I[2], John Jacob[1]) was born April 18, 1939, and died the same day.

2944 VAL LINK MILSARK (Juliette[7], Walter[6], Thomas[5], Alexander[4], John Adam II[3], John Adam I[2], John Jacob[1]) was born September 7, 1929. He studied at West Virginia State University.

2945 JULIETTE JOANNE MILSARK (Juliette[7], Walter[6], Thomas[5], Alexander[4], John Adam II[3], John Adam I[2], John Jacob[1]) was born April 22, 1932. She studied at De Sales Heights Academy and Stephens College.

2946 ELIZABETH BALLENGER HARMAN (Walter[7], Walter[6], Ann[5], Alexander[4], John Adam II[3], John Adam I[2], John Jacob[1]) was born June 6, 1923, at Baltimore, Maryland. She graduated at Goucher College in 1946 and became a teacher. On November 27, 1946, she married James Melcher Aycock, who was the son of Joseph Felix and Edna Maude King Aycock. James was born March 13, 1922, at Melcher, Honduras, and received his advanced education in the United States, graduating from Washington College in 1943 with an A. B. degree, and at the University of Baltimore where he was awarded his law degree in 1949.

(Sup) 2947 JANET FLORENCE HARMAN (Charles[7], Walter[6], Ann[5], Alexander[4], John Adam II[3], John Adam I[2], John Jacob[1]) was the daughter of Charles Henry and Gladys Miles Harman [The Link Family, page 465, No. 1496]. Janet was born September 2, 1922, at Baltimore, Maryland. She became a secretary for a major airline. She married William Hurle Collier September 10, 1949, at Fort Meade, Maryland. He was the son of Brigadier General and Mrs. William A. Collier. Bill served as a captain in the U.S. Army with the Second Armored Division in Germany. He and Janet owned and operated a small beef cattle farm in Orange County, Virginia. He was business manager of Woodberry Forest School (a private preparatory boarding school for boys), and she was parish secretary of St. Thomas Episcopal Church.

(Sup) 5245   i   Gail Sharon Collier, born August 5, 1953.

(Sup) 2948 CHARLES WILLIAM HARMAN (Charles[7], Walter[6], Ann[5], Alexander[4], John AdamII[3], John Adam I[2], John Jacob[1]) was the son of Charles Henry and Dorothy Steedman Harman [The Link Family, page 465, No. 1496]. Charles William was born July 11, 1942, at Baltimore, Maryland. He married Georgianna Mae Efford, September 1, 1960. She was the daughter of Harry and Lillian Efford.

(Sup) 5245A   i   Denise Lynn Harman, born February 1, 1961.
(Sup) 5245B   ii   Tab William Harman, born June 3, 1963.

2949 NANCY HARMAN BLACKFORD (Henry[7], Nancy[6], Ann[5], Alexander[4], John Adam II[3], John Adam I[2], John Jacob[1]) was born March 3, 1921. She married Paul Culbert Metcalf, May 30, 1942. Paul was born at East Milton, Massachusetts, November 7, 1917. He was the son of Henry Knight and Eleanor Melville Thomas Metcalf.

(Sup) 5246   i   Anne Harman Metcalf, born June 29, 1945.

2950 HENRY JACKSON BLACKFORD, JR. (Henry[7], Nancy[6], Ann[5], Alexander[4], John Adam II[3], John Adam I[2], John Jacob[1]) was born January 6, 1913, at Spartanburg, South Carolina. He married Jean Charlotte Price, September 7, 1946. Jean was the daughter of Leo James and Borghild Amolia Gran Price and was born January 24, 1924, at Milwaukee, Wisconsin.

(Sup) 5247   i   Elizabeth Jean Blackford, born November 14, 1947.
(Sup) 5248   ii   Henry Jackson Blackford III, born March 5, 1949.

2951 GEORGE WILLIAM BLACKFORD (Henry[7], Nancy[6], Ann[5], Alexander[4], John Adam II[3], John Adam I[2], John Jacob[1]) was born September 22, 1925, at Spartanburg, South Carolina. He studied at the University of South Carolina and served in the U. S. Navy during World War II. George married Carolyn Wayne Deschamps, October 15, 1948. Carolyn was born June 7, 1927, at Bishopville, South Carolina. Her parents were Carrol Green and Virginia Aiken Gray Deschamps.

(Sup) 2952 LINDA DIANNE BALDWIN (Elsie[7], James[6], Ann[5], Alexander[4], John Adam II[3], John Adam I[2], John Jacob[1]) was the daughter of Edwin Francis and Elsie Harman Baldwin [The Link Family, page 466, No. 1501]. Linda was born March 29, 1943, at Keyser, West Virginia. She married David Carder Trimmier August 26, 1966.

(Sup) 5249   i   Robert Ravenel Trimmier, born May 20, 1976.
(Sup) 5250   ii   James Gignilliat Trimmier, born May 16, 1980.

(Sup) 2953 NANCY CAROL BALDWIN (Elsie[7], James[6], Ann[5], Alexander[4], John Adam II[3], John Adam I[2], John Jacob[1]) was the daughter of Edwin Francis and Elsie Harman Baldwin [The Link Family, page 466, No. 1501]. Nancy was born May 17, 1945, at Keyser, West Virginia.

(Sup) 2954 LAWRENCE EDWIN BALDWIN (Elsie[7], James[6], Ann[5], Alexander[4], John Adam II[3], John Adam I[2], John Jacob[1]) was the son of Edwin Francis and Elsie Harman Baldwin [The Link Family, page 466, No. 1501]. Lawrence was born January 25, 1947, at Keyser, West Virginia. He married Juetta Jane Michael in 1966.

(Sup) 5251   i   Daniel Heath Baldwin, born April 20, 1967.
(Sup) 5252   ii   Autumn Dawn Baldwin, born October 29, 1971.

2955 LEWIS WRIGHT GROVE (Lewis[7], Angeline[6], Emmanuel[5], Mary[4], John Adam II[3], John Adam I[2], John Jacob[1]) was born June 4, 1903, at Denver, Colorado. He married Clara Renk, November 3, 1928, at Denver. They had no children.

2956 WILLIAM CROWELL GROVE (Lewis[7], Angeline[6], Emmanuel[5], Mary[4], John Adam II[3], John Adam I[2], John Jacob[1]) was born December 6, 1905, at Brighton, Colorado. He married Eva Richardson at Denver, Colorado. William became general manager of a large broadcasting company at Cheyenne, Wyoming. He and Eva had a son, named William Crowell Grove, Jr., born February 29, 1932.

2957 WINFIELD CLARK GROVE (Lewis[7], Angeline[6], Emmanuel[5], Mary[4], John Adam II[3], John Adam I[2], John Jacob[1]) was born July 5, 1913, at Denver, Colorado. He graduated from the Colorado School of Mines at Golden, Colorado, in 1935, and served in World War II from 1943 to 1946 as a Lieutenant in the U. S. Navy. He served in the Pacific Theater. Winfield married Peggy Amelia De Andra, May 8, 1948, at Cheyenne, Wyoming. Peggy was born September 5, 1926. After the war Winfield built a radio station at Rawlins, Wyoming, and then entered geophysical research work.

2958 WILLIAM REMSBURG GROVE, JR. (William7, Angeline6, Emmanuel5, Mary4, John Adam II3, John Adam I2, John Jacob1) was born May 5, 1902, at Omaha, Nebraska. After elementary and high school, William received an appointment to the United States Military Academy at West Point, where he graduated June 12, 1923. He rose in rank to that of Colonel in 1942. During World War II he served in the European Theater. At the war's end he was a member of the Command and General Staff College at Fort Leavenworth, Kansas, for some years until the Korean War, when he was assigned as a member of Army Field Forces Board No. 1 at Fort Bragg, North Carolina. William married Elizabeth Winans Carroll, October 16, 1928, at Leavenworth, Kansas. On December 5, 1941, he married Elizabeth Savage Hartnell.

CHILD OF WILLIAM AND ELIZABETH CARROLL

(Sup) 5253   i   William Remsburg Grove III, born February 3, 1931.

CHILD OF WILLIAM AND ELIZABETH HARTNELL

(Sup) 5254   ii   Madge Campbell Grove, born August 22, 1946.

2958A GRAHAM CROWELL GROVE (William7, Angeline6, Emmanuel5, Mary4, John Adam II3, John Adam I2, John Jacob1) was born September 11, 1904. He died December 30, 1915, at Canal Zone, Panama.

2959 CARLA MINNIE SMITH (Hazel7, Angeline6, Emmanuel5, Mary4, John Adam II3, John Adam I2, John Jacob1) was the daughter of Homer A. A. and Hazel Grove Smith [The Link Family, page 468, No. 1505]. Carla was born July 25, 1903, at Washington, D.C. She graduated from Holyoke College in June, 1924. She married Donald LeRoy Turner September 1, 1927, at Takoma Park, Maryland. He was the son of John William and Mary Penn Turner and was born December 15, 1899, at Baltimore Maryland. After a successful teaching career especially in remedial and speed reading in Sarasota, Florida, Carla died July 24, 1976, in La Mesa California. Donald died in San Diego, California, April 28, 1978.

(Sup) 5255   i   Carla Lee Turner, born December 15, 1928.

2960 FRANCES WINFIELD SMITH (Hazel7, Angeline6, Emmanuel5, Mary4, John Adam II3, John Adam I2, John Jacob1) was the daughter of Homer A. A. and Hazel Grove Smith [The Link Family, page 468, No. 1505]. Frances was born March 30, 1907, at Washington, D.C. She graduated from Wilson Normal School. While teaching in the District of Columbia schools she graduated from George Washington University and received her M.A. degree from the University of Maryland. Frances married Edward David Haas August 7, 1933, at Washington, D.C. He was born May 23, 1903, at Tacoma Park, Maryland. Frances retired after thirty-six years as a teacher and principal to accompany her husband to Asheville, North Carolina. He died there July 16, 1966, after which she returned to the Washington area to lead an active life in family and church work. She moved to Daytona Beach, Florida, in 1981, and in 1988 entered a retirement home at Port Orange, Florida.

(Sup) 5256   i   Robert Homer Haas, born May 14, 1934.

2961 HOMER GROVE SMITH (Hazel7, Angeline6, Emmanuel5, Mary4, John Adam II3, John Adam I2, John Jacob1) was the son of Homer A. A. and Hazel Grove Smith [The Link Family, page 468, No. 1505]. Homer was born November 26, 1909, at Washington, D.C. He married Elsa Tavenner August 27, 1938, at Washington. She was the daughter of Clyde Tavenner and was born September 1, 1914, at Moline, Illinois. Homer was employed by the Farm Credit Administration as a Federal Land Bank examiner and then as an official of the Production Credit Division. In 1954 he became director of the Cooperative Bank Service of the F.C.A. and from 1956 to 1974 was president of the Central Bank for Cooperatives, first at Washington, D.C. and then at Denver, Colorado, where he retired. Homer and Elsa moved to Chevy Chase, Maryland. He remained active in the Presbyterian Church. Homer G. Smith authored The 13th Bank, published in 1976; A Challenge to U.S. Agriculture, in 1987; and other publications of interest to the farm credit community.

(Sup) 5257   i   Linda Ann Smith, born August 21, 1940.
(Sup) 5258   ii   Carla Frances Smith, born July 17, 1943.
(Sup) 5259   iii Greta Kathleen Smith, born January 28, 1945.
(Sup) 5260   iv   Martin Homer Smith, born November 16, 1949.

2962 ANGELINE CLARA SMITH (Hazel7, Angeline6, Emmanuel5, Mary4, John Adam II3, John Adam I2, John Jacob1) was the daughter of Homer A. A. and Hazel Grove Smith [The Link Family, page 468, No. 1505]. Angeline was born May 28, 1912, at Denver, Colorado. She married James William Eastwood October 22, 1936, at Washington, D.C. He was the son of Charles S. Eastwood and was born January 24, 1914, at Roanoke, Virginia. James died February 26, 1971, at Washington. After his death Angeline worked as a secretary at the National Institutes of Health. When she retired, she resided at White Oak, Maryland, where she remained very active in tennis, bowling, duplicate bridge, and her church.

(Sup) 5261   i   Elsa Ann Eastwood, born January 3, 1939.

2963 WINIFRED MARGARET BISHOP (Minnie7, Angeline6, Emmanuel5, Mary4, John Adam II3, John Adam I2, John Jacob1) was born January 20, 1908, at Denver, Colorado. She married Leslie John Welch, November 9, 1946, at Denver. Leslie, son of James Timothy Welch, was born June 12, 1904, at Hartford, Connecticut.

2964 THOMAS GROVE BISHOP (Minnie7, Angeline6, Emmanuel5, Mary4, John Adam II3, John Adam I2, John Jacob1) was born May 29, 1910, at Denver, Colorado. He married Althea H. Finn, September 22, 1934, at Los Angeles, California. Althea was the daughter of Arthur Finn and was born July 4, 1908, at Cripple Creek, Colorado.

(Sup) 5262   i   Byron Grove Bishop, born September 22, 1937.

2965 BEATRICE MARY BISHOP (Minnie7, Angeline6, Emmanuel5, Mary4, John Adam II3, John Adam I2, John Jacob1) was born July 5, 1912, at Denver, Colorado. She married Clarence R. Petersen, January 27, 1933, at Kimball, Nebraska. Clarence was the son of Peter Petersen and was born November 20, 1910, at Rawlins, Wyoming.

2966 FRANKLIN ANDREW BISHOP, JR. (Minnie7, Angeline6, Emmanuel5, Mary4, John Adam II3, John Adam I2, John Jacob1) was born January 21, 1916. He served in World War II.

2967 ARAVESTA VIRGINIA JOHNSON (Susan[6], Angeline[5], Emmanuel[5], Mary[4], John Adam II[3], John Adam I[2], John Jacob[1]) was born November 10, 1915, at Denver, Colorado. She married Richard Clyde Soll, March 3, 1934, at Golden, Colorado. She died January 9, 1940.

2968 EARL ZWEILY (Sarah[7], George[6], Emmanuel[5], Mary[4], John Adam II[3], John Adam I[2], John Jacob[1]) was born November 17, 1886, in Sandusky County, Ohio. He married Estella Engler, June 20, 1910. Estella was born November 12, 1889.
(Sup) 5263   i   Lucille Zweily, born June 5, 1911.
(Sup) 5264   ii   Raymond Zweily, born February 21, 1936.
(Sup) 5265   iii Marian Zweily, born March 22, 1918.
(Sup) 5266   iv   Joan Hazel Zweily, born October 19, 1930.

2969 REUBEN LEROY ZWEILY (Sarah[7], George[6], Emmanuel[5], Mary[4], John Adam II[3], John Adam I[2], John Jacob[1]) was born August 13, 1888, in Sandusky County, Ohio He married Maud Kiser, February 12, 1913, at Fremont, Ohio. Maud was born in Sandusky County, September 17, 1893.
(Sup) 5267   i   Walter William Zweily, born April 26, 1914.
(Sup) 5268   ii   Kathryn Winona Zweily, born May 26, 1917.
(Sup) 5269   iii Doris Arlene Zweily, born April 15, 1923.
(Sup) 5270   iv   Alvin Eugene Zweily, born October 22, 1928.

2970 FRANK ZWEILY (Sarah[7], George[6], Emmanuel[5], Mary[4], John Adam II[3], John Adam I[2], John Jacob[1]) was born April 15, 1890, in Sandusky County, Ohio. He died January 15, 1911.

2971 CLARA ZWEILY (Sarah[7], George[6], Emmanuel[5], Mary[4], John Adam II[3], John Adam I[2], John Jacob[1]) was born August 28, 1896, at Fremont, Ohio. She married Howard Shafer, March 29, 1921. Howard was born June 18, 1898, at Old Fort, Ohio. son of John H. Shafer.
(Sup) 5271   i   Melvin Shafer, born December 28, 1921.
(Sup) 5272   ii   Donald Shafer, born January 15, 1924.
(Sup) 5273   iii Lois Shafer, born May 28, 1928.

2972 CLAUDE ZWEILY (Sarah[7], George[6], Emmanuel[5], Mary[4], John Adam II[3], John Adam I[2], John Jacob[1]) was born October 10, 1900, in Sandusky County, Ohio. He married Carol Emick at Fremont, Ohio, December 2, 1921. Carol, daughter of Charles Emick, was born March 24, 1903.
(Sup) 5274   i   Kenneth Zweily, born May 14, 1922.

2973 HATTIE ZWEILY (Sarah[7], George[6], Emmanuel[5], Mary[4], John Adam II[3], John Adam I[2], John Jacob[1]) was born September 22, 1902, in Sandusky County, Ohio. She married George Zilles, August 29, 1923.
(Sup) 5275   i   Joyce Zilles, born June 12, 1926.
(Sup) 5276   ii   Norma Jane Zilles, born February 24, 1928.
(Sup) 5277   iii Paul Zilles, born August 22, 1931.
(Sup) 5278   iv   Dorothy Zilles, born May 24, 1934.
(Sup) 5279   v   Robert Zilles, born October 28, 1935.
(Sup) 5280   vi   Leonard Zilles, born August 29, 1937.

2974 HARRY RAEHRS (Estella[7], Mary[6], Samuel[5], Mary[4], John Adam II[3], John Adam I[2], John Jacob[1]) was born September 3, 1891, in Sandusky County, Ohio. He married Mildred Bahnsen there, February 2, 1921. Mildred was the daughter of Sinke Bahnsen and was born in Sandusky County, August 23, 1899.
(Sup) 5281   i   Doris Raehrs, born April 30, 1922.
(Sup) 5282   ii   Lois Raehrs, born October 25, 1927.

2975 CARL RAEHRS (Estella[7], Mary[6], Samuel[5], Mary[4], John Adam II[3], John Adam I[2], John Jacob[1]) was born October 14, 1895, in Sandusky County, Ohio. He married Beatrice Gressman, January 21, 1939. Beatrice was the daughter of Adam Gressman and was born May 28, 1902, in Sandusky County, Ohio.

2976 MILDRED MAY RAEHRS (Estella[7], Mary[6], Samuel[5], Mary[4], John Adam II[3], John Adam I[2], John Jacob[1]) was born May 29, 1901, in Sandusky County, Ohio. She married Howard Leaser, February 3, 1926. Howard, son of C. W. Leaser, was born November 20, 1902, in Sandusky County, Ohio.
(Sup) 5283   i   Wayne Leaser, born April 3, 1928.
(Sup) 5284   ii   Marlene Leaser, born January 31, 1933.

2977 PEARL KISER (Clara[7], Mary[6], Samuel[5], Mary[4], John Adam II[3], John Adam I[2], John Jacob[1]) was born May 23, 1896, at Fremont, Ohio. She married Robert Smith there, April 18, 1924. Robert was born in Sandusky County, February 26, 1900. Pearl died in Sandusky County, February 24, 1937.
(Sup) 5285   i   Clarabelle Smith, born March 20, 1925.
(Sup) 5286   ii   Vernell Smith, born July 5, 1926.
(Sup) 5287   iii Margaret Ann Smith, born July 20, 1928.

2978 CLARENCE KISER (Clara[7], Mary[6], Samuel[5], Mary[4], John Adam II[3], John Adam I[2], John Jacob[1]) was born May 14, 1900, in Sandusky County, Ohio. He married Lulu K. Beckman, November 4, 1924. Lulu was the daughter of Charles Beckman and was born October 30, 1901. She died November 16, 1935, in Sandusky County, Ohio. Clarence married Lillian Winters, October 22, 1938. Lillian was born January 23, 1902, in Sandusky County, Ohio. She was the daughter of Moritz A. Gessner.

CHILDREN OF CLARENCE AND LULU
(Sup) 5288   i   June Elizabeth Kiser, born June 4, 1926.
(Sup) 5289   ii   Richard Glenn Kiser, born November 11, 1928.

2979 HARRY A. KISER (Clara[7], Mary[6], Samuel[5], Mary[4], John Adam II[3], John Adam I[2], John Jacob[1]) was born January 17, 1902, at Fremont, Ohio. He died there August 26, 1902.

2989 MILDRED HETRICK (Abner^7, Mary^6, Samuel^5, Mary^4, John Adam II^3, John Adam I^2, John Jacob^1) was born July 7, 1908, in Sandusky County, Ohio. She married Glennis Lamalie there, February 22, 1928. Glennis, son of Charles Lamalie, was born March 20, 1906, in Sandusky County.

(Sup) 5299   i   Burdell Lamalie, born March 8, 1930.
(Sup) 5300   ii   Robert Lamalie, born June 3, 1931.
(Sup) 5301   iii Marilyn Lamalie, born March 4, 1935.

2990 THELMA HETRICK (Abner^7, Mary^6, Samuel^5, Mary^4, John Adam II^3, John Adam I^2, John Jacob^1) was born January 15, 1911, in Sandusky County, Ohio. She married Herbert Nickel, son of Julius Nickel, January 11, 1933. Herbert was born September 9, 1911, in Sandusky County.

(Sup) 5302   i   Janet Nickel, born May 5, 1934.
(Sup) 5303   ii   Ronald Nickel, born January 8, 1936.

2991 DOROTHY HETRICK (Abner^7, Mary^6, Samuel^5, Mary^4, John Adam II^3, John Adam I^2, John Jacob^1) was born June 13, 1913, in Sandusky County, Ohio. She married Earl Nickel, June 22, 1935. Earl, son of Julius Nickel, was born March 18, 1913, in Sandusky County.

(Sup) 5304   i   Deanna Marion Nickel, born March 29, 1940.

2992 EVELYN HETRICK (Abner^7, Mary^6, Samuel^5, Mary^4, John Adam II^3, John Adam I^2, John Jacob^1) was born September 7, 1915, in Sandusky County, Ohio, where she died February 26, 1942.

2993 MILTON HETRICK (Abner^7, Mary^6, Samuel^5, Mary^4, John Adam II^3, John Adam I^2, John Jacob^1) was born March 23, 1918, in Sandusky County, Ohio. He married Garnetta Lucille Sours, daughter of Thurman Sours, October 15, 1941, at Lindsey, Ohio. Garnetta was born August 27, 1917, in Wyandotte County, Ohio.

(Sup) 5305   i   Milton A. Hetrick, Jr.
(Sup) 5306   ii   Cathy Ann Hetrick.

2994 VINCENT THEODORE HETRICK (Abner^7, Mary^6, Samuel^5, Mary^4, John Adam II^3, John Adam I^2, John Jacob^1) was born May 27, 1922, in Sandusky County, Ohio. He married Matilda May Sours, June 29, 1944, at Lindsey, Ohio.

(Sup) 5307   i   Connie Sue Hetrick, born January 25, 1947.

2995 CARROLL HETRICK (Abner^7, Mary^6, Samuel^5, Mary^4, John Adam II^3, John Adam I^2, John Jacob^1) was born December 24, 1924, in Sandusky County, Ohio.

2996 ESTHER LUCILE HETRICK (Theodore^7, Mary^6, Samuel^5, Mary^4, John Adam II^3, John Adam I^2, John Jacob^1) was born August 22, 1910, at Toledo, Ohio. She married Gordon A. Blaine, son of Harry Blaine, February 12, 1937. Gordon was born at Willard, Ohio, November 20, 1912.

(Sup) 5308   i   Carol Lee Blaine, born September 30, 1937.
(Sup) 5309   ii   Nancy Jeanne Blaine, born March 27, 1941.
(Sup) 5310   iii Sandra Anne Blaine, born January 31, 1943.

2997 WALTER CROWELL (Charles^7, Samuel^6, Samuel^5, Mary^4, John Adam II^3, John Adam I^2, John Jacob^1) was born January 6, 1900, in McClure County, Ohio. He became an ordained minister. Walter married Eunice Hansen, daughter of Hans A. Hansen, September 11, 1921, at Jersey City, New Jersey. Eunice was born June 9, 1900.

(Sup) 5311   i   Arlo Crowell, born October 16, 1924.
(Sup) 5312   ii   Erlene Crowell, born September 16, 1935.

2980 VIOLA KISER (Clara^7, Mary^6, Samuel^5, Mary^4, John Adam II^3, John Adam I^2, John Jacob^1) was born August 19, 1903, in Sandusky County, Ohio. She married Allen J. Curliss, May 20, 1929. Allen was the son of Marion D. Curliss and was born in Wood County, Ohio, March 21, 1903.

(Sup) 5290   i   Jeannine Norman Curliss, born March 1, 1931.

2981 THEODORE B. KISER (Clara^7, Mary^6, Samuel^5, Mary^4, John Adam II^3, John Adam I^2, John Jacob^1) was born March 15, 1908, at Fremont, Ohio. He married Estell Schindlin, February 16, 1933. Estell, daughter of Reuben J. Schindlin, was born September 22, 1909, at Toledo, Ohio.

(Sup) 5291   i   Theodore Benton Kiser, Jr., born September 16, 1933.

2982 IRA HETRICK (Chester^7, Mary^6, Samuel^5, Mary^4, John Adam II^3, John Adam I^2, John Jacob^1) was born May 3, 1898. He married Florence Bertholf, September 5, 1925.

2983 HAROLD HETRICK (Chester^7, Mary^6, Samuel^5, Mary^4, John Adam II^3, John Adam I^2, John Jacob^1) was born January 5, 1900. He married Catherine J. Wirries, October 25, 1930.

2984 LEONA HETRICK (Chester^7, Mary^6, Samuel^5, Mary^4, John Adam II^3, John Adam I^2, John Jacob^1) was born January 29, 1901. She married Max Griest, December 6, 1922.

(Sup) 5292   i   Elizabeth Ann Griest, born December 17, 1928.

2985 ETHEL OTERMAT (Bertha^7, Mary^6, Samuel^5, Mary^4, John Adam II^3, John Adam I^2, John Jacob^1) was born March 19, 1899, in Sandusky County, Ohio. She married George Shammo, October 14, 1919. George was born March 1, 1890. He was the son of Henry Shammo.

(Sup) 5293   i   Carl Shammo, born August 6, 1920.
(Sup) 5294   ii   Merl Shammo, born March 19, 1922.
(Sup) 5295   iii Viola Shammo, born August 25, 1925.

2986 ORVILLE OTERMAT (Bertha^7, Mary^6, Samuel^5, Mary^4, John Adam II^3, John Adam I^2, John Jacob^1) was born March 17, 1903, in Sandusky County, Ohio. He married Pearl Glasser, July 25, 1925. Pearl, daughter of Joseph Glasser, was born in Sandusky County, Ohio. On June 1, 1935, Orville married Ida Gracemeyer, daughter of Alvin Gracemeyer. Ida was born January 29, 1913, at Fremont, Ohio.

CHILD OF ORVILLE AND PEARL

(Sup) 5296   i   Joan Otermat, born November 4, 1926.

CHILDREN OF ORVILLE AND IDA

(Sup) 5297   i   Larry Lynn Otermat, born December 8, 1939.
(Sup) 5298   ii   Robert Otermat, born April 10, 1945.

2987 NOAH OTERMAT (Bertha^7, Mary^6, Samuel^5, Mary^4, John Adam II^3, John Adam I^2, John Jacob^1) was born August 23, 1907, in Sandusky County, Ohio, where he died November 25, 1915.

2988 WILBUR OTERMAT (Bertha^7, Mary^6, Samuel^5, Mary^4, John Adam II^3, John Adam I^2, John Jacob^1) was born December 9, 1909, in Sandusky County, Ohio.

2998 VIRGIL CROWELL, (Charles^7, Samuel^6, Samuel^5, Mary^4, John Adam II^3, John Adam I^2, John Jacob^1) was born December 9, 1901, at West Hope, Ohio. He died October 11, 1918, and was buried at Waugeon, Ohio.

2999 DELOROUS CROWELL, (Charles^7, Samuel^6, Samuel^5, Mary^4, John Adam II^3, John Adam I^2, John Jacob^1) was born February 21, 1911, at Continental, Ohio. She married Harris Kardatzke, son of Fred Kardatzke, October 8, 1928. Harris was born August 4, 1903, at Elmore, Ohio.

(Sup) 5313 i Elmer Kardatzke, born October 30, 1929.
(Sup) 5314 ii Elaine Kardatzke, born November 14, 1937.

3000 SAMUEL ARTHUR CROWELL, (Frank^7, Samuel^6, Samuel^5, Mary^4, John Adam II^3, John Adam I^2, John Jacob^1) was born June 30, 1904, in Henry County, Ohio.

3001 FRIEDA CROWELL, (Frank^7, Samuel^6, Samuel^5, Mary^4, John Adam II^3, John Adam I^2, John Jacob^1) was born July 27, 1905, in Henry County, Ohio, where she died September 13, 1905.

3002 ALVIRDA CROWELL, (Frank^7, Samuel^6, Samuel^5, Mary^4, John Adam II^3, John Adam I^2, John Jacob^1) was born December 5, 1906, in Henry County, Ohio. She married Walter T. Spicer, March 21, 1939, at Liberty Center, Ohio. Walter, son of Charles C. Spicer, was born April 8, 1906, in Lucas County, Ohio.

(Sup) 5315 i Lauren David Spicer, born January 14, 1940.
(Sup) 5316 ii Alvin Leroy Spicer, born February 17, 1944.

3003 ALICE CROWELL, (Frank^7, Samuel^6, Samuel^5, Mary^4, John Adam II^3, John Adam I^2, John Jacob^1) was born January 19, 1913, in Henry County, Ohio. She married John Armbruster, February 15, 1938, at Columbus Grove, Ohio. John, son of George F. Armbruster, was born January 20, 1907, in Wood County, Ohio.

(Sup) 5317 i Arthur Rudolph Armbruster, born March 28, 1939.
(Sup) 5318 ii Ellen Jane Armbruster, born December 28, 1946.

3004 NORMA IONA CROWELL, (Frank^7, Samuel^6, Samuel^5, Mary^4, John Adam II^3, John Adam I^2, John Jacob^1) was born April 7, 1917, in Henry County, Ohio.

3005 MABEL E. KING, (Clara^7, Eugene^6, Samuel^5, Mary^4, John Adam II^3, John Adam I^2, John Jacob^1) was born October 30, 1897. She married Carl Hasselbach, June 23, 1917.

(Sup) 5319 i Theodore Hasselbach, born September 16, 1918.
(Sup) 5320 ii Robert Hasselbach, born December 8, 1923.

3006 HAZEL R. KING, (Clara^7, Eugene^6, Samuel^5, Mary^4, John Adam II^3, John Adam I^2, John Jacob^1) was born November 21, 1899. She married Harry Gross, June 24, 1922.

(Sup) 5321 i Pearl Adelade Gross, born March 4, 1926.
(Sup) 5322 ii Nolan Christian Gross, born February 26, 1930.

3007 ZELLA M. KING, (Clara^7, Eugene^6, Samuel^5, Mary^4, John Adam II^3, John Adam I^2, John Jacob^1) was born August 6, 1903. She married John Bender, June 12, 1926.

(Sup) 5323 i Myron Dale Bender, born December 4, 1939.

3008 HARVEY NEAL KING (Clara^7, Eugene^6, Samuel^5, Mary^4, John Adam II^3, John Adam I^2, John Jacob^1) was born November 6, 1905. He married Estella Hetrick, November 8, 1928.

(Sup) 5324 i Walter Neal King, born November 6, 1929.
(Sup) 5325 ii Lamar Jacob King, born April 6, 1932.
(Sup) 5326 iii Donald Irwin King, born August 17, 1934.
(Sup) 5327 iv Howard Richard King, born November 30, 1939.

3009 MARY M. KING, (Clara^7, Eugene^6, Samuel^5, Mary^4, John Adam II^3, John Adam I^2, John Jacob^1) was born December 13, 1908. She married Kenneth Winters, March 24, 1934.

(Sup) 5328 i Betty Lou Winters, born February 4, 1936.
(Sup) 5329 ii Doris May Winters, born May 4, 1939.

3010 IRENE SARAH OBERST (Mary^7, Eugene^6, Samuel^5, Mary^4, John Adam II^3, John Adam I^2, John Jacob^1) was born June 12, 1905. She married William Dexter, April 12, 1930.

3011 EARL OBERST (Mary^7, Eugene^6, Samuel^5, Mary^4, John Adam II^3, John Adam I^2, John Jacob^1) was born July 4, 1918.

3012 EUGENE OBERST (Mary^7, Eugene^6, Samuel^5, Mary^4, John Adam II^3, John Adam I^2, John Jacob^1) was born July 4, 1918.

3013 WALTER NEIL LONGANBACH (Ida^7, Eugene^6, Samuel^5, Mary^4, John Adam II^3, John Adam I^2, John Jacob^1) was born January 22, 1902. He married Lois Shellhars, January 8, 1924.

(Sup) 5330 i Walter N. Longanbach, Jr., born May 28, 1927.
(Sup) 5331 ii Wesley Martin Longanbach, born January 6, 1929.
(Sup) 5332 iii Ann Louise Longanbach, born July 1, 1930.
(Sup) 5333 iv John Thomas Longanbach, born April 9, 1932.
(Sup) 5334 v Lewis James Longanbach, born October 14, 1933.

3014 GLADYS ELLEN LONGANBACH (Ida^7, Eugene^6, Samuel^5, Mary^4, John Adam II^3, John Adam I^2, John Jacob^1) was born January 21, 1904. She married William Glenn Boyd, October 9, 1923.

(Sup) 5335 i William Allen Boyd, born October 28, 1924.
(Sup) 5336 ii Donald Elwin Boyd, born September 4, 1926.
(Sup) 5337 iii Constance Joan Boyd, born August 7, 1928.
(Sup) 5338 iv Della Mae Boyd, born November 5, 1930.

3015 IVA KATHERINE LONGANBACH (Ida^7, Eugene^6, Samuel^5, Mary^4, John Adam II^3, John Adam I^2, John Jacob^1) was born March 15, 1905. She married Martin Bebou, March 4, 1926.

(Sup) 5339 i Carolina A. Bebou, born December 14, 1926.
(Sup) 5340 ii Alice Marie Bebou, born January 28, 1933.
(Sup) 5341 iii James Allen Bebou, born March 6, 1940.
(Sup) 5342 iv Judith Ann Bebou, born March 6, 1940.
(Sup) 5343 v Russell Bebou, born January 23, 1941.

3016 RUSSELL LONGANBACH (Ida^7, Eugene^6, Samuel^5, Mary^4, John Adam II^3, John Adam I^2, John Jacob^1) was born January 23, 1907. He died August 20, 1908.

3017 ESTHER LUCILLE LONGANBACH (Ida^7, Eugene^6, Samuel^5, Mary^4, John Adam II^3, John Adam I^2, John Jacob^1) was born August 16, 1908. She married George Ralph Smith, March 18, 1933.

(Sup) 5344 i Margaret Esther Smith, born March 9, 1935.
(Sup) 5345 ii Martin George B. Smith, born June 9, 1937.

3018 LESLIE EUGENE LONGANBACH (Ida[7], Eugene[6], Samuel[5], Mary[4], John Adam II[3], John Adam I[2], John Jacob[1]) was born March 13, 1910. He married Lois Hoyt, August 15, 1936.

3019 DOROTHY MAY LONGANBACH (Ida[7], Eugene[6], Samuel[5], Mary[4], John Adam II[3], John Adam I[2], John Jacob[1]) was born July 16, 1912. She married Harry Acker, February 27, 1931.

(Sup) 5346   i   Gaylord Nelson Acker, born September 19, 1931.
(Sup) 5347   ii   Everett Leroy Acker, born September 19, 1932.
(Sup) 5348   iii   Gerald Acker, born May 16, 1935.
(Sup) 5349   iv   Bonnie Lou Acker, born June 27, 1938.
(Sup) 5350   v   Virginia Mae Acker, born November 25, 1939.

3020 PAUL MARTIN LONGANBACH (Ida[7], Eugene[6], Samuel[5], Mary[4], John Adam II[3], John Adam I[2], John Jacob[1]) was born July 7, 1914. He married Wilma Babier, July 24, 1937.

(Sup) 5351   i   Karon Sue Longanbach, born June 8, 1938.

3021 ROBERT DALE LONGANBACH (Ida[7], Eugene[6], Samuel[5], Mary[4], John Adam II[3], John Adam I[2], John Jacob[1]) was born January 26, 1917. He married Ethel Leutz, January 26, 1940.

3022 BERNICE FAY LONGANBACH (Ida[7], Eugene[6], Samuel[5], Mary[4], John Adam II[3], John Adam I[2], John Jacob[1]) was born February 13, 1919. She married Edwin Roslund, March 15, 1937.

3023 JACK CROWELL (Harrison[7], Eugene[6], Samuel[5], Mary[4], John Adam II[3], John Adam I[2], John Jacob[1]) was born May 2, 1917. He married Mary Johnson, August 8, 1938, at Detroit, Michigan.

3024 HARRISON CROWELL, JR. (Harrison[7], Eugene[6], Samuel[5], Mary[4], John Adam II[3], John Adam I[2], John Jacob[1]) was born April 10, 1928. He died October 3, 1936.

3025 RICHARD D. HEBERLING (Esther[7], Eugene[6], Samuel[5], Mary[4], John Adam II[3], John Adam I[2], John Jacob[1]) was born July 23, 1923.

3026 KENNETH EUGENE HEBERLING (Esther[7], Eugene[6], Samuel[5], Mary[4], John Adam II[3], John Adam I[2], John Jacob[1]) was born July 18, 1927.

3027 IRA WILSON CROWELL (Robert[7], Sardis[6], Samuel[5], Mary[4], John Adam II[3], John Adam I[2], John Jacob[1]) was born August 23, 1913, in Sandusky County, Ohio. He married Julia Heberling, January 80, 1936. Julia was born August 29, 1908.

(Sup) 5352   i   Melvin Earl Crowell, born September 14, 1936.
(Sup) 5353   ii   Janet Mae Crowell, born June 25, 1939.
(Sup) 5354   iii   Carol Ann Crowell, born February 27, 1943.

3028 PAUL H. CROWELL (Robert[7], Sardis[6], Samuel[5], Mary[4], John Adam II[3], John Adam I[2], John Jacob[1]) was born June 12, 1915, in Sandusky County, Ohio. He died there June 5, 1919.

3029 MARTHA LOUISE WRIGHT (Rella[7], Martha[6], Samuel[5], Mary[4], John Adam II[3], John Adam I[2], John Jacob[1]) was born December 18, 1936, at Cleveland, Ohio.

3030 KENNETH HENRY SWINT (Norbert[7], Martha[6], Samuel[5], Mary[4], John Adam II[3], John Adam I[2], John Jacob[1]) was born November 26, 1929, at Fremont, Ohio.

3031 MARY PATRICIA SWINT (Norbert[7], Martha[6], Samuel[5], Mary[4], John Adam II[3], John Adam I[2], John Jacob[1]) was born May 14, 1947, at Cleveland, Ohio.

3032 BARBARA JEAN WOLFE (Alta[7], William[6], Samuel[5], Mary[4], John Adam II[3], John Adam I[2], John Jacob[1]) was born March 4, 1931, at Alma, Michigan.

3033 RONALD THERON WOLFE (Alta[7], William[6], Samuel[5], Mary[4], John Adam II[3], John Adam I[2], John Jacob[1]) was born July 12, 1934, at Alma, Michigan.

3034 PHYLLIS·ANN WOLFE (Alta[7], William[6], Samuel[5], Mary[4], John Adam II[3], John Adam I[2], John Jacob[1]) was born January 16, 1986, at Alma, Michigan.

3035 WAYNE NESBIT (Jane[7], John[6], Samuel[5], Mary[4], John Adam II[3], John Adam I[2], John Jacob[1]) was born February 12, 1931, at Fremont, Ohio.

3036 JANET NESBIT (Jane[7], John[6], Samuel[5], Mary[4], John Adam II[3], John Adam I[2], John Jacob[1]) was born July 21, 1935, at Fremont, Ohio.

3037 MARILYN FABRIAN (Mildred[7], John[6], Samuel[5], Mary[4], John Adam II[3], John Adam I[2], John Jacob[1]) was born January 6, 1941, at Fremont, Ohio.

3038 DONALD LEE FABRIAN (Mildred[7], John[6], Samuel[5], Mary[4], John Adam II[3], John Adam I[2], John Jacob[1]) was born October 18, 1944, at Fremont, Ohio.

3039 RUTH ANN TWISS (Mary[7], John[6], Samuel[5], Mary[4], John Adam II[3], John Adam I[2], John Jacob[1]) was born April 1, 1934, at Fremont, Ohio.

3040 FRANK TWISS (Mary[7], John[6], Samuel[5], Mary[4], John Adam II[3], John Adam I[2], John Jacob[1]) was born June 17, 1937, at Fremont, Ohio.

3041 JAMES ALLEN TWISS (Mary[7], John[6], Samuel[5], Mary[4], John Adam II[3], John Adam I[2], John Jacob[1]) was born March 2, 1940, at Fremont, Ohio.

3042 JOHN EDWARD TWISS (Mary[7], John[6], Samuel[5], Mary[4], John Adam II[3], John Adam I[2], John Jacob[1]) was born December 15, 1943, at Fremont, Ohio.

3043 ROSE MARY HELEN TWISS (Mary[7], John[6], Samuel[5], Mary[4], John Adam II[3], John Adam I[2], John Jacob[1]) was born September 15, 1946, at Fremont, Ohio.

3044 WILLIAM RICHARD NOVITSKI (Sally[7], John[6], Samuel[5], Mary[4], John Adam II[3], John Adam I[2], John Jacob[1]) was born October 30, 1942.

3045 KENNETH LEE NOVITSKI (Sally[7], John[6], Samuel[5], Mary[4], John Adam II[3], John Adam I[2], John Jacob[1]) was born January 13, 1947.

3046 MAXINE MAE SCHOOLEY (Leah[7], Sarah[6], Samuel[5], Mary[4], John Adam II[3], John Adam I[2], John Jacob[1]) was born July 15, 1923, at Fenton, Michigan. She married Harold Dean Jones, March 17, 1946.

3047 GEORGE T. SCHOOLEY, JR. (Leah[7], Sarah[6], Samuel[5], Mary[4], John Adam II[3], John Adam I[2], John Jacob[1]) was born October 9, 1925, at Fenton, Michigan. He married Virginia Slocum, February 22, 1947.

3048 RICHARD EDWIN WARD (Clifford[7], Sarah[6], Samuel[5], Mary[4], John Adam II[3], John Adam I[2], John Jacob[1]) was born November 22, 1941, at Terre Haute, Indiana.

3049 DONALD EUGENE WARD (Clifford[7], Sarah[6], Samuel[5], Mary[4], John Adam II[3], John Adam I[2], John Jacob[1]) was born February 1, 1943, at Terre Haute, Indiana.

3050 LOIS EVELYN WARD (Clifford[7], Sarah[6], Samuel[5], Mary[4], John Adam II[3], John Adam I[2], John Jacob[1]) was born August 8, 1944, at Terre Haute, Indiana.

3051 PATRICIA ANN WARD (James[7], Sarah[6], Samuel[5], Mary[4], John Adam II[3], John Adam I[2], John Jacob[1]) was born May 28, 1934, at Holly, Michigan.

3052 BARBARA JEAN WARD (James[7], Sarah[6], Samuel[5], Mary[4], John Adam II[3], John Adam I[2], John Jacob[1]) was born February 16, 1936, at Holly, Michigan.

3053 DAVID IRVING CLARK (Blanche[7], Sarah[6], Samuel[5], Mary[4], John Adam II[3], John Adam I[2], John Jacob[1]) was born August 9, 1938.

3054 PAUL FREDERICK CLARK (Blanche[7], Sarah[6], Samuel[5], Mary[4], John Adam II[3], John Adam I[2], John Jacob[1]).

3055 SARAH MYRTLE CLARK (Blanche[7], Sarah[6], Samuel[5], Mary[4], John Adam II[3], John Adam I[2], John Jacob[1]).

3056 ELON LAVERNE CLARK, JR. (Blanche[7], Sarah[6], Samuel[5], Mary[4], John Adam II[3], John Adam I[2], John Jacob[1]).

3057 ROBERT ENOS MORDEN (Ruth[7], Sarah[6], Samuel[5], Mary[4], John Adam II[3], John Adam I[2], John Jacob[1]) was born October 4, 1936, at Owosso, Michigan.

3058 HAROLD EDWARD MORDEN (Ruth[7], Sarah[6], Samuel[5], Mary[4], John Adam II[3], John Adam I[2], John Jacob[1]) was born July 20, 1941, at Owosso, Michigan.

3059 ALICE FORGY (Glenn[7], Alice[6], George[5], Mary[4], John Adam II[3], John Adam I[2], John Jacob[1]) was born April 19, 1908, at Chicago, Illinois. She married Glenn Smith, March 14, 1931.

(Sup) 5360   i   Jean Wilson, born February 20, 1931.

3060 BERYL ERNESTINE CROWELL (Letus[7], Abner[6], John[5], Mary[4], John Adam II[3], John Adam I[2], John Jacob[1]) was born June 8, 1909. She married Jerome Oliver Wilson.

3061 ELLA MAY CROWELL (Charles[7], Abner[6], John[5], Mary[4], John Adam II[3], John Adam I[2], John Jacob[1]) was born March 15, 1902, at Hanford, California. She married Sidney Thomas Lee, son of James Lee, July 2, 1927. Sidney died January 17, 1948.

(Sup) 5361   i   Donald Richard Lee, born September 21, 1931.

3062 ORVAL CHESTER CROWELL (Charles[7], Abner[6], John[5], Mary[4], John Adam II[3], John Adam I[2], John Jacob[1]) was born May 11, 1903, at Hanford, California. He married Estelle Logan in 1924. She was the daughter of Matthew Logan and was born April 12, 1933, in New Mexico.

(Sup) 5362   i   Vivian Estelle Crowell, born March 5, 1925.
(Sup) 5363   ii   Ronald Orval Crowell, born August 8, 1931.

3063 ABNER MELVIN CROWELL (Charles[7], Abner[6], John[5], Mary[4], John Adam II[3], John Adam I[2], John Jacob[1]) was born February 24, 1905, at Turlock, California. He married Beth Ione Cleland, June 5, 1928. Beth was the daughter of Ervin A. Cleland and was born at Edgerton, Minnesota, July 28, 1907.

(Sup) 5364   i   Betty Arlene Crowell, born March 15, 1931.
(Sup) 5365   ii   Geraldine Elaine Crowell, born October 17, 1933.
(Sup) 5366   iii   Verna Mae Crowell, born February 22, 1936.

3064 LOREN EUGENE CROWELL (Charles[7], Abner[6], John[5], Mary[4], John Adam II[3], John Adam I[2], John Jacob[1]) was born January 3, 1907, at Turlock, California. He married Agnes Clarabelle Chamberlain, daughter of Leroy Chamberlain. Agnes was born January 3, 1907, at Springfield, Illinois.

(Sup) 5367   i   Beverly Loraine Crowell, born January 13, 1935.
(Sup) 5368   ii   Loren Dale Crowell, born April 26, 1939.

3065 VIRGIL LLOYD CROWELL, (Charles[7], Abner[6], John[5], Mary[4], John Adam II[3], John Adam I[2], John Jacob[1]) was born May 7, 1909, at Turlock, California. He married Della Evelyn Convers, daughter of Ralph Convers. Della was born at LaGrange, California, in 1909.

(Sup) 5369   i   Janet Lea Crowell, born March 23, 1933.
(Sup) 5370   ii   Verle Jean Crowell, born June 6, 1935.
(Sup) 5371   iii   Convers Crowell, born March 12, 1938.

3066 CHARLES COLEMAN CROWELL (Charles[7], Abner[6], John[5], Mary[4], John Adam II[3], John Adam I[2], John Jacob[1]) was born December 14, 1911, at Turlock, California. He married Virginia Louise Davis, daughter of Leroy Davis. Virginia was born at Springfield, Illinois.

(Sup) 5372   i   Robert Coleman Crowell, born September 5, 1935.
(Sup) 5373   ii   Barbara Dale Crowell, born February 27, 1939.

3067 LEILA JOYCE CROWELL (Arthur[7], Abner[6], John[5], Mary[4], John Adam II[3], John Adam I[2], John Jacob[1]) was born October 24, 1908, at Turlock, California. She married Frank Herbert Lang II, August 30, 1939. Frank, son of Frank Herbert Lang, was born May 16, 1908, Salinas, California.

(Sup) 5374   i   Peter Crowell Lang, born February 18, 1932.
(Sup) 5375   ii   Frank Herbert Lang III, born June 27, 1936.
(Sup) 5376   iii   Richard Arthur Lang, born June 22, 1937.

3068 GLADYS MARIAN CROWELL (Arthur[7], Abner[6], John[5], Mary[4], John Adam II[3], John Adam I[2], John Jacob[1]) was born October 28, 1910, at Turlock, California. She married James M. Buchanan, July 18, 1936. James was born July 26, 1909, at Idaho Falls, Idaho.

(Sup) 5377   i   James Douglas Buchanan, born August 7, 1941.
(Sup) 5378   ii   Joan Gale Buchanan, born February 10, 1943.

3069 ARTHUR VERNE CROWELL (Arthur[7], Abner[6], John[5], Mary[4], John Adam II[3], John Adam I[2], John Jacob[1]) was born July 8, 1917, at Turlock, California. He married Barbara Whitaker, August 10, 1937. Barbara, daughter of William Whitaker, was born September 23, 1919, at Turlock, California.

(Sup) 5379   i   Barbara Lynne Crowell, born February 18, 1941.
(Sup) 5380   ii   Michael Verne Crowell, born August 12, 1942.

3070 MARY ELIZABETH CROWELL BURCH (Mary[7], Abner[6], John[5], Mary[4], John Adam II[3], John Adam I[2], John Jacob[1]) was born May 27, 1911, at Raymond, California. She married Frederick Donnell Bennett, October 9, 1938, at Mills College Chapel, Oakland, California. Frederick was born May 3, 1911, at San Francisco, California.

    (Sup) 5381   i Mary Elizabeth Bennett, born September 27, 1942.
    (Sup) 5382   ii Catherine Anne Bennett, born March 7, 1945.

3071 ELMER CROWELL BURCH (Mary[7], Abner[6], John[5], Mary[4], John Adam II[3], John Adam I[2], John Jacob[1]) was born November 11, 1912, at Raymond, California. He married Helen Elizabeth Daetz, April 2, 1938, at Syracuse, New York. Helen was born November 5, 1916, at Two Rivers, Wisconsin. Elmer became an agriculture engineer in Hawaii.

    (Sup) 5383   i Phyllis Elizabeth Burch, born October 6, 1942.
    (Sup) 5384   ii Terry Lee Burch, born December 19, 1945.

3072 CHARLES WILLIAM KOLB (Elizabeth[7], Abner[6], John[5], Mary[4], John Adam II[3], John Adam I[2], John Jacob[1]) was born November 19, 1918, at Madera, California.

3073 ALBERT CROWELL KOLB (Elizabeth[7], Abner[6], John[5], Mary[4], John Adam II[3], John Adam I[2], John Jacob[1]) was born November 7, 1920, at Madera, California.

3074 ELEANOR ESTELLE CROWELL (Clarence[7], Abner[6], John[5], Mary[4], John Adam II[3], John Adam I[2], John Jacob[1]) was born December 30, 1911. She died December 28, 1913.

3075 WILLIAM TURNER CROWELL (Clarence[7], Abner[6], John[5], Mary[4], John Adam II[3], John Adam I[2], John Jacob[1]) was born October 1, 1913. He married Audrey Delmege, May 31, 1937.

    (Sup) 5385   i Catherine LaVerne Crowell, born July 23, 1938.

3076 VERNON ALEXANDER CROWELL (Clarence[7], Abner[6], John[5], Mary[4], John Adam II[3], John Adam I[2], John Jacob[1]) was born November 28, 1915.

3077 IVAN CLARENCE CROWELL (Clarence[7], Abner[6], John[5], Mary[4], John Adam II[3], John Adam I[2], John Jacob[1]) was born November 23, 1919.

3078 IRENE FLORENCE CROWELL (Clarence[7], Abner[6], John[5], Mary[4], John Adam II[3], John Adam I[2], John Jacob[1]) was born November 23, 1919. She married Paul Fuselier, December 17, 1939.

3079 BEULAH T. SCHINDLER (Beulah[7], Abner[6], John[5], Mary[4], John Adam II[3], John Adam I[2], John Jacob[1]) was born February 14, 1912, at Seattle, Washington. She married Cyril Wherry Gilcrest, November 2, 1935. Cyril was the son of John Gilcrest and was born at San Mateo, California, in 1904.

    (Sup) 5386   i Mary Louise Gilcrest, born April 7, 1938.
    (Sup) 5387   ii Richard John Gilcrest, born January 21, 1940.

3080 MARY LOUISE SCHINDLER (Beulah[7], Abner[6], John[5], Mary[4], John Adam II[3], John Adam I[2], John Jacob[1]) was born August 19, 1913. She married John Boucher, January 7, 1939, at Burlingame, California.

    (Sup) 5388   i Laurie Bernard Boucher, born December 7, 1942.
    (Sup) 5389   ii John Thomas Boucher, born February 20, 1944.
    (Sup) 5390   iii Teresa Louise Boucher, born August 16, 1946.

3081 BERNARD CROWELL SCHINDLER (Beulah[7], Abner[6], John[5], Mary[4], John Adam II[3], John Adam I[2], John Jacob[1]) was born August 10, 1916. He married Caroline Anderson, June 27, 1942.

    (Sup) 5391   i George Andrew Schindler, born February 10, 1946.

3082 MARILLA MARY WILLIAMS (Mary[7], Mary[6], John[5], Mary[4], John Adam II[3], John Adam I[2], John Jacob[1]) was born November 11, 1897. She married a Mr. Stannard and they had no children.

3083 HOWARD R. WILLIAMS (Mary[7], Mary[6], John[5], Mary[4], John Adam II[3], John Adam I[2], John Jacob[1]) was born July 5, 1899. He married.

    (Sup) 5396   i Marjorie Williams, born October 4, 1932.

3083A VERDA WILLIAMS (Mary[7], Mary[6], John[5], Mary[4], John Adam II[3], John Adam I[2], John Jacob[1]) was born October 1, 1901. She married a Mr. McKeckin. No children were born to them.

3084 CLARENCE KENNADY (Carroll[7], Mary[6], John[5], Mary[4], John Adam II[3], John Adam I[2], John Jacob[1]) was born September 26, 1906. He married Pearl Brook, February 9, 1932.

3085 ALVIN KENNADY (Carroll[7], Mary[6], John[5], Mary[4], John Adam II[3], John Adam I[2], John Jacob[1]) was born July 9, 1908. He married Mabel Harley, May 16, 1936.

    (Sup) 5397   i Richard Kennady, born July 17, 1937.

3086 JOHN KENNADY (Carroll[7], Mary[6], John[5], Mary[4], John Adam II[3], John Adam I[2], John Jacob[1]) was born August 16, 1910.

3087 MYRTLE KENNADY (Carroll[7], Mary[6], John[5], Mary[4], John Adam II[3], John Adam I[2], John Jacob[1]) was born May 29, 1912.

3088 CHARLES KENNADY (Carroll[7], Mary[6], John[5], Mary[4], John Adam II[3], John Adam I[2], John Jacob[1]) was born January 30, 1914.

3089 CLAYTON KENNADY (Carroll[7], Mary[6], John[5], Mary[4], John Adam II[3], John Adam I[2], John Jacob[1]) was born in November, 1915.

3090 EDITH KENNADY (Carroll[7], Mary[6], John[5], Mary[4], John Adam II[3], John Adam I[2], John Jacob[1]) was born August 2, 1917. She married Robert Morris, July 5, 1936.

    (Sup) 5398   i Marilyn Morris, born January 6, 1937.

3091 MARGARET KENNADY (Carroll[7], Mary[6], John[5], Mary[4], John Adam II[3], John Adam I[2], John Jacob[1]) was born June 24, 1919. She married Eugene Gentles, November 5, 1937.

    (Sup) 5399   i Sandra Gentles, born January 5, 1939.

3092 ABNER BUEL KENNADY, JR. (Abner[7], Mary[6], John[5], Mary[4], John Adam II[3], John Adam I[2], John Jacob[1]) was born April 20, 1921, at Berkeley, California. He married Geraldine Flannigan, August 2, 1947. In 1942 he enlisted in the U. S. Marine Corps and served through World War II in the Pacific Theater, first at Guadalcanal. He was discharged a Staff Sergeant, December 4, 1945.

3093 RALPH LE ROY KENNADY (Abner[7], Mary[6], John[5], Mary[4], John Adam II[3], John Adam I[2], John Jacob[1]) was born March 1, 1924, at Berkeley, California. He married Beulah Trichell, July 14, 1944. Ralph enlisted in the U. S. Navy, December 24, 1941, at the outbreak of World War II. He served nineteen months on New Caledonia in the Pacific Theater and eighteen months on board the Destroyer Escort, "Doyle E. Bannas." He was discharged as a Ship's Fitter, First Class, November 28, 1945.

3094 MARIAN LA VERNA KENNADY (Abner[7], Mary[6], John[5], Mary[4], John Adam II[3], John Adam I[2], John Jacob[1]) was born January 29, 1926, at Berkeley, California.

3095 GEORGE LESTER KENNADY (Abner[7], Mary[6], John[5], Mary[4], John Adam II[3], John Adam I[2], John Jacob[1]) was born December 24, 1931, at Berkeley, California.

3096 ELIZABETH BUHLER (Mary[7], Ella[6], Moses[5], Mary[4], John Adam II[3], John Adam I[2], John Jacob[1]) was born August 30, 1903, at New Orleans, Louisiana. She was educated in the public schools of Victoria, Texas, and in high schools at Cincinnati, Philadelphia, Washington, Chicago, and Louisville, while her father was auditing railroad war accounts for the government. She took her college entrance examination at Louisville and entered Rice Institute at Houston, Texas, in 1921, graduating with an A. B. degree in 1925. In the summer of 1924 she studied geology in Colorado and the next year had another period of study in the Alps with a group from Harvard. She was an assistant to geophysicists in Houston from 1924 to 1934. On September 16, 1929, Elizabeth married Elmer Lee Summers at Victoria, Texas. Elmer was born at Keno, Texas, August 17, 1898. He was a newspaper writer at Houston, Texas, and rose to the agriculture editorship of Houston's largest daily paper.

(Sup) 5400   i   Edward L. Summers, born August 24, 1937.
(Sup) 5401   ii   Charles Dean Summers, born January 22, 1940.
(Sup) 5402   iii Jess William Summers, born October 18, 1941.

3097 CHARLES MICHAEL BUHLER, JR. (Mary[7], Ella[6], Moses[5], Mary[4], John Adam II[3], John Adam I[2], John Jacob[1]) was born December 13, 1905, at New Orleans, Louisiana. He was educated in the public schools of Victoria, Texas, Cincinnati, St. Louis, Washington, Philadelphia, and Louisville. He graduated from Rice Institute, Houston, Texas, in 1928, with an A. B. degree, and entered the cotton business, later becoming manager of a large distributing firm. He married Dorcas Allison Eldredge, October 26, 1935, at Baton Rouge, Louisiana. Dorcas was born at Grand Junction, Colorado. She died July 20, 1949, at Houston, Texas. Charles married Mary Louise Kimball Powers at Houston, March 14, 1950.

3098 MARY ALICE BUHLER (Mary[7], Ella[6], Moses[5], Mary[4], John Adam II[3], John Adam I[2], John Jacob[1]) was born February 5, 1908, at New Orleans, Louisiana, where she died November 11, 1909.

3099 THEODORE BUHLER (Mary[7], Ella[6], Moses[5], Mary[4], John Adam II[3], John Adam I[2], John Jacob[1]) was born December 29, 1915, at Victoria, Texas. He died October 22, 1932, at Edna, Texas.

3100 MARTHA BUHLER (Mary[7], Ella[6], Moses[5], Mary[4], John Adam II[3], John Adam I[2], John Jacob[1]) was born June 21, 1917, at Victoria, Texas. She was educated in the public schools there and entered Rice Institute Houston, Texas, with one summer session at the University of Colorado and another at Northwestern University (where she studied primary school teaching methods), graduating from Rice with an A. B. degree in 1939. She taught in the Victoria (Texas) elementary schools from 1939 to 1942. On June 26, 1942, she married Bromley Francis Cooper at Victoria. Bromley served in World War II as an instructor in flying. He was a Major and after the war became associated with a large oil company in Houston, Texas.

(Sup) 5403   i   David Rotsch Cooper, born October 21, 1943.
(Sup) 5404   ii   Anne Elizabeth Cooper, born November 3, 1945.

3101 WILLIAM VENABLE BURFORD (Jessie[7], Ella[6], Moses[5], Mary[4], John Adam II[3], John Adam I[2], John Jacob[1]) was born October 26, 1909, at Port Lavaca, Texas, where he died July 11, 1911.

3102 REYBURN DEAN BURFORD (Jessie[7], Ella[6], Moses[5], Mary[4], John Adam II[3], John Adam I[2], John Jacob[1]) was born December 6, 1911, at Belton, Texas. He was educated in the public schools at Houston and graduated from Rice Institute with an A. B. degree in 1934. During college he majored in physics and later did graduate work at Rice in mechanical engineering. He became associated with a large gas producing and distributing company at Shreveport, Louisiana, as a physicist. Reyburn married Margaret Regena Gayle, February 2, 1939, at Houston, Texas. Margaret was the daughter of Francis Alexander and Essie Leathers Gayle and was born September 20, 1919, at Edna, Texas.

(Sup) 5405   i   William Gayle Burford, born March 19, 1941.
(Sup) 5406   ii   Katherine Anne Burford, July 30, 1943.

3103 ELBERT DEAN, JR. (Elbert[7], Ella[6], Moses[5], Mary[4], John Adam II[3], John Adam I[2], John Jacob[1]) was born September 29, 1919, at Beaumont, Texas. After graduating from high school, he entered the U. S. Navy during World War II. He married Dorothy Blanche Robinson, May 19, 1938, at Port Arthur, Texas. After the end of World War II Elbert entered business with his uncle in Houston, Texas.

(Sup) 5407   i   James Harold Dean, born October 21, 1939.
(Sup) 5408   ii   William Elbert Dean, born August 17, 1944.

3104 HARRY REYBURN DEAN (Elbert[7], Ella[6], Moses[5], Mary[4], John Adam II[3], John Adam I[2], John Jacob[1]) was born June 12, 1923, at Beaumont, Texas. He was educated in the public schools at Port Neches, and from January 20, 1943, for a little more than three years, he served in the U. S. Marines. After his discharge from military service, Harry entered the University of Texas in 1946, where he graduated in 1950. He married Norma Jean Wolf, June 8, 1943, at Houston, Texas.

(Sup) 5409   i   Dale Thomas Dean, born March 24, 1946.
(Sup) 5410   ii   Diana Jane Dean, born December 22, 1947.

3105 MARION YOUNG (Justin^7, Annie^6, Mary^5, Mary^4, John Adam II^3, John Adam I^2, John Jacob^1) was born May 13, 1907, in Sandusky County, Ohio. She married Keith Selvey, July 6, 1926. Keith was the son of Guy M. Selvey and was born May 17, 1903, at Bellevue, Ohio.

(Sup) 5411   i   Millard Dale Selvey, born April 25, 1928.
(Sup) 5412   ii   Laurel Edward Selvey, born June 2, 1930.
(Sup) 5413   iii   Betty Jean Selvey, born December 10, 1938.
(Sup) 5414   iv   William Robert Selvey, born November 23, 1941.

3106 CHARLES YOUNG (Justin^7, Annie^6, Mary^5, Mary^4, John Adam II^3, John Adam I^2, John Jacob^1) was born October 20, 1910, in Sandusky County, Ohio. He married Mildred Miller, December 24, 1934. Mildred, daughter of Lewis Miller, was born April 27, 1910, at Sandusky, Ohio.

(Sup) 5415   i   Donald Charles Young, born June 29, 1944.

3107 PAULINE YOUNG (Justin^7, Annie^6, Mary^5, Mary^4, John Adam II^3, John Adam I^2, John Jacob^1) was born February 12, 1914, in Sandusky County, Ohio. She married John Coon, son of John S. Coon, March 1, 1933. John was born in Sandusky County, Ohio.

(Sup) 5416   i   Mary Ellen Coon, born December 23, 1933.
(Sup) 5417   ii   Phyllis Mae Coon, born December 17, 1935.
(Sup) 5418   iii   Carol Ann Coon, born May 6, 1938.

3108 JOHN DAWLEY, JR. (Elsie^7, Annie^6, Mary^5, Mary^4, John Adam II^3, John Adam I^2, John Jacob^1) was born September 12, 1915. He married Arletta Duignan in May, 1941. In March of that year he entered the U. S. Army and served through World War II in the 627th Medical Clearing Company in Holland, France, Belgium, and Germany. He was awarded the Certificate of Merit for meritorious and outstanding performance of duty.

(Sup) 5419   i   Patricia Ann Dawley, born November 17, 1941.
(Sup) 5420   ii   Barbara Lou Dawley, born November 2, 1946.

3109 ROBERT HENRY SOMMER (Wilbur^7, Ida^6, Mary^5, Mary^4, John Adam II^3, John Adam I^2, John Jacob^1) was the son of Wilbur and Aimee (Decker) Sommer [The Link Family, pages 481-482, No. 1581]. Robert was born December 22, 1905, in Sandusky County, Ohio. He married Marie Smith, October 6, 1935. She was the daughter of Howard Smith and was born March 18, 1912.

3110 STANLEY SOMMER (Wilbur^7, Ida^6, Mary^5, Mary^4, John Adam II^3, John Adam I^2, John Jacob^1) was the son of Wilbur and Aimee (Decker) Sommer [The Link Family, pages 481-482, No. 1581]. Stanley was born April 10, 1907, in Sandusky County, Ohio. He married Jean E. Lyman, August 29, 1929. Jean was the daughter of Roy Lyman and was born February 1, 1908.

3111 ELIZABETH SOMMER (Wilbur^7, Ida^6, Mary^5, Mary^4, John Adam II^3, John Adam I^2, John Jacob^1) was the daughter of Wilbur and Aimee (Decker) Sommer [The Link Family, pages 481-482, No. 1581]. Elizabeth was born May 9, 1915, in Sandusky County, Ohio.

3112 MERRITT SOMMER (Wilbur^7, Ida^6, Mary^5, Mary^4, John Adam II^3, John Adam I^2, John Jacob^1) was the son of Wilbur and Aimee (Decker) Sommer [The Link Family, pages 481-482, No. 1581]. Merritt was born July 30, 1917, in Sandusky County, Ohio. He married Mary Ellen Laux. She was the daughter of Jerome L. Laux and was born April 12, 1920.

3113 SUSANNAH SOMMER (Wilbur^7, Ida^6, Mary^5, Mary^4, John Adam II^3, John Adam I^2, John Jacob^1) was the daughter of Wilbur and Aimee Decker Sommer [The Link Family, pages 481-482, No. 1581]. Susannah was born September 6, 1923, in Sandusky County, Ohio. She married Robert E. Betson. He was the son of Fred Betson and was born May 14, 1922.

3114 BARBARA THOMSEN (Barbara^7, Ida^6, Mary^5, Mary^4, John Adam II^3, John Adam I^2, John Jacob^1) was the daughter of George and Barbara (Sommer) Thomsen [The Link Family, page 480, No. 1583]. Barbara was born in 1911 and died the same year.

3115 GEORGE HENRY THOMSEN (Barbara^7, Ida^6, Mary^5, Mary^4, John Adam II^3, John Adam I^2, John Jacob^1) was the son of George and Barbara (Sommer) Thomsen [The Link Family, page 480, No. 1583]. George was born October 13, 1913. He married Genevieve Meyer, May 2, 1936.

(Sup) 5425   i   Marlyn Thomsen, born May 4, 1937.
(Sup) 5426   ii   Karol Thomsen, born October 13, 1913.

3116 MAY KATHERINE THOMSEN (Barbara^7, Ida^6, Mary^5, Mary^4, John Adam II^3, John Adam I^2, John Jacob^1) was the daughter of George and Barbara (Sommer) Thomsen [The Link Family, page 480, No. 1583]. She was born May 29, 1918. She married Raymond Thomas, August 29, 1936.

3117 LILLIAN EDNA BAILY (Barbara^7, Ida^6, Mary^5, Mary^4, John Adam II^3, John Adam I^2, John Jacob^1) was the daughter of Frank and Barbara (Sommer Thomsen) Bailey [The Link Family, page 480, No. 1583]. Lillian was born February 1, 1929.

(Sup) 3118 JAMES GOOD (Corine[7], Ida[6], Mary[5], Mary[4], John Adam II[3], John Adam I[2], John Jacob[1]) was the son of Richard and Corine (Sommer) Good [The Link Family, page 480, No. 1585]. James was born February 2, 1915, in Seneca County, Ohio. He married Esther Hintz, June 22, 1940. She was the daughter of Joseph Hintz and was born in Seneca County, June 16, 1913.

(Sup) 5427   i James Alton Good, born September 25, 1941.
(Sup) 5428   ii Joyce Eileen Good, born November 13, 1944.

(Sup) 3119 LUCILLE GOOD (Corine[7], Ida[6], Mary[5], Mary[4], John Adam II[3], John Adam I[2], John Jacob[1]) was the daughter of Richard and Corine (Sommer) Good [The Link Family, page 480, No. 1585]. Lucille was born October 18, 1917, in Seneca County Ohio. She married Daryl Orivig, March 5, 1938. He was the son of George D. Orivig and was born in Seneca County, March 18, 1913.

(Sup) 5428A i Melvin Daryl Orivig, born April 6, 1940.
(Sup) 5428B ii Nancy Sue Orivig, born April 26, 1943.

(Sup) 3120 JEANNE SOMMER (James[7], Ida[6], Mary,[5], Mary[4], John Adam II[3], John Adam I[2], John Jacob[1]) was the daughter of James and Gertrude (Bauman) Sommer [The Link Family, page 480, No. 1586. Jeanne was born September 27, 1921, at Fremont, Ohio. She married Charles Beatty Hartley. He was the son of Kyle and Julia Hartley and was born March 31, 1917, at Huron, Ohio.

(Sup) 5429   i Barbara Jeanne Hartley, born August 10, 1945.
(Sup) 5429A ii Suzanne Marie Hartley, born August 15, 1949.

(Sup) 3121 RUTH E. SOMMER (James[7], Ida[6], Mary[5], Mary[4], John Adam II[3], John Adam I[2], John Jacob[1]) was the daughter of James and Gertrude (Bauman) Sommer [The Link Family, page 480, No. 1586]. Ruth was born February 6, 1925, at Fremont, Ohio. She married, first, Donald D. Meeker April 22, 1944; they were divorced September, 1959, and Donald died June 26, 1982. Ruth married, second, John F. Beckert May, 1968. Ruth and John were divorced May, 1973.

(Sup) 5429B i Margaret K. Meeker, born November 5, 1944.
(Sup) 5429C ii Martha Ruth Meeker, born June 13, 1951.

(Sup) 3122 WAYNE FRANKLIN SOMMER (James[7], Ida[6], Mary[5], Mary[4], John Adam II[3], John Adam I[2], John Jacob[1]) was the son of James and Gertrude (Bauman) Sommer [The Link Family, page 480, No. 1586]. Wayne was born February 27, 1926, at Huron, Ohio. He married Ruth Janet Schaefer June 23, 1951, at Sandusky, Ohio. She was born March 16, 1927, at Sandusky. He and Ruth resided in Erie County, Ohio, where he was a building contractor, and her avocation was working with the Humane Society.

(Sup) 5429D   i   Scott James Sommer, born May 13, 1952.
(Sup) 5429E   ii Sandy Joan Sommer, born November 20, 1953.
(Sup) 5429F   iii Todd Clark Sommer, born November 23, 1956.

(Sup) 3123 WILLIAM WELKER THRAVES (William[7], Meade[6], Mary[5], Mary[4], John Adam II[3], John Adam I[2], John Jacob[1]) was the son of William and Betty Belle (Welker) Thraves [The Link Family, page 480, No. 1589]. William was born July 10, 1945, at Cleveland, Ohio.

(Sup) 3124 MERRITT C. HAVENS-BIXLER (Marilla[7], Lillie[6], Mary[5], Mary[4], John Adam II[3], John Adam I[2], John Jacob[1]) was the son of Willis and Marilla (Huber) Havens [The Link Family, No. 1590, page 481; and Supplement No. 1590]. Merritt was born February 17, 1923, at Fremont, Ohio. He was adopted by his step-father, Marshall Bixler. Merritt married Shirley Jean Wheeler September 13, 1947. She was the adopted daughter of Lorance D. and Margaret Meyer Wheeler and was born in 1925. Merritt died of cancer May 27, 1960, at age thirty-seven. Shirley Jean died in 1968.

(Sup) 5430   i   Merritt C. Bixler, Jr., born June 7, 1948.
(Sup) 5430A   ii Martha Jean Bixler, born July 3, 1950.
(Sup) 5430B   iii Margaret Ann Bixler, born July 27, 1953.
(Sup) 5430C   iv Lorance H. Bixler, born May 3, 1955.

3125 ANNA MARIE COLLINS (Ella[7], Martha[6], Isabella[5], Rebecca[4], John Adam II[3], John Adam I[2], John Jacob[1]) was born May 23, 1888. She married John L. Allen, June 1, 1920. He was the son of Moses Ray Allen and was born October 4, 1888. They had no children.

3126 JESSIE ALICE COLLINS (Ella[7], Martha[6], Isabella[5], Rebecca[4], John Adam I[2], John Jacob[1]) was born March 2, 1891. She married Henry H. Johnston, son of Charles Ernest Johnston, January 9, 1924. Henry was born June 29, 1890.

(Sup) 5431   i Jean Ann Johnston, born May 24, 1927.
(Sup) 5432   ii Nancy Lou Johnston, born January 24, 1930.

3127 MINOR BAUMGARDNER (Charles[7], Martha[6], Isabella[5], Rebecca[4], John Adam II[3], John Adam I[2], John Jacob[1]) was born January 2, 1890. He married Mary Silvers, daughter of John Silvers, November 24, 1912.

(Sup) 5433   i   Dorothy Baumgardner, born November 9, 1914.
(Sup) 5434   ii   Phillip Baumgardner, born April 10, 1921.
(Sup) 5435   iii   Patricia Ann Baumgardner, born February 2, 1932.

3128 WILLARD BAUMGARDNER (Charles[7], Martha[6], Isabella[5], Rebecca[4], John Adam II[3], John Adam I[2], John Jacob[1]) was born September 29, 1891. He married Anna Hardman, December 25, 1913.

3129 EVELYN BAUMGARDNER (Charles[7], Martha[6], Isabella[5], Rebecca[4], John Adam II[3], John Adam I[2], John Jacob[1]) was born April 5, 1906. She married W. Arthur Faus, July 26, 1933. Arthur was born February 24, 1907.

3130 EDGAR BAUMGARDNER (Edward[7], Martha[6], Isabella[5], Rebecca[4], John Adam II[3], John Adam I[2], John Jacob[1]) was born October 19, 1896.

3131 MARTHA EVELEY BAUMGARDNER (Albert[7], Martha[6], Isabella[5], Rebecca[4], John Adam II[3], John Adam I[2], John Jacob[1]) was born November 8, 1890. She married Harry Startzman, son of Lloyd Harrison Startzman, April 5, 1916. Harry was born July 23, 1892.

(Sup) 5436   i   John Startzman, born August 23, 1921.

3132 MARY ELIZABETH BAUMGARDNER (Albert[7], Martha[6], Isabella[5], Rebecca[4], John Adam II[3], John Adam I[2], John Jacob[1]) was born October 6, 1898. She married Robert Orth, January 1, 1920. Robert was the son of Charles Orth and was born January 8, 1898.

3133 JOHN HODGE PLATTENBURG (Nellie[7], Charles[6], Isabella[5], Rebecca[4], John Adam II[3], John Adam I[2], John Jacob[1]) was born December 7, 1900, at Springfield, Ohio. He married Alice A. Paullin, October 26, 1925, at Cleveland, Ohio. Alice, daughter of Herman L. Paullin, was born June 26, 1905, at Mount Sterling, Ohio.

3134 ELIZABETH PAGE PLATTENBURG (Nellie[7], Charles[6], Isabella[5], Rebecca[4], John Adam II[3], John Adam I[2], John Jacob[1]) was born August 23, 1902, at Columbus, Ohio. She married Donald William De Vere, September 4, 1924, at Hudson, Ohio. Donald, son of Joseph De Vere, was born February 11, 1900, at Columbus, Ohio.

(Sup) 5437   i   William Donald De Vere, born October 12, 1927.
(Sup) 5438   ii   Richard Page De Vere, bor May 19, 1929.

3135 LOIS LYNCH (Virma[7], Charles[6], Isabella[5], Rebecca[4], John Adam II[3], John Adam I[2], John Jacob[1]) was born January 13, 1917, at Cleveland, Ohio. She married Arthur G. Koepke, April 25, 1942.

3136 SHIRLEY MAE LYNCH (Virma[7], Charles[6], Isabella[5], Rebecca[4], John Adam II[3], John Adam I[2], John Jacob[1]) was born December 28, 1924, at Cleveland, Ohio.

3137 CHARLES ALVIN ROPP (Eldon[7], Charles[6], Isabella[5], Rebecca[4], John Adam II[3], John Adam I[2], John Jacob[1]) was born October 30, 1914, at Bellefontaine, Ohio. He died May 14, 1935.

3138 ELDON JAY ROPP, JR. (Eldon[7], Charles[6], Isabella[5], Rebecca[4], John Adam II[3], John Adam I[2], John Jacob[1]) was born in June, 1922.

3139 DEMORY ROMAINE COLLIS (Emma[7], Fountain[6], Adam[5], Rebecca[4], John Adam II[3], John Adam I[2], John Jacob[1]) was born December 23, 1942.

3140 GEORGE HOMER COLLIS (Emma[7], Fountain[6], Adam[5], Rebecca[4], John Adam II[3], John Adam I[2], John Jacob[1]) was born September 28, 1944.

3141 SUSAN JANE COLLIS (Emma[7], Fountain[6], Adam[5], Rebecca[4], John Adam II[3], John Adam I[2], John Jacob[1]) was born August 1, 1947.

3142 JOHN LEON SCARLET (George[7], Minnie[6], Adam[5], Rebecca[4], John Adam II[3], John Adam I[2], John Jacob[1]) was born March 28, 1905. Thelma was the daughter of John Wesley and Mettie Lelia Widmyer Rice and was born June 1, 1910.
He married Thelma Lee Rice, June 14, 1930.

(Sup) 5439   i   John Norman Rice Scarlet, born February 19, 1933.
(Sup) 5440   ii   Jo Ann Rice Scarlet, born February 18, 1936.

3143 ANNA MARIE CORNELIA SCARLET (George[7], Minnie[6], Adam[5], Rebecca[4], John Adam II[3], John Adam I[2], John Jacob[1]) was born November 13, 1907. She married Homer William Wagley, August 9, 1930. Homer was the son of John William and Olive Moore Wagley and was born June 25, 1902. Anna and Homer had no children.

3144 GEORGE WILLIAM SCARLET, JR. (George[7], Minnie[6], Adam[5], Rebecca[4], John Adam II[3], John Adam I[2], John Jacob[1]) was born December 5, 1910. He did not marry.

3145 CHARLES DEMORY SCARLET (George[7], Minnie[6], Adam[5], Rebecca[4], John Adam II[3], John Adam I[2], John Jacob[1]) was born March 18, 1915. He married Ester Armbrester, April 17, 1942. Ester was the daughter of Edward Stephens and Rebecca Jane Mason Armbrester and was born January 19, 1918.

3146 HAROLD BERNARD SCARLET (George[7], Minnie[6], Adam[5], Rebecca[4], John Adam II[3], John Adam I[2], John Jacob[1]) was born December 1, 1920.

3147 MARY ELIZABETH SCARLET (George[7], Minnie[6], Adam[5], Rebecca[4], John Adam II[3], John Adam I[2], John Jacob[1]) was born December 7, 1922. She married Henry Clayton Gaver, Jr., November 4, 1942. Henry was the son of Henry Clayton Gaver and was born November 24, 1921. He entered the military forces of his country and died in service, September 24, 1944.

3148 EUGENE THOMAS SCARLET (George[7], Minnie[6], Adam[5], Rebecca[4], John Adam II[3], John Adam I[2], John Jacob[1]) was born August 13, 1924. He married Theresa Virginia Miller, October 24, 1942. Theresa was the daughter of Herbert Wesley and May Elizabeth Keyes Miller and was born February 27, 1926.

(Sup) 5441   i   Eugene Thomas Scarlet, Jr., born August 14, 1943.
(Sup) 5442   ii   Mark Wayne Scarlet, born July 10, 1945.
(Sup) 5443   iii   Gala Louise Scarlet, born July 24, 1946.

3149 MARTIN FRANCIS SCARLET (George^7, Minnie^6, Adam^5, Rebecca^4, John Adam II^3, John Adam I^2, John Jacob^1) was born June 28, 1927.

3150 OSCAR MULLENDORE (Bertha^7, Minnie^6, Adam^5, Rebecca^4, John Adam II^3, John Adam I^2, John Jacob^1) was born September 3, 1908. He married Louise Casey, July 26, 1941. Louise was born October 26, 1915.

(Sup) 3150.1A ROSS EARL DEMORY (Ralph^7, Daniel^6, Adam^5, Rebecca^4, John Adam II^3, John Adam I^2, John Jacob^1) was the son of Ralph Earl and Esse (Ratcliff) Demory [Supplement No. 1616B]. Ross was born November 5, 1928, at Wann, Oklahoma. He married Lucille Young, August 4, 1950. She was the daughter of John Allen and Ada Ansley Young and was born April 25, 1929, at Rockport, Texas.

(Sup) 5448   i   Ada Jean Demory, born June 29, 1952.
(Sup) 5448A   ii   Annette Faye Demory, born July 27, 1954 (twin).
(Sup) 5448B   iii Jeanette Kaye Demory, born July 27, 1954 (twin).
(Sup) 5448C   iv   Sherry Lynn Demory, born June 22, 1958.

(Sup) 3150.1B INA ZOE DEMORY (Ralph^7, Daniel^6, Adam^5, Rebecca^4, John Adam II^3, John Adam I^2, John Jacob^1) was the daughter of Ralph Earl and Esse (Ratcliff) Demory [Supplement No. 1616B]. She was born December 22, 1932, in Bee County, Texas. Ina Zoe married Martin Emmett (Buddy) Harper (brother of Lonnie), January 3, 1952, at Cotulla, Texas. He was a son of Earle and Winnie Jane (Essory) Harper and was born July 8, 1930, at Cotulla.

(Sup) 5449   i   Martin Earl Harper, born March 24, 1953.
(Sup) 5450   ii   Clairece Lynn Harper, born December 31, 1956.

(Sup) 3150.1C GENA BETH DEMORY (Ralph^7, Daniel^6, Adam^5, Rebecca^4, John Adam II^3, John Adam I^2, John Jacob^1) was the daughter of Ralph Earl and Esse (Ratcliff) Demory [Supplement No. 1616B]. Gena was born January 24, 1935, in Bee County, Texas. She married Lonnie Burdwell Harper (brother of Buddy), December 25, 1952. Lonnie was a son of Earle and Winnie Jane (Essory) Harper and was born June 27, 1933, at Cotulla, Texas.

(Sup) 5451   i   Lona Jean Harper, born March 3, 1956.
(Sup) 5452   ii   Jo Ann Harper, born September 14, 1960.

(Sup) 3150.2A MARGIE FAY JAKEWAY (Alma^7, Daniel^6, Adam^5, Rebecca^4, John Adam II^3, John Adam I^2, John Jacob^1) was the daughter of Thomas G. and Alma Lizzie (Demory) Jakeway [Supplement No. 1616D]. Margie was born September 1, 1921, at Wildhorse, Oklahoma. She married James Mack Acree, October 13, 1950. He was born November 8, 1924.

(Sup) 5453   i   Melissa Jane Acree, born October 9, 1951.
(Sup) 5454   ii   Robin Lee Acree, born October 1, 1957.

(Sup) 3150.2B EARL THOMAS JAKEWAY (Alma^7, Daniel^6, Adam^5, Rebecca^4, John Adam II^3, John Adam I^2, John Jacob^1) was the son of Thomas G. and Alma Lizzie (Demory) Jakeway [Supplement No. 1616E]. Earl was born November 10, 1923, at Wildhorse, Oklahoma. He married Lorraine Wikel, August 15, 1947. Lorraine was born May 27, 1925. She died November 14, 1978, and Earl died February 15, 1979.

(Sup) 5455   i   Earl Glen Jakeway, born 17, 1947.
(Sup) 5455A   ii   James Douglas Jakeway, born December 29, 1948.
(Sup) 5455B   iii Nancy Ann Jakeway, born January 8, 1950.
(Sup) 5455C   iv   Joyce Lynn Jakeway, born May 22, 1954.

(Sup) 3150.2C MARILYN MAXINE JAKEWAY (Alma^7, Daniel^6, Adam^5, Rebecca^4, John Adam II^3, John Adam I^2, John Jacob^1) was the daughter of Thomas G. and Alma Lizzie (Demory) Jakeway [Supplement No. 1616F]. Marilyn was born December 13, 1924, at Wildhorse, Oklahoma. Marilyn married William Henry Dillon, April 15, 1950. Bill was born September 11, 1927.

(Sup) 3150.2D LUETTA LEON JAKEWAY (Alma^7, Daniel^6, Adam^5, Rebecca^4, John Adam II^3, John Adam I^2, John Jacob^1) was the daughter of Thomas G. and Alma Lizzie (Demory) Jakeway [Supplement No. 1616D]. Luetta was born October 27, 1926, at Wildhorse, Oklahoma. She married Donald Green Vowell, September 3, 1954. Don was the son of Green Nathaniel and Jewell Amanda Vowell and was born August 31, 1927, at Weleetka, Oklahoma.

(Sup) 5456   i   Donald Gregory Vowell, born January 4, 1956.
(Sup) 5457   ii   Julia Anne Vowell, born April 19, 1958.

(Sup) 3150.3E RAYMOND FRANK HACKLER (Sarah[7], Daniel[6], Adam[5], Rebecca[4], John Adam II[3], John Adam I[2], John Jacob[1]) was the son of Arthur L. and Sarah (Demory) Hackler [Supplement No. 1616E]. Frank was born October 12, 1927, at Cloud Chief, Oklahoma. He married Gaynall Rosalie Norrie, July 20, 1956. She was the daughter of Glen W. and Mildred (Line) Norrie and was born February 3, 1938, at Sabetha, Kansas.

(Sup) 5462   i   Roger Frank Hackler, born July 23, 1961.
(Sup) 5462A ii Rex Glen Hackler, born March 21, 1963.
(Sup) 5462B iii Natalie Sue Hackler, born November 17, 1971.

(Sup) 3150.3F ARTHUR LEROY HACKLER (Sarah[7], Daniel[6], Adam[5], Rebecca[4], John Adam II[3], John Adam I[2], John Jacob[1]) was the son of Arthur L. and Sarah (Demory) Hackler [Supplement No. 1616E]. Art was born June 18, 1929, at Cordell, Oklahoma. He married Edna Rainbow. June 2, 1956, at Oklahoma City, Oklahoma. She was the daughter of Lyle C. and Jo Ella (Witt) Rainbow and was born June 14, 1929, at Oklahoma City.

(Sup) 5463   i   Tamara Jo Hackler, born March 28, 1959.
(Sup) 5464   ii Pamala Sue Hackler, born January 21, 1964.

(Sup) 3150.3G EDITH GOLDEN HACKLER (Sarah[7], Daniel[6], Adam[5], Rebecca[4], John Adam II[3], John Adam I[2], John Jacob[1]) was the daughter of Arthur L. and Sarah (Demory) Hackler [Supplement No. 1616E]. Edie was born August 31, 1931, at Clinton, Oklahoma. She married Robert Lafayette Tulloss, January 4, 1952, at Clinton. He was the son of Murray Pollard and Ethel (Jenkins) Tulloss and was born February 1, 1929, Williamson County, Tennessee.

(Sup) 5465   i   Brett Alan Tulloss, born April 29, 1964.

(Sup) 3150.3H LILLIAN MAXINE HACKLER (Sarah[7], Daniel[6], Adam[5], Rebecca[4], John Adam II[3], John Adam I[2], John Jacob[1]) was the daughter of Arthur L. and Sarah (Demory) Hackler [Supplement No. 1616E]. Maxine was born August 17, 1933, at Clinton, Oklahoma. She married Joseph Messina, November 3, 1951, at Detroit Michigan. He was the son of Gasper and Retrina (Angello) Messina and was born August 20, 1936, at Detroit. Joseph died January 22, 1983, and is buried at Detroit.

(Sup) 5466   i   Deborah Joan Messina, born May 25, 1954.
(Sup) 5466A ii   Sandra Diane Messina, born August 7, 1956.
(Sup) 5466B iii David Joseph Messina, born November 9, 1960.
(Sup) 5466C iv   Donald Dean Messina, born March 17, 1963.
(Sup) 5466D v   Douglas Drew Messina, born March 17, 1963.
(Sup) 5466E vi   Susan Marie Messina, born July 16, 1964.
(Sup) 5466F vii Joseph Patrick Messina, born August 16, 1965.
(Sup) 5466G viii Robert Glen Messina, born January 1, 1968.

(Sup) 3150.2E RICHARD EUGENE JAKEWAY (Alma[7], Daniel[6], Adam[5], Rebecca[4], John Adam II[3], John Adam I[2], John Jacob[1]) was the son of Thomas G. and Alma Lizzie (Demory) Jakeway [Supplement No. 1616D]. Richard was born October 4, 1928, at Wildhorse, Oklahoma. He married Lynetta Mikel.

(Sup) 5458   i   Richard Thomas Jakeway, born October 13, 1951.
(Sup) 5459   ii Mark Anthony Jakeway, born August 8, 1953.

(Sup) 3150.3A OLIVE LEE HACKLER (Sarah[7], Daniel[6], Adam[5], Rebecca[4], John Adam II[3], John Adam I[2], John Jacob[1]) was the daughter of Arthur L. and Sarah (Demory) Hackler [Supplement No. 1616E]. Lee was born September 18, 1922, at Cloud Chief, Oklahoma. She married, first, Edwin Walfred (Joe?) Matson, February, 1950. He was the son of Herman Walfred and Maria Kokko Matson and was born September 5, 1916, at Brooklyn, New York. Lee and Edwin were divorced in 1973. He died April 21, 1983, at Arlington, Texas. She married, second, Adolf David Weiss, January 13, 1979. He was born March 23, 1913.

(Sup) 5460   i   Edwin Lee Matson, born July 7, 1951.
(Sup) 5460A ii Martti Maria Matson, born May 1, 1953.
(Sup) 5460B iii John Alan Matson, born February 21, 1960.

(Sup) 3150.3B DANIEL LAWRENCE HACKLER (Sarah[7], Daniel[6], Adam[5], Rebecca[4], John Adam II[3], John Adam I[2], John Jacob[1]) was the son of Arthur L. and Sarah (Demory) Hackler [Supplement No. 1616E]. He was born November 4, 1923, at Cloud Chief, Oklahoma, and died July 18, 1933.

(Sup) 3150.3C GLEN ELWOOD HACKLER (Sarah[7], Daniel[6], Adam[5], Rebecca[4], John Adam II[3], John Adam I[2], John Jacob[1]) was the son of Arthur L. and Sarah (Demory) Hackler [Supplement No. 1616E]. He was born December 12, 1924, at Cloud Chief, Oklahoma, and died in action in World War II March 8, 1945.

(Sup) 3150.3D LOYD JUNIOR HACKLER (Sarah[7], Daniel[6], Adam[5], Rebecca[4], John Adam II[3], John Adam I[2], John Jacob[1]) was the son of Arthur L. and Sarah (Demory) Hackler [Supplement No. 1616E]. Loyd was born March 23, 1926, at Cloud Chief, Oklahoma. He married Norma Jean Conley, August 31, 1947, at Tulsa, Oklahoma. She was the daughter of Theodore R. and Alma (Quigley) Conley and was born November 21, 1927, at Tulsa.

(Sup) 5461   i   George Conley Hackler, born June 24, 1948.
(Sup) 5461A ii Patricia Hackler, born November 10, 1952.
(Sup) 5461B iii Warren Craig Hackler, born February 3, 1953.

(Sup) 3150.4A ALTA MAY PUTNAM (Hattie[7], Daniel[6], Adam[5], Rebecca[4], John Adam II[3], John Adam I[2], John Jacob[1]) was the daughter of Alfred Lee and Hattie Edith (Demory) Putnam [Supplement No. 1616F]. Alta was born August 1, 1918, Washington County, Oklahoma. She married R. B. Worrell, August 5, 1939, at Tulsa, Oklahoma. He was the son of Robert Wesley and Jewell Beatrice (Williams) Worrell and was born October 26, 1915, at Harmon, Oklahoma. R. B. died December 3, 1969, at Oklahoma City, where he is buried.

(Sup) 5467   i   Carolyn Sue Worrell, born March 6, 1941.

(Sup) 3150.4B LEE ALVIN PUTNAM (Hattie[7], Daniel[6], Adam[5], Rebecca[4], John Adam II[3], John Adam I[2], John Jacob[1]) was the son of Alfred Lee and Hattie Edith (Demory) Putnam [Supplement No. 1616F]. Lee was born May 18, 1920, in Osage County, Oklahoma. He married Florence Jean Folsom, August 31, 1946, at Tulsa, Oklahoma. She was the daughter of Archie LeRoy and Mildred May (Whiston) Flosom and was born February 12, 1925, at Alva, Oklahoma.

(Sup) 5468   i   Patricia Lynn Putnam, born June 1, 1950.
(Sup) 5469   ii   Richard Lee Putnam, born August 4, 1952.

(Sup) 3150.4C DAISY PEARL PUTNAM (Hattie[7], Daniel[6], Adam[5], Rebecca[4], John Adam II[3], John Adam I[2], John Jacob[1]) was the daughter of Alfred Lee and Hattie Edith (Demory) Putnam [Supplement No. 1616F]. She was born February 18, 1922, Osage County, Oklahoma. Daisy married Robert Jean Rogers, December 7, 1944, at Tulsa, Oklahoma. He was the son of Robert Jean and Clyde Elizabeth (Taylor) Rogers and was born November 7, 1921, at Bartlesville, Oklahoma.

(Sup) 5470   i   Elizabeth Rogers, born February 7, 1945.
(Sup) 5470A   ii   Kathryn Rogers, born June 2, 1949.
(Sup) 5470B   iii Robert Jean Rogers, Jr., born January 9, 1954.

(Sup) 3150.4D ROY FRANK PUTNAM (Hattie[7], Daniel[6], Adam[5], Rebecca[4], John Adam II[3], John Adam I[2], John Jacob[1]) was the son of Alfred Lee and Hattie Edith (Demory) Putnam [Supplement No. 1616F]. Roy was born May 10, 1924, Osage County, Oklahoma. He married Kathleen Audrey Nicholls, March 11, 1946, at Enfield, England. She was the daughter of Rederick William and Catherine Lillian (Braid) Nicholls and was born November 11, 1927, at Ford City, Windors, Ontario, Canada.

(Sup) 5471   i   Judith Anne Putnam, born March 2, 1947.
(Sup) 5471A   ii   James Roy Putnam, born January 19, 1949.
(Sup) 5471B   iii Michael Charles Putnam, born September 3, 1952.
(Sup) 5471C   iv   Cynthia Kay Putnam, born November 11, 1955.

(Sup) 3150.4E BEVERLY RUTH PUTNAM (Hattie[7], Daniel[6], Adam[5], Rebecca[4], John Adam II[3], John Adam I[2], John Jacob[1]) was the daughter of Alfred Lee and Hattie Edith (Demory) Putnam [Supplement No. 1616F]. Beverly was born July 7, 1935, at Tulsa, Oklahoma. She married Harold Kermit Fehnel, June 27, 1959, at Tulsa, Oklahoma. He was the son of Leo Lavene and Anna Elizabeth (Newhard) Fehnel and was born October 23, 1933, at Northamton, Pennsylvania.

(Sup) 5472   i   Timothy Duane Fehnel, born November 10, 1963.
(Sup) 5472A   ii   Mark Allen Fehnel, born December, 1965.
(Sup) 5472B   iii Matthew Dale Fehnel, born August 21, 1967.
(Sup) 5472C   iv   Mary Ann Fehnel, born February 18, 1969.

(Sup) 3150.5A LLOYD HUBERT DEMORY (John[7], Daniel[6], Adam[5], Rebecca[4], John Adam II[3], John Adam I[2], John Jacob[1]) was the son of John Daniel Link and Alta (Grey) Demory [Supplement No. 1616G]. Lloyd was born November 29, 1924, in Washington County, Oklahoma. He married Dorothy Faye Holland, December 21, 1949. Lloyd died December 9, 1962, Washington County.

(Sup) 5473   i   Lloyd Hubert Demory, Jr., born December 28, 1951.
(Sup) 5473A   ii   Daniel Richard Demory, born August 9, 1953.
(Sup) 5473B   iii Stephen Perry Demory, born September 5, 1954.
(Sup) 5473C   iv   Janet Lee Demory, born May 16, 1960.

(Sup) 3150.5B ROSALIE FAYE DEMORY (John[7], Daniel[6], Adam[5], Rebecca[4], John Adam II[3], John Adam I[2], John Jacob[1]) was the daughter of John Daniel Link and Alta (Grey) Demory [Supplement No. 1616G]. Rosalie was born December 10, 1927, Washington County, Oklahoma, and died June 10, 1966, in Washington County. She married Robert Woodrow Large, December 24, 1946, at Independence, Kansas. He was the son of William Clinton and Katie Bell (Garrison) Large and was born August 5, 1928, at Flint, Michigan.

(Sup) 5474   i   Stanley Michael Large, born September 30, 1947.
(Sup) 5474A   ii   John Clinton Large, born December 12, 1950.
(Sup) 5474B   iii Kaye Lynn Large, born August 12, 1952.

(Sup) 3150.5C VIVIAN EDITH DEMORY (John[7], Daniel[6], Adam[5], Rebecca[4], John Adam II[3], John Adam I[2], John Jacob[1]) was the daughter of John Daniel Link and Alta (Grey) Demory [Supplement No. 1616G]. Vivian was born June 7, 1933, in Washington County, Oklahoma. She married John Edward Inda, February 2, 1952, at Dewey, Oklahoma. He was born October 28, 1927.

(Sup) 5475   i   John Edward Inda, Jr., born September 7, 1952.
(Sup) 5475A   ii   David Link Inda, born November 21, 1953.
(Sup) 5475B   iii Frank Edward Inda, born December 24, 1955.
(Sup) 5475C   iv   Paul Inda, born November 5, 1968.

(Sup) 3150.6A NETTIE MAY DEMORY (Floyd[7], Daniel[6], Adam[5], Rebecca[4], John Adam II[3], John Adam I[2], John Jacob[1]) was the daughter of Floyd Albert and Lorene (Harris) Demory [Supplement No. 1616H]. Nettie May was born May 25, 1929, at Aransas Pass, Texas. She married James F. Mayfield, June 18, 1948. He was born November 16, 1926.

(Sup) 5476   i   William Floyd Mayfield, born August 1, 1949.
(Sup) 5476A   ii Julie May Mayfield, born September 5, 1952.
(Sup) 5476B   iii Richard James Mayfield, born May 10, 1954.
(Sup) 5476C   iv Peggy Lee Mayfield, born January 30, 1962.

(Sup) 3150.6B JESSIE PEARL DEMORY (Floyd[7], Daniel[6], Adam[5], Rebecca[4], John Adam II[3], John Adam I[2], John Jacob[1]) was the daughter of Floyd Albert and Lorene (Harris) Demory [Supplement No. 1616H]. Jessie was born December 14, 1930, at Aransas Pass, Texas. She married, first, Joe Kenneth Thompson, September 29, 1950. He was born February 5, 1931. They were divorced June, 1961. Jessie married, second, Leo Joseph Gaubert, November 1, 1962.

(Sup) 5477   i   Joe David Thompson, born March 13, 1953.
(Sup) 5477A   ii Lisbeth Rose Thompson, born April 29, 1955.
(Sup) 5477B   iii Timothy Floyd Thompson, born November 28, 1960.

(Sup) 3150.6C GEORGIA FAY DEMORY (Floyd[7], Daniel[6], Adam[5], Rebecca[4], John Adam II[3], John Adam I[2], John Jacob[1]) was the daughter of Floyd Albert and Lorene (Harris) Demory [Supplement No. 1616H]. Georgia was born October 3, 1932, at Aransas Pass, Texas. She married Patrick Lee Welch, January 5, 1951.

(Sup) 5478   i   Daniel Lee Welch, born November 9, 1951.
(Sup) 5478A   ii Dean Walter Welch, born Nov. 22, 1954 (twin).
(Sup) 5478B   iii Damon Wayne Welch, born Nov. 22, 1954 (twin).
(Sup) 5478C   iv Paul Clinton Welch, born November 5, 1958.

(Sup) 3150.6D BETTY JANE DEMORY (Floyd[7], Daniel[6], Adam[5], Rebecca[4], John Adam II[3], John Adam I[2], John Jacob[1]) was the daughter of Floyd Albert and Lorene (Harris) Demory [Supplement No. 1616H]. Betty was born July 25, 1936, at Aransas Pass, Texas. She married Clinton Alvin Rubottom, November 22, 1955. He was born October 9, 1957.

(Sup) 5479   i   Jeffery Clinton Rubottom, born October 9, 1957.

(Sup) 3150.6E MARGIE RAY DEMORY (Floyd[7], Daniel[6], Adam[5], Rebecca[4], John Adam II[3], John Adam I[2], John Jacob[1]) was the daughter of Floyd Albert and Lorene (Harris) Demory [Supplement No. 1616H]. Margie was born December 3, 1940, at Aransas Pass, Texas, and died September 22, 1942.

(Sup) 3150.6F JOHN ALBERT DEMORY (Floyd[7], Daniel[6], Adam[5], Rebecca[4], John Adam II[3], John Adam I[2], John Jacob[1]) was the son of Floyd Albert and Lorene (Harris) Demory [Supplement No. 1616H]. John was born December 2, 1943, at Aransas Pass, Texas. He married Patricia Darlene Harris, September 16, 1967. She was born April 2, 1947.

(Sup) 5480   i   Elizabeth Ann Demory, born November 24, 1968.

(Sup) 3150.6G RAYMOND FRANK DEMORY (Floyd[7], Daniel[6], Adam[5], Rebecca[4], John Adam II[3], John Adam[2], John Jacob[1]) was the son of Floyd Albert and Lorene (Harris) Demory [Supplement No. 1616H]. Frank was born November 27, 1945, at Aransas Pass, Texas. He married Helen Lori Haney, October 9, 1965. Frank died in the service in Vietnam February 3, 1967.

(Sup) 3150.7A VELMA BLANCHE PUTNAM (Pearl[7], Daniel[6], Adam[5], Rebecca[4], John Adam II[3], John Adam I[2], John Jacob[1]) was the daughter of Jesse George and Pearl Ella (Demory) Putnam [Supplement No. 1616I]. She was born November 8, 1923, at Shidler, Osage County, Oklahoma.

(Sup) 3150.7B BONNIE ELLA PUTNAM (Pearl[7], Daniel[6], Adam[5], Rebecca[4], John Adam II[3], John Adam I[2], John Jacob[1]) was the daughter of Jesse George and Pearl Ella (Demory) Putnam [Supplement No. 1616I]. Bonnie was born April 12, 1926, at Shidler, Osage County, Oklahoma. She married Richard Frederick Cullison, February 10, 1946, at Shidler. He was the son of Roy Ancil and Gladys Ryel Cullison and was born October 1, 1921, at Chandler, Oklahoma.

(Sup) 5481   i   Richard Frederick Cullison, Jr., born November 10, 1946.
(Sup) 5482   ii Lyra Ann Cullison, born August 25, 1948.

(Sup) 3150.8C   BARBARA JANE HARRELL (Grace[7], Daniel[6], Adam[5], Rebecca[4], John Adam II[3], John Adam I[2], John Jacob[1]) was the daughter of Luby and Grace May (Demory) Harrell [Supplement No. 1616K]. Barbara was born January 28, 1939, Bee County, Texas. She married Jay Francis Lawson, April 9, 1960. He was born December 21, 1937.

(Sup) 5489   i   Jay Scott Lawson, born January 12, 1961.

(Sup) 3150.8D   ROBERT MARTIN HARRELL (Grace[7], Daniel[6], Adam[5], Rebecca[4], John Adam II[3], John Adam I[2], John Jacob[1]) was the son of Luby and Grace May (Demory) Harrell [Supplement No. 1616K]. Robert was born November 11, 1940, Bee County, Texas. He married Marylin Morrison, November 21, 1964.

3161   GARLAND RALEIGH DEMORY (Elwood[7], George[6], John[5], Rebecca[4], John Adam II[3], John Adam I[2], John Jacob[1]) was born in 1936.

3162   ELWOOD AGLIONBY DEMORY, JR. (Elwood[7], George[6], John[5], Rebecca[4], John Adam II[3], John Adam I[2], John Jacob[1]) was born in 1936.

3163   JOHN EDGAR DEMORY (Garland[7], George[6], John[5], Rebecca[4], John Adam II[3], John Adam I[2], John Jacob[1]) was born September 13, 1928.

3164   FRANCIS LESTER DEMORY (Garland[7], George[6], John[5], Rebecca[4], John Adam II[3], John Adam I[2], John Jacob[1]) was born December 25, 1932.

3155   EMMA MARIE DEMORY (Garland[7], George[6], John[5], Rebecca[4], John Adam II[3], John Adam I[2], John Jacob[1]) was born February 18, 1935.

3156   RUBY CATHERINE DEMORY (Garland[7], George[6], John[5], Rebecca[4], John Adam II[3], John Adam I[2], John Jacob[1]) was born August 8, 1937.

3157   MARVIN CHARLES DEMORY (Garland[7], George[6], John[5], Rebecca[4], John Adam II[3], John Adam I[2], John Jacob[1]) was born March 17, 1940.

3158   ELMER M. DEMORY (William[7], Luther[6], John[5], Rebecca[4], John Adam II[3], John Adam I[2], John Jacob[1]) was born September 13, 1912. He married Fannie Doolinger in August, 1939. Fannie was the daughter of Shaler and Nancy Henderson Doolinger.

(Sup) 3150.7C   JESSE ROBERT PUTNAM (Pearl[7], Daniel[6], Adam[5], Rebecca[4], John Adam II[3], John Adam I[2], John Jacob[1]) was the son of Jesse George and Pearl Ella (Demory) Putnam [Supplement No. 1616I]. Jesse was born December 31, 1927, at Shidler, Osage County, Oklahoma. He married Dorothy Marie York, September 4, 1949, at Sandsprings, Oklahoma. She was the daughter of James Aubrey and Stella Holden York and was born February 16, 1927, at Kellyville Oklahoma.

(Sup) 5483   i   John Lawrence Putnam, born April 1, 1950.
(Sup) 5483A   ii   Linda Marie Putnam, born January 23, 1952.
(Sup) 5483B   iii Jessica Ann Putnam, born August 1, 1954.
(Sup) 5483C   iv   Georgia Lee Putnam, born March 16, 1956.
(Sup) 5483D   v   Roberta Jane Putnam, born July 29, 1961.

(Sup) 3150.7D   GEORGIA MAY PUTNAM (Pearl[7], Daniel[6], Adam[5], Rebecca[4], John Adam II[3], John Adam I[2], John Jacob[1]) was the daughter of Jesse George and Pearl Ella (Demory) Putnam [Supplement No. 1616I]. Georgia was born February 7, 1929, at Shidler, Osage County, Oklahoma. She married Joseph Franklin Jones, June 7, 1951, at Tulsa, Oklahoma. He was the son of Onis and Georgia Naples Jones and was born September 7, 1926, at Miami, Oklahoma.

(Sup) 5486   i   Ella Fay Jones, born June 6, 1952.
(Sup) 5487   ii   Anna Jeanne Jones, born December 29, 1953.

(Sup) 3150.8A   LUBY ALLAN HARRELL (Grace[7], Daniel[6], Adam[5], Rebecca[4], John Adam II[3], John Adam I[2], John Jacob[1]) was the son of Luby and Grace May (Demory) Harrell [Supplement No. 1616K]. Allan was born November 29, 1931. He married Amy Lou O'Neal, January 21, 1954. She was born December 21, 1934.

(Sup) 5484   i   David Allan Harrell, born January 19, 1957.
(Sup) 5485   ii   Cheryl Beth Harrell, born February 7, 1961.

(Sup) 3150.8B   JAMES EDWARD HARRELL (Grace[7], Daniel[6], Adam[5], Rebecca[4], John Adam II[3], John Adam I[2], John Jacob[1]) was the son of Luby and Grace May (Demory) Harrell [Supplement No. 1616K]. James was born February 4, 1934. He married Frances Davis Smith, August 8, 1964. James died May 10, 1981.

(Sup) 5488   i   Karri Lynn Harrell, born May 25, 1966.

3159 NELLIE M. DEMORY (William[7], Luther[6], John[5], Rebecca[4], John Adam II[3], John Adam I[2], John Jacob[1]) was born April 28, 1914. She married Donald Rodenhi in October, 1941. Donald, son of Irvin Lee and Mary Elizabeth Bockelman Rodenhi, was born August 20, 1920.

(Sup) 5498 i Donald Rodenhi, Jr., born July 28, 1943.
(Sup) 5499 ii William Bryant Rodenhi, born January 23, 1947.

3160 RALPH E. DEMORY (William[7], Luther[6], John[5], Rebecca[4], John Adam II[3], John Adam I[2], John Jacob[1]) was born November 18, 1916. He died June 23, 1940.

3161 CARL F. DEMORY (William[7], Luther[6], John[5], Rebecca[4], John Adam II[3], John Adam I[2], John Jacob[1]) was born July 30, 1917. In September, 1943, he married Eunice Johnson.

3162 KENYON LINK DEMORY (William[7], Luther[6], John[5], Rebecca[4], John Adam II[3], John Adam I[2], John Jacob[1]) was born July 21, 1920. He married Mary Mattingly in October, 1945. Mary was the daughter of Lewis Kempt and Della Eleanor Henderson Mattingly.

(Sup) 5500 i James Edward Demory, born January 6, 1947.

3163 CALVIN H. DEMORY (William[7], Luther[6], John[5], Rebecca[4], John Adam II[3], John Adam I[2], John Jacob[1]) was born April 18, 1927.

3164 BETTY LOU DEMORY (Howard[7], Luther[6], John[5], Rebecca[4], John Adam II[3], John Adam I[2], John Jacob[1]) was born May 17, 1935.

3165 DONALD WESLEY DEMORY (Howard[7], Luther[6], John[5], Rebecca[4], John Adam II[3], John Adam I[2], John Jacob[1]) was born March 4, 1939.

3166 HOWARD LEE DEMORY (Howard[7], Luther[6], John[5], Rebecca[4], John Adam II[3], John Adam I[2], John Jacob[1]) was born March 14, 1941.

3167 VIRGINIA DEMORY (Roger[7], Luther[6], John[5], Rebecca[4], John Adam II[3], John Adam I[2], John Jacob[1]) was born September 26, 1932.

3168 LUTHER RAYMOND DEMORY, JR. (Luther[7], Luther[6], John[5], Rebecca[4], John Adam II[3], John Adam I[2], John Jacob[1]) was born June 9, 1943.

3169 WILLARD LINK DEMORY (James[7], Luther[6], John[5], Rebecca[4], John Adam II[3], John Adam I[2], John Jacob[1]) was born July 24, 1944.

3170 SHIRLEY LEE DEMORY (James[7], Luther[6], John[5], Rebecca[4], John Adam II[3], John Adam I[2], John Jacob[1]) was born November 29, 1945.

3171 DELORES JUANITA DEMORY (Leo[7], Henry[6], John[5], Rebecca[4], John Adam II[3], John Adam I[2], John Jacob[1]) was born March 23, 1934.

3172 JAMES WILLIAM DEMORY (Leo[7], Henry[6], John[5], Rebecca[4], John Adam II[3], John Adam I[2], John Jacob[1]) was born January 6, 1936.

(Sup) 3173 PRISCILLA DIANE DEMORY (Charles[7], Henry[6], John[5], Rebecca[4], John Adam II[3], John Adam I[2], John Jacob[1]) was the daughter of Charles William and Erma Carnes Demory [The Link Family, page 485, No. 1629; and Supplement No. 1629]. Priscilla was a registered nurse, a president of the Lawrence County Medical Auxiliary of New Castle, Pennsylvania, and founder of the Lawrence County Future Physicians Club. She married Lawrence Charles Marcella October 8, 1960. He was the son of Charles H. and Pearl Panella Marcella and was born November 6, 1929, at New Castle, Pennsylvania.

(Sup) 5501 i Stephen Andrew Marcella, born August 27, 1961.
(Sup) 5502 ii Jeffrey Charles Marcella, born January 13, 1968.

(Sup) 3174 CHARLES WILLIAM DEMORY, JR. (Charles[7], Henry[6], John[5], Rebecca[4], John Adam II[3], John Adam I[2], John Jacob[1]) was the son of Charles William and Erma Carnes Demory [The Link Family, page 485, No. 1629; and Supplement No. 1629]. William was born November 17, 1939, at Gaithersburg, Maryland. He was a building contractor (William Demory Construction, Gaithersburg, Maryland) and secretary of the National Associated Builders and Contractors. He married Judith Elaine Sebek August 18, 1962, at Parma, Ohio. She was the daughter of Milo and Betty Morris Sebek and was born June 19, 1941, at Cleveland, Ohio.

(Sup) 5503 i   Patricia Joan Demory, born May 26, 1964.
(Sup) 5504 ii Charles William Demory III, born May 21, 1974.
(Sup) 5505 iii Michael Alan Demory, born October 3, 1976.

(Sup) 3175 LARRY SIDNEY DEMORY (Charles[7], Henry[6], John[5], Rebecca[4], John Adam II[3], John Adam I[2], John Jacob[1]) was the son of Charles William and Erma Carnes Demory [The Link Family, page 485, No. 1629; and Supplement No. 1629]. Larry was born January 7, 1942, at Gaithersburg, Maryland. He was a professional barber and owned the American Way Cleaning Company in Gaithers-burg. He married Barbara Ann Moore May 29, 1966, at Gaithersburg, Maryland. She was the daughter of Raymond Jennings and Gladys Frank Moore, and was born January 30, 1945, at Richland, Washington.

(Sup) 5506 i   Eddie Michael Demory, born November 24, 1966.
(Sup) 5507 ii Aaron Matthew Demory, born October 18, 1968.
(Sup) 5508 iii Nancy Christine Demory, born March 24, 1975.

(Sup) 3176 EDWIN FRANKLIN DEMORY (Charles[7], Henry[6], John[5], Rebecca[4], John Adam II[3], John Adam I[2], John Jacob[1]) was the son of Charles William and Erma Carnes Demory [The Link Family, page 485, No. 1629; and Supplement No. 1629]. Edwin was born March 3, 1945, at Gaithersburg, Maryland. He served 4-1/2 years in the U.S. Navy, after which he managed service stations in Gaithersburg and Takoma Park, Maryland. He married Sheila Jean Bentley August 29, 1975, at Damascus, Maryland. She was the daughter of Charles and Eileen Burns Bentley, and was born October 29, 1957, at Norton, Virginia.

(Sup) 5509 i Edwin Franklin Demory, Jr., born Nov 22, 1977.
(Sup) 5510 ii Shannon Marie Demory, born March 11, 1980.

(Sup) 3185 LARRY WILLIAM OSBOURN (Annabel[7], Walter[6], John[5], Rebecca[4], Adam II[3], John Adam I[2], John Jacob[1]) was the son of Charles William and (Iris) Annabel Demory Osbourn [The Link Family, page 486, No. 1639; and Supplement No. 1639]. Larry was born September 25, 1943. He married Linda Lou Willingham June 1, 1968. She was the daughter of Julian Kenneth and June Elizabeth Willingham and was born November 29, 1948. Larry was employed by the General Telephone Company.

(Sup) 5513   i   Joy Lynn Osbourn, born May 28, 1969.
(Sup) 5514   ii Jennifer Jo Osbourn, born December 14, 1972.

(Sup) 3186 NANCY CAROLINE OSBOURN (Annabel[7], Walter[6], John[5], Rebecca[4], John Adam II[3], John Adam I[2], John Jacob[1]) was the daughter of Charles William and Annabel Demory Osbourn [The Link Family, page 486, No. 1639; and Supplement No. 1639]. Nancy was born February 27, 1945. She married Terry Allan Sarra August 25, 1966. He was the son of Marion Albert and Mary Wilma Wintermeyer and was born September 13, 1945. Nancy received a B.S. degree in elementary education from Shepherd College, West Virginia, in 1966 and taught in Jefferson County. Terry attended Shepherd College and worked for the Automobile Association of America in Washington, D.C.

(Sup) 5515   i   Scott Allen Sarra, born August 23, 1967.
(Sup) 5516   ii Matthew Craig Sarra, born May 24, 1973.

(Sup) 3186A MARK EUGENE OSBOURN (Annabel[7], Walter[6], John[5], Rebecca[4], John Adam II[3], John Adam I[2], John Jacob[1]) was the third child of Charles W. and Iris Annabel Demory Osbourn [The Link Family, page 486, No. 1639; and Supplement No. 1639]. Mark was born October 18, 1951. He received a B.S. degree in elementary education from Shepherd College, West Virginia, in 1974 and did graduate work at West Virginia University. He married Sharon Lescallect April 6, 1954. She was the daughter of Earl Louis and Mary Ann Michael Lescallect.

(Sup) 3187 PAMELA JEAN DEMORY (Howard[7], Walter[6], John[5], Rebecca[4], John Adam II[3], John Adam I[2], John Jacob[1]) was the daughter of Howard Griffith and Marguerite Staubs Demory [The Link Family, page 486, No. 1640; and Supplement No. 1640]. Pamela was born September 14, 1947. She married Luther James Nichols March 30, 1968, at Charles Town, West Virginia. He was the son of Nelson and Rosalie Alger Nichols and was born December 6, 1945, at Martinsburg, West Virginia. He served in the U.S. Navy, stationed in Hawaii.

(Sup) 5517   i   Kelly Margaret Nichols, born June 27, 1974.

(Sup) 3176A LINDA CAROL DEMORY (Charles[7], Henry[6], John[5], Rebecca[4], John Adam II[3], John Adam I[2], John Jacob[1]) was the fifth child of Charles William and Erma Carnes Demory; see The Link Family, page 485, No. 1629; and Supplement No. 1629]. Linda was born December 28, 1948, at Olney, Maryland. She was a graduate of the Gardner School of Business. She worked as a secretary at IBM and at Bechtel Engineering in Gaithersburg. Linda married Gale Floyd Graham June 14, 1969, at Gaithersburg, Maryland. The son of Floyd and Barbara Gilman Graham, he was born May 13, 1948, at Binghamton, New York. They were divorced in 1977.

(Sup) 5511   i   Amy Michele Graham, born September 30, 1971.
(Sup) 5512   ii Kelly Elizabeth Graham, born June 15, 1974.

(Sup) 3176B Sup. STEPHEN ERIC DEMORY (Charles[7], Henry[6], John[5], Rebecca[4], John Adam II[3], John Adam I[2], John Jacob[1]) was born July 15, 1951, at Olney, Maryland. [He was the sixth child of Charles William and Erma Carnes Demory [The Link Family, page 485, No. 1629; and Supplement No. 1629]. Stephen was born July 15, 1951, at Olney, Maryland. He worked as an assistant manager for Montgomery Ward at Frederick, Maryland. He married Mona Yvonne Castle May 24, 1975, at Frederick. She was the daughter of Robert and Margaret Bowers Castle and was born March 26, 1953.

3177   DONALD LEO BRIGGS (Beulah[7], Henry[6], John[5], Rebecca[4], John Adam II[3], John Adam I[2], John Jacob[1]) was born November 2, 1943.

3178   ROBERT MILTON CARR, JR. (Gladys[7], Decora[6], John[5], Rebecca[4], John Adam II[3], John Adam I[2], John Jacob[1]) was born December 21, 1928.

3179   MARTIN ALLAN CARR (Gladys[7], Decora[6], John[5], Rebecca[4], John Adam II[3], John Adam I[2], John Jacob[1]) was born December 6, 1931.

3180   EDDY COLBERT CARR (Gladys[7], Decora[6], John[5], Rebecca[4], John Adam II[3], John Adam I[2], John Jacob[1]) was born December 24, 1932.

3181   JOHN HARRY CARR (Gladys[7], Decora[6], John[5], Rebecca[4], John Adam II[3], John Adam I[2], John Jacob[1]) was born January 26, 1934.

3182   JOHN GALE HUFFER (Marguerite[7], Walter[6], John[5], Rebecca[4], John Adam II[3], John Adam I[2], John Jacob[1]) was born June 17, 1940.

3183   RONNIE EUGENE HUFFER (Marguerite[7], Walter[6], John[5], Rebecca[4], John Adam II[3], John Adam I[2], John Jacob[1]) was born May 18, 1943.

3184   KATHERINE LA RUE HUFFER (Marguerite[7], Walter[6], John[5], Rebecca[4], John Adam II[3], John Adam I[2], John Jacob[1]) was born July 20, 1948.

(Sup) 3190A GEORGE ALLEN MILLER (Naomi[7], Walter[6], John[5], Rebecca[4], John Adam II[3], John Adam I[2], John Jacob[1]) was the son of Harvey Allen and Naomi Demory Keesecker Miller [The Link Family, page 486, No. 1641; and Supplement No. 1641]. George was born March 21, 1956. He married Brenda Ann Byers June 13, 1976. She was the daughter of Benjamin and Barbara Hobday Byers and was born December 3, 1955. George studied at West Virginia University, Morgantown. Brenda was a graduate of Shepherd College's Nursing Program in 1976.

(Sup) 3190B MIDA VIRGINIA MILLER (Naomi[7], Walter[6], John[5], Rebecca[4], John Adam II[3], John Adam I[2], John Jacob[1]) was the daughter of Harvey Allen and Naomi Demory Keesecker Miller [The Link Family, page 486, No. 1641; and Supplement No. 1641]. She was born February 12, 1969.

(Sup) 3190C FRANK NICK DEMORY (Milton[7], Walter[6], John[5], Rebecca[4], John Adam II[3], John Adam I[2], John Jacob[1]) was the son of Milton Dale and Ann Custer Demory [The Link Family, page 486, No. 1642; and Supplement No. 1642]. Frank was born January 2, 1948. He married Patpi Ann James September 4, 1976. Patpi was the daughter of Edward B. and Pauline Manning James and was born September 28, 1955.

(Sup) 3190D WALTER DALE DEMORY (Milton[7], Walter[6], John[5], Rebecca[4], John Adam II[3], John Adam I[2], John Jacob[1]) was the son of Milton Dale and Ann Custer Demory [The Link Family, page 486, No. 1642; and Supplement No. 1642]. Walter was born September 24, 1953. He married Ronda Sue Grona March 3, 1973. She was the daughter of William R. and Louise Payne Grona and was born September 25, 1956.

    (Sup) 5524   i Shawn Dale Demory, born September 6, 1973.

(Sup) 3190E JOHN JEFFERY CHARLES MOLER (Juanita[7], Walter[6], John[5], Rebecca[4], John Adam II[3], John Adam I[2], John Jacob[1]) was the son of Charles Griffin and Juanita Demory Moler [The Link Family, page 486, No. 1643; and Supplement No. 1643]. John was born August 9, 1954. He graduated from Lord Fairfax Community College, Middletown, Virginia, with an A.A. degree in history in 1975; and from Virginia Polytechnic Institute with a B.A. degree in history and geography in 1977. He was employed by the U.S. Government.

(Sup) 3188 SHARON DIAN DEMORY (Howard[7], Walter[6], John[5], Rebecca[4], John Adam II[3], John Adam I[2], John Jacob[1]) was the daughter of Howard Griffith and Marguerite Staubs Demory [The Link Family, page 486, No. 1640; and Supplement No.1640]. Sharon was born December 13, 1948. She married Michael Patrick McGuinn June 26, 1971, at Charles Town, West Virginia. He was the son of Claude Wilson and Mary Catherine McGuinn and was born January 6, 1950.

    (Sup) 5518   i   Michael Brian McGuinn, born September 26, 1973.
    (Sup) 5519   ii Teresa Dian McGuinn, born November 17, 1975.

(Sup) 3188A CHERYL LYNN DEMORY (Howard[7], Walter[6], John[5], Rebecca[4], John Adam II[3], John Adam I[2], John Jacob[1]) was the daughter of Howard Griffith and Marguerite Staubs Demory [The Link Family, page 486, No. 1640; and Supplement No. 1640]. Cheryl married Richard Dale Bartles June 16, 1972, at Charles Town, West Virginia. He was the son of Carlton Lee and Vivian Sencindiver Bartles and was born January 29, 1953.

    (Sup) 5520   i   Neil Paul Bartles, born November 21, 1973.
    (Sup) 5521   ii Amy Beth Bartles, born November 3, 1975.

(Sup) 3189 REBECCA JANE KEESECKER (Naomi[7], Walter[6], John[5], Rebecca[4], John Adam II[3], John Adam I[2], John Jacob[1]) was the daughter of William Bernard and Naomi Demory Keesecker [The Link Family, page 486, No. 1641; and Supplement No. 1641]. Rebecca was born June 5, 1945. She married Norman Lee Hall July 2, 1970. He was the son of Austin Mearle and Eunice Barb Hall and was born March 3, 1948.

    (Sup) 5522   i William Lee Hall, born July 25, 1975.

(Sup) 3190 MARY LOUISE KEESECKER (Naomi[7], Walter[6], John[5], Rebecca[4], John Adam II[3], John Adam I[2], John Jacob[1]) was the daughter of William Bernard and Naomi Demory Keesecker [The Link Family, page 486, No. 1641; and Supplement No. 1641]. Mary was born February 23, 1947. She married Russell William Butts, Jr., January 10, 1968. He was born June 1, 1944, the son of Russell William and Beulah Fay Triggs Butts.

    (Sup) 5523   i Katina Jo Butts, born November 19, 1972.

(Sup) 3190F CHARMAYNE DANITA MOLER (Juanita^7, Walter^6, John^5, Rebecca^4, John Adam II^3, John Adam I^2, John Jacob^1) was the daughter of Charles Griffin and Juanita Demory Moler [The Link Family, page 486, No. 1643; and Supplement No. 1643]. Charmayne was born March 14, 1957. She married Daniel Ross Denson December 19, 1975. He was the son of Paul Ross and Carolyn Solenberger Denson and was born December 27, 1955.

(Sup) 3190G LISA DENISE MOLER (Juanita^7, Walter^6, John^5, Rebecca^4, John Adam II^3, John Adam I^2, John Jacob^1) was the daughter of Charles Griffin and Juanita Demory Moler [The Link Family, page 486, No. 1643; and Supplement No. 1643]. Lisa was born October 20, 1959, at Winchester, Virginia. She attended Handley High School and was an outstanding member of the 4H Club.

(Sup) 3190H TINA MARIE MOLER (Juanita^7, Walter^6, John^5, Rebecca^4, John Adam II^3, John Adam I^2, John Jacob^1) was the daughter of Charles Griffin and Juanita Demory Moler [The Link Family, page 486, No. 1643; and Supplement No. 1643]. She was born October 18, 1965, at Winchester, Virginia.

(Sup) 3190I JAMES ARTHUR PRATHER, IV (Rebecca^7, Walter^6, John^5, Rebecca^4, John Adam II^3, John Adam I^2, John Jacob^1) was the son of James Arthur and Rebecca Demory Prather, III [The Link Family, page 487, No. 1645; and Supplement No. 1645]. James, IV, was born October 31, 1951. He married Cynthia Dawn Rouark, November 27, 1971. The daughter of William Hensel and Margaret Schill Lemon Rouark, Cindy was born August 4, 1952.

(Sup) 5525   i   Crystal Lark Prather, born May 11, 1977.

(Sup) 3190J DEBORAH JANE PRATHER (Rebecca^7, Walter^6, John^5, Rebecca^4, John Adam II^3, John Adam I^2, John Jacob^1) was the daughter of James Arthur and Rebecca Demory Prather [The Link Family, page 487, No. 1645; and Supplement No. 1645]. Deborah was born October 18, 1953. She married James Dewey Fritts, September 14, 1973. He was born November 23, 1950.

(Sup) 5526   i   James Dewey Fritts, Jr., born Sept 22, 1975.

(Sup) 3190K CORRINE REBECCA PRATHER (Rebecca^7, Walter^6, John^5, Rebecca^4, John Adam II^3, John Adam I^2, John Jacob^1) was the daughter of James Arthur and Rebecca Demory Prather [The Link Family, page 487, No. 1645]. Corrine was born October 18, 1956. She married Dennis Dinkels May 13, 1976. He was born April 14, 1952, the son of Lewis and Edith Denkels from Brooklyn, New York.

(Sup) 3190L MELISSA BETH PRATHER (Rebecca^7, Walter^6, John^5, Rebecca^4, John Adam II^3, John Adam I^2, John Jacob^1) was the daughter of James Arthur and Rebecca Demory Prather [The Link Family, page 487, No. 1645; and Supplement No. 1645]. Melissa was born April 22, 1964.

3191 FANNIE ALBERTA SCHRYVER (Fannie^7, Almacie^6, John^5, Rebecca^4, John Adam II^3, John Adam I^2, John Jacob^1) was born December 12, 1916. She married Denton Kenyon Swartnout, September 28, 1940. Denton was the son of Denton Kenyon and Frances Pryer Swartnout and was born April 12, 1918.

(Sup) 5527   i   Barbara Swartnout, born November 4, 1942.

3192 GEORGE WHITNEY SCHRYVER (Fannie^7, Almacie^6, John^5, Rebecca^4, John Adam II^3, John Adam I^2, John Jacob^1) was born June 1, 1918. He married Ruth E. Corl, January 1, 1946. Ruth was born November 14, 1916.

(Sup) 5528   i   John Whitney Schryver, born January 29, 1946.
(Sup) 5529   ii   George Hapgood Schryver, born March 24, 1947.

3193 HELEN LOUISE SCHRYVER (Fannie^7, Almacie^6, John^5, Rebecca^4, John Adam II^3, John Adam I^2, John Jacob^1) was born October 15, 1920. She married William Arthur Robishaw, December 13, 1942. William was the son of William F. and Belle Wallace Robishaw and was born January 10, 1918.

(Sup) 5530   i   Judith Anne Robishaw, born February 21, 1943.
(Sup) 5531   ii   William Arthur Robishaw, Jr., born Nov 30, 1946.

3194 WILLIAM STANLEY SHEPPARD (Stanley^7, Almacie^6, John^5, Rebecca^4, John Adam II^3, John Adam I^2, John Jacob^1) was born March 23, 1923.

3195 WILLIAM ERMON SHEPPARD (Stanley^7, Almacie^6, John^5, Rebecca^4, John Adam II^3, John Adam I^2, John Jacob^1) was born June 10, 1924.

(Sup) 3196 PHYLLIS JANE DEMORY (Lilbern^7, Wilmer^6, John^5, Rebecca^4, John Adam I^2, John Jacob^1) was the daughter of Lilbern William and Mary Louise Frye Demory [The Link Family, page 487, No. 1651]. Phyllis was born November 2, 1924. She married Lloyd Albert Wayne, April 3, 1946. Lloyd was born June 17, 1922.

(Sup) 5532   i   Pamela Colleen Wayne, born January 25, 1947.
(Sup) 5533   ii   Nancy Faye Wayne, born April 11, 1955.

3197 THELMA JUANITA DEMORY (Lilbern^7, Wilmer^6, John^5, Rebecca^4, John Adam II^3, John Adam I^2, John Jacob^1) was born March 3, 1929. She married Robert E. Van Gilder, March 12, 1947. Robert was born July 31, 1927.

3198 NANCY BARBARA DEMORY (Lilbern[7], Wilmer[6], John[5], Rebecca[4], John Adam II[3], John Adam I[2], John Jacob[1]) was born November 14, 1933.

3199 PATRICIA DEMORY (Lilbern[7], Wilmer[6], John[5], Rebecca[4], John Adam II[3], John Adam I[2], John Jacob[1]) was born March 24, 1940.

3200 KAY MARLENIA DEMORY (Lilbern[7], Wilmer[6], John[5], Rebecca[4], John Adam II[3], John Adam I[2], John Jacob[1]) was born July 23, 1941.

3201 MARY LEE DEMORY (Lilbern[7], Wilmer[6], John[5], Rebecca[4], John Adam II[3], John Adam I[2], John Jacob[1]) was born March 17, 1944.

3202 PERLA GERALDINE DEMORY (Lilbern[7], Wilmer[6], John[5], Rebecca[4], John Adam II[3], John Adam I[2], John Jacob[1]) was born March 19, 1946.

3203 JAMES CARLETON BAKER (Mary[7], Wilmer[6], John[5], Rebecca[4], John Adam II[3], John Adam I[2], John Jacob[1]) was born December 14, 1926, and died December 15, 1926.

3204 CLARK ADOLPHUS BAKER, JR. (Mary[7], Wilmer[6], John[5], Rebecca[4], John Adam II[3], John Adam I[2], John Jacob[1]) was born January 20, 1929.

3205 ALLEN EDWARD BAKER (Mary[7], Wilmer[6], John[5], Rebecca[4], John Adam II[3], John Adam I[2], John Jacob[1]) was born March 14, 1931.

3206 RENNICE EUGENE BAKER (Mary[7], Wilmer[6], John[5], Rebecca[4], John Adam II[3], John Adam I[2], John Jacob[1]) was born May 31, 1942.

3207 ETHEL MAY DEMORY (Wilmer[7], Wilmer[6], John[5], Rebecca[4], John Adam II[3], John Adam I[2], John Jacob[1]) was born September 19, 1934.

3208 BARBARA ALLINE DEMORY (Wilmer[7], Wilmer[6], John[5], Rebecca[4], John Adam II[3], John Adam I[2], John Jacob[1]) was born July 6, 1937.

3209 WILMER GLENDEN DEMORY (Wilmer[7], Wilmer[6], John[5], Rebecca[4], John Adam II[3], John Adam I[2], John Jacob[1]) was born April 1, 1940.

3210 SHIRLEY LEE DEMORY (Wilmer[7], Wilmer[6], John[5], Rebecca[4], John Adam II[3], John Adam I[2], John Jacob[1]) was born September 1, 1941.

3211 JAMES RICHARD DEMORY (Wilmer[7], Wilmer[6], John[5], Rebecca[4], John Adam II[3], John Adam I[2], John Jacob[1]) was born November 1, 1943.

3212 LESSIE ALLEN DEMORY (Wilmer[7], Wilmer[6], John[5], Rebecca[4], John Adam II[3], John Adam I[2], John Jacob[1]) was born January 1, 1947.

3213 ROBERT LEE DEMORY (Carol[7], Wilmer[6], John[5], Rebecca[4], John Adam II[3], John Adam I[2], John Jacob[1]) was born April 26, 1937.

3214 PEGGY ELIZABETH DEMORY (Carol[7], Wilmer[6], John[5], Rebecca[4], John Adam II[3], John Adam I[2], John Jacob[1]) was born February 23, 1939.

3215 DENNIS WAYNE DEMORY (Floyd[7], Wilmer[6], John[5], Rebecca[4], John Adam II[3], John Adam I[2], John Jacob[1]) was born August 19, 1942.

3216 VIRGINIA MAXINE DEMORY (Floyd[7], Wilmer[6], John[5], Rebecca[4], John Adam II[3], John Adam I[2], John Jacob[1]) was born October 26, 1943.

3217 CHERRY LEE DEMORY (Floyd[7], Wilmer[6], John[5], Rebecca[4], John Adam II[3], John Adam I[2], John Jacob[1]) was born October 20, 1945.

3218 SAUNDRA DARLENE DEMORY (Floyd[7], Wilmer[6], John[5], Rebecca[4], John Adam II[3], John Adam I[2], John Jacob[1]) was born March 9, 1947.

3219 ANNIE LENORA FUNK (John[7], Anne[6], John[5], Rebecca[4], John Adam II[3], John Adam I[2], John Jacob[1]) was born May 27, 1932.

3220 WILLIAM BENJAMIN FUNK (John[7], Anne[6], John[5], Rebecca[4], John Adam II[3], John Adam I[2], John Jacob[1]) was born February 21, 1934.

3221 JOHN DEMORY FUNK (John[7], Anne[6], John[5], Rebecca[4], John Adam II[3], John Adam I[2], John Jacob[1]) was born April 16, 1943.

3222 LINDA KAY MAGAILIS (Eva[7], Anne[6], John[5], Rebecca[4], John Adam II[3], John Adam I[2], John Jacob[1]) was born July 8, 1937.

3223 RUTH AMES BURGES (Ann[7], Annie[6], Margaret[5], Rebecca[4], John Adam II[3], John Adam I[2], John Jacob[1]) was born June 10, 1911. She married Everett Wyman, March 3, 1935. Everett was born August 5, 1892.
(Sup) 5540   i Ann Lindley Wyman, born July 1, 1936.

3224 EVELYN DALE BURGES (Ann[7], Annie[6], Margaret[5], Rebecca[4], John Adam II[3], John Adam I[2], John Jacob[1]) was born September 14, 1913. .She married Gilbert L. Keith, May 23, 1942. Gilbert was born December 8, 1912.
(Sup) 5541   i Karen Paisley Keith, born December 13, 1944.
(Sup) 5542   ii Gilbert L. Keith, Jr., born March 7, 1946.

3225 DOROTHY DAVIS BURGES (Ann[7], Annie[6], Margaret[5], Rebecca[4], John Adam II[3], John Adam I[2], John Jacob[1]) was born October 11, 1915. She married Thomas Murray, October 19, 1937. Thomas was born March 14, 1914.
(Sup) 5543   i James Thomas Murray, born November 19, 1944.

3226 RALPH McCRADY WILBUR (Margaret[7], Annie[6], Margaret[5], Rebecca[4], John Adam II[3], John Adam I[2], John Jacob[1]) was born December 23, 1917. He married Gloria Summerville, November 17, 1942. Gloria was born April 7, 1922.
(Sup) 5544   i Gloria June Wilbur, born February 10, 1944.
(Sup) 5545   ii Sharon Wilbur, born March 26, 1947.

3227 MARGARET CATHERINE WILBUR (Margaret[7], Annie[6], Margaret[5], Rebecca[4], John Adam II[3], John Adam I[2], John Jacob[1]) was born February 15, 1922.

(Sup) 3228 RHODERICK DAVIS WILBUR (Margaret^7, Annie^6, Margaret^5, Rebecca^4, John Adam II^3, John Adam^2, John Jacob^1) was the son of John and Margaret Davis Wilbur [The Link Family, page 489, No. 1660]. Rhoderick was born July 31, 1923. He married Margaret Waldrop March 24, 1942. She was born August 24, 1921. Rhoderick died March 11, 1944.

(Sup) 5546   i   Rhoderick David Wilbur, Jr., born June 27, 1944.

(Sup) 3229 THOMAS PAUL DAVIS, JR. (Thomas^7, Annie^6, Margaret^5, Rebecca^4, John Adam II^3, John Adam^2, John Jacob^1) was the son of Thomas Paul and Betty Harlan Davis [The Link Family, page 489, No. 1662]. Thomas, Jr., was born August 20, 1926.

(Sup) 3230 JUDITH DAVIS (Thomas^7, Annie^6, Margaret^5, Rebecca^4, John Adam II^3, John Adam^2, John Jacob^1) was the daughter of Thomas Paul and Betty Harlan Davis [The Link Family, page 489, No. 1662]. Judith was born April 1, 1931.

(Sup) 3231 RALPH DOUGLAS MORRIS (Clara^7, Adam^6, Ruhama^5, John Adam III^4, John Adam II^3, John Adam^2, John Jacob^1) was the son of Wilbur Alonza and Clara Hendricks Morris [The Link Family, page 489, No. 1664]. Ralph was born April 17, 1893. He married, first, Inez Myers. Ralph married, second, Virginia Charlotte Lawson February 27, 1920. Virginia was the daughter of George Edward and Olivia Anna Lawson and was born December 19, 1900. Ralph died October 24, 1943.

CHILD OF RALPH AND INEZ

(Sup) 5547   i   Violet Virginia Morris, born May 14, 1916.

(Sup) 3232 FLEDA GERTRUDE MORRIS (Clara^7, Adam^6, Ruhama^5, John Adam III^4, John Adam II^3, John Adam^2, John Jacob^1) was the daughter of Wilbur Alonza and Clara Hendricks Morris [The Link Family, page 489, No. 1664]. Fleda was born October 22, 1895. She married Harry Hoover. They resided at Hagerstown, Maryland. Fleda died October 21, 1919.

(Sup) 5548   i   Carole Winston Hoover, born March 21, 1916.

(Sup) 3233 MARY ELLEN MORRIS (Clara^7, Adam^6, Ruhama^5, John Adam III^4, John Adam II^3, John Adam^2, John Jacob^1) was the daughter of Wilbur Alonza and Clara Hendricks Morris [The Link Family, page 489, No. 1664]. She was born April 9, 1897, and died July 21, 1898.

(Sup) 3234 HELEN CLARENE MORRIS (Clara^7, Adam^6, Ruhama^5, John Adam III^4, John Adam II^3, John Adam^2, John Jacob^1) was the daughter of Wilbur Alonza and Clara Hendricks Morris [The Link Family, page 489, No. 1664]. Helen was born July 8, 1903. She married Robert Raymond Darr July 12, 1943. He was born August 28, 1901, the son of Samuel Gilmore and Louise Figgins Darr of Shenandoah Junction, Jefferson County, West Virginia. Robert died in 1979.

(Sup) 3235 MAY BELL MORRIS (Clara^7, Adam^6, Ruhama^5, John Adam III^4, John Adam II^3, John Adam^2, John Jacob^1) was the daughter of Wilbur Alonza and Clara Hendricks Morris [The Link Family, page 489, No. 1664]. May Bell was born August 19, 1905.

(Sup) 3236 FUDORA MORRIS (Clara^7, Adam^6, Ruhama^5, John Adam III^4, John Adam II^3, John Adam^2, John Jacob^1) was the daughter of Wilbur Alonza and Clara Hendricks Morris [The Link Family, page 489, No. 1664]. She was born December 16, 1907, and died the same day.

(Sup) 3237 ROBERT MORRIS (Clara^7, Adam^6, Ruhama^5, John Adam III^4, John Adam II^3, John Adam^2, John Jacob^1) was the son of Wilbur Alonza and Clara Hendricks Morris [The Link Family, page 489, No. 1664]. Robert was born July 28, 1909, and died the same day.

(Sup) 3238 AUDREY ELLEN BELL HENDRICKS (William^7, Adam^6, Ruhama^5, John Adam III^4, John Adam II^3, John Adam^2, John Jacob^1) was the daughter of William Henry and Helen Stribling Hendricks [The Link Family, page 489, No. 1665]. Audrey was born May 21, 1913. She married Vernon Francis Cross July 15, 1933. He was the son of Robert Waldo and Mabel Neill Bell Cross and was born August 14, 1912. Vernon worked at the Maritime Company, Washington, D.C. On his retirement in 1965 Audrey and Vernon moved to Ormond Beach, Florida.

(Sup) 5549   i   Barbara Ellen Cross, born February 13, 1948.
(SuP) 5550   ii   Jay Vernon Cross, born October 31, 1951.

(Sup) 3238A WILLIAM CORNELIUS HENDRICKS (William[7], Adam[6], Ruhama[5], John Adam III[4], John Adam II[3], John Adam[2], John Jacob[1]) was the son of William Henry and Helen Stribling Hendricks [The Link Family, page 489, No. 1665]. He was born April 21, 1922, at Shenandoah Junction, Jefferson County, West Virginia, and moved with his parents to Arlington, Virginia. William joined the Air Force and saw service in World War II at Guam. In 1954 he moved to Daytona Beach, Florida, where he was employed by the Federal Aviation Administration as an electronics engineer, until his retirement in 1974. William married Charlotte McGuffy Davis, a widow with four children. She was born April 11, 1934, at Cincinnati, Ohio.

(Sup) 3239 MILDRED IOLA CONARD (Edith[7], Ambrose[6], Ruhama[5], John Adam III[4], John Adam II[3], John Adam[2], John Jacob[1]) was the daughter of Charles Elbert and Edith Hendricks Conard [The Link Family, page 489, No. 1666]. Mildred was born December 8, 1903. She received her A.B. degree from Shepherd College, West Virginia. She did post-graduate work at Drexel Institute, Philadelphia, and became a librarian at Martinsburg (Virginia) High School. After retirement she resided with her brothers Charles and John and sister Emma at their farm near Shepherdstown, West Virginia, where she died August 19, 1987.

(Sup) 3240 MARY EMMA CONARD (Edith[7], Ambrose[6], Ruhama[5], John Adam III[4], John Adam II[3], John Adam[2], John Jacob[1]) was the daughter of Charles Elbert and Edith Hendricks Conard [The Link Family, page 489, No. 1666]. Emma was born December 20, 1905. She received her A.B. degree from Shepherd College, West Virginia, and became a teacher. After retirement she resided with her brothers Charles and John and sister Mildred at their farm near Shepherdstown, West Virginia.

(Sup) 3241 LESTER HENDRICKS CONARD (Edith[7], Ambrose[6], Ruhama[5], John Adam III[4], John Adam II[3], John Adam[2], John Jacob[1]) was the son of Charles Elbert and Edith Hendricks Conard [The Link Family, page 489, No. 1666]. Lester was born June 27, 1908, in Jefferson County, West Virginia. He married Laura Mae Riggs October 4, 1953, at Hagerstown, Maryland. She was the daughter of Charles Edgar and Nelle Maud Newcomer Riggs and was born August 20, 1909, near Hagerstown. Lester and Laura resided at Maugensville, Washington County, Maryland. He died February 25, 1981, and is buried in St. Paul's Lutheran Cemetery at Clear Springs, Maryland.

(Sup) 3242 RALPH WILLIAM CONARD (Edith[7], Ambrose[6], Ruhama[5], John Adam III[4], John Adam II[3], John Adam[2], John Jacob[1]) was the son of Charles Elbert and Edith Hendricks Conard [The Link Family, page 489, No. 1666]. Ralph was born February 24, 1911, near Shepherdstown, West Virginia. He graduated from Shepherd College with an A.B. degree. During World War I he was an instructor at Yale University in physics and radio. He then received an appointment as assistant professor of physics at West Virginia University. He married Elizabeth Hope Richard May 29, 1943. She was born April 3, 1922, the daughter of George Harry and Daisy Riner Richard. Ralph and Elizabeth resided at Wayland, Massachusetts.

(Sup) 5551   i   Ralph Richard Conard.

(Sup) 3243 CHARLES ELBERT CONARD, JR (Edith[7], Ambrose[6], Ruhama[5], John Adam III[4], John Adam II[3], John Adam[2], John Jacob[1]) was the son of Charles Elbert and Edith Hendricks Conard [The Link Family, page 489, No. 1666]. Charles, Jr., was born June 4, 1914. He became a farmer. His farm was located three miles south of Shepherdstown, West Virginia.

(Sup) 3244 JOHN ROBERT CONARD (Edith[7], Ambrose[6], Ruhama[5], John Adam III[4], John Adam II[3], John Adam[2], John Jacob[1]) was the son of Charles Elbert and Edith Hendricks Conard [The Link Family, page 489, No. 1666]. John was born February 21, 1917. He received an A.B. degree from West Virginia State University and became a commercial chemist at Charleston, West Virginia. After retiring, he resided with his brother Charles and sisters Mildred and Emma at their farm near Shepherdstown, West Virginia.

(Sup) 3245 RETA VIRGINIA CONARD (Edith[7], Ambrose[6], Ruhama[5], John Adam III[4], John Adam II[3], John Adam[2], John Jacob[1]) was the daughter of Charles Elbert and Edith Hendricks Conard [The Link Family, page 489, No. 1666]. Reta was born December 11, 1919. She graduated from Madison College, Harrisonburg, Virginia, with a B.S. degree in home economics. She married Kenneth Pershing Hiett September 25, 1943. He was the son of Edgar Guy and Laura Bartys Hiett and was born September 22, 1919. Reta and Kenneth resided at Hagerstown, Maryland.

(Sup) 5552   i   Jan Kenneth Hiett, born February 29, 1952.
(Sup) 5553   ii   Susan Joy Hiett, born December 27, 1956.

(Sup) 3246 RUTH MARIE CONARD (Edith[7], Ambrose[6], Ruhama[5], John Adam III[4], John Adam II[3], John Adam[2], John Jacob[1]) was the daughter of Charles Elbert and Edith Hendricks Conard [The Link Family, page 489, No. 1666]. Ruth was born May 31, 1923. She received her A.B. degree in physical education from Shepherd State Teachers College and became assistant professor of physical education. She moved to Towson, Maryland, where she taught school.

3247 ALBERT GRIFFITH MOLER (Albert[7], Martha[6], Adam[5], John Adam III[4], John Adam II[3], John Adam I[2], John Jacob[1]) was born June 18, 1910. He died December 28, 1928.

(Sup) 3256 HARRIET ELIZABETH NICHOLS (Edgar⁷, Nora⁶, Daniel⁵, John Adam III⁴, John Adam II³, John Adam I², John Jacob¹) was the daughter of Edgar Holland and Julia Bane Nichols [The Link Family, page 491, No. 1675]. Harriett was born June 5, 1921. She married Ralph W. Binkley May 24, 1957, at Frederick, Maryland. He was the son of Jacob Allen and Lillie Mae Shank Binkley and was born March 13, 1921, at State Line, Pennsylvania. Ralph died August 22, 1973, and is buried in Edge Hill Cemetery at Charles Town, West Virginia.

(Sup) 5564A   i   William David Binkley, born December 5, 1958.
(Sup) 5564B   ii Jacob Holland Binkley, born December 8, 1961.

(Sup) 3257 DAVID HOLLAND NICHOLS (Edgar⁷, Nora⁶, Daniel⁵, John Adam III⁴, John Adam II³, John Adam I², John Jacob¹) was the son of Edgar Holland and Julia Bane Nichols [The Link Family, page 491, No. 1675]. David was born April 7, 1923. He married Reba Florence Ryman July 3, 1951, at Boonsboro, Maryland. She was the daughter of Otto A. and Annie Rebecca Helsley Ryman and was born April 7, 1919, at Mount Jackson, Shenandoah County, Virginia. Reba died February 24, 1969, and is buried in Edge Hill Cemetery at Charles Town, West Virginia.

(Sup) 3258 ELEANOR ANN SHIRLEY (Esther⁷, Nora⁶, Daniel⁵, John Adam III⁴, John Adam II³, John Adam I², John Jacob¹) was the daughter of Roy Jefferson and Esther Nichols Shirley [The Link Family, page 491, No. 1677]. She was born September 7, 1930.

(Sup) 3259 DANIEL RUSSELL NICHOLS, JR. (Daniel⁷, Nora⁶, Daniel⁵, John Adam III⁴, John Adam II³, John Adam I², John Jacob¹) was the son of Daniel Russell and Mildred Maddox Nichols [The Link Family, page 491, No. 1678]. Daniel, Jr., was born September 12, 1929, at Uvilla, Jefferson County, West Virginia. He married Peggy Lou Dorsey November 11, 1950, at Sharpsburg, Maryland. She was the daughter of Paul Richard and Mary Ramey Dorsey and was born April 3, 1932. Daniel and Peggy were divorced.

(Sup) 5565   i   Saundra Ann Nichols, born June 26, 1951.
(Sup) 5566   ii Deborah Dianne Nichols, born March 28, 1953.
(Sup) 5567   iii Daniel Russell Nichols, III, born Dec 29, 1961.

(Sup) 3260 JOYCE JEAN NICHOLS (Daniel⁷, Nora⁶, Daniel⁵, John Adam III⁴, John Adam II³, John Adam I², John Jacob¹) was the daughter of Daniel Russell and Mildred Maddox Nichols [The Link Family, page 491, No. 1678]. Joyce was born April 13, 1931, at Uvilla, Jefferson County, West Virginia. She married Emmett Euen Moore July 31, 1954, at Shepherdstown, West Virginia. He was the son of Marion Lexington and Iva Freeman Moore and was born September 16, 1916, at Fredonia, Kentucky.

(Sup) 5568   i   Karen Kay Moore, born February 14, 1956.
(Sup) 5569   ii Sheeree Sue Moore, born April 3 1957.
(Sup) 5570   iii David Dirk Moore, born November 29, 1959.

3248 KELLAR LINK MOLER (Albert⁷, Martha⁶, Adam⁵, John Adam III⁴, John Adam II³, John Adam I², John Jacob¹) was born November 9, 1913. He married Mary Eugenia Sloan, January 27, 1940.

(Sup) 5554   i   David Link Moler, born July 5, 1942.
(Sup) 5555   ii Nancy Jean Moler, born August 26, 1946.

3249 JULIA LINK MOLER (Ada⁷, Martha⁶, Adam⁵, John Adam III⁴, John Adam II³, John Adam I², John Jacob¹) was born September 10, 1903. She married James Bernard Moler, November 12, 1921. James, son of Raleigh William and Annie Frances Flanagan Moler, was born July 28, 1896. Julia died November 2, 1929.

(Sup) 5556   i   Clifford Greggs Moler, born May 4, 1924.
(Sup) 5557   ii Julia Link Moler, born November 2, 1929.

3250 FRANCES GREGGS MOLER (Ada⁷, Martha⁶, Adam⁵, John Adam III⁴, John Adam II³, John Adam I², John Jacob¹) was born January 29, 1905. She married Gilbert Leadington Storey, June 2, 1928. Gilbert was the son of Thomas and Lilly Mae Storey and was born November 27, 1907.

(Sup) 5558   i   John Gilbert Storey, born April 17, 1929.

3251 GUY MAXWELL MOLER (Ada⁷, Martha⁶, Adam⁵, John Adam III⁴, John Adam II³, John Adam I², John Jacob¹) was born April 6, 1907. He married Charlotte Fern Hill, December 31, 1928. Charlotte was born October 8, 1905. She was the daughter of James Craven and Florence Brantner Hill.

(Sup) 5559   i   Mary Ann Moler, born November 22, 1932.
(Sup) 5560   ii James Douglass Moler, born October 18, 1934.

3252 MARGARET MARIE MOLER (Ada⁷, Martha⁶, Adam⁵, John Adam III⁴, John Adam II³, John Adam I², John Jacob¹) was born June 29, 1909. She died September 23, 1909.

3253 ANNA CATHERINE MOLER (Ada⁷, Martha⁶, Adam⁵, John Adam III⁴, John Adam II³, John Adam I², John Jacob¹) was born May 14, 1911. She married Irvin Hallowell Jones, Jr., April 27, 1941. Irvin, son of Irvin Hallowell and Emma Jones, was born April 16, 1882. Irvin adopted Anna's daughter, Lucile, after his marriage to Anna.

(Sup) 5561   i   Lucille Moler-Jones, born April 2, 1929.

3254 WILLARD JACOB MOLER (Ada⁷, Martha⁶, Adam⁵, John Adam III⁴, John Adam II³, John Adam I², John Jacob¹) was born December 28, 1916. He married Ruth Virginia Phillips, December 26, 1936. Ruth was the daughter of Charles Benjamin and Nellie Winters Phillips and was born August 12, 1914.

(Sup) 5562   i   Patsy Lee Moler, born July 28, 1938.
(Sup) 5563   ii Catherine Eleanor Moler, born August 15, 1945.

3255 ROBERT ARMSTEAD LUCAS (Mary⁷, William⁶, Adam⁵, John Adam III⁴, John Adam II³, John Adam I², John Jacob¹) was born November 4, 1919. After his public schooling, he entered West Virginia University where he graduated with an A.B. in Chemistry in 1941. He earned his M.S. degree in chemistry there in 1942. During World War II he served from 1944 to 1946 and was commissioned a lieutenant (j.g.) in the U.S. Navy. After the war he became a research chemist at Mellon Institute. On August 28, 1948, he married Constance Beatrice Sharp. Constance was the daughter of John D. and Constance Southerland Sharp and was born December 28, 1923.

(Sup) 5564   i   Constance Southerland Lucas, born May 5, 1950.

(Sup) 3261 CLARISSA ELLEN NICHOLS (Daniel[7], Nora[6], Daniel[5], John Adam III[4], John Adam II[3] John Adam I[2], John Jacob[1]) was the daughter of Daniel Russell and Mildred Maddox Nichols [The Link Family, page 491, No. 1678]. Clarissa was born March 26, 1942, at Uvilla, Jefferson County, West Virginia. She married, first, Robert Lee Abshire June 1, 1958. He was the son of Boyd and Mae Abshire. Clarissa married, second, Larry Edward Thatcher February 1, 1965. They were divorced. She married, third, Frederick Gordon Colhard of Quincy, Massachusetts, May 10, 1984.

CHILDREN OF CLARISSA AND ROBERT

(Sup) 5571 i   Bret Alan Abshire, born June 1, 1959.
(Sup) 5572 ii   Kymberlee Kay Abshire, born August 11, 1960.
(Sup) 5573 iii Sheryl Lynne Abshire, born May 20, 1963.

CHILDREN OF CLARISSA AND LARRY

(Sup) 5574 iv   Tonja Renee Thatcher, born July 5, 1965.
(Sup) 5575 v   Kye Nicole Thatcher, born October 30, 1969.
(Sup) 5576 vi   Kelly Marie Thatcher, born September 16, 1970.

(Sup) 3262 WILLIAM PRESTON LINK, JR. (William[7], Adam[6], Daniel[5], John Adam III[4], John Adam II[3], John Adam I[2], John Jacob[1]) was the son of William Preston and Ruth Boyer Link [The Link Family, page 491, No. 1679]. William, Jr., was born August 25, 1936. He married Minerva Jane Abshire, a widow with two children. Minerva was born November 18, 1946. They resided near Shepherdstown, West Virginia.

(Sup) 3263 SARAH ELIZABETH LINK (William[7], Adam[6], Daniel[5], John Adam III[4], John Adam II[3], John Adam I[2], John Jacob[1]) was the daughter of William Preston and Ruth Boyer Link [The Link Family, page 491, No. 1679]. Sarah was born August 14, 1938. She did not marry.

(Sup) 5577 i   Beverly Diane Link, born February 21, 1964.
(Sup) 5578 ii   Kelly Renee Link, born December 21, 1965.

(Sup) 3264 DANIEL CRUZEN LINK, JR., (Daniel[7], Adam[6], Daniel[5], John Adam III[4], John Adam II[3] John Adam I[2], John Jacob[1]) was the son of Daniel Cruzen and Helen Ellis Link [The Link Family, page 492, No. 1681; and Supplement No. 1681]. Daniel, Jr., was born March 30, 1940. He married Elizabeth June Hartsaw June 24, 1967. She was born June 1, 1941.

(Sup) 5579 i   David Cruzen Link, born September 11, 1968.
(Sup) 5580 ii   Kevin Andrew Link, born June 13, 1970.
(Sup) 5581 iii Kristin Elizabeth Link, born November 20, 1977.

(Sup) 3265 MARGARET ELLIS LINK (Daniel[7], Adam[6], Daniel[5], John Adam III[4], John Adam II[3], John Adam I[2], John Jacob[1]) was the daughter of Daniel Cruzen and Helen Ellis Link [The Link Family, page 492, No. 1681; and Supplement No. 1681]. Margaret was born November 14, 1942. She married Terry Allen Bryan December 4, 1983. He was born June 24, 1945. Dr. Bryan was a dentist. Margaret and Terry resided at Dover, Delaware.

(Sup) 3266 DAVID ALLEN LINK (Boteler[7], John[6], Daniel[5], John Adam III[4], John Adam II[3], John Adam I[2], John Jacob[1]) was the son of Boteler Moore and Eva Nichols Link [The Link Family, page 492, No. 1683; and Supplement No. 1683]. David was born October 22, 1932, in Jefferson County, West Virginia. He married Joyce Juanita Athey January 10, 1952, at Frederick, Maryland. The daughter of Irvin Wallis and Lella Frances Shipe Athey, she was born January 10, 1933, at Berryville, Clarke County, Virginia.

(Sup) 5582 i   David Allen Link, Jr., born January 20, 1953.
(Sup) 5583 ii   Irvin Moore Link, born October 31, 1954.

(Sup) 3267 HOWARD SNYDER LINK (Boteler[7], John[6], Daniel[5], John Adam III[4], John Adam II[3], John Adam I[2], John Jacob[1]) was the son of Boteler Moore and Eva Nichols Link [The Link Family, page 492, No. 1683; and Supplement No. 1683]. Howard was born February 10, 1935, in Jefferson County, West Virginia. He married, first, Mary Ann Elizabeth Frye July 21, 1958, at Sharpsburg, Maryland. She was the daughter of William Pittman and Josephine Elizabeth (Breeden) Frye and was born August 3, 1941, at Shepherdstown, West Virginia, the daughter of William Pittman and Josephine Elizabeth Breeden Frye. Howard and Mary Ann were divorced in 1978. He married, second, Fannie Butts Decker, September 20, 1983.

(Sup) 5584 i   Howard Snyder Link, Jr., born March 20, 1959.
(Sup) 5585 ii   Rhonda Gail Link, born November 8, 1961.
(Sup) 5586 iii Kevin Scott Link, born November 7, 1971.
(Sup) 5587 iv   Brian Matthew Link, born December 7, 1977.

(Sup) 3268 BOTELER MOORE LINK JR. (Boteler[7], John[6], Daniel[5], John Adam III[4], John Adam II[3], John Adam I[2], John Jacob[1]) was the son of Boteler Moore and Eva Nichols Link [The Link Family, page 492, No. 1683; and Supplement No. 1683]. Boteler, Jr., was born July 24, 1940, in Jefferson County, West Virginia. He married Geraldine Ann Fritts January 17, 1964, at Duffields, Jefferson County. She was the daughter of Kenneth Trussell and Eunice Elliott Fritts and was born October 1, 1941, at Charles Town, West Virginia.

(Sup) 5588 i   Dawn Lynn Link, born January 8, 1968.
(Sup) 5589 ii   Boteler Moore Link, III, born July 24, 1970.
(Sup) 5590 iii Amanda Lee Link, born October 19, 1971.
(Sup) 5591 iv   Kenneth Jason Link, born September 8, 1976.

(Sup) 3268A JOHN WILLIAM LINK (Boteler[7], John[6], Daniel[5], John Adam III[4], John Adam I[2], John Jacob[1]) was the fourth child of Boteler Moore and Eva Nichols Link [The Link Family, page 492, No. 1683; and Supplement No. 1683]. John was born September 28, 1950, at Charles Town, West Virginia. He died October 2, 1968, and is buried in Pleasant View Cemetery near Martinsburg, West Virginia.

(Sup) 3269 JOHN WALTER WOODSON (Madaline[7], John[6], Daniel[5], John Adam III[4], John Adam II[3], John Adam I[2], John Jacob[1]) was the son of Walter Eldridge and Madaline Link Woodson [The Link Family, page 492, No. 1685; and Supplement No. 1685]. John was born September 2, 1941, at Charles Town, West Virginia.

(Sup) 3269A ALLEN LINK JACKSON (Madaline[7], John[6], Daniel[5], John Adam III[4], John Adam II[3], John Adam I[2], John Jacob[1]) was the son of John Herbert and Madaline Link Woodson Jackson [The Link Family, page 492, No. 1685; and Supplement No.1685.] Allen was born March 3, 1952, at Detroit, Michigan.

(Sup) 3270 MADLYN VAN MOORE LALLY (Florence[7], John[6], Daniel[5], John Adam III[4], John ADam II[3], John Adam I[2], John Jacob[1]) was the daughter of John Paul and Florence Link Lally [The Link Family, page 492, No. 1686; and Supplement No. 1686]. Madlyn was born October 8, 1942, at Martinsburg, West Virginia.

(Sup) 3270A JOHN PAUL LALLY, JR. (Florence[7], John[6], Daniel[5], John Adam III[4], John Adam II[3], John Adam I[2], John Jacob[1]) was the son of John Paul and Florence Link Lally [The Link Family, page 492, No. 1686; and Supplement No. 1686]. John, Jr., was born September 19, 1951, at Youngstown, Ohio. He married Francine Worrellia, who was born August 1, 1955, at Youngstown.

(Sup) 5592 i John Paul Lally, III, born May 20, 1980.

(Sup) 3271 VAUGHEN HARWOOD LINK, JR. (Vaughen[7], Elbert[6], Daniel[5], John Adam III[4], John Adam II[3], John Adam I[2], John Jacob[1]) was the son of Vaughen Harwood and Helen Snively Link [The Link Family, page 492, No. 1687; and Supplement No. 1687]. Vaughen, Jr., was born January 29, 1943, at Shepherdstown, West Virginia. He graduated from the University of Maryland with a B.S. degree in 1965 and was in the U.S. Air Force Reserve as an Air Intelligence Specialist. He was employed as a sales manager for Ciba Gelgy in Allendale, New Jersey. Vaughen married Sandrya Ann Schaefer June 29, 1968. She was the daughter of Bert Fred and Jessie Keith Schaefer.

(Sup) 5593 i Heather Elizabeth Link, born October 19, 1973.

(Sup) 3272 NANCY HELEN LINK (Vaughen[7], Elbert[6], Daniel[5], John Adam III[4], John Adam II[3], John Adam I[2], John Jacob[1]) was the daughter of Vaughen Harwood and Helen Snively Link [The Link Family, page 492, No. 1687; and Supplement No. 1687]. Nancy was born February 14, 1950, at Hagerstown, Maryland.

(Sup) 3272A JAMES ANDREW LINK (Vaughen[7], Elbert[6], Daniel[5], John Adam III[4], John Adam II[3], John Adam I[2], John Jacob[1]) was the son of Vaughen Harwood and Helen Louise Snively Link [The Link Family, page 492, No. 1687; and Supplement No. 1687.] James was born January 17, 1952, at Hagerstown, Maryland. He received a B.A. degree in government and politics in 1974, and a B.S. degree in horticulture in 1980 from the University of Maryland. James married Claudia Ruth Gilcreast October 20, 1979, at College Park, Maryland. She was the daughter of James Everett and Mary Frances Dillon Gilcreast and was born May 28, 1950, at Quincy, Massachusetts.

(Sup) 3273 MARY CATHERINE DUKE (Mabel[7], Walter[6], Sarah[5], John Adam III[4], John ADam II[3], John Adam I[2], John Jacob[1]) was the daughter of Leslie Daniel and Mabel Hendricks Duke [The Link Family, page 492, No. 1688; and Supplement No. 1688]. Mary was born June 7, 1915. She married Edward Collins Enright December 28, 1946. Edward was born September 5, 1909.

(Sup) 3274 ROBERT NEWTON DUKE (Mabel[7], Walter[6], Sarah[5], John Adam III[4], John Adam II[3], John Adam I[2], John Jacob[1]) was the son of Leslie Daniel and Mabel Hendricks Duke [The Link Family, page, No. 1688]. Robert was born March 20, 1919. He married Mildred Ingram.

(Sup) 3275 MARGARET ELIZABETH DUKE (Mabel[7], Walter[6], Daniel[5], John Adam III[4], John Adam II[3], John Adam I[2], John Jacob[1]) was the daughter of Leslie Daniel and Mabel Hendricks Duke [The Link Family, page 493, No. 1688]. Margaret was born May 2, 1922. She married, first, Mr. Oche, and second, Eugene Bledsoe.

3276 JULIA CATHERINE HENDRICKS (Lester[7], Walter[6], Sarah[5], John Adam III[4], John Adam II[3], John Adam I[2], John Jacob[1]) was born July 26, 1941.

3277 ETHYLN ADELL DECK (William[7], Annie[6], Sarah[5], John Adam III[4], John Adam II[3], John Adam I[2], John Jacob[1]) was born July 29, 1909.

(Sup) 3281   WILLIAM HAMPTON HENDRICKS (Garland[7], Harvey[6], Sarah[5], John Adam III[4], John Adam III[3], John Adam[2], John Jacob[1]) was the son of Garland Wilson and Gertrude Willis Hendricks [The Link Family, page 494, No. 1697; and Supplement No. 1697]. William was born September 16, 1934. He was a victim of polio when young but recovered to lead a normal life. He graduated from West Virginia University and was employed by the Potomac Edison Company. William married Ida Elizabeht Hodges August 10, 1963. She was the daughter of Samuel and Nannie Needy Hodges and was born August 13, 1941. Ida graduated from Shepherd College, West Virginia, and was a teacher of mathematics.

(Sup) 5594   i   William Hodges Hendricks, born Dec 23, 1977.

(Sup) 3282   ELIZABETH MARGERY RYDER (Margery[7], Harvey[6], Sarah[5], John Adam III[4], John Adam III[3], John Adam III[2], John Jacob[1]) was the daughter of David Charles and Margery Hendricks Ryder [The Link Family, page 494, No. 1698; and Supplement No. 1698]. Elizabeth was born March 11, 1924. She resided in Maine, where she was in the jewelry business.

(Sup) 3283   PATRICIA ANN RYDER (Margery[7], Harvey[6], Sarah[5], John Adam III[4], John Adam III[3], John Adam III[2], John Jacob[1]) was the daughter of David Charles and Margery Hendricks Ryder [The Link Family, page 494, No. 1698; and Supplement No. 1698]. Patricia was born June 22, 1930, at Washington, D.C. She married Charles Huber October 15, 1949, at Washington. He received a master's degree in engineering from Oklahoma University in 1952.

(Sup) 5594A   i   Janis Huber, born June 4, 1950.
(Sup) 5594B   ii   David Charles Huber,born April 3, 1961.

(Sup) 3284   JOHN WILLIAM HENDRICKS, JR.   (John[7], Harvey[6], Sarah[5], John Adam III[4], John Adam III[3], John Adam III[2], John Jacob[1]) was the son of John William and Bessie Osbourn Hendricks [The Link Family, page 494, No. 1700; and Supplement No. 1700]. John, Jr., was born February 11, 1938, near Shepherdstown, West Virginia. He married Carole Elizabeth Buhrman August 9, 1959, at Kearneysville, Jefferson County, West Virginia. She was the daughter of Harold U. and Hilda Cliff Buhrman and was born December 23, 1940, in Jefferson County. John became a farmer and was employed by the Agricultural Research Center at Bardane, Jefferson County.

(Sup) 5595   i   John William Hendricks, III, born Nov 3, 1960.
(Sup) 5596   ii   Michael Alan Hendricks, born October 28, 1965.
(Sup) 5594A   iii   Elizabeth Kaye Hendricks, born Nov, 13, 1979.

(Sup) 3278   FREDERICK WEBSTER DECK, JR. (Frederick[7], Annie[6], Sarah[5], John Adam III[4], John Adam III[3], John Adam[2], John Jacob[1]) was the son of Frederick Webster and Mary Jolls Deck [The Link Family, page 494, No. 1696; and Supplement No. 1696]. Frederick, Jr., was born December 14, 1925, at Washington, D.C. He graduated from Ursinus College and Jefferson Medical College, Philadelphia. Dr. Deck was intern, resident and instructor in radiology at New York Hospital. From 1956 to 1960 he served as assistant attending radiologist at Memorial Hospital in New York. He was at Fairfax County Hospital, Virginia, from 1960 to 1967, where he became chief radiologist. From 1967 to 1971 Dr. Deck was associate radiologist at St. Agnes Hospital in Baltimore and consultant radiologist to the D.C. correctional system and the National Security Agency. He taught at Cornell University Medical School, at George Washington University, and at the hospitals at which he worked. He was also assistant professor at the Georgetown University Scool of Medicine. As a member of the Naval Reserve he served at the Navy School of Radiology, Bethesda Naval Hospital, and was radiologist at the Norfolk Naval Base. Frederick married Katherine Grieve March 1, 1952. She was born January 22, 1930. They resided at Annandale, Virginia. Frederick died March 17, 1975, in Fairfax County, Virginia.

(Sup) 5593A   i   Evelyn Deck, born December 21, 1952.
(Sup) 5593B   ii   Alison Deck, born August 28, 1955.
(Sup) 5593B   iii   Frederick Webster Deck, III, born Sep 20, 1963.

(Sup) 3279   WILLIAM MEADE DECK (Frederick[7], Annie[6], Sarah[5], John Adam III[4], John Adam III[3], John Adam[2], John Jacob[1]) was the son of Frederick Webster and Mary Jolls Deck [The Link Family, page 494, No. 1696; and Supplement No. 1696]. William was born July 22, 1928, at Washington, D.C. He served in the U.S. Army as a sergeant from October, 1945, to April, 1948. He received his A.B. degree in 1952 and his M.B.A. degree in 1956 from George Washington University. He became District Manager of Maintenance for the Chesapeake and Potomac Telephone Company in the Washington suburban area. William married Elizabeth Freiburghouse. She was the daughter of Rear Admiral Leonard F. and Elizabeth Carroll Freiburghouse.

(Sup) 5593D   i   Linda Ann Deck, born May 5, 1957.
(Sup) 5593E   ii   William meade Deck, Jr., born August 27, 1959.
(Sup) 5593F   iii   Susan Elizabeth deck, born December 30, 1961.

(Sup) 3280   JOHN WHEATON DECK (Frederick[7], Annie[6], Sarah[5], John Adam III[4], John Adam III[3], John Adam[2], John Jacob[1]) was the son of Frederick Webster and Mary Jolls Deck [The Link Family, page 494, No. 1696; and Supplement No. 1696]. John was born March 28, 1932. He married Valerie Stewart September 10, 1955. She was born April 23, 1934.

(Sup) 5593G   i   John Wheaton Deck, Jr., born March 31, 1957.
(Sup) 5593H   ii   Lorraine Deck, born June 12, 1961.
(Sup) 5593J   iii   Cynthia Deck, born July 19, 1966.

(Sup) 3285 RUTH MARIE HENDRICKS (John[7], Harvey[6], Sarah[5], John Adam II[4], John Adam II[3], John Adam I[2], John Jacob[1]) was the daughter of John William and Bessie Osbourn Hendricks [The Link Family, page 494, No. 1700; and Supplement No. 1700]. Ruth was born January 17, 1941. She received a B.A. degree in music education from Shepherd College in 1962 and taught instumental music for nine years in the public schools of Calvert County, Maryland. On December 13, 1970, she married Charles Winfield Denton. He was born April 17, 1921. Charles was an oyster planter and packer. He was the president and owner of Warren Denton and Company, Broomes Island, Maryland. He died April 5, 1976.

(Sup) 5597   i   Mark Edward Denton, born September 30, 1973.
(Sup) 5598   ii Julie Anne Denton, born May 30, 1975.

(Sup) 3285A MARY CATHERINE HENDRICKS (John[7], Harvey[6], Sarah[5], John Adam II[4], John Adam II[3], John Adam I[2], John Jacob[1]) was the third child of John William and Bessie Osbourn Hendricks [The Link Family, page 494, No. 1700; and Supplement No. 1700]. Mary was born December 5, 1950, at Martinsburg, West Virginia. She attended Shepherd College and then West Virginia University from which she obtained a B.S. degree in May 1972. She was employed as a dietitian at Ohio Valley Medical Center, Wheeling, West Virginia. Mary married Charles Stephen Handzo August 15, 1971 at Shepherdstown, West Virginia. He was the son of John and Julia Myers Handzo and was born April 28, 1947, at Martinsburg. Charles graduated from Shepherd College in 1969. He received a Ph.D. degree in analytical chemistry from West Virginia University May 1975 and was employed as a research chemist by Mobay Chemical Company, New Martinsville, West Virginia.

(Sup) 3286 MARGARET LOUISE HENDRICKS (Allen[7], James[6], Sarah[5], John Adam II[4], John Adam II[3], John Adam I[2], John Jacob[1]) was the daughter of Allen Lemen and Caroline Branham Hendricks [The Link Family, page 495, No. 1702; and Supplement No. 1702]. Margaret was born October 15, 1929, at Martinsburg, West Virginia. She attended Shepherd College, West Virginia, then Marshall University where she received her B.S. degree, then West Virginia University where she received an M.A. degree in 1954. She worked as personnel director for the Pennsylvania Hospital. Peggy married Paul Randolph Noyes April 22, 1961, at Martinsburg. He was the son of Edgar and Rosa Doak Noyes and was born in Shreveport, Louisiana. Paul received a B.S. degree from Centenary College of Louisiana, and M.S. and Ph.D. degrees from the university of Texas. He worked for DuPont. Peggy and Paul resided at Philadelphia, Pennsylvania.

(Sup) 5599   i   Caroline Randolph Noyes, born May 17, 1964.
(Sup) 5600   ii Martha Hendricks Noyes, born May 20, 1968.

(Sup) 3287 JANICE MARIE ENGLE (Kenneth[7], Esther[6], Sarah[5], John Adam II[4], John Adam II[3], John Adam I[2], John Jacob[1]) was the daughter of Kenneth Hendricks and Vera Mae Young Engle [The Link Family, page 495, No. 1703; and Supplement No. 1703]. Janice was born November 1, 1928. She married Edward Russell Tabor September 6, 1947. Janice was born May 24, 1924, at Zanesville, Ohio. Janice and Edward resided at Akron, Ohio, where she was a supervisor for Firestone Tire and Rubber, and he was a bank employee.

(Sup) 5600A   i   Deborah Lynn Tabor, born September 20, 1952.
(Sup) 5600B   ii Sandra Lee Tabor, born March 26, 1955.

(Sup) 3288 ANN CONSIDINE ENGLE (Kenneth[7], Esther[6], Sarah[5], John Adam II[4], John Adam II[3], John Adam I[2], John Jacob[1]) was the daughter of Kenneth Hendricks and Vera Mae Young Engle [The Link Family, page 495, No. 1703; and Supplement No. 1703]. Ann was born May 6, 1931, at Charles Town, West Virginia. She married Kenneth Frederick Herchenroeder May 17, 1952. He was the son of George M. and Ada Pfaffle Herchenroeder and was born June 3, 1933, at Akron, Ohio. Kenneth was administrator of a nursing home, and Ann was a special English teacher. They were divorced in 1979.

(Sup) 5600C   i   David Kenneth Herchenroeder, born June 8, 1953.
(Sup) 5600D   ii Michael Lee Herchenroeder, born Dec 29, 1954.
(Sup) 5600E   iii Timothy Alan Herchenroeder, born Nov 2, 1957.
(Sup) 5600F   iv Jefferry Lynn Herchenroeder, born Jan 9, 1959.
(Sup) 5600G   v   James Stephen Herchenroeder, born Sep 21, 1961.
(Sup) 5600H   vi Scott Allen Herchenroeder, born August 15, 1965.

(Sup) 3289 BARBARA JEAN ENGLE (Daniel[7], Esther[6], Sarah[5], John Adam II[4], John Adam II[3], John Adam I[2], John Jacob[1]) was the daughter of Daniel Evans and Jean Linton Engle [The Link Family, page 495, No. 1704; and Supplement No. 1704]. Barbara was born January 29, 1939, at Akron, Ohio. She graduated from Smith College, Massachusetts, in 1960, received her master's degree from the University of Idaho, and performed graduate studies at the University of Wisconsin. Barbara married Gene Lightner of Lincoln, Nebraska, in 1959. He received his doctor's degree in chemistry from the University of Idaho in 1963 and was employed by Weyerhauser Products in the state of Washington.

(Sup) 5600J   i   Scott Richard Lightner, born July 29, 1961.

(Sup) 3290 PRESTON MURRAY ENGLE (James[7], Esther[6], Sarah[5], John Adam II[4], John Adam II[3], John Adam I[2], John Jacob[1]) was the son of James Preston Murray and Ann McMillan Engle [The Link Family, page 495, No. 1706; and Supplement No. 1706]. Murray was born April 12, 1939, at Charleston, West Virginia. He received a B.S. degree in chemical engineering from Tulsa University and a medical degree from Kirksville Osteopathic College, Missouri. He practiced gynecology at Wagoner, Oklahoma. Murray married Diane Olsen July 2, 1966, at Tulsa.

(Sup) 5600K   i   Lori Ann Engle, born December 2, 1967.
(Sup) 5600L   ii Debra Jean Engle, born July 3, 1969.
(Sup) 5600M   iii Heather Diane Engle, born September 4, 1974.

(Sup) 3291 JEAN CATHERINE ENGLE (James P.[7], Esther[6], Sarah[5], John Adam III[4], John Adam II[3], John Adam I[2], John Jacob[1]) was the daughter of James Preston Murray and Ann McMillan Hendricks [The Link Family, page 495, No. 1706; and Supplement No. 1706]. Jean was born August 5, 1943, at Charleston, West Virginia. She married James R. Ballard of Michigan. Jean and James resided four years at London, England, where he was chief engineer for Amoco International, and then at Houston, Texas.

(Sup) 5600N   i   Barbara Ann Ballard, born May 5, 1969.
(Sup) 5600P   ii Elizabeth Jane Ballard, born June 16, 1971.

(Sup) 3292 BRUCE ALLEN ENGLE (James A.[7], Esther[6], Sarah[5], John Adam III[4], John Adam II[3], John Adam I[2], John Jacob[1]) was the son of James Allen Madison and Betty Joe Knapp Engle [The Link Family, page 495, No. 1707; and Supplement No. 1707.]. Bruce was born November 14, 1941. He resided in Kansas.

(Sup) 3293 REBECCA LEE MOLER (Rebecca[7], LeRoy[6], Sarah[5], John Adam III[4], John Adam II[3], John Adam I[2], John Jacob[1]) was the daughter of Kenneth Brooks and Rebecca Hendricks Moler [The Link Family, page 495, No. 1709; and Supplement No. 1709]. Rebecca was born October 24, 1926, at Charles Town, West Virginia. She worked for the National Savings and Trust Company and became assistant vice president and branch manager at Washington, D.C. Rebecca married Douglas Woody Stevens. He was the son of George Benjamin and Clara Mae Wade Stevens and was born December 3, 1920. Rebecca and Douglas resided at Takoma Park, Maryland. He retired in 1972 from his post on the staff of the Joint Chiefs of Staff at the Pentagon, Washington, D.C.

(Sup) 5601   i   Douglas Woody Stevens, Jr., born Dec 16, 1947.
(Sup) 5601A   ii Debra Lee Stevens, born October 5, 1956.

(Sup) 3294 EVELYN MADDOX HENDRICKS (Gilbert[7], Daniel[6], Sarah[5], John Adam III[4], John Adam II[3], John Adam I[2], John Jacob[1]) was the daughter of Gilbert Leo and Evelyn Maddox Hendricks [The Link Family, page 495, No. 1711; and Supplement No. 1711]. Evelyn (Betty) was born May 19, 1929, at Duffields, Jefferson County, West Virginia. She graduated from Shepherd College in 1951 with a B.A. degree in education, from Gallaudet College in 1962 with an M.S. degree in education for the deaf, and from George Washington University with an Ed.S. in special education. She taught and supervised programs for the handicapped and was a school administrator at Hagerstown, Maryland. Betty married James Philip Reinhart on October 17, 1974, at Shepherdstown, West Virginia. He was the son of Charles Hugh and Irma Idella Snyder Reinhart and was born April 14, 1931. They lived at Sharpsburg, Maryland, where James was a prominent orchardist and farmer.

(Sup) 3295 GILBERT LEO HENDRICKS, JR. (Gilbert[7], Daniel[6], Sarah[5], John Adam III[4], John Adam II[3], John Adam I[2], John Jacob[1]) was the son of Gilbert Leo and Evelyn Maddox Hendricks [The Link Family, page 495, No. 1711; and Supplement No. 1711]. Gilbert, Jr., was born July 10, 1931 at Duffields, Jefferson County, West Virginia. He married Ina Mae Williamson, June 5, 1958, at Rockingham, North Carolina. She was the daughter of James Perry and Ina Hayes Williamson of Florence, South Carolina, and was born October 8, 1930, at Florence. Gilbert, Jr., known as Jay, graduated from Shepherd College, West Virginia, in 1952. He received his M.D. degree from the Medical College of Virginia, Richmond, in May 1957. He served his residency in thoracic and cardiovascular surgery at Cleveland Clinic (Ohio) and at Good Samaritan Hospital, Los Angeles, California. He worked in his specialty for ten years at the Giesinger Medical Clinic at Danville, Pennsylvania, and then in private practice at State College, Pennsylvania. Jay became a diplomat to the American College of Surgeons in 1963, and to the American College of Thoracic and Cardio-Vasculary Surgery in 1964. Ina was a graduate of the University of South Carolina with a major in nursing.

(Sup) 5602   i   Gilbert Leo Hendricks III, born June 23, 1959.
(Sup) 5603   ii   James Perry Hendricks, born February 27, 1961.
(Sup) 5604   iii Leslie Ann Hendricks, born September 5, 1963.

(Sup) 3296 DANIEL EWELL HENDRICKS (Gilbert[7], Daniel[6], Sarah[5], John Adam III[4], John Adam II[3], John Adam I[2], John Jacob[1]) was the son of Gilbert Leo and Evelyn Maddox Hendricks [The Link Family, page 495, No. 1711; and Supplement No. 1711]. Ewell was born April 23, 1934, at Duffields, Jefferson County, West Virginia. He attended Shepherd College from 1951 to 1953, and received a B.S. degree from the School of Medicine at West Virginia University in 1955. Ewell earned his M.D. degree from the Medical College of Virginia, Richmond, in 1957. His internship was at Bellevue Hospital, New York, and his residency at the Medical College of Virginia. Dr. Hendricks opened a general surgery practice in 1963 at Martinsburg, West Virginia. During the Vietnam conflict he served in the army as a lieutenant-colonel and was assigned as Chief of Surgery at the Specialized Treatment Center, Fort Gordon, Augusta, Georgia, 1967-1969; for that service he was awarded the Army Commendation Medal. Dr. Hendricks was treasurer, secretary, vice president, and president of the Eastern Panhandle Medical Society at Martinsburg. He served on the Board of Trustees of Kings Daughter Hospital from 1969 until its merger with City Hospital and since that time on the Board of Trustees of City Hospital. Ewell married, first, Barbara Ruth Lightner June 20, 1957, in Augusta County, Virginia. She was the daughter of William Jerome and Baumgardner Lightner and was born January 6, 1936. They were divorced in 1975. He married, second, Barbara Ellen Painter July 1, 1976, at Inwood, Berkeley County, West Virginia. Barbara was the daughter of Paul Jackson and Ruth Ann Fishpaw Painter and was born November 6, 1951 at Martinsburg. She graduated from Virginia Computer College, Alexandria, Virginia, and until her marriage to Ewell had worked in the Department of Surgery at Kings Daughter Hospital at Martinsburg.

CHILDREN OF EWELL AND BARBARA RUTH
(Sup) 5605   i   Susan Ramona Hendricks, born November 17, 1958.

CHILDREN OF EWELL AND BARBARA ELLEN
(Sup) 5606   i   Daniel Ewell Hendricks, Jr., born Feb 14, 1977.
(Sup) 5607   ii   Elizabeth Ann Hendricks, born August 14, 1979.
(Sup) 5607A   iii James Brian Hendricks, born June 21, 1981.
(Sup) 5607B   iv   Mary Ellen Hendricks, born June 17,1982.

(Sup) 3300 EDWARD CRAWFORD McAMIS, JR. (Anna[7], Daniel[6], Sarah[5], John Adam III[4], John Adam II[3], John Adam I[2], John Jacob[1].) was the son of Edward Crawford and Anna Hendricks McAmis [The Link Family, page 496, No. 1713; and Supplement No. 1713]. Edward, Jr., was born August 10, 1926, at Washington, D.C. He married Eleanor Pearl Bickford February 4, 1949, at Washington. She was the daughter of Eben Atherton and Fannie Ursula Brown Bickford and was born November 2, 1927, at Floral Park, New York.

(Sup) 5616   i   Daniel Edward McAmis, born December 30, 1952.
(Sup) 5617   ii   Diana Lynn McAmis, born January 30, 1954.

(Sup) 3301 JAMES EDGAR EDWARDS, JR. (Anna[7], Daniel[6], Sarah[5], John Adam III[4], John Adam II[3], John Adam I[2], John Jacob[1]) was the son of James Edgar and Anna Hendricks McAmis Edwards [The Link Family, page 496, No. 1713; and Supplement No. 1713]. James, Jr., was born April 20, 1943, at Washington, D.C. He married Phyllis Mae Davis July 26, 1962, at Silver Spring, Maryland. She was the daughter of Winfred K. and Dorothy Tobin Davis and was born May 2, 1943, at Alexandria, Virginia. James and Phyllis resided at Front Royal, Virginia.

(Sup) 5618   i   Kimberly Maye Edwards, born December 2, 1966.

(Sup) 3302 BRUCE MELVIN CRANE (Esther[7], Daniel[6], Sarah[5], John Adam III[4], John Adam II[3], John Adam I[2], John Jacob[1]) was the son of Glenn Elmo and Esther Hendricks Crane [The Link Family, page 496, No. 1714; and Supplement No. 1714]. Bruce was born January 4, 1928. There is no record of his first wife, nor were there any children. Bruce married, second, Emma Elvina Weise, August 13, 1952. She was the daughter of Robert and Grace Weise and was born December 28, 1929, at Myersdale, Pennsylvania. Emma died July 17, 1974, and three days later her husband, Bruce, died on July 20, 1974. They are buried in Rest Haven Cemetery, Hagerstown, Maryland.

(Sup) 5619   i   Cynthia Diane Crane, born January 2, 1957.
(Sup) 5620   ii   Glen Elmo Crane, born August 13, 1960.

(Sup) 3303 REVA JEAN CRANE (Esther[7], Daniel[6], Sarah[5], John Adam III[4], John Adam II[3], John Adam I[2], John Jacob[1]) was the daughter of Glenn Elmo and Esther Hendricks Crane [The Link Family, page 496, No. 1714; and Supplement No. 1714]. Reva Jean was born August 24, 1929, at Hagerstown, Maryland. She married Franklin James Hoover October 17, 1947. Franklin was the son of Leon R. and Lillian Hoover and was born September 22, 1924, at Hagerstown.

(Sup) 5621   i   Margaret Ann Hoover, born May 8, 1948.
(Sup) 5622   ii   Sandra Christine Hoover, born May 17, 1949.

(Sup) 3297 SARAH VIRGINIA ANN HENDRICKS (Gilbert[7], Daniel[6], Sarah[5], John Adam III[4], John Adam II[3], John Adam I[2], John Jacob[1]) was the daughter of Gilbert Leo and Evelyn Maddox Hendricks [The Link Family, page 495, No. 1711; and Supplement No. 1711]. Sarah, who was named for her grandmother, was known as Sally. She was born July 27, 1936, at Duffields, Jefferson County, West Virginia. She married Thomas Franklin Anderson, Jr., April 14, 1963, at Dillon, South Carolina. He was the son of Thomas Franklin and Gladys Genevieve Gephart Anderson and was born February 15, 1935, at Richmond, Virginia. Sally graduated from Shepherd College, West Virginia, in 1957 with a B.A. degree in biology and in 1977 received a degree in accounting from Virginia Commonwealth University. Tom graduated from William and Mary College with a B.S. degree in business administration and from Virginia Commonwealth University with a M.A. degree in hospital administration and a postgraduate degree in accounting. Between 1960 and 1962 he served in the Air Force as a first lieutenant. Sally and Tom were employed in public accounting in Richmond, Virginia.

(Sup) 5608   i   Pamela Lynn Anderson, born December 16, 1963.
(Sup) 5609   ii   Kimberly Karyl Anderson, born June 16, 1965.
(Sup) 5610   iii   Sarah Ann Anderson, born March 10, 1969.
(Sup) 5611   iv   Laura Lee Anderson, born May 1, 1970.
(Sup) 5612   v   Mary Elizabeth Anderson, born December 16, 1972.

(Sup) 3298 PEARL HENDRICKS ENNIS (Mary[7], Daniel[6], Sarah[5], John Adam III[4], John Adam II[3], John Adam I[2], John Jacob[1]) was the daughter of Alvin Meredith and Mary Virginia Hendricks Ennis [The Link Family, page 496, No. 1712; and Supplement No. 1712]. Pearl was born March 30, 1921, at Charles Town, West Virginia. She married, first, Paul Whitacre, April 9, 1940. She married, second, Thomas Guy Reynolds, February 1, 1950, at Charles Town. He was the son of Thomas Guy and Lora Stotler Reynolds and was born November 30, 1912, at Martinsburg, West Virginia. He was a teacher in vocational education. Pearl died April 3, 1979, and is buried in Rosedale Cemetery at Martinsburg, West Virginia.

(Sup) 5613   i   Vanda Kay Reynolds, born October 29, 1951.
(Sup) 5614   ii   Ann Meredith Reynolds, born December 15, 1958.

(Sup) 3299 ALVIN MEREDITH ENNIS, JR. (Mary[7], Daniel[6], Sarah[5], John Adam III[4], John Adam II[3], John Adam I[2], John Jacob[1]) was the son of Alvin Meredith and Mary Virginia Hendricks Ennis [The Link Family, page 496, No. 1712; and Supplement No. 1712]. Alvin, Jr., was born March 21, 1924 at Charles Town, West Virginia. He married Betty Cooper November 27, 1952, at Charles Town. She was born July 31, 1929, at Washington, D.C. and was the daughter of Robert and Kathryn Alwin Cooper.

(Sup) 5615   i   Robert Meredith Ennis, born October 24, 1957.

(Sup) 3304 HILDA JOYCE CRANE (Esther[7], Daniel[6], Sarah[5], John Adam III[4], John Adam III[3], John Adam I[2], John Jacob[1]) was the daughter of Glenn Elmo and Esther Hendricks Crane [The Link Family, page 496, No. 1714; and Supplement No. 1714]. Hilda was born October 26, 1931. She married Frank Lowell Brewer, January 7, 1950 at Hagerstown, Maryland. Frank was the son of Charles Edward and Eva Viola Slick Brewer and was born September 15, 1932.

(Sup) 5623 i   Patrick Lowell Brewer, born August 26, 1950.
(Sup) 5624 ii   Michael Glen Brewer, born June 22, 1954.
(Sup) 5625 iii Eric Scott Brewer, born December 19, 1960.
(Sup) 5626 iv   Curtis Lee Brewer, born May 24, 1962.

(Sup) 3305 RICHARD LEE CRANE (Esther[7], Daniel[6], Sarah[5], John Adam III[4], John Adam III[3], John Adam I[2], John Jacob[1]) was the son of Glenn Elmo and Esther Hendricks Crane [The Link Family, page 496, No. 1714; and Supplement No. 1714]. Richard was born October 8, 1935. He married Martha Jane Newkirk August 18, 1962. She was born December 31, 1938. Richard graduated from Virginia Polytechnic Institute with a degree in mechanical engineering and was employed as superintendent of operations for West Penn Power Company, Hatfield Plant, Uniontown, Pennsylvania. Martha received a degree in secondary education from Towson Normal School, Maryland.

(Sup) 5627 i   Melanie Lynn Crane, born September 25, 1963.
(Sup) 5628 ii   Julia Irena Crane, born September 14, 1964.
(Sup) 5629 iii Richard Denton Crane, born July 1, 1967.
(Sup) 5630 iv   Russell Gilbert Crane, born October 9, 1971.

(Sup) 3306 ROBERT CURTIS CRANE (Esther[7], Daniel[6], Sarah[5], John Adam III[4], John Adam III[3], John Adam I[2], John Jacob[1]) was the son of Glenn Elmo and Esther Hendricks Crane [The Link Family, page 496, No. 1714; and Supplement No. 1714]. Robert was born November 6, 1945, at Hagerstown, Maryland. He married Mary Katherine Griffiths August 26, 1969. She was born December 13, 1947, at Clarksburg, West Virginia. Robert received a B.S. degree in accounting from Salem College, West Virginia, and an M.B.A. degree from St. Bonaventure University, New York. He was a plant manager for Cummins Fleetguard, Lake Mills, Iowa.

(Sup) 5631 i   Robert Curtis Crane, Jr., born October 16, 1970.
(Sup) 5632 ii   Amy Marie Crane, born April 24, 1972.

(Sup) 3307 SARA LEE MOORE (Florence[7], Daniel[6], Sarah[5], John Adam III[4], John Adam III[3], John Adam I[2], John Jacob[1]) was the daughter of Charles William and Florence Hendricks Moore [The Link Family, page 496, No. 1715; and Supplement No. 1715]. Sara was born October 1, 1937 at Charles Town, West Virginia. She married, first, Paul Thomas Foley March 21, 1959. He was born March 7, 1938, the son of Joseph W. Foley of Arlington, Virginia. Sara and Paul were both graduates of Shepherd College, West Virginia. She was a librarian in the Arlington and Fairfax County Libraries. Sara and Paul were divorced April, 1967. She married, second, Carroll E. Bond October 23, 1970. He was born March 11, 1926, at Arlington, Virginia.

(Sup) 5633 i   Kimberly Moore Foley, born January 12, 1960.
(Sup) 5634 ii   Patrick William Foley, born April 1, 1961.
(Sup) 5635 iii Colleen Frances Foley, born February 27, 1963.

(Sup) 3308 LOU ELLEN MOORE (Florence[7], Daniel[6], Sarah[5], John Adam III[4], John Adam III[3], John Adam I[2], John Jacob[1]) was the daughter of Charles William and Florence Hendricks Moore [The Link Family, page 496, No. 1715; and Supplement No. 1715]. Lou Ellen was born September 1, 1941 at Charles Town, West Virginia. She was a graduate of Marjorie Webster Junior College, Washington, D.C. She worked as a medical secretary for several years before going into real estate sales. Lou Ellen married Thomas Baille Olin April 24, 1965, at the National Cathedral in Washington, D.C., where Thomas was employed as assistant verger, then as purchasing agent. He was born July 28, 1938, the son of Philip Jenks and Katherine Baille Olin of Washington, D.C.

(Sup) 5636 i   William Philip Olin, born July 26, 1966.
(Sup) 5637 ii   Thomas Scott Olin, born September 7, 1967.

(Sup) 3309 MARY ALICE MOORE (Florence[7], Daniel[6], Sarah[5], John Adam III[4], John Adam III[3], John Adam I[2], John Jacob[1]) was the daughter of Charles William and Florence Hendricks Moore [The Link Family, page 496, No. 1715; and Supplement No. 1715]. Mary Alice was born July 1, 1944 at Charles Town, West Virginia. After attending local schools, she spent a year at the Sorbonne in Paris, France. She married James Henry Lemen [Supplement No. 5006] of Summit Point, Jefferson County, West Virginia, May 10, 1965. James was born February 4, 1944 at Charles Town, West Virginia, the son of Thomas Henry and Nancy Elizabeth Osbourn Lemen of Jefferson County [Supplement No. 2781]. James owned and operated a lamp and brass business at Summit Point, West Virginia. Mary was employed in the insurance department of Jefferson Memorial Hospital. Their two children of are listed under James Henry Lemen [see Supplement No. 5006].

(Sup) 3310 LUCY HENDRICKS MOORE (Florence[7], Daniel[6], Sarah[5], John Adam III[4], John Adam III[3], John Adam I[2], John Jacob[1]) was the daughter of Charles William and Florence Hendricks Moore [The Link Family, page 496, No. 1715; and Supplement No. 1715]. Lucy was born January 11, 1949, at Charles Town, West Virginia. She attended Marjorie Webster Junior College, Washington, D.C., and West Virginia University. She was employed in the academic division of the University of Virginia Rehabilitation Center. Lucy married Richard Dulany Whiting June 12, 1982, at Charles Town. He was the son of Lt. Col. Carlyle Fairfax and Mary Testerman Whiting and was born December 12, 1947. Richard received a B.S.M.E. degree from Michigan State University and M.S. and Ph.D degrees from the University of Rochester. He was a senior engineer at Johns Hopkins University Applied Physics Laboratory.

(Sup) 5638 i   Sarah Carlyle Whiting, born February 29, 1984.

(Sup) 3314   JOHN ROBERT SIMS (Sarah[7], Daniel[6], Sarah[5], John Adam III[4], John Adam II[3], John Adam I[2], John Jacob[1]) was the son of Woodrow Wilson and Sarah Hendricks Sims [The Link Family, page 497, No. 1717; and Supplement No. 1717]. John was born March 17, 1944. He died in an automobile accident October 27, 1976, in North Carolina and is buried in Elmwood Cemetery at Shepherdstown, West Virginia.

(Sup) 3315   REBECCA ANN HENDRICKS (William[7], Daniel[6], Sarah[5], John Adam III[4], John Adam II[3], John Adam I[2], John Jacob[1]) was the daughter of William Knox and Dorothy Foxworth Hendricks [The Link Family, page 497, No. 1718; and Supplement No. 1718]. Rebecca was born August 10, 1942 at Hopewell, Virginia. She married James Alan Parmenter of Red Gate, Maine, September 27, 1960. James was born October 28, 1939, at Boston, Massachusetts and was adopted by his grandmother Mary Ann Parmenter. He was an engineer for Allied Chemical Corporation at Hopewell, Virginia.

(Sup) 5647   i   Marie Antoinette Parmenter, born Oct 20, 1961.

(Sup) 3316   WILLIAM KNOX HENDRICKS, JR. (William[7], Daniel[6], Sarah[5], John Adam III[4], John Adam II[3], John Adam I[2], John Jacob[1]) was the son of William Knox and Dorothy Foxworth Hendricks [The Link Family, page 497, No. 1718; and Supplement No. 1718]. William, Jr., was born March 17, 1944 at Hopewell, Virginia. He married Doris Jean Lowe October 5, 1967. She was the daughter of John David and Ruby Virginia Toombs Lowe and was born November 16, 1949, at Gates, North Carolina. William was employed by Firestone Synthetic Fibers at Hopewell, Virginia.

(Sup) 5648   i   William Wayne Hendricks, born October 7, 1972.
(Sup) 5649   ii   Melanie Dawn Hendricks, born September 9, 1976.

(Sup) 3317   JOHN WAYNE HENDRICKS (William[7], Daniel[6], Sarah[5], John Adam III[4], John Adam II[3], John Adam I[2], John Jacob[1]) was the son of William Knox and Dorothy Foxworth Hendricks [The Link Family, page 497, No. 1718; and Supplement No. 1718]. John was born May 31, 1946 at Hopewell, Virginia. He married Carrolyn Marie Hood of Machias, Maine, November 27, 1970. Carrolyn was born August 5, 1954, the daughter of Carroll Edward and Norma Adell Ramsdell Hood. Wayne was employed by the Phillips Petroleum Company at Whitneyville, Maine.

(Sup) 5650   i   Christopher Allen Hendricks, born June 19, 1972.
(Sup) 5651   ii   Shawn Wayne Hendricks, born June 12, 1976.

(Sup) 3311   DANIEL WEBSTER HENDRICKS, IV (Daniel[7], Daniel[6], Sarah[5], John Adam III[4], John Adam II[3], John Adam I[2], John Jacob[1]) was the son of Daniel Webster and Margaret Polhamus Hendricks, III [The Link Family, page 496, No. 1716; and Supplement No. 1716]. Daniel, IV, was born May 30, 1935, at Shenandoah Junction, Jefferson County, West Virginia. He married Peggy Louise Boyd August 1, 1953. She was the daughter of Herbert L. and Elizabeth Creamer Boyd. Daniel and Peggy owned and operated a country store.

(Sup) 5640   i   Cynthia Lynn Hendricks, born April 1, 1955.
(Sup) 5641   ii   Dana Louise Hendricks, born March 4, 1958.

(Sup) 3312   SARAH MARGARET HENDRICKS (Daniel[7], Daniel[6], Sarah[5], John Adam III[4], John Adam II[3], John Adam I[2], John Jacob[1]) was the daughter of Daniel Webster and Sarah Polhamus Hendricks [The Link Family, page 496, No. 1716; and Supplement No.1716]. Sarah Margaret was born January 3, 1938, at Charles Town, West Virginia. She trained as a nurse at Washington, D.C., and Los Angeles, California. Sarah married Marvin John Potter July 27, 1957, at Uvilla, Jefferson County, West Virginia. John was the son of Frederick Cecil and Maryd Bell Potter and was born in 1933 in Pershing County, Nevada. He performed his undergraduate work at Stanford University, California, medical training at George Washington University, and specialty training at Cleveland Clinic, Ohio. John served in the Medical Corps of the U.S. Navy, where he was Chief of Dependent Services. He then practiced obstetrics and gynecology at Monterey Park and Marina del Ray, California.

(Sup) 5642   i   Jeffrey Glenn Potter, born January 14, 1959.
(Sup) 5643   ii   Daniel Allan Potter, born February 4, 1964.
(Sup) 5644   iii   Mark Christopher Potter, born December 3, 1968.

(Sup) 3313   MARY ELLEN HENDRICKS (Daniel[7], Daniel[6], Sarah[5], John Adam III[4], John Adam II[3], John Adam I[2], John Jacob[1]) was the daughter of Daniel Webster and Sarah Polhamus Webster [The Link Family, page 496, No. 1716; and Supplement No. 1716]. Mary Ellen was born October 11, 1945, at Charles Town, West Virginia. She attended Shepherd College, West Virginia, and received a B.S. degree in dietetics from the University of California at Los Angeles. Mary Ellen married Stephen Peter Pastor December 30, 1972, at Las Vegas, Nevada. He was the son of Peter Paul and Marcella Bromenscheukel Pastor and was born at La Puente, California. Stephen received a B.A. degree in psychology from the University of California at Los Angele and was employed as head of commercial loans by the Federal Deposit Insurance Company.

(Sup) 5645   i   Stephanie Marie Pastor, born August 4, 1975.
(Sup) 5646   ii   Christopher Steven Pastor, born July 20, 1977.

(Sup) 3317A   KENNETH LEE HENDRICKS (William[7], Daniel[6], Sarah[5], John Adam III[4], John Adam II[3], John Adam I[2], John Jacob[1]) the son of William Knox and Dorothy Foxworth Hendricks [The Link Family, page 497, No. 1718; and Supplement No. 1718]. Kenneth was born January 26, 1950, at Hopewell, Virginia. He married Carol Ann Bergeron August 12, 1969. She was the daughter of Rosario and Constance Marie Terault Bergeron and was born April 15, 1951, at Holyoke, Massachusetts. Kenneth attended Southeastern Baptist Seminary, North Carolina, and became a Baptist minister.

(Sup) 5652   i   Jeffery David Hendricks, born February 7, 1970.
(Sup) 5653   ii   Daniel Joseph Hendricks, born December 31, 1977.

(Sup) 3318   MARTHA ANN BLY (Rebecca[7], Daniel[6], Sarah[5], John Adam III[4], John Adam II[3], John Adam I[2], John Jacob[1]) was the daughter of Walter Merlin and Rebecca Hendricks Bly [The Link Family, page 497, No. 1719; and Supplement No. 1719]. Martha was born April 10, 1941 at Winchester, Virginia. She attended Madison College and the University of Virginia. She was a teacher of Latin in the Frederick County Virginia Schools. Martha married Wolfgang Rudolph Schmeller August 24, 1963, at Winchester, Virginia. He was the son of Rudolph Schmeller and Liska Lydia Bergmann Schmeller and was born September 10, 1935, at Johnson City, New York. Wolfgang attended Madison College and Bates College, Lewiston, Maine, where he was a Phi Beta Kappa. He became a teacher of government in the Winchester (Virginia) Public School System.

(Sup) 5654   i   Rachel Hendricks Schmeller, born Aug 19, 1969.
(Sup) 5655   ii   Sara Bergmann Schmeller, born November 1, 1972.

(Sup) 3319   DONALD MAXWELL WALTER, III (Genevieve[7], Daniel[6], Sarah[5], John Adam III[4], John Adam II[3], John Adam I[2], John Jacob[1]) was the son of Donald Maxwell and Genevieve Hendricks Walter, Jr. [The Link Family, page 497, No. 1720; and Supplement No. 1720]. Donald, III, was born June 7, 1947 at Winchester, Virginia. He attended Augusta Military Academy at Fort Defiance, Virginia. In October 1964 Donald enlisted in the U.S. Navy and served in the USS Chemung (AO-30) until his discharge in 1968. He married, first, Rebecca Jane Travers October 4, 1969, at Stephenson, Virginia. She was the daughter of Lewis A. and Margaret Travers of Clarke County. Donald and Rebecca were divorced August, 1976. He married, second, Francine Patricia Boisvert. She was the daughter of Camille and Lillianne Pepin Boisvert and was born October 22, 1950, at Rock Island, Quebec. Donald operated an ambulance service with his parents at Winchester.

CHILDREN OF DONALD AND REBECCA

(Sup) 5656   i   Donald Maxwell Walter IV, born May 12, 1970.
(Sup) 5657   ii   Carol Ann Walter, born March 14, 1971.

CHILD OF DONALD AND FRANCINE

(Sup) 5658   iii Michael Anthony Walter, born July 31, 1981.

(Sup) 3320   JULIA ANN WALTER (Genevieve[7], Daniel[6], Sarah[5], John Adam III[4], John Adam II[3], John Adam I[2], John Jacob[1]) was the daughter of Donald Maxwell and Genevieve Hendricks Walter, Jr. [The Link Family, page 497, No. 1720; and Supplement No. 1720]. Julia was born July 24, 1949 at Winchester, Virginia. She received an Associate in Science degree from Southern Seminary College, Buena Vista, Virginia. She married George Frederick Linne at Winchester on October 14, 1972. He was born October 4, 1942, the son of George Francis and Audria Marie Unger Linne of St. Louis, Missouri. George received his education at the University of Missouri. He was employed as vice president of the Central States Products Company, St. Louis, Missouri, and then established a business consulting company.

(Sup) 5658A   i   Scott Bryan Linne, born September 26, 1977.
(Sup) 5658B   ii   Laura Ann Linne, born December 14, 1981.

(Sup) 3321   DONALD ALLEN LINK (Daniel[7], Daniel[6], John[5], John Adam III[4], John Adam II[3], John Adam I[2], John Jacob[1]) was the son of Daniel Tanner and Elizabeth Gartrell Link [The Link Family, page 497, No. 1721]. Donald was born October 12, 1942, at Washington, D.C.

(Sup) 3322   RICHARD GALE DOLLY (Eleanor[7], Edith[6], John[5], John Adam III[4], John Adam II[3], John Adam I[2], John Jacob[1]) was the son of Woodrow and Eleanor Myers Dolly [The Link Family, page 497, No. 1723]. Richard was born July 24, 1943.

(Sup) 3323   SANDRA LEE EYE (Dorothy[7], Edith[6], John[5], John Adam III[4], John Adam II[3], John Adam I[2], John Jacob[1]) was the daughter of Stanley Earl and Dorothy Myers Eye [The Link Family, page 497, No. 1724]. Sandra was born June 20, 1946. She married Andrew Cavalier.

3324   NEVA SUE REINHART (James[7], Alvey[6], Mary[5], John Adam III[4], John Adam II[3], John Adam I[2], John Jacob[1]) was born October 21, 1920. She married James E. Miller, June 21, 1941. James, son of Emil Miller, was born September 19, 1918.

(Sup) 5659   i   Barbara Jean Miller, born September 1, 1944.
(Sup) 5660   ii   Sandra Sue Miller, born October 5, 1946.

3325   JAMES ANDREW REINHART, JR. (James[7], Alvey[6], Mary[5], John Adam III[4], John Adam II[3], John Adam I[2], John Jacob[1]) was born November 3, 1921. James enlisted in the flying service during World War II His plane was shot down in the Pacific, April 16, 1945. He parachuted to safety but was captured at once by the Japanese, who put him on trial May 12, 1945, and sentenced him to death. His captors executed him about May 15, 1945.

3326   PEGGY SUE McNEIL (Neva[7], Alvey[6], Mary[5], John Adam III[4], John Adam II[3], John Adam I[2], John Jacob[1]) was born March b, 1925. She married James Gordon Curry, March 7, 1945. James was the son of James and Jane Curry and was born November 15, 1924.

(Sup) 5661   i   Susan Gay Curry, born December 22, 1945.
(Sup) 5662   ii   Elizabeth Ann Curry, born January 15, 1947.

3327 DONALD EUGENE REINHART (Harry[7], Alvey[6], Mary[5], John Adam III[4], John Adam II[3], John Adam I[2], John Jacob[1]) was born March 19, 1933.

3328 GARY DEAN REINHART (Harry[7], Alvey[6], Mary[5], John Adam III[4], John Adam II[3], John Adam I[2], John Jacob[1]) was born May 6, 1936.

3329 CHARLES PRESTON BALES, JR. (Deborah[7], John Enoch[6], John[5], Susannah[4], Jacob[3], John Adam I[2], John Jacob[1]) was born March 2, 1900. He died August 8, 1931.

3330 ANDERSON RHODES STONE (Henry[7], John Enoch[6], John[5], Susannah[4], Jacob[3], John Adam I[2], John Jacob[1]) was born in May, 1905. He had no children.

3331 ONALEE STONE (Henry[7], John Enoch[6], John[5], Susannah[4], Jacob[3], John Adam I[2], John Jacob[1]) was born in July, 1906. She married Earl Vogt.

3332 ROBERT L. ZIMMERMAN, JR. (Katherine[7], John Enoch[6], John[5], Susannah[4], Jacob[3], John Adam I[2], John Jacob[1]) was born March 6, 1908.

3333 GEORGE WELLINGTON STONE (George[7], John Enoch[6], John[5], Susannah[4], Jacob[3], John Adam I[2], John Jacob[1]) was born October 15, 1944, at Lexington, Kentucky.

3334 HUGH BENJAMIN THOMAS, JR. (Sara[7], John Enoch[6], John[5], Susannah[4], Jacob[3], John Adam I[2], John Jacob[1]) was born September 14, 1918, at Springfield, Ohio.

3335 LAURA MAE THOMAS (Sara[7], John Enoch[6], John[5], Susannah[4], Jacob[3], John Adam I[2], John Jacob[1]) was born February 21, 1921, at Dayton, Ohio.

3336 BETTY STONE THOMAS (Sara[7], John Enoch[6], John[5], Susannah[4], Jacob[3], John Adam I[2], John Jacob[1]) was born February 18, 1929, at Paris, Kentucky.

3337 OLLIE LINK TARPLEY (Ethelyn[7], Iva[6], Eli[5], Israel[4], Jacob[3], John Adam I[2], John Jacob[1]) was born April 12, 1900, in Nodaway County, Missouri, where she died February 20, 1914.

3338 SARAH ELLEN TARPLEY (Ethelyn[7], Iva[6], Eli[5], Israel[4], Jacob[3], John Adam I[2], John Jacob[1]) was born May 1, 1902, in Nodaway County, Missouri. She married Harry Edwin McPherron, June 4, 1922.
(Sup) 5663   i   Louis Albert McPherson, born November 6, 1923.
(Sup) 5664   ii   Faye Edwyna McPherson, born October 19, 1926.
(Sup) 5665   iii   Marion Dale McPherson, born September 29, 1928.

3339 ROXIE MAY TARPLEY (Ethelyn[7], Iva[6], Eli[5], Israel[4], Jacob[3], John Adam I[2], John Jacob[1]) was born May 29, 1904, in Nodaway County, Missouri. She married Rexford Blaine Whitt, January 10, 1925.
(Sup) 5666   i   Sally May Whitt, born September 11, 1930.

3340 - PAULINE LINK (Alvah[7], John[6], Eli[5], Israel[4], Jacob[3], John Adam I[2], John Jacob[1]) was born July 14, 1910, in Platte County, Missouri. She married Charles R. Steincross, November 17, 1915, at San Diego, California. Charles was born November 17, 1918, in Vernon County, Missouri.

3341 IRENE LINK (Alvah[7], John[6], Eli[5], Israel[4], Jacob[3], John Adam I[2], John Jacob[1]) was born January 5, 1912, in Platte County, Missouri. She married Joseph Travis McCormick, January 29, 1932, at Kansas City, Missouri. Joseph was born November 22, 1907, at Waldron, Missouri.
(Sup) 5667   i   Mary Jo McCormick, born March 17, 1937.

3342 ALVA LAVOYD LINK (Alvah[7], John[6], Eli[5], Israel[4], Jacob[3], John Adam I[2], John Jacob[1]) was born June 8, 1914.

3343 M. FORD LINK (Alvah[7], John[6], Eli[5], Israel[4], Jacob[3], John Adam I[2], John Jacob[1]) was born March 7, 1916. He married Jeanette Smith.

3344 OLA MARGUERITE LINK (Mahlon[7], Jefferson[6], Eli[5], Israel[4], Jacob[3], John Adam I[2], John Jacob[1]) was born December 25, 1916, at Cyril, Oklahoma. She married James Clinton McQuary, May 14, 1936, at Seligman, Missouri. James was born at Seligman, May 14, 1913.
(Sup) 5668   i   Sandra Lee McQuary, born March 8, 1944.
(Sup) 5669   ii   Terry Lee McQuary, born March 28, 1948.

3345 BONNAS ULYSSES RUDY (Lucy[7], Jefferson[6], Eli[5], Israel[4], Jacob[3], John Adam I[2], John Jacob[1]) was born April 15, 1917, at Cyril, Oklahoma. He married Charlotte Jeanne Merritt, April 21, 1946, at Oklahoma City, Oklahoma. Charlotte was the daughter of John W. and Carolyn G. Hawkinson Merritt and was born August 10, 1923, at Oklahoma City.
(Sup) 5670   i   Clifford Merritt Rudy, born June 10, 1947.

3346 BONITA BELLE RUDY (Lucy[7], Jefferson[6], Eli[5], Israel[4], Jacob[3], John Adam I[2], John Jacob[1]) was born August 31, 1918, at Cyril, Oklahoma. She married Clifford Warren Bernard, September 13, 1936. Clifford was born December 11, 1917, at Yukon, Oklahoma, and was the son of Rex and Ollie Bales Bernard.
(Sup) 5671   i   Sue Ellen Bernard, born February 10, 1938.
(Sup) 5672   ii   Rudy Warren Bernard, born August 2, 1943.

3347 DORA MAE RUDY (Lucy[7], Jefferson[6], Eli[5], Israel[4], Jacob[3], John Adam I[2], John Jacob[1]) was born December 3, 1925, at El Reno, Oklahoma. She married Lonnie E. Dalton, August 7, 1944, at Long Beach, California. Lonnie was born January 15, 1924, at Holiday, Texas, and was the son of Rawling T. and Mary Spencer Dalton.

3348 JOHN WALTER CLEMENTS (Frances[7], Eliza[6], Eli[5], Israel[4], Jacob[3], John Adam I[2], John Jacob[1]) was born September 1, 1918. He married Eunice Stover, August 17, 1939.

3349 HAROLD LINK CLEMENTS (Frances[7], Eliza[6], Eli[5], Israel[4], Jacob[3], John Adam I[2], John Jacob[1]) was born August 9, 1920. He married Lenore Blalock, July 30, 1940. On October 25, 1942, Harold married Bonnie Whisler.

CHILD OF HAROLD AND LENORE
(Sup) 5673   i   Linda Sue Clements, born September 16, 1941.

CHILDREN OF HAROLD AND BONNIE
(Sup) 5674   ii   Donald Ray Clements, born November 23, 1943.
(Sup) 5675   iii   Kay Darlene Clements, born September 16, 1946.

3350 WILLIAM RAY CLEMENTS (Frances[7], Eliza[6], Eli[5], Israel[4], Jacob[3], John Adam I[2], John Jacob[1]) was born November 29, 1926. He died June 2, 1943.

3351 NELSON WAYNE CLEMENTS (Frances[7], Eliza[6], Eli[5], Israel[4], Jacob[3], John Adam I[2], John Jacob[1]) was born August 10, 1928.

3352 PHILLIP D. EYER (Veleda[7], David[6], Eli[5], Israel[4], Jacob[3], John Adam I[2], John Jacob[1]) was born February 2, 1940.

3353 PATRICIA ANN LINK (David[7], David[6], Eli[5], Israel[4], Jacob[3], John Adam I[2], John Jacob[1]) was born April 5, 1945, at Kansas City, Missouri.

3354 PAUL ALLEN LINK (David[7], David[6], Eli[5], Israel[4], Jacob[3], John Adam I[2], John Jacob[1]) was born October 30, 1946, at Kansas City, Missouri.

3355 ROBERT OSCAR BROWN (Ira[7], Katherine[6], Sarah[5], Israel[4], Jacob[3], John Adam I[2], John Jacob[1]) was born April 6, 1908, at Kansas City, Kansas. He married Luella Belle Butler, December 2, 1930, at Liberty, Missouri. Luella was the daughter of Charles James and May Belle Young Butler and was born January 22, 1907, at Seneca, Kansas.

3356 EDNA RUBY BROWN (Ira[7], Katherine[6], Sarah[5], Israel[4], Jacob[3], John Adam I[2], John Jacob[1]) was born July 11, 1910, at Kansas City, Kansas. She married Harold R. Guinn, October 29, 1930, at Leavenworth, Kansas.

3357 LAWRENCE LEE BROWN (Ira[7], Katherine[6], Sarah[5], Israel[4], Jacob[3], John Adam I[2], John Jacob[1]) was born November 9, 1912, at Kansas City Kansas. He married June De Vault, July 10, 1933.

3358 HARVEY WINFIELD BROWN (Ira[7], Katherine[6], Sarah[5], Israel[4], Jacob[3], John Adam I[2], John Jacob[1]) was born August 2, 1916, at Kansas City, Kansas.

3359 EARL REYNOLDS BROWN (Ira[7], Katherine[6], Sarah[5], Israel[4], Jacob[3], John Adam I[2], John Jacob[1]) was born November 10, 1917, at Kansas City, Kansas. He married Helen Mitchell, October 29, 1940, at Kansas City, Kansas. Helen, daughter of Walter E. and Freda Clara Arndt Mitchell, was born September 9, 1921. Earl was a pilot and flight instructor.

3360 FLOYD KENNETH BROWN (Ira[7], Katherine[6], Sarah[5], Israel[4], Jacob[3], John Adam I[2], John Jacob[1]) was born January 12, 1919, at Kansas City, Kansas.

3361 IRIS EMMA JEANE BROWN (Ira[7], Katherine[6], Sarah[5], Israel[4], Jacob[3], John Adam I[2], John Jacob[1]) was born September 9, 1922, at Kansas City, Kansas. She married Warren David Griffith, December 21, 1942, at Kansas City, Kansas. Warren was the son of Thomas John and Emma Shaw Griffith and was born February 28, 1921, at Kansas City, Kansas.

(Sup) 5681   i   Warren David Griffith, Jr., born March 7, 1946.

3362 ESTHER VIOLA BROWN (Ira[7], Katherine[6], Sarah[5], Israel[4], Jacob[3], John Adam I[2], John Jacob[1]) was born March 27, 1925, at Kansas City, Kansas, where she married Harlan LeRoy Smith, December 7, 1944. Harlan was born November 27, 1925, at Kansas City, Kansas.

(Sup) 5682   i   D'Arlynn Kay Smith, born September 1, 1947.

3363 WAYNE PERRY BROWN (Ira[7], Katherine[6], Sarah[5], Israel[4], Jacob[3], John Adam I[2], John Jacob[1]) was born February 26, 1928, at Kansas City, Kansas.

3364 JACK NORMAN BROWN (Ira[7], Katherine[6], Sarah[5], Israel[4], Jacob[3], John Adam I[2], John Jacob[1]) was born July 2, 1929, at Kansas City, Kansas.

3365 LEVINA KUYKENDALL (James[7], John[6], Sarah[5], Israel[4], Jacob[3], John Adam I[2], John Jacob[1]) was born December 21, 1918, in Platte County, Missouri. She married Phillip Orman.

3366 MARIE JOSEPHINE KUYKENDALL (James[7], John[6], Sarah[5], Israel[4], Jacob[3], John Adam I[2], John Jacob[1]) was born January 13, 1921, in Platte County, Missouri.

3367 ANABEL KUYKENDALL (James[7], John[6], Sarah[5], Israel[4], Jacob[3], John Adam I[2], John Jacob[1]) was born September 29, 1924, in Platte County, Missouri. She married James Park.

3368 CALVIN STEINER BURRIER (Daniel[7], Calvin[6], Daniel[5], Elizabeth[4], Thomas[3], John Adam I[2], John Jacob[1]) was born November 8, 1907, at Walkersville, Maryland. He married Margaret Bossard, June 2, 1928, at Thurmont, Maryland. Margaret was born April 26, 1910, at Ellicott City, Maryland.

(Sup) 5683   i   Calvin Steiner Burrier, Jr., born August 20, 1929.
(Sup) 5684   ii   George Carrol Burrier, born March 16, 1931.
(Sup) 5685   iii Howard Grayson Burrier, born September 9, 1932.
(Sup) 5686   iv   Margaret Elizabeth Burrier, born August 3, 1935.
(Sup) 5687   v   Ann Wesley Burrier, born July 23, 1938.
(Sup) 5688   vi   Nancy Elaine Burrier, born January 25, 1940.
(Sup) 5689   vii Mary Jane Burrier, born January 25, 1940.
(Sup) 5690   viii Barbara Mae Burrier, born July 11, 1941.
(Sup) 5691   ix   James Stevens Burrier, born October 19, 1943.
(Sup) 5692   x   Cheryl Revelle Burrier, born March 18, 1945.
(Sup) 5693   xi   Kenneth Eugene Burrier, born June 28, 1946.

3369 MARY ELIZABETH BURRIER (Daniel[7], Calvin[6], Daniel[5], Elizabeth[4], Thomas[3], John Adam I[2], John Jacob[1]) was born October 21, 1909, at Walkersville, Maryland. She married Elroy Grimes, September 22 1928, at Walkersville. Elroy was the son of C. Frank Grimes and was born July 25, 1911, at Walkersville.

(Sup) 5694   i   John Grayson Grimes, born October 29, 1935.
(Sup) 5695   ii   Alverda Mae Grimes, born December 29, 1936.
(Sup) 5696   iii Ruth Florence Grimes, born March 25, 1938.
(Sup) 5697   iv   James Staley Grimes, born September 9, 1939.
(Sup) 5698   v   Robert Donald Grimes, born December 19, 1941.

3370 KATHRYN MAE BURRIER (Daniel[7], Calvin[6], Daniel[5], Elizabeth[4], Thomas[3], John Adam I[2], John Jacob[1]) was born December 19, 1910, at Walkersville, Maryland. She married Harold Stull, October 2, 1935, at Walkersville. Harold was born April 3, 1908, at Lewistown, Maryland.

3371 WILMA ALVERDA BURRIER (Daniel[7], Calvin[6], Daniel[5], Elizabeth[4], Thomas[3], John Adam I[2], John Jacob[1]) was born March 20, 1913, near Woodsboro, Maryland. She married Ira Staley Grimes, March 14, 1934, at Ellicott City, Maryland. Ira was born December 22, 1913, at Frederick, Maryland.

3372 MILDRED IRENE BURRIER (Daniel[7], Calvin[6], Daniel[5], Elizabeth[4], Thomas[3], John Adam I[2], John Jacob[1]) was born March 2, 1916, near Walkersville, Maryland.

3373 CHARLES DANIEL BURRIER (Daniel[7], Calvin[6], Daniel[5], Elizabeth[4], Thomas[3], John Adam I[2], John Jacob[1]) was born June 2, 1916, at Walkersville, Maryland. He married Mabel Wright, October 9, 1936, at Walkersville. Mabel, daughter of Clinton Wright, was born March 2, 1913, at Farnville, Virginia.

    (Sup) 5699 i Mary Louise Burrier, born October 25, 1939.
    (Sup) 5700 ii Betty Wright Burrier, born April 4, 1943.

3374 GRAYSON SYLVESTER BURRIER (Daniel[7], Calvin[6], Daniel[5], Elizabeth[4], Thomas[3], John Adam I[2], John Jacob[1]) was born March 14, 1918, at Walkersville, Maryland. He married Charlotte Eader, April 3, 1947. She was the daughter of Charles Eader and was born September 26, 1911, at Frederick, Maryland.

3375 GILMER RAMSBURG BURRIER (Daniel[7], Calvin[6], Daniel[5], Elizabeth[4], Thomas[3], John Adam I[2], John Jacob[1]) was born March 27, 1919, at Walkersville, Maryland. He married Ethel Corrine Baer, March 28, 1942, at Frederick, Maryland. Ethel was born at Utica, Maryland, September 24, 1923.

    (Sup) 5701 i William Grayson Burrier, born December 23, 1946.

3376 HAROLD JOSEPH BURRIER (Daniel[7], Calvin[6], Daniel[5], Elizabeth[4], Thomas[3], John Adam I[2], John Jacob[1]) was born March 29, 1922, near Walkersville, Maryland. He married Martha Flickinger, February 17, 1947. She was the daughter of Howard Flickinger and was born March 12, 1923, near Woodsboro, Maryland.

3377 PAUL MEREDITH BURRIER (Daniel[7], Calvin[6], Daniel[5], Elizabeth[4], Thomas[3], John Adam I[2], John Jacob[1]) was born January 30, 1924, at Walkersville, Maryland. He married Grace Kathleen Albaugh, May 1, 1945, at Mount Pleasant, Maryland. Grace was the daughter of Guy Milton Albaugh and was born May 5, 1923, at Bloomfield, Maryland.

    (Sup) 5702 i Marsha Faith Burrier, born July 24, 1946.

3378 GLENN MONROE BURRIER (Daniel[7], Calvin[6], Daniel[5], Elizabeth[4], Thomas[3], John Adam I[2], John Jacob[1]) was born January 10, 1925, at Walkersville, Maryland. He married Betty Kathleen Shelton, January 26, 1946, at Monrovia, Maryland. Betty was born December 10, 1925, at Frederick, Maryland.

3379 EDITH BURRIER (Mabel[7], Calvin[6], Daniel[5], Elizabeth[4], Thomas[3], John Adam I[2], John Jacob[1]) was born June 12, 1903, at Libertytown, Maryland. She married David Paul Greene, June 22, 1922, at Libertytown. David was born May 30, 1901, near New Windsor, Maryland.

    (Sup) 5703 i David Paul Greene, Jr., born January 26, 1923.
    (Sup) 5704 ii James Arnold Greene, born August 16, 1930.
    (Sup) 5705 iii Arvin Lloyd Greene, born December 28, 1936.

3380 EDITH GRACE BURRIER (Charles[7], Charles[6], Daniel[5], Elizabeth[4], Thomas[3], John Adam I[2], John Jacob[1]) was born May 16, 1897, at Doublin, Maryland. She married Edward Russell Gearinger, July 30, 1921, at Frederick, Maryland. Edward was born December 20, 1900, at Sharpsburg, Maryland.

    (Sup) 5706 i Anne Jane Gearinger, born July 3, 1922.
    (Sup) 5707 ii Charles Gearinger, born January 9, 1924.
    (Sup) 5708 iii Mary Alice Gearinger, born July 3, 1927.
    (Sup) 5709 iv Robert Gearinger, born November 3, 1931.

3381 CECELIA KATHERINE MURPHY (Nannie[7], Charles[6], Daniel[5], Elizabeth[4], Thomas[3], John Adam I[2], John Jacob[1]) was born April 13, 1898, at Walkersville, Maryland. She married Chester Clarence Mosier, January 11, 1922, at Indianapolis, Indiana. Chester was born July 20, 1898, at New Albany, Indiana. He was the son of Arthur Mosier.

    (Sup) 5710 i Chester Mosier, Jr., born March 8, 1923.

3382 CHARLES JOSEPH MURPHY (Nannie[7], Charles[6], Daniel[5], Elizabeth[4], Thomas[3], John Adam I[2], John Jacob[1]) was born April 8, 1900, at Walkersville, Maryland. He attended grade schools at Walkersville, high school at Kentland, Indiana, and entered Purdue University in 1920, graduating in 1924. At Purdue he played varsity football and coached high school football for four years after graduation. In 1928 he joined the Purdue University faculty and went into agricultural extension work with the university and the U. S. Department of Agriculture. Charles married June Hesler, December 25, 1926, at Westfield, Indiana. June was born June 26, 1907, at Altoona, Pennsylvania.

    (Sup) 5711 i Patricia June Murphy, born July 23, 1928.
    (Sup) 5712 ii Dorothy Ann Murphy, born December 30, 1929.
    (Sup) 5713 iii Joseph Murphy, born April 7, 1931.
    (Sup) 5714 iv Virginia Mabel Murphy, born March 29, 1933.
    (Sup) 5715 v Robert Murphy, born March 29, 1935.
    (Sup) 5716 vi Rose Mary Murphy, born June 14, 1938.
    (Sup) 5717 vii Nancy Lee Murphy, born January 10, 1940.

3383 LAWSON WINFIELD MURPHY (Nannie[7], Charles[6], Daniel[5], Elizabeth[4], Thomas[3], John Adam I[2], John Jacob[1]). He married Maurine Stewart.

    (Sup) 5718 i Betty Lou Murphy.
    (Sup) 5719 ii George Elmer Murphy.
    (Sup) 5720 iii Phyllis Ann Murphy.
    (Sup) 5721 iv Richard Lee Murphy.

3384 HELEN EUGENE MURPHY (Nannie[7], Charles[6], Daniel[5], Elizabeth[4], Thomas[3], John Adam I[2], John Jacob[1]) was born May 1, 1903, at Walkersville, Maryland. She married Howard H. Rasher, April 23, 1924, at Chicago, Illinois. Howard was the son of William John Rasher and was born January 31, 1900, at Logansport, Indiana.

    (Sup) 5722 i Howard Lewis Rasher, born February 27, 1925.
    (Sup) 5723 ii William Elmer Rasher, born November 25, 1927.

3385 CHARLES EDWIN OLAND (Nellie[7], Charles[6], Daniel[7], Elizabeth[4], Thomas[3], John Adam I[2], John Jacob[1]) was born October 5, 1896, near Walkersville, Maryland. He married Ethel Holt, January 12, 1916.

3385A THOMAS ROGER OLAND (Nellie[7], Charles[6], Daniel[7], Elizabeth[4], Thomas[3], John Adam I[2], John Jacob[1]) was born February 5, 1899, near Walkersville, Maryland. He died March 3, 1899.

3386 FRANCIS MONROE MUSSER (Fannie[7], Charles[6], Daniel[7], Elizabeth[4], Thomas[3], John Adam I[2], John Jacob[1]) was born October 27, 1917, at Baltimore, Maryland. He married Mary Rose Dukchant, November 1, 1941. Mary, daughter of John M. Dukchant, was born April 27, 1921, at Baltimore, Maryland.

3387 DOLORES SHIRLEY PATRICIA MERCER (Daniel[7], Catherine[6], Daniel[5], Elizabeth[4], Daniel[3], John Adam I[2], John Jacob[1]) was born January 24, 1927. She married James Francis Carver, August 9, 1947.

(Sup) 5724 i Michael Francis Carver, born April 28, 1948.

3388 DANIEL WILLIAM FRANCIS MERCER, JR. (Daniel[7], Catherine[6], Daniel[5], Elizabeth[4], Daniel[3], John Adam I[2], John Jacob[1]) was born May 26, 1934, at Baltimore, Maryland.

3389 JOSEPHINE AMELIA CRAMER (Ellis[7], Catherine[6], Daniel[5], Elizabeth[4], Daniel[3], John Adam I[2], John Jacob[1]) was born January 19, 1929, in Frederick County, Maryland.

3390 SHIRLEY ANN CRAMER (Ellis[7], Catherine[6], Daniel[5], Elizabeth[4], Daniel[3], John Adam I[2], John Jacob[1]) was born January 8, 1932, in Frederick County, Maryland.

3391 FRANK RIDGELEY CRAMER II (Ellis[7], Catherine[6], Daniel[5], Elizabeth[4], Daniel[3], John Adam I[2], John Jacob[1]) was born November 7, 1933, in Frederick County, Maryland.

3392 RICHARD ALLEN CRAMER (Ellis[7], Catherine[6], Daniel[5], Elizabeth[4], Daniel[3], John Adam I[2], John Jacob[1]) was born November 18, 1934, in Frederick County, Maryland.

3393 VIRGINIA ANN DAUGHERTY (Kathryn[7], Catherine[6], Daniel[5], Elizabeth[4], Daniel[3], John Adam I[2], John Jacob[1]) was born February 23, 1936, at Frederick, Maryland.

3394 EDWARD JACOB DAUGHERTY, JR. (Kathryn[7], Catherine[6], Daniel[5], Elizabeth[4], Daniel[3], John Adam I[2], John Jacob[1]) was born June 13, 1939, at Frederick, Maryland.

3394A CHARLES VICTOR MERCER (Charles[7], Catherine[6], Daniel[5], Elizabeth[4], Daniel[3], John Adam I[2], John Jacob[1]) was born February 10, 1940, at Frederick, Maryland.

3395 JOHN MILTON MERCER (Joseph[7], Catherine[6], Daniel[5], Elizabeth[4], Daniel[3], John Adam I[2], John Jacob[1]) was born January 25, 1941, at Frederick, Maryland.

3396 LARRY EUGENE MERCER (Joseph[7], Catherine[6], Daniel[5], Elizabeth[4], Daniel[3], John Adam I[2], John Jacob[1]) was born February 26, 1942, at Frederick, Maryland.

3397 DONNA LEA MERCER (Joseph[7], Catherine[6], Daniel[5], Elizabeth[4], Daniel[3], John Adam I[2], John Jacob[1]) was born August 7, 1943, at Frederick, Maryland.

3398 MAUDE IRENE HAHN (Nellie[7], Thomas[6], Sophia[5], Elizabeth[4], Daniel[3], John Adam I[2], John Jacob[1]) was born October 17, 1905, in Frederick County, Maryland. She married Harvey Franklin Shank, March 15, 1924, at Frederick, Maryland. Harvey was born December 2, 1903, in Frederick County. He was the son of Howard Franklin and Viola Virginia Killian Shank.

(Sup) 5725 i Anna Margaret Shank.
(Sup) 5726 ii Harvey Franklin Shank, Jr.
(Sup) 5727 iii Catherine Violet Shank.
(Sup) 5728 iv Richard Lee Shank.
(Sup) 5729 v Wayne Eugene Shank.

3399 AGNES MAE HAHN (Nellie[7], Thomas[6], Sohpia[5], Elizabeth[4], Daniel[3], John Adam I[2], John Jacob[1]) was born in Frederick County, Maryland. She married a Mr. Smith.

3400 CATHERINE LOUISE HAHN (Nellie[7], Thomas[6], Sophia[5], Elizabeth[4], Daniel[3], John Adam I[2], John Jacob[1]) was born in Frederick County, Maryland. She married a Mr. Strube.

3401 EDWARD MICHAEL HAHN (Nellie[7], Thomas[6], Sophia[5], Elizabeth[4], Daniel[3], John Adam I[2], John Jacob[1]) was born in Frederick County, Maryland.

3402 WILLIAM STEVEN HAHN, JR. (Nellie[7], Thomas[6], Sophia[5], Elizabeth[4], Daniel[3], John Adam I[2], John Jacob[1]) was born May 9, 1911, in Frederick County, Maryland.

3403 BERTHA DELORES HAHN (Nellie[7], Thomas[6], Sophia[5], Elizabeth[4], Daniel[3], John Adam I[2], John Jacob[1]) was born in Frederick County, Maryland. She married Constant Betson, October 22, 1948.

3404 ROLAND LAVERE HAHN (Nellie[7], Thomas[6], Sophia[5], Elizabeth[4], Daniel[3], John Adam I[2], John Jacob[1]) was born March 7, 1914, in Frederick County, Maryland, where he died August 17, 1914.

3405 MARIETTA INEZ HAHN (Nellie[7], Thomas[6], Sophia[5], Elizabeth[4], Daniel[3], John Adam I[2], John Jacob[1]) was born in Frederick County, Maryland. She married a Mr. Kinsey.

3406 CLYTHNIA VIOLETTE HAHN (Nellie[7], Thomas[6], Sophia[5], Elizabeth[4], Daniel[3], John Adam I[2], John Jacob[1]) was born August 25, 1917, at Frederick, Maryland. She married a Mr. DeLashmit, May 24, 1938, at Frederick.

(Sup) 5730 i Wanda Anita DeLashmit.
(Sup) 5731 ii Maurice Eugene DeLashmit.
(Sup) 5732 iii James William DeLashmit.
(Sup) 5733 iv Claudetta Yanice DeLashmit.

3407 JOHN ARTHUR HAHN (Nellie[7], Thomas[6], Sophia[5], Elizabeth[4], Daniel[3], John Adam I[2], John Jacob[1]) was born December 3, 1921, at Frederick, Maryland, where he died April 24, 1924.

3408 DONALD ANTHONY HAHN (Nellie[7], Thomas[6], Sophia[5], Elizabeth[4], Daniel[3], John Adam I[2], John Jacob[1]) was born at Frederick, Maryland.

3423 MARGARET FRANCES GREEN (Goldie[7], Annie[6], Sophia[5], Elizabeth[4], Daniel[3], John Adam I[2], John Jacob[1]) was born November 7, 1920, at Mount Pleasant, Maryland. She married Carl Lockner at Randlestown, Maryland, in 1936.

3424 CHARLES EDWARD GREEN (Goldie[7], Annie[6], Sophia[5], Elizabeth[4], Daniel[3], John Adam I[2], John Jacob[1]) was born April 18, 1922, at Mount Pleasant, Maryland. He married Grace Rebecca Moss, June 19, 1943, at San Luis Obispo, California.

3425 LUCILLE FLORENCE GREEN (Goldie[7], Annie[6], Sophia[5], Elizabeth[4], Daniel[3], John Adam I[2], John Jacob[1]) was born April 14, 1926, at Mount Pleasant, Maryland.

3426 CHARLES LEWIS GEISINGER (Lewis[7], Charles[6], Sophia[5], Elizabeth[4], Daniel[3], John Adam I[2], John Jacob[1]) was born May 3, 1926, at Ceresville, Maryland. He married Mary Louise Sauerwein, April 4, 1948.

3427 JOSEPH DANIEL GEISINGER (Lewis[7], Charles[6], Sophia[5], Elizabeth[4], Daniel[3], John Adam I[2], John Jacob[1]) was born January 16, 1929, near Walkersville, Maryland.

3428 HELEN BERYL GEISINGER (Lewis[7], Charles[6], Sophia[5], Elizabeth[4], Daniel[3], John Adam I[2], John Jacob[1]) was born October 8, 1931, near Walkersville, Maryland.

3429 LOUIS PHILLIP GREENWALD (Kent[7], Mary[6], Sarah[5], Adam[4], Daniel[3], John Adam I[2], John Jacob[1]) was born February 14, 1914, in Frederick County, Maryland.

3430 SARAH KATHERINE STITELY (Laura[7], Mary[6], Sarah[5], Adam[4], Daniel[3], John Adam I[2], John Jacob[1]) was born August 20, 1913, at Frederick, Maryland. She married Ernest Weddle, August 24, 1931, at Frederick.

3431 OSCAR BEATTY STITELY, JR. (Laura[7], Mary[6], Sarah[5], Adam[4], Daniel[3], John Adam I[2], John Jacob[1]) was born September 4, 1917, at Frederick, Maryland. He married Pauline Masser, May 28, 1939.
(Sup) 5735 † Ernest Oliver Stitely, born February 16, 1941.
(Sup) 5736 †† William Allen Stitely, born November 1, 1944.

3432 LOUIS ALBERT STITELY (Laura[7], Mary[6], Sarah[5], Adam[4], Daniel[3], John Adam I[2], John Jacob[1]) was born September 8, 1919, at Frederick, Maryland, where he died February 22, 1920.

3433 ALLEN HERBERT STITELY (Laura[7], Mary[6], Sarah[5], Adam[4], Daniel[3], John Adam I[2], John Jacob[1]) was born April 17, 1921, at Frederick, Maryland.

3434 MARY LOUISE WAESCHE (Sarah[7], Mary[6], Sarah[5], Adam[4], Daniel[3], John Adam I[2], John Jacob[1]) was born September 17, 1920, at Frederick, Maryland. She married Charles N. Davie, March 28, 1942.

3435 SARAH MAGDALENE WAESCHE (Sarah[7], Mary[6], Sarah[5], Adam[4], Daniel[3], John Adam I[2], John Jacob[1]) was born April 24, 1923, at Frederick, Maryland. She married William H. Benjamin, June 25, 1943.

3436 LEONARD RANDOLPH WAESCHE (Sarah[7], Mary[6], Sarah[5], Adam[4], Daniel[3], John Adam I[2], John Jacob[1]) was born July 25, 1927, at Frederick, Maryland.

3409 CAROLYN ELIZABETH HAHN (Nellie[7], Thomas[6], Sophia[5], Elizabeth[4], Daniel[3], John Adam I[2], John Jacob[1]) was born May 7, 1925, at Frederick, Maryland.

3410 NELLIE ANN HAHN (Nellie[7], Thomas[6], Sophia[5], Elizabeth[4], Daniel[3], John Adam I[2], John Jacob[1]) was born December 30, 1929, at Frederick, Maryland, where she died April 4, 1935.

3411 JOHN FRANCIS HAHN (Nellie[7], Thomas[6], Sophia[5], Elizabeth[4], Daniel[3], John Adam I[2], John Jacob[1]) was born November 29, 1933, at Frederick, Maryland.

3412 ANNIE INEZ HANSEN (Ollie[7], Thomas[6], Sophia[5], Elizabeth[4], Daniel[3], John Adam I[2], John Jacob[1]) was born April 18, 1906, at Frederick, Maryland. She married Lester Elliott Orrison, July 10, 1929, at Hagerstown, Maryland. Lester, son of Harry and Oda Shafer Orrison, was born September 6, 1907, at Frederick.

3413 JOHN ANDREW HANSEN, JR. (Ollie[7], Thomas[6], Sophia[5], Elizabeth[4], Daniel[3], John Adam I[2], John Jacob[1]) was born June 22, 1908, at Frederick, Maryland.

3414 BERNARD HAROLD HANSEN (Ollie[7], Thomas[6], Sophia[5], Elizabeth[4], Daniel[3], John Adam I[2], John Jacob[1]) was born December 23, 1917, at Frederick, Maryland, where he died December 23, 1917.

3415 JOHN H. CREAGER (Leslie[7], Ida[6], Sophia[5], Elizabeth[4], Daniel[3], John Adam I[2], John Jacob[1]) was born in October, 1920.

(Sup) 5734 † Frank Carlton Fiery, born June 12, 1948.

3416 WILLIAM S. CREAGER (Leslie[7], Ida[6], Sophia[5], Elizabeth[4], Daniel[3], John Adam I[2], John Jacob[1]) was born in January, 1922.

3417 WILLIAM CREAGER THIEDE (Mary[7], Ida[6], Sophia[5], Elizabeth[4], Daniel[3], John Adam I[2], John Jacob[1]) was born at Baltimore, Maryland. He married Madeline Elizabeth Motley, August 7, 1928. William died May 6, 1929, at Baltimore. He and Madeline had no children.

3418 DOROTHY LOUISE HAHN (Maude[7], Ida[6], Sophia[5], Elizabeth[4], Daniel[3], John Adam I[2], John Jacob[1]) was born June 7, 1913, at Woodsboro, Maryland. She married Frank Luther Fiery, June 19, 1943. Frank was born March 15, 1909.

3419 LENA MAE HAHN (Maude[7], Ida[6], Sophia[5], Elizabeth[4], Daniel[3], John Adam I[2], John Jacob[1]) was born February 21, 1915, at Woodsboro, Maryland. She married Timothy James Dressell, February 15, 1941, at Grand Rapids, Michigan.

3420 MAUDE ETHEL HAHN (Maude[7], Ida[6], Sophia[5], Elizabeth[4], Daniel[3], John Adam I[2], John Jacob[1]) was born February 3, 1917, at Frederick, Maryland.

3421 CHARLOTTE LA RUE GREEN (Goldie[7], Annie[6], Sophia[5], Elizabeth[4], Daniel[3], John Adam I[2], John Jacob[1]) was born January 10, 1916, at Mount Pleasant, Maryland. She married Walter Woods at Spartanburg, South Carolina.

3422 HARRY CLIFTON GREEN (Goldie[7], Annie[6], Sophia[5], Elizabeth[4], Daniel[3], John Adam I[2], John Jacob[1]) was born October 3, 1917, at Mount Pleasant, Maryland. He married Bettie Marie Hall at Walkersville, Maryland, August 9, 1946.

3437 MARTHA FOREMAN WAESCHE (Sarah[7], Mary[6], Sarah[5], Adam[4], Daniel[3], John Adam I[2], John Jacob[1]) was born November 24, 1928, at Thurmont, Maryland.

3438 HARRY LEE PEARRE TURNBULL (Isabella[7], Rosina Katherine[6], Sarah[5], Adam[4], Daniel[3], John Adam I[2], John Jacob[1]) was born December 1, 1927, at York, Pennsylvania.

3439 HARRY WARFIELD HUMMER (Katherine[7], Rosina Katherine[6], Sarah[5], Adam[4], Daniel[3], John Adam I[2], John Jacob[1]) was born March 30, 1943, at York, Pennsylvania.

(Sup) 3440 ETHEL HAMILTON LINK (Lewis[7], Adam[6], Daniel[5], Adam[4], Daniel[3], John Adam I[2], John Jacob[1]) was the daughter of Lewis Wilberforce and Ethel Jean (Hamilton) Link [The Link Family, page 511, No. 1862]. Ethel was born March 7, 1920, at Philadelphia, Pennsylvania. She married William G. Poe, February 20, 1943, at Trenton, New Jersey. William was the son of Clarence W. Poe and was born November 12, 1919, at Cleveland, Ohio. Ethel married, second, Andrew S. Petka, January 19, 1966, at Yardley, Pennsylvania. Andrew was the son of Stanley John and Mary Anna Petka and was born April 16, 1917, at Philadelphia.

(Sup) 5737   i Russell William Poe, born January 10, 1946.

(Sup) 3441 MARY ELIZABETH LINK (Eugene[7], Adam[6], Daniel[5], Adam[4], Daniel[3], John Adam I[2], John Jacob[1]) was the daughter of Eugene Bowers and Amanda Virginia (Maccubbin) Link [The Link Family, page 511, No. 1863]. Mary Elizabeth was born August 18, 1919, at Baltimore, Maryland. She married Donald Main Romney, December 14, 1940, at Baltimore. He was the son of Charles Wesley and Mary Jane Romney and was born December 31, 1919, at Baltimore.

(Sup) 5738   i Donald Main Romney, Jr., born December 1, 1942.
(Sup) 5739   ii Nancy Carol Romney, born September 6, 1948.

(Sup) 3442 JEAN ELLEN LINK (Eugene[7], Adam[6], Daniel[5], Adam[4], Daniel[3], John Adam I[2], John Jacob[1]) was the daughter of Eugene Bowers and Amanda Virginia (Maccubbin) Link [The Link Family, page 511, No. 1863]. Jean Ellen was born November 26, 1926, at Baltimore, Maryland. She married Harry Dawson Mitchell, July 9, 1948. He was born April 20, 1926.

(Sup) 5740   i James Dawson Mitchell, born January 10, 1951.
(Sup) 5741   ii David Bowers Mitchell, born March 11, 1953.

(Sup) 3443 GRACE MARIE ZUMSTEIN (Marie[7], Adam[6], Daniel[5], Adam[4], Daniel[3], John Adam I[2], John Jacob[1]) was the daughter of Frederick Allen and Marie Elizabeth (Link) Zumstein [The Link Family, page 511, No. 1864; and Supplement No. 1864]. Grace was born April 9, 1916, at Baltimore, Maryland. She married Alvin E. Leroy December 19, 1942, at Baltimore. He was the son of Paul Godfrey and Wilhelmina Leroy and was born at Baltimore June 24, 1913. Grace and Alvin were divorced in 1953. She married, second, Theodore George Hoster, November 25, 1969, at Annapolis, Maryland. Theodore was the son of Louis and Grace (Hellman) Hoster and was born July 13, 1909, at Columbus, Ohio. Theodore died May 21, 1971, at Easton, Maryland.

(Sup) 3444 JANE WHITE ZUMSTEIN (Marie[7], Adam[6], Daniel[5], Adam[4], Daniel[3], John Adam I[2], John Jacob[1]) was the daughter of Frederick Allen and Marie Link Zumstein [The Link Family, page 511, No. 1864; and Supplement No. 1864]. Jane was born December 25, 1917, at Baltimore, Maryland. She married Henry Adolph Koenig, III, September 20, 1941. He was the son of Henry Adolph Koenig, II, and was born September 14, 1912, at Easton, Maryland. Jane died June 30, 1976.

(Sup) 5742   i Patricia Marie Koenig, born July 4, 1946.
(Sup) 5743   ii Henry Adolph Koenig IV, born September 21, 1956.

(Sup) 3444A GRACE RUTH LINK (Ralph[7], Adam[6], Daniel[5], Adam[4], Daniel[3], John Adam I[2], John Jacob[1]) was the daughter of Ralph Aubry and Frances Perry Link [The Link Family, page 512, No. 1865; and Supplement No. 1865]. Grace was born October 8, 1953. She married Anthony Curtis Leonard November 8, 1971. He was born March 4, 1953.

(Sup) 5744   i Amy Ruth Leonard, born June 4, 1972.
(Sup) 5745   ii Daniel Curtis Leonard, born October 18, 1973.
(Sup) 5746 iii Stephen Anthony Leonard, born February 15, 1976.
(Sup) 5747   iv Matthew James Leonard, born April 30, 1978.

(Sup) 3444B REBEKAH ELIZABETH LINK (Ralph[7], Adam[6], Daniel[5], Adam[4], Daniel[3], John Adam I[2], John Jacob[1]) was the daughter of Ralph Aubrey and Frances Perry Link [The Link Family, page 512, No. 1865; and Supplement No. 1865]. She was born December 23, 1969.

3445 GEORGE TRELSTAD LINK (George[7], John[6], Adam[5], John[4], Peter[3], Matthias[2], John Jacob[1]) was born March 5, 1924, at Buckley, Washington. He studied at Seattle Pacific College and became an ordained minister, as had his Link ancestors for four generations.

3446 JOHN W. FORD III (John[7], Virginia[6], Adam[5], John[4], Peter[3], Matthias[2], John Jacob[1]) was born in Indianapolis. He lost his life in the service of his country during World War II.

3447 ELIZABETH FORD (Mark[7], Virginia[6], Adam[5], John[4], Peter[3], Matthias[2], John Jacob[1]) married J. H. Glenn and lived in Dallas, Texas.

(Sup) 5748   i Elizabeth Glenn.
(Sup) 5749   ii Virginia Glenn.
(Sup) 5750 iii James Glenn.
(Sup) 5751   iv Ruth Glenn.

3448 VIRGINIA FORD (Mark[7], Virginia[6], Adam[5], John[4], Peter[3], Matthias[2], John Jacob[1]) married J. S. Blakeney.

3449 HOMER GARBER (Hannah[7], Martin[6], Elizabeth[5], John[4], Peter[3], Matthias[2], John Jacob[1]) was born in Augusta County, Virginia.

3450 NINA VIOLA GARBER (Hannah^7, Martin^6, Elizabeth^5, John^4, Peter^3, Matthias^2, John Jacob^1) was born October 15, 1881, in Augusta County, Virginia. She married Elvin W. Kerr, December 8, 1901, at Barren Ridge, Virginia.

(Sup) 5752 i Thelma Kerr, born September 12, 1902.
(Sup) 5753 ii Mildred H. Kerr, born December 17, 1904.

3451 MOLLIE GARBER (Hannah^7, Martin^6, Elizabeth^5, John^4, Peter^3, Matthias^2, John Jacob^1) was born in Augusta County, Virginia.

3452 ELMER HENRY PAYNE (Belle^7, Emily^6, Elizabeth^5, John^4, Peter^3, Matthias^2, John Jacob^1) was born May 7, 1894, at Waynesboro, Virginia.

3453 WILLIAM MONTAGUE PAYNE (Belle^7, Emily^6, Elizabeth^5, John^4, Peter^3, Matthias^2, John Jacob^1) was born in December, 1896, in Augusta County, Virginia.

3454 HARRY WHITNEY PAYNE (Belle^7, Emily^6, Elizabeth^5, John^4, Peter^3, Matthias^2, John Jacob^1) was born March 31, 1906, at Staunton, Virginia. He married Reba Mae Crum, who was born May 1, 1908.

(Sup) 5754 i Marie Bell Payne, born September 7, 1931.
(Sup) 5755 ii Nancy Lee Payne, born February 16, 1936.

3455 MARIE LOUISE SELLERS (Rosa^7, Junius^6, Elizabeth^5, John^4, Peter^3, Matthias^2, John Jacob^1) was born in Augusta County, Virginia.

3456 JANIE STUART SELLERS (Rosa^7, Junius^6, Elizabeth^5, John^4, Peter^3, Matthias^2, John Jacob^1) was born in Augusta County, Virginia. She married B. A. Van Pelt.

(Sup) 5756 i B. A. Van Pelt, Jr.
(Sup) 5757 ii Stuart Van Pelt.

3457 HELEN HAMILTON SELLERS (Rosa^7, Junius^6, Elizabeth^5, John^4, Peter^3, Matthias^2, John Jacob^1) was born in Augusta County, Virginia. She married Mark W. Lewis.

3458 VIRGINIA CONNOR (Mary^7, Junius^6, Elizabeth^5, John^4, Peter^3, Matthias^2, John Jacob^1) was born May 18, 1910, at Brooklyn, New York. She married Johannes Tietz, January 31, 1942, at Baltimore, Maryland. Johannes was the son of Franz and Martha Baginski Tietz and was born July 22, 1902, in East Prussia, Germany.

3459 CHARLES DRUEN CONNOR (Mary^7, Junius^6, Elizabeth^5, John^4, Peter^3, Matthias^2, John Jacob^1) was born November 3, 1911, at Oxford, Pennsylvania.

3460 ALFRED JOHN LICKFOLD (Amanda^7, John^6, Elizabeth^5, John^4, Peter^3, Matthias^2, John Jacob^1) was born September 4, 1896, at Gadsden, Alabama. He married Mary Maude Newlen, October 30, 1923, in Augusta County, Virginia. Mary died January 1, 1929, in Augusta County. Alfred married Mary Eliza Talley, May 20, 1930. Mary was born May 17, 1898, at Staunton, Virginia.

CHILDREN OF ALFRED AND MARY NEWLEN
(Sup) 5758 i Mary Ellen Lickfold, born November 26, 1924.
(Sup) 5759 ii Alfred John Lickfold, Jr., born January 25, 1926.

CHILDREN OF ALFRED AND MARY TALLEY
(Sup) 5760 i Robert Edward Lickfold, born December 11, 1935.
(Sup) 5761 ii Anna Lee Lickfold, born May 25, 1938.

3461 EDITH LOUISE LICKFOLD (Amanda^7, John^6, Elizabeth^5, John^4, Peter^3, Matthias^2, John Jacob^1) was born December 2, 1902, at Gadsden, Alabama. She married John Stephens Shumate, August 22, 1928, at Churchville, Virginia. John was born at Mount Sidney, Virginia, July 4, 1888.

(Sup) 5762 i Nellie Louise Shumate, born May 19, 1930.

3462 EVELYN CLARA LAMBETH (Mamie^7, John^6, Elizabeth^5, John^4, Peter^3, Matthias^2, John Jacob^1) was born October 9, 1900, at Thomasville, North Carolina. She married Allen Lyon Penny, October 25, 1925, at Mount Vernon Place, D. C. Allen was the son of Ovid Bernard and Zella Fleming Penny. He was born May 17, 1903, and died April 16, 1942, at Winston-Salem, North Carolina.

(Sup) 5763 i Allen Lyon Penny, Jr., born September 29, 1930.
(Sup) 5764 ii Thomas Lambeth Penny, born May 29, 1932.
(Sup) 5765 iii William Bell Penny, born May 25, 1934.
(Sup) 5766 iv Hugh Fleming Penny, born August 26, 1937.
(Sup) 5767 v John Allen Penny, born August 26, 1937.

3463 EVELYN FRANCES ROOT (Kenneth^7, John^6, Elizabeth^5, John^4, Peter^3, Matthias^2, John Jacob^1) was born April 24, 1912, in Augusta County, Virginia. She married C. J. Wright.

3464 RALPH DONOVAN ROOT (Kenneth^7, John^6, Elizabeth^5, John^4, Peter^3, Matthias^2, John Jacob^1) was born April 8, 1914, in Augusta County, Virginia. He died November 26, 1930.

3465 CLAUDE HUSTON ROOT (Kenneth^7, John^6, Elizabeth^5, John^4, Peter^3, Matthias^2, John Jacob^1) was born April 2, 1916, in Augusta County, Virginia.

3466 HELEN DEW ROOT (Kenneth^7, John^6, Elizabeth^5, John^4, Peter^3, Matthias^2, John Jacob^1) was born April 28, 1918, in Augusta County, Virginia.

3467 EUGENE BURKETT ROOT (Kenneth^7, John^6, Elizabeth^5, John^4, Peter^3, Matthias^2, John Jacob^1) was born May 16, 1920, in Augusta County, Virginia. He married Ethel Harlow.

3468 EDITH MAY ROOT (Kenneth^7, John^6, Elizabeth^5, John^4, Peter^3, Matthias^2, John Jacob^1) was born May 22, 1922, in Augusta County, Virginia. She married William Grimm.

3469 NELLIE LEE ROOT (Kenneth[7], John[6], Elizabeth[5], John[4], Peter[3], Matthias[2], John Jacob[1]) was born January 29, 1925, in Augusta County, Virginia. She married Joseph Hamilton.

3470 JOHN WILLIAM ROOT (Kenneth[7], John[6], Elizabeth[5], John[4], Peter[3], Matthias[2], John Jacob[1]) was born March 14, 1928, in Augusta County, Virginia. He married Beulah Choleo Sheets.

3471 JACK GORDON ROOT (Kenneth[7], John[6], Elizabeth[5], John[4], Peter[3], Matthias[2], John Jacob[1]) was born February 15, 1929, in Augusta County, Virginia.

3472 JOE REDMOND ROOT (Kenneth[7], John[6], Elizabeth[5], John[4], Peter[3], Matthias[2], John Jacob[1]) was born October 27, 1930, in Augusta County, Virginia.

3473 MADELEIN RAY ROOT (Kenneth[7], John[6], Elizabeth[5], John[4], Peter[3], Matthias[2], John Jacob[1]) was born January 4, 1933, in Augusta County, Virginia.

3474 BEULAH NEFF (William[7], Sarah[6], Catherine[5], John[4], Peter[3], Matthias[2], John Jacob[1]) was born June 6, 1895, at Staunton, Virginia. She married Dr. John L. Kable, January 1, 1917, at Youngstown, Ohio. John was the son of Captain William Kabel and was born January 30, 1885, at Staunton, Virginia. He died at Charleston, West Virginia.

3475 JOHN SAMUEL NEFF (William[7], Sarah[6], Catherine[5], John[4], Peter[3], Matthias[2], John Jacob[1]) was born December 28, 1896, at Staunton, Virginia. He married Sylva Pate in 1928. Sylva was born January 14, 1900. John died December 24, 1948.

3476 WILLIAM EARL NEFF (William[7], Sarah[6], Catherine[5], John[4], Peter[3], Matthias[2], John Jacob[1]) was born March 21, 1897, at Staunton, Virginia. He did not marry and died November 18, 1939, at Youngstown, Ohio.

3477 KATHERINE ELIZABETH NEFF (Frank[7], Sarah[6], Catherine[5], John[4], Peter[3], Matthias[2], John Jacob[1]) was born August 23, 1903, in Augusta County, Virginia. She married William Frank Baxter, August 14, 1919. William was born March 1, 1900. Katherine married Maximillian Ware, November 8, 1942, at Baltimore, Maryland. Maximillian was born November 11, 1900.

3478 GARLAND MEREDITH NEFF (David[7], Sarah[6], Catherine[5], John[4], Peter[3], Matthias[2], John Jacob[1]) was born August 19, 1910, at Weyers Cave, Virginia. He married Grace Marian Wehn, December 19, 1932, at Erie, Pennsylvania. During World War II Garland was a Lieutenant of Paratroops and fought in Japan and the Pacific Theater.
(Sup) 5768   i   David Lee Neff, born July 31, 1937.
(Sup) 5769   ii Frank Martin Neff, born June 8, 1942.

3479 SAMUEL FRANK NEFF (David[7], Sarah[6], Catherine[5], John[4], Peter[3], Matthias[2], John Jacob[1]) was born September 28, 1912, at Dayton, Virginia. He married Irene Willis, January 1, 1939, at Lutz, Florida. Samuel was a First Lieutenant of Infantry in World War II and served in Germany and the European Theater.

3480 EDNA QUICK (Alberta[7], Elizabeth[6], Daniel[5], John[4], Peter[3], Matthias[2], John Jacob[1]) was born at Mount Sidney, Virginia. She married W. W. Brown.

3481 TESSA QUICK (Alberta[7], Elizabeth[6], Daniel[5], John[4], Peter[3], Matthias[2], John Jacob[1]) was born at Mount Sidney, Virginia. She married Carl Wilborn.
(Sup) 5770   i   Jack Wilborn.
(Sup) 5771   ii Robert Wilborn.

3482 HAZEL QUICK (Alberta[7], Elizabeth[6], Daniel[5], John[4], Peter[3], Matthias[2], John Jacob[1]) was born May 8, 1891, at Mount Sidney, Virginia. She married William Merrill Sanders, February 1, 1908, at Starkweather, North Dakota. William was born November 11, 1881, at Gary, South Dakota.
(Sup) 5772   i   Dallas Melvin Sanders, born June 28, 1908.
(Sup) 5773   ii Charles Preston Sanders, born January 7, 1911.
(Sup) 5774   iii Velma Louise Sanders, born November 11, 1912.
(Sup) 5775   iv Louella Elizabeth Sanders, born September 14, 1914.

3483 RILLA QUICK (Alberta[7], Elizabeth[6], Daniel[5], John[4], Peter[3], Matthias[2], John Jacob[1]) was born October 22, 1894, at Mount Sidney, Virginia. She married Claude Gibson, February 11, 1914. Claude was the son of Clinton Gibson and was born May 2, 1893, at Starkweather, North Dakota. He died November 10, 1928.
(Sup) 5776   i   Kathryn Alberta Gibson, born December 20, 1914.
(Sup) 5777   ii   Ray Leslie Gibson.
(Sup) 5778   iii Iola May Gibson, born December 1, 1918 (twin).
(Sup) 5779   iv Viola Ethel Gibson, born December 1, 1918 (twin).
(Sup) 5780   v   Bernard Patrick Gibson, born March 17, 1921.
(Sup) 5781   vi   Eileen Isabelle Gibson, born March 6, 1923.
(Sup) 5782   vii Wilma Jean Gibson, born July 17, 1926.

3484 HOBART QUICK (Alberta[7], Elizabeth[6], Daniel[5], John[4], Peter[3], Matthias[2], John Jacob[1]) was born June 7, 1897, in Augusta County, Virginia. He married Orpha Wagoner, November 25, 1920. Orpha was born at Owasco, Indiana, August 17, 1896.
(Sup) 5783   i   Robert Vernon Quick, born August 1, 1921.

3485 VIRGINIA RITCHIE (Albertine[7], Elizabeth[6], Daniel[5], John[4], Peter[3], Matthias[2], John Jacob[1]) was born September 18, 1895, at Mount Sidney, Virginia. She married Emmett F. Fishburne, June 30, 1920. Emmett was born February 6, 1893, at Staunton, Virginia.
(Sup) 5784   i   Frank Allen Fishburne, born March 8, 1922.
(Sup) 5785   ii   Stuart Paxton Fishburne, born September 11, 1924.
(Sup) 5786   iii Emmett Ritchie Fishburne, born August 3, 1932.

3486 ELIZABETH RITCHIE (Albertine[7], Elizabeth[6], Daniel[5], John[4], Peter[3], Matthias[2], John Jacob[1]) was born in July, 1901, at Mount Sidney, Virginia, where she died August 30, 1902.

3487 WILLIAM DALLAS SHUMATE (Annie[7], Elizabeth[6], Daniel[5], John[4], Peter[3], Matthias[2], John Jacob[1]) was born October 20, 1895, at Mount Sidney, Virginia. He married Leta Vianna Coyner, May 6, 1918. Leta was the daughter of B. Frank Coyner and was born at Waynesboro, Virginia, May 5, 1900.
(Sup) 5787   i   Martha Evelyn Shumate, born September 23, 1919.
(Sup) 5788   ii   William Dallas Shumate, Jr., born December 23, 1923.
(Sup) 5789   iii Marrianne K. Shumate, born May 18, 1932.

3488 STANLEY A. SHUMATE (Annie[7], Elizabeth[6], Daniel[5], John[4], Peter[3], Matthias[2], John Jacob[1]) was born September 15, 1897. He married Arlene Hiner in 1920 who died in 1941. Then he married Mattie Perry, November 9, 1942, at Hagerstown, Maryland. Mattie was born August 6, 1913.

(Sup) 5790   i   Anne Belle Shumate.
(Sup) 5791   ii   Carl Shumate.

3489 ALBERT SHUMATE (Annie[7], Elizabeth[6], Daniel[5], John[4], Peter[3], Matthias[2], John Jacob[1]) was born October 20, 1901, at Centerville, Virginia. He married Lottie Taliaferro, June 27, 1929, at Lone Fountain, Virginia. Lottie was born at Lone Fountain, January 10, 1903. Albert was an ordained Lutheran minister.

(Sup) 5792   i   Eleanor Shumate, born August 2, 1932.
(Sup) 5793   ii   George Dallas Shumate, born March 11, 1939.

3490 ALFRED SHUMATE (Annie[7], Elizabeth[6], Daniel[5], John[4], Peter[3], Matthias[2], John Jacob[1]) was born October 20, 1901, at Centerville, Virginia. He married Ellen Hanger Burkholder May 23, 1928 at Staunton, Virginia. Ellen was born February 8, 1904, at Mt. Sidney, Virginia. Alfred was an ordained Lutheran minister and volunteered in World War II. He was commissioned a First Lieutenant and served as Chaplain in the Air Force for 34 months, sixteen of which were with the Eighth Air Force in Europe. He was promoted to Captain and then Major and after the war retained his rank in the Officers Reserve Corps.

(Sup) 5794   i   Thomas Joseph Shumate, born October 15, 1929.
(Sup) 5795   ii   Kathleen Allen Shumate, born June 1, 1931.
(Sup) 5796   iii   Robert Hanger Shumate, born October 27, 1935.

3491 AUDREY SHUMATE (Annie[7], Elizabeth[6], Daniel[5], John[4], Peter[3], Matthias[2], John Jacob[1]) was born June 13, 1903, at Mount Sidney, Virginia. She married Kenneth Yount, June 11, 1929, at Churchville, Virginia. Kenneth, son of David E. and Mary A. Miller Yount, was born January 26, 1902, at Hickory, North Carolina. Kenneth was an ordained Lutheran minister.

3492 PHYLLIS SHUMATE (Annie[7], Elizabeth[6], Daniel[5], John[4], Peter[3], Matthias[2], John Jacob[1]) was born January 6, 1909, in Augusta County, Virginia. She married Charles W. Cupp, July 26, 1933, at Washington, D. C. Charles was born June 5, 1910, near Raphine, Virginia.

(Sup) 5797   i   Jean Annette Cupp, born February 21, 1935.
(Sup) 5798   ii   Thomas Keith Cupp, born February 20, 1946.

3493 RAYMOND LINK (Amanda[7], John[6], Daniel[5], John[4], Peter[3], Matthias[2], John Jacob[1]) was born June 30, 1907, in Augusta County, Virginia. He married Leona Beatrice Wine, September 19, 1931, in Augusta County. Leona was the daughter of Emmett C. and Effie E. Wine and was born September 8, 1910, in Augusta County, Virginia. Raymond was postmaster at Mount Sidney, Virginia. He helped much in gathering genealogical data for this history.

(Sup) 5799   i   Donald Norman Link, born June 23, 1933.

3494 CARL CHALMERS HUDSON (Laura[7], Daniel[6], Daniel[5], John[4], Peter[3], Matthias[2], John Jacob[1]) was born April 30, 1899, in Augusta County, Virginia. He married Marie Helen Warren, October 11, 1925, at Middletown, New York. Helen was born August 11, 1902, at Woodridge, New York.

(Sup) 5800   i   Paula Dawn Hudson, born May 13, 1930.
(Sup) 5801   ii   Glenn Chalmers Hudson, born September 9, 1931.
(Sup) 5802   iii   Mary Joyce Hudson, born April 18, 1934.
(Sup) 5803   iv   Jay Allen Hudson, born July 8, 1938.

3495 RUTH ROSELLA HUDSON (Laura[7], Daniel[6], Daniel[5], John[4], Peter[3], Matthias[2], John Jacob[1]) was born November 12, 1900, in Augusta County, Virginia.

3496 RALPH HUDSON (Laura[7], Daniel[6], Daniel[5], John[4], Peter[3], Matthias[2], John Jacob[1]) was born September 8, 1902, in Augusta County, Virginia, where he died September 28, 1902.

3497 BERKLEY BOWMAN LINK (David[7], Daniel[6], Daniel[5], John[4], Peter[3], Matthias[2], John Jacob[1]) was born March 20, 1907, in Augusta County, Virginia.

3498 DOROTHY PEARL LINK (David[7], Daniel[6], Daniel[5], John[4], Peter[3], Matthias[2], John Jacob[1]) was born September 23, 1908, in Augusta County, Virginia. She married Lacy Crum Boward, October 4, 1930. Lacy, son of John Boward, was born July 27, 1906.

(Sup) 5804   i   Isabell Eudora Boward, born October 23, 1933.

3499 ENDORA MARTHA ALICE LINK (David[7], Daniel[6], Daniel[5], John[4], Peter[3], Matthias[2], John Jacob[1]) was born June 19, 1913, in Augusta County, Virginia. She married David Luther Simmons, July 18, 1936. David, son of William Floyd Simmons, was born September 12, 1910, in Augusta County, Virginia.

(Sup) 5805   i   David Floyd Simmons, born June 8, 1939.
(Sup) 5806   ii   Martha Agnes Simmons, born November 12, 1945.

3500 LACY AUSBERT LINK (David[7], Daniel[6], Daniel[5], John[4], Peter[3], Matthias[2], John Jacob[1]) was born September 28, 1914, in Augusta County, Virginia. He married Daisy Eveline Draine, July 24, 1940.

(Sup) 5807   i   Linda Anne Link, born May 30, 1945.

3501 DAVID DANIEL LINK, JR. (David[7], Daniel[6], Daniel[5], John[4], Peter[3], Matthias[2], John Jacob[1]) was born September 28, 1914, in Augusta County, Virginia. He died there July 6, 1924.

3502 DELPHA VIRGINIA LINK (Samuel[7], Daniel[6], Daniel[5], John[4], Peter[3], Matthias[2], John Jacob[1]) was born March 27, 1905, in Augusta County, Virginia. She married Wade William Meyerhoeffer, April 25, 1923. Wade was born October 5, 1898, in Rockingham County, Virginia.

(Sup) 5808   i   Virginia Lucille Meyerhoeffer, born Dec 4, 1923.
(Sup) 5809   ii   William Wade Meyerhoeffer, born October 6, 1925.
(Sup) 5810   iii   Ellen Elaine Meyerhoeffer, born November 26, 1927.
(Sup) 5811   iv   Martha Lee Meyerhoeffer, born January 18, 1930.
(Sup) 5812   v   Mildred Ann Meyerhoeffer, born November 25, 1932.
(Sup) 5813   vi   Sarah Katheryn Meyerhoeffer, born June 2, 1935.
(Sup) 5814   vii   Nelson B. Meyerhoeffer, born June 11, 1938.

3503 ELIZABETH LUELLA LINK (Samuel[7], Daniel[6], Daniel[5], John[4], Peter[3], Matthias[2], John Jacob[1]) was born January 4, 1909, in Augusta County, Virginia, and died there January 18, 1917.

3504 RAYMOND WALTER LINK (Samuel[7], Daniel[6], Daniel[5], John[4], Peter[3], Matthias[2], John Jacob[1]) was born September 15, 1911, in Augusta County, Virginia. He married Gretchen Hitt, June 18, 1939, at Mint Springs, Augusta County, Virginia. Gretchen was born at Mint Springs, April 25, 1920.

(Sup) 5815 i Patricia Anne Link, born July 10, 1940.

3505 REBA MAE LINK (Samuel[7], Daniel[6], Daniel[5], John[4], Peter[3], Matthias[2], John Jacob[1]) was born November 28, 1913, in Augusta County, Virginia. She married Glenn B. Campbell, February 4, 1935.

3506 KATHERYN V. LINK (Samuel[7], Daniel[6], Daniel[5], John[4], Peter[3], Matthias[2], John Jacob[1]) was born May 20, 1916, in Augusta County, Virginia. She married Tyree Back, March 26, 1938.

3507 PAULINE WINIFRED LINK (Samuel[7], Daniel[6], Daniel[5], John[4], Peter[3], Matthias[2], John Jacob[1]) was born February 12, 1919, in Augusta County, Virginia. She married Sidney L. Stover, August 31, 1940, at Swoope, Virginia. Sidney, son of Edgar Stover, was born November 19, 1910, at Staunton, Virginia.

(Sup) 5816 i Rebecca Joan Stover, born August 31, 1945.

3508 CLETA FRANCES LINK (Samuel[7], Daniel[6], Daniel[5], John[4], Peter[3], Matthias[2], John Jacob[1]) was born August 27, 1923, in Augusta County, Virginia. She married Clarence D. Truxell, January 17, 1942. Clarence, son of Joseph Truxell, was born September 14, 1916, at Lowry, Virginia.

(Sup) 5817 i   Kay Frances Truxell, born August 14, 1943.
(Sup) 5818 ii Fay Douglas Truxell, born August 14, 1943.

3509 HELEN LEORA LINK (George[7], Daniel[6], Daniel[5], John[4], Peter[3], Matthias[2], John Jacob[1]) was born April 25, 1908, in Augusta County, Virginia. She married Golden McClune Smith, December 16, 1926. Golden was born December 28, 1907, in Augusta County, Virginia.

(Sup) 5819 i   Wilfred Link Smith, born September 25, 1929.
(Sup) 5820 ii Goldie Ann Smith, born February 5, 1943.

3510 MARY ELIZABETH LINK (George[7], Daniel[6], Daniel[5], John[4], Peter[3], Matthias[2], John Jacob[1]) was born April 1, 1919, in Augusta County, Virginia. She married G. A. Guyer, June 4, 1938.

3511 MALCOLM VERNIE LINK (George[7], Daniel[6], Daniel[5], John[4], Peter[3], Matthias[2], John Jacob[1]) was born October 20, 1925, in Augusta County, Virginia.

3512 MARGORY RUTH LINK (John[7], Daniel[6], Daniel[5], John[4], Peter[3], Matthias[2], John Jacob[1]) was born in Augusta County, Virginia. She married Arlie Sheets.

3513 EDNA MAY LINK (John[7], Daniel[6], Daniel[5], John[4], Peter[3], Matthias[2], John Jacob[1]) was born May 22, 1911, in Augusta County, Virginia, where she died July 2, 1912.

3514 JOHN PAUL LINK (John[7], Daniel[6], Daniel[5], John[4], Peter[3], Matthias[2], John Jacob[1]) was born August 17, 1914, in Augusta County, Virginia.

3515 MARY COTTA LINK (John[7], Daniel[6], Daniel[5], John[4], Peter[3], Matthias[2], John Jacob[1]) was born October 13, 1916, at Bridgewater, Virginia.

3516 EUNICE CHARLENE LINK (John[7], Daniel[6], Daniel[5], John[4], Peter[3], Matthias[2], John Jacob[1]) was born February 11, 1920, in Augusta County, Virginia. She married Tracy Wenger, December 5, 1942, at Staunton, Virginia.

(Sup) 5821 i Ann Hilton Wenger, born September 13, 1945.

3517 WINIFRED CALVIN LINK (John[7], Daniel[6], Daniel[5], John[4], Peter[3], Matthias[2], John Jacob[1]) was born in Augusta County, Virginia. He married Sue Spitler.

3518 STANLEY RAYBURN LINK (John[7], Daniel[6], Daniel[5], John[4], Peter[3], Matthias[2], John Jacob[1]) was born in Augusta County, Virginia. He married Elizabeth Lindamood.

3519 NATHALEE OCHELTREE (Mary[7], Daniel[6], Daniel[5], John[4], Peter[3], Matthias[2], John Jacob[1]) was born October 2, 1913, in Augusta County, Virginia.

3520 LURTY PAUL OCHELTREE (Mary[7], Daniel[6], Daniel[5], John[4], Peter[3], Matthias[2], John Jacob[1]) was born March 12, 1920, in Augusta County, Virginia. He married Virginia Mae Gilbert, December 19, 1942.

3521 LESTER RAYMOND LINK (Lester[7], Daniel[6], Daniel[5], John[4], Peter[3], Matthias[2], John Jacob[1]) was born July 22, 1921, in Augusta County, Virginia. He married Eleanor Cline.

3522 AUDREY LORRAINE LINK (Lester[7], Daniel[6], Daniel[5], John[4], Peter[3], Matthias[2], John Jacob[1]) was born December 6, 1923, in Augusta County, Virginia. She married James Schreckliss.

3523 ELLEN ELIZABETH LINK (Lester[7], Daniel[6], Daniel[5], John[4], Peter[3], Matthias[2], John Jacob[1]) was born April 13, 1933, in Augusta County, Virginia.

3524 ETHELEEN V. TUTWILER (Emma[7], Margaret[6], Daniel[5], John[4], Peter[3], Matthias[2], John Jacob[1]) was born November 23, 1897, in Augusta County, Virginia. She married Wade O. Whitesell, March 11, 1914.

3525 OTIS HAMPTON TUTWILER (Emma[7], Margaret[6], Daniel[5], John[4], Peter[3], Matthias[2], John Jacob[1]) was born July 23, 1899, at Churchville, Virginia. He married Lillian G. Bauserman, November 18, 1918, at Harrisonburg, Virginia. Lillian was born May 2, 1899, at Montevideo, Virginia. Otis became the Farm Bureau manager at Mount Crawford, Virginia.

(Sup) 5822 i   Edith Barton Tutwiler, born January 3, 1919.
(Sup) 5823 ii   Pauline La Van Tutwiler, born September 6, 1921.
(Sup) 5824 iii Dorothy Marie Tutwiler, born January 14, 1925.
(Sup) 5825 iv   Ruth Adoree Tutwiler, born November 2, 1927.

3526 HOUSTON RUDOLPH FRY (Minor^7, Margaret^6, Daniel^5, John^4, Peter^3, Matthias^2, John Jacob^1) was born March 25, 1907, at Churchville, Virginia. He married Sara Katherine Hall, September 16, 1931.

3527 NATALIE CARLTON FRY (Minor^7, Margaret^6, Daniel^5, John^4, Peter^3, Matthias^2, John Jacob^1) was born August 12, 1920, at Staunton, Virginia. She married Kent Dexter Steele, September 11, 1943.

3528 MARSHALL DAVID FRY (Harvey^7, Margaret^6, Daniel^5, John^4, Peter^3, Matthias^2, John Jacob^1) was born September 19, 1908, in Augusta County, Virginia.

3529 DOROTHY WILSON FRY (Harvey^7, Margaret^6, Daniel^5, John^4, Peter^3, Matthias^2, John Jacob^1) was born May 27, 1911, in Augusta County, Virginia. She married Marshall Bare, June 8, 1935, in Staunton, Virginia.

(Sup) 5826   i   Marshall Bare, Jr., born February 8, 1941.

3530 RAYMOND ROBERT ALEXANDER (Oscar^7, Mary^6, Daniel^5, John^4, Peter^3, Matthias^2, John Jacob^1) was born August 6, 1909, in Augusta County, Virginia. He married Mary Virginia Alexander, daughter of Raymond and Mary Croushorn Alexander, December 24, 1929, in Augusta County, Virginia. Mary was born May 29, 1909, near Stonewall, Virginia.

(Sup) 5827   ii   Virginia Joyce Alexander, born July 8, 1933.

3531 NAOMI ALEXANDER (Oscar^7, Mary^6, Daniel^5, John^4, Peter^3, Matthias^2, John Jacob^1) was born March 14, 1911, at Mount Sidney, Virginia.

3532 MARGARET C. ALEXANDER (Oscar^7, Mary^6, Daniel^5, John^4, Peter^3, Matthias^2, John Jacob^1) was born February 25, 1913, at Mount Sidney, Virginia. She died July 11, 1913, at Bridgewater, Virginia.

3533 MARTHA ALICE ALEXANDER (Oscar^7, Mary^6, Daniel^5, John^4, Peter^3, Matthias^2, John Jacob^1) was born March 8, 1914, at Bridgewater, Virginia. She married Martin Luther Good, November 4, 1933, in Hagerstown, Maryland. Martin was the son of Charles William and Clara Ellen Link Good and was born in Augusta County, March 19, 1915. See No. 3563. Children are listed under this number.

3534 LURTY ALEXANDER (Oscar^7, Mary^6, Daniel^5, John^4, Peter^3, Matthias^2, John Jacob^1) was born November 12, 1915, at Bridgewater, Virginia.

3535 ELVIN GARDELL ALEXANDER (Irenus^7, Mary^6, Daniel^5, John^4, Peter^3, Matthias^2, John Jacob^1) was born March 30, 1912, near Sea Wright Springs, Virginia. He married Reba Frances, June 6, 1931, at Hagerstown, Maryland. Reba was born May 11, 1911, at Montefella, Virginia.

(Sup) 5828   i   Elvin Gardell Alexander, Jr.
(Sup) 5829   ii   Hilda Lee Alexander.
(Sup) 5830   iii   Harold Phillip Alexander.

3536 CATHERINE ALEXANDER (Irenus^7, Mary^6, Daniel^5, John^4, Peter^3, Matthias^2, John Jacob^1) was born July 15, 1914, in Augusta County, Virginia. She married Clyde J. Stockdale, August 29, 1933, in Augusta County. Clyde was born September 5, 1910.

3537 WILLIAM D. ALEXANDER (Irenus^7, Mary^6, Daniel^5, John^4, Peter^3, Matthias^2, John Jacob^1) was born March 2, 1916, in Augusta County, Virginia. He married Maybelle Lyle Ramsey, July 20, 1940, at Staunton, Virginia. Maybelle was born June 12, 1920, in Nelson County, Virginia.

(Sup) 5831   i   Carolyn May Alexander, born July 12, 1942.
(Sup) 5832   ii   Joan Dale Alexander, born December 23, 1945.
(Sup) 5833   iii   Shelvia Jean Alexander, born March 14, 1947.

3538 CHARLES E. ALEXANDER (Irenus^7, Mary^6, Daniel^5, John^4, Peter^3, Matthias^2, John Jacob^1) was born August 18, 1918, at Mount Sidney, Virginia. He was a Lieutenant in the U. S. Army.

3539 DOROTHY L. ALEXANDER (Irenus^7, Mary^6, Daniel^5, John^4, Peter^3, Matthias^2, John Jacob^1) was born in Augusta County, Virginia.

3540 JOHANNA (JONIE) ALEXANDER (Irenus^7, Mary^6, Daniel^5, John^4, Peter^3, Matthias^2, John Jacob^1) was born in Augusta County, Virginia.

3541 BONNIE LOU ALEXANDER (Irenus^7, Mary^6, Daniel^5, John^4, Peter^3, Matthias^2, John Jacob^1) was born September 2, 1933, in Augusta County, Virginia.

3542 MARION RICHARD ALEXANDER (John^7, Mary^6, Daniel^5, John^4, Peter^3, Matthias^2, John Jacob^1) was born December 5, 1914, near Mount Sidney, Virginia.

3543 REDA FRANCES ALEXANDER (John^7, Mary^6, Daniel^5, John^4, Peter^3, Matthias^2, John Jacob^1) was born May 28, 1916, near Mount Sidney, Virginia. She married Hugh Alexander Christian, September 2, 1939, at Newport News, Virginia.

(Sup) 5834   i   Lola Lee Christian, born January 21, 1942.
(Sup) 5835   ii   Hugh Alexander Christian, Jr., born Nov 27, 1945.

3544 STANLEY ROLLER ALEXANDER (John^7, Mary^6, Daniel^5, John^4, Peter^3, Matthias^2, John Jacob^1) was born July 3, 1918, at Weyers Cave, Virginia. He married Kathleen Mowrey Borden at Grottoes, Virginia, December 16, 1945.. Stanley served in the U. S. Army in the European Theater during World War II from March 24, 1941, to October 15, 1945.

3545 JOSEPH ALFRED ALEXANDER (John^7, Mary^6, Daniel^5, John^4, Peter^3, Matthias^2, John Jacob^1) was born September 17, 1920, at Weyers Cave, Virginia. He was in the U. S. Army from September 4, 1942, to March 18, 1943.

3546 PAUL GARDNER ALEXANDER (John^7, Mary^6, Daniel^5, John^4, Peter^3, Matthias^2, John Jacob^1) was born October 23, 1921, at Weyers Cave, Virginia. He was in the U. S. Army from September 16, 1942, to February 14, 1946, and saw service in the Pacific Theater during World War II.

3547 EDWIN GLENN ALEXANDER (John^7, Mary^6, Daniel^5, John^4, Peter^3, Matthias^2, John Jacob^1) was born February 28, 1924, at Weyers Cave, Virginia. He married Sarah Adaline Black, September 1, 1946, at Mount Vernon, New York. During World War II Edwin served in the U. S. Navy from July 3, 1942, to February 14, 1946, much of the time in the Pacific Theater.

3548 NELSON JOHN ROBERT ALEXANDER (John[7], Mary[6], Daniel[5], John[4], Peter[3], Matthias[2], John Jacob[1]) was born November 24, 1925, at Weyers Cave, Virginia. He served in the U. S. Army from March 9, 1944, to May 30, 1946, during World War II.

3549 ROSCOE VERNON ALEXANDER (John[7], Mary[6], Daniel[5], John[4], Peter[3], Matthias[2], John Jacob[1]) was born October 23, 1926, at Weyers Cave, Virginia. He was in the U. S. Army of Occupation in Japan.

3550 LINDBERG CRAWFORD ALEXANDER (John[7], Mary[6], Daniel[5], John[4], Peter[3], Matthias[2], John Jacob[1]) was born May 22, 1928, at Weyers Cave, Virginia.

3551 MELVIN HARRY ALEXANDER (Oney[7], Mary[6], Daniel[5], John[4], Peter[3], Matthias[2], John Jacob[1]) was born July 4, 1921, in Augusta County, Virginia. He married Goldie Elizabeth Readcap, October 19, 1944, at Staunton, Virginia.

(Sup) 5841   i   Robert Milton Alexander, born March 4, 1946.

3552 EDITH CATHERINE ALEXANDER (Hobart[7], Mary[6], Daniel[5], John[4], Peter[3], Matthias[2], John Jacob[1]) married Ray Brubeck, August 8, 1945.

3553 MAHLIN ALEXANDER MOORE (Flossie[7], Mary[6], Daniel[5], John[4], Peter[3], Matthias[2], John Jacob[1]) was born November 4, 1924, at Mount Sidney, Virginia.

3554 ANGELINE CATHERINE LINK (Daniel[7], Martin[6], Daniel[5], John[4], Peter[3], Matthias[2], John Jacob[1]) was born December 31, 1905, in Augusta County, Virginia. She married Joseph Lewis Wenger, son of Joseph W. Wenger, August 8, 1928. Joseph was born at Spring Hill, Virginia, October 6, 1904.

(Sup) 5842   i   Robert Lewis Wenger, born January 27, 1931.
(Sup) 5843   ii   Jennie Ellen Wenger, born May 28, 1933.
(Sup) 5844   iii Mildred Louise Wenger, born December 22, 1940.
(Sup) 5845   iv   Carolyn Kay Wenger, born September 15, 1945.

3555 ELWOOD RALPH LINK (Daniel[7], Martin[6], Daniel[5], John[4], Peter[3], Matthias[2], John Jacob[1]) was born July 3, 1909, in Augusta County, Virginia. He married Mary Alexander, daughter of Minor Alexander, June 2, 1932. Mary was born September 13, 1909, at Hagerstown, Maryland.

(Sup) 5846   i   Anna Jane Link, born March 15, 1933.
(Sup) 5847   ii   Betty Lou Link, born June 7, 1934.
(Sup) 5848   iii Joan Link, born May 10, 1936.
(Sup) 5849   iv   Mary Sue Link, born February 10, 1938.
(Sup) 5850   v   Elwood Ralph Link, Jr., born September 24, 1939.

3556 IRENE FRANCES LINK (Daniel[7], Martin[6], Daniel[5], John[4], Peter[3], Matthias[2], John Jacob[1]) was born October 27, 1913, in Augusta County, Virginia. She married Roy Francis McAllister, son of Lester McAllister, November 20, 1943. Roy was born October 19, 1922, in Augusta County.

(Sup) 5851   i   Roy Clinton McAllister, born December 21, 1944.

3557 DRUSILLA B. HUFFMAN (Elizabeth[7], Martin[6], Daniel[5], John[4], Peter[3], Matthias[2], John Jacob[1]) was born February 9, 1903, at Mount Sidney, Virginia. She married Warren Wright, June 11, 1925. Warren was born January 19, 1903, at Weyers Cave, Virginia.

3558 JOSEPH HUFFMAN (Elizabeth[7], Martin[6], Daniel[5], John[4], Peter[3], Matthias[2], John Jacob[1]) was born in Augusta County, Virginia. He married Eva Perry, August 31, 1931.

3559 ELAINE FRANCES HUFFMAN (Elizabeth[7], Martin[6], Daniel[5], John[4], Peter[3], Matthias[2], John Jacob[1]) was born in Augusta County, Virginia. She married Clinton Dodd, December 31, 1935. Elaine died March 5, 1943.

3560 HILDRED HUFFMAN (Elizabeth[7], Martin[6], Daniel[5], John[4], Peter[3], Matthias[2], John Jacob[1]) was born April 12, 1912, at Mount Sidney, Virginia. She married Garfield Richard Dawson, July 25, 1931, at Rockville, Maryland. Garfield was born March 22, 1913, at Village, Virginia.

(Sup) 5852   i   Jacqueline Doris Dawson, born July 27, 1933.

3561 EUNICE MARGARET HUFFMAN (Elizabeth[7], Martin[6], Daniel[5], John[4], Peter[3], Matthias[2], John Jacob[1]) was born December 5, 1914, at Mount Sidney, Virginia. She married Henry Clay Wright, July 26, 1938, at Alexandria, Virginia. Henry was the son of Martin Luther Wright and was born December 10, 1910.

3562 VIRGINIA CARROL HUFFMAN (Elizabeth[7], Martin[6], Daniel[5], John[4], Peter[3], Matthias[2], John Jacob[1]) was born in Augusta County, Virginia. She married Carl Matthias, May 25, 1946.

3563 MARTIN LUTHER GOOD (Clara[7], Martin[6], Daniel[5], John[4], Peter[3], Matthias[2], John Jacob[1]) was born March 19, 1915, in Augusta County, Virginia. He married Martha Alice Alexander, daughter of Oscar and Carrie Sheets Alexander, November 4, 1933, at Hagerstown, Maryland. Martha was born March 8, 1914, at Bridgewater, Virginia. See No. 3533.

(Sup) 5853   i   Donald Alfred Good, born October 2, 1937.
(Sup) 5854   ii   Norman Eugene Good, born August 31, 1940.
(Sup) 5855   iii Martin Luther Good, Jr., born May 9, 1943.
(Sup) 5856   iv   David Samuel Good, born September 4, 1945.

3564 DANIE GOOD (Clara[7], Martin[6], Daniel[5], John[4], Peter[3], Matthias[2], John Jacob[1]) was born October 22, 1918, in Augusta County, Virginia. She married Eugene N. Wise, May 4, 1945.

(Sup) 5857   i   Nancy Ellen Wise, born February 17, 1947.

3565 AGNES GOOD (Clara[7], Martin[6], Daniel[5], John[4], Peter[3], Matthias[2], John Jacob[1]) was born November 8, 1925, in Augusta County, Virginia. She married Roy B. Powell, October 6, 1946.

3566 CHARLES IVAN GOOD (Clara[7], Martin[6], Daniel[5], John[4], Peter[3], Matthias[2], John Jacob[1]) was born July 31, 1927, in Augusta County, Virginia.

3567 ADELE GOOD (Clara[7], Martin[6], Daniel[5], John[4], Peter[3], Matthias[2], John Jacob[1]) was born June 13, 1929, in Augusta County, Virginia.

3568 SYLVIA EDWARD HICKLIN (Mary^7, Martin^6, Daniel^5, John^4, Peter^3, Matthias^2, John Jacob^1) was born December 24, 1915, at Mount Sidney, Virginia. He married Fleeta Gay Sheets, February 6, 1938. Fleeta was born May 20, 1918, in Augusta County, Virginia.

(Sup) 5858   † Betty Lou Hicklin, born November 12, 1938.

3569 WINSTON BARTH WINE (Jesse^7, Julia^6, Daniel^5, John^4, Peter^3, Matthias^2, John Jacob^1) was born September 21, 1916, at Weyers Cave, Virginia. He married Maude McChesney, August 11, 1941, at Highland Springs, Virginia. Maude was born June 5, 1920, in Hanover County, Virginia.

(Sup) 5859   † Winston Barth Wine, Jr., born February 25, 1943.
(Sup) 5860   †† Joan Carlie Wine, born January 12, 1945.

3570 CHARLOTTE FAY WINE (Jesse^7, Julia^6, Daniel^5, John^4, Peter^3, Matthias^2, John Jacob^1) was born May 28, 1918, at Mount Sidney, Virginia. She married Paul Harman, November 30, 1939.

3571 MAXINE WINE (Jesse^7, Julia^6, Daniel^5, John^4, Peter^3, Matthias^2, John Jacob^1) was born November 2, 1920, at Mount Sidney, Virginia. She married Wade Hawkins, November 17, 1945.

3572 BERNICE WINE (Jesse^7, Julia^6, Daniel^5, John^4, Peter^3, Matthias^2, John Jacob^1) was born April 17, 1923, at Mount Sidney, Virginia. She married Russell Landes, May 30, 1945.

3573 ELLEN LANDES WINE (Jesse^7, Julia^6, Daniel^5, John^4, Peter^3, Matthias^2, John Jacob^1) was born August 2, 1928, at Mount Sidney, Virginia.

3574 JUANITA TINN HARSHBARGER (Margaret^7, Julia^6, Daniel^5, John^4, Peter^3, Matthias^2, John Jacob^1) was born September 14, 1916, in Augusta County, Virginia. She married Charles Dennison, August 14, 1937, at Mount Sidney, Virginia. Charles was born May 26, 1914, at Rockingham, Virginia.

(Sup) 5861   † Judith Tinn Dennison.
(Sup) 5862   †† Sara Sue Dennison.
(Sup) 5863   ††† Jane Ellen Dennison.

3575 CALVIN WINE HARSHBARGER (Margaret^7, Julia^6, Daniel^5, John^4, Peter^3, Matthias^2, John Jacob^1) was born in Augusta County, Virginia. He served in World War II and was killed in action in Germany, March 25, 1945.

3576 ROLLIN MAURICE HARSHBARGER (Margaret^7, Julia^6, Daniel^5, John^4, Peter^3, Matthias^2, John Jacob^1) was born December 27, 1919, at Weyers Cave, Virginia. He married Betty Wayne Wilberger, February 2, 1946, at Mount Solon, Virginia. Betty was born at Moscow, Virginia, October 4, 1921. She was the daughter of Emmett L. and Edna D. Houff Wilberger.

3577 JANET MATILDA HARSHBARGER (Margaret^7, Julia^6, Daniel^5, John^4, Peter^3, Matthias^2, John Jacob^1) was born in Augusta County, Virginia. She married Robert Cash.

3578 JEAN PORTER HARSHBARGER (Margaret^7, Julia^6, Daniel^5, John^4, Peter^3, Matthias^2, John Jacob^1) was born June 22, 1923, in Augusta County, Virginia. She married William Johnson Graham, Jr., son of William J. Graham, April 7, 1946, at Mount Sidney, Virginia. William was born November 26, 1923, at Staunton, Virginia.

3579 DALLAS WILLIAM HARSHBARGER (Margaret^7, Julia^6, Daniel^5, John^4, Peter^3, Matthias^2, John Jacob^1) was born December 13, 1925, in Augusta County, Virginia.

3580 NORMA HOPE WINE (Nelson^7, Julia^6, Daniel^5, John^4, Peter^3, Matthias^2, John Jacob^1) was born January 3, 1925, at Mount Sidney, Virginia. She married Frederick Hamer Berry, August 27, 1944, at Mount Sidney. Frederick was the son of Reginald and Elizabeth Hamer Berry and was born January 3, 1921, at Staunton, Virginia.

3581 PALMER FRANKLIN WINE (Nelson^7, Julia^6, Daniel^5, John^4, Peter^3, Matthias^2, John Jacob^1) was born February 20, 1927, at Mount Sidney, Virginia.

3582 HAROLD HUDSON WINE (Nelson^7, Julia^6, Daniel^5, John^4, Peter^3, Matthias^2, John Jacob^1) was born June 4, 1929, at Mount Sidney, Virginia.

3583 PHILLIP MORTON WINE (Nelson^7, Julia^6, Daniel^5, John^4, Peter^3, Matthias^2, John Jacob^1) was born September 23, 1932, at Mount Sidney, Virginia.

3584 SHELTON GARDNER WINE (Nelson^7, Julia^6, Daniel^5, John^4, Peter^3, Matthias^2, John Jacob^1) was born April 21, 1935, at Mount Sidney, Virginia.

3585 JOHN WENDALL WINE (Nelson^7, Julia^6, Daniel^5, John^4, Peter^3, Matthias^2, John Jacob^1) was born March 20, 1943, at Mount Sidney, Virginia.

3586 CORDELIA WINE (Richard^7, Julia^6, Daniel^5, John^4, Peter^3, Matthias^2, John Jacob^1) was born November 29, 1929, at Verona, Virginia.

3587 RICHARD WAYNE WINE (Richard^7, Julia^6, Daniel^5, John^4, Peter^3, Matthias^2, John Jacob^1) was born September 23, 1940, at Mount Sidney, Virginia.

3588 WILLIAM AUSTIN QUICK, JR. (William^7, Martha^6, Daniel^5, John^4, Peter^3, Matthias^2, John Jacob^1) was born April 10, 1916, in Augusta County, Virginia. He married Anna Tucker, May 28, 1942.

(Sup) 5864   † Brenda Ann Quick.

3589 FAYE NELSON QUICK (William^7, Martha^6, Daniel^5, John^4, Peter^3, Matthias^2, John Jacob^1) was born October 11, 1917, in Augusta County, Virginia. She married Lindsey Rosser, June 16, 1941.

(Sup) 5865   † William Faye Rosser.

3590 RICHARD ROLANDER QUICK (William^7, Martha^6, Daniel^5, John^4, Peter^3, Matthias^2, John Jacob^1) was born October 19, 1921, in Augusta County, Virginia. He married Anita Kefauver, October 12, 1943.

(Sup) 5866   † Stuart Quick.

3591 MARY FRANCES QUICK (William^7, Martha^6, Daniel^5, John^4, Peter^3, Matthias^2, John Jacob^1) was born February 8, 1924, in Augusta County, Virginia. She married Novice Deaver, March 29, 1947.

3592 PHYLLIS OPAL QUICK (Edward^7, Martha^6, Daniel^5, John^4, Peter^3, Matthias^2, John Jacob^1) was born September 2, 1916, in Augusta County, Virginia. She married James Allen Camer, April 4, 1941, at Staunton, Virginia.

(Sup) 5867   † James Allen Camer, Jr., born April 6, 1944.

3593 LEROY GLENWOOD QUICK (Edward[7], Martha[6], Daniel[5], John[4], Peter[3], Matthias[2], John Jacob[1]) was born May 17, 1921, in Augusta County, Virginia. He married Thelma Anderson, April 12, 1944, at Staunton, Virginia.

(Sup) 5868   i Edward Glenn Quick, born September 13, 1946.

3594 EVELYN LEOTA QUICK (Edward[7], Martha[6], Daniel[5], John[4], Peter[3], Matthias[2], John Jacob[1]) was born April 6, 1923, in Augusta County, Virginia. She married Nelson Clay Dotson, June 21, 1944, at Staunton, Virginia.

(Sup) 5869   i William Clay Dotson, born October, 1946.

3595 JAMES WINFREE COX (Alma[7], Martha[6], Daniel[5], John[4], Peter[3], Matthias[2], John Jacob[1]) was born May 5, 1925, in Augusta County, Virginia. He married Elizabeth Knott, December 20, 1946.

3596 WILLIAM DOUGLAS COX (Alma[7], Martha[6], Daniel[5], John[4], Peter[3], Matthias[2], John Jacob[1]) was born May 14, 1926, at Staunton, Virginia.

3597 ELIZABETH KATHRYN COX (Alma[7], Martha[6], Daniel[5], John[4], Peter[3], Matthias[2], John Jacob[1]) was born September 14, 1927, at Staunton, Virginia.

3598 SAMUEL JACKSON COX (Alma[7], Martha[6], Daniel[5], John[4], Peter[3], Matthias[2], John Jacob[1]) was born November 5, 1928, at Staunton, Virginia.

3599 MARTHA ANN COX (Alma[7], Martha[6], Daniel[5], John[4], Peter[3], Matthias[2], John Jacob[1]) was born October 30, 1929, at Staunton, Virginia.

3600 MARY JANE COX (Alma[7], Martha[6], Daniel[5], John[4], Peter[3], Matthias[2], John Jacob[1]) was born December 28, 1934, at Staunton, Virginia.

3601 FRED BERKLEY COX (Alma[7], Martha[6], Daniel[5], John[4], Peter[3], Matthias[2], John Jacob[1]) was born November 11, 1938, at Staunton, Virginia.

3602 ALMA SUE COX (Alma[7], Martha[6], Daniel[5], John[4], Peter[3], Matthias[2], John Jacob[1]) was born July 7, 1942, at Staunton, Virginia.

3603 MARTHA VIRGINIA CRUTE (Virginia[7], Martha[6], Daniel[5], John[4], Peter[3], Matthias[2], John Jacob[1]) was born March 12, 1933, at Stuarts Draft, Virginia.

3604 KAY SPENCER CRUTE (Virginia[7], Martha[6], Daniel[5], John[4], Peter[3], Matthias[2], John Jacob[1]) was born March 28, 1934.

3605 JANE MORTON CRUTE (Virginia[7], Martha[6], Daniel[5], John[4], Peter[3], Matthias[2], John Jacob[1]) was born October 17, 1936.

3606 NANCY BOWMAN QUICK (Bowman[7], Martha[6], Daniel[5], John[4], Peter[3], Matthias[2], John Jacob[1]) was born June 5, 1941, at Waynesboro, Virginia.

3607 JUDITH BENNETT QUICK (Bowman[7], Martha[6], Daniel[5], John[4], Peter[3], Matthias[2], John Jacob[1]) was born November 17, 1944, at Waynesboro, Virginia.

3608 CHARLES LEE QUICK (Jackson[7], Martha[6], Daniel[5], John[4], Peter[3], Matthias[2], John Jacob[1]) was born September 22, 1934, in Augusta County, Virginia, where he died August 10, 1935.

3609 SHIRLEY ANNE QUICK (Jackson[7], Martha[6], Daniel[5], John[4], Peter[3], Matthias[2], John Jacob[1]) was born October 29, 1935, in Augusta County, Virginia.

3610 JACKSON EUTAH QUICK, JR. (Jackson[7], Martha[6], Daniel[5], John[4], Peter[3], Matthias[2], John Jacob[1]) was born February 20, 1937, in Augusta County, Virginia.

3611 BRYA MORRIS QUICK (Jackson[7], Martha[6], Daniel[5], John[4], Peter[3], Matthias[2], John Jacob[1]) was born August 10, 1939, in Augusta County, Virginia.

3612 LOLA JEAN QUICK (Jackson[7], Martha[6], Daniel[5], John[4], Peter[3], Matthias[2], John Jacob[1]) was born January 4, 1943, in Augusta County, Virginia.

3613 BARBARA LEE QUICK (Jackson[7], Martha[6], Daniel[5], John[4], Peter[3], Matthias[2], John Jacob[1]) was born April 17, 1945, in Augusta County, Virginia.

3614 STUART JACKSON WAMSLEY (La Mira[7], Martha[6], Daniel[5], John[4], Peter[3], Matthias[2], John Jacob[1]) was born September 27, 1937, at Staunton, Virginia.

3615 ALICE TOE WAMSLEY (La Mira[7], Martha[6], Daniel[5], John[4], Peter[3], Matthias[2], John Jacob[1]) was born June 9, 1939, at Staunton, Virginia.

3616 CHARLES RAYMOND HOUFF (Joseph[7], John[6], Susan[5], John[4], Peter[3], Matthias[2], John Jacob[1]) was born May 11, 1891, in Augusta County, Virginia. He married Ethel Sheets in 1914.

3617 JOHN FRANKLIN HOUFF (Joseph[7], John[6], Susan[5], John[4], Peter[3], Matthias[2], John Jacob[1]) was born October 25, 1894, in Augusta County, Virginia. He married Roxie Varner, February 14, 1918.

3618 ROY GORDON HOUFF (Joseph[7], John[6], Susan[5], John[4], Peter[3], Matthias[2], John Jacob[1]) was born September 18, 1896, at Mount Sidney, Virginia. He married Cora Pullins at Fort Defiance, Virginia, June 2, 1923. Cora was born August 28, 1897, at Mount Sidney.

(Sup) 5871   † Raymond Maurice Houff.
(Sup) 5872   †† Ethel Annette Houff.

3619 CARL BENJAMIN HOUFF (Joseph[7], John[6], Susan[5], John[4], Peter[3], Matthias[2], John Jacob[1]) was born February 5, 1898, in Augusta County, Virginia. He married Lucille Sampson in 1921.

3620 EVA F. HOUFF (Joseph[7], John[6], Susan[5], John[4], Peter[3], Matthias[2], John Jacob[1]) was born January 30, 1900, in Augusta County, Virginia. She married Forrest Daniel Click, June 15, 1918, at Mount Tabor, Virginia. She married Forrest was the son of Joseph and Cecelia Spreekhise Click and was born May 21, 1894, at Mount Sidney, Virginia.

(Sup) 5873   † Joseph Paul Click, born June 8, 1919.
(Sup) 5874   †† Hardenia Carolyn Click, born September 7, 1923.
(Sup) 5875   ††† Mary Helen Click, born January 29, 1932.

3621 HAZEL RUTH HOUFF (Joseph[7], John[6], Susan[5], John[4], Peter[3], Matthias[2], John Jacob[1]) was born January 3, 1903, at Mount Sidney, Virginia. She married William Austin Landes, May 31, 1922, at Lebanon, Pennsylvania. William was the son of John Alexander and Margaret Moore Landes and was born July 13, 1900, at Mount Sidney, Virginia.

(Sup) 5876 i Charlotte Catherine Landes, born February 15, 1923.
(Sup) 5877 ii Maxine Ellen Landes, born August 14, 1924.
(Sup) 5878 iii Bernice Imogene Landes, born July 23, 1926.
(Sup) 5879 iv Richard Stanly Landes, born September 28, 1930.
(Sup) 5880 v Martha Lucille Landes, born July 26, 1933.
(Sup) 5881 vi Nancy Lee Landes, born February 26, 1936.
(Sup) 5882 vii James Franklin Landes, born April 17, 1938.
(Sup) 5883 viii Helen Ruth Landes, born September 9, 1939.

3622 RICE TATUM SCOTT (Lulu[7], John[6], Susan[5], John[4], Peter[3], Matthias[2], John Jacob[1]) was born January 26, 1900, at Clifton Forge, Virginia. He married Ella Peters there, May 8, 1921.

(Sup) 5884 i Mildred Juanita Scott, born September 30, 1923.
(Sup) 5885 ii Louis Merrian Scott, born March 9, 1927.
(Sup) 5886 iii Mary Lou Scott, born July 1, 1928.

3623 MARGARET VIRGINIA SCOTT (Lulu[7], John[6], Susan[5], John[4], Peter[3], Matthias[2], John Jacob[1]) was born October 24, 1904, at Clifton Forge, Virginia. She died unmarried, September 25, 1920, at Roanoke, Virginia, and was buried at Staunton, Virginia.

3624 ROY HOMER SCOTT (Lulu[7], John[6], Susan[5], John[4], Peter[3], Matthias[2], John Jacob[1]) was born September 15, 1906, at Clifton Forge, Virginia. He married Katherine Matheny, May 28, 1939, at Russell, Kentucky. Katherine was the daughter of George and Gypsey Bartlett Matheny and was born August 3, 1915, at Ronceverte, West Virginia.

(Sup) 5887 i Elizabeth Ann Scott, born September 26, 1940.

3625 IVA MAE SCOTT (Lulu[7], John[6], Susan[5], John[4], Peter[3], Matthias[2], John Jacob[1]) was born October 15, 1909, at Roanoke, Virginia. She married John Carmack, February 26, 1933.

(Sup) 5888 i Margaret Ann Carmack, born July 2, 1935.
(Sup) 5889 ii Nancy Patricia Carmack, born October 30, 1941.

3626 MARY GLADYS SCOTT (Lulu[7], John[6], Susan[5], John[4], Peter[3], Matthias[2], John Jacob[1]) was born August 7, 1911, at Roanoke, Virginia.

3627 LOUIS A. HOUFF (Andrew[7], John[6], Susan[5], John[4], Peter[3], Matthias[2], John Jacob[1]) was born September 27, 1903, at Clifton Forge, Virginia. He married Ethel Bartlett, June 1, 1934, at Clifton Forge. Ethel was the daughter of J. P. and Calla Ward Bartlett and was born October 16, 1912, at Rural Home, Grayson County, Virginia. Louis studied medicine and became a practicing physician at Clifton Forge, Virginia.

(Sup) 5890 i Louis A. Houff, Jr., born February 5, 1936.
(Sup) 5891 ii James Neff Houff, born February 19, 1938.

3628 JAMES H. HOUFF (Andrew[7], John[6], Susan[5], John[4], Peter[3], Matthias[2], John Jacob[1]) was born October 7, 1908. He married Audrey Justice in 1932.

(Sup) 3629 HELEN HULVEY (Otey[7], Elizabeth[6], Susan[5], John[4], Peter[3], Matthias[2], John Jacob[1]) was the daughter of Otey Crawford and Geneva Silling Hulvey [The Link Family, page 523, No. 1953]. Helen married Arthur Barnes.

(Sup) 5892 i Arthur Milton Barnes, Jr., born May 12, 1925.
(Sup) 5893 ii Robert Crawford Barnes.

3630 LOUISE HULVEY (Otey[7], Elizabeth[6], Susan[5], John[4], Peter[3], Matthias[2], John Jacob[1]) married Paul Jones King.

3631 MARGERY HULVEY (Otey[7], Elizabeth[6], Susan[5], John[4], Peter[3], Matthias[2], John Jacob[1]) married Willard P. Bratten.

(Sup) 5894 i Willard P. Bratten, Jr.
(Sup) 5895 ii James Crawford Bratten.

3632 WINIFRED JOHNSON (Florence[7], Elizabeth[6], Susan[5], John[4], Peter[3], Matthias[2], John Jacob[1]) married a Mr. Fogle.

(Sup) 3633 ELIZABETH DRUEN JOHNSON (Florence[7], Elizabeth[6], Susan[5], John[4], Peter[3], Matthias[2], John Jacob[1]) was the daughter of James Crossman and Florence Hulvey Johnson [The Link Family, page 523, No. 1955]. Elizabeth was born June 19, 1909, in Augusta County, Virginia.

3634 WILBUR HULVEY JOHNSON (Florence[7], Elizabeth[6], Susan[5], John[4], Peter[3], Matthias[2], John Jacob[1]) was born May 27, 1912, at Avon, Illinois. He married Catherine Coyner, September 25, 1937, at Waynesboro, Virginia. Catherine was the daughter of Samuel and Myrtle Verner Coyner and was born January 14, 1916, at Waynesboro.

(Sup) 5896 i Jean Palmer Johnson, born August 25, 1945.
(Sup) 5897 ii Robert Michael Johnson, born March 18, 1947.

3635 JAMES CHRISTIAN JOHNSON (Florence[7], Elizabeth[6], Susan[5], John[4], Peter[3], Matthias[2], John Jacob[1]) was born February 20, 1914, at Avon, Illinois. He married Mildred Shaner, September 10, 1945, at Washington, D. C. Mildred was born February 20, 1921, at Staunton, Virginia.

(Sup) 5898 i Nella Roberta Johnson, born June 17, 1946.
(Sup) 5899 ii Wanda Joanne Johnson, born July 2, 1947.

3636 HARRY CRAWFORD JOHNSON (Florence[7], Elizabeth[6], Susan[5], John[4], Peter[3], Matthias[2], John Jacob[1]) was born August 19, 1916, at Avon, Illinois. He married Virginia Daniel.

(Sup) 5900 Harry Coyt Johnson.

(Sup) 3636A VIRGINIA HULVEY (John[7], Elizabeth[6], Susan[5], John[4], Peter[3], Matthias[2], John Jacob[1]) was the daughter of John Christian and Effie Greiner Hulvey, Jr. [The Link Family, page 524, No. 1956]. and Supplement No. 1956]. Virginia was born September 13, 1902. She married Mr. Snead.

(Sup) 3636G GRACE HULVEY (John[7], Elizabeth[6], Susan[5], John[4], Peter[3], Matthias[2], John Jacob[1]) was the daughter of John Christian and Jane Fifer Hulvey, Jr. [The Link Family, page 524, No. 1956; and Supplement No. 1956]. Grace was born December 27, 1928, at Staunton, Virginia. She married John E. Marshall October 28, 1948, at Staunton. He was born January 14, 1916.

(Sup) 3636H BENJAMIN FRANKLIN HULVEY, JR. (Benjamin[7], Elizabeth[6], Susan[5], John[4], Peter[3], Matthias[2], John Jacob[1]) was the son of Benjamin F. and Lucy Sutton Hulvey [The Link Family, page 524, No. 1958; and Supplement No. 1958]. Ben, Jr., was born July 6, 1907, at Staunton, Virginia. He married Virginia Fontaine Thompson June 6, 1931, at Staunton. She was born February 3, 1914, at Staunton. Ben died October 30, 1958.

(Sup) 5911   i   Robert Dale Hulvey, born March 29, 1932.
(Sup) 5912   ii   Nancy Mildred Hulvey, born May 16, 1933.
(Sup) 5913   iii Anna Virginia Hulvey, born January 3, 1935.
(Sup) 5914   iv   Gloria Jean Hulvey, born April 8, 1936.
(Sup) 5915   v   James Franklin Hulvey, born June 21, 1938.

(Sup) 3636I MARY ELIZABETH HULVEY (Benjamin[7], Elizabeth[6], Susan[5], John[4], Peter[3], Matthias[2], John Jacob[1]) was the daughter of Benjamin F. and Lucy Sutton Hulvey [The Link Family, page 524, No. 1958; and Supplement No. 1958]. She was born July 28, 1909, at Staunton, Virginia. She married Russell Lee Wilberger August 4, 1934, at Staunton. Russell was born December 24, 1909. He was a service station owner and operator.

(Sup) 5916   i   Donald Lee Wilberger, born February 13, 1936.

(Sup) 3636J GLADYS MAUDE HULVEY (Benjamin[7], Elizabeth[6], Susan[5], John[4], Peter[3], Matthias[2], John Jacob[1]) was the daughter of Benjamin F. and Lucy Sutton Hulvey [The Link Family, page 524, No. 1958; and Supplement No. 1958]. Gladys was born December 18, 1910, in Augusta County, Virginia. She married Bruce Eugene Windham November 19, 1937. Bruce was employed by the Texaco Company. He died March 8, 1969.

(Sup) 5917   i   Lucy Anna Windham, born September 27, 1938.
(Sup) 5918   ii   Carol Bruce Windham, born August 24, 1943.

(Sup) 3636K MARGARET CHRISTINE HULVEY (Benjamin[7], Elizabeth[6], Susan[5], John[4], Peter[3], Matthias[2], John Jacob[1]) was the daughter of Benjamin F. and Lucy Sutton Hulvey [The Link Family, page 524, No. 1958; and Supplement No. 1958]. She was born July 1, 1913, in Augusta County, Virginia. In 1934 she married Jess Willard Vines, who was born April 9, 1912. They were divorced.

(Sup) 5919   i   Patricia Ann Vines, born August 6, 1935.
(Sup) 5920   ii   Jacquelyn Burns Vines, born February 7, 1940.

(Sup) 3636B EFFIE THELMA HULVEY (John[7], Elizabeth[6], Susan[5], John[4], Peter[3], Matthias[2], John Jacob[1]) was the daughter of John Christian and Effie Greiner Hulvey, Jr. [The Link Family, page 524, No. 1956; and Supplement No. 1956]. Thelma was born November 9, 1908, at Staunton, Virginia. She received her A.B. degree from Mary Baldwin College, Staunton. She married Frank Charles Meyer, III, June 18, 1938, at Charlottesville, Virginia. He was the son of Frank C. and Pauline Pfeifle Meyer, Jr., and was born April 5, 1917, at Brooklyn, New York. Frank, III, was a doctor of medicine. He and Thelma resided at Oswego, New York.

(Sup) 5901   i   Barbara Anne Meyer, born May 28, 1940.
(Sup) 5902   ii   Virginia Hulvey Meyer, born June 18, 1941.
(Sup) 5903   iii Martha Mowry Meyer, born February 7, 1944.
(Sup) 5904   iv   Mary Elizabeth Meyer, born September 24, 1947.
(Sup) 5905   v   Frank Charles Meyer, IV, born January 6, 1950.

(Sup) 3636C TULULU HULVEY (John[7], Elizabeth[6], Susan[5], John[4], Peter[3], Matthias[2], John Jacob[1]) was the daughter of John Christian and Effie Greiner Hulvey, Jr. [The Link Family, page 524, No. 1956; and Supplement No. 1956]. Tululu was born November 9, 1908, the twin of Thelma. She died an infant in 1908, a few days after her mother, and is buried at Pleasant View Lutheran Cemetery in Augusta County, Virginia.

(Sup) 3636D JOHN WILLIAM HULVEY (John[7], Elizabeth[6], Susan[5], John[4], Peter[3], Matthias[2], John Jacob[1]) was the son of John Christian and Jane Fifer Hulvey, Jr. [The Link Family, page 524, No. 1956; and Supplement No. 1956]. John William was born October 21, 1914, at Staunton, Virginia. He married Lelia Radford, and they lived in Roanoke, Virginia. He died February 6, 1960.

(Sup) 5906   i   John Thomas Hulvey, born November 15, 1935.
(Sup) 5907   ii   Larry William Hulvey, born May 16, 1943.

(Sup) 3636E MARGARET HULVEY (John[7], Elizabeth[6], Susan[5], John[4], Peter[3], Matthias[2], John Jacob[1]) was the daughter of John Christian and Jane Fifer Hulvey, Jr. [The Link Family, page 524, No. 1956; and Supplement No. 1956]. Margaret was born October 21, 1915, at Staunton, Virginia. She married Charles Henry Hamlett March 10, 1934, at Covington, Virginia. He was the son of James Robert and Cora Lee Smith Hamlett and was born September 2, 1912, at Ronceverte, West Virginia. He died May 2, 1982.

(Sup) 3636F HELEN HULVEY (John[7], Elizabeth[6], Susan[5], John[4], Peter[3], Matthias[2], John Jacob[1]) was the daughter of John Christian and Jane Fifer Hulvey, Jr. [The Link Family, page 524, No. 1956; and Supplement No. 1956]. Helen was born January 28, 1925, at Staunton, Virginia. She married Samuel Alexander.

(Sup) 5908   i   Constance Elaine Alexander, born June 10, 1952.
(Sup) 5909   ii   Steven Scott Alexander, born July 25, 1956.
(Sup) 5910   iii Sue Ann Alexander, born March 4, 1963.

born August 5, 1924, at Wenatchee, Washington. He died January 22, 1983, at Charlottesville.

(Sup) 5925   i   John William Hulvey, Jr., born January 24, 1949.
(Sup) 5926   ii Elizabeth Cullen Hulvey, born May 18, 1951.
(Sup) 5927   iii Charles Newton Hulvey III, born Dec 17, 1957.
(Sup) 5928   iv Sarah Archer Hulvey, born November 2, 1959.

3637 INA IOPHA SHEETS (Otto[7], Sarah[6], Susan[5], John[4], Peter[3], Matthias[2], John Jacob[1]) was born December 21, 1897, at Mount Sidney, Virginia. She died December 26, 1911, in Augusta County, Virginia.

3638 HERBERT DWIGHT SHEETS (Otto[7], Sarah[6], Susan[5], John[4], Peter[3], Matthias[2], John Jacob[1]) was born December 21, 1899, at Mount Sidney, Virginia. He married Crystal Wiseman, July 14, 1926, at Hagerstown, Maryland. Crystal was the daughter of William and Belle Frink Wiseman.

(Sup) 5929   1   Herbert Dwight Sheets, Jr.
(Sup) 5930   11 Eugene Earl Sheets.

3639 VIOLA CHRISTINA SHEETS (Otto[7], Sarah[6], Susan[5], John[4], Peter[3], Matthias[2], John Jacob[1]) was born October 26, 1904, at Mount Sidney, Virginia.

3640 EVA VIRGINIA SHEETS (Otto[7], Sarah[6], Susan[5], John[4], Peter[3], Matthias[2], John Jacob[1]) was born January 20, 1906, at Mount Sidney, Virginia. She married James Shattuck, February 11, 1928.

(Sup) 5931   1   Audrey La Verne Shattuck.
(Sup) 5932   11 Mary Lou Shattuck.

3641 MINNIE BELL SHEETS (Otto[7], Sarah[6], Susan[5], John[4], Peter[3], Matthias[2], John Jacob[1]) was born August 31, 1909, at Mount Sidney, Virginia. She married Medford Wright, November 4, 1929, at Rockville, Maryland. Medford was the son of Ocle B. and Violetta Wheeler Wright and was born April 2, 1906, at Rayo, Virginia.

(Sup) 5933   i   Joan Christine Wright.

3642 MARY ELIZABETH SHEETS (Otto[7], Sarah[6], Susan[5], John[4], Peter[3], Matthias[2], John Jacob[1]) was born October 28, 1911, at Mount Sidney, Virginia. She married Lester Rhinehart, October 21, 1933, at Verona, Virginia. Lester, son of John and Evalina Weller Rhinehart, was born August 3, 1907, near Bullville, New York.

(Sup) 5934   i   Kenneth Lester Rhinehart, born August 8, 1936.
(Sup) 5935   ii William Otto Rhinehart, born June 21, 1939.

3643 MEREDITH WAYNE SHEETS (Mary[7], Sarah[6], Susan[5], John[4], Peter[3], Matthias[2], John Jacob[1]) was born November 22, 1907, at Brooklyn, Iowa. He married Mary Daisy Downing, February 6, 1937. Mary, daughter of Daniel A. and Laura Croft Downing, was born October 7, 1910, at Green City, Missouri.

(Sup) 5936   i   Ivan Wayne Sheets, born May 7, 1938.
(Sup) 5937   ii Melvin Robert Sheets, born June 22, 1940.
(Sup) 5938   iii James Dwight Sheets, born December 8, 1944.

(Sup) 3636L HOWARD M. HULVEY (Benjamin[7], Elizabeth[6], Susan[5], John[4], Peter[3], Matthias[2], John Jacob[1]) was the son of Benjamin F. and Lucy Sutton Hulvey [The Link Family, page 524, No. 1958; and Supplement No. 1958]. Howard was born June 21, 1915, in Augusta county, Virginia. He married Genevieve Ellinger August 24, 1936, in Maryland. She was the daughter of Earl E. and Lottie Lucas Ellinger and was born June 6, 1916, in Augusta County, Virginia. They owned and operated Arcade Dry Cleaners, Fredericksburg, Virginia.

(Sup) 5921   i   Wanda Louise Hulvey, born October 26, 1939.
(Sup) 5922   ii Benjamin Earl Hulvey, born November 5, 1943.

(Sup) 3636M CHARLES NEWTON HULVEY, JR. (Charles[7], Elizabeth[6], Susan[5], John[4], Peter[3], Matthias[2], John Jacob[1]) was the son of Charles Newton and Pearl Pickel Hulvey [The Link Family, page 524, No. 1959]. Charles was born May 13, 1913, at Sweetwater, Tennessee. He received the B.S. degree from the University of Virginia in 1936 and became an attorney in 1950. He married Jean Meredith Sprague May 31, 1949, at Amherst, Virginia. She was the daughter of George Finley and Anna Rose Robertson Sprague and was born September 10, 1912, at Twin Falls, Idaho. The Hon. Charles N. Hulvey retired as Substitute Judge for the General District Court, Arlington, Virginia. Jean died January 25, 1978.

(Sup) 5923   i   Jean Meredith Hulvey, born October 31, 1952.

(Sup) 3636N MARGARET ANN HULVEY (Charles[7], Elizabeth[6], Susan[5], John[4], Peter[3], Matthias[2], John Jacob[1]) was the daughter of Charles Newton and Pearl Pickel Hulvey [The Link Family, page 524, No. 1959; and Supplement No. 1959]. Margaret was born November 6, 1915, at Sweetwater, Tennessee. She married John Henry Wright, Jr., January 5, 1936, at Coral Gables, Florida. He was the son of John Henry and Jeanette Whitmore Wright and was born July 27, 1913, at Lynchburg, Virginia. Margaret received a B.A. degree from the University of Miami in 1937 and was a real estate agent in Charlottesville, Virginia. John died November 14, 1946.

(Sup) 5924   i   John Henry Wright, III, born April 25, 1939.

(Sup) 3636P JOHN WILLIAM HULVEY (Charles[7], Elizabeth[6], Susan[5], John[4], Peter[3], Matthias[2], John Jacob[1]) was the son of Charles Newton and Pearl Pickel Hulvey [The Link Family, page 524, No. 1959]. Bill was born April 5, 1922, at Charlottesville, Virginia. He served in the U.S. Marine Corps during World War II, both as enlisted and officer. He received a B.S. degree in commerce from the University of Virginia in 1948. He was in the wholesale lumber business. He married Virginia Lee Broome October 11, 1946, at Charlottesville. She was the daughter of Nathaniel Wilson and Elizabeth Cullen Anderson Broome and was

3644 RAYMOND SHEETS (Mary[7], Sarah[6], Susan[5], John[4], Peter[3], Matthias[2], John Jacob[1]) was born January 7, 1909, at Brooklyn, Iowa. He married Edna Vogt, May 25, 1938, at Gilman, Iowa. Edna was born June 27, 1914, at Melbourne, Iowa, and was the daughter of Henry and Henrietta Abraham Vogt.

3645 STOVER McCLAIN SHEETS (Mary[7], Sarah[6], Susan[5], John[4], Peter[3], Matthias[2], John Jacob[1]) was born March 16, 1910, at Brooklyn, Iowa. He married Mabel Irene Parker, December 9, 1933, at Des Moines, Iowa. Mabel was the daughter of Melvin and Margaret Kendall Parker and was born August 3, 1908, at Muncie, Indiana.

(Sup) 5939 † Patsy Ann Sheets, born and died May 27, 1937.
(Sup) 5940 †† Yvonne Kay Sheets, born May 1, 1939.
(Sup) 5941 ††† Robert Le Roy Sheets, born January 25, 1941.

3646 ORNA RUTH SHEETS (Arvil[7], Sarah[6], Susan[5], John[4], Peter[3], Matthias[2], John Jacob[1]) was born October 14, 1906, at Mount Sidney, Virginia.

3647 ISA VIRGINIA SHEETS (Arvil[7], Sarah[6], Susan[5], John[4], Peter[3], Matthias[2], John Jacob[1]) was born September 2, 1908, at Mount Sidney, Virginia. She married Roy B. Simmons, August 1, 1933, in Augusta County, Virginia.

(Sup) 5942 † Sallie Jane Simmons, born September 11, 1936.
(Sup) 5943 †† William Arvil Simmons, born November 29, 1938.

3648 PAUL STICKLEY SHEETS (Arvil[7], Sarah[6], Susan[5], John[4], Peter[3], Matthias[2], John Jacob[1]) was born July 27, 1910, in Augusta County, Virginia. He married Joanna Grey Bright, June 16, 1936, at Churchville, Virginia. Joanna was born December 7, 1912, at Deerfield, Bath County, Virginia.

(Sup) 5944 † Dorothy Lee Sheets, born January 6, 1938.
(Sup) 5945 †† Rebecca Sue Sheets, born September 28, 1946.
(Sup) 5946 ††† Carolyn Anne Sheets, born April 13, 1948.

3649 ARTHUR WAYNE SHEETS (Arvil[7], Sarah[6], Susan[5], John[4], Peter[3], Matthias[2], John Jacob[1]) was born August 2, 1912, at Mount Sidney, Virginia. He married Gladys May Switzer, April 30, 1940, at Mount Sidney, Virginia.

3650 ARVIL HAMLIN SHEETS (Arvil[7], Sarah[6], Susan[5], John[4], Peter[3], Matthias[2], John Jacob[1]) was born April 24, 1920, at Mount Sidney, Virginia.

3651 JOSEPH HOWARD SHEETS (Bernard[7], Sarah[6], Susan[5], John[4], Peter[3], Matthias[2], John Jacob[1]) was born November 11, 1913, at Brooklyn, Iowa. He married Pauletta Horn.

3652 BERNARD CLAUDE SHEETS (Bernard[7], Sarah[6], Susan[5], John[4], Peter[3], Matthias[2], John Jacob[1]) was born July 13, 1915, at Brooklyn, Iowa. He married Erma Evalee Sandy, September 20, 1941, at Mount Solon, Virginia.

(Sup) 5947 † Robert Milton Sheets.
(Sup) 5948 †† Linda Anne Sheets.

3653 LAURA PEARL SHEETS (Bernard[7], Sarah[6], Susan[5], John[4], Peter[3], Matthias[2], John Jacob[1]) was born February 5, 1917, at Brooklyn, Iowa. She married Haven William Kessel, June 14, 1941, at Mount Pisgah, Virginia. Haven was born October 30, 1915, at Fisher, West Virginia.

(Sup) 5949 † Jeanette Marie Kessel, born May 29, 1943.
(Sup) 5950 †† Sylvia Jean Kessel, born December 19, 1947.

3654 LOIS VIRGINIA SHEETS (Bernard[7], Sarah[6], Susan[5], John[4], Peter[3], Matthias[2], John Jacob[1]) was born July 25, 1919, at Mount Sidney, Virginia. She married Randall Fletcher Gwin, July 17, 1943, at Mount Sidney. Randall was the son of William T. and Maude Gwin and was born July 10, 1917.

(Sup) 5951 † Joan Patricia Gwin, born May 17, 1944.
(Sup) 5952 †† Carlyle Evans Gwin, born August 2, 1945.
(Sup) 5953 ††† Alvin Lloyd Gwin, born September 16, 1946.
(Sup) 5954 †v Leslie Wayne Gwin, born August 24, 1947.

3655 CHARLOTTE MAY SHEETS (Bernard[7], Sarah[6], Susan[5], John[4], Peter[3], Matthias[2], John Jacob[1]) was born October 1, 1923, in Augusta County, Virginia.

3656 EVELYN WENGER SHEETS (Bernard[7], Sarah[6], Susan[5], John[4], Peter[3], Matthias[2], John Jacob[1]) was born May 22, 1926, in Augusta County, Virginia.

3657 BEULAH CHLOE SHEETS (Bernard[7], Sarah[6], Susan[5], John[4], Peter[3], Matthias[2], John Jacob[1]) was born August 28, 1928, in Augusta County, Virginia. She married John Root.

3658 CASPER W. GARBER (Sada[7], William[6], Susan[5], John[4], Peter[3], Matthias[2], John Jacob[1]) was born August 2, 1908, at Mount Sidney, Virginia. He married Helen Clemmer, July 2, 1930.

3659 MERLIN E. GARBER (Sada[7], William[6], Susan[5], John[4], Peter[3], Matthias[2], John Jacob[1]) was born March 26, 1912, at Fort Defiance, Virginia. He married Dorothy Faw, June 3, 1934, at Roanoke, Virginia. Dorothy was the daughter of Ross Amos and Georgianna Hatter Faw and was born February 4, 1912.

(Sup) 5957 † Leland Faw Garber, born August 9, 1937.
(Sup) 5958 †† Elaine Estella Garber, born March 9, 1940.

3660 ELVA OTITIA GARBER (Sada[7], William[6], Susan[5], John[4], Peter[3], Matthias[2], John Jacob[1]) was born January 28, 1916, at Buena Vista, Virginia. She married Warren Justus Huffman, August 20, 1938, at Staunton, Virginia. Warren, son of Wade J. and Ruth Esther Shiflett Huffman, was born October 14, 1916, at Harrisonburg, Virginia.

(Sup) 5959 † James Warren Huffman, born October 28, 1940.
(Sup) 5960 †† Larry Richard Huffman, born November 14, 1942.

3661 MAYNARD A. GARBER (Sada[7], William[6], Susan[5], John[4], Peter[3], Matthias[2], John Jacob[1]) was born February 23, 1920, in Augusta County, Virginia.

3662 FRANCIS HOUFF (William^7, William^6, Susan^5, John^4, Peter^3, Matthias^2, John Jacob^1) was born August 31, 1912, in Augusta County, Virginia.

3663 KATHLEEN HOUFF (William^7, William^6, Susan^5, John^4, Peter^3, Matthias^2, John Jacob^1) was born May 19, 1917, in Augusta County, Virginia. She married a Mr. Michael.

3664 MILDRED HOUFF (William^7, William^6, Susan^5, John^4, Peter^3, Matthias^2, John Jacob^1) was born March 28, 1921, in Augusta County, Virginia. She married a Mr. Cason.

3665 WILLIAM A. HOUFF, JR. (William^7, William^6, Susan^5, John^4, Peter^3, Matthias^2, John Jacob^1) was born December 31, 1925, in Augusta County, Virginia.

3666 WILLIAM A. GEORGE (Iva^7, Sarah^6, John^5, John^4, Peter^3, Matthias^2, John Jacob^1) married Maxine Freeman, December 13, 1924. William married Meryl Reynolds, July 14, 1931.

CHILD OF WILLIAM AND MAXINE

(Sup) 5961 i Margaret Mae George, born April 28, 1926.

CHILD OF WILLIAM AND MERYL

(Sup) 5962 ii Wilford George, born March 5, 1935.

3667 OLIVER EDWIN PECK (Ora^7, John^6, John^5, John^4, Peter^3, Matthias^2, John Jacob^1) was born April 7, 1903, at La Harpe, Illinois. He married Lucille Barbe, April 5, 1926. Oliver died at La Harpe, November 3, 1931.

(Sup) 5963 i Doran Willis Peck, born December 24, 1926.
(Sup) 5964 ii Loren Edwin Peck, born January 17, 1928.

3668 LOLA ELVA LINK (Sidney^7, John^6, John^5, John^4, Peter^3, Matthias^2, John Jacob^1) was born March 30, 1911, at La Harpe. She married Orville Theodore Cooper, December 21, 1929, at Macomb, Illinois. Orville, son of John Cooper, was born June 21, 1904, at La Harpe, Illinois. Orville served in the U. S. Navy in World War II.

(Sup) 5965 i Richard Theodore Cooper, born April 3, 1931.
(Sup) 5966 ii Dolores Jean Cooper, born July 7, 1932.
(Sup) 5967 iii Hazelmae Cooper, born June 6, 1934.

(Sup) 3669 JOHN EDWIN LINK (Sidney^7, John^6, John^5, John^4, Peter^3, Matthias^2, John Jacob^1) was the son of Sidney Chester and Sophronia McCord Link [The Link Family, page 526, No. 1984]. John was born March 23, 1913, in Durham Township, Hancock County, Illinois. He married Kathryn Jane Manifold, May 11, 1942. She was the daughter of A. R. Manifold and was born May 11, 1918, at La Harpe, Illinois.

(Sup) 5968 i John Leonard Link, born May 3, 1944.
(Sup) 5969 ii Nina Eleanor Link, born November 24, 1945.
(Sup) 5970 iii Edwina Jane Link, born January 9, 1947.
(Sup) 5971 iv Lyle Arthur Link, born July 31, 1948.
(Sup) 5972 v Rex Eugene Link, born December 23, 1949.
(Sup) 5973 vi Ann Elizabeth Link, born October 6, 1951.

(Sup) 3670 VERNON CHESTER LINK (Sidney^7, John^6, John^5, John^4, Peter^3, Matthias^2, John Jacob^1) was the son of Sidney Chester and Sophronia McCord Link [The Link Family, page 526, No. 1984]. He was born April, 1914, and died in infancy.

(Sup) 3671 ELDON EARL LINK (Sidney^7, John^6, John^5, John^4, Peter^3, Matthias^2, John Jacob^1) was the son of Sidney Chester and Sophronia McCord Link [The Link Family, page 526, No. 1984]. Eldon was born June 22, 1916, at Courtney, North Dakota. He married Hazel Pauline Brewer August 1, 1938.

(Sup) 5974 i Edwin Earl Link, born February 12, 1939.
(Sup) 5975 ii David Paul Link, born March 30, 1941.
(Sup) 5976 iii Carolyn Sue Link, born October 14, 1945.
(Sup) 5977 iv Becky Jean Link, born November 8, 1959.

(Sup) 3672 KATHERINE MAE LINK (Sidney^7, John^6, John^5, John^4, Peter^3, Matthias^2, John Jacob^1) was the daughter of Sidney Chester and Sophronia McCord Link [The Link Family, page 526, No. 1984]. Katherine was born October 20, 1918, at Disco, Illinois. She married Robert Glendal Glisan, February 27, 1936, at Macomb, Illinois. Robert was born August 22, 1914, at Williams Town, Missouri.

(Sup) 5978 i Patricia Joan Glisan, born July 7, 1937.
(Sup) 5979 ii Marjorie Catherine Glisan, born October 7, 1939.
(Sup) 5980 iii Jaunita Farrell Glisan, born December 22, 1945.
(Sup) 5981 iv Ronald Gregory Glisan, born March 28, 1949.
(Sup) 5982 v Roger Mason Glisan, born December 19, 1950.

(Sup) 3673 HERMAN GEORGE LINK (Sidney^7, John^6, John^5, John^4, Peter^3, Matthias^2, John Jacob^1) was the son of Sidney Chester and Sophronia McCord Link [The Link Family, page 526, No. 1984]. Herman was born October 20, 1918, at Disco, Illinois. He served in World War II and was taken prisoner off Corregidor Island; he was held for three years and three months and was released in 1945. Herman married Virginia Lou France July 11, 1948, at La Harpe, Illinois. She was the daughter of Hardy and Lillie Johnson France and was born July 2, 1930, at Ipava, Illinois. Virginia died March 28, 1976, and is buried at Ursa, Illinois.

(Sup) 5983 i George Kenneth Link, born June 7, 1949.
(Sup) 5984 ii Phillip Allen Link, born March 13, 1951.
(Sup) 5985 iii Judy Adelle Link, born March 16, 1953
(Sup) 5986 iv Peggy Diane Link, born April 13, 1954 (twin).
(Sup) 5987 v Nancy Joann Link, born April 13, 1954 (twin).
(Sup) 5988 vi William Andrew Link, born August 20, 1955.
(Sup) 5989 vii James Francis Link, born March 23, 1957.
(Sup) 5990 viii Marion Katherine Link, born March 18, 1959.

(Sup) 3674 KENNETH RAY LINK (Sidney[7], John[6], John[5], John[4], Peter[3], Matthias[2], John Jacob[1]) was the son of Sidney Chester and Sophronia McCord Link [The Link Family, page 526, No. 1984]. Kenneth was born January 16, 1921, at La Harpe, Illinois. He married Wilma Idaline Burford, June, 1942, at Kahoka, Missouri. She was the daughter of Cecil Ray Burford and was born November 16, 1924. Wilma died September 8, 1963, leaving Ken to raise their eight children. On May 5, 1984 he married, second, Betty Gillet Hensly, May 5, 1984. She had four sons: Robert, Roger, Randall, and Richard. Ken and Betty lived at La Harpe.

(Sup) 5991   i   Rodney Ray Link, born May 28, 1943.
(Sup) 5992   ii   Galen Michael Link, born April 2, 1948.
(Sup) 5993   iii Sidney Cecil Link, born October 31, 1949.
(Sup) 5994   iv   Kennetta Faye Link, born March 22, 1952.
(Sup) 5995   v   Miriam Jane Link, born January 12, 1955.
(Sup) 5996   vi   Twyla Jean Link, born May 11, 1956.
(Sup) 5997   vii Ezra Lee Link, born December 16, 1957.
(Sup) 5998   viii Julie Luan Link, born January 15, 1959.

(Sup) 3675 HELEN RUTH LINK (Sidney[7], John[6], John[5], John[4], Peter[3], Matthias[2], John Jacob[1]) was the daughter of Sidney Chester and Sophronia McCord Link [The Link Family, page 526, No. 1984]. Helen was born October 14, 1923, at La Harpe, Illinois. She married Lyle Robert White, May 1, 1943, at Kakoka, Missouri. Lyle was born September 8, 1923, at Bladinsville, Illinois. They were divorced in 1976. Helen resided at Rockford, Illinois.

(Sup) 5999   i   Lyla Kay White, born December 3, 1943.
(Sup) 6000   ii   Marlene Ruth White, born September 7, 1952.
(Sup) 6001   iii Robin Lodella White, born October 31, 1961.

(Sup) 3676 LOIS IDEL LINK (Sidney[7], John[6], John[5], John[4], Peter[3], Matthias[2], John Jacob[1]) was the daughter of Sidney Chester and Sophronia McCord Link [The Link Family, page 526, No. 1984]. Lois was born July 24, 1926, at La Harpe, Illinois. She married George Donald Kreps, October 24, 1943, at Memphis, Missouri. Donald was born September 8, 1923, at Blandinsville, Illinois.

(Sup) 6002   i   George Delbert Kreps, born May 21, 1944.
(Sup) 6003   ii   Allen Keith Kreps, born December 28, 1947.
(Sup) 6004   iii Karen Kathleen Kreps, born September 2, 1949.
(Sup) 6005   iv   Steven Neal Kreps, born May 26, 1952.
(Sup) 6006   v   Lillian Gayle Kreps, born June 9, 1955.
(Sup) 6007   vi   Rita Kristine Kreps, born April 4, 1958.
(Sup) 6008   vii Melvin Dean Kreps, born December 13, 1961.
(Sup) 6009   viii Diana Dawn Kreps, February 22, 1964.

(Sup) 3677 VIVIAN HAZEL LINK (Sidney[7], John[6], John[5], John[4], Peter[3], Matthias[2], John Jacob[1]) was the daughter of Sidney Chester and Sophronia McCord Link [The Link Family, page 526, No. 1984]. Vivian was born January 11, 1929, at La Harpe, Illinois, and died in infancy.

(Sup) 3678 VELMA VERLEE LINK (Frank[7], John[6], John[5], John[4], Peter[3], Matthias[2], John Jacob[1]) was the daughter of Frank Elsworth and Pearl Starkey Link [The Link Family, page 527, No. 1985]. Velma was born June 22, 1910, in Hancock County, Illinois. She married Robert McConnell Gittings June 22, 1945, at Rochester, Illinois. He was the son of Robert and Mary Ellen Judd Gittings and was born January 22, 1896, at La Harpe, Illinois.

(Sup) 3679 GAIL ELSWORTH LINK (Frank[7], John[6], John[5], John[4], Peter[3], Matthias[2], John Jacob[1]) was the son of Frank Elsworth and Pearl Starkey Link [The Link Family, page 527, No. 1985]. Gail was born January 14, 1920, at La Harpe, Illinois. He married Pauline Delores Bundy, March 16, 1946, at La Harpe. Pauline was the daughter of Amos Bundy and was born January 2, 1927, at La Harpe.

(Sup) 6010   i   Jerry Gail Link, born November 3, 1946.
(Sup) 6011   ii   Larry Paul Link, born October 26, 1948.
(Sup) 6012   iii Thomas Merrill Link, born March 10, 1955.

3680 DELMA GENEVIEVE BRADFIELD (Daisy[7], John[6], John[5], John[4], Peter[3], Matthias[2], John Jacob[1]) was born December 4, 1909, near La Harpe, Illinois. She married Arthur Clinton Gillett, August 23, 1929, at Peoria, Illinois. Arthur was born November 12, 1909, at Galesburg, Illinois.

(Sup) 6013   i   Donald Arthur Gillet, born December 3, 1929.
(Sup) 6014   ii   Darrell Clinton Gillett, born May 30, 1934.
(Sup) 6015   iii Delbert Gene Gillett, born February 23, 1944.

3681 OLIVE EILEEN BRADFIELD (Daisy[7], John[6], John[5], John[4], Peter[3], Matthias[2], John Jacob[1]) was born August 24, 1913, near La Harpe, Illinois. She married Stace Lawrence Schutte, November 7, 1943, at Fort Madison, Iowa. Stace was born January 7, 1904, near St. Paul, Iowa.

(Sup) 6016   i   Jerry Lee Schutte, born August 22, 1945.

3682 FLORENCE LOUISE LINK (Lewis[7], John[6], John[5], John[4], Peter[3], Matthias[2], John Jacob[1]) was born May 3, 1919, near La Harpe, Illinois.

3683 MERRILL ROBERT LINK (Lewis[7], John[6], John[5], John[4], Peter[3], Matthias[2], John Jacob[1]) was born September 20, 1920, near La Harpe, Illinois. He served in the U. S. military forces during World War II.

3684 LUELLA MAE LINK (Lewis[7], John[6], John[5], John[4], Peter[3], Matthias[2], John Jacob[1]) was born May 23, 1922, near La Harpe, Illinois. She married Roy Bowen, Jr., April 5, 1941, at Burlington, Iowa. Roy was the son of Roy Bowen and born December 6, 1921, at Colchester, Illinois.

(Sup) 6017   i   Larry Eugene Bowen, born October 11, 1941.
(Sup) 6018   ii   Deanne Jane Bowen, born April 7, 1944.

3685 BARBARA JEAN LINK (Lewis[7], John[6], John[5], John[4], Peter[3], Matthias[2], John Jacob[1]) was born May 27, 1923, near La Harpe, Illinois. She married Franklin Louden in January, 1946.

3686 DONALD PAUL LINK (Lewis[7], John[6], John[5], John[4], Peter[3], Matthias[2], John Jacob[1]) was born May 7, 1925, near La Harpe, Illinois. He married Elizabeth Hobby, September 14, 1946. Donald served in the U. S. military forces during World War II.

3687 DOROTHY MARIE LINK (Lewis[7], John[6], John[5], John[4], Peter[3], Matthias[2], John Jacob[1]) was born October 27, 1927, near La Harpe, Illinois.

(Sup) 3688 WENDELL LAYBOURNE LINK (Lewis[7], John[6], John[5], John[4], Peter[3], Matthias[2], John Jacob was the son of Lewis Paul and Eva Laybourne Link [The Link Family, page 527, No. 1987]. Wendell was born October 13, 1930, near La Harpe, Illinois. He married Eleanor Annabelle Klossing July 27, 1951, at Dallas City, Illinois. She was the daughter of Floyd Edward and Alma Mae (Kaminski) Klossing and was born April 4, 1933, at Dallas City.

(Sup) 6019 i Bradley Wendell Link, born September 16, 1955.
(Sup) 6020 ii Barbara Ann Link, born April 30, 1958.
(Sup) 6021 iii Susan Marie Link, born January 1, 1964.

3689 WESLEY WAYNE LINK (Lewis[7], John[6], John[5], John[4], Peter[3], Matthias[2], John Jacob[1]) was born June 16, 1932, near La Harpe, Illinois.

3690 LEAH BELLE LINK (Lewis[7], John[6], John[5], John[4], Peter[3], Matthias[2], John Jacob[1]) was born May 4, 1934, near La Harpe, Illinois.

3691 THOMAS FREDERICK LINK (Fred[7], Thomas[6], John[5], John[4], Peter[3], Matthias[2], John Jacob[1]) was born August 19, 1922. He married Marjorie Neves, March 20, 1943.

3692 RUTH LUELLA COOVERT (Marie[7], Thomas[6], John[5], John[4], Peter[3], Matthias[2], John Jacob[1]) was born November 29, 1927, at Warsaw, Illinois.

3693 JOHN WESLEY COOVERT, JR. (Marie[7], Thomas[6], John[5], John[4], Peter[3], Matthias[2], John Jacob[1]) was born February 18, 1934, at Warsaw, Illinois.

(Sup) 3693A JAMES EDWIN BAKER (Pearl[7], Frank[6], John[5], John[4], Peter[3], Matthias[2], John Jacob[1]) was the son of Theodore and Pearl Link Baker [The Link Family, page 528, No. 1994; and Supplement No. 1994.] James was born December 27, 1921, in Delaware County, Ohio. He married Irene McNamee June 30, 1945. She was born January 3, 1921. They lived at Columbus, Ohio.

(Sup) 6022 i Kathryn Irene Baker, born May 2, 1946.
(Sup) 6023 ii Kenneth James Baker, born July 16, 1948.
(Sup) 6024 iii Neil Douglas Baker, born February 9, 1950.
(Sup) 6025 iv Melanie Ann Baker, born February 27, 1955.

(Sup) 3693B DAVID THEODORE BAKER (Pearl[7], Frank[6], John[5], John[4], Peter[3], Matthias[2], John Jacob[1]) was the son of Theodore and Pearl Link Baker [The Link Family, page 528, No. 1994.] David was born August 28, 1924. He married Virginia Peters February 19, 1946. They lived at Gahanna, Ohio.

(Sup) 6026 i John L. Baker, born November 24, 1953.
(Sup) 6027 ii Wayne Steven Baker, born February 9, 1955.
(Sup) 6028 iii William Scott Baker, born December 19, 1960.

(Sup) 3693C CARL WILFRED BAKER (Pearl[7], Frank[6], John[5], John[4], Peter[3], Matthias[2], John Jacob[1]) was the son of Theodore and Pearl Link Baker [The Link Family, page 528, No. 1994; and Supplement No. 1994.] Carl was born September 24, 1925. He married Marie Niles, November 3, 1957, at Newburgh, New York. They resided at Syracuse, New York.

(Sup) 3693D ALFRED WALLACE BAKER (Pearl[7], Frank[6], John[5], John[4], Peter[3], Matthias[2], John Jacob[1]) was the son of Theodore and Pearl Link Baker [The Link Family, page 528, No. 1994; and Supplement No. 1994]. Alfred was born February 19, 1929, in Delaware County, Ohio. He married Mary Ann Rawson, November 2, 1950. She was born June 7, 1926, Champaign County, Ohio. They lived at Conyers, Georgia.

(Sup) 6029 i Douglas Alfred Baker, born May 21, 1961.
(Sup) 6030 ii Laura Ruth Baker, born December 4, 1962.

(Sup) 3693E THOMAS QUENTIN BAKER (Pearl[7], Frank[6], John[5], John[4], Peter[3], Matthias[2], John Jacob[1]) was the son of Theodore and Pearl Link Baker [The Link Family, page 528, No. 1994; and Supplement No. 1994]. Thomas was born March 23, 1931. He lived at Tampa, Florida.

(Sup) 3693F MARILYN JEAN BAKER (Pearl[7], Frank[6], John[5], John[4], Peter[3], Matthias[2], John Jacob[1]) was the daughter of Theodore and Pearl Link Baker [The Link Family, page 528, No. 1994; and Supplement No. 1994]. Marilyn was born May 29, 1933. She married Ronald Francis Kinsella, September 17, 1955. He was born August 22, 1932, and died September 2, 1986.

(Sup) 6031 i Kathleen Susan Kinsella, born November 10, 1956.
(Sup) 6032 ii Ronald Francis Kinsella, Jr., born Nov 5, 1958.
(Sup) 6033 iii Joseph Patrick Kinsella, born December 16, 1962.

(Sup) 3693G RITA CAROLY BAKER (Pearl[7], Frank[6], John[5], John[4], Peter[3], Matthias[2], John Jacob[1]) was the daughter of Theodore and Pearl Link Baker [The Link Family, page 528, No. 1994; and Supplement No. 1994]. She was born January 25, 1936. She married Coyt Hamilton, November 30, 1970. He was born May 9, 1925. They lived at Tampa, Florida.

(Sup) 3693H SHARON ELIZABETH BAKER (Pearl[7], Frank[6], John[5], John[4], Peter[3], Matthias[2], John Jacob[1]) was the daughter of Theodore and Pearl Link Baker [The Link Family, page 528, No. 1994; and Supplement No. 1994]. Sharon was born August 31, 1942. She married Cecil Hayman Tillis, June 16, 1962. He was born February 11, 1942. They lived Wauchula, Florida.

(Sup) 6034   i Nathan Andrew Tillis, born September 5, 1967.

(Sup) 3693I IVOR FLOYD TERRY (Zella[7], Frank[6], John[5], John[4], Peter[3], Matthias[2], John Jacob[1]) was the son of Arnold and Zella Link Terry [The Link Family, page 528, No. 1995; and Supplement No. 1995]. He was born April 13, 1923, and died August 13, 1938.

(Sup) 3693J HAROLD HENRY TERRY (Zella[7], Frank[6], John[5], John[4], Peter[3], Matthias[2], John Jacob[1]) was the son of Arnold and Zella Link Terry [The Link Family, page 528, No. 1995; and Supplement No. 1995]. Harrold was born June 2, 1924. He married, first, Ollie Hines, February 5, 1946. She died November 29, 1946. Harold married, second, Alma Maxine Sims, who was born January 30, 1925; she died February 22, 1977. He married, third, Nancy Ruth Puckett Davis, January 14, 1983; she was born October 15, 1932.

CHILDREN OF HAROLD AND ALMA MAXINE
(Sup) 6035   i   Cheryl Ann Terry, born May 30, 1950.
(Sup) 6036   ii   James Steven Terry, born December 22, 1957.
(Sup) 6037   iii Charlene Louise Terry, born August 19, 1961.

(Sup) 3693K FRANK LEE TERRY (Zella[7], Frank[6], John[5], John[4], Peter[3], Matthias[2], John Jacob[1]) was the son of Arnold and Zella Link Terry [The Link Family, page 528, No. 1995; and Supplement No. 1995]. Frank was born August 13, 1926. He married Alice Eileen Knotts, May 5, 1950. She was born October 1, 1925. Frank served in the U.S. Air Force. After he retired, they lived at Mt. Dora, Florida.

Stepdaughter   i   Kandace Ann Terry, born December 8, 1946.
(Sup) 6038   ii   Paul A. Terry, born January 7, 1952.
(Sup) 6039   iii Linda K. Terry, born April 15, 1960.

(Sup) 3693L ELSIE ELIZABETH TERRY (Zella[7], Frank[6], John[5], John[4], Peter[3], Matthias[2], John Jacob[1]) was the daughter of Arnold and Zella Link Terry [The Link Family, page 528, No. 1995; and Supplement No. 1995]. Elsie was born August 24, 1928, at Marion, Ohio. She married, first, Irvin Ross Jones, March 15, 1945; they were divorced. Elsie married, second, Charles Anderson, June 22, 1973. Charles was born July 1, 1925.

(Sup) 6040   i   Charles Irvin Jones, born December 16, 1945.
(Sup) 6041   ii Carol Ann Jones, born May 30, 1947.

(Sup) 3693M PAUL EARL TERRY (Zella[7], Frank[6], John[5], John[4], Peter[3], Matthias[2], John Jacob[1]) was the son of Arnold and Zella Link Terry [The Link Family, page 528, No. 1995; and Supplement No. 1995]. Paul was born April 26, 1932. He died in the Korean War July 14, 1950.

(Sup) 3693N KENNETH ELDON TERRY (Zella[7], Frank[6], John[5], John[4], Peter[3], Matthias[2], John Jacob[1]) was the son of Arnold and Zella Link Terry [The Link Family, page 528, No. 1995; and Supplement No. 1995]. Kenneth was born April 2, 1933, and died March 15, 1934.

(Sup) 3693P DALE ARNOLD TERRY (Zella[7], Frank[6], John[5], John[4], Peter[3], Matthias[2], John Jacob[1]) was the son of Arnold and Zella Link Terry [The Link Family, page 528, No. 1995; and Supplement No. 1995]. Dale was born September 5, 1935. He married, first, Patricia Chapman, September 7, 1956. She was born July 16, 1938. Dale and Patricia were divorced. He married, second, Debra Stine, September 1, 1982. Dale and Debra lived at Lancaster, South Carolina.

CHILDREN OF DALE AND PATRICIA
(Sup) 6042   i   Nancy Lynn Terry, born October 20, 1957.
(Sup) 6043   ii   Matthew Dale Terry, born January 10, 1959.
(Sup) 6044   iii Christopher Allen Terry, born Sept 17, 1961.
(Sup) 6045   iv   Jill Terry, born April 25, 1966.
(Sup) 6046   v   Tom Terry, born October 11, 1969.

CHILDREN OF DALE AND DEBRA
(Sup) 6046A   vi   Gene Link Terry, born August 18, 1983.
(Sup) 6046B   vii Jacob Dale Terry, born June 10, 1985.

(Sup) 3693Q ESTHER JUNE TERRY (Zella[7], Frank[6], John[5], John[4], Peter[3], Matthias[2], John Jacob[1]) was the daughter of Arnold and Zella Link Terry [The Link Family, page 528, No. 1995; and Supplement No. 1995]. Esther was born March 21, 1938. She married, first, Richard Allen Groves, December 29, 1954; they were divorced. She married, second, Charles Raymond Pierce, June 17, 1965. Charles was born July 28, 1929, and was a farmer.

(Sup) 6047   i   Terri Sue Groves, born January 13, 1956.
(Sup) 6048   ii   Vicki Lee Groves, born May 30, 1957.
(Sup) 6049   iii   Richard Allen Groves, Jr., born May 4, 1960.
(Sup) 6050   iv   Tami Lynn Groves, born April 17, 1962.

(Sup) 3693R VINAL RAY TERRY (Zella[7], Frank[6], John[5], John[4], Peter[3], Matthias[2], John Jacob[1]) was the son of Arnold and Zella Link Terry [The Link Family, page 528, No. 1995; and Supplement No. 1995]. He was born October 1, 1940. He married Carol Burche, October 1, 1958. She was born November 15, 1940.

(Sup) 6051   i   Penny Ann Terry, born May 10, 1959.
(Sup) 6052   ii   Paula Irene Terry, born August 2, 1960.
(Sup) 6053   iii   Kelly Marie Terry, born September 3, 1965.
(Sup) 6054   iv   Kathleen Rae Terry, born May 23, 1971.

(Sup) 3693S DONALD ALVIN TERRY (Zella[7], Frank[6], John[5], John[4], Peter[3], Matthias[2], John Jacob[1]) was the son of Arnold and Zella Link Terry [The Link Family, page 528, No. 1995; and Supplement No. 1995]. Donald was born October 31, 1941. He married, first, Claudette Dechesne, June 10, 1961. She was born October 1, 1941. They were divorced. He married, second, Sarah Brawley July 16, 1964; she had one child by a previous marriage, Shiela, born March 14, 1963. Donald and Sarah were divorced, 1982. He married, third, Lisa Powell, February 27, 1982. Lisa was born November 24, 1958. Donald served in the U.S. Army, and Lisa was a school teacher. They lived at Lancaster, South Carolina.

CHILD OF DONALD AND CLAUDETTE
(Sup) 6055   i   Brenda Irene Terry, born August 11, 1962.

CHILD OF DONALD AND SARAH
(Sup) 6056   ii   Donald Alvin Terry, Jr., born September 6, 1966.

CHILD OF DONALD AND LISA
(Sup) 6056A   iii   Christopher Shawn Terry, born March 2, 1984.

(Sup) 3693T SANDRA LEE TERRY (Zella[7], Frank[6], John[5], John[4], Peter[3], Matthias[2], John Jacob[1]) was the daughter of Arnold and Zella Link Terry [The Link Family, page 528, No. 1995; and Supplement No. 1995]. Sandra was born January 3, 1944. She married, first, Thomas Hardin June 17, 1961. They were divorced. She married, second, David Eckman July 30, 1967. He was born January 6, 1938. Sandra and David lived at Vero Beach, Florida, where he was employed by the Gulf Company.

CHILDREN OF SANDRA AND THOMAS
(Sup) 6057   i   Melinda Kay Hardin, born April 9, 1962.
(Sup) 6058   ii   Jeff Alan Hardin, born January 15, 1964.

CHILDREN OF SANDRA AND DAVID
(Sup) 6059   iii   Amy Sue Eckman, born January 6, 1969.
(Sup) 6060   iv   Brian Bradford Eckman, born June 5, 1972.

(Sup) 3694 JOHN CARROLL WELCH (Carrie[7], Frank[6], John[5], John[4], Peter[3], Matthias[2], John Jacob[1]) was the son of Carroll C. and Carrie Link Welch [The Link Family, page 528, No. 1996; and Supplement No. 1996]. John was born August 18, 1930, in Union County, Ohio. He married Dorothy Ruth Armstrong, September 9, 1955. She was born April 11, 1929. John was employed by the Engineering Division of Rockwell International. He and Dorothy lived at Howard, Ohio.

(Sup) 6061   i   John Timothy Welch, born April 23, 1956.
(Sup) 6062   ii   Judith Lynn Welch, born May 23, 1957.

(Sup) 3695 JERRY LINK WELCH (Carrie[7], Frank[6], John[5], John[4], Peter[3], Matthias[2], John Jacob[1]) was the son of Carroll C. and Carrie Link Welch [The Link Family, page 528, No. 1996; and Supplement No. 1996]. Jerry was born October 27, 1935, in Union County, Ohio. He was an electronic technician with Lockheed Missile and Space Corp., Kennedy Space Center, Florida.

(Sup) 3695A JOHN RAYMOND LINK, JR. (Raymond[7], Frank[6], John[5], John[4], Peter[3], Matthias[2], John Jacob[1]) was the son of John Raymond and Lucille Mooney Link [The Link Family, page 528, No. 1997; and Supplement No. 1997]. John, Jr., was born June 10, 1933. He married Beverly Joan Davenport, April 23, 1953. John died May 21, 1955.

(Sup) 6063   i   John Raymond Link, III, born January 5, 1955.

(Sup) 3695B ROBERT EUGENE LINK (Raymond[7], Frank[6], John[5], John[4], Peter[3], Matthias[2], John Jacob[1]) was the son of John Raymond and Lucille Mooney Link [The Link Family, page 528, No. 1997; and Supplement No. 1997]. Bob was born December 27, 1936, at Ashley, Ohio. He married, first, Luella Mullins, July 15, 1956, at Bennettsville, South Carolina. She was born June 19, 1935, at Ada, Ohio, the daughter of Eda and Kenneth Mullins. Robert and Luella were divorced. He married, second, Inis Ann Mullins, July 12, 1979, at Westerville, Ohio; she was the daughter of Pridemore and Virgie Lee (Moore) Mullins. Bob married, third, Ann Powell, in April, 1981. Bob and Ann lived at Sunbury, Ohio, where they owned and operated Annie's Log Cabin Crafts.

CHILDREN OF ROBERT AND LUELLA

(Sup) 6064 i   Robert Eugene Link, Jr., born August 5, 1957.
(Sup) 6065 ii   William Dennis Link, born September 1, 1959.
(Sup) 6066 iii Brenda Louise Link, born July 11, 1960.
(Sup) 6067 iv   Bryon Wayne Link, born November 17, 1965.

(Sup) 3695C NANCY MURIEL LINK (Raymond[7], Frank[6], John[5], John[4], Peter[3], Matthias[2], John Jacob[1]) was the daughter of John Raymond and Lucille Mooney Link [The Link Family, page 528, No. 1997; and Supplement No. 1997]. Nancy was born June 22, 1939, in Delaware County, Ohio. She married Fred Lee Stults, October 18, 1959, at Kilbourne, Ohio. Fred was born February 15, 1937, in Union County, Ohio, the son of Loran F. and Imogene Farrand Stults. Nancy worked at Ohio Wesleyan University as Secretary to the Dean of Academic Affairs, and Fred was the Delaware County Engineer.

(Sup) 6068 i   Timothy Jon Link Stults, born June 16, 1964.
(Sup) 6069 ii   Loren Kelly Stults, born July 18, 1967.

(Sup) 3695D PHILIP ALLEN LINK (Raymond[7], Frank[6], John[5], John[4], Peter[3], Matthias[2], John Jacob[1]) was the son of John Raymond and Lucille Mooney Link [The Link Family, page 528, No. 1997; and Supplement No. 1997]. Philip was born September 24, 1941, at Olive Green, Ohio. He married Joyce Darlene Doane, July 9, 1960, at Kilbourne, Ohio. Joyce was born November 28, 1941, at Berkshire, Ohio, the oldest daughter of Raymond Kenneth and Tina Belle (Webb) Doans. Philip owned an electrical business in Sunbury, Ohio. He became Superintendent of the Delaware County Home, Ohio. Later Philip and Joyce moved to Fort Myers Beach, Florida, where he was a radio dispatcher for the fire department, and she was a secretary.

(Sup) 6070   i   Philip Michael Link, born August 13, 1961.
(Sup) 6071   ii   Steven Allen Link, born August 8, 1966.
      Adopted iii Melissa Link, born February 22, 1968.
(Sup) 6072   iv   Scott Andrew Link, born August 13, 1971.

(Sup) 3695E NITA LOUISE LINK (Raymond[7], Frank[6], John[5], John[4], Peter[3], Matthias[2], John Jacob[1]) was the daughter of John Raymond and Lucille Mooney Link [The Link Family, page 528, No. 1997; and Supplement No. 1997]. Nita was born July 8, 1945, at Delaware, Ohio. She married Ronald Russell Teeter, June 19, 1966, at Kilbourne, Ohio. He was the son of Francis Kaylor and Lulu Agnes (Woodruff) Teeter and was born November 20, 1942, at Youngstown, Ohio. Ronald was an aeronautical engineer in Delaware County, Ohio.

(Sup) 6073 i   Ronald Russell Teeter, Jr., born June 12, 1967.
(Sup) 6074 ii   John Kaylor Teeter, born May 4, 1969.
(Sup) 6075 iii Daniel Link Teeter, born January 9, 1972.

(Sup) 3695F PHILIP LEE DAUGHERTY (Anna Marie[7], Frank[6], John[5], John[4], Peter[3], Matthias[2], John Jacob[1]) was the son of Harry and Anna Marie Link Daugherty [The Link Family, page 528, No. 1998; and Supplement No. 1998]. Philip was born February 3, 1947, at Columbus, Ohio. He married Patricia Ileene Commiskey, February 6, 1971. She was born August 22, 1950. Philip was vice president of Manufacturers Hanover Trust Co., and they lived at Hauppauge, New York.

(Sup) 6075A i   Meagan Allison Daugherty, born April 4, 1986.

(Sup) 3695G SUSAN JANE DAUGHERTY (Anna Marie[7], Frank[6], John[5], John[4], Peter[3], Matthias[2], John Jacob[1]) was the daughter of Harry and Anna Marie Link Daugherty [The Link Family, page 528, No. 1998; and Supplement No. 1998]. Susan was born July 8, 1948, at Columbus, Ohio. She married John Paul Oberdier, September 7, 1968. He was born July 31, 1947, at Richwood, Ohio. Susan and John lived at Grayslake, Illinois. He was manager of the Analytical Research Department, Abbott Laboratories.

(Sup) 6076   i   Eva Marie Oberdier, born May 30, 1971.
(Sup) 6077   ii   Nathan John Oberdier, born November 23, 1974.
(Sup) 6077A iii Andrew Caleb Oberdier, born January 10, 1981.

(Sup) 3696 SUZANNE JANE LINK (Kenneth[7], Frank[6], John[5], John[4], Peter[3], Matthias[2], John Jacob[1]) was the daughter of Kenneth Ivan and Maxine Perfect Link [The Link Family, page 528, No. 1999]. Suzanne was born September 5, 1937. She married Duane Van Sickle. They were divorced. Suzanne was a learning-disabilities teacher, and she raised horses. She lived at Cardington, Ohio.

(Sup) 6078 i   John Allan Van Sickle, born October 16, 1957.
(Sup) 6079 ii   Joyce Ann Van Sickle, born February 27, 1959.
(Sup) 6080 iii Jeffrey Duane Van Sickle, born Feb 11, 1963.

(Sup) 3697 SHERRY LYNNE LINK (Kenneth[7], Frank[6], John[5], John[4], Peter[3], Matthias[2], John Jacob[1]) was the daughter of Kenneth Ivan and Maxine Perfect Link [The Link Family, page 528, No. 1999]. Sherry was born August 5, 1939. She married Thomas Buel, September 30, 1961. He was born June 12, 1936.

(Sup) 6081   i   Krista Kay Buel, born January 13, 1963.
(Sup) 6082   ii Karla Rea Buel, born May 28, 1971.

(Sup) 3698 STEPHEN KENNETH LINK (Kenneth[7], Frank[6], John[5], John[4], Peter[3], Matthias[2], John Jacob[1]) was the son of Kenneth Ivan and Maxine Perfect Link [The Link Family, page 528, No. 1999]. Stephen was born August 24, 1943. He married, first, Jeanne Hunter, 1962. They were divorced. Stephen married, second, Debra King, October 1970; they were divorced. He married, third, Teresa Bovard in 1979. Stephen and Teresa lived at Bennington, Indiana, where he was a cattle representative.

CHILD OF STEPHEN AND JEANNE
(Sup) 6082A   i   Lisa Jeanne Link, born October 10, 1962.

CHILDREN OF STEPHEN AND DEBRA
(Sup) 6083   ii   Sara Jo Link, born July 7, 1971.
(Sup) 6084   iii Jamie Lynn Link, born April 10, 1975.

CHILD OF STEPHEN AND TERESA
(Sup) 6085   iv Annie Marie Link, born March 2, 1980.

(Sup) 3699 LINDA ELAINE LINK (Kenneth[7], Frank[6], John[5], John[4], Peter[3], Matthias[2], John Jacob[1]) was the daughter of Kenneth Ivan and Maxine Perfect Link [The Link Family, page 528, No. 1999]. Linda was born December 9, 1945. She married, first, Ronald Glaze, January 24, 1966. They were divorced. Linda married, second, James Murray, August 12, 1977. James was vice president of the Electric Power Equipment Company, and Linda was a hair dresser.

(Sup) 6086   i   Richard Dean Glaze, born November 4, 1969.
(Sup) 6087   ii Robert Michael Glaze, born April 19, 1972.

(Sup) 3700 RICHARD LOUIS LINK (Vinal[7], Frank[6], John[5], John[4], Peter[3], Matthias[2], John Jacob[1]) was the son of Vinal Thurston and Edna Krieger Link [The Link Family, page 528, No. 2000]. Richard was born June 1, 1941, at Columbus, Ohio. He married Mary Anna Shaw, June 10, 1961. Richard was an assistant school superintendent, and she was a school teacher.

(Sup) 6088   i   Lizabeth Sue Link, born October 23, 1969.

(Sup) 3701 DONNA KAY LINK (Vinal[7], Frank[6], John[5], John[4], Peter[3], Matthias[2], John Jacob[1]) was the daughter of Vinal Thurston and Edna Krieger Link [The Link Family, page 528, No. 2000]. Donna was born October 4, 1944, at Columbus, Ohio. She married Elwood Caudill, Jr., June 13, 1965. They lived at Sunbury, Ohio.

(Sup) 6089   i   Kevin Andrew Caudill, born April 7, 1970.
(Sup) 6090   ii Kathleen Ann Caudill, born September 21, 1971.

(Sup) 3702 CAROLYN JUNE PITTMAN (Charlotte[7], Frank[6], John[5], John[4], Peter[3], Matthias[2], John Jacob[1]) was the daughter of Harold and Charlotte Link Pittman [The Link Family, page 523, No. 2001]. Carolyn was born May 9, 1939, in Delaware County, Ohio. She married Gary Ferrell, July 1, 1961. He was born June 30, 1940. They lived at Franklin, Ohio, where Gary was employed as a machinist.

(Sup) 6091   i   Kelli Sue Ferrell, born April 22, 1963.
(Sup) 6092   ii Timothy Wayne Ferrell, born January 9, 1966.

(Sup) 3703 HAROLD EDGAR PITTMAN, JR. (Charlotte[7], Frank[6], John[5], John[4], Peter[3], Matthias[2], John Jacob[1]) was the son of Harold and Charlotte Link Pittman [The Link Family, page 523, No. 2001]. Ed was born July 21, 1941, in Delaware County, Ohio. He married Beverly Borchers, April 8, 1962. She was born February 4, 1943. They lived at Ashley, Ohio, where Ed was a farmer.

(Sup) 6093   i   Dawn E'Lyn Pittman, born June 28, 1965
(Sup) 6094   ii Craig Alan Pittman, born May 17, 1967.

(Sup) 3704 PAMELA JO LINK (James[7], Frank[6], John[5], John[4], Peter[3], Matthias[2], John Jacob[1]) was the daughter of James Franklin and Betty Postle Link [The Link Family, page 529, No. 2002; and Supplement No. 2002]. Pamela was born November 6, 1944, at Kilbourne, Ohio. She married Larry Hillard, May 21, 1966. He was born July 26, 1943.

(Sup) 6095   i   Angie Lynn Hillard, born November 8, 1968.
(Sup) 6096   ii Rodd L. Hillard, born December 12, 1970.

3706 RAY PALMER WINGATE (Arthur^7, Susan^6, David^5, John^4, Peter^3, Matthias^2, John Jacob^1) was born March 15, 1898, in Warren County, Illinois. He married Mary Hites, December 24, 1919.

(Sup) 6099 † Elizabeth Ann Wingate, born March 9, 1921.
(Sup) 6100 †† Mary Elinor Wingate, born October 17, 1926.

3707 FERN IONE WINGATE (Arthur^7, Susan^6, David^5, John^4, Peter^3, Matthias^2, John Jacob^1) was born July 13, 1902, in Warren County, Illinois. She married Clarence Watt, June 21, 1923. Fern died August 4, 1939.

(Sup) 6101 † Jean Iris Watt, born April 2, 1924.
(Sup) 6102 †† James Arthur Watt, born October 9, 1925.

3708 ETHEL MAY WINGATE (Martin^7, Susan^6, David^5, John^4, Peter^3, Matthias^2, John Jacob^1) was born November 23, 1900, in Warren County, Illinois. She married Herbert Wilkins, August 25, 1919.

(Sup) 6103 † Marjorie Evelyn Wilkins, born March 28, 1920.
(Sup) 6104 †† Ralph Dale Wilkins, born February 16, 1922.

3709 ORVAL MILO WINGATE (John^7, Susan^6, David^5, John^4, Peter^3, Matthias^2, John Jacob^1) was born April 3, 1913, in Warren County, Illinois. He married Pauline Vidas, December 4, 1937.

(Sup) 6105 † Wesley Orval Wingate, born June 18, 1938.
(Sup) 6106 †† Mryna Elaine Wingate, born April 18, 1941.

3710 ARNOLD JAY SIMMONS (Effie^7, Susan^6, David^5, John^4, Peter^3, Matthias^2, John Jacob^1) was born September 16, 1907, in Warren County, Illinois, where he died October 24, 1907.

3711 RAYMOND ALLEN SIMMONS (Effie^7, Susan^6, David^5, John^4, Peter^3, Matthias^2, John Jacob^1) was born January 11, 1909, in Warren County, Illinois. He married Evelyn Hendricks, December 20, 1930. Raymond died July 13, 1936.

(Sup) 6107 † Robert Lee Simmons, born March 19, 1934.
(Sup) 6108 †† Rodney Allen Simmons, born July 28, 1935.

3712 LEONA MARIE YOUNG (Lulu^7, Susan^6, David^5, John^4, Peter^3, Matthias^2, John Jacob^1) was born October 9, 1904, in Warren County, Illinois. She married Raymond Reihm, September 27, 1922.

(Sup) 6109 † Lyle Werton Reihm, born June 10, 1924.
(Sup) 6110 †† Betty Lou Reihm, born February 13, 1926.
(Sup) 6111 ††† Lowell Lee Reihm, born September 13, 1928.

(Sup) 3704A WENDY SUE LINK (James^7, Frank^6, John^5, John^4, Peter^3, Matthias^2, John Jacob^1) was the second daughter of James and Betty Postle Link [The Link Family, page 529, No. 2002; and Supplement No. 2002]. Wendy Sue was born April 9, 1949. She married Larry Floyd Wilson, February 19, 1972. He was born April 7, 1949.

(Sup) 6097 † James Link Wilson, born June 16, 1980.
(Sup) 6097A †† Kyle Lewis Wilson, born October 13, 1983.

(Sup) 3705 VICTORIA ANN LINK (William^7, Frank^6, John^5, John^4, Peter^3, Matthias^2, John Jacob^1) was the daughter of William Lloyd and Sarah Jean Arthur Link [The Link Family, page 529, No. 2003; and Supplement No. 2003]. Vickie Ann was born March 3, 1947, at Delaware, Ohio. She married Richard Applegate, May 28, 1976; they were divorced. She married, second, Michael Rife.

(Sup) 6098 † Aaron Lloyd Buell, born May 16, 1969.

(Sup) 3705A WILLIAM LLOYD LINK, JR. (William^7, Frank^6, John^5, John^4, Peter^3, Matthias^2, John Jacob^1) was the second child of William Lloyd and Sarah Jean Arthur Link [The Link Family, page 529, No. 2003; and Supplement No. 2003]. William Jr., was born January 9, 1952. He married Tammie Lantz, December 22, 1974. They were divorced.

(Sup) 3705B KENNETH ALAN LEFLER (Emery^7, Ethel^6, John^5, John^4, Peter^3, Matthias^2, John Jacob^1) was the son of Emery Dale and Jo Ann Penn Lefler [The Link Family, page 530, No. 2018; and Supplement No. 2018]. Kenneth was born June 12, 1953, at Dayton, Ohio. He received a Ph.D. degree in high energy physics from the University of Maryland.

(Sup) 3705C RANDALL EUGENE LEFLER (Emery^7, Ethel^6, John^5, John^4, Peter^3, Matthias^2, John Jacob^1) was the son of Emery Dale and Jo Ann Penn Lefler [The Link Family, page 530; No. 2018; and Supplement No. 2018]. Randall was born April 9, 1956, at Dayton, Ohio. He did graduate work at the University of Michigan.

3713 DWIGHT R. THOMAS (Rosa7, Susan6, David5, John4, Peter3, Matthias2, John Jacob1) was born February 18, 1909, in Warren County, Illinois.

3714 HELEN CLARA THOMAS (Rosa7, Susan6, David5, John4, Peter3, Matthias2, John Jacob1) was born May 27, 1914, in Warren County, Illinois.

3715 ROBERTA CHAMBERS (Emma7, Susan6, David5, John4, Peter3, Matthias2, John Jacob1) was born March 15, 1919, at Raymond, Washington. She married William Gilbert, January 12, 1944.

3716 JOSEPHINE IRENE WINGATE (Edwin7, Susan6, David5, John4, Peter3, Matthias2, John Jacob1) was born March 19, 1912, in Warren County, Illinois, and died September 12, 1921.

3717 LOIS LEIGH WINGATE (Edwin7, Susan6, David5, John4, Peter3, Matthias2, John Jacob1) was born February 5, 1915, in Warren County, Illinois. She married Ivan Peach, September 21, 1935.

(Sup) 6112   i   Josephine Irene Peach, born May 15, 1938.
(Sup) 6113   ii   Judy Ann Peach, born January 30, 1940.
(Sup) 6114   iii   Jerri Lynn Peach, born November 21, 1945.

3718 DEAN MILTON SIMMONS (Alta7, Susan6, David5, John4, Peter3, Matthias2, John Jacob1) was born October 24, 1914, in Warren County, Illinois. He married Montique Kathryn Dean, December 11, 1945.

3719 DAVID KUTCHLER WINGATE (David7, Susan6, David5, John4, Peter3, Matthias2, John Jacob1) was born October 2, 1921, in Knox County, Illinois.

3720 MARILYN ARDIS WINGATE (David7, Susan6, David5, John4, Peter3, Matthias2, John Jacob1) was born August 12, 1924, in Knox County, Illinois. She married Charles Donaldson, December 29, 1946.

3720A JOHN LEE WINGATE (David7, Susan6, David5, John4, Peter3, Matthias2, John Jacob1) was born July 14, 1929, in Fulton County, Illinois.

3721 BLANCHE A. HEWETT (Harvey7, Sarah6, David5, John4, Peter3, Matthias2, John Jacob1) was born February 24, 1904, in Taylor County, Iowa. She married Herbert P. Neumann, April 7, 1922, at Miles City, Montana. Herbert was born July 26, 1886, in Custer County, Montana. He died January 27, 1937, at Portland, Oregon. Blanche married Harry J. Reinhart, July 14, 1938, at Wheatland, Wyoming. Harry was born April 24, 1906, at Pesham, Minnesota.

CHILDREN OF BLANCHE AND HERBERT
(Sup) 6115   i   Ella Florence Neumann, born October 19, 1923.
(Sup) 6116   ii   Edna Fay Neumann, born September 16, 1926.
(Sup) 6117   iii   Herbert H. Neumann, born March 3, 1931.
(Sup) 6118   iv   Hugh Ronald Neumann, born October 10, 1933.

CHILDREN OF BLANCHE AND HARRY
(Sup) 6119   v   Mary Irene Reinhart, born April 30, 1939.
(Sup) 6120   vi   Raymond Lee Reinhart, born April 28, 1940.
(Sup) 6121   vii   Marjory Jean Reinhart, born July 31, 1944.
(Sup) 6122   viii   Howard Joseph Reinhart, born May 1, 1946.

3722 FLORENCE MAE HEWETT (Harvey7, Sarah6, David5, John4, Peter3, Matthias2, John Jacob1) was born September 13, 1906, in Taylor County, Iowa. She married Louis K. Hobbs, November 7, 1924, at Miles City, Montana. Louis was born November 21, 1903, in Missouri.

(Sup) 6123   i   Roy Troy Hobbs, born October 8, 1925.
(Sup) 6124   ii   Evelyn Mae Hobbs, born February 15, 1928.
(Sup) 6125   iii   Sherry Ann Hobbs, born March 5, 1944.

3723 HELEN IRENE HEWETT (Harvey7, Sarah6, David5, John4, Peter3, Matthias2, John Jacob1) was born August 24, 1907, in Taylor County, Iowa. She married Charles V. Lawrence, March 13, 1926, at Glendine, Montana. Charles was born January 18, 1904, in Warren County, Illinois, and died August 24, 1927. Helen married Ralph Gilmore, November 29, 1929, at Baker, Montana. Ralph was born March 15, 1882, in Custer County, Montana. He died March 1, 1940. Helen married Alvin E. Beusley, August 15, 1942, at Miles City, Montana. He was born May 15, 1896, in Custer County, Montana.

CHILDREN OF HELEN AND RALPH
(Sup) 6126   i   Opal Jean Gilmore, born August 10, 1930.
(Sup) 6127   ii   Katherine Davis Gilmore, born November 18, 1932.

CHILD OF HELEN AND ALVIN
(Sup) 6128   iii   Allen Lee Buesley, born July 15, 1943.

3724 HARLAN DALE HEWETT (Harvey7, Sarah6, David5, John4, Peter3, Matthias2, John Jacob1) was born February 2, 1913, in Taylor County, Iowa. He married Marguerite McMullen, April 29, 1933, at Bedford, Iowa. Marguerite was born in Nodaway County, Missouri, August 28, 1916.

(Sup) 6129   i   Harold Dean Hewett, born January 27, 1934.
(Sup) 6130   ii   Richard Lee Hewett, born December 22, 1935.

3725 NOEL ARCHIE ANDERSON (Mary7, Elizabeth6, David5, John4, Peter3, Matthias2, John Jacob1) was born November 28, 1902, at Sloan, Iowa.

(Sup) 6131   i   Mary Lou Anderson, born May 11, 1930.
(Sup) 6132   ii   Dwight Albert Anderson, born July 10, 1934.
(Sup) 6133   iii   Ronald James Anderson, born February 15, 1937.
(Sup) 6134   iv   Judith Edna Anderson, born October 13, 1939.
(Sup) 6135   v   Larry Le Roy Anderson, born March 2, 1943.

3726 BRADD BENNETT COONS (John7, Elizabeth6, David5, John4, Peter3, Matthias2, John Jacob1) was born November 17, 1914, at Onawa, Iowa. He married Barbara Stauch, June 14, 1941, at Rockport, Missouri. Barbara was the daughter of Martin O. and Lida Simons Stauch and was born August 21, 1917, at Whiting, Iowa. Bradd was a captain in the U.S. Army and served through World War II and the Korean campaign.

3728 JOHN J. COONS, JR. (John7, Elizabeth6, David5, John4, Peter3, Matthias2, John Jacob1) married Phylis Pratt.

3729 DONALD MAC COONS (John^7, Elizabeth^6, David^5, John^4, Peter^3, Matthias^2, John Jacob^1) was born June 23, 1924, at Sioux City, Iowa. He married Glenna Laura Thompson, June 28, 1946, at Elk Point, South Dakota. Glenna was the daughter of Glenn Thompson and was born October 12, 1928, at Oto, Iowa.

(Sup) 6136   i   Linda Kay Coons, born August 28, 1947.

3730 LILLIAN BEATRICE KRON (Zulah^7, Elizabeth^6, David^5, John^4, Peter^3, Matthias^2, John Jacob^1) was born April 30, 1907, at Homer, Nebraska. She married Ralph Bigelow, November 13, 1926, at Elk Point, South Dakota. Ralph died April 17, 1944, at North Halland, California. Lillian then married J. R. Hechenlively.

(Sup) 6137   i   Warren Leslie Bigelow, born February 9, 1927.
(Sup) 6138   ii   Robert Gene Bigelow, born March 6, 1928.
(Sup) 6139   iii Alton Wayne Bigelow, born May 30, 1930.
(Sup) 6140   iv   Billie Joe Bigelow, born November 22, 1942.

3731 LULAH GERTRUDE KRON (Zulah^7, Elizabeth^6, David^5, John^4, Peter^3, Matthias^2, John Jacob^1) was born April 10, 1910, at Whiting, Iowa. She married Coral C. Highsmith, February 4, 1944, at Sioux City, Iowa.

3732 DOLORES KATHLEEN STAGGS (Aerie^7, William^6, David^5, John^4, Peter^3, Matthias^2, John Jacob^1) was born March 30, 1917, at Avon, Illinois. She married Wright R. Hinkley, April 28, 1945, at Bryant, Ohio.

(Sup) 6141   i   Craig Wright Hinkley, born January 10, 1947.

3733 JAMES MARVIN LEE STAGGS (Aerie^7, William^6, David^5, John^4, Peter^3, Matthias^2, John Jacob^1) was born July 3, 1927, at Avon, Illinois.

3734 PHILLIP LEWIS MOWERY (Pearl^7, Eliza^6, David^5, John^4, Peter^3, Matthias^2, John Jacob^1) was born November 21, 1925, at Seattle, Washington. He married Carolyn Ann Kuns, June 20, 1947. Carolyn was the daughter of Irl Everett Kuns and was born May 25, 1927, at Seattle, Washington.

3735 ANNE ELIZABETH MOWERY (Pearl^7, Eliza^6, David^5, John^4, Peter^3, Matthias^2, John Jacob^1) was born January 4, 1932, at Seattle, Washington.

3736 DEAN HATHAWAY PREWITT (Bessie^7, Jennetta^6, David^5, John^4, Peter^3, Matthias^2, John Jacob^1) was born September 8, 1911, at Fort Morgan, Colorado. He married Audrey King, August 27, 1937, at Lone Pine, California.

3738 ROBERT LEE PREWITT (Bessie^7, Jennetta^6, David^5, John^4, Peter^3, Matthias^2, John Jacob^1) was born October 23, 1915, at Fort Morgan, Colorado.

3739 ALICE JANET HATHAWAY (Howard^7, Jennetta^6, David^5, John^4, Peter^3, Matthias^2, John Jacob^1) was born July 9, 1925, at Trinidad, Colorado. She married Qwin Lorraine Walker, February 17, 1946, at Long Beach, California. Qwin was born July 22, 1921, at Corona, California. He was a Lieutenant in the U. S. Armed Forces.

(Sup) 6142   i   Alan Ray Walker, born September 22, 1946.

3740 DONALD WILLARD HATHAWAY (Howard^7, Jennetta^6, David^5, John^4, Peter^3, Matthias^2, John Jacob^1).

3741 WILLIAM H. ASH (Gertrude^7, Ora^6, David^5, John^4, Peter^3, Matthias^2, John Jacob^1) was born December 24, 1913, at Boise, Idaho. He married Ruth Chastain, January 11, 1941. Ruth was the daughter of Carl Chastain and was born January 19, 1922, at Twin Falls, Idaho.

(Sup) 6143   i   Pamela Ash, born May 11, 1947.

3742 MILDRED MARIAN ASH (Gertrude^7, Ora^6, David^5, John^4, Peter^3, Matthias^2, John Jacob^1) was born September 22, 1915, at Boise, Idaho. She married George W. Thornbrough, February 1, 1939, at San Antonio, Texas. George was born July 7, 1914, at Lincoln, Nebraska. He graduated from Kansas State College, was a member of Sigma Phi Epsilon, and after graduation became a reserve officer in the U. S. Cavalry at Fort Riley, Kansas. He went to flying school at Randolph and Kelly Fields and won his wings February 1, 1939, the day of his marriage. He was commissioned a captain in the regular army and in March, 1941, was sent to Alaska. He lost his life June 4, 1942, in action against Japanese ships in the Aleutians while torpedo bombing them. He was awarded the Distinguished Service Cross, posthumously, for "extraordinary heroism in action." Mildred and George, with their small daughter, lived at Anchorage, Alaska, from March, 1941, until February, 1942, when she and the child were evacuated to the States. On September 8, 1945, Mildred married Justin G. Knowlton, son of J. G. Knowlton. Justin was born June 8, 1914. He adopted Judith Thornbrough, the daughter of Mildred and George.

(Sup) 6144   i   Judith Thornbrough-Knowlton, born May 16, 1940.

3743 PAUL HACKETT KYBURZ (Lucy^7, Frances^6, Adam^5, Phillip^4, Peter^3, Matthias^2, John Jacob^1) was born November 9, 1908, at Woodburn, Indiana. He married Helen Mabel Millard, June 20, 1936. Helen was born January 13, 1910, at Medina, Michigan.

(Sup) 6145   i   Bruce Allan Kyburz, born May 2, 1937.
(Sup) 6146   ii   Carolyn Jean Kyburz, born October 12, 1939.
(Sup) 6147   iii Dean Howard Kyburz, born December 28, 1943.

3744 FRANCES ELIZABETH KYBURZ (Lucy^7, Frances^6, Adam^5, Phillip^4, Peter^3, Matthias^2, John Jacob^1) was born June 21, 1911, at Woodburn, Indiana. She married Harold Darwin Caswell, September 13, 1930, at Kinderhook, Michigan. Harold, son of William Worden and Nellie Gertrude Caswell, was born October 11, 1906, near Rossford, Ohio.

(Sup) 6148   i   Paul James Caswell, born September 3, 1931.
(Sup) 6149   ii   Russell Robert Caswell, born July 3, 1933.
(Sup) 6150   iii Irving Harold Caswell, born September 6, 1935.
(Sup) 6151   iv   Dorothy Lee Caswell, born November 15, 1938.
(Sup) 6152   v   Eugene William Caswell, born December 20, 1939.
(Sup) 6153   vi   Joy Ann Caswell, born October 15, 1943.

3745 HENRY HUGH McMAKEN (Henry^7, Frances^6, Adam^5, Phillip^4, Peter^3, Matthias^2, John Jacob^1) was born July 19, 1902, in Allen County, Indiana. He married Maude Essy Long, September 15, 1928, at Rocky Comfort, Missouri.

(Sup) 6154   i   Joan Ruth McMaken, born November 15, 1933.

3746 RUTH LUCILE McMAKEN (Henry[7], Frances[6], Adam[5], Phillip[4], Peter[3], Matthias[2], John Jacob[1]) was born January 15, 1904, in Allen County, Indiana. She married Lloyd Forsythe, April 8, 1934, at Fort Wayne, Indiana. Lloyd was the son of Frank and Ava May Taylor Forsythe and was born in Allen County, January 8, 1904.

(Sup) 6155   i   Adelia Ruth Forsythe, born March 26, 1935.
(Sup) 6156   ii William Lloyd Forsythe, born January 6, 1940.
(Sup) 6157   iii Anna Mae Forsythe, born October 20, 1943.

3747 HERBERT ROSS McMAKEN (Henry[7], Frances[6], Adam[5], Phillip[4], Peter[3], Matthias[2], John Jacob[1]) was born October 17, 1906, in Allen County, Indiana. He married Justine Corby Ward, June 25, 1932, at Washington, D. C. Justine, daughter of Rufus and Ettie Ernst Ward, was born May 25, 1910, near Rockville, Maryland.

(Sup) 6158   i   Herbert Ross McMaken, Jr., born May 29, 1937.
(Sup) 6159   ii Ward McMaken, born November 18, 1941.
(Sup) 6160   iii Peter William McMaken, born November 26, 1948.

3748 MARGARET EVA McMAKEN (Henry[7], Frances[6], Adam[5], Phillip[4], Peter[3], Matthias[2], John Jacob[1]) was born December 11, 1908, in Allen County, Indiana. She married Doris D. Van Hoozen, February 26, 1933, in Whitley County, Indiana. Doris was born October 10, 1903, in Allen County, Indiana. He was the son of Henry and Eleta Hays Van Hoozen.

(Sup) 6161   i   Barbara Ann Van Hoozen, born October 26, 1934.
(Sup) 6162   ii Joyce Elaine Van Hoozen, born May 3, 1939.
(Sup) 6163   iii Richard Henry Van Hoozen, born December 4, 1943.

3749 JESSIE WILMA McMAKEN (Henry[7], Frances[6], Adam[5], Phillip[4], Peter[3], Matthias[2], John Jacob[1]) was born January 14, 1912, in Allen County, Indiana. She married Joseph George Carroll, November 6, 1941, at Auburn, Indiana. Joseph was the son of John and Mary Carroll and was born November 24, 1912, at Durango, Colorado.

(Sup) 6164   i   Lorraine Jo Carroll, born July 4, 1942.
(Sup) 6165   ii Mary Louise Carroll, born December 16, 1943.
(Sup) 6166   iii Norma Anita Carroll, born May 6, 1947
(Sup) 6167   iv Janice Gail Carroll, born September 23, 1949.

3750 EDITH JANE McMAKEN (Henry[7], Frances[6], Adam[5], Phillip[4], Peter[3], Matthias[2], John Jacob[1]) was born September 16, 1914, in Allen County, Indiana.

3751 RALPH HARRY JACKSON (Helen[7], Frances[6], Adam[5], Phillip[4], Peter[3], Matthias[2], John Jacob[1]) was born February 12, 1901, at Fort Wayne, Indiana. He married Freda Emilia Grothe, September 11, 1921, at Omaha, Nebraska. Freda was the daughter of Emil Grothe and was born September 30, 1900, at Pappillion, Nebraska.

(Sup) 6168   i   Marguerite Helen Jackson, born December 20, 1922.
(Sup) 6169   ii Alice Louise Jackson, born May 19, 1924.
(Sup) 6170   iii Freda Ilene Jackson, born June 12, 1928.
(Sup) 6171   iv Mary Ellen Jackson, born May 9, 1931.
(Sup) 6172   v   Dona Jean Jackson, born June 30, 1933.

3752 ISAAC LEWIS JACKSON (Helen[7], Frances[6], Adam[5], Phillip[4], Peter[3], Matthias[2], John Jacob[1]) was born January 3, 1903, at Pellston, Michigan.

3753 PLUMA ELIZABETH JACKSON (Helen[7], Frances[6], Adam[5], Phillip[4], Peter[3], Matthias[2], John Jacob[1]) was born August 28, 1904, at Pellston, Michigan. She married Herschel Orville Orcutt, September 3, 1933, at Cleveland, Ohio. Herschel was born September 3, 1900, at Nappanee, Indiana, and died at Fort Wayne, July 9, 1936.

6173   i   Pluma Adelia Orcutt, born July 28, 1934.

3754 MERLE BYRON JACKSON (Helen[7], Frances[6], Adam[5], Phillip[4], Peter[3], Matthias[2], John Jacob[1]) was born May 14, 1907, at Pellston, Michigan.

3755 JOHN GOUTY (Elizabeth[7], Frances[6], Adam[5], Phillip[4], Peter[3], Matthias[2], John Jacob[1]). His wife's first name was Caroline.

3756 ARTHUR GOUTY (Elizabeth[7], Frances[6], Adam[5], Phillip[4], Peter[3], Matthias[2], John Jacob[1]). He died unmarried.

3757 EMMA ALEMITH GOUTY (Elizabeth[7], Frances[6], Adam[5], Phillip[4], Peter[3], Matthias[2], John Jacob[1]) was born May 2, 1904, at Fort Wayne, Indiana. She married Vearl Osborn Pontius, July 19, 1922, at Fort Wayne. Vearl was born October 12, 1898, at Marion, Indiana.

(Sup) 6174   i   Earl Pontius, born 1937.
(Sup) 6175   ii Ruth Ann Pontius, born 1939.
(Sup) 6176   iii Carole Jean Pontius, born 1940.
(Sup) 6177   iv Dale Edward Pontius, born 1942.
(Sup) 6178   v   Judith Arlene Pontius, born 1945.
(Sup) 6179   vi Sharon Jane Pontius, born 1948.

3758 WALTER GOUTY (Elizabeth[7], Frances[6], Adam[5], Phillip[4], Peter[3], Matthias[2], John Jacob[1]) was born May 9, 1906, at Fort Wayne, Indiana. He married Elizabeth Jane Robertson, October 17, 1936, at Fort Wayne. Elizabeth was born October 11, 1914, at Fort Wayne.

(Sup) 6180   i   Carl Douglas Gouty, born 1939.
(Sup) 6181   ii Doyle Keith Gouty, born 1944.
(Sup) 6182   iii Lee Walter Gouty, born 1947.

3759 THOMAS ALEXANDER GOUTY (Elizabeth[7], Frances[6], Adam[5], Phillip[4], Peter[3], Matthias[2], John Jacob[1]) was born March 9, 1913, near Fort Wayne, Indiana. He married Grace Lois Davis, October 12, 1933, at Rochester, Indiana. Grace was the daughter of Vibert and Mary Irelan Davis and was born November 28, 1914, at Philadelphia, Pennsylvania.

(Sup) 6183   i   Susan Lynn Gouty, born June 2, 1935.
(Sup) 6184   ii Mary Elizabeth Gouty, born March 5, 1937.
(Sup) 6185   iii Helen Anita Gouty, born July 4, 1938.
(Sup) 6186   iv Phyllis Dianne Gouty, born March 17, 1942.
(Sup) 6187   v   Thomas Richard Gouty, born August 26, 1944.
(Sup) 6188   vi James Paul Gouty, born January 7, 1948.

3760 WILLIAM GOUTY (Elizabeth[7], Frances[6], Adam[5], Phillip[4], Peter[3], Matthias[2], John Jacob[1]). His wife's name was Julie.

3761 HENRI BROWNELL VIDAL (Jennie[7], Helen[6], Adam[5], Phillip[4], Peter[3], Matthias[2], John Jacob[1]) was born January 16, 1901, at Holly, Colorado. He married Eddah Hillier James, September 6, 1923. Eddah was the daughter of Henry James and was born August 4, 1900, at Altoona, Pennsylvania. She died May 12, 1942, at Buffalo, New York.

(Sup) 6189 i Ellen Jane Vidal, born August 25, 1924.

3762 NUMA FERDINAND VIDAL II (Jennie[7], Helen[6], Adam[5], Phillip[4], Peter[3], Matthias[2], John Jacob[1]) was born November 20, 1902, at Holly, Colorado. He married Arabel Truog, September 22, 1928. Arabel was the daughter of Christ Truog and was born December 2, 1902, at Youngstown, Ohio.

(Sup) 6190 i Numa Ferdinand Vidal, III, born May 23, 1931.

3763 RICHARD WILSON VIDAL (Jennie[7], Helen[6], Adam[5], Phillip[4], Peter[3], Matthias[2], John Jacob[1]) was born June 24, 1909, at Denver, Colorado. He married Barbara Wilson, June 24, 1935, at Crown Point, Indiana. Barbara was born at Chicago, Illinois.

(Sup) 6191 i Gay Vidal, born August 14, 1936.

3764 ELIZABETH LA VERNE PARKS (Myrtle[7], Adam[6], Adam[5], Phillip[4], Peter[3], Matthias[2], John Jacob[1]) was born March 21, 1925, at Bend, Oregon. She married Leo Perkins, October 13, 1944.

(Sup) 6192 i Sandra Rae Perkins, born October 20, 1944.
(Sup) 6193 ii Linda Lee Perkins, born January 11, 1946.

3765 WILLIAM EDWARD PARKS (Myrtle[7], Adam[6], Adam[5], Phillip[4], Peter[3], Matthias[2], John Jacob[1]) was born October 12, 1929, at St. Helena, California.

3766 ROBERT CLARENCE PARKS (Myrtle[7], Adam[6], Adam[5], Phillip[4], Peter[3], Matthias[2], John Jacob[1]) was born August 19, 1931, at Bend, Oregon.

3767 GLADYS ELIZABETH HULVEY (George[7], Elizabeth[6], Rebecca[5], William[4], Peter[3], Matthias[2], John Jacob[1]) was born October 28, 1901, at Fort Defiance, Virginia. She married Harry Hamilton Hanger, August 15, 1931, at Staunton, Virginia. Harry was born September 7, 1907, at Staunton.

3768 HERBERT SAMUEL HULVEY (George[7], Elizabeth[6], Rebecca[5], William[4], Peter[3], Matthias[2], John Jacob[1]) was born October 27, 1903, in Augusta County, Virginia. He married Louise Catherine Shiflette, August 27, 1931, in Augusta County. Louise was the daughter of E. H. and Myrtle Rohr Shiflette and was born at Staunton, February 28, 1913.

(Sup) 6194 i Christie Lou Hulvey, born April 30, 1936.

3769 RUTH JONES HULVEY (George[7], Elizabeth[6], Rebecca[5], William[4], Peter[3], Matthias[2], John Jacob[1]) was born October 31, 1905, in Augusta County, Virginia. She married Richard Ruff, November 27, 1933.

3770 MERLIN CRAWFORD HULVEY (George[7], Elizabeth[6], Rebecca[5], William[4], Peter[3], Matthias[2], John Jacob[1]) was born August 21, 1912, in Augusta County, Virginia. He married Margaret Carr in April, 1941.

3771 ARLENE WINTERS HUDSON (Alice[7], Elizabeth[6], Rebecca[5], William[4], Peter[3], Matthias[2], John Jacob[1]) was born June 3, 1903, in Augusta County, Virginia. She married Harold M. Hevener. Arlene died March 31, 1948.

3772 THELMA LEOLA HUDSON (Alice[7], Elizabeth[6], Rebecca[5], William[4], Peter[3], Matthias[2], John Jacob[1]) was born February 20, 1905, in Augusta County, Virginia. She married Warren E. Breth, July 1, 1944.

3773 VIRGINIA CAROLINE HUDSON (Alice[7], Elizabeth[6], Rebecca[5], William[4], Peter[3], Matthias[2], John Jacob[1]) was born August 22, 1906, in Augusta County, Virginia. She married Nelson P. Wine, son of Julia Link and John W. Wine. Nelson was born in Augusta County, August 28, 1901. See No. 1935. Children are listed under this number.

3774 ALVIN EYLER DAVIS (Hester[7], Elizabeth[6], Rebecca[5], William[4], Peter[3], Matthias[2], John Jacob[1]) was born June 4, 1907, at Fort Defiance, Virginia. He married Virginia Kirkpatrick Obenschain.

3775 ORPHA LOUISE DAVIS (Hester[7], Elizabeth[6], Rebecca[5], William[4], Peter[3], Matthias[2], John Jacob[1]) was born March 6, 1914, at New Hope, Virginia.

3776 VERNON THOMAS DAVIS (Hester[7], Elizabeth[6], Rebecca[5], William[4], Peter[3], Matthias[2], John Jacob[1]) was born August 5, 1917, at New Hope, Virginia. He married Helen Louise Crickenberger, June 4, 1949, at New Hope. Helen was born March 18, 1919, and was the daughter of Lloyd and Ethel Wright Crickenberger.

3777 CHRISTINE VIRGINIA DAVIS (Hester[7], Elizabeth[6], Rebecca[5], William[4], Peter[3], Matthias[2], John Jacob[1]) was born October 2, 1920, at New Hope, Virginia. She married Richard Wendall Leighton, May 25, 1946.

3778. CARMEN SAMUEL DAVIS (Hester[7], Elizabeth[6], Rebecca[5], William[4], Peter[3], Matthias[2], John Jacob[1]) was born September 23, 1922, at New Hope, Virginia. She married Burdine Hyden, June 21, 1947.

3779 MARJORIE RUTH HOUFF (Arthur[7], Erasmus[6], Rebecca[5], William[4], Peter[3], Matthias[2], John Jacob[1]) was born August 3, 1911, at Waynesboro, Virginia. She married Russell M. Shank, January 28, 1927, at Waynesboro, Virginia. Russell was born there in December, 1906.

(Sup) 6195 i Russell M. Shank, Jr., born July 6, 1932.
(Sup) 6196 ii Helen Janet Shank, born March 17, 1937.

3780 DAVID EARL HOUFF (Arthur[7], Erasmus[6], Rebecca[5], William[4], Peter[3], Matthias[2], John Jacob[1]) was born May 22, 1918, at Waynesboro, Virginia. He married Wilhelmina Grove, May 27, 1939, at Waynesboro. Wilhelmina was born February 20, 1913.

(Sup) 6197 i David Earl Houff, Jr., born August 3, 1942.
(Sup) 6198 ii Diane Elizabeth Houff, born September 25, 1946.

3781 RAYMOND LEROY HOUFF (Arthur[7], Erasmus[6], Rebecca[5], William[4], Peter[3], Matthias[2], John Jacob[1]) was born in Augusta County, Virginia. He married Frances Willard Sayre, December 24, 1941.

3782 ARTHUR GORDON HOUFF (Arthur[7], Erasmus[6], Rebecca[5], William[4], Peter[3], Matthias[2], John Jacob[1]) was born in Augusta County, Virginia. He married Frances Joy Paynter, April 30, 1949.

3783 HAROLD M. HOUFF (Elsie[7], Walter[6], Rebecca[5], William[4], Peter[3], Matthias[2], John Jacob[1]) was born March 26, 1921, at Staunton, Virginia. He married Maxine McMichael, April 14, 1946. Maxine was born November 9, 1919, at Lowry City, Missouri.

3784 FLOYD LINK HOUFF (Emmett[7], Walter[6], Rebecca[5], William[4], Peter[3], Matthias[2], John Jacob[1]) was born April 14, 1932, in Ford County, Kansas.

3785 ALPHADINE LEOTA MEYERHOEFFER (Myrtle[7], Walter[6], Rebecca[5], William[4], Peter[3], Matthias[2], John Jacob[1]) was born August 31, 1924, in Augusta County, Virginia. She married Harry R. McCray, June 18, 1943.

3786 MILDRED PAULINE HOUFF (Edgar[7], Walter[6], Rebecca[5], William[4], Peter[3], Matthias[2], John Jacob[1]) was born November 1, 1918, in Augusta County, Virginia. She married Eugene Twigg, October 16, 1937.

3787 WALTER LINK HOUFF II (Edgar[7], Walter[6], Rebecca[5], William[4], Peter[3], Matthias[2], John Jacob[1]) was born October 19, 1921, in Augusta County, Virginia. He married Phyllis Ellinger, October 19, 1946.

3788 KATHERINE ALICE HOUFF (Edgar[7], Walter[6], Rebecca[5], William[4], Peter[3], Matthias[2], John Jacob[1]) was born April 17, 1927, at Akron, Ohio. She married Dewey Warren Sensabaugh, September 7, 1947, in Augusta County, Virginia. Dewey was the son of Dewey Clemmer and Mary Frances Lindsay Sensabaugh and was born at Staunton, Virginia, September 28, 1928.

3789 BURTON LEE HOUFF (Edgar[7], Walter[6], Rebecca[5], William[4], Peter[3], Matthias[2], John Jacob[1]) was born April 5, 1935, in Augusta County, Virginia.

3790 LOEY EDWARD HOUFF (Loey[7], Walter[6], Rebecca[5], William[4], Peter[3], Matthias[2], John Jacob[1]) was born January 29, 1930, at Akron, Ohio.

3791 RAYMOND LUTHER STOVER (George[7], William[6], Elizabeth[5], William[4], Peter[3], Matthias[2], John Jacob[1]) was born May 19, 1900, near Topeka, Kansas. He married Myrtle Grace Foltz, June 4, 1924, at Topeka, Kansas. Myrtle, daughter of Edwin Foltz, was born July 12, 1902. Raymond was the Extension Dairyman for Kansas State College at Manhattan.

(Sup) 6201   i   Donald Austin Stover, born April 28, 1925.
(Sup) 6202   ii   Robert Raymond Stover, born December 1, 1926.
(Sup) 6203 iii   Dorothy Stover, born April 2, 1928.
(Sup) 6204   iv   Wilbur Dean Stover, born September 27, 1929.
(Sup) 6205   v   Marjorie Jean Stover, born October 3, 1934.
(Sup) 6206   vi   James Richard Stover, born June 24, 1940.

3792 AUSTIN WILLIAM STOVER (George[7], William[6], Elizabeth[5], William[4], Peter[3], Matthias[2], John Jacob[1]) was born January 4, 1902, at Topeka, Kansas. He married Opal Ellen Campbell, March 16, 1936, at Bozeman, Montana. Opal was born November 19, 1916. She was the daughter of Clarence Campbell.

(Sup) 6207   i   Gene Austin Stover, born November 13, 1933.
(Sup) 6208   ii   Ronald William Stover, born January 19, 1942.
(Sup) 6209 iii   Marilyn Dee Stover, born October 7, 1944.

3793 GLADYS MIRIAM STOVER (George[7], William[6], Elizabeth[5], William[4], Peter[3], Matthias[2], John Jacob[1]) was born February 23, 1904, at Topeka, Kansas. She married Duane Everette Wollner, June 27, 1929, at Manhattan, Kansas. Duane was the son of George Wollner and was born December 20, 1902, at Wakeeney, Kansas.

(Sup) 6210   i   Patricia Jean Wollner, born September 28, 1934.

3794 EDITH LOUISE STOVER (Arthur[7], Jacob[6], Elizabeth[5], William[4], Peter[3], Matthias[2], John Jacob[1]) was born September 29, 1911, at Seattle, Washington. She married John Richard Wiley, October 29, 1935, at Seattle, Washington.

(Sup) 6211   i   Paul Richard Wiley, born October 4, 1941.
(Sup) 6212   ii   Roger Stover Wiley, born September 27, 1943.

3795 KATHRYN JUNE STOVER (Arthur[7], Jacob[6], Elizabeth[5], William[4], Peter[3], Matthias[2], John Jacob[1]) was born June 4, 1914, at Seattle, Washington.

3796 ETHEL LUCILLE STOVER (James William[7], Jacob[6], Elizabeth[5], William[4], Peter[3], Matthias[2], John Jacob[1]) was born January 29, 1918, at Seattle, Washington. She married Alvin J. Lawson, August 20, 1942, at Seattle, Washington.

(Sup) 6213   i   Alvin Eugene Lawson, born December 25, 1944.

3797 PHILLIP EUGENE AUER (Ethel[7], Jacob[6], Elizabeth[5], William[4], Peter[3], Matthias[2], John Jacob[1]) was born October 2, 1912, at Seattle, Washington. He married Frances Eleanor Barney, November 8, 1942, at Reno, Nevada. Frances was the daughter of William Martin and Eleanor C. Nesbund Barney and was born November 19, 1920, at Everett, Washington.

(Sup) 6214   i   Lynn Christine Auer, born August 8, 1946.

3798 RICHARD BRUCE AUER (Ethel[7], Jacob[6], Elizabeth[5], William[4], Peter[3], Matthias[2], John Jacob[1]) was born September 5, 1916, at Seattle, Washington.

3799 DWIGHT WAIN HANSEN (Maude[7], Jacob[6], Elizabeth[5], William[4], Peter[3], Matthias[2], John Jacob[1]) was born July 30, 1916, at Seattle, Washington. He married Halgero Synovë Oversen, May 7, 1941, at Seattle, Washington.

3800 MARGARET IONE HANSEN (Maude[7], Jacob[6], Elizabeth[5], William[4], Peter[3], Matthias[2], John Jacob[1]) was born April 16, 1920, at Seattle, Washington. She married Alfred Anthony Aries, October 25, 1940, at Seattle, Washington.

3801 DONALD HANSEN (Maude[7], Jacob[6], Elizabeth[5], William[4], Peter[3], Matthias[2], John Jacob[1]) was born September 2, 1922, at Seattle, Washington. He married Laura Jean Craig, February 13, 1943, at Decatur, Alabama. Donald was a Lieutenant in the U. S. Air Corps in World War II and was killed in a bomber crash at Attleboro, Sherwood, England. He was a pilot.

3802 ANNA STOVER (Robert[7], Charles[6], Elizabeth[5], William[4], Peter[3], Matthias[2], John Jacob[1]) was born December 8, 1914, at Topeka, Kansas, where she died the same day.

3803 FREDA FAY STOVER (Robert[7], Charles[6], Elizabeth[5], William[4], Peter[3], Matthias[2], John Jacob[1]) was born March 1, 1917, at Topeka, Kansas. She married Alexander Jacob Damme, April 19, 1938, at Topeka. Alexander was born July 29, 1911, in Russia.

(Sup) 6215   i   Francis Glenn Damme, born January 12, 1939.

3804 CHARLES WESLEY STOVER II (Robert[7], Charles[6], Elizabeth[5], William[4], Peter[3], Matthias[2], John Jacob[1]) was born February 4, 1920. He married Lucile Kathryn Wigington.

3805 PHILLIP MILTON STOVER (Robert[7], Charles[6], Elizabeth[5], William[4], Peter[3], Matthias[2], John Jacob[1]) was born December 26, 1921, at Topeka, Kansas, where he died March 1, 1922.

3806 WAYNE DELBERT STOVER (Robert[7], Charles[6], Elizabeth[5], William[4], Peter[3], Matthias[2], John Jacob[1]) was born May 2, 1923. He married Dorothy Darlene Walker, May 6, 1944.

3807 ROBERT HARRY STOVER, JR. (Robert[7], Charles[6], Elizabeth[5], William[4], Peter[3], Matthias[2], John Jacob[1]) was born December 5, 1925, at Topeka, Kansas, where he died October 20, 1928.

3808 JOSEPH DEAN STOVER (Robert[7], Charles[6], Elizabeth[5], William[4], Peter[3], Matthias[2], John Jacob[1]) was born March 9, 1928, at Topeka, Kansas.

3809 CHARLOTTE JOAN STOVER (Robert[7], Charles[6], Elizabeth[5], William[4], Peter[3], Matthias[2], John Jacob[1]) was born July 28, 1931, at Topeka, Kansas.

3810 KATHRYN JANE STOVER (Charles[7], Charles[6], Elizabeth[5], William[4], Peter[3], Matthias[2], John Jacob[1]) was born December 25, 1929, near Topeka, Kansas.

3811 ROBERT LESTER DISTER (Anna[7], Charles[6], Elizabeth[5], William[4], Peter[3], Matthias[2], John Jacob[1]) was born January 22, 1919, at North Topeka, Kansas. He married Evelyn Reedy, July 26, 1941.

3812 ANNE GERTRUDE DISTER (Anna[7], Charles[6], Elizabeth[5], William[4], Peter[3], Matthias[2], John Jacob[1]) was born April 21, 1920, at North Topeka, Kansas. She married Donald Ostrander in July, 1939.

3813 MARJORIE ELIZABETH DISTER (Anna[7], Charles[6], Elizabeth[5], William[4], Peter[3], Matthias[2], John Jacob[1]) was born December 30, 1922, at North Topeka, Kansas. She married Daniel Iwig, June 30, 1944.

3814 MARTHA JANE DISTER (Anna[7], Charles[6], Elizabeth[5], William[4], Peter[3], Matthias[2], John Jacob[1]) was born September 29, 1933, at North Topeka, Kansas.

3815 DANIEL STOVER DISTER (Anna[7], Charles[6], Elizabeth[5], William[4], Peter[3], Matthias[2], John Jacob[1]) was born June 22, 1937, at North Topeka, Kansas.

3816 RALPH CECIL FLOWERS, JR. (Florence[7], Simon[6], Elizabeth[5], William[4], Peter[3], Matthias[2], John Jacob[1]) was born July 16, 1918.

3817 MARY ELOISE FLOWERS (Florence[7], Simon[6], Elizabeth[5], William[4], Peter[3], Matthias[2], John Jacob[1]) was born December 27, 1921. She married Delmar R. Lawrence, June 30, 1943.

3818 NOEL STOVER (Leonard[7], Simon[6], Elizabeth[5], William[4], Peter[3], Matthias[2], John Jacob[1]) was born February 22, 1936, in Shawnee County, Kansas. He died July 25, 1936.

3819 DELMAR STOVER (Leonard[7], Simon[6], Elizabeth[5], William[4], Peter[3], Matthias[2], John Jacob[1]) was born November 20, 1937, in Shawnee County, Kansas.

3820 JACK EISENHOWER (Edgar[7], Ida[6], Elizabeth[5], William[4], Peter[3], Matthias[2], John Jacob[1]) was born May 30, 1916, at Tacoma, Washington. He married Muriel Menadue, whose father was Sidney Menadue, February 13, 1946, at Laguna Beach, California.

3821 JANIS EISENHOWER (Edgar[7], Ida[6], Elizabeth[5], William[4], Peter[3], Matthias[2], John Jacob[1]) was born April 5, 1922, at Tacoma, Washington. She married William Oliver Causin, August 31, 1946, at Tacoma, Washington. William, son of William Causin, was born July 4, 1922, at Tacoma, Washington.

3822 DOUD DWIGHT EISENHOWER (Dwight[7], Ida[6], Elizabeth[5], William[4], Peter[3], Matthias[2], John Jacob[1]) was born September 24, 1917, at Denver, Colorado. He died January 2, 1921, at Camp Meade, Maryland, and is buried at Denver, Colorado.

3823 JOHN SHELDON DOUD EISENHOWER (Dwight[7], Ida[6], Elizabeth[5], William[4], Peter[3], Matthias[2], John Jacob[1]) was born August 3, 1922, at Denver, Colorado. John graduated from the U. S. Military Academy in 1944 with a Bachelor of Science degree. He served twenty-eight months overseas in World War II and in the occupation. He did post-graduate work at Columbia University, where he was awarded his Master of Arts degree in English in 1950. He was then appointed professor of English at United States Military Academy. On June 10, 1947, John married Barbara Jean Thompson at Fort Monroe, Virginia. Barbara was the daughter of Colonel Percy W. Thompson and was born June 15, 1926, at Fort Knox, Kentucky. After her public schooling Barbara studied at Purdue University.

(Sup) 6216   i   Dwight David Eisenhower II, born March 31, 1948.
(Sup) 6217   ii Barbara Anne Eisenhower, born May 30, 1949.

3824 PATRICIA EISENHOWER (Roy[7], Ida[6], Elizabeth[5], William[4], Peter[3], Matthias[2], John Jacob[1]) was born June 17, 1918, at Ellsworth, Kansas. She married Thomas B. Feagan, February 14, 1941. Thomas was the son of Robert Benjamin and Marian R. Lewis Feagan and was born June 29, 1916.

(Sup) 6218   †   Thomas Benjamin Feagan, Jr., born Dec 8, 1941.
(Sup) 6219   ii Robert Roy Feagan, born July 2, 1945.
(Sup) 6220   iii Thomas Michael Feagan, born February 9, 1949.

3825 ROY JACK EISENHOWER (Roy[7], Ida[6], Elizabeth[5], William[4], Peter[3], Matthias[2], John Jacob[1]) was born April 20, 1921, at Junction City, Kansas, where he died April 24, 1921.

3826 PEGGY JANE EISENHOWER (Roy[7], Ida[6], Elizabeth[5], William[4], Peter[3], Matthias[2], John Jacob[1]) was born April 12, 1923, at Junction City, Kansas. She married Oliver Jackson Bryan, Jr., July 25, 1943, at Bay City, Texas. Oliver was the son of Oliver Jackson and Linnie Luce Bryan, Sr., and was born September 28, 1921, at Atchison, Kansas.

(Sup) 6225   †   Dina Jane Bryan, born August 13, 1949.

3827 LLOYD EDGAR EISENHOWER (Roy[7], Ida[6], Elizabeth[5], William[4], Peter[3], Matthias[2], John Jacob[1]) was born March 21, 1925, at Junction City, Kansas.

3828 KATHRYN SNYDER EISENHOWER (Earl[7], Ida[6], Elizabeth[5], William[4], Peter[3], Matthias[2], John Jacob[1]) was born September 20, 1934, at Charleroi, Pennsylvania.

3829 EARL DEWEY EISENHOWER, JR. (Earl[7], Ida[6], Elizabeth[5], William[4], Peter[3], Matthias[2], John Jacob[1]) was born September 6, 1936, at Charleroi, Pennsylvania.

3830 **MILTON STOVER EISENHOWER, JR.** (Milton[7], Ida[6], Elizabeth[5], William[4], Peter[3], Matthias[2], John Jacob[1]) was born December 11, 1930, at Washington, D. C.

3831 **RUTH EAKIN EISENHOWER** (Milton[7], Ida[6], Elizabeth[5], William[4], Peter[3], Matthias[2], John Jacob[1]) was born July 21, 1938, at Washington, D. C.

3832 **ELEANOR WALLACE LANDES** (Warrick[7], Hester[6], Peter[5], William[4], Peter[3], Matthias[2], John Jacob[1]) was born November 8, 1921, at Houston, Texas. She married Joseph Whitfield Outlaw II, November 9, 1942. Joseph was the son of Joseph Whitfield Outlaw I and was born at Beaumont, Texas.

   (Sup) 6226   i   Joseph Whitfield Outlaw, III, born Dec 20, 1943.
   (Sup) 6227   ii   Warrick Bell Outlaw, born February 12, 1946.
   (Sup) 6228   iii   Daniel Carter Outlaw, born December 16, 1948.

3833 **BETTY LOU TURNER** (Thomas[7], David[6], Nancy[5], Peter[4], Peter[3], Matthias[2], John Jacob[1]) was born May 14, 1920, at Paris, Illinois. She married Charles Whitton, June 19, 1938. Charles was born October 26, 1918.

   (Sup) 6229   i   Charles Whitton, Jr., born July 26, 1939.
   (Sup) 6230   ii   Sandra Lynn Whitton, born June 24, 1941.
   (Sup) 6231   iii   Thomas Whitton, born September 7, 1942.
   (Sup) 6232   iv   Edward Whitton, born August 17, 1943.

3834 **JOSEPH MARION TURNER** (Thomas[7], David[6], Nancy[5], Peter[4], Peter[3], Matthias[2], John Jacob[1]) was born July 2, 1921, at Paris, Illinois, and died there July 3, 1921.

3835 **ROBERT HERMAN TURNER** (Thomas[7], David[6], Nancy[5], Peter[4], Peter[3], Matthias[2], John Jacob[1]) was born July 8, 1924, at Paris, Illinois. He married Alice Andrews, December 4, 1943. Alice was born March 20, 1919.

   (Sup) 6233   i   Linda Kay Turner, born August 15, 1944.

3836 **JOANNE TURNER** (Thomas[7], David[6], Nancy[5], Peter[4], Peter[3], Matthias[2], John Jacob[1]) was born April 22, 1931, at Paris, Illinois.

3837 **KATHLEEN SUE TURNER** (William[7], Booth[6], Nancy[5], Peter[4], Peter[3], Matthias[2], John Jacob[1]) was born December 31, 1915, at Bloomington, Indiana. She married Reverend Herbert H. Fuller, July 22, 1934. Herbert was born June 8, 1905, at Sterling, Illinois.

   (Sup) 6234   i   William Hugh Fuller, born July 27, 1938.

3838 **WILLIAM RAYMOND TURNER** (William[7], Booth[6], Nancy[5], Peter[4], Peter[3], Matthias[2], John Jacob[1]) was born September 24, 1921, at Bloomington, Indiana. He married Mary Jane Harper, June 9, 1946. Mary was the daughter of W. Carl Harper and was born February 5, 1922, at Sharpsville, Indiana.

3839 **BETTY LOU TURNER** (William[7], Booth[6], Nancy[5], Peter[4], Peter[3], Matthias[2], John Jacob[1]) was born October 14, 1925, at Lafayette, Indiana.

3840 **CHARLOTTE JUNE TURNER** (Norman[7], Booth[6], Nancy[5], Peter[4], Peter[3], Matthias[2], John Jacob[1]) was born September 9, 1922, at Bloomington, Indiana, where she died October 15, 1922.

3841 **SHIRLEY JEAN TURNER** (Norman[7], Booth[6], Nancy[5], Peter[4], Peter[3], Matthias[2], John Jacob[1]) was born September 9, 1922, at Bloomington, Indiana, where she died October 16, 1922.

3842 **MARY VIRGINIA TURNER** (Norman[7], Booth[6], Nancy[5], Peter[4], Peter[3], Matthias[2], John Jacob[1]) was born November 5, 1923, at Bloomington, Indiana. She married James A. Wisehart, April 23, 1944. James was the son of Roy P. Wisehart and was born July 18, 1920, at Union City, Indiana.

   (Sup) 6235   i   Pamela Ann Wisehart, born May 12, 1945.

3843 **RICHARD NORMAN TURNER** (Norman[7], Booth[6], Nancy[5], Peter[4], Peter[3], Matthias[2], John Jacob[1]) was born October 10, 1925, at Bloomington, Indiana.

3844 **MIRIAM CALLAWAY** (Llewellyn[7], Mary[6], Nethaniah[5], Peter[4], Peter[3], Matthias[2], John Jacob[1]) was born July 6, 1894, at Virginia City, Montana. She married William Harper Jones, son of Edwin Ashton Jones, in 1921. William was born March 8, 1895.

   (Sup) 6236   i   William Harper Jones, Jr., born 1925.
   (Sup) 6237   ii   Llewellyn Callaway Jones, born November 17, 1927.

3845 **JAMES EDMUND CALLAWAY** (Llewellyn[7], Mary[6], Nethaniah[5], Peter[4], Peter[3], Matthias[2], John Jacob[1]) was born March 6, 1899, at Virginia City, Montana. He graduated in law from the University of Nebraska in 1922. James married Ruth Lapp, August 21, 1920. Ruth was the daughter of William Lapp and was born March 4, 1900, at Great Falls, Montana. James married Florence Elizabeth Svieven, daughter of Martin O. Svieven. Florence was born May 1, 1902. James died in November, 1945, at Helena, Montana.

   (Sup) 6238   i   James Edmund Callaway, Jr., born March 21, 1921.
   (Sup) 6239   ii   George Link Callaway, born December 22, 1930.

3846 **FRANCES LATHROP CALLAWAY** (Llewellyn[7], Mary[6], Nethaniah[5], Peter[4], Peter[3], Matthias[2], John Jacob[1]) was born October 21, 1902, at Virginia City, Montana. She married Sam Dupuy Goza IV, July 10, 1928. Sam was the son of Sam Dupuy Goza III. Frances died June 4. 1931, at Helena, Montana.

   (Sup) 6240   i   Sam Dupuy Goza, V, born April 28, 1929.

3847 **LLEWELLYN LINK CALLAWAY, JR.** (Llewellyn[7], Mary[6], Nethaniah[5], Peter[4], Peter[3], Matthias[2], John Jacob[1]) was born September 12, 1907, at Virginia City, Montana. He married Helene Louise Anderson, October 10, 1937, at Westport, Connecticut. Helene was the daughter of Peter Anderson and was born December 2, 1907, at Denver, Colorado. Llewellyn, after completing his formal education, went into advertising and rose to the position of Advertising Manager of *Fortune Magazine*.

   (Sup) 6241   i   Peter Anderson Callaway, born January 8, 1941.
   (Sup) 6242   ii   Elizabeth Woodson Callaway, born October 16, 1942.

3848 MARY ELIZABETH CALLAWAY (Llewellyn[7], Mary[6], Nethaniah[5], Peter[4], Peter[3], Matthias[2], John Jacob[1]) was born March 21, 1917, at Great Falls, Montana. She married Dr. Gordon L. Doering, September 14, 1939. Gordon was the son of Julius D. Doering and was born November 9, 1913, at Goodrich, North Dakota.

(Sup) 6243   i   Charles Gordon Doering, born April 7, 1941.
(Sup) 6244   ii   Bruce Callaway Doering, born October 10, 1947.
(Sup) 6245   iii Mary Ellen Doering, born February 19, 1950.

3849 CATHERINE CALLAWAY (Edmund[7], Mary[6], Nethaniah[5], Peter[4], Peter[3], Matthias[2], John Jacob[1]) was born October 2, 1917, at Dillon, Montana. She married William F. Freese, August 29, 1946. William was born June 20, 1920. Catherine graduated from the University of Oregon with a B.S. degree. During World War II she served in the U.S. Navy as a civil service supervisor of Fleet Survey from 1942 to 1945.

3850 EDMUND JAMES CALLAWAY, JR. (Edmund[7], Mary[6], Nethaniah[5], Peter[4], Peter[3], Matthias[2], John Jacob[1]) was born June 26, 1925. He died July 25, 1939.

3851 CLINTON CALLAWAY (Edmund[7], Mary[8], Nethaniah[5], Peter[4], Peter[3], Matthias[2], John Jacob[1]) was born October 2, 1927.

3852 ALICE ESTHER DONALDSON (Burt[7], Alice[6], Nethaniah[5], Peter[4], Peter[3], Matthias[2], John Jacob[1]) was born November 16, 1907, at Seattle, Washington. She married Thomas Etherington, December 31, 1927.

(Sup) 6249   i   Donn Etherington, born January 31, 1932.

3853 HELEN PEARL DONALDSON (Burt[7], Alice[6], Nethaniah[5], Peter[4], Peter[3], Matthias[2], John Jacob[1]) was born May 8, 1916, at Seattle, Washington. She married Carl Straight, December 8, 1940.

(Sup) 6250   i   Stephen Carl Straight, born October 21, 1941.
(Sup) 6251   ii   William Burt Straight, born November 21, 1944.

3854 FREDERICK PAUL ZSCHEILE, JR. (Esther[7], Virginia[6], Nethaniah[5], Peter[4], Peter[3], Matthias[2], John Jacob[1]) was born May 11, 1907, at Burlington, Kansas. He married Emily Di Silvestro, October 14, 1933. Emily was the daughter of Gerinaro Di Silvestro and was born February 29, 1912, at Chicago, Illinois.

(Sup) 6252   i   Fredrick Paul Zscheile, III, born Sept 5, 1934.
(Sup) 6253   ii   Richard Zscheile, born May 27, 1937.
(Sup) 6254   iii Elizabeth Therese Zscheile, born July 8, 1941.

3855 CARL EUGENE ZSCHEILE (Esther[7], Virginia[6], Nethaniah[5], Peter[4], Peter[3], Matthias[2], John Jacob[1]) was born December 14, 1914, at Burlington, Kansas. He married Eleanor Parker, July 21, 1945. Eleanor was the daughter of George Parker and was born November 5, 1923, at Fresno, California.

3856 JESSIE VIRGINIA ZSCHEILE (Esther[7], Virginia[6], Nethaniah[5], Peter[4], Peter[3], Matthias[2], John Jacob[1]) was born August 7, 1922, at Burlington, Kansas.

3857 MEREDITH MOREAU WARD (Jessie[7], Virginia[6], Nethaniah[5], Peter[4], Peter[3], Matthias[2], John Jacob[1]) was born February 5, 1913, at Burlington, Kansas. He married Rosalie Louise Springman, October 4, 1932.

3858 MIRIAM WARD (Jessie[7], Virginia[6], Nethaniah[5], Peter[4], Peter[3], Matthias[2], John Jacob[1]) was born September 17, 1914, at Burlington, Kansas. She married Dr. R. G. Nichols, May 3, 1946.

(Sup) 3859 PAXSON RUDE LINK (Horace[7], James[6], Christopher[5], Peter[4], Peter[3], Matthias[2], John Jacob[1]) was born January 29, 1897, at Paris, Illinois. He was educated in the public schools of Paris and attended De Pauw University, where he studied three years majoring in sociology, until the spring of 1918, when he enlisted in the Army. He was assigned, first, to the Ordnance Corps and, later, to an Infantry Officers' Training Battalion from which he was discharged after the war's end in December, 1918. Entering his father's business, he purchased an interest from his father's partner in 1920 and became active in extending the volume and scope of the business until it included four retail stores, a wholesale distributorship, and three plants manufacturing carbonated beverages. These were located in Paris and Danville, Illinois; Brazil and Greencastle, Indiana; Nashville, Tennessee; Houston, Texas; and Charlotte, North Carolina. From 1928 through 1930 Paxson was president of the Paris Chamber of Commerce, during which time a substantial new industry was brought to Paris and 4-H Clubs were established throughout Edgar County. He was a member of Rotary. With others, he organized the Community Chest at Paris, formed the Community Nurse Association, and financed the first school lunch programs. He, his father, and brother gave the city a recreational park in 1942, and he was a member of the Paris Park Board for many years. Paxson married Louise Cole, February 2, 1922, at Paris, Illinois. She was the daughter of Warren David and Ella Hennasy Cole and was born January 8, 1902, at Paris, Illinois. Louise was educated in the Paris public schools and at Penn Hall, Chambersburg, Pennsylvania, where she graduated in 1921. Louise helped organize the Paris Woman's Club and, with others, sponsored and supervised the landscaping of a park at Paris in 1932 to provide employment and to beautify a large tract which became an important recreational center in the middle west. Louise was a charter member of the Paris Park Board. She was active in garden and art club work, as well as in the Girl Scouts, serving as council president. Her avocation was painting. In 1971, Paxson and Louise gave the city a park honoring her ancestor Samuel Vance, founder of Paris, Illinois. Louise died May 14, 1975. In her memory Paxson donated to the Bicentennial Art Center a historical building with funds to adapt it for galleries and studios. Paxson was principal author of this history. He was a community leader in developing an industrial park, building a new community hospital, and establishing a YMCA. His last gift was a fountain for the court house square. Paxson was a member of Beta Theta Pi, and his clubs were Paris Country Club, Country Club of Terre Haute, Belle Meade Country Club of Nashville, Tennessee, and The Houston Club of Houston, Texas. He was a 32nd-degree Mason and a member of B.P.O.E. Paxson died August 19, 1983. He and Louise are buried in Edgar Cemetery at Paris, Illinois.

(Sup) 6255   i   James Cole Link, born May 11, 1924.
(Sup) 6256   ii   Martha Jane Link, born March 30, 1927.
(Sup) 6257   iii Joanna Christie Link, born January 2, 1935.

(Sup) 3862 ARTHUR KESSLER LINK (Foster[7], Arthur[6], Christopher[5], Peter[4], Peter[3], Matthias[2], John Jacob[1]) was the son of Foster H. and Carrie Kessler Link [The Link Family, page 551, No. 2156]. Arthur was born August 1, 1904, at Florence, Alabama.

(Sup) 3863 RACHEL CATHERINE LINK (Foster[7], Arthur[6], Christopher[5], Peter[4], Peter[3], Matthias[2], John Jacob[1]) was the daughter of Foster H. and Carrie Kessler Link [The Link Family, page 551, No. 2156]. Rachel was born December 1, 1906, at Robinson, Illinois. She married Thomas Clayton Donahoe at Los Angeles, California, November 24, 1925.

(Sup) 6260	i	Thomas Link Donahoe, born March 9, 1929.
(Sup) 6261	ii	Jack Foster Donahoe, born September 29, 1932.
(Sup) 6262	iii	Jerry Edward Donahoe, born October 22, 1946.

(Sup) 3864 MARJORIE LINK APPLE (Mabel[7], Arthur[6], Christopher[5], Peter[4], Peter[3], Matthias[2], John Jacob[1]) was the daughter of Emerson and Mable Link Apple [The Link Family, page 551, No. 2158]. Marjorie was born December 24, 1909, at Robinson, Illinois, where she died December 26, 1909.

(Sup) 3865 ROBERT WILLIAM APPLE (Mabel[7], Arthur[6], Christopher[5], Peter[4], Peter[3], Matthias[2], John Jacob[1]) was the son of Emerson and Mabel Apple Link [The Link Family, page 551, No. 2158]. Robert was born August 18, 1914, at Houston, Texas. He died September 25, 1927, at Robinson, Illinois.

(Sup) 3866 MIRIAM COLE YOUNG (Edith[7], Arthur[6], Christopher[5], Peter[4], Peter[3], Matthias[2], John Jacob[1]) was the daughter of Edwin S. and Edith Christine (Link) Young [The Link Family, page 551, No. 2160]. Miriam was born August 26, 1915, at Tulsa, Oklahoma. She married Henry M. Pack, July 7, 1937. He was the son of Arvilla Garrett Pack and was born January 15, 1915, at Kansas City, Missouri.

| (Sup) 6263 | i | Garrett Edwin Pack, born November 25, 1938. |
| (Sup) 6264 | ii | David Joseph Pack, born March 28, 1945. |

(Sup) 3867 DAVID EDWIN YOUNG (Edith[7], Arthur[6], Christopher[5], Peter[4], Peter[3], Matthias[2], John Jacob[1]) was the son of Edwin S. and Edith Christine (Link) Young [The Link Family, page 551, No. 2160]. David was born April 14, 1918, at Robinson, Illinois. He served in World War II overseas as a bomber pilot in the U.S. Air Corps. David married Helen Elizabeth Heard, April 25, 1942. She was the daughter of John E. Heard and was born October 23, 1918, at Arkansas City, Arkansas.

| (Sup) 6265 | i | Christine Young, born August 10, 1945. |
| (Sup) 6266 | ii | John Timothy Young, born September 23, 1946. |

3860 RICHARD MIDDLETON LINK (Horace[7], James[6], Christopher[5], Peter[4], Peter[3], Matthias[2], John Jacob[1]) was born January 30, 1900, at Paris, Illinois. He was educated in the Paris public schools and at De Pauw University until his induction in the S. A. T. C. At the war's end he entered his father's business and, with his brother, purchased the interest of a partner. The business grew into four retail branches, a wholesale business, and three manufacturing plants. He operated a retail branch of the business at Brazil, Indiana, until 1934, when he took over the supervision of three of the retail units with his headquarters at Paris, Illinois. While at Brazil he served two terms as president of the Chamber of Commerce. At Paris he became active in community affairs, serving as president of the Rotary Club and director of the Chamber of Commerce. After his appointment to the board of the Edgar County Children's Home, a privately financed orphanage, he became the board's president and secured considerable increase in the home's endowment as well as initiated modern methods of operation and child care. In 1940 he was elected to the board of directors of the National Retail Furniture Association and later became a vice president, in which capacity he served for many years. Dick, as he was known, with his father and brother, gave the City of Paris a large recreational park in 1942. During World War II he was Director of Civilian Defense for Edgar County. He married Dorothy Carter, February 6, 1937, at Paris, Illinois. Dorothy was the daughter of James Everett and Anna Carter Carter and was born April 3, 1909, at Patterson, Iowa. After her public schooling Dorothy became a graduate nurse, having graduated from Mercy Hospital School of Nurses, Des Moines, Iowa, in 1931. Dick was a member of Beta Theta Pi, the Masonic Orders (he was a 32nd-degree Mason), B. P. O. E., Paris Country Club, Country Club of Terre Haute, and Indian Creek Country Club of Miami, Florida.

| (Sup) 6258 | i | Linda Ann Link, born May 8, 1938. |
| (Sup) 6259 | ii | Lucy Link, born November 7, 1943. |

(Sup) 3861 REBECCA LINK JONES (Tatt[7], James[6], Christopher[5], Peter[4], Peter[3], Matthew[2], John Jacob[1]) was the daughter of Arthur W. and Tatt (Link) Jones [The Link Family, pages 550-551, No. 2155]. Rebecca was born July 30, 1922, at Paris, Illinois. She received a degree in art from Miami University, Ohio. She pursued graduate studies in art at the University of Chicago and the Institute of Design, and taught in public schools in Ohio and Indiana. She received an M.A. degree in library science from Indiana University in 1953 and became head of the Crawfordsville Public Library. She married Aquilla Webb Groves, May 14, 1960. He was born February 26, 1910, at Wingate, Indiana, son of David Arthur and Mary Jane (Webb) Groves. Aquilla graduated from Wabash College, from Harvard Law School, and Indiana University. He was assistant to the General Counsel of Lumbermans Mutual Casualty Company at Chicago and served from 1942 to 1946 in the U.S. Air Force, attaining the rank of major. He was appointed deputy attorney general for the State of Indiana and then entered general practice of law at Crawfordsville, Indiana. Rebecca was active in the church, in music and art events, and was a founding director of the Old Jail Museum of local history and art.

(Sup) 6259A i Charles Arthur Groves, born January 20, 1964.

(Sup) 3871 MARY MARGARET BARR (Bess[7], Frank[6], Simon[5], Peter[4], Peter[4], Matthew[2], John Jacob[1]) was the daughter of Frank (Link) Barr [The Link Family, page 553, No. 2167]. She was born December 2, 1915, at Paris, Illinois. She married Eric Roughton, August 19, 1944. He was the son of Ernest and Lucy Summerbell Roughton of England.

(Sup) 6269B   i   Anne Roughton, born August 14, 1946.
(Sup) 6269C   ii Julie Roughton, born June 3, 1949.

(Sup) 3872 CHARLES MAX SMITH (Hugh[7], Charles[6], Mary[5], Peter[4], Peter[3], Matthias[2], John Jacob[1]) was the son of Hugh and Elfie Faught Smith [The Link Family, page 553, No. 2168]. Charles was born September 9, 1899, at Annapolis, Illinois. He married Naomi Engle, March 3, 1927. Naomi was the daughter of Jasper Engle and was born December 23, 1900.

(Sup) 3873 MERLE SMITH (Hugh[7], Charles[6], Mary[5], Peter[4], Peter[3], Matthias[2], John Jacob[1]) was the daughter of Hugh and Elfie Faught Smith [The Link Family, page 553, No. 2168]. Merle was born March 31, 1902, at Annapolis, Illinois. She married Arthur B. Colliflower, September 4, 1926. He was the son of Lawrence G. Colliflower and was born March 7, 1899.

(Sup) 6270   i   Jetta Lee Colliflower, born Oct. 1, 1928.
(Sup) 6271   ii   Lawrence H. Colliflower, born Dec. 24, 1932.
(Sup) 6272   iii Marilyn Jean Colliflower, born Jul. 19, 1935.
(Sup) 6273   iv   Sue Ellen Colliflower, born Jun. 22, 1940.
(Sup) 6274   v   David Arthur Colliflower, born Nov. 1942.

(Sup) 3874 MAYME SMITH (Hugh[7], Charles[6], Mary[5], Peter[4], Peter[3], Matthias[2], John Jacob[1]) was the daughter of Hugh and Elfie Faught Smith [The Link Family, page 553, No. 2168]. Mayme was born June 16, 1910, at Annapolis, Illinois. She married Alexander S. Wilson, May 20, 1934. Alexander was the son of William George Wilson and was born December 1, 1907.

(Sup) 6275   i   Patricia Jean Wilson, born January 18, 1938.
(Sup) 6276   ii   William A. Wilson, born April 24, 1939.
(Sup) 6277   iii Robert Kenneth Wilson, born June 25, 1940 (twin).
(Sup) 6278   iv   Richard Keith Wilson, born June 25, 1940 (twin).

(Sup) 3867A SUSANNE CHAMBERS (Kathryn[7], Ivan[6], Christopher[5], Peter[4], Peter[4], Matthias[2], John Jacob[1]) was the daughter of Frank Patterson and Kathryn (Link) Chambers [The Link Family, No. 2164]. Susanne was born December 18, 1925, at Indianapolis, Indiana. She was educated at Tudor Hall, Indianapolis; Greenwood High School, Springfield, Missouri; and Drury College, Springfield, where she graduated with an A.B. degree. She was a member of Pi Beta Phi and University Women. She wrote a column on the arts for a Springfield newspaper. Susanne married Wilson Marion Wheat, November 15, 1952. They were divorced in 1954. She continued her career as a writer and editor. Her novel, Mother of Mine, was published in 1988.

(Sup) 6266A   1   Christopher Chambers Wheat, born Oct. 6, 1953.

(Sup) 3868 CHARLES MILTON LINK, JR. (Charles[7], Charles[6], Simon[5], Peter[4], Peter[3], Matthias[2], John Jacob[1]) was the son of Charles Milton and Nellie (Brooks) Link [The Link Family, page 552, No. 2165]. Charles, Jr., was born September 15, 1919, at Salt Lake City, Utah. He married Marjorie Featherstone, May 10, 1943, at Glendale, California. She was the daughter of Ralph Wilson Featherstone and was born December 10, 1920, at Seattle, Washington.

(Sup) 6267   1   Susan Carol Link, born January 7, 1947.

(Sup) 3869 JOHN B. LINK (Charles[7], Charles[6], Simon[5], Peter[4], Matthias[2], John Jacob[1]) was the son of Charles Milton and Nellie (Brooks) Link [The Link Family, page 552, No. 2165]. John was born January 27, 1927, at Salt Lake City, Utah.

(Sup) 3870 ROBERT LINK BARR (Bess[7], Frank[6], Simon[5], Peter[4], Peter[3], Matthias[2], John Jacob[1]) was the son of Karl and Bess (Link) Barr [The Link Family, page 553, No. 2167]. Robert was born May 28, 1910, at Paris, Illinois. He received a degree in electrical engineering from Rose Poly Institute of Technology at Terre Haute, Indiana, in 1932. He began his own business, making plastic manufacturing parts. Robert married Dorothy Russell, August 12, 1940. She died August, 1974. Robert married, second, Marcelle Gagnon, February, 1978. After retirement he made a hobby building or repairing homes in various places including Michigan, Florida, and Canada.

(Sup) 6268   i   Robert Link Barr, Jr., born May 28, 1943.
(Sup) 6269   ii   Jean Gibbs Barr, born February 25, 1946.
(Sup) 6269A   iii Kathryn Lenore Barr, born June 16, 1955.

(Sup) 3875   MADGE SMITH (Hugh[7], Charles[6], Mary[5], Peter[4], Peter[3], Matthias[2], John Jacob[1]) was the daughter of Hugh and Elfie Faught Smith [The Link Family, page 553, No. 2168]. Madge was born September 9, 1916, at Annapolis, Illinois. She married Clarence F. Schroeder, September 29, 1936. He was the son of Frederick Carl Schroeder and was born April 1, 1907.

(Sup) 6279   i   Clarence Max Schroeder, born April 17, 1938.
(Sup) 6280   ii   Donna Naomi Schroeder, born January 18, 1941.
(Sup) 6281   iii James F. Schroeder, born December 10, 1943.

(Sup) 3876   MARY ELIZABETH PARRISH (Mary[7], Cary[6], Mary[5], Peter[4], Peter[3], Matthias[2], John Jacob[1]) was the daughter of Robert Nevins and Mary Magdalene (Smith) Parrish [The Link Family, page 553, No. 2171]. Elizabeth was born June 24, 1909, at Paris, Illinois. She was educated in the public schools at Paris and at the University of Wisconsin and the University of Illinois, graduating from the former. She was a member of Delta Gamma. Betty, as she was known, married George Halsey Beddoe, June 24, 1935, at Paris. He was the son of George K. Beddoe and was born July 18, 1908.

(Sup) 6282   i   Mary Inglis Beddoe, born December 30, 1938.
(Sup) 6283   ii   Elizabeth Crawford Beddoe, born June 19, 1940.
(Sup) 6284   iii George Beddoe, born February 1, 1943.

(Sup) 3877   JAMES EDWARD PARRISH (Mary[7], Cary[6], Mary[5], Peter[4], Peter[3], Matthias[2], John Jacob[1]) was the son of Robert Nevins and Mary Magdalene (Smith) Parrish [The Link Family, page 553, No. 2171]. James was born October 23, 1912, at Paris, Illinois. He was educated in the Paris public schools and studied at Northwestern University. He married Alma Sorenson, May 7, 1942. Alma was the daughter of Hans Sorenson and was born February 7, 1919. James was an executive of Marathon Oil Company at Casper, Wyoming; Findlay, Ohio; and Tulsa, Oklahoma. He served as head of Elks (national) and was a water color artist. James died November, 1974, in an automobile accident near Tulsa, Oklahoma.

(Sup) 6285   i   Constance Elizabeth Parrish, born Aug. 15, 1945.
(Sup) 6285A   ii   Janet Kaye Parrish, born June 18, 1948.

(Sup) 3878   ROBERT NEVINS PARRISH JR. (Mary[7], Cary[6], Mary[5], Peter[4], Peter[3], Matthias[2], John Jacob[1]) was the son of Robert Nevins and Mary Magdalene (Smith) Parrish [The Family Link, page 553, No. 2171]. Robert was born July 9, 1925, at Paris, Illinois. He received his education in: the public schools at Paris; Appleby College (prep) at Oakville, Ontario; Darlington School, Rome, Georgia; Casper College, Wyoming; and the Parsons School of Design, New York City. He married Bonnie Jo Huffer, June 27, 1959, at Indianapolis, Indiana. She was the daughter of Walter and Mary (Swackhammer) Huffer and was born August 21, 1935.

(Sup) 6285B   i   Mary Jennifer Parrish, born Apr. 6, 1960.
(Sup) 6285C   ii   Jane Shoppard Parrish, born Nov. 15, 1961.
(Sup) 6285D   iii Robert Nevins Parrish, III, born Jan. 4, 1963.

(Sup) 3879   ISAAC DICKSON LINK (Francis[7], Ruez[6], Francis Marion[5], Peter[4], Peter[3], Matthias[2], John Jacob[1]) the son of Francis Warner and Hallie (Sheppard) Link [The Link Family, page 554, No. 2178]. Isaac was born August 31, 1899, at Paris, Illinois. He moved to California with his parents when young and there married Elizabeth Edmonds, June 16, 1922. She was the daughter of the Reverend Walter Edmonds and was born January 31, 1902.

(Sup) 6286   i   Paul Warner Link, born October 18, 1922.
(Sup) 6287   ii   John Link, born June 11, 1930.

(Sup) 3880   HILAH JANE KIRK (Hilah[7], Ruez[6], Francis Marion[5], Peter[4], Peter[3], Matthias[2], John Jacob[1]) the daughter of Haddon Spurgeon and Hilah Jane (Link) Kirk [The Link Family, pages 554-555, No. 2181]. Hilah was born June 20, 1918, at Paris, Illinois. She was educated at Salem College, North Carolina, where she graduated with an A.B. degree in 1940. Hilah married Carrol Rollins Wood, November 17, 1943. He who was the son of A. N. Wood.

(Sup) 6288   i   Carrol Rollins Wood, Jr., born May 28, 1945.
(Sup) 6288A   ii   Hilah Jane Wood, born January 11, 1949.
(Sup) 6288B   iii John Wood, born October 13, 1956.

(Sup) 3881   HADDON SPURGEON KIRK, JR. (Hilah[7], Ruez[6], Francis Marion[5], Peter[4], Peter[3], Matthias[2], John Jacob[1]) the son of Haddon Spurgeon and Hilah Jane (Link) Kirk [The Link Family, pages 554-555, No. 2181]. Haddon, Jr., was born March 30, 1921, at Paris, Illinois. He was educated at Princeton University, where he graduated, cum laude, with an A.B. degree in 1943. He was a member of Tiger Inn at Princeton. Haddon married Charlotte Byrd Clarke at New Orleans, Louisiana, November 8, 1946. She was the daughter of Oliver Lyons Clarke.

(Sup) 6288C   i   Charlotte Link Kirk, born August 10, 1947.
(Sup) 6288D   ii   Haddon Spurgeon Kirk, III, born March 5, 1949.
(Sup) 6288E   iii Catherine Clarke Kirk, born March 10, 1952.
(Sup) 6288F   iv   Elizabeth Godwin Kirk, born December 14, 1954.

(Sup) 3882   ROBERT LINK KIRK (Hilah[7], Ruez[6], Francis Marion[5], Peter[4], Peter[3], Matthias[2], John Jacob[1]) was the son of Haddon Spurgeon and Hilah Jane (Link) Kirk [The Link Family, pages 554-555, No. 2181]. Robert was born March 7, 1928, at Winston-Salem, North Carolina. He received an A.B. degree from the University of North Carolina in 1950 and earned his track letter all four years. He became Eastern U.S. champion in javelin throwing in 1949, which title he held also in 1950. He was a member of Sigma Alpha Epsilon fraternity. Robert married Laura Hyman Harvey, 1953, at Kinston, North Carolina. She was the daughter of Leo H. Harvey. Robert and Laura were divorced, 1965.

(Sup) 6288G   i   Leo Harvey Kirk, born August 26, 1955.
(Sup) 6288H   ii   Robert Link Kirk, Jr., born December 10, 1956.

(Sup) 3883 MARY OSBORNE DOLE (Pearl7, John6, Francis Marion5, Peter4, Peter3, Matthias2, John Jacob1] the daughter of George and Pearl (Link) Dole Jr., [The Link Family, page 555, No. 2182]. Mary was born March 20, 1906, at Paris, Illinois. She was educated in the public schools of Paris, at North Cathedral School for Girls at Washington, D.C., and at Wellesley College, where she graduated with an A.B. degree in 1928. After further specialized study, Mary Osborne became librarian for the high school at Paris. She married Frank Bryan, October 18, 1928, at Paris.

(Sup) 6289   i   Ann Dole Bryan, born October 1, 1929.

(Sup) 3884 GEORGE DOLE III (Pearl7, John6, Francis Marion5, Peter4, Peter3, Matthias2, John Jacob1] was the son of George and Pearl (Link) Dole, Jr., [The Link Family, page 555, No. 2182]. George was born September 3, 1914, at Paris, Illinois. He attended public schools at Paris and entered Dartmouth College, where he graduated in 1935 with an A.B. degree. He was awarded an LL.B. degree from the Law School of Harvard University. From 1938 until 1941 he practiced law. In May 1941 George was appointed Special Agent for the Federal Bureau of Investigation. He spent most of the time in war security investigations of a secret and perilous nature which resulted in many cases being brought to justice. After 1946 he opened a law practice at Paris, Illinois. George married Dorothy Thomas, May 11, 1940, at Paris. She was the daughter of Claud and Myrtle Harris Thomas, and was born November 12, 1913, at Paris, Illinois. Dorothy attended public schools there and spent two years at Tudor Hall, Indianapolis, Indiana, before entering college. She studied at Randolph Macon College for Women, De Pauw University, Rockford College (Illinois), and the University of Wisconsin.

(Sup) 6290   i   Elizabeth Dole, born August 22, 1942.
(Sup) 6291   ii Peter Thomas Dole, born June 15, 1944.

(Sup) 3885 ALLEN A. PARRISH (Fred7, Susan6, Francis Marion5, Peter4, Peter3, Matthias2, John Jacob1] was the son of Fred and Mabel (Siders) Parrish [Supplement No. 2183]. Allen was born May 8, 1907, at Paris, Illinois, and was educated in the schools there. He married, first, Dorothy Koho, June 24, 1928, at Paris. She was the daughter of A. B. Koho and was born at Vermillion, Illinois, July 24, 1904. Dorothy died March 1, 1929, at Paris. Allen married, second, Minnie Bovill, daughter of M. C. Bovill, June 11, 1939, at Paris, Illinois. Minnie was born October 24, 1907, at Crystal Springs, Mississippi. She was educated at the Paris schools, De Pauw University and the University of Illinois from which she graduated in 1928 with an A.B. degree. Allen married, third, LeVon (Cross) Vance, October 16, 1987, at Paris. LeVon was born March 9, 1914, at Windsor, Illinois. Allen engaged in specialty promotion and farming.

(Sup) 6292   i   Mary Jane Parrish, born February 3, 1929.

(Sup) 3886 WILLIAM PARRISH (Harry7, Susan6, Francis Marion5, Peter4, Peter3, Matthias2, John Jacob1] the son of Harry and Della (Carnahan) Parrish [Supplement No. 2184]. William was born January 12, 1915, at Paris, Illinois. He received a B.S. degree from the University of Illinois in 1936 and earned a C.P.A. degree in 1939. He was associated with a large Chicago accounting firm for five years and then was appointed Comptroller of Illinois Institute of Technology at Chicago; that position he held until 1946, when William opened his own accounting office at Paris, Illinois. He married Hilah Huffman, July 27, 1937, at Paris, Illinois. She was the daughter of Frank and Mary Stuart Huffman and was born at Paris, January 16, 1916. Hilah was educated in the Paris schools and studied at the University of Indiana three years, where she was a member of Delta Gamma and Pleiades. Hilah died February 24, 1986.

(Sup) 6293   i   John Arthur Parrish, born May 1, 1941.
(Sup) 6294   ii William Lee Parrish, born July 31, 1945.

(Sup) 3887 HARRY CURTIS PARRISH (Edgar7, Susan6, Francis Marion5, Peter4, Peter3, Matthias2, John Jacob1] was the son of Edgar and Ruth Curtis Parrish [Supplement No. 2186]. Harry was born January 29, 1914, at Paris, Illinois. He graduated form Paris High School and entered De Pauw University where he studied two years, after which he entered his father's insurance business and became a partner. Harry was active in civic affairs and served as a director of the Chamber of Commerce, the Community Chest, and other civic organizations. He was a member of Exchange, Kiwanis, Beta Theta Pi, B.P.O.E. and the Masonic order. During World War II Harry wa commissioned a lieutenant of infantry. He married Frances Steidl, February 11, 1939, at Paris. She was the daughter of Benjamin and Anna Connery Steidl and was born November 3, 1913, also at Paris. Frances received an A.B. degree from St. Mary-of-the-Woods, Indiana, in 1935.

(Sup) 6295   i   Harry Curtis Parrish, Jr., born April 19, 1942.
(Sup) 6296   ii   Pamela Anne Parrish, born November 1, 1945.
(Sup) 6297   iii Frances Sharon Parrish, born August 22, 1948.

(Sup) 3888 JOSEPH PARRISH (Edgar7, Susan6, Francis Marion5, Peter4, Peter3, Matthias2, John Jacob1] was the son of Edgar and Ruth Curtis Parrish [Supplement No. 2186]. Joseph was born January 20, 1918, at Paris, Illinois. He attended public schools there and served during World War II overseas in the European Theater for thirty-four months. He married Kathleen Noyes, December 12, 1948, at Paris. She was the daughter of Lester Olin and Opal Patchett Noyes and was born October 7, 1921, at Martinsville, Illinois. Kathleen was educated in the Martinsville public schools and took specialized work as a beautician at the Excello Beauty School, St. Louis, Missouri. Joseph was a farmer in Edgar County, Illinois.

(Sup) 6298   i   James Arthur Parrish, born April 2, 1950.

(Sup) 3889 CATHARINE JANE WINN (Nila[7], Christopher[6], Francis Marion[5], Peter[4], Peter[3], Matthias[2], John Jacob[1]) was the daughter of Homer and Nila Link Winn [Supplement No. 2187]. Catharine was born August 10, 1917, at Louisville, Kentucky. She was educated in the public schools at DeKalb, Illinois, and at Cleveland, Ohio. She received an A.B. degree from the North State Teachers College at DeKalb. She became a teacher and later went to Washington, D.C., where she was in the Signal Corps during World War II. In 1950 she became a teacher in the Paris, Illinois, schools. She received a master's degree from Indiana State Teachers College, and she served as an instructor in English and as a member of the Dean of Women's Staff at Miami University, Ohio.

(Sup) 3890 JO ANN LINK (Marion[7], Christopher[6], Francis Marion[5], Peter[4], Peter[3], Matthias[2], John Jacob[1]) was the daughter of Marion Henry and Alma Mills Link [The Link Family, page 556, No. 2188]. Jo Ann was born January 5, 1923, at Paris, Illinois. She married Dr. Louis Johnson, April 5, 1945. He was the son of Arthur J. and Maude (Bandy) Johnson and was born June 1, 1922, Terre Haute, Indiana. Louis served in the U.S. Navy during World War II in the South Pacific. He graduated from Illinois College of Optometry in 1948. Jo Ann and Louis resided at Fairfield Illinois, where he practiced optometry. She was active in the Parent Teacher Association and served as President. Active in politics, she was president of the Wayne County League of Republican Women. She served as chairman of the Daughters of the American Revolution Essay Contest. Dr. Johnson was president of the Fairfield Rotary Club.

(Sup) 6299   i   Jo Lynne Johnson, born March 31, 1946.
(Sup) 6299A   ii   Gregory Louis Johnson, born October 29, 1950.
(Sup) 6299B   iii Michael Link Johnson, born December 29, 1955.
(Sup) 6299C   iv   Mark Francis Johnson, born September 4, 1963.

(Sup) 3891 PATRICIA LINK (Marion[7], Christopher[6], Francis Marion[5], Peter[4], Peter[3], Matthias[2], John Jacob[1]) was the daughter of Marion Henry and Alma Mills Link [The Link Family, page 556, No. 2188]. Patricia was born March 17, 1925, at Paris, Illinois. She married Merle Anker, September 1, 1948 at Soto, Iowa. He was born April 7, 1924. Merle served in the U.S. Army and Air Force for twenty-one years and then was employed by Louis County, Missouri.

(Sup) 6300   i   Steven Earl Anker, born September 6, 1951.
(Sup) 6300A   ii   David Patrick Anker, born August 7, 1953.
(Sup) 6300B   iii Jenise Ann Anker, born January 5, 1959.

(Sup) 3892 WENDELL HUBBARD LINK (Wendell[7], Nethaniah[6], Francis Marion[5], Peter[4], Peter[3], Matthias[2], John Jacob[1]) was the son of Wendell A. and Alline Hubbard Link [The Link Family, page 557, No. 2189]. Wendell was born September 27, 1922, at Emporia, Kansas. He married Barbara Ford, August 8, 1947. She was the daughter of Eustace Ford.

(Sup) 6301   i   Stacey Ford Link, born December 21, 1952.
(Sup) 6302   ii   Wendell Anthony Link, born February 6, 1957.

(Sup) 3893 PATRICIA ALLINE LINK (Wendell[7], Nethaniah[6], Francis Marion[5], Peter[4], Peter[3], Matthias[2], John Jacob[1]) was the daughter of Wendell A. and Alline Hubbard Link [The Link Family, page 557, No. 2189]. Patricia was born August 12, 1928 at Houston, Texas. She received a B.A. degree in social work from the University of Kansas in 1944. Patricia married Dale R. Marshall, June 8, 1949. He was the son of William A. and Stella F. Marshall and was born August 28, 1924, at Parsons, Kansas. Dale received a B.S. degree in business from the University of Kansas, 1950. Patricia and Dale lived at Kansas City, Missouri, where he owned and was president of SD Corporation, a business supply company.

(Sup) 6303   i   Janet Emily Marshall, born August 25, 1950.
(Sup) 6303A   ii   Susan Patricia Marshall, born January 17, 1952.
(Sup) 6303B   iii Debra Dale Marshall, born October 4, 1953.
(Sup) 6303C   iv   Rebecca Lyn Marshall, born January 20, 1957.
(Sup) 6303D   v   Nancy Ann Marshall, born October 6, 1959.

(Sup) 3894 MARTHA TANYA LINK (Eugene[7], Nethaniah[6], Francis Marion[5], Peter[4], Peter[3], Matthias[2], John Jacob[1]) was the daughter of Eugene Perry and Beulah Meyer Link [The Link Family, page 557, No. 2190]. Martha was born June 14, 1942, at Gaffney, South Carolina. She married Charles Phillip Casey, July 20, 1968. Martha and Charles both graduated from Massachusetts Institute of Technology with PhD's in chemistry. Both taught at the University of Wisonsin, where Charles was Chairman of Organic Chemistry, and Martha was Director of Future Planning.

(Sup) 6304   i   Jennifer M. Casey, born August 10, 1969.

(Sup) 3895 EUGENE PERRY LINK, JR. (Eugene[7], Nethaniah[6], Francis Marion[5], Peter[4], Peter[3], Matthias[2], John Jacob[1]) was the son of Eugene Perry and Beulah Meyer Link [The Link Family, page 557, No. 2190]. Eugene, Jr., was born August 6, 1944, at Gaffney, South Carolina. He was educated at Deerfield Academy and then Harvard University where he was a member of Phi Beta Kappa and from which he received the B.A. degree in philosophy. He received higher degrees in regional studies and Asian languages from Harvard. He taught at Harvard four years, at Princeton University four years, and then at the University of California at Los Angeles where he was assistant professor of Oriental languages. He was a member of the National Academy of Sciences and noted for his scholarly publications in Chinese literature. On 23 August 1978 he married Sue Jean Wong at Cambridge, Massachusetts. She was the daughter of Bing Yue and Sun Yan Quan Wong and was born May 5, 1951, at Boston, Massachusetts. Jean graduated with highest honors from Connecticut College in 1971 and worked as a journalist, researcher, and teacher of English. Dr. Link was noted for his scholarly works in Chinese literature. His many articles and translations appeared in Chinese as well as English-language publications, and he served as a distinguished panelist at numerous conferences and colloquiums.

(Sup) 6304A   i   Monica Link, born March 27, 1981.
(Sup) 6304B   ii   Nathan Link, born Febuary 22, 1985.

(Sup) 3895A   BRUCE GEORGE LINK (Eugene7, Nethaniah6, Marion5, Peter4, Peter3, Matthias2, John Jacob1) was the third child of Eugene Perry and Beulah Meyer Link [The Link Family, page 558, No. 2190]. Bruce was born September 5, 1949, at Denver, Colorado. He received his B.A. degree from Earlham College, and his Ph.D. from Columbia University where he did research and taught. He became Professor of Sociology in Epidemiology Studies at Columbia University and published numerous articles in professional journals on the scope of mental diseases. Bruce married Serena Deutsch, the daughter of Louis and Jean Deutsch.

(Sup) 6304C   1   Sasha Deutsch-Link, born January 6, 1988.

(Sup) 3896   ROBERT GEORGE SCHWEGLER   (Lida7, Nethaniah6, Francis Marion5, Peter4, Peter3, Matthias2, John Jacob1) was the son of George and Lida Link Schwegler [The Link Family, page 558, No. 2191]. Robert was born August 11, 1945, at Kansas City, Missouri. He graduated from De Pauw University, Indiana. In 1967 and received an M.D. degree from Kansas University in 1971, completing his residency in Radiology at the Medical Center in 1975. He served in the U.S. Army Medical Corps, 1975-77, with the rank of major. Robert married Martha Louise Stitt, September 12, 1970. She was the daughter of Ronald and Kathryn Stitt and was born October 29, 1947, at Kansas City, Missouri.

(Sup) 6304D   1   Amanda Kathryn Schwegler, born April 28, 1975.
(Sup) 6304E   11   Cara Elizabeth Schwegler, born July 29, 1979.

(Sup) 3897   JOHN STEPHAN SCHWEGLER   (Lida7, Nethaniah6, Francis Marion5, Peter4, Peter3, Matthias2, John Jacob1) was the son of George and Lida Link Schwegler [The Link Family, page 558, No. 2191]. John was born November 8, 1947, at Kansas City, Missouri. He received a bachelor's degree from the University of Missouri; a master's degree in Russian Area Studies from Kansas University; and a doctorate degree from the Teachers' College, Columbia University, New York. He was a member of the Peace Corps in Thailand, 1972-76, and he taught at Chulalongkorn University, Bangkok. John married Napaporn Poltecha of Bangkok, September 20, 1975, at Kansas City.

(Sup) 6304F   1   Lawrence Allen Schwegler, born July 13, 1980.
(Sup) 6304G   11   John Phillip Schwegler, born November 18, 1984.

(Sup) 3897A   THOMAS LINK SCHWEGLER   (Lida7, Nethaniah6, Francis Marion5, Peter4, Peter3, Matthias2, John Jacob1) was the son of George and Lida Link Schwegler [The Link Family, page 558, No. 2191]. Thomas attended Coe College, Iowa, and graduated from Kansas University in communications, 1978. He organized and performed with a band in the Kansas/Missouri area and was employed in the public relations field.

(Sup) 3898   WILLIAM FOLEY   (Blanche7, William6, Francis Marion5, Peter4, Peter3, Matthias2, John Jacob1) was the son of William and Blanche Link Foley [The Link Family, page 559, No. 2194]. William was born January 1, 1916, at Paris, Illinois. He was educated in the Paris schools. He married, first, Ruth Strohm, January 1, 1916, at West Union, Illinois. She was the daughter of Charles and Nell Strohm and was born November 15, 1916, at West Union. William was in the U.S. Army during World War 11. Ruth graduated with a B.S. degree in home economics from the University of Illinois in 1938. She taught at Westfield and Martinsville, Illinois, and was a home demonstration agent at Washington, Indiana. William operated a glass business at Paris. William and Ruth were divorced, April, 1961. He married, second, Pat Sager, June, 1961. William died February, 1984.

(Sup) 6305   1   Carla Lee Foley, born June 12, 1944.
(Sup) 6306   11   Joan Foley, born December 13, 1946.
(Sup) 6307   111 William Mack Foley, born July 21, 1950.
(Sup) 6307A   1v   Jane Elizabeth Foley, born September 26, 1952.

(Sup) 3899   JACK BEECHER FOLEY   (Blanche7, William6, Francis Marion5, Peter4, Peter3, Matthias2, John Jacob1) was the son of William and Blanche Link Foley [The Link Family, page 559, No. 2194]. Jack was born June 19, 1920, at Paris Illinois. He married, first, Gloria Maxine Joseph, August 11, 1946, at Paris, Illinois. She was the daughter of Charles and Mary (Heady) Joseph and was born in Jasper County, Illinois, August 12, 1927. She was educated in Paris public schools. Jack and Gloria were divorced. He married, second, Betty Graham, February 15, 1959.

(Sup) 6308   1   Jack Franklin Foley, born March 12, 1949.

(Sup) 3900 CONRAD LEE FOLEY (Blanche[3], William[6], Francis Marion[5], Peter[4], Peter[3], Matthias[2], John Jacob[1]) was the son of William and Blanche Link Foley [The Link Family, page 559, No. 2194]. Conrad was born June 18, 1923, at Paris, Illinois. He was educated in the Paris schools and during World War II was in the U.S. Navy Air Corps as an air gunner. During his youth he held the Boys National Championship for trap shooting. He married Polly Etta Kersey, August 1, 1948, at Dana, Indiana. She was the daughter of Raleigh Hoyt and Mary Jane (Doidge) Kersey and was born June 9, 1925, at Fairbanks, Indiana. She was educated in the Dana schools and studied at Indiana State Teachers College and at Central Business College, Indianapolis, Indiana. Conrad joined the Illinois Department of Conservation and became district supervisor of eight Illinois counties. In 1975 he received the "Officer of the Year" award for outstanding service in conservation. He retired in 1983 with the rank of sergeant. Conrad died April 1, 1986.

(Sup) 6309 i Cheryl Anne Foley, born May 11, 1949.
(Sup) 6310 ii Polly Catherine Foley, born December 18, 1950.

(Sup) 3901 ROBERT ALLEN FOLEY (Blanche[7], William[6], Francis Marion[5], Peter[4], Peter[3], Matthias[2], John Jacob[1]) was the son of William and Blanche Link Foley [The Link Family, page 559, No. 2194]. Robert was born July 23, 1930, at Paris, Illinois. He received an M.D. degree from the University of Illinois in 1955; he interned at the Presbyterian Hospital and completed his residency in Internal Medicine at Presbyterian and St. Lukes Hospitals, Chicago. He married Patricia Joan Crowe, June 27, 1953, at Hammond, Indiana. She was the daughter of Howard Murten and Suzanne Chizmar Crowe. Dr. Foley served two years in the U.S. Navy Medical Corps as a lieutenant-commander. He then went into private practice in the Doctors Clinic at Bremerton, Washington. Robert died November 15, 1983, at Bremerton and is buried in Maple Leaf Cemetery at Oak Harbor, Washington.

(Sup) 6311 i Blythe Patrice Foley, born August 12, 1954.
(Sup) 6311A ii Guy Franklin Foley, born July 21, 1955.
(Sup) 6311B iii Neal Robert Foley, born August 24, 1956.
(Sup) 6311C iv Maureen Ruth Foley, born October 29, 1957.
(Sup) 6311D v Bryan Howard Foley, born May 15, 1959.
(Sup) 6311E vi Meredyth Suzanne Foley, born June 14, 1960.
(Sup) 6311F vii Myles Richard Foley, born March 29, 1963.
(Sup) 6311G viii Suzanne Paige Foley, born April 26, 1965.

(Sup) 3902 LARRY ROBERT ROSS (Florence[7], William[6], Francis Marion[5], Peter[4], Peter[3], Matthias[2], John Jacob[1]) was the son of Charles T. and Florence Link Ross [The Link Family, page 559, No. 2195]. Larry was born November 30, 1938, at Springfield, Illinois.

(Sup) 3903 WILLIAM RICHARD LINK (William[7], Francis[6], Francis Marion[5], Peter[4], Peter[3], Matthias[2], John Jacob[1]) was the son of William Francis and Ruth Lemon Link [The Link Family, page 559, No. 2196]. He was born September 16, 1930, at Paris, Illinois. He received an A.B. degree from Harvard University in 1953, and an A.M. degree in 1954. William served in the U.S. Army 1954-56. He married Emily Cosslett Putnam in 1953.

(Sup) 6312 i Cynthia Link, August 4, 1959.
(Sup) 6312A ii Stephen Link, born February 1, 1963.
(Sup) 6312B iii Anthony Link, born January 22, 1965.
(Sup) 6312C iv Matthew Link, born August 30, 1966.

3904 DOROTHY PEARL JOSEPHINE CHESNEY (Edith[7], Mary[6], Sarah[5], Peter[4], Peter[3], Matthias[2], John Jacob[1]) was born February 12, 1905, at Kansas City, Missouri. She married John Wylie Loop, October 31, 1931. John was the son of John Joseph Loop and was born February 11, 1904. They had no children.

3905 ANNA MARIE HOVEY (Martha[7], Anna[6], Sarah[5], Peter[4], Peter[3], Matthias[2], John Jacob[1]) was born November 15, 1918, at Kansas City, Kansas. She married a Mr. Dodds.

3906 RUTH HOVEY (Martha[7], Anna[6], Sarah[5], Peter[4], Peter[3], Matthias[2], John Jacob[1]) was born November 12, 1928, at St. Louis, Missouri.

3907 THEODORE C. HENDERSON, JR. (Ruth[7], Anna[6], Sarah[5], Peter[4], Peter[3], Matthias[2], John Jacob[1]) was born May 18, 1933, at Glendale, California.

3908 RALPH F. HUNTSBERGER (Aileen[7], Nancy[6], Sarah[5], Peter[4], Peter[3], Matthias[2], John Jacob[1]) was born September 12, 1915, at Los Angeles, California. He married Margaret Kroener, February 21, 1942. Margaret was the daughter of William Frederick Kroener and was born February 14, 1920.

(Sup) 6314 i Diane Elizabeth Huntsberger, born Sep 12, 1943.
(Sup) 6315 i James Ralph Huntsberger, born February 25, 1946.

3909 ELIZABETH LA GRANGE HUNTSBERGER (Aileen[7], Nancy[6], Sarah[5], Peter[4], Peter[3], Matthias[2], John Jacob[1]) was born January 28, 1918, at Los Angeles, California. She married Robert Dwight Fenn, September 20, 1941. Robert was the son of Burton Dwight Fenn and was born November 23, 1914.

(Sup) 6316 i Nancy Jane Fenn, born May 6, 1944.

3910 GEORGE EDWARD HUNTSBERGER (Aileen[7], Nancy[6], Sarah[5], Peter[4], Peter[3], Matthias[2], John Jacob[1]) was born March 4, 1920; at Los Angeles, California. He married Margaret Ann Carr, December 2, 1944. Margaret was the daughter of Garcy William Carr and was born November 25, 1922.

3911 CLEMENT RICHARD HUNTSBERGER (Aileen[7], Nancy[6], Sarah[5], Peter[4], Peter[3], Matthias[2], John Jacob[1]) was born July 18, 1922, at Los Angeles, California.

3912 PAUL H. MATTHIAS (Charles[7], Ellen[6], Zedekiah[5], Matthias[4], Peter[3], Matthias[2], John Jacob[1]) was born March 12, 1905, at Gordonsville, Virginia. He married Margaret Bean.

3913 HARRY E. MATTHIAS (Charles[7], Ellen[6], Zedekiah[5], Matthias[4], Peter[3], Matthias[2], John Jacob[1]) was born December 28, 1906, at Gordonsville, Virginia. He married Mary Wilson.

(Sup) 6317 i Stephen Matthias, born March 18, 1935.
(Sup) 6318 ii Paul Matthias, born April 4, 1938.

3914 CHARLES WILLARD MATTHIAS, JR. (Charles[7], Ellen[6], Zedekiah[5], Matthias[4], Peter[3], Matthias[2], John Jacob[1]).

3915 JOHN GILMOUR SNAPP (Fred[7], Flora[6], Zedekiah[5], Matthias[4], Peter[3], Matthias[2], John Jacob[1]) was born October 24, 1921, at Terre Haute, Indiana.

3916 IVAN LEON KAUFMAN (Ivan[7], Ida[6], Zedekiah[5], Matthias[4], Peter[3], Matthias[2], John Jacob[1]) was born July 13, 1922, at Minneapolis, Minnesota. He married Janet Elizabeth Toy, January 5, 1943. Janet was the daughter of Howard Toy and was born June 6, 1922.

(Sup) 6319 i John Howard Kaufman, born December 2, 1943.
(Sup) 6320 ii David Leon Kaufman, born June 17, 1946.

3917 PATRICIA LORAINE KAUFMAN (Ivan[7], Ida[6], Zedekiah[5], Matthias[4], Peter[3], Matthias[2], John Jacob[1]) was born July 10, 1928, at Minneapolis, Minnesota.

3918 BARBARA ANN KAUFMAN (Ivan[7], Ida[6], Zedekiah[5], Matthias[4], Peter[3], Matthias[2], John Jacob[1]) was born January 29, 1933, at Minneapolis, Minnesota.

3919 DOROTHY C. PROX (Amie[7], Ida[6], Zedekiah[5], Matthias[4], Peter[3], Matthias[2], John Jacob[1]) was born April 19, 1919, at Terre Haute, Indiana. She married Richard Arling Williamson, April 26, 1943. Richard was the son of Adam Williamson.

(Sup) 6321 i Nancy A. Williamson, born March 22, 1944.
(Sup) 6322 ii Stephen Michael Williamson, born June 8, 1946.

3920 BETTIE MARIE PROX (Amie[7], Ida[6], Zedekiah[5], Matthias[4], Peter[3], Matthias[2], John Jacob[1]) was born September 3, 1920, at Terre Haute, Indiana. She married Albert Dudley Parish, August 6, 1943, son of William Raymond Parish.

3921 ROBERT F. PROX (Amie[7], Ida[6], Zedekiah[5], Matthias[4], Peter[3], Matthias[2], John Jacob[1]) was born May 24, 1926, at Terre Haute, Indiana.

3922 JULIA JANE KEYES (Esther[7], Amy[6], Zedekiah[5], Matthias[4], Peter[3], Matthias[2], John Jacob[1]) was born April 1, 1908, at Terre Haute, Indiana.

3923 JOHN COLLIER KEYES (Esther[7], Amy[6], Zedekiah[5], Matthias[4], Peter[3], Matthias[2], John Jacob[1]) was born March 8, 1909, at Dana, Indiana. He married Mary Fox Greenland, December 24, 1945. Mary, daughter of Samuel Wilson and Mary Fox Greenland, was born June 10, 1916.

3924 JOSEPHINE ANNE WEIDELY (Helen[7], Frank[6], John[5], Matthias[4], Peter[3], Matthias[2], John Jacob[1]) was the daughter of Walter Albert and Helen Link Weidely [The Link Family, page 563, No. 2238]. Jo Anne was born March 14, 1927, at Cleveland, Ohio. She married Stanley Matthew Rogge on June 10, 1950, at Binghamton, New York.

(Sup) 6323 i Susan Lafoe Rogge, born April 12, 1951.
(Sup) 6324 ii Phillip Christian Rogge, born April 12, 1954.

3925 SALLY LA FOE WEIDELY (Helen[7], Frank[6], John[5], Matthias[4], Peter[3], Matthias[2], John Jacob[1]) was the daughter of Walter Albert and Helen Link Weidely [The Link Family, page 563, No. 2238]. Sally was born March 10, 1933, at Cleveland, Ohio. She married Clarence Theodore Darrah, Jr., April 12, 1952, at Binghamton, New York.

(Sup) 6325 i Scott Bethel Darrah, born November 19, 1954.
(Sup) 6326 ii David Link Darrah, born October 31, 1955.
(Sup) 6327 iii Todd Matthew Darrah, born January 27, 1958.
(Sup) 6328 iv Craig Theodore Darrah, born October 17, 1959.

3926 JANICE HELEN RECKER (Josephine[7], Frank[6], John[5], Matthias[4], Peter[3], Matthias[2], John Jacob[1]) was the daughter of Max and Josephine Link Recker [The Link Family, page 563, No. 2239]. Janice was born December 13, 1922, at Indianapolis, Indiana. She married John Hartwell Slinde, November 8, 1942. He was he son of Francis Leonal Slinde and was born May 20, 1920, at Cleveland, Ohio.

(Sup) 6329 i Philip Hartwell Slinde.
(Sup) 6330 ii Alexander Slinde.

3927 ANDREW ALEXANDER NESBITT (Josephine[7], Frank[6], John[5], Matthias[4], Peter[3], Matthias[2], John Jacob[1]) was the son of Clarence R. and Josephine Link Recker Nesbitt [The Link Family, page 563, No. 2239]. Andrew was born June 24, 1933, at Pittsburgh, Pennsylvania. He won a scholarship to Oxford University. Alexander's first marriage was in England; he was divorced and returned to the U.S. He married second, Elenore Peyton Sinclaire, and they were divorced. Alexander married and divorced a third time. He married, fourth, Brenda Hicks, from North Carolina.

CHILDREN OF ALEXANDER AND ELENORE
(Sup) 6331 i Ian Peyton Nesbitt.
Adopted ii Anne Alexandra Nesbitt.

CHILD OF ALEXANDER AND THIRD WIFE
(Sup) 6332 iii Benjamin Owen Nesbitt.

3928 ARTHUR BRADY BALL (Frances[7], Bonnie[6], John[5], Matthias[4], Peter[3], Matthias[2], John Jacob[1]) was born January 22, 1921, at Indianapolis, Indiana. He died at San Antonio, Texas, March 9, 1929.

3929 BARBARA HELEN BALL (Frances[7], Bonnie[6], John[5], Matthias[4], Peter[3], Matthias[2], John Jacob[1]) was born February 22, 1923, at Indianapolis, Indiana. She married William Thomas Foley, June 29, 1946, at Muncie, Indiana. William was the son of Edward Foley.

3930 DOROTHY ANNE BALL (Frances[7], Bonnie[6], John[5], Matthias[4], Peter[3], Matthias[2], John Jacob[1]) was born December 6, 1925, at Indianapolis, Indiana. She married Wallace Friestedt.

Matthias[1], Peter[3], Matthias[2], John Jacob[1]) was born March 28, 1931, at Indianapolis, Indiana. He was educated at Williams College.

3932 MARY LOUISE MANSON (John[7], Mary[6], John[5], Matthias[4], Peter[3], Matthias[2], John Jacob[1]) was born March 27, 1943, at Akron, Ohio.

(Sup) 3933 VIRGINIA ELLINGTON LINK (George[7], Edwin[6], George[5], Matthias[4], Peter[3], Matthias[2], John Jacob[1]) was the daughter of George Theron and Virginia Ellington Link [The Link Family, page 565, No. 2247]. Virginia was born January 28, 1924, at Binghamton, New York. She married Joseph E. Murray, June 2, 1945. He was the son of William Andrew and Mary D. Murray and was born April 1, 1919, at Milford, Massachusetts. During World War II Joseph was a major in the U.S. Medical Corps, and before and after the war he was a practicing physician. A professor of plastic surgery at Harvard University, Dr. Murray performed the first kidney transplant at Peter Brent Brigham Hospital in Boston. Virginia and Joseph resided at Wellesley Hills, Massachusetts.

(Sup) 6333   i   Virginia Maria Murray, born May 7, 1946.
(Sup) 6334   ii   Margaret Joan Murray, born September 30, 1949.
(Sup) 6335   iii Joseph Link Murray, born July 31, 1951.
(Sup) 6336   iv   Katherine Ann Murray, born September 30, 1952.
(Sup) 6337   v   Thomas George Murray, born March 12, 1958.
(Sup) 6338   vi   Richard William Murray, born September 18, 1963.

(Sup) 3934   WILLIAM MARTIN LINK (Edwin[7], Edwin[6], George[5], Matthias[4], Peter[3], John Jacob[1]) was the son of Edwin Albert and Marion Elizabeth Clayton Link [The Link Family, page 565, No. 2248]. William was born January 1, 1938, at Binghamton, New York. He married first, Juliet Ann Ridley, April 15, 1961. They were divorced. He married, second, Joyce Ann Edrinn, June 23, 1979.

CHILDREN OF WILLIAM AND JULIET

(Sup) 6339   i   Mary Catherine Link, born January 8, 1969.
(Sup) 6340   ii   Thomas Edwin Link, born May 12, 1971.

CHILD OF WILLIAM AND JOYCE

Stepdaughter iii Julie Ann Link, born November 5, 1969.

(Sup) 3935   EDWIN CLAYTON LINK (Edwin[7], Edwin[6], George[5], Matthias[4], Peter[3], Matthias[2], John Jacob[1]) was the son of Edwin Albert and Marion Elizabeth Clayton Link [The Link Family, page 565, No. 2248]. He was born November 30, 1941, at Binghamton, New York. In 1964 he graduated from Colgate University, where he was a member of Lambda Chi Alpha social fraternity. He was commissioned in the U.S. Naval Reserve in 1964 through the Reserve Officers Candidate School, and resigned in 1968 as a lieutenant. He married Maurine Lee Muzzy March 11, 1967, at Pearl Harbor, Hawaii. Maurine was born April 3, 1945, in Seattle, Washington. She was an airline stewardess. Edwin Clayton died while conducting undersea explorations June 18, 1973, near Key West, Florida.

(Sup) 6341   i   Stephen Clayton Link, born January 15, 1972.

(Sup) 3936   ALICE MILLER (Joseph[7], Peter[6], Peter[5], Peter[3], Matthias[2], John Jacob[1]) was the daughter of Joseph Rupert and Edith Schmogrow Miller [The Link Family, page 567, No. 2261]. Alice was born March 2, 1912, at Cincinnati, Ohio. She married Don G. Shaw, May 3, 1940.

(Sup) 6341A   i   Sandra Shaw.
(Sup) 6341B   ii   John Douglas Shaw.

(Sup) 3937   PAUL LINK MILLER (Joseph[7], Peter[6], Peter[5], Elizabeth[4], Peter[3], Matthias[2], John Jacob[1]) was the son of Joseph Rupert and Edith Schmogrow Miller [The Link Family, page 567, No. 2261]. Paul was born January 4, 1914, at Cincinnati, Ohio. He married Gladys Ullery in July, 1940.

(Sup) 6342   i   Judith Miller.
(Sup) 6343   ii   Mary Dee Miller.
(Sup) 6344   iii Paul Link Miller, Jr., born January 25, 1947.
(Sup) 6345   iv   Peter Link Miller, III, born January 25, 1947.

(Sup) 3938   WILLIAM MILLER FRYE, JR. (William[7], Mary[6], Peter[5], Elizabeth[4], Peter[3], Matthias[2], John Jacob[1]) was the son of William Miller and Hilda Heischman Frye [The Link Family, page 568, No. 2263]. William was born September 17, 1919, at Wardersville, West Virginia. He married Lorraine Johnson, September 5, 1942, at Kelly Lake, Minnesota.

(Sup) 3939   BENJAMIN LINK FRYE (William[7], Mary[6], Peter[5], Elizabeth[4], Peter[3], Matthias[2], John Jacob[1]) was the son of William Miller and Hilda Heischman Frye [The Link Family, page 568, No. 2263]. Benjamin was born October 9, 1920, at Wardersville, West Virginia.

(Sup) 3940   JAMES KENNETH FRYE (William[7], Mary[6], Peter[5], Elizabeth[4], Peter[3], Matthias[2], John Jacob[1]) was the son of William Miller and Hilda Heischman Frye [The Link Family, page 568, No. 2263]. James was born December 5, 1921, at Wardersville, West Virginia.

(Sup) 3941 HENRY LEE FRYE (William[7], Mary[6], Peter[5], Elizabeth[4], Peter[3], Matthias[2], John Jacob[1]) was the son of William Miller and Hilda Heischman Frye [The Link Family, page 568, No. 2263]. Henry was born May 9, 1923, at Wardersville, West Virginia, where he died July 29, 1923.

(Sup) 3942 HILDA ROBERTA FRYE (William[7], Mary[6], Peter[5], Elizabeth[4], Peter[3], Matthias[2], John Jacob[1]) was the daughter of William Miller and Hilda Heischman Frye [The Link Family, page 568, No. 2263]. Hilda was born February 24, 1925, at Wardersville, West Virginia. She married M. R. Cappiello, May 18, 1946, at Boston, Massachusetts.

(Sup) 3943 ROBERT OGDEN FRYE (William[7], Mary[6], Peter[5], Elizabeth[4], Peter[3], Matthias[2], John Jacob[1]) was the son of William Miller and Hilda Heischman Frye [The Link Family, page 568, No. 2263]. Robert was born February 24, 1925, at Wardersville, West Virginia. He married Evelyn Fletcher at Winchester, Virginia, August 20, 1945.

(Sup) 3944 MARY LOU FRYE (William[7], Mary[6], Peter[5], Elizabeth[4], Peter[3], Matthias[2], John Jacob[1]) was the daughter of William Miller and Hilda Heischman Frye [The Link Family, page 568, No. 2263]. Mary Lou was born February 17, 1930, (twin of Martha Lynn) at Wardersville, West Virginia, where she died the same day.

(Sup) 3945 MARTHA LYNN FRYE (William[7], Mary[6], Peter[5], Elizabeth[4], Peter[3], Matthias[2], John Jacob[1]) was the daughter of William Miller and Hilda Heischman Frye [The Link Family, page 568, No. 2263]. Martha Lynn was born February 17, 1930, (twin of Mary Lou) at Wardersville, West Virginia, where she died the same day.

(Sup) 3946 PEGGY ANNE FRYE (William[7], Mary[6], Peter[5], Elizabeth[4], Peter[3], Matthias[2], John Jacob[1]) was the daughter of William Miller and Hilda Heischman Frye [The Link Family, page 568, No. 2263]. Peggy Anne was born February 26, 1931, at Wardersville, West Virginia. She married A. L. Halterman at Needmore, West Virginia.

(Sup) 3947 EULA ADELL FRYE (Lutz[7], Mary[6], Peter[5], Elizabeth[4], Peter[3], Matthias[2], John Jacob[1]) was the daughter of Lutz and Olive Elizabeth (McNally) Frye [The Link Family, page 568, No. 2264]. She was born May 11, 1916, at Sessums, Mississippi. She married Robert E. Lavy, May 27, 1937.

(Sup) 3948 CHARLES LUTZ FRYE (Lutz[7], Mary[6], Peter[5], Elizabeth[4], Peter[3], Matthias[2], John Jacob[1]) was the son of Lutz and Olive Elizabeth (McNally) Frye [The Link Family, page 568, No. 2264]. Charles was born June 10, 1918, at Sessums, Mississippi. He married Mary Agnes Burns, April 3, 1943.

(Sup) 3949 ADELAIDE BELL FRYE (Lutz[7], Mary[6], Peter[5], Elizabeth[4], Peter[3], Matthias[2], John Jacob[1]) was the daughter of Lutz and Olive Elizabeth (McNally) Frye [The Link Family, page 568, No. 2264]. Adelaide was born December 16, 1919, at Sessums, Mississippi. She married Phillip A. Stubblefield.

3950 JOHN MILLER DREHER, JR. (John^7, Margaret^6, Peter^5, Elizabeth^4, Peter^3, Matthias^2, John Jacob^1) was born May 24, 1919. He married Gaynelle Hornsby, September 6, 1941.

(Sup) 6349   i   Margaret Naomi Dreher, born March 10, 1947.

3951 JOHN THADDEUS DREHER (Martha^7, Margaret^6, Peter^5, Elizabeth^4, Peter^3, Matthias^2, John Jacob^1) was born March 29, 1914. He married Mary Hamilton, December 26, 1940.

(Sup) 6350   i   Mary Ann Dreher, born May 2, 1946.

3952 MARGARET ELIZABETH DREHER (Martha^7, Margaret^6, Peter^5, Elizabeth^4, Peter^3, Matthias^2, John Jacob^1) was born November 14, 1916. She married Arthur M. Morton, Jr., December 22, 1945.

3953 MARTHA HELEN DREHER (Martha^7, Margaret^6, Peter^5, Elizabeth^4, Peter^3, Matthias^2, John Jacob^1) was born September 14, 1918. She married William Ellerbe Rogers, Jr., August 17, 1946.

3954 WILFRED RIVERS CLAYTOR (Virginia^7, Margaret^6, Peter^5, Elizabeth^4, Peter^3, Matthias^2, John Jacob^1) was born March 21, 1919. He married Frances Wells, January 17, 1946.

(Sup) 6351   i   Wilfred Rivers Claytor, Jr., born December 24, 1946.

3955 VIRGINIA CAROLINE CLAYTOR (Virginia^7, Margaret^6, Peter^5, Elizabeth^4, Peter^3, Matthias^2, John Jacob^1) was born March 9, 1920. She married Gerald Guy Edward Manning, June 19, 1943.

(Sup) 6352   i   Gerald Guy Manning II, born February 2, 1945.
(Sup) 6353   ii   Marguerite Chapman Manning, born Nov 14, 1947.

3956 ARCHIBALD MILLER LYNN (Elsie^7, Joseph II^6, Adam^5, Elizabeth^4, Peter^3, Matthias^2, John Jacob^1) was born June 4, 1916, at Staunton, Virginia. He married Edith Wilson Curry, July 29, 1941, at Staunton. Edith was born March 12, 1919, at Staunton.

(Sup) 6354   i   Archibald Miller Lynn, Jr., born Oct 27, 1942.

3957 THOMAS WATSON LYNN (Elsie^7, Joseph II^6, Adam^5, Elizabeth^4, Peter^3, Matthias^2, John Jacob^1) was born June 30, 1918, in Augusta County, Virginia. He married Ruth Barkley, August 4, 1945, at Waynesboro, Virginia. Ruth was the daughter of Frank Barkley and was born September 18, 1927, in Augusta County.

(Sup) 6355   i   Yvonne Watson Lynn, born March 2, 1946.
(Sup) 6356   ii   Thomas Cooper Lynn, born January 14, 1948.

3958 SARAH ELIZABETH LYNN (Elsie^7, Joseph II^6, Adam^5, Elizabeth^4, Peter^3, Matthias^2, John Jacob^1) was born July 8, 1921, at Staunton, Virginia. She married J. A. Lorentzson, December 15, 1942, at Palatka, Florida. J. A. Lorentzson was the son of Alex Lorentzson and was born July 15, 1918, at Brunswick, Georgia.

3959 ARMAND SHERMAN MILLER, JR. (Armand^7, Armand^6, Joseph^5, Elizabeth^4, Peter^3, Matthias^2, John Jacob^1) was born April 4, 1920, at Rockford, Illinois. He married Ruth Moulik, September 18, 1948, at Geneva, Switzerland. Armand was a member of the United Nations staff of the U. S. Government.

3960 ROGER SHERMAN MILLER (Karl^7, Armand^6, Joseph^5, Elizabeth^4, Peter^3, Matthias^2, John Jacob^1) was born July 11, 1923, at Philadelphia, Pennsylvania. He graduated from Episcopal Academy in Philadelphia in 1941 and from the University of Pennsylvania in 1944 with an A. B. degree. He was commissioned an Ensign in the U. S. Navy at graduation and served two years on a destroyer in the Atlantic and Pacific and was discharged as Lieutenant, j. g., in 1946. He did graduate work in physics at the University of Pennsylvania, receiving the degree of Master of Science in June, 1948. He was then appointed to the faculty of Episcopal Academy, teaching mathematics and physics.

3961 ELLIS PAUL DINKLE (Iva^7, Peter^6, Judith Rebecca^5, Elizabeth^4, Peter^3, Matthias^2, John Jacob^1) was born January 16, 1907. He married Ruth Virginia McCutchan, April 16, 1927, at Springfield, Ohio. Ruth was born November 18, 1905, at Sangerville, Virginia.

(Sup) 6357   i   Mary Louise Dinkle, born July 4, 1928.
(Sup) 6358   ii   Betty Lee Dinkle, born Augst 25, 1929.
(Sup) 6359   iii   Nancy Jane Dinkle, born November 1, 1930.

3962 PAULINE RODGERS DINKLE (Iva^7, Peter^6, Judith Rebecca^5, Elizabeth^4, Peter^3, Matthias^2, John Jacob^1) was born in 1910. She married Randolph Showker.

3963 BURTON M. DINKLE (Iva^7, Peter^6, Judith Rebecca^5, Elizabeth^4, Peter^3, Matthias^2, John Jacob^1) was born June 12, 1914, at Mount Solon, Virginia. He married Annie Mae Hall, November 1, 1939, at Washington, D. C. Annie was born October 22, 1921, at Washington.

(Sup) 6360   i   Charlotte Marie Dinkle, born July 11, 1941.

3964 ROBERT W. DINKLE (Iva^7, Peter^6, Judith Rebecca^5, Elizabeth^4, Peter^3, Matthias^2, John Jacob^1) was born September 6, 1926, at Mount Solon, Virginia. He married Marjorie Elizabeth Yancey, April 23, 1949, at Waynesboro, Virginia. Marjorie, daughter of John and Margaret Perry Yancey, was born September 7, 1926, at Waynesboro.

3965 RAYMOND OLIVER NEWBY (Lillian^7, Robert^6, Judith Rebecca^5, Elizabeth^4, Peter^3, Matthias^2, John Jacob^1) was born October 25, 1921, at Washington, D. C. He married Helen Rainey, September 17, 1943.

3966 DOROTHY MATILDA NEWBY (Lillian^7, Robert^6, Judith Rebecca^5, Elizabeth^4, Peter^3, Matthias^2, John Jacob^1) was born March 29, 1923, at Washington, D. C. She married Delbert Kirk Campbell, who was the son of Delbert A. and Edna Crosby Campbell Delbert was born May 27, 1922, at Carthage, Missouri.

(Sup) 6361   i   Donna Marie Campbell, born December 2, 1946.

3967 AUDREY NEWBY (Lillian^7, Robert^6, Judith Rebecca^5, Elizabeth^4, Peter^3, Matthias^2, John Jacob^1) was born April 13, 1926, at Washington, D. C. She married William Phillip Souderman, October 16, 1948, at Baltimore, Maryland. William was born June 10, 1925, at Baltimore, Maryland.

3968 RUSSELL WAYNE AUGSPURGER (Elsie[7], Walker[6], Melanchthon[5], Elizabeth[4], Peter[3], Matthias[2], John Jacob[1]) was born June 5, 1903, at Pulaski, Iowa. He married Nellie Ernestine Bohi, September 3, 1924, at Pulaski, Iowa. Nellie was born at Bloomfield, Iowa, January 9, 1906.

(Sup) 6362 i   Byron Bohi Augspurger, born February 14, 1926.
(Sup) 6363 ii Roger Lee Augspurger, born August 22, 1927.
(Sup) 6364 iii Keith William Augspurger, born May 12, 1929.
(Sup) 6365 iv Russell Dwayne Augspurger, born December 14, 1930.
(Sup) 6366 v   Arden Paul Augspurger, born May 7, 1934.
(Sup) 6367 vi Rose Marie Augspurger, born July 7, 1946.

3969 GERALD W. AUGSPURGER (Elsie[7], Walker[6], Melanchthon[5], Elizabeth[4], Peter[3], Matthias[2], John Jacob[1]) was born September 10, 1904, at Pulaski, Iowa. He married Cleo Tillie Ogden, June 15, 1935, at Pulaski. Cleo was born April 19, 1910, in Davis County, Iowa.

(Sup) 6368 i   J. Ogden Augspurger.
(Sup) 6369 ii Gerald Edwin Augspurger.
(Sup) 6370 iii Samuel Dee Augspurger.

3970 LUCILLE ETHEL AUGSPURGER (Elsie[7], Walker[6], Melanchthon[5], Elizabeth[4], Peter[3], Matthias[2], John Jacob[1]) was born February 11, 1907, at Pulaski, Iowa. She married Arthur Edward Blasi, August 12, 1926, at Pulaski. Arthur was the son of Edward Blasi and was born April 13, 1906, at Knoxville, Iowa.

(Sup) 6371 i   Jerald Den Blasi, born January 30, 1928.
(Sup) 6372 ii Dwight Arthur Blasi, born January 29, 1929.
(Sup) 6373 iii Robert Dwayne Blasi, born November 26, 1933.

3971 VERA JUNE MASSEY (Ethel[7], Walker[6], Melanchthon[5], Elizabeth[4], Peter[3], Matthias[2], John Jacob[1]) was born June 23, 1918, at Chicago, Illinois. She married William Percy Slonaker, June 19, 1938, at Pulaski, Iowa. William, son of Homer and Ruth Slonaker, was born July 30, 1913, at Milton, Iowa.

(Sup) 6374 i   Frederick Lee Slonaker, born August 29, 1939.
(Sup) 6375 ii Janet Sue Slonaker, born October 12, 1943.
(Sup) 6376 iii Linda Kay Slonaker, born July 26, 1947.

3972 WILLIAM ARTHUR MASSEY, JR. (Ethel[7], Walker[6], Melanchthon[5], Elizabeth[4], Peter[3], Matthias[2], John Jacob[1]) was born August 4, 1919, at Goshen, Indiana. He married Virginia Jane Morello, April 13, 1940, at Muscatine, Iowa. Virginia was born September 2, 1920, at Marseilles, Illinois.

3973 ROBERT RUSSELL LE ROY MASSEY (Ethel[7], Walker[6], Melanchthon[5], Elizabeth[4], Peter[3], Matthias[2], John Jacob[1]) was born December 15, 1920, at Goshen, Indiana. He married Edith Yetti Dornfeld, April 23, 1946, at Reno, Nevada. Edith was born May 28, 1918, at New York, New York.

3974 PAUL RAYMOND MASSEY (Ethel[7], Walker[6], Melanchthon[5], Elizabeth[4], Peter[3], Matthias[2], John Jacob[1]).

3975 EUGENE MASSEY (Ethel[7], Walker[6], Melanchthon[5], Elizabeth[4], Peter[3], Matthias[2], John Jacob[1])

3976 MARCELLA MILDRED HERALD (Maurice[7], Arresta[6], Melanchthon[5], Elizabeth[4], Peter[3], Matthias[2], John Jacob[1]) was born May 4, 1917. She married C. W. Moyers.

3977 LUELLA MAY HERALD (Maurice[7], Arresta[6], Melanchthon[5], Elizabeth[4], Peter[3], Matthias[2], John Jacob[1]) was born July 17, 1918. She died January 10, 1919.

3978 LOYD MAURICE HERALD (Maurice[7], Arresta[6], Melanchthon[5], Elizabeth[4], Peter[3], Matthias[2], John Jacob[1]) was born January 4, 1920. He died April 4, 1920.

3979 DONALD WARD HERALD (Maurice[7], Arresta[6], Melanchthon[5], Elizabeth[4], Peter[3], Matthias[2], John Jacob[1]) was born March 4, 1921. He died July 4, 1921.

3980 RUSSELL JAY HERALD (Maurice[7], Arresta[6], Melanchthon[5], Elizabeth[4], Peter[3], Matthias[2], John Jacob[1]) was born May 28, 1922. He was killed in action, March 28, 1945, while fighting with U. S. forces in Germany in World War II.

3981 KENNETH WAYNE HERALD (Maurice[7], Arresta[6], Melanchthon[5], Elizabeth[4], Peter[3], Matthias[2], John Jacob[1]) was born January 28, 1925.

3982 CARL DEAN HERALD (Maurice[7], Arresta[6], Melanchthon[5], Elizabeth[4], Peter[3], Matthias[2], John Jacob[1]) was born October 28, 1927.

3983 RICHARD EARL HERALD (Maurice[7], Arresta[6], Melanchthon[5], Elizabeth[4], Peter[3], Matthias[2], John Jacob[1]) was born July 17, 1929.

3984 CLAUDE LAVERNE CROSBY (Beulah[7], Arresta[6], Melanchthon[5], Elizabeth[4], Peter[3], Matthias[2], John Jacob[1]) was born November 18, 1916, at Fredericksburg, Ohio. He married Marie Roen, January 20, 1945.

3985 ALDENE ARRESTA CROSBY (Beulah[7], Arresta[6], Melanchthon[5], Elizabeth[4], Peter[3], Matthias[2], John Jacob[1]) was born December 15, 1919, at Fredericksburg, Ohio. She married John Floyd Vogt, August 10, 1938.

(Sup) 6377 i   Glenn Bruce Vogt, born August 21, 1939.
(Sup) 6378 ii John Floyd Vogt, Jr., born June 25, 1941.
(Sup) 6379 iii Lynda Karen Vogt, born October 26, 1943.
(Sup) 6380 iv Garyn Burl Vogt, born October 13, 1947.

3986 KATHERYNE CHAFIN (Florence[7], Joseph[6], Mary Ann[5], Elizabeth[4], Peter[3], Matthias[2], John Jacob[1]) was born October 4, 1920. She married Charles L. Aldredge, and on June 21, 1947, she married James Morrison Hale. James was the son of Eugene and Mabel Hale.

3987 MARY CATHERINE HEMP (Otis[7], John[6], Evalena[5], Rebecca[4], Peter[3], Matthias[2], John Jacob[1]) was born February 12, 1919, in Augusta County, Virginia. She married B. E. Hutchans, February 27, 1940.

3988 EVALYN LAVEINA HEMP (Otis[7], John[6], Evalena[5], Rebecca[4], Peter[3], Matthias[2], John Jacob[1]) was born January 1, 1922, in Augusta County, Virginia. She married Lester E. Switzer, November 12, 1940.

3989 RUBY PAULINE HEMP (Otis[7], John[6], Evalena[5], Rebecca[4], Peter[3], Matthias[2], John Jacob[1]) was born October 7, 1923, in Augusta County, Virginia. She married Marvin E. Switzer, December 25, 1941.

3990 IVA VIOLA HEMP (Otis^7, John^6, Evalena^5, Rebecca^4, Peter^3, Matthias^2, John Jacob^1) was born February 12, 1926, in Augusta County, Virginia. She married Millard B. English, August 27, 1946.

3991 BERRY McCUTCHAN HEMP (Otis^7, John^6, Evalena^5, Rebecca^4, Peter^3, Matthias^2, John Jacob^1) was born November 3, 1927, in Augusta County, Virginia.

3992 DALLAS MONROE HEMP (Otis^7, John^6, Evalena^5, Rebecca^4, Peter^3, Matthias^2, John Jacob^1) was born October 7, 1929, in Augusta County, Virginia.

3993 JOE LESTER HEMP (Otis^7, John^6, Evalena^5, Rebecca^4, Peter^3, Matthias^2, John Jacob^1) was born May 10, 1936, in Augusta County, Virginia.

3994 KATHERINE JANE SPITLER (Charles^7, Alice^6, Mary^5, Rebecca^4, Peter^3, Matthias^2, John Jacob^1) was born October 3, 1914, at Huntington, West Virginia. She married Frank Moore Deacon, October 7, 1936.

3995 MARY HAGAN SPITLER (Charles^7, Alice^6, Mary^5, Rebecca^4, Peter^3, Matthias^2, John Jacob^1) was born August 9, 1920, at Huntington, West Virginia. She married Jack Norvell Staton, September 1, 1940.

3996 WILLIAM EDWARD WINN (William^7, Daisy^6, James^5, Rebecca^4, Peter^3, Matthias^2, John Jacob^1) was born December 21, 1920, and died at the age of six months.

3997 FRANKLIN ELMER WINN (William^7, Daisy^6, James^5, Rebecca^4, Peter^3, Matthias^2, John Jacob^1) was born December 21, 1922.

(Sup) 6384   1 Raymond O'Brien Ball II, born November 26, 1946.

3998 IVY KATHLEEN WINN (William^7, Daisy^6, James^5, Rebecca^4, Peter^3, Matthias^2, John Jacob^1) was born June 27, 1924, at Philadelphia, Pennsylvania. She married Ray O'Brien Ball, June 4, 1934, at San Francisco, California. Ray was born June 10, 1925, Perry, Florida.

3999 RICHARD WILLIAM WINN (William^7, Daisy^6, James^5, Rebecca^4, Peter^3, Matthias^2, John Jacob^1) was born November 4, 1927.

4000 ROBERT EDWARD WINN (William^7, Daisy^6, James^5, Rebecca^4, Peter^3, Matthias^2, John Jacob^1) was born November 4, 1927.

4001 PATRICIA MARY SPRING (Ruth^7, Daisy^6, James^5, Rebecca^4, Peter^3, Matthias^2, John Jacob^1) was born November 10, 1940, at Peoria, Illinois.

4002 SHARON MARIE SPRING (Ruth^7, Daisy^6, James^5, Rebecca^4, Peter^3, Matthias^2, John Jacob^1) was born December 10, 1943, at Springfield, Illinois.

4003 MARY CALENE CLINE (Merle^7, Frances^6, James^5, Rebecca^4, Peter^3, Matthias^2, John Jacob^1) was born January 16, 1937, at Decatur, Illinois.

4004 SHARON LYNNE TUNNICLIFF (Richard^7, Carolyn^6, James^5, Rebecca^4, Peter^3, Matthias^2, John Jacob^1) was born January 23, 1943, at Oklahoma City, Oklahoma.

4005 SOPHIA MAE PALMER (Fleming^7, Andrew^6, Hannah^5, David^4, Catherine^3, Matthias^2, John Jacob^1) was born March 16, 1886. She married Herman Kraleman, May 16, 1917.

4006 FANNIE BESSIE PALMER (Fleming^7, Andrew^6, Hannah^5, David^4, Catherine^3, Matthias^2, John Jacob^1) was born June 20, 1890. She married Leander Pinson, September 11, 1909, and later, John Carlson.

(Sup) 6385   i Milford Pinson.
(Sup) 6386   ii Robert Pinson.

4007 DAISY PALMER (Fleming^7, Andrew^6, Hannah^5, David^4, Catherine^3, Matthias^2, John Jacob^1) was born May 30, 1900, at Bellview, Missouri. She married Millard Edward Fridley, August 24, 1933, at Waterloo, Iowa.

4008 GRACE ELIZABETH PALMER (Harvey^7, Andrew^6, Hannah^5, David^4, Catherine^3, Matthias^2, John Jacob^1) was born August 30, 1896, at Murphysboro, Illinois. She married Frank Axel Larsen, November 8, 1916, at Long Beach, California. Frank was born January 9, 1895, at Minneapolis, Minnesota.

(Sup) 6387   i Kent Palmer Larsen, born December 8, 1922.
(Sup) 6388   ii Alexia Louise Larsen, born September 24, 1926.

4009 ELECTRA PALMER (Harvey^7, Andrew^6, Hannah^5, David^4, Catherine^3, Matthias^2, John Jacob^1) was born February 15, 1908, at Murphysboro, Illinois. She first married a Mr. Powell. On September 3, 1939, she married Donald George Walker.

(Sup) 6389   i Marilynne Diana Powell.
(Sup) 6390   ii Harold Webb Powell.

4010 JOSEPHINE MARIE PALMER (Roy^7, Andrew^6, Hannah^5, David^4, Catherine^3, Matthias^2, John Jacob^1) was born May 19, 1903, at Murphysboro, Illinois. Josephine provided valuable assistance in gathering family data for this history.

4011 ROBERT JACKSON PALMER (Roy^7, Andrew^6, Hannah^5, David^4, Catherine^3, Matthias^2, John Jacob^1) was born December 5, 1904, at Murphysboro, Illinois. He entered the Order of St. Benedict and became Father Jerome. He lived at the Abbey at St. Meinrad, Indiana.

4012 ETTA LOUISE PALMER (Roy^7, Andrew^6, Hannah^5, David^4, Catherine^3, Matthias^2, John Jacob^1) was born June 29, 1906, at Murphysboro, Illinois. She entered the Order of St. Benedict, became Sister Mary Robert and lived at the Sisters' monastery at Ferdinand, Indiana.

4013 PAUL MUNIER PALMER (Roy^7, Andrew^6, Hannah^5, David^4, Catherine^3, Matthias^2, John Jacob^1) was born August 19, 1907, at Murphysboro, Illinois. He married Ruth Gilvarry, November 2, 1931, at Clayton, Missouri. Ruth was the daughter of Michael Gilvarry and was born September 20, 1912, at St. Louis, Missouri.

(Sup) 6391   i Dorothy Marie Palmer, born September 21, 1932.
(Sup) 6392   ii Paul Michael Palmer, born December 24, 1934.
(Sup) 6393   iii James Thomas Palmer, born September 24, 1938.
(Sup) 6394   iv Robert Frances Palmer, born July 26, 1940.
(Sup) 6395   v John Anthony Palmer, born February 18, 1942.

4014 MARTIN ANDREW PALMER (Roy^7, Andrew^6, Hannah^5, David^4, Catherine^3, Matthias^2, John Jacob^1) was born January 19, 1909, at Murphysboro, Illinois. He died there February 11, 1910.

4015 JAMES THOMAS PALMER (Roy[7], Andrew[6], Hannah[5], David[4], Catherine[3], Matthias[2], John Jacob[1]) was born November 3, 1914, at Murphysboro, Illinois. He entered the Order of St. Benedict, became Father Herbert and lived at St. Meinrad, Indiana.

4016 JESSIE ANDREW AU BUCHON (Sophia[7], Mary Ann[6], Hannah[5], David[4], Catherine[3], Matthias[2], John Jacob[1]) was born June 28, 1901, at Bonne Terre, Missouri, where he died October 18, 1901.

4017 ANTHY MARY AU BUCHON (Sophia[7], Mary Ann[6], Hannah[5], David[4], Catherine[3], Matthias[2], John Jacob[1]) was born February 24, 1903, at Bonne Terre, Missouri, where she died March 9, 1921.

4018 BERNICE LORRAINE AU BUCHON (Sophia[7], Mary Ann[6], Hannah[5], David[4], Catherine[3], Matthias[2], John Jacob[1]) was born March 20, 1906, at Bonne Terre, Missouri.

4019 VERDIE L. KING (Mary[7], Peter[6], Hannah[5], David[4], Catherine[3], Matthias[2], John Jacob[1]) was born April 24, 1886, at Magnolia, Arkansas. She married William Bradford Toland, December 15, 1901, at Magnolia. William was born at Milner, Arkansas, in 1875.

(Sup) 6396 i Fred Toland.
(Sup) 6397 ii Audrey Toland.
(Sup) 6398 iii Princess Olga Toland, born August 2, 1917.

4020 MARY GRACE HENDRICKS (Susan[7], Peter[6], Hannah[5], David[4], Catherine[3], Matthias[2], John Jacob[1]) was born August 3, 1897, at Waldo, Arkansas. She married William H. Arnold, Jr., December 31, 1921. William was the son of William H. Arnold and was born at Texarkana, Arkansas. William was a graduate in law and a partner with his father in a large practice in east Texas and southern Arkansas. After his father's death, William continued the practice of law under the firm name at Texarkana. See No. 2404.

(Sup) 6399 i William H. Arnold, III, born November 2, 1923.
(Sup) 6400 ii Thomas Saxon Arnold, born August 3, 1928.

4021 CATHERINE EDNA LEWIS (Arthur[7], Peter[6], Hannah[5], David[4], Catherine[3], Matthias[2], John Jacob[1]) was born December 15, 1900, at Magnolia, Arkansas. She married J. F. Jones, December 16, 1915.

4022 FLORENCE DORNBY LEWIS (Arthur[7], Peter[6], Hannah[5], David[4], Catherine[3], Matthias[2], John Jacob[1]) was born July 18, 1902, at Lewisville, Arkansas. She married Edgar Roberts, April 27, 1925, at Stamps, Arkansas. Edgar was the son of Luther Calvin Roberts and was born January 31, 1904, at Stamps, Arkansas.

4023 PITZEL HOWARD LEWIS (Arthur[7], Peter[6], Hannah[5], David[4], Catherine[3], Matthias[2], John Jacob[1]) was born May 16, 1904, at Magnolia, Arkansas. He married Alma Davidson, December 31, 1927, at Minden, Louisiana. Alma, daughter of F. N. Davidson, was born December 20, 1907, at Dry Prong, Louisiana.

(Sup) 6401 i Helen Laverne Lewis, born November 25, 1929.
(Sup) 6402 ii Shirley Nell Lewis, born November 18, 1935.
(Sup) 6403 iii Donna Fay Lewis, born February 22, 1943.
(Sup) 6404 iv Terry Howard Lewis, born October 6, 1945.

4024 MARY VIVIAN LEWIS (Arthur[7], Peter[6], Hannah[5], David[4], Catherine[3], Matthias[2], John Jacob[1]) was born August 2, 1907, at Honduras, Arkansas. She married Oscar Mitchell, December 13, 1930, at Minden, Louisiana. Oscar was born January 14, 1900, at Homer, Louisiana.

(Sup) 6405 i Patsy Faye Mitchell, born January 24, 1932.
(Sup) 6406 ii Donald Oscar Mitchell, born March 23, 1934.

4025 LUCY VIRGINIA LEWIS (Arthur[7], Peter[6], Hannah[5], David[4], Catherine[3], Matthias[2], John Jacob[1]) was born December 22, 1909, at Magnolia, Arkansas. She married John Daniel Mitchell, April 3, 1937, at Minden, Louisiana. John was the son of Daniel Mitchell and was born December 1, 1912.

(Sup) 6407 i Virginia Kay Mitchell.

4026 CARNELL LEWIS (Arthur[7], Peter[6], Hannah[5], David[4], Catherine[3], Matthias[2], John Jacob[1]) was born November 9, 1912, at Magnolia, Arkansas. She married James Plell Hilburn, May 12, 1930, at Minden, Louisiana. James was born April 22, 1908, at Shongaloo, Louisiana.

(Sup) 6408 i James Lewis Hilburn.
(Sup) 6409 ii William Dwain Hilburn.
(Sup) 6410 iii Robert Gerald Hilburn.

4027 WILLIAM ARTHUR LEWIS (Arthur[7], Peter[6], Hannah[5], David[4], Catherine[3], Matthias[2], John Jacob[1]) was born September 15, 1913, at Magnolia, Arkansas. He married Marie Upshaw, June 28, 1942, at Conshatta, Louisiana. Marie, daughter of James Upshaw, was born April 3, 1924, at Conshatta, Louisiana.

(Sup) 6411 i Charlotte Marie Lewis, born March 2, 1945.
(Sup) 6412 ii Sharon Idella Lewis, born August 30, 1936.

4028 SAMUEL BROOKS LEWIS (Arthur[7], Peter[6], Hannah[5], David[4], Catherine[3], Matthias[2], John Jacob[1]) was born March 31, 1918, at Magnolia, Arkansas. He married Emma Lee Nix, December 26, 1938. Emma was born January 15, 1916, at Buckner, Arkansas. She was the daughter of Frank Nix.

(Sup) 6413 i Carolyn Florence Lewis, born December 5, 1937.
(Sup) 6414 ii Ronald Brook Lewis, born February 19, 1940.
(Sup) 6415 iii Norma Joyce Lewis, born September 10, 1946.

4029 THOMAS EMMETT LOFTEN (Anna[7], Samuel[6], Hannah[5], David[4], Catherine[3], Matthias[2], John Jacob[1]) was born November 5, 1895, at Atlanta, Arkansas. He died February 9, 1949, at Magnolia, Arkansas. Thomas married Frances Onnie Mabel Awbrey, November 9, 1924, at Calhoun, Arkansas. Frances was the daughter of Rufus Pinckney and Mary Enfaula Kirkpatrick Awbrey and was born March 3, 1908, at Bienville, Louisiana.

(Sup) 6416 i Ruby Edell Loften, born May 8, 1926.
(Sup) 6417 ii Frances De Maurice Loften, born Nov 18, 1931.
(Sup) 6418 iii Loye Emmett Loften, born November 20, 1939.

4030 WALTER ERNEST LOFTEN (Anna[7], Samuel[6], Hannah[5], David[4], Catherine[3], Matthias[2], John Jacob[1]) was born December 4, 1896, at Atlanta, Arkansas. From August, 1918, to September, 1919, he served in the U. S. armed forces in World War I. He married Wyllie Mae Fuller, March 17, 1918. Walter died December 11, 1948, and was buried at Holly Grove Cemetery, Junction City, Arkansas.

(Sup) 6419　i　Mahdeen Loften, born January 12, 1919.
(Sup) 6420　ii　John Thurbyn Loften, born June 28, 1921.
(Sup) 6421　iii　Christine Loften, born November 24, 1924.
(Sup) 6422　iv　James Geneva Loften, born March 28, 1930.

4031 PARRIE GENEVA LOFTEN (Anna[7], Samuel[6], Hannah[5], David[4], Catherine[3], Matthias[2], John Jacob[1]) was born July 26, 1898. She married Asie Leonard Reid, November 11, 1916. Parrie died August 16, 1940, and was buried at the Old Cemetery, Magnolia, Arkansas.

(Sup) 6423　i　Mary Syble Reid, born May 22, 1918.
(Sup) 6424　ii　Frederick Samuel Reid, born September 23, 1924.

4032 DELLA BURLEY (Ella[7], Samuel[6], Hannah[5], David[4], Catherine[3], Matthias[2], John Jacob[1]) was born April 11, 1892. She married Samuel Arthur Griffin at Wesson, Arkansas. Samuel was born April 11, 1892, near Atlanta, Arkansas.

4033 CHARLES AUGUSTUS BURDINE (Mary[7], Samuel[6], Hannah[5], David[4], Catherine[3], Matthias[2], John Jacob[1]) was born November 12, 1892, at Magnolia, Arkansas. He married Mabel Elizabeth Garrett, November 3, 1920, at Minden, Louisiana. Mabel was born April 6, 1893, at Haynesville, Louisiana, and died September 16, 1936, at Minden. Charles married Susie McNeely Herman, December 24, 1937, at Minden. He was a building contractor.

(Sup) 6425　i　Charles Augustus Burdine, Jr., born August 14, 1922.
(Sup) 6426　ii　John Rhon Burdine, born January 6, 1928.

4034 ELLA AGNES BURDINE (Mary[7], Samuel[6], Hannah[5], David[4], Catherine[3], Matthias[2], John Jacob[1]) was born August 19, 1894, at Magnolia, Arkansas. She died in infancy.

4035 RUFUS EARLIE BURDINE (Mary[7], Samuel[6], Hannah[5], David[4], Catherine[3], Matthias[2], John Jacob[1]) was born July 31, 1895, at Magnolia, Arkansas. He married Gladys Mac Nouts, April 24, 1923, at Pine Bluff, Arkansas. Gladys was born December 24, 1898, at Hope, Arkansas.

4036 JESSE GUY BURDINE (Mary[7], Samuel[6], Hannah[5], David[4], Catherine[3], Matthias[2], John Jacob[1]) was born November 28, 1899, at Tubal, Arkansas. He married Tessie May Davis, July 18, 1926, at Camden, Arkansas. Tessie was the daughter of Jasper Newton and Julia R. Davis and was born December 16, 1908, at Logansport, Indiana.

(Sup) 6427　i　Gladys Alline Burdine, born December 10, 1926.
(Sup) 6428　ii　Evelyn Juanita Burdine, born June 22, 1929.
(Sup) 6429　iii　Ralph Albert Burdine, born March 8, 1931.
(Sup) 6430　iv　Guy Lewis Burdine, born June 6, 1935.
(Sup) 6431　v　Willie Eugene Burdine, born December 7, 1938.
(Sup) 6432　vi　Billie Ray Burdine, born March 9, 1940.

4037 CORBIN STEVENS BURDINE (Mary[7], Samuel[6], Hannah[5], David[4], Catherine[3], Matthias[2], John Jacob[1]) was born January 7, 1904, at Magnolia, Arkansas. He died in infancy.

4038 MABEL SALOME BURDINE (Mary[7], Samuel[6], Hannah[5], David[4], Catherine[3], Matthias[2], John Jacob[1]) was born October 11, 1906, at Magnolia, Arkansas. She married Baker William Yeates, June 21, 1931, at Antioch, Louisiana. Baker was born April 28, 1907, at Waldo, Arkansas. Baker was a Nazarene minister.

(Sup) 6433　i　Martha Anne Yeates, born November 21, 1936.

4039 TRUMAN CECIL BURDINE (Mary[7], Samuel[6], Hannah[5], David[4], Catherine[3], Matthias[2], John Jacob[1]) was born July 7, 1907, in Columbia County, Arkansas. He married Othelle Carter, December 29, 1931, at Summerfield, Louisiana. Othelle was the daughter of W. H. and Maggie Oxford Carter and was born July 1, 1912, at Ilico, Louisiana.

(Sup) 6434　i　Janet Gaynor Burdine, born June 14, 1936.
(Sup) 6435　ii　Rose Margaret Burdine, born December 28, 1940.

4040 CLYDE VINCENT BURDINE (Mary[7], Samuel[6], Hannah[5], David[4], Catherine[3], Matthias[2], John Jacob[1]) was born November 6, 1913, at Summerfield, Louisiana. He married Georgia Mae Collier, November 24, 1934, at Rayville, Louisiana. Georgia was born September 24, 1917, at Magnolia, Arkansas. She was the daughter of Walter Albertis and Susie Yeates Collier.

(Sup) 6436　i　Mary Olive Burdine, born December 2, 1935.
(Sup) 6437　ii　Anita Joan Burdine, born February 7, 1938.
(Sup) 6438　iii　Robert Terrell Burdine, born September 4, 1944.

4041 A. Z. EILAND (Katherine[7], Samuel[6], Hannah[5], David[4], Catherine[3], Matthias[2], John Jacob[1]) was born December 30, 1899, at El Dorado, Arkansas. He married Olive Pepper in 1924.

4042 J. D. EILAND (Katherine[7], Samuel[6], Hannah[5], David[4], Catherine[3], Matthias[2], John Jacob[1]) was born November 4, 1904, at Junction City, Arkansas. He married Ruby Dell Ball, in 1929.

4043 OREN OLIN BAKER (Jessie[7], Samuel[6], Hannah[5], David[4], Catherine[3], Matthias[2], John Jacob[1]) was born February 19, 1901. He married Carmellar Huison, April 24, 1922. Carmellar was born March 18, 1901. Oren died October 6, 1948.

(Sup) 6439　i　Rodney Lee Baker, born April 12, 1923.
(Sup) 6440　ii　Donald Gene Baker, born July 4, 1928.

4043A ERMA INEZ LEWIS (Sterling[7], Samuel[6], Hannah[5], David[4], Catherine[3], Matthias[2], John Jacob[1]) was born October 14, 1906, in Columbia County, Arkansas. She died February 3, 1908.

4044 LAURA LUCILLE LEWIS (Sterling[7], Samuel[6], Hannah[5], David[4], Catherine[3], Matthias[2], John Jacob[1]) was born December 11, 1908. She married Thornton Nicklas, July 28, 1944.

4045 STETSON RAYFORD LEWIS (Sterling[7], Samuel[6], Hannah[5], David[4], Catherine[3], Matthias[2], John Jacob[1]) was born November 29, 1910. He married Evelyn Hull, October 6, 1931.

4054A EDITH J. VAUGHAN (Dora[7], Nancy[6], Minerva[5], Hannah[4], Catherine[3], Matthias[2], John Jacob[1]) was born January 21, 1900.

4054B EVA A. VAUGHAN (Dora[7], Nancy[6], Minerva[5], Hannah[4], Catherine[3], Matthias[2], John Jacob[1]) was born June 3, 1902.

4054C MINERVA D. VAUGHAN (Dora[7], Nancy[6], Minerva[5], Hannah[4], Catherine[3], Matthias[2], John Jacob[1]) was born November 29, 1905.

4054D DOROTHY K. VAUGHAN (Dora[7], Nancy[6], Minerva[5], Hannah[4], Catherine[3], Matthias[2], John Jacob[1]) was born December 18, 1907.

4054E GENEVIEVE C. VAUGHAN (Dora[7], Nancy[6], Minerva[5], Hannah[4], Catherine[3], Matthias[2], John Jacob[1]) was born March 1, 1909.

4054F DARRELL VAUGHAN (Dora[7], Nancy[6], Minerva[5], Hannah[4], Catherine[3], Matthias[2], John Jacob[1]) was born September 13, 1914.

4054G SARAH ELIZABETH VAUGHAN (Dora[7], Nancy[6], Minerva[5], Hannah[4], Catherine[3], Matthias[2], John Jacob[1]) was born February 21, 1916.

4055 AUDLEY MAURICE DONHAM (Audley[7], Nancy[6], Minerva[5], Hannah[4], Catherine[3], Matthias[2], John Jacob[1]) was born November 17, 1912. He married Leta F. McCaskey, August 28, 1944. Leta was born May 4, 1911.

4056 JOHN BURTON DONHAM (Audley[7], Nancy[6], Minerva[5], Hannah[4], Catherine[3], Matthias[2], John Jacob[1]) was born December 9, 1917.

4057 ALICIA LLOYD MOORE (Thomas[7], Laura[6], Peter[5], Hannah[4], Catherine[3], Matthias[2], John Jacob[1]) was born in February, 1922, and died the same month.

4058 ADRIENNE MOORE (Thomas[7], Laura[6], Peter[5], Hannah[4], Catherine[3], Matthias[2], John Jacob[1]) was born March 30, 1923, at New York, New York. She married Stuart Eldred Hutchings, June 4, 1949.

4059 GEORGE TAYLOR SINCLAIR (Katherine[7], Katherine[6], Henry[5], Peter[4], Catherine[3], Matthias[2], John Jacob[1]) was born October 26, 1921, at Newport News, Virginia.

4060 CARTER ASHTON SINCLAIR (Katherine[7], Katherine[6], Henry[5], Peter[4], Catherine[3], Matthias[2], John Jacob[1]) was born August 28, 1924, at Bluefield, West Virginia. He married Betty Irene Bush, May 31, 1947.

(Sup) 6457   1   John Marshall Sinclair, born October 27, 1948.

4061 HARRIET ECHOLS HANGER (Franklin[7], Franklin[6], David[5], Peter[4], Catherine[3], Matthias[2], John Jacob[1]) was born December 13, 1944.

4062 CLAY HANGER (Irwin[7], Franklin[6], David[5], Peter[4], Catherine[3], Matthias[2], John Jacob[1]) was born February 19, 1935, at Cleveland, Ohio.

4063 SALLY HANGER (Irwin[7], Franklin[6], David[5], Peter[4], Catherine[3], Matthias[2], John Jacob[1]) was born November 14, 1936, at Cleveland, Ohio.

4064 MARTHA LOUISE HANGER (Irwin[7], Franklin[6], David[5], Peter[4], Catherine[3], Matthias[2], John Jacob[1]) was born March 7, 1941, at Cleveland, Ohio.

4046 CLINTON KELLY McWILLIAMS (Beulah[7], Samuel[6], Hannah[5], David[4], Catherine[3], Matthias[2], John Jacob[1]) was born September 25, 1910, at Calhoun, Arkansas. He married Emma Lee Blasingame, May 30, 1931, at Texarkana, Arkansas. Emma was the daughter of W. James and Bernie Smith Blasingame and was born August 9, 1914, at Magnolia, Arkansas.

(Sup) 6441   i   James Donald McWilliams, born September 8, 1933.
(Sup) 6442   ii   Anita Kay McWilliams, born November 21, 1936.
(Sup) 6443   iii Frances Jan McWilliams, born July 18, 1946.

4047 MABELLE WALLACE MILLER (John[7], Sarah[6], Minerva[5], Hannah[4], Catherine[3], Matthias[2], John Jacob[1]) was born October 2, 1916, at Tulsa, Oklahoma. She graduated from the University of Oklahoma and married William C. Bell.

(Sup) 6444   i   Anne Kathryn Bell, born November 14, 1945.
(Sup) 6445   ii   Lee Ellen Bell, born November 16, 1948.
(Sup) 6446   iii Margaret Wallace Bell, born December 9, 1949.

4048 KATHRYN MILLER (John[7], Sarah[6], Minerva[5], Hannah[4], Catherine[3], Matthias[2], John Jacob[1]) was born November 4, 1924, at Tulsa, Oklahoma. She married Claude James Pierce, Jr. Kathryn was a graduate of the University of Oklahoma.

4049 MARY ELIZABETH MILLER (Darrell[7], Sarah[6], Minerva[5], Hannah[4], Catherine[3], Matthias[2], John Jacob[1]) was born December 15, 1912, at Tulsa, Oklahoma. She married Travers Sparks Mahan, June 14, 1935, at Tulsa. Mary graduated from the University of Oklahoma.

(Sup) 6447   i   Mazilu Mahan, born April 4, 1936.
(Sup) 6448   ii   Travers S. Mahan, Jr., born April 22, 1947.

4050 MARY ELLEN MILLER (Darrell[7], Sarah[6], Minerva[5], Hannah[4], Catherine[3], Matthias[2], John Jacob[1]) was born January 18, 1915, at Tulsa, Oklahoma, where she died August 13, 1920.

4051 MAZIE ANN MILLER (Darrell[7], Sarah[6], Minerva[5], Hannah[4], Catherine[3], Matthias[2], John Jacob[1]) was born September 8, 1921, at Tulsa, Oklahoma. She married Lieutenant Colonel Edwin Forrest Harding, Jr., October 27, 1941, at Tulsa. Mazie was a graduate of the University of Oklahoma.

(Sup) 6449   i   Eleanor Elizabeth Harding, born October 21, 1942.
(Sup) 6450   ii   Edwin Forrest Harding, III, born November 7, 1943.
(Sup) 6451   iii Ann Miller Harding, born August 12, 1946.
(Sup) 6452   iv   Jonathan Wayne Harding, born January 14, 1948.

4052 DARRELL CHASTAIN MILLER (Darrell[7], Sarah[6], Minerva[5], Hannah[4], Catherine[3], Matthias[2], John Jacob[1]) was born July 13, 1928.

4053 SARAH ANN HILL (Edith[7], Sarah[6], Minerva[5], Hannah[4], Catherine[3], Matthias[2], John Jacob[1]) was born May 23, 1924, at Tulsa, Oklahoma. She married Robert Nelson Bonner, February 18, 1948, at Tulsa. Sarah graduated from Wellesley College.

4064 VERNON IRVING HILL, JR. (Edith[7], Sarah[6], Minerva[5], Hannah[4], Catherine[3], Matthias[2], John Jacob[1]) was born February 25, 1931, at Tulsa, Oklahoma.

4065 TAYLOR MANSFIELD BOXLEY, JR. (Mildred[7], Bessie[6], David[5], Peter[4], Catherine[3], Matthias[2], John Jacob[1]) was born June 17, 1925. He served in World War II in the European Theater, was a German prisoner of war, won the Purple Heart, Combat Infantry Badge, Presidential Unit Citation with Cluster. Three Bronze Stars and Allied Colors for Service with the Russians. Taylor married Anne Irvine Brown, September 7, 1946, at Swoope, Virginia.

(Sup) 6458   i Taylor Mansfield Boxley, III, born July 15, 1947.

4066 DOROTHY DOUGLAS BOXLEY (Mildred[7], Bessie[6], David[5], Peter[4], Catherine[3], Matthias[2], John Jacob[1]) was born April 26, 1930, at Louisa, Virginia.

4067 MARY TAYLOR HANGER (Harry[7], Percy[6], David[5], Peter[4], Catherine[3], Matthias[2], John Jacob[1]) was born March 6, 1945, at Charlottesville, Virginia.

4068 SARA IRVINE HANGER (Harry[7], Percy[6], David[5], Peter[4], Catherine[3], Matthias[2], John Jacob[1]) was born April 13, 1948, at Mather Field, Sacramento, California.

4069 FRANCES LELIA WOODWARD (Harry[7], Joseph[6], Peter[5], Mary[4], Catherine[3], Matthias[2], John Jacob[1]) was born January 11, 1904, at Richmond, Virginia. She married William Thomas Bryan, Jr.

(Sup) 6459   i Frances Woodward Bryan, born April 1, 1926.
(Sup) 6460   ii William T. Bryan, III, born November 19, 1931.
(Sup) 6461   iii Harry Woodward Bryan, born November 7, 1933.
(Sup) 6462   iv John Proctor Bryan, born March 17, 1946.

4070 HARRY BEERS WOODWARD, JR. (Harry[7], Joseph[6], Peter[5], Mary[4], Catherine[3], Matthias[2], John Jacob[1]) was born in April, 1906, at Richmond, Virginia, where he died in November the same year.

4071 JOSEPH BARNES WOODWARD (Harry[7], Joseph[6], Peter[5], Mary[4], Catherine[3], Matthias[2], John Jacob[1]) was born December 21, 1907, at Staunton, Virginia. He married Eleanor Hilton.

4072 MILDRED MERCEREAU (Anna[7], Joseph[6], Peter[5], Mary[4], Catherine[3], Matthias[2], John Jacob[1]) was born April 28, 1906, at Staunton, Virginia. She married Percival Loth, Jr., May 31, 1928, at Staunton. Percival, son of Percival Loth, was born August 17, 1898.

(Sup) 6463   i Wallace De Hart Mercereau, born December 25, 1943.
(Sup) 6464   ii Edward Findley Mercereau, born August 1946.

4073 WALLACE WOODWARD MERCEREAU (Anna[7], Joseph[6], Peter[5], Mary[4], Catherine[3], Matthias[2], John Jacob[1]) was born December 7, 1909, at Staunton, Virginia. He married Florine De Hart.

4074 ANNE MONTGOMERY WOODWARD (Edward[7], Joseph[6], Peter[5], Mary[4], Catherine[3], Matthias[2], John Jacob[1]) was born April 16, 1917, at Staunton, Virginia.

4075 EDWARD WOODWARD, JR. (Edward[7], Joseph[6], Peter[5], Mary[4], Catherine[3], Matthias[2], John Jacob[1]) was born March 10, 1922, at Staunton, Virginia.

4076 WILLIAM GAMBLE WOODWARD, JR. (William[7], Joseph[6], Peter[5], Mary[4], Catherine[3], Matthias[2], John Jacob[1]) was born July 19, 1911, at Baltimore, Maryland. He attended Exeter and Choate schools and entered military service. During World War II he became a Major and Aide to General Hayes, Commander of Second Service Command, U. S. Army, at Baltimore. He married Elaine Richardson Smith, December 7, 1940, at Glen Cove, Long Island.

4077 HARMON WOODWARD, JR. (Harmon[7], Samuel[6], Peter[5], Mary[4], Catherine[3], Matthias[2], John Jacob[1]) was born January 9, 1916, at Bluefields, West Virginia. He married June Witt Rish, November 25, 1939, at Bluefields. June was born September 9, at Keystone, West Virginia.

(Sup) 6465   i Harmon Rish Woodward, born March 6, 1943.
(Sup) 6466   ii Thomas Hale Woodward, born March 31, 1947.
(Sup) 6467   iii Crissie Jane Woodware, born June 14, 1949.

4078 SAMUEL MILLER WOODWARD (Harmon[7], Samuel[6], Peter[5], Mary[4], Catherine[3], Matthias[2], John Jacob[1]) was born December 8, 1919, at Bluefields, West Virginia. He married Belle Atha, August 1, 1946.

4079 DANIEL WENTWORTH RICHARDS (Katherine[7], Samuel[6], Peter[5], Mary[4], Catherine[3], Matthias[2], John Jacob[1]) was born July 6, 1910, at Roanoke, Virginia. He married Helen Cox, December 25, 1942, in Floyd County, Virginia. Helen was born in Floyd County, May 8, 1914.

(Sup) 6468   i Daniel Wentworth Richards, Jr., born 1944.
(Sup) 6469   ii Katharine Woodward Richards, born 1949.

4080 MARTHA ANNE KING (Janet[7], Effie[6], Catherine[5], Mary[4], Catherine[3], Matthias[2], John Jacob[1]) was born January 21, 1918, at Raleigh, North Carolina. She married Richard B. Castell, December 23, 1940, at Washington, D. C.

4081 WILLIAM BURNETT MILLER, JR. (William[7], Effie[6], Catherine[5], Mary[4], Catherine[3], Matthias[2], John Jacob[1]) was born September 6, 1930, at Asheville, North Carolina.

4082 DAVID WILLIAMSON MILLER (William[7], Effie[6], Catherine[5], Mary[4], Catherine[3], Matthias[2], John Jacob[1]) was born May 15, 1934, at Glen Ridge, New Jersey.

4083 BILLY JANE CROSBY (Ralph[7], Janet[6], Catherine[5], Mary[4], Catherine[3], Matthias[2], John Jacob[1]) was born May 29, 1921, at Bramwell, West Virginia. She was educated at Mary Baldwin Primary School and Stuart Hall, Staunton, Virginia, and in the public schools of Richmond, Virginia. She graduated from Westhampton College, Richmond, with an A. B. degree in 1944. She was a member of Mortar Board and American Federation of University Women. After college she went into secretarial work.

4084 MARY BROOKS McCHESNEY (Francis[7], John[6], Mary[5], Eveline[4], Catherine[3], Matthias[2], John Jacob[1]) was born February 15, 1918, at Seattle, Washington. She married Lancaster Rigby Fontaine.

4085 JOHN TAYLOR McCHESNEY II (Francis[7], John[6], Mary[5], Eveline[4], Catherine[3], Matthias[2], John Jacob[1]) was born June 10, 1919. He married Alice Blake Bropy, May 26, 1943, at Phoenix, Arizona. Alice was the daughter of Frank Bropy and was born May 10, 1920, at Seattle, Washington.

4086 FRANCIS WILLIAM McCHESNEY, JR. (Francis[7], John[6], Mary[5], Eveline[4], Catherine[3], Matthias[2], John Jacob[1]) was born November 19, 1921, at Seattle, Washington. He married Jean Ellen Coghlan.

4087 HENRY P. SCOTT III (Virginia[7], John[6], Mary[5], Eveline[4], Catherine[3], Matthias[2], John Jacob[1]) was born January 5, 1916, at Wilmington, Delaware. He married Elizabeth Shepherd in March, 1943, at Wilmington.

4088 VIRGINIA SCOTT (Virginia[7], John[6], Mary[5], Eveline[4], Catherine[3], Matthias[2], John Jacob[1]) was born October 27, 1917, at Wilmington, Delaware. She married Edmund G. Laird in November, 1940, at Wilmington.

4089 MARY McCHESNEY SCOTT (Virginia[7], John[6], Mary[5], Eveline[4], Catherine[3], Matthias[2], John Jacob[1]) was born January 17, 1919, at Wilmington, Delaware. She married Edward C. Kirkpatrick in January, 1941, at Wilmington.

4090 MARGARET SCOTT (Virginia[7], John[6], Mary[5], Eveline[4], Catherine[3], Matthias[2], John Jacob[1]) was born December 11, 1920, at Wilmington, Delaware. She married Paul E. Wilson in April, 1940, at Wilmington.

4091 JACOB BAYLOR VAN METER, JR. (Jacob[6], Eveline[5], Eveline[4], Catherine[3], Matthias[2], John Jacob[1]) was born September 21, 1925, at Lexington, Kentucky.

4092 LOUISE BROWNELL VAN METER (Jacob[6], Eveline[5], Eveline[4], Catherine[3], Matthias[2], John Jacob[1]) was born November 17, 1928, at Lexington, Kentucky. She married Peter A. B. Widener III, October 24, 1947, at Lexington. Peter was the son of Peter A. B. Widener II and was born August 12, 1925, at New York, New York. Peter, besides other interests, had a well-known and large farm near Lexington which was famous for the thoroughbred horses that were bred and trained there.

4093 ELLISON VAN METER CAPERS (Margaret[7], Eveline[6], Catherine[5], Eveline[4], Catherine[3], Matthias[2], John Jacob[1]) was born March 30, 1919, at High River, Alberta, Canada. He married Rose Marie Doherty, August 26, 1946, at Leghorn, Italy.

(Sup) 6470   i   Ellison Douglas Capers, born September 5, 1947.

4094 BAYLOR VAN METER CAPERS (Margaret[7], Eveline[6], Catherine[5], Eveline[4], Catherine[3], Matthias[2], John Jacob[1]) was born June 7, 1921, at High River, Alberta, Canada. He married Eleanor Agnes Vail, December 21, 1946, at Poughkeepsie, New York. He studied law and graduated at the University of Virginia.

4095 MARGARET BAYLOR VAN METER CAPERS (Margaret[7], Eveline[6], Catherine[5], Eveline[4], Catherine[3], Matthias[2], John Jacob[1]) was born May 31, 1928, at High River, Alberta, Canada. She graduated from Vassar College.

4096 EVELYN SWOOPE BERRYMAN (Evelyn[7], Evaline[6], Margaret[5], Eveline[4], Catherine[3], Matthias[2], John Jacob[1]) was born June 18, 1921, at Lexington, Kentucky. She married Carlisle Kirkpatrick II, October 16, 1941, at Lexington. Carlisle, son of Carlisle and Lucy Haden Kirkpatrick, was born June 21, 1919, at Greenville, Kentucky.

(Sup) 6473   i   Carlisle Kirkpatrick III, born April 18, 1944.

4097 MARGARET BROWNELL BERRYMAN (Evelyn[7], Evaline[6], Margaret[5], Eveline[4], Catherine[3], Matthias[2], John Jacob[1]) was born October 13, 1927, at Lexington, Kentucky. She married William Hughes Bronston, Jr., December 19, 1947, at Lexington. William was the son of William and Nadine Snyder Bronston and was born at Lexington, Kentucky, February 25, 1923.

4098 FITZHUGH SCOTT, JR. (Ella[7], Charlotte[6], William[5], Eveline[4], Catherine[3], Matthias[2], John Jacob[1]) was born January 13, 1910, at Milwaukee, Wisconsin. He became an architect. Fitzhugh married Eileen Schlesinger, January 11, 1937, at Milwaukee. Eileen was the daughter of Arman and Kathleen McCullough Schlesinger and was born October 17, 1910, at Milwaukee.

(Sup) 6474   i   Fitzhugh Scott III, born December 27, 1937.
(Sup) 6475   ii   Eileen McGregor Scott, born December 27, 1938.
(Sup) 6476   iii Lorna Landrum Scott, born December 27, 1938.

4099 WILLIAM FREDERICK SCOTT (Ella[7], Charlotte[6], William[5], Eveline[4], Catherine[3], Matthias[2], John Jacob[1]) was born October 24, 1911, at Milwaukee, Wisconsin. He married Janet Blish, October 3, 1936, at Seymour, Indiana. Janet was born at Seymour, July 16, 1914. She was the daughter of Tipton and Agnes Andrews Blish. William was a Manager of Sales.

(Sup) 6477   i   Susan Fitzhugh Scott, born August 7, 1939.
(Sup) 6478   ii   Stuart Landrum Scott, born August 14, 1947.

4100 ELSIE WARREN SCOTT (Ella[7], Charlotte[6], William[5], Eveline[4], Catherine[3], Matthias[2], John Jacob[1]) was born June 10, 1914, at Milwaukee, Wisconsin. She married George William Fox, Jr., December 21, 1935. George was the son of George William and Mary Romadka Fox. He was born November 28, 1906, at Milwaukee, Wisconsin. After his graduation from college he studied medicine and received his M. D. degree. He entered the Navy at the beginning of World War II as a naval surgeon and was killed in action aboard the U. S. Carrier "Franklin" in the Pacific, March 19, 1945. Elsie married Robert Coleman Swansen, December 7, 1946. Robert was the son of Samuel T. and Jessie Nelson Swansen and was born July 18, 1915, at Madison, Wisconsin.

4101 BAYLOR LANDRUM, JR. (Baylor[7], Charlotte[6], William[5], Eveline[4], Catherine[3], Matthias[2], John Jacob[1]) was born November 1, 1918, at Louisville, Kentucky. He married Mary Wallis Evans, September 14, 1946, at Pineville, Kentucky. Mary was the daughter of Herndon J. and Mary Elizabeth Downing Evans and was born at Louisville, Kentucky, May 15, 1921.

(Sup) 6479   i   Baylor Landrum, III, born June 17, 1949.

4102 ROBERT K. LANDRUM (Baylor[7], Charlotte[6], William[5], Eveline[4], Catherine[3], Matthias[2], John Jacob[1]) was born November 7, 1922, at Lexington, Kentucky.

4103 JULIA GRINSTEAD LANDRUM (Baylor[7], Charlotte[6], William[5], Eveline[4], Catherine[3], Matthias[2], John Jacob[1]) was born August 31, 1924, at Louisville, Kentucky. Julia married Stanley Parker McGee, Jr., July 13, 1946, at Lexington, Kentucky. Stanley, son of Stanley Parker McGee, was born October 14, 1918, at Louisville.

(Sup) 6480 i Stanley Parker McGee, III, born February 13, 1947.
(Sup) 6481 ii Robert Baylor McGee, born November 1, 1948.

4104 STANLEY BRYCE JOHNSON, JR. (Mary[7], Charlotte[6], William[5], Eveline[4], Catherine[3], Matthias[2], John Jacob[1]) was born March 11, 1920, at Columbus, Ohio.

4105 CHARLOTTE BAYLOR JOHNSON (Mary[7], Charlotte[6], William[5], Eveline[4], Catherine[3], Matthias[2], John Jacob[1]) was born November 20, 1922, at Columbus, Ohio. She married William Harvey Barrett, March 27, 1943.

4106 TIMOTHY LANDRUM JOHNSON (Mary[7], Charlotte[6], William[5], Eveline[4], Catherine[3], Matthias[2], John Jacob[1]) was born November 13, 1930, at Columbus, Ohio.

4107 ERNESTINE HARRIS (Frank[7], Ida[6], Franklin[5], Adam[4], Adam[3], Matthias[2], John Jacob[1]). She married Harry W. Miller, April 30, 1927, at Covington, Indiana.

(Sup) 6482 i Elizabeth Ann Miller, born May 27, 1929.
(Sup) 6483 ii Harry W. Miller, Jr., born July 8, 1930.
(Sup) 6484 iii Frank Harris Miller, born January 5, 1933.

(Sup) 4108 ROBERT WILLIAMSON HARRIS, JR. (Robert[7], Ida[6], Franklin[5], Adam[4], Adam[3], Matthias[2], John Jacob[1]) was the son of Robert Williamson and Lydia Chambers Harris [The Link Family, page 597, No. 2510]. Robert, Jr., was born January 13, 1906, at Middleport, Ohio. He married Frances Faye Dye, June 15, 1939, at Pomeroy, Ohio. Frances was the daughter of Harry and Marjorie (Gilmore) Dye and was born September 29, 1912, at Harrisonville, Ohio. Robert and Frances resided at Columbus, Ohio, where he was an auditor. Frances was a graduate of Ohio University, where she was a member of Alpha Delta Pi sorority. She taught school at Grandview Heights near Columbus, Ohio, 1964-72. Frances died August 15, 1987.

(Sup) 6485 i Susan Dye Harris, born October 24, 1943.

(Sup) 4109 MARTHA MARJORIE HARRIS (Robert[7], Ida[6], Franklin[5], Adam[4], Adam[3], Matthias[2], John Jacob[1]) was the daughter of Robert Williamson and Lydia Chambers Harris [The Link Family, page 597, No. 2510]. Martha was born July 16, 1907, at Middleport, Ohio. She was a U.S. Government clerk at Washington, D.C. Martha died September 18, 1980, and is memorialized in Riverview Cemetery, Middleport, Ohio.

(Sup) 4110 GORDON KENNETH HARRIS (Robert[7], Ida[6], Franklin[5], Adam[4], Adam[3], Matthias[2], John Jacob[1]) was the son of Robert Williamson and Lydia Chambers Harris [The Link Family, page 597, No. 2510]. Gordon was born July 7, 1913, at Middleport, Ohio. He was a school administrator. He married Mary Eunice Hennesy June 4, 1939, at Middleport, Ohio. She was the daughter of Charles M. and Clara Crary Hennesy and was born November 23, 1918, at Middleport.

(Sup) 6486 i Gordon Kenneth Harris, Jr., born Oct 20, 1942.
(Sup) 6487 ii James Richard Harris, born August 28, 1946.

(Sup) 4111 EUGENE M. HARRIS (Robert[7], Ida[6], Franklin[5], Adam[4], Adam[3], Matthias[2], John Jacob[1]) was the son of Robert Williamson and Lydia Chambers Harris [The Link Family, page 597, No. 2510]. Eugene was born June 4, 1922, at Middleport, Ohio. He married Janet Hecox, December 27, 1946. She was the daughter of Raymond and Norma Lewis Hecox and was born January 21, 1923, at Columbus, Ohio. Eugene was an engineer.

(Sup) 6488 i Kenneth Eugene Harris, born March 13, 1948.
(Sup) 6489 ii Marjorie Ellen Harris, born October 25, 1949.
(Sup) 6490 iii Nancy Jean Harris, born May 21, 1951.
(Sup) 6491 iv Patricia Ann Harris, born April 5, 1954.
(Sup) 6492 v Robert Williamson Harris, born Feb 14, 1956.
(Sup) 6493 vi Kathryn Elizabeth Harris, born March 30, 1958.

(Sup) 4111A WALTER BURNS HARRIS (Walter[7], Ida[6], Franklin[5], Adam[4], Adam[3], Matthias[2], John Jacob[1]) was the fifth child of Walter Frazer and Mayme Burns Harris [The Link Family, page 597, No. 2511; and Supplement No. 2511]. Walter was born June 16, 1910, at Middleport, Ohio. He married Hilda J. Russell, October 29, 1936, at Pomeroy, Ohio. She was the daughter of Harry Andrew and Lula Hall Russell and was born August 27, 1911, at Clifton, West Virginia. Walter was engaged in various business enter- prises in the Middleport, Ohio area. He died October 18, 1971, and is buried in Sacred Heart Cemetery, Pomeroy, Ohio.

(Sup) 6494 i Jane Harris, born September 5, 1939.
(Sup) 6495 ii Catherine Jill Harris, born March 1, 1954.

(Sup) 4112 VIRGINIA ADELINE LINK (Paul[7], Herndon[6], Franklin[5], Adam[4], Adam[3], Matthias[2], John Jacob[1]) was the daughter of Paul Davis and Cora Morgan Link [The Link Family, page 597, No. 2513]. Virginia was born July 7, 1914, at Ronceverte, West Virginia. She married Russell Wilbur Johnson, July 18, 1936, at Ronceverte. Russell was born January 14, 1915, at Lawton, West Virginia, the son of Sidney F. and Eliza Johnson. Russell died July 26, 1978, and is buried in Riverview Cemetery, Roncevert, West Virginia.

(Sup) 6496 i Judith Lynn Johnson, born July 9, 1946.

(Sup) 4113   FRANCES PAULINE LINK (Paul[7], Herndon[6], Franklin[5], Adam[4], Adam[3], Matthias[2], John Jacob[1]) was the daughter of Paul Davis and Cora Morgan Link [The Link Family, page 597, No. 2513]. Frances was born April 19, 1917, at Ronceverte, West Virginia. She married, first, John William Wise, May 14, 1948, at Salem Virginia. John was the son of Robert Johnson and Virginia Marguerite Wise and was born October 18, 1911, at Ronceverte, West Virginia. She married, second, Perry William Baker, September 13, 1972, at Lewisburg, West Virginia. Perry was the son of William Lake and Maggie Cleveland (Clevie) Arbaugh Baker and was born April 29, 1913, at Fort Spring, West Virginia.

(Sup) 6497   1   Barbara Mary Frances Wise, born January 6, 1951.

(Sup) 4114   ROGER LEE LINK (Paul[7], Herndon[6], Franklin[5], Adam[4], Adam[3], Matthias[2], John Jacob[1]) was the son of Paul Davis and Cora Morgan Link [The Link Family, page 597, No. 2513]. Roger was born March 24, 1922, at Ronceverte, West Virginia. He married Ida Maxine Miller, July 3, 1943. Ida was the daughter of William Rufus and Mary Jane Miller and was born June 13, 1925, at Alderson, West Virginia. Roger died February 6, 1978, in Decatur, Georgia, and is buried at Riverview Cemetery, Ronceverte, West Virginia.

(Sup) 6498   1   Donna Lee Link, born January 24, 1944.
(Sup) 6499   11   Beverly Jean Link, born October 22, 1946.
(Sup) 6500   111 Martha Lou Link, born December 15, 1947.

(Sup) 4115   MARY LEE LINK (Gordon[7], Herndon[6], Franklin[5], Adam[4], Adam[3], Matthias[2], John Jacob[1]) was the daughter of Gordon Lee and Mary Littlepage Link [The Link Family, page 597, No. 2515]. Mary was born September 28, 1927, at Charles Town, West Virginia. She married Ashby Bridgforth Allen in 1950.

(Sup) 6501   1   Ashby Bridgforth Allen, Jr., born Mar. 18, 1951.
(Sup) 6501A   11   Rebecca Warren Allen, born May 27, 1952.
(Sup) 6501B   111 Charles Littlepage Allen, born Jun. 1, 1954.
(Sup) 6501C   1v   Mary Frances Allen, born Jun. 10, 1958.

(Sup) 4116   JOYCE WARREN LINK (Gordon[7], Herndon[6], Franklin[5], Adam[4], Adam[3], Matthias[2], John Jacob[1]) was the daughter of Gordon Lee and Mary Littlepage Link [The Link Family, page 597, No. 2515]. Joyce was born March 12, 1929, at Charleston, West Virginia. She married Armistead Taylor Harvie, Jr., May 16, 1953, at Richmond, Virginia. He was the son of Armistead and Alice Lee Harvie and was born December 14, 1922. He was a graduate of Virginia Military Institute in 1944. Joyce died March 18, 1973, and Armistead died September 5, 1974.

(Sup) 6502   1   Maria Warren Harvie, born June 8, 1955.
(Sup) 6502A   11   Armistead Taylor Harvie III, born Sept 26, 1956.
(Sup) 6502B   111 Gordon Link Harvie, born November 20, 1958.
(Sup) 6502C   1v   Lewis Edwin Harvie, born May 13, 1960.
(Sup) 6502D   v   Rebecca Littlepage Harvie, born Jan 10, 1972.

(Sup) 4117   GORDON LITTLEPAGE LINK (Gordon[7], Herndon[6], Franklin[5], Adam[4], Adam[3], Matthias[2], John Jacob[1]) was the son of Gordon Lee and Mary Littlepage Link [The Link Family, page 597, No. 2515]. He was born February 9, 1932, at Charleston, West Virginia. Gordon married Sarah Dean Spangler, June 1955.

(Sup) 6503   1   Gordon Lee Link, III, born August 8, 1963.

(Sup) 4118   REBECCA ELEANOR LINK (Gordon[7], Herndon[6], Franklin[5], Adam[4], Adam[3], Matthias[2], John Jacob[1]) was the daughter of Gordon Lee and Mary Littlepage Link [The Link Family, page 597, No. 2515]. Rebecca was born June 30, 1937, at Columbus, Ohio. She married, first, Charles Vincent Panettiere, July 9, 1960. Rebecca married, second, Kevin Rooney.

(Sup) 6504   1   Angela Kellett Panettiere, born May 4, 1961.
(Sup) 6504A   11   Tracy Lee Panettiere, born November 3, 1962.
(Sup) 6504B   111 Charles Link Panettiere, born August 10, 1967.

(Sup) 4119   MARY ALICE LINK (Arthur[7], James[6], James[5], Adam[4], Adam[3], Matthias[2], John Jacob[1]) was the daughter of Arthur Finley and Sarah Arnold Link [The Link Family, page 598, No. 2521]. Mary Alice was born December 14, 1933, at Atlanta, Georgia. She studied at Emory University, Atlanta. On May 20, 1947, Mary won the U.S. Junior National Swimming Championship in 220-yard free-style and broke the pool record in the All Southern 100-yard breast stroke. She also won the Senior A.A.U. 100-meter breast stroke at Athens, Georgia.

(Sup) 4120   JAMES ALLEN LINK IV (James[7], James[6], James[5], Adam[4], Adam[3], Matthias[2], John Jacob[1]) was the son of James Allen and Mary Thomas (Bethea) Link, III [The Link Family, page 598, No. 2523]. James, IV, was born March 4, 1942, at Corpus Christi, Texas.

(Sup) 4121   MARY CATHERINE LINK (James[7], James[6], James[5], Adam[4], Adam[3], Matthias[2], John Jacob[1]) was the daughter of James Allen and Mary Thomas (Bethea) Link, III [The Link Family, page 598, No. 2523]. Mary Catherine was born July 9, 1945, at Tampa, Florida.

(Sup) 4122   RUTH WAYNE RIPLEY (Allen[7], Fannie[6], James[5], Adam[4], Adam[3], Matthias[2], John Jacob[1]) was the daughter of Allen Weeks and Ruth Wayne (Williams) Ripley [The Link Family, page 599, No. 2524]. Ruth was born September 30, 1925, at Atlanta, Georgia. She married Foster Lalor in 1946.

4123 ALLEN WEEKS RIPLEY III (Allen^7, Fannie^6, James^5, Adam^4, Adam^3, Matthias^2, John Jacob^1) was the son of Allen Weeks and Ruth Wayne (Williams) Ripley [The Link Family, page 599, No. 2524]. Allen, III, was born November 16, 1926, at Atlanta, Georgia.

(Sup) 4124 DOROTHY ANNE RIPLEY (William^7, Fannie^6, James^5, Adam^4, Adam^3, Matthias^2, John Jacob^1) was the daughter of William Conner and Dorothy (Dickson) Ripley [The Link Family, page 599, No. 2525]. Dorothy was born in 1937.

(Sup) 4125 WILLIAM CONNER RIPLEY, JR. (William^7, Fannie^6, James^5, Adam,^{4}, Adam^3, Matthias^2, John Jacob^1) was the son of William Conner and Dorothy (Dickson) Ripley [The Link Family, page 599, No. 2525]. William, Jr., was born in 1941.

4126 FRANCIS MARTIN RIPLEY, JR. (Francis^7, Fannie^6, James^5, Adam^4, Adam^3, Matthias^2, John Jacob^1) was born March 14, 1942, at Atlanta, Georgia.

4127 MARY LILLIAN RIPLEY (Francis^7, Fannie^6, James^5, Adam^4, Adam^3, Matthias^2, John Jacob^1) was born March 14, 1943, at Atlanta, Georgia.

4128 GEORGE BREWSTER McCONNELL, JR. (Miriam^7, Roger^6, James^5, Adam^4, Adam^3, Matthias^2, John Jacob^1) was born July 19, 1930, at Tampa, Florida.

4129 OWEN LINK McCONNELL (Miriam^7, Roger^6, James^5, Adam^4, Adam^3, Matthias^2, John Jacob^1) was born July 8, 1933, at Tampa, Florida.

4130 NANCY JEAN McCONNELL (Miriam^7, Roger^6, James^5, Adam^4, Adam^3, Matthias^2, John Jacob^1) was born September 17, 1935, at Tampa, Florida.

(Sup) 4131 DENZIL MORTON FERGUSON, JR. (Mary^7, Alice^6, Samuel^5, Lewis^4, Christian^3, Matthias^2, John Jacob^1) was the son of Denzil Morton and Margaret Whitacre Ferguson [The Link Family, pages 599-600, No. 2532]. Denzil, Jr., was born February 13, 1918, at La Grange, Missouri. He married Eleanor Thomas, June 28, 1945. Eleanor was the daughter of Seth C. Thomas and was born September 24, 1923, at Kirksville, Missouri. Denzil graduated from the College of Osteopathy at Kirksville and established a practice with his father at Terre Haute, Indiana.

(Sup) 6506   i   Denzil Morton Ferguson, III, born Sep. 21, 1946.
(Sup) 6507   ii   Seth Thomas Ferguson, born Sep. 29, 1948.

(Sup) 4132 MARGARET LOUISE FERGUSON (Mary^7, Alice^6, Samuel^5, Lewis^4, Christian^3, Matthias^2, John Jacob^1) was the daughter of Denzil Morton and Margaret Whitacre Ferguson [The Link Family, pages 599-600, No. 2532]. Margaret was born October 29, 1919, at Kirksville, Missouri. She married Benjamin Crawford, Jr., December 27, 1947, at Terre Haute, Indiana. Benjamin was the son of Benjamin and Nell (Gregg) Crawford and was born at Terre Haute, June 26, 1919. Benjamin engaged in the insurance business at Terre Haute.

(Sup) 6508   i   Gregg Whitacre Crawford, born November 29, 1948.

(Sup) 4133 JAMES EDWARD WHITACRE (Marion^7, Alice^6, Samuel^5, Lewis^4, Christian^3, Matthias^2, John Jacob^1) was the son of Marion Edward and Alberta Wilson Whitacre [The Link Family, page 600, No. 2533]. James was born October 23, 1936, at Kirksville, Missouri.

(Sup) 4134 SARAH ALICE WHITACRE (Marion^1, Alice^6, Samuel^5, Lewis^4, Christian^3, Matthias^2, John Jacob^1) was the daughter of Marion Edward and Alberta Wilson Whitacre [The Link Family, page 600, No. 2533]. Sarah Alice was born November 19, 1940, at Kirksville, Missouri.

(Sup) 4135 EUGENE CROSS LINK (Vergil^7, Eugene^6, Samuel^5, Lewis^4, Christian^3, Matthias^2, John Jacob^1) was the son of Vergil Gentry and Doretta Gross Link [The Link Family, page 600, No. 2536]. Eugene was born May 10, 1918, at Stamford, Connecticut. He joined the U.S. Air Corps and graduated a pilot and commissioned second lieutenant in February, 1943, at Albany, Georgia. In August of that year he was promoted to first lieutenant and sent to the South Pacific as pilot of a Liberator B-24 bomber. He saw much action, fifty-five missions, in the Pacific theater and was decorated with the Distinguished Service Medal with several Oak Clusters. In August, 1944, he was promoted to captain and returned to the States as an instructor until the war's end. He was later promoted to major. On June 5, 1943, at Del Monte, California, he married Patricia Ann Smith. She was born January 19, 1920, at Portland, Oregon.

(Sup) 6509   i   Peter Jackson Link, born April 3, 1944.
(Sup) 6510   ii   Roger Mark Link, born September 22, 1946.

(Sup) 4136 MARY LOUISE LINK (Vergil^7, Eugene^6, Samuel^5, Lewis^4, Christian^3, Matthias^2, John Jacob^1) was the daughter of Vergil Gentry and Doretta Gross Link, III [The Link Family, page 600, No. 2536]. Mary was born August 24, 1920, at Stamford, Connecticut. She married George Ashton Pattison, November 17, 1945. He was born in June, 1916.

(Sup) 6511   i   Nancy Link Pattison, born April 15, 1947.

4137 JULIE ELIZABETH LINK (Vergil[7], Eugene[6], Samuel[5], Lewis[4], Christian[3], Matthias[2], John Jacob[1]) was born August 24, 1920, at Stamford, Connecticut. She married Stewart Lane Whitman, Jr., November 6, 1938. Stewart was born March 10, 1917.

(Sup) 6512   i   Elizabeth Emily Whitman, born August 2, 1939.
(Sup) 6513   ii Barbara Link Whitman, born November 30, 1940.

4138 SYBIL CLAIRBORNE LINK (Vergil[7], Eugene[6], Samuel[5], Lewis[4], Christian[3], Matthias[2], John Jacob[1]) was born March 7, 1929, at Stamford, Connecticut.

4139 PATRICIA ANN LINK (Samuel[7], Eugene[6], Samuel[5], Lewis[4], Christian[3], Matthias[2], John Jacob[1]) was born October 31, 1924, at Kirksville, Missouri. She married Robert Joseph Cavanaugh at Greeneville, South Carolina, May 1, 1944. Robert was the son of George H. Cavanaugh and was born March 10, 1919. He served overseas in World War II and was killed in action December 26, 1944. Patricia married Thomas Christopher Murphy, November 30, 1947. Thomas was born December 9, 1914, at New York, New York.

(Sup) 6514   i   Thomas Christopher Murphy, Jr., born Aug 26, 1948.

4140 SALLY ELIZABETH LINK (Samuel[7], Eugene[6], Samuel[5], Lewis[4], Christian[3], Matthias[2], John Jacob[1]) was born January 17, 1927, at Kirksville, Missouri. She married Robert Bilder, March 22, 1947. Robert was born in New York, New York.

4141 SAMUEL ADAMS LINK (Samuel[7], Eugene[6], Samuel[5], Lewis[4], Christian[3], Matthias[2], John Jacob[1]) was born June 29, 1932, at Stamford, Connecticut.

4142 WALKER GORDON LINK (Samuel[7], Eugene[6], Samuel[5], Lewis[4], Christian[3], Matthias[2], John Jacob[1]) was born August 11, 1934, at Stamford, Connecticut.

4143 RICHARD LINK TYERS III (Eugenia[7], Eugene[6], Samuel[5], Lewis[4], Christian[3], Matthias[2], John Jacob[1]) was born November 1, 1929, at Stamford, Connecticut.

4144 ROBERT DEWITT TYERS (Eugenia[7], Eugene[6], Samuel[5], Lewis[4], Christian[3], Matthias[2], John Jacob[1]) was born December 1, 1932, at Stamford, Connecticut.

4145 JEAN ELIZABETH TYERS (Eugenia[7], Eugene[6], Samuel[5], Lewis[4], Christian[3], Matthias[2], John Jacob[1]) was born February 17, 1937, at Stamford, Connecticut.

4146 FRANCES LYNNE TYERS (Eugenia[7], Eugene[6], Samuel[5], Lewis[4], Christian[3], Matthias[2], John Jacob[1]) was born September 30, 1941.

(Sup) 4147 JAMES EMMETT III (Frances[7], Elizabeth[6], Samuel[5], Lewis[4], Christian[3], Matthias[2], John Jacob[1]) was the son of James and Frances (Longpré) Emmett, Jr. [The Link Family, page 601, No. 2542]. James, III, was born February 22, 1940, at Hinsdale, Illinois. He married Judy Gibbs, August 25, 1962. She was born April 12, 1941.

(Sup) 6515   i   Thomas James Emmett.
(Sup) 6515A   ii Elizabeth Ann Emmett, born June 24, 1964.

(Sup) 4148 RICHARD LONGPRE EMMETT (Frances[7], Elizabeth[6], Samuel[5], Lewis[4], Christian[3], Matthias[2], John Jacob[1]) was the son of James and Frances (Longpré) Emmett [The Link Family, page 601, No. 2542]. Richard was born April 4, 1943, at Hinsdale, Illinois. He married Patricia Joanne Yeager, December 30, 1972.

(Sup) 6515B   i   Aspen Christine Emmett, born February 1, 1976.
(Sup) 6515C   ii   Hillary Leora Emmett, born June 14, 1978.
(Sup) 6515D   iii Bethany Yeager Emmett, born March 1, 1982.

(Sup) 4148A MARY SHAUN EMMETT (Frances[7], Elizabeth[6], Francis[5], Lewis[4], Christian[3], Matthias[2], John Jacob[1]) was the daughter of James and Frances (Longpré) Emmett, Jr. [The Link Family, page 601, No. 2543]. Mary was born November 9, 1950, at Hinsdale, Illinois.

(Sup) 4148B JEANNE LONGPRE GUNNING (Mary[7], Elizabeth[6], Francis[5], Lewis[4], Christian[3], Matthias[2], John Jacob[1]) was the daughter of Thomas David and Mary (Longpré) Gunning [The Link Family, page 601, No. 2546]. Jeanne was born October 27, 1952 (twin of David), at Chicago, Illinois. She married Kent McDaniel, June 23, 1983, at Hinsdale, Illinois. He was the son of Kelsey L. and Marguerite (Berning) McDaniel and was born August 9, 1951, at Douglas, Arizona. Kent was Project Director of Indiana University Institute for Urban Transportation and the Center for Transit Research and Management Development.

(Sup) 6516   i   Matthew Gunning McDaniel, born February 2, 1987.

(Sup) 4148C DAVID LAVERY GUNNING (Mary[7], Elizabeth[6], Francis[5], Lewis[4], Christian[3], Matthias[2], John Jacob[1]) was the son of Thomas David and Mary (Longpré) Gunning [The Link Family, page 601, No. 2546]. David was born October 27, 1952 (twin of Jeanne), at Chicago, Illinois. He died January 16, 1977.

4155 CARL PEOPLES SMYTHE (Carl[7], Agnes[6], Jane[5], Matthias[4], Christian[3], Matthias[2], John Jacob[1]) was born December 30, 1915. His wife's name was Mary Elizabeth.

(Sup) 6520 i Mary Elizabeth Smythe, born September 28, 1938.
(Sup) 6521 ii Carol Ann Smythe, born August 9, 1946.

4156 VERNE C. FRYKLUND, JR. (Adah[7], Agnes[6], Jane[5], Matthias[4], Christian[3], Matthias[2], John Jacob[1]) was born July 2, 1920. He married Shirley Marie Zimmerman.

(Sup) 6522 i Karen Inge Fryklund, born June 8, 1946.

4157 JOHN RICHARD FRYKLUND (Adah[7], Agnes[6], Jane[5], Matthias[4], Christian[3], Matthias[2], John Jacob[1]) was born September 17, 1921.

4158 KENNETH STRONG CAMPBELL (John[7], Agnes[6], Jane[5], Matthias[4], Christian[3], Matthias[2], John Jacob[1]) was born December 5, 1941, at Denver, Colorado.

4158A THOMAS EDWARD LINK (John[7], Thomas[6], John[5], Thomas[4], John[3], Matthias[2], John Jacob[1]) was born October 5, 1928, at Detroit, Michigan.

4159 DOROTHY JEAN MILLIKIN (Sara[7], Thomas[6], John[5], Thomas[4], John[3], Matthias[2], John Jacob[1]) was born October 11, 1931, in Grundy County, Iowa.

4160 KENT A. LINK (Thomas[7], Thomas[6], John[5], Thomas[4], John[3], Matthias[2], John Jacob[1]) was born February 25, 1935, at Algona, Iowa.

4161 KERMIT J. LINK (Thomas[7], Thomas[6], John[5], Thomas[4], John[3], Matthias[2], John Jacob[1]) was born February 25, 1935, at Algona, Iowa.

4162 THOMAS KLEMET LINK (Thomas[7], Thomas[6], John[5], Thomas[4], John[3], Matthias[2], John Jacob[1]) was born May 27, 1937, at Algona, Iowa.

4163 JULIAN THOMAS DIETER (Thelma[7], Nannie[6], John[5], Thomas[4], John[3], Matthias[2], John Jacob[1]) was born November 17, 1935, at Elizabeth, New Jersey.

4164 WILLIAM MICHAEL DIETER (Thelma[7], Nannie[6], John[5], Thomas[4], John[3], Matthias[2], John Jacob[1]) was born February 6, 1937, at Elizabeth, New Jersey.

4165 SUSAN KALE DIETER (Thelma[7], Nannie[6], John[5], Thomas[4], John[3], Matthias[2], John Jacob[1]) was born September 30, 1938, at Elizabeth, New Jersey.

4166 MARY RUTH DIETER (Thelma[7], Nannie[6], John[5], Thomas[4], John[3], Matthias[2], John Jacob[1]) was born May 10, 1941, at Elizabeth, New Jersey.

4167 BARBARA JEAN DIETER (Thelma[7], Nannie[6], John[5], Thomas[4], John[3], Matthias[2], John Jacob[1]) was born March 14, 1944, at Elizabeth, New Jersey.

(Sup) 41480 PATRICK JAMES GUNNING (Mary[7], Elizabeth[6], Francis[5], Lewis[4], Christian[3], Matthias[2], John Jacob[1]) was the son of Thomas David and Mary (Longpré) Gunning [The Link Family, page 601, No. 2546]. Patrick was born August 4, 1955, at Chicago, Illinois.

(Sup) 4149 MARY ELIZABETH LINK (Robert[7], Charles[6], Francis[5], Lewis[4], Christian[3], Matthias[2], John Jacob[1]) was the daughter of Robert Lewis and Mary Elizabeth (Garth) Link [The Link Family, page 602, No. 2556]. She was born March 12, 1936, at Jacksonville, Illinois.

(Sup) 4150 JULIA ANN LINK (Robert[7], Charles[6], Frances[5], Lewis[4], Christian[3], Matthias[2], John Jacob[1]) was the daughter of Robert Lewis and Mary Elizabeth (Garth) Link [The Link Family, page 602, No. 2556]. She was born January 13, 1941, at Kirksville, Missouri.

(Sup) 4151 CHARLES ROBERT LINK (Robert[7], Charles[6], Francis[5], Lewis[4], Christian[3], Matthias[2], John Jacob[1]) was the son of Robert Lewis and Mary Elizabeth (Garth) Link [The Link Family, page 602, No. 2556]. He was born December 8, 1944, at Kirksville, Missouri.

(Sup) 4152 GEORGANNA MUSSON (Anna[7], Charles[6], Francis[5], Lewis[4], Christian[3], Matthias[2], John Jacob[1]) was the daughter of Nelson Joseph and Anna Margaret (Link) Musson [The Link Family, page 602, No. 2557]. Georganna was born October 29, 1934, at Sandusky, Ohio.

(Sup) 4153 LINDA LOUISE MUSSON (Anna[7], Charles[6], Francis[5], Lewis[4], Christian[3], Matthias[2], John Jacob[1]) was the daughter of Nelson Joseph and Anna Margaet (Link) Musson [The Link Family, page 602, No. 2557]. Linda was born August 25, 1940, at Sandusky, Ohio.

(Sup) 4154 PATRICIA ELIZABETH BAUGHMAN (Mary[7], Sarah[6], John[5], Matthias[4], John Jacob[1]) was the daughter of John Joseph and Mary Elma (Langdon) Baughman [The Link Family, page 603, No. 2570]. Patricia was born February 8, 1921. She married Donald James Monson, June 4, 1939.

(Sup) 6517 i David Clay Monson, born October 27, 1941.
(Sup) 6518 ii Mary Louise Monson, born October 2, 1944.
(Sup) 6519 iii Diana Lynn Monson, born May 28, 1949.

4168 CATHERINE DIETER (Thelma[7], Nannie[6], John[5], Thomas[4], John[3], Matthias[2], John Jacob[1]) was born November 26, 1945, at Elizabeth, New Jersey.

4169 GORDON WYATT WILES (Mary[7], Mary[6], Leonidas[5], Thomas[4], John[3], Matthias[2], John Jacob[1]) was the son of Ivan L. and Mary Wyatt Wiles [The Link Family, page 605, No. 2590]. Gordon was born June 20, 1929, at Pontiac, Michigan. He attended Wabash College, where he was a member of Beta Theta Pi fraternity. Gordon married Eve Hunter, July 1955. They lived at Los Angeles, California, where he was a television and movie director.

(Sup) 6522A i Wendy Hunter Wiles, born February 12, 1955.
(Sup) 6522B ii Gordon Wyatt Wiles, Jr., born January 9, 1960.

4170 MARTHA LINK WILES (Mary[7], Mary[6], Leonidas[5], Thomas[4], John[3], Matthias[2], John Jacob[1]) was the daughter of Ivan L. and Mary Wyatt Wiles [The Link Family, page 605, No. 2590; and Supplement No. 2590]. Martha was born June 15, 1935, at Flint, Michigan. She received a B.A. degree in 1958 from the University of Michigan, where she was a member of Kappa Alpha Theta sorority. Martha married David Christian Krimendahl, May 9, 1959. He was the son of Herbert Frederick and Mary Bess (Christian) Krimendahl and was born November 29, 1926, at Cincinnati, Ohio. David graduated from the U.S. Military Academy in 1949. He served as a pilot in the Korean War with the 17th Bomber Wing, where he received an Air Medal and the Distinguished Flying Cross. He was later employed with Stokely Van Camp, Indianapolis.

(Sup) 6522C i Elizabeth Link Krimendahl, born April 14, 1960.
(Sup) 6522D ii David Christian Krimendahl, Jr., born February 22, 1962.
(Sup) 6522E iii Mary Katrine Krimendahl, born October 17, 1964.

4171 JOHN LINK WYATT (John[7], Mary[6], Leonidas[5], Thomas[4], John[3], Matthias[2], John Jacob[1]) was the son of John Burt and Catherine (Willis) Wyatt [The Link Family, page 605, No. 2591]. John was born August 15, 1936, at Crawfordsville, Indiana. He married Beverly Campbell, September 5, 1965. She was the daughter of Robert and Ruth Campbell and was born January 29, 1944, at Crawfordsville. John was a district agent for Northwestern Mutual Life Insurance Company. He was a member of Beta Theta Pi fraternity, an elder in the Presbyterian Church, and active in the Boy Scout movement.

(Sup) 6522F i Marabeth Link Wyatt, born February 19, 1970.
(Sup) 6522G ii John Campbell Wyatt, born July 10, 1973.

4172 CONSTANCE WYATT (John[7], Mary[6], Leonidas[5], Thomas[4], John[3], Matthias[2], John Jacob[1]) daughter of John Burt and Catherine (Willis) Wyatt [The Link Family, page 605, No. 2591]. Constance was born July 13, 1939, at Crawfordsville, Indiana. She attended Indiana University, where she was a member of Kappa Kappa Gamma, and she worked in real estate at Carmel, Indiana. Constance married Mason Crocker Price, June 16, 1962. He was the son of Delmas and Hila Price and was born November 15, 1937.

(Sup) 6522H i Adam Crocker Price, born July 31, 1966.
(Sup) 6522J ii Mason Wyatt Price, born November 4, 1968.

4173 PHILLIP WARDER WYATT (John[7], Mary[6], Leonidas[5], Thomas[4], John[3], Matthias[2], John Jacob[1]) son of John Burt and Catherine (Willis) Wyatt [The Link Family, page 605, No. 2591]. Phillip was born April 9, 1943, at Crawfordsville, Indiana. He graduated from Dennison University, where he was a member of Sigma Alpha Epsilon fraternity. He was vice president and general manager of Migada Ltd. at Glendale, California. Phillip married Cythia. She was born April 9, 1954.

(Sup) 5622K i Michael P. Wyatt, born November 4, 1986.

4174 BEVERLY JEANNE BROWN (James[7], Albert[6], Clomanthe[5], Ephraim[4], John[3], Matthias[2], John Jacob[1]) was born July 19, 1924, at Keokuk, Iowa. She married Matthew J. Bonas, Jr., September 22, 1945. Matthew, son of Matthew J. Bonas, was born September 22, 1921.

(Sup) 6523 i Melinda Bonas, born June 11, 1946.

4175 ROBERT HAYNES BROWN (James[7], Albert[6], Clomanthe[5], Ephraim[4], John[3], Matthias[2], John Jacob[1]) was born June 13, 1925, at Keokuk, Iowa.

4176 WARREN J. HUGHES, JR. (Louise[7], Albert[6], Clomanthe[5], Ephraim[4], John[3], Matthias[2], John Jacob[1]) was born November 25, 1932, at New Haven, Connecticut.

4177 RICHARD BROWN HUGHES (Louise[7], Albert[6], Clomanthe[5], Ephraim[4], John[3], Matthias[2], John Jacob[1]) was born April 21, 1935, at New Haven, Connecticut.

4178 BONNIE RACHEL STUDEBAKER (Marion[7], Bonnie[6], Emma[5], Mary[4], John[3], Matthias[2], John Jacob[1]) was born December 25, 1916, at Des Moines, Iowa. She married Ernest Renner, January 4, 1943. Ernest was born at Altoona, Pennsylvania, in 1912.

(Sup) 6524 i Patricia Diana Renner, born June 21, 1945.

4179 NANCY ALICE STUDEBAKER (Marion[7], Bonnie[6], Emma[5], Mary[4], John[3], Matthias[2], John Jacob[1]) was born June 17, 1921. She became a graduate nurse and lived in Honolulu.

4180 ROBERT S. MILNUE, JR. (Marion[7], Bonnie[6], Emma[5], Mary[4], John[3], Matthias[2], John Jacob[1]) was born January 19, 1928. He served in the U. S. Navy in World War II.

4181 JAMES AUSTEN MORRISON (Martha[7], Bonnie[6], Emma[5], Mary[4], John[3], Matthias[2], John Jacob[1]) was born August 7, 1925, at Honduras, Central America. He was an ensign in the U. S. Navy in World War II.

4182 ANNE MORRISON (Martha[7], Bonnie[6], Emma[5], Mary[4], John[3], Matthias[2], John Jacob[1]) was born November 12, 1931, at Greensburg, Indiana.

4183 MARION GIRDNER THACKER (Anna[7], Bonnie[6], Emma[5], Mary[4], John[3], Matthias[2], John Jacob[1]) was born November 29, 1935, at Memphis, Tennessee.

4184 MARTHA IDORA THACKER (Anna[7], Bonnie[6], Emma[5], Mary[4], John[3], Matthias[2], John Jacob[1]) was born April 21, 1940, at Atlanta, Georgia.

4185 MARY ETHEL THACKER (Anna[7], Bonnie[6], Emma[5], Mary[4], John[3], Matthias[2], John Jacob[1]) was born April 21, 1940, at Atlanta, Georgia.

4186 LAURIE MAY BUHRER (Edith[7], Penelope[6], John[5], Mary[4], John[3], Matthias[2], John Jacob[1]) was born May 10, 1934, at New York, New York.

4187 ELIZABETH ANN LINK FLANAGAN (Grace[7], Grace[6], Henry[5], Henry[4], John[3], Matthias[2], John Jacob[1]) was born February 10, 1944, at Palestine, Texas.

4188 JAMES ROLLIE CHITTICK (Gerayne[7], Rollie[6], Mary[5], Harvey[4], John[3], Matthias[2], John Jacob[1]) was born May 23, 1939.

4189 STEPHANIE ANN CHITTICK (Gerayne[7], Rollie[6], Mary[5], Harvey[4], John[3], Matthias[2], John Jacob[1]) was born March 2, 1947.

4190 DUANE LLOYD CRAWFORD (Lloyd[7], Sidney[6], Mary[5], Harvey[4], John[3], Matthias[2], John Jacob[1]) was born October 6, 1939, at Omaha, Nebraska.

4191 TERRY JOE LINK (Robert[7], Leonard[6], Leonidas[5], Harvey[4], John[3], Matthias[2], John Jacob[1]) was born October 5, 1943, at Denver, Colorado.

4192 PENELOPE RAE LINK (Robert[7], Leonard[6], Leonidas[5], Harvey[4], John[3], Matthias[2], John Jacob[1]) was born February 8, 1946, at Denver, Colorado.

4193 ROLAND DICKES (Theodore[7], Mabel[6], Leonidas[5], Harvey[4], John[3], Matthias[2], John Jacob[1]) was born August 3, 1940, at Silverton, Oregon.

4194 BEVERLY DICKES (Theodore[7], Mabel[6], Leonidas[5], Harvey[4], John[3], Matthias[2], John Jacob[1]) was born February 13, 1942, at Randolph, Nebraska.

4195 DAVID DICKES (Theodore[7], Mabel[6], Leonidas[5], Harvey[4], John[3], Matthias[2], John Jacob[1]) was born March 10, 1947, at Harlan, Iowa.

4196 GARY LEE DICKES (Leo[7], Mabel[6], Leonidas[5], Harvey[4], John[3], Matthias[2], John Jacob[1]) was born February 22, 1944, at Randolph, Nebraska.

4197 JEROME LINN DICKES (Leo[7], Mabel[6], Leonidas[5], Harvey[4], John[3], Matthias[2], John Jacob[1]) was born January 28, 1946, at Randolph, Nebraska.

4198 SHARON KAY DICKES (Leo[7], Mabel[6], Leonidas[5], Harvey[4], John[3], Matthias[2], John Jacob[1]) was born October 9, 1947, at Randolph, Nebraska.

4199 ALLEN LEROY DICKES (Raymond[7], Mabel[6], Leonidas[5], Harvey[4], John[3], Matthias[2], John Jacob[1]) was born August 4, 1943, at Coleridge, Nebraska.

4200 BARBARA LOUISE DICKES (Raymond[7], Mabel[6], Leonidas[5], Harvey[4], John[3], Matthias[2], John Jacob[1]) was born November 24, 1946, at Bellevue, Nebraska.

4201 LAWRENCE RAYMOND DICKES (Raymond[7], Mabel[6], Leonidas[5], Harvey[4], John[3], Matthias[2], John Jacob[1]) was born March 19, 1948, at Blair, Nebraska.

4202 JUDY ANN DICKES (Eugene[7], Mabel[6], Leonidas[5], Harvey[4], John[3], Matthias[2], John Jacob[1]) was born November 13, 1947, at Harlan, Iowa.

4203 MARGERY KAY DICKES (Herbert[7], Gladys[6], Leonidas[5], Harvey[4], John[3], Matthias[2], John Jacob[1]) was born January 9, 1943, at Long Beach, California.

4204 ALBERT ALLEN PARVU (Loretta[7], Gladys[6], Leonidas[5], Harvey[4], John[3], Matthias[2], John Jacob[1]) was born May 18, 1938, at Sioux City, Iowa.

4205 ROBERTA RAE PARVU (Loretta[7], Gladys[6], Leonidas[5], Harvey[4], John[3], Matthias[2], John Jacob[1]) was born September 1, 1940, at Sioux City, Iowa.

4206 ROCHELLE MAE PARVU (Loretta[7], Gladys[6], Leonidas[5], Harvey[4], John[3], Matthias[2], John Jacob[1]) was born November 9, 1942, at Sioux City, Iowa.

4207 RICHARD HENRY SCOTT (Mildred[7], Gladys[6], Leonidas[5], Harvey[4], John[3], Matthias[2], John Jacob[1]) was born October 30, 1942, at Sioux City, Iowa.

4208 DOROTHY IRENE SCOTT (Mildred[7], Gladys[6], Leonidas[5], Harvey[4], John[3], Matthias[2], John Jacob[1]) was born October 29, 1945, at Sioux City, Iowa.

4209 DOUGLAS RAY STOUT (Alverna[7], Ethel[6], Leonidas[5], Harvey[4], John[3], Matthias[2], John Jacob[1]) was born September 4, 1938, at Huntington, Oregon. He died May 14, 1941, at Baker, Oregon.

4210 PHYLLIS KAREN STOUT (Alverna[7], Ethel[6], Leonidas[5], Harvey[4], John[3], Matthias[2], John Jacob[1]) was born January 27, 1940, at Huntington, Oregon.

4211 DONALD GALEN STOUT (Alverna[7], Ethel[6], Leonidas[5], Harvey[4], John[3], Matthias[2], John Jacob[1]) was born July 7, 1941, at Huntington, Oregon.

4212 GENA ANNE STOUT (Alverna[7], Ethel[6], Leonidas[5], Harvey[4], John[3], Matthias[2], John Jacob[1]) was born July 7, 1948, at Boise, Idaho.

4213 LUELLA BETTIE SMITH (Lulu[7], Elizabeth[6], Felix[5], David[4], Elizabeth[3], Matthias[2], John Jacob[1]) was born December 25, 1892, in Knox County, Tennessee. She married John R. Walker, June 15, 1924. John was born September 22, 1891.
(Sup) 6525   i Vernon Allison Walker, born April 10, 1925.
(Sup) 6526   ii Emma Jenevra Walker, born September 23, 1928.

4214 HUEBERT BROWN SMITH (Lulu[7], Elizabeth[6], Felix[5], David[4], Elizabeth[3], Matthias[2], John Jacob[1]) was born October 13, 1894, in Knox County, Tennessee, where he died July 28, 1896.

4215 GEORGE ARNOLD SMITH (Lulu[7], Elizabeth[6], Felix[5], David[4], Elizabeth[3], Matthias[2], John Jacob[1]) was born October 24, 1900, in Knox County, Tennessee. He died there September 1, 1919.

4216 HELEN IRENE SMITH (Lulu[7], Elizabeth[6], Felix[5], David[4], Elizabeth[3], Matthias[2], John Jacob[1]) was born November 22, 1903, in Knox County, Tennessee.

4217 HARRY PERRY SMITH (Lulu[7], Elizabeth[6], Felix[5], David[4], Elizabeth[3], Matthias[2], John Jacob[1]) was born April 21, 1913, in Knox County, Tennessee. He died there September 20, 1913.

4218 FLOYD RUGGLES (Carrie[7], Elizabeth[6], Felix[5], David[4], Elizabeth[3], Matthias[2], John Jacob[1]) was born April 2, 1898, in Knox County, Tennessee. He died there the same day.

4219 ELAH MAY RUGGLES (Carrie[7], Elizabeth[6], Felix[5], David[4], Elizabeth[3], Matthias[2], John Jacob[1]) was born January 23, 1900, in Knox County, Tennessee.

4220 JOHN MORRIS RUGGLES (Carrie[7], Elizabeth[6], Felix[5], David[4], Elizabeth[3], Matthias[2], John Jacob[1]) was born July 15, 1902, in Knox County, Tennessee. He married Lola Mae Caldwell, March 20, 1926, in Knox County, Tennessee.
(Sup) 6527   i Clyde Lowe Ruggles, born August 14, 1930.

4221 NINA ALLENA RUGGLES (Carrie[7], Elizabeth[6], Felix[5], David[4], Elizabeth[3], Matthias[2], John Jacob[1]) was born May 9, 1905, in Knox County, Tennessee. She married Orville Edgar Caldwell, June 16, 1923, in Knox County.
(Sup) 6528   i Carl Leonard Caldwell, born April 25, 1925.
(Sup) 6529   ii Betty Jo Caldwell, born July 10, 1927.
(Sup) 6530   iii William Howard Caldwell, born November 30, 1929.

4222 JAMES WESLEY RUGGLES (Carrie[7], Elizabeth[6], Felix[5], David[4], Elizabeth[3], Matthias[2], John Jacob[1]) was born September 23, 1908, in Knox County, Tennessee.

4223 WILLIAM FRANKLIN RUGGLES (Carrie[7], Elizabeth[6], Felix[5], David[4], Elizabeth[3], Matthias[2], John Jacob[1]) was born May 14, 1911, in Knox County, Tennessee.

4224 OLLIE AGNES RUGGLES (Carrie[7], Elizabeth[6], Felix[5], David[4], Elizabeth[3], Matthias[2], John Jacob[1]) was born May 16, 1914, in Knox County, Tennessee.

4225 KATHERINE BELLE RUGGLES (Carrie[7], Elizabeth[6], Felix[5], David[4], Elizabeth[3], Matthias[2], John Jacob[1]) was born June 1, 1917, in Knox County, Tennessee.

4226 PETER DAVIS RUGGLES (Carrie[7], Elizabeth[6], Felix[5], David[4], Elizabeth[3], Matthias[2], John Jacob[1]) was born October 6, 1920, in Knox County, Tennessee.

4227 NOLA JUNE RUGGLES (Carrie[7], Elizabeth[6], Felix[5], David[4], Elizabeth[3], Matthias[2], John Jacob[1]) was born July 10, 1922, in Knox County, Tennessee.

4228 CHARLES ERNEST CATE (Mary[7], Elizabeth[6], Felix[5], David[4], Elizabeth[3], Matthias[2], John Jacob[1]) was born August 16, 1907, in Knox County, Tennessee. He married Ina Jolly, November 1, 1926, in Knox County.
(Sup) 6531   i   Charles Edgar Cate, born October 9, 1927.
(Sup) 6532   ii William Horace Cate, born July 20, 1929.
(Sup) 6533   iii Mary Ellen Cate, born January 15, 1930.

4229 HOMER ARVEL CATE (Mary[7], Elizabeth[6], Felix[5], David[4], Elizabeth[3], Matthias[2], John Jacob[1]) was born March 12, 1911, in Knox County, Tennessee.

4230 WILLIE LEOLA CATE (Mary[7], Elizabeth[6], Felix[5], David[4], Elizabeth[3], Matthias[2], John Jacob[1]) was born June 28, 1913, in Knox County, Tennessee.

4231 HORACE EDGAR CATE (Mary[7], Elizabeth[6], Felix[5], David[4], Elizabeth[3], Matthias[2], John Jacob[1]) was born June 4, 1919.

4232 FREDERICK ROTH CHANDLER (Murta[7], William[6], Felix[5], David[4], Elizabeth[3], Matthias[2], John Jacob[1]) was born September 14, 1900, at Knoxville, Tennessee. He married Frances Katherine Aaron, August 8, 1935. Frances was the daughter of John Marshall Aaron and was born November 12, 1911.
(Sup) 6534   i Evelyn Ann Chandler, born June 16, 1936.

4233 HARRY HOUSTON CHANDLER (Murta[7], William[6], Felix[5], David[4], Elizabeth[3], Matthias[2], John Jacob[1]) was born May 22, 1906, at Knoxville, Tennessee. He married Stella Scheyer, September 14, 1934, at New Orleans, Louisiana. Stella was born September 14, 1912. She was the daughter of S. O. Scheyer. Harry married Pauline Elizabeth Cooke, December 1, 1938, at Rossville, Georgia. Pauline was the daughter of Bose Cooke. She died at Chattanooga, Tennessee, in 1940. Harry married Mary Elizabeth Martin at Nashville, Tennessee, in July, 1942.

4234 CHARLES FRANKLIN WAYLAND, JR. (Charles[7], William[6], Felix[5], David[4], Elizabeth[3], Matthias[2], John Jacob[1]) was born February 28, 1909, at Birmingham, Alabama. He married Margaret Luttrell Mitchell, October 9, 1934. Margaret was the daughter of Charles M. Mitchell and was born March 19, 1910, at Knoxville, Tennessee. Charles served in the U. S. Army during World War II, twenty-one months of his duty being overseas in Ireland, England and North Africa. He was returned to the States and appointed Director of Training at Camp Lee, Virginia, where he was also a Staff Officer with the rank of Major. He won the European, African, Middle Eastern, American Defense and Service medals. He lived at Knoxville and became Commissioner of Roads for the State of Tennessee in 1948.
(Sup) 6535   i Mary Goodman Wayland, born July 15, 1938.
(Sup) 6536   ii Jennie Luttrell Wayland, born November 16, 1942.

4235 BENJAMIN JACKSON WAYLAND (Charles7, William6, Felix5, David4, Elizabeth3, Matthias2, John Jacob1) was born September 25, 1910, at Knoxville, Tennessee. He married Argus Artilla Huffacre, August 2, 1940. Argus, daughter of Elmer R. Huffacre, was born April 24, 1919.

(Sup) 6537   i   Benjamin Jackson Wayland, Jr., born Aug 2, 1940.
(Sup) 6538   ii   William Frazier Wayland, born January 12, 1942.
(Sup) 6539   iii Bobbie Jean Wayland, born June 18, 1943.

4236 HERMAN HOUSTON WAYLAND (Charles7, William6, Felix5, David4, Elizabeth3, Matthias2, John Jacob1) was born January 10, 1913, at Knoxville, Tennessee. He married Anna Lou Thompson, December 15, 1934. On January 16, 1938, he married Virginia Lee Weber. Virginia was born at Denver, Colorado. During World War II Herman joined the U. S. Navy, serving from November 10, 1942, until January 2, 1946.

(Sup) 6540   i   Herman Houston Wayland, Jr., born Sep 28, 1939.
(Sup) 6541   ii   Marion Lee Wayland, born October 15, 1940.

4237 CLIFFORD HYDER WAYLAND (Charles7, William6, Felix5, David4, Elizabeth3, Matthias2, John Jacob1) was born November 27, 1914, at Knoxville, Tennessee. He married Mary Emma Perry, September 2, 1938, at Knoxville. Mary was the daughter of George Sergeant Perry and was born November 11, 1916, in York County, Pennsylvania. Clifford was a Major of Artillery in World War II and served from February 25, 1941, to March 12, 1946—eighteen months of this period overseas. He was with Headquarters Group of 191st Field Artillery. He won Occupational Specialty Supply and Evacuation Staff Officer. He won the American Theater Medal, World War II Victory Medal, Philippine Liberation Medal with one Bronze Star for Lingayen Gulf, Asiatic Theater Medal with three Bronze Stars for Northern Butian, New Guinea and Philippine campaigns.

(Sup) 6542   i   Stephenia Carol Wayland, born May 2, 1942.
(Sup) 6543   ii   Gregory Sergeant Wayland, born October 15, 1946.
(Sup) 6544   iii Eric Richard Wayland, born October 15, 1946.

4238 HARRY RICHARD WAYLAND (Charles7, William6, Felix5, David4, Elizabeth3, Matthias2, John Jacob1) was born May 22, 1919, at Knoxville, Tennessee. He was a pilot, with rank of First Lieutenant, of a B-17 bomber in World War II and was killed in a crash at Church Lawford, England, June 14, 1944. He was commissioned September 29, 1942, having enlisted in August, 1940. His overseas service began April 27, 1943, with the 96th Bombardment Group, Eighth Bomber Command, Eighth Air Force. His citations were the Air Medal, June 10, 1943; Oak Leaf Cluster, October 16, 1943; Oak Leaf Cluster, August, 1943; Oak Leaf Cluster, September 7, 1943, and Distinguished Flying Cross, November 5, 1943.

4239 ERNEST TEDFORD WAYLAND (Charles7, William6, Felix5, David4, Elizabeth3, Matthias2, John Jacob1) was born June 22, 1923, at Knoxville, Tennessee. He married Beulah Butler Denton, May 11, 1946.

4240 ANNA CATHERINE WAYLAND (Charles7, William6, Felix5, David4, Elizabeth3, Matthias2, John Jacob1) was born July 31, 1928, at Knoxville, Tennessee.

4241 WANITA ELIZABETH GRIFFIN (Annie7, William6, Felix5, David4, Elizabeth3, Matthias2, John Jacob1) was born February 22, 1900, at Knoxville, Tennessee. She married Horace Lenard Waters, October 16, 1919, at Knoxville. Horace was the son of John Wesley Waters and was born April 27, 1899, at Knoxville. Wanita died December 21, 1927, at Knoxville, Tennessee.

(Sup) 6545   i   Dorothy Lavern Waters, born August 16, 1921.
(Sup) 6546   ii   John Franklin Waters, born December 17, 1922.
(Sup) 6547   iii Barbara June Waters, born May 20, 1926.

4242 LILLIAN CHRISTINE GRIFFIN (Annie7, William6, Felix5, David4, Elizabeth3, Matthias2, John Jacob1) was born May 12, 1902, at Knoxville, Tennessee. She married James Douglass Flynn, August 29, 1919, at Knoxville. James was born April 7, 1900. In November, 1946, Lillian married Carl Dunn.

(Sup) 6548   i   James Douglass Flynn, Jr., born August 27, 1920.

4243 FRANK WAYLAND GRIFFIN (Annie7, William6, Felix5, David4, Elizabeth3, Matthias2, John Jacob1) was born August 30, 1904, at Knoxville, Tennessee. He married Annie Lee Edwards, November 25, 1925, at Knoxville, Tennessee. Annie was born March 15, 1905.

(Sup) 6549   i   Joycelyn Lee Griffin, born January 2, 1927.
(Sup) 6550   ii   Ote Edward Griffin, born October 15, 1929.

4244 WILLIAM CLABORN GRIFFIN (Annie7, William6, Felix5, David4, Elizabeth3, Matthias2, John Jacob1) was born August 3, 1907, at Knoxville, Tennessee. He married Lennis Haggard, July 2, 1930, at Knoxville. Lennis was born at Knoxville, February 8, 1906.

(Sup) 6551   i   Gordon Gene Griffin, born February 27, 1931.
(Sup) 6552   ii   Nanette Griffin, born December 15, 1932.

4245 JAMES LAFAYETTE GRIFFIN (Annie7, William6, Felix5, David4, Elizabeth3, Matthias2, John Jacob1) was born July 17, 1910, at Knoxville, Tennessee. He married Alice Elizabeth Leedy, December 31, 1935. Alice was the daughter of Charles Allen Leedy and was born May 17, 1910.

4246 ROY CLIFTON GRIFFIN (Annie7, William6, Felix5, David4, Elizabeth3, Matthias2, John Jacob1) was born March 6, 1916, at Knoxville, Tennessee.

4247 HOWARD MAYNARD WAYLAND (William7, William6, Felix5, David4, Elizabeth3, Matthias2, John Jacob1) was born June 16, 1922, at Knoxville, Tennessee. He served in the U. S. Army during World War II.

4248 BETTIE LOUISE WAYLAND (William7, William6, Felix5, David4, Elizabeth3, Matthias2, John Jacob1) was born February 26, 1924, at Knoxville, Tennessee.

4249 GLENN HEATH WHITE (Mary[7], William[6], Felix[5], David[4], Elizabeth[3], Matthias[2], John Jacob[1]) was born December 20, 1902, at Knoxville, Tennessee. He married Carrie Lee Pickell, November 22, 1922. Carrie was born August 9, 1904, at Knoxville, Tennessee.

(Sup) 6553   † Jack Edward White, born November 22, 1923.
(Sup) 6554   †† Dorothy Elizabeth White, born April 18, 1926.

4250 CHARLES LEE WHITE (Mary[7], William[6], Felix[5], David[4], Elizabeth[3], Matthias[2], John Jacob[1]) was born June 12, 1905, at Knoxville, Tennessee. He married Mary Eleanor Griffin, June 12, 1929, at Knoxville. Mary was the daughter of J. D. Griffin and was born at Knoxville.

4251 JOSEPH WAYLAND WHITE (Mary[7], William[6], Felix[5], David[4], Elizabeth[3], Matthias[2], John Jacob[1]) was born August 11, 1907, at Knoxville, Tennessee.

4252 KATHERINE EVELYN WHITE (Mary[7], William[6], Felix[5], David[4], Elizabeth[3], Matthias[2], John Jacob[1]) was born February 26, 1910, at Knoxville, Tennessee.

4253 EDWARD JUDSON WHITE, JR. (Mary[7], William[6], Felix[5], David[4], Elizabeth[3], Matthias[2], John Jacob[1]) was born March 21, 1916, at Knoxville, Tennessee.

4254 WANDA ROSE WHITE (Mary[7], William[6], Felix[5], David[4], Elizabeth[3], Matthias[2], John Jacob[1]) was born July 22, 1921, at Knoxville, Tennessee.

4255 RUTH CATHERINE WAYLAND (Addlebert[7], William[6], Felix[5], David[4], Elizabeth[3], Matthias[2], John Jacob[1]) was born November 29, 1913.

4256 VIRGINIA JANE WAYLAND (Addlebert[7], William[6], Felix[5], David[4], Elizabeth[3], Matthias[2], John Jacob[1]) was born June 10, 1917.

4257 HELEN McIVOR WAYLAND (Addlebert[7], William[6], Felix[5], David[4], Elizabeth[3], Matthias[2], John Jacob[1]) was born February 7, 1919.

4258 WILLIFORD WAYLAND (Benjamin[7], William[6], Felix[5], David[4], Elizabeth[3], Matthias[2], John Jacob[1]) was born September 12, 1912, at Knoxville, Tennessee.

4259 ELIZABETH GERTRUDE WAYLAND (Lloyd[7], William[6], Felix[5], David[4], Elizabeth[3], Matthias[2], John Jacob[1]) was born March 8, 1924.

4260 HUBERT WEIR NEUBERT (Appilonia[7], James[6], Felix[5], David[4], Elizabeth[3], Matthias[2], John Jacob[1]) was born October 5, 1896, in Knox County, Tennessee. He married Katie Lucile Fisher, May 22, 1927, in Knox County. Katie was the daughter of William Fisher and was born September 4, 1893, in Knox County, Tennessee.

4261 GRACE WILHELMINA NEUBERT (Appilonia[7], James[6], Felix[5], David[4], Elizabeth[3], Matthias[2], John Jacob[1]) was born June 5, 1898, in Knox County, Tennessee.

4262 EARNEST VANCE NEUBERT (Appilonia[7], James[6], Felix[5], David[4], Elizabeth[3], Matthias[2], John Jacob[1]) was born September 28, 1900.

4263 HOPE LENORA NEUBERT (Appilonia[7], James[6], Felix[5], David[4], Elizabeth[3], Matthias[2], John Jacob[1]) was born November 26, 1902, in Knox County, Tennessee. She married Claud McPherson, July 20, 1924, in Knox County, Tennessee. Claud was born April 15, 1904, at Knoxville, Tennessee.

(Sup) 6555   † Barbour Daun McPherson, born December 29, 1929.
(Sup) 6556   †† Ronald Claude McPherson, born October 27, 1932.

4264 FLETA MARIAM NEUBERT (Appilonia[7], James[6], Felix[5], David[4], Elizabeth[3], Matthias[2], John Jacob[1]) was born September 26, 1908, in Knox County, Tennessee.

(Sup) 4265 CLARENCE JACOBS (John[7], Martin[6], Elizabeth[5], Martha[4], John Adam I1[3], John Adam I[2], John Jacob[1]) was the son of John Adam and Anne Pumphrey Jacobs [Supplement No. 1392A]. He died and is buried at Fort Wayne, Indiana.

(Sup) 4266 DONNA JACOBS (John[7], Martin[6], Elizabeth[5], Martha[4], John Adam I1[3], John Adam I[2], John Jacob[1]) was the daughter of John Adam and Anne Pumphrey Jacobs [Supplement No. 1392A]. Donna married Mr. Stonebraker. She died and is buried in Crown Hill Cemetery at Indianapolis, Indiana.

(Sup) 6561   † Garnett Stonebraker.
(Sup) 6562   †† Ruth Stonebraker.

(Sup) 4267 LEHMAN JACOBS (John[7], Martin[6], Elizabeth[5], Martha[4], John Adam I1[3], John Adam I[2], John Jacob[1]) was the son of John Adam and Anne Pumphrey Jacobs [Supplement No. 1392A]. Lehman married Edrea _____. He died and is buried at Huntington, Indiana.

(Sup) 6563   † Maxine Jacobs.
(Sup) 6564   †† Homer Jacobs.

(Sup) 4268 ETHEL HILDEBRAND (Elizabeth[7], Martin[6], Elizabeth[5], Martha[4], John Adam I1[3], John Adam I[2], John Jacob[1]) was the daughter of Martin and Elizabeth Jacobs Hildebrand [Supplement No. 1392B]. Ethel married Mr. Steinhagen. She died and is buried at Huntington, Indiana.

(Sup) 4269 JOHN HILDEBRAND (Elizabeth[7], Martin[6], Elizabeth[5], Martha[4], John Adam I1[3], John Adam I[2], John Jacob[1]) was the son of Martin and Elizabeth Jacobs Hildebrand [Supplement No. 1392B]. He died and is buried at South Bend, Indiana.

(Sup) 4270 PAUL HILDEBRAND (Elizabeth^7, Martin^6, Elizabeth^5, Martha^4, John Adam II^3, John Adam I^2, John Jacob^1) was the son of Martin and Elizabeth Jacobs Hildebrand [Supplement No. 1392B]. Paul married, first, Jamilia _____. They were divorced. He married, second, Dorothy _____. Paul died and is buried at Clearwater, Florida.

CHILDREN OF PAUL AND JAMILIA
(Sup) 6568 i Paul Hildebrand, Jr.
(Sup) 6569 ii Stanley Hildebrand.

CHILDREN OF PAUL AND DOROTHY
(Sup) 6570 ii Robert Hildebrand.
(Sup) 6571 iii Gloria Hildebrand.

(Sup) 4271 ALMA JACOBS (Franklin^7, Martin^6, Elizabeth^5, Martha^4, John Adam II^3, John Adam I^2, John Jacob^1) was the daughter of Franklin Fonrose and Minnie Schwicho Jacobs [Supplement No. 1392C]. Alma was born in 1895 and died in 1909. She is buried in Crown Hill Cemetery at Indianapolis, Indiana.

(Sup) 4272 CHARLOTTE JACOBS (Franklin^7, Martin^6, Elizabeth^5, Martha^4, John Adam II^3, John Adam I^2, John Jacob^1) was the daughter of Franklin Fonrose and Minnie Schwicho Jacobs [Supplement No. 1392C]. Charlotte was born in 1896. She married Fred Schmidt. Charlotte died and is buried at Dallas, Texas.

(Sup) 6572 i Jean Schmidt.
(Sup) 6573 ii Marilyn Schmidt.
(Sup) 6574 iii Carol Schmidt.

(Sup) 4273 MARIETTA JACOBS (Franklin^7, Martin^6, Elizabeth^5, Martha^4, John Adam II^3, John Adam I^2, John Jacob^1) was the daughter of Franklin Fonrose and Minnie Schwicho Jacobs [Supplement No. 1392C]. Marietta was born in 1898. She married Louis William Bonsib, Jr. He was the son of Louis Bonsib. Marietta died in 1979.

(Sup) 6576 i Louis William Bonsib, III, born 1918.
(Sup) 6577 ii Joan Bonsib.
(Sup) 6578 iii John Frank Bonsib.
(Sup) 6579 iv Richard E. Bonsib.

(Sup) 4274 EDNA JACOBS (Franklin^7, Martin^6, Elizabeth^5, Martha^4, John Adam II^3, John Adam I^2, John Jacob^1) was the daughter of Franklin Fonrose and Minnie Schwicho Jacobs [Supplement No. 1392C]. Edna was born in 1900. She died in 1928 and is buried in Crown Hill Cemetery at Indianapolis, Indiana.

(Sup) 4275 FRANK LOWELL JACOBS (Franklin^7, Martin^6, Elizabeth^5, Martha^4, John Adam II^3, John Adam I^2, John Jacob^1) was the son of Franklin Fonrose and Minnie Schwicho Jacobs [Supplement No. 1392C]. Frank was born in 1902 and died in 1904. He is buried in Crown Hill Cemetery at Indianapolis, Indiana.

(Sup) 4276 IRVIN JACOBS (Franklin^7, Martin^6, Elizabeth^5, Martha^4, John Adam II^3, John Adam I^2, John Jacob^1) was the son of Franklin Fonrose and Minnie Schwicho Jacobs [Supplement No. 1392C]. Irvin was born in 1904 and died in 1950. He is buried in Crown Hill Cemetery at Indianapolis, Indiana.

(Sup) 4277 ROBERT JACOBS (Franklin^7, Martin^6, Elizabeth^5, Martha^4, John Adam II^3, John Adam I^2, John Jacob^1) was the son of Franklin Fonrose and Minnie Schwicho Jacobs [Supplement No. 1392C]. Robert was born in 1906. He married Evelyn (Betty) Davis in 1930. Robert died in 1981.

(Sup) 6580 i John Robert Jacobs.
(Sup) 6581 ii Richard Jacobs.

(Sup) 4278 LILLIAN JACOBS (Franklin^7, Martin^6, Elizabeth^5, Martha^4, John Adam II^3, John Adam I^2, John Jacob^1) was the daughter of Franklin Fonrose and Minnie Schwicho Jacobs [Supplement No. 1392C]. Lillian was born in 1907. She married William Everett Hauck. He was employed as General Manager of the F&P Division of the Inland Container Company, Indianapolis, Indiana. Lillian died February, 1983, at Niranja Beach, Florida.

(Sup) 6582 i William Everett Hauck, Jr., born July 5, 1930.
(Sup) 6583 ii Ronald Lee Hauck, born November 15, 1932.
(Sup) 6584 iii David Allen Hauck, born January 21, 1934.
(Sup) 6585 iv Barbara Jean Hauck, born December 9, 1941.
(Sup) 6586 v Robert Reed Hauck, born October 9, 1946 (twin).
(Sup) 6587 vi Ralph Richard Hauck, born October 9, 1946 (twin).

(Sup) 4279 RALPH REED JACOBS (Franklin^7, Martin^6, Elizabeth^5, Martha^4, John Adam II^3, John Adam I^2, John Jacob^1) was the son of Franklin Fonrose and Minnie Schwicho Jacobs [Supplement No. 1392C]. Ralph was born September 15, 1909, at Indianapolis, Indiana. He married Edwina Evelyn Longest at Indianapolis September 15, 1943. She was the daughter of Clovia Basil and Helen Longest and was born October 23, 1917, at Indianapolis.

(Sup) 6588 i Frank Charles Jacobs, born April 9, 1944.
(Sup) 6589 ii Gene R. Jacobs, born November 2, 1945.
(Sup) 6590 iii James Edward Jacobs, born March 25, 1949.
(Sup) 6591 iv Jeffrey Leon Jacobs, July 9, 1954.

(Sup) 4280 CLARABELL JACOBS (Franklin^7, Martin^6, Elizabeth^5, Martha^4, John Adam II^3, John Adam I^2, John Jacob^1) was the daughter of Franklin Fonrose and Minnie Schwicho Jacobs [Supplement No. 1392C]. Clarabell was born in 1911. She married Hubert H. Smallwood in 1933. She and Hubert both died in 1967 at North Miami, Florida.

(Sup) 6592   i   Susan Smallwood.

(Sup) 4281 NORWELL JACOBS (Martin^7, Martin^6, Elizabeth^5, Martha^4, John Adam II^3, John Adam I^2, John Jacob^1) was the son of Martin A. and Merle Reed Jacobs [Supplement No. 1392D]. Norwell married Esther _____. He died and is buried in Crown Hill Cemetery at Indianapolis, Indiana.

(Sup) 6593   i   Richard Jacobs.

(Sup) 4282 AMY LEE JACOBS (George^7, Martin^6, Elizabeth^5, Martha^4, John Adam II^3, John Adam I^2, John Jacob^1) was the daughter of George Lowell and Virgie S. Ricketts Jacobs [Supplement No. 1392E]. Amy was born September 21, 1898, at Portsmouth, Virginia. She attended the University of Maryland and American University, and she continued courses elsewhere in religion, art, interior decoration, fashion design, and photography. She was a member of the Daughters of the American Revolution and the Colonial Dames. Amy married Ralph Homer Tibbs October 25, 1925, at West Brighton, on Staten Island, New York. He was the son of Harry Albert and Mattie Essie Florence Holt Tibbs and was born April 1, 1900, at Columbus, Georgia. He died May 20, 1974, at Paris, France. Amy retired after thirty-nine years from the U.S. Government and continued to participate actively in sports, the arts, and family genealogy. She performed the extensive research for this Supplement on the numerous descendents of John George and Martha Link [Supplement Nos. 16, 51, 179A-G, 557A-K, 1392A-H, and 4265-4292].

(Sup) 6594   i   Ralph Homer Tibbs, Jr., born May 9, 1928.

(Sup) 4283 RICHARD VAN BUREN JACOBS (George^7, Martin^6, Elizabeth^5, Martha^4, John Adam II^3, John Adam I^2, John Jacob^1) was the son of George Lowell and Virgie Ricketts Jacobs [Supplement No. 1392E]. Richard died young.

(Sup) 4284 VIRGIE LOUISE JACOBS (George^7, Martin^6, Elizabeth^5, Martha^4, John Adam II^3, John Adam I^2, John Jacob^1) was the daughter of George Lowell and Virgie Ricketts Jacobs [Supplement No. 1392E] and was born February 19, 1901, at Washington, DC. She married Henry Dempsey Salley at New York City, New York.

(Sup) 4285 ESTHER De ETTA JACOBS (George^7, Martin^6, Elizabeth^5, Martha^4, John Adam II^3, John Adam I^2, John Jacob^1) was the daughter of George Lowell and Virgie Ricketts Jacobs [Supplement No. 1392E]. She was born in 1903 and died when one year old.

(Sup) 4286 GEORGE LOWELL JACOBS, JR. (George^7, Martin^6, Elizabeth^5, Martha^4, John Adam II^3, John Adam I^2, John Jacob^1) was the son of George Lowell and Virgie Ricketts Jacobs [Supplement No. 1392E]. George, Jr., was born March 22, 1906, at Arlington, New York. He married Ruth Alda Lester September 20, 1930, at Port Richmond, New York. She was born January 16, 1909, at Islip, Long Island, New York.

(Sup) 6595   i   Joan Ellen Jacobs, born April 13, 1932.
(Sup) 6596   ii   Ruth Marilyn Jacobs, born November 6, 1935.
(Sup) 6597   iii Beverly Ann Jacobs, born December 28, 1941.

(Sup) 4287 MABLE YOPST (Minnie^7, Martin^6, Elizabeth^5, Martha^4, John Adam II^3, John Adam I^2, John Jacob^1) was the daughter of George and Minnie Jacobs Yopst [Supplement No. 1392F].

(Sup) 4288 WILLIS YOPST (Minnie^7, Martin^6, Elizabeth^5, Martha^4, John Adam II^3, John Adam I^2, John Jacob^1) was the son of George and Minnie Jacobs Yopst [Supplement No. 1392F]. Willis died during World War I.

(Sup) 4289 WALTER YOPST (Minnie^7, Martin^6, Elizabeth^5, Martha^4, John Adam II^3, John Adam I^2, John Jacob^1) was the son of George and Minnie Jacobs Yopst [Supplement No. 1392F].

(Sup) 4290 MARGUERITE YOPST (Minnie^7, Martin^6, Elizabeth^5, Martha^4, John Adam II^3, John Adam I^2, John Jacob^1) was the daughter of George and Minnie Jacobs Yopst [Supplement No. 1392F].

(Sup) 4291 JAY YOPST (Minnie^7, Martin^6, Elizabeth^5, Martha^4, John Adam II^3, John Adam I^2, John Jacob^1) was the son of George and Minnie Jacobs Yopst [Supplement No. 1392F].

(Sup) 4292 MILDRED YOPST (Minnie^7, Martin^6, Elizabeth^5, Martha^4, John Adam II^3, John Adam I^2, John Jacob^1) was the daughter of George and Minnie Jacobs Yopst [Supplement No. 1392F].

Chapter 3

Ninth Generation

This chapter contains (new) entries for all those members of the
Ninth Generation of descendants of John Jacob Link for whom
information was received for the 1988 Supplement.

Generation	*Entry Numbers*
Ninth	5000-6000 series

The biographies in this section of the Supplement are for the Ninth Generation of the descendants of John Jacob Link (1682-1738).

The information here includes entries for many individuals who were not listed in The Link Family book, as well as information on the children of members of the Eighth Generation who were listed on pages 620-774 of the book.

Each member of the Ninth Generation in this Supplement, both old (TLF) and new, is given a (Sup) serial number for identification. (In the book, the Ninth Generation members are not identified by serial numbers.)

(Sup) 5001 MARJORIE LOUISE STONER (Lloyd^8, Raleigh^7, Dennis^5, John^4, Elizabeth^3, John Adam I^2, John Jacob^1) was the daughter of Lloyd Gordon and Edith Dauer Stoner [Supplement No. 2759]. Marjorie was born April 25, 1920, at Liberal, Kansas. She married Charles Elliott August 23, 1947, at Liberal.

(Sup) 5002 DONNA LEE STONER (Lee^8, Lee^7, Thomas^6, Dennis^5, John^4, Elizabeth^3, John Adam I^2, John Jacob^1) was the daughter of Lee Rowland and Ruth Hafley Stoner [Supplement No. 2764]. She was born September 30, 1945, at Albany, New York.

(Sup) 5003 PATRICIA GAYLE STONER (Lee^8, Lee^7, Thomas^6, Dennis^5, John^4, Elizabeth^3, John Adam I^2, John Jacob^1) was the daughter of Lee Rowland and Ruth Hafley Stoner, Jr. [Supplement No. 2764]. Patricia was born December 11, 1947, at Cleveland, Ohio.

(Sup) 5004 DANIEL GAVER HARVEY (Lydia^8, Clayton^7, Theodore^6, Margaret^5, Catherine^4, John Adam II^3, John Adam I^2, John Jacob^1) was the son of Ruben Comer and Lydia Gaver Harvey [Supplement No. 2780]. Daniel was born December 3, 1945.

(Sup) 5005 JOANNE STUART LEMEN (Thomas^8, Mamie^7, Thomas^6, Adam^5, Alexander^4, John Adam II^3, John Adam I^2, John Jacob^1) was the daughter of Thomas Henry and Nancy Elizabeth Osbourn Lemen [Supplement No. 2781]. Joanne was born February 6, 1942, at Duffields, Jefferson County, West Virginia. She graduated from Winchester Memorial Hospital Nursing School, Winchester, Virginia, in 1963, and was a registered nurse there.

(Sup) 5006 JAMES HENRY LEMEN (Thomas^8, Mamie^7, Thomas^6, Adam^5, Alexander^4, John Adam II^3, John Adam I^2, John Jacob^1) was the son of Thomas Henry and Nancy Elizabeth Osbourn Lemen [Supplement No. 2781]. James was born February 4, 1944, at Charles Town, West Virginia. He graduated from Charles Town High School in 1961. He married Mary Alice Moore May 10, 1965, at Rockville, Maryland [see Supplement No. 3309]. She was the daughter of Charles William and Florence Gertrude Hendricks Moore [The Link Family, No. 1715] and was born July 1, 1944. James owned and operated a lamp and brass business at Summit Point, West Virginia. The children of James and Mary Alice have an apparently unique distinction in that they are descended from the immigrant John Jacob Link in three lines: (1) James^9, Thomas^8, Mamie^7, Thomas^6, Adam^5, Alexander^4, Adam II^3, Adam I^2, John Jacob^1; (2) Mary Alice^9, Florence^8, Sarah^7, William^6, Adam^5, Alexander^4, Adam II^3, Adam I^2, John Jacob^1; and (3) Mary Alice^8, Florence^7, Daniel^6, Sarah^5, Adam III^4, Adam II^3, Adam I^2, John Jacob^1.

(Sup) 7001   i Thomas William Lemen, born September 7, 1970.
(Sup) 7002   ii Sarah Elizabeth Lemen, born April 29, 1974.

(Sup) 5007 BARBARA ELLEN JONES (Franklin^8, Adam^7, Mary^6, Adam^5, Alexander^4, John Adam II^3, John Adam I^2, John Jacob^1) was the daughter of Franklin Hager and Agnes Trussell Jones [Supplement No. 2782]. Barbara was born January 21, 1931, at Bakerton, Jefferson County, West Virginia. She married, first, Robert James Macnamara July 4, 1952, at Washington, D.C. He was the son of Hubert M. and Agnes Ione Lundy Macnamara and was born December 1, 1932, at Bonner's Ferry, Idaho. Robert served in the Marine Corps. Barbara married, second, James Gus Sardelis January 21, 1969, at Hagerstown, Maryland. He was the son of Gus Baker and Marie Geanious Sardelis and was born April 2, 1937, at Winchester, Virginia. James served in the Air Force 1959-1962.

CHILDREN OF BARBARA AND ROBERT

(Sup) 7003   i Michael Patrick Macnamara, born October 7, 1953.
(Sup) 7004   ii Teresa Lynn Macnamara, born October 8, 1954.
(Sup) 7005   iii Maureen Ann Macnamara, born February 27, 1960.
(Sup) 7006   iv Mary Colleen Macnamara, born December 23, 1961.

CHILD OF BARBARA AND JAMES

(Sup) 7007   v Christopher James Sardelis, born October 16, 1969.

(Sup) 5008   CHARLOTTE   RAE JONES   (Franklin[8], Adam[7], Mary[6], Adam[5],
Alexander[4], John Adam II[3], John Adam I[2], John Jacob[1]) was the daughter
of Franklin Hager and Agnes Trussell Jones [Supplement No. 2782]. Charlotte
was born March 31, 1939, at Bakerton, West Virginia. She married Harry Compher
September 7, 1960, at Bolivar, Jefferson County, West Virginia. He was the son
of Ebeneezer and Lula Mae George Compher and was born June 1, 1930, at Purcell-
ville, Virginia. Harry served for two years in the U.S. Army, 1955-1957.

(Sup) 7008   i Dean Conard Compher, born August 27, 1963.

(Sup) 5009   MARY NORMA TRUSSELL   (Mary[8], Adam[7], Mary[6], Adam[5], Alexan-
der[4], John Adam II[3], John Adam I[2], John Jacob[1]) was the daughter of
Frank William and Mary Margaret Jones Trussell [Supplement No. 2783]. She was
born August 11, 1931, at Charles Town, West Virginia. Norma graduated from a
Hill High School in Cumberland, Maryland, and was employed by the C&P Telephone
Company in 1949. She retired in 1982. Norma married Harold Luther Senkbeil,
Jr., July 25, 1953, at Cumberland. He was the son of Harold Luther and Virginia
Kenney Senkbeil, and was born March 28, 1931.

(Sup) 5010   JOYCE LEE TRUSSELL   (Mary[8], Adam[2], John Jacob[1]) was the
der[4], John Adam II[3], John Adam[2], John Jacob[1]) was the daughter of Frank
William and Mary Margaret Jones Trussell [Supplement No. 2783]. Joyce was born
March 26, 1936, at Halltown, Jefferson County, West Virginia. She married,
first, Elmer Stanton Smith, Jr., May 12, 1955, at Cumberland, Maryland. He was
the son of Elmer Stanton and Dorothy Twigg Smith and was born August 26, 1933,
at Cumberland. Elmer served in the U.S. Navy during the Korean conflict. Joyce
married, second, Edward L. McFadden November 21, 1962, at Cumberland. He was
the son of James and Grace Bradley McFadden and was born April 8, 1934, at
Ridgley, West Virginia. Edward also served in the U.S. Navy during the Korean
conflict.

         CHILD OF JOYCE AND FRANK

(Sup) 7009   i Stephen Scott Smith, born November 12, 1955.

         CHILD OF JOYCE AND EDWARD

(Sup) 7010   ii Bradley William McFadden, born August 31, 1963.

(Sup) 5011   LARRY WILLIAM JONES   (David[8], Adam[7], Mary[6], Adam[5], Alex-
ander[4], John Adam II[3], John Adam I[2], John Jacob[1]) was the son of David
Martin and Minno Staubs Jones [Supplement No. 2784]. Larry was born September
29, 1936, at Bolivar, Jefferson County, West Virginia. He married Sara DeLawter
July 23, 1961, at Brunswick, Maryland. She was the daughter of Edgar and Clara
Spitzer DeLawter and was born August 12, 1943, at Charles Town, West Virginia.
Larry and Sara resided at Jefferson, Maryland.

(Sup) 7011   i Larry William Jones, Jr., born December 7, 1961.
(Sup) 7012   ii Timothy Wayne Jones, born July 9, 1965.
(Sup) 7013   iii Jeffrey Allen Jones, born January 24, 1967.

(Sup) 5012   MARTIN DAVID JONES   (David[8], Adam[7], Mary[6], Adam[5], Alexan-
der[4], John Adam II[3], John Adam I[2], John Jacob[1]) was the son of David
Martin and Minno Staubs Jones [Supplement No. 2784]. Martin was born May 13,
1939, at Bolivar, Jefferson County, West Virginia. He married Bertie Lea Goins
January 14, 1961, at Frederick, Maryland. She was the daughter of Homer and
Lillie Houndshell Goins and was born October 26, 1938, at Woodsboro, Maryland.

(Sup) 7014   i Keith Michael Jones, born November 10, 1962.
(Sup) 7015   ii Traci Lyne Jones, born December 30, 1965.

(Sup) 5013   VIRGINIA MAE JONES   (David[8], Adam[7], Mary[6], Adam[5], Alexan-
der[4], John Adam II[3], John Adam I[2], John Jacob[1]) was the daughter of
David Martin and Minno Staubs Jones [Supplement No. 2784]. Virginia was born
December 29, 1941, at Bolivar, Jefferson County, West Virginia. She was a
professional cosmetologist. She married Maurice Franklin Hoffmaster May 9,
1959, at Brunswick, Maryland. He was the son of George Franklin and Leoda
Sweeney Hoffmaster and was born July 22, 1937, at Weaverton, Washington County,
Maryland. Maurice served in the U.S. Marine Corps 1954-1959.

(Sup) 7016   i Maurice Franklin Hoffmaster, Jr., born May 24, 1960.
(Sup) 7017   ii Yvonne Rene' Hoffmaster, born August 11, 1961.
(Sup) 7018   iii David Dwayne Hoffmaster, born August 4, 1962.

(Sup) 5014   MARY LOUISE JONES   (David[8], Adam[7], Mary[6], Adam[5], Alexan-
der[4], John Adam II[3], John Adam I[2], John Jacob[1]) was the daughter of
David Martin and Minno Staubs Jones [Supplement No. 2784]. Mary Louise was born
September 5, 1945, at Bolivar, Jefferson County, West Virginia. She married
Melvin McClure Bartlett June 29, 1963, at Brunswick, Maryland. He was the son
of Mervin Isaac and Gaynelle Carroll Bartlett and was born November 1, 1942, at
Stanley, Virginia.

(Sup) 7019   i Michelle Denise Bartlett, born February 11, 1966.
(Sup) 7020   ii Michael Scott Bartlett, born January 31, 1968.
(Sup) 7021   iii Leslie Dawn Bartlett, born September 12, 1969.

(Sup) 5015   RALPH JERRY JONES   (Ralph[8], Adam[7], Mary[6], Adam[5], Alexan-
der[4], John Adam II[3], John Adam I[2], John Jacob[1]) was the son of Ralph
Banks and Blanche James Jones [Supplement No. 2785]. Ralph was born August 19,
1936, at Millville, Jefferson County, West Virginia. He married Rosemary Boyd
February 10, 1954, at Brunswick, Maryland. She was the daughter of Charles
Clarence and Bertie Mae Wagamon Boyd and was born July 31, 1935, at Charles
Town, West Virginia.

(Sup) 7022   i Donald Steven Jones, born September 6, 1954.
(Sup) 7023   ii Jerry Wayne Jones, born August 19, 1956.

(Sup) 5020 JOHN CLARENCE RUNION (Sarah[8], Adam[7], Mary[6], Adam[5], Alexander[4], John Adam II[3], John Adam I[2], John Jacob[1]) was the son of Roy William and Sarah Jones Runion [Supplement No. 2786]. John was born April 8, 1950, at Charles Town, West Virginia. He married Virginia Bell Kenney April 10, 1970, at Antietem, Maryland. She was the daughter of Lewis Melton and Norma Lee Smallwood Kenney and was born February 5, 1952, in Jefferson County, West Virginia.

(Sup) 7033   i   Dustin Conrad Runion, born November 24, 1970.
(Sup) 7034   ii Trista Nikole Runion, born February 3, 1975.

(Sup) 5021 CHARLES ROBERT RUNION (Sarah[8], Adam[7], Mary[6], Adam[5], Alexander[4], John Adam II[3], John Adam I[2], John Jacob[1]) was the son of of Roy William and Sarah Jones Runion [Supplement No. 2786]. Charles was born October 17, 1951, at Charles Town, West Virginia. He married Lovada Nadene Hardy, May 4, 1973, at Harper's Ferry, West Virginia. She was the daughter of William and Shirley Hawkins Hardy and was born January 8, 1956.

(Sup) 7035   i   Melinda Darnell Runion, born February 26, 1974.
(Sup) 7036   ii Susanne Marie Runion, born June 25, 1976.

(Sup) 5022 MARSHALL RONEMOUS JONES (Robert[8], Robert[7], Mary[6], Adam[5], Alexander[4], John Adam II[3], John Adam I[2], John Jacob[1]) was the son of Robert Luther and Virginia Lee Smallwood Jones [Supplement No. 2788]. Marshall was born July 16, 1932, at Duffields, Jefferson County, West Virginia. He married Sylvia Irene Housden Harrison June 24, 1967, at Charles Town, West Virginia. She was the daughter of Millard Sylvester and Parthenia Cubbage Housden and was born August 15, 1927, in Page County, Virginia.

(Sup) 5023 CATHERINE LOUISE HANSON (Elise[8], Ernest[7], Mary[6], Adam[5], Alexander[4], John Adam II[3], John Adam I[2], John Jacob[1]) was the daughter of Jennings Linton and Elsie Catherine Jones Hanson [Supplement No. 2790]. Kitty Lou was born February 11, 1940, at La Plata, Maryland. She graduated magna cum laude from Shepherd College, West Virginia, with a B.S. degree in English and a B.A. degree in business education. She received an M.A. degree from the University of South Florida, and served in 1981 as president of the Florida State Business Education Association. Catherine married Kenneth James Etterman December 22, 1962, at Sarasota, Florida. He was the son of Edmund and Pearl Kennedy Etterman and was born August 26, 1939, at Detroit, Michigan. Kenneth received a B.A. degree in education from the University of Florida and an M.A. degree in education from Eastern Michigan University. He was Executive Director of the Education Association of Collier and Hendrey Counties, Florida.

(Sup) 7037   i   Kenneth James Etterman, Jr., born March 4, 1968.
(Sup) 7038   ii Kimberly Kay Etterman, born September 30, 1969.

(Sup) 5016 GARY EUGENE JONES (Ralph[8], Adam[7], Mary[6], Adam[5], Alexander[4], John Adam II[3], John Adam I[2], John Jacob[1]) was the son of Ralph Banks and Blanche James Jones [Supplement No. 2785]. He was born December 14, 1939, at Milville, Jefferson County, West Virginia.

(Sup) 5017 BENJAMIN ROGER JONES (Ralph[8], Adam[7], Mary[6], Adam[5], Alexander[4], John Adam II[3], John Adam I[2], John Jacob[1]) was the son of Ralph Banks and Blanche James Jones [Supplement No. 2785]. Benjamin was born January 19, 1943, at Millville, Jefferson County, West Virginia. He married Nancy Mower August 18, 1962, at Cumberland, Maryland. She was the daughter of John Harris and Bertha Elizabeth Lewis Mower and was born July 26, 1944, at Cumberland.

(Sup) 7024   i   Roger Harris Jones, born August 12, 1963.
(Sup) 7025   ii   Traci Michelle Jones, born June 14, 1966.
(Sup) 7026   iii Rebecca Elizabeth Jones, born January 25, 1974.

(Sup) 5018 NANCY LEE RUNION (Sarah[8], Adam[7], Mary[6], Adam[5], Alexander[4], John Adam II[3], John Adam I[2], John Jacob[1]) was the daughter of Roy William and Sarah Jones Runion [Supplement No. 2786]. Nancy was born April 20, 1946, at Bollvar, Jefferson County, West Virginia. She married Lester Carlton Dillow April 25, 1964, at Winchester, Virginia. He was the son of Thomas William and Nannie Elizabeth Myers Dillow and was born January 14, 1935, in Jefferson County.

(Sup) 7027   i   Judith Darlene Dillow, born September 7, 1964.
(Sup) 7028   ii   Lester William Dillow, born May 10, 1966.
(Sup) 7029   iii John Roy Scott Dillow, born July 14, 1967.

(Sup) 5019 DONALD WILLIAM RUNION (Sarah[8], Adam[7], Mary[6], Adam[5], Alexander[4], John Adam II[3], John Adam I[2], John Jacob[1]) was the son of Roy William and Sarah Jones Runion [Supplement No. 2786]. Donald was born August 7, 1947, at Halltown, Jefferson County, West Virginia. He was in the U.S. Army 1967-70, receiving basic training at Fort Bragg, North Carolina, and serving in the 82nd Airborne. He married Patsy Marie Jenkins May 14, 1971, at Hagerstown, Maryland. She was the daughter of Luther C. and Hazel Mills Jenkins and was born October 15, 1950, in Jefferson County, West Virginia. Donald and Patsy Marie resided at Kearneysville, Jefferson County.

(Sup) 7030   i   Timothy William Runion, born December 9, 1971.
(Sup) 7031   ii   Jeffrey Dwayne Runion, born September 14, 1974.
(Sup) 7032   iii Wendy Michelle Runion, born February 23, 1977.

(Sup) 5024 JENNINGS LINTON HANSON, JR. (Elise[8], Ernest[7], Mary[6], Adam[5], Alexander[4], John Adam II[3], John Adam I[2], John Jacob[1]) was the son of Jennings Linton and Elsie Catherine Jones [Supplement No. 2790]. He served in the U.S. Army 1958-1964, including a year in Korea providing artillery support to the 101st Airborne Division. He operated a barber shop at Martinsburg, West Virginia, for several years and then moved to Florida, where he attended Sarasota Vocational Technical Center and became a television service technician. He owned and operated Hanson's TV Service at Venice, Florida. Jennings married Iris Ann Dunbar March 24, 1962, at Huntington, West Virginia. The daughter of C. Richard and Florence Gertrude Conkle Dunbar, she was born September 1, 1945, at Ameagle, West Virginia.

(Sup) 7039 i Karen Renée Hanson, born September 25, 1963.
(Sup) 7040 ii Melissa Ann Hanson, born January 4, 1968 (twin).
(Sup) 7041 iii Jennings Linton Hanson III, born January 4, 1968 (twin).

(Sup) 5025 ERNEST MERCER JONES, JR. (Ernest[8], Ernest[7], Mary[6], Adam[5], Alexander[4], John Adam II[3], John Adam I[2], John Jacob[1]) was the son of Ernest Mercer and Mary Young Jones [Supplement No. 2791]. Ernest, Jr., was born January 11, 1946, at Newport News, Virginia, and attended public schools in Jefferson County, West Virginia. He received a B.S. degree from the University of Maryland in chemical engineering in 1967 and did graduate work in business administration at Indiana Central University. Ernest married Patricia Ann Bernadyn June 10, 1967, at Hagerstown, Maryland. The daughter of Stephen and Madelyn Gozora Bernadyn, Pat was born October 6, 1944, at Perth Amboy, New Jersey. She was an artist.

(Sup) 7042 i Ernest Mercer Jones, III, born January 5, 1969.
(Sup) 7043 ii Timothy Wayne Jones, born January 16, 1972.
(Sup) 7044 iii Caroline Elizabeth Jones, born April 12, 1974.

(Sup) 5026 WILLIAM MICHAEL JONES (Ernest[8], Ernest[7], Mary[6], Adam[5], Alexander[4], John Adam II[3], John Adam I[2], John Jacob[1]) was the son of Ernest Mercer and Mary Young Jones [Supplement No. 2791]. William was born January 2, 1953, at Charles Town, West Virginia. He attended the University of West Virginia and received a B.S. degree in mathematics from Florida Atlantic University. After serving in the U.S. Navy, William became a school teacher.

(Sup) 5027 DOUGLAS LEE CURRIER, JR. (Patricia[8], Ernest[7], Mary[6], Adam[5], Alexander[4], John Adam II[3], John Adam I[2], John Jacob[1]) was the son of Douglas Lee and Patricia Ann Jones Currier [Supplement No. 2792]. Douglas, Jr., was born August 6, 1947, at St. Johnsbury, Vermont. He studied aeronautical engineering at the Pittsburgh Institute of Technology, Pennsylvania, and became a foreman at East Alcoa Aluminum Company, near Frederick, Maryland. He married Cheryl Lee Byers January 28, 1967, at Newcastle, Pennsylvania. She was the daughter of John Hamilton and Doris June Boallck Byers and was born October 11, 1945, at Newcastle.

(Sup) 7045 i Michelle Lynn Currier, born August 2, 1967.
(Sup) 7046 ii Erin Lee Currier, born May 27, 1969.

(Sup) 5028 PEGGY ANN CURRIER (Patricia[8], Ernest[7], Mary[6], Adam[5], Alexander[4], John Adam II[3], John Adam I[2], John Jacob[1]) was the daughter of Douglas Lee and Patricia Ann Jones Currier [Supplement No. 2792]. Peggy was born November 23, 1948, at Martinsburg, West Virginia. She received a B.A. degree in secondary education from Shepherd College, West Virginia, in 1948, and an M.S. degree in vocational education from John Marshall University at Huntington, West Virginia. She was employed as a teacher at James Rumsey Vocational Technical Center, Martinsburg, and served as leader of the 4-H Club in the area of Bakerton, Jefferson County, West Virginia. Peggy married Larry Edwin Talley June 7, 1970, at Uvilla, Jefferson County, West Virginia. He was the son of Hunter Edwin and Margaret Louise Jamison Talley and was born November 24, 1945, at Martinsburg. He served with the U.S. Army in Germany 1965-1967.

(Sup) 7047 i Jody Lynn Talley, born May 28, 1973.
(Sup) 7048 ii Amy Beth Talley, born February 9, 1975.

(Sup) 5029 CYNTHIA KAREN JONES (John[8], Ernest[7], Mary[6], Adam[5], Alexander[4], John Adam II[3], John Adam I[2], John Jacob[1]) was the daughter of John Link and Mary Jane McLaney Jones [Supplement No. 2793]. She was born May 20, 1963, at Laurel, Maryland. Cindy received a B.S. degree with highest honors in history from Shepherd College, West Virginia. She married Steven Lyle Nicewarner, March 22, 1986, at Columbia, Maryland. He was the son of Lyle L. and Dorothy (Billmyer) Nicewarner and was born August 31, 1962, at Arlington, Virginia. Steve graduated from Shepherd College, West Virginia, in 1984, and worked as an accountant for Giant Food, Inc.

(Sup) 5030 JOHN LINK JONES, JR. (John[8], Ernest[7], Mary[6], Adam[5], Alexander[4], John Adam II[3], John Adam I[2], John Jacob[1]) was the son of John Link and Mary Jane McLaney Jones [Supplement No. 2793]. John, Jr., was born August 9, 1966, at Laurel, Maryland. He studied electrical engineering at Shepherd College, West Virginia.

(Sup) 5031 RUDOLPH LOUIS WEYEL, JR. (Katherine[8], Henry[7], Adam[6], Adam[5], Alexander[4], John Adam II[3], John Adam I[2], John Jacob[1]) was the son of Rudolph Louis and Katherine Link Weyel [Supplement No. 2798]. Rudolph, Jr., was born October 6, 1931, at San Antonio, Texas. He married Orvetta Lee McNelly September 3, 1954, at Houston, Texas. She was born December 7, 1932, at Iraan, Texas. Rudolph died September 1, 1974, and is buried at Houston.

(Sup) 7048A i Deborah Lee Weyel, born December 11, 1953.
(Sup) 7048B ii Susan Lynn Weyel, born September 19, 1956.
(Sup) 7048C iii Karen Louise Weyel, born February 26, 1961.

(Sup) 5032 FRANCES LOUISE WEYEL (Katherine[8], Henry[7], Adam[6], Adam[5], Alexander[4], John Adam II[3], John Adam I[2], John Jacob[1]) was the daughter of Rudolph Louis and Katherine Link Weyel [Supplement No. 2798]. Frances was born June 17, 1936, at San Antonio, Texas. (She was the twin of Foster). She married, first, Jesse L. Howington. He was born May 15, 1935, at Monroe, Louisiana. Frances married, second, Thomas Wayne Bilbo. He was born September 3, 1932, at Houston, Texas. Frances was vice president of a savings and loan company at Corpus Christi, Texas, and Thomas was a petroleum engineer.

(Sup) 7049   i   Kevin Lewis Howington, born April 26, 1960.
(Sup) 7049A ii Katherine Jeanine Howington, born June 11, 1968.

(Sup) 5033 FOSTER LINK WEYEL (Katherine[8], Henry[7], Adam[6], Adam[5], Alexander[4], John Adam II[3], John Adam I[2], John Jacob[1]) was the son of Rudolph Louis and Katherine Link Weyel [Supplement No. 2798]. Foster was born June 17, 1936, at San Antonio, Texas (the twin of Frances). He married Mary Ann Signe Ruthstrom January 27, at Richmond, Texas. She was born April 22, 1939, at Houston, Texas. Foster owned a vending machine company.

(Sup) 7050   i   Cynthia Link Weyel, born December 8, 1956.
(Sup) 7050A ii Keith Foster Weyel, born October 5, 1960.
(Sup) 7050B iii Steven Louis Weyel, born January 7, 1963.

(Sup) 5034 GLORIA LEE GLASER (Martha[8], Ann[7], William[6], Adam[5], Alexander[4], John Adam II[3], John Adam I[2], John Jacob[1]) was the daughter of Arthur Raymond and Martha Mae Hough Glaser [Supplement No. 2804]. Gloria was born March 9, 1928, at Martinsburg, West Virginia. She married Wilmer McKendree Mumma October 25, 1947. He was the son of Victor Richard and Beulah Wilson Mumma and was born April 14, 1920, at Hagerstown, Maryland.

(Sup) 7050C i   Sue Ellen Mumma, born March 8, 1950.
(Sup) 7050D ii Dwight David E. Mumma, born August 12, 1955.

(Sup) 5035 JOSEPH BURTON BRUNK (Mary[8], Ann[7], William[6], Adam[5], Alexander[4], John Adam II[3], John Adam I[2], John Jacob[1]) was the son of Joseph Abraham and Mary Hough Brunk [Supplement No. 2805]. Joseph was born January 6, 1925, in Martinsburg, West Virginia. He married, first, Frances Ward Sperow, February 7, 1946. The daughter of Frank and Hilda Hardy Sperow, she was born May 28, 1930, at Martinsburg, West Virginia. Joseph served three years in the Navy Medical Corps as a pharmacists mate during World War II in the Alaskan and Pacific theaters. His second marriage was to Anna McGee; they had no children. Joseph died December 27, 1973, and is buried in Rosedale Cemetery, Martinsburg, West Virginia.

(Sup) 7051   i   Joseph Burton Brunk, Jr., born October 4, 1946.
(Sup) 7052   ii Grace Carolyn Brunk, born March 31, 1948.

(Sup) 7053   iii Steven Victor Brunk, born August 30, 1949.
(Sup) 7054   iv   Julia Kay Brunk, born July 7, 1951.
(Sup) 7055   v   Mark Thomas Brunk, born August 21, 1953.
(Sup) 7056   vi   Matthew Taylor Brunk, born July 31, 1957.
(Sup) 7057   vii Ann Elizabeth Brunk, born January 29, 1960.

(Sup) 5036 BETTY JUNE BRUNK (Mary[8], Ann[7], William[6], Adam[5], Alexander[4], John Adam II[3], John Adam I[2], John Jacob[1]) was the daughter of Joseph Abraham and Mary Hough Brunk [Supplement No. 2805]. She was born March 8, 1926, at Martinsburg, West Virginia. She married Willard Hunter Grimes, Jr., on June 25, 1948. He was the son of Willard Hunter and Ella Rose Marshall Grimes and was born December 24, 1918. He served four years in the Army Medical Corps during World War II and was very active in the Boy Scout movement. Willard died September 26, 1973, and is buried in Pleasant View Memory Gardens, Martinsburg, West Virginia.

(Sup) 7058   i   Willard Hunter Grimes III, born March 2, 1956.

(Sup) 5037 JOHN HENRY BRUNK (Mary[8], Ann[7], William[6], Adam[5], Alexander[4], John Adam II[3], John Adam I[2], John Jacob[1]) was the son of Joseph Abraham and Mary Hough Brunk [Supplement No. 2805]. John was born November 28, 1928, at Martinsburg. He married Elsie Ann Roberts August 3, 1952, at Martinsburg. The daughter of Henry Silcer and Clara Virginia Keedy Roberts, she was born May 7, 1931, at Martinsburg. John and Ann resided at Wheaton, Maryland, where John was a quality control supervisor.

(Sup) 7059   i   Michael Douglas Brunk, born October 30, 1954.
(Sup) 7060   ii Jonathan Wayne Brunk, born December 27, 1959.

(Sup) 5038 BARBARA JEAN BRUNK (Mary[8], Ann[7], William[6], Adam[5], Alexander[4], John Adam II[3], John Adam I[2], John Jacob[1]) was the daughter of Joseph Abraham and Mary Hough Brunk [Supplement No. 2805]. Barbara was born April 17, 1932, at Bedington, West Virginia. She married Gene L. Neff January 8, 1955, at Martinsburg, West Virginia. Gene was the son of William and Gladys See Neff and was born August 9, 1930. He served in the Army during the Korean War and chose Army service as a career. After his retirement Barbara and Gene operated a farm and orchard at Troy, Idaho.

(Sup) 7061   i   Susan Gwen Neff, born December 30, 1955.
(Sup) 7062   ii   Carol Lynn Neff, born February 10, 1961.
(Sup) 7063   iii John David Neff, born April 8, 1963.
(Sup) 7064   iv   Mary Catherine Neff, born November 1, 1964.

(Sup) 5039 VIRGINIA ANN BRUNK (Mary⁸, Ann⁷, William⁶, Adam⁵, Alexander⁴, John Adam II³, John Adam I², John Jacob¹) was the daughter of Joseph Abraham and Mary Hough Brunk [Supplement No. 2805]. Virginia was born September 6, 1933, at Martinsburg, West Virginia. She married, first, Garland McCormack Sencindiver September 1, 1952, at Martinsburg. He was the son of Ernest Hunter and Lee Sencindiver and was born June 13, 1933. Virginia married, second, Otho Gesford March 1, 1969. Otho was the son of Otho and Cecelia Gesford and was born March 21, 1922, at Williamsport, Maryland.

CHILDREN OF VIRGINIA ANN AND GARLAND SENCINDIVER

(Sup) 7065 i Pamela Kay Sencindiver, born January 10, 1953.
(Sup) 7066 ii Paula Ann Sencindiver, born September 5, 1956.
(Sup) 7067 iii Diane Elaine Sencindiver, born January 25, 1961.

CHILD OF VIRGINIA ANN AND OTHO GESFORD

(Sup) 7068 iv Phyliss Jean Gesford, born February 2, 1970.

(Sup) 5040 ROBERT KENNETH BRUNK (Mary⁸, Ann⁷, William⁶, Adam⁵, Alexander⁴, John Adam II³, John Adam I², John Jacob¹) was the son of Joseph Abraham and Mary Hough Brunk [Supplement No. 2805]. Robert was born November 23, 1938, at Martinsburg, West Virginia. He married Dorothy J. Gantarz September 24, 1960. She was the daughter of Stephen and Genevieve Gantarz and was born March 11, 1941, at Utica, New York. Robert served four years in the U.S. Air Force.

(Sup) 7069 i Teresa Joan Brunk, born November 21, 1961.
(Sup) 7070 ii Lori Jean Brunk, born April 12, 1963.

(Sup) 5041 CHARLES JOSEPH HOUGH, III (Charles⁸, Ann⁷, William⁶, Adam⁵, Alexander⁴, John Adam II³, John Adam I², John Jacob¹) was the son of Charles Joseph and Ella Brown Hough, Jr. [Supplement No. 2806]. Charles, III, was born February 17, 1927, at Baltimore, Maryland. He owned and operated a garage at Middleway, Jefferson County, West Virginia, for fifteen years before moving to Florida in 1965, where he worked at the University of Florida. Charles married Emily Elizabeth Shamburg September 22, 1945, at Hagerstown, Maryland. She was the daughter of Henry F. and Rose Effie Coffman Shamburg and was born September 8, 1927, at Inwood, West Virginia.

(Sup) 7070A i Charles Hubert Hough, born September 12, 1946.
(Sup) 7070B ii Sherry Brown Hough, born March 2, 1948.
(Sup) 7070C iii Robert Lee Hough, born April 26, 1955.

(Sup) 5042 PAULA ROSEMARY HOUGH (Charles⁸, Ann⁷, William⁶, Adam⁵, Alexander⁴, John Adam II³, John Adam I², John Jacob¹) was the daughter of Charles Joseph and Elo Elizabeth Myrick Hough, Jr. [Supplement No. 2806]. Paula was born July 18, 1949, at Martinsburg, West Virginia. She died May 20, 1969, and is buried in Rosedale Cemetery at Martinsburg.

(Sup) 5042A CHARLES RICHARD HOUGH (Charles⁸, Ann⁷, William⁶, Adam⁵, Alexander⁴, John Adam II³, John Adam I², John Jacob¹) was the son of Charles Joseph and Elo Elizabeth Myrick Hough, Jr. [Supplement No. 2806]. He was born April 16, 1951, at Martinsburg, West Virginia. Charles married Cheri Lynn Beadle April 14, 1976, at New Boston, Ohio. She was the daughter of Ernest H. and Margaret Neace Beadle and was born July 26, 1947, at Portsmouth, Ohio. Cheri received a nursing degree from Eastern Kentucky University in 1970 and became a cardiac care nurse at the Veterans Administration Medical Center, Martinsburg. Richard received a bachelors degree in business administration in 1948 and was a member of Alpha Kappa Psi Business Honorary Fraternity. He was employed as an accountant and financial planner.

(Sup) 7071 i Chad E. Hough, born June 14, 1972.

(Sup) 5042B WILLIAM JOSEPH HOUGH (Charles⁸, Ann⁷, William⁶, Adam⁵, Alexander⁴, John Adam II³, John Adam I², John Jacob¹) was the son of Charles Joseph and Elo Elizabeth Myrick Hough, Jr. [Supplement No. 2806]. William was born December 17, 1952, at Martinsburg, West Virginia. He married Brenda Joyce Foster January 19, 1975, at Martinsburg. She was the daughter of John E. and Vera Joyce Foster and was born January 5, 1957. William was a track foreman for the Chessie Railroad System.

(Sup) 7071A i William Joseph Hough, Jr., born June 16, 1975.
(Sup) 7071B ii Christopher Wilkes Hough, born October 1, 1980.

(Sup) 5043 FRANK LOUIS SAVILLE, JR. (Grace⁸, Ann⁷, William⁶, Adam⁵, Alexander⁴, John Adam II³, John Adam I², John Jacob¹) was the son of Frank Louis and Grace Cornelia Hough Saville [Supplement No. 2807]. Frank, Jr., was born January 2, 1941, at Martinsburg, West Virginia. He married Nancy Rebecca Taylor August 19, 1961. She was the daughter of Wilson Samuel and Ida Rebecca Smith Taylor and was born May 8, 1943, at Baltimore, Maryland. Frank joined the U.S. Navy June, 1960; he served aboard USS Sierra 1960-62, USS Dewey 1962-63, and USS Loeser 1963-64.

(Sup) 7071C i Rebecca Ann Saville, born September 10, 1963.

(Sup) 5044 VICTOR LESLIE GLOVER SAVILLE (Grace⁸, Ann⁷, William⁶, Adam⁵, Alexander⁴, John Adam II³, John Adam I², John Jacob¹) was the son of Frank Louis and Grace Cornelia Hough Saville [Supplement No. 2807]. Victor was born January 3, 1942, at Baltimore, Maryland. He married Sandra Lynn Kerner September 7, 1968. She was the daughter of Albert Paul Kerner and was born May 21, 1948, at Baltimore.

(Sup) 5045 SALLYE ANN SAVILLE (Grace[8], Ann[7], William[6], Adam[5], Alexander[4], John Adam II[3], John Adam I[2], John Jacob[1]) was the daughter of Frank Louis and Grace Cornelia Hough Saville [Supplement No. 2807]. Sallye Ann was born February 3, 1945, at Martinsburg, West Virginia. She married Donald Herbert Hoover June 19, 1971. He was the son of Benjamin Henry and Edna Leonard Frey Hoover and was born August 20, 1939, at Baltimore, Maryland.

(Sup) 5046 HENRY PAUL SAVILLE (Grace[8], Ann[7], William[6], Adam[5], Alexander[4], John Adam II[3], John Adam I[2], John Jacob[1]) was the son of Frank Louis and Grace Cornelia Hough Saville [Supplement No. 2807]. Henry was born August 21, 1949, at Parkville, Maryland. He died December 5, 1949, and is buried in St. James Lutheran Cemetery, Uvilla, Jefferson County, West Virginia.

(Sup) 5047 JOAN SANDRA HOUGH (John[8], Ann[7], William[6], Adam[5], Alexander[4], John Adam II[3], John Adam I[2], John Jacob[1]) was the daughter of John Hugo and Virginia Fisher Hough [Supplement No. 2808]. Sandra was born September 11, 1933, at Charles Town, West Virginia. She married Paul Craig Westlein August 23, 1952, at Washington, D.C. He was the son of Joseph Clifford and Rose Marie Majulian Westlein and was born February 1, 1931, at Washington. Paul was a plumbing and heating contractor.

(Sup) 7072   i   Deborah Marie Westlein, born December 8, 1955.
(Sup) 7072A ii   Sandra Jean Westlein, born May 6, 1959.
(Sup) 7072B iii Patricia Irene Westlein, born May 13, 1960.
(Sup) 7072C iv   Paul Craig Westlein, born June 10, 1961.
(Sup) 7072D v   Joan Teresa Westlein, born August 3, 1964.
(Sup) 7072E vi   Linda Susan Westlein, born September 26, 1965.
(Sup) 7072F vii Nancy Alice Westlein, born September 10, 1970.

(Sup) 5048 JOHN HUGO HOUGH, JR. (John[8], Ann[7], William[6], Adam[5], Alexander[4], John Adam II[3], John Adam I[2], John Jacob[1]) was the son of John Hugo and Virginia Fisher Hough [Supplement No. 2808]. John, Jr., was born June 2, 1937, at Charles Town, West Virginia. He married, first, Joan Marie Marceron September 26, 1956, at Arlington, Virginia. She was the daughter of Elmer and Doris Marceron and was born May 26, 1937, at Washington, D.C. John and Joan were divorced December, 1974. He married, second, Delores Ann Pugh March 23, 1975, at Riverdale, Maryland. She was the daughter of Keith and Geraldine Pugh and was born November 27, 1942, at Washington, D.C.

(Sup) 7073   i   David Craig Hough, born June 30, 1957.
(Sup) 7074   ii   John Richard Hough, born June 27, 1958.
(Sup) 7075   iii Paul Jeffrey Hough, born December 23, 1959.
(Sup) 7076   iv   Karen Lynn Hough, born March 12, 1963.
Stepdaughter v   Catherine Marie Parezo, born February 18, 1961.
Stepdaughter vi   Christine Ann Parezo, born November 14, 1962.

(Sup) 5049 JOYCE ANN HOUGH (Woodrow[8], Ann[7], William[6], Adam[5], Alexander[4], John Adam II[3], John Adam I[2], John Jacob[1]) was the daughter of Woodrow Wilson and Genevieve Ruby Downs Hough [Supplement No. 2809]. Joyce was born November 20, 1936, at Martinsburg, West Virginia. She received a B.S. degree in nursing from Shepherd College, West Virginia, and was employed as a nurse and doctor's office manager at Martinsburg. Joyce married, first, Frank Edward Johnson June 13, 1955, at Martinsburg. He was the son of John Frank and Marie Johnson. Joyce and Frank were divorced. She married, second, Floyd Maynard McDowell. Floyd was born May 1, 1910, at Midway, Pennsylvania. Joyce and Floyd adopted her granddaughter, the daughter of Frank Edward and Tammie Evans Johnson, Jr. [Supplement No. 7077A].

(Sup) 7077   i   Cynthia Marie Johnson, born June 13, 1956.
(Sup) 7077A ii   Frank Edward Johnson, Jr., born August 18, 1957.
(Sup) 8040T iii Jan Augusta Johnson McDowell, born Sept 4, 1980. (adopted)

(Sup) 5050 WOODROW WILSON HOUGH (Woodrow[8], Ann[7], William[6], Adam[5], Alexander[4], John Adam II[3], John Adam I[2], John Jacob[1]) was the son of Woodrow Wilson and Thelma Turner Hough [Supplement No. 2809]. Woodrow, Jr., was born April 14, 1946, at Martinsburg, West Virginia. He married Lee Bailey in May, 1977, and they resided at Chula Vista, California.

(Sup) 5050A DEBRA KAY HOUGH (Woodrow[8], Ann[7], William[6], Adam[5], Alexander[4], John Adam II[3], John Adam I[2], John Jacob[1]) was the daughter of Woodrow Wilson and Thelma Turner Hough [Supplement No. 2809]. Debra was born August 2, 1952, at Martinsburg, West Virginia. She was employed at City Hospital, Martinsburg, while studying toward a degree in nursing. Debra married Richard Stone April 23, 1982, at Hagerstown, Maryland. He was the son of Ulyses G. and Bertha Jane Stone and was born June 30, 1954, at Hagerstown.

(Sup) 7077B i   Eric Strobridge, born December 17, 1978.

(Sup) 5051 PATRICIA ANN SAVILLE (Woodrow[8], Ann[7], William[6], Adam[5], Alexander[4], John Adam II[3], John Adam I[2], John Jacob[1]) was the daughter of Woodrow Pearell and Frances Irene Hough Saville [Supplement No. 2810]. Patricia was born November 9, 1935, at Martinsburg, West Virginia. She married Douglas Eugene Golliday March 1, 1954, at Hagerstown, Maryland. He was the son of Henry Eugene and Margaret Kitchen Golliday. Patricia was supervisor at Potomac Sportswear, Martinsburg.

(Sup) 7078   i   Douglas Eugene Golliday, Jr., born Sept 6, 1954.
(Sup) 7078A ii   Clark Wayne Golliday, born January 18, 1958.
(Sup) 7078B iii Bertie Lynn Golliday, born April 15, 1961.

(Sup) 5052 JO ANN SAVILLE (Frances[8], Ann[7], William[6], Adam[5], Alexander[4], John Adam II[3], John Adam I[2], John Jacob[1]) was the daughter of Woodrow Pearell and Frances Irene Hough Saville [Supplement No. 2810]. Jo Ann was born May 24, 1939, at Martinsburg, West Virginia. She married Jacob Lee Cave September 5, 1958, at Martinsburg, West Virginia. He was the son of Charles Claude and Leah Virginia Coates Cave and was born December 28, 1935, at Blairton, West Virginia. Jo Ann was a medical assistant, and Lee was a painter.

(Sup) 7078C   i   Mark Anthony Cave, born December 25, 1959.
(Sup) 7078D   ii   Brian Andrew Cave, born September 24, 1966.
(Sup) 7078E iii   Chad Matthew Cave, born November 18, 1976.

(Sup) 5053 WOODROW PEARELL SAVILLE, JR. (Frances[8], Ann[7], William[6], Adam[5], Alexander[4], John Adam II[3], John Adam I[2], John Jacob[1]) was the son of Woodrow Pearell and Frances Irene Hough Saville [Supplement No. 2810]. Woodrow, Jr., was born March 5, 1942, at Martinsburg, West Virginia. He married Carol Leigh Skidmore June 5, 1965, at South Charleston, West Virginia. She was the daughter of Virgil Floyd and Leona Ann Humphrey Skidmore and was born January 1, 1946, at Richmond, Virginia. Woodrow was in the contracting and development business with his brother Richard at Martinsburg (Saville Brothers). They developed and owned "Clifton Square Shopping and Professional Village" and were owners of "Kwik Chek" stores at Martinsburg.

(Sup) 7078F   i   Sherri Lynn Saville, born November 20, 1968.
(Sup) 7078G   ii   Scott Robert Saville, born February 16, 1972.
(Sup) 7078H iii   Shawn Matthew Saville, born April 22, 1978.
(Sup) 7078J   iv   Sara Beth Saville, born July 2, 1981.

(Sup) 5054 RICHARD TAYLOR SAVILLE (Frances[8], Ann[7], William[6], Adam[5], Alexander[4], John Adam II[3], John Adam I[2], John Jacob[1]) was the son of Woodrow Pearell and Frances Irene Hough Saville [Supplement No. 2810]. Richard was born March 9, 1945, at Martinsburg, West Virginia. He married Mary Lou Flores March 18, 1967, in Guam. She was the daughter of Joaquin T. and Louisa M. Flores and was born September 21, 1944, at Agana Heights, Guam. Richard was in the contracting and development business with his brother Woodrow at Martinsburg. Mary was a senior data processor.

(Sup) 7078K   i   Freddie L. Saville, born February 6, 1965.
(Sup) 7078L   ii   Lisa A. Saville, born January 16, 1971.

(Sup) 5055 FRANCES IRENE SAVILLE (Frances[8], Ann[7], William[6], Adam[5], Alexander[4], John Adam II[3], John Adam I[2], John Jacob[1]) was the daughter of Woodrow Pearell and Frances Irene Hough Saville [Supplement No. 2810]. Frances was born March 29, 1947, at Martinsburg, West Virginia. She married Raymond Bruce Myers September 29, 1967, at Williamsport, Maryland. He was the son of Vernon Odell and Frances Catherine Myers and was born July 25, 1947, at Martinsburg. Raymond was an upholsterer.

(Sup) 7078M   i   Sandra Kaye Myers, born March 17, 1969.
(Sup) 7078N   ii   Raymond Bruce Myers, born September 27, 1973.

(Sup) 5056 DANIELS PERSHING BAKER HOUGH, JR. (Daniels[8], Ann[7], William[6], Adam[5], Alexander[4], John Adam II[3], John Adam I[2], John Jacob[1]) was the son of Danniels Pershing Baker and Gladys Clark Hough [Supplement No. 2811]. Daniels, Jr., was born December 10, 1940, at Martinsburg, West Virginia. He married Janet Jean Davis Hanson October 10, 1963, at San Diego, California. She was the daughter of Samuel and Margarete Davis Hanson and was born in 1933. Daniels was employed by the U.S. Government. He and Janet were divorced August, 1981.

(Sup) 7079   i   Pamela Marie Hough, born August 25, 1962.

(Sup) 5057 REBECCA ANN HOUGH (Daniels[8], Ann[7], William[6], Adam[5], Alexander[4], John Adam II[3], John Adam I[2], John Jacob[1]) was the daughter of Daniels Pershing Baker and Gladys Clark Hough [Supplement No. 2811]. Rebecca was born August 20, 1947, at Martinsburg, West Virginia. She married Patrick Wallace Larkin, Jr., June 10, 1967, at Parkville, Maryland. He was the son of Patrick Wallace and Martha Hall Larkin and was born April 11, 1943, at Baltimore, Maryland. Rebecca was a school teacher, and Patrick was a stock broker.

(Sup) 7079A   i   Kathleen Elizabeth Larkin, born March 22, 1973.
(Sup) 7079B   ii   Patrick Wallace Larkin, III, born Sept 20, 1975.

(Sup) 5058 SALLY VIRGINIA HOUGH (Daniels[8], Ann[7], William[6], Adam[5], Alexander[4], John Adam II[3], John Adam I[2], John Jacob[1]) was the daughter of Danniels Pershing Baker and Gladys Clark Hough [Supplement No. 2811]. Sally was born November 12, 1949, at Martinsburg, West Virginia. She married John Douglas Smith September 2, 1967, at Parkville, Maryland. He was the son of John Abert and Theresa Fickert Smith and was born June 25, 1949, at Parkville. Sally was a secretary, and John worked for General Motors. They resided at Delta, Pennsylvania.

(Sup) 7079C   i   Ann Marie Smith, born December 12, 1968.
(Sup) 7079D   ii   Jaye Dea Smith, born February 27, 1970.

(Sup) 5058A CORNELIA JUANITA HOUGH (Daniels^8, Ann^7, William^6, Adam^5, Alexander^4, John Adam II^3, John Adam I^2, John Jacob^1) was the daughter of Daniels Pershing Baker and Gladys Clark Hough [Supplement No. 2811]. Cornelia was born June 16, 1950, at Martinsburg, West Virginia. She married Jerry Michael Ritz November 5, 1967, at Parkville, Maryland. He was the the son of Milton Michael and Elsie Miller Ritz and was born October 13, 1946, at Baltimore. Cornelia was a dental laboratory technician, and Jerry was a carpenter.

(Sup) 7079E i Michael Daniel Ritz, born September 27, 1968.
(Sup) 7079F ii Michelle Lynn Ritz, born June 23, 1971.

(Sup) 5058B ROBERT JEROME HOUGH (Daniels^8, Ann^7, William^6, Adam^5, Alexander^4, John Adam II^3, John Adam I^2, John Jacob^1) was the son of Daniels Pershing Baker and Gladys Clark Hough [Supplement No. 2811]. Robert was born November 6, 1952, at Parkville, Maryland. He married Susan Marie Kappes March 26, 1972, at Parkville. She was the daughter of Egon Karl and Ann Bem Kappes and was born November 29, 1952, at Parkville. Robert and Susan resided at Joppatowne, Maryland.

(Sup) 7079G i Karley Jean Hough, born October 20, 1976.
(Sup) 7079H ii Daniel Robert Houh, born November 5, 1983.

(Sup) 5058C JOHN WILLIAM HOUGH (Daniels^8, Ann^7, William^6, Adam^5, Alexander^4, John Adam II^3, John Adam I^2, John Jacob^1) was the son of Daniels Pershing Baker and Gladys Clark Hough [Supplement No. 2811]. John was born July 13, 1956, at Baltimore, Maryland. He married Terri Ann Wall July 30, 1976, at Parkville, Maryland. She was the daughter of James Green and Carol Sherri Wall and was born November 16, 1960, in South Carolina. John was a carpenter, and Sherri was a grocery store clerk, at Perry Hall, Maryland.

(Sup) 7079J i Christy Ann Hough, born October 10, 1978.

(Sup) 5059 PHILLIP VAN HOUGH (Paul^8, Ann^7, William^6, Adam^5, Alexander^4, John Adam II^3, John Adam I^2, John Jacob^1) was the son of Paul Vincent and Pauline Shiver Hough [Supplement No. 2812]. Phillip was born October 22, 1945, at Martinsburg, West Virginia. He received his B.S. degree from Towson State University, Maryland, and his M.S. degree from Johns Hopkins University. Phillip married Andrea Jean Guzick July 21, 1968, at Baltimore, Maryland. She was the daughter of John and Jean Mary Cramblitt Guzick of Baltimore and was born November 1, 1947.

(Sup) 7080 i Tara Lynn Hough, born January 9, 1977.

(Sup) 5060 MARY CULLEEN HOUGH (Paul^8, Ann^7, William^6, Adam^5, Alexander^4, John Adam II^3, John Adam I^2, John Jacob^1) was the daughter of Paul Vincent and Pauline Shiver Hough [Supplement No. 2812]. Mary was born January 12, 1948, at Parkville, Maryland. She married, first, Ronald Stephen Elliot March 17, 1968. Ronald was the son of Joseph Hunter and Euphemia Tyson Rotering Elliot and was born July 15, 1947, at Gettysburg, Pennsylvania. He was a carpenter and cabinet maker. Mary and Ronald were divorced October, 1980. She married, second, James Kelly Carrigan February 14, 1981. James was the son of John Donley and Marian Joy Silman Carrigan and was born July 29, 1955, at Cheverly, Maryland. He was a construction supervisor.

CHILD OF MARY AND RONALD
(Sup) 7080A i Clinton Christopher Elliot, born October 10, 1973.

CHILD OF MARY AND JAMES
(Sup) 7080B ii David Corey Carrigan, born August 28, 1981.

(Sup) 5060A PAULA JEANENETTE HOUGH (Paul^8, Ann^7, William^6, Adam^5, Alexander^4, John Adam II^3, John Adam I^2, John Jacob^1) was the daughter of Paul Vincent and Paula Shiver Hough [Supplement No. 2812]. She was born January 16, 1951, at Parkville, Maryland. After graduating from Parkville High School, Paula moved to Fairbanks, Alaska, where she was employed as an accounts payable technician by Fairbanks North Star Borough.

(Sup) 5060B KAREN ELAINE HOUGH (Paul^8, Ann^7, William^6, Adam^5, Alexander^4, John Adam II^3, John Adam I^2, John Jacob^1) was the daughter of Paul Vincent and Paula Shivers Hough [Supplement No. 2812]. Karen was born March 21, 1957, at Parkville, Maryland. She was a taxidermist. Karen married, first, Charles Benjamin Payne June 9, 1973. He was the son of Williamson and Mary Catherine Cloud Payne and was born March 12, 1953, at Martinsburg, West Virginia. Karen and Charles were divorced March, 1977. She married, second, Willard Shriver.

(Sup) 7080C i Jason Matthew Payne, born April 18, 1974.
(Sup) 7080D ii Timothy Paul Payne, born September 29, 1975.

(Sup) 5061 JOHN WILLIAM LINK, III (John William^8, John^7, William^6, Adam^5, Alexander^4, John Adam II^3, John Adam I^2, John Jacob^1) was the son of John William and Verna Mae Hahn Link, Jr. [Supplement No. 2813]. John William, III, was born September 12, 1953, at Concord, North Carolina. He lived most of his early years with his father, at Grants, New Mexico. He married Peggy Diane Wilson of Odessa, Texas on March 18, 1971, at Juarez, Mexico. She was the daughter of Willie Lee and Eula Nell Norton Wilson and was born November 6, 1955, at Grand Junction, Colorado. John William was an electronics specialist in the Air Force. He and Peggy lived in Germany, New Mexico, Idaho, Texas, and Florida.

(Sup) 7081 i Cynthia Diane Link, born May 25, 1972.
(Sup) 7082 ii John William Link, IV, born September 29, 1976.

(Sup) 5062 ELIZABETH JUNE RUSSELL (Elizabeth[8], John[7], William[6], Adam[5], Alexander[4], John Adam II[3], John Adam I[2], John Jacob[1]) was the daughter of Charles Richard and Elizabeth Link Russell [Supplement No. 2814]. Elizabeth was born April 29, 1942, at Granite Falls, North Carolina. She married Noel Herbert Dentner June 17, 1972, at Monroe, Michigan. Elizabeth and Noel resided at Petersburg, Michigan.

(Sup) 5063 MARTHA LINK RUSSELL (Elizabeth[8], John[7], William[6], Adam[5], Alexander[4], John Adam II[3], John Adam I[2], John Jacob[1]) was the daughter of Charles Richard and Elizabeth Link Russell [Supplement No. 2814]. Martha was born January 13, 1947, at Granite Falls, North Carolina.

(Sup) 5064 CHARLES RICHARD RUSSELL III (Elizabeth[8], John[7], William[6], Adam[5], Alexander[4], John Adam II[3], John Adam I[2], John Jacob[1]) was the son of Charles Richard and Elizabeth Melvin Link Russell, Jr. [Supplement No. 2814]. Charles, III, was born September 9, 1948, at Charles Town, West Virginia. He was in the U.S. Army from July 1969 to April 1971, and served in Vietnam. He married Diane Marie Cameron January 20, 1973, at Hillsdale, Michigan. Charles graduated from Hillsdale College in May 1974, and Diane graduated in June 1972. They were divorced.

(Sup) 7083 i Karen Marie Russell, born August 11, 1976.
(Sup) 7084 ii Andrea Link Russell, born July 5, 1978.

(Sup) 5065 ARTHUR STANLEY LINK, Jr. (Arthur[8], John[7], William[6], Adam[5], Alexander[4], John Adam II[3], John Adam I[2], John Jacob[1]) was the son of Arthur Stanley and Margaret McDowell Douglas Link [Supplement No. 2815]. Arthur, Jr., was born November 2, 1946, at Princeton, New Jersey. He received his B.S. degree from Davidson College, Davidson, North Carolina, in June, 1968, and the M.D. degree from Columbia University College of Physicians and Surgeons, New York, in June, 1972. He performed his medical internship in internal medicine at North Carolina Baptist Hospital (Bowman Gray School of Medicine), Winston-Salem, North Carolina, in 1972-1973 and his second year residency at Harlem Hospital Center, New York, in 1973-1974. He was on active duty in the U.S. Army at Lyster Hospital, Fort Rucker, Alabama, 1974-1976. He performed his third year residency in internal medicine at North Carolina Baptist Hospital, Winston-Salem, North Carolina in 1977, where he conducted research in infectious diseases. Dr. Link was in the private practice of internal medicine. On June 9, 1973 he married Mary Margaret Brown from Winston-Salem, North Carolina. She was the daughter of Oscar Underwood and Johnsie Shore Brown.

(Sup) 7085 i Arthur Stanley Link, III, born May 12, 1974.

(Sup) 5066 JAMES DOUGLAS LINK (Arthur[8], John[7], William[6], Adam[5], Alexander[4], John Adam II[3], John Adam I[2], John Jacob[1]) was the son of Arthur Stanley and Margaret McDonald Douglas Link [Supplement No. 2815]. James was born April 20, 1950, at Evanston, Illinois. He attended the University of North Carolina and became a writer, residing at Princeton, New Jersey.

(Sup) 5066A MARGARET McDOWELL LINK (Arthur[8], John[7], William[6], Adam[5], Alexander[4], John Adam II[3], John Adam I[2], John Jacob[1]) was the daughter of Arthur Stanley and Margaret McDowell Douglas Link [Supplement No. 2815]. She was born August 30, 1951, at Charlotte, North Carolina. Margaret graduated from the University of North Carolina and worked as a travel agent at Winston-Salem and Boston. After attending hotel management school, she was employed as a sales manager for Marriot and Hyatt Hotels in the Washington, D.C. area.

(Sup) 5066B WILLIAM ALLEN LINK (Arthur[8], John[7], William[6], Adam[5], Alexander[4], John Adam II[3], John Adam I[2], John Jacob[1]) was the son of Arthur Stanley and Margaret McDowell Douglas Link [Supplement No. 2815]. William was born August 18, 1954, at Evanston, Illinois. He graduated from Davidson College, where he was a Phi Beta Kappa. He received his Ph.D. degree in American history from the University of Virginia and taught American history at the University of North Carolina. William married Susannah Hopkins Jones June 21, 1980. She was the daughter of Arthur Cummings and Dorothy Brothers Jones.

(Sup) 7085A i Percy Anne Link, born May 31, 1983.

(Sup) 5066C DOUGLAS LINK COSTA (Elinor[8], John[7], William[6], Adam[5], Alexander[4], John Adam II[3], John Adam I[2], John Jacob[1]) was the son of Anthony Paul and Elinor Link Costa [Supplement No. 2816]. Douglas was born March 8, 1948, at New York, New York. He received a B.S. degree in mathematics in 1968 from Oberlin College, Ohio, where he was a president of the Young Democrats. He received M.S. and Ph.D. degrees in mathematics from the University of Kansas in 1974 and was associate professor of mathematics at the University of Virginia. Douglas married Laurel Lynn Pierce of Orleans, Cape Cod, Massachusetts, June 7, 1969. She was the daughter of Bion Clifford and Charlotte Woodward Pierce. Laurel received a B.A. degree in French from Oberlin College in May 1969 and M.A. degrees in French and linguistics from the University of Kansas. (She descends on her mother's side from Daniel Webster, and on her father's side from the late Prime Minister Churchill of England.)

(Sup) 7086 i Jason Churchill Costa, born January 19, 1974.
(Sup) 7087 ii Thomas Woodward Costa, born August 23, 1979.

(Sup) 5067 PAUL EDWARD COFFINBERGER (Holland[8], Margaret[7], William[6], Adam[5], Alexander[4], John Adam II[3], John Adam I[2], John Jacob[1]) was the son of Holland Rocky and Hester Virginia Braithwaite Coffinberger [Supplement No. 2817]. Paul was born October 30, 1923, at Martinsburg, West Virginia. He married Margaret Elizabeth Rowell March 29, 1947. She was the daughter of Charles T. and Jane Harris Rowell and was born July 7, 1925, at Milwaukee, Wisconsin. Paul and Margaret resided at Millville, Pennsylvania.

(Sup) 7088 i Dennis Link Coffinberger, born February 5, 1948.
(Sup) 7089 ii Diane Louise Coffinberger, born May 20, 1951.

(Sup) 5068 MARY HESTER COFFINBERGER (Holland[8], Margaret[7], William[6], Adam[5], Alexander[4], John Adam II[3], John Adam I[2], John Jacob[1]) was the daughter of Holland Rocky and Hester Virginia Braithwaite Coffinberger [Supplement No. 2817]. Mary was born June 4, 1926, at Martinsburg, West Virginia. She married, first, Lewis Benton Rothgeb January 4, 1947. He was the son of Benton E. and Myra Payne Rothgeb and was born June 9, 1926, at Washington, D.C. Mary and Lewis were divorced in 1966. She married, second, Edward B. Booth. He was the son of Edward Benjamin and Lucy Ann Colley Booth and was born February 6, 1909, at Milton, North Carolina.

(Sup) 7090   i Benton Rocky Rothgeb, born January 3, 1948.
(Sup) 7091   ii David Earl Rothgeb, born March 31, 1952.

(Sup) 5069 LUCY MAE PATTERSON (Grace[8], Margaret[7], William[6], Adam[5], Alexander[4], John Adam II[3], John Adam I[2], John Jacob[1]) was the daughter of John William and Grace Coffinberger Patterson [Supplement No. 2818]. Lucy was born January 9, 1921, at Martinsburg, West Virginia. She died January 4, 1964, and is buried in Rosedale Cemetery at Martinsburg.

(Sup) 5070 VIRGINIA LEE PATTERSON (Grace[8], Margaret[7], William[6], Adam[5], Alexander[4], John Adam II[3], John Adam I[2], John Jacob[1]) was the daughter of John William and Grace Coffinberger Patterson [Supplement No. 2818]. She married Jessie Edwin Crumbacker December 26, 1945, at Martinsburg, West Virginia. She married Jessie Edwin Crumbacker and was born July 16, 1917, at Hagerstown, Maryland.

(Sup) 7092   i Robert Link Crumbacker, born August 19, 1947.
(Sup) 7093   ii Richard Lee Crumbacker, born March 9, 1949.
(Sup) 7093A iii Jesse Edwin Crumbacker, Jr., born October 6, 1958.

(Sup) 5071 ROSE ELAINE PATTERSON (Grace[8], Margaret[7], William[6], Adam[5], Alexander[4], John Adam II[3], John Adam I[2], John Jacob[1]) was the daughter of John William and Grace Coffinberger Patterson [Supplement No. 2818]. Rose Elaine was born August 24, 1927, at Martinsburg, West Virginia. She married Vincent Paul Noll June 28, 1947. He was the son of Roy Clarence and Sarah E. Koontz Noll and was born August 19, 1924, at Martinsburg, West Virginia. Elaine was employed by the Sheriff's Office at Martinsburg, and Vincent worked for the DuPont Company.

(Sup) 7094   i Lawrence Patterson Noll, born July 19, 1950.
(Sup) 7095   ii Ann Marie Noll, born July 23, 1953.
(Sup) 7096 iii Marcia Lou Noll, born December 15, 1954.
(Sup) 7097   iv Jeffery Michael Noll, born October 8, 1956.
(Sup) 7098   v Melissa Sue Noll, born May 1, 1961.

(Sup) 5072 JAMES WALTER COFFINBERGER (Walter[8], Margaret[7], William[6], Adam[5], Alexander[4], John Adam II[3], John Adam I[2], John Jacob[1]) was the son of Walter and Mildred Fogle Coffinberger [Supplement No. 2819]. James was born June 28, 1945, at Fort Wayne, Indiana.

(Sup) 5073 ROSE ELAINE COFFINBERGER (Walter[8], Margaret[7], William[6], Adam[5], Alexander[4], John Adam II[3], John Adam I[2], John Jacob[1]) was the daughter of Walter Welligton Sperow and Mildred Elnora Fogle Coffinberger [Supplement No. 2819]. Rose was born December 28, 1946, at Baltimore, Maryland. She married, first, George Edward Hohman, Jr., May 30, 1964, at Baltimore. He was the son of George Edward and Ruby Fialkewicz Hohman, and was born March 16, 1947, at Baltimore. Rose and George were divorced in 1970. She married, second, George Francis Haskell, Jr., January 17, 1976. The son of George Francis and Lorraine Fitzgerald Haskell, he was born January 12, 1952.

(Sup) 7099   i George Edward Hohman, III, born May 23, 1964.
(Sup) 7100   ii Stanley Chester Hohman, born June 3, 1965.

(Sup) 5074 WILLIAM FREDERICK COFFINBERGER (Walter[8], Margaret[7], William[6], Adam[5], Alexander[4], John Adam II[3], John Adam I[2], John Jacob[1]) was the son of Walter and Mildred Fogel Coffinberger [Supplement No. 2819]. William was born August 20, 1949, at Baltimore, Maryland. He married Patricia Ann Hutzler June 1, 1969, at Baltimore. She was the daughter of Norman and Mary Jane Thomson Hutzler and was born May 18, 1951, at Baltimore. William was an electronic repairman, and Patricia was a cosmetologist.

(Sup) 7101   i Tanya Renee Coffinberger, born February 6, 1974.
(Sup) 7102   ii April Dawn Coffinberger, born April 30, 1976.
(Sup) 7103 iii Tamela Joy Coffinberger, born June 6, 1979.
(Sup) 7104   iv Christopher William Coffinberger, born June 6, 1979.

(Sup) 5075 DORIS LINK CLOUD (Elmer Mae[8], Margaret[7], William[6], Adam[5], Alexander[4], John Adam II[3], John Adam I[2], John Jacob[1]) was the daughter of James Franklin and Elmer Mae Coffinberger Cloud [Supplement No. 2820]. Doris was born February 24, 1936, at Martinsburg, West Virginia. She married Leroy William Miller June 15, 1957. He was the son of George William and Beulah Ramsburg Miller.

(Sup) 5076 NANCY LOU CLOUD (Elmer Mae[8], Margaret[7], William[6], Adam[5], Alexander[4], John Adam II[3], John Adam I[2], John Jacob[1]) was the daughter of James Franklin and Elmer Mae Coffinberger Cloud [Supplement No. 2820]. Nancy was born February 28, 1939, and died October 1, 1939, at Martinsburg, West Virginia. She is buried in Elmwood Cemetery at Shepherdstown, West Virginia.

(Sup) 5081 BETTY JEANENE NEIBERT (Cornelia[8], Margaret[7], William[6], Adam[5], Alexander[4], John Adam II[3], John Adam I[2], John Jacob[1]) was the daughter of Scott Alvy and Cornelia Coffinberger Neibert [Supplement No. 2821]. Betty was born May 26, 1933, at Hagerstown, Maryland. She married, first, Wayne Steward Crider May 22, 1954. He was the son of Dr. Wayne F. and Ida Mae Lehman Crider and was born May 30, 1931, at Hagerstown. Betty and Wayne were divorced. She married, second, John Richard Crowe February 2, 1979. He was the son of Patrick and Elizabeth Thome Crowe and was born April 16, 1925, at Magnolia, Ohio. John received his B.S. degree from the University of Detroit in 1966.

(Sup) 7109   i   Wayne Stewart Crider, Jr., born May 30, 1955.
(Sup) 7110   ii   Catherine Carol Crider, born January 21, 1958.

(Sup) 5082 RICHARD DUANE NEIBERT (Cornelia[8], Margaret[7], William[6], Adam[5], Alexander[4], John Adam II[3], John Adam I[2], John Jacob[1]) was the son of Scott Alvy and Cornelia Coffinberger Neibert [Supplement No. 2821]. Richard was born October 20, 1934, at Hagerstown, Maryland. He married Hazel Louise Farris April 7, 1962, at Clearspring, Maryland. She was the daughter of Floyd Roosevelt and Mildred Elizabeth Shafer Farris and was born April 15, 1938, at Cumberland, Maryland.

(Sup) 5083 FAYE RENE NEIBERT (Cornelia[8], Margaret[7], William[6], Adam[5], Alexander[4], John Adam II[3], John Adam I[2], John Jacob[1]) was the daughter of Scott Alvy and Cornelia Coffinberger Neibert [Supplement No. 2821]. Fay Rene was born April 29, 1938, at Hagerstown, Maryland. She married, first, Robert Leon Elgin October 20, 1959. He was the son of Leon M. and Margarette Houser Elgin and was born June 21, 1930, at Hagerstown. Faye and Robert were divorced in 1963. She married, second, David W. Fowler March 1, 1966. He was the son of Oscar and Nellie Rockwell Fowler and was born December 1, 1929, at Martinsburg, West Virginia.

(Sup) 7111   i   Karen Sue Elgin, born April 2, 1962.

(Sup) 5084 JO ANN WHITTINGTON (Bertha[8], Margaret[7], William[6], Adam[5], Alexander[4], John Adam II[3], John Adam I[2], John Jacob[1]) was the daughter of Bernard Nelson and Bertha Link Coffinberger Whittington [Supplement No. 2822]. Jo Ann was born September 7, 1933, at Martinsburg, West Virginia. She married Frazier Clayborn Worley August 15, 1952, at Dunn Loring, Fairfax County, Virginia. He was the son of Gilbert Frazier and Bessie DeHart Worley and was born September 27, 1932, in Fairfax County.

(Sup) 7111A   i   Sheila Link Worley, born February 17, 1954.
(Sup) 7111B   ii   Gilbert Frazier Worley, born March 3, 1958.
(Sup) 7111C iii   Ann Michelle Worley, born March 2, 1963.

(Sup) 5077 JAMES DOUGLAS CLOUD (Elmer Mae[8], Margaret[7], William[6], Adam[5], Alexander[4], John Adam II[3], John Adam I[2], John Jacob[1]) was the son of James Franklin and Elmer Mae Coffinberger Cloud [Supplement No. 2820]. James was born November 23, 1941, at Martinsburg, West Virginia. He was employed as an electrician by the Board of Education of Berkeley County, West Virginia. James married Hilda Diana Grove. She was the daughter of Charles and Hilda Grove and was born May 11, 1945.

(Sup) 7105   i   Kimberly Ann Cloud, born January 7, 1964.
(Sup) 7106   ii   Stephen Douglas Cloud, born January 3, 1965.
(Sup) 7107 iii   Jeanette Lynn Cloud, born August 30, 1972.

(Sup) 5078 WILLIAM CALVIN CLOUD (Elmer Mae[8], Margaret[7], William[6], Adam[5], Alexander[4], John Adam II[3], John Adam I[2], John Jacob[1]) was the son of James Franklin and Elmer Mae Coffinberger Cloud [Supplement No. 2820]. William was born September 4, 1943, and died December 17, 1943, at Martinsburg, West Virginia. He is buried in Rosedale Cemetery at Martinsburg.

(Sup) 5079 DAVID MARTIN CLOUD (Elmer Mae[8], Margaret[7], William[6], Adam[5], Alexander[4], John Adam II[3], John Adam I[2], John Jacob[1]) was the son of James Franklin and Elmer Mae Coffinberger Cloud [Supplement No. 2820]. David was born October 4, 1944, at Martinsburg, West Virginia. He worked for a plastics firm at Herndon, Virginia. David married, first, Gwendolyn Edwards of Hedgesville, West Virginia. She was the daughter of Leroy Edwards. David married, second, Elizabeth Ann Myers of Shepherdstown, West Virginia. She was the daughter of Walter and Lou Ella Sheetz Myers and was born November 11, 1947.

CHILD OF DAVID AND GWENDOLYN

(Sup) 7108   i   David Martin Cloud, Jr., born July 22, 1964.

(Sup) 5080 CORNELIA DIANNE CLOUD (Elmer Mae[8], Margaret[7], William[6], Adam[5], Alexander[4], John Adam II[3], John Adam I[2], John Jacob[1]) was the daughter of James Franklin and Elmer Mae Coffinberger Cloud [Supplement No. 2820]. Cornelia was born March 21, 1948, at Martinsburg, West Virginia. She married Vernon Lee Kidwiler. Vernon was the son of Wade and Florence Griffin Kidwiler. He was employed at Dixie-Narco at Charles Town, West Virginia.

(Sup) 7108A   i   Michael Todd Kidwiler, born March 2, 1964.
(Sup) 7108B   ii   Valerie Ann Kidwiler, born June 29, 1965.

Anne was born August 29, 1931, at Martinsburg, West Virginia. She married, first, Richard Dix Shimp September 16, 1949. He was the son of Harry H. and Mary Ellen Ridenhour Shimp and was born April 12, 1927, at Martinsburg. Anne and Richard were divorced. She married, second, Kenneth Martin Rutherford January 9, 1955. Kenneth was the son of Thomas Miller and Bessie Thompson Rutherford and was born November 14, 1924, at Martinsburg. Anne was a motel clerk, and Kenneth was a licensed nurse at City Hospital in Martinsburg.

CHILD OF ANNE AND RICHARD

(Sup) 7112   i   James Richard Shimp, born September 7, 1950.

CHILDREN OF ANNE AND KENNETH

(Sup) 7112A ii   Kenneth Martin Rutherford, Jr., born July 29, 1955.
(Sup) 7112B iii Laura Lee Rutherford, born May 12, 1958.
(Sup) 7112C iv   Priscilla Anne Rutherford, born April 22, 1957.
(Sup) 7112D v   Lisa May Rutherford, born May 29, 1959.
(Sup) 7112E vi   Thomas Clay Rutherford, born July 23, 1960.

(Sup) 5090 JAMES WILLIAM COFFINBERGER (William[8], Martha[7], William[6], Adam[5], Alexander[4], John Adam II[3], John Adam I[2], John Jacob[1]) was the son of William Banks and Amanda Elizabeth Huff Coffinberger [Supplement No. 2827]. James was born August 31, 1935, at Winchester, Virginia. He married, first, Barbara Jean Carpenter of Shepherdstown, West Virginia. James married, second, Mary Jo Pappas of Winchester, Virginia.

CHILDREN OF JAMES AND BARBARA

(Sup) 7112F i   James Scott Coffinberger, born August 23, 1959.
(Sup) 7112G ii   Patricia Kay Coffinberger, born March 5, 1962.

(Sup) 5091 JOAN ELIZABETH COFFINBERGER (William[8], Martha[7], William[6], Adam[5], Alexander[4], John Adam II[3], John Adam I[2], John Jacob[1]) was the daughter of William Banks and Amanda Elizabeth Huff Coffinberger [Supplement No. 2827]. Joan was born October 15, 1937, at Winchester, Virginia. She was a school teacher of history. Joan married Gary Lee Johnson. He was born February 15, 1941, and was a self-employed barber.

(Sup) 7112H i   Andrew Patrick Johnson, born April 14, 1965.
(Sup) 7112J ii   Amy Elizabeth Johnson, born November 23, 1968.

(Sup) 5092 RICHARD LEE COFFINBERGER (William[8], Martha[7], William[6], Adam[5], Alexander[4], John Adam II[3], John Adam I[2], John Jacob[1]) was the son of William Banks and Amanda Elizabeth Huff Coffinberger [Supplement No. 2827]. Richard was born March 27, 1948, at Martinsburg, West Virginia. He married Janet Fletcher, March 5, 1977. She was the daughter of William C. and Mary Anne Fletcher and was born February 2, 1954, at Washington, D.C. Richard and Janet resided at Herndon, Fairfax County, Virginia. He was a lawyer, and associate dean of the School of Business at George Mason University, Virginia.

(Sup) 7112K i   Joseph William Coffinberger, born July 4, 1985.

(Sup) 5085 WILMA ARLENE WHITTINGTON (Bertha[8], Margaret[7], William[6], Adam[5], Alexander[4], John Adam II[3], John Adam I[2], John Jacob[1]) was the daughter of Bernard Nelson and Bertha Link Coffinberger Whittington [Supplement No. 2822]. Wilma was born October 9, 1935, at Martinsburg, West Virginia. She married Morris Beverly Wheeler January 13, 1956, at Dunn Loring, Fairfax County, Virginia. He was the son of Keith and Josephine Lacy Wheeler and was born December 31, 1935, at Falls Church, Virginia.

(Sup) 71110 i   Robin Arlene Wheeler, born June 29, 1958.
(Sup) 7111E ii   Sandra Dawn Wheeler, born October 23, 1962.

(Sup) 5086 BERNARD NELSON WHITTINGTON, JR. (Bertha[8], Margaret[7], William[6], Adam[5], Alexander[4], John Adam II[3], John Adam I[2], John Jacob[1]) was the son of Bernard Nelson and Bertha Link Coffinberger Whittington [Supplement No. 2822]. Bernard, Jr., was born July 1, 1944, at Georgetown, D.C. He married, first, Susan Carol Hoffman October 12, 1961. She was the daughter of Arlie C. and Margaret Bailey Hoffman and was born in 1944. Bernard and Susan were divorced September, 1967. He married, second, Lisa Kaye Fisher August 6, 1977, at Woodbridge, Virginia. Lisa was the daughter of Wilson and Lucy Walker Fisher and was born May 27, 1956.

CHILDREN OF BERNARD AND SUSAN

(Sup) 7111F i   David Lee Whittington, born January 4, 1963.
(Sup) 7111G ii   Daniel Nelson Whittington, born January 21, 1964.
(Sup) 7111H iii Hope Virginia Whittington, born December 29, 1966.

CHILDREN OF BERNARD AND LISA

(Sup) 7111J iv   Anna Kazimiera Whittington, born February 25, 1982.

(Sup) 5087 CHERYL ANN COFFINBERGER (William[8], Margaret[7], William[6], Adam[5], Alexander[4], John Adam II[3], John Adam I[2], John Jacob[1]) was the daughter of William Calvin and Kathleen Mae Cooper Coffinberger [Supplement No. 2823]. Cheryl was born April 8, 1945, at Hagerstown, Maryland. She married Phillip Ross Snodderly June 13, 1964, at Hagerstown. He was the son of Sherman Eugene and Evelyn Bachtell Snodderly and was born June 12, 1941.

(Sup) 7111K i   Kristy Ann Snodderly, born November 22, 1963.
(Sup) 7111L ii   Deanna Kay Snodderly, born January 2, 1968.

(Sup) 5088 DAVID CLIFTON COFFINBERGER (Martha[8], Martha[7], William[6], Adam[5], Alexander[4], John Adam II[3], John Adam I[2], John Jacob[1]) was the son of James Link and Ida Mae Gageby Coffinberger [Supplement No. 2824]. David was born November 15, 1927, at Martinsburg, West Virginia, and died that day.

(Sup) 5089 ANNE VIRGINIA COFFINBERGER (Martha[8], Martha[7], William[6], Adam[5], Alexander[4], John Adam II[3], John Adam I[2], John Jacob[1]) was the daughter of James Link and Ida Mae Gageby Coffinberger [Supplement No. 2824].

(Sup) 5093   SANDRA LOU COFFINBERGER (Daniel[8], Martha[7], William[6], Adam[5], Alexander[4], John Adam II[3], John Adam I[2], John Jacob[1]) was the daughter of Daniel Henry and Marguerite Johnston Coffinberger [Supplement No. 2828]. Sandra was born July 15, 1936, at Winchester, Virginia. She married Clifton Charles Keller December 15, 1956. He was the son of Charles and Angela Keller. Sandra and Clifton resided at Littlestown, Pennsylvania.

(Sup) 7113   i   Clifton Daniel Keller, born January 9, 1958.
(Sup) 7114   ii   Steven Mark Keller, born November 4, 1959.
(Sup) 7115   iii   Michael John Keller, born January 23, 1965.
(Sup) 7116   iv   Toni Nicole Keller, born January 3, 1975.

(Sup) 5094   DEANE LEE COFFINBERGER (Daniel[8], Martha[7], William[6], Adam[5], Alexander[4], John Adam II[3], John Adam I[2], John Jacob[1]) was the daughter of Daniel Henry and Marguerite Johnson Coffinberger [Supplement No. 2828]. Deanne was born October 24, 1942, at Winchester, Virginia. She married Earl Lee Nelson, III, December 3, 1960. He was the son of Earl Lee and Mary Nelson. Deane and Earl were divorced June, 1970.

(Sup) 7117   i   Earl Lee Nelson, IV, born August 15, 1961.
(Sup) 7118   ii   Denene Michelle Nelson, born February 15, 1966.

(Sup) 5095   RONALD LEE EVANS (Eunice[8], Martha[7], William[6], Adam[5], Alexander[4] John Adam II[3], John Adam I[2], John Jacob[1]) was the son of Lee French and Eunice Coffinberger Evans [Supplement No. 2829]. Ronald was born June 16, 1938, at Cumberland, Maryland. He married, first, Mary Elizabeth Prather June 15, 1958. She was the daughter of William E. and Clara Rhodes Prather and was born Decmber 25, 1939. Ronald and Mary Elizabeth were divorced. He married, second, Mary Frances Creamer December 29, 1979. She was the daughter of William G. and Isabel Lloyd Creamer of Kearneysville, West Virginia, and was born June 19, 1950. Ronald was an insurance agent for Smith-Nadenbousch Insurance Inc., Charles Town, West Virginia.

(Sup) 7118A   i   Scott Ashley Evans, born April 26, 1959.
(Sup) 7118B   ii   Kimberly Annette Evans, born November 6, 1960.
(Sup) 7118C   iii   Maria Leigh Evans, born October 29, 1966.

(Sup) 5096   SAMUEL WAYNE EVANS (Eunice[8], Martha[7], William[6], Adam[5], Alexander[4], John Adam II[3], John Adam I[2], John Jacob[1]) was the son of Lee French and Eunice Coffinberger Evans [Supplement No. 2829]. William was born March 19, 1940, at Cumberland, Maryland. He graduated from public schools in Martinsburg, West Virginia; obtained a B.S. degree in physics from St. Mary's University, San Antonio, Texas, in 1975; and served in the U.S. Air Force. Samuel married Minnette Elizabeth Jones August 2, 1963, at San Antonio, Texas. She was the daughter of Ishmael R. and Annie L. Brodbeck Jones and was born November 18, 1939, at San Antonio.

Stepdaughter   i   Karen Elizabeth Spurling, born January 2, 1961.
(Sup) 7119   ii   James Lee Evans, born June 13, 1964.
(Sup) 7120   iii   Cynthia Diane Evans, born September 6, 1965.

(Sup) 5097   EUNICE DIANE EVANS (Eunice[8], Martha[7], William[6], Adam[5], Alexander[4], John Adam II[3], John Adam I[2], John Jacob[1]) was the daughter of Lee French and Eunice Coffinberger Evans [Supplement No. 2829]. Diane was born March 27, 1942, at Martinsburg, West Virginia. She married Clayton August Brandt August 28, 1971, at Steelton, Pennsylvania. He was the son of Clayton Aaron and Edna Baughman Brandt and was born November 23, 1940, at Newport News Virginia. Eunice and Clayton lived at Harrisburg, Pennsylvania, where he was TV cable technician.

(Sup) 7121   i   Marcus Ryan Brandt, born February 16, 1972.
(Sup) 7122   ii   Matthew French Brandt, born September 12, 1973.

(Sup) 5098   DAVID LEE COFFINBERGER (Lee[8], Martha[7], William[6], Adam[5], Alexander[4], John Adam II[3], John Adam I[2], John Jacob[1]) was the son of Lee Matthias and Helen Russler Coffinberger [Supplement No. 2830]. David was born September 9, 1949, at Martinsburg, West Virginia. He attended Shepherd College, West Virginia, and was employed by the U.S. Postal Service.

(Sup) 5099   SHERLYN KAY COFFINBERGER (Lee[8], Martha[7], William[6], Adam[5], Alexander[4], John Adam II[3], John Adam I[2], John Jacob[1]) was the daughter of Lee Matthias and Helen Russler Coffinberger [Supplement No. 2830]. Sherlyn was born July 23, 1954, at Martinsburg, West Virgina. She married Russell Dean Clarke January 8, 1977. He was the son of William Dean and Dorothy Mae Tyre Clarke and was born November 29, 1955, at Leesburg, Virginia. Russell served in the U.S. Army. stationed in the United States and Germany.

(Sup) 7122A   i   Deanna Marie Clarke, born February 21, 1978.
(Sup) 7122B   ii   Daniel Matthew Clarke, born May 30, 1980.

(Sup) 5100   SUSAN MARIE COFFINBERGER (John[8], Martha[7], William[6], Adam[5], Alexander[4], John Adam II[3], John Adam I[2], John Jacob[1]) was the daughter of John Harman and Evelyn Lee Cammer Coffinberger [Supplement No. 2831]. Susan was born March 12, 1949, at Martinsburg, West Virginia. She married Ronald Lee Wenger June 1, 1969. He was born February 26, 1946, at Harrisonburg, Virginia. Ronald was employed by International Guard and Susan was a bank teller for Merchants and Farmers Bank at Martinsburg.

(Sup) 7123   i   Gregory Lee Wenger, born April 8, 1970.
(Sup) 7124   ii   Hilary Ann Wenger, Born January 12, 1973.

(Sup) 5101   JOHN BRADLEY COFFINBERGER (John[8], Martha[7], William[6], Adam[5], Alexander[4], John Adam II[3], John Adam I[2], John Jacob[1]) was the son of John Harman and Evelyn Lee Cammer Coffinberger [see Supplement No. 2831]. Brad was born October 29, 1957, at Martinsburg, West Virginia. He owned and operated a catering business in Martinsburg, West Virginia.

(Sup) 5102 BABETH LORRAINE KIPE (Nannie[8], Martha[7], William[6], Adam[5], Alexander[4], John Adam II[3], John Adam I[2], John Jacob[1]) was the daughter of Howard Philiphert and Nannie Coffinberger Leber [Supplement No. 2832]. Babeth was born October 25, 1946, at Memphis, Tennessee. She married, first, Walter Ross Pearson. He was born March 29, 1942, at Hagerstown, Maryland. Babeth and Walter were divorced. She married, second, John J. Craig. John was born April 1, 1945, at Richmond, Virginia.

(Sup) 7125 i Walter Ross Pearson, Jr., born May 25, 1966.
(Sup) 7126 ii Chance Allen Pearson, born June 2, 1969.

(Sup) 5103 MARY ELIZABETH KIPE (Nannie[8], Martha[7], William[6], Adam[5], Alexander[4], John Adam II[3], John Adam I[2], John Jacob[1]) was the daughter of Samuel Washington and Nannie Coffinberger Leber Kipe [Supplement No. 2832]. Mary was born March 29, 1945, at Hagerstown, Maryland. She married Eldon Lee Strite. He was born March 11, 1949, at Waynesboro, Pennsylvania.

(Sup) 7126A i Michael Kevin Strite, born April 23, 1968.
(Sup) 7126B ii Michelle Renee Strite, born September 15, 1970.

(Sup) 5104 JOHN KENNETH KIPE (Nannie[8], Martha[7], William[6], Adam[5], Alexander[4], John Adam II[3], John Adam I[2], John Jacob[1]) was the son of Samuel and Nannie Coffinberger Leber Kipe [Supplement No. 2832]. John was born April 17, 1954, at Waynesboro, Pennsylvania. He married, first, Erin Marie Eberly. She was born June 12, 1957. Erin died February, 1980, and is buried at Waynesboro. John married, second, Elenor Voth. Elenor was born October 16, 1963, in Canada.

CHILDREN OF JOHN AND ERIN

(Sup) 7127 i Mandy Marie Kipe, born May 26, 1977.
(Sup) 7127A ii Emily Ann Kipe, born January 19, 1980.

CHILD OF JOHN AND ELENOR

(Sup) 7127B iii Brandon Alexander Kipe, born October 22, 1983.

(Sup) 5105 MARK STEVEN CALDWELL (Mary[8], Martha[7], William[6], Adam[5], Alexander[4], John Adam II[3], John Adam I[2], John Jacob[1]) was the son of Calvin McKown and Mary Edna Coffinberger Caldwell [Supplement No. 2833]. Mark was born March 17, 1951.

(Sup) 5106 ELIZABETH PAIGE CALDWELL (Mary[8], Martha[7], William[6], Adam[5], Alexander[4], John Adam II[3], John Adam I[2], John Jacob[1]) was the daughter of Calvin McKown and Mary Edna Coffinberger Caldwell [Supplement No. 2833]. Elizabeth was born June 3, 1952. She married Gary Kevin McCauley September 1, 1973, at Martinsburg, West Virginia.

(Sup) 5107 MARY MARTHA CALDWELL (Mary[8], Martha[7], William[6], Adam[5], Alexander[4], John Adam II[3], John Adam I[2], John Jacob[1]) was the daughter of Calvin McKown and Mary Edna Coffinberger Caldwell [Supplement No. 2833]. Mary was born January 16, 1954. She was married February 28, 1976, at Martinsburg, West Virginia.

(Sup) 5108 CALVIN WILLIAM CALDWELL (Mary[8], Martha[7], William[6], Adam[5], Alexander[4], John Adam II[3], John Adam I[2], John Jacob[1]) was the son of Calvin McKown and Mary Edna Coffinberger Caldwell [Supplement No. 2833]. William was born February 28, 1957. He attended Concord and Fairmont College, majoring in business administration. He became associated with his parents' jewelry store.

(Sup) 5109 BEVERLY JEAN COFFINBERGER (Dennis[8], Martha[7], William[6], Adam[5], Alexander[4], John Adam II[3], John Adam I[2], John Jacob[1]) was the daughter of Dennis Clifton and Frances Louise Sine Coffinberger [Supplement No. 2834]. Beverly was born September 5, 1949, at Martinsburg, West Virginia. She married Patrick Hale Murphy June 7, 1969. He was the son of Thomas P. and Darlene Sherman Murphy and was born February 26, 1948. Beverly and Patrick both graduated from Shepherd College, West Virginia, with B.S. degrees in elementary education. Patrick served in the U.S. Marine Corps.

(Sup) 7127C i Tonya Marie Murphy, born October 1, 1970.
(Sup) 7127D ii Michael Patrick Murphy, born April 2, 1975.

(Sup) 5110 DENNIS CLIFTON COFFINBERGER, JR. (Dennis[8], Martha[7], William[6], Adam[5], Alexander[4], John Adam II[3], John Adam I[2], John Jacob[1]) was the son of Dennis Clifton and Frances Louise Sine Coffinberger [Supplement No. 2834]. Dennis, Jr., was born August 30, 1951, at Martinsburg, West Virginia. He married Christina Lynn Mickey February 23, 1974. She was the daughter of Andrew Dean and Sally Mae Frances Mickey. Dennis and Christina graduated from James Rumsey Vocational Technical Center, Hedgesville, West Virginia.

(Sup) 5111 DREW STEVEN COFFINBERGER (Dennis[8], Martha[7], William[6], Adam[5], Alexander[4], John Adam II[3], John Adam I[2], John Jacob[1]) was the son of Dennis Clifton and Frances Louise Sine Coffinberger [Supplement No. 2834]. Drew was born February 1, 1955, at Martinsburg, West Virginia. He married Barbara Jean Kenney May 4, 1975. She was the daughter of Floyd E. and Gertrude Czaykowski Kenney.

(Sup) 7128E i Stephanie Marcia Coffinberger, born Nov 28, 1975.
(Sup) 7128F ii Christi Anna Leigh Coffinberger, born July 14, 1980.
(Sup) 7128G iii Megann Renee Coffinberger, born August 8, 1983.

University. He became associated with his father in the Whitman Exterminating Company in 1972. Linda and Richard resided at Beckley, West Virginia.

(Sup) 7132　　i　Brian Keith Whitman, born January 22, 1975.
(Sup) 7133　　ii　Julie Marie Whitman, born March 1, 1978.

(Sup) 5517　PAMELA MARLOW LINK (Adam[8], Adam[7], William[6], Adam[5], Alexander[4], John Adam II[3], John Adam I[2], John Jacob[1]) was the daughter of Adam Baker and Margaret Marlow Link, Jr. [Supplement No. 2836]. Pamela was born September 28, 1946, at Winchester, Virginia. She studied at Marion College, Virginia, then transferred to Shepherd College where she received her B.S. degree in secondary education in 1968. She earned a master's degree in vocational education from Marshall University in 1978. Pamela was Miss Jefferson County in 1964 and West Virginia State Dairy Princess in 1965. She married, first, Calvin Herman Peterson, Jr., September 2, 1967, at Shepherdstown, West Virginia. He was the son of Calvin Herman and Phyllis Aubin Peterson and was born January 6, 1947, at Providence, Rhode Island. He received a B.S. degree in secondary education from Shepherd College and his master's degree in physical education from the University of Maryland. Pamela and Calvin were divorced December, 1975. She married, second, John Robert Wilmer, July 24, 1976, at Shenandoah Junction, Jefferson County, West Virginia. John was born November 24, 1952, at Washington, D.C. He was the son of Henry Banks and Marian Lynn Wilmer.

(Sup) 7134　　i　Tamara Lynn Peterson, born August 21, 1970.
(Sup) 7135　　ii　Calvin Herman Peterson III, born October 21, 1973.

(Sup) 5118　ADAM BAKER LINK, III (Adam[8], Adam[7], William[6], Adam[5], Alexander[4], John Adam II[3], John Adam I[2], John Jacob[1]) was the son of Adam Baker and Margaret Isabel Marlow Link, Jr. [Supplement No. 2836]. Adam, III, was born April 5, 1951, at Charles Town, West Virginia. He graduated from Shepherd College with a degree in business administration in 1973. He was employed by Acme Markets. Adam married Anita Louise Ramey June 12, 1976, at Charles Town, West Virginia. She was the daughter of Turner Allen and Louise Ware Ramey and was born July 12, 1952, at Charles Town. Anita graduated from Shepherd College, West Virginia. She and Adam lived on their "Broad View" farm near Uvilla, Jefferson County, West Virginia.

(Sup) 7135A　　i　Adam Baker Link, IV, born February 2, 1986.

(Sup) 5119　GLENDA GAIL FROCKE (Hildred[8], Samuel[7], William[6], Adam[5], Alexander[4], John Adam II[3], John Adam I[2], John Jacob[1]) was the daughter of George Gilbert and Hildred Link Frocke [Supplement No. 2840]. Glenda was born March 6, 1940, at Washington, D.C. She married Dennis Peter Spoto August 11, 1962, at Washington. He was the son of Peter and Dorothy Megis Spoto of New York and was born January 9, 1943, at Brooklyn, New York.

(Sup) 7136　　i　Susan Marie Spoto, born March 21, 1963.
(Sup) 7137　　ii　Deborah Ann Spoto, born August 30, 1966.

(Sup) 5512　TIMOTHY DANIEL COFFINBERGER (Dennis[8], Martha[7], William[6], Adam[5], Alexander[4], John Adam II[3], John Adam I[2], John Jacob[1]) was the son of Dennis Clifton and Frances Louise Sine Coffinberger [Supplement No. 2834]. Timothy was born October 31, 1959, at Martinsburg, West Virginia. He married Tamela Jean Roberts June 14, 1979. She was the daughter of James N. and Bonnie Beard Roberts and was born February 6, 1963.

(Sup) 7129　　i　Shannon Renee Coffinberger, born September 2, 1979.
(Sup) 7130　　ii　Daniel Lee Coffinberger, born August 31, 1983.

(Sup) 5513　MILDRED FRANCES COFFINBERGER (Dennis[8], Martha[7], William[6], Adam[5], Alexander[4], John Adam II[3], John Adam I[2], John Jacob[1]) was the daughter of Dennis Clifton and Frances Louise Sine Coffinberger [Supplement No. 2834]. She studied secondary education at Shepherd College, West Virginia.

(Sup) 5514　HOWARD BAYRLE LINK, JR. (Bayrle[8], Adam[7], William[6], Adam[5], Alexander[4], John Adam II[3], John Adam I[2], John Jacob[1]) was the son of Howard Bayrle and Alice Polhamus Link, Sr. [Supplement No. 2835]. Howard, Jr., was born September 3, 1943, at Indio, California. He died June 9, 1952, from a farming accident in Jefferson County, West Virginia, and is buried in Edge Hill Cemetery at Charles Town, West Virginia.

(Sup) 5515　KITTY KARYL LINK (Bayrle[8], Adam[7], William[6], Adam[5], Alexander[4], John Adam II[3], John Adam I[2], John Jacob[1]) was the daughter of Howard Bayrle and Alice Polhamus Link [Supplement No. 2835]. Kitty was born May 2, 1947, at Charles Town, West Virginia. She received her B.S. degree from West Virginia University in 1969. She worked as a medical technologist at Emory University Hospital in Atlanta, Georgia, and at the National Institutes of Health in Bethesda, Maryland. Kitty married Neil Alan Kaplan, August 16, 1975. He was the son of Sol and Louise Kaplan of Vienna, West Virginia, and was born October 17, 1947. Neil received a B.S. degree in chemical engineering from West Virginia University in 1969 and was a graduate of Georgetown Law School. Kitty and Neil resided at Sandy, Utah.

(Sup) 7131　　i　David Asher Kaplan, born May 5, 1981.

(Sup) 5516　LINDA LOUISE LINK (Bayrle[8], Adam[7], William[6], Adam[5], Alexander[4], John Adam II[3], John Adam I[2], John Jacob[1]) was the daughter of Howard Bayrle and Alice Polhamus Link [Supplement No. 2835]. Linda was born October 26, 1948, at Charles Town, West Virginia. She received a B.S. degree in language arts in 1970 and the M.S. degree in remedial reading in 1978 from West Virginia University, where she was a member of Pi Beta Phi social fraternity. She taught in Jefferson and Raleigh County public schools. Linda married Richard Charles Whitman August 8, 1970, at Leetown, West Virginia. He was the son of Charles Mason and Maxine Nettie Bryant Whitman and was born January 26, 1947, at Charleston, West Virginia. Richard received a B.A. degree from West Virginia University and did graduate work in fish pathology with Fordham

(Sup) 5120 PATRICIA LEE FROCKE (Hildred[8], Samuel[7], William[6], Adam[5], Alexander[4], John Adam II[3], John Adam I[2], John Jacob[1]) was the daughter of George Gilbert and Hildred Link Frocke [Supplement No. 2840]. Patricia was born May 15, 1942, at Washington, D.C. She married Fredrick Harvey Roll March 5, 1960, at Wichita and was born December 28, 1940, at Eskridge, Kansas.

(Sup) 7138   i   Doris Jean Roll, born December 5, 1960.
(Sup) 7139   ii   Michael Fredrick Roll, born March 13, 1967.

(Sup) 5121 GEORGE GILBERT FROCKE, JR. (Hildred[8], Samuel[7], William[6], Adam[5], Alexander[4], John Adam II[3], John Adam I[2], John Jacob[1]) was the son of George Gilbert and Hildred Link Frocke [Supplement No. 2840]. George, Jr., was born January 17, 1944, at Washington, D.C. He attended George Washington University, 1961 to 1965. He served in the U.S. Army 1965-1967 and was then employed by the City of Dallas, Texas. George married Martha Louise Bennett May 18, 1968, at Powell, Texas. She was the daughter of Buren Benard and Myrtle Mason Estelle Bennett of Kerens, Texas, and was born August 4, 1943, at Corsicana, Texas.

(Sup) 7140   i   Martha Celeste Frocke, born August 6, 1975.

(Sup) 5122 FRANCES DEE OWENS (Frances[8], Samuel[7], William[6], Adam[5], Alexander[4], John Adam II[3], John Adam I[2], John Jacob[1]) was the daughter of Richard Vern and Frances Link Owens [Supplement No. 2841]. Frances was born July 24, 1945, at San Francisco, California. She married, first, Edward Joseph Frey, Jr., December 14, 1964, at Boise, Idaho. He was the son of Edward Joseph and Flora Frey. Frances and Edward were divorced January, 1971. She married, second, Jay Lee Curtiss July 27, 1972, at Vancouver, Washington. He was the son of Jay and Margaret McCarter Curtiss.

CHILDREN OF FRANCES AND EDWARD
(Sup) 7141   i   Patricia Denise Frey, born February 23, 1966.
(Sup) 7141A   ii   Jennifer Dee Frey, born May 6, 1969.

CHILDREN OF FRANCES AND JAY
(Sup) 7171B   iii Jay Lee Curtiss, Jr., born September 7, 1971.
(Sup) 7171C   iv   Jason Vernon Curtiss, born July 4, 1973.

(Sup) 5123 SANDRA JEAN OWENS (Frances[8], Samuel[7], William[6], Adam[5], Alexander[4], John Adam II[3], John Adam I[2], John Jacob[1]) was the daughter of Richard Vern and Frances Link Owens [Supplement No. 2841]. Sandra was born October 29, 1946, at Portland, Oregon. She married Clois Wade Bellah, June 6, 1968, at Nocona, Texas. He was the son of Henry Allen and Josie Jean Benson Bellah and was born June 2, 1947, at Nocona.

(Sup) 7142   i   Rebecca Diane Bellah, born April 30, 1971.
(Sup) 7142A   ii   Misty Dawn Bellah, born June 28, 1973.
(Sup) 7142B   iii Cynthia Marie Bellah, born April 11, 1975.
(Sup) 7142C   iv   Amanda Irene Bellah, born October 4, 1977.
(Sup) 7142D   v   Clois Wade Bellah, Jr., born January 13, 1981.

(Sup) 5123A DEBORAH ANN OWENS (Frances[8], Samuel[7], William[6], Adam[5], Alexander[4], John Adam II[3], John Adam I[2], John Jacob[1]) was the daughter of Richard Vern and Frances Link Owens [Supplement No. 2840]. Debbie was born February 21, 1951, at Portland, Oregon. She married Daniel David Senften, Jr., August 24, 1970, at Gresham, Oregon. He was the son of Daniel David and Elsia Caroline Edmonston Senften and was born November 14, 1951, at Portland.

(Sup) 7143   i   Lucinda Grace Senften, born September 26, 1972.
(Sup) 7143A   ii   Sarah DeAnn Senften, born January 6, 1975.
(Sup) 7143B   iii Daniel David Senften, III, born October 20, 1976.

(Sup) 5123B RICHARD FREDERICK OWENS (Frances[8], Samuel[7], William[6], Adam[5], Alexander[4], John Adam II[3], John Adam I[2], John Jacob[1]) was the son of Richard Vern and Frances Link Owens [Supplement No. 2841]. Rick was born September 5, 1952, at Portland, Oregon. He married Weslyn Janine Russell June 21, 1975, at Milwaukie, Oregon. She was the daughter of Wesley William and Joan Schaffer Russell and was born August 29, 1954, at Portland.

(Sup) 7144   i   Erica Bril Owens, born November 28, 1980.
(Sup) 7144A   ii   Corin Rochelle Owens, born November 29, 1984.

(Sup) 5124 WESLEY BRIAN LINK (William[8], Samuel[7], William[6], Adam[5], Alexander[4], John Adam II[3], John Adam I[2], John Jacob[1]) was the son of William Byron and Ruby Jean Burton Link [Supplement No. 2844]. Wesley was born July 16, 1957, at Washington, D.C. He received B.S. and M.S. degrees in applied mathematics from the University of Virginia, 1975-1980, and was employed by the Mitre Corporation, McLean, Virginia.

(Sup) 5125 GREGORY CHARLES LINK (William[8], Samuel[7], William[6], Adam[5], Alexander[4], John Adam II[3], John Adam I[2], John Jacob[1]) was the son of William Byron and Ruby Jean Burton Link [Supplement No. 2844]. Gregory was born April 27, 1959, at Arlington, Virginia. He obtained a B.S. degree in aeronautical science from Embry-Riddle Aeronautical University in 1981 and trained to become an air controller.

(Sup) 5126 DAVID GORDON LINK (William[8], Samuel[7], William[6], Adam[5], Alexander[4], John Adam II[3], John Adam I[2], John Jacob[1]) was the son of William Byron and Ruby Jean Burton Link [Supplement No. 2844]. David was born April 6, 1961, at Arlington, Virginia. After public schools in Fairfax City, Virginia, he attended George Mason University, 1979-1984. He received a B.S. degree in electronic engineering in 1985 and was employed by the U.S. Army Center for Night Vision and Electro-Optics.

(Sup) 5127 RONALD NEAL WALTERS (Betty[8], Samuel[7], William[6], Adam[5], Alexander[4], John Adam II[3], John Adam I[2], John Jacob[1]) was the son of Harry Neil and Betty Geneva Link Walters [Supplement No. 2845]. Ronald was born June 29, 1950, at Washington, D.C. He became Vice President and Director of Employee Benefits for Silverstein DeVan Insurance Agency at Charleston, West Virginia. He married, first, Rashell Ann Yanero. She was the daughter of Michael T. and Peggy Fortney Yanero and was born July 3, 1953, at Fairmont, West Virginia. Ronald and Rashell were divorced in 1978. He married, second, Debra Lynn Cantees May 21, 1982, at Uvilla, Jefferson County, West Virginia. Debra was the daughter of John J. and Cleta B. Cantees and was born March 7, 1954, at Williamson, West Virginia.

CHILD OF RONALD AND RASHELL ANN

(Sup) 7145   i   Michael Jason Walters, born March 1, 1973.

CHILDREN OF RONALD AND DEBRA

(Sup) 7145A   ii Ronald Neal Walters, Jr., born June 7, 1984.
(Sup) 7145B   iii Christopher Wesley Walters, born May 1, 1986.

(Sup) 5128 LUCINDA STARR WALTERS (Betty[8], Samuel[7], William[6], Adam[5], Alexander[4], John Adam II[3], John Adam I[2], John Jacob[1]) was the daughter of Harry Neil and Betty Geneva Link Walters [Supplement No. 2845]. Lucinda was born November 15, 1951 at Washington, D.C. She married Robert Eugene Collis October 6, 1980, at Ranson, Jefferson County, West Virginia. He was the son of Jack Ellis and Patricia Blais Collis and was born March 23, 1952, at Martinsburg, West Virginia.

(Sup) 7146   i   Shannon Hope Walters, born January 23, 1974.

(Sup) 5129 HARRY PAUL WALTERS (Betty[8], Samuel[7], William[6], Adam[5], Alexander[4], John Adam II[3], John Adam I[2], John Jacob[1]) was the son of Harry Neil and Betty Geneva Link Walters [Supplement No. 2845]. He was born June 3, 1954, at Charles Town, West Virginia. He married Glenna Fay Carr April 7, 1973, at Hagerstown, Maryland. She was the daughter of Glen and Edna Carr and was born July 17, 1955, at Keyser, West Virginia.

(Sup) 7147   i   Dawn Hope Walters, born June 21, 1975.
(Sup) 7148   ii Glen Samuel Walters, born September 29, 1978.

(Sup) 5130 JOSEPH THOMAS WALTERS (Betty[8], Samuel[7], William[6], Adam[5], Alexander[4], John Adam II[3], John Adam I[2], John Jacob[1]) was the son of Harry Neil and Betty Geneva Link Walters [Supplement No. 2845]. Joseph was born April 29, 1956 at Charles Town, West Virginia. He married Shirley Mae Edwards April 22, 1978, at Ranson, Jefferson County, West Virginia. She was the daughter of Charles Robert and Nancy Hardy Edwards and was born November 25, 1962, at Charles Town.

(Sup) 7149   i   Ruby Mae Walters, born December 3, 1978.
(Sup) 7150   ii April Geneva Walters, born February 15, 1984.

(Sup) 5131 JOHN STEWART LINK (Samuel[8], Samuel[7], William[6], Adam[5], Alexander[4], John Adam II[3], John Adam I[2], John Jacob[1]) was the son of Samuel Wesley and Donna Collins Link, Jr. [Supplement No. 2846]. John was born April 17, 1959, at Martinsburg, West Virginia. He graduated from James Madison University, Harrisonburg, Virginia, in 1981. He was employed by Satellite Business Systems and then by Planning Research Company. In 1985, John married Terri Rae Johnston. She was the daughter of Gary Eugene and Patricia Geraldine Johnston of Sterling, Virginia.

(Sup) 7151   i   Sean Christopher Stewart Link, born Nov 5, 1987.

(Sup) 5132 RHONDA JEAN LINK (Samuel[8], Samuel[7], William[6], Adam[5], Alexander[4], John Adam II[3], John Adam I[2], John Jacob[1]) was the daughter of Samuel Wesley and Donna Collins Link, Jr. [Supplement No. 2846]. She was born April 30, 1965, at Falls Church, Virginia. Rhonda graduated from Radford University, Virginia, in 1987 and was employed as a teacher in the Loudon County, Virginia, public schools. In 1987 she married David James Allen. He was the son of Theodore and Sarah Allen of Sterling, Virginia.

(Sup) 5133 SUSAN CHRISTINE LINK (William[8], James[7], William[6], Adam[5], Alexander[4], John Adam II[3], John Adam I[2], John Jacob[1]) was the daughter of William Homer and Kathryn Anne Cooper Link [Supplement No. 2848]. Christine was born September 12, 1963, at Abingdon, Washington County, Virginia. She graduated from Lenoir-Rhyne College, North Carolina. Christine married Tommy Louis Lowman, June 29, 1985, at Richfield, Rowan County, North Carolina. He was the son of Samuel Martin and Peggy Ann (Haynes) Lowman and was born March 4, 1963, at Salisbury, Rowan County. Christine and Tommy resided at Newton, North Carolina.

(Sup) 7152   i   Benjamin Lee Lowman, born October 30, 1987.

(Sup) 5134 MARY VIRGINIA LINK (William[8], James[7], William[6], Adam[5], Alexander[4], John Adam II[3], John Adam I[2], John Jacob[1]) was the daughter of William Homer and Kathryn Anne Cooper Link [Supplement No. 2848]. Virginia born April 30, 1965, at Prosperity, Newberry County, South Carolina. Virginia graduated from Lenoir-Rhyne College and was employed as a teacher at Charlotte, North Carolina.

(Sup) 5135 DAVID JONATHAN LINK (William[8], James[7], William[6], Adam[5], Alexander[4], John Adam II[3], John Adam I[2], John Jacob[1]) was the son of William Homer and Kathryn Anne Cooper Link [Supplement No. 2848]. David was born May 16, 1968, at Prosperity, Newberry County, South Carolina. He attended Lenoir-Rhyne College, North Carolina.

(Sup) 5136 JONATHAN MARK BRUCE (Martha[8], James[7], William[6], Adam[5], Alexander[4], John Adam II[3], John Adam I[2], John Jacob[1]) was the son of Jimmy Lane and Martha Susan Link Bruce [Supplement No. 2849]. Jonathan was born September 16, 1961, at Columbia, South Carolina. He graduated from Lenoir-Rhyne College, North Carolina, May, 1986, with a degree in business administration. He married Nancy Jean Howard March 17, 1984, at Startown, Catawba County, North Carolina. She was the daughter of Samuel H. Howard, of Hickory, North Carolina, and was born June 21, 1962.

(Sup) 5137 MARTHA CONSTANCE BRUCE (Martha[8], James[7], William[6], Adam[5], Alexander[4], John Adam II[3], John Adam I[2], John Jacob[1]) was the daughter of Jimmy Lane and Martha Susan Link Bruce [Supplement No. 2849]. She was born March 20, 1964, at Abingdon, Washington County, Virginia. Connie graduated from Kings Business College, Charlotte, North Carolina, in 1983. She joined the U.S. Navy and became a photographer.

(Sup) 5138 DAVID LAWRENCE MOOSE (Sarah[8], James[7], William[6], Adam[5], Alexander[4], John Adam II[3], John Adam I[2], John Jacob[1]) was the son of Paul Lawrence and Sarah Constance Link Moose [Supplement No. 2850]. David was born December 3, 1963, at Charlottesville, Virginia.

(Sup) 5139 JOHN EDWARD MOOSE (Sarah[8], James[7], William[6], Adam[5], Alexander[4], John Adam II[3], John Adam I[2], John Jacob[1]) was the son of Paul Lawrence and Sarah Constance Link Moose [Supplement No. 2850]. John was born May 1, 1968, at Lexington, Virginia (the twin of Philip).

(Sup) 5140 PHILLIP JAMES MOOSE (Sarah[8], James[7], William[6], Adam[5], Alexander[4], John Adam II[3], John Adam I[2], John Jacob[1]) was the son of Paul Lawrence and Sarah Constance link Moose [Supplement No. 2850]. Phillip was born May 1, 1968, at Lexington, Virginia (the twin of John).

(Sup) 5141 CYNTHIA CHRISTINE DAVIS (Janet[8], James[7], William[6], Adam[5], Alexander[4], John Adam II[3], John Adam I[2], John Jacob[1]) was the daughter of Robert Washington and Janet Christine Link Davis [Supplement No. 2851]. Cynthia was born October 21, 1964, at Staunton, Virginia.

(Sup) 5142 ROBERT TIMOTHY DAVIS (Janet[8], James[7], William[6], Adam[5], Alexander[4], John Adam II[3], John Adam I[2], John Jacob[1]) was the son of Robert Washington and Janet Christine Link Davis [Supplement No. 2851]. Robert was born November 16, 1967, at Staunton, Virginia.

(Sup) 5143 ANDREA ELAINE DAVIS (Janet[8], James[7], William[6], Adam[5], Alexander[4], John Adam II[3], John Adam I[2], John Jacob[1]) was the son of Robert Washington and Janet Christine Link Davis [Supplement No. 2851]. Andrea was born April 6, 1972, at Staunton, Virginia.

(Sup) 5144 LEROY STUART ZIDER, III (Eleanor[8], Albert[7], John[6], Adam[5], Alexander[4], John Adam II[3], John Adam I[2], John Jacob[1]) was the son of LeRoy Stuart and Eleanor Anne Link Zider, Jr. [Supplement No. 2852]. LeRoy, III, was born May 13, 1942, at Brooklyn, New York. He graduated from Princeton University and received his M.B.A. from Harvard Business School. He married Linda Elliott October 18, 1981, at San Francisco, California. She was the daughter of Donald and Janice Condit Elliott and was born October 7, 1950, at San Francisco. Linda graduated from the University of California at Berkeley.

(Sup) 7161   i   Alexander David Zider, born January 24, 1982.
(Sup) 7162   ii   Jacqueline Elliott Zider, born May 17, 1984.

(Sup) 5145 ROBERT BRUCE ZIDER (Eleanor[8], Albert[7], John[6], Adam[5], Alexander[4], John Adam II[3], John Adam I[2], John Jacob[1]) was the son of LeRoy Stuart and Eleanor Anne Link Zider, Jr. [Supplement No. 2852]. Robert was born April 1, 1948, at Brooklyn, New York. He graduated from the University of Virginia and received his M.B.A. degree from Harvard Business School. He married Cheryl Anne Faulconer June 14, 1969, at Charlottesville, Virginia. She was the daughter of Angus Leslie and Sarah Norman Faulconer and was born June 3, 1947, at Lynchburg, Virginia. Cheryl Anne graduated from the University of Virginia.

(Sup) 7163   i   Christopher Stuart Zider, born April 20, 1971.
(Sup) 7164   ii   Allison Leslie Zider, born February 2, 1979.
(Sup) 7165   iii   John Robert Zider, born May 17, 1982.
(Sup) 7166   iv   Grant Thompson Zider, born December 1, 1983.

(Sup) 5140 PHILLIP JAMES MOOSE (Sarah[8], James[7], William[6], Adam[5], Alexander[4], John Adam II[3], John Adam I[2], John Jacob[1]) was the son of Paul Lawrence and Sarah Constance link Moose [Supplement No. 2850]. Phillip was born May 1, 1968, at Lexington, Virginia (the twin of John).

(Sup) 5141 CYNTHIA CHRISTINE DAVIS (Janet[8], James[7], William[6], Adam[5], Alexander[4], John Adam II[3], John Adam I[2], John Jacob[1]) was the daughter of Robert Washington and Janet Christine Link Davis [Supplement No. 2851]. Cynthia was born October 21, 1964, at Staunton, Virginia.

(Sup) 5142   ROBERT TIMOTHY DAVIS (Janet[8], James[7], William[6], Adam[5], Alexander[4], John Adam II[3], John Adam I[2], John Jacob[1]) was the son of Robert Washington and Janet Christine Link Davis [Supplement No. 2851]. Robert was born November 16, 1967, at Staunton, Virginia.

(Sup) 5143   ANDREA ELAINE DAVIS (Janet[8], James[7], William[6], Adam[5], Alexander[4], John Adam II[3], John Adam I[2], John Jacob[1]) was the son of Robert Washington and Janet Christine Link Davis [Supplement No. 2851]. Andrea was born April 6, 1972, at Staunton, Virginia.

(Sup) 5144   LEROY STUART ZIDER, III (Eleanor[8], Albert[7], John[6], Adam[5], Alexander[4], John Adam II[3], John Adam I[2], John Jacob[1]) was the son of LeRoy Stuart and Eleanore Anne Link Zider, Jr. [Supplement No. 2852]. LeRoy, III, was born May 13, 1942, at Brooklyn, New York. He graduated from Princeton University and received his M.B.A. from Harvard Business School. He married Linda Elliott October 18, 1981, at San Francisco, California. She was the daughter of Donald and Janice Condit Elliott and was born October 7, 1950, at San Francisco. Linda graduated from the University of California at Berkeley.

(Sup) 7161   i   Alexander David Zider, born January 24, 1982.
(Sup) 7162   ii   Jacqueline Elliott Zider, born May 17, 1984.

(Sup) 5145   ROBERT BRUCE ZIDER (Eleanor[8], Albert[7], John[6], Adam[5], Alexander[4], John Adam II[3], John Adam I[2], John Jacob[1]) was the son of LeRoy Stuart and Eleanore Anne Link Zider, Jr. [Supplement No. 2852]. Robert was born April 1, 1948, at Brooklyn, New York. He graduated from the University of Virginia and received his M.B.A. degree from Harvard Business School. He married Cheryl Anne Faulconer June 14, 1969, at Charlottesville, Virginia. She was the daughter of Angus Leslie and Sarah Norman Faulconer and was born June 3, 1947, at Lynchburg, Virginia. Cheryl Anne graduated from the University of Virginia.

(Sup) 7163   i   Christopher Stuart Zider, born April 20, 1977.
(Sup) 7164   ii   Allison Leslie Zider, born February 2, 1979.
(Sup) 7165 iii   John Robert Zider, born May 17, 1982.
(Sup) 7166   iv   Grant Thompson Zider, born December 1, 1983.

(Sup) 5146   WINSTON CONWAY LINK (Ogle Winston[8], Albert[7], John[6], Adam[5], Alexander[4], John Adam II[3], John Adam I[2], John Jacob[1]) was the son of Ogle Winston and Vonda Marteal Oglesby Link [Supplement No. 2853]. He was born April 2, 1945, at Mineola, New York. He received his B.S. degree in mathematics from Louisiana Tech University in 1967, and an M.A. degree in mathematics from the University of Oklahoma in 1970. His interests were old cars and model trains. He married Marilyn Frances Madden August 24, 1968, at Ruston, Louisiana. She was the daughter of Ragan Duprec and Margaret Elizabeth Burt Madden and was born October 29, 1946, at Ruston.

(Sup) 7167   i   Anne Stampley Link, born September 10, 1971.

(Sup) 5147   LUCINDA ANNE LINK (Albert[8], Albert[7], John[6], Adam[5], Alexander[4], John Adam II[3], John Adam I[2], John Jacob[1]) was the daughter of Albert and Elizabeth Margaret Dennison Link, Jr. [Supplement No. 2855]. Lucinda Anne was born July 19, 1955, at Brooklyn, New York. She graduated from Somers High School, Somers, New York, in 1973. In 1977 she received a B.S. degree in business administration from Central Connecticut State College, where she was a member of Phi Beta Lambda.

(Sup) 5148   ALBERT DENNIS LINK (Albert[8], Albert[7], John[6], Adam[5], Alexander[4], John Adam II[3], John Adam I[2], John Jacob[1]) was the son of Albert and Elizabeth Margaret Dennison Link, Jr. [Supplement No. 2855]. He was born October 1, 1958, at Brooklyn, New York. Albert graduated from Somers High School, Somers, New York, in 1976, and received a B.S. degree in business administration from The State University of New York at Oswego, where he was a member of the National Honor Society.

(Sup) 5149   MICHAEL ROBERT GEHRET (Barbara[8], Lester[7], John[6], Adam[5], Alexander[4], John Adam II[3], John Adam I[2], John Jacob[1]) was the son of Robert Edward and Barbara Anne Link Gehret [Supplement No. 2856]. Michael was born June 18, 1953, at Reading, Pennsylvania. He graduated from Berks Vo-Tech, where he studied automotive engineering. He married Sylvia Louise Wentzel September 29, 1973, at Reading. She was the daughter of Earl and Myrtle Ruth Wentzel and was born June 8, 1953, at Reading.

(Sup) 7168   i   Michael Robert Gehret, Jr., born March 4, 1974.

(Sup) 5150   NANCY EILEEN GEHRET (Barbara[8], Lester[7], John[6], Adam[5], Alexander[4], John Adam II[3], John Adam I[2], John Jacob[1]) was the daughter of Robert Edward and Barbara Anne Link Gehret [Supplement No. 2856]. Nancy was born March 3, 1955, at Reading, Pennsylvania. She married, first, Michael Henry Arndt November 6, 1971, at Reading. He was the son of Victor and Marie McGargle Arndt and was born March 5, 1953. Nancy and Michael were divorced. She married, second, Steven Max Renner July 10, 1981, at Oley, Pennsylvania. He was the son of Leonard G. and Mabel Stabolepazy Renner and was born May 20, 1957.

(Sup) 7169   i   Shannon Marie Arndt, born May 13, 1972.

(Sup) 5151 JO ANNE GEHRET (Barbara[8], Lester[7], John[6], Adam[5], Alexander[4], John Adam II[3], John Adam I[2], John Jacob[1]) was the daughter of Robert Edward and Barbara Anne Link Gehret [Supplement No. 2856]. Jo Anne was born March 27, 1956, at Reading, Pennsylvania. She graduated from York Academy of Arts in York, Pennsylvania.

(Sup) 5152 KATHLEEN KAY GEHRET (Barbara[8], Lester[7], John[6], Adam[5], Alexander[4], John Adam II[3], John Adam I[2], John Jacob[1]) was the daughter of Robert Edward and Barbara Anne Link Gehret [Supplement No. 2856]. She was born May 28, 1960, at Reading, Pennsylvania, and graduated from high school in Hamburg, Pennsylvania.

(Sup) 5153 STEPHEN ALAN LINK (Robert[8], Lester[7], John[6], Adam[5], Alexander[4], John Adam II[3], John Adam I[2], John Jacob[1]) was the son of Robert Ogle and Blanche Ailene Clauser Link [Supplement No. 2857]. Stephen was born May 20, 1952, at Baltimore, Maryland. He received a degree in business administration from Old Dominion University, Norfolk, Virginia, in 1975 and worked for K-Mart and Trailways. He married Debra Jean Turner September 17, 1977, at Johnston, South Carolina. She was the daughter of Richard Clark and Cleo Turner and was born April 25, 1956, at Augusta, Georgia.

(Sup) 7170 i Christopher Stephen Link, born June 17, 1981.

(Sup) 5154 JOHN ROBERT LINK (Robert[8], Lester[7], John[6], Adam[5], Alexander[4], John Adam II[3], John Adam I[2], John Jacob[1]) was the son of Robert Ogle and Blanche Ailene Clauser Link [Supplement No. 2857]. John was born April 8, 1955, at Baltimore, Maryland. He received a B.S. degree from Old Dominion University and performed cancer research at Meloy Laboratories, Springfield, Virginia. He married Donna Sue Anstine May 3, 1980, at Arlington, Virginia. She was the daughter of Monroe and Alva Anstine and was born May 3, 1954, at Arlinton, Virginia.

(Sup) 7171 i Gregory John Link, born March 16, 1981.

(Sup) 5155 RUSSELL DUANE RUGH (Margaret[8], Samuel[7], Nancy[6], Elizabeth[5], Alexander[4], John Adam II[3], John Adam I[2], John Jacob[1]) was the son of Oscar Oliver and Margaret Gardner Rugh [TLF No. 2858]. Russell was born June 8, 1938, at Logansport, Pennsylvania.

(Sup) 5156 WILLIAM ROBERT GARDNER (William[8], Samuel[7], Nancy[6], Elizabeth[5], Alexander[4], John Adam II[3], John Adam I[2], John Jacob[1]) was the son of William Fontaine and Verna Weston Gardner [TLF No. 2859]. He was born December 1, 1946, at Swissvale, Pennsylvania.

(Sup) 5157 LARRY WAYNE GARDNER (John[8], Samuel[7], Nancy[6], Elizabeth[5], Alexander[4], John Adam II[3], John Adam I[2], John Jacob[1]) was the son of John William and Alma Cline Gardner [TLF No. 2861]. Larry was born April 23, 1946, at Pitcairn, Pennsylvania.

(Sup) 5158 JAMES CHARLES GARDNER (John[8], Samuel[7], Nancy[6], Elizabeth[5], Alexander[4], John Adam II[3], John Adam I[2], John Jacob[1]) was the son of John William and Alma Cline Gardner [TLF No. 2861]. James was born October 1, 1947, at Pitcairn, Pennsylvania.

(Sup) 5159 MARY LOUISE COLE (Mary[8], Samuel[7], Nancy[6], Elizabeth[5], Alexander[4], John Adam II[3], John Adam I[2], John Jacob[1]) was the daughter of Frederick and Mary Gardner Cole [TLF No. 2864]. Mary was born June 16, 1947, at Pitcairn, Pennsylvania.

(Sup) 5160 JOHN IRVING HESS (John[8], Irving[7], John[6], Elizabeth[5], Alexander[4], John Adam II[3], John Adam I[2], John Jacob[1]) was the son of John Dawson and Cleo Garra Hess [Supplement No. 2873]. John was born October 11, 1949, at San Diego, California, and was raised at El Centro, California, and Phoenix, Arizona. He attended Arizona State University, the University of California at Irvine, and the University of Santa Clara where he received the B.S. degree in chemical engineering. These were followed by graduate studies in chemical engineering, physics, and business administration. He married Kimberly Ann Dougan, September 17, 1977. She was the daughter of Barbara Ann Del Pesco and Harry Charles Zurowski. John Irving and Kimberly lived at Santa Clara, California where John was operations manager for an electronics firm.

(Sup) 7175 i Adrienne Denise Hess, born June 30, 1980.
(Sup) 7176 ii Jordan Matthew Hess, born September 1, 1982.
(Sup) 7177 iii Kimberly Janelle Hess, born June 26, 1984.

(Sup) 5161 CATHARINE ANNE HESS (John[8], Irving[7], John[6], Elizabeth[5], Alexander[4], John Adam II[3], John Adam I[2], John Jacob[1]) was the daughter of John Dawson and Cleo Garra Hess [Supplement No. 2873]. Catharine was born March 10, 1951, at Fresno, California. Raised at El Centro and Phoenix, Arizona, she married Edwin Perry on June 26, 1971. His parents were Jesse Thomas and Barbara Ahlstrom Perry. Catharine and Edwin lived at Chino, California, where Ed was employed as a supervisor for General Motors Corporation.

(Sup) 7178   i   Jarred Christopher Perry, born November 27, 1972.
(Sup) 7179   ii   Ryan Edwin Perry, born August 25, 1976.
(Sup) 7180   iii   Justin Michael Perry, born September 19, 1979.
(Sup) 7181   iv   Lauren Elizabeth Perry, born July 18, 1981.

(Sup) 5162 MARY TERESA HESS (John[8], Irving[7], John[6], Elizabeth[5], Alexander[4], John Adam II[3], John Adam I[2], John Jacob[1]) was the daughter of John Dawson and Cleo Garra Hess [Supplement No. 2873]. She was born July 17, 1952, at San Diego, California, and was raised at El Centro and Phoenix, Arizona. On June 29, 1973, she married Anthony Kersh, the son of Leonard Richard and Loretta Thorn Kersh. Anthony and Mary Teresa lived at Phoenix, where Tony was senior vice president of Structural Behavior Engineering Laboratories.

(Sup) 7182   i   Marissa Michele Kersh, born May 20, 1974.
(Sup) 7183   ii   Tara Denise Kersh, born February 20, 1976.
(Sup) 7184   iii   Bridgette Teresa Kersh, born October 20, 1978.
(Sup) 7185   iv   Richard Dawson Kersh, born July 23, 1980.

(Sup) 5163 PATRICIA IRENE HESS (John[8], Irving[7], John[6], Elizabeth[5], Alexander[4], John Adam II[3], John Adam I[2], John Jacob[1]) was the daughter of John Dawson and Cleo Garra Hess [Supplement No. 2873]. Patricia was born January 28, 1954, and was raised in El Centro, California, and Phoenix, Arizona. On May 24, 1975, she married Stephen Silva, the son of Vernon Sousa and Beverly Bragg Silva. Steven and Patricia lived in Phoenix, where Stephen was employed by Mountain Bell Telephone Company.

(Sup) 7186   i   Sean Michael Silva, born April 29, 1976.
(Sup) 7187   ii   Alicia Kimberly Silva, born June 14, 1979.

(Sup) 5164 PAULA EVELYN HESS (John[8], Irving[7], John[6], Elizabeth[5], Alexander[4], John Adam II[3], John Adam I[2], John Jacob[1]) was the daughter of John Dawson and Cleo Garra Hess [Supplement No. 2873]. Paula was born January 28, 1954 (twin sister of Patricia). She married Lawrence Ray February 14, 1982. They resided in Colorado Springs, Colorado, where he was an Air Force master sergeant assigned to the Space Systems Command.

(Sup) 7188   i   Damien John Hess, born December 25, 1977.

(Sup) 5165 DENISE ELLEN HESS (John[8], Irving[7], John[6], Elizabeth[5], Alexander[4], John Adam II[3], John Adam I[2], John Jacob[1]) was the daughter of John Dawson and Cleo Garra Hess [Supplement No. 2873]. Denise was born June 26, 1955 and raised in El Centro, California, and Phoenix, Arizona. On October 18, 1980, she married Daniel Kuemmerle, the son of Herman Joseph and Evelyn Dorsey Kuemmerle. Daniel was an accountant with the State of Arizona Auditors Office.

(Sup) 7189   i   Danielle Denise Kuemmerle, born November 30, 1981.

(Sup) 5166 CLEO MICHELE HESS (John[8], Irving[7], John[6], Elizabeth[5], Alexander[4], John Adam II[3], John Adam I[2], John Jacob[1]) was the daughter of John Dawson and Cleo Garra Hess [Supplement No. 2873]. Cleo was born August 28, 1958, and raised in El Centro, California, and Phoenix, Arizona. She married Gary Vickers on November 19, 1977. He was the son of Virgil Thomas and Betty Anne Rolan Vickers. Gary was employed by G.V. Masonry, Inc., of Phoenix.

(Sup) 7190   i   Adam Manley Vickers, born March 31, 1979.
(Sup) 7191   ii   Christa Michele Vickers, born December 17, 1982.

(Sup) 5167 SANDRA CATHARINE HESS (Joseph[8], Irving[7], John[6], Elizabeth[5], Alexander[4], John Adam II[3], John Adam I[2], John Jacob[1]) was the daughter of Joseph Irving and Rosemarie Cohen Hess [Supplement No. 2874]. Sandi was born October 25, 1960, at San Francisco, California. After attending private schools in San Francisco, she received the B.A. degree in 1983 from Loyola Marymount University, Los Angeles. She lived in Los Angeles where she worked as a fund raiser for the Republican Party.

(Sup) 5168 GREGORY DAWSON HESS (Joseph[8], Irving[7], John[6], Elizabeth[5], Alexander[4], John Adam II[3], John Adam I[2], John Jacob[1]) was the son of Joseph Irving and Rosemarie Cohen Hess [Supplement No. 2874]. Greg was born August 6, 1962, at San Francisco, California. He graduated in June 1984 in economics from the University of California at Davis after having attended a year at the London School of Economics, London, England.

(Sup) 5169 ROBERT BARRINGER HESS (John[8], Guy[7], John[6], Elizabeth[5], Alexander[4], John Adam II[3], John Adam I[2], John Jacob[1]) was the son of John Thomas and Katherine Davis Hess [Supplement No. 2875]. Robert was born April 15, 1948, at Houston, Texas. He accompanied his parents to southern California, and attended California State, Long Beach. He married Elaine Olson December 21, 1968.

(Sup) 5170 KATHRYN JANEEN JONES (Helen[8], Guy[7], John[6], Elizabeth[5], Alexander[4], John Adam II[3], John Adam I[2], John Jacob[1]) was the daughter of Clayton Valentine and Helen Marie Hess Jones [Supplement No. 2876]. Kathryn was born February 7, 1940, at Bryan, Texas. She married William Drake in 1961. They resided in Pearland, Texas.

(Sup) 7194 i Laureen Kathryn Drake, born November 6, 1962.
(Sup) 7195 ii Brian William Drake, born October 25, 1963.
(Sup) 7196 iii Cheryl Marie Drake, born October 16, 1966.

(Sup) 5171 CLAYLENE MARIE JONES (Helen[8], Guy[7], John[6], Elizabeth[5], Alexander[4], John Adam II[3], John Adam I[2], John Jacob[1]) was the daughter of Clayton Valentine and Helen Marie Hess Jones [Supplement No. 2876]. Claylene was born July 13, 1942, at Galveston, Texas. She resided at North Hollywood, a free lance writer-producer.

(Sup) 5172 JACK ALTON JONES (Helen[8], Guy[7], John[6], Elizabeth[5], Alexander[4], John Adam II[3], John Adam I[2], John Jacob[1]) was the son of Clayton Valentine and Helen Marie Hess Jones [Supplement No. 2876]. Jack was born March 31, 1946, at Blanco, Texas. He married Gloria Pao in May, 1975. They resided at Bellaire, Texas, where he was a senior petroleum geophysicist for Exxon. They were divorced in 1982. He married, second, Mona Kaye McGarrah, December 7, 1983, at Norman, Oklahoma. They resided at Mandeville, Louisiana.

(Sup) 7196A i Ryan Jordan Jones, born October 25, 1984.
(Sup) 7196B ii Devin Jacob Jones, born January 9, 1987.

(Sup) 5173 DEBORAH JILL JONES (Helen[8], Guy[7], John[6], Elizabeth[5], Alexander[4], John Adam II[3], John Adam I[2], John Jacob[1]) was the daughter of Clayton Valentine and Helen Marie Hess Jones [Supplement No. 2876]. Deborah was born January 18, 1950, at Galveston, Texas. She married Mr. McCormick September 12, 1929. They were divorced.

(Sup) 7197 i Robert Clayton McCormick, born February 13, 1970.

(Sup) 5174 GUY LAWRENCE HESS (Lewis[8], Guy[7], John[6], Elizabeth[5], Alexander[4], John Adam II[3], John Adam I[2], John Jacob[1]) was the son of Lewis Lee and Orlean Fretwell Hess [Supplement No. 2877]. Lewis was born August 2, 1934, at Houston, Texas. He was a certified public accountant.

(Sup) 5175 LEWIS LEE HESS, JR. (Lewis[8], Guy[7], John[6], Elizabeth[5], Alexander[4], John Adam II[3], John Adam I[2], John Jacob[1]) was the son of Lewis Lee and Orlean Fretwell Hess [Supplement No. 2877]. Lewis was born January 6, 1938, at Houston, Texas. He was a teacher at Austin, Texas.

(Sup) 5176 NEIL WATSON (Katherine[8], Guy[7], John[6], Elizabeth[5], Alexander[4], John Adam II[3], John Adam I[2], John Jacob[1]) was the son of Neil Edward and Katherine Hess Watson [Supplement No. 2878]. Neil, Jr., was born October 28, 1949.

(Sup) 5177 DEBORAH GAIL WATSON (Katherine[8], Guy[7], John[6], Elizabeth[5], Alexander[4], John Adam II[3], John Adam I[2], John Jacob[1]) was the daughter of Neil Edward and Katherine Hess Watson [Supplement No. 2828]. Deborah was born September 3, 1952, at Houston, Texas. She married David Jay Schuren, April 1, 1970. They were divorced.

(Sup) 7197A i Jason Barringer Schuren, born October 9, 1971.

(Sup) 5178 BARRY THOMAS HESS (Guy[8], Guy[7], John[6], Elizabeth[5], Alexander[4], John Adam II[3], John Adam I[2], John Jacob[1]) was the son of Guy Link and Margaret Johnson Hess, Jr. [Supplement No. 2879]. He was born January 20, 1947, at Houston, Texas. He married Cynthia Trammel June 23, 1973.

(Sup) 7198 i Lori Joanne Hess, born October 31, 1977.
(Sup) 7199 ii Terri Suzanne Hess, born August 9, 1979.

(Sup) 5179 DANIEL STEPHEN HESS (Guy[8], Guy[7], John[6], Elizabeth[5], Alexander[4], John Adam II[3], John Adam I[2], John Jacob[1]) was the son of Guy Link and Margaret Johnson Hess, Jr. [Supplement No. 2879]. He was born February 13, 1949, at Houston, Texas. He married, first, Debra Greenland, October 23, 1976. They were divorced in 1981. He married, second, Vicki Sharp, March 14, 1985.

(Sup) 7200 i Christopher Stephen Hess, born August 13, 1986.

(Sup) 5180 PAMELA RUTH HESS (Guy[8], Guy[7], John[6], Elizabeth[5], Alexander[4], John Adam II[3], John Adam I[2], John Jacob[1]) was the daughter of Guy Link and Margaret Johnson Hess, Jr. [Supplement No. 2879]. She was born March 11, 1953, at Clark Air Force Base, Philippine Islands. She married Charles Faulkner July 30, 1971.

(Sup) 5181 GUY LINK HESS, III (Guy[8], Guy[7], John[6], Elizabeth[5], Alexander[4], John Adam II[3], John Adam I[2], John Jacob[1]) was the son of Guy Link and Margaret Johnson Hess, Jr. [Supplement No. 2879]. He was born December 4, 1964, at San Antonio, Texas. He received a bachelor's degree in business administration from Stephen Faustin State University in 1987.

(Sup) 5182 CATHERINE ANN HESS (Robert[8], Harry[7], John[6], Elizabeth[5], Alexander[4], John Adam II[3], John Adam I[2], John Jacob[1]) was the daughter of Robert Lee and Rebecca Yingling Hess [Supplement No. 2880]. Cathy was born May 27, 1966, in Fairfax County, Virginia. She received a bachelor's degree in mathematics in 1988 from the University of Virginia, where she becamea member of Phi Beta Kappa, and she attended graduate school at Pennsylvania State University.

(Sup) 5183 ELIZABETH LEE HESS (Robert[8], Harry[7], John[6], Elizabeth[5], Alexander[4], John Adam II[3], John Adam I[2], John Jacob[1]) was the daughter of Robert Lee and Rebecca Yingling Hess [Supplement No. 2880]. Lizzie was born April 1, 1968, in Fairfax County, Virginia. She studied English and biology at the University of Virginia.

(Sup) 5184 MARTHA SUE HESS (Robert[8], Harry[7], John[6], Elizabeth[5], Alexander[4], John Adam II[3], John Adam I[2], John Jacob[1]) was the daughter of Robert Lee and Rebecca Yingling Hess [Supplement No. 2880]. Martha was born June 21, 1970, in Fairfax County, Virginia. She studied at the Northern Virginia Community College, Annandale.

(Sup) 5185 NANCY LEE GLASS (John[8], Florence[7], John[6], Elizabeth[5], Alexander[4], John Adam II[3], John Adam I[2], John Jacob[1]) was the daughter of John Strider and Margaret Ewing Glass [Supplement No. 2882]. Nancy was born August 1, 1954, at Albuquerque, New Mexico. She attended public schools in Albuquerque, Truth or Consequences, and Santa Fe, New Mexico. She received a bachelors degree in psychology from Willamette in 1976, and a masters degree in special education from Oregon College.

(Sup) 5186 MARY KATHERINE RAY (Walter[8], Mary[7], Thomas[6], Elizabeth[5], Alexander[4], John Adam II[3], John Adam I[2], John Jacob[1]) was the daughter of Walter Franklin and Louise Fuller Ray [TLF No. 2883]. She was born October 7, 1943, at Santa Monica, California.

(Sup) 5187 MARY AGNES RAY (Walter[8], Mary[7], Thomas[6], Elizabeth[5], Alexander[4], John Adam II[3], John Adam I[2], John Jacob[1]) was the daughter of Walter Franklin and Louise Fuller Ray [TLF No. 2883]. She was born March 25, 1946, at Santa Monica, California.

(Sup) 5188 THOMAS WATSON RAY (Thomas[8], Mary[7], Thomas[6], Elizabeth[5], Alexander[4], John Adam II[3], John Adam I[2], John Jacob[1]) was the son of Thomas Rudolph and Gretchen Watson Ray [TLF No. 2884]. He was born September 29, 1933, at Santa Barbara, California.

(Sup) 5189 SALLY RAY (Thomas[8], Mary[7], Thomas[6], Elizabeth[5], Alexander[4], John Adam II[3], John Adam I[2], John Jacob[1]) was the daughter of Thomas Rudolph and Gretchen Watson Ray [TLF No. 2884]. She was born July 27, 1936, at Long Beach, California.

(Sup) 5190 CHERYL FRANCES JOHNSON (Mary Elizabeth[8], Gordon[7], Frank[6], Elizabeth[5], Alexander[4], John Adam II[3], John Adam I[2], John Jacob[1]) was the daughter of Robert Gordon and Mary Elizabeth Hess Johnson [Supplement No. 2898]. Cheryl was born in May 1950 at San Carlos, California. She was a nurse. She married Edwin D. Bliss.

(Sup) 7211   i David Bliss.
(Sup) 7212   ii Michael Bliss.

(Sup) 5191 ROBERT GORDON JOHNSON (Mary Elizabeth[8], Gordon[7], Frank[6], Elizabeth[5], Alexander[4], John Adam II[3], John Adam I[2], John Jacob[1]) was the son of Robert Gordon and Mary Elizabeth Hess Johnson [Supplement No. 2898]. He was born in April, 1952, at San Carlos, California. He married Diane Ammerman of Burlingame, California. Robert was the assistant harbor master at Pillar Point near Half Moon Bay, California, and Diane taught pre-school classes.

(Sup) 5192 SCOTT WARREN GOLDSMITH (Virginia[8], Gordon[7], Frank[6], Elizabeth[5], Alexander[4], John Adam II[3], John Adam I[2], John Jacob[1]) was the son of John and Virginia Hess Goldsmith [Supplement No. 2899]. Scott was born September 24, 1947, at Palo Alto, California. He graduated from the School of Architecture of the University of California, Berkeley, in 1970. He died May 25, 1977, at San Francisco, California.

(Sup) 5193 JOHN BERNARD GOLDSMITH (Virginia[8], Gordon[7], Frank[6], Elizabeth[5], Alexander[4], John Adam II[3], John Adam I[2], John Jacob[1]) was the son of John and Virginia Hess Goldsmith [Supplement No. 2899]. He was born March 3, 1950, at Palo Alto, California. Jay, as he was called, graduated from the University of California, Berkeley, in 1972. He became an environmental planner for the Federal Bureau of Outdoor Recreation and the National Park Service in San Francisco. Jay married Diahnn Jolene Caracciolo, June 21, 1980, at Berkeley, California. She was the daughter of Joseph Edmund and Pauline Evangeline Paul Caracciolo and was born September 21, 1954, at Hayward, California. Jay and Diahnn lived at Walnut Creek, California.

(Sup) 7215   1 Lindsay Diahnn Goldsmith, born April 24, 1982.
(Sup) 7216   11 Anne Jaylene Goldsmith, born February 28, 1985.

(Sup) 5194 LYNN ELIZABETH GOLDSMITH (Virginia[8], Gordon[7], Frank[6], Elizabeth[5], Alexander[4], John Adam II[3], John Adam I[2], John Jacob[1]) was the daughter of John and Virginia Hess Goldsmith [Supplement No. 2899]. Lynn was born December 7, 1956, at San Francisco, California. She graduated from the University of California, Davis, in 1979 and pursued a career as a singer in southern California.

(Sup) 5195 WILLIAM THOMAS MINKLER (Beatrice Ann 8, Beatrice[7], Frank[6], Elizabeth[5], Alexander[4], John Adam II[3], John Adam I[2], John Jacob[1]) was the son of William Sausman and Beatrice Ann MacGinitie Minkler [Supplement No. 2901]. He was born April 3, 1963, at Pittsburgh, Pennsylvania.

(Sup) 5196 DONALD BURTON MINKLER (Beatrice Ann 8, Beatrice[7], Frank[6], Elizabeth[5], Alexander[4], John Adam II[3], John Adam I[2], John Jacob[1]) was the son of William Sausman and Beatrice Ann MacGinitie Minkler [Supplement No. 2901]. Donald was born April 23, 1965, at Pittsburgh, Pennsylvania.

(Sup) 5197 MARJORIE ALICE MINKLER (Beatrice Ann 8, Beatrice[7], Frank[6], Elizabeth[5], Alexander[4], John Adam II[3], John Adam I[2], John Jacob[1]) was the daughter of William Sausman and Beatrice Ann MacGinitie Minkler [Supplement No. 2901]. Marjorie was born July 12, 1967, at Pittsburgh, Pennsylvania.

(Sup) 5198 SHARON ANDREA MINKLER (Beatrice Ann 8, Beatrice[7], Frank[6], Elizabeth[5], Alexander[4], John Adam II[3], John Adam I[2], John Jacob[1]) was the daughter of William Sausman and Beatrice Ann MacGinitie Minkler [Supplement No. 2901]. She was born January 6, 1969, at Pittsburgh, Pennsylvania.

(Sup) 5199 ROBERT E. MUDGE (Harriett[8], Jeanette[7], Mary[6], Elizabeth[5], Alexander[4], John Adam II[3], John Adam I[2], John Jacob[1]) was the son of David C. and Harriett Leach Mudge [Supplement No. 2902]. Robert was born December 24, 1954, at Martinsburg, West Virginia.

(Sup) 5200 SUSAN ANN McKEE (John[8], John[7], Mary[6], Elizabeth[5], Alexander[4], John Adam II[3], John Adam I[2], John Jacob[1]) was the daughter of John Strother and Jean Chandler McKee [TLF No. 2904]. She was born May 6, 1944, at Chicago, Illinois.

(Sup) 5201 JOHN DOUGLAS McKEE (John[8], John Adam I[2], John Jacob[1]) was the son of John Strother and Jean Chandler McKee [TLF No. 2904]. He was born May 3, 1947, at Welch, West Virginia.

(Sup) 5202 SHERRY ANN McKEE (Douglas[8], Ernest[7], Mary[6], Elizabeth[5], Alexander[4], John Adam II[3], John Adam I[2], John Jacob[1]) was the daughter of Douglas Parker and Frances Langford McKee [TLF No. 2907]. Sherry was born May 6, 1940, at Martinsburg, West Virginia.

(Sup) 5202A VICTORIA LYNN PHILLIPS (Iris[8], Harriet[7], Mary[6], Elizabeth[5], Alexander[4], John Adam II[3] John Adam I[2], John Jacob[1]) was the daughter of John David and Iris Hawk Phillips [Supplement No. 2910]. Victoria was born May 6, 1958, at Petersburg, Virginia. She graduated from Stockton State College, New Jersey, in June, 1981, and was Director of Volunteers for Atlantic County, New Jersey.

(Sup) 5202B MARY KATHERINE HAWK (John[8], Harriet[7], Mary[6], Elizabeth[5], Alexander[4], John Adam II[3] John Adam I[2], John Jacob[1]) was the daughter of John Marvin and Katherine Grant Hawk, Jr. [Supplement No. 2911]. Mary Katherine was born April 1, 1961, at Martinsburg, West Virginia. She married Charles R. Brown, Jr., June 9, 1982, at Williamsport, Maryland. He was the son of Charles R. and Connie Gearhart Brown and was born March 2, 1961, at Martinsburg. Mary Katherine received a bachelor's degree from Shippensburg State College, Pennsylvania, in 1982, and Charles attended Hagerstown Junior College, Maryland.

(Sup) 7220   i Jennifer Lynn Brown, born November 2, 1984.

(Sup) 5202C   LAURA JON HAWK   (John[8], Harriet[7], Mary[6], Elizabeth[5], Alexander[4], John Adam II[3], John Adam I[2], John Jacob[1]) was the daughter of John Marvin and Katherine Grant Hawk, Jr. [Supplement No. 2911]. Laura was born June 29, 1963, at Martinsburg, West Virginia. She married Andrew Patrick Short February 14, 1986, at Williamsport, Maryland. He was the son of Nevin A. and Sherry West Short and was born March 19, 1964, at Greencastle, Pennsylvania. Laura and Andrew both graduated from Shepherd College, West Virginia.

(Sup) 5203   KENNETH VINCENT DUCKSON   (Frances[8], Herbert[7], Alexander[6], Jane[5], Alexander[4], John Adam II[3], John Adam I[2], John Jacob[1]) was the son of Russell Harrison and Frances Osbourn Duckson [TLF No. 2912]. Kenneth was born July 19, 1928, at Washington, D.C.

(Sup) 5204   JOHN EDWARD BOEHM   (Frances[8], Herbert[7], Alexander[6], Jane[5], Alexander[4], John Adam II[3], John Adam I[2], John Jacob[1]) was the son of Arthur John and Frances Osbourn Duckson Boehm [TLF No. 2912]. John was born July 17, 1940.

(Sup) 5205   ARTHUR JOHN BOEHM, JR.   (Frances[8], Herbert[7], Alexander[6], Jane[5], Alexander[4], John Adam II[3], John Adam I[2], John Jacob[1]) was the son of Arthur John and Frances Osbourn Duckson Boehm [TLF No. 2912]. Arthur, Jr., was born October 19, 1944.

(Sup) 5206   WILLIAM JOSEPH BOEHM   (Frances[8], Herbert[7], Alexander[6], Jane[5], Alexander[4], John Adam II[3], John Adam I[2], John Jacob[1]) was the son of Arthur John and Frances Osbourn Duckson Boehm [TLF No. 2912]. William was born December 30, 1947.

(Sup) 5207   JAMES CLEMENT CAWOOD, III   (Ruth[8], Herbert[7], Alexander[6], Jane[5], Alexander[4], John Adam II[3], John Adam I[2], John Jacob[1]) was the son of James Clement and Ruth Osbourn Cawood, Jr. [TLF No. 2913]. James, III, born June 4, 1936, at Washington, D.C.

(Sup) 5208   JUNE MATIE CAWOOD   (Ruth[8], Herbert[7], Alexander[6], Jane[5], Alexander[4], John Adam II[3], John Adam I[2], John Jacob[1]) was the daughter of James Clement and Ruth Osbourn Cawood, Jr. [TLF No. 2913]. June was born June 25, 1940, at Washington, D.C.

(Sup) 5209   VALENTINE MARK CAWOOD   (Ruth[8], Herbert[7], Alexander[6], Jane[5], Alexander[4], John Adam II[3], John Adam I[2], John Jacob[1]) was the son of James Clement and Ruth Osbourn Cawood, Jr. [TLF No. 2914]. He was born December 30, 1943, at Washington, D.C.

(Sup) 5210   RAYMOND VOLL OSBOURN   (Raymond[8], Herbert[7], Alexander[6], Jane[5], Alexander[4], John Adam II[3], John Adam I[2], John Jacob[1]) was the son of Raymond Allen and Dorothea Schumann Osbourn [TLF No. 2914]. He was born September 10, 1945, at White Sulphur Springs, West Virginia.

(Sup) 5211   DOROTHEA ELISE OSBOURN   (Raymond[8], Herbert[7], Alexander[6], Jane[5], Alexander[4], John Adam II[3], John Adam I[2], John Jacob[1]) was the daughter of Raymond Allen and Dorothea Schumann Osbourn [TLF No. 2914]. She was born February 4, 1948, at Washington, D.C.

(Sup) 5212   SAMUEL EDMUND OSBOURN, III   (Samuel[8], Samuel[7], Nancy[6], John[5], Alexander[4], John Adam II[3], John Adam I[2], John Jacob[1]) was the son of Samuel Edmund and Doris Evelíne Baker Osbourn, Jr. [Supplement No. 2925]. Samuel was born September 23, 1961, at Drexel Hills, Pennsylvania. He received a B.A. degree from Geneva College. Samuel married Devona Lorene Sams, August 6, 1983, at New Brighton, Delaware. She was the daughter of Aubrey and Mildred Sams and was born May 25, 1959. Sam and Devona resided at Wilmington, Delaware, where he taught social studies at Wilmington Christian School. He was a deacon of the Baptist Church and a member of the Delaware Council of Social Studies and the Brookland Terrace Civic Club.

(Sup) 5213   DEAN BAKER OSBOURN   (Samuel[8], Samuel[7], Nancy[6], John[5], Alexander[4], John Adam II[3], John Adam I[2], John Jacob[1]) was the son of Samuel Edmund and Doris Eveline Baker Osbourn, Jr. [Supplement No. 2925]. He was born on August 18, 1965, at Bryn Mawr, Pennsylvania. Dean received an associate degree from Montgomery County Community College, Pennsylvania.

(Sup) 5214   JAMES OSBOURN HUNTER, JR.   (James[8], Ann[7], Nancy[6], John[5], Alexander[4], John Adam II[3], John Adam I[2], John Jacob[1]) was the son of James Osbourn and Betty McKee Hunter [Supplement No. 2931]. James, Jr., was born March 14, 1949, at Martinsburg, West Virginia. He received a B.S. degree in civil engineering from Virginia Polytechnic Institute in 1971. He served as a first lieutenant in the U.S. Air Force until 1973. He was employed as a civilian by the Army Corps of Engineers in Huntington, West Virginia from 1975 to 1981, and then by the Federal Regulatory Commission in Washington, D.C. James married Joan Swindall June 24, 1972, at Clintwood, Virginia. She was the daughter of Arnold Joseph and Dorothy Owens Swindall and was born March 31, 1949, at Clintwood.

(Sup) 7225   i   Jennifer Elizabeth Hunter, born June 27, 1978.
(Sup) 7226   ii   Juliet Kathryn Hunter, born November 4, 1981.

(Sup) 5215 ERNEST McKEE HUNTER (James[8], Ann[7], Nancy[6], John[5], Alexander[4], John Adam II[3], John Adam I[2], John Jacob[1]) was the son of James Osbourn and Betty McKee Hunter [Supplement No. 2931]. Ernest was born August 16, 1950, at Martinsburg, West Virginia. He graduated from Virginia Polytechnic Institute in 1972 and from the Oklahoma State University in 1975 with a doctor's degree in veterinary medicine. He practiced veterinary medicine at Durango, Colorado.

(Sup) 5216 ANN HAMPTON HUNTER (James[8], Ann[7], Nancy[6], John[5], Alexander[4], John Adam II[3], John Adam I[2], John Jacob[1]) was the daughter of James Osbourn and Betty McKee Hunter [Supplement No. 2931]. Ann was born September 4, 1952, at Martinsburg, West Virginia. She received an A.B. degree in elementary education from Shepherd College, West Virginia, in 1974 and taught school in Jefferson County, West Virginia.

(Sup) 5217 FRANCES WYATT LYNCH (Helen[8], Walter[7], Nancy[6], John[5], Alexander[4], John Adam II[3], John Adam I[2], John Jacob[1]) was the daughter of James and Helen Wyatt Osbourn Lynch, Jr. [Supplement No. 2933]. Frances was born January 30, 1949, at Washington, D.C. She graduated from the University of Maryland in accounting.

(Sup) 5218 NANCY GAYLE LYNCH (Helen[8], Walter[7], Nancy[6], John[5], Alexander[4], John Adam II[3], John Adam I[2], John Jacob[1]) was the daughter of James and Helen Wyatt Osbourn Lynch, Jr. [Supplement No. 2933]. Nancy was born May 27, 1962, at Bethesda, Maryland. She received a B.S. degree in accounting from the University of Delaware in 1984. She married Jeffrey Alan Dyer, September 13, 1986, at Chevy Chase, Maryland. He was the son of James L. and V. Joanne Dyer of Archbold, Ohio.

(Sup) 5219 JASON FEREBEE SIMPSON (Sallie[8], Margaret[7], Jacob[6], Thomas[5], Alexander[4], John Adam II[3], John Adam I[2], John Jacob[1]) was the son of Eugene Myers and Sallie Corbett O'Keef Simpson, Jr. [Supplement No. 2936A]. Jason was born October 8, 1974, at Winston-Salem, North Carolina.

(Sup) 5220 ANDREW LINK SIMPSON (Sallie[8], Margaret[7], Jacob[6], Thomas[5], Alexander[4], John Adam II[3], John Adam I[2], John Jacob[1]) was the son of Eugene Myers and Sallie Corbett O'Keef Simpson, Jr. [Supplement No. 2936A]. Andrew was born on October 16, 1978, at Winston-Salem, North Carolina.

(Sup) 5221 MARGARET FRANCES DAVENPORT (Nancy Ann[8], Wallace[7], Adam[6], Thomas[5], Alexander[4], John Adam II[3], John Adam I[2], John Jacob[1]) was the daughter of Charles Carlyle and Nancy Ann Link Davenport, Jr. [Supplement No. 2937]. She was born March 24, 1961, at Sierra Vista, Arizona.

(Sup) 5222 CHARLES CARLYLE DAVENPORT, III (Nancy Ann[8], Wallace[7], Adam[6], Thomas[5], Alexander[4], John Adam II[3], John Adam I[2], John Jacob[1]) was the son of Charles Carlyle and Nancy Ann Link Davenport, Jr. [Supplement No. 2937]. Charles, III, was born January 24, 1964, at Montgomery, Alabama.

(Sup) 5223 WILLARD KENT BAKER, JR. (Elizabeth[8], Wallace[7], Adam[6], Thomas[5], Alexander[4], John Adam II[3], John Adam I[2], John Jacob[1]) was the son of Willard Kent and Elizabeth Irene Link Baker [Supplement No. 2938]. Willard, Jr., was born November 26, 1963, at Fayetteville, North Carolina.

(Sup) 5224 WALLACE LINK BAKER (Elizabeth[8], Wallace[7], Adam[6], Thomas[5], Alexander[4], John Adam II[3], John Adam I[2], John Jacob[1]) was the son of Willard Kent and Elizabeth Irene Link Baker [Supplement No. 2938]. Wallace was born May 15, 1967, Fulton County, Georgia.

(Sup) 5225 WILLIAM SCOTT BAKER (Elizabeth[8], Wallace[7], Adam[6], Thomas[5], Alexander[4], John Adam II[3], John Adam I[2], John Jacob[1]) was the son of Willard Kent and Elizabeth Irene Link Baker [Supplement No. 2938]. William was born April 23, 1973, at Dekalb County, Georgia.

(Sup) 5226 KATHRYN ELIZABETH WHITE (Harriett[8], Wallace[7], Adam[6], Thomas[5], Alexander[4], John Adam II[3], John Adam I[2], John Jacob[1]) was the daughter of Charles Ellis and Harriett link White [Supplement No. 2938A]. Kathryn was born March 8, 1971, at Sylva, North Carolina.

(Sup) 5227 CHRISTIE ELLIS WHITE (Harriett[8], Wallace[7], Adam[6], Thomas[5], Alexander[4], John Adam II[3], John Adam I[2], John Jacob[1]) was the son of Charles Ellis and Harriett Link White [Supplement No. 2938A]. Christie was born February 2, 1975, at Wilmington, North Carolina, the twin of Ashley.

(Sup) 5228 ASHLEY ANN WHITE (Harriett^8, Wallace^7, Adam^6, Thomas^5, Alexander^4, John Adam II^3, John Adam I^2, John Jacob^1) was the daughter of Charles Ellis and Harriett Link White [Supplement No. 2938A]. She was born February 2, 1975, at Wilmington, North Carolina, the twin of Christie.

(Sup) 5229 MICHELE deFOREST BOUVE' (Grace^8, Nancy^7, Adam^6, Thomas^5, Alexander^4, John Adam II^3, John Adam I^2, John Jacob^1) was the daughter of Warren Lincoln and Grace Powars Bouvé [Supplement No. 2939]. Michele was born December 15, 1962, at Washington, D.C. She married Ariel Dan Kerner June 5, 1982, at Alexandria, Virginia.

(Sup) 7235 † Grace Ashley Kerner, born January 14, 1983.
(Sup) 7236 †† Kaitlyn Marie Kerner, born May 14, 1984.

(Sup) 5230 ELIZABETH ASHTON BANKS (Grace^8, Nancy^7, Adam^6, Thomas^5, Alexander^4, John Adam II^3, John Adam I^2, John Jacob^1) was the daughter of William Ashton and Grace Powars Bouvé Banks [Supplement No. 2939.] Elizabeth was born July 3, 1970, at Alexandria, Virginia.

(Sup) 5231 NANCY LINK BANKS (Grace^8, Nancy^7, Adam^6, Thomas^5, Alexander^4, John Adam II^3, John Adam I^2, John Jacob^1) was the daughter of William Ashton and Grace Powars Bouvé Banks [Supplement No. 2939]. Nancy was born March 14, 1972, at Alexandria, Virginia.

(Sup) 5232 KATHRYN STURTEVANT BANKS (Grace^8, Nancy^7, Adam^6, Thomas^5, Alexander^4, John Adam II^3, John Adam I^2, John Jacob^1) was the daughter of William Ashton and Grace Powars Bouvé Banks [Supplement No. 2939]. Kathryn was born April 17, 1978, at Alexandria, Virginia.

(Sup) 5233 ELIZABETH LINDSEY POWARS (Mason^8, Nancy^7, Adam^6, Thomas^5, Alexander^4, John Adam II^3, John Adam I^2, John Jacob^1) was the daughter of Forrest Mason and Linda Krogmann Powars [Supplement No. 2939A]. Lindsey was born June 26, 1977, at Arlington, Virginia.

(Sup) 5234 MARY LAURA POWARS (Mason^8, Nancy^7, Adam^6, Thomas^5, Alexander^4, John Adam II^3, John Adam I^2, John Jacob^1) was the daughter of Forrest Mason and Linda Krogmann Powars [Supplement No. 2939A]. Laura was born July 8, 1981, at Arlington, Virginia.

(Sup) 5234A CATHERINE VIRGINIA POWARS (Mason^8, Nancy^7, Adam^6, Thomas^5, Alexander^4, John Adam II^3, John Adam I^2, John Jacob^1) was the daughter of Forrest Mason and Linda (Krogmann) Powars [Supplement No. 2939A]. Catherine was born April 14, 1987, at Arlington, Virginia.

(Sup) 5235 ADAM LINK POWARS (Link^8, Nancy^7, Adam^6, Thomas^5, Alexander^4, John Adam II^3, John Adam I^2, John Jacob^1) was the son of Wayne Link and Susan Behrens Powars [Supplement No. 2939B]. He was born March 30, 1974, at Miami, Florida.

(Sup) 5236 VIRGINIA LEE POWARS (Link^8, Nancy^7, Adam^6, Thomas^5, Alexander^4, John Adam II^3, John Adam I^2, John Jacob^1) was the daughter of Wayne Link and Susan Behrens Powars [Supplement No. 2939B]. Virginia was born April 15, 1976, at Coral Gables, Florida.

(Sup) 5237 MARY KATHERINE ELIZABETH POWARS (Link^8, Nancy^7, Adam^6, Thomas^5, Alexander^4, John Adam II^3, John Adam I^2, John Jacob^1) was the daughter of Wayne Link and Susan Behrens Powars [Supplement No. 2939B]. She was born January 22, 1978, at Miami, Florida.

(Sup) 5238 ANDREW SCOTT POWARS (Link^8, Nancy^7, Adam^6, Thomas^5, Alexander^4, John Adam II^3, John Adam I^2, John Jacob^1) was the son of Wayne Link and Susan Behrens Powars [Supplement No. 2939B]. He was born November 1, 1980, at Miami, Florida.

(Sup) 5239 FORREST EDWARD POWARS (Link^8, Nancy^7, Adam^6, Thomas^5, Alexander^4, John Adam II^3, John Adam I^2, John Jacob^1) was the son of Wayne Link and Susan Behrens Powars [Supplement No. 2939B]. He was born July 6, 1983, at Miami, Florida.

(Sup) 5239A WILLIAM WALLACE POWARS (Link^8, Nancy^7, Adam^6, Thomas^5, Alexander^4, John Adam II^3, John Adam I^2, John Jacob^1) was the son of Wayne Link and Susan Behrens Powars [Supplement No. 2939B]. William was born September -, 1985, at Miami, Florida.

(Sup) 5240 JENNIFER LEE FINNEY (Judith^8, Charles^7, Adam^6, Thomas^5, Alexander^4, John Adam II^3, John Adam I^2, John Jacob^1) was the daughter of Dennis Harlan and Judith Kathryn Link Finney [Supplement No. 2940]. Jennifer was born September 1, 1973, at Edmonds, Washington.

(Sup) 5241   CHRISTOPHER LINK FINNEY (Judith^8, Charles^7, Adam^6, Thomas^5, Alexander^4, John Adam II^3, John Adam I^2, John Jacob^1) was the son of Dennis Harlan and Judith Kathryn Link Finney [Supplement No. 2940]. Christopher was born August 28, 1976, at Edmonds, Washington.

(Sup) 5242   JEFFREY CHARLES LINK (Robert^8, Charles^7, Adam^6, Thomas^5, Alexander^4, John Adam II^3, John Adam I^2, John Jacob^1) was the son of Robert Gibson and Jacklyn Burrier Link [Supplement No. 2940A]. Jeffrey was born July 14, 1967, at Edmonds, Washington.

(Sup) 5243   GREGORY THOMAS LINK (Robert^8, Charles^7, Adam^6, Thomas^5, Alexander^4, John Adam II^3, John Adam I^2, John Jacob^1) was the son of Robert Gibson and Jacklyn Burrier Link [Supplement No. 2940A]. Gregory was born March 29, 1971, at Edmonds, Washington.

(Sup) 5244   BRYAN GIBSON LINK (Robert^8, Charles^7, Adam^6, Thomas^5, Alexander^4, John Adam II^3, John Adam I^2, John Jacob^1) was the son of Robert Gibson and Jacklyn Burrier Link [Supplement No. 2940A]. Bryan was born September 27, 1981, at Edmonds, Washington.

(Sup) 5245   GAIL SHARON COLLIER (Janet^8, Charles^7, Walter^6, Ann^5, Alexander^4, John Adam II^3, John Adam I^2, John Jacob^1) was the daughter of William Hurle and Janet Harman Collier [Supplement No. 2947]. She was born August 5, 1953, at Heidelberg, Germany. She lived three years in Hawaii, attended high school in McLean, Virginia, and worked with TRW as a computer programmer. She married Allen Hunting Burr, February 3, 1973, at McLean, Virginia. He was the son of Howard Ellsworth and Jeanette Biller Burr of Fairfax County, Virginia, and was born February 15, 1954, at Washington, D.C.

(Sup) 7237   † Stacy Lynn Burr, born January 10, 1985.
(Sup) 7238   †† Justin Allen Burr, born October 14, 1987.

(Su) 5245A   DENISE LYNN HARMAN (Charles^8, Charles^7, Walter^6, Ann^5, Alexander^4, John Adam II^3, John Adam I^2, John Jacob^1) was the daughter of Charles William and Georgianna (Efford) Harman [Supplement No. 2948]. She was born February 1, 1961, at Baltimore, Maryland. She married John Robert Patrick Bell, Septemberr 22, 1984, at Horsham, Pennsylvania. He was the son of

John Robert and Margaret Shirley Bell and was born March 17, 1945, at Valley Forge, Pennsylvania.

(Sup) 7239   † Samantha Ashley Bell, born August 28, 1986.

(Sup) 5245B   TAB WILLIAM HARMAN (Charles^8, Charles^7, Walter^6, Ann^5, Alexander^4, hn Adam II^3, John Adam I^2, John Jacob^1) was the son of Charles William and Georgianna (Efford) Harman [Supplement No. 2948]. He was born June 3, 1963, at Baltimore, Maryland. He married Julie Ann MacEwen, March 9, 1985, at Dundalk, Maryland.

(Sup) 5246   ANNE HARMAN METCALF (Nancy^8, Henry^7, Nancy^6, Ann^5, Alexander^4, John Adam II^3, John Adam I^2, John Jacob^1) was the daughter of Paul Culbert and Nancy Blackford Metcalf [TLF No. 2949]. Anne was born June 29, 1945.

(Sup) 5247   ELIZABETH JEAN BLACKFORD (Henry^8, Henry^7, Nancy^6, Ann^5, Alexander^4, John Adam II^3, John Adam I^2, John Jacob^1) was the daughter of Henry Jackson and Jean Price Blackford, Jr. [TLF No. 2950]. Elizabeth was born November 14, 1947, at Tenafly, New Jersey.

(Sup) 5248   HENRY JACKSON BLACKFORD, III (Henry^7, Nancy^6, Ann^5, Alexander^4, John Adam II^3, John Adam I^2, John Jacob^1) was the son of Henry Jackson and Jean Price Blackford, Jr. [TLF No. 2950]. Henry, III, was born March 5, 1949, at Spartanburg, South Carolina.

(Sup) 5249   ROBERT RAVENAL TRIMMIER (Linda^8, Elsie^7, James^6, Ann^5, Alexander^4, John Adam II^3, John Adam I^2, John Jacob^1) was the son of David Carder and Linda Dianne Baldwin Trimmier [Supplement No. 2952]. Robert was born May 20, 1976, at Cumberland, Maryland.

(Sup) 5250   JAMES GIGNILLIAT TRIMMIER (Linda^8, Elsie^7, James^6, Ann^5, Alexander^4, John Adam II^3, John Adam I^2, John Jacob^1) was the son of David Carder and Linda Dianne Baldwin Trimmier [Supplement No. 2952]. James was born May 16, 1980, at Cumberland, Maryland.

(Sup) 5251 DANIEL HEATH BALDWIN (Lawrence^8, Elsie^7, James^6, Ann^5, Alexander^4, John Adam II^3, John Adam I^2, John Jacob^1) was the son of Lawrence Edwin and Juetta Jane Michael Baldwin [Supplement No. 2954]. Daniel was born April 20, 1967, at Cumberland, Maryland.

(Sup) 5252 AUTUMN DAWN BALDWIN (Lawrence^8, Elsie^7, James^6, Ann^5, Alexander^4, John Adam II^3, John Adam I^2, John Jacob^1) was the daughter of Lawrence Edwin and Juetta Jane Michael Baldwin [Supplement No. 2954]. She was born October 29, 1971, at Keyser, West Virginia.

(Sup) 5253 WILLIAM REMSBURG GROVE, III (William^8, William^7, Angeline^6, Emmanuel^5, Mary^4, John Adam II^3, John Adam I^2, John Jacob^1) was the son of William Remsburg and Elizabeth Carroll Grove, Jr. [ILF No. 2958]. William, III, was born February 3, 1931, at Fort Ethan Allen, Vermont. He was a cadet at the U.S. Military Academy.

(Sup) 5254 MADGE CAMPBELL GROVE (William^8, William^7, Angeline^6, Emmanuel^5, Mary^4, John Adam II^3, John Adam I^2, John Jacob^1) was the daughter of William Remsburg and Elizabeth Hartnell Grove [ILF No. 2958]. Madge was born August 22, 1946, at Fort Leavenworth, Kansas.

(Sup) 5255 CARLA LEE TURNER (Carla^8, Hazel^7, Angeline^6, Emmanuel^5, Mary^4, John Adam II^3, John Adam I^2, John Jacob^1) was the daughter of Donald Le Roy and Carla Minnie Smith Turner [Supplement No. 2959]. Carla was born December 15, 1928, at Washington, D.C. She graduated from Wheaton College in June 1950. She married Richard Carl Thommen June 27, 1953. His parents were Wilda Keck and Carl Albert Thomme. Carla and Richard resided in San Marino, California.

(Sup) 7251   i   Robert Clark Thommen, born June 3, 1954.
(Sup) 7252   ii Linda Mary Thommen, born January 28, 1957.
(Sup) 7253   iii Lisa Margaret Thommen, born December 13, 1965.

(Sup) 5256 ROBERT HOMER HAAS (Frances^8, Hazel^7, Angeline^6, Emmanuel^5, Mary^4, John Adam II^3, John Adam I^2, John Jacob^1) was the son of Edward Davis and Frances Smith Haas [Supplement No. 2960]. Robert was born May 14, 1934, at Washington, DC. He graduated from the College of Wooster, Ohio, and McCormick Theological Seminary. He married Mary Alice Jewell on August 29, 1958. She was the daughter of Bill and Eula Bass Jewell of Athens, Texas. Robert served as pastor of the Presbyterian Church in Niobrara and Verdel, Nebraska; Sioux City, Iowa; Wayne, Nebraska; and as Director of the Tennessee Region for the National Conference of Christians and Jews. Robert and Mary Alice resided at Marshall, Missouri, where he was pastor of the First Presbyterian Church, and she was assistant manager of the bookstore at Missouri Valley College.

(Sup) 7254   i   Katherine Ann Haas, born September 14, 1959.
(Sup) 7255   ii William David Haas, born June 2, 1962.

(Sup) 5257 LINDA ANN SMITH (Homer^8, Hazel^7, Angeline^6, Emmanuel^5, Mary^4, John Adam II^3, John Adam I^2, John Jacob^1) was the daughter of Homer Grove and Elsa Tavenner Smith [Supplement No. 2961]. She was born August 21, 1940, at Washington, D.C. After teaching history for a number of years in Maryland and Virginia, she left teaching to work in the computer field and toward a Master's Degree in computer science.

(Sup) 5258 CARLA FRANCES SMITH (Homer^8, Hazel^7, Angeline^6, Emmanuel^5, Mary^4, John Adam II^3, John Adam I^2, John Jacob^1) was the daughter of Homer Grove and Elsa Tavenner Smith [Supplement No. 2961]. She was born July 17, 1943, at Kansas City, Kansas. Carla worked as a chemist at the National Institute of Health and became active in the Church of Scientology where she was employed. She married Kendrick Lichty Moxon, May 5, 1974, at Washington, D.C. Rick was the son of Leslie Neal and Winifred Lichty Moxon. Carla and Rick resided at Los Angeles, California, where he was an attorney.

(Sup) 7256   i   Brian Tavenner Moxon, born May 21, 1978.
(Sup) 7257   ii Stacy Grove Moxon, born December 4, 1979.
(Sup) 7257A   iii Audrey Margaret Moxon, born February 8, 1984.

(Sup) 5259 GRETA KATHLEEN SMITH (Homer^8, Hazel^7, Angeline^6, Emmanuel^5, Mary^4, John Adam II^3, John Adam I^2, John Jacob^1) was the daughter of Homer Grove and Elsa Tavenner Smith [Supplement No. 2961]. She was born January 28, 1945, at Kansas City, Missouri. Greta married Milton Kotler in Washington, D.C., on July 11, 1976. Milton was the son of Maurice and Rebecca Bubar Kotler. By a former marriage he had two sons, Anthony and Joshua Kotler. Both Greta and Milton were active in Social Welfare work, specializing in helping neighborhoods to help themselves to improve social conditions. Greta was then employed by the Society for Training and Development, while she studied in a doctoral program in adult/human resources development. Milton became co-director of CRG Communications Corporation providing institutional marketing services to hospitals and colleges.

(Sup) 7258   i   Jonathan Smith Kotler, born August 31, 1977.
(Sup) 7259   ii Rebecca Tavenner Kotler, born June 4, 1979.

(Sup) 5260 MARTIN HOMER SMITH (Homer[8], Hazel[7], Angeline[6], Emmanuel[5], Mary[4], John Adam II[3], John Adam I[2], John Jacob[1]) was the son of Homer Grove and Elsa Tavenner Smith [Supplement No. 3961]. Martin was born November 16, 1949. He attended the University of Washington, interrupted by a tour of service overseas in the Vietnam War. He returned to graduate from the University and subsequently took additional courses in printing and photography. After considerable experience in the field, he established his own firm, the Chesapeake Press, Seattle, Washington.

(Sup) 5261 ELSA ANN EASTWOOD (Angeline[8], Hazel[7], Angeline[6], Emmanuel[5], Mary[4], John Adam II[3], John Adam I[2], John Jacob[1]) was the daughter of James William and Angeline Clara Smith Eastwood [Supplement No. 2962]. Elsa was born January 3, 1939. She married Allen Shue Norris on March 3, 1961, at Silver Spring, Maryland. Allen was the son of Chalmers Gail and Margaret Henrietta Shue Norris and was born August 25, 1936, in Bellefonte, Pennsylvania. A multi-talented woman, Elsa put creative talents to use as director of public information for a public television station in Virginia. She later became Program Coordinator for the Fairfax County Schools Community Cable TV Channels. Allen, with a master's degree in public administration from American University, was employed in management training and executive research.

(Sup) 7260 i   Gregory Allen Norris, born March 10, 1963.
(Sup) 7261 ii Andrew William Norris, born January 10, 1965.
(Sup) 7262 iii Kathleen Sue Norris, born December 3, 1969.

(Sup) 5262 BYRON GROVE BISHOP (Thomas[8], Minnie[7], Angeline[6], Emmanuel[5], Mary[4], John Adam II[3], John Adam I[2], John Jacob[1]) was the son of Thomas Grove and Althea Finn Bishop [ILF No. 2964]. Byron was born September 22, 1937, at Los Angeles, California.

(Sup) 5263 LUCILLE ZWEILY (Earl[8], Sarah[7], George[6], Emmanuel[5], Mary[4], John Adam II[3], John Adam I[2], John Jacob[1]) was the daughter of Earl and Estella Engler Zweily [TLF No. 2968]. Lucille was born June 5, 1911. She married Ralph Voss June 30, 1939.

(Sup) 7263 i Janet Elizabeth Voss, born September 15, 1940.
(Sup) 7264 ii Ralph Gary Voss, born September 19, 1941.

(Sup) 5264 RAYMOND ZWEILY (Earl[8], Sarah[7], George[6], Emmanuel[5], Mary[4], John Adam II[3], John Adam I[2], John Jacob[1]) was the son of Earl and Estella Engler Zweily [TLF No. 2968]. Raymond was born February 5, 1914. He married Elizabeth Blum November 21, 1936.

(Sup) 7265 i Barbara Beith Zweily, born October 19, 1942.

(Sup) 5265 MARIAN ZWEILY (Earl[8], Sarah[7], George[6], Emmanuel[5], Mary[4], John Adam II[3], John Adam I[2], John Jacob[1]) was the daughter of Earl and Estella Engler Zweily [TLF No. 2968]. Marian was born March 22, 1918. She married Robert Earl Karlovetz August 23, 1941.

(Sup) 7266 i Thomas Earl Karlovetz, born December 16, 1944.
(Sup) 7267 ii Patricia Ann Karlovetz, born December 5, 1946.

(Sup) 5266 JOAN HAZEL ZWEILY (Earl[8], Sarah[7], George[6], Emmanuel[5], Mary[4], John Adam II[3], John Adam I[2], John Jacob[1]) was the daughter of Earl and Estella Engler Zweily [TLF No. 2968]. Joan was born October 19, 1930.

(Sup) 5267 WALTER WILLIAM ZWEILY (Reuben[8], Sarah[7], George[6], Emmanuel[5], Mary[4], John Adam II[3], John Adam I[2], John Jacob[1]) was the son of Reuben Leroy and Maud Kiser Zweily [TLF No. 2969]. Walter was born April 26, 1914.

(Sup) 5268 KATHRYN WINONA ZWEILY (Reuben[8], Sarah[7], George[6], Emmanuel[5], Mary[4], John Adam II[3], John Adam I[2], John Jacob[1]) was the daughter of Reuben Leroy and Maud Kiser Zweily [TLF No. 2969]. Kathryn was born May 26, 1917. She married Thomas Duff November 7, 1942.

(Sup) 5269 DORIS ARLENE ZWEILY (Reuben[8], Sarah[7], George[6], Emmanuel[5], Mary[4], John Adam II[3], John Adam I[2], John Jacob[1]) was the daughter of Reuben Leroy and Maud Kiser Zweily [TLF No. 2969]. Doris was born April 15, 1923. She married Earl E. Smith, June 25, 1941.

(Sup) 5270 ALVIN EUGENE ZWEILY (Reuben[8], Sarah[7], George[6], Emmanuel[5], Mary[4], John Adam II[3], John Adam I[2], John Jacob[1]) was the son of Reuben Leroy and Maud Kiser Zweily [ILF No. 2969]. Alvin was born October 22, 1928. died January 8, 1929.

(Sup) 5271 MELVIN SHAFER (Clara[8], Sarah[7], George[6], Emmanuel[5], Mary[4], John Adam II[3], John Adam I[2], John Jacob[1]) was the son of Howard and Clara Zweily Shafer [TLF No. 2971]. Melvin was born December 28, 1921, at Fremont, Ohio. He was a first lieutenant in the U.S. Air Corps during World War II and served in Italy.

(Sup) 5272 DONALD SHAFER (Clara[8], Sarah[7], George[6], Emmanuel[5], Mary[4], John Adam II[3], John Adam I[2], John Jacob[1]) was the son of Howard and Clara Zweily Shafer [TLF No. 2971]. Donald was born January 15, 1924, at Fremont, Ohio. He served during World War II in the U.S. Navy on amphibious landing craft in the Pacific. He married Frances M. Schnitke, December 20, 1943. She was the daughter of Albert H. Schnitke and was born December 8, 1924, at Fremont, Ohio.

(Sup) 7268   i   June Arthur Shafer, born December 29, 1946.

(Sup) 5273 LOIS SHAFER (Clara[8], Sarah[7], George[6], Emmanuel[5], Mary[4], John Adam II[3], John Adam I[2], John Jacob[1]) was the daughter of Howard and Clara Zweily Shafer [TLF No. 2971]. Lois was born May 28, 1928, at Fremont, Ohio.

(Sup) 5274 KENNETH ZWEILY (Claude[8], Sarah[7], George[6], Emmanuel[5], Mary[4], John Adam II[3], John Adam I[2], John Jacob[1]) was the son of Claude and Carol Emick Zweily [TLF No. 2972]. Kenneth was born May 14, 1922, at Fremont, Ohio. He served three years in the U.S. Army during World War II, in the First Cavalry Division overseas. He married Janis Martha Zartman, September 10, 1942.

(Sup) 7269   i   Pamela Ann Zweily.

(Sup) 5275 JOYCE ZILLES (Hattie[8], Sarah[7], George[6], Emmanuel[5], Mary[4], John Adam II[3], John Adam I[2], John Jacob[1]) was born June 12, 1926.

(Sup) 5276 NORMA JANE ZILLES (Hattie[8], Sarah[7], George[6], Emmanuel[5], Mary[4], John Adam II[3], John Adam I[2], John Jacob[1]) was the daughter of George and Hattie Zweily Zilles [TLF No. 2973]. Norma was born February 24, 1928.

(Sup) 5277 PAUL ZILLES (Hattie[8], Sarah[7], George[6], Emmanuel[5], Mary[4], John Adam II[3], John Adam I[2], John Jacob[1]) was the daughter of George and Hattie Zweily Zilles [TLF No. 2973]. Paul was born August 22, 1931.

(Sup) 5278 DOROTHY ZILLES (Hattie[8], Sarah[7], George[6], Emmanuel[5], Mary[4], John Adam II[3], John Adam I[2], John Jacob[1]) was the daughter of George and Hattie Zweily Zilles [TLF No. 2973]. Dorothy was born May 24, 1934.

(Sup) 5279 ROBERT ZILLES (Hattie[8], Sarah[7], George[6], Emmanuel[5], Mary[4], John Adam II[3], John Adam I[2], John Jacob[1]) was the daughter of George and Hattie Zweily Zilles [TLF No. 2973]. Robert was born October 28, 1935.

(Sup) 5280 LEONARD ZILLES (Hattie[8], Sarah[7], George[6], Emmanuel[5], Mary[4], John Adam II[3], John Adam I[2], John Jacob[1]) was the daughter of George and Hattie Zweily Zilles [TLF No. 2973]. Leonard was born August 29, 1937.

(Sup) 5281 DORIS RAEHRS (Harry[8], Estella[7], Mary[6], Samuel[5], Mary[4], John Adam II[3], John Adam I[2], John Jacob[1]) was the daughter of Harry and Mildred Bahnsen Raehrs [TLF No. 2974]. Doris was born April 30, 1922, in Sandusky County, Ohio.

(Sup) 5282 LOIS RAEHRS (Harry[8], Estella[7], Mary[6], Samuel[5], Mary[4], John Adam II[3], John Adam I[2], John Jacob[1]) was the daughter of Harry and Mildred Bahnsen Raehrs [TLF No. 2974]. Lois was born October 25, 1927, in Sandusky Co., Ohio.

(Sup) 5283 WAYNE LEASER (Mildred[8], Estella[7], Mary[6], Samuel[5], Mary[4], John Adam II[3], John Adam I[2], John Jacob[1]) was the son of Howard and Mildred Raehrs Leaser [TLF No. 2976]. Wayne was born April 3, 1928, in Sandusky County, Ohio.

(Sup) 5284 MARLENE LEASER (Mildred[8], Estella[7], Mary[6], Samuel[5], Mary[4], John Adam II[3], John Adam I[2], John Jacob[1]) was the daughter of Howard and Mildred Raehrs Leaser [TLF No. 2976]. Marlene was born January 31, 1933, in Sandusky County, Ohio.

(Sup) 5285 CLARABELLE SMITH (Pearl[8], Clara[7], Mary[6], Samuel[5], Mary[4], John Adam II[3], John Adam I[2], John Jacob[1]) was the daughter of Robert and Pearl Kiser Smith [TLF No. 2977]. Clarabelle was born March 20, 1925, in Sandusky County, Ohio.

(Sup) 5286 VERNELL SMITH (Pearl[8], Clara[7], Mary[6], Samuel[5], Mary[4], John Adam II[3], John Adam I[2], John Adam[1]) was the child of Robert and Pearl Kiser Smith [TLF NO. 2977]. Vernell was born July 5, 1926, in Sandusky County, Ohio.

(Sup) 5287 MARGARET ANN SMITH (Pearl[8], Clara[7], Mary[6], Samuel[5], Mary[4], John Adam II[3], John Adam I[2], John Jacob[1]) was the daughter of Robert and Pearl Kiser Smith [TLF No. 2977]. Margaret was born July 20, 1928, in Sandusky County, Ohio.

(Sup) 5288 JUNE ELIZABETH KISER (Clarence[8], Clara[7], Mary[6], Samuel[5], Mary[4], John Adam II[3], John Adam I[2], John Jacob[1]) was the daughter of Clarence and Lulu Beckman Kiser [TLF No. 2978]. June was born June 4, 1926, in Sandusky County, Ohio.

(Sup) 5289 RICHARD GLENN KISER (Clarence^8, Clara^7, Mary^6, Samuel^5, Mary^4, John Adam II^3, John Adam I^2, John Jacob^1) was the son of Clarence and Lulu Beckman Kiser [TLF No. 2978]. Richard was born November 11, 1928, in Sandusky County, Ohio.

(Sup) 5290 JEANNINE NORMAN CURLISS (Viola^8, Clara^7, Mary^6, Samuel^5, Mary^4, John Adam II^3, John Adam I^2, John Jacob^1) was the daughter of Allen J. and Viola Kiser Curliss [TLF No. 2980]. Jeannine was born March 1, 1931, at Sandusky County, Ohio.

[Sup) 5291 THEODORE BENTON KISER, JR. (Theodore^8, Clara^7, Mary^6, Samuel^5, Mary^4, John Adam II^3, John Adam I^2, John Jacob^1) was the son of Theodore B. and Estell Schindlin Kiser [TLF No. 2981]. Theodore, Jr., was born September 16, 1933, at Fremont, Ohio.

(Sup) 5292 ELIZABETH ANN GRIEST (Leona^8, Chester^7, Mary^6, Samuel^5, Mary^4, John Adam II^3, John Adam I^2, John Jacob^1) was the daughter of Max and Leona Hetrick Griest [TLF No. 2984]. Elizabeth was born December 17, 1928.

(Sup) 5293 CARL SHAMMO (Ethel^8, Bertha^7, Mary^6, Samuel^5, Mary^4, John Adam II^3, John Adam I^2, John Jacob^1) was the child of George and Ethel Otermat Shammo [TLF No. 2985]. Carl was born August 6, 1920, at Fremont, Ohio.

(Sup) 5294 MERL SHAMMO (Ethel^8, Bertha^7, Mary^6, Samuel^5, Mary^4, John Adam II^3, John Adam I^2, John Jacob^1) was the child of George and Ethel Otermat Shammo [TLF No. 2985]. Merl was born March 19, 1922, at Fremont, Ohio.

(Sup) 5295 VIOLA SHAMMO (Ethel^8, Bertha^7, Mary^6, Samuel^5, Mary^4, John Adam II^3, John Adam I^2, John Jacob^1) was the child of George and Ehtel Etermat Shammo [TLF No. 2985]. Viola was born August 25, 1925, at Fremont, Ohio.

(Sup) 5296 JOAN OTERMAT (Orville^8, Bertha^7, Mary^6, Samuel^5, Mary^4, John Adam II^3, John Adam I^2, John Jacob^1) was the daughter of Orville and Pearl Glasser Otermat [TLF No. 2986]. Joan was born November 4, 1926, at Fremont, Ohio.

(Sup) 5297 LARRY LYNN OTERMAT (Orville^8, Bertha^7, Mary^6, Samuel^5, Mary^4, John Adam II^3, John Adam I^2, John Jacob^1) was the child of Orville and Ida Gracemeyer Otermat [TLF No. 2986]. Larry was born December 8, 1939, at Fremont, Ohio.

(Sup) 5298 ROBERT OTERMAT (Orville^8, Bertha^7, Mary^6, Samuel^5, Mary^4, John Adam II^3, John Adam I^2, John Jacob^1) was the son of Orville and Ida Gracemerey Otermat [TLF No. 2986]. Robert was born April 10, 1945, at Fremont, Ohio.

(Sup) 5299 BURDELL LAMALIE (Mildred^8, Abner^7, Mary^6, Samuel^5, Mary^4, John Adam II^3, John Adam I^2, John Jacob^1) was the son of Glennis and Mildred Hetrick Lamalie [TLF No. 2989]. Burdell was born March 8, 1930, at Fremont, Ohio.

(Sup) 5300 ROBERT LAMALIE (Mildred^8, Abner^7, Mary^6, Samuel^5, Mary^4, John Adam II^3, John Adam I^2, John Jacob^1) was the son of Glennis and Mildred Hetrick Lamalie [TLF No. 2989]. Robert was born June 3, 1931, at Fremont, Ohio.

(Sup) 5301 MARILYN LAMALIE (Mildred^8, Abner^7, Mary^6, Samuel^5, Mary^4, John Adam II^3, John Adam I^2, John Jacob^1) was the daughter of Glennis and Mildred Hetrick Lamalie [TLF No. 2989]. Marilyn was born March 3, 1935, at Fremont, Ohio.

(Sup) 5302 JANET NICKEL (Thelma^8, Abner^7, Mary^6, Samuel^5, Mary^4, John Adam II^3, John Adam I^2, John Jacob^1) was the daughter of Herbert and Thelma Hetrick Nickel [TLF No. 2990]. Janet was born May 5, 1934, at Cleveland, Ohio.

(Sup) 5303 RONALD NICKEL (Thelma^8, Abner^7, Mary^6, Samuel^5, Mary^4, John Adam II^3, John Adam I^2, John Jacob^1) was the son of Herbert and Thelma Hetrick Nickel [TLF No. 2990]. Ronald was born January 8, 1936, at Cleveland, Ohio.

(Sup) 5304 DEANNA MARION NICKEL (Dorothy^8, Abner^7, Mary^6, Samuel^5, Mary^4, John Adam II^3, John Adam I^2, John Jacob^1) was the daughter of Earl and Dorothy Hetrick Nickel [TLF No. 2991]. Deanna was born March 29, 1940, at Lakewood, Ohio.

(Sup) 5305 MILTON A. HETRICK, JR. (Milton^8, Abner^7, Mary^6, Samuel^5, Mary^4, John Adam II^3, John Adam I^2, John Jacob^1) was the son of Milton and Garnetta Sours Hetrick [TLF No. 2993].

(Sup) 5306 CATHY ANN HETRICK (Milton^8, Abner^7, Mary^6, Samuel^5, Mary^4, John Adam II^3, John Adam I^2, John Jacob^1) was the daughter of Milton and Garnetta Sours Hetrick [TLF No. 2993].

(Sup) 5307 CONNIE SUE HETRICK (Vincent^8, Abner^7, Mary^6, Samuel^5, Mary^4, John Adam II^3, John Adam I^2, John Jacob^1) was the daughter of Vincent Theodore and Matilda Masy Sours Hetrick [TLF No. 2994]. Connie was born January 25, 1947, at Fremont, Ohio.

(Sup) 5308 CAROL LEE BLAINE (Esther^8, Theodore^7, Mary^6, Samuel^5, Mary^4, John Adam II^3, John Adam I^2, John Jacob^1) was the daughter of Gordon A. and Esther Hetrick Blaine [TLF No. 2996]. Carol was born September 30, 1937, at Toledo, Ohio.

(Sup) 5309 NANCY JEANNE BLAINE (Esther[8], Theodore[7], Mary[6], Samuel[5], Mary[4], John Adam II[3], John Adam I[2], John Jacob[1]) was the daughter of Gordon A. and Esther Hetrick Blaine [TLF No. 2996]. Nancy was born March 27, 1941, at Toledo, Ohio.

(Sup) 5310 SANDRA ANNE BLAINE (Esther[8], Theodore[7], Mary[6], Samuel[5], Mary[4], John Adam II[3], John Adam I[2], John Jacob[1]) was the daughter of Gordon A. and Esther Hetrick Blaine [TLF No. 2996]. Sandra was born January 31, 1943, at Toledo, Ohio.

(Sup) 5311 ARLO CROWELL (Walter[8], Charles[7], Samuel[6], Samuel[5], Mary[4], John Adam II[3], John Adam I[2], John Jacob[1]) was the son of Walter and Eunice Hansen Crowell [TLF No. 2997]. Arlo was born October 16, 1924, at Bellingham, Washington.

(Sup) 5312 ERLENE CROWELL (Walter[8], Charles[7], Samuel[6], Samuel[5], Mary[4], John Adam II[3], John Adam I[2], John Jacob[1]) was the daughter of Walter and Eunice Hansen Crowell [TLF No. 2997]. Erlene was born September 16, 1935, at St. Louis, Missouri.

(Sup) 5313 ELMER KARDATZKE (Delorous[8], Charles[7], Samuel[6], Samuel[5], Mary[4], John Adam II[3], John Adam I[2], John Jacob[1]) was the son of Harris and Delorous Crowell Kardatzke [TLF No. 2999]. Elmer was born October 30, 1929, at Detroit, Michigan.

(Sup) 5314 ELAINE KARDATZKE (Delorous[8], Charles[7], Samuel[6], Samuel[5], Mary[4], John Adam II[3], John Adam I[2], John Jacob[1]) was the daughter of Harris and Delorous Crowell Kardatzke [TLF No. 2999]. Elaine was born November 14, 1937, at Elmore, Ohio.

(Sup) 5315 LAUREN DAVID SPICER (Alvida[8], Frank[7], Samuel[6], Samuel[5], Mary[4], John Adam II[3], John Adam I[2], John Jacob[1]) was the son of Walter T. and Alvida Crowell Spicer [TLF No. 3002]. He was born January 14, 1940, in Wood County, Ohio.

(Sup) 5316 ALVIN LEROY SPICER (Alvida[8], Frank[7], Samuel[6], Samuel[5], Mary[4], John Adam II[3], John Adam I[2], John Jacob[1]) was the son of Walter T. and Alvida Crowell Spicer [TLF No. 3002]. He was born February 17, 1944, in Wood County, Ohio.

(Sup) 5317 ARTHUR RUDOLPH ARMBRUSTER (Alice[8], Frank[7], Samuel[6], Samuel[5], Mary[4], John Adam II[3], John Adam I[2], John Jacob[1]) was the son of John and Alice Crowell Armbruster [TLF No. 3003]. Arthur was born March 28, 1939, at Perrysburg, Ohio.

(Sup) 5318 ELLEN JANE ARMBRUSTER (Alice[8], Frank[7], Samuel[6], Samuel[5], Mary[4], John Adam II[3], John Adam I[2], John Jacob[1]) was the daughter of John and Alice Crowell Armbruster [TLF No. 3003]. Ellen was born December 28, 1946, at Perrysburg, Ohio.

(Sup) 5319 THEODORE HASSELBACH (Mabel[8], Clara[7], Eugene[6], Samuel[5], Mary[4], John Adam II[3], John Adam I[2], John Jacob[1]) was the son of Carl and Mabel King Hasselbach [TLF No. 3005]. Theodore was born September 16, 1918.

(Sup) 5320 ROBERT HASSELBACH (Mabel[8], Clara[7], Eugene[6], Samuel[5], Mary[4], John Adam II[3], John Adam I[2], John Jacob[1]) was the son of Carl and Mabel King Hasselbach [TLF No. 3005]. Robert was born December 8, 1923.

(Sup) 5321 PEARL ADELADE GROSS (Hazel[8], Clara[7], Eugene[6], Samuel[5], Mary[4], John Adam II[3], John Adam I[2], John Jacob[1]) was the daughter of Harry and Hazel King Gross [TLF No. 3005]. Pearl was born March 4, 1926.

(Sup) 5322 NOLAN CHRISTIAN GROSS (Hazel[8], Clara[7], Eugene[6], Samuel[5], Mary[4], John Adam II[3], John Adam I[2], John Jacob[1]) was the son of Harry and Hazel King Gross [TLF No. 3005]. Nolan was born February 26, 1930.

(Sup) 5323 MYRON DALE BENDER (Zella[8], Clara[7], Eugene[6], Samuel[5], Mary[4], John Adam II[3], John Adam I[2], John Jacob[1]) was the son of John and Zella King Bender [TLF No. 3006]. Myron was born December 4, 1939.

(Sup) 5324 WALTER NEAL KING (Harvey[8], Clara[7], Eugene[6], Samuel[5], Mary[4], John Adam II[3], John Adam I[2], John Jacob[1]) was the son of Harvey Neal and Estella Hetrick King [TLF No. 3008]. Walter was born November 6, 1929.

(Sup) 5325 LAMAR JACOB KING (Harvey[8], Chara[7], Eugene[6], Samuel[5], Mary[4], John Adam II[3], John Adam I[2], John Jacob[1]) was the son of Harvey Neal and Estella Hetrick King [TLF No. 3008]. He was born April 6, 1932.

(Sup) 5326 DONALD IRWIN KING (Harvey[8], Clara[7], Eugene[6], Samuel[5], Mary[4], John Adam II[3], John Adam I[2], John Jacob[1]) was the son of Harvey Neal and Estella Hetrick King [TLF No. 3008]. Donald was born August 17, 1934.

(Sup) 5327 HOWARD RICHARD KING (Harvey[8], Clara[7], Eugene[6], Samuel[5], Mary[4], John Adam II[3], John Adam I[2], John Jacob[1]) was the son of Harvey Neal and Estella Hetrick King [TLF No. 3008]. Howard was born November 30, 1939.

(Sup) 5328 BETTY LOU WINTERS (Mary[8], Clara[7], Eugene[6], Samuel[5], Mary[4], John Adam II[3], John Adam I[2], John Jacob[1]) was the daughter of Kenneth and Mary King Winters [TLF No. 3009]. Betty Lou was born February 4, 1936.

(Sup) 5329 DORIS MAY WINTERS (Mary[8], Clara[7], Eugene[6], Samuel[5], Mary[4], John Adam II[3], John Adam I[2], John Jacob[1]) was the daughter of Kenneth and Mary King Winters [TLF No. 3009]. Doris was born May 4, 1939.

(Sup) 5330 WALTER NEIL LONGANBACH, JR. (Walter[8], Ida[7], Eugene[6], Samuel[5], Mary[4], John Adam II[3], John Adam I[2], John Jacob[1]) was the son of Walter Neil and Lois Shellhass Longanbach [TLF No. 3013]. Walter, Jr., was born May 18, 1927.

(Sup) 5331 WESLEY MARTIN LONGANBACH (Walter[8], Ida[7], Eugene[6], Samuel[5], Mary[4], John Adam II[3], John Adam I[2], John Jacob[1]) was the son of Walter Neil and Lois Shellhass Longanbach [TLF No. 3013]. Wesley was born January 6, 1929.

(Sup) 5332 ANN LOUISE LONGANBACH (Walter[8], Ida[7], Eugene[6], Samuel[5], Mary[4], John Adam II[3], John Adam I[2], John Jacob[1]) was the daughter of Walter Neil and Lois Shellhass Longanbach [TLF No. 3013]. She was born July 1, 1930.

(Sup) 5333 JOHN THOMAS LONGANBACH (Walter[8], Ida[7], Eugene[6], Samuel[5], Mary[4], John Adam II[3], John Adam I[2], John Jacob[1]) was the son of Walter Neil and Lois Shellhass Longanbach [TLF No. 3013]. He was born April 9, 1932.

(Sup) 5334 LEWIS JAMES LONGANBACH (Walter[8], Ida[7], Eugene[6], Samuel[5], Mary[4], John Adam II[3], John Adam I[2], John Jacob[1]) was the son of Walter Neil and Lois Shellhass Longanbach [TLF No. 3013]. Lewis was born October 14, 1933.

(Sup) 5335 WILLIAM ALLEN BOYD (Gladys[8], Ida[7], Eugene[6], Samuel[5], Mary[4], John Adam II[3], John Adam I[2], John Jacob[1]) was the son of William Glenn and Gladys Longanbach Boyd [TLF No. 3014]. William was born October 28, 1924.

(Sup) 5336 DONALD ELWIN BOYD (Gladys[8], Ida[7], Eugene[6], Samuel[5], Mary[4], John Adam II[3], John Adam I[2], John Jacob[1]) was the son of William Glenn and Gladys Longanbach Boyd [TLF No. 3014]. Donald was born September 4, 1926.

(Sup) 5337 CONSTANCE JOAN BOYD (Gladys[8], Ida[7], Eugene[6], Samuel[5], Mary[4], John Adam II[3], John Adam I[2], John Jacob[1]) was the daughter of William Glenn and Gladys Longanbach Boyd [TLF No. 3014]. Constance was born August 7, 1928.

(Sup) 5338 DELLA MAE BOYD (Gladys[8], Ida[7], Eugene[6], Samuel[5], Mary[4], John Adam II[3], John Adam I[2], John Jacob[1]) was the daughter of William Glenn and Gladys Longanbach Boyd [TLF No. 3014]. Della was born November 5, 1930.

(Sup) 5339 CAROLINE A. BEBOU (Iva[8], Ida[7], Eugene[6], Samuel[5], Mary[4], John Adam II[3], John Adam I[2], John Jacob[1]) was the daughter of Martin and Iva Katherine Longanbach Bebou [TLF No. 3015]. Caroline was born December 14, 1926.

(Sup) 5340 ALICE MARIE BEBOU (Iva[8], Ida[7], Eugene[6], Samuel[5], Mary[4], John Adam II[3], John Adam I[2], John Jacob[1]) was the daughter of Martin and Iva Katherine Longanbach Bebou [TLF No. 3015]. Alice was born January 28, 1933.

(Sup) 5341 JAMES ALLEN BEBOU (Iva[8], Ida[7], Eugene[6], Samuel[5], Mary[4], John Adam II[3], John Adam I[2], John Jacob[1]) was the son of Martin and Iva Katherine Longanbach Bebou [TLF No. 3015]. James was born March 6, 1940 (twin of Judith).

(Sup) 5342 JUDITH ANN BEBOU (Iva[8], Ida[7], Eugene[6], Samuel[5], Mary[4], John Adam II[3], John Adam I[2], John Jacob[1]) was the daughter of Martin and Iva Katherine Longanbach Bebou [TLF No. 3015]. Judith was born March 6, 1940 (twin of James).

(Sup) 5343 RUSSELL BEBOU (Iva[8], Ida[7], Eugene[6], Samuel[5], Mary[4], John Adam II[3], John Adam I[2], John Jacob[1]) was the son of Martin and Iva Katherine Longanbach Bebou [TLF No. 3015]. Russell was born January 23, 1941.

(Sup) 5344 MARGARET ESTHER SMITH (Esther[8], Ida[7], Eugene[6], Samuel[5], Mary[4], John Adam II[3], John Adam I[2], John Jacob[1]) was the daughter of George Ralph and Esther Longanbach Smith [TLF No. 3017]. Margaret was born March 9, 1935, and died March 11, 1935.

(Sup) 5345 MARTIN GEORGE B. SMITH (Esther[8], Ida[7], Eugene[6], Samuel[5], Mary[4], John Adam II[3], John Adam I[2], John Jacob[1]) was the son of George Ralph and Esther Longanbach Smith [TLF No. 3017]. Martin was born June 9, 1937.

(Sup) 5346 GAYLORD NELSON ACKER (Dorothy[8], Ida[7], Eugene[6], Samuel[5], Mary[4], John Adam II[3], John Adam I[2], John Jacob[1]) was the son of Harry and Dorothy Longanbach Acker [TLF No. 3019]. He was born September 19, 1931.

(Sup) 5347 EVERETT LEROY ACKER (Dorothy[8], Ida[7], Eugene[6], Samuel[5], Mary[4], John Adam II[3], John Adam I[2], John Jacob[1]) was the son of Harry and Dorothy Longanbach Acker [TLF No. 3019]. He was born September 19, 1932.

(Sup) 5348 GERALD ACKER (Dorothy[8], Ida[7], Eugene[6], Samuel[5], Mary[4], John Adam II[3], John Adam I[2], John Jacob[1]) was the son of Harry and Dorothy Longanbach Acker [TLF No. 3019]. Gerald was born May 16, 1935.

(Sup) 5349 BONNIE LOU ACKER (Dorothy[8], Ida[7], Eugene[6], Samuel[5], Mary[4], John Adam II[3], John Adam I[2], John Jacob[1]) was the daughter of Harry and Dorothy Longanbach Acker [TLF No. 3019]. She was born June 27, 1938.

(Sup) 5350 VIRGINIA MAE ACKER (Dorothy[8], Ida[7], Eugene[6], Samuel[5], Mary[4], John Adam II[3], John Adam I[2], John Jacob[1]) was the daughter of Harry and Dorothy Longanbach Acker [TLF No. 3019]. She was born November 25, 1939.

(Sup) 5351 KARON SUE LONGANBACH (Paul[8], Ida[7], Eugene[6], Samuel[5], Mary[4], John Adam II[3], John Adam I[2], John Jacob[1]) was the daughter of Paul Martin and Wilma Babler Longanbach [TLF No. 3020]. She was born June 8, 1938.

(Sup) 5352 MELVIN EARL CROWELL (Ira[8], Robert[7], Sardis[6], Samuel[5], Mary[4], John Adam II[3], John Adam I[2], John Jacob[1]) was the son of Ira Wilson and Julia Heberling Crowell [TLF No. 3027]. Melvin was born September 14, 1936, in Sandusky County, Ohio.

(Sup) 5353 JANET MAE CROWELL (Ira[8], Robert[7], Sardis[6], Samuel[5], Mary[4], John Adam II[3], John Adam I[2], John Jacob[1]) was the daughter of Ira Wilson and Julia Heberling Crowell [TLF No. 3027]. Janet was born June 25, 1939, in Sandusky County, Ohio.

(Sup) 5354 CAROL ANN CROWELL (Ira[8], Robert[7], Sardis[6], Samuel[5], Mary[4], John Adam II[3], John Adam I[2], John Jacob[1]) was the daughter of Ira Wilson and Julia Heberling Crowell [TLF No. 3027]. Carol was born February 27, 1943, in Sandusky County, Ohio.

- - - - - - - - - - - - - - - -

(Sup) 5360 JEAN WILSON (Beryl[8], Letus[7], Abner[6], John[5], Mary[4], John Adam II[3], John Adam I[2], John Jacob[1]) was the daughter of Jerome Oliver and Beryl Ernestine Crowell Wilson [TLF No. 3060]. Jean was born February 20, 1931, at New Orleans, Louisiana.

(Sup) 5361 DONALD RICHARD LEE (Ella[8], Charles[7], Abner[6], John[5], Mary[4], John Adam II[3], John Adam I[2], John Jacob[1]) was the son of Sidney Thomas and Ella May Crowell Lee [TLF No. 3061]. Donald was born September 21, 1931, at Turlock, California.

(Sup) 5362 VIVIAN ESTELLE CROWELL (Orval[8], Charles[7], Abner[6], John[5], Mary[4], John Adam II[3], John Adam I[2], John Jacob[1]) was the daughter of Orval Chester and Estelle Logan Crowell [TLF No. 3062]. Vivian was born March 5, 1925, at Los Angeles, California.

(Sup) 5363 RONALD ORVAL CROWELL (Orval[8], Charles[7], Abner[6], John[5], Mary[4], John Adam II[3], John Adam I[2], John Jacob[1]) was the son of Orval Chester and Estelle Logan Crowell [TLF No. 3062]. Ronald was born August 8, 1931, at Sacramento, California.

(Sup) 5364 BETTY ARLENE CROWELL (Abner[8], Charles[7], Abner[6], John[5], Mary[4], John Adam II[3], John Adam I[2], John Jacob[1]) was the daughter of Abner Melvin and Beth Cleland Crowell [TLF No. 3063]. Betty was born March 15, 1931, and died March 15, 1931, at Turlock, California.

(Sup) 5365 GERALDINE ELAINE CROWELL (Abner[8], Charles[7], Abner[6], John[5], Mary[4], John Adam II[3], John Adam I[2], John Jacob[1]) was the daughter of Abner Melvin and Beth Cleland Crowell [TLF No. 3063]. She was born October 17, 1933, at Turlock, California.

(Sup) 5366 VERNA MAE CROWELL (Abner[8], Charles[7], Abner[6], John[5], Mary[4], John Adam II[3], John Adam I[2], John Jacob[1]) was the daughter of Abner Melvin and Beth Cleland Crowell [TLF No. 3063]. Verna Mae was born February 22, 1936, at Turlock, California.

(Sup) 5367 BEVERLY LORAINE CROWELL (Loren[8], Charles[7], Abner[6], John[5], Mary[4], John Adam II[3], John Adam I[2], John Jacob[1]) was the daughter of Loren Eugene and Agnes Chamberlain Crowell [TLF No. 3064]. Beverly was born January 13, 1935, at Turlock, California.

(Sup) 5368 LOREN DALE CROWELL (Loren[8], Charles[7], Abner[6], John[5], Mary[4], John Adam II[3], John Adam I[2], John Jacob[1]) was the son of Loren Eugene and Agnes Chamberlain Crowell [TLF No. 3064]. He was born April 26, 1939, and died May 18, 1939, at Turlock, California.

(Sup) 5369 JANET LEA CROWELL (Virgil[8], Charles[7], Abner[6], John[5], Mary[4], John Adam II[3], John Adam I[2], John Jacob[1]) was the child of Virgil Lloyd and Della Convers Crowell [TLF No. 3065]. Janet was born March 23, 1933, at Turlock, California.

(Sup) 5370 VERLE JEAN CROWELL (Virgil[8], Charles[7], Abner[6], John[5], Mary[4], John Adam II[3], John Adam I[2], John Jacob[1]) was the child of Virgil Lloyd and Della Convers Crowell [TLF No. 3065]. She was born June 6, 1935, and died November 6, 1936, at Turlock, California.

(Sup) 5371 CONVERS CROWELL (Virgil[8], Charles[7], Abner[6], John[5], Mary[4], John Adam II[3], John Adam I[2], John Jacob[1]) was the child of Virgil Lloyd and Della Convers Crowell [TLF No. 3065]. Convers was born March 12, 1938, at Turlock, California.

(Sup) 5372 ROBERT COLEMAN CROWELL (Charles^8, Charles^7, Abner^6, John^5, Mary^4, John Adam II^3, John Adam I^2, John Jacob^1) was the son of Charles Coleman and Virginia David Crowell [TLF No. 3066]. Robert was born September 5, 1935, at Turlock, California.

(Sup) 5373 BARBARA DALE CROWELL (Charles^8, Charles^7, Abner^6, John^5, Mary^4, John Adam II^3, John Adam I^2, John Jacob^1) was the daughter of Charles Coleman and Virginia David Crowell [TLF No. 3066]. Barbara was born February 27, 1939, at Turlock, California.

(Sup) 5374 PETER CROWELL LANG (Leila^8, Arthur^7, Abner^6, John^5, Mary^4, John Adam II^3, John Adam I^2, John Jacob^1) was the son of Frank Herbert and Leila Crowell Lang, Jr. [TLF No. 3067]. Peter was born February 18, 1932, at Turlock, California.

(Sup) 5375 FRANK HERBERT LANG, III (Leila^8, Arthur^7, Abner^6, John^5, Mary^4, John Adam II^3, John Adam I^2, John Jacob^1) was the son of Frank Herbert and Leila Crowell Lang, Jr. [TLF No. 3067]. Frank, III, was born June 27, 1936, at Modesto, California.

(Sup) 5376 RICHARD ARTHUR LANG (Leila^8, Arthur^7, Abner^6, John^5, Mary^4, John Adam II^3, John Adam I^2, John Jacob^1) was the son of Frank Herbert and Leila Crowell Lang, Jr. [TLF No. 3067]. Richard was born June 22, 1937, at Modesto, California.

(Sup) 5377 JAMES DOUGLAS BUCHANAN (Gladys^8, Arthur^7, Abner^6, John^5, Mary^4, John Adam II^3, John Adam I^2, John Jacob^1) was the son of James M. and Gladys Crowell Buchanan [TLF No. 3068]. He was born August 7, 1941, at Modesto, California.

(Sup) 5378 JOAN GALE BUCHANAN (Gladys^8, Arthur^7, Abner^6, John^5, Mary^4, John Adam II^3, John Adam I^2, John Jacob^1) was the daughter of James M. and Gladys Crowell Buchanan [TLF No. 3068]. Joan was born February 10, 1943, at Oakland, California.

(Sup) 5379 BARBARA LYNNE CROWELL (Arthur^8, Arthur^7, Abner^6, John^5, Mary^4, John Adam II^3, John Adam I^2, John Jacob^1) was the daughter of Arthur Verne and Barbara Whitaker Crowell [TLF No. 3069]. Barbara was born February 18, 1941, at Modesto, California.

(Sup) 5380 MICHAEL VERNE CROWELL (Arthur^8, Arthur^7, Abner^6, John^5, Mary^4, John Adam II^3, John Adam I^2, John Jacob^1) was the son of Arthur Verne and Barbara Whitaker Crowell [TLF No. 3069]. Michael was born August 12, 1942, at Modesto, California.

(Sup) 5381 MARY ELIZABETH BENNETT (Mary^8, Arthur^7, Abner^6, John^5, Mary^4, John Adam II^3, John Adam I^2, John Jacob^1) was the daughter of Frederick Donell and Mary Elizabeth Crowell Burch Bennett [TLF No. 3070]. She was born September 27, 1942, at San Francisco, California.

(Sup) 5382 CATHERINE ANNE BENNETT (Mary^8, Mary^7, Abner^6, John^5, Mary^4, John Adam II^3, John Adam I^2, John Jacob^1) was the daughter of Frederick Donell and Mary Elizabeth Crowell Burch Bennett [TLF No. 3070]. Catherine was born March 7, 1945, at San Francisco, California.

(Sup) 5383 PHYLLIS ELIZABETH BURCH (Elmer^8, Mary^7, Abner^6, John^5, Mary^4, John Adam II^3, John Adam I^2, John Jacob^1) was the child of Elmer Crowell and Helen Daetz Burch [TLF No. 3071]. Phyllis was born October 6, 1942, at Syracuse, New York.

(Sup) 5384 TERRY LEE BURCH (Elmer^8, Mary^7, Abner^6, John^5, Mary^4, John Adam II^3, John Adam I^2, John Jacob^1) was the child of Elmer Crowell and Helen Daetz Burch [TLF No. 3071]. Terry Lee was born December 19, 1945, at Alameda, California.

(Sup) 5385 CATHERINE LAVERNE CROWELL (William^8, Clarence^7, Abner^6, John^5, Mary^4, John Adam II^3, John Adam I^2, John Jacob^1) was the daughter of William Turner and Audrey Delmege Crowell [TLF No. 3075]. Catherine was born July 23, 1938.

(Sup) 5386 MARY LOUISE GILCREST (Beulah^8, Beulah^7, Abner^6, John^5, Mary^4, John Adam II^3, John Adam I^2, John Jacob^1) was the daughter of Cyril Wherry and Beulah Schindler Gilcrest [TLF No. 3079]. She was born April 7, 1938, at San Mateo, California.

(Sup) 5387 RICHARD JOHN GILCREST (Beulah^8, Beulah^7, Abner^6, John^5, Mary^4, John Adam II^3, John Adam I^2, John Jacob^1) was the son of Cyril Wherry and Beulah Schindler Gilcrest [TLF No. 3079]. Richard was born January 21, 1940, at San Mateo, California.

(Sup) 5388 LAURIE BERNARD BOUCHER (Mary^8, Beulah^7, Abner^6, John^5, Mary^4, John Adam II^3, John Adam I^2, John Jacob^1) was the child of John and Mary Schindler Boucher [TLF No. 3080]. Laurie was born December 7, 1942, at San Mateo, California.

(Sup) 5389 JOHN THOMAS BOUCHER (Mary^8, Beulah^7, Abner^6, John^5, Mary^4, John Adam II^3, John Adam I^2, John Jacob^1) was the child of John and Mary Schindler Boucher [TLF No. 3080]. He was born February 20, 1944, at San Mateo, California.

(Sup) 5390 TERESA LOUISE BOUCHER (Mary[8], Beulah[7], Abner[6], John[5], Mary[4], John Adam II[3], John Adam I[2], John Jacob[1]) was the child of John and Mary Schindler Boucher [TLF No. 3080]. She was born August 16, 1946, at San Mateo, California.

(Sup) 5391 GEORGE ANDREW SCHINDLER (Bernard[8], Beulah[7], Abner[6], John[5], Mary[4], John Adam II[3], John Adam I[2], John Jacob[1]) was the son of Bernard Crowell and Caroline Anderson Schindler [ILF No. 3081]. George was born February 10, 1946, at Long Beach, California.

- - - - - - - - - - - - - - - -

(Sup) 5396 MARJORIE WILLIAMS (Howard[8], Mary[7], Mary[6], John[5], Mary[4], John Adam II[3], John Adam I[2], John Jacob[1]) was the daughter of Howard R. Williams [ILF No. 3083]. Marjorie was born October 4, 1932.

(Sup) 5397 RICHARD KENNADY (Alvin[8], Carroll[7], Mary[6], John[5], Mary[4], John Adam II[3], John Adam I[2], John Jacob[1]) was the son of Alvin and Mabel Harley Kennady [TLF No. 3085]. Richard was born July 17, 1937.

(Sup) 5398 MARLYN MORRIS (Edith[8], Carroll[7], Mary[6], John[5], Mary[4], John Adam II[3], John Adam I[2], John Jacob[1]) was the daughter of Robert and Edith Kennady Morris [ILF No. 3090]. Marlyn was born January 6, 1937.

(Sup) 5399 SANDRA GENTLES (Margaret[8], Carroll[7], Mary[6], John[5], Mary[4], John Adam II[3], John Adam I[2], John Jacob[1]) was the daughter of Eugene and Margaret Kennady Gentles [TLF No. 3091]. Sandra was born January 5, 1939.

(Sup) 5400 EDWARD L. SUMMERS (Elizabeth[8], Mary[7], Ella[6], Moses[5], Mary[4], John Adam II[3], John Adam I[2], John Jacob[1]) was the son of Elmer Lee and Elizabeth Buhler Summers [TLF No. 3096]. Edward was born August 24, 1937, at Houston, Texas.

(Sup) 5401 CHARLES DEAN SUMMERS (Elizabeth[8], Mary[7], Ella[6], Moses[5], Mary[4], John Adam II[3], John Adam I[2], John Jacob[1]) was the son of Elmer Lee and Elizabeth Buhler Summers [TLF No. 3096]. Charles was born January 22, 1940, at Houston, Texas.

(Sup) 5402 JESS WILLIAM SUMMERS (Elizabeth[8], Mary[7], Ella[6], Moses[5], Mary[4], John Adam II[3], John Adam I[2], John Jacob[1]) was the son of Elmer Lee and Elizabeth Buhler Summers [TLF No. 3096]. He was born October 18, 1941, at Houston, Texas.

(Sup) 5403 DAVID ROTSCH COOPER (Martha[8], Mary[7], Ella[6], Moses[5], Mary[4], John Adam II[3], John Adam I[2], John Jacob[1]) was the son of Bromley Francis and Martha Buhler Cooper [TLF No. 3100]. David was born October 21, 1943, at Victoria, Texas.

(Sup) 5404 ANNE ELIZABETH COOPER (Martha[8], Mary[7], Ella[6], Moses[5], Mary[4], John Adam II[3], John Adam I[2], John Jacob[1]) was the daughter of Bromley Francis and Martha Buhler Cooper [TLF No. 3100]. She was born November 3, 1945, at Victoria, Texas.

(Sup) 5405 WILLIAM GAYLE BURFORD (Reyburn[8], Jessie[7], Ella[6], Moses[5], Mary[4], John Adam II[3], John Adam I[2], John Jacob[1]) was the son of Reyburn Dean and Margaret Gayle Burford [TLF No. 3102]. William was born March 19, 1941, at Shreveport, Louisiana.

(Sup) 5406 KATHERINE ANNE BURFORD (Reyburn[8], Jessie[7], Ella[6], Moses[5], Mary[4], John Adam II[3], John Adam I[2], John Jacob[1]) was the daughter of Reyburn Dean and Margaret Gayle Burford [TLF No. 3102]. Katherine was born July 30, 1943, at Shreveport, Louisiana.

(Sup) 5407 JAMES HAROLD DEAN (Elbert[8], Elbert[7], Ella[6], Moses[5], Mary[4], John Adam II[3], John Adam I[2], John Jacob[1]) was the son of Elbert and Dorothy Robinson Dean [TLF No. 3103]. James was born October 21, 1939, at Port Neches, Texas.

(Sup) 5408 WILLIAM ELBERT DEAN (Elbert[8], Elbert[7], Ella[6], Moses[5], Mary[4], John Adam II[3], John Adam I[2], John Jacob[1]) was the son of Elbert and Dorothy Robinson Dean [TLF No. 3103]. William was born August 17, 1944, at Port Neches, Texas.

(Sup) 5409 DALE THOMAS DEAN (Harry[8], Elbert[7], Ella[6], Moses[5], Mary[4], John Adam II[3], John Adam I[2], John Jacob[1]) was the son of Harry Reyburn and Norma Jean Wolf Dean [TLF No. 3104]. He was born March 24, 1946, at Beaumont, Texas.

(Sup) 5410 DIANA JANE DEAN (Harry[8], Elbert[7], Ella[6], Moses[5], Mary[4], John Adam II[3], John Adam I[2], John Jacob[1]) was the daughter of Harry Reyburn and Norma Jean Wolf Dean [TLF No. 3104]. She was born December 22, 1947, at Houston, Texas.

(Sup) 5411 MILLARD DALE SELVEY (Marion[8], Justin[7], Annie[6], Mary[5], Mary[4], John Adam II[3], John Adam I[2], John Jacob[1]) was the son of Keith and Marion Young Selvey [TLF No. 3105]. He was born April 5, 1928, in Sandusky County, Ohio.

(Sup) 5412 LAUREL EDWARD SELVEY (Marion[8], Justin[7], Annie[6], Mary[5], Mary[4], John Adam II[3], John Adam I[2], John Jacob[1]) was the son of Keith and Marion Young Selvey [ILF No. 3105]. He was born June 2, 1930, in Sandusky County, Ohio.

(Sup) 5413 BETTY JEAN SELVEY (Marion[8], Justin[7], Annie[6], Mary[5], Mary[4], John Adam II[3], John Adam I[2], John Jacob[1]) was the daughter of Keith and Marion Young Selvey [ILF No. 3105]. She was born December 10, 1938, in Sandusky, Ohio.

(Sup) 5414 WILLIAM ROBERT SELVEY (Marion[8], Justin[7], Annie[6], Mary[5], Mary[4], John Adam II[3], John Adam I[2], John Jacob[1]) was the son of Keith and Marion Young Selvey [ILF No. 3105]. William was born November 23, 1941, in Sandusky, Ohio.

(Sup) 5415 DONALD CHARLES YOUNG (Charles[8], Justin[7], Annie[6], Mary[5], Mary[4], John Adam II[3], John Adam I[2], John Jacob[1]) was the son of Charles and Mildred Miller Young [ILF No. 3106]. Donald was born June 29, 1944, at Clyde, Ohio.

(Sup) 5416 MARY ELLEN COON (Pauline[8], Justin[7], Annie[6], Mary[5], Mary[4], John Adam II[3], John Adam I[2], John Jacob[1]) was the daughter of John and Pauline Young Coon [ILF No. 3107]. Mary was born December 23, 1933, at Fremont, Ohio.

(Sup) 5417 PHYLLIS MAE COON (Pauline[8], Justin[7], Annie[6], Mary[5], Mary[4], John Adam II[3], John Adam I[2], John Jacob[1]) was the daughter of John and Pauline Young Coon [ILF No. 3107]. Phyllis was born December 17, 1935, at Fremont, Ohio.

(Sup) 5418 CAROL ANN COON (Pauline[8], Justin[7], Annie[6], Mary[5], Mary[4], John Adam II[3], John Adam I[2], John Jacob[1]) was the daughter of John and Pauline Young Coon [ILF No. 3107]. Carol was born May 6, 1938, at Fremont, Ohio.

(Sup) 5419 PATRICIA ANN DAWLEY (John[8], Elsie[7], Annie[6], Mary[5], Mary[4], John Adam II[3], John Adam I[2], John Jacob[1]) was the daughter of John and Arletta Duignan Dawley [ILF No. 3108]. Patricia was born November 17, 1941.

(Sup) 5420 BARBARA LOU DAWLEY (John[8], Elsie[7], Annie[6], Mary[5], Mary[4], John Adam II[3], John Adam I[2], John Jacob[1]) was the daughter of John and Arletta Duignan Dawley [ILF No. 3108]. Barbara was born November 2, 1946.

(Sup) 5425 MARLYN THOMSEN (George[8], Barbara[7], Ida[6], Mary[5], Mary[4], John Adam II[3], John Adam I[2], John Jacob[1]) was the daughter of George Henry and Genevieve Meyer Thomsen [ILF No. 3115]. Marlyn was born May 4, 1937.

(Sup) 5426 KAROL THOMSEN (George[8], Barbara[7], Ida[6], Mary[5], Mary[4], John Adam II[3], John Adam I[2], John Jacob[1]) was the daughter of George Henry and Genevieve Meyer Thomsen [ILF No. 3115]. Karol was born October 2, 1938.

(Sup) 5427 JAMES ALTON GOOD (James[8], Corine[7], Ida[6], Mary[5], Mary[4], John Adam II[3], John Adam I[2], John Jacob[1]) was the son of James and Esther Hintz Good [ILF No. 3118]. James was born September 25, 1941, in Seneca County, Ohio.

(Sup) 5428 JOYCE EILEEN GOOD (James[8], Corine[7], Ida[6], Mary[5], Mary[4], John Adam II[3], John Adam I[2], John Jacob[1]) was the daughter of James and Esther Hintz Good [ILF No. 3118]. Joyce was born November 13, 1944, in Seneca County, Ohio.

(Sup) 5428A MELVIN DARYL ORIVIG (Lucille[8], Corine[7], Ida[6], Mary[5], Mary[4], John Adam II[3], John Adam I[2], John Jacob[1]) was the son of Daryl and Lucille Good Orivig [ILF No. 3119]. Melvin was born April 6, 1940, in Seneca County, Ohio.

(Sup) 5428B NANCY SUE ORIVIG (Lucille[8], Corine[7], Ida[6], Mary[5], Mary[4], John Adam II[3], John Adam I[2], John Jacob[1]) was the daughter of Daryl and Lucille Good Orivig [ILF No. 3119]. Nancy was born April 26, 1943, at Tiffin Ohio.

(Sup) 5429 BARBARA JEANNE HARTLEY (Jeanne[8], James[7], Ida[6], Mary[5], Mary[4], John Adam II[3], John Adam I[2], John Jacob[1]) was the daughter of Charles Beatty and Jeanne (Sommer) Hartley [Supplement No. 3120]. Barbara was born August 10, 1945, at Huron, Ohio. She married Melvin Harlan Schlachter, August 24, 1968, at Huron. He was the son of Melvin and Mildred Schlachter and was born February 2, 1946, at San Pedro, California.

(Sup) 7275   1 Erika Ellen Hartley, born August 11, 1975.
(Sup) 7276 11 Jacob Thomas Hartley, born May 1, 1980.

(Sup) 5429A SUZANNE MARIE HARTLEY (Jeanne[8], James[7], Ida[6], Mary[5], Mary[4], John Adam II[3], John Adam I[2], John Jacob[1]) was the daughter of Charles Beatty and Jeanne (Sommer) Hartley [Supplement No. 3120]. Suzanne was born August 15, 1949, at Huron, Ohio.

(Sup) 5429B MARGARET K. MEEKER (Ruth^8, James^7, Ida^6, Mary^5, Mary^4, John Adam II^3, John Adam I^2, John Jacob^1) was the daughter of Donald D. and Ruth (Sommer) Meeker [Supplement No. 3121]. Margaret was born November 5, 1944, at Huron, Erie County, Ohio. She married Rex C. Clay, November 23, 1974. He was born June 30, 1930, in Huron County, Ohio.

Stepchild   i Todd C. Clay, born May 15, 1962.
Stepchild   ii Marilyn Ann Clay, born July 22, 1964.

(Sup) 5429C MARTHA RUTH MEEKER (Ruth^8, James^7, Ida^6, Mary^5, Mary^4, John Adam II^3, John Adam I^2, John Jacob^1) was the daughter of Donald D. and Ruth (Sommer) Meeker [Supplement No. 3121]. Martha was born June 13, 1951, at Huron, Erie County, Ohio. She married, first, Merv Clemons in 1969. He was born October 21, 1948, in Kentucky. Martha and Merv were divorced in 1972. She married, second, Rick Stanfield, 1973; they were divorced in 1974. Ruth remarried Merv Clemons, April 13, 1974. Merv served with the First Battalion, 2nd Armored Division of the U.S. Army. He died April 19, 1975, in Germany.

(Sup) 7277   i Melissa R. Clemons, born April 20, 1970.
(Sup) 7278   ii Jason C. Stanfied, born September 29, 1973.

(Sup) 5429D SCOTT JAMES SOMMER (Wayne^8, James^7, Ida^6, Mary^5, Mary^4, John Adam II^3, John Adam I^2, John Jacob^1) was the son of Wayne Franklin and Ruth (Schaefer) Sommer [Supplement No. 3122]. Scott was born May 13, 1952, at Sandusky, Ohio. He married Bette Lee Becker, June 29, 1980, at Milan, Ohio. She was the daughter of David Harrison and Eveline (Burke) Becker and was born at Hanover, Illinois. Scott was a building contractor, and Bette Lee was a saleslady.

(Sup) 5429E SANDY JOAN SOMMER (Wayne^8, James^7, Ida^6, Mary^5, Mary^4, John Adam II^3, John Adam I^2, John Jacob^1) was the daughter of Wayne Franklin and Ruth (Schaefer) Sommer [Supplement No. 3122]. Sandy was born November 20, 1953, at Sandusky, Ohio. She married Karl Lloyd Stierhoff, November 20, 1976, at Huron, Ohio. He was the son of Karl and Jeanne Marie (Conrad) Stierhoff and was born July 6, 1953, at Sandusky. Sandy and Karl resided at Sandusky, where he was a mechanic for the city, and she served as a saleslady for the Creative Circle Corp.

(Sup) 7279   i Jamie D. Stierhoff, born March 25, 1974.
(Sup) 7279A ii Benjamin Karl Stierhoff, born January 25, 1980.
(Sup) 7279B iii Casey Marie Stierhoff, born March 7, 1982.

(Sup) 5429F TODD CLARK SOMMER (Wayne^8, James^7, Ida^6, Mary^5, Mary^4, John Adam II^3, John Adam I^2, John Jacob^1) was the son of Wayne Franklin and Ruth (Schaefer) Sommer [Supplement No. 3122]. Todd was born November 23, 1956, at Sandusky, Ohio. He married Miriam Eileen Grunden, September 4, 1976, at Sandusky. She was the daughter of Robert Eugene and Rosemary (Hill) Grunden and was born February 25, 1958, at Sandusky. Todd was in construction work, and Miriam was a nurse.

(Sup) 7280   i Nicole Marie Sommer, born July 21, 1978.
(Sup) 7280A ii Rachel Arien Sommer, born October 16, 1980.
(Sup) 7280B iii Kailee Elizabeth Sommer, born October 24, 1985.

(Sup) 5430 MERRITT C. BIXLER, JR. (Merritt^8, Marilla^7, Lillie^6, Mary^5, Mary^4, John Adam II^3, John Adam I^2, John Jacob^1) was the son of Merritt C. and Shirley Wheeler Havens-Bixler [Supplement No. 3124]. Merritt, Jr., was born June 7, 1948, at Fremont, Ohio. He married Jill L. Hannon, August 3, 1974. She was the daughter of Richard and Dee Hannon and was born May 12, 1947. Merritt and Jill were divorced in 1985.

(Sup) 7281   i Aimée Lynn Bixler, born January 24, 1976.

(Sup) 5430A MARTHA JEAN BIXLER (Merritt^8, Marilla^7, Lillie^6, Mary^5, Mary^4, John Adam II^3, John Adam I^2, John Jacob^1) was the daughter of Merritt C. and Shirley Wheeler Havens-Bixler [Supplement No. 3124]. Martha was born July 3, 1950, at Fremont, Ohio. She married Roger C. Poole, April 19, 1985. He was the son of James E. and Hilda M. (Hammond) Poole and was born October 28, 1947.

(Sup) 5430B MARGARET ANN BIXLER (Merritt^8, Marilla^7, Lillie^6, Mary^5, Mary^4, John Adam II^3, John Adam I^2, John Jacob^1) was the daughter of Merritt C. and Shirley Wheeler Havens-Bixler [Supplement No. 3124]. Margie was born July 27, 1953, at Fremont, Ohio. She married John R. Foster, October 1, 1981. He was the son of Richard P. and Ruth E. (Meyer) Foster and was born January 26, 1951. Margie graduated from Columbus College of Art and Design, Ohio. She and John received masters' degrees from Bowling Green State University, Ohio, where they taught. Margie worked also as an illustrator and stained-glass artist.

(Sup) 7282   i Philip J. Foster, born February 11, 1985.
(Sup) 7283   ii Cara Jean Foster, born March 9, 1987.

(Sup) 5430C LORANCE H. BIXLER (Merritt^8, Marilla^7, Lillie^6, Mary^5, Mary^4, John Adam II^3, John Adam I^2, John Jacob^1) was the son of Merritt C. and Shirley Wheeler Havens-Bixler [Supplement No. 3124]. Lorance was born May 3, 1955, at Fremont, Ohio. He married Laura A. Lorenz, April 24, 1976. She was the daughter of Robert H. and Beatrice A. (Cronin) Lorenz and was born October 5, 1956.

(Sup) 7284   i Leslie A. Bixler, born February 6, 1984.

(Sup) 5431 JEAN ANN JOHNSTON (Jessie[8], Ella[7], Martha[6], Isabella[5], Rebecca[4], John Adam II[3], John Adam I[2], John Jacob[1]) was the daughter of Henry H. and Jessie Collins Johnston [ILF No. 3126]. Jean was born May 24, 1927, at Columbus, Ohio.

(Sup) 5432 NANCY LOU JOHNSTON (Jessie[8], Ella[7], Martha[6], Isabella[5], Rebecca[4], John Adam II[3], John Adam I[2], John Jacob[1]) was the daughter of Henry H. and Jessie Collins Johnston [ILF No. 3126]. Nancy was born January 24, 1930, at Columbus, Ohio.

(Sup) 5433 DOROTHY BAUMGARDNER (Minor[8], Charles[7], Martha[6], Isabella[5], Rebecca[4], John Adam II[3], John Adam I[2], John Jacob[1]) was the daughter of Minor and Mary Silvers Baumgardner [ILF No. 3127]. Dorothy was born November 9, 1914.

(Sup) 5434 PHILLIP BAUMGARDNER (Minor[8], Charles[7], Martha[6], Isabella[5], Rebecca[4], John Adam II[3], John Adam I[2], John Jacob[1]) was the son of Minor and Mary Silvers Baumgardner [ILF No. 3127]. Phillip was born April 10, 1921.

(Sup) 5435 PATRICIA ANN BAUMGARDNER (Minor[8], Charles[7], Martha[6], Isabella[5], Rebecca[4], John Adam II[3], John Adam I[2], John Jacob[1]) was the daughter of Minor and Mary Silvers Baumgardner [ILF No. 3127]. Patricia was born February 2, 1932.

(Sup) 5436 JOHN STARTZMAN (Martha[8], Albert[7], Martha[6], Isabella[5], Rebecca[4], John Adam II[3], John Adam I[2], John Jacob[1]) was the son of Harry and Martha Baumgardner Startzman [ILF No. 3131]. John was born August 23, 1921. He married Acacia Sharp June 13, 1945. She was the daughter of James Burton Sharp and was born June 1, 1922, at Nappanee, Indiana.

(Sup) 5437 WILLIAM DONALD De VERE (Elizabeth[8], Nellie[7], Charles, Isabella[5], Rebecca[4], John Adam II[3], John Adam I[2], John Jacob[1]) was the son of Donald William and Elizabeth Page Plattenburg De Vere [ILF No. 3134]. William was born October 12, 1927, at Columbus, Ohio.

(Sup) 5438 RICHARD PAGE De VERE (Elizabeth[8], Nellie[7], Charles[6], Isabella[5], Rebecca[4], John Adam II[3], John Adam I[2], John Jacob[1]) was the son of Donald William and Elizabeth Page Plattenburg De Vere [ILF No. 3134]. Richard was born May 19, 1929, at Columbus, Ohio.

(Sup) 5439 JOHN NORMAN RICE SCARLET (John[8], George[7], Minnie[6], Adam[5], Rebecca[4], John Adam II[3], John Adam I[2], John Jacob[1]) was the son of John Leon and Thelma Rice Scarlet [ILF No. 3142]. John Norman was born February 19, 1933.

(Sup) 5440 JO ANN RICE SCARLET (John[8], George[7], Minnie[6], Adam[5], Rebecca[4], John Adam II[3], John Adam I[2], John Jacob[1]) was the daughter of John Leon and Thelma Rice Scarlet [ILF No. 3142]. Jo Ann was born February 18, 1936.

(Sup) 5441 EUGENE THOMAS SCARLET, JR. (Eugene[8], George[7], Minnie[6], Adam[5], Rebecca[4], John Adam II[3], John Adam I[2], John Jacob[1]) was the son of Eugene Thomas and Theresa Miller Scarlet [ILF No. 3148]. Eugene, Jr., was born August 14, 1943.

(Sup) 5442 MARK WAYNE SCARLET (Eugene[8], George[7], Minnie[6], Adam[5], Rebecca[4], John Adam II[3], John Adam I[2], John Jacob[1]) was the son of Eugene Thomas and Theresa Miller Scarlet [ILF No. 3148]. Mark was born July 10, 1945.

(Sup) 5443 GALA LOUISE SCARLET (Eugene[8], George[7], Minnie[6], Adam[5], Rebecca[4], John Adam II[3], John Adam I[2], John Jacob[1]) was the daughter of Eugene Thomas and Theresa Miller Scarlet [ILF No. 3148]. She was born July 24, 1946.

- -

(Sup) 5448 ADA JEAN DEMORY (Ross[8], Ralph[7], Daniel[6], Adam[5], Rebecca[4], John Adam II[3], John Adam I[2], John Jacob[1]) was the daughter of Ross Earl and Lucille (Young) Demory [Supplement No. 3150.1A]. Ada Jean was born June 29, 1952, at Aransas Pass, Texas. She married Wayne Gamelin, September 4, 1971, at Aransas Pass. He was born November 13, 1950, at Sault Ste. Marie, Michigan.

(Sup) 7287 i Jenny Wynette Gamelin, born February 25, 1972.
(Sup) 7288 ii Michael Shayne Gamelin, born May 31, 1975.

(Sup) 5448A ANNETTE FAYE DEMORY (Ross[8], Ralph[7], Daniel[6], Adam[5], Rebecca[4], John Adam II[3], John Adam I[2], John Jacob[1]) was the daughter of Ross Earl and Lucille (Young) Demory [Supplement No. 3150.1A]. Annette was born July 27, 1954 (twin of Jeanette) at Aransas Pass, Texas. She married Gary Wolf, December 26, 1978. He was the son of Jim Darrell and Rilda (Baker) Wolf and was born August 2, 1951, at Stellwater, Oklahoma.

(Sup) 7289 i Christine Nicole Wolf, born May 27, 1981.
(Sup) 7289A ii Angela Marie Wolf, born October 25, 1984.
(Sup) 7289B iii Sarah Ann Wolf, born December 27, 1987.

(Sup) 5448B   JEANETTE KAYE DEMORY (Ross[8], Ralph[7], Daniel[6], Adam[5], Rebecca[4], John Adam II[3], John Adam I[2], John Jacob[1]) was the daughter of Ross Earl and Lucille (Young) Demory [Supplement No. 3150.1A]. Jeanette was born July 27, 1954 (twin of Annette), at Aransas Pass, Texas. She married Grayson Tillman Hodges, June 14, 1980. He was the son of Edward Doll and Zenoma (Archer) Hodges and was born March 24, 1952, at Houston, Texas.

(Sup) 7290   i   Brady Gray Hodges, born June 9, 1981.
(Sup) 7291   ii   Heather Diane Hodges, born November 12, 1987.

(Sup) 5448C   SHERRY LYNN DEMORY (Ross[8], Ralph[7], Daniel[6], Adam[5], Rebecca[4], John Adam II[3], John Adam I[2], John Jacob[1]) was the daughter of Ross Earl and Lucille (Young) Demory [Supplement No. 3150.1A]. Sherry was born June 22, 1958, at Aransas Pass, Texas. She married James Douglas Woodrum, August 1, 1981. He was the son of James Francis and Ruby (Roberts) Woodrum and was born February 6, 1956, at Portsmouth, Ohio.

(Sup) 5449   MARTIN EARL HARPER (Ina Zoe[8], Ralph[7], Daniel[6], Adam[5], Rebecca[4], John Adam II[3], John Adam I[2], John Jacob[1]) was the son of Martin Emmett and Ina Zoe (Demory) Harper [Supplement No. 3150.1B]. He was born March 24, 1953, at Cotulla, Texas. He married Donna Hatfield, February 21, 1978, at Cotulla.

(Sup) 5450   CLAIRECE LYNN HARPER (Ina Zoe[8], Ralph[7], Daniel[6], Adam[5], Rebecca[4], John Adam II[3], John Adam I[2], John Jacob[1]) was the daughter of Martin Emmett and Ina Zoe (Demory) Harper [Supplement No. 3150.1B]. She was born December 31, 1956, at Cotulla, Texas. Clairece married Glen Megason.

(Sup) 7292   i   Christopher Glen Megason, born February 24, 1978.

(Sup) 5451   LONA JEAN HARPER (Gena[8], Ralph[7], Daniel[6], Adam[5], Rebecca[4], John Adam II[3], John Adam I[2], John Jacob[1]) was the daughter of Lonnie Burdwell and Gena (Demory) Harper [Supplement No. 3150.1C]. She was born March 3, 1956, at Victory, Texas. She married Chris Bergman, July 7, 1985. He was the son of William and Wynette Bergman and was born December 10, 1962.

(Sup) 5452   JOANN HARPER (Gena[8], Ralph[7], Daniel[6], Adam[5], Rebecca[4], John Adam II[3], John Adam I[2], John Jacob[1]) was the daughter of Lonnie Burdwell and Gena (Demory) Harper [Supplement No. 3150.1C]. Joann was born September 14, 1960, at Victoria, Texas. She married Leon V. Erdelt, Jr., March 23, 1981. He was the son of Leon V. and Nettie Bell (Miller) Erdelt and was born March 13, 1954.

(Sup) 7293   i   Steffanie Anne Erdelt, born May 27, 1983.

(Sup) 5453   MELISSA JANE ACREE (Margie[8], Alma[7], Daniel[6], Adam[5], Rebecca[4], John Adam II[3], John Adam I[2], John Jacob[1]) was the daughter of James Mack and Margie Fay (Jakeway) Acree [Supplement No. 3150.2A]. Melissa was born October 9, 1951, at Tulsa, Oklahoma.

(Sup) 5454   ROBIN LEE ACREE (Margie[8], Alma[7], Daniel[6], Adam[5], Rebecca[4], John Adam II[3], John Adam I[2], John Jacob[1]) was the daughter of James Mack and Margie Fay (Jakeway) Acree [Supplement No. 3150.2A]. Robin was born October 1, 1957, at Irving, Texas. She married Wesley Neeper, September 4, 1984.

(Sup) 5455   EARL GLEN JAKEWAY (Earl[8], Alma[7], Daniel[6], Adam[5], Rebecca[4], John Adam II[3], John Adam I[2], John Jacob[1]) was the son of Earl Thomas and Lorraine (Mikel) Jakeway [Supplement No. 3150.2B]. He was born June 17, 1947, at Skiatook, Oklahoma. He married Deborah Lee Hunt Davis, May 24, 1986. She was born May 14, 1957.

(Sup) 5455A   JAMES DOUGLAS JAKEWAY (Earl[8], Alma[7], Daniel[6], Adam[5], Rebecca[4], John Adam II[3], John Adam I[2], John Jacob[1]) was the son of Earl Thomas and Lorraine (Mikel) Jakeway [Supplement No. 3150.2B]. James was born December 29, 1948, at Tulsa, Oklahoma. He married Helga Michaelis, June 14, 1969.

(Sup) 7294   i   Stephanie Jakeway, born 1970.

(Sup) 5455B   NANCY ANN JAKEWAY (Earl[8], Alma[7], Daniel[6], Adam[5], Rebecca[4], John Adam II[3], John Adam I[2], John Jacob[1]) was the daughter of Earl Thomas and Lorraine (Mikel) Jakeway [Supplement No. 3150.2B]. Nancy was born January 8, 1950, at Tulsa, Oklahoma. She married Harry John Ogilvie, June 29, 1968.

(Sup) 7295   i   Nichole Erin Ogilvie, born August 10, 1975.

(Sup) 5455C   JOYCE LYNN JAKEWAY (Earl[8], Alma[7], Daniel[6], Adam[5], Rebecca[4], John Adam II[3], John Adam I[2], John Jacob[1]) was the daughter of Earl Thomas and Lorraine (Mikel) Jakeway [Supplement No. 3150.2B]. Joyce was born May 22, 1954, at Tulsa, Oklahoma. She married Michael Howard Ferguson. He was born July 4, 1953.

(Sup) 7296   i   Michael Howard Ferguson, Jr., born Nov 11, 1974.
(Sup) 7297   ii   Benjamin Douglas Ferguson, born Aug 15, 1978.

(Sup) 5456   DONALD GREGORY VOWELL (Luetta^8, Alma^7, Daniel^6, Adam^5, Rebecca^4, John Adam II^3, John Adam I^2, John Jacob^1) was the son of Donald Green and Luetta (Jakeway) Vowell [Supplement No. 3150.2D]. He was born April 19, 1958, at Tulsa, Oklahoma. He married Nancy Rose Selsor, April 27, 1985. She was the daughter of Jerry Lee and Pauline (Henley) Selsor.

(Sup) 5457   JULIA ANNE VOWELL (Luetta^8, Alma^7, Daniel^6, Adam^5, Rebecca^4, John Adam II^3, John Adam I^2, John Jacob^1) was the daughter of Donald Green and Luetta (Jakeway) Vowell [Supplement No. 3150.2D]. Julia was born April 10, 1981, at Tulsa, Oklahoma. She married Dennis Alvin Powders, April 10, 1981, at Tulsa. He was the son of Alvin LeRoy and Donna Jo (Stubbs) Powders and was born March 29, 1961.

(Sup) 7298   1 Tiffany Renee Powders, born October 4, 1984.

(Sup) 5458   RICHARD THOMAS JAKEWAY (Richard^8, Alma^7, Daniel^6, Adam^5, Rebecca^4, John Adam II^3, John Adam I^2, John Jacob^1) was the son of Richard Eugene and Lynetta (Wikel) Jakeway [Supplement No. 3150.2E]. He was born October 13, 1951. His wife was Corrine.

(Sup) 7299   1 Joshua Jakeway.
(Sup) 7300   11 Sarah Jakeway.

(Sup) 5459   MARK ANTHONY JAKEWAY (Richard^8, Alma^7, Daniel^6, Adam^5, Rebecca^4, John Adam II^3, John Adam I^2, John Jacob^1) was the son of Richard Eugene and Lynetta (Wikel) Jakeway [Supplement No. 3150.2E]. Mark was born August 8, 1953. His wife was Sherry.

(Sup) 7301   1 Raylene Marie Jakeway, born September 13, 1986.

(Sup) 5460   EDWIN LEE MATSON (Lee^8, Sarah^7, Daniel^6, Adam^5, Rebecca^4, John Adam II^3, John Adam I^2, John Jacob^1) was the son of Edwin Walfred and Olive Lee (Hackler) Matson [Supplement No. 3150.3A]. Edwin was born July 7, 1951, at Chicago, Illinois.

(Sup) 5460A   MARTTI MARIA MATSON (Lee^8, Sarah^7, Daniel^6, Adam^5, Rebecca^4, John Adam II^3, John Adam I^2, John Jacob^1) ws the daughter of Edwin Walfred and Olive Lee (Hackler) Matson [Supplement No. 3150.3A]. She was born May 1, 1953. She married Randall Wesley Cade, December 10, 1983. He was the son of Leland Paul and Janet (Elliott) Cade and was born January 19, 1955, at Havre, Montana.

(Sup) 7302   i Lindsay Rachel Cade, born May 26, 1985.

(Sup) 5460B   JOHN ALAN MATSON (Lee^8, Sarah^7, Daniel^6, Adam^5, Rebecca^4, John Adam II^3, John Adam I^2, John Jacob^1) was the son of Edwin Walfred and Olive Lee (Hackler) Matson [Supplement No. 3150.3A]. John was born February 21, 1960, at Arlington, Texas.

(Sup) 5461   GEORGE CONLEY HACKLER (Loyd^8, Sarah^7, Daniel^6, Adam^5, Rebecca^4, John Adam II^3, John Adam I^2, John Jacob^1) was the son of Loyd Junior and Norma (Conley) Hackler [Supplement No. 3150.3D]. George was born June 24, 1948, at Stillwater, Oklahoma. He married Shelly Perra.

(Sup) 7303   1 Jason Loyd Hackler, born April 27, 1975.

(Sup) 5461A   PATRICIA HACKLER (Loyd^8, Sarah^7, Daniel^6, Adam^5, Rebecca^4, John Adam II^3, John Adam I^2, John Jacob^1) was the daughter of Loyd Junior and Norma (Conley) Hackler [Supplement No. 3150.3D]. Patricia was born November 10, 1952, at San Angelo, Texas. She married Thomas Reed Brown, June 5, 1982. He was the son of Thomas Augustine and Marianna (Forrest) Brown and was born May 5, 1982, at Austin, Texas.

(Sup) 5461B   WARREN CRAIG HACKLER (Loyd^8, Sarah^7, Daniel^6, Adam^5, Rebecca^4, John Adam II^3, John Adam I^2, John Jacob^1) was the son of Loyd Junior and Norma (Conley) Hackler [Supplement No. 3150.3D]. Warren was born February 3, 1953, at San Angelo, Texas.

(Sup) 5462   ROGER FRANK HACKLER (Frank^8, Sarah^7, Daniel^6, Adam^5, Rebecca^4, John Adam II^3, John Adam I^2, John Jacob^1) was the son of Raymond Frank and Gaynall (Norrie) Hackler [Supplement No. 3150.3E]. He was born July 23, 1961, at Paola, Kansas.

(Sup) 5462A   REX GLEN HACKLER (Frank^8, Sarah^7, Daniel^6, Adam^5, Rebecca^4, John Adam II^3, John Adam I^2, John Jacob^1) was the son of Raymond Frank and Gaynall (Norrie) Hackler [Supplement No. 3150.3E]. He was born March 21, 1963, at Hiawatha, Kansas.

(Sup) 5462B   NATALIE SUE HACKLER (Frank^8, Sarah^7, Daniel^6, Adam^5, Rebecca^4, John Adam II^3, John Adam I^2, John Jacob^1) was the daughter of Raymond Frank and Gaynall (Norrie) Hackler [Supplement No. 3150.3E]. She was born November 17, 1971, at Hiawatha, Kansas.

(Sup) 5463   TAMARA JO HACKLER (Arthur[8], Sarah[7], Daniel[6], Adam[5], Rebecca[4], John Adam II[3], John Adam I[2], John Jacob[1]) was the daughter of Arthur Leroy and Edna (Rainbow) Hackler [Supplement No. 3150.3F]. Tamara was born March 28, 1959, at Oklahoma City, Oklahoma. She married Dallas Wayne Scribner, Jr., June 29, 1979, at Kingston, Oklahoma. He was the son of Dallas Wayne and Violet (Wagoner) Scribner and was born May 25, 1959, at Madill, Oklahoma.

(Sup) 7304   i   Dallas Wayne Scribner, III, born June 14, 1981.
(Sup) 7305   ii   Bobbie Rachel Scribner, born July 26, 1985.

(Sup) 5464   PAMALA SUE HACKLER (Arthur[8], Sarah[7], Daniel[6], Adam[5], Rebecca[4], John Adam II[3], John Adam I[2], John Jacob[1]) was the daughter of Arthur Leroy and Edna (Rainbow) Hackler [Supplement No. 3150.3F]. Pamala was born January 21, 1964, at Oklahoma City, Oklahoma. She married Don Michael Allen, December 18, 1987, at Madill, Oklahoma. He was the son of Donald Wayne and Theresa (Girouad) Allen and was born June 19, 1963, at New Iberia, Louisiana.

(Sup) 5465   BRETT ALAN TULLOSS (Edith[8], Sarah[7], Daniel[6], Adam[5], Rebecca[4], John Adam II[3], John Adam I[2], John Jacob[1]) was the son of Robert Lafayette and Edith (Hackler) Tulloss [Supplement No. 3150.3G]. He was born April 24, 1959, at San Antonio, Texas.

(Sup) 5466   DEBORAH JOAN MESSINA (Maxine[8], Sarah[7], Daniel[6], Adam[5], Rebecca[4], John Adam II[3], John Adam I[2], John Jacob[1]) was the daughter of Joseph and Maxine (Hackler) Messina [Supplement No. 3150.3H]. Deborah was born May 25, 1954, at Detroit, Michigan. She married Peter Bernard Moceri, June 1, 1973, at Mt. Clemens, Michigan. He was the son of Joseph and Geraldine (Pokrieska) Moceri and was born August 29, 1951, at Detroit.

(Sup) 7306   i   Anthony Joseph Moceri, born October 27, 1978.
(Sup) 7307   ii   Lisa Marie Moceri, born August 7, 1983.

(Sup) 5466A   SANDRA DIANE MESSINA (Maxine[8], Sarah[7], Daniel[6], Adam[5], Rebecca[4], John Adam II[3], John Adam I[2], John Jacob[1]) was the daughter of Joseph and Maxine (Hackler) Messina [Supplement No. 3150.3H]. Sandra was born August 7, 1956, at Detroit, Michigan. She married Michael Joseph Venditti, May 11, 1979. He was the son of Levio and Doris (Collier) Venditti and was born July 26, 1953, at Detroit.

(Sup) 5466B   DAVID JOSEPH MESSINA (Maxine[8], Sarah[7], Daniel[6], Adam[5], Rebecca[4], John Adam II[3], John Adam I[2], John Jacob[1]) was the son of Joseph and Maxine (Hackler) Messina [Supplement No. 3150.3H]. David was born

November 9, 1960, at Detroit, Michigan. He married Linda Marie Yates, June, 1982. She was born August 31, 1964.

(Sup) 7308   i   Jaqueline Marie Messina, born May 31, 1982.

(Sup) 5466C   DONALD DEAN MESSINA (Maxine[8], Sarah[7], Daniel[6], Adam[5], Rebecca[4], John Adam II[3], John Adam I[2], John Jacob[1]) was the son of Joseph and Maxine (Hackler) Messina [Supplement No. 3150.3H]. Donald was born March 12, 1963 (twin of Douglas), at Mt. Clemens, Michigan. He married Vicki Marie Thompson.

(Sup) 7309   i   Andrea Christine Messina, born November 24, 1985.

(Sup) 5466D   DOUGLAS DREW MESSINA (Maxine[8], Sarah[7], Daniel[6], Adam[5], Rebecca[4], John Adam II[3], John Adam I[2], John Jacob[1]) was the son of Joseph and Maxine (Hackler) Messina [Supplement No. 3150.3H]. Douglas was born March 12, 1963 (twin of Donald), at Mt. Clemens, Michigan. He married Visa Marie Lemore.

(Sup) 7310   i   Ashley Lauren Messina, born December 12, 1985.

(Sup) 6466E   SUSAN MARIE MESSINE (Maxine[8], Sarah[7], Daniel[6], Adam[5], Rebecca[4], John Adam II[3], John Adam I[2], John Jacob[1]) was the daughter of Joseph and Maxine (Hackler) Messina [Supplement No. 3150.3H]. She was born July 16, 1964, at Mt. Clemens, Michigan.

(Sup) 5466F   JOSEPH PATRICK MESSINA (Maxine[8], Sarah[7], Daniel[6], Adam[5], Rebecca[4], John Adam II[3], John Adam I[2], John Jacob[1]) was the son of Joseph and Maxine (Hackler) Messina [Supplement No. 3150.3H]. He was born August 16, 1965, at Mt. Clemens, Michigan.

(Sup) 5466G   ROBERT GLEN MESSINA (Maxine[8], Sarah[7], Daniel[6], Adam[5], Rebecca[4], John Adam II[3], John Adam I[2], John Jacob[1]) was the son of Joseph and Maxine (Hackler) Messina [Supplement No. 3150.3H]. He was born January 1, 1968, at Mt. Clemens, Michigan.

(Sup) 5467   CAROLYN SUE MORRELL (Alta[8], Hattie[7], Daniel[6], Adam[5], Rebecca[4], John Adam II[3], John Adam I[2], John Jacob[1]) was the daughter of R.B. and Alta (Putnam) Morrell [Supplement No. 3150.4A]. Carolyn was born March 6, 1941, at Purcell, Oklahoma. She married Glenn Albert Reding, June 8, 1963, at Tulsa, Oklahoma. He was the son of Albert Peter and Mary Alberta (Brack) Reding and was born December 25, 1941, at Geary, Oklahoma.

(Sup) 7311   i   Shelly Lynn Reding, born March 11, 1966.
(Sup) 7311A   ii   Scott Allen Reding, born March 30, 1967.
(Sup) 7311B   iii   Shannon Elaine Reding, born October 14, 1970.

(Sup) 5468 PATRICIA LYNN PUTNAM (Lee^3, Hattie^7, Daniel^6, Adam^5, Rebecca^4, John Adam II^3, John Adam I^2, John Jacob^1) was the daughter of Lee Alvin and Florence (Folsom) Putnam [Supplement No. 3150.4B]. Patricia was born June 1, 1950, at Corsicana, Texas.

(Sup) 5469 RICHARD LEE PUTNAM (Lee^8, Hattie^7, Daniel^6, Adam^5, Rebecca^4, John Adam II^3, John Adam I^2, John Jacob^1) was the son of Lee Alvin and Florence (Folsom) Putnam [Supplement No. 3150.4B]. Richard was born August 4, 1952, at Corsicana, Texas. He married Debra Elizabeth Murphy. She was the daughter of Thomas Eugene and Lois Elizabeth (Hayes) Murphy and was born December 30, 1957, at Tunica, Mississippi.

(Sup) 7312   i Eric Shane Putnam, born November 26, 1986.

(Sup) 5470 ELIZABETH ROGERS (Daisy^8, Hattie^7, Daniel^6, Adam^5, Rebecca^4, John Adam II^3, John Adam I^2, John Jacob^1) was the daughter of Robert Jean and Daisy (Putnam) Rogers [Supplement No. 5130.4C]. Elizabeth was born February 7, 1945, at Tulsa, Oklahoma. She married Raymond Lee Fletcher, Jr.. September 24, 1965, at Denton, Texas. He was the son of Raymond Lee and Bonnie (Boyd) Fletcher and was born December 1, 1945, at Denton.

(Sup) 7313   i Brian Lee Fletcher, born April 14, 1966.
(Sup) 7314   ii Elisabeth Fletcher, born August 20, 1970.

(Sup) 4570A KATHRYN ROGERS (Daisy^8, Hattie^7, Daniel^6, Adam^5, Rebecca^4, John Adam II^3, John Adam I^2, John Jacob^1) was the daughter of Robert Jean and Daisy (Putnam) Rogers [Supplement No. 5130.4C]. Kathryn was born June 2, 1949, at Denton, Texas. She married Chris Harry Rhoads, December 5, 1980, at San Antonio, Texas. He was the son of Kenneth Harry and Lucille Edna (Walker) Rhoads and was born June 4, 1950, at Houston, Texas.

(Sup) 5470B ROBERT JEAN ROGERS, JR., (Daisy^8, Hattie^7, Daniel^6, Adam^5, Rebecca^4, John Adam II^3, John Adam I^2, John Jacob^1) was the son of Robert Jean and Daisy (Putnam) Rogers [Supplement No. 5130.4C]. Robert, Jr., was born January 9, 1954, at Denton, Texas. He married Mildren Ellen Hopkins, August 7, 1976, at Denton. She was the daughter of George and Jane Hopkins and was born January 13, 1954, at Fort Worth, Texas.

(Sup) 7315   i Samuel Hopkins Rogers, born September 1, 1984.
(Sup) 7316   ii Rebella Jane Rogers, born September 15, 1987.

(Sup) 5471 JUDITH ANNE PUTNAM (Roy^8, Hattie^7, Daniel^6, Adam^5, Rebecca^4, John Adam II^3, John Adam I^2, John Jacob^1) was the daughter of Roy Frank and Kathleen (Nicholls) Putnam [Supplement No. 3150.4D]. Judith was born March 2, 1947, at Stillwater, Oklahoma. She married James Koenig Lewis, July 21, 1968, at Sacramento, California. He was the son of James Atkinson and Berneace Alma (Koenig) Lewis and was born October 11, 1945, at Hanford, California.

(Sup) 7317   i James Braid Lewis, born May 19, 1971.
(Sup) 7318   ii Justin Koenig Lewis, born June 30, 1975.

(Sup) 5471A JAMES ROY PUTNAM (Roy^8, Hattie^7, Daniel^6, Adam^5, Rebecca^4, John Adam II^3, John Adam I^2, John Jacob^1) was the son of Roy Frank and Kathleen (Nicholls) Putnam [Supplement No. 3150.4D]. James was born January 19, 1949, at Stillwater, Oklahoma. He married Laura Claire Johnson, July 8, 1972, at Redwood City, California. She was the daughter of Gerald Clark and Helene (Vostroff) Johnson and was born June 4, 1949, at San Francisco.

(Sup) 7319   i Jennifer Nicole Putnam, born July 20, 1977.
(Sup) 7320   ii Gregory Michael Putnam, born July 12, 1981.

(Sup) 5471B MICHAEL CHARLES PUTNAM (Roy^8, Hattie^7, Daniel^6, Adam^5, Rebecca^4, John Adam II^3, John Adam I^2, John Jacob^1) was the son of Roy Frank and Kathleen (Nicholls) Putnam [Supplement No. 3150.4D]. Michael was born September 3, 1952, at Corpus Christi, Texas. He married Dorothy Edith Hanson, May 5, 1943, at Fair Oaks, California. She was the daughter of Walter Frank and Glorie Edith (Wilcox) Hanson and was born August 3, 1953, at Dearborn, Michigan. Michael died February 8, 1981, at Sacramento, California.

(Sup) 7321   i Daniel Michael Putnam, born December 22, 1977.
(Sup) 7322   ii Erick Frank Putnam, born May 28, 1980.

(Sup) 5471C CYNTHIA KAY PUTNAM (Roy^8, Hattie^7, Daniel^6, Adam^5, Rebecca^4, John Adam II^3, John Adam I^2, John Jacob^1) was the daughter of Roy Frank and Kathleen (Nicholls) Putnam [Supplement no. 3150.4D]. Cynthia was born November 11, 1955, at Corpus Christi, Texas. She married Tom Burgardt at Sacramento, California.

(Sup) 7323   i Megan Michelle Burgardt, born September 3, 1986.

(Sup) 5472 TIMOTHY DUANE FEHNEL (Beverly^8, Hattie^7, Daniel^6, Adam^5, Rebecca^4, John Adam II^3, John Adam I^2, John Jacob^1) was the son of Harold Kermit and Beverly (Putnam) Fehnel [Supplement No. 3150.4E]. Timothy was born November 10, 1963, at Tucson, Arizona.

(Sup) 5472A MARK ALLEN FEHNEL (Beverly^8, Hattie^7, Daniel^6, Adam^5, Rebecca^4, John Adam II^3, John Adam I^2, John Jacob^1) was the son of Harold Kermit and Beverly (Putnam) Fehnel [Supplement No. 3150.4E]. Mark was born December 6, 1965, at Tucson, Arizona.

(Sup) 5472B MATTHEW DALE FEHNEL (Beverly^8, Hattie^7, Daniel^6, Adam^5, Rebecca^4, John Adam II^3, John Adam I^2, John Jacob^1) was the son of Harold Kermit and Beverly (Putnam) Fehnel [Supplement No. 3150.4E]. Matthew was born August 21, 1967, at Scottsdale, Arizona.

(Sup) 5472C MARY ANN FEHNEL (Beverly^8, Hattie^7, Daniel^6, Adam^5, Rebecca^4, John Adam II^3, John Adam I^2, John Jacob^1) was the daughter of Harold Kermit and Beverly (Putnam) Fehnel [Supplement No. 3150.4E]. Mary Ann was born February 18, 1969, at Hillsboro, Texas.

(Sup) 5473 LLOYD HUBERT DEMORY, JR., (Lloyd^8, John^7, Daniel^6, Adam^5, Rebecca^4, John Adam II^3, John Adam I^2, John Jacob^1) was the son of Lloyd Hubert and Dorothy (Holland) Demory [Supplement No. 3150.5A]. Lloyd, Jr., was born December 28, 1951.

(Sup) 5473A DANIEL RICHARD DEMORY (Lloyd^8, John^7, Daniel^6, Adam^5, Rebecca^4, John Adam II^3, John Adam I^2, John Jacob^1) was the son of Lloyd Hubert and Dorothy (Holland) Demory [Supplement No. 3150.5A]. Daniel was born August 9, 1953.

(Sup) 5473B STEPHEN PERRY DEMORY (Lloyd^8, John^7, Daniel^6, Adam^5, Rebecca^4, John Adam II^3, John Adam I^2, John Jacob^1) was the son of Lloyd Hubert and Dorothy (Holland) Demory [Supplement No. 3150.5A]. Stephen was born September 5, 1954.

(Sup) 5473C JANET LEE DEMORY (Lloyd^8, John^7, Daniel^6, Adam^5, Rebecca^4, John Adam II^3, John Adam I^2, John Jacob^1) was the daughter of Lloyd Hubert and Dorothy (Holland) Demory [Supplement No. 3150.5A]. Janet was born May 16, 1960.

(Sup) 5474 STANLEY MICHAEL LARGE (Rosalie^8, John^7, Daniel^6, Adam^5, Rebecca^4, John Adam II^3, John Adam I^2, John Jacob^1) was the son of Robert Woodrow and Rosalie (Demory) Large [Supplement No. 3150.5B]. Stanley was born September 30, 1947, in Michigan. He married Patricia Price at Houma, Louisiana.

(Sup) 5474A JOHN CLINTON LARGE (Rosalie^8, John^7, Daniel^6, Adam^5, Rebecca^4, John Adam II^3, John Adam I^2, John Jacob^1) was the son of Robert Woodrow and Rosalie (Demory) Large [Supplement No. 3150.5B]. John was born December 12, 1950, at Bartlesville, Oklahoma. He married Catherine Mire, June 10, 1973, at Houma, Louisiana.

(Sup) 5474B KAYE LYNN LARGE (Rosalie^8, John^7, Daniel^6, Adam^5, Rebecca^4, John Adam II^3, John Adam I^2, John Jacob^1) was the daughter of Robert Woodrow and Rosalie (Demory) Large [Supplement No. 3150.5B]. Kaye Lynn was born August 12, 1952, at Bartlesville, Oklahoma. She married Verlon Martin Davis, June 10, 1978, at Raceland, Louisiana. He was the son of Robert Alpus and Sarah (Meadows) Davis and was born January 12, 1952, at Andalusia, Alabama.

(Sup) 7326 † Daniel Raymond Davis, born Jun 12, 1972. (adopted by Verlon Martin Davis, Nov 17, 1981)

(Sup) 5475 JOHN EDWARD INDA, JR., (Vivian^8, John^7, Daniel^6, Adam^5, Rebecca^4, John Adam II^3, John Adam I^2, John Jacob^1) was the son of John Edward and Vivian (Demory) Inda [Supplement No. 3150.5C]. John Edward, Jr., was born September 7, 1952, and died October, 1952, at Dewey, Oklahoma.

(Sup) 5475A DAVID LINK INDA (Vivian^8, John^7, Daniel^6, Adam^5, Rebecca^4, John Adam II^3, John Adam I^2, John Jacob^1) was the son of John Edward and Vivian (Demory) Inda [Supplement No. 3150.5C]. David was born November 21, 1953, at Dewey, Oklahoma.

(Sup) 5475B FRANK EDWARD INDA (Vivian^8, John^7, Daniel^6, Adam^5, Rebecca^4, John Adam II^3, John Adam I^2, John Jacob^1) was the son of John Edward and Vivian (Demory) Inda [Supplement No. 3150.5C]. Frank was born December 24, 1955, at Dewey, Oklahoma.

(Sup) 5475C PAUL INDA (Vivian^8, John^7, Daniel^6, Adam^5, Rebecca^4, John Adam II^3, John Adam I^2, John Jacob^1) was the son of John Edward and Vivian (Demory) Inda [Supplement No. 3150.5C]. Paul was born November 5, 1968, at Dewey, Oklahoma.

(Sup) 5476 WILLIAM FLOYD MAYFIELD (Nettie May^8, Floyd^7, Daniel^6, Adam^5, Rebecca^4, John Adam II^3, John Adam I^2, John Jacob^1) was the son of James F. and Nettie May (Demory) Mayfield [Supplement No. 3150.6A]. He was born August 1, 1949.

(Sup) 5476A JULIE MAY MAYFIELD (Nettie May[8], Floyd[7], Daniel[6], Adam[5], Rebecca[4], John Adam II[3], John Adam I[2], John Jacob[1]) was the daughter of James F. and Nettie May (Demory) Mayfield [Supplement No. 3150.6A]. She was born September 5, 1952.

(Sup) 5476B RICHARD JAMES MAYFIELD (Nettie May[8], Floyd[7], Daniel[6], Adam[5], Rebecca[4], John Adam II[3], John Adam I[2], John Jacob[1]) was the son of James F. and Nettie May (Demory) Mayfield [Supplement No. 3150.6A]. He was born May 10, 1954.

(Sup) 5476C PEGGY LEE MAYFIELD (Nettie May[8], Floyd[7], Daniel[6], Adam[5], Rebecca[4], John Adam II[3], John Adam I[2], John Jacob[1]) was the daughter of James F. and Nettie May (Demory) Mayfield [Supplement No. 3150.6A]. She was born January 30, 1962.

(Sup) 5477 JOE DAVID THOMPSON (Jessie[8], Floyd[7], Daniel[6], Adam[5], Rebecca[4], John Adam II[3], John Adam I[2], John Jacob[1]) was the son of Joe Kenneth and Jessie (Demory) Thompson [Supplement No. 3150.6B]. He was born March 13, 1953.

(Sup) 5477A LISBETH ROSE THOMPSON (Jessie[8], Floyd[7], Daniel[6], Adam[5], Rebecca[4], John Adam II[3], John Adam I[2], John Jacob[1]) was the daughter of Joe Kenneth and Jessie (Demory) Thompson [Supplement No. 3150.6B]. She was born April 29, 1955.

(Sup) 5477B TIMOTHY FLOYD THOMPSON (Jessie[8], Floyd[7], Daniel[6], Adam[5], Rebecca[4], John Adam II[3], John Adam I[2], John Jacob[1]) was the son of Joe Kenneth and Jessie (Demory) Thompson [Supplement No. 3150.6B]. He was born November 28, 1960.

(Sup) 5478 DANIEL LEE WELCH (Georgia[8], Floyd[7], Daniel[6], Adam[5], Rebecca[4], John Adam II[3], John Adam I[2], John Jacob[1]) was the son of Patrick Lee and Georgia (Demory) Welch [Supplement No. 3150.6C]. He was born November 9, 1951.

(Sup) 5478A DEAN WALTER WELCH (Georgia[8], Floyd[7], Daniel[6], Adam[5], Rebecca[4], John Adam II[3], John Adam I[2], John Jacob[1]) was the son of Patrick Lee and Georgia (Demory) Welch [Supplement No. 3150.6C]. He was born November 22, 1954 (twin of Damon Wayne).

(Sup) 5478B DAMON WAYNE WELCH (Georgia[8], Floyd[7], Daniel[6], Adam[5], Rebecca[4], John Adam II[3], John Adam I[2], John Jacob[1]) was the son of Patrick Lee and Georgia (Demory) Welch [Supplement No. 3150.6C]. He was born November 22, 1954 (twin of Dean Walter).

(Sup) 5478C PAUL CLINTON WELCH (Georgia[8], Floyd[7], Daniel[6], Adam[5], Rebecca[4], John Adam II[3], John Adam I[2], John Jacob[1]) was the son of Patrick Lee and Georgia (Demory) Welch [Supplement No. 3150.6C]. He was born November 5, 1958.

(Sup) 5479 JEFFERY CLINTON RUBOTTOM (Betty[8], Floyd[7], Daniel[6], Adam[5], Rebecca[4], John Adam II[3], John Adam I[2], John Jacob[1]) was the son of Clinton Alvin and Betty Jane (Demory) Rubottom [Supplement No. 3150.6D]. He was born October 9, 1957.

(Sup) 5480 ELIZABETH ANN DEMORY (John[8], Floyd[7], Daniel[6], Adam[5], Rebecca[4], John Adam II[3], John Adam I[2], John Jacob[1]) was the daughter of John Albert and Patricia (Harris) Demory [Supplement No. 3150.6F]. Elizabeth was born November 24, 1968.

(Sup) 5481 RICHARD FREDERICK CULLISON, JR., (Bonnie[8], Pearl[7], Daniel[6], Adam[5], Rebecca[4], John Adam II[3], John Adam I[2], John Jacob[1]) was the son of Richard Frederick and Bonnie (Putnam) Cullison [Supplement No. 3150.7B]. Richard, Jr., was born November 10, 1946, at Chula Vista, California. He married Patricia Ellen Sommers, June 17, 1978, at Sandsprings, Oklahoma. She was the daughter of Warren Albert and Shari (Hill) Sommers, and was born March 9, 1955, at Danville, Illinois.

(Sup) 7332 1 Sarah Elizabeth Cullison, born August 12, 1982.

(Sup) 5482 LYRA ANN CULLISON (Bonnie[8], Pearl[7], Daniel[6], Adam[5], Rebecca[4], John Adam II[3], John Adam I[2], John Jacob[1]) was the daughter of Richard Frederick and Bonnie (Putnam) Cullison [Supplement No. 3150.7B]. Lyra Ann was born August 25, 1948, at Ponca City, Oklahoma.

(Sup) 5483 JOHN LAWRENCE PUTNAM (Jesse[8], Pearl[7], Daniel[6], Adam[5], Rebecca[4], John Adam II[3], John Adam I[2], John Jacob[1]) was the son of Jesse Robert and Dorothy (York) Putnam [Supplement No. 3150.7C]. John was born April 1, 1950, and died April 3, 1950, at Stillwater, Oklahoma. He is buried at Kellyville, Oklahoma.

(Sup) 5483A LINDA MARIE PUTNAM (Jesse[8], Pearl[7], Daniel[6], Adam[5], Rebecca[4], John Adam II[3], John Adam I[2], John Jacob[1]) was the daughter of Jesse Robert and Dorothy (York) Putnam [Supplement No. 3150.7C]. Linda was born January 23, 1952, at Schenectady, New York. She married Walter William McCollom, III, June 1, 1974, at Oklahoma City, Oklahoma. He was the son of Walter William and Virginia (Miller) McCollom, Jr., and was born April 13, 1953, at Stillwater, Oklahoma.

(Sup) 7333   i Megan Marie McCollom, born March 30, 1976.
(Sup) 7334   ii Virginia Victoria McCollom, born May 9, 1981.

(Sup) 5483B JESSICA ANN PUTNAM (Jesse[8], Pearl[7], Daniel[6], Adam[5], Rebecca[4], John Adam II[3], John Adam I[2], John Jacob[1]) was the daughter of Jesse Robert and Dorothy (York) Putnam [Supplement No. 3150.7C]. Jessica was born August 1, 1954, at Sherman, Texas. She married Robert Marvin Jones, May 26, 1973, at Oklahoma City, Oklahoma.

(Sup) 5483C GEORGIA LEE PUTNAM (Jesse[8], Pearl[7], Daniel[6], Adam[5], Rebecca[4], John Adam II[3], John Adam I[2], John Jacob[1]) was the daughter of Jesse Robert and Dorothy (York) Putnam [Supplement No. 3150.7C]. Georgia was born March 16, 1956, at Sherman, Texas.

(Sup) 5483D ROBERTA JANE PUTNAM (Jesse[8], Pearl[7], Daniel[6], Adam[5], Rebecca[4], John Adam II[3], John Adam I[2], John Jacob[1]) was the daughter of Jesse Robert and Dorothy (York) Putnam [Supplement no. 3150.7C]. Roberta was born July 26, 1961, at Oklahoma City, Oklahoma. She married Bruce Michael Wright, September 27, 1984, at Oklahoma City. He was the son of Jimmie Lee and Mary (Morgan) Wright and was born May 10, 1958, at Tulsa, Oklahoma.

(Sup) 5484 ELLA FAY JONES (Georgia[8], Pearl[7], Daniel[6], Adam[5], Rebecca[4], John Adam II[3], John Adam I[2], John Jacob[1]) was the daughter of Joseph Franklin and Georgia (Putnam) Jones [Supplement No. 3150.7D]. Ella was born June 6, 1952, at Oklahoma City, Oklahoma. She married John Richard Starnes, August 16, 1977, at Bonham, Texas. He was the son of John R. and Frances (Golden) Starnes and was born November 10, 1951, at Sherman, Texas.

(Sup) 7335   i Eric Richard Starnes, born December 6, 1978.
(Sup) 7336   ii Zachary Paul Starnes, born June 15, 1984.

(Sup) 5485 ANNA JEANNE JONES (Georgia[8], Pearl[7], Daniel[6], Adam[5], Rebecca[4], John Adam II[3], John Adam I[2], John Jacob[1]) was the daughter of Joseph Franklin and Georgia (Putnam) Jones [Supplement No. 3150.7D]. She was born December 29, 1953, at Oklahoma City, Oklahoma. She married David Evans Reed, March 24, 1972, at Oklahoma City. He was the son of David Evans (Beck) Reed, and was born March 24, 1972, at Oklahoma City.

(Sup) 7337   i David Evans Reed, Jr., born October 8, 1972.
(Sup) 7338   ii Josephine Rebecca Reed, born September 13, 1975.

(Sup) 5486 DAVID ALLAN HARRELL (Allan[8], Grace[7], Daniel[6], Adam[5], Rebecca[4], John Adam II[3], John Adam I[2], John Jacob[1]) was the son of Luby Allan and Amy Lou (O'Neal) Harrell [Supplement No. 3150.8A]. David was born January 19, 1957.

(Sup) 5487 CHERYL BETH HARRELL (Allan[8], Grace[7], Daniel[6], Adam[5], Rebecca[4], John Adam II[3], John Adam I[2], John Jacob[1]) was the daughter of Luby Allan and Amy Lou (O'Neal) Harrell [Supplement No. 3150.8A]. Cheryl was born February 7, 1961.

(Sup) 5488 KARRI LYNN HARRELL (James[8], Grace[7], Daniel[6], Adam[5], Rebecca[4], John Adam II[3], John Adam I[2], John Jacob[1]) daughter of James Edward and Frances (Smith) Harrell [Supplement No. 3150.8B]. Karri Lynn was born May 25, 1966.

(Sup) 5489 JAY SCOTT LAWSON (Barbara[8], Grace[7], Daniel[6], Adam[5], Rebecca[4], John Adam II[3], John Adam I[2], John Jacob[1]) son of Jay Francis and Barbara (Harrell) Lawson [Supplement No. 3150.8D]. Jay was born January 12, 1961.

- -

(Sup) 5498 DONALD RODENHI, JR. (Nellie[8], William[7], Luther[6], John[5], Rebecca[4], John Adam II[3], John Adam I[2], John Jacob[1]) was the son of Donald and Nellie Demory Rodenhi [TLF No. 3159]. Donald, Jr., was born July 28, 1943.

(Sup) 5499 WILLIAM BRYANT RODENHI (Nellie[8], William[7], Luther[6], John[5], Rebecca[4], John Adam II[3], John Adam I[2], John Jacob[1]) was the son of Donald and Nellie Demory Rodenhi [TLF No. 3159]. William was born January 23, 1947.

(Sup) 5500 JAMES EDWARD DEMORY (Kenyon[8], William[7], Luther[6], John[5], Rebecca[4], John Adam II[3], John Adam I[2], John Jacob[1]) was the son of Kenyon Link and Mary Mattingly Demory [TLF No. 3162]. James was born January 6, 1947.

(Sup) 5501 STEPHEN ANDREW MARCELLA (Priscilla[8], Charles[7], Henry[6], John[5], Rebecca[4], John Adam II[3], John Adam I[2], John Jacob[1]) was the son of Lawrence Charles and Priscilla Diane Demory Marcella [Supplement No. 3173]. He was born August 27, 1961, at Newcastle, Pennsylvania.

(Sup) 5502 JEFFREY CHARLES MARCELLA (Priscilla[8], Charles[7], Henry[6], John[5], Rebecca[4], John Adam II[3], John Adam I[2], John Jacob[1]) was the son of Lawrence Charles and Priscilla Diane Demory Marcella [Supplement No. 3173]. He was born January 13, 1968, at Newcastle, Pennsylvania.

(Sup) 5503 PATRICIA JOAN DEMORY (Charles[8], Charles[7], Henry[6], John[5], Rebecca[4], John Adam II[3], John Adam I[2], John Jacob[1]) was the daughter of William and Judith Elaine Sebek Demory, Jr. [Supplement No. 3174]. She was born May 26, 1964, at Bethesda, Maryland.

(Sup) 5504 CHARLES WILLIAM DEMORY III (Charles[8], Charles[7], Henry[6], John[5], Rebecca[4], John Adam II[3], John Adam I[2], John Jacob[1]) was the son of Charles William and Judith Elaine Sebek Demory, Jr. [Supplement No. 3174]. He was born May 21, 1974, at Bethesda, Maryland.

(Sup) 5505 MICHAEL ALAN DEMORY (Charles[8], Charles[7], Henry[6], John[5], Rebecca[4], John Adam II[3], John Adam I[2], John Jacob[1]) was the son of Charles William and Judith Elaine Sebek Demory, Jr. [Supplement No. 3174]. He was born October 3, 1976, at Silver Spring, Maryland.

(Sup) 5506 EDDIE MICHAEL DEMORY (Larry[8], Charles[7], Henry[6], John[5], Rebecca[4], John Adam II[3], John Adam I[2], John Jacob[1]) was the son of Larry Sidney and Barbara Ann Moore Demory [Supplement No. 3175]. He was born November 24, 1966, at Bethesda, Maryland.

(Sup) 5507 AARON MATTHEW DEMORY (Larry[8], Charles[7], Henry[6], John[5], Rebecca[4], John Adam II[3], John Adam I[2], John Jacob[1]) was the son of Larry Sidney and Barbara Ann Moore Demory [Supplement No. 3175]. He was born October 18, 1968, at Bethesda, Maryland.

(Sup) 5508 NANCY CHRISTINE DEMORY (Larry[8], Charles[7], Henry[6], John[5], Rebecca[4], John Adam II[3], John ADam I[2], John Jacob[1]) was the daughter of Larry Sidney and Barbara Ann Moore Demory [Supplement No. 3175]. She was born March 24, 1975, at Bethesda, Maryland.

(Sup) 5509 EDWIN FRANKLIN DEMORY, JR. (Edwin[8], Charles[7], Henry[6], John[5], Rebecca[4], John Adam II[3], John Adam I[2], John Jacob[1]) was the son of Edwin Franklin and Sheila Jean Bentley Demory [Supplement No. 3176]. He was born November 22, 1977, at Silver Spring, Maryland.

(Sup) 5510 SHANNON MARIE DEMORY (Edwin[8], Charles[7], Henry[6], John[5], Rebecca[4], John Adam II[3], John Adam I[2], John Jacob[1]) was the daughter of Edwin Franklin and Sheila Jean Bentley Demory [Supplement No. 3176]. She was born March 11, 1980, at Silver Spring, Maryland.

(Sup) 5511 AMY MICHELE GRAHAM (Linda[8], Charles[7], Henry[6], John[5], Rebecca[4], John Adam II[3], John Adam I[2], John Jacob[1]) was the daughter of Gale Floyd and Linda Carol Demory Graham [Supplement No. 3176A]. She was born September 30, 1971, at Bethesda, Maryland.

(Sup) 5512 KELLY ELIZABETH GRAHAM (Linda[8], Charles[7], Henry[6], John[5], Rebecca[4], John Adam II[3], John Adam I[2], John Jacob[1]) was the daughter of Gale Floyd and Linda Carol Demory Graham [Supplement No. 3176A]. She was born June 15, 1974, at Bethesda, Maryland.

(Sup) 5513 JOY LYNN OSBOURN (Larry[8], Iris[7], Walter[6], John[5], Rebecca[4], John Adam II[3], John Adam I[2], John Jacob[1]) was the daughter of Larry William and Linda Lou Willingham Osbourn [Supplement No. 3185]. She was born May 28, 1969.

(Sup) 5514 JENNIFER JO OSBOURN (Larry[8], Iris[7], Walter[6], John[5], Rebecca[4], John Adam II[3], John Adam I[2], John Jacob[1]) was the daughter of Larry William and Linda Lou Willingham Osbourn [Supplement No. 3185]. Jennifer was born December 14, 1972.

(Sup) 5515 SCOTT ALLEN SARRA (Nancy[8], Iris[7], Walter[6], John[5], Rebecca[4], John Adam II[3], John Adam I[2], John Jacob[1]) was the son of Terry Allan and Nancy Osbourn Sarra [Supplement No. 3186]. Scott was born August 23, 1967.

(Sup) 5516 MATTHEW CRAIG SARRA (Nancy[8], Iris[7], Walter[6], John[5], Rebecca[4], John Adam II[3], John Adam I[2], John Jacob[1]) was the son of Terry Allan and Nancy Osbourn Sarra [Supplement No. 3186]. Matthew was born May 24, 1973.

(Sup) 5517 KELLY MARGARET NICHOLS (Pamela[8], Howard[7], Walter[6], John[5], Rebecca[4], John Adam II[3], John Adam I[2], John Jacob[1]) was the daughter of Luther James and Pamela Demory Nichols [Supplement No. 3187]. She was born June 27, 1974, at Martinsburg, West Virginia.

(Sup) 5518 MICHAEL BRIAN McGUINN (Sharon[8], Howard[7], Walter[6], John[5], Rebecca[4], John Adam II[3], John Adam I[2], John Jacob[1]) was the son of Michael Patrick and Sharon Dian Demory McGuinn [Supplement No. 3188]. Michael was born September 26, 1973, at Winchester, Virginia.

(Sup) 5519 TERESA DIAN McGUINN (Sharon[8], Howard[7], Walter[6], John[5], Rebecca[4], John Adam II[3], John Adam I[2], John Jacob[1]) was the daughter of Michael Patrick and Sharon Dian Demory McGuinn [Supplement No. 3188]. She was born November 17, 1975.

(Sup) 5520 NEIL PAUL BARTLES (Cheryl[8], Howard[7], Walter[6], John[5], Rebecca[4], John Adam II[3], John Adam I[2], John Jacob[1]) was the son of Richard Dale and Cheryl Lynn Demory Bartles [Supplement No. 3188A]. He was born November 21, 1973, at Winchester, Virginia.

(Sup) 5521 AMY BETH BARTLES (Cheryl[8], Howard[7], Walter[6], John[5], Rebecca[4], John Adam II[3], John Adam I[2], John Jacob[1]) was the daughter of Richard Dale and Cheryl Lynn Demory Bartles [Supplement No. 3188A]. She was born November 3, 1975, at Winchester, Virginia.

(Sup) 5522 WILLIAM LEE HALL (Rebecca[8], Naomi[7], Walter[6], John[5], Rebecca[4], John Adam II[3], John Adam I[2], John Jacob[1]) was the son of Norman Lee and Rebecca Jane Keesecker Hall [Supplement No. 3189]. William was born July 5, 1975.

(Sup) 5523 KATINA JO BUTTS (Mary[8], Naomi[7], Walter[6], John[5], Rebecca[4], John Adam II4y3, John Adam I[2], John Jacob[1]) was the daughter of Terry William and Louise Keesecker Butts, Jr. [Supplement No. 3190]. She was born November 19, 1972.

(Sup) 5524 SHAWN DALE DEMORY (Walter[8], Milton[7], Walter[6], John[5], Rebecca[4], John Adam II[3], John Adam I[2], John Jacob[1]) was the child of Walter Dale and Sue Grona Demory [Supplement No. 3190D]. Shawn was born September 6, 1973.

(Sup) 5525 CRYSTAL LARK PRATHER (James[8], Rebecca[7], Walter[6], John[5], Rebecca[4], John Adam II[3], John Adam I[2], John Jacob[1]) was the daughter of Arthur and Cynthia Rouark Prather [Supplement No. 3190I]. She was born May 11, 1977.

(Sup) 5526 JAMES DEWEY FRITTS, JR. (Deborah[8], Rebecca[7], Walter[6], John[5], Rebecca[4], John Adam II[3], John Adam I[2], John Jacob[1]) was the son of James and Deborah Prather Fritts [Supplement No. 3190J]. He was born September 22, 1975.

(Sup) 5527 BARBARA SWARTNOUT (Fannie[8], Fannie[7], Almacie[6], John[5], Rebecca[4], John Adam II[3], John Adam I[2], John Jacob[1]) was the daughter of Denton Kenyon and Fannie Schryver Swartnout [ILF No. 3191]. Barbara was born November 4, 1942.

(Sup) 5528 JOHN WHITNEY SCHRYVER (George[8], Fannie[7], Almacie[6], John[5], Rebecca[4], John Adam II[3], John Adam I[2], John Jacob[1]) was the son of George Whitney and Ruth Carl Schryver [ILF No. 3192]. John was born January 29, 1946.

(Sup) 5529 GEORGE HAPGOOD SCHRYVER (George[8], Fannie[7], Almacie[6], John[5], Rebecca[4], John Adam II[3], John Adam I[2], John Jacob[1]) was the son of George Whitney and Ruth Carl Schryver [ILF No. 3192]. George was born March 24, 1947.

(Sup) 5530 JUDITH ANNE ROBISHAW (Helen[8], Fannie[7], Almacie[6], John[5], Rebecca[4], John Adam II[3], John Adam I[2], John Jacob[1]) was the daughter of William Arthur and Helen Schryver Robishaw [ILF No. 3193]. Judith was born February 21, 1943.

(Sup) 5531 WILLIAM ARTHUR ROBISHAW, JR. (Helen[8], Fannie[7], Almacie[6], John[5], Rebecca[4], John Adam II[3], John Adam I[2], John Jacob[1]) was the son of William Arthur and Helen Schryver Robishaw [ILF No. 3193]. William, Jr., was born November 30, 1946.

(Sup) 5532 PAMELA COLLEEN WAYNE (Phyllis[8], Lilbern[7], Wilmer[6], John[5], Rebecca[4], John Adam II[3], John Adam I[2], John Jacob[1]) was the daughter of Albert and Phyllis Jane Demory Wayne [Supplement No. 3196]. Pamela was born on January 25, 1947, at Bethesda, Maryland. She married Roger James Bogley on September 3, 1966, at Gaithersburg, Maryland. He was the son of William and Margaret Bogley and was born October 16, 1943, at Olney, Maryland.

(Sup) 7341   i Ian Wayne Bogley, born September 30, 1971.
(Sup) 7342   ii Justin Thomas Bogley, born September 23, 1972.

(Sup) 5533 NANCY FAYE WAYNE (Phyllis[8], Lilbern[7], Wilmer[6], John[5], Rebecca[4], John Adam II[3], John Adam I[2], John Jacob[1]) was the daughter of Lloyd Albert and Phyllis Jane Demory Wayne [Supplement No. 3196]. Nancy was born April 11, 1955, at Olney, Maryland. She married Craig Franklin Matovich September 14, 1974, at Gaithersburg, Maryland. He was the son of Stephan and Thelma Lenore Matovich and was born March 22, 1955, at Cincinnati, Ohio.

- -

(Sup) 5540 ANN LINDLEY WYMAN (Ruth[8], Ann[7], Annie[6], Margaret[5], Rebecca[4], John Adam II[3], John Adam I[2], John Jacob[1]) was the daughter of Everett and Ruth Burges Wyman [ILF No. 3223]. Ann was born July 1, 1936.

(Sup) 5541 KAREN PAISLEY KEITH (Evelyn[8], Ann[7], Annie[6], Margaret[5], Rebecca[4], John Adam II[3], John Adam I[2], John Jacob[1]) was the daughter of Gilbert L. and Evelyn Burges Keith [ILF No. 3224]. Karen was born December 13, 1944.

(Sup) 5542 GILBERT L. KEITH, JR. (Evelyn[8], Ann[7], Annie[6], Margaret[5], Rebecca[4], John Adam II[3], John Adam I[2], John Jacob[1]) was the son of Gilbert L. and Evelyn Burges Keith [ILF No. 3224]. Gilbert, Jr., was born March 7, 1946.

(Sup) 5543 JAMES THOMAS MURRAY (Dorothy[8], Ann[7], Annie[6], Margaret[5], Rebecca[4], John Adam II[3], John Adam I[2], John Jacob[1]) was the son of Thomas and Dorothy Burges Murray [ILF No. 3225]. James was born November 19, 1944.

(Sup) 5544 GLORIA JUNE WILBUR (Ralph[8], Margaret[7], Annie[6], Margaret[5], Rebecca[4], John Adam II[3], John Adam I[2], John Jacob[1]) was the daughter of Ralph McCrady Wilbur [ILF No. 3226]. Gloria was born February 10, 1944.

(Sup) 5545 SHARON WILBUR (Ralph[8], Margaret[7], Annie[6], Margaret[5], Rebecca[4], John Adam II[3], John Adam I[2], John Jacob[1]) was the daughter of Ralph McCrady Wilbur [ILF No. 3226]. Sharon was born March 26, 1947.

(Sup) 5546 RHODERICK DAVIS WILBUR, JR. (Rhoderick[8], Margaret[7], Annie[6], Margaret[5], Rebecca[4], John Adam II[3], John Adam I[2], John Jacob[1]) was the son of Rhoderick David and Margaret Waldrop Wilbur [Supplement No. 3228]. Rhoderick, Jr., was born June 27, 1944.

(Sup) 5547 VIOLET VIRGINIA MORRIS (Ralph[8], Clara[7], Adam[6], Ruhama[5], John Adam II[3], John Adam I[2], John Jacob[1]) was the daughter of Ralph Douglas and Inez Myers Morris [Supplement No. 3231]. Violet was born May 14, 1916. She married Claude C. Harris July 8, 1940.

(Sup) 5548 CAROL WINSTON HOOVER (Fleda[8], Clara[7], Adam[6], Ruhama[5], John Adam II[3], John Adam I[2], John Jacob[1]) was the daughter of Harry and Fleda Gertrude (Morris) Hoover [Supplement No. 3232]. Carol was born March 21, 1916.

(Sup) 5549 BARBARA ELLEN CROSS (Audrey[8], William[7], Adam[6], Ruhama[5], John Adam II[3], John Adam I[2], John Jacob[1]) was the daughter of Vernon Francis and Audrey Ellen (Hendricks) Cross [Supplement No. 3238]. Barbara was born February 13, 1948, at Arlington, Virginia. She married Joseph Orlando Gionfriddo May 17, 1969. The son of Orlando and Esther Alloco Gionfriddo from Sicily, he was born May 17, 1969. Barabara worked as a dental assistant and a bank teller, and Joseph was assistant manager of a 7-11 store at Daytona Beach, Florida.

(Sup) 7343   i Matthew George Gionfriddo, born February 2, 1977.
(Sup) 7343A   ii Jennifer Ellen Gionfriddo, born February 23, 1979.
(Sup) 7343B   iii Lindsey Rae Gionfriddo, born August 4, 1981.

(Sup) 5550 JAY VERNON CROSS (Audrey[8], William[7], Adam[6], Ruhama[5], John Adam III[4], John Adam III[3], John Adam I[2], John Jacob[1]) was the son of Vernon Francis and Audrey Ellen (Hendricks) Cross [Supplement No. 3238]. Jay was born October 31, 1951, at Arlington, Virginia. He married Peggy Wentz, October 31, 1971. Jay was a deputy sherriff in Valasia County, Florida.

7344   i   Benjamin Jay Cross, born July 27, 1973.
7344A ii René Marie Cross, born December 3, 1978.
7344B iii Rachel Nicole Cross, born June 10, 1981.
7344C iv Jesse William Cross, born January 27, 1983.

(Sup) 5551 RALPH RICHARD CONARD (Ralph[8], Edith[7], Ambrose[6], Ruhama[5], John Adam III[4], John Adam III[3], John Adam I[2], John Jacob[1]) was the son of Ralph William and Elizabeth Hope (Richard) Conard [Supplement No. 3242]. Ralph, Jr., was born August 7, 1952, at Boston, Massachusetts. He graduated from Hartwick College, Oneonta, New York, in 1974 and did graduate work at Northwestern University, Evanston, Illinois, 1979-1981.

(Sup) 5552 JAN KENNETH HIETT (Reta[8], Edith[7], Ambrose[6], Ruhama[5], John Adam II III[4], John Adam III[3], John Adam I[2], John Jacob[1]) was the son of Kenneth Pershing and Reta Virginia (Conard) Hiett [Supplement No. 3245]. Jan was born February 29, 1952, at Hagerstown, Maryland. He graduated from Eastern Kentucky University, Lexington. Jan married Victoria McAllister September 5, 1975, at Hagerstown. The daughter of Lloyd B. and Mabel Stine McAllister, she was born December 1, 1953, at Hagerstown, Maryland.

(Sup) 7345   i   Jeremy Shawn Hiett, born October 7, 1977.
(Sup) 7346 ii Christina Leigh Hiett, born August 11, 1981.

(Sup) 5553 SUSAN JOY HIETT (Reta[8], Edith[7], Ambrose[6], Ruhama[5], John Adam III[4], John Adam III[3], John Adam I[2], John Jacob[1]) was the daughter of Kenneth Pershing and Reta Virginia (Conard) Hiett [Supplement No. 3245]. Susan was born December 27, 1956, at Hagerstown, Maryland. She graduated from Towson University, Towson, Maryland in June, 1978, and was employed at Baltimore, Maryland. Susan married Jules Marc Siskind, August 7, 1983.

(Sup) 7347   i   Zachary Alexander Siskind, born February 12, 1987.

(Sup) 5554 DAVID LINK MOLER (Kellar[8], Albert[7], Martha[6], Adam[5], John Adam III[4], John Adam III[3], John Adam I[2], John Jacob[1]) was the son of Kellar Link and Mary Sloan Moler [TLF No. 3248]. David was born July 5, 1942.

(Sup) 5555 NANCY JEAN MOLER (Kellar[8], Albert[7], Martha[6], Adam[5], John Adam III[4], John Adam III[3], John Adam I[2], John Jacob[1]) was the daughter of Kellar Link and Mary Sloan Moler [TLF No. 3248]. Nancy was born August 26, 1946.

(Sup) 5556 CLIFFORD GREGGS MOLER (Julia[8], Adam[7], Martha[6], Adam[5], John Adam III[4], John Adam III[3], John Adam I[2], John Jacob[1]) was the son of James Bernard and Julia Link Moler [TLF No. 3249]. Clifford was born May 4, 1924, and died February 1, 1926.

(Sup) 5557 JULIA LINK MOLER (Julia[8], Ada[7], Martha[6], Adam[5], John Adam III[4], John Adam III[3], John Adam I[2], John Jacob[1]) was the daughter of James Bernard and Julia Link Moler [TLF No. 3249]. She was born November 2, 1929.

(Sup) 5558 JOHN GILBERT STOREY (Frances[8], Ada[7], Martha[6], Adam[5], John Adam III[4], John Adam III[3], John Adam I[2], John Jacob[1]) was the son of Gilbert Leadington and Frances Moler Storey [TLF No. 3250]. John was born April 17, 1929.

(Sup) 5559 MARY ANN MOLER (Guy[8], Ada[7], Martha[6], Adam[5], John Adam III[4], John Adam III[3], John Adam I[2], John Jacob[1]) was the daughter of Guy Maxwell and Charlotte Hill Moler [TLF No. 3251]. Mary Ann was born November 22, 1932.

(Sup) 5560 JAMES DOUGLASS MOLER (Guy[8], Ada[7], Martha[6], Adam[5], John Adam III[4], John Adam III[3], John Adam I[2], John Jacob[1]) was the son of Guy Maxwell and Charlotte Hill Moler [TLF No. 3251]. James was born October 18, 1934.

(Sup) 5561 LUCILLE MOLER JONES (Anna[8], Ada[7], Martha[6], Adam[5], John Adam III[4], John Adam III[3], John Adam I[2], John Jacob[1]) was the daughter of Anna Moler Jones [TLF No. 3253]. Lucille was born April 2, 1929.

(Sup) 5562 PATSY LEE MOLER (Willard[8], Ada[7], Martha[6], Adam[5], John Adam III[4], John Adam III[3], John Adam I[2], John Jacob[1]) was the daughter of Willard Jacob and Ruth Phillips Moler [TLF No. 3254]. Patsy was born July 28, 1938.

(Sup) 5563 CATHERINE ELEANOR MOLER (Willard[8], Ada[7], Martha[6], Adam[5], John Adam III[4], John Adam I[2], John Jacob[1]) was the daughter of Willard Jacob and Ruth Phillips Moler [TLF No. 3254]. Catherine was born August 15, 1945.

(Sup) 5568   KAREN KAY MOORE (Joyce^8, Daniel^7, Nora^6, Daniel^5, John Adam III^4, John Adam II^3, John Adam I^2, John Jacob^1) was the daughter of Emmett and Joyce Jean (Nichols) Moore [Supplement No. 3260]. Karen was born February 14, 1956, at Hagerstown, Maryland. She married Roy Robert Mackert May 25, 1975, at Sterling, Virginia. They were divorced.

(Sup) 5569   SHEEREE SUE MOORE (Joyce^8, Daniel^7, Nora^6, Daniel^5, John Adam III^4, John Adam II^3, John Adam I^2, John Jacob^1) was the daughter of Emmett and Joyce Jean (Nichols) Moore [Supplement No. 3260]. Sheeree was born April 3, 1957, at Hagerstown, Maryland. She married Stanley Robert Henriksen September 20, 1980, at Sterling, Virginia. He was born December 23, 1953.

(Sup) 7352   i   Matthew Robert Henriksen, born Mat 8, 1984.

(Sup) 5570   DAVID DIRK MOORE (Joyce^8, Daniel^7, Nora^6, Daniel^5, John Adam III^4, John Adam II^3, John Adam I^2, John Jacob^1) was the son of Emmett and Joyce Jean (Nichols) Moore [Supplement No. 3260]. David was born November 29, 1959, at Hagerstown, Maryland. He married Pamela Lynn Abel, June 19, 1981, at Washington, D.C.

(Sup) 5571   BRET ALAN ABSHIRE (Clarissa^8, Daniel^7, Nora^6, Daniel^5, John Adam III^4, John Adam II^3, John Adam I^2, John Jacob^1) was the son of Robert and Clarissa Ellen (Nichols) Abshire [Supplement No. 3261]. He was born June 1, 1959.

(Sup) 5572   KYMBERLEE KAY ABSHIRE (Clarissa^8, Daniel^7, Nora^6, Daniel^5, John Adam III^4, John Adam II^3, John Adam I^2, John Jacob^1) was the daughter of Robert and Clarissa Ellen (Nichols) Abshire [Supplement No. 3261]. Kymberlee was born August 11, 1960. She married Gary Parella of Gloversville, New York. They resided at Hollywood, Florida.

(Sup) 5573   SHERYL LYNNE ABSHIRE (Clarissa^8, Daniel^7, Nora^6, Daniel^5, John Adam III^4, John Adam II^3, John Adam I^2, John Jacob^1) was the daughter of Robert and Clarissa Ellen (Nichols) Abshire [Supplement No. 3261]. Sheryl was born May 20, 1963.

(Sup) 5574   TONYA RENEE THATCHER (Clarissa^8, Daniel^7, Nora^6, Daniel^5, John Adam III^4, John Adam II^3, John Adam I^2, John Jacob^1) was the daughter of Robert and Clarissa Ellen (Nichols) (Abshire) Thatcher [Supplement No. 3261]. Tonya was born July 5, 1965. She married Samuel Shawyer of Hedgesville, West Virginia.

(Sup) 5564   CONSTANCE SOUTHERLAND LUCAS (Robert^8, Mary^7, William^6, Adam^5, John Adam III^4, John Adam II^3, John Adam I^2, John Jacob^1) was the daughter of Robert Armstead and Constance Sharp Lucas [ILF No. 3255]. She was born May 5, 1950, at Pittsburgh, Pennsylvania.

(Sup) 5564A   WILLIAM DAVID BINKLEY (Harriet^8, Edgar^7, Nora^6, Daniel^5, John Adam III^4, John Adam II^3, John Adam I^2, John Jacob^1) was the son of Ralph W. and Harriet Nichols Binkley [Supplement No. 3256]. William was born December 5, 1958.

(Sup) 5564B   JACOB HOLLAND BINKLEY (Harriet^8, Edgar^7, Nora^6, Daniel^5, John Adam III^4, John Adam II^3, John Adam I^2, John Jacob^1) was the son of Ralph W. and Harriet Nichols Binkley [Supplement No. 3256]. Jacob was born December 8, 1961.

(Sup) 5565   SAUNDRA ANN NICHOLS (Daniel^8, Daniel^7, Nora^6, Daniel^5, John Adam III^4, John Adam II^3, John Adam I^2, John Jacob^1) was the daughter of Daniel Russell and Peggy Dorsey Nichols, Jr. [Supplement No. 3259]. Saundra Ann was born June 26, 1951, at Charles Town, West Virginia. She married, first, Larry Boyd of Jefferson County, West Virginia, August 18, 1968. Saundra and Larry were divorced. She married, second, David Ash of Charleston, West Virginia.

(Sup) 7349   i   Lisa Leigh Boyd, born October 24, 1968.

(Sup) 5566   DEBORAH DIANNE NICHOLS (Daniel^8, Daniel^7, Nora^6, Daniel^5, John Adam III^4, John Adam II^3, John Adam I^2, John Jacob^1) was the daughter of Daniel Russell and Peggy Dorsey Nichols, Jr. [Supplement No. 3259]. Deborah was born March 28, 1953, at Charles Town, West Virginia. She married Gary Wayne Thomas of Kearneysville, West Virginia, September 25, 1971.

(Sup) 7350   i   Michelle Thomas, born May 1972.
(Sup) 7351   ii   Clint Daniel Thomas, born August 26, 1974.

(Sup) 5567   DANIEL RUSSELL NICHOLS, III (Daniel^8, Daniel^7, Nora^6, Daniel^5, John Adam III^4, John Adam II^3, John Adam I^2, John Jacob^1) was the son of Daniel Russell and Peggy Dorsey Nichols, Jr. [Supplement No. 3259]. Daniel, III, was born December 29, 1961, at Hagerstown, Maryland.

(Sup) 5575 KYE NICOLE THATCHER (Clarissa^8, Daniel^7, Nora^6, Daniel^5, John Adam III^4, John Adam I^2, John Jacob^1) was the daughter of Larry and Clarissa Ellen (Nichols) (Abshire) Thatcher Thatcher [Supplement No. 3261]. She was born October 30, 1969.

(Sup) 5576 KELLY MARIE THATCHER (Clarissa^8, Daniel^7, Nora^6, Daniel^5, John Adam III^4, John Adam I^2, John Jacob^1) was the daughter of Larry and Clarissa Ellen (Nichols) (Abshire) Thatcher [Supplement No. 3261]. She was born and died September 16, 1970.

(Sup) 5577 BEVERLY DIANE LINK (Sarah^8, William^7, Adam^6, Daniel^5, John Adam III^4, John Adam I^2, John Jacob^1) was the daughter of Sarah Elizabeth Link [Supplement No. 3263]. Beverly was born February 21, 1964, at Martinsburg, West Virginia.

(Sup) 5578 KELLY RENEE LINK (Sarah^8, William^7, Adam^6, Daniel^5, John Adam III^4, John Adam I^2, John Jacob^1) was the daughter of Sarah Elizabeth Link [Supplement No. 3263]. Kelly was born December 21, 1965, at Martinsburg, West Virginia.

(Sup) 5579 DAVID CRUZEN LINK (Daniel^8, Daniel^7, Adam^6, Daniel^5, John Adam III^4, John Adam I^2, John Jacob^1) was the son of Daniel Cruzen and Elizabeth June (Hartsaw) Link [Supplement No. 3264]. David was born September 11, 1968, at Charlottesville, Virginia.

(Sup) 5580 KEVIN ANDREW LINK (Daniel^8, Daniel^7, Adam^6, Daniel^5, John Adam III^4, John Adam I^2, John Jacob^1) was the son of Daniel Cruzen and Elizabeth June (Hartsaw) Link [Supplement No. 3264]. Kevin was born June 13, 1970, at Richmond, Virginia.

(Sup) 5581 KRISTIN ELIZABETH LINK (Daniel^8, Daniel^7, Adam^6, Daniel^5, John Adam III^4, John Adam I^2, John Jacob^1) was the daughter of Daniel Cruzen and Elizabeth June (Hartsaw) Link [Supplement No. 3264]. She was born November 20, 1977, at Fairfax, Virginia.

(Sup) 5582 DAVID ALLEN LINK, JR. (David^8, Boteler^7, John^6, Daniel^5, John Adam III^4, John Adam I^2, John Jacob^1) was the son of David Allen and Joyce Juanita (Athey) Link [Supplement No. 3266]. David, Jr., was born January 20, 1953, at Charles Town, West Virginia.

(Sup) 5583 IRVIN MOORE LINK (David^8, Boteler^7, John^6, Daniel^5, John Adam III^4, John Adam I^2, John Jacob^1) was the son of David Allen and Joyce Juanita (Athey) Link [Supplement No. 3266]. Irvin was born October 31, 1954, at Charles Town, West Virginia.

(Sup) 5584 HOWARD SNYDER LINK, JR. (Howard^8, Boteler^7, John^6, Daniel^5, John Adam III^4, John Adam I^2, John Jacob^1) was the son of Howard Snyder and Mary Ann (Frye) Link [Supplement No. 3267]. Howard, Jr., was born March 20, 1959, in Jefferson County, West Virginia. He married Pamela Joy Mazotas. She was born August 8, 1966, at Trenton, New Jersey. Howard was a heavy equipment construction operator, and Pamela was a beautician.

(Sup) 5585 RHONDA GAIL LINK (Howard^8, Boteler^7, John^6, Daniel^5, John Adam III^4, John Adam I^2, John Jacob^1) was the daughter of Howard Snyder and Mary Ann (Frye) Link [Supplement No. 3267]. Rhonda was born November 8, 1961, at Martinsburg, West Virginia. She married, first, Kevin Day Banks June 23, 1979, at Uvilla, in Jefferson County, West Virginia. He was the son of Gordon W. and Clara V. Day Banks and was born January 24, 1959, at Martinsburg, Berkeley County, West Virginia. Rhonda and Kevin were divorced. She married, second, Paul Martin Miller, II, August 29, 1987, at Shepherdstown, West Virginia. He was the son of Paul Martin and Eileen (Small) Miller. Paul was a dairy farmer in Jefferson County.

(Sup) 5586 KEVIN SCOTT LINK (Howard^8, Boteler^7, John^6, Daniel^5, John Adam III^4, John Adam I^2, John Jacob^1) was the son of Howard Snyder and Mary Ann (Frye) Link [Supplement No. 3267]. He was born November 7, 1971, at Martinsburg, West Virginia.

(Sup) 5587 BRIAN MATTHEW LINK (Howard^8, Boteler^7, John^6, Daniel^5, John Adam III^4, John Adam I^2, John Jacob^1) was the son of Howard Snyder and Mary Ann (Frye) Link [Supplement No. 3267]. He was born December 7, 1977, at Martinsburg, West Virginia.

(Sup) 5588 DAWN LYNN LINK (Boteler^8, Boteler^7, John^6, Daniel^5, John Adam III^4, John Adam III^3, John Adam I^2, John Jacob^1) was the son of Boteler Moore and Geraldine Ann Fritts Link, Jr. [Supplement No. 3268]. She was born January 8, 1968, at Martinsburg, West Virginia.

(Sup) 5589 BOTELER MOORE LINK, III (Boteler^8, Boteler^7, John^6, Daniel^5, John Adam III^4, John Adam III^3, John Adam I^2, John Jacob^1) was the son of Boteler Moore and Geraldine Ann Fritts Link, Jr. [Supplement No. 3268]. He was born July 24, 1970, at Martinsburg, West Virginia.

(Sup) 5590 AMANDA LEE LINK (Boteler^8, Boteler^7, John^6, Daniel^5, John Adam III^4, John Adam III^3, John Adam I^2, John Jacob^1) was the daughter of Boteler Moore and Geraldine Ann Fritts Link, Jr. [Supplement No. 3268]. Amanda was born October 19, 1971, at Martinsburg, West Virginia.

(Sup) 5591 KENNETH JASON LINK (Boteler^8, Boteler^7, John^6, Daniel^5, John Adam III^4, John Adam III^3, John Adam I^2, John Jacob^1) was the son of Boteler Moore and Geraldine Ann Fritts Link, Jr. [Supplement No. 3268]. Kenneth was born September 8, 1976, at Martinsburg, West Virginia.

(Sup) 5592 JOHN PAUL LALLY, III (John Paul^8, Florence^7, John^6, Daniel^5, John Adam III^4, John Adam III^3, John Adam I^2, John Jacob^1) was the son of John Paul and Francine Worrellia Lally [Supplement No. 3270A]. He was born May 20, 1980, at Youngstown, Ohio.

(Sup) 5593 HEATHER ELIZABETH LINK (Vaughen^8, Vaughen^7, Elbert^6, Daniel^5, John Adam III^4, John Adam III^3, John Adam I^2, John Jacob^1) was the daughter of Vaughen Harwood and Sandrya Ann Schaeffer Link, Jr. [Supplement No. 3271]. She was born October 19, 1973, at Arlington Heights, Illinois.

(Sup) 5593A EVELYN DECK (Frederick^8, Frederick^7, Annie^6, Sarah^5, John Adam III^4, John Adam III^3, John Adam I^2, John Jacob^1) was the daughter of Frederick Webster and Katherine Grieve Deck, Jr. [Supplement No. 3278]. Evelyn was born December 21, 1952.

(Sup) 5593B ALISON DECK (Frederick^8, Frederick^7, Annie^6, Sarah^5, John Adam III^4, John Adam III^3, John Adam I^2, John Jacob^1) was the daughter of Frederick Webster and Katherine Grieve Deck, Jr. [Supplement No. 3278]. Alison was born August 28, 1955.

(Sup) 5593C FREDERICK WEBSTER DECK, III (Frederick^8, Frederick^7, Annie^6, Sarah^5, John Adam III^4, John Adam III^3, John Adam I^2, John Jacob^1) was the son of Frederick Webster and Katherine Grieve Deck, Jr. [Supplement No. 3278]. Frederick, III, was born September 20, 1963.

(Sup) 5593D LINDA ANNE DECK (William^8, Frederick^7, Annie^6, Sarah^5, John Adam III^4, John Adam III^3, John Adam I^2, John Jacob^1) was the daughter of William Meade and Elizabeth Freiburg Deck [Supplement No. 3279]. Linda was born May 5, 1957. She received a B.A. degree in communications from Virginia Polytechnic Institute June 9, 1979, and married Donald J. Woodbridge that same date. They resided at Williamsburg, Virginia, where Linda managed the sweater outlet at the Williamsburg Pottery.

(Sup) 5593E WILLIAM MEADE DECK, JR. (William^8, Frederick^7, Annie^6, Sarah^5, John Adam III^4, John Adam III^3, John Adam I^2, John Jacob^1) was the son of William Meade and Elizabeth Freiburg Deck [Supplement No. 3279]. William, Jr., was born August 27, 1959. He received a B.S. degree in industrial engineering from Virginia Polytechnic Institute with honors June, 1981. He was employed by Cost Engineering Banking Machines, IBM, Charlotte, North Carolina.

(Sup) 5593F SUSAN ELIZABETH DECK (William^8, Frederick^7, Annie^6, Sarah^5, John Adam III^4, John Adam III^3, John Adam I^2, John Jacob^1) was the daughter of William Meade and Elizabeth Freiburg Deck [Supplement No. 3279]. Susan was born December 30, 1961. She graduated from James Madison University with a teaching degree in music.

(Sup) 5594 WILLIAM HODGES HENDRICKS (William^8, Garland^7, Harvey^6, Sarah^5, John Adam III^4, John Adam III^3, John Adam I^2, John Jacob^1) was the son of William Hampton and _____ Hodges Hendricks [Supplement No. 3281].

(Sup) 5594A JANIS HUBER (Patricia^8, Margery^7, Harvey^6, Sarah^5, John Adam III^4, John Adam III^3, John Adam I^2, John Jacob^1) was the daughter of Charles and Patricia Ann Ryder Huber [Supplement No. 3283]. Janis was born June 4, 1950. She married Paul Ackerman. She was employed by the U.S. Government.

(Sup) 7370 1 Matthew Paul Ackerman, born May 30, 1981.

(Sup) 5594B DAVID CHARLES HUBER (Patricia^8, Margery^7, Harvey^6, Sarah^5, John Adam III^4, John Adam III^3, John Adam I^2, John Jacob^1) was the son of Charles and Patricia Ann Ryder Huber [Supplement No. 3283]. David was born April 3, 1961. He graduated from Lincoln Tech and worked for the U.S. Government.

(Sup) 5600B SANDRA LEE TABER (Janice^8, Kenneth^7, Esther^6, Sarah^5, John Adam III^4, John Adam III^3, John Adam I^2, John Jacob^1) was the daughter of Edward Russell and Janice Engle Taber [Supplement No. 3287]. Sandra was born March 26, 1955, at Akron, Ohio. She married Gregory John Felber June 4, 1983. He was born June 4, 1955, at Akron.

(Sup) 5600C DAVID KENNETH HERCHENROEDER (Ann^8, Kenneth^7, Esther^6, Sarah^5, John Adam III^4, John Adam III^3, John Adam I^2, John Jacob^1) was the son of Kenneth Frederick and Ann Engle Herchenroeder [Supplement No. 3288]. David was born June 8, 1953. He married Georganna Rogers.

(Sup) 7375   i   Laurie Lyn Herchenroeder, born March 22, 1977.
(Sup) 7376   ii   Lisa Marie Herchenroeder, born August 8, 1979.
(Sup) 7377 iii   Douglas David Herchenroeder, born July 16, 1983.

(Sup) 5600D MICHAEL LEE HERCHENROEDER (Ann^8, Kenneth^7, Esther^6, Sarah^5, John Adam III^4, John Adam III^3, John Adam I^2, John Jacob^1) was the son of Kenneth Frederick and Ann Engle Herchenroeder [Supplement No. 3288]. Michael was born December 29, 1954. He married Rita Joseph.

(Sup) 7378   i   Ann Marie Herchenroeder, born January 1, 1979.

(Sup) 5600E TIMOTHY ALAN HERCHENROEDER (Ann^8, Kenneth^7, Esther^6, Sarah^5, John Adam III^4, John Adam III^3, John Adam I^2, John Jacob^1) was the son of Kenneth Frederick and Ann Engle Herchenroeder [Supplement No. 3288]. Timothy was born November 9, 1959.

(Sup) 5600F JEFFERY LYNN HERCHENROEDER (Ann^8, Kenneth^7, Esther^6, Sarah^5, John Adam III^4, John Adam III^3, John Adam I^2, John Jacob^1) was the son of Kenneth Frederick and Ann Engle Herchenroeder [Supplement No. 3288]. Jeffery was born January 9, 1959.

(Sup) 5600G JAMES STEPHEN HERCHENROEDER (Ann^8, Kenneth^7, Esther^6, Sarah^5, John Adam III^4, John Adam III^3, John Adam I^2, John Jacob^1) was the son of Kenneth Frederick and Ann Engle Herchenroeder [Supplement No. 3288]. James was born September 21, 1961. He married Rita Osterfeld.

(Sup) 7379   i   Daniel James Herchenroeder, born May 5, 1981.
(Sup) 7380   ii   William Stephen Herchenroeder, born July 20, 1984.

(Sup) 5600H SCOTT ALLEN HERCHENROEDER (Ann^8, Kenneth^7, Esther^6, Sarah^5, John Adam III^4, John Adam III^3, John Adam I^2, John Jacob^1) was the son of Kenneth Frederick and Ann Engle Herchenroeder [Supplement No. 3288]. Scott was born August 15, 1965.

(Sup) 5595 JOHN WILLIAM HENDRICKS, III (John^8, John^7, Harvey^6, Sarah^5, John Adam III^4, John Adam III^3, John Adam I^2, John Jacob^1) was the son of John William and Carole Buhrman Hendricks, Jr. [Supplement No. 3284]. John William, Jr., was born November 3, 1960. He graduated from West Virginia University, where he was drum major of the marching band and majored in music.

(Sup) 5596 MICHAEL ALAN HENDRICKS (John^8, John^7, Harvey^6, Sarah^5, John Adam III^4, John Adam III^3, John Adam I^2, John Jacob^1) was the son of John William and Carole Buhrman Hendricks, Jr. [Supplement No. 3284]. Michael was born October 28, 1965.

(Sup) 5596A ELIZABETH KAYE HENDRICKS (John^8, John^7, Harvey^6, Sarah^5, John Adam III^4, John Adam III^3, John Adam I^2, John Jacob^1) was the daughter of John William and Carole Buhrman Hendricks, Jr. [Supplement No. 3284]. Elizabeth was born November 13, 1979.

(Sup) 5597 MARK EDWARD DENTON (Ruth^8, John^7, Harvey^6, Sarah^5, John Adam III^4, John Adam III^3, John Adam I^2, John Jacob^1) was the son of Charles Winfield and Ruth Marie Hendricks Denton [Supplement No. 3285]. Mark was born September 30, 1973.

(Sup) 5598 JULIE ANNE DENTON (Ruth^8, John^7, Harvey^6, Sarah^5, John Adam III^4, John Adam III^3, John Adam I^2, John Jacob^1) was the daughter of Charles Winfield and Ruth Marie Hendricks Denton [Supplement No. 3285]. Julie was born May 30, 1975.

(Sup) 5599 CAROLINE RANDOLPH NOYES (Margaret^8, Allen^7, James^6, Sarah^5, John Adam III^4, John Adam III^3, John Adam I^2, John Jacob^1) was the daughter of Paul Randolph and Margaret Louise Hendricks Noyes [Supplement No. 3286]. Caroline was born May 17, 1964, at Philadelphia, Pennsylvania. She attended Randolph Macon College, Lynchburg, Virginia.

(Sup) 5600 MARTHA HENDRICKS NOYES (Margaret^8, Allen^7, James^6, Sarah^5, John Adam III^4, John Adam III^3, John Adam I^2, John Jacob^1) was the daughter of Paul Randolph and Margaret Louise Hendricks Noyes [Supplement No. 3286]. Martha was born May 20, 1968, at Philadelphia, Pennsylvania. She attended Friends Select School at Philadelphia.

(Sup) 5600A DEBORAH LYNN TABER (Janice^8, Kenneth^7, Esther^6, Sarah^5, John Adam III^4, John Adam III^3, John Adam I^2, John Jacob^1) was the daughter of Edward Russell and Janice Engle Taber [Supplement No. 3287]. Deborah was born September 20, 1952, at Akron, Ohio.

(Sup) 5600J   SCOTT RICHARD LIGHTNER (Barbara^8, Daniel^7, Esther^6, Sarah^5, John Adam III^4, John Adam III^3, John Adam I^2, John Jacob^1) was the son of Gene and Barbara Jean Engle Lightner [Supplement No. 3289]. Scott was born July 29, 1961. He was employed as an electronics engineer by a company at Winslow, Illinois. Scott married Marrianne Ter Loww October 1, 1983. After graduating from the University of Wisconsin she continued the study of law.

(Sup) 5600K   LORI ANNE ENGLE (Murray^8, James^7, Esther^6, Sarah^5, John Adam III^4, John Adam III^3, John Adam I^2, John Jacob^1) was the daughter of Preston Murray and Diane Olsen Engle [Supplement No. 3290]. She was born December 2, 1967.

(Sup) 5600L   DEBRA JEAN ENGLE (Murray^8, James^7, Esther^6, Sarah^5, John Adam III^4, John Adam III^3, John Adam I^2, John Jacob^1) was the daughter of Preston Murray and Diane Olsen Engle [Supplement No. 3290]. She was born July 3, 1969.

(Sup) 5600M   HEATHER DIANE ENGLE (Murray^8, James^7, Esther^6, Sarah^5, John Adam III^4, John Adam III^3, John Adam I^2, John Jacob^1) was the daughter of Preston Murray and Diane Olsen Engle [Supplement No. 3290]. She was born September 4, 1974.

(Sup) 5600N   BARBARA ANNE BALLARD (Jean^8, James^7, Esther^6, Sarah^5, John Adam III^4, John Adam III^3, John Adam I^2, John Jacob^1) was the daughter of James R. and Jean Catherine Engle Ballard [Supplement No. 3291]. Barbara was born May 5, 1969, at Fort Worth, Texas.

(Sup) 5600P   ELIZABETH JANE BALLARD (Jean^8, James^7, Esther^6, Sarah^5, John Adam III^4, John Adam III^3, John Adam I^2, John Jacob^1) was the daughter of James R. and Jean Catherine Engle Ballard [Supplement No. 3291]. Elizabeth was born June 16, 1971, at Tulsa, Oklahoma.

(Sup) 5601   DOUGLAS WOODY STEVENS, JR. (Rebecca^8, Rebecca^7, LeRoy^6, Sarah^5, John Adam III^4, John Adam III^3, John Adam I^2, John Jacob^1) was the son of Douglas Woody and Rebecca Moler Stevens [Supplement No. 3293]. Douglas, Jr., was born December 16, 1947. He received a B.S. degree from the University of Maryland and a master's degree in theology from Loiusville Seminary. He was a Presbyterian minister at Philadelphia, Pennsylvania. Douglas married Penelope Ann Secord of Hyattsville, Maryland. She received a B.S. degree in education from the University of Maryland.

(Sup) 7381   1 Kymberly Lynn Stevens, born July 10, 1982.

(Sup) 5601A   DEBRA LEE STEVENS (Rebecca^8, Rebecca^7, LeRoy^6, Sarah^5, John Adam III^4, John Adam III^3, John Adam I^2, John Jacob^1) was the daughter of Douglas Woody and Rebecca Moler Stevens [Supplement No. 3293]. Debra was born October 5, 1956, at Washington, D.C. She received a B.S. degree from the University of Maryland. Debra married Charles Alexander Measday. He was born July 31, 1955, at College Park, Maryland. Charles received a B.S. degree in computer science from the University of Maryland and was employed by General Electric.

(Sup) 5602   GILBERT LEO HENDRICKS, III (Gilbert^8, Gilbert^7, Daniel^6, Sarah^5, John Adam III^4, John Adam III^3, John Adam I^2, John Jacob^1) was the son of Gilbert Leo and Ina Mae Williamson Hendricks, Jr. [Supplement No. 3295]. Gilbert, III, was born June 23, 1959, at Richmond, Virginia.

(Sup) 5603   JAMES PERRY HENDRICKS (Gilbert^8, Gilbert^7, Daniel^6, Sarah^5, John Adam III^4, John Adam III^3, John Adam I^2, John Jacob^1) was the son of Gilbert Leo and Ina Mae Williamson Hendricks, Jr. [Supplement No. 3295]. James was born February 27, 1961, at Richmond Virginia.

(Sup) 5604   LESLIE ANN HENDRICKS (Gilbert^8, Gilbert^7, Daniel^6, Sarah^5, John Adam III^4, John Adam III^3, John Adam I^2, John Jacob^1) was the daughter of Gilbert Leo and Ina Mae Williamson Hendricks, Jr. [Supplement No. 3295]. Leslie was born September 5, 1963 at Los Angeles, California.

(Sup) 5605   SUSAN RAMONA HENDRICKS (Daniel^8, Gilbert^7, Daniel^6, Sarah^5, John Adam III^4, John Adam III^3, John Adam I^2, John Jacob^1) was the daughter of Daniel Ewell and Barbara Lightner Hendricks [Supplement No. 3296]. She was born November 17, 1958, in Augusta County, Virginia.

(Sup) 5606   DANIEL EWELL HENDRICKS, JR. (Daniel^8, Gilbert^7, Daniel^6, Sarah^5, John Adam III^4, John Adam III^3, John Adam I^2, John Jacob^1) was the son of Daniel Ewell and Barbara Painter Hendricks [Supplement No. 3296]. Daniel was born February 14, 1977, at Martinsburg, West Virginia.

(Sup) 5607   ELIZABETH ANN HENDRICKS (Daniel^8, Gilbert^7, Daniel^6, Sarah^5, John Adam III^4, John Adam III^3, John Adam I^2, John Jacob^1) was the daughter of Daniel Ewell and Barbara Painter Hendricks [Supplement No. 3296]. Elizabeth was born August 14, 1979, at Martinsburg, West Virginia.

(Sup) 5607A JAMES BRIAN HENDRICKS (Daniel[8], Gilbert[7], Daniel[6], Sarah[5], John Adam III[4], John Adam II[3], John Adam I[2], John Jacob[1]) was the son of Daniel Ewell and Barbara Painter Hendricks [Supplement No. 3296]. James was born and died June 21, 1981, at Martinsburg, West Virginia. He is buried in Elmwood Cemetery at Shepherdstown, West Virginia.

(Sup) 5607B MARY ELLEN HENDRICKS (Daniel[8], Gilbert[7], Daniel[6], Sarah[5], John Adam III[4], John Adam II[3], John Adam I[2], John Jacob[1]) was the daughter of Daniel Ewell and Barbara Painter Hendricks [Supplement No. 3296]. She was born and died June 17, 1982, at Martinsburg, West Virginia. She is buried in Elmwood Cemetery at Shepherdstown, West Virginia.

(Sup) 5608 PAMELA LYNN ANDERSON (Sarah[8], Gilbert[7], Daniel[6], Sarah[5], John Adam III[4], John Adam II[3], John Adam I[2], John Jacob[1]) was the daughter of Thomas Franklin and Sarah Virginia Hendricks Anderson, Jr. [Supplement No. 3297]. She was born December 16, 1963, at Richmond, Virginia.

(Sup) 5609 KIMBERLY KARYL ANDERSON (Sarah[8], Gilbert[7], Daniel[6], Sarah[5], John Adam III[4], John Adam II[3], John Adam I[2], John Jacob[1]) was the daughter of Thomas Franklin and Sarah Virginia Hendricks Anderson, Jr. [Supplement No. 3297]. She was born June 16, 1965, at Richmond, Virginia.

(Sup) 5610 SARAH ANN ANDERSON (Sarah[8], Gilbert[7], Daniel[6], Sarah[5], John Adam III[4], John Adam II[3], John Adam I[2], John Jacob[1]) was the daughter of Thomas Franklin and Sarah Virginia Hendricks Anderson, Jr. [Supplement No. 3297]. Sarah was born March 10, 1969, at Richmond, Virginia.

(Sup) 5611 LAURA LEE ANDERSON (Sarah[8], Gilbert[7], Daniel[6], Sarah[5], John Adam III[4], John Adam II[3], John Adam I[2], John Jacob[1]) was the daughter of Thomas Franklin and Sarah Virginia Hendricks Anderson, Jr. [Supplement No. 3297]. Laura was born May 1, 1970, at Richmond, Virginia.

(Sup) 5612 MARY ELIZABETH ANDERSON. (Sarah[8], Gilbert[7], Daniel[6], Sarah[5], John Adam III[4], John Adam II[3], John Adam I[2], John Jacob[1]) was the daughter of Thomas Franklin and Sarah Virginia Hendricks Anderson, Jr. [Supplement No. 3297]. Mary was born December 16, 1972, at Richmond, Virginia.

(Sup) 5613 VANDA KAY REYNOLDS (Pearl[8], Mary[7], Daniel[6], Sarah[5], John Adam III[4], John Adam II[3], John Adam I[2], John Jacob[1]) was the daughter of Thomas Guy and Pearl Ennis Reynolds [Supplement No. 3298]. Vanda Kay was born October 29, 1951 at Martinsburg, West Virginia. She married Grady Spruce White December 29, 1973, at Martinsburg, West Virginia. He was born February 22, 1950, at Waco, Texas, the son of Warren Travis and Genevieve Greer White. Vanda received a B.A. degree in mathematics from the College of William and Mary, where she was a member of Kappa Delta social sorority and Phi Beta Kappa. Grady received his B.S. degree from the College of William and Mary and his M.S. and Ph.D. from the University of North Carolina at Chapel Hill, where he was a member of the Sigma Xi scientific honor society. He was employed by the National Bureau of Standards.

(Sup) 5614 ANN MEREDITH REYNOLDS (Pearl[8], Mary[7], Daniel[6], Sarah[5], John Adam III[4], John Adam II[3], John Adam I[2], John Jacob[1]) was the daughter of Thomas Guy and Pearl Hendricks Ennis Reynolds [Supplement No. 3298]. Ann was born December 15, 1958, at Martinsburg, West Virginia. She graduated with honors from West Virginia University, Morgantown, West Virginia, where she was a member of Sigma Delta Chi and received a B.S. degree in communications. She received the West Virginia Broadcasters award in 1979. Ann moved to Buffalo, New York, where she worked for radio and television stations.

(Sup) 5615 ROBERT MEREDITH ENNIS (Alvin[8], Mary[7], Daniel[6], Sarah[5], John Adam III[4], John Adam II[3], John Adam I[2], John Jacob[1]) was the son of Alvin Meredith and Betty Cooper Ennis, Jr. [Supplement No. 3299]. Robert was born October 24, 1957, at Charles Town, West Virginia. He married Tina Rene Smallwood August 17, 1981, at Winchester, Virginia. She was the daughter of Lloyd and Gail Petrucci Smallwood and was born June 20, 1963, in Jefferson County, West Virginia. Robert was employed as an electrician at Ranson, West Virginia, and Tina was employed at Shepherd College in Shepherdstown.

(Sup) 7391 i Meredith Nicole Ennis, born November 20, 1983.

(Sup) 5616 DANIEL EDWARD McAMIS (Edward[8], Anna[7], Daniel[6], Sarah[5], John Adam III[4], John Adam II[3], John Adam I[2], John Jacob[1]) was the son of Edward Crawford and Eleanor Bickford McAmis, Jr. [Supplement No. 3300]. Daniel was born December 30, 1952, at Takoma Park, Maryland.

(Sup) 5617 DIANA LYNN McAMIS (Edward[8], Anna[7], Daniel[6], Sarah[5], John Adam III[4], John Adam II[3], John Adam I[2], John Jacob[1]) was the daughter of Edward Crawford and Eleanor Bickford McAmis, Jr. [Supplement No. 3300]. Diana was born January 30, 1954, at Takoma Park, Maryland. She married Richard Allen Pond December 1, 1976, at Arlington, Virginia. He was born March 7, 1940, at Schoolcraft, Michigan.

(Sup) 7391A i Rebecca McAmis Pond, born March 18, 1979.

(Sup) 5618 KIMBERLY MAYE EDWARDS (James[8], Anna[7], Daniel[6], Sarah[5], John Adam III[4], John Adam II[3], John Adam I[2], John Jacob[1]) was the daughter of James Edgar and Phyllis David Edwards, Jr. [Supplement No. 3301]. Kimberly was born December 2, 1966, at Washington, D.C.

(Sup) 5619 CYNTHIA DIANE CRANE (Bruce[8], Esther[7], Daniel[6], Sarah[5], John Adam III[4], John Adam II[3], John Adam I[2], John Jacob[1]) was the daughter of Bruce Melvin and Emma Weise Crane [Supplement No. 3302]. Cynthia was born January 2, 1957, at Martinsburg, West Virginia. She married John Mark Wallmeyer December, 1978. He was the son of Ignatius Herman and Virginia M. Dart Wallmeyer.

(Sup) 7392   i Christine Marie Wallmeyer, born May 21, 1979.

(Sup) 5620 GLEN ELMO CRANE (Bruce[8], Esther[7], Daniel[6], Sarah[5], John Adam III[4], John Adam II[3], John Adam I[2], John Jacob[1]) was the son of Bruce Melvin and Emma Weise Crane [Supplement No. 3302]. Glen was born August 13, 1960, at Manassa, Virginia. He married Tamela Kaye Wright August, 1978. She was the daughter of Dalton L. and Patsy F. Nealy Wright.

(Sup) 7393   i Stephanie Lynn Crane, born June 16, 1979.

(Sup) 5621 MARGARET ANN HOOVER (Reva[8], Esther[7], Daniel[6], Sarah[5], John Adam III[4], John Adam II[3], John Adam I[2], John Jacob[1]) was the daughter of Franklin James and Reva Jean Crane Hoover [Supplement No. 3303]. Margaret was born May 8, 1948, at Hagerstown, Maryland. She married, first, William E. Henry, Jr. He was the son of William E. Henry. Margaret and William were divorced January, 1970. She married, second, Philip J. Bray April 26, 1975. He was the son of Henry G. Small and Mary Miller Bray and was born February 24, 1943.

(Sup) 7394   i Douglas Truen Henry, born October 27, 1966.

(Sup) 5622 SANDRA CHRISTINE HOOVER (Reva[8], Esther[7], Daniel[6], Sarah[5], John Adam III[4], John Adam II[3], John Adam I[2], John Jacob[1]) was the daughter of Franklin James and Reva Jean Crane Hoover [Supplement No. 3303]. Sandra was born May 17, 1949, at Hagerstown, Maryland.

(Sup) 5623 PATRICK LOWELL BREWER (Hilda[8], Esther[7], Daniel[6], Sarah[5], John Adam III[4], John Adam II[3], John Adam I[2], John Jacob[1]) was the son of Frank Lowell and Hilda Joyce Crane Brewer [Supplement No. 3304]. Patrick was born August 26, 1950, at Hagerstown, Maryland. He married Elizabeth Catherine Haney of Pittsburgh, Pennsylvania. She was the daughter of Philip Clement and Elizabeth Lant Haney.

(Sup) 7395   i Christopher Lowell Brewer, born June 29, 1973.

(Sup) 5624 MICHAEL GLEN BREWER (Hilda[8], Esther[7], Daniel[6], Sarah[5], John Adam III[4], John Adam II[3], John Adam I[2], John Jacob[1]) was the son of Frank Lowell and Hilda Joyce Crane Brewer [Supplement No. 3304]. Michael was born June 22, 1954, at Hagerstown, Maryland. He married Mary Hoeschen September 29, 1979. She was born October 20, 1955, the daughter of Jerome William and Joyce Juanita Often Hoeschen.

(Sup) 5625 ERIC SCOTT BREWER (Hilda[8], Esther[7], Daniel[6], Sarah[5], John Adam III[4], John Adam II[3], John Adam I[2], John Jacob[1]) was the son of Frank Lowell and Hilda Joyce Crane Brewer [Supplement No. 3304]. Eric was born December 19, 1960.

(Sup) 5626 CURTIS LEE BREWER (Hilda[8], Esther[7], Daniel[6], Sarah[5], John Adam III[4], John Adam II[3], John Adam I[2], John Jacob[1]) was the son of Frank Lowell and Hilda Joyce Crane Brewer [Supplement No. 3304]. Curtis was born May 24, 1962.

(Sup) 5627 MELANIE LYNN CRANE (Richard[8], Esther[7], Daniel[6], Sarah[5], John Adam III[4], John Adam II[3], John Adam I[2], John Jacob[1]) was the daughter of Richard Lee and Martha Jane Newkirk Crane [Supplement No. 3305]. She was born September 25, 1963.

(Sup) 5628 JULIA IRENE CRANE (Richard[8], Esther[7], Daniel[6], Sarah[5], John Adam III[4], John Adam II[3], John Adam I[2], John Jacob[1]) was the daughter of Richard Lee and Martha Jane Newkirk Crane [Supplement No. 3305]. She was born September 14, 1964.

(Sup) 5629 RICHARD DENTON CRANE (Richard[8], Esther[7], Daniel[6], Sarah[5], John Adam III[4], John Adam II[3], John Adam I[2], John Jacob[1]) was the son of Richard Lee and Martha Jane Newkirk Crane [Supplement No. 3305]. Richard was born July 1, 1967.

(Sup) 5630 RUSSELL GILBERT CRANE (Richard[8], Esther[7], Daniel[6], Sarah[5], John Adam III[4], John Adam II[3], John Adam I[2], John Jacob[1]) was the son of Richard Lee and Martha Jane Newkirk Crane [Supplement No. 3305]. He was born October 9, 1971.

(Sup) 5631 ROBERT CURTIS CRANE, JR. (Robert[8], Esther[7], Daniel[6], Sarah[5], John Adam III[4], John Adam II[3], John Adam I[2], John Jacob[1]) was the son of Robert Curtis and Mary Katherine Griffiths Crane, Sr. [Supplement No. 3306]. He was born October 16, 1970, at Hagerstown, Maryland.

(Sup) 5632   AMY MARIE CRANE (Robert[8], Esther[7], Daniel[6], Sarah[5], John Adam II[4], John Adam I[3], John Adam I[2], John Jacob[1]) was the daughter of Robert Curtis and Mary Katherine Griffiths Crane, Sr. [Supplement No. 3306]. She was born April 24, 1972, at Hagerstown, Maryland.

(Sup) 5633   KIMBERLY MOORE FOLEY (Sara[8], Florence[7], Daniel[6], Sarah[5], John Adam II[4], John Adam I[3], John Adam I[2], John Jacob[1]) was the daughter of Paul Thomas and Sara Lee Moore Foley [Supplement No. 3307]. She was born January 12, 1960 at Martinsburg, West Virginia. She was empoyed at a heart clinic in Washington, D.C.

(Sup) 5634   PATRICK WILLIAM FOLEY (Sara[8], Florence[7], Daniel[6], Sarah[5], John Adam II[4], John Adam I[3], John Adam I[2], John Jacob[1]) was the son of Paul Thomas and Sara Lee Moore Foley [Supplement No. 3307]. Patrick was born April 1, 1961, at Arlington, Virginia.

(Sup) 5635   COLLEEN FRANCES FOLEY (Sara[8], Florence[7], Daniel[6], Sarah[5], John Adam II[4], John Adam I[3], John Adam I[2], John Jacob[1]) was the daughter of Paul Thomas and Sara Lee Moore Foley [Supplement No. 3307]. Colleen was born February 27, 1963, at Arlington, Virginia. She was a dental assistant.

(Sup) 5636   WILLIAM PHILIP OLIN (Lou Ellen[8], Florence[7], Daniel[6], Sarah[5], John Adam II[4], John Adam I[3], John Adam I[2], John Jacob[1]) was the son of Thomas Baille and Lou Ellen Moore Olin [Supplement No. 3308]. He was born July 26, 1966, at Bethesda, Maryland.

(Sup) 5637   THOMAS SCOTT OLIN (Lou Ellen[8], Florence[7], Daniel[6], Sarah[5], John Adam II[4], John Adam I[3], John Adam I[2], John Jacob[1]) was the son of Thomas Baille and Lou Ellen Moore Olin [Supplement No. 3308]. He was born September 7, 1967, at Bethesda, Maryland.

(Sup) 5638   SARAH CARLYLE WHITING (Lucy[8], Florence[7], Daniel[6], Sarah[5], John Adam II[4], John Adam I[3], John Adam I[2], John Jacob[1]) was the daughter of Richard Dulaney and Lucy Moore Hendricks [Supplement No. 3310]. Sarah was born February 29, 1984, at Columbia, Maryland.

- -

(Sup) 5640   CYNTHIA LYNN HENDRICKS (Daniel[8], Daniel[7], Daniel[6], Sarah[5], John Adam II[4], John Adam I[3], John Adam I[2], John Jacob[1]) was the daughter of Daniel Webster and Peggy Louise Boyd Hendricks, IV [Supplement No. 3311]. Cynthia was born April 1, 1955, at Shenandoah Junction, Jefferson County, West Virginia. She married, first, David Wayne Lawrence July 12, 1975. He was the son of Glenville and Ann Fulk Lawrence and was born June 7, 1953, at Brooklyn, New York. Cynthia and David were divorced. She married, second, Kevin Englebright of Martinsburg, West Virginia. Kevin was a store clerk, and Cynthia was a nurse.

(Sup) 7410   i Dara Lane Englebright, born December 4, 1982.

(Sup) 5641   DANA LOUISE HENDRICKS (Daniel[8], Daniel[7], Daniel[6], Sarah[5], John Adam II[4], John Adam I[3], John Adam I[2], John Jacob[1]) was the daughter of Daniel Webster and Peggy Louise Boyd Hendricks, IV [Supplement No. 3311]. Dana was born March 4, 1958, at Shenandoah Junction, Jefferson County, West Virginia. She married Clayton A. Anders of Charles Town, West Virginia, July 24, 1982. Dana graduated from Shepherd College, West Virginia, and was a computer operator. Clayton graduated from West Virginia University and was a teacher and coach at Boonsboro High School, Maryland.

(Sup) 5642   JEFFREY GLENN POTTER (Sarah[8], Daniel[7], Daniel[6], Sarah[5], John Adam II[4], John Adam I[3], John Adam I[2], John Jacob[1]) was the son of Marvin John and Sarah Margaret Hendricks Potter [Supplement No. 3312]. Jeffrey was born January 14, 1959, at Los Angeles, California. He married Carol Lemka of Pasadena, California.

(Sup) 7411   i Martha Glenn Potter, born July 24, 1983.

(Sup) 5643   DANIEL ALLEN POTTER (Sarah[8], Daniel[7], Daniel[6], Sarah[5], John Adam II[4], John Adam I[3], John Adam I[2], John Jacob[1]) was the son of Marvin John and Sarah Margaret Hendricks Potter [Supplement No. 3312]. Daniel was born February 4, 1964, at Los Angeles, California.

(Sup) 5644   MARK CHRISTOPHER POTTER (Sarah[8], Daniel[7], Daniel[6], Sarah[5], John Adam II[4], John Adam I[3], John Adam I[2], John Jacob[1]) was the son of Marvin John and Sarah Margaret Hendricks Potter [Supplement No. 3312]. Mark was born December 3, 1968, at Los Angeles, California.

(Sup) 5645   STEPHANIE MARIE PASTOR (Mary Ellen[8], Daniel[7], Daniel[6], Sarah[5], John Adam II[4], John Adam I[3], John Adam I[2], John Jacob[1]) was the daughter of Stephen Peter and Mary Ellen Hendricks Pastor [Supplement No. 3313]. Stephanie was born August 4, 1975.

(Sup) 5646   CHRISTOPHER STEVEN PASTOR (Mary Ellen[8], Daniel[7], Daniel[6], Sarah[5], John Adam II[4], John Adam I[3], John Adam I[2], John Jacob[1]) was the son of Stephen Peter and Mary Ellen Hendricks Pastor [Supplement No. 3313]. He was born July 20, 1977, at Covina, California.

(Sup) 5647 MARIE ANTOINETTE PARMENTER (Rebecca^8, William^7, Daniel^6, Sarah^5, John Adam III^4, John Adam II^3, John Adam I^2, John Jacob^1) was the daughter of James Alan and Rebecca Ann Hendricks Parmenter [Supplement No. 3315]. She was born October 20, 1961, at Hopewell, Virginia.

(Sup) 5648 WILLIAM WAYNE HENDRICKS (William^8, William^7, Daniel^6, Sarah^5, John Adam III^4, John Adam II^3, John Adam I^2, John Jacob^1) was the son of William Knox and Doris Jean Lowe Hendricks, Jr. [Supplement No. 3316]. He was born October 7, 1972, at Hopewell, Virginia.

(Sup) 5649 MELANIE DAWN HENDRICKS (William^8, William^7, Daniel^6, Sarah^5, John Adam III^4, John Adam II^3, John Adam I^2, John Jacob^1) was the daughter of William Knox and Doris Jean Lowe Hendricks, Jr. [Supplement No. 3316]. She was born September 9, 1976, at Hopewell, Virginia.

(Sup) 5650 CHRISTOPHER ALEN HENDRICKS (John^8, William^7, Daniel^6, Sarah^5, John Adam III^4, John Adam II^3, John Adam I^2, John Jacob^1) was the son of John Wayne and Carrolyn Marie Hood Hendricks [Supplement No. 3317]. He was born June 19, 1972, at Machias, Maine.

(Sup) 5651 SHAWN WAYNE HENDRICKS (John^8, William^7, Daniel^6, Sarah^5, John Adam III^4, John Adam II^3, John Adam I^2, John Jacob^1) was the son of John Wayne and Carrolyn Marie Hood Hendricks [Supplement No. 3317]. Shawn was born June 12, 1976, at Machias, Maine.

(Sup) 5652 JEFFERY DAVID HENDRICKS (Kenneth^8, William^7, Daniel^6, Sarah^5, John Adam III^4, John Adam II^3, John Adam I^2, John Jacob^1) was the son of Kenneth Lee and Carol Ann Bergeron Hendricks [Supplement No. 3317A]. He was born February 7, 1970, at Holyoke, Massachusetts.

(Sup) 5653 DANIEL JOSEPH HENDRICKS (Kenneth^8, William^7, Daniel^6, Sarah^5, John Adam III^4, John Adam II^3, John Adam I^2, John Jacob^1) was the son of Kenneth Lee and Carol Ann Bergeron Hendricks [Sup- plement No. 3317A]. He was born December 31, 1977, at Hopewell, Virginia.

(Sup) 5654 RACHEL HENDRICKS SCHMELLER (Martha^8, Rebecca^7, Daniel^6, Sarah^5, John Adam III^4, John Adam II^3, John Adam I^2, John Jacob^1) was the daughter of Wolfgang Rudolph and Martha Ann Bly Schmeller [Supplement No. 3318]. Rachel was born August 19, 1969, at Winchester, Virginia.

(Sup) 5655 SARA BERGMANN SCHMELLER (Martha^8, Rebecca^7, Daniel^6, Sarah^5, John Adam III^4, John Adam II^3, John Adam I^2, John Jacob^1) was the daughter of Wolfgang Rudolph and Martha Ann Bly Schmeller [Supplement No. 3318]. Sara was born November 1, 1972, at Winchester, Virginia.

(Sup) 5656 DONALD MAXWELL WALTER, IV (Donald^8, Genevieve^7, Daniel^6, Sarah^5, John Adam III^4, John Adam II^3, John Adam I^2, John Jacob^1) was the son of Donald Maxwell and Rebecca Jane Travers Walter, III [Supplement No. 3319]. Donald, IV. was born May 12, 1970, at Winchester, Virginia.

(Sup) 5657 CAROL ANN WALTER (Donald^8, Genevieve^7, Daniel^6, Sarah^5, John Adam III^4, John Adam II^3, John Adam I^2, John Jacob^1) was the daughter of Donald Maxwell and Rebecca Jane Travers Walter, III [Supplement No. 3319]. Carol Ann was born March 14, 1971, at Winchester, Virginia.

(Sup) 5658 MICHAEL ANTHONY WALTER (Donald^8, Genevieve^7, Daniel^6, Sarah^5, John Adam III^4, John Adam II^3, John Adam I^2, John Jacob^1) was the son of Donald Maxwell and Francine Boisvert Walter [Supplement No. 3319]. Michael was born July 31, 1981, at Leeburg, Florida.

(Sup) 5658A SCOTT BRYAN LINNE (Julia^8, Genevieve^7, Daniel^6, Sarah^5, John Adam III^4, John Adam II^3, John Adam I^2, John Jacob^1) was the son of George Frederick and Julia Ann Walter Linne [Supplement No. 3320]. Scott was born September 26, 1977, at St. Louis, Missouri.

(Sup) 5658B LAURA ANN LINNE (Julia^8, Genevieve^7, Daniel^6, Sarah^5, John Adam III^4, John Adam II^3, John Adam I^2, John Jacob^1) was the daughter of George Frederick and Julia Ann Walter Linne [Supplement No. 3320]. Laura was born December 14, 1981, at St. John's, Missouri.

(Sup) 5659 BARBARA JEAN MILLER (Neva^8, James^7, Alvey^6, Mary^5, John Adam III^4, John Adam II^3, John Adam I^2, John Jacob^1) was the daughter of James E. and Neva Sue Reinhart Miller [TLF, No. 3324]. Barbara was born September 1, 1944.

(Sup) 5660 SANDRA SUE MILLER (Neva^8, James^7, Alvey^6, Mary^5, John Adam III^4, John Adam II^3, John Adam I^2, John Jacob^1) was the daughter of James E. and Neva Sue Reinhart Miller [TLF, No. 3324]. Sandra was born October 5, 1946.

(Sup) 5661 SUSAN GAY CURRY (Peggy[8], Neva[7], Alvey[6], Mary[5], John Adam III[4], John Adam II[3], John Adam I[2], John Jacob[1]) was the daughter of James Gordon and Peggy Sue McNeil Curry [TLF, No. 3326]. Susan was born December 22, 1945.

(Sup) 5662 ELIZABETH ANN CURRY (Peggy[8], Neva[7], Alvey[6], Mary[5], John Adam III[4], John Adam II[3], John Adam I[2], John Jacob[1]) was the daughter of James Gordon and Peggy Sue McNeil Curry [TLF No. 3326]. Elizabeth was born January 15, 1947.

(Sup) 5663 LOUIS ALBERT McPHERSON (Sarah[8], Ethelyn[7], Iva[6], Eli[5], Israel[4], Jacob[3], John Adam I[2], John Jacob[1]) was the son of Harry Edwin and Sarah Tarpley McPherson [TLF No. 3338]. He was born November 6, 1923, in Gentry County, Missouri. He married.

(Sup) 7430   i Beverly Jean McPherson, born July 3, 1946.

(Sup) 5664 FAYE EDWYNA McPHERSON (Sarah[8], Ethelyn[7], Iva[6], Eli[5], Israel[4], Jacob[3], John Adam I[2], John Jacob[1]) was the daughter of Harry Edwin and Sarah Tarpley McPherson [TLF No. 3338]. She was born October 19, 1926, in Caddo County, Oklahoma.

(Sup) 5665 MARION DALE McPHERSON (Sarah[8], Ethelyn[7], Iva[6], Eli[5], Israel[4], Jacob[3], John Adam I[2], John Jacob[1]) was the child of Harry Edwin and Sarah Tarpley McPherson [TLF No. 3338]. Marion was born September 29, 1928, in Caddo County, Oklahoma.

(Sup) 5666 SALLY MAY WHITT (Roxie[8], Ethelyn[7], Iva[6], Eli[5], Israel[4], Jacob[3], John Adam I[2], John Jacob[1]) was the daughter of Rexford Blaine and Roxie May Tarpley Whitt [TLF No. 3339]. Sally May was born September 11, 1930, at Cyril, Ohio.

(Sup) 5667 MARY JO McCORMICK (Irene[8], Alvah[7], John[6], Eli[5], Israel[4], Jacob[3], John Adam I[2], John Jacob[1]) was the daughter of Joseph Travis and Irene Link McCormick [TLF No. 3341]. Mary Jo was born March 17, 1937, at Kansas City, Missouri.

(Sup) 5668 SANDRA LEE McQUARY (Ola[8], Mahlon[7], Jefferson[6], Eli[5], Israel[4], Jacob[3], John Adam I[2], John Jacob[1]) was the daughter of James Clinton and Ola Marguerite Link McQuary [TLF No. 3344]. Sandra was born March 8, 1941.

(Sup) 5669 TERRY LEE McQUARY (Ola[8], Mahlon[7], Jefferson[6], Eli[5], Israel[4], Jacob[3], John Adam I[2], John Jacob[1]) was the child of James Clinton and Ola Marguerite Link McQuary [TLF No. 3344]. Terry was born March 28, 1948.

(Sup) 5670 CLIFFORD MERRITT RUDY (Bonnas[8], Lucy[7], Jefferson[6], Eli[5], Israel[4], Jacob[3], John Adam I[2], John Jacob[1]) was the son of Bonnas Ulyses and Charlotte Merritt Rudy [TLF No. 3345]. Clifford was born June 10, 1947, at Wichita, Kansas.

(Sup) 5671 SUE ELLEN BERNARD (Bonita[8], Lucy[7], Jefferson[6], Eli[5], Israel[4], Jacob[3], John Adam I[2], John Jacob[1]) was the daughter of Clifford Warren and Bonita Rudy Bernard [TLF No. 3346]. She was born February 10, 1938, at Yukon, Oklahoma.

(Sup) 5672 RUDY WARREN BERNARD (Bonita[8], Lucy[7], Jefferson[6], Eli[5], Israel[4], Jacob[3], John Adam I[2], John Jacob[1]) was the son of Clifford Warren and Bonita Rudy Bernard [TLF No. 3346]. He was born August 2, 1943, at Hawthorne, California.

(Sup) 5673 LINDA SUE CLEMENTS (Harold[8], Frances[7], Eliza[6], Eli[5], Israel[4], Jacob[3], John Adam I[2], John Jacob[1]) was the daughter of Harold Link and Lenore Blalock Clements [TLF No. 3349]. Linda was born September 16, 1943.

(Sup) 5674 DONALD RAY CLEMENTS (Harold[8], Frances[7], Eliza[6], Eli[5], Israel[4], Jacob[3], John Adam I[2], John Jacob[1]) was the son of Harold Link and Bonnie Whisler Clements [TLF No. 3349]. Donald was born November 23, 1943.

(Sup) 5675 KAY DARLENE CLEMENTS (Harold[8], Frances[7], Eliza[6], Eli[5], Israel[4], Jacob[3], John Adam I[2], John Jacob[1]) was the daughter of Harold Link and Bonnie Whisler Clements [TLF No. 3349]. She was born September 16, 1946.

- -

(Sup) 5681 WARREN DAVID GRIFFITH (Iris[8], Ira[7], Katherine[6], Sarah[5], Israel[4], Jacob[3], John Adam I[2], John Jacob[1]) was the son of Warren David and Iris Brown Griffith [TLF No. 3361]. Warren, Jr., was born March 7, 1946, at Kansas City, Kansas.

(Sup) 5682 D'ARLYNN KAY SMITH (Esther[8], Ira[7], Katherine[6], Sarah[5], Israel[4], Jacob[3], John Adam I[2], John Jacob[1]) was the daughter of Harlan LeRoy and Esther Brown Smith [TLF No. 3362]. D'Arlynn was born September 1, 1947.

(Sup) 5683 CALVIN STEINER BURRIER, JR. (Calvin[8], Daniel[7], Calvin[6], Daniel[5], Elizabeth[4], Thomas[3], John Adam I[2], John Jacob[1]) was the son of Calvin Steiner and Margaret Bossard Burrier [TLF No. 3368]. Calvin, Jr., was born August 20, 1929, at Walkersville, Maryland.

(Sup) 5684 GEORGE CARROL BURRIER (Calvin[8], Daniel[7], Calvin[6], Daniel[5], Elizabeth[4], Thomas[3], John Adam I[2], John Jacob[1]) was the son of Calvin Steiner and Margaret Bossard Burrier [TLF No. 3368]. George was born March 16, 1931, at Thurmont, Maryland.

(Sup) 5685 HOWARD GRAYSON BURRIER (Calvin[8], Daniel[7], Calvin[6], Daniel[5], Elizabeth[4], Thomas[3], John Adam I[2], John Jacob[1]) was the son of Calvin Steiner and Margaret Bossard Burrier [TLF No. 3368]. Howard was born September 9, 1932, at Walkersville, Maryland.

(Sup) 5686 MARGARET ELIZABETH BURRIER (Calvin[8], Daniel[7], Calvin[6], Daniel[5], Elizabeth[4], Thomas[3], John Adam I[2], John Jacob[1]) was the daughter of Calvin Steiner and Margaret Bossard Burrier [TLF No. 3368]. Margaret was born August 3, 1935, at Thurmont, Maryland.

(Sup) 5687 ANN WESLEY BURRIER (Calvin[8], Daniel[7], Calvin[6], Daniel[5], Elizabeth[4], Thomas[3], John Adam I[2], John Jacob[1]) was the daughter of Calvin Steiner and Margaret Bossard Burrier [TLF No. 3368]. Ann was born July 23, 1938, at Frederick, Maryland.

(Sup) 5688 NANCY ELAINE BURRIER (Calvin[8], Daniel[7], Calvin[6], Daniel[5], Elizabeth[4], Thomas[3], John Adam I[2], John Jacob[1]) was the daughter of Calvin Steiner and Margaret Bossard Burrier [TLF No. 3368]. Nancy was born January 25, 1940, at Frederick, Maryland (twin of Mary Jane).

(Sup) 5689 MARY JANE BURRIER (Calvin[8], Daniel[7], Calvin[6], Daniel[5], Elizabeth[4], Thomas[3], John Adam I[2], John Jacob[1]) was the daughter of Calvin Steiner and Margaret Bossard Burrier [TLF No. 3368]. Mary Jane was born January 25, 1940, at Frederick, Maryland (twin of Nancy Elaine).

(Sup) 5690 BARBARA MAE BURRIER (Calvin[8], Daniel[7], Calvin[6], Daniel[5], Elizabeth[4], Thomas[3], John Adam I[2], John Jacob[1]) was the daughter of Calvin Steiner and Margaret Bossard Burrier [TLF No. 3368]. Barbara was born July 11, 1941, at Frederick, Maryland.

(Sup) 5691 JAMES STEVENS BURRIER (Calvin[8], Daniel[7], Calvin[6], Daniel[5], Elizabeth[4], Thomas[3], John Adam I[2], John Jacob[1]) was the son of Calvin Steiner and Margaret Bossard Burrier [TLF No. 3368]. James was born October 19, 1943, at Frederick, Maryland.

(Sup) 5692 CHERYL REVELLE BURRIER (Calvin[8], Daniel[7], Calvin[6], Daniel[5], Elizabeth[4], Thomas[3], John Adam I[2], John Jacob[1]) was the daughter of Calvin Steiner and Margaret Bossard Burrier [TLF No. 3368]. Cheryl was born March 18, 1945, at Frederick, Maryland.

(Sup) 5693 KENNETH EUGENE BURRIER (Calvin[8], Daniel[7], Calvin[6], Daniel[5], Elizabeth[4], Thomas[3], John Adam I[2], John Jacob[1]) was the son of Calvin Steiner and Margaret Bossard Burrier [TLF No. 3368]. Kenneth was born June 28, 1946, at Frederick, Maryland.

(Sup) 5694 JOHN GRAYSON GRIMES (Wilma[8], Daniel[7], Calvin[6], Daniel[5], Elizabeth[4], Thomas[3], John Adam I[2], John Jacob[1]) was the son of Ira Staley and Wilma Burrier Grimes [TLF No. 3371]. John was born October 29, 1935, at Frederick, Maryland.

(Sup) 5695 ALVERDA MAE GRIMES (Wilma[8], Daniel[7], Calvin[6], Daniel[5], Elizabeth[4], Thomas[3], John Adam I[2], John Jacob[1]) was the daughter of Ira Staley and Wilma Burrier Grimes [TLF No. 3371]. Alverda was born December 29, 1936, near Frederick, Maryland.

(Sup) 5696 RUTH FLORENCE GRIMES (Wilma[8], Daniel[7], Calvin[6], Daniel[5], Elizabeth[4], Thomas[3], John Adam I[2], John Jacob[1]) was the daughter of Ira Staley and Wilma Burrier Grimes [TLF No. 3371]. Ruth was born March 25, 1938, near Frederick, Maryland.

(Sup) 5697 JAMES STALEY GRIMES (Wilma[8], Daniel[7], Calvin[6], Daniel[5], Elizabeth[4], Thomas[3], John Adam I[2], John Jacob[1]) was the son of Ira Staley and Wilma Burrier Grimes [TLF No. 3371]. James was born September 9, 1939, near Frederick, Maryland.

(Sup) 5698 ROBERT DONALD GRIMES (Wilma[8], Daniel[7], Calvin[6], Daniel[5], Elizabeth[4], Thomas[3], John Adam I[2], John Jacob[1]) was the son of Ira Staley and Wilma Burrier Grimes [TLF No. 3371]. Robert was born December 19, 1941, near Frederick, Maryland.

(Sup) 5699 MARY LOUISE BURRIER (Charles[8], Daniel[7], Calvin[6], Daniel[5], Elizabeth[4], Thomas[3], John Adam I[2], John Jacob[1]) was the daughter of Charles Daniel and Mabel Wright Burrier [TLF No. 3373]. Mary was born October 25, 1939, at Frederick, Maryland.

(Sup) 5700 BETTY WRIGHT BURRIER (Charles[8], Daniel[7], Calvin[6], Daniel[5], Elizabeth[4], Thomas[3], John Adam I[2], John Jacob[1]) was the daughter of Charles Daniel and Mabel Wright Burrier [TLF No. 3373]. Betty was born April 4, 1943, at Walkersville, Maryland.

(Sup) 5701 WILLIAM GRAYSON BURRIER, JR. (Gilmer[8], Daniel[7], Calvin[6], Daniel[5], Elizabeth[4], Thomas[3], John Adam I[2], John Jacob[1]) was the son of Gilmer Ramsburg and Ethel Baer Burrier [TLF No. 3375]. William was born December 23, 1946, at Frederick, Maryland.

(Sup) 5702   MARSHA FAITH BURRIER (Paul[8], Daniel[7], Calvin[6], Daniel[5], Elizabeth[4], Thomas[3], John Adam I[2], John Jacob[1]) was the daughter of Paul Meredith and Grace Albaugh Burrier [TLF No. 3377]. Marsha was born July 24, 1946, at Frederick, Maryland.

(Sup) 5703   DAVID PAUL GREENE, JR. (Edith[8], Mabel[7], Calvin[6], Daniel[5], Elizabeth[4], Thomas[3], John Adam I[2], John Jacob[1]) was the son of David Paul and Edith Burrier Greene [TLF No. 3379]. David, Jr., was born January 26, 1923, in Frederick County, Maryland. He married Margaret Louise Garner. David was a graduate of Bridgewater College and became an ordained minister.

(Sup) 7436   i   Byron Paul Greene, born August 1, 1945.
(Sup) 7437   ii   Carol Ann Greene, born January 4, 1947.

(Sup) 5704   JAMES ARNOLD GREENE (Edith[8], Mabel[7], Calvin[6], Daniel[5], Elizabeth[4], Thomas[3], John Adam I[2], John Jacob[1]) was the son of David Paul and Edith Burrier Greene [TLF No. 3379]. James was born August 16, 1930, in Carroll County, Maryland.

(Sup) 5705   ARVIN LLOYD GREENE (Edith[8], Mabel[7], Calvin[6], Daniel[5], Elizabeth[4], Thomas[3], John Adam I[2], John Jacob[1]) was the son of David Paul and Edith Burrier Greene [TLF No. 3379]. Arvin was born December 28, 1936, in Carroll County, Maryland.

(Sup) 5706   ANNE JANE GEARINGER (Edith[8], Charles[7], Charles[6], Daniel[5], Elizabeth[4], Thomas[3], John Adam I[2], John Jacob[1]) was the daughter of Edward Russeell and Edith Grace Burrier Gearinger [TLF No. 3380]. Anne was born July 3, 1922, at Frederick, Maryland. She married Thomas Cramer Michael, October 6, 1940, at Frederick. He was the son of Mantz Michael and was born February 17, 1921.

(Sup) 7438   i   Thomas Cramer Michael, Jr., born May 18, 1941.
(Sup) 7439   ii   Connie Sue Michael, born June 1, 1942.

(Sup) 5707   CHARLES GEARINGER (Edith[8], Charles[7], Charles[6], Daniel[5], Elizabeth[4], Thomas[3], John Adam I[2], John Jacob[1]) was the son of Edward Russel and Edith Burrier Gearinger [TLF No. 3380]. Charles was born January 9, 1924, at Frederick, Maryland. He married Martha Jeanne Biser June 13, 1946, at Frederick. Martha was the daughter of Glenn O. Biser and was born October 18, 1926, at Piqua, Ohio.

(Sup) 7440   i   Charles Michael Gearinger, born July 4, 1947.

(Sup) 5708   MARY ALICE GEARINGER (Edith[8], Charles[7], Charles[6], Daniel[5], Elizabeth[4], Thomas[3], John Adam I[2], John Jacob[1]) was the daughter of Edward Russel and Edith Burrier Gearinger [TLF No. 3380]. Mary Alice was born July 3, 1927, at Frederick, Maryland. She married Paul B. Hammond, Jr., June 7, 1947, at Frederick. He was the son of Paul B. Hammond and was born January 31, 1927, at Frederick.

(Sup) 5709   ROBERT GEARINGER (Edith[8], Charles[7], Charles[6], Daniel[5], Elizabeth[4], Thomas[3], John Adam I[2], John Jacob[1]) was the son of Edward Russel and Edith Burrier Gearinger [TLF No. 3380]. Robert was born November 3, 1931, at Frederick, Maryland.

(Sup) 5710   CHESTER MOSIER, JR. (Cecelia[8], Nannie[7], Charles[6], Daniel[5], Elizabeth[4], Thomas[3], John Adam I[2], John Jacob[1]) was the son of Chester Clarence and Cecelia Murphy Mosier [TLF No. 3381]. Chester, Jr., was born March 8, 1923. He married Doris Hogenbaugh May 9, 1945.

(Sup) 7441   1   Donnie Dean Mosier, born October 23, 1946.

(Sup) 5711   PATRICIA JUNE MURPHY (Charles[8], Nannie[7], Charles[6], Daniel[5], Elizabeth[4], Thomas[3], John Adam I[2], John Jacob[1]) was the daughter of Charles Joseph and June Hesler Murphy [TLF No. 3382]. Patricia was born July 23, 1928, at Indianapolis, Indiana.

(Sup) 5712   DOROTHY ANN MURPHY (Charles[8], Nannie[7], Charles[6], Daniel[5], Elizabeth[4], Thomas[3], John Adam I[2], John Jacob[1]) was the daughter of Charles Joseph and June Hesler Murphy [TLF No. 3382]. Dorothy was born December 30, 1929, at Indianapolis, Indiana.

(Sup) 5713   JOSEPH MURPHY (Charles[8], Nannie[7], Charles[6], Daniel[5], Elizabeth[4], Thomas[3], John Adam I[2], John Jacob[1]) was the son of Charles Joseph and June Hesler Murphy [TLF No. 3382]. Joseph was born April 7, 1931, at Indianapolis, Indiana.

(Sup) 5714   VIRGINIA MABEL MURPHY (Charles[8], Nannie[7], Charles[6], Daniel[5], Elizabeth[4], Thomas[3], John Adam I[2], John Jacob[1]) was the daughter of Charles Joseph and June Hesler Murphy [TLF No. 3382]. Virginia was born March 29, 1933, at Indianapolis, Indiana.

(Sup) 5715   ROBERT MURPHY (Charles[8], Nannie[7], Charles[6], Daniel[5], Elizabeth[4], Thomas[3], John Adam I[2], John Jacob[1]) was the son of Charles Joseph and June Hesler Murphy [TLF No. 3382]. Robert was born March 29, 1935, at Indianapolis, Indiana.

(Sup) 5716   ROSE MARY MURPHY (Charles[8], Nannie[7], Charles[6], Daniel[5], Elizabeth[4], Thomas[3], John Adam I[2], John Jacob[1]) was the daughter of Charles Joseph and June Hesler Murphy [TLF No. 3382]. Rose Mary was born June 14, 1938, at Indianapolis, Indiana.

(Sup) 5717 NANCY LEE MURPHY (Charles^8, Nannie^7, Charles^6, Daniel^5, Elizabeth^4, Thomas^3, John Adam I^2, John Jacob^1) was the daughter of Charles Joseph and June Hesler Murphy [TLF No. 3382]. Nancy Lee was born January 10, 1940, at Indianapolis, Indiana.

(Sup) 5718 BETTY LOU MURPHY (Lawson^8, Nannie^7, Charles^6, Daniel^5, Elizabeth^4, Thomas^3, John Adam I^2, John Jacob^1) was the daughter of Lawson Winfield and Maurine Stewart Murphy [TLF No. 3383].

(Sup) 5719 GEORGE ELMER MURPHY (Lawson^8, Nannie^7, Charles^6, Daniel^5, Elizabeth^4, Thomas^3, John Adam I^2, John Jacob^1) was the son of Lawson Winfield and Maurine Stewart Murphy [TLF No. 3383].

(Sup) 5720 PHYLLIS ANN MURPHY (Lawson^8, Nannie^7, Charles^6, Daniel^5, Elizabeth^4, Thomas^3, John Adam I^2, John Jacob^1) was the daughter of Lawson Winfield and Maurine Stewart Murphy [TLF No. 3383].

(Sup) 5721 RICHARD LEE MURPHY (Lawson^8, Nannie^7, Charles^6, Daniel^5, Elizabeth^4, Thomas^3, John Adam I^2, John Jacob^1) was the son of Lawson Winfield and Maurine Stewart Murphy [TLF No. 3383].

(Sup) 5722 HOWARD LEWIS RASHER (Helen^8, Nannie^7, Charles^6, Daniel^5, Elizabeth^4, Thomas^3, John Adam I^2, John Jacob^1) was the son of William John and Helen Murphy Rasher [TLF No. 3384]. Howard was born February 27, 1925, at Logansport, Indiana.

(Sup) 5723 WILLIAM ELMER RASHER (Helen^8, Nannie^7, Charles^6, Daniel^5, Elizabeth^4, Thomas^3, John Adam I^2, John Jacob^1) was the son of William John and Helen Murphy Rasher [TLF No. 3384]. William Elmer was born November 25, 1927, at Logansport, Indiana.

(Sup) 5724 MICHAEL FRANCIS CARVER (Dolores^8, Daniel^7, Catherine^6, Daniel^5, Elizabeth^4, Daniel^3, John Adam I^2, John Jacob^1) was the son of James Francis and Dolores Mercer Carver [TLF No. 3387]. Michael was born April 28, 1948.

(Sup) 5725 ANNA MARGARET SHANK (Maude^8, Nellie^7, Thomas^6, Sophia^5, Elizabeth^4, Daniel^3, John Adam I^2, John Jacob^1) was the daughter of Harvey Franklin and Maude Hahn Shank [TLF No. 3398]. She married James Grimes June 19, 1943.

(Sup) 5726 HARVEY FRANKLIN SHANK, JR. (Maude^8, Nellie^7, Thomas^6, Sophia^5, Elizabeth^4, Thomas^3, John Adam I^2, John Jacob^1) was the son of Harvey Franklin and Maude Hahn Shank [TLF No. 3398]. Harvey, Jr., died in infancy.

(Sup) 5727 CATHERINE VIOLET SHANK (Maude^8, Nellie^7, Thomas^6, Sophia^5, Elizabeth^4, Thomas^3, John Adam I^2, John Jacob^1) was the daughter of Harvey Franklin and Maude Hahn Shank [TLF No. 3398].

(Sup) 5728 RICHARD LEE SHANK (Maude^8, Nellie^7, Thomas^6, Sophia^5, Elizabeth^4, Thomas^3, John Adam I^2, John Jacob^1) was the son of Harvey Franklin and Maude Hahn Shank [TLF No. 3398].

(Sup) 5729 WAYNE EUGENE SHANK (Maude^8, Nellie^7, Thomas^6, Sophia^5, Elizabeth^4, Thomas^3, John Adam I^2, John Jacob^1) was the son of Harvey Franklin and Maude Hahn Shank [TLF No. 3398].

(Sup) 5730 WANDA ANITA DeLASHMIT (Clythnia^8, Nellie^7, Thomas^6, Sophia^5, Elizabeth^4, Thomas^3, John Adam I^2, John Jacob^1) was the daughter of Clythnia Hahn DeLashmit [TLF No. 3406].

(Sup) 5731 MAURICE EUGENE DeLASHMIT (Clythnia^8, Nellie^7, Thomas^6, Sophia^5, Elizabeth^4, Thomas^3, John Adam I^2, John Jacob^1) was the son of Clythnia Hahn DeLashmit [TLF No. 3406].

(Sup) 5732 JAMES WILLIAM DeLASHMIT (Clythnia^8, Nellie^7, Thomas^6, Sophia^5, Elizabeth^4, Thomas^3, John Adam I^2, John Jacob^1) was the son of Clythnia Hahn DeLashmit [TLF No. 3406].

(Sup) 5733 CLAUDETTA YANICE DeLASHMIT (Clythnia^8, Nellie^7, Thomas^6, Sophia^5, Elizabeth^4, Thomas^3, John Adam I^2, John Jacob^1) was the daughter of Clythnia Hahn DeLashmit [TLF No. 3406].

(Sup) 5734 FRANK CARLTON FIERY (Dorothy^8, Maude^7, Ida^6, Sophia^5, Elizabeth^4, Daniel^3, John Adam I^2, John Jacob^1) was the son of Frank Luther and Dorothy Hahn Fiery [TLF No. 3418]. Frank Carlton was born June 12, 1948, at Hagerstown, Maryland.

(Sup) 5735 ERNEST OLIVER STITELY (Oscar^8, Laura^7, Mary^6, Sarah^5, Adam^4, Daniel^3, John Adam I^2, John Jacob^1) was the son of Oscar Beatty and Pauline Masser Stitely [TLF No. 3431]. Ernest was born February 16, 1941.

(Sup) 5736 WILLIAM ALLEN STITELY (Oscar^8, Laura^7, Mary^6, Sarah^5, Adam^4, Daniel^3, John Adam I^2, John Jacob^1) was the son of Oscar Beatty and Pauline Masser Stitely [TLF No. 3431]. William was born November 1, 1944.

(Sup) 5742   PATRICIA MARIE KOENIG (Jane[8], Marie[7], Adam[6], Daniel[5], Adam[4], Daniel[3], John Adam I[2], John Jacob[1]) was the daughter of Henry Adolph and Jane White (Zumstein) Koenig, III [Supplement No. 3444]. Patricia was born July 4, 1946, at Baltimore, Maryland. She married Faris Lee Worthington, May 20, 1972, at Easton, Maryland. He was born June 16, 1946, at Baltimore.

(Sup) 5743   HENRY ADOLPH KOENIG, IV (Jane[8], Marie[7], Adam[6], Daniel[5], Adam[4], Daniel[3], John Adam I[2], John Jacob[1]) was the son of Henry Adolph and Jane White (Zumstein) Koenig, III [Supplement No. 3444]. Henry, IV, was born September 21, 1956, at Baltimore, Maryland. He married Julia Anne Walls, May 5, 1983, at Easton, Maryland. She was the daughter of Edward Lee and Lois Ann (McGuire) Walls and was born April 5, 1956, at Bussac, France. Henry and Julia Ann resided at Berlin, Maryland.

(Sup) 7451   ī Lindsay Jane Koenig, born May 7, 1987.

(Sup) 5744   AMY RUTH LEONARD (Grace[8], Ralph[7], Adam[6], Daniel[5], Adam[4], Daniel[3], John Adam I[2], John Jacob[1]) was the daughter of Anthony Curtis and Grace Ruth (Link) Leonard [Supplement No. 3444A]. Amy was born June 4, 1972.

(Sup) 5745   DANIEL CURTIS LEONARD (Grace[8], Ralph[7], Adam[6], Daniel[5], Adam[4], Daniel[3], John Adam I[2], John Jacob[1]) was the son of Anthony Curtis and Grace Ruth (Link) Leonard [Supplement No. 3444A]. He was born October 18, 1973.

(Sup) 5746   STEPHEN ANTHONY LEONARD (Grace[8], Ralph[7], Adam[6], Daniel[5], Adam[4], Daniel[3], John Adam I[2], John Jacob[1]) was the son of Anthony Curtis and Grace Ruth (Link) Leonard [Supplement No. 3444A]. He was born February 15, 1976.

(Sup) 5747   MATTHEW JAMES LEONARD (Grace[8], Ralph[7], Adam[6], Daniel[5], Adam[4], Daniel[3], John Adam I[2], John Jacob[1]) was the son of Anthony Curtis and Grace Ruth (Link) Leonard [Supplement No. 3444A]. He was born April 30, 1978.

(Sup) 5748   ELIZABETH GLENN (Elizabeth[8], Mark[7], Virginia[6], Adam[5], John[4], Peter[3], Matthias[2], John Jacob[1]) was the daughter of J. H. and Elizabeth Ford Glenn [ILF No. 3447]. She married Mr. Bigham.

(Sup) 5737   RUSSELL WILLIAM POE (Ethel[8], Lewis[7], Adam[6], Daniel[5], Adam[4], Daniel[3], John Adam I[2], John Jacob[1]) was the son of William George and Ethel (Link) Poe [Supplement No. 3440]. He was born January 10, 1946, at Bridgeport, Connecticut. He married Victoria Ann Margo April 17, 1969.

(Sup) 7446   ī Melinda Jean Poe, born 1978.

(Sup) 5738   DONALD MAIN ROMNEY, JR. (Mary[8], Eugene[7], Adam[6], Daniel[5], Adam[4], Daniel[3], John Adam I[2], John Jacob[1]) was the son of Donald Main and Mary Elizabeth (Link) Romney [Supplement No. 3441]. Donald was born December 1, 1942, at Baltimore, Maryland. He married, first, Jean Sauter, June 27, 1964; they were divorced. He married, second, Paula Patch Prescott, September 30, 1972; they divorced. He married, third, Audrey Ann King, October 15, 1977, at Vienna, Virginia. She was the daughter of John Heister and Audrey King, and was born December 28, 1947, at Warrenton, Virginia.

            CHILD OF DONALD AND AUDREY

(Sup) 7447   ī Aaron Link Romney, born May 26, 1978.

(Sup) 5739   NANCY CAROL ROMNEY (Mary[8], Eugene[7], Adam[6], Daniel[5], Adam[4], Daniel[3], John Adam I[2], John Jacob[1]) was the daughter of Donald Main and Mary Elizabeth (Link) Romney [Supplement No. 3441]. Nancy was born September 6, 1948. She married, first, Thomas Browning Saylor, May 6, 1972. They were divorced. Nancy married, second, James Vincent Fitzgibbons, April 11, 1987, at Margate, New Jersey. He was the son of Walter and Jane Fitzgibbons and was born June 5, 1951, at Philadelphia, Pennsylvania.

(Sup) 5740   JAMES DAWSON MITCHELL (Jean Ellen[8], Eugene[7], Adam[6], Daniel[5], Adam[4], Daniel[3], John Adam I[2], John Jacob[1]) was the son of Harry Dawson and Jean Ellen (Link) Mitchell [Supplement No. 3442]. James was born January 10, 1951. He married Judy Louise Russell, October 4, 1980, at Baltimore, Maryland. She was born January 8, 1953.

(Sup) 7448   ī Kyle James Mitchell, born January 21, 1983.
(Sup) 7449   īī Carly Janeen Mitchell, born January 11, 1985.

(Sup) 5741   DAVID BOWERS MITCHELL (Jean Ellen[8], Eugene[7], Adam[6], Daniel[5], Adam[4], Daniel[3], John Adam I[2], John Jacob[1]) was the son of Harry Dawson and Jean Ellen (Link) Mitchell [Supplement No. 3442]. David was born March 11, 1953. He married Barbara Ann Casciotti, August 22, 1981, in Baltimore County, Maryland. She was born April 22, 1956.

(Sup) 7450   ī Kenneth David Mitchell, born April 24, 1986.

(Sup) 5749   VIRGINIA GLENN (Elizabeth^8, Mark^7, Virginia^6, Adam^5, John^4, Peter^3, Matthias^2, John Jacob^1) was the daughter of J. H. and Elizabeth Ford Glenn [TLF No. 3447].

(Sup) 5750   JAMES GLENN (Elizabeth^8, Mark^7, Virginia^6, Adam^5, John^4, Peter^3, Matthias^2, John Jacob^1) was the son of J. H. and Elizabeth Ford Glenn [TLF No. 3447].

(Sup) 5751   RUTH GLENN (Elizabeth^8, Mark^7, Virginia^6, Adam^5, John^4, Peter^3, Matthias^2, John Jacob^1) was the daughter of J. H. and Elizabeth Ford Glenn [TLF No. 3447].

(Sup) 5752   THELMA KERR (Nina^8, Hannah^7, Martin^6, Elizabeth^5, John^4, Peter^3, Matthias^2, John Jacob^1) was was the daughter of Elvin W. and Nina Garber Kerr [TLF No. 3450]. Thelma was born September 12, 1902.

(Sup) 5753   MILDRED H. KERR (Nina^8, Hannah^7, Martin^6, Elizabeth^5, John^4, Peter^3, Matthias^2, John Jacob^1) was the daughter of Elvin W. and Nina Garber Kerr [TLF No. 3450]. Mildred was born December 17, 1904.

(Sup) 5754   MARIE BELL PAYNE (Harry^8, Belle^7, Emily^6, Elizabeth^5, John^4, Peter^3, Matthias^2, John Jacob^1) was the daughter of Harry Whitney and Reba Mae Crum Payne [TLF No. 3454]. Marie was born September 7, 1931, in Augusta County, Virginia.

(Sup) 5755   NANCY LEE PAYNE (Harry^8, Belle^7, Emily^6, Elizabeth^5, John^4, Peter^3, Matthias^2, John Jacob^1) was the daughter of Harry Whitney and Reba Mae Crum Payne [TLF No. 3454]. Nancy was born February 16, 1936, in Augusta County, Virginia.

(Sup) 5756   B.A. VAN PELT, JR. (Janie^8, Rosa^7, Junius^6, Elizabeth^5, John^4, Peter^3, Matthias^2, John Jacob^1) was the son of B.A. and Janie Sellers Van Pelt [TLF No. 3456].

(Sup) 7460   i   B.A. Van Pelt, III.
(Sup) 7461   ii Barry Neil Van Pelt.

(Sup) 5757   STUART VAN PELT (Janie^8, Rosa^7, Junius^6, Elizabeth^5, John^4, Peter^3, Matthias^2, John Jacob^1) was the son of B.A. and Janie Sellsers Van Pelt [TLF No. 3456].

(Sup) 7462   i   Stuart Van Pelt, Jr.

(Sup) 5758   MARY ELLEN LICKFOLD (Alfred^8, Amanda^7, John^6, Elizabeth^5, John^4, Peter^3, Matthias^2, John Jacob^1) was the daughter of Alfred John and Mary Newlen Lickfold [TLF No. 3460]. Mary Ellen was born November 26, 1924.

(Sup) 5759   ALFRED JOHN LICKFOLD, JR. (Alfred^8, Amanda^7, John^6, Elizabeth^5, John^4, Peter^3, Matthias^2, John Jacob^1) was the son of Alfred John and Mary Newlen Lickfold [TLF No. 3460]. Alfred, Jr., was born January 25, 1927. He died June 15, 1948.

(Sup) 5760   ROBERT EDWARD LICKFOLD (Alfred^8, Amanda^7, John^6, Elizabeth^5, John^4, Peter^3, Matthias^2, John Jacob^1) was the son of Alfred John and Mary Talley Lickfold [TLF No. 3460]. Robert was born December 11, 1935, at Staunton, Virginia.

(Sup) 5761   ANNA LEE LICKFOLD (Alfred^8, Amanda^7, John^6, Elizabeth^5, John^4, Peter^3, Matthias^2, John Jacob^1) was the daughter of Alfred John and Mary Talley Lickfold [TLF No. 3460]. Anna was born May 25, 1938, at Staunton, Virginia.

(Sup) 5762   NELLIE LOUISE SHUMATE (Edith^8, Amanda^7, John^6, Elizabeth^5, John^4, Peter^3, Matthias^2, John Jacob^1) was the daughter of John Stephens and Edith Lickfold Shumate [TLF No. 3461]. She was born May 19, 1930, near Grottoes, Virginia.

(Sup) 5763   ALLEN LYON PENNY, JR. (Evelyn^8, Mamie^7, John^6, Elizabeth^5, John^4, Peter^3, Matthias^2, John Jacob^1) was the son of Allen Lyon and Evelyn Lambeth Penny [TLF No. 3462]. Allen, Jr., was born September 29, 1930, at Goldsboro, North Carolina.

(Sup) 5764   THOMAS LAMBETH PENNY (Evelyn^8, Mamie^7, John^6, Elizabeth^5, John^4, Peter^3, Matthias^2, John Jacob^1) was the son of Allen Lyon and Evelyn Lambeth Penny [TLF No. 3462]. Thomas was born May 29, 1932, at Leaksville, North Carolina.

(Sup) 5765   WILLIAM BELL PENNY (Evelyn^8, Mamie^7, John^6, Elizabeth^5, John^4, Peter^3, Matthias^2, John Jacob^1) was the son of Allen Lyon and Evelyn Lambeth Penny [TLF No. 3462]. William was born May 25, 1934, at Leaksville, North Carolina.

(Sup) 5766   HUGH FLEMING PENNY (Evelyn^8, Mamie^7, John^6, Elizabeth^5, John^4, Peter^3, Matthias^2, John Jacob^1) was the son of Allen Lyon and Evelyn Lambeth Penny [TLF No. 3462]. Hugh was born August 26, 1937, at Winston-Salem, North Carolina.

(Sup) 5767   JOHN ALLEN PENNY (Evelyn^8, Mamie^7, John^6, Elizabeth^5, John^4, Peter^3, Matthias^2, John Jacob^1) was the son of Allen Lyon and Evelyn Lambeth Penny [TLF No. 3462]. John was born August 26, 1937, at Winston-Salem, North Carolina, and died in infancy.

(Sup) 5768   DAVID LEE NEFF (Garland^8, David^7, Sarah^6, Catherine^5, John^4, Peter^3, Matthias^2, John Jacob^1) was the son of Garland Meredith and Grace Wehn Neff [TLF No. 3478]. David was born July 31, 1937, at Columbia, South Carolina.

(Sup) 5769   FRANK MARTIN NEFF (Garland^8, David^7, Sarah^6, Catherine^5, John^4, Peter^3, Matthias^2, John Jacob^1) was the son of Garland Meredith and Grace Wehn Neff [TLF No. 3478]. Frank was born June 8, 1942, at Miami, Florida.

(Sup) 5770   JACK WILBORN (Tessa^8, Alberta^7, Elizabeth^6, Daniel^5, John^4, Peter^3, Matthias^2, John Jacob^1) was the son of Carl and Tessa Quick Wilborn [TLF No. 3481].

(Sup) 5771   ROBERT WILBORN (Tessa^8, Alberta^7, Elizabeth^6, Daniel^5, John^4, Peter^3, Matthias^2, John Jacob^1) was the son of Carl and Tessa Quick Wilborn [TLF No. 3481].

(Sup) 5772   DALLAS MELVIN SANDERS (Hazel^8, Alberta^7, Elizabeth^6, Daniel^5, John^4, Peter^3, Matthias^2, John Jacob^1) was the son of William Merrill and Hazel Quick Sanders [TLF No. 3482]. Dallas was born June 28, 1908, at Starkweather, North Dakota. He married Sybella Eileen Sloniker May 30, 1934, at Emmetsburg, Iowa. Sybella was the daughter of William L. Sloniker and was born March 27, 1918, at Emmetsburg.

(Sup) 7466   i Donna Mae Sanders, born in 1936.
(Sup) 7467   ii Jo Anne Sanders, born in 1937.

(Sup) 5773   CHARLES PRESTON SANDERS (Hazel^8, Alberta^7, Elizabeth^6, Daniel^5, John^4, Peter^3, Matthias^2, John Jacob^1) was the son of William Merrill and Hazel Quick Sanders [TLF No. 3482]. Charles was born January 7, 1911, at Starkweather, North Dakota. He married Magaret Kathryn Quain September 27, 1929. Margaret was the daughter of John Quain and was born October 26, 1907, at Cando, North Dakota.

(Sup) 7468   i Elizabeth Sanders, born in 1930.

(Sup) 5774   VELMA LOUISE SANDERS (Hazel^8, Alberta^7, Elizabeth^6, Daniel^5, John^4, Peter^3, Matthias^2, John Jacob^1) was the daughter of William Merrill and Hazel Quick Sanders [TLF No. 3482]. Velma was born November 11, 1912, in Ramsey County, North Dakota. She married Paul Louis Axtman June 11, 1934, at Devils Lake, North Dakota. Paul was the son of Michael Felix Axtman and was born near Odessa, Russia, October 7, 1907. Velma and Paul adopted her cousin's son David [Supplement No. 5781].

Adopted   i David Louis Gibson Axtman, born April 19, 1942.

(Sup) 5775   LOUELLA ELIZABETH SANDERS (Hazel^8, Alberta^7, Elizabeth^6, Daniel^5, John^4, Peter^3, Matthias^2, John Jacob^1) was the daughter of William Merrill and Hazel Quick Sanders [TLF No. 3482]. Louella was born September 14, 1914 in Ramsey County, North Dakota. She married Lars Russell Duhn April 23, 1932, at Devils Lake, North Dakota. He was the son of Peter Larsen Duhn and was born April 18, 1898, in Palo Alto County, Iowa.

(Sup) 7469   i   Carol Ann Duhn, born October 12, 1932.
(Sup) 7470   ii Clifford Allen Duhn, born August 5, 1935.
(Sup) 7471   iii Larry Reno Duhn, born June 20, 1945.

(Sup) 5776 KATHRYN ALBERTA GIBSON (Rilla[8], Alberta[7], Elizabeth[6], Daniel[5], John[4], Peter[3], Matthias[2], John Jacob[1]) was the daughter of Claude and Rilla Quick Gibson [TLF No. 3483]. Kathryn was born December 20, 1914, at Starkweather, North Dakota. She married William Monaghan March 6, 1937, at Devils Lake, North Dakota. He was the son of William Monaghan and was born July 22, 1916, at Oberon, North Dakota.

(Sup) 7472   i   Ilaine Marie Monaghan, born March 21, 1936.
(Sup) 7473   ii   William Duane Monaghan, born September 12, 1937.
(Sup) 7474 iii   Shirley Ann Monaghan, born October 25, 1938.
(Sup) 7475   iv   Douglas Le Roy Monaghan, born and died Mar 1, 1944.
(Sup) 7476   v   Gerald Jerome Monaghan, born May 15, 1947.

(Sup) 5777 RAY LESLIE GIBSON (Rilla[8], Alberta[7], Elizabeth[6], Daniel[5], John[4], Peter[3], Matthias[2], John Jacob[1]) was the son of Claude and Rilla Quick Gibson [TLF No. 3483]. Ray married Edith Tweeten at Starkweather, North Dakota.

(Sup) 5778 IOLA MAY GIBSON (Rilla[8], Alberta[7], Elizabeth[6], Daniel[5], John[4], Peter[3], Matthias[2], John Jacob[1]) was the daughter of Claude and Rilla Quick Gibson [TLF No. 3483]. Iola was born December 1, 1918, in Cavalier County, North Dakota (twin of Viola). She died July 14, 1919.

(Sup) 5779 VIOLA ETHEL GIBSON (Rilla[8], Alberta[7], Elizabeth[6], Daniel[5], John[4], Peter[3], Matthias[2], John Jacob[1]) was the daughter of Claude and Rilla Quick Gibson [TLF No. 3483]. Viola was born December 1, 1918, in Cavalier County, North Dakota (twin of Iola).

(Sup) 5780 BERNARD PATRICK GIBSON (Rilla[8], Alberta[7], Elizabeth[6], Daniel[5], John[4], Peter[3], Matthias[2], John Jacob[1]) was the son of Claude and Rilla Quick Gibson [TLF No. 3483]. Bernard was born March 17, 1921, near Starkweather, North Dakota. He served three years and six months overseas in the U.S. military forces during World War II.

(Sup) 5781 EILEEN ISABELLE GIBSON (Rilla[8], Alberta[7], Elizabeth[6], Daniel[5], John[4], Peter[3], Matthias[2], John Jacob[1]) was the daughter of Claude and Rilla Quick Gibson [TLF No. 3483]. Eileen was born March 6, 1923.

(Sup) 7477   i   David Louis Gibson Axtman, born April 19 1942.

(Sup) 5782 WILMA JEAN GIBSON (Rilla[8], Alberta[7], Elizabeth[6], Daniel[5], John[4], Peter[3], Matthias[2], John Jacob[1]) was the daughter of Claude and Rilla Quick Gibson [TLF No. 3483]. Wilma Jean was born July 17, 1926, in Ramsey County, North Dakota.

(Sup) 5783 ROBERT VERNON QUICK (Hobart[8], Alberta[7], Elizabeth[6], Daniel[5], John[4], Peter[3], Matthias[2], John Jacob[1]) was the son of Hobart and Orpha Wagoner [TLF No. 3484]. Robert was born August 1, 1921.

(Sup) 5784 FRANK ALLEN FISHBURNE (Virginia[8], Albertine[7], Elizabeth[6], Daniel[5], John[4], Peter[3], Matthias[2], John Jacob[1]) was the son of Emmett F. and Virginia Ritchie Fishburne [TLF No. 3485]. Frank was born March 8, 1922, at Staunton, Virginia. He married Elaine Bailey October 18, 1943.

(Sup) 7478   i   Frank Allen Fishburne II, born April 1, 1946.

(Sup) 5785 STUART PAXTON FISHBURNE (Virginia[8], Albertine[7], Elizabeth[6], Daniel[5], John[4], Peter[3], Matthias[2], John Jacob[1]) was the son of Emmett F. and Virginia Ritchie Fishburne [TLF No. 3485]. Stuart was born September 11, 1924, at Staunton, Virginia.

(Sup) 5786 EMMETT RITCHIE FISHBURNE (Virginia[8], (Albertine[7], Eliza-beth[6], Daniel[5], John[4], Peter[3], Matthias[2], John Jacob[1]) was the son of Emmett F. and Virginia Ritchie Fishburne [TLF No. 3485]. He was born August 3, 1932, at Staunton, Virginia.

(Sup) 5787 MARTHA EVELYN SHUMATE (William[8], Annie[7], Elizabeth[6], Daniel[5], John[4], Peter[3], Matthias[2], John Jacob[1]) was the daughter of William Dallas and Leta Coyner Shumate [TLF No. 3487]. Martha was born September 23, 1919, at Waynesboro, Virginia. She married Robert Anderson September 14, 1938, at Emmettsburg, Maryland. Robert was the son of Reuben Nathaniel Anderson and was born March 8, 1919, at Youngstown, Ohio.

(Sup) 7479   i   Robert Paul Anderson, Jr., born September 24, 1939.

(Sup) 5788 WILLIAM DALLAS SHUMATE, JR. (William[8], Annie[7], Elizabeth[6], Daniel[5], John[4], Peter[3], Matthias[2], John Jacob[1]) was the son of William Dallas and Leta Coyner Shumate [TLF No. 3487]. William, Jr., was born December 23, 1923, at Waynesboro, Virginia.

(Sup) 5789   MARRIANE K. SHUMATE (William[8], Annie[7], Elizabeth[6], Daniel[5], John[4], Peter[3], Matthias[2], John Jacob[1]) was the daughter of William Dallas and Leta Coyner Shumate [TLF No. 3487]. Marriane was born May 18, 1932, at Waynesboro, Virginia.

(Sup) 5790   ANNE BELLE SHUMATE (Stanley[8], Annie[7], Elizabeth[6], Daniel[5], John[4], Peter[3], Matthias[2], John Jacob[1]) was the daughter of Stanley A. and Arlene Hiner Shumate [TLF No. 3488]. She was born at Waynesboro, Virginia.

(Sup) 5791   CARL SHUMATE (Stanley[8], Annie[7], Elizabeth[6], Daniel[5], John[4], Peter[3], Matthias[2], John Jacob[1]) was the son of Stanley A. and Arlene Hiner Shumate [TLF No. 3488].

(Sup) 5792   ELEANOR SHUMATE (Albert[8], Annie[7], Elizabeth[6], Daniel[5], John[4], Peter[3], Matthias[2], John Jacob[1]) was the daughter of Albert and Lottie Talliaferro Shumate [TLF No. 3489]. Eleanor was born August 2, 1932, at Staunton, Virginia.

(Sup) 5793   GEORGE DALLAS SHUMATE (Albert[8], Annie[7], Elizabeth[6], Daniel[5], John[4], Peter[3], Matthias[2], John Jacob[1]) was the son of Albert and Lottie Talliaferro Shumate [TLF No. 3489]. George was born March 11, 1939, at Harrisonburg, Virginia.

(Sup) 5794   THOMAS JOSEPH SHUMATE (Alfred[8], Annie[7], Elizabeth[6], Daniel[5], John[4], Peter[3], Matthias[2], John Jacob[1]) was the son of Alfred and Ellen Hanger Burkholder Shumate [TLF No. 3490]. Thomas was born October 15, 1929, at Staunton, Virginia.

(Sup) 5795   KATHLEEN ALLEN SHUMATE (Alfred[8], Annie[7], Elizabeth[6], Daniel[5], John[4], Peter[3], Matthias[2], John Jacob[1]) was the daughter of Alfred and Ellen Hanger Burkholder Shumate [TLF No. 3490]. Kathleen was born June 1, 1931, at Staunton, Virginia.

(Sup) 5796   ROBERT HANGER SHUMATE (Alfred[8], Annie[7], Elizabeth[6], Daniel[5], John[4], Peter[3], Matthias[2], John Jacob[1]) was the son of Alfred and Ellen Hanger Burkholder Shumate [TLF No. 3490]. Robert was born October 27, 1935, at Staunton, Virginia.

(Sup) 5797   JEAN ANNETTE CUPP (Phyllis[8], Annie[7], Elizabeth[6], Daniel[5], John[4], Peter[3], Matthias[2], John Jacob[1]) was the daughter of Charles W. and Phyllis Shumate Cupp [TLF No. 3492]. Jean was born February 21, 1935, near Raphine, Virginia.

(Sup) 5798   THOMAS KEITH CUPP (Phyllis[8], Annie[7], Elizabeth[6], Daniel[5], John[4], Peter[3], Matthias[2], John Jacob[1]) was the son of Charles W. and Phyllis Shumate Cupp [TLF No. 3492]. Thomas was born February 20, 1946, at Staunton, Virginia.

(Sup) 5799   DONALD NORMAN LINK (Raymond[8], Amanda[7], John[6], Daniel[5], John[4], Peter[3], Matthias[2], John Jacob[1]) was the son of Raymond and Leona Wine Link [TLF No. 3493]. Donald was born June 23, 1933, in Augusta County, Virginia.

(Sup) 5800   PAULA DAWN HUDSON (Carl[8], Laura[7], Daniel[6], Daniel[5], John[4], Peter[3], Matthias[2], John Jacob[1]) was the daughter of Carl Chalmers and Marie Warren Hudson [TLF No. 3494]. Paula was born May 13, 1930, at Middletown, New York.

(Sup) 5801   GLENN CHALMERS HUDSON (Carl[8], Laura[7], Daniel[6], Daniel[5], John[4], Peter[3], Matthias[2], John Jacob[1]) was the son of Carl Chalmers and Marie Warren Hudson [TLF No. 3494]. Glenn was born September 9, 1931, at Middletown, New York.

(Sup) 5802   MARY JOYCE HUDSON (Carl[8], Laura[7], Daniel[6], Daniel[5], John[4], Peter[3], Matthias[2], John Jacob[1]) was the daughter of Carl Chalmers and Marie Warren Hudson [TLF No. 3494]. Mary was born April 18, 1934, at Middletown, New York.

(Sup) 5803   JAY ALLEN HUDSON (Carl[8], Laura[7], Daniel[6], Daniel[5], John[4], Peter[3], Matthias[2], John Jacob[1]) was the son of Carl Chalmers and Marie Warren Hudson [TLF No. 3494]. Jay was born July 8, 1938, at Middletown, New York.

(Sup) 5804   ISABELL EUDORA BOWARD (Dorothy[8], David[7], Daniel[6], Daniel[5], John[4], Peter[3], Matthias[2], John Jacob[1]) was the daughter of Lacy Crum and Dorothy Link Boward [TLF No. 3498]. Isabell was born October 23, 1933, in Augusta County, Virginia.

(Sup) 5805 DAVID FLOYD SIMMONS (Endora[8], David[7], Daniel[5], John[4], Peter[3], Matthias[2], John Jacob[1]) was the son of David Luther and Endora Link Simmons [TLF No. 3499]. He was born June 8, 1939, in Augusta County, Virginia.

(Sup) 5806 MARTHA AGNES SIMMONS (Endora[8], David[7], Daniel[5], John[4], Peter[3], Matthias[2], John Jacob[1]) was the daughter of David Luther and Endora Link Simmons [TLF No. 3499]. Martha was born November 12, 1945, in Augusta County, Virginia.

(Sup) 5807 LINDA ANNE LINK (Lacy[8], David[7], Daniel[5], John[4], Peter[3], Matthias[2], John Jacob[1]) was the daughter of Lacy Ausbert and Daisy Draine Link [TLF No. 3500]. Linda was born May 30, 1945.

(Sup) 5808 VIRGINIA LUCILLE MEYERHOEFFER (Delpha[8], Samuel[7], Daniel[6], Daniel[5], John[4], Peter[3], Matthias[2], John Jacob[1]) was the daughter of Wade William and Delpha Virginia Link Meyerhoeffer [TLF No. 3502]. Virginia was born December 4, 1923, in Augusta County, Virginia. She married Harry Weaver March 17, 1945.

(Sup) 5809 WILLIAM WADE MEYERHOEFFER (Delpha[8], Samuel[7], Daniel[6], Daniel[5], John[4], Peter[3], Matthias[2], John Jacob[1]) was the son of Wade William and Delpha Virginia Link Meyerhoeffer [TLF No. 3502]. William was born October 6, 1925, in Augusta County, Virginia. He married Lois Weaver May 30, 1947.

(Sup) 5810 ELLEN ELLAINE MEYERHOEFFER (Delpha[8], Samuel[7], Daniel[6], Daniel[5], John[4], Peter[3], Matthias[2], John Jacob[1]) was the daughter of Wade William and Delpha Virginia Link Meyerhoeffer [TLF No. 3502]. Ellen was born November 26, 1927, in Augusta County, Virginia. She married Warren Drumheller November 19, 1946.

(Sup) 5811 MARTHA LEE MEYERHOEFFER (Delpha[8], Samuel[7], Daniel[6], Daniel[5], John[4], Peter[3], Matthias[2], John Jacob[1]) was the daughter of Wade William and Delpha Virginia Link Meyerhoeffer [TLF No. 3502]. Martha was born January 18, 1930, in Augusta County, Virginia.

(Sup) 5812 MILDRED ANN MEYERHOEFFER (Delpha[8], Samuel[7], Daniel[6], Daniel[5], John[4], Peter[3], Matthias[2], John Jacob[1]) was the daughter of Wade William and Delpha Virginia Link Meyerhoeffer [TLF No. 3502]. Mildred was born November 25, 1932, in Augusta County, Virginia.

(Sup) 5813 SARAH KATHERYN MEYERHOEFFER (Delpha[8], Samuel[7], Daniel[6], Daniel[5], John[4], Peter[3], Matthias[2], John Jacob[1]) was the daughter of Wade William and Delpha Virginia Link Meyerhoeffer [TLF No. 3502]. Sarah was born June 2, 1935, in Augusta County, Virginia.

(Sup) 5814 NELSON B. MEYERHOEFFER (Delpha[8], Samuel[7], Daniel[6], Daniel[5], John[4], Peter[3], Matthias[2], John Jacob[1]) was the son of Wade William and Delpha Virginia Link Meyerhoeffer [TLF No. 3502]. Nelson was born June 11, 1938, in Augusta County, Virginia.

(Sup) 5815 PATRICIA ANNE LINK (Raymond[8], Samuel[7], Daniel[6], Daniel[5], John[4], Peter[3], Matthias[2], John Jacob[1]) was the daughter of Raymond Walter and Gretchen Hitt Link [TLF No. 3504]. Patricia was born July 10, 1940, at Staunton, Virginia.

(Sup) 5816 REBECCA JOAN STOVER (Pauline[8], Samuel[7], Daniel[6], Daniel[5], John[4], Peter[3], Matthias[2], John Jacob[1]) was the daughter of Sidney L. and Pauline Link Stover [TLF No. 3507]. Rebecca was born August 31, 1945, at Staunton, Virginia.

(Sup) 5817 KAY FRANCES TRUXELL (Cleta[8], Samuel[7], Daniel[6], Daniel[5], John[4], Peter[3], Matthias[2], John Jacob[1]) was the daughter of Clarence D. and Cleta Frances Link Truxell [TLF No. 3508]. Kay was born August 14, 1943, at Baltimore, Maryland (twin of Fay).

(Sup) 5818 FAY DOUGLAS TRUXELL (Cleta[8], Samuel[7], Daniel[6], Daniel[5], John[4], Peter[3], Matthias[2], John Jacob[1]) was the daughter of Clarence D. and Cleta Frances Link Truxell [TLF No. 3508]. Fay was born August 14, 1943, at Baltimore, Maryland (twin of Kay).

(Sup) 5819 WILFRED LINK SMITH (Helen[8], George[7], Daniel[6], Daniel[5], John[4], Peter[3], Matthias[2], John Jacob[1]) was the son of Golden McClune and Helen Link Smith [TLF No. 3509]. Wilfred was born September 25, 1929, in Augusta County, Virginia.

(Sup) 5820 GOLDIE ANN SMITH (Helen[8], George[7], Daniel[6], Daniel[5], John[4], Peter[3], Matthias[2], John Jacob[1]) was the daughter of Golden McClune and Helen Link Smith [TLF No. 3509]. Goldie Ann was born February 5, 1943, in Augusta County, Virginia.

(Sup) 5821 ANN HILTON WENGER (Eunice^8, John^7, Daniel^6, Daniel^5, John^4, Peter^3, Matthias^2, John Jacob^1) was the daughter of Tracy and Eunice Link Wenger [TLF No. 3516]. Ann was born September 13, 1945, at Staunton, Virginia.

(Sup) 5822 EDITH BARTON TUTWILER (Otis^8, Emma^7, Margaret^6, Daniel^5, John^4, Peter^3, Matthias^2, John Jacob^1) was the daughter of Otis Hampton and Lillian Bauserman Tutwiler [TLF No. 3525]. Edith was born January 3, 1919, in Augusta County, Virginia. She married Jack Evans Kincheloe December 24, 1940, at Mount Crawford, Virginia. Jack was the son of Phillip R. Kincheloe and was born September 4, 1918, at Harrisonburg, Virginia.

(Sup) 7484   i Robert Evans Kincheloe, born September 18, 1941.
(Sup) 7485   ii Stephen Richard Kincheloe, born August 2, 1946.

(Sup) 5823 PAULINE La VAN TUTWILER (Otis^8, Emma^7, Margaret^6, Daniel^5, John^4, Peter^3, Matthias^2, John Jacob^1) was the daughter of Otis Hampton and Lillian Bauserman Tutwiler [TLF No.3525]. Pauline was born September 6, 1921, in Augusta County, Virginia. She married Mervil James Hensley in 1941.

(Sup) 5824 DOROTHY MARIE TUTWILER (Otis^8, Emma^7, Margaret^6, Daniel^5, John^4, Peter^3, Matthias^2, John Jacob^1) was the daughter of Otis Hampton and Lillian Bauserman Tutwiler [TLF No. 3525]. Dorothy was born January 14, 1925, in Augusta County, Virginia. She married James Edward Chaplin in 1944.

(Sup) 5825 RUTH ADOREE TUTWILER (Otis^8, Emma^7, Margaret^6, Daniel^5, John^4, Peter^3, Matthias^2, John Jacob^1) was the daughter of Otis Hampton and Lillian Bauserman Tutwiler [TLF No. 3525]. Ruth was born November 2, 1927, in Augusta County, Virginia. She married Tribbett Hall Painer, Jr., in 1954.

(Sup) 5826 MARSHALL BARE, JR. (Dorothy^8, Harvey^7, Margaret^6, Daniel^5, John^4, Peter^3, Matthias^2, John Jacob^1) was the son of Marshall and Dorothy Fry Bare [TLF No. 3529]. Marshall, Jr., was born July 8, 1933, at Augusta County, Virginia.

(Sup) 5827 VIRGINIA JOYCE ALEXANDER (Raymond^8, Oscar^7, Mary^6, Daniel^5, John^4, Peter^3, Matthias^2, John Jacob^1) was the daughter of Raymond Robert and Mary Alexander [TLF No. 3530]. Virginia was born July 8, 1933, in Augusta County, Virginia.

(Sup) 5828 ELVIN GARDELL ALEXANDER, JR. (Elvin^8, Irenus^7, Mary^6, Daniel^5, John^4, Peter^3, Matthias^2, John Jacob^1) was the son of Elvin Gardell and Reba Francs Alexander [TLF No. 3535].

(Sup) 5829 HILDA LEE ALEXANDER (Elvin^8, Irenus^7, Mary^6, Daniel^5, John^4, Peter^3, Matthias^2, John Jacob^1) was the daughter of Elvin Gardell and Reba Frances Alexander [TLF No. 3535].

(Sup) 5830 HAROLD PHILLIP ALEXANDER (Elvin^8, Irenus^7, Mary^6, Daniel^5, John^4, Peter^3, Matthias^2, John Jacob^1) was the son of Elvin Gardell and Reba Frances Alexander [TLF No. 3535].

(Sup) 5831 CAROLYN MAY ALEXANDER (William^8, Irenus^7, Mary^6, Daniel^5, John^4, Peter^3, Matthias^2, John Jacob^1) was the daughter of William D. and Maybelle Ramsey Alexander [TLF No. 3537]. Carolyn was born July 12, 1942, at Staunton, Virginia.

(Sup) 5832 JOAN DALE ALEXANDER (William^8, Irenus^7, Mary^6, Daniel^5, John^4, Peter^3, Matthias^2, John Jacob^1) was the daughter of William D. and Maybelle Ramsey Alexander [TLF No. 3537]. Joan was born December 23, 1945, at Staunton, Virginia.

(Sup) 5833 SHELVIA JEAN ALEXANDER (William^8, Irenus^7, Mary^6, Daniel^5, John^4, Peter^3, Matthias^2, John Jacob^1) was the daughter of William D. and Maybellee Ramsey Alexander [TLF No. 3537]. She was born March 14, 1947, at Staunton, Virginia.

(Sup) 5834 LOLA LEE CHRISTIAN (Reda^8, John^7, Mary^6, Daniel^5, John^4, Peter^3, Matthias^2, John Jacob^1) was the daughter of Hugh Alexander and Reda Alexander Christian [TLF No. 3543]. Lola was born January 21, 1942, at Weyers Cave, Virginia.

(Sup) 5835 HUGH ALEXANDER CHRISTIAN, JR. (Reda^8, John^7, Mary^6, Daniel^5, John^4, Peter^3, Matthias^2, John Jacob^1) was the son of Hugh Alexander and Reda Alexander Christian [TLF No. 3543]. Hugh was born November 27, 1945, at Centerville, Virginia.

- -

(Sup) 5841 ROGER MILTON ALEXANDER (Melvin[8], Oney[7], Mary[6], Daniel[5], John[4], Peter[3], Matthias[2], John Jacob[1]) was the son of Melvin Harry and Goldie Elizabeth Roadcap Alexander [TLF No. 3551]. Roger was born March 4, 1946, in Augusta County, Virginia.

(Sup) 5842 ROBERT LEWIS WENGER (Angeline[8], Daniel[7], Martin[6], Daniel[5], John[4], Peter[3], Matthias[2], John Jacob[1]) was the son of Joseph Lewis and Angeline Link Wenger [TLF No. 3554]. Robert was born January 27, 1931, in Augusta County, Virginia.

(Sup) 5843 JENNIE ELLEN WENGER (Angeline[8], Daniel[7], Martin[6], Daniel[5], John[4], Peter[3], Matthias[2], John Jacob[1]) was the daughter of Joseph Lewis and Angeline Link Wenger [TLF No. 3554]. Jennie was born May 28, 1933, in Augusta County, Virginia.

(Sup) 5844 MILDRED LOUISE WENGER (Angeline[8], Daniel[7], Martin[6], Daniel[5], John[4], Peter[3], Matthias[2], John Jacob[1]) was the daughter of Joseph Lewis and Angeline Link Wenger [TLF No. 3554]. Mildred was born December 22, 1940, in Augusta County, Virginia.

(Sup) 5845 CAROLYN KAY WENGER (Angeline[8], Daniel[7], Martin[6], Daniel[5], John[4], Peter[3], Matthias[2], John Jacob[1]) was the daughter of Joseph Lewis and Angeline Link Wenger [TLF No. 3554]. Carolyn was born September 15, 1945, in Augusta County, Virginia.

(Sup) 5846 ANNA JANE LINK (Elwood[8], Daniel[7], Martin[6], Daniel[5], John[4], Peter[3], Matthias[2], John Jacob[1]) was the daughter of Elwood Ralph and Mary Alexander Link [TLF No. 3555]. Anna Jane was born March 15, 1933, in Augusta County, Virginia.

(Sup) 5847 BETTY LOU LINK (Elwood[8], Daniel[7], Martin[6], Daniel[5], John[4], Peter[3], Matthias[2], John Jacob[1]) was the daughter of Elwood Ralph and Mary Alexander Link [TLF No. 3555]. Betty Lou was born June 7, 1934, in Augusta County, Virginia.

(Sup) 5848 JOAN LINK (Elwood[8], Daniel[7], Martin[6], Daniel[5], John[4], Peter[3], Matthias[2], John Jacob[1]) was the daughter of Elwood Ralph and Mary Alexander Link [TLF No. 3555]. Joan was born May 10, 1936, in Augusta County, Virginia.

(Sup) 5849 MARY SUE LINK (Elwood[8], Daniel[7], Martin[6], Daniel[5], John[4], Peter[3], Matthias[2], John Jacob[1]) was the daughter of Elwood Ralph and Mary Alexander Link [TLF No. 3555]. Mary Sue was born February 10, 1938, in Augusta County, Virginia.

(Sup) 5850 ELWOOD RALPH LINK, JR. (Elwood[8], Daniel[7], Martin[6], Daniel[5], John[4], Peter[3], Matthias[2], John Jacob[1]) was the son of Elwood Ralph and Mary Alexander Link [TLF No. 3555]. Elwood, Jr., was born September 24, 1939, in Augusta County, Virginia.

(Sup) 5851 ROY CLINTON McALLISTER (Irene[8], Daniel[7], Martin[6], Daniel[5], John[4], Peter[3], Matthias[2], John Jacob[1]) was the son of Roy Francis and Irene Link McAllister [TLF No. 3556]. He was born December 21, 1944, in Augusta County, Virginia.

(Sup) 5852 JACQUELINE DORIS DAWSON (Hildred[8], Elizabeth[7], Martin[6], Daniel[5], John[4], Peter[3], Matthias[2], John Jacob[1]) was the daughter of Garfield Richard and Hildred Huffman Dawson [TLF No. 3560]. Jacqueline was born July 27, 1933.

(Sup) 5853 DONALD ALFRED GOOD (Martin[8], Clara[7], Martin[6], Daniel[5], John[4], Peter[3], Matthias[2], John Jacob[1]) was the son of Martin Luther and Martha Alexander Good [TLF No. 3563]. Donald was born October 2, 1937, at Mount Sidney, Virginia.

(Sup) 5854 NORMAN EUGENE GOOD (Martin[8], Clara[7], Martin[6], Daniel[5], John[4], Peter[3], Matthias[2], John Jacob[1]) was the son of Martin Luther and Martha Alexander Good [TLF No. 3563]. Norman was born August 31, 1940, at Mount Sidney, Virginia.

(Sup) 5855 MARTIN LUTHER GOOD, JR. (Martin[8], Clara[7], Martin[6], Daniel[5], John[4], Peter[3], Matthias[2], John Jacob[1]) was the son of Martin Luther and Martha Alexander Good [TLF No. 3563]. Martin, Jr., was born May 9, 1943, at Mount Sidney, Virginia.

(Sup) 5856 DAVID SAMUEL GOOD (Martin[8], Clara[7], Martin[6], Daniel[5], John[4], Peter[3], Matthias[2], John Jacob[1]) was the son of Martin Luther and Martha Alexander Good [TLF No. 3563]. David was born September 4, 1945, at Mount Sidney, Virginia.

(Sup) 5857 NANCY ELLEN WISE (Danie[8], Clara[7], Martin[6], Daniel[5], John[4], Peter[3], Matthias[2], John Jacob[1]) was the daughter of Eugene N. and Danie Good Wise [TLF No. 3564]. Nancy was born February 17, 1947, in Augusta County, Virginia.

(Sup) 5858 BETTY LOU HICKLIN (Edward[8], Mary[7], Martin[6], Daniel[5], John[4], Peter[3], Matthias[2], John Jacob[1]) was the daughter of Sylvia Edward and Fleeta Sheets Hicklin [TLF No. 3568]. Betty Lou was born November 13, 1938, in Augusta County, VA.

(Sup) 5859 WINSTON BARTH WINE, JR. (Winston[8], Jesse[7], Julia[6], Daniel[5], John[4], Peter[3], Matthias[2], John Jacob[1]) was the son of Winston Barth and Maude McChesney Wine [TLF No. 3569]. Winston, Jr., was born February 25, 1943, at Temple, Texas.

(Sup) 5860 JOAN CARLIE WINE (Winston[8], Jesse[7], Julia[6], Daniel[5], John[4], Peter[3], Matthias[2], John Jacob[1]) was the daughter of Winston Barth and Maude McChesney Wine [TLF No. 3569]. Joan was born January 12, 1945, at Richmond, Virginia.

(Sup) 5861 JUDITH TINN DENNISON (Juanita[8], Margaret[7], Julia[6], Daniel[5], John[4], Peter[3], Matthias[2], John Jacob[1]) was the daughter of Charles and Juanita Tinn Harshburger Dennison [TLF No. 3574].

(Sup) 5862 SARA SUE DENNISON (Juanita[8], Margaret[7], Julia[6], Daniel[5], John[4], Peter[3], Matthias[2], John Jacob[1]) was the daughter of Charles and Juanita Tinn Harshburger Dennison [TLF No. 3574].

(Sup) 5863 JANE ELLEN DENNISON (Juanita[8], Margaret[7], Julia[6], Daniel[5], John[4], Peter[3], Matthias[2], John Jacob[1]) was the daughter of Charles and Juanita Tinn Harshburger Dennison [TLF No. 3574].

(Sup) 5864 BRENDA ANN QUICK (William[8], William[7], Martha[6], Daniel[5], John[4], Peter[3], Matthias[2], John Jacob[1]) was the daughter of William Austin and Anna Tucker Quick [TLF No. 3588].

(Sup) 5865 WILLIAM FAYE ROSSER (Faye[8], William[7], Martha[6], Daniel[5], John[4], Peter[3], Matthias[2], John Jacob[1]) was the son of Lindsey and Faye Quick Rosser [TLF No. 3589].

(Sup) 5866 STUART QUICK (Richard[8], William[7], Martha[6], Daniel[5], John[4], Peter[3], Matthias[2], John Jacob[1]) was the son of Richard Rolander and Anita Kefauver Quick [TLF No. 3590].

(Sup) 5867 JAMES ALLEN CAMER, JR. (Phyllis[8], Edward[7], Martha[6], Daniel[5], John[4], Peter[3], Matthias[2], John Jacob[1]) was the son of James Allen and Phyllis Quick Camer [TLF No. 3592]. James, Jr., was born April 6, 1944, at Staunton, Virginia.

(Sup) 5868 EDWARD GLENN QUICK (Leroy[8], Edward[7], Martha[6], Daniel[5], John[4], Peter[3], Matthias[2], John Jacob[1]) was the son of LeRoy Glenwood and Thelma Anderson Quick [TLF No. 3593]. Edward was born September 13, 1946, at Staunton, Virginia.

(Sup) 5869 WILLIAM CLAY DOTSON (Evelyn[8], Edward[7], Martha[6], Daniel[5], John[4], Peter[3], Matthia[2], John Jacob[1]) was the son of Nelson Clay and Evelyn Quick Dotson [TLF No. 3594]. William was born October, 1946, at Staunton, Virginia.

- - - - - - - - - - - - - - - - - -

(Sup) 5871 RAYMOND MAURICE HOUFF (Roy[8], Joseph[7], John[6], Susan[5], John[4], Peter[3], Matthias[2], John Jacob[1]) was the son of Roy Gordon and Cora Pullins Houff [TLF No. 3618]. Raymond married Sarah Venable.

(Sup) 5872 ETHEL ANETTE HOUFF (Roy[8], Joseph[7], John[6], Susan[5], John[4], Peter[3], Matthias[2], John Jacob[1]) was the daughter of Roy Gordon and Cora Pullina Houff [TLF No. 3618].

(Sup) 5873 JOSEPH PAUL CLICK (Eva[8], Joseph[7], John[6], Susan[5], John[4], Peter[3], Matthias[2], John Jacob[1]) was the son of Forrest Daniel and Eva Houff Click [TLF No. 3620]. Joseph was born June 8, 1919, in Augusta County, Virginia. He married Catherine Smiley August 13, 1949.

(Sup) 5874 HARDENIS CAROLYN CLICK (Eva[8], Joseph[7], John[6], Susan[5], John[4], Peter[3], Matthias[2], John Jacob[1]) was the daughter of Forrest Daniel and Eva Houff Click [TLF No. 3620]. She was born September 7, 1923, In Augusta County, Virginia. She married John Hiram Zibler July 27, 1946.

(Sup) 5875 MARY HELEN CLICK (Eva[8], Joseph[7], John[6], Susan[5], John[4], Peter[3], Matthias[2], John Jacob[1]) was the daughter of Forrest Daniel and Eva Houff Click [TLF No. 3620]. She was born January 29, 1932, in Augusta County, Virginia.

(Sup) 5876 CHARLOTTE CATHERINE LANDES (Hazel[8], Joseph[7], John[6], Susan[5], John[4], Peter[3], Matthias[2], John Jacob[1]) was the daughter of William Austin and Hazel Houff Landes [TLF No. 3621]. Charlotte was born February 15, 1923, at Mount Sidney, Virginia.

(Sup) 5877 MAXINE ELLEN LANDES (Hazel[8], Joseph[7], John[6], Susan[5], John[4], Peter[3], Matthias[2], John Jacob[1]) was the daughter of William Austin and Hazel Houff Landes [TLF No. 3621]. Maxine was born August 14, 1924, at Mount Sidney, Virginia. She married William Harlan Dean April 17, 1947, at Harrisonburg, Virginia. He was the son of Samuel W. and Beulah Shiflett Dean and was born June 20, 1920.

(Sup) 7494   i William Harlan Dean, Jr.

(Sup) 5878 BERNICE IMOGENE LANDES (Hazel[8], Joseph[7], John[6], Susan[5], John[4], Peter[3], Matthias[2], John Jacob[1]) was the daughter of William Austin and Hazel Houff Landes [TLF No. 3621]. Bernice was born July 23, 1926, at Mount Sidney, Virginia. She married Hugh Berkley Snyder August 30, 1947, at Harrisonburg, Virginia. He was the son of Stanley F. and Ada Browning Snyder and was born July 17, 1916, at Staunton, Virginia.

(Sup) 7495   i Larry Berkley Snyder, born June 3, 1949.

(Sup) 5879 RICHARD STANLEY LANDES (Hazel[8], Joseph[7], John[6], Susan[5], John[4], Peter[3], Matthias[2], John Jacob[1]) was the son of William Austin and Hazel Houff Landes [TLF No. 3621].

(Sup) 5880 MARTHA LUCILLE LANDES (Hazel[8], Joseph[7], John[6], Susan[5], John[4], Peter[3], Matthias[2], John Jacob[1]) was the daughter of William Austin and Hazel Houff Landes [TLF No. 3621].

(Sup) 5881 NANCY LEE LANDES (Hazel[8], Joseph[7], John[6], Susan[5], John[4], Peter[3], Matthias[2], John Jacob[1]) was the daughter of William Austin and Hazel Houff Landes [TLF No. 3621].

(Sup) 5882 JAMES FRANKLIN LANDES (Hazel[8], Joseph[7], John[6], Susan[5], John[4], Peter[3], Matthias[2], John Jacob[1]) was the son of William Austin and Hazel Houff Landes [TLF No. 3621].

(Sup) 5883 HELEN RUTH LANDES (Hazel[8], Joseph[7], John[6], Susan[5], John[4], Peter[3], Matthias[2], John Jacob[1]) was the daughter of William Austin and Hazel Houff Landes [TLF No. 3621].

(Sup) 5884 MILDRED JUANITA SCOTT (Rice[8], Lulu[7], John[6], Susan[5], John[4], Peter[3], Matthias[2], John Jacob[1]) was the daughter of Rice Tatum and Ella Peters Scott [TLF No. 3622]. Mildred was born September 30, 1923, at Clifton Forge, Virginia.

(Sup) 5885 LOUIS MERRIAN SCOTT (Rice[8], Lulu[7], John[6], Susan[5], John[4], Peter[3], Matthias[2], John Jacob[1]) was the son of Rice Tatum and Ella Peters Scott [TLF No. 3622]. He was born March 9, 1927, at Clifton Forge, Virginia.

(Sup) 5886 MARY LOU SCOTT (Rice[8], Lulu[7], John[6], Susan[5], John[4], Peter[3], Matthias[2], John Jacob[1]) was the daughter of Rice Tatum and Ella Peters Scott [TLF No. 3622]. She was born January 26, 1900, at Clifton Forge, Virginia.

(Sup) 5887 ELIZABETH ANN SCOTT (Roy[8], Lulu[7], John[6], Susan[5], John[4], Peter[3], Matthias[2], John Jacob[1]) was the daughter of Roy Homer and Katherine Matheny Scott [TLF No. 3625]. Elizabeth was born September 26, 1940, at Kingston, West Virginia.

(Sup) 5888 MARGARET ANN CARMACK (Iva[8], Lulu[7], John[6], Susan[5], John[4], Peter[3], Matthias[2], John Jacob[1]) was the daughter of John and Iva Mae Scott Carmack [TLF No. 3625]. She was born July 2 1935.

(Sup) 5889 NANCY PATRICIA CARMACK (Iva[8], Lulu[7], John[6], Susan[5], John[4], Peter[3], Matthias[2], John Jacob[1]) was the daughter of John and Iva Mae Scott Carmack [TLF No. 3625]. She was born October 30, 1941.

(Sup) 5890 LOUIS A. HOUFF, JR. (Louis[8], Andrew[7], John[6], Susan[5], John[4], Peter[3], Matthias[2], John Jacob[1]) was the son of Louis A. and Ethel Bartlett Houff [TLF No. 3627]. Louis, Jr., was born February 5, 1936, at Clifton Forge, Virginia.

(Sup) 5891 JAMES NEFF HOUFF (Louis[8], Andrew[7], John[6], Susan[5], John[4], Peter[3], Matthias[2], John Jacob[1]) was the son of Louis A. and Ethel Bartlett Houff [TLF No. 3627]. James was born February 19, 1938, at Clifton Forge, Virginia.

(Sup) 5892 ARTHUR MILTON BARNES, JR. (Helen[8], Otey[7], Elizabeth[6], Susan[5], John[4], Peter[3], Matthias[2], John Jacob[1]) was the son of Arthur and Helen Hulvey Barnes [Supplement No. 3629]. Arthur, Jr., was born May 12, 1925, at Pittsburgh, Pennsylvania. He married Grace Miller September 4, 1948, at Verona, Pennsylvania. The daughter of Watt and Bess Ritchey Miller, she was born January 31, 1927, at Verona, Pennsylvania.

(Sup) 7498   i   Susan Barnes, born January 12, 1950.
(Sup) 7499   ii   Donald Barnes, born April 28, 1952.
(Sup) 7500   iii Vicki Barnes, born May 8, 1959.

(Sup) 5893 ROBERT CRANFORD BARNES (Helen[8], Otey[7], Elizabeth[6], Susan[5], John[4], Peter[3], Matthias[2], John Jacob[1]) was the son of Arthur and Helen Hulvey Barnes [Supplement No. 3629]. Robert married Frances Stridinger April 1958, at Long Island, New York. She was the daughter of Ferdinand and Freida Kolak Stridinger and was born February 23, 1934, at Salix, Pennsylvania.

(Sup) 7501   i Laura Barnes, born January 19, 1959.
(Sup) 7502   ii Jeffrey Barnes, born August 11, 1962.

(Sup) 5894 WILLARD P. BRATTEN, JR. (Margery[8], Otey[7], Elizabeth[6], Susan[5], John[4], Peter[3], Matthias[2], John Jacob[1]) was the son of Willard P. and Margery Hulvey Bratten [TLF No. 3631].

(Sup) 5895 JAMES CRAWFORD BRATTEN (Margery[8], Otey[7], Elizabeth[6], Susan[5], John[4], Peter[3], Matthias[2], John Jacob[1]) was the son of Willard P. and Margery Hulvey Bratten [TLF No. 3631].

(Sup) 5896 JEAN PALMER JOHNSON (Wilbur[8], Florence[7], Elizabeth[6], Susan[5], John[4], Peter[3], Matthias[2], John Jacob[1]) was the daughter of Wilbur Hulvey and Catherine Coyner Johnson [TLF No. 3634]. She was born August 25, 1945, at Charlottesville, Virginia.

(Sup) 5897 ROBERT MICHAEL JOHNSON (Wilbur[8], Florence[7], Elizabeth[6], Susan[5], John[4], Peter[3], Matthias[2], John Jacob[1]) was the son of Wilbur Hulvey and Catherine Coyner Johnson [TLF No. 3634]. He was born March 18, 1947, at Charlottesville, Virginia.

(Sup) 5898 NEILA ROBERTA JOHNSON (James[8], Florence[7], Elizabeth[6], Susan[5], John[4], Peter[3], Matthias[2], John Jacob[1]) was the daughter of James Christian and Mildred Shaner Johnson [TLF No. 3635]. She was born June 17, 1946.

(Sup) 5899 WANDA JOANNE JOHNSON (James[8], Florence[7], Elizabeth[6], Susan[5], John[4], Peter[3], Matthias[2], John Jacob[1]) was the daughter of James Christian and Mildred Shaner Johnson [TLF No. 3635]. She was born July 2, 1947.

(Sup) 5900 HARRY COYT JOHNSON (Harry[8], Lulu[7], John[6], Susan[5], John[4], Peter[3], Matthias[2], John Jacob[1]) was the son of Harry Crawford and Virginia Daniel Johnson [TLF No. 3636]. Harry was born September 26, 1940, at Kingston, West Virginia.

(Sup) 5901 BARBARA ANNE MEYER (Thelma[8], John[7], Elizabeth[6], Susan[5], John[4], Peter[3], Matthias[2], John Jacob[1]) was the daughter of Frank C. and Thelma Hulvey Meyer [Supplement No. 3636B]. Barbara was born May 28, 1940, at

Brooklyn, New York. She was a Doctor of Medicine at the George Washington University, College of Medicine. She married Norman Marshall Meyers May 30, 1964, at Fulton, New York. Norman was the son of Norman and Catherine Meyers and was born October 14, 1938. He was a Doctor of Jurisprudence. Barbara and Norman lived at Washington, D.C.

(Sup) 7505   † John Marshall Meyers, born March 24, 1970.
(Sup) 7506   †i Edward Hulvey Meyers, born October 7, 1972.

(Sup) 5902 VIRGINIA HULVEY MEYER (Thelma[8], John[7], Elizabeth[6], Susan[5], John[4], Peter[3], Matthias[2], John Jacob[1]) was the daughter of Frank C. and Thelma Hulvey Meyer [Supplement No. 3636B]. Virginia was born June 18, 1941, at Brooklyn, New York. She attained the Doctor of Jurisprudence degree at the Delaware Law School, Widener University. She married Michael Joseph Morris, Jr., November 29, 1962, at Cherry Point, North Carolina. He was the son of Michael Joseph and Dollie Morris and was born January 18, 1938.

(Sup) 7507   † Michael Joseph Morris, III, born October 21, 1968.

(Sup) 5903 MARTHA MOWRY MEYER (Thelma[8], John[7], Elizabeth[6], Susan[5], John[4], Peter[3], Matthias[2], John Jacob[1]) was the daughter of Frank C. and Thelma Hulvey Meyer [Supplement No. 3636B]. Martha was born February 7, 1944, at Syracuse, New York. She married Robert Arthur Steinbach, III, December 18, 1965, at Oswego, New York. He was the son of Lester and Evelyn Woodward Steinbach and was born October 20, 1942, at Wausau, Wisconsin.

(Sup) 7508   † Christopher Mohr Steinbach, born February 3, 1968.
(Sup) 7509   ii Lesley Woodward Steinbach, born February 3, 1968.
(Sup) 7510 iii Sarah Meyer Steinbach, born December 17, 1973.

(Sup) 5904 MARY ELIZABETH MEYER (Thelma[8], John[7], Elizabeth[6], Susan[5], John[4], Peter[3], Matthias[2], John Jacob[1]) was the daughter of Frank C. and Thelma Hulvey Meyer [Supplement No. 36368]. Mary was born September 24, 1947, at Syracuse, New York.

(Sup) 5905 FRANK CHARLES MEYER, IV (Thelma[8], John[7], Elizabeth[6], Susan[5], John[4], Peter[3], Matthias[2], John Jacob[1]) was the son of Frank C. and Thelma Hulvey Meyer, III [Supplement No. 36368]. Frank. IV. was born January 6, 1950, at Syracuse, New York. He received the Doctor of Jurisprudence degree from McGeorge Law School, University of the Pacific (Sacramento, California). He married Elizabeth Anne Dressler November 17, 1972, at Portland, Oregon. She was the daughter of Robert Lyle and Margaret Dawn O'Day Dressler and was born July 16, 1950, at Portland.

(Sup) 7511   i Frank Charles Meyer V, born April 22, 1983.

(Sup) 5906 JOHN THOMAS HULVEY (John William[8], John[7], Elizabeth[6], Susan[5], John[4], Peter[3], Matthias[2], John Jacob[1]) was the son of John William and Lelia Radford Hulvey [Supplement No. 3636D]. He was born November 15, 1935, at Staunton, Virginia. John Thomas resided in Abingdon, Virginia, where he practiced orthopedic surgery. He married Elizabeth Kelsey February 8, 1964, at Salem, Virginia. She was the daughter of Paul Victor Kelsey.

(Sup) 7512 i   Elizabeth Kelsey Hulvey, born April 2, 1969.
(Sup) 7513 ii   Margaret Lewis Hulvey, born March 2, 1971.
(Sup) 7514 iii John Thomas Hulvey, Jr., born June 18, 1972.

(Sup) 5907 LARRY WILLIAM HULVEY (John William[8], John[7], Elizabeth[6], Susan[5], John[4], Peter[3], Matthias[2], John Jacob[1]) was the son of John William and Lelia Radford Hulvey [Supplement No. 3636D]. Larry was born May 16, 1943, at Staunton, Virginia. He married Judy Hensley June 6, 1966. They resided in Jesup, Georgia.

(Sup) 7515 i   Michael Hulvey, born November 9, 1973.
(Sup) 7516 ii   Jonathan Patrick Hulvey, born October 31,   .

(Sup) 5908 CONSTANCE ELAINE ALEXANDER (Helen[8], John[7], Elizabeth[6], Susan[5], John[4], Peter[3], Matthias[2], John Jacob[1]) was the daughter of Samuel and Helen Hulvey Alexander [Supplement No. 3636F]. She was born June 10, 1952, at Carlisle, Pennsylvania.

(Sup) 5909 STEVEN SCOTT ALEXANDER (Helen[8], John[7], Elizabeth[6], Susan[5], John[4], Peter[3], Matthias[2], John Jacob[1]) was the son of Samuel and Helen Hulvey Alexander [Supplement No. 3636F]. He was born July 25, 1956, at Carlisle, Pennsylvania.

(Sup) 5910 SUE ANN ALEXANDER (Helen[8], John[7], Elizabeth[6], Susan[5], John[4], Peter[3], Matthias[2], John Jacob[1]) was the daughter of Samuel and Helen Hulvey Alexander [Supplement No. 3636F]. She was born March 4, 1963, at Carlisle, Pennsylvania.

(Sup) 5911 ROBERT DALE HULVEY (Benjamin[8], Benjamin[7], Elizabeth[6], Susan[5], John[4], Peter[3], Matthias[2], John Jacob[1]) was the son of Benjamin F. and Virginia Thompson Hulvey [Supplement No. 3636H]. Robert was born March 29, 1932, at Staunton, Virginia. He married Joyce Yvonne Wine, October 11, 1951, at Fishersville, Virginia.

(Sup) 7519 i   Alan Dale Hulvey.
(Sup) 7520 ii   Kemper Franklin Hulvey.
(Sup) 7521 iii Judith Lee Hulvey.

(Sup) 5912 NANCY MILDRED HULVEY (Benjamin[8], Benjamin[7], Elizabeth[6], Susan[5], John[4], Peter[3], Matthias[2], John Jacob[1]) was the daughter of Benjamin F. and Virginia Thompson Hulvey [Supplement No. 3636H]. Nancy was born May 16, 1933, at Staunton, Virginia. She married Clay Edward Hewitt August 22, 1953, at Staunton.

(Sup) 7522 i   Neal Edward Hewitt.
(Sup) 7523 ii   Dennis Clay Hewitt.
(Sup) 7524 iii Jerry Nelson Hewitt.
(Sup) 7525 iv   Kathy Hewitt.

(Sup) 5913 ANNA VIRGINIA HULVEY (Benjamin[8], Benjamin[7], Elizabeth[6], Susan[5], John[4], Peter[3], Matthias[2], John Jacob[1]) was the daughter of Benjamin F. and Virginia Thompson Hulvey [Supplement No. 3636H]. She was born January 3, 1935, at Staunton, Virginia. She married Willis Earl McCray October 1, 1954, at Staunton.

(Sup) 7526 i   Janice Christine McCray.
(Sup) 7527 ii   Willis Earl McCray, Jr.
(Sup) 7528 iii Julia Ann McCray.
(Sup) 7529 iv   Stephen Scott McCray.
(Sup) 7530 v   Kevin Brian McCray.
(Sup) 7531 vi   Eric Clyde McCray.

(Sup) 5914 GLORIA JEAN HULVEY (Benjamin[8], Benjamin[7], Elizabeth[6], Susan[5], John[4], Peter[3], Matthias[2], John Jacob[1]) was the daughter of Benjamin F. and Virginia Thompson Hulvey [Supplement No. 3636H]. Gloria was born April 8, 1936, at Staunton, Virginia. She married James William Collins June 4, 1955, at Staunton. They were divorced.

(Sup) 7532 i   Kenneth Wayne Collins.
(Sup) 7533 ii   Beatrice Ann Collins.

(Sup) 5915 JAMES FRANKLIN HULVEY (Benjamin[8], Benjamin[7], Elizabeth[6], Susan[5], John[4], Peter[3], Matthias[2], John Jacob[1]) was the son of Benjamin F. and Virginia Thompson Hulvey [Supplement No. 3636H]. James was born June 21, 1938, at Staunton, Virginia. He married Shirley Sandy March 10, 1961, at Churchville, Virginia.

(Sup) 7534 i   Jennifer Lynn Hulvey.
(Sup) 7535 ii   Benjamin Price Hulvey.
(Sup) 7536 iii Kenneth Scott Hulvey.

(Sup) 5916   DONALD LEE WILBERGER (Mary^8, Benjamin^7, Elizabeth^6, Susan^5, John^4, Peter^3, Matthias^2, John Jacob^1) was the son of Russell Lee and Mary Elizabeth Hulvey Wilberger [Supplement No. 3636I]. Donald was born February 13, 1936, at Staunton, Virginia. He married Becky Harris October 18, 1957, at Staunton. She was born August 1, 1914.

(Sup) 7537   i   Tamany Lee Wilberger, born May 29, 1958.
(Sup) 7538   ii   Donna Sue Wilberger, born March 16, 1961.
(Sup) 7539   iii Christina Wilberger, born August 20, 1966.

(Sup) 5917   LUCY ANNA WINDHAM (Gladys^8, Benjamin^7, Elizabeth^6, Susan^5, Peter^3, Matthias^2, John Jacob^1) was the daughter of Bruce Eugene and Gladys Hulvey Windham [Supplement No. 3636J]. Lucy Anna was born September 27, 1938. She married, first, Jimmy R. Fleming in 1959. They were divorced in 1976. She married, second, Robert Dale Sipe.

CHILDREN OF LUCY ANNA AND JIMMY
(Sup) 7540   i   Franklin Eugene Fleming, born September 2, 1960.
(Sup) 7541   ii   Yvonne Lenora Fleming, born October 14, 1965.

CHILDREN OF LUCY ANNA AND ROBERT
(Sup) 7542   iii Bruce Eugene Sipe, born September 19, 1977.

(Sup) 5918   CAROL BRUCE WINDHAM (Gladys^8, Benjamin^7, Elizabeth^6, Susan^5, John^4, Peter^3, Matthias^2, John Jacob^1) was the daughter of Bruce Eugene and Gladys Hulvey Windham [Supplement No. 3636J]. Carol was born August 24, 1943. She married Wayne E. Stevens, who was born July 6, 1937.

(Sup) 7543   i   Wayne E. Stevens, Jr., born August 27, 1963.
(Sup) 7544   ii   James Franklin Stevens, born March 11, 1965.

(Sup) 5919   PATRICIA ANN VINES (Margaret^8, Benjamin^7, Elizabeth^6, Susan^5, John^4, Peter^3, Matthias^2, John Jacob^1) was the daughter of Jess Willard and Margaret Hulvey Vines [Supplement No. 3636K]. Patsy was born August 6, 1935. She married Simon Welcome Knapp September 28, 1951. He was born February 10, 1933.

(Sup) 7545   i   Deborah Kay Knapp, born April 30, 1952.
(Sup) 7546   ii   Diane Lee Knapp, born July 19, 1956.
(Sup) 7547   iii Jenny Elder Knapp, born February 15, 1964.
(Sup) 7548   iv   Patricia Studley Knapp, born March 1, 1969.

(Sup) 5920   JACQUELYN BURNS VINES (Margaret^8, Benjamin^7, Elizabeth^6, Susan^5, John^4, Peter^3, Matthias^2, John Jacob^1) was the daughter of Jess Willard and Margaret Hulvey Vines [Supplement No. 3636K]. Jacquelyn was born February 7, 1940. She married Mack Chapman Kester March 27, 1959. He was born February 24, 1934.

(Sup) 7549   i   Renee Carianne Kester, born March 11, 1961.
(Sup) 7550   ii   Mack Chapman Kester, Jr., born March 24, 1966.

(Sup) 5921   WANDA LOUISE HULVEY (Howard^8, Benjamin^7, Elizabeth^6, Susan^5, John^4, Peter^3, Matthias^2, John Jacob^1) was the daughter of Howard M. and Genevieve Ellinger Hulvey [Supplement No. 3636L]. She was born October 26, 1939, at Fredericksburg, Virginia. She married Leslie F. Swift.

(Sup) 7551   i   Matthew Thomas Swift, born August 24, 1965.

(Sup) 5922   BENJAMIN EARL HULVEY (Howard^8, Benjamin^7, Elizabeth^6, Susan^5, John^4, Peter^3, Matthias^2, John Jacob^1) was the son of Howard M. and Genevieve Ellinger Hulvey [Supplement No. 3636L]. He was born November 5, 1953, at Staunton, Virginia. He married Barbara Ann Lotts.

(Sup) 7552   i   Sherry Ann Hulvey, born November 24, 1965.
(Sup) 7553   ii   Christopher Earl Hulvey, born August 26, 1969.

(Sup) 5923   JEAN MEREDITH HULVEY (Charles^8, Charles^7, Elizabeth^6, Susan^5, John^4, Peter^3, Matthias^2, John Jacob^1) was the daughter of Charles Newton and Jean Meredith Sprague Hulvey [Supplement No. 3636H]. Jean was born October 31, 1952, at Washington, D.C., and died November 17, 1952.

(Sup) 5924   JOHN HENRY WRIGHT, III (Margaret^8, Charles^7, Elizabeth^6, Susan^5, John^4, Peter^3, Matthias^2, John Jacob^1) was the son of John Henry and Margaret Hulvey Wright, Jr. [Supplement No. 3636N]. John Henry, III, was born April 25, 1939, at Charlottesville, Virginia. He attended the University of Virginia, from which he received the B.S. and M.B.A. degrees. He was president of the John H. Wright Co. in Columbus, South Carolina. He married Trida Leventis, May 8, 1965. She was the daughter of Chris P. and Catherine Leventis.

(Sup) 7554   i   Catherine Margaret Wright, born June 5, 1972.
(Sup) 7555   ii   John Henry Wright, IV, born February 9, 1975.

(Sup) 5925   JOHN WILLIAM HULVEY, JR. (William^8, Charles^7, Elizabeth^6, Susan^5, John^4, peter^3, Matthias^2, John Jacob^1) was the son of John William and Virginia Lee Broome Hulvey [Supplement No. 3636K]. John William, Jr., was born January 24, 1949, at Lewiston, Idaho. He received a B.A. degree in English literature from the University of North Florida. He married Shirley Refuse June 9, 1973, at Jacksonville, Florida. She was the daughter of James and Myako Conger and was born August 21, 1949, at Tokyo, Japan. John William and Shirley lived at Berkeley, California.

(Sup) 5926 ELIZABETH CULLEN HULVEY (William[8], Charles[7], Elizabeth[6], Sarah[5], John[4], Peter[3], Matthias[2], John Jacob[1]) was the daughter of John William and Virginia Lee Broome Hulvey [Supplement No. 3636K]. Elizabeth was born May 18, 1951, at Jersey City, New Jersey. She received a bachelors degree in fine arts from Jacksonville University. She married Mr. Hupp. They were divorced. Elizabeth resided at Mesa, Arizona.

(Sup) 7556   1 Christian Archer Hupp, born May 4, 1975.

(Sup) 5927 CHARLES NEWTON HULVEY, III (William[8], Charles[7], Elizabeth[6], Sarah[5], John[4], Peter[3], Matthias[2], John Jacob[1]) was the son of John William and Virginia Lee Broome Hulvey [Supplement No. 3636K]. Charles was named after his uncle Charles Newton Hulvey, and was born December 17, 1957, at Bryn Mawr, Pennsylvania. He received a B.A. degree in political science from Old Dominion University and resided at Virginia Beach, Virginia.

(Sup) 5928 SARAH ARCHER HULVEY (William[8], Charles[7], Elizabeth[6], Susan[5], John[4], Peter[3], Matthias[2], John Jacob[1]) was the daughter of John William and Virginia Lee Broome Hulvey [Supplement No. 3636K]. Sarah was born November 2, 1959, at Bryn Mawr, Pennsylvania. She received a B.S. degree in business management from Marymount Manhattan College (New York City). She resided at Toronto, Ontario, Canada.

(Sup) 5929 HERBERT DWIGHT SHEETS, JR. (Herbert[8], Otto[7], Sarah[6], Susan[5], John[4], Peter[3], Matthias[2], John Jacob[1]) was the son of Herbert Dwight and Crystal Wiseman Sheets [TLF No. 3638].

(Sup) 5930 EUGENE EARL SHEETS (Herbert[8], Otto[7], Sarah[6], Susan[5], John[4], Peter[3], Matthias[2], John Jacob[1]) was the son of Herbert Dwight and Crystal Wiseman Sheets [TLF No. 3638].

(Sup) 5931 AUDREY LA VERNE SHATTUCK (Eva[8], Otto[7], Sarah[6], Susan[5], John[4], Peter[3], Matthias[2], John Jacob[1]) was the daughter of James and Eva Virginia Sheets Shattuck [TLF No. 3640]. Audrey married a Mr. Sinton.

(Sup) 7559   1 Carol Anne Sinton.

(Sup) 5932 MARY LOU SHATTUCK (Eva[8], Otto[7], Sarah[6], Susan[5], John[4], Peter[3], Matthias[2], John Jacob[1]) was the daughter of James and Eva Virginia Sheets Shattuck [TLF No. 3640].

(Sup) 5933 JOAN CHRISTINE WRIGHT (Minnie[8], Otto[7], Sarah[6], Susan[5], John[4], Peter[3], Matthias[2], John Jacob[1]) was the daughter of Medford and Minnie Bell Sheets Wright [TLF No. 3641].

(Sup) 5934 KENNETH LESTER RHINEHART (Mary[8], Otto[7], Sarah[6], Susan[5], John[4], Peter[3], Matthias[2], John Jacob[1]) was the son of Lester and Mary Elizabeth Sheets Rhinehart [TLF No. 3642]. Kenneth was born August 8, 1936, at Middletown, New York.

(Sup) 5935 WILLIAM OTTO RHINEHART (Mary[8], Otto[7], Sarah[6], Susan[5], John[4], Peter[3], Matthias[2], John Jacob[1]) was the son of Lester and Mary Elizabeth Sheets Rhinehart [TLF No. 3642]. William was born June 21, 1939, at Middletown, New York.

(Sup) 5936 IVAN WAYNE SHEETS (Meredith[8], Mary[7], Sarah[6], Susan[5], John[4], Peter[3], Matthias[2], John Jacob[1]) was the son of Meredith Wayne and Mary Daisy Dowring Sheets [TLF No. 3643]. He was born May 7, 1938, at Grinnell, Iowa.

(Sup) 5937 MELVIN ROBERT SHEETS (Meredith[8], Mary[7], Sarah[6], Susan[5], John[4], Peter[3], Matthias[2], John Jacob[1]) was the son of Meredith Wayne and Mary Daisy Dowring Sheets [TLF No. 3643]. He was born June 22, 1940, at Grinnell, Iowa.

(Sup) 5938 JAMES DWIGHT SHEETS (Meredith[8], Mary[7], Sarah[6], Susan[5], John[4], Peter[3], Matthias[2], John Jacob[1]) was the son of Meredith Wayne and Mary Daisy Dowring Sheets [TLF No. 3643]. He was born December 8, 1944, at Grinnell, Iowa.

(Sup) 5939 PATSY ANN SHEETS (Stover[8], Mary[7], Sarah[6], Susan[5], John[4], Peter[3], Matthias[2], John Jacob[1]) was the daughter of Stover McClain and Mabel Irene Parker Sheets [TLF No. 3645]. She was born and died May 27, 1937, at Deep River, Iowa.

(Sup) 5940 YVONNE KAY SHEETS (Stover[8], Mary[7], Sarah[6], Susan[5], John[4], Peter[3], Matthias[2], John Jacob[1]) was the daughter of Stover McClain and Mabel Irene Parker Sheets [TLF No. 3645]. She was born May 1, 1939, at Deep River, Iowa.

(Sup) 5941 ROBERT LE ROY SHEETS (Stover[8], Mary[7], Sarah[6], Susan[5], John[4], Peter[3], Matthias[2], John Jacob[1]) was the son of Stover McClain and Mabel Irene Parker Sheets [TLF No. 3645]. He was born January 25, 1941, at Deep River, Iowa.

(Sup) 5942 SALLIE JANE SIMMONS (Isa[8], Arvil[7], Sarah[6], Susan[5], John[4], Peter[3], Matthias[2], John Jacob[1]) was the daughter of Roy B. and Isa Virginia Sheets Simmons [TLF No. 3647]. She was born September 11, 1936, in Augusta County, Virginia.

(Sup) 5943 WILLIAM ARVIL SIMMONS (Isa[8], Arvil[7], Sarah[6], Susan[5], John[4], Peter[3], Matthias[2], John Jacob[1]) was the son of Roy B. and Isa Virginia Sheets Simmons [TLF No. 3647]. He was born November 29, 1938, in Augusta County, Virginia.

(Sup) 5944 DOROTHY LEE SHEETS (Paul[8], Arvil[7], Sarah[6], Susan[5], John[4], Peter[3], Matthias[2], John Jacob[1]) was the son of Paul Stickley and Joanna Bright Sheets [TLF No. 3648]. Dorothy was born January 6, 1938, at Staunton, Virginia.

(Sup) 5945 REBECCA SUE SHEETS (Paul[8], Arvil[7], Sarah[6], Susan[5], John[4], Peter[3], Matthias[2], John Jacob[1]) was the daughter of Paul Stickley and Joanna Bright Sheets [TLF No. 3648]. Rebecca was born September 28, 1946, at Staunton, Virginia.

(Sup) 5946 CAROLYN ANNE SHEETS (Paul[8], Arvil[7], Sarah[6], Susan[5], John[4], Peter[3], Matthias[2], John Jacob[1]) was the daughter of Paul Stickley and Joanna Bright Sheets [TLF No. 3648]. Carolyn was born April 13, 1948, at Staunton, Virginia.

(Sup) 5947 ROBERT MILTON SHEETS (Bernard[8], Bernard[7], Sarah[6], Susan[5], John[4], Peter[3], Matthias[2], John Jacob[1]) was the son of Bernard Claude and Erma Sandy Sheets [TLF No. 3652].

(Sup) 5948 LINDA ANNE SHEETS (Bernard[8], Bernard[7], Sarah[6], Susan[5], John[4], Peter[3], Matthias[2], John Jacob[1]) was the daughter of Bernard Claude and Erma Sandy Sheets [TLF No. 3652].

(Sup) 5949 JEANETTE MARIE KESSEL (Laura[8], Bernard[7], Sarah[6], Susan[5], John[4], Peter[3], Matthias[2], John Jacob[1]) was the daughter of Haven William and Laura Sheets Kessel [TLF No. 3653]. She was born May 29, 1943, at Harrisonburg, Virginia.

(Sup) 5950 SYLVIA JEAN KESSEL (Laura[8], Bernard[7], Sarah[6], Susan[5], John[4], Peter[3], Matthias[2], John Jacob[1]) was the daughter of Haven William and Laura Sheets Kessel [TLF No. 3653]. She was born December 19, 1947, at Sanford, Florida.

(Sup) 5951 JOAN PATRICIA GWIN (Lois[8], Bernard[7], Sarah[6], Susan[5], John[4], Peter[3], Matthias[2], John Jacob[1]) was the daughter of Randall Fletcher and Lois Virginia Sheets Gwin [TLF No. 3654]. She was born May 17, 1944, at Lakeland, Florida.

(Sup) 5952 CARLYLE EVANS GWIN (Lois[8], Bernard[7], Sarah[6], Susan[5], John[4], Peter[3], Matthias[2], John Jacob[1]) was the son of Randall Fletcher and Lois Virginia Sheets Gwin [TLF No. 3654]. He was born August 2, 1945, at Harrisonburg, Virginia.

(Sup) 5953 ALVIN LLOYD GWIN (Lois[8], Bernard[7], Sarah[6], Susan[5], John[4], Peter[3], Matthias[2], John Jacob[1]) was the son of Randall Fletcher and Lois Virginia Sheets Gwin [TLF No. 3654]. He was born September 16, 1946, at Sanford, Florida.

(Sup) 5954 LESLIE WAYNE GWIN (Lois[8], Bernard[7], Sarah[6], Susan[5], John[4], Peter[3], Matthias[2], John Jacob[1]) was the son of Randall Fletcher and Lois Virginia Sheets Gwin [TLF No. 3654]. He was born August 24, 1947, at Sanford, Florida.

- - - - - - - - - - - - - - - -

(Sup) 5957 LELAND FAW GARBER (Merlin[8], Sada[7], William[6], Susan[5], John[4], Peter[3], Matthias[2], John Jacob[1]) was the son of Merlin E. and Dorothy Faw Garber [TLF No. 3659]. Leland was born August 9, 1937, at Champaign, Illinois.

(Sup) 5958 ELAINE ESTELLA GARBER (Merlin[8], Sada[7], William[6], Susan[5], John[4], Peter[3], Matthias[2], John Jacob[1]) was the daughter of Merlin E. and Dorothy Faw Garber [TLF No. 3659]. Elaine was born March 9, 1940, at Chicago, Illinois.

(Sup) 5959 JAMES WARREN HUFFMAN (Elva[8], Sada[7], William[6], Susan[5], John[4], Peter[3], Matthias[2], John Jacob[1]) was the son of Warren Justus and Elva Garber Huffman [TLF No. 3660]. He was born October 28, 1940, at Champaign, Illinois.

(Sup) 5960 LARRY RICHARD HUFFMAN (Elva[8], Sada[7], William[6], Susan[5], John[4], Peter[3], Matthias[2], John Jacob[1]) was the son of Warren Justus and Elva Barger Huffman [TLF No. 3660]. He was born November 14, 1942, at Champaign, Illinois.

(Sup) 5961 MARGARET MAE GEORGE (William[8], Iva[7], Sarah[6], Susan[5], John[4], Peter[3], Matthias[2], John Jacob[1]) was the daughter of William A. and Maxine Freeman George [TLF No. 3666]. Margaret was born April 28, 1926.

(Sup) 5962 WILFORD GEORGE (William[8], Iva[7], Sarah[6], Susan[5], John[4], Peter[3], Matthias[2], John Jacob[1]) was the son of William A. and Meryl Reynolds George [TLF No. 3666]. He was born March 5, 1935.

(Sup) 5963 DORAN WILLIS PECK (Oliver[8], Ora[7], John[6], Susan[5], John[4], Peter[3], Matthias[2], John Jacob[1]) was the son of Oliver Edwin and Lucille Barbe Peck [TLF No. 3667]. He was born December 24, 1926, at La Harpe, Illinois.

(Sup) 5964 LOREN EDWIN PECK (Oliver[8], Ora[7], John[6], Susan[5], John[4], Peter[3], Matthias[2], John Jacob[1]) was the son of Oliver Edwin and Lucille Barbe Peck [TLF No. 3667]. He was born January 17, 1928, at La Harpe, Illinois.

(Sup) 5965 RICHARD THEODORE COOPER (Lola[8], Sidney[8], John[6], John[5], John[4], Peter[3], Matthias[2], John Jacob[1]) was the son of Orville Theodore and Lola Elva Link Cooper [TLF No. 3668]. Richard was born April 3, 1931, at Washington, D.C.

(Sup) 5966 DOLORES JEAN COOPER (Lola[8], Sidney[7], John[6], John[5], John[4], Peter[3], Matthias[2], John Jacob[1]) was the daughter of Orville Theodore and Lola Elva Link Cooper [TLF No. 3668]. She was born July 7, 1932, at San Diego, California.

(Sup) 5967 HAZELMAE COOPER (Lola[8], Sidney[7], John[6], John[5], John[4], Peter[3], Matthias[2], John Jacob[1]) was the daughter of Orville Theodore and Lola Elva Link Cooper [TLF No. 3668]. She was born June 6, 1934, at La Harpe, Illinois.

(Sup) 5968 JOHN LEONARD LINK (John[8], Sidney[7], John[6], John[5], John[4], Peter[3], Matthias[2], John Jacob[1]) was the son of John Edwin and Kathryn Jane Manifold Link [Supplement No. 3669]. He was born May 3, 1944, at La Harpe, Illinois. After graduating from La Harpe High School in 1962, he engaged in farming, trucking, soil service business, and carpentry and in 1980 became a licensed plumber. He married Leila Marie Burrell June 20, 1965, at Burlington, Iowa. She was the daughter of Melvin and Elizabeth Marie Schaumleffel Burrell and was born June 22, 1945, at Burlington, Iowa. They lived at La Harpe, Illinois.

(Sup) 7566   † Joani Marie Link, born June 22, 1966.
(Sup) 7567   †† Lisa Kay Link, born February 20, 1969.

(Sup) 5969 NINA ELEANOR LINK (John[8], Sidney[7], John[6], John[5], John[4], Peter[3], Matthias[2], John Jacob[1]) was the daughter of John Edwin and Kathryn Jane Manifold Link [Supplement No. 3669]. She was born November 24, 1945, at La Harpe, Illinois. She attended Burlington Business College and was employed at Farmers' State Bank, Ferris, Illinois. She was a member of the Daughters of the American Revolution. She married Arnold Eugene Boyer October 7, 1967, at La Harpe, Illinois. He was the son of Hubert and Arlene Bell Boyer and was born November 12, 1941, at Carthage, Illinois.

(Sup) 7568   † Susan Kathlene Boyer, born April 8, 1968.
(Sup) 7569   †† Steven Eugene Boyer, born May 16, 1969.

(Sup) 5970 EDWINA JANE LINK (John[8], Sidney[7], John[6], John[5], John[4], Peter[3], Matthias[2], John Jacob[1]) was the daughter of John Edwin and Kathryn Jane Manifold Link [Supplement No. 3669]. She was born January 9, 1947, at La Harpe, Illinois. She attended the University of Illinois and was a member of the Daughters of the American Revolution. She married Edwin Lyle Goldhammer May 1, 1965, at La Harpe. The son of Eldon and Wilma Lentfer Goldhammer, he was born May 24, 1944, at Peoria, Illinois.

(Sup) 7570   † Janet Lynn Goldhammer, born August 10, 1966.
(Sup) 7571   †† Jennifer Dawn Goldhammer, born October 2, 1971.

(Sup) 5971 LYLE ARTHUR LINK (John[8], Sidney[7], John[6], John[5], John[4], Peter[3], Matthias[2], John Jacob[1]) was the son of John Edwin and Kathryn Jane Manifold Link [Supplement No. 3669]. He was born July 31, 1948, at La Harpe, Illinois. After attending La Harpe schools, he joined the United States Army for four years, serving in Germany and Viet Nam. He attended Carl Sandburg College. He married Beverly Jane Garrett June 9, 1972, at La Harpe, Illinois. The daughter of Mary Garrett, she was born July 14, 1954, at La Harpe. They were divorced in 1980.

(Sup) 7572   i Karen Renee Link, born October 3, 1972.
(Sup) 7573   ii Mary Ellen Link, born February 28, 1976.
(Sup) 7574   iii John Waylon Link, born August 17, 1977.

(Sup) 5972 REX EUGENE LINK (John[8], Sidney[7], John[6], John[5], John[4], Peter[3], Matthias[2], John Jacob[1]) was the son of John Edwin and Kathryn Jane Manifold Link [Supplement No. 3669]. He was born December 23, 1949, at La Harpe, Illinois. He attended Park College and Springfield (Missouri) Bible Baptist College. He married Wanda Mae Wear July 13, 1973, at Quincy, Illinois. The daughter of Donald and Ilena Stewart Wear, she was born January 2, 1954, at Quincy, Illinois. They were divorced in 1980.

Stepson
              i Steven J. Link, born October 1, 1972.
(Sup) 7575   ii Anthony Ray Link, born September 28, 1975.
(Sup) 7576   iii Joshua Wayne Link, born August 19, 1977.

(Sup) 5973 ANN ELIZABETH LINK (John[8], Sidney[7], John[6], John[5], John[4], Peter[3], Matthias[2], John Jacob[1]) was the daughter of John Edwin and Kathryn Jane Manifold Link [Supplement No. 3669]. She was born October 6, 1951, at La Harpe, Illinois. A graduate of La Harpe High School in 1969, she attended business college and was an active member of the Daughters of the American Revolution. She married Roger Neil Jackson November 28, 1969, at La Harpe, Illinois. He was the son of Robert and June Bouseman Jackson and was born June 24, 1951, at La Harpe.

(Sup) 7577   i Lori Ann Jackson, born July 11, 1970.
(Sup) 7578   ii Gary Neil Jackson, born August 30, 1972.

(Sup) 5974   EDWIN EARL LINK (Eldon[8], Sidney[7], John[6], John[5], John[4], Peter[3], Matthias[2], John Jacob[1]) was the son of Eldon Earl and Hazel Brewer Link [Supplement No. 3671]. Edwin was born February 12, 1939, at La Harpe, Illinois. He married Madeline Carol Garrett September 3, 1960, at Carthage, Illinois. She was the daughter of Estel and Emily Garrett and was born July 3, 1943, at Fort Madison, Iowa.

(Sup) 7579   i   Cathy Lynn Link, born March 4, 1961.
(Sup) 7580   ii   Ava Joan Link, born December 28, 1962.
(Sup) 7581   iii Stephen Craig Link, born February 3, 1965.
(Sup) 7582   iv   Bradley Earl Link, born October 20, 1966.
(Sup) 7583   v   Christina Beth Link, born April 22, 1968.

(Sup) 5975   DAVID PAUL LINK (Eldon[8], Sidney[7], John[6], John[5], John[4], Peter[3], Matthias[2], John Jacob[1]) was the son of Eldon Earl and Hazel Brewer Link [Supplement No. 3671]. David was born March 30, 1941, at La Harpe, Illinois. He married Constance Josephine Meyer April 30, 1962, at West Point, Iowa. She was the daughter of Jerry Meyer and was born at Fort Madison, Iowa.

(Sup) 7584   i   Kelley Kay Link, born December 16, 1963.
(Sup) 7585   ii   Tammy Sue Link, born January 15, 1965.
(Sup) 7586   iii Barbara Ann Link, born October 8, 1966.
(Sup) 7587   iv   David Paul Link, born October 17, 1968.
(Sup) 7588   v   Heather Renee Link, born March 7, 1979.
(Sup) 7589   vi   Shannon Nicole Link, born April 15, 1980.

(Sup) 5976   CAROLYN SUE LINK (Eldon[8], Sidney[7], John[6], John[5], John[4], Peter[3], Matthias[2], John Jacob[1]) was the daughter of Eldon Earl and Hazel Brewer Link [Supplement No. 3671]. Carolyn Sue was born October 14, 1945, at La Harpe, Illinois.

(Sup) 5977   BECKY JEAN LINK (Eldon[8], Sidney[7], John[6], John[5], John[4], Peter[3], Matthias[2], John Jacob[1]) was the daughter of Eldon Earl and Hazel Brewer Link [Supplement No. 3671]. She was born November 8, 1959, at La Harpe, Illinois. She married Gary Thomas Griggs May 12, 1979, at Quincy, Illinois. He was the son of Thomas R. and Norma L. Griggs and was born July 22, 1957, at Quincy, Illinois.

(Sup) 7590   i   Thomas Eldon Griggs, born October 3, 1979.

(Sup) 5978   PATRICIA JOAN GLISAN (Katherine[8], Sidney[7], John[6], John[5], John[4], Peter[3], Matthias[2], John Jacob[1]) was the daughter of Robert Glendal and Kathrine Mae (Link) Glisan [Supplement No. 3672]. Patsy was born July 7, 1937, at La Harpe, Illinois. She graduated from Western Illinois University with a degree in nursing. She married, first, James Peter Goad November 28, 1957, at Galesburg, Illinois. He was the son of Miles and Hazel Coffey Goad and was born January 20, 1936, at Galesburg. She married, second, Ronald Allen Cox July 22, 1979, at Indianapolis, Indiana. He was born October 21, 1954.

(Sup) 7591   i   Jeffery Mark Goad, born June 3, 1960.
(Sup) 7592   ii   David Allan Goad, born August 26, 1961.
(Sup) 7593   iii Bradley James Goad, born March 25, 1965.
(Sup) 7594   iv   Eric Mathew Goad, born October 31, 1969.

(Sup) 5979   MARJORIE CATHERINE GLISAN (Katherine[8], Sidney[7], John[6], John[5], John[4], Peter[3], Matthias[2], John Jacob[1]) was the daughter of Robert Glendal and Katherine Mae (Link) Glisan [Supplement No. 3672]. Marjorie was born October 4, 1939, at La Harpe, Illinois. She married Richard Paul Ruebush January 23, 1957, at Fort Madison, Iowa. He was the son of Robert and Idelle Barker Ruebush and was born June 29, 1939, at Macomb, Illinois.

(Sup) 7595   i   Deborah Kaye Ruebush, born August 2, 1957.
(Sup) 7596   ii   Laurie Rene Ruebush, born October 25, 1960.
(Sup) 7597   iii Shelley Faye Ruebush, born November 3, 1962.

(Sup) 5980   JUANITA FARRELL GLISAN (Katherine[8], Sidney[7], John[6], John[5], John[4], Peter[3], Matthias[2], John Jacob[1]) was the daughter of Robert Glendal and Kathrine Mae (Link) Glisan [Supplement No. 3672]. Juanita was born December 22, 1945, at La Harpe, Illinois. She married Kenneth Marvin Anderson September 20, 1963, at Fort Madison, Iowa. He was the son of Kenneth Mahlon and Mary Lela Poe Anderson and was born July 17, 1942, at Fort Madison, Iowa.

(Sup) 7598   i   Donna Lynn Anderson, born June 23, 1965.
(Sup) 7599   ii   Diana Carol Anderson, born September 21, 1967.
(Sup) 7600   iii Darren Wade Anderson, born March 21, 1974.

(Sup) 5981   RONALD GREGORY GLISAN (Katherine[8], Sidney[7], John[6], John[5], John[4], Peter[3], Matthias[2], John Jacob[1]) was the son of Robert Glendal and Kathrine Mae (Link) Glisan [Supplement No. 3672]. Ronald was born March 28, 1949, at La Harpe, Illinois. He graduated from Western Illinois University in business administration. He married Katherine Ann Hulick July 31, 1971, at Rockford, Illinois. She is the daughter of Harry and Dorothy Hulick and was born April 3, 1949, at Rockford.

(Sup) 7601   i   Michelle Adria Glisan, born October 16, 1980.

(Sup) 5982   ROGER MASON GLISAN   (Katherine[8], Sidney[7], John[6], John[5], John[4], Peter[3], Matthias[2], John Jacob[1]) was the son of Robert Glendal and Kathrine Mae (Link) Glisan [Supplement No. 3672]. Roger was born December 19, 1950, at La Harpe, Illinois. He graduated from Western Illinois University in parks and recreation. He married Ellen McPeek January 29, 1977, at Stockton, Illinois. She was the daughter of Kenneth McPeek and was born June 27,1954, at Stockton.

(Sup) 7601A   i   Abigail Lane Glisan, born March 23, 1983.
(Sup) 7601B   ii   Rebecca Jane Glisan, born July 22, 1985.

(Sup) 5983   GEORGE KENNETH LINK   (Herman[8], Sidney[7], John[6], John[5], John[4], Peter[3], Matthias[2], John Jacob[1]) was the son of Herman George and Virginia Lou France Link [Supplement No. 3673]. George was born June 7, 1949, at La Harpe, Illinois. He resided in La Harpe.

(Sup) 5984   PHILLIP ALLEN LINK   (Herman[8], Sidney[7], John[6], John[5], John[4], Peter[3], Matthias[2], John Jacob[1]) was the son of Herman George and Virginia Lou France Link [Supplement No. 3673]. Phillip was born March 13, 1951, at La Harpe, Illinois. He married Ethel Parson, at Oquawka, Illinois. The daughter of Harold Parson, she was born November 3, 1958, at Oquawka.

(Sup) 7602   i   Ronald Allen Link, born March 16, 1977.
(Sup) 7603   ii   Roger Eugene Link, born November 10, 1979.

(Sup) 5985   JUDY ADELLE LINK   (Herman[8], Sidney[7], John[6], John[5], John[4], Peter[3], Matthias[2], John Jacob[1]) was the daughter of Herman George and Virginia Lou France Link [Supplement No. 3673]. Judy was born March 16, 1963, at La Harpe, Illinois. She married Darrell Taylor March 4, 1972, at Quincy, Illinois.

(Sup) 7604   i   Katherine Adelle Taylor, born September 11, 1972.
(Sup) 7605   ii   Michael Lee Taylor, born August 5, 1977.

(Sup) 5986   PEGGY DIANE LINK   (Herman[8], Sidney[7], John[6], John[5], John[4], Peter[3], Matthias[2], John Jacob[1]) was the daughter of Herman George and Virginia Lou (France) Link [Supplement No. 3673]. She was born April 13, 1954, at La Harpe, Illinois (twin of Nancy Joann Link). She married Howard Roy Leonard, May 27, 1972, at Quincy, Illinois. The son of George Howard Taft and Maxine Rae (Pridmore) Leonard, he was born April 7, 1954, at Quincy.

(Sup) 7606   i   George Lyndell Leonard, born September 8, 1972.
(Sup) 7607   ii   Ginny Rae Leonard, born October 15, 1974.
(Sup) 7608   iii Bobbi Renae Leonard, born October 27, 1977.

(Sup) 5987   NANCY JOANN LINK   (Herman[8], Sidney[7], John[6], John[5], John[4], Peter[3], Matthias[2], John Jacob[1]) was the daughter of Herman George and Virginia Lou (France) Link [Supplement No. 3673]. She was born April 13, 1954, at La Harpe, Illinois (twin of Peggy Diane Link). She married E. Joseph Todd, August 19, 1972, at Hannibal, Missouri. He was the son of Virgil Leon and Roberta Ruth Benedict Todd and was born February 14, 1954, at Hannibal, Missouri.

(Sup) 7609   i   Jeffery Todd, born June 20, 1972.
(Sup) 7610   ii   Michelle Todd, born August 26, 1976.

(Sup) 5988   WILLIAM ANDREW LINK   (Herman[8], Sidney[7], John[6], John[5], John[4], Peter[3], Matthias[2], John Jacob[1]) was the son of Herman George and Virginia Lou (France) Link [Supplement No. 3673]. William was born August 20, 1955, at La Harpe, Illinois. He lived in Quincy, Illinois.

(Sup) 5989   JAMES FRANCIS LINK   (Herman[8], Sidney[7], John[6], John[5], John[4], Peter[3], Matthias[2], John Jacob[1]) was the son of Herman George and Virginia Lou (France) Link [Supplement No. 3673]. James was born March 28, 1957, at La Harpe, Illinois. He served in the U.S. Marine Corps.

(Sup) 5990   MARION KATHRINE LINK   (Herman[8], Sidney[7], John[6], John[5], John[4], Peter[3], Matthias[2], John Jacob[1]) was the daughter of Herman George and Virginia Lou (France) Link [Supplement No. 3673]. She was born March 18, 1959, at La Harpe, Illinois. She died at the age of twenty on December 31, 1979, and was buried at Ursa, Illinois.

(Sup) 5991   RODNEY RAY LINK   (Kenneth[8], Sidney[7], John[6], John[5], John[4], Peter[3], Matthias[2], John Jacob[1]) was the son of Kenneth Ray and Idaline Burford Link [Supplement No. 3674]. Rodney was born May 28, 1943, at La Harpe, Illinois. He married Mary Ellen Reese, September 14, 1963, at Oscaloosa, Iowa. The daughter of Ralph and Ruby Johnson Reese, she was born July 31, 1945, at Oscaloosa.

(Sup) 7611   i   Rodney Ray Link, Jr., born April 2, 1964.
(Sup) 7612   ii   Gregory Scott link, born November 12, 1966.
(Sup) 7613   iii Jacob Reese Link, born April 10, 1974.

(Sup) 5992 GALEN MICHAEL LINK (Kenneth[8], Sidney[7], John[6], John[5], John[4], Peter[3], Matthias[2], John Jacob[1]) was the son of Kenneth Ray and Idaline Burford Link [Supplement No. 3674]. He was born April 2, 1948, at Mt. Pleasant, Iowa. He married Linda Sue Ganzer, November 21, 1970, at Walcott, Iowa. The daughter of Max and Valeria Papen Ganzer, she was born February 10, 1950, at Davenport, Iowa. They were divorced January 1977. He remarried May 7, 1977.

(Sup) 7614   i   Gerard Michael Link, born September 30, 1972.
(Sup) 7614A   ii   Ginger Michelle Link, born October 24, 1977.
(Sup) 7615   iii Jessica Marie Link, born September 4, 1979.

(Sup) 5993 SIDNEY CECIL LINK (Kenneth[8], Sidney[7], John[6], John[5], John[4], Peter[3], Matthias[2], John Jacob[1]) was the son of Kenneth Ray and Idaline Burford Link [Supplement No. 3674]. He was born October 31, 1949, at Mt. Pleasant, Iowa. He married Mary Susan Melton, August 8, 1971, at Seaton, Illinois. She was the daughter of Jerry and Virginia Bocke Melton and was born February 21, 1951, at Monmouth, Illinois. They were divorced April 1980.

(Sup) 7616   i   James Ty Link, born October 17, 1974.
(Sup) 7617   ii   Erin Danielle Link, born December 18, 1977.

(Sup) 5994 KENNETTA FAYE LINK (Kenneth[8], Sidney[7], John[6], John[5], John[4], Peter[3], Matthias[2], John Jacob[1]) was the daughter of Kenneth Ray and Idaline Burford Link [Supplement No. 3674]. She was born March 22, 1952, at Little York, Illinois. She married Earl James Scott, August 30, 1975, at Mt. Pleasant, Iowa. He was the son of Clarence Sylvenster and Gladys Elizabeth Dingman Scott and was born September 27, 1942, at Webster City, Iowa. She adopted his first three children.

Stepson   i   Kenneth Paul Scott, born November 16, 1963.
Stepson   ii   Jeffery Allen Scott, born May 31, 1966.
Stepdaughter   iii Christine Beth Scott, born April 16, 1973.
(Sup) 7618   iv   Deena Marie Scott, born April 23, 1979.

(Sup) 5995 MIRIAM JANE LINK (Kenneth[8], Sidney[7], John[6], John[5], John[4], Peter[3], Matthias[2], John Jacob[1]) was the daughter of Kenneth Ray and Idaline Burford Link [Supplement No. 3674]. She was born January 12, 1955, at Mt. Pleasant, Iowa. She married Donald Dean Mullison, February 26, 1977, at Ames, Iowa. He was the son of Harold and Gloria (Wright) (Barnett) Mullison and was born December 13, 1954, at Lincoln, Nebraska. Miriam was engaged in the nursing profession. Don received a Ph.D. degree in psychology from the University of Utah and became a professor and staff psychologist at the University of Maryland. Miriam and Don lived at Columbia, Maryland.

(Sup) 7618A   i   Amanda Link Mullison, born October 14, 1985.
(Sup) 7618B   ii   Benjamin Daniel Link Mullison, born July 14, 1988.

(Sup) 5996 TWYLA JEAN LINK (Kenneth[8], Sidney[7], John[6], John[5], John[4], Peter[3], Matthias[2], John Jacob[1]) was the daughter of Kenneth Ray and Idaline (Burford) Link [Supplement No. 3674]. She was born May 11, 1956, at Mt. Pleasant, Iowa. She married Gerald Allen Kain, June 25, 1977, at Davenport, Iowa. The son of Lester Harvey and Eloise Magdalene Kain, he was born January 7, 1955, at Rock Island, Illinois.

(Sup) 7619   i   Kelli Jean Kain, born October 10, 1980.

(Sup) 5997 EZRA LEE LINK (Kenneth[8], Sidney[7], John[6], John[5], John[4], Peter[3], Matthias[2], John Jacob[1]) was the son of Kenneth Ray and Idaline (Burford) Link [Supplement No. 3674]. Ezra was born December 16, 1957, at Mt. Pleasant, Iowa. He married Tracey Electa Wittstruck, September 1977 at Davenport, Iowa. She was the daughter of Lawerence and Joyce Wittstruck and was born August 8, 1959, at Omaha, Nebraska.

(Sup) 7620   i   Allen Ray Link, born June 15, 1980.

(Sup) 5998 JULIE LUAN LINK (Kenneth[8], Sidney[7], John[6], John[5], John[4], Peter[3], Matthias[2], John Jacob[1]) was the daughter of Kenneth Ray and Idaline (Burford) Link [Supplement No. 3674]. Julie was born January 15, 1959, at Mt. Pleasant, Iowa.

(Sup) 5999 LYLA KAY WHITE (Helen[8], Sidney[7], John[6], John[5], John[4], Peter[3], Matthias[2], John Jacob[1]) was the daughter of Lyle Robert and Helen Ruth (Link) White [Supplement No. 3675]. She was born December 3, 1943, at La Harpe, Illinois. She graduated from the Swedish American Hospital School of Nursing and was a Registered Nurse in Illinois. She married Jimmie Lynn Stinnett, September 12, 1964 at Rockford, Illinois. He was the son of Charles and Virgie (Hall) Stinnett and was born February 7, 1943, at Carlinville, Illinois.

(Sup) 7621   i   Amy Lynn Stinnett, burn December 10, 1967.
(Sup) 7622   ii   Jay Patrick Stinnett, born December 22, 1972.

(Sup) 6000 MARLENE RUTH WHITE (Helen[8], Sidney[7], John[6], John[5], John[4], Peter[3], Matthias[2], John Jacob[1]) was the daughter of Lyle Robert and Helen Ruth (Link) White [Supplement No. 3675]. She was born September 7, 1952, at La Harpe, Illinois. She graduated from Rockford Memorial Hospital School of Radiology and worked at the Swedish American Hospital in Special Procedures. Marlene married Randy Paul Kramer, March 17, 1973, at St. Joseph, Michigan. He was the son of Leonard Franklin and Dora Jane (Rubly) Kramer and was born March 17, 1953, at Rockford, Illinois.

September 6, 1952, at La Harpe. Steve made the Air Force a career and was stationed in Texas, England, and at Scott Air Force Base in Illinois.

(Sup) 7629   i   Alecs Jonathan Kreps, born September 10, 1974.
(Sup) 7630   ii Stacey Leann Kreps, born March 7, 1978.

(Sup) 6006 LILLIAN GAYLE KREPS (Lois[8], Sidney[7], John[6], John[5], John[4], Peter[3], Matthias[2], John Jacob[1]) was the daughter of George Donald and Lois Idel (Link) Kreps [Supplement No. 3676]. Gayle was born June 9, 1955, at La Harpe, Illinois. She was employed at the Blandinsville Meat Locker.

(Sup) 6007 RITA KRISTINE KREPS (Lois[8], Sidney[7], John[6], John[5], John[4], Peter[3], Matthias[2], John Jacob[1]) was the daughter of George Donald and Lois Idel (Link) Kreps [Supplement No. 3676]. Rita was born April 4, 1958, at La Harpe, Illinois. She married Gregory Leon Siegworth, November 1, 1980, at La Harpe. He was the son of John Foster and Joan Marie (Bell) Siegworth and was born August 17, 1956, at La Harpe. Rita was a meat cutter in a grocery store, and Greg was a farmer.

(Sup) 7631   i   Jason Michael Siegworth, born November 16, 1983.

(Sup) 6008 MELVIN DEAN KREPS (Lois[8], Sidney[7], John[6], John[5], John[4], Peter[3], Matthias[2], John Jacob[1]) was the son of George Donald and Lois Idel (Link) Kreps [Supplement No. 3676]. Dean was born December 13, 1961, at La Harpe, Illinois. He received a B.A. degree from Monmouth College, Illinois, and an M.S. degree from the University of Illinois. He became a college educator and football coach. Dean married Kathryn Pitcher Smith, May 16, 1987, at Mountain Lakes, New Jersey. She was the daughter of Henley Little and Bernardine (Gill) Smith, and was born March 9, 1961, at Houston, Texas. Kathy was a teacher and coach in public schools.

(Sup) 6009 DIANA DAWN KREPS (Lois[8], Sidney[7], John[6], John[5], John[4], Peter[3], Matthias[2], John Jacob[1]) ws the daughter of George Donald and Lois Idel (Link) Kreps [Supplement No. 3676]. Diane was born February 22, 1964, at La Harpe, Illinois.

(Sup) 6010 JERRY GAIL LINK (Gail[8], Frank[7], John[6], John[5], John[4], Peter[3], Matthias[2], John Jacob[1]) was the son of Gail Ellsworth and Pauline (Bundy) Link [Supplement No. 3679]. Jerry was born November 3, 1946, at La Harpe, Illinois. He married Mary Irsik, October 29, 1968, at Colorado Springs, Colorado. The daughter of Ed and Phyllis Irsik, she was born January 20, 1950.

(Sup) 7634   i   Geri Marie Link, born August 19, 1969.
(Sup) 7635   ii   Karen Louise Link, born November 17, 1970.
(Sup) 7636   iii Laurie Denise Link, born September 21, 1973.

(Sup) 6001 ROBIN LODELLE WHITE (Helen[8], Sidney[7], John[6], John[5], John[4], Peter[3], Matthias[2], John Jacob[1]) was the daughter of Lyle Robert and Helen Ruth (Link) White [Supplement No. 3675]. She was born October 31, 1961, at Rockford, Illinois. Robin attended Milton College and Rock Valley College.

(Sup) 6002 GEORGE DELBERT KREPS (Lois[8], Sidney[7], John[6], John[5], John[4], Peter[3], Matthias[2], John Jacob[1]) was the son of George Donald and Lois (Link) Kreps [Supplement No. 3676]. He was born May 21, 1944, at La Harpe, Illinois. George married Donna Lee Hillyer, September 14, 1963, at Sciota, Illinois. She was the daughter of Herschel Eugene and Betty Darlene (Schlegel) Hillyer and was born November 11, 1944, at Macomb, Illinois. George owned and operated a grocery store at Good Hope, Illinois; Donna was a surgical assistant at McDonough District Hospital in Macomb.

(Sup) 7623   i   Debra Leanne Kreps, born November 18, 1964.
(Sup) 7624   ii Kimberlee Denise Kreps, born June 4, 1968.

(Sup) 6003 ALLEN KEITH KREPS (Lois[8], Sidney[7], Elizabeth[6], Susan[5], John[4], Peter[3], Matthias[2], John Jacob[1]) was the son of George Donald and Lois (Link) Kreps [Supplement No. 3676]. Keith was born December 28, 1947, at La Harpe, Illinois. He served in the Vietnam conflict and was stationed at Long Binh. He married Wendy Jo Haymack, July 21, 1972, at Good Hope, Illinois. She was the daughter of Kenneth Jake and Marie Francis (Guarin) Haymack and was born June 20, 1954, at Macomb.

(Sup) 7625   i   Christopher Donald Kreps, born December 31, 1974.
(Sup) 7626   ii   Brian Keith Kreps, born October 13, 1978.
(Sup) 7626A iii Jacob Todd Kreps, born June 11, 1981.

(Sup) 6004 KAREN KATHLEEN KREPS (Lois[8], Sidney[7], John[6], John[5], John[4], Peter[3], Matthias[2], John Jacob[1]) was the daughter of George Donald and Lois (Link) Kreps [Supplement No. 3676]. Karen was born September 2, 1949, at Dixon, Illinois. She married Gregory Robert Bratton, September 1, 1971, at Burlington, Iowa. He was the son of Robert William and Rose Anna (Smith) Bratton and was born October 31, 1951, at Burlington. Karen was a licensed beautician, and Greg was a factory employee.

(Sup) 7627   i   Michelle Marie Bratton, born December 22, 1968.
(Sup) 7628   ii Teresa Dawn Bratton, born March 11, 1972.

(Sup) 6005 STEVEN NEAL KREPS (Lois[8], Sidney[7], John[6], John[5], John[4], Peter[3], Matthias[2], John Jacob[1]) was the son of George Donald and Lois (Link) Kreps [Supplement No. 3676]. Steve was born May 26, 1952, at La Harpe, Illinois. He married Peggy Jo Harper, January 8, 1972, at Sciota, Illinois. She was the daughter of Robert Lee and Julia Mae (Colberg) Harper and was born

(Sup) 6011 LARRY PAUL LINK (Gail[8], Frank[7], John[6], John[5], John[4], Peter[3], Matthias[2], John Jacob[1]) was the son of Gail Ellsworth and Pauline (Bundy) Link [Supplement No. 3679]. He was born October 26, 1948, at La Harpe, Illinois. He died from an automobile accident February 22, 1955.

(Sup), 6012 THOMAS MERRILL LINK (Gail[8], Frank[7], John[6], John[5], John[4], Peter[3], Matthias[2], John Jacob[1]) was the son of Gail Ellsworth and Pauline (Bundy) Link [Supplement No. 3679]. Thomas was born March 10, 1955, at La Harpe, Illinois. He married, first, Debbie Ann Swain, August 15, 1975, at La Harpe. The daughter of Earl and Mary Ann Swain, she was born August 25, 1957, at Carthage, Illinois. Thomas and Debbie were divorced, May, 1983. He married, second, Teresa Lynn Hopping, June 25, 1983. She was the daughter of Jack Hopping, and was born January 2, 1966. She had two children: Heather Lynn, born October 25, 1980; and Cody Alan, born June 3, 1982.

CHILDREN OF THOMAS AND DEBBIE
(Sup) 7637   i   Tommie Gail Link, born March 8, 1977.
(Sup) 7638   ii Jamie Nicole Link, born December 19, 1981.

CHILDREN OF THOMAS AND TERESA
(Sup) 7639   iii Jennifer LeAnne Link, born July 11, 1984.
(Sup) 7639A iv   Paula Dianna Link, born November 9, 1985.

(Sup) 6013 DONALD ARTHUR GILLETT (Delma[8], Daisy[7], John[6], John[5], John[4], Peter[3], Matthias[2], John Jacob[1]) was the son of Arthur Clinton and Delma Genevieve (Bradfield) Gillett [TLF No. 3680]. He was born December 3, 1929, at La Harpe, Illinois.

(Sup) 6014 DARRELL CLINTON GILLETT (Delma[8], Daisy[7], John[6], John[5], John[4], Peter[3], Matthias[2], John Jacob[1]) was the son of Arthur Clinton and Delma Genevieve (Bradfield) Gillett [TLF No. 3680]. He was born May 30, 1934, at La Harpe, Illinois.

(Sup) 6015 DELBERT GENE GILLETT (Delma[8], Daisy[7], John[6], John[5], John[4], Peter[3], Matthias[2], John Jacob[1]) was the son of Arthur Clinton and Delma Genevieve (Bradfield) Gillett [TLF No. 3680]. He was born February 23, 1944, and died March 1, 1944, at La Harpe, Illinois.

(Sup) 6016 JERRY LEE SCHUTTE (Olive[8], Daisy[7], John[6], John[5], John[4], Peter[3], Matthias[2], John Jacob[1]) was the son of Stace Lawrence and Olive Eileen (Bradford) Schutte [TLF No. 3681]. Jerry was born August 22, 1945, at Fort Madison, Iowa.

(Sup) 6017 LARRY EUGENE BOWEN (Luella[8], Lewis[7], John[6], John[5], John[4], Peter[3], Matthias[2], John Jacob[1]) was the son of Roy and Luella Mae (Link) Bowen [TLF No. 3684]. He was born October 11, 1941, at La Harpe, Illinois.

(Sup) 6018 DEANNE JANE BOWEN (Luella[8], Lewis[7], John[6], John[5], John[4], Peter[3], Matthias[2], John Jacob[1]) was the daughter of Roy and Luella Mae (Link) Bowen [TLF No. 3684]. She was born April 7, 1944, at La Harpe, Illinois.

(Sup) 6019 BRADLEY WENDELL LINK (Wendell[8], Lewis[7], John[6], John[5], John[4], Peter[3], Matthias[2], John Jacob[1]) was the son of Wendell Laybourne and Eleanor Annabelle (Klossing) Link [Supplement No. 3688]. Bradley was born September 16, 1955, at La Harpe, Illinois. He married Sheila Lynn McConnell, March 15, 1975, at Fountain Green, Illinois. She was the daughter of Robert Wayne and Linda Lea (Patch) McConnell and was born November 26, 1958, at La Harpe.

(Sup) 7640   1   Amy Jo Link, born July 14, 1978.

(Sup) 6020 BARBARA ANN LINK (Wendell[8], Lewis[7], John[6], John[5], John[4], Peter[3], Matthias[2], John Jacob[1]) was the daughter of Wendell Laybourne and Eleanor Annabelle (Klossing) Link [Supplement No. 3688]. Barbara Ann was born April 30, 1958, at La Harpe, Illinois. She married Rex David Mynatt, August 27, 1977, at La Harpe. He was the son of Rex and Dorothy (Hill) Mynatt and was born May 17, 1957.

(Sup) 6021 SUSAN MARIE LINK (Wendell[8], Lewis[7], John[6], John[5], John[4], Peter[3], Matthias[2], John Jacob[1]) was the daughter of Wendell Laybourne and Eleanor Annabelle (Klossing) Link [Supplement No. 3688]. She was born January 1, 1964, at La Harpe, Illinois.

(Sup) 6022 KATHRYN IRENE BAKER (James[8], Pearl[7], Frank[6], John[5], John[4], Peter[3], Matthias[2], John Jacob[1]) was the daughter of James Edwin and Irene (McNamee) Baker [Supplement No. 3693A]. Kathryn was born May 2, 1946. She married David Dicke, June 11, 1966. They lived at Manchester, Missouri.

(Sup) 7641   i   Amy Kristine Dicke, born December 19, 1969.
(Sup) 7642   ii Susan Jennifer Dicke, born February 17, 1972.

(Sup) 6023 KENNETH JAMES BAKER (James[8], Pearl[7], Frank[6], John[5], John[4], Peter[3], Matthias[2], John Jacob[1]) was the son of James Edwin and Irene (McName) Baker [Supplement No. 3693A]. Ken was born July 16, 1948. He married Dr. Ellen Shulman, May 25, 1986. She was born April 27, 1953. They resided at Houston, Texas; both worked for the National Aeronautics and Space Administration.

(Sup) 6024 NEIL DOUGLAS BAKER (James[8], Pearl[7], Frank[6], John[5], John[4], Peter[3], Matthias[2], John Jacob[1]) was the son of James Edwin and Irene (McName) Baker [Supplement No. 3693A]. Neil was born February 9, 1950. He married Kathy Farr, June 17, 1972. She was born August 30, 1950. They lived at Wadsworth, Ohio.

(Sup) 7643 i Kelly Ann Baker, born July 20, 1975.
(Sup) 7644 ii Megan Elizabeth Baker, born August 20, 1977.

(Sup) 6025 MELANIE ANN BAKER (James[8], Pearl[7], Frank[6], John[5], John[4], Peter[3], Matthias[2], John Jacob[1]) was the daughter of Jamed Edwin and Irene (McName) Baker [Supplement No. 3693A]. Melanie Ann was born February 27, 1955. She married Steven Francavilla, October 29, 1978. He was born August 6, 1953. They lived at Baldwin, New York.

(Sup) 7645 i Justin James Francavilla, born September 17, 1979.
(Sup) 7645A ii Tyler Andrew Francavilla, born July 26, 1980.
(Sup) 7645B iii Stefan John Francavilla, born November 22, 1985.

(Sup) 6026 JOHN L. BAKER (David[8], Pearl[7], Frank[6], John[5], John[4], Peter[3], Matthias[2], John Jacob[1]) was the son of David Theodore and Virginia (Peters) Baker [Supplement No. 3693B]. John was born November 24, 1953. He married, first, Anna Marie Dean, April 23, 1977. She was born January 24, 1958. They were divorced. John married, second, Janice Lorene Miller, July 5, 1986. She was born November 27, 1958.

(Sup) 6027 WAYNE STEVEN BAKER (David[8], Pearl[7], Frank[6], John[5], John[4], Peter[3], Matthias[2], John Jacob[1]) was the son of David Theodore and Virginia (Peters) Baker [Supplement No. 3693B]. Wayne was born February 9, 1955. He married, first, Rhonda Sue Brockman, October 8, 1977. She was born June 15, 1954. They lived at Westerville, Ohio. They were divorced. Wayne married, second, Anne Judith Morris, August 15, 1987. She was born July 20, 1963.

(Sup) 7646 i Kari Lynn Baker, born April 16, 1978.
(Sup) 7647 ii Crystal Lee Baker, born August 7, 1980.

(Sup) 6028 WILLIAM SCOTT BAKER (David[8], Pearl[7], Frank[6], John[5], John[4], Peter[3], Matthias[2], John Jacob[1]) was the son of David Theodore and Virginia (Peters) Baker [Supplement No. 3693B]. William was born December 19, 1960. He married Deborah Ann Cameely, November 10, 1979. She was born August 9, 1960. They lived at Westerville, Ohio. William and Deborah were divorced.

(Sup) 7648 i Bradley Scott Baker, born August 8, 1980.

(Sup) 6029 DOUGLAS ALFRED BAKER (Alfred[8], Pearl[7], Frank[6], John[5], John[4], Peter[3], Matthias[2], John Jacob[1]) was the son of Alfred Wallace and Mary Ann (Rawson) Baker [Supplement No. 3693D]. Douglas was born May 21, 1961.

(Sup) 6030 LAURA RUTH BAKER (Alfred[8], Pearl[7], Frank[6], John[5], John[4], Peter[3], Matthias[2], John Jacob[1]) was the daughter of Alfred Wallace and Mary Ann (Rawson) Baker [Supplement No. 3693D]. Laura was born December 4, 1962. She married Robert Stanley Burton, December 31, 1987, at Conyers, Georgia. He was born October 8, 1963, at Atlanta, Georgia.

(Sup) 6031 KATHLEEN SUSAN KINSELLA (Marilyn[8], Pearl[7], Frank[6], John[5], John[4], Peter[3], Matthias[2], John Jacob[1]) was the daughter of Ronald Francis and Marilyn Jean (Baker) Kinsella [Supplement No. 3693F]. Kathleen was born November 10, 1956. She married Mario Ricardo Montane, February 26, 1977. He was born June 9, 1947. They lived at Odessa, Florida.

(Sup) 7649 i Ryan Francis Montane, born March 12, 1978.
(Sup) 7650 ii Carmen Elizabeth Montane, born 1980.
(Sup) 7651 iii Yvette Montane.

(Sup) 6032 RONALD FRANCIS KINSELLA, JR. (Marilyn[8], Pearl[7], Frank[6], John[5], John[4], Peter[3], Matthias[2], John Jacob[1]) was the son of Ronald Francis and Marilyn Jean (Baker) Kinsella [Supplement No. 3693F]. Ronald was born November 5, 1958.

(Sup) 6033 JOSEPH PATRICK KINSELLA (Marilyn[8], Pearl[7], Frank[6], John[5], John[4], Peter[3], Matthias[2], John Jacob[1]) was the son of Ronald Francis and Marilyn Jean (Baker) Kinsella [Supplement No. 3693F]. Joe was born December 16, 1962. He lived at Tampa, Florida.

(Sup) 6034 NATHAN ANDREW TILLIS (Sharon[8], Pearl[7], Frank[6], John[5], John[4], Peter[3], Matthias[2], John Jacob[1]) was the son of Cecil Hayman and Sharon Elizabeth (Baker) Tillis [Supplement N. 3693H]. Nathan was born September 5, 1967. He served in the 82nd Airborne Division in Georgia.

(Sup) 6035 CHERYL ANN TERRY (Harold^8, Zella^7, Frank^6, John^5, John^4, Peter^3, Matthias^2, John Jacob^1) was the daughter of Harold Henry and Alma Maxine (Sims) Terry [Supplement No. 3693J]. Cheryl Ann was born May 30, 1950. She lived at Delaware, Ohio.

(Sup) 6036 JAMES STEVEN TERRY (Harold^8, Zella^7, Frank^6, John^5, John^4, Peter^3, Matthias^2, John Jacob^1) was the son of Harold Henry and Alma Maxine (Sims) Terry [Supplement No. 3693J]. James was born December 22, 1957. He married Sandra Lee Massey November 25, 1977. They lived at Marion, Ohio.

(Sup) 7652　i　James Michael Terry, born August 19, 1979.
(Sup) 7653　ii　Bobbi Marie Terry, born March 14, 1981.

(Sup) 6037 CHARLENE LOUISE TERRY (Harold^8, Zella^7, Frank^6, John^5, John^4, Peter^3, Matthias^2, John Jacob^1) was the daughter of Harold Henry and Alma Maxine (Sims) Terry [Supplement No.3693J]. Charlene was born August 19, 1961. She married Philip Textor. They lived at Pittsburgh, Pennsylvania.

(Sup) 7654　i　Alexandra Megham Sasha Textor, born March 29, 1984.

(Sup) 6038 PAUL A. TERRY (Frank^8, Zella^7, Frank^6, John^5, John^4, Peter^3, Matthias^2, John Jacob^1) was the son of Frank Lee and Alice Eileen (Knotts) Terry [Supplement No. 3693K]. Paul was born January 7, 1952. He married, first, Patricia Marie Murphy, April 25, 1976. She was born August 12, 1956. They were divorced. Paul married, second, Pamela Kimes, March 28, 1982.

(Sup) 7657　i　Joshua Paul Terry, born December 5, 1978.

(Sup) 6039 LINDA KAY TERRY (Frank^8, Zella^7, Frank^6, John^5, John^4, Peter^3, Matthias^2, John Jacob^1) was the daughter of Frank Lee and Alice Eileen (Knotts) Terry [Supplement No. 3693K]. Linda was born April 15, 1960. She married Ronald Ray Philips, June 10, 1978. He was born January 29, 1958.

(Sup) 7658　i　Fawn K. Philips, born January 1, 1979.
(Sup) 7658A　ii　Bambi Eileen Philips, born October 17, 1980.

(Sup) 6040 CHARLES IRVIN JONES (Elsie^8, Zella^7, Frank^6, John^5, John^4, Peter^3, Matthias^2, John Jacob^1) was the son of Irvin Ross and Elsie Elizabeth (Terry) Jones [Supplement No. 3693L]. Charles was born December 16, 1945. He married Jeanne Borland, August, 1963. She died December 1, 1986.

(Sup) 7659　i　Christopher Charles Jones, born August 12, 1967.
(Sup) 7660　ii　Jon Lynn Jones, born April 18, 1970.

(Sup) 6041 CAROL ANN JONES (Elsie^8, Zella^7, Frank^6, John^5, John^4, Peter^3, Matthias^2, John Jacob^1) was the daughter of Irvin Ross and Elsie Elizabeth (Terry) Jones [Supplement No. 3693L]. Carol Ann was born May 30, 1947. She married Ronald Pettit.

(Sup) 7661　i　Mark Erwin Pettit, born June 22, 1974.

(Sup) 6042 NANCY LYNN TERRY (Dale^8, Zella^7, Frank^6, John^5, John^4, Peter^3, Matthias^2, John Jacob^1) was the daughter of Dale Arnold and Patricia (Chapman) Terry [Supplement No. 3693P]. Nancy was born October 20, 1957. She married, first, Daniel Hughes, December 3, 1975. He was born January 6, 1956. They were divorced. Nancy married, second, James Brookband.

(Sup) 7662　i　Andy Ray Hughes, born September 8, 1976.
(Sup) 7663　ii　Stacey Lynn Hughes, born February 23, 1978.

(Sup) 6043 MATTHEW DALE TERRY (Dale^8, Zella^7, Frank^6, John^5, John^4, Peter^3, Matthias^2, John Jacob^1) was the son of Dale Arnold and Patricia (Chapman) Terry [Supplement No. 3693P]. Matthew was born January 10, 1959. He married Barbara Smith, October 20, 1978.

(Sup) 7664　i　Emily Michelle Terry, born October 7, 1981.
(Sup) 7664A　ii　Megan Elizabeth Terry, born May 23, 1983.
(Sup) 7664B　iii　Laurie Terry, born April 28, 1986.

(Sup) 6044 CHRISTOPHER ALLEN TERRY (Dale^8, Zella^7, Frank^6, John^5, John^4, Peter^3, Matthias^2, John Jacob^1) was the son of Dale Arnold and Patricia (Chapman) Terry [Supplement No. 3693P]. Christopher was born September 17, 1961.

(Sup) 6045 JILL ELIZABETH TERRY (Dale^8, Zella^7, Frank^6, John^5, John^4, Peter^3, Matthias^2, John Jacob^1) was the daughter of Dale Arnold and Patricia (Chapman) Terry [Supplement No. 3693P]. Jill was born April 25, 1966. She married Michael Behnken, August 10, 1983.

(Sup) 7665　i　Jennifer Irene Behnken, born May 12, 1986.

(Sup) 6046 TOM TERRY (Dale^8, Zella^7, Frank^6, John^5, John^4, Peter^3, Matthias^2, John Jacob^1) was the son of Dale Arnold and Patricia (Chapman) Terry [Supplement No. 3693P]. Tom was born October 11, 1969.

(Sup) 6051 PENNY ANN TERRY (Vinal Ray[8], Zella[7], Frank[6], John[5], John[4], Peter[3], Matthias[2], John Jacob[1]) was the daughter of Vinal Ray and Carol (Burche) Terry [Supplement No. 3693R]. Penny Ann was born May 10, 1959. She married Greg Condron.

(Sup) 7672 i Aaron Joseph Condron, born September 11, 1978.
(Sup) 7673 ii Casey Elizabeth Condron, born September 23, 1982.
(Sup) 7674 iii Jennifer Maureen Condron, born January 22, 1984.
(Sup) 7675 iv Christopher Vinal Condron, born October 22, 1985.

(Sup) 6052 PAULA IRENE TERRY (Vinal Ray[8], Zella[7], Frank[6], John[5], John[4], Peter[3], Matthias[2], John Jacob[1]) was the daughter of Vinal Ray and Carol (Burche) Terry [Supplement No. 3693R]. Paula was born August 2, 1960. She married Richard Stevens.

(Sup) 7676 i Richard Charles Stevens, born February 18, 1979.
(Sup) 7677 ii Laura Lynn Stevens, born September 26, 1981.

(Sup) 6053 KELLY MARIE TERRY (Vinal Ray[8], Zella[7], Frank[6], John[5], John[4], Peter[3], Matthias[2], John Jacob[1]) was the daughter of Vinal Ray and Carol (Burche) Terry [Supplement No. 3693R]. Kelly was born September 3, 1965. She married Patrick O'Quinn, December 10, 1985.

(Sup) 7678 i Andrew O'Quinn, born September 11, 1986.

(Sup) 6054 KATHLEEN RAE TERRY (Vinal Ray[8], Zella[7], Frank[6], John[5], John[4], Peter[3], Matthias[2], John Jacob[1]) was the daughter of Vinal Ray and Carol (Burche) Terry [Supplement No. 3693R]. Kathleen was born May 23, 1971.

(Sup) 6055 BRENDA IRENE TERRY (Donald[8], Zella[7], Frank[6], John[5], John[4], Peter[3], Matthias[2], John Jacob[1]) was the daughter of Donald Alvin and Claudette (Dechesne) Terry [Supplement No. 3693S]. Brenda was born August 11, 1962. She married Dan Green.

(Sup) 7679 i Jenny Irene Green, born August 11, 1980.
(Sup) 7680 ii _____ Green.

(Sup) 6056 DONALD ALVIN TERRY, JR. (Donald[8], Zella[7], Frank[6], John[5], John[4], Peter[3], Matthias[2], John Jacob[1]) was the son of Donald Alvin and Sarah (Brawley) Terry [Supplement No. 3693S]. Donald, Jr., was born September 6, 1966.

(Sup) 6046A GENE LINK TERRY (Dale[8], Zella[7], Frank[6], John[5], John[4], Peter[3], Matthias[2], John Jacob[1]) was the son of Dale Arnold and Debra (Stone) Terry [Supplement No. 3693P]. Gene was born August 18, 1983.

(Sup) 6046B JACOB DALE TERRY (Dale[8], Zella[7], Frank[6], John[5], John[4], Peter[3], Matthias[2], John Jacob[1]) was the son of Dale Arnold and Debra (Stone) Terry [Supplement No. 3693P]. Jacob was born June 10, 1985.

(Sup) 6047 TERRI SUE GROVES (Esther[8], Zella[7], Frank[6], John[5], John[4], Peter[3], Matthias[2], John Jacob[1]) was the daughter of Richard Allen and Esther June (Terry) Groves [Supplement No. 3693Q]. Terri was born January 13, 1956. She married William Craig Eisenbrandt, September 1, 1974. He was born September 30, 1954. They lived at Feelemere, Florida, where William was a farm manager.

(Sup) 7667 i Christy Sue Eisenbrandt, born November 30, 1975.
(Sup) 7668 ii Dana Michelle Eisenbrandt, Born June 23, 1979.
(Sup) 7669 iii Melissa Kay Eisenbrandt, born May 5, 1982.

(Sup) 6048 VICKI LEE GROVES (Esther[8], Zella[7], Frank[6], John[5], John[4], Peter[3], Matthias[2], John Jacob[1]) was the daughter of Richard Allen and Esther June (Terry) Groves [Supplement No. 3693Q]. Vicki was born May 30, 1957. She married Ronnie Lamar Gamble, December 31, 1974. He was born October 22, 1951. They lived at Leesburg, Florida, where Ronnie was a detective.

(Sup) 7670 i Angel Irene Gamble, born February 16, 1978.
(Sup) 7671 ii Amanda Jane Gamble, born August 1, 1981.

(Sup) 6049 RICHARD ALLEN GROVES, JR. (Esther[8], Zella[7], Frank[6], John[5], John[4], Peter[3], Matthias[2], John Jacob[1]) was the son of Richard Allen and Esther June (Terry) Groves [Supplement No. 3693Q]. Richard, Jr., was born May 4, 1960. He married Sukie Cheng, July 4, 1981. They lived at Fayetteville, North Carolina, where he operated a landscaping business, and she was a waitress.

(Sup) 6050 TAMI LYNN GROVES (Esther[8], Zella[7], Frank[6], John[5], John[4], Peter[3], Matthias[2], John Jacob[1]) was the daughter of Richard Allen and Esther June (Terry) Groves [Supplement No. 3693Q]. She was born April 17, 1962. She married Rick Ceman, July 4, 1981. They were divorced. She lived at Grant, Florida, where she was employed as a mechanical draftswoman.

(Sup) 6056A   CHRISTOPHER SHAWN TERRY (Donald[8], Zella[7], Frank[6], John[5], John[4], Peter[3], Matthias[2], John Jacob[1]) was the son of Donald Alvin and Lisa (Powell) Terry [Supplement No. 3693S]. Christopher was born March 2, 1984.

(Sup) 6057   MELINDA KAY HARDIN (Sandra[8], Zella[7], Frank[6], John[5], John[4], Peter[3], Matthias[2], John Jacob[1]) was the daughter of Thomas and Sandra Lee Terry Hardin [Supplement No. 3693T]. Melinda was born April 9, 1962.

(Sup) 6058   JEFF ALAN HARDIN (Sandra[8], Zella[7], Frank[6], John[5], John[4], Peter[3], Matthias[2], John Jacob[1]) was the son of Thomas and Sandra Lee (Terry) Hardin [Supplement No. 3693T]. Jeff was born January 15, 1964. He married Wendy Rader, August 10, 1985.

(Sup) 6059   AMY SUE ECKMAN (Sandra[8], Zella[7], Frank[6], John[5], John[4], Peter[3], Matthias[2], John Jacob[1]) was the daughter of David and Sandra Lee Terry Hardin Eckman [Supplement No. 3693T]. Amy was born January 6, 1969. She married Michael Cragin, December 28, 1986.

(Sup) 6060   BRIAN BRADFORD ECKMAN (Sandra[8], Zella[7], Frank[6], John[5], John[4], Peter[3], Matthias[2], John Jacob[1]) was the son of David and Sandra Lee Terry Hardin Eckman [Supplement No. 3693T]. Brian was born June 5, 1972.

(Sup) 6061   JOHN TIMOTHY WELCH (John[8], Carrie[7], Frank[6], John[5], John[4], Peter[3], Matthias[2], John Jacob[1]) was the son of John Carroll and Dorothy Ruth (Armstrong) Welch [Supplement No. 3694]. John was born April 23, 1956. He was an electronic technician, employed by ITT Corporation.

(Sup) 6062   JUDITH LYNN WELCH (John[8], Carrie[7], Frank[6], John[5], John[4], Peter[3], Matthias[2], John Jacob[1]) was the daughter of John Carroll and Dorothy Ruth (Armstrong) Welch [Supplement No. 3694]. Judith was born May 23, 1957. She married Mark A. Newman, April 12, 1986. They lived at Pataskala, Ohio.

(Sup) 7681   i Elizabeth Nicole Newman, born December 30, 1986.

(Sup) 6063   JOHN RAYMOND LINK, III (John[8], Raymond[7], Frank[6], John[5], John[4], Peter[3], Matthias[2], John Jacob[1]) was the son of John Raymond and Joan (Davenport) Link, Jr. [Supplement No. 3695A]. John Raymond, III, was born January 5, 1955. He married Shirley Alane Lowe, May 12, 1974, at Shawnee Hills, Ohio. She was the daughter of Henry and Iva Eunice (Fowler) Lowe, and was born July 10, 1956, at Columbus, Ohio. He was an auto mechanic for the county after serving three years in the U.S. Army. She worked as a clerk in the Delaware County Bank. John and Shirley resided in Ashley County, Ohio.

(Sup) 7682   i Amy Alane Link, born November 10, 1984.

(Sup) 6064   ROBERT EUGENE LINK, JR. (Robert[8], Raymond[7], Frank[6], John[5], John[4], Peter[3], Matthias[2], John Jacob[1]) was the son of Robert Eugene and Loueilla (Mullins) Link [Supplement No. 3695B]. Robert, Jr., was born August 5, 1957, at Columbus, Ohio. He married Kathy Lynette Baxter, October 9, 1977. She was the daughter of David E. and Sara G. (Daughtery) Baxter, and was born October 2, 1957. Robert and Kathy both attended Ohio State University, Ohio Technical Institute and Moody Bible Institute.

(Sup) 7683   i Bethany Link, born October 19, 1983.

(Sup) 6065   WILLIAM DENNIS LINK (Robert[8], Raymond[7], Frank[6], John[5], John[4], Peter[3], Matthias[2], John Jacob[1]) was the son of Robert Eugene and Louella (Mullins) Link [Supplement No. 3695B]. William was born September 1, 1959, at Kilbourne, Ohio.

(Sup) 6066   BRENDA LOUISE LINK (Robert[8], Raymond[7], Frank[6], John[5], John[4], Peter[3], Matthias[2], John Jacob[1]) was the daughter of Robert Eugene and Louella (Mullins) Link [Supplement No. 3695B]. Brenda was born July 11, 1960, at Columbus, Ohio. She married Brett William Wilson, September 8, 1979. He was the son of William Hilton and Gloria Jean Wilson and was born May 11, 1979, at Columbus. Brett managed his father's truck stop, and Brenda worked at Citizens Federal Savings and Loan, Delaware County, Ohio. They were divorced. Brenda married, second, Kent Manley, June, 1986. Kent was born June 17, 1958. Brenda and Kent resided at Delaware, Ohio.

(Sup) 6067   BRYON WAYNE LINK (Robert[8], Raymond[7], Frank[6], John[5], John[4], Peter[3], Matthias[2], John Jacob[1]) was the son of Robert Eugene and Louella (Mullins) Link [Supplement No. 3695B]. He was born November 17, 1965, at Kilbourne, Ohio. He married Peggy Cole, July, 1985. They lived at Delaware, Ohio.

(Sup) 6068 TIMOTHY JON LINK STULTS (Nancy[8], Raymond[7], Frank[6], John[5], John[4], Peter[3], Matthias[2], John Jacob[1]) was the son of Fred Lee and Nancy Muriel (Link) Stults [Supplement No. 3695C]. He was born June 16, 1964, at Lancaster, Ohio. He studied at Ohio Wesleyan University.

(Sup) 6069 LOREN KELLY STULTS (Nancy[8], Raymond[7], Frank[6], John[5], John[4], Peter[3], Matthias[2], John Jacob[1]) was the daughter of Fred Lee and Nancy Muriel (Link) Stults [Supplement No. 3695C]. She was born July 18, 1967, at Delaware, Ohio.

(Sup) 6070 PHILIP MICHAEL LINK (Philip[8], Raymond[7], Frank[6], John[5], John[4], Peter[3], Matthias[2], John Jacob[1]) was the son of Philip Allen and Joyce Darlene (Doane) Link [Supplement No. 3695D]. Philip was born August 13, 1961, at Columbus, Ohio. He married Patsy Denise Tackett, February 14, 1981. She was born September 11, 1961, the daughter of Emma Mae (Oiler) and Sterling Tackett. Philip and Patsy lived at Ostrander, Ohio.

(Sup) 7684   i Joshua Michael Link, born May 2, 1985.

(Sup) 6071 STEVEN ALLEN LINK (Philip[8], Raymond[7], Frank[6], John[5], John[4], Peter[3], Matthias[2], John Jacob[1]) was the son of Philip Allen and Joyce Darlene (Doane) Link [Supplement No. 3695D]. Steven was born August 8, 1966, at Columbus, Ohio. He married Kerry Lynn Keatley; she was the daughter of Robert Lee and Constance Lee (Yuenger) Keatley, and was born June 5, 1966. Steven and Kerry were divorced, 1987.

(Sup) 7685   i Kierra Lynn Link, born February 2, 1984.

(Sup) 6072 SCOTT ANDREW LINK (Philip[8], Raymond[7], Frank[6], John[5], John[4], Peter[3], Matthias[2], John Jacob[1]) was the son of Philip Allen and Joyce Darlene (Doane) Link [Supplement No. 3695D]. Scott was born August 13, 1971, at Columbus, Ohio.

(Sup) 6073 RONALD RUSSELL TEETER, JR., (Nita[8], Raymond[7], Frank[6], John[5], John[4], Peter[3], Matthias[2], John Jacob[1]) was the son of Ronald Russell and Nita Louise (Link) Teeter [Supplement No. 3695E]. Ronald was born June 12, 1967, at Columbus, Ohio. He served in the U.S. Air Force.

(Sup) 6074 JOHN KAYLOR TEETER (Nita[8], Raymond[7], Frank[6], John[5], John[4], Peter[3], Matthias[2], John Jacob[1]) was the son of Ronald Russell and Nita Louise (Link) Teeter [Supplement No. 3695E]. John was born May 4, 1969, at Columbus, Ohio.

(Sup) 6075 DANIEL LINK TEETER (Nita[8], Raymond[7], Frank[6], John[5], John[4], Peter[3], Matthias[2], John Jacob[1]) was the son of Ronald Russell and Nita Louise (Link) Teeter [Supplement No. 3695E]. Daniel was born January 9, 1972, at Columbus, Ohio.

(Sup) 6075A MEAGAN ALLISON DAUGHERTY (Philip[8], Anna Marie[7], Frank[6], John[5], John[4], Peter[3], Matthias[2], John Jacob[1]) was the daughter of Philip Lee and Patricia (Commiskey) Daugherty [Supplement No. 3695F]. Meagan was born April 4, 1986, at Hauppauge, New York.

(Sup) 6076 EVA MARIE OBERDIER (Susan[8], Anna Marie[7], Frank[6], John[5], John[4], Peter[3], Matthias[2], John Jacob[1]) was the daughter of John Paul and Susan Jane (Daugherty) Oberdier [Supplement No. 3695G]. She was born May 30, 1971, at Bloomington, Indiana.

(Sup) 6077 NATHAN JOHN OBERDIER (Susan[8], Anna Marie[7], Frank[6], John[5], John[4], Peter[3], Matthias[2], John Jacob[1]) was the son of John Paul and Susan Jane (Daugherty) Oberdier [Supplement No. 3695G]. Nathan was born November 23, 1974, at Lake Villa, Illinois.

(Sup) 6077A ANDREW CALEB OBERDIER (Susan[8], Anna Marie[7], Frank[6], John[5], John[4], Peter[3], Matthias[2], John Jacob[1]) was the son of John Paul and Susan Jane (Daugherty) Oberdier [Supplement No. 3695G]. Andrew was born January 10, 1981, at Grayslake, Illinois.

(Sup) 6078 JOHN ALLEN VAN SICKLE (Suzanne[8], Kenneth[7], Frank[6], John[5], John[4], Peter[3], Matthias[2], John Jacob[1]) was the son of Suzanne Jane (Link) Van Sickle [Supplement No. 3696]. John was born October 16, 1957. He married Patricia Rowe June 10, 1978. They lived at Delaware, Ohio, where he was an attorney, and she was a hair dresser.

(Sup) 6079 JOYCE ANN VAN SICKLE (Suzanne[8], Kenneth[7], Frank[6], John[5], John[4], Peter[3], Matthias[2], John Jacob[1]) was the daughter of Suzanne Jane (Link) Van Sickle [Supplement No. 3696]. Joyce was born February 27, 1959. She married Roger Harris, July 11, 1981. Joyce worked with standard bred horses.

(Sup) 6080 JEFFREY DUANE VAN SICKLE (Suzanne[8], Kenneth[7], Frank[6], John[5], John[4], Peter[3], Matthias[2], John Jacob[1]) was the son of Suzanne Jane (Link) Van Sickle [Supplement No. 3696]. Jeffrey was born February 11, 1963. He married Dana Hankinson. They were divorced.

(Sup) 7686   i Justin Colt Van Sickle, born March, 1985.

(Sup) 6081 KRISTA KAY BUEL (Sherry[8], Kenneth[7], Frank[6], John[5], John[4], Peter[3], Matthias[2], John Jacob[1]) was the daughter of Thomas and Sherry Lynne (Link) Buel [Supplement No. 3697]. Krista was born January 13, 1963.

(Sup) 6082 KARLA REA BUEL (Sherry[8], Kenneth[7], Frank[6], John[5], John[4], Peter[3], Matthias[2], John Jacob[1]) was the daughter of Thomas and Sherry Lynn (Link) Buel [Supplement No. 3697]. Karla was born May 28, 1971.

(Sup) 6082A LISA JEANNE LINK (Stephen[8], Kenneth[7], Frank[6], John[5], John[4], Peter[3], Matthias[2], John Jacob[1]) was the daughter of Stephen Kenneth and Jeanne (Hunter) Link [Supplement No. 3698]. Lisa Jeanne was born October 10, 1962, at Mount Vernon, Ohio. She married, first, James Brad Fielding, 1979. They were divorced. Lisa married, second, Victor Boreau. They lived at Valdosta, Georgia, where she was a fashion consultant.

(Sup) 7697   1 Coby Jeanne Fielding, born April 6, 1980.

(Sup) 6083 SARA JO LINK (Stephen[8], Kenneth[7], Frank[6], John[5], John[4], Peter[3], Matthias[2], John Jacob[1]) was the daughter of Stephen Kenneth and Debra (King) Link [Supplement No. 3698]. Sara Jo was born July 7, 1971.

(Sup) 6084 JAMIE LYNN LINK (Stephen[8], Kenneth[7], Frank[6], John[5], John[4], Peter[3], Matthias[2], John Jacob[1]) was the daughter of Stephen Kenneth and Debra (King) Link [Supplement No. 3698]. Jamie Lynn was born April 10, 1975.

(Sup) 6085 ANNIE MARIE LINK (Stephen[8], Kenneth[7], Frank[6], John[5], John[4], Peter[3], Matthias[2], John Jacob[1]) was the daughter of Stephen Kenneth and Teresa (Bovard) Link [Supplement No. 3698]. She was born March 2, 1980.

(Sup) 6086 RICHARD DEAN GLAZE (Linda[8], Kenneth[7], Frank[6], John[5], John[4], Peter[3], Matthias[2], John Jacob[1]) was the son of Ronald and Linda Claire (Link) Glaze [Supplement No. 3699]. Richard was born November 4, 1969.

(Sup) 6087 ROBERT MICHAEL GLAZE (Linda[8], Kenneth[7], Frank[6], John[5], John[4], Peter[3], Matthias[2], John Jacob[1]) was the son of Ronald and Linda Claire (Link) Glaze [Supplement No. 3699]. Robert was born April 19, 1972.

(Sup) 6088 LIZABETH SUE LINK (Richard[8], Vinal[7], Frank[6], John[5], John[4], Peter[3], Matthias[2], John Jacob[1]) was the daughter of Richard Louis and Mary Anna (Shaw) Link [Supplement No. 3700]. She was born October 23, 1969.

(Sup) 6089 KEVIN ANDREW CAUDILL (Donna[8], Vinal[7], Frank[6], John[5], John[4], Peter[3], Matthias[2], John Jacob[1]) was the son of Elwood and Donna Kay (Link) Caudill [Supplement No. 3701]. Kevin was born April 7, 1970.

(Sup) 6090 KATHLEEN ANN CAUDILL (Donna[8], Vinal[7], Frank[6], John[5], John[4], Peter[3], Matthias[2], John Jacob[1]) was the daughter of Elwood and Donna Kay (Link) Caudill [Supplement No. 3701]. Kathleen was born September 21, 1971.

(Sup) 6091 KELLI SUE FERRELL (Carolyn[8], Charlotte[7], Frank[6], John[5], John[4], Peter[3], Matthias[2], John Jacob[1]) was the daughter of Gary and Carolyn June (Pittman) Ferrell [Supplement No. 3702]. Kelli was born April 22, 1963. She married David Charles London, February 17, 1984. They lived at Middletown, Ohio, where Kelli and David were employed.

(Sup) 6092 TIMOTHY WAYNE FERRELL (Carolyn[8], Charlotte[7], Frank[6], John[5], John[4], Peter[3], Matthias[2], John Jacob[1]) was the son of Gary and Carolyn June (Pittman) Ferrell [Supplement No. 3702]. Timothy was born January 9, 1966. He studied at Sinclair University.

(Sup) 6093 DAWN E'LYN PITTMAN (Harold[8], Charlotte[7], Frank[6], John[5], John[4], Peter[3], Matthias[2], John Jacob[1]) was the daughter of Harold Edgar and Beverly (Borchers) Pittman [Supplement No. 3703]. Dawn was born June 28, 1965. She engaged to marry Peter Michael Bermudez. He was born February 24, 1963.

(Sup) 6094 CRAIG ALAN PITTMAN (Harold[8], Charlotte[7], Frank[6], John[5], John[4], Peter[3], Matthias[2], John Jacob[1]) was the son of Harold Edgar and Beverly (Borchers) Pittman [Supplement No. 3703]. Craig was born May 17, 1967. He farmed with his father at Ashley, Ohio.

(Sup) 6095 ANGIE LYNN HILLARD (Pamela[8], James[7], Frank[6], John[5], John[4], Peter[3], Matthias[2], John Jacob[1]) was the daughter of Larry and Pamela Jo (Link) Hillard [Supplement No. 3704]. She was born November 8, 1968.

(Sup) 6096 RODD L. HILLARD (Pamela[8], James[7], Frank[6], John[5], John[4], Peter[3], Matthias[2], John Jacob[1]) was the son of Larry and Pamela Jo (Link) Hillard [Supplement No. 3704]. Rodd was born December 12, 1970.

(Sup) 6097 JAMES LINK WILSON (Wendy[8], James[7], Frank[6], John[5], John[4], Peter[3], Matthias[2], John Jacob[1]) was the son of Larry and Wendy Sue (Link) Wilson [Supplement No. 3704A]. James was born June 16, 1980.

(Sup) 6097A KYLE LEWIS WILSON (Wendy[8], James[7], Frank[6], John[5], John[4], Peter[3], Matthias[2], John Jacob[1]) was the son of Larry and Wendy Sue (Link) Wilson [Supplement No. 3704A]. Kyle was born October 13, 1983.

(Sup) 6098 AARON LLOYD BUELL (Victoria[8], William[7], Frank[6], John[5], John[4], Peter[3], Matthias[2], John Jacob[1]) was the son of Vickie Anne (Link) Buell [Supplement No. 3705]. Aaron was born May 16, 1969.

(Sup) 6099 ELIZABETH ANN WINGATE (Ray[8], Arthur[7], Susan[6], David[5], John[4], Peter[3], Matthias[2], John Jacob[1]) was the daughter of Ray Palmer and Mary (Hites) Wingate [TLF No. 3706]. Elizabeth was was born March 9, 1921, in McDonough County, Illinois. She married James Reynolds December 24, 1944.

(Sup) 7719   1 Jane Ann Reynolds, born June 29, 1946.

(Sup) 6100 MARY ELINOR WINGATE (Ray[8], Arthur[7], Susan[6], David[5], John[4], Peter[3], Matthias[2], John Jacob[1]) was the daughter of Ray Palmer and Mary (Hites) Wingate [TLF No. 3706]. Mary was born October 17, 1926, at McDonough, Illinois.

(Sup) 6101 JEAN IRIS WATT (Fern[8], Arthur[7], Susan[6], David[5], John[4], Peter[3], Matthias[2], John Jacob[1]) was the daughter of Clarence and Fern (Wingate) Watt [TLF No. 3707]. Jean was born April 2, 1924, in McDonough County, Illinois. She married Paul Robinson August 23, 1943.

(Sup) 6102 JAMES ARTHUR WATT (Fern[8], Arthur[7], Susan[6], David[5], John[4], Peter[3], Matthias[2], John Jacob[1]) was the son of Clarence and Fern (Wingate) Watt [TLF No. 3707]. James was born October 9, 1925, in Peoria County, Illinois; he married Mary Ruth Mobley March 30, 1947.

(Sup) 6103 MARJORIE EVELYN WILKINS (Ethel[8], Martin[7], Susan[6], David[5], John[4], Peter[3], Matthias[2], John Jacob[1]) was the daughter of Herbert and Ethel May (Wingate) Wilkins [TLF No. 3708]. Marjorie was born March 28, 1920, in McDonough County, Illinois. She married Robert Erwin May 18, 1943.

(Sup) 6104 RALPH DALE WILKINS (Ethel[8], Martin[7], Susan[6], David[5], John[4], Peter[3], Matthias[2], John Jacob[1]) was the son of Herbert and Ethel May Wingate Wilkins [TLF No. 3708]. Ralph was born February 16, 1922, in Warren County, Illinois. He married Arlene Anderson July 25, 1943.

(Sup) 6105 WESLEY ORVAL WINGATE (Orval[8], John[7], Susan[6], David[5], John[4], Peter[3], Matthias[2], John Jacob[1]) was the son of Orval Milo and Paulina Vidas Wingate [TLF No. 3709]. Wesley was born June 18, 1938, at Kalamazoo, Michigan.

(Sup) 6106 MYRNA ELAINE WINGATE (Orval[8], John[7], Susan[6], David[5], John[4], Peter[3], Matthias[2], John Jacob[1]) was the daughter of Orval Milo and Pauline Vidas Wingate [TLF No. 3709]. Myrna was born April 18, 1941, at Sault Ste. Marie, Michigan.

(Sup) 6107 ROBERT LEE SIMMONS (Raymond[8], Effie[7], Susan[6], David[5], John[4], Peter[3], Matthias[2], John Jacob[1]) was the son of Raymond Allen and Evelyn Hendricks Simmons [TLF No. 3711]. He was born and died March 19, 1934, in Fulton County, Illinois.

(Sup) 6108 RODNEY ALLEN SIMMONS (Raymond[8], Effie[7], Susan[6], David[5], John[4], Peter[3], Matthias[2], John Jacob[1]) was the son of Raymond Allen and Evelyn Hendricks Simmons [TLF No. 3711]. He was born July 28, 1935, in Warren County, Illinois.

(Sup) 6109 LYLE MERTON REIHM (Leona[8], Lulu[7], Susan[6], David[5], John[4], Peter[3], Matthias[2], John Jacob[1]) was the son of Raymond and Leona Marie Young Reihm [TLF No. 3712]. Lyle was born June 10, 1924, in Knox County, Illinois. He married Barbara Malley January 25, 1945.

(Sup) 6110 BETTY LOU REIHM (Leona[8], Lulu[7], Susan[6], David[5], John[4], Peter[3], Matthias[2], John Jacob[1]) was the daughter of Raymond and Leona Marie Young Reihm [TLF No. 3712]. Betty Lou was born February 13, 1926, in Warren County, Illinois. She married Robert Lyon April 18, 1947.

(Sup) 7722   † Susan Marie Reihm, born May 8, 1944.

(Sup) 6111 LOWELL LEE REIHM (Leona[8], Lulu[7], Susan[6], David[5], John[4], Peter[3], Matthias[2], John Jacob[1]) was the son of Raymond and Leona Marie Young Reihm [TLF No. 3712]. Lowell was born September 13, 1928, in Warren County, Illinois.

(Sup) 6112 JOSEPHINE IRENE PEACH (Lois[8], Edwin[7], Susan[6], David[5], John[4], Peter[3], Matthias[2], John Jacob[1]) was the daughter of Ivan and Lois Wingate Peach [TLF No. 3717]. She was born May 15, 1938, in Bureau County, Illinois.

(Sup) 6113 JUDY ANN PEACH (Lois[8], Edwin[7], Susan[6], David[5], John[4], Peter[3], Matthias[2], John Jacob[1]) was the daughter of Ivan and Lois Wingate Peach [TLF No. 3717]. She was born January 30, 1940, in Bureau County, Illinois.

(Sup) 6114 JERRI LYNN PEACH (Lois[8], Edwin[7], Susan[6], David[5], John[4], Peter[3], Matthias[2], John Jacob[1]) was the daughter of Ivan and Lois Wingate Peach [TLF No. 3717]. She was born November 21, 1945, in Bureau County, Illinois.

(Sup) 6115 ELLA FLORENCE NEUMANN (Blanche[8], Harvey[7], Sarah[6], David[5], John[4], Peter[3], Matthias[2], John Jacob[1]) was the daughter of Herbert P. and Blanche Hewett Neumann [TLF No. 3721]. Ella was born October 19, 1923, in Custer County, Montana. She married Henry Melvin Grau July 11, 1942, at Miles City, Montana. He was born August 17, 1917, at Glassglow, Montana.

(Sup) 7723   † Gordon Paul Grau, born December 2, 1946.

(Sup) 6116 EDNA FAY NEUMANN (Blanche[8], Harvey[7], Sarah[6], David[5], John[4], Peter[3], Matthias[2], John Jacob[1]) was the daughter of Herbert P. and Blanche Hewett Neumann [TLF No. 3721]. Edna was born September 16, 1926, in Custer County, Montana. She married Clarence Erwin Mendenhall February 10, 1945, at Miles City, Montana. He was born July 6, 1923, at Paris, Montana.

(Sup) 6117 HERBERT H. NEUMANN (Blanche[8], Harvey[7], Sarah[6], David[5], John[4], Peter[3], Matthias[2], John Jacob[1]) was the son of Herbert P. and Blanche Hewett Neumann [TLF No. 3721]. Herbert born March 3, 1931, in Custer County, Montana.

(Sup) 6118 HUGH RONALD NEUMANN (Blanche[8], Harvey[7], Sarah[6], David[5], John[4], Peter[3], Matthias[2], John Jacob[1]) was the son of Herbert P. and Blanche Hewett Neumann [TLF No. 3721]. Hugh was born October 10, 1933, at Custer County, Montana.

(Sup) 6119 MARY IRENE REINHART (Blanche[8], Harvey[7], Sarah[6], David[5], John[4], Peter[3], Matthias[2], John Jacob[1]) was the daughter of Harry J. and Blanche Hewett Neumann Reinhart [TLF No. 3721]. She was born April 30, 1939, at Miles City, Montana.

(Sup) 6120 RAYMOND LEE REINHART (Blanche[8], Harvey[7], Sarah[6], David[5], John[4], Peter[3], Matthias[2], John Jacob[1]) was the son of Harry J. and Blanche Hewett Neumann Reinhart [TLF No. 3721]. Raymond was born April 28, 1940, at Miles City, Montana.

(Sup) 6121 MARJORY JEAN REINHART (Blanche[8], Harvey[7], Sarah[6], David[5], John[4], Peter[3], Matthias[2], John Jacob[1]) was the daughter of Harry J. and Blanche Hewett Neumann Reinhart [TLF No. 3721]. Marjory was born July 31, 1944, at Miles City, Montana.

(Sup) 6122 HOWARD JOSEPH REINHART (Blanche[8], Harvey[7], Sarah[6], David[5], John[4], Peter[3], Matthias[2], John Jacob[1]) was the son of Harry J. and Blanche Hewett Neumann Reinhart [TLF No. 3721]. Howard was born May 1, 1946, at Miles City, Montana.

(Sup) 6123 ROY TROY HOBBS (Florence[8], Harvey[7], Sarah[6], David[5], John[4], Peter[3], Matthias[2], John Jacob[1]) was the son of Louis J. and Florence Mae Hewett Hobbs [TLF No. 3722]. Roy was born October 8, 1925, in Custer County, Montana.

(Sup) 6124 EVELYN MAE HOBBS (Florence[8], Harvey[7], Sarah[6], David[5], John[4], Peter[3], Matthias[2], John Jacob[1]) was the daughter of Louis K. and Florence Mae Hewett Hobbs [TLF No. 3722]. Evelyn was born February 15, 1928, in Custer County, Montana. She married Mervil Pope January 3, 1946, at Miles City, Montana. He was born June 17, 1920, at Harrison, Arkansas.

(Sup) 7726   † Sandra Jean Pope, born January 26, 1947.

(Sup) 6125 SHERRY ANN HOBBS (Florence^8, Harvey^7, Sarah^6, David^5, John^4, Peter^3, Matthias^2, John Jacob^1) was the daughter of Louis K. and Florence Mae Hewett Hobbs [TLF No. 3722]. She was born March 5, 1944, in Custer County, Montana.

(Sup) 6126 OPAL JEAN GILMORE (Helen^8, Harvey^7, Sarah^6, David^5, John^4, Peter^3, Matthias^2, John Jacob^1) was the daughter of Ralph and Helen Hewett Gilmore [TLF No. 3723]. She was born August 10, 1930, at Glendine, Montana.

(Sup) 6127 KATHERINE DAVID GILMORE (Helen^8, Harvey^7, Sarah^6, David^5, John^4, Peter^3, Matthias^2, John Jacob^1) was the daughter of Ralph and Helen Hewett Gilmore [TLF No. 3723]. She was born November 18, 1932, at Ismay, Montana.

(Sup) 6128 ALLEN LEE BEUSLEY (Helen^8, Harvey^7, Sarah^6, David^5, John^4, Peter^3, Matthias^2, John Jacob^1) was the son of Alvin E. and Helen Hewett Gilmore Beusley [TLF No. 3723]. Allen was born July 15, 1943, at Miles City, Montana.

(Sup) 6129 HAROLD DEAN HEWETT (Harlan^8, Harvey^7, Sarah^6, David^5, John^4, Peter^3, Matthias^2, John Jacob^1) was the son of Harlan Dale and Marguerite McMullen Hewett [TLF No. 3724]. Harold was born January 27, 1934, in South Taylor County, Iowa.

(Sup) 6130 RICHARD LEE HEWETT (Harlan^8, Harvey^7, Sarah^6, David^5, John^4, Peter^3, Matthias^2, John Jacob^1) was the son of Harlan Dale and Marguerite McMullen Hewett [TLF No. 3724]. Richard was born December 22, 1935, in Nodaway County, Missouri.

(Sup) 6131 MARY LOU ANDERSON (Noel^8, Mary^7, Elizabeth^6, David^5, John^4, Peter^3, Matthias^2, John Jacob^1) was the daughter of Noel Archie Anderson [TLF No. 3725]. She was born May 11, 1930, at Sioux City, Iowa.

(Sup) 6132 DWIGHT ALBERT ANDERSON (Noel^8, Mary^7, Elizabeth^6, David^5, John^4, Peter^3, Matthias^2, John Jacob^1) was the son of Noel Archie Anderson [TLF No. 3725]. Dwight was born July 10, 1934, at Woodland, Washington.

(Sup) 6133 RONALD JAMES ANDERSON (Noel^8, Mary^7, Elizabeth^6, David^5, John^4, Peter^3, Matthias^2, John Jacob^1) was the son of Noel Archie Anderson [TLF No. 3725]. Ronald was born February 15, 1937, at Vancouver, Washington.

(Sup) 6134 JUDITH EDNA ANDERSON (Noel^8, Mary^7, Elizabeth^6, David^5, John^4, Peter^3, Matthias^2, John Jacob^1) was the daughter of Noel Archie Anderson [TLF No. 3725]. Judith was born October 13, 1939, at Vancouver, Washington.

(Sup) 6135 LARRY LE ROY ANDERSON (Noel^8, Mary^7, Elizabeth^6, David^5, John^4, Peter^3, Matthias^2, John Jacob^1) was the son of Noel Archie Anderson [TLF No. 3725]. Larry was born March 2, 1943, at Vancouver, Washington.

(Sup) 6136 LINDA KAY COONS (Donald^8, John^7, Elizabeth^6, David^5, John^4, Peter^3, Matthias^2, John Jacob^1) was the daughter of Donald Mac and Glenna Thompson Coons [TLF No. 3729]. She was born August 28, 1947, at Sioux City, Iowa.

(Sup) 6137 WARREN LESLIE BIGELOW (Lillian^8, Zulah^7, Elizabeth^6, David^5, John^4, Peter^3, Matthias^2, John Jacob^1) was the son of Ralph and Lillian Kron Bigelow [TLF No. 3730]. Warren was born February 9, 1927, at Whiting, Iowa.

(Sup) 6138 ROBERT GENE BIGELOW (Lillian^8, Zulah^7, Elizabeth^6, David^5, John^4, Peter^3, Matthias^2, John Jacob^1) was the son of Ralph and Lillian Kron Bigelow [TLF No. 3730]. Robert was born March 6, 1928, at South Sioux City, Iowa.

(Sup) 6139 ALTON WAYNE BIGELOW (Lillian^8, Zulah^7, Elizabeth^6, David^5, John^4, Peter^3, Matthias^2, John Jacob^1) was the son of Ralph and Lillian Kron Bigelow [TLF No. 3730]. He was born May 30, 1930, at Whiting, Iowa.

(Sup) 6140 BILLIE JOE BIGELOW (Lillian^8, Zulah^7, Elizabeth^6, David^5, John^4, Peter^3, Matthias^2, John Jacob^1) was the child of Ralph and Lillian Kron Bigelow [TLF No. 3730]. Billie Joe was born November 22, 1942, at North Hollywood, California.

(Sup) 6141 CRAIG WRIGHT HINKLEY (Dolores^8, Aerie^7, William^6, David^5, John^4, Peter^3, Matthias^2, John Jacob^1) was the son of Wright R. and Dolores Staggs Hinkley [TLF No. 3732]. Craig was born January 10, 1947, at Glendale, California.

(Sup) 6142 ALAN RAY WALKER (Alice^8, Howard^7, Jennetta^6, David^5, John^4, Peter^3, Matthias^2, John Jacob^1) was the son of Qwin Lorraine and Alice Hathaway Walker [TLF No. 3739]. Alan was born September 22, 1946, at Fullerton, California.

(Sup) 6143 PAMELA ASH (William^8, Gertrude^7, Ora^6, David^5, John^4, Peter^3, Matthias^2, John Jacob^1) was the daughter of William H. and Ruth Chastain Ash [TLF No. 3741]. Pamela was born May 11, 1947.

(Sup) 6144 JUDITH THORNBROUGH KNOWLTON (Mildred^8, Gertrude^7, Ora^6, David^5, John^4, Peter^3, Matthias^2, John Jacob^1) was the daughter of George W. and Mildred Ash Thornbrough [TLF No. 3742]. Judith was born May 16, 1940. After the death of her father in 1942 and her mother's remarriage, she was adopted by her stepfather Justin G. Knowlton.

(Sup) 6145 BRUCE ALLAN KYBURZ (Paul^8, Lucy^7, Frances^6, Adam^5, Phillip^4, Peter^3, Matthias^2, John Jacob^1) was the son of Paul Hackett and Helen Millard Kyburz [TLF No. 3743]. Bruce was born May 2, 1937, at Battle Creek, Michigan.

(Sup) 6146 CAROLYN JEAN KYBURZ (Paul^8, Lucy^7, Frances^6, Adam^5, Phillip^4, Peter^3, Matthias^2, John Jacob^1) was the daughter of Paul Hackett and Helen Millard Kyburz [TLF No. 3743]. She was born October 12, 1939, at Battle Creek, Michigan.

(Sup) 6147 DEAN HOWARD KYBURZ (Paul^8, Lucy^7, Frances^6, Adam^5, Phillip^4, Peter^3, Matthias^2, John Jacob^1) was the son of Paul Hackett and Helen Millard Kyburz [TLF No. 3743]. He was born December 28, 1943, at Lansing, Michigan.

(Sup) 6148 PAUL JAMES CASWELL (Frances^8, Lucy^7, Frances^6, Adam^5, Phillip^4, Peter^3, Matthias^2, John Jacob^1) was the son of Harold Darwin and Frances Kyburz Caswell [TLF No. 3744]. Paul was born September 3, 1931, at Kinderhook, Michigan.

(Sup) 6149 RUSSELL ROBERT CASWELL (Frances^8, Lucy^7, Frances^6, Adam^5, Phillip^4, Peter^3, Matthias^2, John Jacob^1) was the son of Harold Darwin and Frances Kyburz Caswell [TLF No. 3744]. He was born July 3, 1933, at Kinderhook, Michigan.

(Sup) 6150 IRVING HAROLD CASWELL (Frances^8, Lucy^7, Frances^6, Adam^5, Phillip^4, Peter^3, Matthias^2, John Jacob^1) was the son of Harold Darwin and Frances Kyburz Caswell [TLF No. 3744]. He was born September 6, 1935, at Kinderhook, Michigan.

(Sup) 6151 DOROTHY LEE CASWELL (Frances^8, Lucy^7, Frances^6, Adam^5, Phillip^4, Peter^3, Matthias^2, John Jacob^1) was the daughter of Harold Darwin and Frances Kyburz Caswell [TLF No. 3744]. She was born November 15, 1938, at Kinderhook, Michigan.

(Sup) 6152 EUGENE WILLIAM CASWELL (Frances^8, Lucy^7, Frances^6, Adam^5, Phillip^4, Peter^3, Matthias^2, John Jacob^1) was the son of Harold Darwin and Frances Kyburz Caswell [TLF No. 3744]. He was born December 20, 1939, at Kinderhook, Michigan.

(Sup) 6153 JOY ANN CASWELL (Frances^8, Lucy^7, Frances^6, Adam^5, Phillip^4, Peter^3, Matthias^2, John Jacob^1) was the daughter of Harold Darwin and Frances Kyburz Caswell [TLF No. 3744]. She was born October 15, 1943, at Kinderhook, Michigan.

(Sup) 6154 JOAN RUTH McMAKEN (Henry^8, Henry^7, Frances^6, Adam^5, John^4, Peter^3, Matthias^2, John Jacob^1) was the daughter of Henry Hugh and Maude Long McMaken [TLF No. 3745]. Joan was born November 15, 1933.

(Sup) 6155 ADELIA RUTH FORSYTHE (Ruth^8, Henry^7, Frances^6, Adam^5, Phillip^4, Peter^3, Matthias^2, John Jacob^1) was the daughter of Lloyd and Ruth McMaken Forsythe [TLF No. 3746]. She was born March 26, 1935, at Fort Wayne, Indiana.

(Sup) 6156 WILLIAM LLOYD FORSYTHE (Ruth^8, Henry^7, Frances^6, Adam^5, Phillip^4, Peter^3, Matthias^2, John Jacob^1) was the son of Lloyd and Ruth McMaken Forsythe [TLF No. 3746]. He was born January 6, 1940, in Whitley County, Indiana.

(Sup) 6157 ANNA MAE FORSYTHE (Ruth^8, Henry^7, Frances^6, Adam^5, Phillip^4, Peter^3, Matthias^2, John Jacob^1) was the daughter of Lloyd and Ruth McMaken Forsythe [TLF No. 3746]. She was born October 20, 1943, at Fort Wayne, Indiana.

(Sup) 6158 HERBERT ROSS McMAKEN, JR. (Herbert[8], Henry[7], Frances[6], Adam[5], Phillip[4], Peter[3], Matthias[2], John Jacob[1]) was the son of Herbert Ross and Justine Ward McMaken [TLF No. 3747]. Herbert, Jr., was born May 29, 1937, at Hartford, Connecticut.

(Sup) 6159 WARD McMAKEN (Herbert[8], Henry[7], Frances[6], Adam[5], Phillip[4], Peter[3], Matthias[2], John Jacob[1]) was the son of Herbert Ross and Justine Ward McMaken [TLF No. 3747]. Ward was born November 18, 1941, at San Diego, California.

(Sup) 6160 PETER WILLIAM McMAKEN (Herbert[8], Henry[7], Frances[6], Adam[5], Phillip[4], Peter[3], Matthias[2], John Jacob[1]) was the son of Herbert Ross and Justine Ward McMaken [TLF No. 3747]. Peter was born November 26, 1948, at San Diego, California.

(Sup) 6161 BARBARA ANN VAN HOOZEN (Margaret[8], Henry[7], Frances[6], Adam[5], Phillip[4], Peter[3], Matthias[2], John Jacob[1]) was the daughter of D. and Margaret McMaken Van Hoozen [TLF No. 3748]. Barbara was born October 26, 1934.

(Sup) 6162 JOYCE ELAINE VAN HOOZEN (Margaret[8], Henry[7], Frances[6], Adam[5], Phillip[4], Peter[3], Matthias[2], John Jacob[1]) was the daughter of D. and Margaret McMaken Van Hoozen [TLF No. 3748]. Joyce was born May 3, 1939.

(Sup) 6163 RICHARD HENRY VAN HOOZEN (Margaret[8], Henry[7], Frances[6], Adam[5], Phillip[4], John[4], Peter[3], Matthias[2], John Jacob[1]) was the son of D. and Margaret McMaken Van Hoozen [TLF No. 3748]. Richard was born December 4, 1943.

(Sup) 6164 LORRAINE JO CARROLL (Jessie[8], Henry[7], Frances[6], Adam[5], Phillip[4], John[4], Peter[3], Matthias[2], John Jacob[1]) was the daughter of George and Jessie McMaken Carroll [TLF No. 3749]. She was born July 4, 1942, at Fort Wayne, Indiana.

(Sup) 6165 MARY LOUISE CARROLL (Jessie[8], Henry[7], Frances[6], Adam[5], Phillip[4], Peter[3], Matthias[2], John Jacob[1]) was the daughter of George and Jessie McMaken Carroll [TLF No. 3749]. She was born December 16, 1943, at Fort Wayne, Indiana.

(Sup) 6166 NORMA ANITA CARROLL (Jessie[8], Henry[7], Frances[6], Adam[5], Phillip[4], Peter[3], Matthias[2], John Jacob[1]) was the daughter of George and Jessie McMaken Carroll [TLF No. 3749]. She was born May 6, 1947, at Fort Wayne, Indiana.

(Sup) 6167 JANICE GAIL CARROLL (Jessie[8], Henry[7], Frances[6], Adam[5], Phillip[4], Peter[3], Matthias[2], John Jacob[1]) was the daughter of George and Jessie McMaken Carroll [TLF No. 3749]. She was born September 23, 1949, at Fort Wayne, Indiana.

(Sup) 6168 MARGUERITE HELEN JACKSON (Ralph[8], Helen[7], Frances[6], Adam[5], Phillip[4], Peter[3], Matthias[2], John Jacob[1]) was the daughter of Ralph Harry and Freda Grothe Jackson [TLF No. 3751]. Marguerite was born December 20, 1922, at Detroit, Michigan. She married Don Will June 23, 1939.

(Sup) 6169 ALICE LOUISE JACKSON (Ralph[8], Helen[7], Frances[6], Adam[5], Phillip[4], Peter[3], Matthias[2], John Jacob[1]) was the daughter of Ralph Harry and Freda Grothe Jackson [TLF No. 3751]. Alice was born May 19, 1924, at Detroit, Michigan. She married Therald Fleming April 12, 1946.

(Sup) 6170 FREDA ILENE JACKSON (Ralph[8], Helen[7], Frances[6], Adam[5], Phillip[4], Peter[3], Matthias[2], John Jacob[1]) was the daughter of Ralph Harry and Freda Grothe Jackson [TLF No. 3751]. Freda was born June 12, 1928, and died November 29, 1928, at Detroit, Michigan.

(Sup) 6171 MARY ELLEN JACKSON (Ralph[8], Helen[7], Frances[6], Adam[5], Phillip[4], Peter[3], Matthias[2], John Jacob[1]) was the daughter of Ralph Harry and Freda Grothe Jackson [TLF No. 3751]. She was born May 9, 1931, at Detroit, Michigan, and died April 4, 1932, at Berkley, Michigan.

(Sup) 6172 DONA JEAN JACKSON (Ralph[8], Helen[7], Frances[6], Adam[5], Phillip[4], Peter[3], Matthias[2], John Jacob[1]) was the daughter of Ralph Harry and Freda Grothe Jackson [TLF No. 3751]. She was born June 30, 1933, at Omaha, Nebraska.

(Sup) 6173 PLUMA ADELIA ORCUTT (Pluma[8], Helen[7], Frances[6], Adam[5], Phillip[4], John[4], Peter[3], Matthias[2], John Jacob[1]) was the daughter of Herschel Orville and Pluma Elizabeth Jackson Orcutt [TLF No. 3753]. She was born July 28, 1934.

(Sup) 6174 EARL PONTIUS (Emma[8], Elizabeth[7], Frances[6], Adam[4], Phillip[4], Peter[3], Matthias[2], John Jacob[1]) was the son of Yearl Osborn and Emma Gouty Pontius [TLF No. 3757]. Earl was born in 1937.

(Sup) 6175 RUTH ANN PONTIUS (Emma[8], Elizabeth[7], Frances[6], Adam[5], Phillip[4], Peter[3], Matthias[2], John Jacob[1]) was the daughter of Yearl Osborn and Emma Gouty Pontius [TLF No. 3757]. She was born in 1939.

(Sup) 6176 CAROLE JEAN PONTIUS (Emma[8], Elizabeth[7], Frances[6], Adam[5], Phillip[4], Peter[3], Matthias[2], John Jacob[1]) was the daughter of Yearl Osborn and Emma Gouty Pontius [TLF No. 3757]. She was born in 1940.

(Sup) 6177 DALE EDWARD PONTIUS (Emma[8], Elizabeth[7], Frances[6], Adam[5], Phillip[4], Peter[3], Matthias[2], John Jacob[1]) was the son of Yearl Osborn and Emma Gouty Pontius [TLF No. 3757]. He was born in 1942.

(Sup) 6178 JUDITH ARLENE PONTIUS (Emma[8], Elizabeth[7], Frances[6], Adam[5], Phillip[4], Peter[3], Matthias[2], John Jacob[1]) was the daughter of Yearl Osborn and Emma Gouty Pontius [TLF No. 3757]. She was born in 1945.

(Sup) 6179 SHARON JANE PONTIUS (Emma[8], Elizabeth[7], Frances[6], Adam[5], Phillip[4], Peter[3], Matthias[2], John Jacob[1]) was the daughter of Yearl Osborn and Emma Gouty Pontius [TLF No. 3757]. She was born in 1948.

(Sup) 6180 CARL DOUGLAS GOUTY (Walter[8], Elizabeth[7], Frances[6], Adam[5], Phillip[4], Peter[3], Matthias[2], John Jacob[1]) was the son of Walter and Elizabeth Robertson Gouty [TLF No. 3758]. Carl was born in 1939.

(Sup) 6181 DOYLE KEITH GOUTY (Walter[8], Elizabeth[7], Frances[6], Adam[5], Phillip[4], Peter[3], Matthias[2], John Jacob[1]) was the son of Walter and Elizabeth Robertson Gouty [TLF No. 3758]. He was born in 1944.

(Sup) 6182 LEE WALTER GOUTY (Walter[8], Elizabeth[7], Frances[6], Adam[5], Phillip[4], Peter[3], Matthias[2], John Jacob[1]) was the son of Walter and Elizabeth Robertson Gouty [TLF No. 3758]. Lee was born in 1947.

(Sup) 6183 SUSAN LYNN GOUTY (Thomas[8], Elizabeth[7], Frances[6], Adam[5], Phillip[4], John[4], Peter[3], Matthias[2], John Jacob[1]) was the daughter of Thomas Alexander and Grace Davis Gouty [TLF No. 3759]. She was born June 2, 1935, at Fort Wayne, Indiana.

(Sup) 6184 MARY ELIZABETH GOUTY (Thomas[8], Elizabeth[7], Frances[6], Adam[4], Phillip[4], Peter[3], Matthias[2], John Jacob[1]) was the daughter of Thomas Alexander and Grace Davis Gouty [TLF No. 3759]. She was born March 5, 1937, at Fort Wayne, Indiana.

(Sup) 6185 HELEN ANITA GOUTY (Thomas[8], Elizabeth[7], Frances[6], Adam[5], Phillip[4], Peter[3], Matthias[2], John Jacob[1]) was the daughter of Thomas Alexander and Grace Davis Gouty [TLF No. 3759]. Helen was born July 4, 1938, at Fort Wayne, Indiana.

(Sup) 6186 PHYLLIS DIANE GOUTY (Thomas[8], Elizabeth[7], Frances[6], Adam[5], Phillip[4], Peter[3], Matthias[2], John Jacob[1]) was the daughter of Thomas Alexander and Grace Davis Gouty [TLF No. 3759]. Phyllis was born March 17, 1942, at Fort Wayne, Indiana.

(Sup) 6187 THOMAS RICHARD GOUTY (Thomas[8], Elizabeth[7], Frances[6], Adam[5], Phillip[4], Peter[3], Matthias[2], John Jacob[1]) was the son of Thomas Alexander and Grace David Gouty [TLF No. 3759]. He was born August 26, 1944, at Fort Wayne, Indiana.

(Sup) 6188 JAMES PAUL GOUTY (Thomas[8], Elizabeth[7], Frances[6], Adam[5], Phillip[4], Peter[3], Matthias[2], John Jacob[1]) was the son of Thomas Alexander and Grace Davis Gouty [TLF No. 3759]. James was born January 7, 1948, at Fort Wayne, Indiana.

(Sup) 6189 ELLEN JANE VIDAL (Henri[8], Jennie[7], Helen[6], Adam[5], Phillip[4], Peter[3], Matthias[2], John Jacob[1]) was the daughter of Henri Brownell and Eddah James Vidal [TLF No. 3761]. Ellen was born August 25, 1924, at Niagara Falls, New York. She married Arthur Letcher Jones September 21, 1946.

(Sup) 6190 NUMA FERDINAND VIDAL, III (Numa[8], Jennie[7], Helen[6], Adam[5], Phillip[4], Peter[3], Matthias[2], John Jacob[1]) was the son of Numa Ferdinand and Arabel Truog Vidal [TLF No. 3762]. He was born May 23, 1931.

(Sup) 6191 GAY VIDAL (Richard[8], Jennie[7], Helen[6], Adam[5], Phillip[4], Peter[3], Matthias[2], John Jacob[1]) was the daughter of Richard Wilson and Barbara Wilson Vidal [TLF No. 3763]. Gay was born August 14, 1936, at Chicago, Illinois.

(Sup) 6192 SANDRA RAE PERKINS (Elizabeth[8], Myrtle[7], Adam[6], Adam[5], Phillip[4], Peter[3], Matthias[2], John Jacob[1]) was the daughter of Leo and Elizabeth Parks Perkins [TLF No. 3764]. She was born October 20, 1944.

(Sup) 6193 LINDA LEE PERKINS (Elizabeth[8], Myrtle[7], Adam[6], Adam[5], Phillip[4], Peter[3], Matthias[2], John Jacob[1]) was the daughter of Leo and Elizabeth Parks Perkins [TLF No. 3764]. She was born January 11, 1946.

(Sup) 6194 CHRISTIE LOU HULVEY (Herbert[8], George[7], Elizabeth[6], Rebecca[5], William[4], Peter[3], Matthias[2], John Jacob[1]) was the daughter of Herbert Samuel and Louise Shiflette Hulvey [TLF No. 3768]. She was born April 30, 1936, at Staunton, Virginia.

(Sup) 6195 RUSSELL M. SHANK, JR. (Marjorie[8], Arthur[7], Erasmus[6], Rebecca[5], William[4], Peter[3], Matthias[2], John Jacob[1]) was the son of Russell M. and Marjorie Houff Shank [TLF No. 3779]. Russell, Jr., was born July 6, 1932, at Waynesboro, Virginia.

(Sup) 6196 HELEN JANET SHANK (Marjorie[8], Arthur[7], Erasmus[6], Rebecca[5], William[4], Peter[3], Matthias[2], John Jacob[1]) was the daughter of Russell M. and Marjorie Houff Shank [TLF No. 3779]. Helen was born March 17, 1937, at Waynesboro, Virginia.

(Sup) 6197   DAVID EARL HOUFF, JR. (David^8, Arthur^7, Erasmus^6, Rebecca^5, William^4, Peter^3, Matthias^2, John Jacob^1) was the son of David Earl and Wilhelmina Grove Houff [TLF No. 3780]. David, Jr., was born August 3, 1942, at Waynesboro, Virginia.

(Sup) 6198   DIANE ELIZABETH HOUFF (David^8, Arthur^7, Erasmus^6, Rebecca^5, William^4, Peter^3, Matthias^2, John Jacob^1) was the daughter of David Earl and Wilhelmina Grove Houff [TLF No. 3780]. Diane was born September 25, 1946, at Waynesboro, Virginia.

- -

(Sup) 6201   DONALD AUSTIN STOVER (Raymond^8, George^7, William^6, Elizabeth^5, William^4, Peter^3, Matthias^2, John Jacob^1) was the son of Raymond Luther and Myrtle Foltz Stover [TLF No. 3791]. Donald was born April 28, 1925, at Altoona, Kansas. He married Ann Warren in 1944.

(Sup) 6202   ROBERT RAYMOND STOVER (Raymond^8, George^7, William^6, Elizabeth^5, William^4, Peter^3, Matthias^2, John Jacob^1) was the son of Raymond Luther and Myrtle Foltz Stover [TLF No. 3791]. Robert was born December 1, 1926, at Corvallis, Oregon.

(Sup) 6203   DOROTHY STOVER (Raymond^8, George^7, William^6, Elizabeth^5, William^4, Peter^3, Matthias^2, John Jacob^1) was the daughter of Raymond Luther and Myrtle Foltz Stover [TLF No. 3791]. Dorothy was born April 2, 1928, at Lincoln, Kansas.

(Sup) 6204   WILBUR DEAN STOVER (Raymond^8, George^7, William^6, Elizabeth^5, William^4, Peter^3, Matthias^2, John Jacob^1) was the son of Raymond Luther and Myrtle Foltz Stover [TLF No. 3791]. Wilbur was born September 27, 1929, at Lincoln, Kansas.

(Sup) 6205   MARJORIE JEAN STOVER (Raymond^8, George^7, William^6, Elizabeth^5, William^4, Peter^3, Matthias^2, John Jacob^1) was the daughter of Raymond Luther and Myrtle Foltz Stover [TLF No. 3791]. Marjorie was born October 3, 1934, at Hiawatha, Kansas.

(Sup) 6206   JAMES RICHARD STOVER (Raymond^8, George^7, William^6, Elizabeth^5, William^4, Peter^3, Matthias^2, John Jacob^1) was the son of Raymond Luther and Myrtle Foltz Stover [TLF No. 3791]. James was born June 24, 1940, at Hiawatha, Kansas. He died from drowning on February 16, 1947.

(Sup) 6207   GENE AUSTIN STOVER (Austin^8, George^7, William^6, Elizabeth^5, William^4, Peter^3, Matthias^2, John Jacob^1) was the son of Austin William and Opal Campbell Stover [TLF No. 3792]. He was born November 13, 1938, at Pocatello, Idaho.

(Sup) 6208   RONALD WILLIAM STOVER (Austin^8, George^7, William^6, Elizabeth^5, William^4, Peter^3, Matthias^2, John Jacob^1) was the son of Austin William and Opal Campbell Stover [TLF No. 3792]. He was born January 19, 1942, at Pocatello, Idaho.

(Sup) 6209   MARILYN DEE STOVER (Austin^8, George^7, William^6, Elizabeth^5, William^4, Peter^3, Matthias^2, John Jacob^1) was the daughter of Austin William and Opal Campbell Stover [TLF No. 3792]. Marilyn was born October 7, 1944, at Pocatello, Idaho.

(Sup) 6210   PATRICIA JEAN WOLLNER (Gladys^8, George^7, William^6, Elizabeth^5, William^4, Peter^3, Matthias^2, John Jacob^1) was the daughter of Duane Everette and Gladys Stover Wollner [TLF No. 3793]. Patricia was born September 28, 1934, at Manhattan, Kansas.

(Sup) 6211   PAUL RICHARD WILEY (Edith^8, George^7, William^6, Elizabeth^5, William^4, Peter^3, Matthias^2, John Jacob^1) was the son of John Richard and Edith Stover Wiley [TLF No. 3794]. Paul was born October 4, 1941, at Portland, Oregon.

(Sup) 6212   ROGER STOVER WILEY (Edith^8, George^7, William^6, Elizabeth^5, William^4, Peter^3, Matthias^2, John Jacob^1) was the son of John Richard and Edith Stover Wiley [TLF No. 3794]. Roger was born September 27, 1943, at Seattle, Washington.

(Sup) 6213   ALVIN EUGENE LAWSON (Ethel^8, James William^7, Jacob^6, Elizabeth^5, William^4, Peter^3, Matthias^2, John Jacob^1) was the son of Alvin J. and Ethel Stover Lawson [TLF No. 3796]. Alvin was born December 25, 1944, at Seattle, Washington.

(Sup) 6214   LYNN CHRISTINE AUER (Phillip^8, Ethel^7, Jacob^6, Elizabeth^5, William^4, Peter^3, Matthias^2, John Jacob^1) was the daughter of Phillip Eugene and Frances Barney Auer [TLF No. 7215]. Lynn was born August 8, 1946.

(Sup) 6215   FRANCIS GLENN DAMME (Freda^8, Robert^7, Charles^6, Elizabeth^5, William^4, Peter^3, Matthias^2, John Jacob^1) was the son of Alexander Jacob and Freda Stover Damme [TLF No. 3803]. He was born January 12, 1939, at Topeka, Kansas.

(Sup) 6216   DWIGHT DAVID EISENHOWER, II (John^8, Dwight^7, Ida^6, Elizabeth^5, William^4, Peter^3, Matthias^2, John Jacob^1) was the son of John Sheldon and Barbara Jean Thompson Eisenhower [TLF No. 3823]. Dwight David II, was born March 31, 1948, at West Point, New York.

(Sup) 6217 BARBARA ANNE EISENHOWER (John[8], Dwight[7], Ida[6], Elizabeth[5], William[4], Peter[3], Matthias[2], John Jacob[1]) was the daughter of John Sheldon and Barbara Jean Thompson Eisenhower [TLF No. 3823]. She was born May 30, 1949, at West Point, New York.

(Sup) 6218 THOMAS BENJAMIN FEAGAN, JR. (Patricia[8], Roy[7], Ida[6], Elizabeth[5], William[4], Peter[3], Matthias[2], John Jacob[1]) was the son of Thomas Benjamin and Patricia Eisenhower Feagan [TLF No. 3824]. Thomas, Jr., was born December 8, 1941, and died December 25, 1943.

(Sup) 6219 ROBERT ROY FEAGAN (Patricia[8], Roy[7], Ida[6], Elizabeth[5], William[4], Peter[3], Matthias[2], John Jacob[1]) was the son of Thomas Benjamin and Patricia Eisenhower Feagan [TLF No. 3824]. Robert was born July 2, 1945.

(Sup) 6220 THOMAS MICHAEL FEAGAN (Patricia[8], Roy[7], Ida[6], Elizabeth[5], William[4], Peter[3], Matthias[2], John Jacob[1]) was the son of Thomas Benjamin and Patricia Eisenhower Feagan [TLF No. 3824]. Thomas was born February 9, 1949.

- - - - - - - - - - - - - - - -

(Sup) 6225 DINA JANE BRYAN (Peggy[8], Roy[7], Ida[6], Elizabeth[5], William[4], Peter[3], Matthias[2], John Jacob[1]) was the daughter of Oliver Jackson and Peggy Jane Eisenhower Bryan [TLF No. 3826]. She was born August 13, 1949, at Denver, Colorado.

(Sup) 6226 JOSEPH WHITFIELD OUTLAW, III (Eleanor[8], Warrick[7], Hester[6], Peter[5], William[4], Peter[3], Matthias[2], John Jacob[1]) was the son of Joseph Whitfield and Eleanor Landes Outlaw, Jr., [TLF No. 3832]. Joseph Whitfield and Eleanor Landes Outlaw, Jr., was born December 20, 1943, at Beaumont, Texas.

(Sup) 6227 WARRICK BELL OUTLAW (Eleanor[8], Warrick[7], Hester[6], Peter[5], William[4], Peter[3], Matthias[2], John Jacob[1]) was the son of Joseph Whitfield and Eleanor Landes Outlaw, Jr. [TLF No. 3832]. Warrick was born February 12, 1946, at Beaumont, Texas.

(Sup) 6228 DANIEL CARTER OUTLAW (Eleanor[8], Warrick[7], Hester[6], Peter[5], William[4], Peter[3], Matthias[2], John Jacob[1]) was the son of Joseph Whitfield and Eleanor Landes Outlaw, Jr. [TLF No. 3832]. Daniel was born December 16, 1948, at Beaumont, Texas.

(Sup) 6229 CHARLES WHITTON, JR. (Betty Lou[8], Thomas[7], David[6], Nancy[5], Peter[4], Peter[3], Matthias[2], John Jacob[1]) was the son of Charles and Betty Lou Turner Whitton [TLF No. 3833]. Charles, Jr., was born July 26 1939, at Paris, Illinois.

(Sup) 6230 SANDRA LYNN WHITTON (Betty Lou[8], Thomas[7], David[6], Nancy[5], Peter[4], Peter[3], Matthias[2], John Jacob[1]) was the daughter of Charles and Betty Lou Turner Whitton [TLF No. 3833]. She was born June 25, 1941, at Paris, Illinois.

(Sup) 6231 THOMAS WHITTON (Betty Lou[8], Thomas[7], David[6], Nancy[5], Peter[4], Peter[3], Matthias[2], John Jacob[1]) was the son of Charles and Betty Lou Turner Whitton [TLF No. 3833]. Thomas was born September 7, 1942, at Paris, Illinois.

(Sup) 6232 EDWARD WHITTON (Betty Lou[8], Thomas[7], David[6], Nancy[5], Peter[4], Peter[3], Matthias[2], John Jacob[1]) was the son of Charles and Betty Lou Turner Whitton [TLF No. 3833]. Edward was born August 17, 1943, at Paris, Illinois.

(Sup) 6233 LINDA KAY TURNER (Robert[8], Thomas[7], David[6], Nancy[5], Peter[4], Peter[3], Matthias[2], John Jacob[1]) was the daughter of Robert Herman and Alici Andrews Turner [TLF No. 3835]. She was born August 15, 1944.

(Sup) 6234 WILLIAM HUGH FULLER (Kathleen[8], William[7], Booth[6], Nancy[5], Peter[4], Peter[3], Matthias[2], John Jacob[1]) was the son of Herbert H. and Kathleen Turner Fuller [TLF No. 3837]. William was born July 27, 1938, at Bozeman, Montana.

(Sup) 6235 PAMELA ANN WISEHART (Mary[8], Norman[7], Booth[6], Nancy[5], Peter[4], Peter[3], Matthias[2], John Jacob[1]) was the daughter of James A. and Mary Turner Wisehart [TLF No. 3842]. Pamela was born May 12, 1945, at Bloomington, Indiana.

(Sup) 6236 WILLIAM HARPER JONES, JR. (Miriam[8], Llewellyn[7], Mary[6], Nethaniah[5], Peter[4], Peter[3], Matthias[2], John Jacob[1]) was the son of William Harper and Miriam Callaway Jones [TLF No. 3844]. William, Jr., was born in 1925 at Great Falls, Montana. He served in the Navy during World War II.

(Sup) 6237 LLEWELLYN CALLAWAY JONES (Miriam[8], Llewellyn[7], Mary[6], Nethaniah[5], Peter[4], Peter[3], Matthias[2], John Jacob[1]) was the child of William Harper and Miriam Callaway Jones [TLF No. 3844]. Llewellyn was born November 17, 1927, at Great Falls, Montana.

(Sup) 6238 JAMES EDMUND CALLAWAY, JR. (James[8], Llewellyn[7], Mary[6], Nethaniah[5], Peter[4], Peter[3], Matthias[2], John Jacob[1]) was the son of James Edmund and Ruth Lapp Callaway [TLF No. 3845]. James, Jr., was born March 21, 1921.

(Sup) 6239 GEORGE LINK CALLAWAY (James[8], Llewellyn[7], Mary[6], Nethaniah[5], Peter[4], Peter[3], Matthias[2], John Jacob[1]) was the son of James Edmund and Ruth Lapp Callaway [TLF No. 3845]. George was born December 22, 1930.

(Sup) 6240 SAM DUPUY GOZA, V (Frances[8], Llewellyn[7], Mary[6], Nethaniah[5], Peter[4], Peter[3], Matthias[2], John Jacob[1]) was the son of Sam Dupuy and Frances Callaway Goza, IV [TLF No. 3846]. Sam, V, was born April 28, 1929, at Helena, Montana.

(Sup) 6241 PETER ANDERSON CALLAWAY (Llewellyn[8], Llewellyn[7], Mary[6], Nethaniah[5], Peter[4], Peter[3], Matthias[2], John Jacob[1]) was the son of Llewellyn Link and Helene Anderson Callaway [TLF No. 3847]. Peter was born January 8, 1941, at New York, New York.

(Sup) 6242 ELIZABETH WOODSON CALLAWAY (Llewellyn[8], Llewellyn[7], Mary[6], Nethaniah[5], Peter[4], Peter[3], Matthias[2], John Jacob[1]) was the daughter of Llewellyn Link and Helene Anderson Callaway [TLF No. 3847]. Elizabeth was born October 16, 1942, at New York, New York.

(Sup) 6243 CHARLES GORDON DOERING (Mary[8], Llewellyn[7], Mary[6], Nethaniah[5], Peter[4], Peter[3], Matthias[2], John Jacob[1]) was the son of Gordon L. and Mary Callaway Doering [TLF No. 3848]. Charles was born April 7, 1941, at Helena, Montana.

(Sup) 6244 BRUCE CALLAWAY DOERING (Mary[8], Llewellyn[7], Mary[6], Nethaniah[5], Peter[4], Peter[3], Matthias[2], John Jacob[1]) was the son of Gordon L. and Mary Callaway Doering [TLF No. 3848]. Bruce was born October 10, 1947, at Helena, Montana.

- - - - - - - - - - - - - - - - - - -

(Sup) 6245 MARY ELLEN DOERING (Mary[8], Llewellyn[7], Mary[6], Nethaniah[5], Peter[3], Matthias[2], John Jacob[1]) was the daughter of Gordon L. and Mary Callaway Doering [TLF No. 3848]. She was born February 19, 1950, at Helena, Montana.

(Sup) 6249 DONN ETHERINGTON (Alice[8], Burt[7], Alice[6], Nethaniah[5], Peter[4], Peter[3], Matthias[2], John Jacob[1]) was the son of Thomas and Alice (Donaldson) Etherington [TLF No. 3852]. Donn was born January 31, 1932, at Seattle, Washington.

(Sup) 6250 STEPHEN CARL STRAIGHT (Helen[8], Burt[7], Alice[6], Nethaniah[5], Peter[4], Peter[3], Matthias[2], John Jacob[1]) was the son of Carl and Helen (Donaldson) Straight [TLF No. 3853]. Stephen was born October 21, 1941, at Seattle, Washington.

(Sup) 6251 WILLIAM BURT STRAIGHT (Helen[8], Burt[7], Alice[6], Nethaniah[5], Peter[4], Peter[3], Matthias[2], John Jacob[1]) was the son of Carl and Helen (Donaldson) Straight [TLF No. 3853]. William was born November 21, 1944, at Seattle, Washington.

(Sup) 6252 FREDERICK PAUL ZSCHEILE, III (Frederick[8], Esther[7], Virginia[6], Nethaniah[5], Peter[4], Peter[3], Matthias[2], John Jacob[1]) was the son of Frederick Paul and Emily (Di Silvestro) Zscheile, Jr. [TLF No. 3854]. Frederick, III, was born September 5, 1934, at Chicago, Illinois.

(Sup) 6253 RICHARD ZSCHEILE (Frederick[8], Esther[7], Virginia[6], Nethaniah[5], Peter[4], Peter[3], Matthias[2], John Jacob[1]) was the son of Frederick Paul and Emily (Di Silvestro) Zscheile [TLF No. 3854]. Richard was born May 27, 1937, at Lafayette, Indiana.

(Sup) 6254 ELIZABETH THERESE ZSCHEILE (Frederick[8], Esther[7], Virginia[6], Foster[7], Virginia[6], Nethaniah[5], Peter[4], Peter[3], Matthias[2], John Jacob[1]) was the daughter of Frederick Paul and Emily (Di Silvestro) Zscheile [TLF No. 3854]. She was born July 8, 1941, at Lafayette, Indiana.

(Sup) 6255 JAMES COLE LINK (Paxson[8], Horace[7], James[6], Christopher[5], Peter[4], Peter[3], Matthias[2], John Jacob[1]) was the son of Paxson Rude and Louise (Cole) Link [Supplement No. 3859]. James was born May 11, 1924, at Paris, Illinois. An Eagle Scout, he was educated at De Pauw University and the University of Illinois where he received a B.S. degree in 1947. He served in the U.S. Navy for thirty-two months in the Pacific Theater during World War II. James married Blythe McCradie on October 21, 1948, at Chicago, Illinois. She was the daughter of Dr. Ray and Kathleen Jacobs McCradie and was born February 16, 1928, at Chicago, Illinois. Blythe graduated cum laude in 1950 from the University of Illinois, where she was a member of Gamma Phi Beta, Alpha Lambda Delta, and Torch. James operated a carbonated beverage plant at Charlotte, North Carolina, until 1973. He then served as a consultant for bottling plants in South America, Africa, and Jamaica. He was a member of the Charlotte City Club, Myers Park Country Club, and Beta Theta Pi. James and Blythe were divorced in 1972. He married, second, Laura Ann (Robinson) Jones, November 23, 1973, at Charlotte, North Carolina. She was the daughter of O.A. and Katherine (Hargrave) Robinson and was born June 16, 1934, at Charlotte. James and Laura resided at Banner Elk, North Carolina.

CHILDREN OF JAMES AND BLYTHE

(Sup) 7735   i   Christopher Ross Link, born March 26, 1952.
(Sup) 7735A   ii   David Stuart Link, born January 10, 1954.
(Sup) 7735B   iii   Blythe Andrea Link, born February 19, 1957.

Webb and Rebecca (Jones) Groves [Supplement No. 3861]. Charles was born January 20, 1964, at Crawfordsville, Indiana. An Eagle Scout, he graduated magna cum laude from Knox College, Illinois, and studied medicine at Indiana University School of Medicine. He was a member of Phi Delta Theta social fraternity and Phi Beta Kappa.

(Sup) 6260 THOMAS LINK DONAHOE (Rachel[8], Foster[7], Arthur[6], Christopher[5], Peter[4], Peter[3], Matthias[2], John Jacob[1]) was the son of Thomas Clayton and Rachel (Link) Donahoe [TLF No. 3863]. Thomas was born March 9, 1929, at Oakland, California.

(Sup) 6261 JACK FOSTER DONAHOE (Rachel[8], Foster[7], Arthur[6], Christopher[5], Peter[4], Peter[3], Matthias[2], John Jacob[1]) was the son of Thomas Clayton and Rachel (Link) [TLF No. 3863]. Jack was born September 29, 1932, at Los Angeles, California.

(Sup) 6262 JERRY EDWARD DONAHOE (Rachel[8], Foster[7], Arthur[6], Christopher[5], Peter[4], Peter[3], Matthias[2], John Jacob[1]) was the son of Thomas Clayton and Rachel (Link) Donahoe [TLF No. 3863]. Jerry was born October 22, 1946, at Long Beach, California.

(Sup) 6263 GARRETT EDWIN PACK (Miriam[8], Edith[7], Arthur[6], Christopher[5], Peter[4], Peter[3], Matthias[2], John Jacob[1]) was the son of Henry M. and Miriam (Young) Pack [TLF No. 3866]. He was born November 25, 1938, at Wichita, Kansas.

(Sup) 6264 DAVID JOSEPH PACK (Miriam[8], Edith[7], Arthur[6], Christopher[5], Peter[4], Peter[3], Matthias[2], John Jacob[1]) was the son of Henry H. and Miriam Young Pack [TLF No. 3866]. David was born March 28, 1945, at Baton Rouge, Louisiana.

(Sup) 6265 CHRISTINE YOUNG (David[8], Edith[7], Arthur[6], Christopher[5], Peter[4], Peter[3], Matthias[2], John Jacob[1]) was the daughter of David Edwin and Helen Heard Young [TLF No. 3867]. Christine was born August 10, 1945, at Moody Field, Valdosta, Georgia.

(Sup) 6266 JOHN TIMOTHY YOUNG (David[8], Edith[7], Arthur[6], Christopher[5], Peter[4], Peter[3], Matthias[2], John Jacob[1]) was the son of David Edwin and Helen Heard Young [TLF No. 3867]. He was born September 23, 1946, at Evansville, Indiana.

(Sup) 6256 MARTHA JANE LINK (Paxson[8], Horace[7], James[6], Christopher[5], Peter[4], Peter[3], Matthias[2], John Jacob[1]) was the daughter of Paxson Rude and Louise Cole Link [Supplement No. 3859]. She was born March 30, 1927, at Paris, Illinois, where she died May 8, 1935.

(Sup) 6257 JOANNA CHRISTIE LINK (Paxson[8], Horace[7], James[6], Christopher[5], Peter[4], Peter[3], Matthias[2], John Jacob[1]) was the daughter of Paxson Rude and Louise Cole Link [Supplement No. 3859]. Christie was born January 2, 1935, at Paris, Illinois. She received her education in Paris public schools and graduated from Westbrook Junior College, Portland, Maine. She married John Richard Spung, March 8, 1959, at Corpus Christi, Texas. John was the son of William Earl and Ruby Ellen (Dickson) Spung, and was born January 8, 1933, at Paris, Illinois. He was educated in Paris public schools and graduated from Indiana State Teachers College, Terre Haute, Indiana in 1956. He served as a Navy pilot and in 1967 entered the retail furniture business at Paris, Illinois. Christie served on the board of the Edgar County Red Cross, the Edgar County Children's Home and the Bicentennial Art Center and Museum.

(Sup) 7736 i Richard Cole Spung, born June 8, 1959.
(Sup) 7736A ii Peter Link Spung, born September 11, 1961.
(Sup) 7736B iii John Dickson Spung, born February 2, 1964.

(Sup) 6258 LINDA ANN LINK (Richard[8], Horace[7], James[6], Christopher[5], Peter[4], Peter[3], Matthias[2], John Jacob[1]) was the daughter of Richard Middleton and Dorothy Carter Link [Supplement No. 3860]. Linda was born May 3, 1938. She studied at DePauw University two years (where she was a member of Alpha Chi Omega sorority, as had her grandmother Link); graduated in 1960 from Indiana State Teachers College, Terre Haute, Indiana, with a B.A. degree in art education, and taught art in the schools of Prince Georges County, Maryland. In 1958 Linda married Noble Franklin Huff. He was the son of Theodore and Nathalie Jennings Huff. Frank graduated cum laude from Rose Polytechnic Institute wiyh a B.S. degree in chemical engineering in 1960. He joined Dow Chemical Company and then served in the U.S. Army 1961-1963. In 1964 he received the MBA degree from George Washington University and became Vice President of Productivity and Quality for Dow Chemical Europe, at Zürich, Switzerland.

(Sup) 7737 i Laura Jennings Huff, born July 4, 1964.
(Sup) 7738 ii Matthew Link Huff, born April 29, 1967.

(Sup) 6259 LUCY LINK (Richard[8], Horace[7], James[6], Christopher[5], Peter[4], Peter[3], Matthias[2], John Jacob[1]) was the daughter of Richard Middleton and Dorothy Carter Link [Supplement No. 3860]. Lucy was born November 7, 1943.

(Sup) 6259A CHARLES ARTHUR GROVES (Rebecca[8], Tatt[7], James[6], Christopher[5], Peter[4], Peter[3], Matthias[2], John Jacob[1]) was the son of Aquilla

(Sup) 6266A CHRISTOPHER CHAMBERS WHEAT (Susanne[8], Kathryn[7], Ivan[6], Christopher[5], Peter[4], Peter[3], Matthias[2], John Jacob[1]) was the son of Wilson Marion and Susanne Chambers Wheat [Supplement No. 3867A]. Christopher was born October 6, 1953, at Springfield, Missouri. He received an A.B. degree from Drury College, Missouri, in 1976. He received a masters degree in counseling from Missouri State University and was employed as a counselor at Park Central Hospital in Springfield. Christopher married Letha Welch, July 9, 1983. She was the daughter of Bernal Russell and Atha Welch and was born March 17, 1959, at Mountain Grove, Missouri. Letha earned an A.B. degree in interior design from Southwest Missouri State University and was employed by a retail furniture store.

(Sup) 7742   i   Jenna Marie Wheat, born March 23, 1987.

(Sup) 6267 SUSAN CAROL LINK (Charles[8], Charles[7], Charles[6], Simon[5], Peter[4], Peter[3], Matthias[2], John Jacob[1]) was the daughter of Charles Milton and Marjorie (Featherstone) Link [ILF No. 3868]. Susan was born January 7, 1947, at Glendale, California.

(Sup) 6268 ROBERT LINK BARR, JR. (Robert[8], Bess[7], Frank[6], Simon[5], Peter[4], Peter[3], Matthias[2], John Jacob[1]) was the son of Robert Link and Dorothy (Russell) Barr [Supplement No. 3870]. Robert Jr., was born May 28, 1943, at Evanston, Illinois. He attended Rose Poly Institute, Terra Haute, Indiana, and joined the U.S. Air Force 1964-69. On his return he took over his father's plastic business. Robert Married JoAnne _____, December 1979, at Dunedin, Florida. Robert and JoAnne resided in Florida.

(Sup) Adopted i Paul Barr.

(Sup) 6269 JEAN GIBBS BARR (Robert[8], Bess[7], Frank[6], Simon[5], Peter[4], Peter[3], Matthias[2], John Jacob[1]) was the daughter of Robert Link and Dorothy (Russell) Barr [Supplement No. 3870]. Jean was born February 25, 1946, at Evanston, Illinois. She received a B.A. degree from Beloit College in 1968. She worked at Citicorp Savings as records manager and at the Chicago Board of Trade as a records supervisor. She became a Certified Records Manager in 1985 and practiced as a consultant in the field of records and information management.

(Sup) 6269A KATHRYN LENORE BARR (Robert[8], Bess[7], Frank[6], Simon[5], Peter[4], Peter[3], Matthias[2], John Jacob[1]) was the daughter of Robert Link and Dorothy (Russell) Barr [Supplement No. 3870]. "Taffy" was born June 16, 1955, at Lake Forest, Illinois. She married Gerald "Mike" Smith, March 25, 1981, at Atlanta, Georgia. He was born October 17, 1946. Mike was a geography teacher and then an information analyst.

(Sup) 6269B ANNE ROUGHTON (Mary[8], Bess[7], Frank[6], Simon[5], Peter[4], Peter[3], Matthias[2], John Jacob[1]) was the daughter of Eric and Mary Margaret (Barr) Roughton [Supplement No. 3867A]. Anne was born August 14, 1946, at Rhinelander, Wisconsin. She received from the University of Wisonsin (Madison) a B.A. degree in 1968 and an M.A. degree in library science in 1969. Anne married Charles Richard Frihart, June 13, 1970, at Prairie du Lac, Wisconsin. He was the son of Arlington Leonard and Helen Gale (Waffenschmidt) Frihart, and was born September 24, 1947, at Madison, Wisconsin.

(Sup) 7743   i   Eric Arlington Frihart, born August 25, 1977.
(Sup) 7743A   ii   Rebecca Elizabeth Frihart, born May 26, 1979.
(Sup) 7743B   iii Karl Richard Frihart, born September 19, 1981.

(Sup) 6269C JULIE ROUGHTON (Mary[8], Bess[7], Frank[6], Simon[5], Peter[4], Peter[3], Matthias[2], John Jacob[1]) was the daughter of Eric and Mary Margaret (Barr) Roughton [Supplement No. 3871]. Julie was born June 3, 1949, at Rhinelander, Wisconsin. She graduated from the University of Wisconsin, Madison, in June, 1971. Julie married Gerald Lawrence Shidell, June 21, 1969, at Wausau, Wisconsin. He was the son of Lawrence and Ruth Shidell and was born May 1, 1947, at Wausau.

(Sup) 7743C i   Christine Louise Shidell, born October 25, 1969.
(Sup) 7743D ii Alison Marie Shidell, born May 1, 1973.

(Sup) 6270 JETTA LEE COLLIFLOWER (Merle[8], Hugh[7], Charles[6], Mary[5], Peter[4], Peter[3], Matthias[2], John Jacob[1]) was the daughter of Arthur B. and Merle Smith Colliflower [ILF No. 3873]. She was born October 1, 1928, at Robinson, Illinois.

(Sup) 6271 LAWRENCE H. COLLIFLOWER (Merle[8], Hugh[7], Charles[6], Mary[5], Peter[4], Peter[3], Matthias[2], John Jacob[1]) was the son of Arthur B. and Merle Smith Colliflower [ILF No. 3873]. Lawrence was born December 24, 1932, at Robinson, Illinois.

(Sup) 6272 MARILYN JEAN COLLIFLOWER (Merle[8], Hugh[7], Charles[6], Mary[5], Peter[4], Peter[3], Matthias[2], John Jacob[1]) was the daughter of Arthur B. and Merle Smith Colliflower [ILF No. 3873]. Marilyn was born July 19, 1935, at Robinson, Illinois.

(Sup) 6273 SUE ELLEN COLLIFLOWER (Merle[8], Hugh[7], Charles[6], Mary[5], Peter[4], Peter[3], Matthias[2], John Jacob[1]) was the daughter of Arthur B. and Merle Smith Colliflower [ILF No. 3873]. She was born June 22, 1940, at Robinson, Illinois.

(Sup) 6274 DAVID ARTHUR COLLIFLOWER (Merle[8], Hugh[7], Charles[6], Mary[5], Peter[4], Peter[3], Matthias[2], John Jacob[1]) was the son of Arthur B. and Merle Smith Colliflower [TLF No. 3873]. He was born November 16, 1942, at Robinson, Illinois.

(Sup) 6275 PATRICIA JEAN WILSON (Mayme[8], Hugh[7], Charles[6], Mary[5], Peter[4], Peter[3], Matthias[2], John Jacob[1]) was the daughter of Alexander S. and Mayme Smith Wilson [TLF No. 3874]. Patricia was born January 18, 1938, at Chicago, Illinois.

(Sup) 6276 WILLIAM A. WILSON (Mayme[8], Hugh[7], Charles[6], Mary[5], Peter[4], Peter[3], Matthias[2], John Jacob[1]) was the son of Alexander S. and Mayme Smith Wilson [TLF No. 3874]. William was born April 24, 1939, at Chicago, Illinois.

(Sup) 6277 ROBERT KENNETH WILSON (Mayme[8], Hugh[7], Charles[6], Mary[5], Peter[4], Peter[3], Matthias[2], John Jacob[1]) was the son of Alexander S. and Mayme Smith Wilson [TLF No. 3874]. Robert was born June 25, 1940, at Chicago, Illinois.

(Sup) 6278 RICHARD KEITH WILSON (Mayme[8], Hugh[7], Charles[6], Mary[5], Peter[4], Peter[3], Matthias[2], John Jacob[1]) was the son of Alexander S. and Mayme Smith Wilson [TLF No. 3874]. Richard was born June 25, 1940, at Chicago, Illinois.

(Sup) 6279 CLARENCE MAX SCHROEDER (Madge[8], Hugh[7], Charles[6], Mary[5], Peter[4], Peter[3], Matthias[2], John Jacob[1]) was the son of Clarence F. and Madge Smith Schroeder [TLF No. 3875]. Clarence was born April 17, 1938, at South Bend, Indiana.

(Sup) 6280 DONNA NAOMI SCHROEDER (Madge[8], Hugh[7], Charles[6], Mary[5], Peter[4], Peter[3], Matthias[2], John Jacob[1]) was the daughter of Clarence F. and Madge Smith Schroeder [TLF No. 3875]. Donna was born January 18, 1941, at South Bend, Indiana.

(Sup) 6281 JAMES F. SCHROEDER (Madge[8], Hugh[7], Charles[6], Mary[5], Peter[4], Peter[3], Matthias[2], John Jacob[1]) was the son of Clarence F. and Madge Smith Schroeder [TLF No. 3875]. James was born December 10, 1943, at South Bend, Indiana.

(Sup) 6282 MARY INGLIS BEDDOE (Mary[8], Mary[7], Cary[6], Mary[5], Peter[4], Peter[3], Matthias[2], John Jacob[1]) was the daughter of George Halsey and Mary Elizabeth (Parrish) Beddoe [Supplement No. 3876]. Mary was born December 30, 1937, at Toronto, Ontario, Canada. Polly, as she was known, graduated from Stuart Hall in Staunton, Virginia, in 1956 and attended Duke University 1956-57. She married George William Jett, August 3, 1958, at Ashland, Kentucky. He was the son of Curtis Beach and Jalia Mae (Noland) Jett of Winchester, Kentucky, and was born July 29, 1938, at Winchester. George attended Duke University and graduated from the University of Kentucky in 1961 and then from the George Washington Law School in 1965. He was admitted to the Virginia Bar. He was employed in various government positions, serving as the minority counsel, Senate Government Affairs Committee; Intergovernmental Relations Subcommittee, General Counsel of the Defense Civil Preparedness Agency, and last as general counsel of the Federal Emergency Management Administration. Mary was active in the Episcopal Church. They had four children.

(Sup) 7747 i Mary Noland Jett, born July 9, 1959.
(Sup) 7747A ii George William Jett, Jr., born June 1, 1960.
(Sup) 7747B iii John Beach Jett, born February 18, 1963.
(Sup) 7748C iv Elizabeth Parrish Jett, born October 25, 1967.

(Sup) 6283 ELIZABETH CRAWFORD BEDDOE (Mary[8], Mary[7], Cary[6], Mary[5], Peter[4], Peter[3], Matthias[2], John Jacob[1]) was the daughter of George Halsey and Mary Elizabeth (Parrish) Beddoe [Supplement No. 3876]. Betsy was born June 19, 1940, at Toronto, Ontario, Canada. She married Stephen Ernest Berger, June 9, 1962, at Ashland, Kentucky. He was the son of George Adam and Amelia Berger and was born April 17, 1931, at Baltimore, Maryland. Stephen was in the business of petroleum sales.

(Sup) 7747D i George Adam Berger, born October 27, 1964.
(Sup) 7747E ii Mary Elizabeth Berger, born June 6, 1966.
(Sup) 7747F iii Robert Parrish Berger, born September 26, 1967.

(Sup) 6284 GEORGE BEDDOE (Mary[8], Mary[7], Cary[6], Mary[5], Peter[4], Peter[3], Matthias[2], John Jacob[1]) was the son of George Halsey and Mary Elizabeth (Parrish) Beddoe [Supplement No. 3876]. George was born February 1, 1943, at Miami, Florida. He married, first, Carol Amelia Barrow, September 4, 1972, at Ellicott City, Maryland. They were divorced June 4, 1975. George married, second, Penelope Upshur Pritchard on August 13, 1977, at Fairfax, Virginia. She was the daughter of Charles Austin and Martha Lee (Upshur) Pritchard and was born July 22, 1943, at Baltimore, Maryland. George graduated from Christ School, Arden, North Carolina, in 1960; received his B.A. from Ohio Wesleyan University in 1964; his master's degree from University of Miami in 1968; and attended the graduate school of business at George Washington University. He was employed by the Office of the Secretary of Defense. Penelope graduated from Hollins College in 1965. She had two children by a previous marriage, Elizabeth Page Logsdon and Michael Cary Logsdon.

CHILDREN OF GEORGE AND PENELOPE

(Sup) 7747G i George Halsey Beddoe, Jr., born July 3, 1978.
(Sup) 7747H ii Sarah Pritchard Beddoe, born May 8, 1982.

(Sup) 6285 CONSTANCE ELIZABETH PARRISH (James[8], Mary[7], Cary[6], Mary[5], Peter[4], Peter[3], Matthias[2], John Jacob[1]) was the daughter of James Edward and Alma (Sorensen) Parrish [Supplement No. 3877]. Constance was born August 15, 1945, at Blair, Nebraska. She married Gail Pershing Norstrom, Jr. He was the son of Gail Pershing and Elizabeth Lee Norstrom, and was born September 8, 1945, at Washington, D.C. Constance and Gail were both educated at Tulsa University. He was an executive in the insurance industry at Hartford, Connecticut; they resided at Simsby, Connecticut.

(Sup) 7748   i   Rebecca Gail Norstrom, born Dec 22, 1976.
(Sup) 7748A ii Gregory James Parrish Norstrom, born Jan 27, 1983.

(Sup) 6285A JANET KAYE PARRISH (James[8], Mary[7], Cary[6], Mary[5], Peter[4], Peter[3], Matthias[2], John Jacob[1]) was the daughter of James Edward and Alma (Sorensen) Parrish [Supplement No. 3877]. Janet was born June 18, 1948, at Casper, Wyoming. She married Charles Louis Rogers, III, December 21, 1969, at Tulsa, Oklahoma. Janet and Charles resided at Tulsa.

(Sup) 7748B i   Jeffery Michael Rogers, born August 13, 1974.
(Sup) 7748C ii Chad Edward Rogers, born December 17, 1978.

(Sup) 6285B MARY JENNIFER PARRISH (Robert[8], Mary[7], Cary[6], Mary[5], Peter[4], Peter[3], Matthias[2], John Jacob[1]) was the daughter of Robert Nevins and Bonnie (Huffer) Parrish [Supplement No. 3878]. Mary was born April 6, 1960, at Indianapolis, Indiana. She was a graduate of Saint Richard's School and Park Tudor School at Indianapolis, and she received a B.A. degree in 1982 from College of Wooster, Ohio. She was employed as editorial assistant at Franklin Watts Publishing Co., New York. Mary married John Rakos, Jr., September 19, 1987, at Madison, New Jersey. He was the son of John and Eva Rakos.

(Sup) 6285C JANE SHEPPARD PARRISH (Robert[8], Mary[7], Cary[6], Mary[5], Peter[4], Peter[3], Matthias[2], John Jacob[1]) was the daughter of Robert Nevins and Bonnie (Huffer) Parrish [Supplement No. 3878]. Jane was born November 15, 1961, at Indianapolis, Indiana.

(Sup) 6285D ROBERT NEVINS PARRISH, III (Robert[8], Mary[7], Cary[6], Mary[5], Peter[4], Peter[3], Matthias[2], John Jacob[1]) was the son of Robert Nevins and Bonnie (Huffer) Parrish [Supplement No. 3878]. Robert, III, was born January 4, 1963, at Indianapolis, Indiana.

(Sup) 6286 PAUL WARNER LINK (Isaac[8], Francis[7], Ruez[6], Francis Marion[5], Peter[4], Peter[3], Matthias[2], John Jacob[1]) was the son of Isaac Dickson and Elizabeth Edmonds Link [TLF No. 3879]. Paul was born October 18, 1922, at Los Angeles, California,

(Sup) 6287 JOHN LINK (Isaac[8], Francis[7], Ruez[6], Francis Marion[5], Peter[4], Peter[3], Matthias[2], John Jacob[1]) was the son of Isaac Dickson and Elizabeth (Edmonds) Link [TLF No. 3879]. John was born June 11, 1930, at Los Angeles, California.

(Sup) 6288 CARROL ROLLINS WOOD, JR. (Hilah[8], Hilah[7], Ruez[6], Francis Marion[5], Peter[4], Peter[3], Matthias[2], John Jacob[1]) was the son of Carrol Rollins and Hilah Jane (Kirk) Wood [Supplement No. 3880]. Carrol, Jr., was born May 28, 1945, at Winston-Salem, North Carolina.

(Sup) 6288A HILAH JANE WOOD (Hilah[8], Hilah[7], Ruez[6], Francis Marion[5], Peter[4], Peter[3], Matthias[2], John Jacob[1]) was the daughter of Carrol Rollins and Hilah Jane (Kirk) Wood [Supplement No. 3880]. Hilah was born January 11, 1949, at Atlanta, Georgia. She received from the University of Georgia a bachelor's degree in 1970 and a master's degree in 1972. Hilah married James Fender Watson, June 12, 1970, at Atlanta. He was the son of William Albert and Sarah (Fender) Watson, and was born October 6, 1948, at Jesup, Georgia.

(Sup) 7749   i   James Justin Watson, born February 20, 1974.
(Sup) 7749A ii Thad Kirk Watson, born June 6, 1976.
(Sup) 7749B iii Kathryn Jane Watson, born March 30, 1981.

(Sup) 6288B JOHN WOOD (Hilah[8], Hilah[7], Ruez[6], Francis Marion[5], Peter[4], Peter[3], Matthias[2], John Jacob[1]) was the son of Carrol Rollins and Hilah Jane (Kirk) Wood [Supplement No. 3380]. John was born October 13, 1956, at Plainfield, New Jersey.

(Sup) 6288C CHARLOTTE LINK KIRK (Haddon[8], Hilah[7], Ruez[6], Francis Marion[5], Peter[4], Peter[3], Matthias[2], John Jacob[1]) was the daughter of Haddon Spurgeon and Charlotte (Clarke) Kirk, Jr. [Supplement No. 3881]. Charlotte was born August 10, 1947, at Winston-Salem, North Carolina. She graduated from Chatham Hall and Vassar College. Charlotte married Jonathan Randolph Reynolds, June 10, 1978, at New York City. He was the son of Donald Worthington and Edith (Remick) Reynolds, and was born February 13, 1942.

(Sup) 7750   i   Frank Worthington Reynolds, born June 5, 1980.
(Sup) 7750A ii Edward Kirk Reynolds, born August 5, 1983.

School and the University of North Carolina. He became a fashion photographer in New York City, New York.

(Sup) 6289 ANN DOLE BRYAN (Mary[8], Pearl[7], John[6], Francis Marion[5], Peter[4], Peter[3], Matthias[2], John Jacob[1]) was the daughter of Frank and Mary (Dole) Bryan [Supplement No. 3883]. Ann was born October 1, 1929, at St. Louis, Missouri. She studied at De Pauw University and graduated from Skidmore College. In 1951. She married Walter R. Steidl, 1951, at West Point Military Academy. They owned the Burgess Falls Nursery at Cookeville, Tennessee.

(Sup) 7753   1 Catherine Steidl, born July 23, 1952.
(Sup) 7753A   ii Phillip Andrew Steidl, born February 6, 1954.
(Sup) 7753B   iii Carrie Beth Steidl, born February 23, 1970.

(Sup) 6290 ELIZABETH DOLE (George[8], Pearl[7], John[6], Francis Marion[5], Peter[4], Peter[3], Matthias[2], John Jacob[1]) was the daughter of George and Dorothy (Thomas) Dole [Supplement No. 3884]. Elizabeth was born August 22, 1942, at Wilkes-Barre, Pennsylvania. She married, first, Jerome Akin. Elizabeth married, second, Robert Gardner. She married, third, Douglas Weigelt. Elizabeth was head of volunteers for Swedish Hospital, Seattle, Washington.

(Sup) 7754   1 Christine Akin.
(Sup) 7754A   ii Jerome Eric Akin.
(Sup) 7754B   iii Erika Akin, born October 26, 1970.

(Sup) 6291 PETER THOMAS DOLE (George[8], Pearl[7], John[6], Francis Marion[5], Peter[4], Peter[3], Matthias[2], John Jacob[1]) was the son of George and Dorothy (Thomas) Dole [Supplement No. 3884]. Peter was born June 15, 1944, at Buffalo, New York. He served as a Green Beret in Vietnam. He graduated from Dartmouth College, 1966, and Vanderbilt Law School. He practiced law with the lawfirm of Dillavou, Overaker, Asher, Smith, & Dole at Paris, Illinois. Peter married, first, Barbara Ann Robertaccio. He married, second, Rebecca Welch.

CHILDREN OF PETER AND BARBARA
(Sup) 7754C   1 Polly Dole, born October 28, 1975.
(Sup) 7754D   ii Anna Apphia Dole, born February 11, 1979.

(Sup) 6292 MARY JANE PARRISH (Allen[8], Fred[7], Susan[6], Francis Marion[5], Peter[4], Peter[3], Matthias[2], John Jacob[1]) was the daughter of Allen and Dorothy (Koho) Parrish [Supplement No. 3885]. Mary was born February 3, 1929, at Paris, Illinois. After graduating from Paris High School, she worked as a secretary. She married Gene L. Amacher, September 9, 1950, at Marshall, Illinois. He was the son of John L. and Nell (Gross) Amacher and was born August 31, 1929, at Terry Haute, Indiana. Gene graduated in electrical engineering from the Milwaukee School of Engineering, 1956, and was employed by National Cash Register at Dayton and Cambridge, Ohio.

(Sup) 7755   1 Carol Sue Amacher, born October 10, 1952.

(Sup) 6288D HADDON SPURGEON KIRK, III (Haddon[8], Hilah[7], Ruez[6], Francis Marion[5], Peter[4], Peter[3], Matthias[2], John Jacob[1]) was the son of Haddon Spurgeon and Charlotte (Clarke) Kirk, Jr., [Supplement No. 3881]. Haddon III was born March 5, 1949, at Plainfield, New Jersey. He graduated from Woodberry Forest School and Yale University, and was employed in advertizing for cable TV. He married Mary Ruth Marsh, June 11, 1977, at Elkin, North Carolina. She was the daughter of James and Mary Ruth Marsh, and was born June 20, 1954, at Elkin.

(Sup) 7750B   1 Emily Kirk, born May 31, 1981.
(Sup) 7750C   ii Haddon Clarke Kirk, born August 24, 1983.

(Sup) 6288E CATHERINE CLARKE KIRK (Haddon[8], Hilah[7], Ruez[6], Francis Marion[5], Peter[4], Peter[3], Matthias[2], John Jacob[1]) was the daughter of Haddon Spurgeon and Charlotte (Clarke) Kirk, Jr., [Supplement No. 3881]. Catherine was born March 10, 1952, at Plainfield, New Jersey. She graduated from Chatham Hall and Sophie Newcombe. Catherine married Michael Allen Fogarty, Jr., September 17, 1977, at Roaring Gap, North Carolina. He was the son of Michael Allen and Sandra Fogarty. Catherine and Michael resided at New Orleans, Louisiana.

(Sup) 7751   1 Cecily Fogarty, born April 10, 1979.
(Sup) 7751A   ii Michael Shane Fogarty, born August 26, 1982.
(Sup) 7751B   iii Joshua Neal Fogarty, born January 7, 1986.

(Sup) 6288F ELIZABETH GODWIN KIRK (Haddon[8], Hilah[7], Ruez[6], Francis Marion[5], Peter[4], Peter[3], Matthias[2], John Jacob[1]) was the daughter of Haddon Spurgeon and Charlotte (Clarke) Kirk, Jr., [Supplement No. 3881]. Elizabeth was born December 14, 1954, at Plainfield, New Jersey. She graduated from Chatham Hall and Williams College. Elizabeth married Peter Reppert Unger, June 7, 1980, at Roaring Gap, North Carolina. He was the son of Richard and Laura (Reppert) Unger, and was born April 26, 1956, at Paoli, Pennsylvania. Elizabeth and Peter resided at Paoli.

(Sup) 7752   1 Edward Reppert Unger, born March 8, 1984.
(Sup) 7752A   ii Sarah Elizabeth Unger, born July 21, 1986.

(Sup) 6288G LEO HARVEY KIRK (Robert[7], Hilah[7], Ruez[6], Francis Marion[5], Peter[4], Peter[3], Matthias[2], John Jacob[1]) was the son of Robert Link and Laura (Harvey) Kirk [Supplement No. 3882]. Leo was born August 26, 1955, at Kinston, North Carolina. He was a free-lance travel agent at Charlotte, North Carolina.

(Sup) 6288H ROBERT LINK KIRK, JR. (Robert[7], Hilah[7], Ruez[6], Francis Marion[5], Peter[4], Peter[3], Matthias[2], John Jacob[1]) was the son of Robert Link and Laura (Harvey) Kirk [Supplement No. 3882]. Robert, Jr., was born December 10, 1956, at Kinston, North Carolina. He attended Woodberry Forest

(Sup) 6293 JOHN ARTHUR PARRISH (William^8, Harry^7, Susan^6, Francis Marion^5, Peter^4, Peter^3, Matthias^2, John Jacob^1) was the son of William and Hilah (Huffman) Parrish [Supplement No. 3886]. John was born May 1, 1941. He married Lona Rae Sandilands. She was the daughter of Jay and Pauline (Zea) Sandilands. John and Lona lived at Overland Park, Kansas, where he was a CPA in private practice.

(Sup) 7756   i   Kimberly Lynn Parrish, born April 11, 1964.
(Sup) 7757   ii   Michael Parrish, born August 25, 1966.

(Sup) 6294 WILLIAM LEE PARRISH (William^8, Harry^7, Susan^6, Francis Marion^5, Peter^4, Peter^3, Matthias^2, John Jacob^1) was the son of William and Hilah Huffman Parrish [Supplement No. 3886]. William was born July 31, 1945. He married Fredrica Fazio. She was the daughter of Harry and Emily (Wolfe) Fazio.

(Sup) 6295 HARRY CURTIS PARRISH, JR. (Harry^8, Edgar^7, Susan^6, Francis Marion^5, Peter^4, Peter^3, Matthias^2, John Jacob^1) was the son of Harry Curtis and Frances Steidl Parrish [TLF No. 3887]. Harry was born April 19, 1942, at Paris, Illinois.

(Sup) 6296 PAMELA ANNE PARRISH (Harry^8, Edgar^7, Susan^6, Francis Marion^5, Peter^4, Peter^3, Matthias^2, John Jacob^1) was the daughter of Harry Curtis and Frances Steidl Parrish [TLF No. 3887]. Pamela Anne was born November 1, 1945, at Paris, Illinois.

(Sup) 6297 FRANCES SHARON PARRISH (Harry^8, Edgar^7, Susan^6, Francis Marion^5, Peter^4, Peter^3, Matthias^2, John Jacob^1) was the daughter of Harry Curtis and Frances Steidl Parrish [TLF No. 3887]. She was born August 22, 1948, at Paris, Illinois.

(Sup) 6298 JAMES ARTHUR PARRISH (Joseph^8, Edgar^7, Susan^6, Francis Marion^5, Peter^4, Peter^3, Matthias^2, John Jacob^1) was the son of Joseph and Kathleen Noyes Parrish [TLF No. 3888]. James was born April 2, 1950, at Paris, Illinois.

(Sup) 6299 JO LYNNE JOHNSON (Jo Ann^8, Marion^7, Christopher^6, Francis Marion^5, Peter^4, Peter^3, Matthias^2, John Jacob^1) was the daughter of Louis F. and Jo Ann Link Johnson [Supplement No. 3890]. Jo Lynn was born March 31, 1946, at Terre Haute, Indiana. She attended Indiana State University and graduated with a degree in Criminal Justice from Southern Illinois University in 1971. Jo Lynne married Patrick G. Wohlwend, August 16, 1971, at Carbondale, Illinois. He was the son of Jacob A. and Bess Wyman Wohlwend, and was born January 25, 1950, near Chicago, Illinois. Jo Lynne and Patrick resided at Lompac, California, where he was employed with the Justice Department of the Federal Penitentiary.

(Sup) 7758   i   Jennifer Jo Wohlwend, born July 25, 1973.
(Sup) 7758A   ii Julie Wohlwend, born July 16, 1977.

(Sup) 6299A GREGORY LOUIS JOHNSON (Jo Ann^8, Marion^7, Christopher^6, Francis Marion^5, Peter^4, Peter^3, Matthias^2, John Jacob^1) was the son of Louis F. and Jo Ann Link Johnson [Supplemet No. 3890]. Gregory was born October 29, 1950, at Fairfield, Illinois. He graduated form Augustinian Academy at St. Louis, Missouri, and later attended several junior colleges. He resided at Naples, Florida, wehre he was employed by a construction company.

(Sup) 6299B MICHAEL LINK JOHNSON (Jo Ann^8, Marion^7, Christopher^6, Francis Marion^5, Peter^4, Peter^3, Matthias^2, John Jacob^1) was the son of Louis F. and Jo Ann Link Johnson [Supplement No. 3890]. Michael was born September 29, 1955, at Fairfield, Illinois. He received a B.S. degree in 1978 from Murray State University, Kentucky, where he was active in Alpha Tau Omega fraternity. Michael married Deborah Walker, November 8, 1980, at Calvert City, Kentucky. She was the daughter of Daniel Johnson and Janice Bowling Walker and was born January 20, 1962, at Murray, Kentucky. Michael and Deborah lived at Arlington Heights, Illinois, where he was the regional manager of the Midwest Division of Siemen's.

(Sup) 7758B   i   Danielle Marie Johnson, born February 28, 1981.
(Sup) 7758C   ii   Megan Christine Johnson, born March 6, 1986.

(Sup) 6299C MARK FRANCIS JOHNSON (Jo Ann^8, Marion^7, Christopher^6, Francis Marion^5, Peter^4, Peter^3, Matthias^2, John Jacob^1) was the son of Louis F. and Jo Ann Link Johnson [Supplement No. 3890]. Mark was born September 4, 1963, at Fairfield, Illinois. He studied petroleum technology at Lincoln Trail Junior College, Illinois, and received a Bachelor's degree in geology from Eastern Illinois University. Mark married Rae Ellen Owen, August 8, 1987, at Fairfield. She was the daughter of Bob C. and Kay Ellen (Hill) Owen and was born September 14, 1967, at Fairfield.

(Sup) 6300 STEVEN EARL ANKER (Patricia^8, Marion^7, Christopher^6, Francis Marion^5, Peter^4, Peter^3, Matthias^2, John Jacob^1) was the son of Merle and Patricia Link Anker [Supplement No. 3891]. Steven was born September 6, 1951, at Fort Riley, Kansas. He died December 21, 1981.

(Sup) 6300A DAVID PATRICK ANKER (Patricia^8, Marion^7, Christopher^6, Francis Marion^5, Peter^4, Peter^3, Matthias^2, John Jacob^1) was the son of Merle and Patricia Link Anker [Supplement No. 3891]. David was born August 7, 1953, at Fairfield, Illinois. He died November 3, 1971.

(Sup) 6300B JENISE ANN ANKER (Patricia^8, Marion^7, Christopher^6, Francis Marion^5, Peter^4, Peter^3, Matthias^2, John Jacob^1) was the daughter of Merle and Patricia Link Anker [Supplement No. 3891]. Jenise was born January 5, 1959, at St. Louis, Missouri.

(Sup) 6301 STACEY FORD LINK (Wendell^8, Wendell^7, Nethaniah^6, Francis Marion^5, Peter^4, Peter^3, Matthias^2, John Jacob^1) was the daughter of Wendell Hubbard and Barbara Ford Link [Supplement No. 3892]. Stacey was born December 21, 1952, at New York City. She married Kunio Kobiyama, August 9, 1980, at Denver, Colorado.

(Sup) 6302 WENDEL ANTHONY LINK (Wendell^8, Wendell^7, Nethaniah^6, Francis Marion^5, Peter^4, Peter^3, Matthias^2, John Jacob^1) was the son of Wendell Hubbard and Barbara Ford Link [Supplement No. 3892]. Wendell was born February 6, 1957, at Freeport, New York. He married Margaret Hall, August 2, 1986, at Grant Junction, Colorado.

(Sup) 6303 JANET EMILY MARSHALL (Patricia^8, Peter^4, Peter^3, Matthias^2, John Jacob^1) was the daughter of Dale R. and Patricia Link Marshall [Supplement No. 3893]. Janet was born August 25, 1950, at Kansas City, Kansas. She graduated from Cornell College, Iowa, in 1972. Janet married, first, Andrew J. Kostrog, June 8, 1974. She married, second, Scott M. Anderson, September 2, 1982. He was the son of Rod and Darlene Anderson of Rockford, Illinois. Janet and Scott resided at Kansas City, Missouri, where they were employed at Business Supply Company.

CHILD OF JANET AND ANDREW

(Sup) 7759 i Christine Michele Kostrog, born January 18, 1978.

CHILD OF JANET AND SCOTT

(Sup) 7760 ii Jessica Kathleen Anderson, born January 25, 1987.

(Sup) 6303A SUSAN PATRICIA MARSHALL (Patricia^8, Wendell^7, Nethaniah^6, Francis Marion^5, Peter^4, Peter^3, Matthias^2, John Jacob^1) was the daughter of Dale R. and Patricia Link Marshall [Supplement No. 3893]. Susan was born January 17, 1952, at Kansas City, Kansas. She married Mark A. Lagergren, September 13, 1980. He was the son of Gil and Lorraine Lagergren of Kansas City. He graduated from the University of Missouri. Susan and Mark lived at Kansas City, where he worked for North Supply Co., and she worked for Ford Motor Credit.

(Sup) 6303B DEBRA DALE MARSHALL (Patricia^8, Wendell^7, Nethaniah^6, Francis Marion^5, Peter^4, Peter^3, Matthias^2, John Jacob^1) was the daughter of Dale R. and Patricia Link Marshall [Supplement No. 3893]. Debra was born October 4, 1953, at Kansas City, Kansas. She married James W. Stephens,

March 20, 1976. He was the son of "Spiz" and Billie Ann Stephens of Cassville, Missouri. James was a gunnery sergeant in the U.S. Marine Corps.

(Sup) 7761 i Christopher Wiliam Stephens, born July 18, 1978.
(Sup) 7761A ii Jeffrey Dale Stephens, born December 2, 1980.

(Sup) 6303C REBECCA LYN MARSHALL (Patricia^8, Wendell^7, Nethaniah^6, Francis Marion^5, Peter^4, Peter^3, Matthias^2, John Jacob^1) was the daughter of Dale R. and Patricia Link Marshall [Supplement No. 3893]. Rebecca was born January 20, 1957, at Kansas City, Missouri. She married James Carmean, January 25, 1975. They lived at Belton, Missouri.

(Sup) 7761B i Erin Lyn Carmean, born July 22, 1975.

(Sup) 6303D NANCY ANN MARSHALL (Patricia^8, Peter^4, Peter^3, Matthias^2, John Jacob^1) was the daughter of Dale R. and Patricia Link Marshall [Supplement No. 3893]. Nancy was born October 6, 1959, at Kansas City, Missouri. She married, first, Patrick A. Lumb, June 17, 1978. Nancy married, second, Michael C. Miller, February 8, 1985. They lived at Belton, Missouri.

CHILD OF NANCY AND PATRICK

(Sup) 7761C i Patricia Ann Lumb, born September 12, 1985.

CHILD OF NANCY AND MICHAEL

(Sup) 7761D ii Joshua Michael Miller, born January 20, 1986.

(Sup) 6304 JENNIFER M. CASEY (Martha^8, Eugene^7, Nethaniah^6, Francis Marion^5, Peter^4, Peter^3, Matthias^2, John Jacob^1) was the daughter of Charles Phillip and Martha (Link) Casey [Supplement No. 3894]. Jennifer was born August 10, 1969, at Madison, Wisconsin. She attended Pomona College, California.

(Sup) 6304A MONICA LINK (Martha^8, Eugene^7, Nethaniah^6, Francis Marion^5, Peter^4, Peter^3, Matthias^2, John Jacob^1) was the daughter of Charles Phillip and Martha (Link) Casey [Supplement No. 3894]. Monica was born March 27, 1981.

(Sup) 6304B NATHAN LINK (Martha^8, Eugene^7, Nethaniah^6, Francis Marion^5, Peter^4, Peter^3, Matthias^2, John Jacob^1) was the son of Charles Phillip and Martha (Link) Casey [Supplement No. 3894]. Nathan was born February 22, 1985.

(Sup) 6304C SASHA DEUTSCH-LINK (Bruce[8], Eugene[7], Nethaniah[7], Francis Marion[5], Peter[4], Peter[3], Matthias[2], John Jacob[1]) was the daughter of William Bruce George and Serena (Deutsch) Link [Supplement No. 3895A]. Sasha was born January 6, 1988, at New York City.

(Sup) 6304D AMANDA KATHRYN SCHWEGLER (Robert[8], Lida[7], Nethaniah[6], Francis Marion[5], Peter[4], Peter[3], Matthias[2], John Jacob[1]) was the daughter of Robert George and Martha (Stitt) Schwegler [Supplement No. 3896]. Amanda was born April 28, 1975, at Kansas City, Kansas.

(Sup) 6304E CARA ELIZABETH SCHWEGLER (Robert[8], Lida[7], Nethaniah[6], Francis Marion[5], Peter[4], Peter[3], Matthias[2], John Jacob[1]) was the daughter of Robert George and Martha (Stitt) Schwegler [Supplement No. 3896]. Cara was born July 29, 1979, at Overland Park, Kansas.

(Sup) 6304F LAWRENCE ALLEN SCHWEGLER (John[8], Lida[7], Nethaniah[6], Francis Marion[5], Peter[4], Peter[3], Matthias[2], John Jacob[1]) was the son of John Stephan and Napaporn (Poltecha) Schwegler [Supplement No. 3897]. Lawrence was born July 13, 1980, at New York, New York.

(Sup) 6304G JOHN PHILLIP SCHWEGLER (John[8], Lida[7], Nethaniah[6], Francis Marion[5], Peter[4], Peter[3], Matthias[2], John Jacob[1]) was the son of John Stephan and Napaporn (Poltecha) Schwegler [Supplement No. 3897]. John was born November 18, 1984, at Kansas City, Missouri.

(Sup) 6305 CARLA LEE FOLEY (William[8], Blanche[7], William[6], Francis Marion[5], Peter[4], Peter[3], Matthias[2], John Jacob[1]) was the daughter of William and Ruth (Strohm) Foley [Supplement No. 3898]. Carla was born June 12, 1944, at Richmond, California. She attended the University of Illinois, Chicago. Carla married Daniel Patrick Proffitt, December 27, 1964, at Mattoon, Illinois. He was the son of Jesse James and Marjorie (Smith) Proffitt. Daniel was vice president of Faison, in the business of leasing commercial real estate.

(Sup) 7762 i   Daniel Patrick Proffitt, Jr., born August 16, 1967.
(Sup) 7762A ii Jason Miles Proffitt, born November 23, 1969.
(Sup) 7762B iii Jessica Jane Proffitt, born July 9, 1974.

(Sup) 6306 JOAN FOLEY (William[8], Blanche[7], William[6], Francis Marion[5], Peter[4], Peter[3], Matthias[2], John Jacob[1]) was the daughter of William and Ruth (Strohm) Foley [Supplement No. 3898]. Joan was born December 13, 1946, at Harris, Illinois. She graduated from Lakeland College as a registered nurse. Joan married William Matherly, July 20, 1966. He was the son of William and Margaret Matherly and was born in 1942. William was an engineer for the Central Illinois Public Service. He died in 1981.

(Sup) 7762C i   Cameron Matherly, born October 30, 1967.
(Sup) 7762D ii Calista Matherly, born May 28, 1971.
(Sup) 7762E iii William Jacob Matherly, born April 16, 1979.

(Sup) 6307 WILLIAM MACK FOLEY (William[8], Blanche[7], William[6], Francis Marion[5], Peter[4], Peter[3], Matthias[2], John Jacob[1]) was the son of William and Ruth (Strohm) Foley [Supplement No. 3898]. William was born July 21, 1950, at Harris, Illinois. He graduated from Southern Illinois University, 1972. He served two years in the U.S. Army, including a year in Korea. He was an autombile salesman. William married Linda Mae Elam, September 8, 1972. She was the daughter of William and Virginia (Van Gilder) Elam and was born November 7, 1951.

(Sup) 7763   i   William Andrew Foley, born May 26, 1976.
(Sup) 7763A ii Alicia Ann Foley, born March 21, 1980.

(Sup) 6307A JANE ELIZABETH FOLEY (William[8], Blanch[7], William[6], Francis Marion[5], Peter[4], Peter[3], Matthias[2], John Jacob[1]) was the daughter of William and Ruth (Strohm) Foley [Supplement No. 3898]. Jane was born September 26, 1952, at Paris, Illinois. She graduated from the University of Illinois as a teacher in 1975. She married Gary Lee Wright, December 28, 1975, at Paris, Illinois. He was the son of Charles and Barbara Wright and was born June 22, 1950. Gary graduated from the University of Illinois, 1980, and was a construction engineer.

(Sup) 7763B i   Lucas Charles Wright, born July 10, 1983.
(Sup) 7763C ii Gary Joseph Wright, born February 25, 1985.
(Sup) 7763D iii David Michael Wright, born February 11, 1987.

(Sup) 6308 JACK FRANKLIN FOLEY (Jack[8], Blanche[7], William[6], Francis Marion[5], Peter[4], Peter[3], Matthias[2], John Jacob[1]) was the son of Jack Beecher and Gloria (Joseph) Foley [Supplement No. 3899]. Jack was born March 12, 1949, at Paris, Illinois. He married Linda Sue Dodd, September 27, 1968, at Vermilion, Illinois. She was the daughter of Homer Francis and Beulah (Anderson) Dodd, and was born January 4, 1949, at Paris, Illinois.

(Sup) 7764   i   Laura Anne-Marie Foley, born January 4, 1971.
(Sup) 7764A ii Damian Patrick Foley, born September 4, 1974.

(Sup) 6309   CHERYL ANNE FOLEY (Conrad[8], Blanche[7], William[6], Francis Marion[5], Peter[4], Peter[3], Matthias[2], John Jacob[1]) was the daughter of Conrad Lee and Polly Etta (Kersey) Foley [Supplement No. 3900]. Cheryl Anne was born May 11, 1949, at Paris, Illinois. She married John Williams, June 10, 1946. He was the son of Glenn and Beulah Williams. Cheryl and John were divorced, August, 1984. She was a correspondent for the Illinois State Police.

(Sup) 7765   1   Dawn Michelle Williams, born January 7, 1970.
(Sup) 7765A   11   Terisa Anne Williams, born May 14, 1971.
(Sup) 7765B   111 Tamara Lyn Williams, born December 29, 1975.

(Sup) 6310   POLLY CATHERINE FOLEY (Conrad[8], Blanche[7], William[6], Fracis Marion[5], Peter[4], Peter[3], Matthias[2], John Jacob[1]) was the daughter of Conrad Lee and Polly Etta (Kersey) Foley [Supplement No. 3900]. Polly was born December 18, 1950, at Paris, Illinois. She married James Lawrence Willis. Larry was the son of Earl Raymond and Mary Ellen (York) Willis and was born November 29, 1949.

(Sup) 7765C   1   Christopher Earl Lee Willis, born Sep 21, 1970.
(Sup) 7765D   11 Brandy Michelle Willis, born Jan 12, 1973.

(Sup) 6311   BLYTHE PATRICE FOLEY (Robert[8], Blanche[7], William[6], Francis Marion[5], Peter[4], Peter[3], Matthias[2], John Jacob[1]) was the daughter of Robert Allen and Patricia (Crowe) Foley [Supplement No. 3901]. Blythe was born August 12, 1954, at Chicago, Illinois. She died May 17, 1962, at Bremerton, Washington, and is buried in Maple Leaf Cemetery at Oak Harbor, Washington.

(Sup) 6311A GUY FRANKLIN FOLEY (Robert[8], Blanche[7], William[6], Francis Marion[5], Peter[4], Peter[3], Matthias[2], John Jacob[1]) was the son of Robert Allen and Patricia (Crowe) Foley [Supplement No. 3901]. Guy was born July 21, 1955, at Chicago, Illinois. He graduated from high school at Bremerton, Washington, and was employed as a welder at the Naval Undersea Warfare Engineering Station, Keyport, Washington. Guy married Carma Laverne Brueckner, December 18, 1982, at Bremerton. She was the daughter of Reuben Fredrick Ernest and Margaret Laverne (Nyers) Breuckner and was born December 5, 1955, at Seattle, Washington.

(Sup) 7766   1   Cara Suzanne Foley, born July 29, 1983.
(Sup) 7766A   11 Margaret Patricia Foley, born May 7, 1986.

(Sup) 6311B NEAL ROBERT FOLEY (Robert[8], Blanche[7], William[6], Francis Marion[5], Peter[4], Peter[3], Matthias[2], John Jacob[1]) was the son of Robert Allen and Patricia (Crowe) Foley [Supplement No. 3901]. Neal was born August 24, 1956, at Chicago, Illinois. He graduated from high school at Bremerton, Washington, and was employed at the Puget Sound Naval Shipyard, Bremerton. Neal married Marla Jean Everist, July 7, 1977, at Bremerton. She was the daughter of Willis James and Ruth (Meisel) Everist and was born July 1, 1957, at Bremerton.

(Sup) 7767   1   Shaina Maureen Foley, born October 4, 1981.
(Sup) 7767A   11 James Willis Foley, born September 18, 1983.

(Sup) 6311C MAUREEN RUTH FOLEY (Robert[8], Blanche[7], William[6], Francis Marion[5], Peter[4], Peter[3], Matthias[2], John Jacob[1]) was the daughter of Robert Allen and Patricia (Crowe) Foley [Supplement No. 3901]. Maureen was born October 29, 1957, at Chicago, Illinois. She attended Olympic College at Bremerton and Washington State University, and was a realtor at Seattle, Washington. Maureen married Michael Joseph Perrone, December 22, 1978, at Suquamish, Washington. He was the son of Tony Adolfo and Teresa (Alfieri) Perrone and was born September 29, 1957.

(Sup) 7767B   1   Nathaniel David Perrone, born October 2, 1981.
(Sup) 7767C   11 Paige Nicole Perrone, born March 11, 1983.

(Sup) 6311D BRYAN HOWARD FOLEY (Robert[8], Blanche[7], William[6], Francis Marion[5], Peter[4], Peter[3], Matthias[2], John Jacob[1]) was the son of Robert Allen and Patricia (Crowe) Foley [Supplement No. 3901]. Bryan was born May 15, 1959, at Chicago, Illinois. He attended Olympic College, Bremerton, Washington, and was employed as an ordinance equipment mechanic at the Naval Undersea Warfare Engineering Station at Keyport, Washington. Bryan married Karen Lynn Broussard, March 1, 1986, at Bremerton. She was the daughter of Kenneth Dale and Helen (Richard) Broussard, and was born August 6, 1961, at Neubrucke, Germany.

(Sup) 7767D   1   Joshua James Foley, born February 7, 1987.

(Sup) 6311E MEREDYTH SUZANNE FOLEY (Robert[8], Blanche[7], William[6], Francis Marion[5], Peter[4], Peter[3], Matthias[2], John Jacob[1]) was the daughter of Robert Allen and Patricia (Crowe) Foley [Supplement No. 3901]. Meredyth was born June 14, 1960, at Oak Harbor, Washington. She died July 19, 1961, at Bremerton, Washington, and is buried in Maple Leaf Cemetery at Oak Harbor.

(Sup) 6311F MYLES RICHARD FOLEY (Robert[8], Blanche[7], William[6], Francis Marion[5], Peter[4], Peter[3], Matthias[2], John Jacob[1]) was the son of Robert Allen and Patricia (Crowe) Foley [Supplement No. 3901]. Myles was born March 29, 1963, at Bremerton, Washington. He attended Seattle Preparatory School, Seattle University, the University of Washington, and Olympic College, receiving an associate in Technical Arts degree, 1985. He was employed as a mechanical engineer technician at the Puget Sound Naval Shipyard, Bremerton.

(Sup) 6311G SUZANNE PAIGE FOLEY (Robert[8], Blanche[7], William[6], Francis Marion[5], Peter[4], Peter[3], Matthias[2], John Jacob[1]) was the daughter of Robert Allen and Patricia (Crowe) Foley [Supplement No. 3901]. Suzanne was born April 26, 1965, at Bremerton, Washington. She graduated from Seattle Preparatory School and attended Western Washington University. Suzanne married David Norman Arnold, December 10, 1983, at Bremerton. He was the son of Norman Eugene and Carol Lynn (Pooley) Arnold, and was born March 5, 1960, at Seattle, Washington.

   (Sup) 7768   1 Benjamin Allen Arnold, born May 8, 1984.
   (Sup) 7768A 11 Zachary David Arnold, born July 27, 1986.

(Sup) 6312 CYNTHIA LINK (William[8], William[7], Francis[6], Francis Marion[5], Peter[4], Peter[3], Matthias[2], John Jacob[1]) was the daughter of William Richard and Ruth (Lemon) Link [Supplement No. 3903]. Cynthia was born August 4, 1959. She died October 10, 1979.

(Sup) 6312A STEPHEN LINK (William[8], William[7], Francis[6], Francis Marion[5], Peter[4], Peter[3], Matthias[2], John Jacob[1]) was the son of William Richard and Ruth (Lemon) Link [Supplement No. 3903]. Stephen was born February 1, 1963. He married Colleen O'Brien, August 18, 1984.

(Sup) 6312B ANTHONY LINK (William[8], William[7], Fracis[6], Francis Marion[5], Peter[4], Peter[3], Matthias[2], John Jacob[1]) was the son of William Richard and Ruth (Lemon) Link [Supplement No. 3903]. Anthony was born January 22, 1965.

(Sup) 6312C MATTHEW LINK (William[8], William[7], Francis[6], Francis Marion[5], Peter[4], Peter[3], Matthias[2], John Jacob[1]) was the son of William Richard and Ruth (Lemon) Link [Supplement No. 3903]. Matthew was born August 30, 1966.

- - - - - - - - - - - - - - - - - -

(Sup) 6314 DIANE ELIZABETH HUNTSBURGER (Ralph[8], Aileen[7], Nancy[6], Sarah[5], Peter[4], Peter[3], Matthias[2], John Jacob[1]) was the daughter of Ralph F. and Margaret (Kroener) Huntsberger [TLF No. 3908]. Diane was born September 12, 1943, at Palo Alto, California.

(Sup) 6315 JAMES RALPH HUNTSBERGER (Ralph[8], Aileen[7], Nancy[6], Sarah[5], Peter[4], Peter[3], Matthias[2], John Jacob[1]) was the son of Ralph F. and Margaret (Kroener) Huntsberger [TLF No. 3908]. James was born February 25, 1946, at Palo Alto, California.

(Sup) 6316 NANCY JANE FENN (Elizabeth[8], Aileen[7], Nancy[6], Sarah[5], Peter[4], Peter[3], Matthias[2], John Jacob[1]) was the daughter of Robert Dwight and Elizabeth (Huntsberger) Fenn [TLF No. 3909]. Nancy was born May 6, 1944, at San Diego, California.

(Sup) 6317 STEPHEN MATTHIAS (Harry[8], Charles[7], Ellen[6], Zedekiah[5], Matthias[4], Peter[3], Matthias[2], John Jacob[1]) was the son of Harry E. and Mary (Wilson) Matthias [TLF No. 3913]. Stephen was born March 18, 1935, at Washington, D.C.

(Sup) 6318 PAUL MATTHIAS (Harry[8], Charles[7], Ellen[6], Zedekiah[5], Matthias[4], Peter[3], Matthias[2], John Jacob[1]) was the son of Harry E. and Mary (Wilson) Matthias [TLF No. 3913]. Paul was born April 4, 1938, at Washington, D.C.

(Sup) 6319 JOHN HOWARD KAUFMAN (Ivan[8], Ivan[7], Ida[6], Zedekiah[5], Matthias[4], Peter[3], Matthias[2], John Jacob[1]) was the son of Ivan Leon and Janet (Toy) Kaufman [TLF No. 3916]. John was born December 2, 1943, at Minneapolis, Minnesota.

(Sup) 6320 DAVID LEON KAUFMAN (Ivan[8], Ivan[7], Ida[6], Zedekiah[5], Matthias[4], Peter[3], Matthias[2], John Jacob[1]) was the son of Ivan Leon and Janet (Toy) Kaufman [TLF No. 3916]. David was born June 17, 1946, at Minneapolis, Minnesota.

(Sup) 6321 NANCY A. WILLIAMSON (Dorothy[8], Amie[7], Ida[6], Zedekiah[5], Matthias[4], Peter[3], Matthias[2], John Jacob[1]) was the daughter of Richard Arling and Dorothy Prox Williamson [TLF No. 3919]. Nancy was born March 22, 1944, at Terre Haute, Illinois.

(Sup) 6322 STEPHEN MICHAEL WILLIAMSON (Dorothy[8], Amie[7], Ida[6], Zedekiah[5], Matthias[4], Peter[3], Matthias[2], John Jacob[1]) was the son of Richard Arling and Dorothy Prox Williamson [TLF No. 3919]. Stephen was born June 8, 1946, at Terre Haute, Indiana.

(Sup) 6323 SUSAN LA FOE ROGGE (Jo Anne[8], Helen[7], Frank[6], John[5], Matthias[4], Peter[3], Matthias[2], John Jacob[1]) was the daughter of Stanley Matthew and Josephine Anne Weldely Rogge [Supplement No. 3924]. Susan was born April 12, 1951, at Johnson City, New York.

(Sup) 6324 PHILIP CHRISTIAN ROGGE (Jo Anne[8], Helen[7], Frank[6], John[5], Matthias[4], Peter[3], Matthias[2], John Jacob[1]) was the son of Stanley Matthew and Josephine Anne Weidely Rogge [Supplement No. 3924]. Philip was born April 12, 1954, at Johnson City, New York.

(Sup) 6325 SCOTT BETHEL DARRAH (Sally[8], Helen[7], Frank[6], John[5], Matthias[4], Peter[3], Matthias[2], John Jacob[1]) was the son of Clarence Theodore and Sally Weidely Darrah, Jr. [Supplement No. 3925]. Scott was born November 19, 1954, at Johnson City, New York.

(Sup) 6326 DAVID LINK DARRAH (Sally[8], Helen[7], Frank[6], John[5], Matthias[4], Peter[3], Matthias[2], John Jacob[1]) was the son of Clarence Theodore and Sally Weidely Darrah, Jr. [Supplement No. 3925]. Daniel was born October 31, 1955, at Binghamton, New York.

(Sup) 6327 TODD MATTHEW DARRAH (Sally[8], Helen[7], Frank[6], John[5], Matthias[4], Peter[3], Matthias[2], John Jacob[1]) was the son of Clarence Theodore and Sally Weidely Darrah, Jr. [Supplement No. 3925]. He was born January 27, 1958, at Binghamton, New York.

(Sup) 6328 CRAIG THEODORE DARRAH (Sally[8], Helen[7], Frank[6], John[5], Matthias[4], Peter[3], Matthias[2], John Jacob[1]) was the son of Clarence Theodore and Sally Weidely Darrah, Jr. [Supplement No. 3925]. He was born October 17, 1959, at Binghamton, New York.

(Sup) 6329 PHILIP HARTWELL SLINDE (Janice[8], Josephine[7], Frank[6], John[5], Matthias[4], Peter[3], Matthias[2], John Jacob[1]) was the son of John Hartwell and Janice Helen Recker Slinde [Supplement No. 3926].

(Sup) 6330 ALEXANDER SLINDE (Janice[8], Josephine[7], Frank[6], John[5], Matthias[4], Peter[3], Matthias[2], John Jacob[1]) was the son of John Hartwell and Janice Helen Recker Slinde [Supplement No. 3926].

(Sup) 6331 IAN PEYTON NESBITT (Alexander[8], Josephine[7], Frank[6], John[5], Matthias[4], Peter[3], Matthias[2], John Jacob[1]) was the son of Andrew Alexander and Elenore (Sinclaire) Nesbitt [Supplement No. 3927].

(Sup) 6332 BENJAMIN OWEN NESBITT (Alexander[8], Josephine[7], Frank[6], John[5], John[4], Peter[3], Matthias[2], John Jacob[1]) was the son of Andrew Alexander and Elenore (Sinclaire) Nesbitt [Supplement No. 3927].

(Sup) 6333 VIRGINIA MARIA MURRAY (Virginia[8], George[7], Edwin[6], George[5], Matthias[4], Peter[3], Matthias[2], John Jacob[1]) was the daughter of Dr. Joseph E. and Virginia E. (Link) Murray [Supplement No. 3933]. She was born May 7, 1946, at Binghamton, New York. Virginia married Leo Boyle.

(Sup) 6334 MARGARET JOAN MURRAY (Virginia[8], George[7], Edwin[6], George[5], Matthias[4], Peter[3], Matthias[2], John Jacob[1]) was the daughter of Joseph E. and Virginia E. (Link) Murray, MD [Supplement No. 3933]. Margaret was born September 30, 1949, at Boston, Massachusetts. She resided at El Cerrito, California.

(Sup) 6335 JOSEPH LINK MURRAY (Virginia[8], George[7], Edwin[6], George[5], Matthias[4], Peter[3], Matthias[2], John Jacob[1]) was the son of Joseph E. and Virginia E. (Link) Murray [Supplement No. 3933]. Joseph was born July 31, 1951, at Boston, Massachusetts.

(Sup) 6336 KATHERINE ANN MURRAY (Virginia[8], George[7], Edwin[6], George[5], Matthias[4], Peter[3], Matthias[2], John Jacob[1]) was the daughter of Joseph E. and Virginia E. (Link) Murray [Supplement No. 3933]. Katherine was born September 30, 1952, at Boston, Massachusetts.

(Sup) 6337 THOMAS GEORGE MURRAY (Virginia[8], George[7], Edwin[6], George[5], Matthias[4], Peter[3], Matthias[2], John Jacob[1]) was the son of Joseph E. and Virginia E. (Link) Murray [Supplement No. 3933]. Thomas was born March 12, 1958, at Boston, Massachusetts. He resided at Wellesley Hills, Massachusetts.

(Sup) 6338 RICHARD WILLIAM MURRAY (Virginia[8], George[7], Edwin[6], George[5], Matthias[4], Peter[3], Matthias[2], John Jacob[1]) was the son of William A. and Virginia E. (Link) Murray [Supplement No. 3933]. Richard was born September 18, 1963, at Boston, Massachusetts. He resided at Wellesley Hills, Massachusetts.

(Sup) 6339 MARY CATHERINE LINK (William[8], Edwin[7], Edwin[6], George[5], Matthias[4], Peter[3], Matthias[2], John Jacob[1]) was the daughter of William Martin and Juliet Ann (Ridley) Link [Supplement No. 3934]. Mary Catherine was born January 8, 1969, at Denver, Colorado.

6340 THOMAS EDWIN LINK (William[8], Edwin[7], Edwin[6], George[5], Matthias[4], Peter[3], Matthias[2], John Jacob[1]) was the son of William Martin and Juliet Ann (Ridley) Link [Supplement No. 3934]. Thomas was born May 12, 1971, at Boulder, Colorado.

(Sup) 6341 STEPHEN CLAYTON LINK (Edwin[8], Edwin[7], Edwin[6], George[5], Matthias[4], Peter[3], Matthias[2], John Jacob[1]) was the son of Edwin Clayton and Maurine Lee (Muzzy) Link [Supplement No. 3935]. Stephen was born January 15, 1972, at Stuart, Florida.

(Sup) 6341A SANDRA SHAW (Alice[8], Joseph[7], Peter[6], Peter[5], Elizabeth[3], Matthias[2], John Jacob[1]) was the daughter of Don G. and Alice (Miller) Shaw [TLF No. 3936].

(Sup) 6341B JOHN DOUGLAS SHAW (Alice[8], Joseph[7], Peter[6], Peter[5], Elizabeth[3], Matthias[2], John Jacob[1]) was the son of Don G. and Alice (Miller) Shaw [TLF No. 3936].

(Sup) 6342 JUDITH MILLER (Paul[8], Joseph[7], Peter[6], Peter[5], Elizabeth[4], Peter[3], Matthias[2], John Jacob[1]) was the daughter of Paul Link and Gladys (Ulery) Miller [TLF No. 3937].

(Sup) 6343 MARY DEE MILLER (Paul[8], Joseph[7], Peter[6], Peter[5], Elizabeth[4], Peter[3], Matthias[2], John Jacob[1]) was the daughter of Paul Link and Gladys (Ulery) Miller [TLF No. 3937].

(Sup) 6344 PAUL LINK MILLER, JR. (Paul[8], Joseph[7], Peter[6], Peter[5], Elizabeth[4], Peter[3], Matthias[2], John Jacob[1]) was the son of Paul Link and Gladys (Ulery) Miller [TLF No. 3937]. Paul, Jr., was born January 25, 1947.

(Sup) 6345 PETER LINK MILLER, III (Paul[8], Joseph[7], Peter[6], Peter[5], Elizabeth[4], Peter[3], Matthias[2], John Jacob[1]) was the son of Paul Link and Gladys (Ulery) Miller [TLF No. 3937]. Peter was born January 25, 1947.

- - - - - - - - - - - - - - - -

(Sup) 6349 MARGARET NAOMI DREHER (John[8], John[7], Margaret[6], Peter[5], Elizabeth[4], Peter[3], Matthias[2], John Jacob[1]) was the daughter of John Miller and Gaynelle (Hornsby) Dreher [TLF No. 3950]. Margaret was born March 10, 1947.

(Sup) 6350 MARY ANN DREHER (John[8], Martha[7], Margaret[6], Peter[5], Elizabeth[4], Peter[3], Matthias[2], John Jacob[1]) was the daughter of John Thaddeus and Mary (Hamilton) Dreher [TLF No. 3951]. Mary Ann was born May 2, 1946.

(Sup) 6351 WILFRED RIVERS CLAYTOR, JR. (Wilfred[8], Virginia[7], Margaret[6], Peter[5], Elizabeth[4], Peter[3], Matthias[2], John Jacob[1]) was the son of Wilfred Rivers and Frances (Wells) Claytor [TLF No. 3954]. Wilfred, Jr., was born December 24, 1946.

(Sup) 6352 GERALD GUY MANNING, II (Virginia[8], Virginia[7], Margaret[6], Peter[5], Elizabeth[4], Peter[3], Matthias[2], John Jacob[1]) was the son of Gerald Guy and Virginia (Claytor) Manning [TLF No. 3955]. Gerald, Jr., was born February 2, 1945.

(Sup) 6353 MARGUERITE CHAPMAN MANNING (Virginia[8], Virginia[7], Margaret[6], Peter[5], Elizabeth[4], Peter[3], Matthias[2], John Jacob[1]) was the daughter of Gerald Guy and Virginia Claytor Manning [TLF No. 3955]. Marguerite was born November 14, 1947.

(Sup) 6354 ARCHIBALD MILLER LYNN, JR. (Archibald[8], Elsie[7], Joseph[6], Adam[5], Elizabeth[4], Peter[3], Matthias[2], John Jacob[1]) was the son of Archibald Miller and Edith Curry Lynn [TLF No. 3956]. Archibald, Jr., was born October 27, 1942, at Staunton, Virginia.

(Sup) 6355 YVONNE WATSON LYNN (Thomas[8], Elsie[7], Joseph[6], Adam[5], Elizabeth[4], Peter[3], Matthias[2], John Jacob[1]) was the daughter of Thomas Watson and Ruth Barkley Lynn [TLF No. 3957]. Yvonne was born March 2, 1946, at Augusta County, Virginia.

(Sup) 6356 THOMAS COOPER LYNN (Thomas[8], Elsie[7], Joseph II[6], Adam[5], Elizabeth[4], Peter[3], Matthias[2], John Jacob[1]) was the son of Thomas Watson and Ruth Barkley Lynn [TLF No. 3957]. He was born January 14, 1948, in Augusta County, Virginia.

(Sup) 6357 MARY LOUISE DINKLE (Ellis[8], Iva[7], Peter[6], Judith Rebecca[5], Elizabeth[4], Peter[3], Matthias[2], John Jacob[1]) was the son of Ellis Paul and Ruth McCutchan Dinkle [TLF No. 3961]. Mary was born July 4, 1928. She married Eddie Claytor in 1948.

(Sup) 6367 ROSE MARIE AUGSPURGER (Russell[8], Elsie[7], Walker[6], Melanc-thon[5], Elizabeth[4], Peter[3], Matthias[2], John Jacob[1]) was the daughter of Russell Wayne and Nellie Bohi Augspurger [TLF No. 3968]. She was born July 7, 1946, at Oskaloosa, Iowa.

(Sup) 6368 J. OGDEN AUGSPURGER (Gerald[8], Elsie[7], Walker[6], Melanc-thon[5], Elizabeth[4], Peter[3], Matthias[2], John Jacob[1]) was the son of Gerald W. and Cleo Ogden Augspurger [TLF No. 3969].

(Sup) 6369 GERALD EDWIN AUGSPURGER (Gerald[8], Elsie[7], Walker[6], Melanc-thon[5], Elizabeth[4], Peter[3], Matthias[2], John Jacob[1]) was the son of Gerald W. and Cleo Ogden Augspurger [TLF No. 3969].

(Sup) 6370 SAMUEL DEE AUGSPURGER (Gerald[8], Elsie[7], Walker[6], Melanc-thon[5], Elizabeth[4], Peter[3], Matthias[2], John Jacob[1]) was the son of Gerald W. and Cleo Ogden Augspurger [TLF No. 3969].

(Sup) 6371 JERALD DEAN BLASI (Lucille[8], Elsie[7], Walker[6], Melanc-thon[5], Elizabeth[4], Peter[3], Matthias[2], John Jacob[1]) was the son of Arthur Edward and Lucille Augspurger Blasi [TLF No. 3970]. Jerald was born January 30, 1928, at Pulaski, Iowa.

(Sup) 6372 DWIGHT ARTHUR BLASI (Lucille[8], Elsie[7], Walker[6], Melanc-thon[5], Elizabeth[4], Peter[3], Matthias[2], John Jacob[1]) was the son of Arthur Edward and Lucille Augspurger Blasi [TLF No. 3970]. Dwight was born January 29, 1929, at Pulaski, Iowa.

(Sup) 6373 ROBERT DWAYNE BLASI (Lucille[8], Elsie[7], Walker[6], Melanc-thon[5], Elizabeth[4], Peter[3], Matthias[2], John Jacob[1]) was the son of Arthur Edward and Lucille Augspurger Blasi [TLF No. 3970]. Robert was born November 26, 1933, at Pulaski, Iowa.

(Sup) 6374 FREDERICK LEE SLONAKER (Vera[8], Ethel[7], Walker[6], Melanc-thon[5], Elizabeth[4], Peter[3], Matthias[2], John Jacob[1]) was the son of William Percy and Vera June Massey Slonaker [TLF No. 3971]. Frederick was born August 29, 1939.

(Sup) 6375 JANET SUE SLONAKER (Vera[8], Ethel[7], Walker[6], Melancthon[5], Elizabeth[4], Peter[3], Matthias[2], John Jacob[1]) was the daughter of William Percy and Vera June Massey Slonaker [TLF No. 3971]. Janet was born October 12, 1943.

(Sup) 6376 LINDA KAY SLONAKER (Vera[8], Ethel[7], Walker[6], Melancthon[5], Elizabeth[4], Peter[3], Matthias[2], John Jacob[1]) was the daughter of William Percy and Vera June Massey Slonaker [TLF No. 3971]. Linda was born July 26, 1947

(Sup) 6358 BETTY LEE DINKLE (Ellis[8], Iva[7], Peter[6], Judith Rebecca[5], Elizabeth[4], Peter[3], Matthias[2], John Jaob[1]) was the daughter of Ellis Paul and Ruth McCutchan Dinkle [TLF No. 3961]. Betty was born August 25, 1929.

(Sup) 6359 NANCY JANE DINKLE (Ellis[8], Iva[7], Peter[6], Rebecca[5], Eliza-beth[4], Peter[3], Matthias[2], John Jacob[1]) was the daughter of Ellis Paul and Ruth McCutchan Dinkle [TLF No. 3961]. Nancy was born November 1, 1930.

(Sup) 6360 CHARLOTTE MARIE DINKLE (Burton[8], Iva[7], Peter[6], Judith Rebecca[5], Elizabeth[4], Peter[3], Matthias[2], John Jacob[1]) was the daughter of Burton M. and Annie Mae Hall Dinkle [TLF No. 3963]. Charlotte was born July 11, 1941, at Washington, D.C.

(Sup) 6361 DONNA MARIE CAMPBELL (Dorothy[8], Lillian[7], Robert[6], Judith Rebecca[5], Elizabeth[4], Peter[3], Matthias[2], John Jacob[1]) was the daughter of Delbert Kirk and Dorothy Newby Campbell [TLF No. 3966]. Donna was born December 2, 1946, at Washington, D.C.

(Sup) 6362 BYRON BOHI AUGSPURGER (Russell[8], Elsie[7], Walker[6], Melanc-thon[5], Elizabeth[4], Peter[3], Matthias[2], John Jacob[1]) was the son of Russell Wayne and Nellie Bohi Augspurger [TLF No. 3968]. Byron was born February 14, 1926, at West Branch, Iowa. He married Anne Henderson July 12, 1947, at Pulaski, Iowa.

(Sup) 6363 ROGER LEE AUGSPURGER (Russell[8], Elsie[7], Walker[6], Melanc-thon[5], Elizabeth[4], Peter[3], Matthias[2], John Jacob[1]) was the son of Russell Wayne and Nellie Bohi Augspurger [TLF No. 3968]. Roger was born August 22, 1927, at West Branch, Iowa.

(Sup) 6364 KEITH WILLIAM AUGSPURGER (Russell[8], Elsie[7], Walker[6], Mel-ancthon[5], Elizabeth[4], Peter[3], Matthias[2], John Jacob[1]) was the son of Russell Wayne and Nellie Bohi Augspurger [TLF No. 3968]. Keith was born May 12, 1929, at Bloomfield, Iowa.

(Sup) 6365 RUSSELL DWAYNE AUGSPURGER (Russell[8], Elsie[7], Walker[6], Melancthon[5], Elizabeth[4], Peter[3], Matthias[2], John Jacob[1]) was the son of Russell Wayne and Nellie Bohi Augspurger [TLF No. 3968]. He was born December 14, 1930, at Pulaski, Iowa.

(Sup) 6366 ARDEN PAUL AUGSPURGER (Russell[8], Elsie[7], Walker[6], Melanc-thon[5], Elizabeth[4], Peter[3], Matthias[2], John Jacob[1]) was the son of Russell Wayne and Nellie Bohi Augspurger [TLF No. 3968]. He was born May 7, 1934, at Pulaski, Iowa.

(Sup) 6377 GLENN BRUCE VOGT (Aldene[8], Elizabeth[4], Peter[3], Matthias[2], John Jacob[1]) was the son of John Floyd and Aldene Crosby Vogt [TLF No. 3985]. Glenn was born August 21, 1939.

(Sup) 6378 JOHN FLOYD VOGT, JR. (Aldene[8], Elizabeth[4], Peter[3], Matthias[2], John Jaob[1]) was the son of John Floyd and Aldene Crosby Vogt [TLF No. 3985]. John, Jr., was born June 25, 1941.

(Sup) 6379 LYNDA KAREN VOGT (Aldene[8], Elizabeth[4], Peter[3], Matthias[2], John Jacob[1]) was the daughter of John Floyd and Aldene Crosby Vogt [TLF No. 3985]. Lynda was born October 26, 1943.

(Sup) 6380 GARY BURL VOGT (Aldene[8], Elizabeth[4], Peter[3], Matthias[2], John Jacob[1]) was the son of John Floyd and Aldene Crosby Vogt [TLF No. 3985]. Gary was born October 13, 1947.

- - - - - - - - - - - - - - -

(Sup) 6384 RAYMOND O'BRIEN BALL, JR. (Ivy[8], William[7], Daisy[6], James[5], Rebecca[4], Peter[3], Matthias[2], John Jacob[1]) was the son of Raymond O'Brien and Ivy Kathleen Winn Ball [TLF No. 3998]. Raymond, Jr., was born November 26, 1946.

(Sup) 6385 MILFORD PINSON (Fannie[8], Flemine[7], Andrew[6], Hannah[5], David[4], Catherine[3], Matthias[2], John Jacob[1]) was the son of Leander and Fannie Palmer Pinson [TLF No. 4006].

(Sup) 6386 ROBERT PINSON (Fannie[8], Flemine[7], Andrew[6], Hannah[5], David[4], Catherine[3], Matthias[2], John Jacob[1]) was the son of Leander and Fannie Palmer Pinson [TLF No. 4006].

(Sup) 6387 KENT PALMER LARSEN (Grace[8], Harvey[7], Andrew[6], Hannah[5], David[4], Catherine[3], Matthias[2], John Jacob[1]) was the son of Frank Axel and Grace Palmer Larsen [TLF No. 4008]. Kent was born December 8, 1922, at Long Beach, California. He married Luella June Brainard January 23, 1943, at San Antonio, Texas. Luella, the daughter of Albert H. Brainard, was born July 31, 1924, at Inglewood, California.

(Sup) 7785   1 Sandra Louise Larsen, born November 16, 1944.

(Sup) 6388 ALEXIA LOUISE LARSEN (Grace[8], Harvey[7], Andrew[6], Hannah[5], David[4], Catherine[3], Matthias[2], John Jacob[1]) was the daughter of Frank Axel and Grace Palmer Larsen [TLF No. 4008]. Alexia was born September 24, 1926, at Long Beach, California. She married James Dobbie Lithgow April 1, 1946. James died April 1, 1946. Alexia married, second, Robert Calvin Hardt May 25, 1947. Robert was the son of Ernest Hardt and was born March 25, 1924, at Wilmette, Illinois.

(Sup) 6389 MARILYNNE DIANA POWELL (Electra[8], Harvey[7], Andrew[6], Hannah[5], David[4], Catherine[3], Matthias[2], John Jacob[1]) was the daughter of Electra Palmer Powell [TLF No. 4009].

(Sup) 6390 HAROLD WEBB POWELL (Electra[8], Harvey[7], Andrew[6], Hannah[5], David[4], Catherine[3], Matthias[2], John Jacob[1]) was the son of Electra Palmer Powell [TLF No. 4009].

(Sup) 6391 DOROTHY MARIE PALMER (Paul[8], Roy[7], Andrew[6], Hannah[5], David[4], Catherine[3], Matthias[2], John Jacob[1]) was the daughter of Paul Munier and Ruth Gilvarry Palmer [TLF No. 4013]. Dorothy was born September 21, 1932, at St. Louis, Missouri.

(Sup) 6392 PAUL MICHAEL PALMER (Paul[8], Roy[7], Andrew[6], Hannah[5], David[4], Catherine[3], Matthias[2], John Jacob[1]) was the son of Paul Munier and Ruth Gilvarry Palmer [TLF No. 4013]. Paul was born December 24, 1934, at St. Louis, Missouri.

(Sup) 6393 JAMES THOMAS PALMER (Paul[8], Roy[7], Andrew[6], Hannah[5], David[4], Catherine[3], Matthias[2], John Jacob[1]) was the son of Paul Munier and Ruth Gilvarry Palmer [TLF No. 4013]. James was born September 24, 1938, at St. Louis, Missouri.

(Sup) 6394 ROBERT FRANCIS PALMER (Paul[8], Roy[7], Andrew[6], Hannah[5], David[4], Catherine[3], Matthias[2], John Jacob[1]) was the son of Paul Munier and Ruth Gilvarry Palmer [TLF No. 4013]. Robert was born July 26, 1940, at St. Louis, Missouri.

(Sup) 6395 JOHN ANTHONY PALMER (Paul[8], Roy[7], Andrew[6], Hannah[5], David[4], Catherine[3], Matthias[2], John Jacob[1]) was the son of Paul Munier and Ruth Gilvarry Palmer [TLF No. 4013]. John was born February 18, 1942, at St. Louis, Missouri.

(Sup) 6396 FRED TOLAND (Verdie[8], Mary[7], Peter[6], Hannah[5], David[4], Catherine[3], Matthias[2], John Jacob[1]) was the son of William Bradford and Verdie King Toland [TLF No. 4019]. Fred was born at Beaumont, Texas. He married Elizabeth Moore.

(Sup) 6397 AUDREY TOLAND (Verdie[8], Mary[7], Peter[6], Hannah[5], David[4], Catherine[3], Matthias[2], John Jacob[1]) was the daughter of William Bradford and Verdie King Toland [TLF No. 4019]. Audrey married Charles W. Gore.

(Sup) 6398 PRINCESS OLGA TOLAND (Verdie[8], Mary[7], Peter[6], Hannah[5], David[4], Catherine[3], Matthias[2], John Jacob[1]) was the daughter of William Bradford and Verdie King Toland [TLF No. 4019]. She was born August 2, 1917, at Magnolia, Arkansas.

(Sup) 6399 WILLIAM H. ARNOLD, III (Mary[8], Susan[7], Peter[6], Hannah[5], David[4], Catherine[3], Matthias[2], John Jacob[1]) was the son of William H. and Mary Grace Hendricks Arnold, Jr. [TLF No. 4020]. William, III, was born November 2, 1923, at Texarkana, Arkansas. He graduated from the University of Texas Law School and served four years in U.S. forces during World War II as a first lieutenant.

(Sup) 6400 THOMAS SAXON ARNOLD (Mary[8], Susan[7], Peter[6], Hannah[5], David[4], Catherine[3], Matthias[2], John Jacob[1]) was the son of William H. and Mary Grace Hendricks Arnold [TLF No. 4020]. Thomas was born August 3, 1928, at Texarkana, Arkansas. He studied at Rice Institute, Houston, Texas.

(Sup) 6401 HELEN LAVERNE LEWIS (Pitzel[8], Arthur[7], Peter[6], Hannah[5], David[4], Catherine[3], Matthias[2], John Jacob[1]) was the daughter of Pitzel Howard and Alma Davidson Lewis [TLF No. 4023]. Helen was born November 25, 1929, at Shreveport, Louisiana.

(Sup) 6402 SHIRLEY NELL LEWIS (Pitzel[8], Arthur[7], Peter[6], Hannah[5], David[4], Catherine[3], Matthias[2], John Jacob[1]) was the daughter of Pitzel Howard and Alma Davidson Lewis [TLF No. 4023]. Shirley was born November 18, 1935, at Zenoria, Louisiana.

(Sup) 6403 DONNA FAY LEWIS (Pitzel[8], Arthur[7], Peter[6], Hannah[5], David[4], Catherine[3], Matthias[2], John Jacob[1]) was the daughter of Pitzel Howard and Alma Davidson Lewis [TLF No. 4023]. Donna was born February 22, 1943, at Georgetown, Louisiana.

(Sup) 6404 TERRY HOWARD LEWIS (Pitzel[8], Arthur[7], Peter[6], Hannah[5], David[4], Catherine[3], Matthias[2], John Jacob[1]) was the son of Pitzel Howard and Alma Davidson Lewis [TLF No. 4023]. Terry was born October 6, 1945, at Georgetown, Louisiana.

(Sup) 6405 PATSY FAYE MITCHELL (Mary[8], Arthur[7], Peter[6], Hannah[5], David[4], Catherine[3], Matthias[2], John Jacob[1]) was the daughter of Oscar and Mary Lewis Mitchell [TLF No. 4024]. Patsy was born January 24, 1932, at Minden, Louisiana.

(Sup) 6406 DONALD OSCAR MITCHELL (Mary[8], Arthur[7], Peter[6], Hannah[5], David[4], Catherine[3], Matthias[2], John Jacob[1]) was the son of Oscar and Mary Lewis Mitchell [TLF No. 4024]. Donald was born March 23, 1934, at Minden, Louisiana.

(Sup) 6407 VIRGINIA KAY MITCHELL (Lucy[8], Arthur[7], Peter[6], Hannah[5], David[4], Catherine[3], Matthias[2], John Jacob[1]) was the daughter of John Daniel and Lucy Virginia Lewis Mitchell [TLF No. 4025].

(Sup) 6408 JAMES LEWIS HILBURN (Carnell[8], Arthur[7], Peter[6], Hannah[5], David[4], Catherine[3], Matthias[2], John Jacob[1]) was the son of James Plell and Carnell Lewis Hilburn [TLF No. 4026].

(Sup) 6409 WILLIAM DWAIN HILBURN (Carnell[8], Arthur[7], Peter[6], Hannah[5], David[4], Catherine[3], Matthias[2], John Jacob[1]) was the son of James Plell and Carnell Lewis Hilburn [TLF No. 4026].

(Sup) 6410 ROBERT GERALD HILBURN (Carnell[8], Arthur[7], Peter[6], Hannah[5], David[4], Catherine[3], Matthias[2], John Jacob[1]) was the son of James Plell and Carnell Lewis Hilburn [TLF No 4026].

(Sup) 6411 CHARLOTTE MARIE LEWIS (William[8], Arthur[7], Peter[6], Hannah[5], David[4], Catherine[3], Matthias[2], John Jacob[1]) was the daughter of William Arthur and Marie Upshaw Lewis [TLF No. 4027]. Charlotte was born March 2, 1945, at Georgetown, Louisiana.

(Sup) 6412 SHARON IDELLA LEWIS (William[8], Arthur[7], Peter[6], Hannah[5], David[4], Catherine[3], Matthias[2], John Jacob[1]) was the daughter of William Arthur and Marie Upshaw Lewis [TLF No. 4027]. Sharon was born August 30, 1936, at Georgetown, Louisiana.

(Sup) 6413 CAROLYN FLORENCE LEWIS (Samuel[8], Arthur[7], Peter[6], Hannah[5], David[4], Catherine[3], Matthias[2], John Jacob[1]) was the daughter of Samuel Brooks and Emma Lee Nix Lewis [TLF No. 4028]. She was born December 5, 1937, at Stamps, Arkansas.

(Sup) 6414 RONALD BROOK LEWIS (Samuel[8], Arthur[7], Peter[6], Hannah[5], David[4], Catherine[3], Matthias[2], John Jacob[1]) was the son of Samuel Brooks and Emma Lee Nix Lewis [TLF No. 4028]. Ronald was born February 19, 1940, at Stamps, Arkansas.

(Sup) 6415 NORMA JOYCE LEWIS (Samuel[8], Arthur[7], Peter[6], Hannah[5], David[4], Catherine[3], Matthias[2], John Jacob[1]) was the daughter of Samuel Brooks and Emma Lee Nix Lewis [TLF No. 4028]. She was born September 10, 1946, at Stamps, Arkansas.

(Sup) 6416   RUBY EDELL LOFTEN (Thomas^8, Anna^7, Samuel^6, Hannah^5, David^4, Catherine^3, Matthias^2, John Jacob^1) was the daughter of Thomas Emmett and Frances Awbrey Loften [TLF No. 4029]. Ruby was born May 8, 1926, at Grove, Louisiana. She married Ralph Edgar Martin November 5, 1942, at Magnolia, Arkansas.

(Sup) 7790   i Bettie Mable Martin, born January 9, 1945.

(Sup) 6417   FRANCES De MAURICE LOFTEN (Thomas^8, Anna^7, Samuel^6, Hannah^5, David^4, Catherine^3, Matthias^2, John Jacob^1) was the daughter of Thomas Emmett and Frances Awbrey Loften [TLF No. 4029]. She was born November 18, 1931, at Magnolia, Arkansas.

(Sup) 6418   LOYE EMMETT LOFTEN (Thomas^8, Anna^7, Samuel^6, Hannah^5, David^4, Catherine^3, Matthias^2, John Jacob^1) was the son of Thomas Emmett and Frances Awbrey Loften [TLF No. 4029]. He was born November 20, 1939, at Magnolia, Arkansas.

(Sup) 6419   MAHDEEN LOFTEN (Thomas^8, Anna^7, Samuel^6, Hannah^5, David^4, Catherine^3, Matthias^2, John Jacob^1) was the daughter of Walter Ernest and Wyllie Mae Fuller Loften [TLF No. 4030]. Mahdeen was born January 12, 1919, at Junction City, Arkansas. She married Haskell Runnels December 21, 1938, at Camden, Arkansas.

(Sup) 7791   i Joseph Dwayne Runnels, born in 1939.

(Sup) 6420   JOHN THURBYN LOFTEN (Walter^8, Anna^7, Samuel^6, Hannah^5, David^4, Catherine^3, Matthias^2, John Jacob^1) was the son of Walter Ernest and Wyllie Mae Fuller Loften [TLF No. 4030]. John was born June 28, 1921, at Magnolia, Arkansas. He married Louise Ponder on March 17, 1941. He served in the U.S. Air Force during World War II and was killed in a bomber crash over the Gulf of Mexico September 12, 1943.

(Sup) 6421   CHRISTINE LOFTEN (Walter^8, Anna^7, Samuel^6, Hannah^5, David^4, Catherine^3, Matthias^2, John Jacob^1) was the daughter of Walter Ernest and Willie Mae Fuller Loften [TLF No. 4030]. Christine was born November 24, 1924. She married William Young May 11, 1943. She married, second, William Bay, February 11, 1947, at Camden, Arkansas. William was a technical sergeant in the U.S. Marines during World War II; he was captured in Guam and spent 45 months as a Japanese prisoner of war.

    CHILD OF CHRISTINE AND WILLIAM YOUNG
(Sup) 7792   i Yvonne Young, born October 5, 1945.

    CHILD OF CHRISTINE AND WILLIAM BAY
(Sup) 7793   ii James Thurbyn Bay, born March 29, 1948.

(Sup) 6422   JAMES GENEVA LOFTEN (Walter^8, Anna^7, Samuel^6, Hannah^5, David^4, Catherine^3, Matthias^2, John Jacob^1) was the son of Walter Ernest and Wyllie Mae Fuller Loften [TLF No. 4030]. James was born March 28, 1930, at Magnolia, Arkansas. He died November 20, 1935.

(Sup) 6423   MARY SYBLE REID (Parrie^8, Anna^7, Samuel^6, Hannah^5, David^4, Catherine^3, Matthias^2, John Jacob^1) was the daughter of Asie Leonard and Parrie Loften Reid [TLF No. 4031]. Mary was born May 22, 1918, at Magnolia, Arkansas. She married Clarence David Keith July, 1939.

(Sup) 7794   i Patricia Ann Keith, born July 16, 1940.
(Sup) 7795   ii David Reid Keith, born August 13, 1949.

(Sup) 6424   FREDERICK SAMUEL REID (Parrie^8, Anna^7, Samuel^6, Hannah^5, David^4, Catherine^3, Matthias^2, John Jacob^1) was the son of Asie Leonard and Parrie Loften Reid [TLF No. 4031]. Frederick was born September 23, 1924. He served three years as an ensign in the U.S. Navy Air Corps.

(Sup) 6425   CHARLES AUGUSTUS BURDINE, JR. (Charles^8, Mary^7, Samuel^6, Hannah^5, David^4, Catherine^3, Matthias^2, John Jacob^1) was the son of Charles Augustine and Mabel Garrett Burdine [TLF No. 4033]. Charles, Jr., was born August 14, 1922.

(Sup) 6426   JOHN RHON BURDINE (Charles^8, Mary^7, Samuel^6, Hannah^5, David^4, Catherine^3, Matthias^2, John Jacob^1) was the son of Charles Augustine and Mabel Garrett Burdine [TLF No. 4033]. John was born January 6, 1928.

(Sup) 6427   GLADYS ALLINE BURDINE (Jesse^8, Mary^7, Samuel^6, Hannah^5, David^4, Catherine^3, Matthias^2, John Jacob^1) was the daughter of Jesse Guy and Tessie May Davis Burdine [TLF No. 4036]. Gladys was born December 10, 1926, at Lowann, Arkansas. She married W. R. Hudson September, 1944.

(Sup) 6428   EVELYN JUANITA BURDINE (Jesse^8, Mary^7, Samuel^6, Hannah^5, David^4, Catherine^3, Matthias^2, John Jacob^1) was the daughter of Jesse Guy and Tessie May David Burdine [TLF No. 4036]. Evelyn was born June 22, 1929, at Monroe, Louisiana.

(Sup) 6429   RALPH ALBERT BURDINE (Jesse^8, Mary^7, Samuel^6, Hannah^5, David^4, Catherine^3, Matthias^2, John Jacob^1) was the son of Jesse Guy and Tessie May Davis Burdine [TLF No. 4036]. Ralph was born March 8, 1931, at Shreveport, Louisiana.

(Sup) 6430 GUY LEWIS BURDINE (Jesse[8], Mary[7], Samuel[6], Hannah[5], David[4], Catherine[3], Matthias[2], John Jacob[1]) was the son of Jesse Guy and Tessie May Davis Burdine [TLF No. 4036]. Guy was born June 6, 1935. He died July 15, 1941, at Logansport, Louisiana.

(Sup) 6431 WILLIE EUGENE BURDINE (Jesse[8], Anna[7], Samuel[6], Hannah[5], David[4], Catherine[3], Matthias[2], John Jacob[1]) was the son of Jesse Guy and Tessie May Davis Burdine [TLF No. 4036]. He was born December 7, 1938, at Antioch, Louisiana.

(Sup) 6432 BILLIE RAY BURDINE (Jesse[8], Anna[7], Samuel[6], Hannah[5], David[4], Catherine[3], Matthias[2], John Jacob[1]) was the son of Jesse Guy and Tessie May Davis Burdine [TLF No. 4036]. He was born March 9, 1940, at Antioch, Louisiana.

(Sup) 6433 MARTHA ANNE YEATES (Mabel[8], Mary[7], Samuel[6], Hannah[5], David[4], Catherine[3], Matthias[2], John Jacob[1]) was the daughter of Backer William and Mabel Burdine Yeates [TLF No. 4038]. Martha was born November 21, 1936, at Shreveport, Louisiana.

(Sup) 6434 JANET GAYNOR BURDINE (Truman[8], Mary[7], Samuel[6], Hannah[5], David[4], Catherine[3], Matthias[2], John Jacob[1]) was the daughter of Truman Cecil and Othelle Carter Burdine [TLF No. 4039]. She was born June 14, 1936.

(Sup) 6435 ROSE MARGARET BURDINE (Truman[8], Mary[7], Samuel[6], Hannah[5], David[4], Catherine[3], Matthias[2], John Jacob[1]) was the daughter of Truman Cecil and Othelle Carter Burdine [TLF 4039]. Rose was born December 28, 1940, and died February 27, 1941.

(Sup) 6436 MARY OLIVE BURDINE (Clyde[8], Mary[7], Samuel[6], Hannah[5], David[4], Catherine[3], Matthias[2], John Jacob[1]) was the daughter of Clyde Vincent and George Mae Collier Burdine [TLF No. 4040]. Mary was born December 2, 1935, at Antioch, California.

(Sup) 6437 ANITA JOAN BURDINE (Clyde[8], Mary[7], Samuel[6], Hannah[5], David[4], Catherine[3], Matthias[2], John Jacob[1]) was the daughter of Clyde Vincent and Georgia Mae Collier Burdine [TLF No. 4040]. Anita was born February 7, 1938, at Antioch, Louisiana.

(Sup) 6438 ROBERT TERRELL BURDINE (Clyde[8], Mary[7], Samuel[6], Hannah[5], David[4], Catherine[3], Matthias[2], John Jacob[1]) was the son of Clyde Vincent and Georgia Mae Collier Burdine [TLF No. 4040]. Robert was born September 4, 1944, at Delhi, Louisiana.

(Sup) 6439 RODNEY LEE BAKER (Oren[8], Jessie[7], Samuel[6], Hannah[5], David[4], Catherine[3], Matthias[2], John Jacob[1]) was the son of Oren Olin and Carmellar Hulson Baker [TLF No. 4043]. Rodney was born April 12, 1923. He married Billy Sue Emerson November 11, 1941. She was born December 24, 1924.

(Sup) 7800   1 Rodney Lee Baker, Jr., born December 3, 1942.

(Sup) 6440 DONALD GENE BAKER (Oren[8], Jessie[7], Samuel[6], Hannah[5], David[4], Catherine[3], Matthias[2], John Jacob[1]) was the son of Oren Olin and Carmellar Hulson Baker [TLF No. 4043]. Donald was born July 4, 1928. He married Mavis Edna Hines September 24, 1949. Mavis was born April 11, 1934.

(Sup) 6441 JAMES DONALD McWILLIAMS (Clinton[8], Beulah[7], Samuel[6], Hannah[5], David[4], Catherine[3], Matthias[2], John Jacob[1]) was the son of Clinton Kelly and Emma Lee Blasingame McWilliams [TLF No. 4046]. James was born September 8, 1933, at Magnolia, Arkansas.

(Sup) 6442 ANITA KAY McWILLIAMS (Clinton[8], Beulah[7], Samuel[6], Hannah[5], David[4], Catherine[3], Matthias[2], John Jacob[1]) was the daughter of Clinton Kelly and Emma Lee Blasingame McWilliams [TLF No. 4046]. Anita was born November 21, 1936, at Magnolia, Arkansas.

(Sup) 6443 FRANCES JAN McWILLIAMS (Clinton[8], Beulah[7], Samuel[6], Hannah[5], David[4], Catherine[3], Matthias[2], John Jacob[1]) was the daughter of Clinton Kelly and Emma Lee Blasingame McWilliams [TLF No. 4046]. Frances was born July 18, 1946, at Springfield, Louisiana.

(Sup) 6444 ANNE KATHRYN BELL (Mabelle[8], John[7], Sarah[6], Minerva[5], Hannah[4], Catherine[3], Matthias[2], John Jacob[1]) was the daughter of William C. and Mabelle Miller Bell [TLF No. 4047]. She was born November 14, 1945.

(Sup) 6445 LEE ELLEN BELL (Mabelle[8], John[7], Sarah[6], Minerva[5], Hannah[4], Catherine[3], Matthias[2], John Jacob[1]) was the daughter of William C. and Mabelle Miller Bell [TLF No. 4047]. Lee Ellen was born November 16, 1948.

(Sup) 6446 MARGARET WALLACE BELL (Mabelle[8], John[7], Sarah[6], Minerva[5], Hannah[4], Catherine[3], Matthias[2], John Jacob[1]) was the daughter of William C. and Mabelle Miller Bell [TLF No. 4047]. Margaret was born December 9, 1949.

(Sup) 6447 MAZILU MAHAN (Mary[8], Darrell[7], Sarah[6], Minerva[5], Hannah[4], Catherine[3], Matthias[2], John Jacob[1]) was the son of Clyde Vincent Sparks and Mary Elizabeth Miller Mahan [TLF No. 4049]. Mazilu was born April 4, 1936.

(Sup) 6448 TRAVERS S. MAHAN, JR. (Mary[8], Darrell[7], Sarah[6], Minerva[5], Hannah[4], Catherine[3], Matthias[2], John Jacob[1]) was the son of Travers Sparks and Mary Elizabeth Miller Mahan [TLF No. 4049]. Travers, Jr., was born April 22, 1947.

(Sup) 6449 ELEANOR ELIZABETH HARDING (Mazie[8], Darrell[7], Sarah[6], Minerva[5], Hannah[4], Catherine[3], Matthias[2], John Jacob[1]) was the daughter of Edwin Forrest and Mazie Ann Miller Harding [TLF No. 4051]. Eleanor was born October 21, 1942.

(Sup) 6450 EDWIN FORREST HARDING, III (Mazie[8], Darrell[7], Sarah[6], Minerva[5], Hannah[4], Catherine[3], Matthias[2], John Jacob[1]) was the son of Edwin Forrest and Mazie Ann Miller Harding, Jr. [TLF No. 4051]. Edwin, III, was born November 7, 1943.

(Sup) 6451 ANN MILLER HARDING (Mazie[8], Darrell[7], Sarah[6], Minerva[5], Hannah[4], Catherine[3], Matthias[2], John Jacob[1]) was the daughter of Edwin Forrest and Mazie Ann Miller Harding [TLF No. 4051]. Ann was born August 12, 1946.

(Sup) 6452 JONATHAN WAYNE HARDING (Mazie[8], Darrell[7], Sarah[6], Minerva[5], Hannah[4], Catherine[3], Matthias[2], John Jacob[1]) was the son of Edwin Forrest and Mazie Ann Miller Harding [TLF No. 4051]. Jonathan was born January 14, 1948.

- - - - - - - - - - - -

(Sup) 6457 JOHN MARSHALL SINCLAIR (Carter[8], Katherine[7], Katherine[6], Henry[5], Peter[4], Catherine[3], Matthias[2], John Jacob[1]) was the son of Carter Ashton and Betty Irene Bush Sinclair [TLF No. 4060]. John was born October 27, 1948.

(Sup) 6458 TAYLOR MANSFIELD BOXLEY, III (Taylor[8], Mildred[7], Bessie[6], David[5], Peter[4], Catherine[3], Matthias[2], John Jacob[1]) was the son of Taylor Mansfield and Anne Brown Boxley, Jr. [TLF No. 4065]. Taylor, III, was born July 15, 1947.

(Sup) 6459 FRANCES WOODWARD BRYAN (Frances[8], Harry[7], Joseph[6], Peter[5], Mary[4], Catherine[3], Matthias[2], John Jacob[1]) was the daughter of William Thomas and Frances Lella Woodward Bryan, Jr. [TLF No. 4069]. Frances was born April 1, 1926, at Athens, Georgia.

(Sup) 6460 WILLIAM T. BRYAN, III (Frances[8], Harry[7], Joseph[6], Peter[5], Mary[4], Catherine[3], Matthias[2], John Jacob[1]) was the son of William Thomas and Frances Lella Woodward Bryan, Jr. [TLF No. 4069]. William, III, was born November 19, 1931, at Athens, Georgia.

(Sup) 6461 HARRY WOODWARD BRYAN (Frances[8], Harry[7], Joseph[6], Peter[5], Mary[4], Catherine[3], Matthias[2], John Jacob[1]) was the son of William Thomas and Frances Woodward Bryan [TLF No. 4069]. Harry was born November 7, 1933, at Athens, Georgia.

(Sup) 6462 JOHN PROCTOR BRYAN (Frances[8], Harry[7], Joseph[6], Peter[5], Mary[4], Catherine[3], Matthias[2], John Jacob[1]) was the son of William Thomas and Frances Woodward Bryan [TLF No. 4069]. John was born March 17, 1946, at Athens, Georgia.

(Sup) 6463 WALLACE De HART MERCEREAU (Wallace[8], Anna[7], Joseph[6], Peter[5], Mary[4], Catherine[3], Matthias[2], John Jacob[1]) was the son of Wallace Woodward and Florine De Hart Mercereau [TLF No. 4073]. Wallace was born December 25, 1943, at Bristol, Virginia.

(Sup) 6464 EDWARD FINDLEY MERCEREAU (Wallace[8], Anna[7], Joseph[6], Peter[5], Mary[4], Catherine[3], Matthias[2], John Jacob[1]) was the son of Wallace Woodward and Florine de Hart Mercereau [TLF No. 4073]. Edward was born August, 1946, at Baltimore, Maryland.

(Sup) 6465 HARMON RISH WOODWARD (Harmon[8], Harmon[7], Samuel[6], Peter[5], Mary[4], Catherine[3], Matthias[2], John Jacob[1]) was the son of Harmon and June Rish Woodward [TLF No. 4077]. He was born March 6, 1943, at Bluefields, West Virginia.

(Sup) 6466 THOMAS HALE WOODWARD (Harmon[8], Harmon[7], Samuel[6], Peter[5], Mary[4], Catherine[3], Matthias[2], John Jacob[1]) was the son of Harmon and June Rish Woodward [TLF No. 4077]. Thomas was born March 31, 1947, at Bluefields, West Virginia.

(Sup) 6467 CHRISSIE JANE WOODWARD (Harmon[8], Harmon[7], Samuel[6], Peter[5], Mary[4], Catherine[3], Matthias[2], John Jacob[1]) was the daughter of Harmon and June Rish Woodward [TLF No. 4077]. Chrissie was born June 14, 1949, at Bluefields, West Virginia.

(Sup) 6468 DANIEL WENTWORTH RICHARDS, JR. (Daniel[8], Katherine[7], Samuel[6], Peter[5], Mary[4], Catherine[3], Matthias[2], John Jacob[1]) was the son of Daniel Wentworth and Helen Cox Richards [TLF No. 4079]. Daniel, Jr., was born in 1944.

(Sup) 6469 KATHARINE WOODWARD RICHARDS (Daniel[8], Katherine[7], Samuel[6], Peter[5], Mary[4], Catherine[3], Matthias[2], John Jacob[1]) was the daughter of Daniel Wentworth and Helen Cox Richards [TLF No. 4079]. Katherine was born in 1949.

(Sup) 6470 ELLISON DOUGLAS CAPERS (Ellison[8], Margaret[7], Eveline[6], Margaret[5], Eveline[4], Catherine[3], Matthias[2], John Jacob[1]) was the son of Ellison Van Meter and Rose Marie Doherty Capers [TLF No. 4093]. He was born September 5, 1947.

(Sup) 6473 CARLISLE KIRKPATRICK, III (Evelyn[8], Evelyn[7], Evaline[6], Margaret[5], Eveline[4], Catherine[3], Matthias[2], John Jacob[1]) was the son of Carlisle and Evelyn Berryman Kirkpatrick, Jr. [TLF No. 4096]. Carlisle, III, was born April 18, 1944, at Lexington, Kentucky.

(Sup) 6474 FITZHUGH SCOTT, III (Fitzhugh[8], Ella[7], Charlotte[6], William[5], Eveline[4], Catherine[3], Matthias[2], John Jacob[1]) was the son of Fitzhugh and Eileen Schlesinger Scott, Jr. [TLF No. 4098]. Fitzhugh, III, was born December 27, 1937, at Milwaukee, Wisconsin.

(Sup) 6475 EILEEN MCGREGOR SCOTT (Fitzhugh[8], Ella[7], Charlotte[6], William[5], Eveline[4], Catherine[3], Matthias[2], John Jacob[1]) was the daughter of Fitzhugh and Eileen Schlesinger Scott [TLF No. 4098]. She was born December 27, 1938, at Milwaukee, Wisconsin.

(Sup) 6476 LORNA LANDRUM SCOTT (Fitzhugh[8], Ella[7], Charlotte[6], William[5], Eveline[4], Catherine[3], Matthias[2], John Jacob[1]) was the daughter of Fitzhugh and Eileen Schlesinger Scott [TLF No. 4098]. Lorna was born

(Sup) 6477 SUSAN FITZHUGH SCOTT (William[8], Ella[7], Charlotte[6], William[5], Eveline[4], Catherine[3], Matthias[2], John Jacob[1]) was the daughter of William Frederick and Janet Blish Scott [TLF No. 4099]. Susan was born August 7, 1939, at Columbus, Ohio.

(Sup) 6478 STUART LANDRUM SCOTT (William[8], Ella[7], Charlotte[6], William[5], Eveline[4], Catherine[3], Matthias[2], John Jacob[1]) was the son of William Frederick and Janet Blish Scott [TLF No. 4099]. Stuart was born August 14, 1947, at Charlottesville, Virginia.

(Sup) 6479 BAYLOR LANDRUM, III (Baylor[8], Baylor[7], Charlotte[6], William[5], Eveline[4], Catherine[3], Matthias[2], John Jacob[1]) was the son of Baylor Landrum and Mary Evans Landrum, Jr. [TLF No. 4101]. Baylor, III, was born June 17, 1949, at Louisville, Kentucky.

(Sup) 6480 STANLEY PARKER McGEE, III (Julia[8], Baylor[7], Charlotte[6], William[5], Eveline[4], Catherine[3], Matthias[2], John Jacob[1]) was the son of Stanley Parker and Julia Landrum McGee, Jr. [TLF No. 4103]. Stanley, III, was born February 13, 1947, at Louisville, Kentucky.

(Sup) 6481 ROBERT BAYLOR McGEE (Julia[8], Baylor[7], Charlotte[6], William[5], Eveline[4], Catherine[3], Matthias[2], John Jacob[1]) was the son of Stanley Parker and Julia Landrum McGee, Jr. [TLF No. 4103]. Robert was born November 1, 1948, at Louisville, Kentucky.

(Sup) 6482 ELIZABETH ANN MILLER (Ernestine[8], Frank[7], Ida[6], Franklin[5], Adam[4], Adam[3], Matthias[2], John Jacob[1]) was the daughter of Harry W. and Ernestine Harris Miller [TLF No. 4107]. Elizabeth was born May 27, 1929.

(Sup) 6483 HARRY W. MILLER, JR. (Ernestine[8], Frank[7], Ida[6], Franklin[5], Adam[4], Adam[3], Matthias[2], John Jacob[1]) was the son of Harry W. and Ernestine Harris Miller [TLF No. 4107]. Harry, Jr., was born July 8, 1930.

(Sup) 6484 FRANK HARRIS MILLER (Ernestine[8], Frank[7], Ida[6], Franklin[5], Adam[4], Adam[3], Matthias[2], John Jacob[1]) was the son of Harry W. and Ernestine Harris Miller [TLF No. 4107]. Frank was born January 5, 1933.

(Sup) 6485 SUSAN DYE HARRIS (Robert[8], Robert[7], Ida[6], Franklin[5], Adam[4], Adam[3], Matthias[2], John Jacob[1]) was the daughter of Robert Williamson and Frances Dye Harris, Jr. [Supplement No. 4108]. Susan was born October 24, 1943, at Columbus, Ohio. She was a school teacher. She married Steven J. Roby June 10, 1967, at Columbus, Ohio. Steven was the son of John Melvin and Lucille Black Roby and was born June 7, 1943, at Bellefontaine, Ohio. He served as a captain in the Air Force Minuteman missile maintenance program during the Vietnam Conflict, and he became a mechanical engineer.

(Sup) 7810   i   Christi Diane Roby, born September 10, 1968.
(Sup) 7811 ii   Robert John Roby, born May 18, 1971.

(Sup) 6486 GORDON KENNETH HARRIS, JR. (Gordon[8], Robert[7], Ida[6], Franklin[5], Adam[4], Adam[3], Matthias[2], John Jacob[1]) was the son of Gordon Kenneth and Mary Eunice Hennesy Harris [Supplement No. 4110]. Gordon, Jr., was born October 20, 1942, at Gallipolis, Ohio.

(Sup) 6487 JAMES RICHARD HARRIS (Gordon[8], Robert[7], Ida[6], Franklin[5], Adam[4], Adam[3], Matthias[2], John Jacob[1]) was the son of Gordon Kenneth and Mary Eunice Hennesy Harris [Supplement No. 4110]. James was born August 28, 1946, at Columbus, Ohio.

(Sup) 6488 KENNETH EUGENE HARRIS (Eugene[8], Robert[7], Ida[6], Franklin[5], Adam[4], Adam[3], Matthias[2], John Jacob[1]) was the son of Eugene M. and Janet Hecox Harris [Supplement No. 4111]. Kenneth was born March 13, 1948, at Wadsworth, Ohio.

Russell W. and Virginia Adeline Johnson [Supplement No. 4112]. She was born July 9, 1946, at Ronceverte, West Virginia. She married Paul Edgar Monroe February 7, 1971, at Covington, Virginia. He was the son of Emory and Inez Monroe and was born July 2, 1931. Judith and Paul resided in Houston, Texas.

(Sup) 7821   i Russell Emory Monroe, born December 18, 1973.
(Sup) 7822   ii Rebecca Virginia Monroe, born October 21, 1976.

(Sup) 6497 BARBARA MARY FRANCES WISE (Frances[8], Paul[7], Herndon[6], Franklin[5], Adam[4], Adam[3], Matthias[2], John Jacob[1]) was the daughter of John William and Frances Pauline (Link) Wise [Supplement No. 4113]. Barbara was born January 6, 1951, at Ronceverte, West Virginia. She resided at Ronceverte.

(Sup) 6498 DONNA LEE LINK (Roger[8], Paul[7], Herndon[6], Franklin[5], Adam[4], Adam[3], Matthias[2], John Jacob[1]) was the daughter of Roger Lee and Ida Maxine (Miller) Link [Supplement No. 4114]. Donna was born January 24, 1944, at Ronceverte, West Virginia. She married William Douglas Cook, June 11, 1966, at Ronceverte. He was the son of Clifford and Josephine Cook, and was born at Birmingham, Alabama. Donna and William resided at Duluth, Georgia.

(Sup) 7823   i Tracy Allson Cook, born October 1, 1970.

(Sup) 6499 BEVERLY JEAN LINK (Roger[8], Paul[7], Herndon[6], Franklin[5], Adam[4], Adam[3], Matthias[2], John Jacob[1]) was the daughter of Roger Lee and Ida Maxine (Miller) Link [Supplement No. 4114]. She was born October 22, 1946, at Ronceverte, West Virginia. She married Kenneth Woodward (Woody) Oden in 1965 at Brunswick, Maryland. He was the son of Kenneth and Kathleen Oden and was born at Charles Town, West Virginia.

(Sup) 7824   i Jeanna Roxanne Oden, born March 4, 1966.
(Sup) 7825   ii Dena Nicole Oden, born September 27, 1967.

(Sup) 6500 MARTHA LOU LINK (Roger[8], Paul[7], Herndon[6], Franklin[5], Adam[4], Adam[3], Matthias[2], John Jacob[1]) was the daughter of Roger Lee and Ida Maxine (Miller) Link [Supplement No. 4114]. Martha Lou was born December 15, 1947, at Ronceverte, West Virginia. She married Delmas Allen Morgan, July 3, 1967, at Staunton, Virginia. He was the son of Orby J. and Isabel Loudermilk Morgan and was born August 16, 1946, at Caldwell, West Virginia.

(Sup) 7826   i   April Dawn Morgan, born April 1, 1968.
(Sup) 7827   ii Heather Lynn Morgan, born August 28, 1970.
(Sup) 7828   iii Tia Ann Morgan, born October 3, 1978.

(Sup) 6489 MARJORIE ELLEN HARRIS (Eugene[8], Robert[7], Ida[6], Franklin[5], Adam[4], Adam[3], Matthias[2], John Jacob[1]) was the daughter of Eugene M. and Janet Hecox Harris [Supplement No. 4111]. Marjorie was born October 25, 1949, at Wadsworth, Ohio.

(Sup) 6490 NANCY JEAN HARRIS (Eugene[8], Robert[7], Ida[6], Franklin[5], Adam[4], Adam[3], Matthias[2], John Jacob[1]) was the daughter of Eugene M. and Janet Hecob Harris [Supplement No. 4111]. Nancy was born May 21, 1951, at Wadsworth, Ohio.

(Sup) 6491 PATRICIA ANN HARRIS (Eugene[8], Robert[7], Ida[6], Franklin[5], Adam[4], Adam[3], Matthias[2], John Jacob[1]) was the daughter of Eugene M. and Janet Hecox Harris [Supplement No. 4111]. Patricia was born April 5, 1954, at Wadsworth, Ohio.

(Sup) 6492 ROBERT WILLIAMSON HARRIS (Eugene[8], Robert[7], Ida[6], Franklin[5], Adam[4], Adam[3], Matthias[2], John Jacob[1]) was the son of Eugene M. and Janet (Hecox) Harris [Supplement No. 4111]. Robert was born February 14, 1956, at Hutchinson, Kansas.

(Sup) 6493 KATHRYN ELIZABETH HARRIS (Eugene[8], Robert[7], Ida[6], Franklin[5], Adam[4], Adam[3], Matthias[2], John Jacob[1]) was the daughter of Eugene M. and Janet (Hecox) Harris [Supplement No. 4111]. Kathryn was born March 30, 1958, at Pomeroy, Ohio.

(Sup) 6494 JANE HARRIS (Walter[8], Walter[7], Ida[6], Franklin[5], Adam[4], Adam[3], Matthias[2], John Jacob[1]) was the daughter of Walter Burns and Hilda (Russell) Harris [Supplement No. 4111A]. Jane was born September 5, 1939, at Middleport, Ohio.

(Sup) 6495 CATHERINE JILL HARRIS (Walter[8], Walter[7], Ida[6], Franklin[5], Adam[4], Adam[3], Matthias[2], John Jacob[1]) was the daughter of Walter Burns and Hilda (Russell) Harris [Supplement No. 4111A]. Catherine was born March 1, 1954, at Gallipolis, Ohio.

(Sup) 6496 JUDITH LYNN JOHNSON (Virginia[8], Paul[7], Herndon[6], Franklin[5], Adam[4], Adam[3], Matthias[2], John Jacob[1]) was the daughter of

(Sup) 6501 ASHBY BRIDGFORTH ALLEN, JR. (Mary^8, Gordon^7, Herndon^6, Franklin^5, Adam^4, Adam^3, Matthias^2, John Jacob^1) was the son of Ashby Bridgforth and Mary Lee (Link) Allen [Supplement No. 4115]. Ashby, Jr., was born March 18, 1951.

(Sup) 6501A REBECCA WARREN ALLEN (Mary^8, Gordon^7, Herndon^6, Franklin^5, Adam^4, Adam^3, Matthias^2, John Jacob^1) was the daughter of Ashby Bridgforth and Mary Lee (Link) Allen [Supplement No. 4115]. Rebecca was born May 27, 1952.

(Sup) 6501B CHARLES LITTLEPAGE ALLEN (Mary^8, Gordon^7, Herndon^6, Franklin^5, Adam^4, Adam^3, Matthias^2, John Jacob^1) was the son of Ashby Bridgforth and Mary Lee (Link) Allen [Supplement No. 4115]. Charles was born June 1, 1954.

(Sup) 6501C MARY FRANCES ALLEN (Mary^8, Gordon^7, Herndon^6, Franklin^5, Adam^4, Adam^3, Matthias^2, John Jacob^1) was the daughter of Ashby Bridgforth and Mary Lee (Link) Allen [Supplement No. 4115]. Mary was born June 10, 1958.

(Sup) 6502 MARIA WARREN HARVIE (Joyce^8, Gordon^7, Herndon^6, Franklin^5, Adam^4, Adam^3, Matthias^2, John Jacob^1) was the daughter of Armistead Taylor and Joyce (Link) Harvie, Jr. [Supplement No. 4116]. Maria was born June 8, 1955, at Richmond, Virginia. She married Mr. Whitaker.

(Sup) 6502A ARMISTEAD TAYLOR HARVIE, III (Joyce^8, Gordon^7, Herndon^6, Franklin^5, Adam^4, Adam^3, Matthias^2, John Jacob^1) was the son of Armistead Taylor and Joyce (Link) Harvie, Jr. [Supplement No. 4116]. He was born September 26, 1956, at Richmond, Virginia.

(Sup) 6502B GORDON LINK HARVIE (Joyce^8, Gordon^7, Herndon^6, Franklin^5, Adam^4, Adam^3, Matthias^2, John Jacob^1) was the son of Armistead Taylor and Joyce (Link) Harvie [Supplement No. 4116]. Gordon was born November 20, 1958, at Richmond, Virginia.

(Sup) 6502C LEWIS EDWIN HARVIE (Joyce^8, Gordon^7, Herndon^6, Franklin^5, Adam^4, Adam^3, Matthias^2, John Jacob^1) was the son of Armistead Taylor and Joyce (Link) Harvie [Supplement No. 4116]. Lewis was born May 13, 1960, at Richmond, Virginia.

(Sup) 6502D REBECCA LITTLEPAGE HARVIE (Joyce^8, Gordon^7, Herndon^6, Franklin^5, Adam^4, Adam^3, Matthias^2, John Jacob^1) was the daughter of Armistead Taylor and Joyce (Link) Harvie [Supplement No. 4116]. Rebecca was born January 18, 1972, at Richmond, Virginia.

(Sup) 6503 GORDON LEE LINK, III (Gordon^8, Gordon^7, Herndon^6, Franklin^5, Adam^4, Adam^3, Matthias^2, John Jacob^1) was the son of Gordon Littlepage and Sarah (Spangler) Link [Supplement No. 4117]. Gordon, III was born August 8, 1963.

(Sup) 6504 ANGELA KELLETT PANETTIERE (Rebecca^8, Gordon^7, Herndon^6, Franklin^5, Adam^4, Adam^3, Matthias^2, John Jacob^1) was the daughter of Charles Vincent and Rebecca (Link) Panettiere [Supplement No. 4118]. Angela was born May 4, 1961.

(Sup) 6504A TRACY LEE PANETTIERE (Rebecca^8, Gordon^7, Herndon^6, Franklin^5, Adam^4, Adam^3, Matthias^2, John Jacob^1) was the daughter of Charles Vincent and Rebecca (Link) Panettiere [Supplement No. 4118]. Tracy was born November 3, 1962.

(Sup) 6504B CHARLES LINK PANETTIERE (Rebecca^8, Gordon^7, Herndon^6, Franklin^5, Adam^4, Adam^3, Matthias^2, John Jacob^1) was the son of Charles Vincent and Rebecca (Link) Panettiere [Supplement No. 4118]. Charles was born August 10, 1967.

- -

(Sup) 6506 DENZIL MORTON FERGUSON, III (Denzil^8, Mary^7, Alice^6, Samuel^5, Lewis^4, Christina^3, Matthias^2, John Jacob^1) was the son of Denzil Morton and Eleanor Thomas Ferguson, Jr. [TLF No. 4131]. D. M., III, was born September 21, 1946, at Terre Haute, Indiana.

(Sup) 6507 SETH THOMAS FERGUSON (Denzil^8, Mary^7, Alice^6, Samuel^5, Lewis^4, Christian^3, Matthias^2, John Jacob^1) was the son of Denzil Morton and Eleanor Thomas Ferguson, Jr. [TLF No. 4131]. He was born September 29, 1948, at Terre Haute, Indiana.

(Sup) 6508 GREGG WHITACRE CRAWFORD (Margaret[8], Mary[7], Alice[6], Samuel[5], Lewis[4], Christina[3], Matthias[2], John Jacob[1]) was the son of Benjamin and Margaret Ferguson Crawford [TLF No. 4132]. Gregg was born November 29, 1948, at Terre Haute, Indiana.

(Sup) 6509 PETER JACKSON LINK (Eugene[8], Virgil[7], Eugene[6], Samuel[5], Lewis[4], Christina[3], Matthias[2], John Jacob[1]) was the son of Eugene Gross and Patricia Ann Smith Link [TLF No. 4135]. Peter was born April 3, 1944, at Portland, Oregon.

(Sup) 6510 ROGER MARK LINK (Eugene[8], Virgil[7], Eugene[6], Samuel[5], Lewis[4], Christina[3], Matthias[2], John Jacob[1]) was the son of Eugene Gross and Patricia Ann Smith Link [TLF No. 4135]. Roger was born September 22, 1946, at Silver Spring, Maryland.

(Sup) 6511 NANCY LINK PATTISON (Mary[8], Virgil[7], Eugene[6], Samuel[5], Lewis[4], Christina[3], Matthias[2], John Jacob[1]) was the daughter of George Ashton and Mary Louise Link Pattison [TLF No. 4136]. Nancy was born April 15, 1947, at Stamford, Connecticut.

(Sup) 6512 ELIZABETH EMILY WHITMAN (Julie[8], Virgil[7], Eugene[6], Samuel[5], Lewis[4], Christian[3], Matthias[2], John Jacob[1]) was the daughter of Stewart Lane and Julie Link Whitman [TLF No. 4137]. Elizabeth was born August 9, 1939, at Stamford, Connecticut.

(Sup) 6513 BARBARA LINK WHITMAN (Julie[8], Virgil[7], Eugene[6], Samuel[5], Lewis[4], Christian[3], Matthias[2], John Jacob[1]) was the daughter of Stewart Lane and Julie Link Whitman [TLF No. 4137]. Barbara was born November 30, 1940, at Stamford, Connecticut.

(Sup) 6514 THOMAS CHRISTOPHER MURPHY, JR. (Patricia[8], Samuel[7], Eugene[6], Samuel[5], Lewis[4], Christian[3], Matthias[2], John Jacob[1]) was the son of Thomas Christopher and Patricia Ann Link Murphy [TLF No. 4139]. Thomas, Jr., was born August 26, 1948, at Stamford, Connecticut.

(Sup) 6515 THOMAS JAMES EMMETT (James[8], Frances[7], Elizabeth[6], Samuel[5], Lewis[4], Christian[3], Matthias[2], John Jacob[1]) was the son of James and Judy (Gibbs) Emmett, Jr. [Supplement No. 4147]. Thomas was born at Greeley, Colorado.

(Sup) 6515A ELIZABETH ANN EMMETT (James[8], Frances[7], Elizabeth[6], Samuel[5], Lewis[4], Christian[3], Matthias[2], John Jacob[1]) was the daughter of James and Judy (Gibbs) Emmett, Jr. [Supplement No. 4147]. Elizabeth was born June 24, 1964, at Greeley, Colorado.

(Sup) 6515B ASPEN CHRISTINE EMMETT (Richard[8], Frances[7], Elizabeth[6], Samuel[5], Lewis[4], Christian[3], Matthias[2], John Jacob[1]) was the daughter of Richard Longpre and Patricia (Yeager) Emmett [Supplement No. 4148]. She was born February 1, 1976.

(Sup) 6515C HILLARY LEORA EMMETT (Richard[8], Frances[7], Elizabeth[6], Samuel[5], Lewis[4], Christian[3], Matthias[2], John Jacob[1]) was the daughter of Richard Longpre and Patricia (Yeager) Emmett [Supplement No. 4148]. She was born June 14, 1978.

(Sup) 6515D BETHANY YEAGER EMMETT (Richard[8], Frances[7], Elizabeth[6], Samuel[5], Lewis[4], Christian[3], Matthias[2], John Jacob[1]) was the daughter of Richard Longpre and Patricia (Yeager) Emmett [Supplement No. 4148]. Bethany was born March 1, 1982, and died May 16, 1984.

(Sup) 6516 MATTHEW GUNNING McDANIEL (Jeanne[8], Mary[7], Elizabeth[6], Frances[5], Lewis[4], Christian[3], Matthias[2], John Jacob[1]) was the son of Kent and Jeanne (Gunning) McDaniel [Supplement No. 4148B]. Matthew was born February 2, 1987, at Bloomington, Intdiana.

(Sup) 6517 DAVID CLAY MONSON (Patricia[8], Mary[7], Sarah[6], John[5], Matthias[4], Christian[3], Matthias[2], John Jacob[1]) was the son of Donald James and Patricia (Baughman) Monson [TLF No. 4154]. David was born October 27, 1941.

(Sup) 6518 MARY LOUISE MONSON (Patricia[8], Mary[7], Sarah[6], John[5], Matthias[4], Christian[3], Matthias[2], John Jacob[1]) was the daughter of Donald James and Patricia (Baughman) Monson [TLF No. 4154]. Mary was born October 2, 1944.

(Sup) 6519 DIANA LYNN MONSON (Patricia[8], Mary[7], Sarah[6], John[5], Matthias[4], Christian[3], Matthias[2], John Jacob[1]) was the daughter of Donald James and Patricia (Baughman) Monson [TLF No. 4154]. Diana was born May 28, 1949.

(Sup) 6520 MARY ELIZABETH SMYTHE (Carl[8], Carl[7], Agnes[6], Jane[5], Matthias[4], Christian[3], Matthias[2], John Jacob[1]) was the daughter of Carl Peoples and Mary Elizabeth Smythe [TLF No. 4155]. She was born September 28, 1938.

(Sup) 6521 CAROL ANN SMYTHE (Carl[8], Carl[7], Agnes, Jane[5], Matthias[4], Christian[3], Matthias[2], John Jacob[1]) was the daughter of Carl Peoples and Mary Elizabeth Smythe [TLF No. 4155]. Carol was born August 9, 1946.

(Sup) 6522 KAREN INGE FRYKLUND (Verne[8], Adah[7], Agnes[6], Jane[5], Matthias[4], Christian[3], Matthias[2], John Jacob[1]) was the daughter of Verne C. and Shirley Zimmerman Fryklund [TLF No. 4156]. Karen was born June 8, 1946.

(Sup) 6522A WENDY HUNTER WILES (Gordon[8], Mary[7], Mary[6], Leonidas[5], Thomas[4], John[3], Matthias[2], John Jacob[1]) was the daughter of Gordon Wyatt and Eve Hunter Wiles [Supplement No. 4169]. Wendy was born February 12, 1955, at Los Angeles, California. She received a B.A. degree in communications and a B.S. degree in business from Pepperdine College and a J.D. degree from Whitter Law School. Wendy married Jeffrey M. Verdon. He was born July 24, 1954, at Miami, Florida, and obtained an L.L.M. degree from Boston College.

(Sup) 7833   i   Ashley Hunter Verdon, born February 21, 1985.
(Sup) 7834   ii Adam Joseph Verdon, born July 7, 1988.

(Sup) 6522B GORDON WYATT WILES, JR. (Gordon[8], Mary[7], Mary[6], Leonidas[5], Thomas[4], John[3], Matthias[2], John Jacob[1]) was the son of Gordon Wyatt and Eve Hunter Wiles [Supplement No. 4169]. Gordon, Jr., was born January 9, 1960, at Encino, California.

(Sup) 6522C ELIZABETH LINK KRIMENDAHL (Martha[8], Mary[7], Mary[6], Leonidas[5], Thomas[4], John[3], Matthias[2], John Jacob[1]) was the daughter of David Christian and Martah Wiles Krimendahl [Supplement No. 4170]. Elizabeth was born April 14, 1960, at Indianapolis, Indiana. She received a B.A. degree in 1982 from Miami University of Ohio, where she was a member of Kappa Alpha Theta and the Miami University Student Foundation. She received an M.B.A. from Kellogg School of Management, Northwestern University, in 1986.

(Sup) 6522D DAVID CHRISTIAN KRIMENDAHL, JR. (Martha[8], Mary[7], Mary[6], Leonidas[5], Thomas[4], John[3], Matthias[2], John Jacob[1]) was the son of David Christian and Martha Wiles Krimendahl [Supplement No. 4170]. David, Jr., was born February 22, 1962, at Indianapolis, Indiana. He received a B.A. degree in 1984 from Hillsdale College, where he was a member of Tau Kappa Epsilon fraternity.

(Sup) 6522E MARY KATHRINE KRIMENDAHL (Martha[8], Mary[7], Mary[6], Leonidas[5], Thomas[4], John[3], Matthias[2], John Jacob[1]) was the daughter of Carl David Christian and Martha Wiles Krimendahl [Supplement No. 4170]. Mary was born October 17, 1964, at Indianapolis, Indiana. She received a B.A. degree in 1987 form the University of Colorado.

(Sup) 6522F MARABETH LINK WYATT (John[8], John[7], Mary[6], Leonidas[5], Thomas[4], John[3], Matthias[2], John Jacob[1]) was the daughter of John Link and Beverly (Campbell) Wyatt [Supplement No. 4171]. Marabeth was born February 19, 1970, at Crawfordsville, Indiana. She lettered four years in high school swimming.

(Sup) 6522G JOHN CAMPBELL WYATT (John[8], John[7], Mary[6], Leonidas[5], Thomas[4], John[3], Matthias[2], John Jacob[1]) was the son of John Link and Beverly (Campbell) Wyatt [Supplement No. 4171]. John Campbell was born July 10, 1973, at Crawfordsville, Indiana. He was an Eagle Scout.

(Sup) 6522H ADAM CROCKER PRICE (Constance[8], John[7], Mary[6], Leonidas[5], Thomas[4], John[3], Matthias[2], John Jacob[1]) was the son of Mason Crocker and Constance (Wyatt) Price [Supplement No. 4172]. Adam was born July 31, 1966, at Indianapolis, Indiana. He studied at Wabash College, Indiana.

(Sup) 6522J MASON WYATT PRICE (Constance[8], John[7], Mary[6], Leonidas[5], Thomas[4], John[3], Matthias[2], John Jacob[1]) was the son of Mason Crocker and Constance (Wyatt) Price [Supplement No. 4172]. Mason was born November 4, 1968, at Indianapolis, Indiana. He attended Indiana State University.

(Sup) 6522K MICHAEL P. WYATT (Phillip[8], John[7], Mary[6], Leonidas[5], Thomas[4], John[3], Matthias[2], John Jacob[1]) was the son of Phillip Warder and Cynthia M. Wyatt [Supplement No. 4173]. Michael was born November 4, 1986, at LaCañada, California.

(Sup) 6523 MELINDA BONAS (Beverly[8], James[7], Albert[6], Clemanthe[5], Ephraim[4], John[3], Matthias[2], John Jacob[1]) was the daughter of Matthew J. and Beverly (Brown) Bonas [TLF No. 4174]. Melinda was born June 11, 1946, at Hollywood, Florida.

(Sup) 6524 PATRICIA DIANA RENNER (Bonnie[8], Marion[7], Bonnie[6], Emma[5], Mary[4], John[3], Matthias[2], John Jacob[1]) was the daughter of Ernest and Bonnie (Studebaker) Renner [TLF No. 4178]. Patricia was born June 21, 1945, at Los Angeles, California.

(Sup) 6525 VERNON ALLISON WALKER (Luella[8], Lulu[7], Elizabeth[6], Felix[5], David[4], Elizabeth[3], Matthias[2], John Jacob[1]) was the son of John R. and Luella (Smith) Walker [TLF No. 4213]. Vernon was born April 10, 1925, in Knox County, Tennessee.

(Sup) 6526 EMMA JENERVA WALKER (Luella[8], Lulu[7], Elizabeth[6], Felix[5], David[4], Elizabeth[3], Matthias[2], John Jacob[1]) was the daughter of John R. and Luella (Smith) Walker [TLF No. 4213]. Emma was born September 23, 1928, in Knox County, Tennessee.

(Sup) 6527 CLYDE LOWE RUGGLES (John[8], Carrie[7], Elizabeth[6], Felix[5], David[4], Elizabeth[3], Matthias[2], John Jacob[1]) was the son of John Morris and Lola Mae Caldwell Ruggles [TLF No. 4220]. Clyde was born and died August 14, 1930, in Knox County, Tennessee.

(Sup) 6528 CARL LEONARD CALDWELL (Nina[8], Carrie[7], Elizabeth[6], Felix[5], David[4], Elizabeth[3], Matthias[2], John Jacob[1]) was the son of Orville Edgar and Nina Ruggles Caldwell [TLF No. 4221]. Carl was born April 25, 1925, in Knox County, Tennessee.

(Sup) 6529 BETTY JO CALDWELL (Nina[8], Carrie[7], Elizabeth[6], Felix[5], David[4], Elizabeth[3], Matthias[2], John Jacob[1]) was the daughter of Orville Edgar and Nina Ruggles Caldwell [TLF No. 4221]. Betty Jo was born July 10, 1927, in Knox County, Tennessee.

(Sup) 6530 WILLIAM HOWARD CALDWELL (Nina[8], Carrie[7], Elizabeth[6], Felix[5], David[4], Elizabeth[3], Matthias[2], John Jacob[1]) was the son of Orville Edgar and Nina Ruggles Caldwell [TLF No. 4221]. William was born November 30, 1929, in Knox County, Tennessee.

(Sup) 6531 CHARLES EDGAR CATE (Charles[8], Mary[7], Elizabeth[6], Felix[5], David[4], Elizabeth[3], Matthias[2], John Jacob[1]) was the son of Charles Ernest and Ina Jolly Cate [TLF No. 4228]. He was born October 9, 1927, in Knox County, Tennessee.

(Sup) 6532 WILLIAM HORACE CATE (Charles[8], Mary[7], Elizabeth[6], Felix[5], David[4], Elizabeth[3], Matthias[2], John Jacob[1]) was the son of Charles Ernest and Ina Jolly Cate [TLF No. 4228]. William was born July 20, 1929, in Knox County, Tennessee.

(Sup) 6533 MARY ELLEN CATE (Charles[8], Mary[7], Elizabeth[6], Felix[5], David[4], Elizabeth[3], Matthias[2], John Jacob[1]) was the daughter of Charles Ernest and Ina Jolly Cate [TLF No. 4228]. Mary Ellen was born January 15, 1930, in Knox County, Tennessee.

(Sup) 6534 EVELYN ANN CHANDLER (Frederick[8], Murta[7], William[6], Felix[5], David[4], Elizabeth[3], Matthias[2], John Jacob[1]) was the daughter of Frederick Roth and Frances Aaron Chandler [TLF No. 4232]. Evelyn was born June 16, 1936.

(Sup) 6535 MARY GOODMAN WAYLAND (Charles[8], Charles[7], William[6], Felix[5], David[4], Elizabeth[3], Matthias[2], John Jacob[1]) was the daughter of Charles Franklin and Margaret Mitchell Wayland [TLF No. 4234]. Mary was born July 15, 1938, at Knoxville, Tennessee.

(Sup) 6536 JENNIE LUTTRELL WAYLAND (Charles[8], Charles[7], William[6], Felix[5], David[4], Elizabeth[3], Matthias[2], John Jacob[1]) was the daughter of Charles Franklin and Margaret Mitchell Wayland [TLF No. 4234]. Jennie was born November 16, 1942, at Knoxville, Tennessee.

(Sup) 6537 BENJAMIN JACKSON WAYLAND, JR. (Benjamin[8], Charles[7], William[6], Felix[5], David[4], Elizabeth[3], Matthias[2], John Jacob[1]) was the son of Benjamin Jackson and Argus Huffacre Wayland [TLF No. 4235]. Benjamin, Jr., was born August 2, 1940, at Knoxville, Tennessee.

(Sup) 6538 WILLIAM FRAZIER WAYLAND (Benjamin[8], Charles[7], William[6], Felix[5], David[4], Elizabeth[3], Matthias[2], John Jacob[1]) was the son of Benjamin Jackson and Argus Huffacre Wayland [TLF No. 4235]. William was born January 12, 1942, at Knoxville, Tennessee.

(Sup) 6539 BOBBIE JEAN WAYLAND (Benjamin[8], Charles[7], William[6], Felix[5], David[4], Elizabeth[3], Matthias[2], John Jacob[1]) was the child of Horace Benjamin Jackson and Argus Huffacre Wayland [TLF No. 4235]. Bobbie Jean was born June 18, 1943, at Knoxville, Tennessee.

(Sup) 6540 HERMAN HOUSTON WAYLAND, JR. (Herman[8], Charles[7], William[6], Felix[5], David[4], Elizabeth[3], Matthias[2], John Jacob[1]) was the child of Herman Houston and Virginia Weber Wayland [TLF No. 4236]. Herman was born September 28, 1939, at Knoxville, Tennessee.

(Sup) 6541 MARION LEE WAYLAND (Herman[8], Charles[7], William[6], Felix[5], David[4], Elizabeth[3], Matthias[2], John Jacob[1]) was the child of Herman Houston and Virginia Weber Wayldn [TLF No. 4236]. Marion was born October 15, 1940, at Knoxville, Tennessee.

(Sup) 6542 STEPHENIA CAROL WAYLAND (Clifford[8], Charles[7], William[6], Felix[5], David[4], Elizabeth[3], Matthias[2], John Jacob[1]) was the daughter of Clifford Hyder and Mary Emma Perry Wayland [TLF No. 4237]. She was born May 2, 1942.

(Sup) 6543 GREGORY SERGEANT WAYLAND (Clifford[8], Charles[7], William[6], Felix[5], David[4], Elizabeth[3], Matthias[2], John Jacob[1]) was the son of Clifford Hyder and Mary Emma Perry Wayldn [TLF No. 4237]. Gregory was born October 15, 1946, at Knoxville, Tennessee.

(Sup) 6544 ERIC RICHARD WAYLAND (Clifford[8], Charles[7], William[6], Felix[5], David[4], Elizabeth[3], Matthias[2], John Jacob[1]) was the son of Clifford Hyder and Mary Emma Perry Wayland [TLF No. 4237]. Eric was born October 15, 1946, at Knoxville, Tennessee.

(Sup) 6545 DOROTHY LAVERN WATERS (Wanita[8], Annie[7], William[6], Felix[5], David[4], Elizabeth[3], Matthias[2], John Jacob[1]) was the daughter of Horace Lenard and Wanita Griffin Waters [TLF No. 4241]. Dorothy was born August 16, 1921, at Knoxville, Tennessee. She married Carol Miller.

(Sup) 7840   i Sharon Jo Miller, born 1946.

(Sup) 6546 JOHN FRANKLIN WATERS (Wanita[8], Annie[7], William[6], Felix[5], David[4], Elizabeth[3], Matthias[2], John Jacob[1]) was the son of Horace Lenard and Wanita Griffin Waters [TLF No. 4241]. John was born December 17, 1922, at Knoxville,. Tennessee.

(Sup) 6547 BARBARA JUNE WATERS (Wanita[8], Annie[7], William[6], Felix[5], David[4], Elizabeth[3], Matthias[2], John Jacob[1]) was the daughter of Horace Lenard and Wanita Griffin Waters [TLF No. 4241]. Barbara was born May 20, 1926, at Knoxville, Tennessee.

(Sup) 6548 JAMES DOUGLASS FLYNN, JR. (Lillian[8], Annie[7], William[6], Felix[5], David[4], Elizabeth[3], Matthias[2], John Jacob[1]) was the son of James Douglass and Lillian Griffin Flynn [TLF No. 4242]. James, Jr., was born August 27, 1920, at Knoxville, Tennessee.

(Sup) 6549 JOYCELYN LEE GRIFFIN (Frank[8], Annie[7], William[6], Felix[5], David[4], Elizabeth[3], Matthias[2], John Jacob[1]) was the daughter of Frank Wayland and Annie Lee Edwards Griffin [TLF No. 4243]. Joycelyn was born January 2, 1927, at Knoxville, Tennessee.

(Sup) 6550 OTE EDWARD GRIFFIN (Frank[8], Annie[7], William[6], Felix[5], David[4], Elizabeth[3], Matthias[2], John Jacob[1]) was the son of Frank Wayland and Annie Lee Edwards Griffin [TLF No. 4243]. Ote was born October 15, 1929, at Knoxville, Tennessee.

(Sup) 6551 GORDON GENE GRIFFIN (William[8], Annie[7], William[6], Felix[5], David[4], Elizabeth[3], Matthias[2], John Jacob[1]) was the son of William Clayborn and Lennis Haggard Griffin [TLF No. 4244]. Gordon was born February 27, 1931.

(Sup) 6552 NANETTE GRIFFIN (William[8], Annie[7], William[6], Felix[5], David[4], Elizabeth[3], Matthias[2], John Jacob[1]) was the daughter of William Clayborn and Lennis Haggard Griffin [TLF No. 4244]. Nanette was born December 1, 1932, at Knoxville, Tennessee.

(Sup) 6553 JACK EDWARD WHITE (Glenn[8], Mary[7], William[6], Felix[5], David[4], Elizabeth[3], Matthias[2], John Jacob[1]) was the son of Glenn Heath and Carrie Lee Pickell White [TLF No 4249]. He was born November 22, 1923, at Knoxville, Tennessee.

(Sup) 6554 DOROTHY ELIZABETH WHITE (Glenn[8], Mary[7], William[6], Felix[5], David[4], Elizabeth[3], Matthias[2], John Jacob[1]) was the daughter of Glenn Heath and Carrie Lee Pickell White [TLF No. 4249]. Dorothy was born April 18, 1926, at Knoxville, Tennessee.

(Sup) 6555 BARBOUR DAUN McPHERSON (Hope[8], Appilonia[7], James[6], Felix[5], David[4], Elizabeth[3], Matthias[2], John Jacob[1]) was the child of Claud and Hope Neubert McPherson [TLF No. 4263]. Barbour was born December 29, 1929, in Knox County, Tennessee.

(Sup) 6556 RONALD CLAUDE McPHERSON (Hope[8], Appilonia[7], James[6], Felix[5], David[4], Elizabeth[3], Matthias[2], John Jacob[1]) was the son of Claud and Hope neubert McPherson [TLF No. 4263]. Ronald was born October 27, 1932, in Knox County, Tennessee.

- - - - - - - - - - - - - - - - - -

(Sup) 6561 GARNETT STONEBREAKER (Donna[8], John[7], Martin[6], Elizabeth[5], Martha[4], John Adam II[3], John Adam I[2], John Jacob[1]) was the daughter of Samuel Donna Jacobs Stonebreaker [Supplement No. 4266].

(Sup) 6562 RUTH STONEBREAKER (Donna[8], John[7], Martin[6], Elizabeth[5], Martha[4], John Adam II[3], John Adam I[2], John Jacob[1]) was the daughter of Donna Jacobs Stonebreaker [Supplement NO. 4266].

(Sup) 6563 MAXINE JACOBS (Lehman[8], John[7], Martin[6], Elizabeth[5], Martha[4], John Adam II[3], John Adam I[2], John Jacob[1]) was the daughter of Lehman and Edrea Jacobs [Supplement No. 4266].

(Sup) 6564 HOMER JACOBS (Lehman[8], John[7], Martin[6], Elizabeth[5], Martha[4], John Adam II[3], John Adam I[2], John Jacob[1]) was the son of Lehman and Edrea Jacobs [Supplement No. 4266].

- - - - - - - - - - - - - - - - - -

(Sup) 6568 PAUL HILDEBRAND, JR. (Paul[8], Elizabeth[7], Martin[6], Elizabeth[5], Martha[4], John Adam II[3], John Adam I[2], John Jacob[1]) was the son of Paul and Jamilia Hildebrand [Supplement No. 4270]. Paul, Jr., lived in California.

(Sup) 6569 STANLEY HILDEBRAND (Paul[8], Elizabeth[7], Martin[6], Elizabeth[5], Martha[4], John Adam II[3], John Adam I[2], John Jacob[1]) was the son of Paul and Jamilia Hildebrand [Supplement No. 4270]. Stanley died at Detroit, Michigan.

(Sup) 6570 ROBERT HILDEBRAND (Paul[8], Elizabeth[7], Martin[6], Elizabeth[5], Martha[4], John Adam II[3], John Adam I[2], John Jacob[1]) was the son of Paul and Dorothy Hildebrand [Supplement No. 4270]. Robert lived at Clearwater, Florida. He married Karen _____.

(Sup) 7845   i Jenny Hildebrand.

(Sup) 6571 GLORIA HILDEBRAND (Paul[8], Elizabeth[7], Martin[6], Elizabeth[5], Martha[4], John Adam II[3], John Adam I[2], John Jacob[1]) was the daughter of Paul and Dorothy Hildebrand [Supplement No. 4270]. Gloria married Charles Whitfield.

(Sup) 6572 JEAN SCHMIDT (Charlotte[8], Franklin[7], Martin[6], Elizabeth[5], Martha[4], John Adam II[3], John Adam I[2], John Jacob[1]) was the daughter of Fred and Charlotte Jacobs Schmidt [Supplement No. 4272]. Jean married Wayne Knipe, Jr..

(Sup) 7846   i Wayne Knipe, III.
(Sup) 7847   ii Rickie Knipe.

(Sup) 6573 MARILYN SCHMIDT (Charlotte[8], Franklin[7], Martin[6], Elizabeth[5], Martha[4], John Adam II[3], John Adam I[2], John Jacob[1]) was the daughter of Fred and Charotte Jacobs Schmidt [Supplement No. 4272]. Marilyn married Paul Planck. They were divorced.

(Sup) 7848   i   Lynette Planck.
(Sup) 7849   ii Grayson Planck.
(Sup) 7850   iii Melanie Planck.
(Sup) 7851   iv Melinda Planck.

(Sup) 6574 CAROL SCHMIDT (Charlotte[8], Franklin[7], Martin[6], Elizabeth[5], Martha[4], John Adam II[3], John Adam I[2], John Jacob[1]) was the daughter of Samuel Fred and Charlotte Jacobs Schmidt [Supplement No. 4272]. She married Mr. McEwan.

(Sup) 7852   i   Jon McEwan.
(Sup) 7853   ii Karen McEwan.
(Sup) 7854   iii Marc McEwan.

- - - - - - - - - - - - - - - - - -

(Sup) 6576 LOUIS WILLIAM BONSIB, III (Marietta^8, Franklin^7, Martin^6, Elizabeth^5, Martha^4, John Adam II^3, John Adam I^2, John Jacob^1) was the son of Louis and Marietta Jacobs Bonsib, Jr. [Supplement No. 4273]. Louis was born in 1918. He married, first, Virginia Gardner, who was born in 1918. He married, second, JoAnn David Diener, born in 1925.

CHILDREN OF LOUIS AND VIRGINIA

(Sup) 7855   i   Judy Bonsib, born in 1941.
(Sup) 7856   ii Susan Gene Bonsib, born in 1942.
(Sup) 7857   iii Betty Virginia Bonsib, born in 1946.
(Sup) 7858   iv Grant Gardner Bonsib, born in 1948 (twin).
(Sup) 7859   v   John McDonald Bonsib, born in 1948 (twin).

(Sup) 6577 JOAN BONSIB (Marietta^8, Franklin^7, Martin^6, Elizabeth^5, Martha^4, John Adam II^3, John Adam I^2, John Jacob^1) was the daughter of Louis and Marietta Jacobs Bonsib [Supplement No. 4273]. She married, first, Carl Lipp. He died in 1982. Joan married, second, Carl Brandt.

(Sup) 7860   i   Sandra Lipp.
(Sup) 7861   ii Pamela Lipp.
(Sup) 7862   iii Terry Lipp.

(Sup) 6578 JOHN FRANK BONSIB (Marietta^8, Franklin^7, Martin^6, Eliza-beth^5, Martha^4, John Adam II^3, John Adam I^2, John Jacob^1) was the son of of Louis and Marietta Jacobs Bonsib [Supplement No. 4273]. He married Nancy Van Arman. She died. John married, second, Patricia. _____

(Sup) 7863   i   Deborah Bonsib.
(Sup) 7864   ii Rebecca Bonsib.

(Sup) 6579 RICHARD E. BONSIB (Marietta^8, Franklin^7, Martin^6, Eliza-beth^5, Martha^4, John Adam II^3, John Adam I^2, John Jacob^1) was the son of Louis and Marietta Jacobs Bonsib [Supplement No. 4273]. He married Gretchen Allen.

(Sup) 7865   i   Gregory Bonsib.
(Sup) 7866   ii Steven Bonsib.

(Sup) 6580 JOHN ROBERT JACOBS (Robert^8, Franklin^7, Martin^6, Eliza-beth^5, Martha^4, John Adam II^3, John Adam I^2, John Jacob^1) was the son of Robert and Betty Davis Jacobs [Supplement No. 4277].

(Sup) 7867   i   Deborah Jacobs.
(Sup) 7868   ii Valeria Jacobs.
(Sup) 7869   iii Kenneth Jacobs.

(Sup) 6581 RICHARD JACOBS (Robert^8, Franklin^7, Martin^6, Elizabeth^5, Martha^4, John Adam II^3, John Adam I^2, John Jacob^1) was the son of Robert and Betty Davis Jacobs [Supplement No. 4277]. He resided at Indianapolis, Indiana.

(Sup) 6582 WILLIAM EVERETT HAUCK, JR. (Lillian^8, Franklin^7, Martin^6, Elizabeth^5, Martha^4, John Adam II^3, John Adam I^2, John Jacob^1) was the son of William E. and Lillian Jacobs Hauck [Supplement No. 4278]. William, Jr., was born July 5, 1930, at Indianapolis, Indiana. He married Jean Alette Jacobi in 1957. She was born October 17 1933.

(Sup) 7870   i   Kathy Hauck.
(Sup) 7871   ii William Hauck, III.
(Sup) 7872   iii Cindy Hauck.
(Sup) 7873   iv Jeannie Hauck.
(Sup) 7874   v   Christina Hauck.

(Sup) 6583 RONALD LEE HAUCK (Lillian^8, Franklin^7, Martin^6, Eliza-beth^4, Martha^4, John Adam II^3, John Adam I^2, John Jacob^1) was the son of William Everett and Lillian Jacobs Hauck [Supplement No. 4278]. Ronald was born November 15, 1932, at Middletown, Ohio. He married Helen Hathorn, April 21, 1956. She was born February 2, 1935.

(Sup) 7875   i   Lillie Hauck.
(Sup) 7876   ii Ronald Hauck, Jr.
(Sup) 7877   iii Becky Hauck.

(Sup) 6584 DAVID ALLEN HAUCK (Lillian^8, Franklin^7, Martin^6, Eliza-beth^5, Martha^4, John Adam II^3, John Adam I^2, John Jacob^1) was the son of William Everett and Lillian Jacobs Hauck [Supplement No. 4278]. David was born January 21, 1934, at Middletown, Ohio. He married Bonnie Allender. She was born June 21, 1941.

(Sup) 7878   i   Pamela Hauck.
(Sup) 7879   ii Douglas Hauck.
(Sup) 7880   iii Dawn Hauck.

(Sup) 6585 BARBARA JEAN HAUCK (Lillian^8, Franklin^7, Martin^6, Eliza-beth^5, John Adam II^3, John Adam I^2, John Jacob^1) was the daughter of William Everett and Lillian Jacobs Hauck [Supplement No. 4278]. Barabara was born December 9, 1941. She married, first, Louis J. Mahern, Jr. He was the son of Louis J. and Elyse Kentwell Mahern and was born November 5, 1941, at Indian-apolis, Indiana. Barbara and Louis were divorced in 1975. She married, second, Daniel B. Mohler July 20, 1985. Barbara and Daniel resided at Colorado Springs, Colorado, where she was employed by the Broadmore Hotel, and he was an attorney.

(Sup) 7881   i   James Michael Mahern, born June 3, 1966.
(Sup) 7882   ii Briam Thomas Mahern, born February 3, 1968.
(Sup) 7883   iii Jennifer Jean Mahern, born September 20, 1970.

(Sup) 6586   ROBERT REED HAUCK (Lillian^8, Franklin^7, Martin^6, Elizabeth^5, Martha^4, John Adam II^3, John Adam I^2, John Jacob^1) was the son of William Everett and Lillian Jacobs Hauck [Supplement No. 4278]. Robert was born October 9, 1946 at Indianapolis, Indiana (twin of Richard). He married Patricia Karen Driskill February 10, 1968. She was born August 12, 1947.

(Sup) 7884   i Ryan Hauck.
(Sup) 7885   ii Cory Hauck.
(Sup) 7886 iii Travis Hauck.

(Sup) 6587   RALPH RICHARD HAUCK (Lillian^8, Franklin^7, Martin^6, Elizabeth^5, Martha^4, John Adam II^3, John Adam I^2, John Jacob^1) was the son of William Everett and Lillian Jacobs Hauck [Supplement No. 4278]. Richard was born October 9, 1946 at Indianapolis, Indiana (twin of Robert). He married Minoo Manavi, March 23, 1950. She was born December 16, 1973.

(Sup) 6588   FRANK CHARLES JACOBS (Ralph^8, Franklin^7, Martin^6, Elizabeth^5, Martha^4, John Adam II^3, John Adam I^2, John Jacob^1) was the son of Ralph Reed and Edwina Longest Jacobs [Supplement No. 4279]. Frank was born April 9, 1944, at Indianapolis, Indiana. He married Arlene Harlow, June 3, 1967, at Tipton, Indiana. She was the daughter of Merlin and Margaret Harlow and was born April 23, 1944, at Tipton.

(Sup) 7887   i Brian D. Jacobs, born November 13, 1971.
(Sup) 7888   ii Eric M. Jacobs, born January 22, 1976.

(Sup) 6589   GENE R. JACOBS (Ralph^8, Franklin^7, Martin^6, Elizabeth^5, Martha^4, John Adam II^3, John Adam I^2, John Jacob^1) was the son of Ralph Reed and Edwina Longest Jacobs [Supplement No. 4279]. Gene was born November 2, 1945, at Indianapolis, Indiana.

(Sup) 6590   JAMES EDWARD JACOBS (Ralph^8, Franklin^7, Martin^6, Elizabeth^5, Martha^4, John Adam II^3, John Adam I^2, John Jacob^1) was the son of Ralph Reed and Edwina Longest Jacobs [Supplement No. 4279]. James was born March 25, 1949, at Indianapolis, Indiana. He married Ruth Ann Tully in 1974.

(Sup) 6591   JEFFREY LEON JACOBS (Ralph^8, Franklin^7, Martin^6, Elizabeth^5, Martha^4, John Adam II^3, John Adam I^2, John Jacob^1) was the son of Ralph Reed and Edwina Longest Jacobs [Supplement No. 4279]. Jeffrey was born July 9, 1954, at Indianapolis, Indiana.

(Sup) 6592   SUSAN SMALLWOOD (Clarabel^8, Franklin^7, Martin^6, Elizabeth^5, Martha^4, John Adam II^3, John Adam I^2, John Jacob^1) was the daughter of Hubert H. and Clarabel Jacobs Smallwood [Supplement No. 4280]. Susan married Jerry Willenborg.

(Sup) 6593   RICHARD JACOBS (Norwell^8, Franklin^7, Martin^6, Elizabeth^5, Martha^4, John Adam II^3, John Adam I^2, John Jacob^1) was the son of Norwell and Esther Jacobs [Supplement No. 4281].

(Sup) 6594   RALPH HOMER TIBBS, JR. (Amy^8, George^7, Martin^6, Elizabeth^5, Martha^4, John Adam II^3, John Adam I^2, John Jacob^1) was the son of Ralph Homer and Amy Jacobs Tibbs [Supplement No. 4282]. Ralph Jr. was born May 9, 1928, at East Orange, New Jersey. He served on active duty in the U.S. Air Force for ten years and later in the Coast Guard Reserve. He attended the University of Virginia and was employed in computer sciences. Ralph married Carol May Suydam September 26, 1953, at Valley Stream, Long Island, New York. She was the daughter of William Lassell and E. Lucille Doughty Suydam and was born October 9, 1932, at Oceanside, New York. Ralph and Carol were divorced August 1960. Carol married, second, Christian C. Westerman. (The children of Ralph and Carol were adopted by their stepfather in July 1969, and their surnames were changed to Westerman.)

(Sup) 7891   i Jeffrey Raymond Westerman, born June 11, 1954.
(Sup) 7892   ii Andrew Lee Westerman, born February 2, 1956.
(Sup) 7893 iii Jill Lucie Westerman, born September 18, 1957.

(Sup) 6595   JOAN ELLEN JACOBS (George^8, George^7, Martin^6, Elizabeth^5, Martha^4, John Adam II^3, John Adam I^2, John Jacob^1) was the daughter of George Lowell and Ruth Lester Jacobs [Supplement No. 4286]. She was born April 13, 1932, and died that year.

(Sup) 6596   RUTH MARILYN JACOBS (George^8, George^7, Martin^6, Elizabeth^5, Martha^4, John Adam II^3, John Adam I^2, John Jacob^1) was the daughter of George Lowell and Ruth Lester Jacobs [Supplement No. 4286]. Ruth was born November 6, 1935, at West Brighton, New York. She married Roy Elwood Jacques, Jr., June 28, 1958, on Staten Island, New York. Roy was born February 13, 1936. He was an aircraft mechanic, employed by the American Cyanamid Company. Ruth and Roy resided in Hazlet, New Jersey.

(Sup) 7894   i Lisa Michelle Jacques, born October 23, 1960.
(Sup) 7895   ii Roy Elwood Jacques III, born December 27, 1962.

(Sup) 6597   BEVERLY ANN JACOBS (George[8], George[7], Martin[6], Elizabeth[5], Martha[4], John Adam[3], John Adam[2], John Jacob[1]) was the daughter
of George Lowell and Ruth Lester Jacobs [Supplement No. 4286]. Beverly was born
December 28, 1941, at West Brighton, New York. She married, first, Gregory S.
Miller. They were divorced. She married, second, R. L. Weise.

(Sup) 7896   i   Donna Lee Miller, born January 24, 1965 (twin).
(Sup) 7897   ii   Deborah Lynn Miller, born January 24, 1965 (twin).

Chapter 4

Tenth Generation

This chapter contains (new) entries for all those members of the
Tenth Generation of descendants of John Jacob Link for whom
information was received for the 1988 Supplement.

Generation	*Entry Numbers*
Tenth	7000 series

SUPPLEMENT TO THE TENTH GENERATION

The biographies in this section of the Supplement are for the Tenth Generation of the descendants of John Jacob Link.

- -

(Sup) 7001   THOMAS WILLIAM LEMEN (James[9], Thomas[8], Mamie[7], Thomas[6], Adam[5], Alexander[4], John Adam[3], John Adam[2], John Jacob[1]) was the son of James Henry and Mary Alice Moore Lemen [Supplement Nos. 3309 and 5006]. Thomas was born September 7, 1970.

(Sup) 7002   SARAH ELIZABETH LEMEN (James[9], Thomas[8], Mamie[7], Thomas[6], Adam[5], Alexander[4], John Adam[3], John Adam[2], John Jacob[1]) was the daughter of James Henry and Mary Alice Moore Lemen [Supplement Nos. 3309 and 5006]. Sarah was born April 29, 1974.

(Sup) 7003   MICHAEL PATRICK MACNAMARA (Barbara[9], Franklin[8], Adam[7], Mary[6], Adam[5], Alexander[4], John Adam[3], John Adam[2], John Jacob[1]) was the son of Robert James and Barbara Jones Macnamara [Supplement No. 5007]. Michael was born October 7, 1953, at Quantico, Virginia.

(Sup) 7004   TERESA LYNN MACNAMARA (Barbara[9], Franklin[8], Adam[7], Mary[6], Adam[5], Alexander[4], John Adam[3], John Adam[2], John Jacob[1]) was the daughter of Robert James and Barbara Jones Macnamara [Supplement No. 5007]. Teresa was born October 8, 1954, at Oceanside, California. She married Michael Wayne Smith July 7, 1979, at Winchester, Virginia. He was the son of John Henry and Martha Smith and was born October 15, 1952, at Winchester.

(Sup) 8011   i Kelley Jo Smith, born January 16, 1980 (twin).
(Sup) 8012   ii Tracy Michelle Smith, born January 18, 1980 (twin).

(Sup) 7005   MAUREEN ANN MACNAMARA (Barbara[9], Franklin[8], Adam[7], Mary[6], Adam[5], Alexander[4], John Adam[3], John Adam[2], John Jacob[1]) was the daughter of Robert James and Barbara Ellen Jones Macnamara [Supplement No. 5007]. Maureen was born February 27, 1960, at Oceanside, California. She married Roger David Webster February 18, 1983, at Winchester, Virginia. He was the son of Terry A. and Rebecca Keeler Webster and was born September 18, 1950, at Winchester.

(Sup) 7006   MARY COLLEEN MACNAMARA (Barbara[9], Franklin[8], Adam[7], Mary[6], Adam[5], Alexander[4], John Adam[3], John Adam[2], John Jacob[1]) was the daughter of Robert James and Barbara Jones Macnamara [Supplement No. 5007]. She was born December 23, 1961, at Oceanside, California. She married Mark Andrew Marple August 2, 1980, at Winchester, Virginia. He was the son of Clifton A. and Norma Joyce Garrett Marple and was born August 12, 1961, at Winchester.

(Sup) 8015   i Jennifer Leigh Marple, born May 5, 1981.

(Sup) 7007   CHRISTOPHER JAMES SARDELIS (Barbara[9], Franklin[8], Adam[7], Mary[6], Adam[5], Alexander[4], John Adam 11[3], John Adam 1[2], John Jacob[1]) was the son of James Gus and Barbara Jones Macnamara Sardelis [Supplement No. 5007]. He was born October 16, 1969, at Winchester, Virginia.

(Sup) 7008   DEAN CONARD COMPHER (Charlotte[9], Franklin[8], Adam[7], Mary[6], Adam[5], Alexander[4], John Adam[3], John Adam[2], John Jacob[1]) was the son of Harry and Charlotte Jones Compher [Supplement No. 5008]. Dean was born August 27, 1963, at Winchester, Virginia.

(Sup) 7009   STEPHEN SCOTT SMITH (Joyce[9], Mary Margaret[8], Adam[7], Mary[6], Adam[5], Alexander[4], John Adam[3], John Adam[2], John Jacob[1]) was the son of Elmer Stanton and Joyce Trussell Smith [Supplement No. 5010]. Stephen was born November 12, 1955, at Annapolis, Maryland. He married, first, Hilda Hensel, March 29, 1974, at Cumberland, Maryland. He married, second, Diane Hott December 21, 1979, at Byron, Illinois. Diane was the daughter of Homer and Pauline Adams Hott and was born November 5, 1955, at Cumberland.

CHILDREN OF STEPHEN AND HILDA

(Sup) 8021   i Autumn Smith, born November 5, 1974.
(Sup) 8022   ii Stacey Smith, born January 26, 1976.

(Sup) 7017 YVONNE RENE' HOFFMASTER (Virginia[9], David[8], Adam[7], Mary[6], Adam[5], Alexander[4], John Adam[3], John Adam[2], John Jacob[1]) was the daughter of Maurice Franklin and Virginia Mae Jones Hoffmaster [Supplement No. 5013]. Yvonne was born August 11, 1961, at Charles Town, West Virginia. She married Vincent Allen Mundy June 19, 1982, at Jefferson, Maryland. He was the son of Martin and Cora Mundy and was born September 4, 1961, at Gaithersburg, Maryland.

(Sup) 8031   i   Jennifer Marie Mundy, born January 31, 1984.

(Sup) 7018 DAVID DWAYNE HOFFMASTER (Virginia[9], David[8], Adam[7], Mary[6], Adam[5], Alexander[4], John Adam[3], John Adam[2], John Jacob[1]) was the son of Maurice Franklin and Virginia Mae Jones Hoffmaster [Supplement No. 5013]. David was born August 4, 1962, at Charles Town, West Virginia.

(Sup) 7019 MICHELLE DENISE BARTLETT (Mary[9], David[8], Adam[7], Mary[6], Adam[5], Alexander[4], John Adam[3], John Adam[2], John Jacob[1]) was the daughter of Melvin McClure and Mary Louise Jones Bartlett [Supplement No. 5014]. Michelle was born February 11, 1966, at Charles Town, West Virginia. She married Oren Codd Smith July 16, 1983, at Jefferson, Maryland. He was the son of Oscar Clayton and Shirley Adkins Smith.

(Sup) 7020 MICHAEL SCOTT BARTLETT (Mary[9], David[8], Adam[7], Mary[6], Adam[5], Alexander[4], John Adam[3], John Adam[2], John Jacob[1]) was the son of Melvin McClure and Mary Louise Jones Bartlett [Supplement No. 5014]. Michael was born January 31, 1968, at Charles Town, West Virginia.

(Sup) 7021 LESLIE DAWN BARTLETT (Mary[9], David[8], Adam[7], Mary[6], Adam[5], Alexander[4], John Adam[3], John Adam[2], John Jacob[1]) was the daughter of Melvin McClure and Mary Louise Jones Bartlett [Supplement No. 5014]. Leslie was born September 12, 1969, at Charles Town, West Virginia.

(Sup) 7022 DONALD STEVEN JONES (Ralph[9], Ralph[8], Adam[7], Mary[6], Adam[5], Alexander[4], John Adam[3], John Adam[2], John Jacob[1]) was the son of Ralph Jerry and Rosemary Boyd Jones [Supplement No. 5015]. Donald was born September 6, 1954, at Charles Town, West Virginia. He married Tina Marie Churchy November 8, 1980, at Harpers Ferry, West Virginia. She was the daughter of George Eugene and June Marie Hoover Churchy and was born December 1, 1959, at Hagerstown, Maryland.

(Sup) 7010 BRADLEY WILLIAM McFADDEN (Joyce[9], Mary Margaret[8], Adam[7], Mary[6], Adam[5], Alexander[4], John Adam[3], John Adam[2], John Jacob[1]) was the son of Edward L. and Joyce Trussell Smith McFadden [Supplement No. 5010]. He was born August 31, 1963, at Cumberland, Maryland. He married Linda Simmons August 12, 1983, at Cumberland. She was the daughter of Eugene and Betty Eaton Simmons and was born October 7, 1962, at Cumberland.

(Sup) 7011 LARRY WILLIAM JONES, JR. (Larry[9], David[8], Adam[7], Mary[6], Adam[5], Alexander[4], John Adam[3], John Adam[2], John Jacob[1]) was the son of Larry William and Sara DeLawter Jones [Supplement No. 5011]. Larry, Jr., was born December 7, 1961, at Charles Town, West Virginia.

(Sup) 7012 TIMOTHY WAYNE JONES (Larry[9], David[8], Adam[7], Mary[6], Adam[5], Alexander[4], John Adam[3], John Adam[2], John Jacob[1]) was the son of Larry William and Sara DeLawter Jones [Supplement No. 5011]. Timothy was born July 9, 1965, at Charles Town, West Virginia.

(Sup) 7013 JEFFREY ALLEN JONES (Larry[9], David[8], Adam[7], Mary[6], Adam[5], Alexander[4], John Adam[3], John Adam[2], John Jacob[1]) was the son of Larry William and Sara DeLawter Jones [Supplement No. 5011]. Jeffrey was born January 24, 1967, at Charles Town, West Virginia.

(Sup) 7014 KEITH MICHAEL JONES (Martin[9], David[8], Adam[7], Mary[6], Adam[5], Alexander[4], John Adam[3], John Adam[2], John Jacob[1]) was the son of Martin David and Bertie Lea Goins Jones [Supplement No. 5012]. Keith was born November 10, 1962, at Frederick, Maryland.

(Sup) 7015 TRACI LYNE JONES (Martin[9], David[8], Adam[7], Mary[6], Adam[5], Alexander[4], John Adam[3], John Adam[2], John Jacob[1]) was the daughter of Martin David and Bertie Lea Goins Jones [Supplement No. 5012]. Traci was born December 30, 1965, at Frederick, Maryland.

(Sup) 7016 MAURICE FRANKLIN HOFFMASTER, JR. (Virginia[9], David[8], Adam[7], Mary[6], Adam[5], Alexander[4], John Adam[3], John Adam[2], John Jacob[1]) was the son of Maurice Franklin and Virginia Mae Jones Hoffmaster [Supplement No. 5013]. He was born May 24, 1960, at Charles Town, West Virginia. He married Laurie Ann Korzendorser May 16, 1981, at Jefferson, Maryland. She was the daughter of William and Becky Korzendorser and was born April, 1960, in New York State.

(Sup) 7023 JERRY WAYNE JONES (Ralph^9, Ralph^8, Adam^7, Mary^6, Adam^5, Alexander^4, John Adam^3, John Adam^2, John Jacob^1) was the son of Ralph Jerry and Rosemary Boyd Jones [Supplement No. 5015]. Jerry was born August 19, 1956, at Charles Town, West Virginia. He married Kimberly D'Angelo June 14, 1975, at Harpers Ferry, West Virginia. She was the daughter of Samuel and Doris Jean Staubs D'Angelo and was born March 17, 1960, at Charles Town, West Virginia.

(Sup) 8041 i Eric Wayne Jones, born May 15, 1976.
(Sup) 8042 ii Christopher Shane Jones, born June 5, 1977.

(Sup) 7024 ROGER HARRIS JONES (Benjamin^9, Ralph^8, Adam^7, Mary^6, Adam^5, Alexander^4, John Adam^3, John Adam^2, John Jacob^1) was the son of Benjamin Roger and Nancy Mower Jones [Supplement No. 5017]. Roger was born August 12, 1963, at Charles Town, West Virginia. He was a draftsman.

(Sup) 7025 TRACI MICHELLE JONES (Benjamin^9, Ralph^8, Adam^7, Mary^6, Adam^5, Alexander^4, John Adam^3, John Adam^2, John Jacob^1) was the daughter of Benjamin Roger and Nancy Mower Jones [Supplement No. 5017]. She was born June 14, 1966, at Martinsburg, West Virginia.

(Sup) 7026 REBECCA ELIZABETH JONES (Benjamin^9, Ralph^8, Adam^7, Mary^6, Adam^5, Alexander^4, John Adam^3, John Adam^2, John Jacob^1) was the daughter of Benjamin Roger and Nancy Mower Jones [Supplement No. 5017]. Rebecca was born January 25, 1974, at York, Pennsylvania.

(Sup) 7027 JUDITH DARLENE DILLOW (Nancy^9, Sarah^8, Adam^7, Mary^6, Adam^5, Alexander^4, John Adam^3, John Adam^2, John Jacob^1) was the daughter of Lester Carlton and Nancy Runion Dillow [Supplement No. 5018]. Judith was born September 7, 1964, at Charles Town, West Virginia.

(Sup) 7028 LESTER WILLIAM DILLOW (Nancy^9, Sarah^8, Adam^7, Mary^6, Adam^5, Alexander^4, John Adam^3, John Adam^2, John Jacob^1) was the son of Lester Carlton and Nancy Runion Dillow [Supplement No. 5018]. He was born May 10, 1966, at Charles Town, West Virginia.

(Sup) 7029 JOHN ROY SCOTT DILLOW (Nancy^9, Sarah^8, Adam^7, Mary^6, Adam^5, Alexander^4, John Adam^3, John Adam^2, John Jacob^1) was the son of Lester Carlton and Nancy Runion Dillow [Supplement No. 5018]. John was born July 14, 1967, at Charles Town, West Virginia.

(Sup) 7030 TIMOTHY WILLIAM RUNION (Donald^9, Sarah^8, Adam^7, Mary^6, Adam^5, Alexander^4, John Adam^3, John Adam^2, John Jacob^1) was the son of Donald William and Patsy Marie Jenkins Runion [Supplement No. 5019]. Timothy was born December 9, 1971, at Charles Town, West Virginia.

(Sup) 7031 JEFFREY DWAYNE RUNION (Donald^9, Sarah^8, Adam^7, Mary^6, Adam^5, Alexander^4, John Adam^3, John Adam^2, John Jacob^1) was the son of Donald William and Patsy Marie Jenkins Runion [Supplement No. 5019]. Jeffrey was born September 14, 1974, at Winchester, Virginia.

(Sup) 7032 WENDY MICHELLE RUNION (Donald^9, Sarah^8, Adam^7, Mary^6, Adam^5, Alexander^4, John Adam^3, John Adam^2, John Jacob^1) was the daughter of Donald William and Patsy Marie Jenkins Runion [Supplement No. 5019]. Wendy was born February 23, 1977, at Winchester, Virginia.

(Sup) 7033 DUSTIN CONRAD RUNION (John^9, Sarah^8, Adam^7, Mary^6, Adam^5, Alexander^4, John Adam^3, John Adam^2, John Jacob^1) was the son of John Clarence and Virginia Kenney Runion [Supplement No. 5020]. He was born November 24, 1970, at Charles Town, West Virginia.

(Sup) 7034 TRISTA NIKOLE RUNION (John^9, Sarah^8, Adam^7, Mary^6, Adam^5, Alexander^4, John Adam^3, John Adam^2, John Jacob^1) was the daughter of John Clarence and Virginia Kenney Runion [Supplement No. 5020]. She was born February 3, 1975, at Charles Town, West Virginia.

(Sup) 7035 MELINDA DARNELL RUNION (Charles^9, Sarah^8, Adam^7, Mary^6, Adam^5, Alexander^4, John Adam^3, John Adam^2, John Jacob^1) was the daughter of Charles Robert and Lovada Nadene Hardy Runion [Supplement No. 5021]. Melinda was born February 26, 1974.

(Sup) 7036 SUSANNE MARIE RUNION (Charles[9], Sarah[8], Adam[7], Mary[6], Adam[5], Alexander[4], John Adam[3], John Adam[2], John Jacob[1]) was the daughter of Charles Robert and Lovada Nadene Hardy Runion [Supplement No. 5021]. Susanne was born June 25, 1976.

(Sup) 7037 KENNETH JAMES ETTERMAN, JR. (Catherine[9], Elsie[8], Ernest[7], Mary[6], Adam[5], Alexander[4], John Adam[3], John Adam[2], John Jacob[1]) was the son of Kenneth James and Catherine Hanson Etterman [Supplement No. 5023]. Kenneth was born March 4, 1968, at Sarasota, Florida.

(Sup) 7038 KIMBERLY KAY ETTERMAN (Catherine[9], Elsie[8], Ernest[7], Mary[6], Adam[5], Alexander[4], John Adam[3], John Adam[2], John Jacob[1]) was the daughter of Kenneth James and Catherine Hanson Etterman [Supplement No. 5023]. Kimberly was born September 30, 1969, at Sarasota, Florida.

(Sup) 7039 KAREN RENEE HANSON (Jennings[9], Elsie[8], Ernest[7], Mary[6], Adam[5], Alexander[4], John Adam[3], John Adam[2], John Jacob[1]) was the daughter of Jennings Linton and Iris Ann Dunbar Jones, Jr. [Supplement No. 5024]. She was born September 25, 1963, at Martinsburg, West Virginia.

(Sup) 7040 MELISSA ANN HANSON (Jennings[9], Elsie[8], Ernest[7], Mary[6], Adam[5], Alexander[4], John Adam[3], John Adam[2], John Jacob[1]) was the daughter of Jennings Linton and Iris Ann Dunbar Hanson, Jr. [Supplement No. 5024]. She was born January 4, 1968, at Venice, Florida (twin of Jennings Linton III).

(Sup) 7041 JENNINGS LINTON HANSON, III (Jennings[9], Elsie[8], Ernest[7], Mary[6], Adam[5], Alexander[4], John Adam[3], John Adam[2], John Jacob[1]) was the son of Jennings Linton and Iris Ann Dunbar Hanson, Jr. [Supplement No. 5024]. He was born January 4, 1968, at Venice, Florida (twin of Melissa Ann).

(Sup) 7042 ERNEST MERCER JONES, III (Ernest[9], Ernest[8], Ernest[7], Mary[6], Adam[5], Alexander[4], John Adam[3], John Adam[2], John Jacob[1]) was the son of Ernest Mercer and Patricia A. Bernadyn Jones, Jr. [Supplement No. 5025]. Ernest, III, was born January 5, 1969, at Plainfield, New Jersey.

(Sup) 7043 TIMOTHY WAYNE JONES (Ernest[9], Ernest[8], Ernest[7], Mary[6], Adam[5], Alexander[4], John Adam[3], John Adam[2], John Jacob[1]) was the son of Ernest Mercer and Patricia A. Bernadyn Jones, Jr. [Supplement No. 5025]. Timothy was born January 16, 1972, at Perth Amboy, New Jersey.

(Sup) 7044 CAROLINE ELIZABETH JONES (Ernest[9], Ernest[8], Ernest[7], Mary[6], Adam[5], Alexander[4], John Adam[3], John Adam[2], John Jacob[1]) was the daughter of Ernest Mercer and Patricia A. Bernadyn Jones, Jr. [Supplement No. 5025]. She was born April 12, 1974, at Hammond, Indiana.

(Sup) 7045 MICHELLE LYNN CURRIER (Douglas[9], Patricia[8], Ernest[7], Mary[6], Adam[5], Alexander[4], John Adam[3], John Adam[2], John Jacob[1]) was the daughter of Douglas Lee and Cheryl Lee Byers Currier, Jr. [Supplement No. 5027]. Michelle was born August 2, 1967, at Charles Town, West Virginia. She married Francis Lloyd Parker, Jr., July 20, 1985, at Bunker Hill, Berkeley County, West Virginia. He was the son of Francis Lloyd and Betty Jo Brand Parker and was born September 15, 1966, at Kingswood, West Virginia.

(Sup) 8061   i Johnathan Rian Parker, born January 9, 1986.

(Sup) 7046 ERIN LEE CURRIER (Douglas[9], Patricia[8], Ernest[7], Mary[6], Adam[5], Alexander[4], John Adam[3], John Adam[2], John Jacob[1]) was the daughter of Douglas Lee and Cheryl Lee Byers Currier, Jr. [Supplement No. 5027]. Erin was born May 27, 1969, at Newcastle, Pennsylvania. She was chairman of the John Augustine Washington Chapter, Children of the American Revolution.

(Sup) 7047 JODY LYNN TALLEY (Peggy[9], Patricia[8], Ernest[7], Mary[6], Adam[5], Alexander[4], John Adam[3], John Adam[2], John Jacob[1]) was the daughter of Larry Edwin and Peggy Ann Currier Talley [Supplement No. 5028]. She was born May 28, 1973, at Winchester, Virginia.

(Sup) 7048 AMY BETH TALLEY (Peggy[9], Patricia[8], Ernest[7], Mary[6], Adam[5], Alexander[4], John Adam[3], John Adam[2], John Jacob[1]) was the daughter of Larry Edwin and Peggy Ann Currier Talley [Supplement No. 5028]. She was born February 9, 1975, at Winchester, Virginia.

(Sup) 7048A DEBORAH LEE WEYEL (Rudolph[9], Katherine[8], Henry[7], Adam[6], Adam[5], Alexander[4], John Adam[3], John Adam[2], John Jacob[1]) was the daughter of Rudolph Louis and Orvetta McNelly Weyel [Supplement No. 5031]. Deborah was born December 11, 1953, at Houston, Texas. She married James William Ramsey. He was born February 12, 1954, at Youngstown, Ohio. James was a petroleum engineer.

(Sup) 8071 i Katherine Marie Ramsey, born July 17, 1984.

(Sup) 7048B SUSAN LYNN WEYEL (Rudolph[9], Katherine[8], Henry[7], Adam[6], Adam[5], Alexander[4], John Adam[3], John Adam[2], John Jacob[1]) was the daughter of Rudolph Louis and Orvetta McNelly Weyel [Supplement No. 5031]. Susan was born September 19, 1956, at Houston, Texas. She married Bennett Ross Morgan. He was born October 8, 1956, at Lubbock, Texas. Bennett was an officer in the U.S. Navy.

(Sup) 8075 i William Rudolph Morgan, born July 21, 1981.
(Sup) 8076 ii Holly Ann Morgan, born November 20, 1983.

(Sup) 7048C KAREN LOUISE WEYEL (Rudolph[9], Katherine[8], Henry[7], Adam[6], Adam[5], Alexander[4], John Adam[3], John Adam[2], John Jacob[1]) was the daughter of Rudolph Louis and Orvetta McNelly Weyel [Supplement No. 5031]. Karen was born February 26, 1961, at Houston, Texas. She studied at the University of Texas.

(Sup) 7049 KEVIN LEWIS HOWINGTON (Frances[9], Katherine[8], Henry[7], Adam[6], Adam[5], Alexander[4], John Adam[3], John Adam[2], John Jacob[1]) was the son of Jesse L. and Frances Weyel Howington [Supplement No. 5032]. Kevin was born April 26, 1960, at Houston, Texas.

(Sup) 7049A KATHERINE JEANINE HOWINGTON (Frances[9], Katherine[8], Henry[7], Adam[6], Adam[5], Alexander[4], John Adam[3], John Adam[2], John Jacob[1]) was the daughter of Jesse L. and Frances Weyel Howington [Supplement No. 5032]. Katherine was born June 11, 1968, at Corpus Christi, Texas.

(Sup) 7050 CYNTHIA LINK WEYEL (Foster[9], Katherine[8], Henry[7], Adam[6], Adam[5], Alexander[4], John Adam[3], John Adam[2], John Jacob[1]) was the daughter of Foster Link and Mary Ann Ruthstrom Weyel [Supplement No. 5033]. Cynthia was born December 8, 1956, at Houston, Texas. She was a buyer for Foley's Department Stores. Cynthia married Thomas Drew Sides.

(Sup) 7050A KEITH FOSTER WEYEL (Foster[9], Katherine[8], Henry[7], Adam[6], Adam[5], Alexander[4], John Adam[3], John Adam[2], John Jacob[1]) was the son of Foster Link and Mary Ann Ruthstrom Weyel [Supplement No. 5033]. Keith was born October 5, 1960, at Houston, Texas. He attended the University of Texas.

(Sup) 7050B STEVEN LOUIS WEYEL (Foster[9], Katherine[8], Henry[7], Adam[6], Adam[5], Alexander[4], John Adam[3], John Adam[2], John Jacob[1]) was the son of Foster Link and Mary Ann Ruthstrom Weyel [Supplement No. 5033]. Steven was born

(Sup) 7050C SUE ELLEN MUMMA (Gloria[9], Martha[8], Ann[7], William[6], Adam[5], Alexander[4], John Adam[3], John Adam[2], John Jacob[1]) was the daughter of Wilmer McKendree and Gloria Glaser Mumma [Supplement No. 5034]. Sue Ellen was born March 8, 1950, at Hagerstown, Maryland. She married Andrew Kardos, Jr., August 3, 1976. He was the son of Andrew and Jeanette Balut Kardos and was born June 12, 1935, at Perth Amboy, New Jersey.

(Sup) 70500 DWIGHT DAVID E. MUMMA (Gloria[9], Martha[8], Ann[7], William[6], Adam[5], Alexander[4], John Adam[3], John Adam[2], John Jacob[1]) was the son of Wilmer McKendree and Gloria Glaser Mumma [Supplement No. 5034]. He was born August 12, 1955, at Hagerstown, Maryland.

(Sup) 7051 JOSEPH BURTON BRUNK, Jr. (Joseph[9], Mary[8], Ann[7], William[6], Adam[5], Alexander[4], John Adam[3], John Adam[2], John Jacob[1]) was the son of Joseph Burton and Frances Sperow Brunk [Supplement No. 5035]. Joseph was born October 4, 1946, at Martinsburg, West Virginia. He married Patricia Autera June 18, 1965, at Hagerstown, Maryland. She was the daughter of Donald Joseph and Mae Wagner Autera and was born November 26, 1945, in Butler Township, Schuylkill County, Pennsylvania.

(Sup) 8091 i Joseph Burton Brunk, III, born May 11, 1966.

(Sup) 7052 GRACE CAROLYN BRUNK (Joseph[9], Mary[8], Ann[7], William[6], Adam[5], Alexander[4], John Adam[3], John Adam[2], John Jacob[1]) was the daughter of Joseph Burton and Frances Sperow Brunk [Supplement No. 5035]. She was born March 31, 1948, and died March 31, 1948, at Martinsburg, West Virginia.

(Sup) 8101   i Christopher Dean Lance, born December 15, 1975.

(Sup) 7058 WILLARD HUNTER GRIMES, III (Betty June^9, Mary^8, Ann^7, William^6, Adam^5, Alexander^4, John Adam^3, John Adam^2, John Jacob^1) was the son of Willard Hunter and Betty June Brunk Grimes [Supplement No. 5036]. Willard was born March 2, 1956, at Martinsburg, West Virginia. He graduated from West Virginia Institute of Technology in electrical engineering, 1979, where he was a member of Alpha Phi Omega, IEEE, Tau Beta Phi, and Eta Kappa Nu. He was an electrical engineer. Willard married Georgia Clay Miller July 17, 1982.

(Sup) 8102   i Holly Louise Grimes, born January 9, 1984.

(Sup) 7059 MICHAEL DOUGLAS BRUNK (John^9, Mary^8, Ann^7, William^6, Adam^5, Alexander^4, John Adam^3, John Adam^2, John Jacob^1) was the son of John Henry and Elsie Ann Roberts Brunk [Supplement No. 5037]. Michael was born October 30, 1954, at Martinsburg, West Virginia. He was a manager of an office supply store at Arlington, Virginia.

(Sup) 7060 JONATHAN WAYNE BRUNK (John^9, Mary^8, Ann^7, William^6, Adam^5, Alexander^4, John Adam^3, John Adam^2, John Adam^1) was the son of John Henry and Elsie Ann Roberts Brunk [Supplement No. 5037]. He was born December 27, 1959, at Shawnee, Oklahoma. He was a laboratory technician residing at Wheaton, Maryland.

(Sup) 7061 SUSAN GWEN NEFF (Barbara Jean^9, Mary^8, Ann^7, William^6, Adam^5, Alexander^4, John Adam^3, John Adam^2, John Adam^1) was the daughter of Gene L. and Barbara Jean Brunk Neff [Supplement No. 5038]. Susan was born December 30, 1955, at Columbus, Georgia. She married Kevin Lon Larsen November 27, 1974, at Firth, Bingham County, Idaho. He was the son of Reid Kay and Janice Clayson Larsen and was born May 29, 1957, at Idaho Falls, Idaho. Susan and Kevin resided at Firth, Idaho, where she was a doctor's receptionist, and he was a truckdriver and mechanic.

(Sup) 8105   i Justin Berkeley Larsen, born August 21, 1982.

(Sup) 7053 STEVEN VICTOR BRUNK (Joseph^9, Mary^8, Ann^7, William^6, Adam^5, Alexander^4, John Adam^3, John Adam^2, John Jacob^1) was the son of Joseph Burton and Frances Sperow Brunk [Supplement No. 5035]. He was born August 30, 1949, and died August 31, 1949, at Bridgeton, New Jersey.

(Sup) 7054 JULIA KAY BRUNK (Joseph^9, Mary^8, Ann^7, William^6, Adam^5, Alexander^4, John Adam^3, John Adam^2, John Jacob^1) was the daughter of Joseph Burton and Frances Sperow Brunk [Supplement No. 5035]. She was born July 7, 1951, at Bloomsburg, Pennsylvania. She married, first, Francis Kenneth Haight December 6, 1969, at St. Petersburg, Florida. He was the son of Mervin and Deloise Irene Haight. Julia and Francis were divorced in 1974. She married, second, Carl Edward Joseph October 26, 1979, at Rockville, Maryland. He was the son of Carl Eugene and Myrtle Virginia Rice Joseph and was born February 20, 1950, at Harrisonburg, Virginia.

CHILD OF JULIA KAY AND FRANCIS

(Sup) 8095   i Francis Kenneth Haight, Jr., born April 29, 1970.

CHILDREN OF JULIA KAY AND CARL

Stepson   ii Carl Edward Joseph, Jr., born January 19, 1974.
(Sup) 8096 iii Sarah Elizabeth Joseph, born January 27, 1981.

(Sup) 7055 MARK THOMAS BRUNK (Joseph^9, Mary^8, Ann^7, William^6, Adam^5, Alexander^4, John Adam^3, John Adam^2, John Jacob^1) was the son of Joseph Burton and Frances (Sperow) Brunk [Supplement No. 5035]. He was born August 21, 1953, at Bloomsburg, Pennsylvania. He married, first, Patty Edwards Stephanie Cacopardo April 3, 1977. She was the daughter of Salvatore and Jeanne Trauning Cacopardo and was born December 5, 1957, on Long Island, New

CHILD OF MARK AND PATTY

(Sup) 8097   i Christina Michelle Brunk, born April 30, 1975.

(Sup) 7056 MATTHEW TAYLOR BRUNK (Joseph^9, Mary^8, Ann^7, William^6, Adam^5, Alexander^4, John Adam^3, John Adam^2, John Adam^1) was the son of Joseph Burton and Frances (Sperow) Brunk [Supplement No. 5035]. He was born July 31, 1957, at Bloomsburg, Pennsylvania. He served in the Navy four years as a radioman.

(Sup) 7057 ANN ELIZABETH BRUNK (Joseph^9, Mary^8, Ann^7, William^6, Adam^5, Alexander^4, John Adam^3. John Adam^2, John Adam^1) was the daughter of Garland McCormack and Virginia Ann Brunk Sencindiver [Supplement No. 5039]. Paula was born September 5, 1956, at Martinsburg, West Virginia. She married Al Sine February 14, 1975, at Martinsburg. He was the son of Lester and Hazel Sine and was born at Martinsburg December 9, 1947.

(Sup) 8118   i   Heather Ann Sencindiver, born October 15, 1973.
(Sup) 8119   ii   Rodney William Sine, born September 12, 1975.

(Sup) 7067 DIANE ELAINE SENCINDIVER (Virginia^9, Mary^8, Ann^7, William^6, Adam^5, Alexander^4, John Adam^3, John Adam^2, John Jacob^1) was the daughter of Garland McCormack and Virginia Ann Brunk Sencindiver [Supplement No. 5039]. Diane was born January 25, 1961, at Martinsburg, West Virginia. She married Gerald D. Hubbard, Jr., July 28, 1979, at Martinsburg. He was the son of Gerald D. and Gwendolyn A. Spurling Hubbard and was born October 10, 1960, at Martinsburg.

(Sup) 8120   i   Jeremy Duane Hubbard, born January 9, 1980.

(Sup) 7068 PHYLISS JEAN GESFORD (Virginia^9, Mary^8, Ann^7, William^6, Adam^5, Alexander^4, John Adam^3, John Adam^2, John Jacob^1) was the daughter of Otho and Virginia Ann Brunk Sencindiver Gesford [Supplement No. 5039]. She was born February 2, 1970, at Martinsburg, West Virginia.

(Sup) 7069 TERESA JOAN BRUNK (Robert^9, Mary^8, Ann^7, William^6, Adam^5, Alexander^4, John Adam^3, John Adam^2, John Jacob^1) was the daughter of Robert Kenneth and Dorothy J. Gantarz Brunk [Supplement No. 5040]. Teresa was born November 21, 1961, at Martinsburg, West Virginia. She married Claude Louis Vignali July 26, 1980, at Poughkeepsie, New York. The son of Wilbur Lee and Betty June Morris Vignali, he was born April 7, 1961, at Seattle, Washington, and attended North Carolina State University in electrical engineering.

(Sup) 8125   i   Michelle Vignali, born September 21, 1981.
(Sup) 8126   ii   Robert Vignali, born December 25, 1983.

(Sup) 7070 LORI JEAN BRUNK (Robert^9, Mary^8, Ann^7, William^6, Adam^5, Alexander^4, John Adam^3, John Adam^2, John Jacob^1) was the daughter of Robert Kenneth and Dorothy J. Gantarz Brunk [Supplement No. 5040]. She was born April 12, 1963, at Utica, New York.

(Sup) 7062 CAROL LYNN NEFF (Barbara Jean^9, Mary^8, Ann^7, William^6, Adam^5, Alexander^4, John Adam^3, John Adam^2, John Jacob^1) was the daughter of Gene L. and Barbara Jean Brunk Neff [Supplement No. 5038]. Carol was born February 10, 1961, at Fort Belvoir, Virginia. She worked as a book-keeper at Moscow, Idaho. Carol married Brett Wiley Proudfit, May 23, 1982. He was born March 3, 1953.

Stepdaughter   i   Sarah Elizabeth Marie Proudfit, born Dec 12, 1972.

(Sup) 7063 JOHN DAVID NEFF (Barbara Jean^9, Mary^8, Ann^7, William^6, Adam^5, Alexander^4, John Adam^3, John Adam^2, John Jacob^1) was the son of Gene L. and Barbara Jean Brunk Neff [Supplement No. 5038]. John was born April 8, 1963, at Berlin, West Germany, and attended high school at Troy, Idaho. He married Shawn Christine Ketchum July 27, 1983. She was born April 8, 1963.

(Sup) 8111   i   Christi Jo Neff, born February 16, 1984.

(Sup) 7064 MARY CATHERINE NEFF (Barbara Jean^9, Mary^8, Ann^7, William^6, Adam^5, Alexander^4, John Adam^3, John Adam^2, John Jacob^1) was the daughter of Gene L. and Barbara Jean Brunk Neff [Supplement No. 5038]. Mary was born November 1, 1964, at Milwaukee, Wisconsin. She marrie John Kyle March 24, 1984. He was born March 13, 1963.

(Sup) 7065 PAMELA KAY SENCINDIVER (Virginia^9, Mary^8, Ann^7, William^6, Adam^5, Alexander^4, John Adam^3, John Adam^2, John Jacob^1) was the daughter of Garland McCormack and Virginia Ann Brunk Sencindiver [Supplement No. 5038]. Pamela was born January 10, 1953, at Chambersburg, Pennsylvania. She married, first, David Orndorf January 17, 1969, at Martinsburg, West Virginia. The son of James Herbert and Mary Orndorf, he was born October 6, 1945, at Martinsburg, West Virginia. Pamela married, second, John Edward Gesford, December 21, 1979, at Hagerstown, Maryland. He was the son of Otho C. and Cecilia Gesford and was born December 14, 1939, at Martinsburg.

(Sup) 8115   i   Kimberly Sue Orndorf, born May 28, 1969.
(Sup) 8116   ii   Mary Beth Orndorf, born January 4, 1974.
(Sup) 8117   iii James David Orndorf, born February 3, 1975.

(Sup) 7066 PAULA ANN SENCINDIVER (Virginia^9, Mary^8, Ann^7, William^6, Adam^5, Alexander^4, John Adam^3, John Adam^2, John Jacob^1) was the daugh-

(Sup) 7070A   CHARLES HUBERT HOUGH   (Charles[9], Charles[8], Ann[7], William[6], Adam[5], Alexander[4], John Adam[3], John Adam[2], John Jacob[1]) was the son of Charles Joseph and Emily Shamburg Hough, III [Supplement No. 5041]. He was born September 12, 1946, at Martinsburg, West Virginia. Charles married Susan Rebecca Ott of Charles Town, West Virginia, August 19, 1966.

(Sup) 8131   i   John David Hough, born November 1, 1968.
(Sup) 8132   ii   Joseph Christopher Hough, born January 22, 1972.

(Sup) 7070B   SHERRY BROWN HOUGH   (Charles[9], Charles[8], Ann[7], William[6], Adam[5], Alexander[4], John Adam[3], John Adam[2], John Jacob[1]) was the daughter of Charles Joseph and Emily Shamburg Hough, III [Supplement No. 5041]. Sherry was born March 2, 1948, at Martinsburg, West Virginia. She married George Phillip Landis of Madison, Tennessee, May 21, 1966.

(Sup) 8133   i   Janet Rene Landis, born February 18, 1967.
(Sup) 8134   ii   Katie Beth Landis, born January 29, 1975.

(Sup) 7070C   ROBERT LEE HOUGH   (Charles[9], Charles[8], Ann[7], William[6], Adam[5], Alexander[4], John Adam[3], John Adam[2], John Jacob[1]) was the son of Charles Joseph and Emily Shamburg Hough, III [Supplement No. 5041]. Robert was born April 26, 1955, at Charles Town, West Virginia. He married Katie Susan Schaffer April 22, 1977, at Sanford, Florida.

(Sup) 8135   i   Matthew Cameron Hough, born January 24, 1984.

(Sup) 7071   CHAD E. HOUGH   (Charles[9], Charles[8], Ann[7], William[6], Adam[5], Alexander[4], John Adam[3], John Adam[2], John Jacob[1]) was the son of Charles Richard and Cheri Lynn Beadle Hough [Supplement No. 5042A]. Chad was born June 14, 1972, at Columbus, Ohio.

(Sup) 7071A   WILLIAM JOSEPH HOUGH, JR. (William[9], Charles[8], Ann[7], William[6], Adam[5], Alexander[4], John Adam[3], John Adam[2], John Jacob[1]) was the son of William Joseph and Brenda Foster Hough [Supplement No. 5042B]. William, Jr., was born June 16, 1975, at Martinsburg, West Virginia.

(Sup) 7071B   CHRISTOPHER WILKES HOUGH   (William[9], Charles[8], Ann[7], William[6], Adam[5], Alexander[4], John Adam[3], John Adam[2], John Jacob[1]) was the son of William Joseph and Brenda Foster Hough [Supplement No. 5042B]. Christopher was born October 1, 1980, at Winchester, Virginia.

(Sup) 7071C   REBECCA ANN SAVILLE   (Frank[9], Grace[8], Ann[7], William[6], Adam[5], Alexander[4], John Adam[3], John Adam[2], John Jacob[1]) was the daughter of Frank Louis and Nancy Taylor Saville [Supplement No. 5043]. Rebecca was born September 10, 1963, at Fort Eustis, Virginia. She married Albert Dominic Miller, III, July 21, 1984. He was the son of Albert Dominic and Jean Dorothy Grenzer Miller, Jr., and was born June 22, 1963, at Baltimore, Maryland.

(Sup) 7072   DEBORAH MARIE WESTLEIN   (Joan[9], John[8], Ann[7], William[6], Adam[5], Alexander[4], John Adam[3], John Adam[2], John Jacob[1]) was the daughter of Paul Craig and Joan Hough Westlein [Supplement No. 5047]. Deborah was born December 8, 1955, at Washington, D.C.

(Sup) 7072A   SANDRA JEAN WESTLEIN   (Joan[9], John[8], Ann[7], William[6], Adam[5], Alexander[4], John Adam[3], John Adam[2], John Jacob[1]) was the daughter of Paul Craig and Joan Hough Westlein [Supplement No. 5047]. Sandra was born May 6, 1959, at Washington, D.C.

(Sup) 7072B   PATRICIA IRENE WESTLEIN   (Joan[9], John[8], Ann[7], William[6], Adam[5], Alexander[4], John Adam[3], John Adam[2], John Jacob[1]) was the daughter of Paul Craig and Joan Hough Westlein [Supplement No. 5047]. Patricia was born May 13, 1960, at Washington, D.C.

(Sup) 7072C   PAUL CRAIG WESTLEIN   (Joan[9], John[8], Ann[7], William[6], Adam[5], Alexander[4], John Adam[3], John Adam[2], John Jacob[1]) was the son of Paul Craig and Joan Hough Westlein [Supplement No. 5047]. Paul was born June 10, 1961, at Arlington, Virginia. He died March 17, 1979, at Alexandria, Virginia.

(Sup) 7072D   JOAN TERESA WESTLEIN   (Joan[9], John[8], Ann[7], William[6], Adam[5], Alexander[4], John Adam[3], John Adam[2], John Jacob[1]) was the daughter of Paul Craig and Joan Hough Westlein [Supplement No. 5047]. Joan was born August 3, 1964, at Alexandria, Virginia.

(Sup) 7072E LINDA SUSAN WESTLEIN (Joan^9, John^8, Ann^7, William^6, Adam^5, Alexander^4, John Adam^3, John Adam^2, John Jacob^1) was the daughter of Paul Craig and Joan Hough Westlein [Supplement No. 5047]. Linda was born September 26, 1965, at Alexandria, Virginia.

(Sup) 7072F NANCY ALICE WESTLEIN (Joan^9, John^8, Ann^7, William^6, Adam^5, Alexander^4, John Adam^3, John Adam^2, John Jacob^1) was the daughter of Paul Craig and Joan Hough Westlein [Supplement No. 5047]. Nancy was born September 10, 1970, at Fairfax, Virginia.

(Sup) 7073 DAVID CRAIG HOUGH (John^9, John^8, Ann^7, William^6, Adam^5, Alexander^4, John Adam^3, John Adam^2, John Jacob^1) was the son of John Hugo and Joan Marie Marceron Hough, Jr. [Supplement No. 5048]. David was born June 30, 1957, at Port Lyauty, Morocco. He married Catherine Marie Dabbs October 4, 1980. She was the daughter of Donald and Marie Dabbs.

(Sup) 7074 JOHN RICHARD HOUGH (John^9, John^8, Ann^7, William^6, Adam^5, Alexander^4, John Adam^3, John Adam^2, John Jacob^1) was the son of John Hugo and Joan Marie Marceron Hough, Jr. [Supplement No. 5048]. John was born June 27, 1958, at Port Lyauty, Morocco. He married Beth Ann Dilley November 25, 1978. She was the daughter of Earl Herbert and Regina May Dilley.

(Sup) 8151 i Michael Joseph Hough, born November 4, 1979.
(Sup) 8152 ii Shannon Marie Hough, born November 23, 1982.

(Sup) 7075 PAUL JEFFREY HOUGH (John^9, John^8, Ann^7, William^6, Adam^5, Alexander^4, John Adam^3, John Adam^2, John Jacob^1) was the son of John Hugo and Joan Marie Marceron Hough, Jr. [Supplement No. 5048]. Paul was born December 23, 1959, at Washington, D.C. He married Deborah Carol Carneal October 2, 1981. She was the daughter of Kenneth and Gladys Carneal.

(Sup) 8153 i Paul Jason Hough, born December 18, 1983.

(Sup) 7076 KAREN LYNN HOUGH (John^9, John^8, Ann^7, William^6, Adam^5, Alexander^4, John Adam^3, John Adam^2, John Jacob^1) was the daughter of John Hugo and Joan Marie Marceron Hough, Jr. [Supplement No. 5048]. Karen was born March 12, 1963, at Tacoma Park, Maryland.

(Sup) 7077 CYNTHIA MARIE JOHNSON (Joyce^9, Woodrow^8, Ann^7, William^6, Adam^5, Alexander^4, John Adam^3, John Adam^2, John Jacob^1) was the daughter of Frank Edward and Joyce Hough Johnson [Supplement No. 5049]. Cynthia was born June 13, 1956, at Martinsburg, West Virginia. She married George Webber Mong, Jr., June 22, 1974, at Martinsburg. He was the son of George Webber and Rosa Belle Lanham Mong and was born December 31, 1952, at Martinsburg.

(Sup) 8161 i Michelle Lynn Mong, born December 17, 1977.
(Sup) 8162 ii Kimberly Lee Mong, born May 23, 1979.
(Sup) 8163 iii Jennifer Marie Mong, born August 30, 1980.
(Sup) 8164 iv Matthew Scott Mong, born June 25, 1983.

(Sup) 7077A FRANK EDWARD JOHNSON, JR. (Joyce^9, Woodrow^8, Ann^7, William^6, Adam^5, Alexander^4, John Adam^3, John Adam^2, John Jacob^1) was the son of Frank Edward and Joyce Hough Johnson [Supplement No. 5049]. Frank, Jr., was born August 18, 1957, at Martinsburg, West Virginia. He served in the U.S. Army Corps of Engineers 1974-76 and then was employed by the Martinsburg Journal. Frank married Tammie Evans, April 23, 1979, at Martinsburg. She was born January 23, 1957, at Dover, Delaware. Tammie died in 1981.

(Sup) 8165 i Jan Augusta Johnson, born September 4, 1980.

(Sup) 7077B ERIC STROBRIDGE (Debra^9, Woodrow^8, Ann^7, William^6, Adam^5, Alexander^4, John Adam^3, John Adam^2, John Jacob^1) was the son of Debra Kay Hough [Supplement No. 5050A]. Eric was born December 17, 1978, at Winchester, Virginia.

(Sup) 7078 DOUGLAS EUGENE GOLLIDAY, JR. (Patricia^9, Frances^8, Ann^7, William^6, Adam^5, Alexander^4, John Adam^3, John Adam^2, John Jacob^1) was the son of Douglas Eugene and Patricia Ann Saville Golliday [Supplement No. 5051]. Douglas, Jr., was born September 6, 1954, at Martinsburg, West Virginia. He was a gunnery sergeant in the U.S. Marine Corps. Douglas married Anna Corrine Jenson August 24, 1974, in Hawaii. She was the daughter of Arthur and Nora Jenson of Long Beach, California.

(Sup) 8171 i Christopher Douglas Golliday, born April 13, 1975.
(Sup) 8172 ii Jonathan Randolph Golliday, born December 19, 1977.
(Sup) 8173 iii Benjamin Eugene Golliday, born April 18, 1980.

(Sup) 7078A   CLARK WAYNE GOLLIDAY (Patricia^9, Frances^8, Ann^7, William^6, Adam^5, Alexander^4, John Adam^3, John Adam^2, John Jacob^1) was the son of Douglas Eugene and Patricia Ann Saville Golliday [Supplement No. 5051]. Clark was born January 18, 1958, at Martinsburg, West Virginia. He married Cynthia Dee Wagner June 17, 1978, at Easton, Maryland. She was the daughter of Carl and Betty Wagner of Easton. Clark was a mechanic, and Cynthia managed a jewelry store at Easton.

(Sup) 8174   i Kimberly Nicole Golliday, born March 5, 1982.

(Sup) 7078B   BERTIE LYNN GOLLIDAY (Patricia^9, Frances^8, Ann^7, William^6, Adam^5, Alexander^4, John Adam^3, John Adam^2, John Jacob^1) was the daughter of Douglas Eugene and Patricia Ann Saville Golliday [Supplement No. 5051]. Bertie Lynn was born April 15, 1961, at Martinsburg, West Virginia. She married Jeffery Alan Erskine June 23, 1979, at Easton, Maryland. He was the son of Huey J. and Betty Erskine. Jeffery was a sergeant in the U.S. Marine Corps.

(Sup) 8175   i   Holly Marie Erskine, born December 29, 1979.
(Sup) 8176   ii Jessica Renee Erskine, born March 27, 1983.

(Sup) 7078C   MARK ANTHONY CAVE (JoAnn^9, Frances^8, Ann^7, William^6, Adam^5, Alexander^4, John Adam^3, John Adam^2, John Jacob^1) was the son of Jacob Lee and JoAnn Saville Cave [Supplement No. 5052]. Mark was born December 25, 1959, at Martinsburg, West Virginia. He was a security guard at the Air National Guard, Martinsburg. Mark married, first, Natalie Dorothea Stickles March 14, 1981, at Martinsburg. She was the daughter of Marshall and Vivian Wetzel Stickles. Mark and Natalie were divorced. He married, second, Penny Marie Grubb February 25, 1984, at Martinsburg. Penny was the daughter of Robert M. and Doris McCarty Grubb.

(Sup) 8177   i   Jennifer Brooke Cave, born October 26, 1981.

(Sup) 7078D   BRIAN ANDREW CAVE (JoAnn^9, Frances^8, Ann^7, William^6, Adam^5, Alexander^4, John Adam^3, John Adam^2, John Jacob^1) was the son of Jacob Lee and JoAnn Saville Cave [Supplement No. 5052]. Brian was born September 24, 1966, at Martinsburg, West Virginia.

(Sup) 7078E   CHAD MATTHEW CAVE (JoAnn^9, Frances^8, Ann^7, William^6, Adam^5, Alexander^4, John Adam^3, John Adam^2, John Jacob^1) was the son of Jacob Lee and JoAnn Saville Cave [Supplement No. 5052]. Chad was born November 18, 1976, at Martinsburg, West Virginia.

(Sup) 7078F   SHERRI LYNN SAVILLE (Woodrow^9, Frances^8, Ann^7, William^6, Adam^5, Alexander^4, John Adam^3, John Adam^2, John Jacob^1) was the daughter of Woodrow Pearell and Carol Skidmore Saville, Jr. [Supplement No. 5053]. Sherri was born November 20, 1968, at Hammond, Indiana.

(Sup) 7078G   SCOTT ROBERT SAVILLE (Woodrow^9, Frances^8, Ann^7, William^6, Adam^5, Alexander^4, John Adam^3, John Adam^2, John Jacob^1) was the son of Woodrow Pearell and Carol Skidmore Saville, Jr. [Supplement No. 5053]. Scott was born February 16, 1972, at Hammond, Indiana.

(Sup) 7078H   SHAWN MATTHEW SAVILLE (Woodrow^9, Frances^8, Ann^7, William^6, Adam^5, Alexander^4, John Adam^3, John Adam^2, John Jacob^1) was the son of Woodrow Pearell and Carol Skidmore Saville, Jr. [Supplement No. 5053]. He was born April 22, 1978, at Martinsburg, West Virginia.

(Sup) 7078J   SARA BETH SAVILLE (Woodrow^9, Frances^8, Ann^7, William^6, Adam^5, Alexander^4, John Adam^3, John Adam^2, John Jacob^1) was the daughter of Woodrow Pearell and Carol Skidmore Saville, Jr. [Supplement No. 5053]. She was born July 2, 1981, at Martinsburg, West Virginia.

(Sup) 7078K   FREDDIE L. SAVILLE (Richard^9, Frances^8, Ann^7, William^6, Adam^5, Alexander^4, John Adam^3, John Adam^2, John Jacob^1) was the son of Richard Taylor and Mary Lou Flores Saville [Supplement No. 5054]. Freddie was born February 6, 1965, at Tamuning, Guam.

(Sup) 7078L   LISA A. SAVILLE (Richard^9, Frances^8, Ann^7, William^6, Adam^5, Alexander^4, John Adam^3, John Adam^2, John Jacob^1) was the daughter of Richard Taylor and Mary Lou Flores Saville [Supplement No. 5054]. Lisa was born January 16, 1971, at Martinsburg, West Virginia.

(Sup) 7078M   SANDRA KAYE MYERS (Frances^9, Frances^8, Ann^7, William^6, Adam^5, Alexander^4, John Adam^3, John Adam^2, John Jacob^1) was the daughter of Raymond Bruce and Frances Saville Myers [Supplement No. 5055]. Sandra was born March 17, 1969, at Martinsburg, West Virginia.

(Sup) 7079F MICHELLE LYNN RITZ (Cornelia[9], Daniels[8], Ann[7], William[6], Adam[5], Alexander[4], John Adam[3], John Adam[2], John Jacob[1]) was the daughter of Jerry Michael and Cornelia Hough Ritz [Supplement No. 5058A]. Michelle was born June 23, 1971, in Baltimore County, Maryland.

(Sup) 7079G KARLEY JEAN HOUGH (Robert[9], Daniels[8], Ann[7], William[6], Adam[5], Alexander[4], John Adam[3], John Adam[2], John Jacob[1]) was the son of Robert Jerome and Susan Kappes Hough [Supplement No. 5058B]. Karley was born October 20, 1976, in Baltimore County, Maryland.

(Sup) 7079H DANIEL ROBERT HOUGH (Robert[9], Daniels[8], Ann[7], William[6], Adam[5], Alexander[4], John Adam[3], John Adam[2], John Jacob[1]) was the son of Robert Jerome and Susan Kappes Hough [Supplement No. 5058B]. Daniel was born November 5, 1983, in Baltimore County, Maryland.

(Sup) 7079J CHRISTY ANN HOUGH (John[9], Daniels[8], Ann[7], William[6], Adam[5], Alexander[4], John Adam[3], John Adam[2], John Jacob[1]) was the daughter of John William and Terri Ann Wall Hough [Supplement No. 5058C]. Christy was born October 10, 1978, in Baltimore County, Maryland.

(Sup) 7080 TARA LYNN HOUGH (Phillip[9], Paul[8], Ann[7], William[6], Adam[5], Alexander[4], John Adam[3], John Adam[2], John Jacob[1]) was the daughter of Phillip Van and Andrea Guzick Hough [Supplement No. 5059]. Tara Lynn was born January 9, 1977, at Baltimore, Maryland.

(Sup) 7080A CLINTON CHRISTOPHER ELLIOTT (Mary[9], Paul[8], Ann[7], William[6], Adam[5], Alexander[4], John Adam[3], John Adam[2], John Jacob[1]) was the son of Ronald Stephen and Mary Hough Elliott [Supplement No. 5060]. Clinton was born October 10, 1973, at Baltimore, Maryland.

(Sup) 7080B DAVID COREY CARRIGAN (Mary[9], Paul[8], Ann[7], William[6], Adam[5], Alexander[4], John Adam[3], John Adam[2], John Jacob[1]) was the son of James Kelly and Mary Hough Eliott Carrigan [Supplement No. 5060]. David was born August 28, 1981, at Lake Wales, Florida.

(Sup) 7078N RAYMOND BRUCE MYERS, JR. (Frances[9], Frances[8], Ann[7], William[6], Adam[5], Alexander[4], John Adam[3], John Adam[2], John Jacob[1]) was the son of Raymond Bruce and Frances Saville Myers [Supplement No. 5055]. Raymond, Jr., was born September 27, 1973, at Martinsburg, West Virginia.

(Sup) 7079 PAMELA MARIE HOUGH (Daniels[9], Daniels[8], Ann[7], William[6], Adam[5], Alexander[4], John Adam[3], John Adam[2], John Jacob[1]) was the daughter of Daniels Pershing Baker and Janet Hanson Hough [Supplement No. 5056]. Pamela was born August 25, 1962, at San Diego, California. She married Anthony Rocco Bonbeno, III, in 1979 at Las Vegas, Nevada. He was the son of Anthony Rocco Bonbeno, Jr., of San Diego.

(Sup) 8191 i Anthony Rocco Bonbeno, IV, born November 10, 1980.
(Sup) 8192 ii Shannon Marie Bonbeno, born March, 1982.

(Sup) 7079A KATHLEEN ELIZABETH LARKIN (Rebecca[9], Daniels[8], Ann[7], William[6], Adam[5], Alexander[4], John Adam[3], John Adam[2], John Jacob[1]) was the daughter of Patrick Wallace and Rebecca Ann Hough Larkin, Jr. [Supplement No. 5057]. Kathleen was born March 22, 1973, at Baltimore, Maryland.

(Sup) 7079B PATRICK WALLACE LARKIN, III (Rebecca[9], Daniels[8], Ann[7], William[6], Adam[5], Alexander[4], John Adam[3], John Adam[2], John Jacob[1]) was the son of Patrick Wallace and Rebecca Ann Hough Larkin, Jr. [Supplement No. 5057]. Patrick, III, was born September 20, 1975, at Baltimore, Maryland.

(Sup) 7079C ANN MARIE SMITH (Sally[9], Daniels[8], Ann[7], William[6], Adam[5], Alexander[4], John Adam[3], John Adam[2], John Jacob[1]) was the daughter of John Douglas and Sally Virginia Hough Smith [Supplement No. 5058]. Ann Marie was born December 12, 1968, in Baltimore County, Maryland.

(Sup) 7079D JAYE DEA SMITH (Sally[9], Daniels[8], Ann[7], William[6], Adam[5], Alexander[4], John Adam[3], John Adam[2], John Jacob[1]) was the daughter of John Douglas and Sally Virginia Hough Smith [Supplement No. 5058]. Jaye Dea was born February 27, 1970, in Baltimore County, Maryland.

(Sup) 7079E MICHAEL DANIEL RITZ (Cornelia[9], Daniels[8], Ann[7], William[6], Adam[5], Alexander[4], John Adam[3], John Adam[2], John Jacob[1]) was the son of Jerry Michael and Cornelia Hough Ritz [Supplement No. 5058A]. Michael was born September 27, 1968, in Baltimore County, Maryland.

(Sup) 7080C JASON MATTHEW PAYNE (Karen^9, Paul^8, Ann^7, William^6, Adam^5, Alexander^4, John Adam^3, John Adam^2, John Jacob^1) was the son of Charles Benjamin and Karen Hough Payne [Supplement No. 5060B]. Jason was born April 18, 1974.

(Sup) 7080D TIMOTHY PAUL PAYNE (Karen^9, Paul^8, Ann^7, William^6, Adam^5, Alexander^4, John Adam^3, John Adam^2, John Jacob^1) was the son of Charles Benjamin and Karen Hough Payne [Supplement No. 5060B]. Timothy was born September 29, 1975.

(Sup) 7081 CYNTHIA DIANE LINK (John William^9, John William^8, John^7, William^6, Adam^5, Alexander^4, John Adam^3, John Adam^2, John Jacob^1) was the daughter of John William and Peggy Diane Wilson Link III [Supplement No. 5061]. Cynthia was born May 25, 1972, at Cannon Air Force Base, New Mexico.

(Sup) 7082 JOHN WILLIAM LINK, IV (John William^9, John William^8, John^7, William^6, Adam^5, Alexander^4, John Adam^3, John Adam^2, John Jacob^1) was the son of John William and Peggy Diane Wilson Link, III [Supplement No. 5061]. John William, IV, was born September 29, 1976, at Mountain Home Air Force Base, Idaho.

(Sup) 7083 KAREN MARIE RUSSELL (Charles^9, Elizabeth^8, John^7, William^6, Adam^5, Alexander^4, John Adam^3, John Adam^2, John Jacob^1) was the daughter of Charles Richard and Diane Marie Cameron Russell [Supplement No. 5064]. Karen was born August 11, 1976, at Coldwater, Michigan.

(Sup) 7084 ANDREA LINK RUSSELL (Charles^9, Elizabeth^8, John^7, William^6, Adam^5, Alexander^4, John Adam^3, John Adam^2, John Jacob^1) was the daughter of Charles Richard and Diane Marie Cameron Russell [Supplement No. 5064]. Andrea was born July 5, 1978, at Coldwater, Michigan.

(Sup) 7085 ARTHUR STANLEY LINK, III (Arthur^9, Arthur^8, John^7, William^6, Adam^5, Alexander^4, John Adam^3, John Adam^2, John Jacob^1) was the son of Arthur Stanley and Mary Margaret Brown Link, Jr. [Supplement No. 5065]. Arthur was born May 12, 1974, at New York City. He was reared at Winston-Salem, North Carolina.

(Sup) 7085A PERCY ANNE LINK (William^9, Arthur^8, John^7, William^6, Adam^5, Alexander^4, John Adam^3, John Adam^2, John Jacob^1) was the daughter of William Allen and Susannah Jones Link [Supplement No. 5066B]. She was born May 31, 1983.

(Sup) 7086 JASON CHURCHILL COSTA (Douglas^9, Elinor^8, John^7, William^6, Adam^5, Alexander^4, John Adam^3, John Adam^2, John Jacob^1) was the son of Douglas Link and Laurel Lynn Pierce Costa [Supplement No. 5066C]. Jason was born January 19, 1974, at Lawrence, Kansas.

(Sup) 7087 THOMAS WOODWARD COSTA (Douglas^9, Elinor^8, John^7, William^6, Adam^5, Alexander^4, John Adam^3, John Adam^2, John Jacob^1) was the son of Douglas Link and Laurel Lynn Pierce Costa [Supplement No. 5066C]. Thomas was born August 23, 1979, at Charlottesville, Virginia.

(Sup) 7088 DENNIS LINK COFFINBERGER (Paul^9, Holland^8, Margaret^7, William^6, Adam^5, Alexander^4, John Adam^3, John Adam^2, John Jacob^1) was the son of Paul Edward and Margaret Rowell Coffinberger [Supplement No. 5067]. Dennis was born February 5, 1948, at Arlington, Virginia. He graduated from Millersville State Teachers College, Pennsylvania, with a B.S. degree in education. He taught high-school industrial art and was coach of the wrestling team at Millville, Pennsylvania. He married, first, Gail Lynn Greenfield November 8, 1969. Gail was the daughter of George Montgomery and Ora Lee Greenfield and was born January 26, 1949, at Coatesville, Pennsylvania. Dennis and Gail were divorced in 1982. He married, second, Cynthia Sue Hawley January 8, 1983. Cynthia was born February 11, 1957, at Portsmouth, Virginia.

(Sup) 8251　i　Gwen Marie Coffinberger, born June 23, 1971.
(Sup) 8252　ii　Erin Leigh Coffinberger, born February 20, 1974.
(Sup) 8253　iii　Adam Link Coffinberger, born June 22, 1975.

(Sup) 7089 DIANE LOUISE COFFINBERGER (Paul^9, Holland^8, Margaret^7, William^6, Adam^5, Alexander^4, John Adam^3, John Adam^2, John Jacob^1) was the daughter of Paul Edward and Margaret Rowell Coffinberger [Supplement No. 5067]. Diane was born May 20, 1951, at Arlington, Virginia. She married Bernard Frederick Shaurette March 15, 1975. He was the son of Bernard Neil and Dorothy Shaurette and was born March 1, 1951, at Milwaukee, Wisconsin. Bernard Frederick died September 30, 1982, and is buried at Culpepper, Virginia.

(Sup) 8254　i　Marie Ann Shaurette, born December 12, 1977.
(Sup) 8255　ii　Jason Allen Shaurette, born April 20, 1980.

(Sup) 7090   BENTON ROCKY ROTHGEB (Mary[9], Holland[8], Margaret[7], William[6], Adam[5], Alexander[4], John Adam[3], John Adam[2], John Jacob[1]) was the son of Lewis Benton and Mary Coffinberger Rothgeb [Supplement No. 5068]. He was born January 3, 1948, at Arlington, Virginia. He married Linda Grant December 4, 1971. She was the daughter of Blain D. and Mary Ann Grant and was born January 7, 1952, at Washington, D.C.

(Sup) 8256   i Brian Lewis Rothgeb, born March 18, 1975.
(Sup) 8257   ii Michael Rothgeb, born April 10, 1978.

(Sup) 7091   DAVID EARL ROTHGEB (Mary[9], Holland[8], Margaret[7], William[6], Adam[5], Alexander[4], John Adam[3], John Adam[2], John Jacob[1]) was the son of Lewis Benton and Mary Coffinberger Rothgeb [Supplement No. 5068]. He was born March 31, 1952, at Arlington, Virginia.

(Sup) 7092   ROBERT LINK CRUMBACKER (Virginia[9], Grace[8], Margaret[7], William[6], Adam[5], Alexander[4], John Adam[3], John Adam[2], John Jacob[1]) was the son of Jesse Edwin and Virginia Lee Patterson Crumbacker [Supplement No. 5070]. Robert was born August 19, 1947, at Martinsburg, West Virginia. He was employed as manager of a janitorial services company. Robert married Theresa Oftedahl.

(Sup) 8261   i   Michael Lee Crumbacker, born May 9, 1972.
(Sup) 8262   ii Matthew Link Crumbacker, born August 11, 1974.
(Sup) 8263   iii Amy Joy Crumbacker, born November 26, 1976.
(Sup) 8264   iv Dawn Michell Crumbacker, born October 8, 1979.

(Sup) 7093   RICHARD LEE CRUMBACKER (Virginia[9], Grace[8], Margaret[7], William[6], Adam[5], Alexander[4], John Adam[3], John Adam[2], John Jacob[1]) was the son of Jesse Edwin and Virginia Lee Patterson Crumbacker [Supplement No. 5070]. Richard was born March 9, 1949, at San Juan, Puerto Rico. He managed one of the Cepak stores. Richard married Patricia Gosen, a widow with four children.

(Sup) 7093A JESSE EDWIN CRUMBACKER, JR. (Virginia[9], Grace[8], Margaret[7], William[6], Adam[5], Alexander[4], John Adam[3], John Adam[2], John Jacob[1]) was the son of Jessie Edwin and Virginia Patterson Crumbacker [Supplement No. 5070]. Jesse, Jr., was born October 6, 1958, at Patuxent River, Maryland. He was employed by Cepak, Inc., as a sales clerk.

(Sup) 7094   LAWRENCE PATTERSON NOLL (Elaine[9], Grace[8], Margaret[7], William[6], Adam[5], Alexander[4], John Adam[3], John Adam[2], John Jacob[1]) was the son of Vincent Paul and Rose Elaine Patterson Noll [Supplement No. 5071]. Lawrence was born July 19, 1950, at Martinsburg, West Virginia. He married Vickie Allright. They were divorced. Lawrence married, second, Connie Sine.

CHILDREN OF LAWRENCE AND VICKIE

(Sup) 8271   i Thomas Vincent Noll, born February 18, 1970.
(Sup) 8272   ii Richard Joseph Noll, born April 28, 1971.

(Sup) 7095   ANN MARIE NOLL (Elaine[9], Grace[8], Margaret[7], William[6], Adam[5], Alexander[4], John Adam[3], John Adam[2], John Jacob[1]) was the daughter of Vincent Paul and Rose Elaine Patterson Noll [Supplement No. 5071]. Ann was born July 23, 1953, at Martinsburg, West Virginia. She married, first, Greg Wachtel; they were divorced. She married, second, Stephen Craig Smallwood. Ann was a schoolteacher, and Steve worked for the Post Office.

(Sup) 7096   MARCIA LOU NOLL (Elaine[9], Grace[8], Margaret[7], William[6], Adam[5], Alexander[4], John Adam[3], John Adam[2], John Jacob[1]) was the daughter of Vincent Paul and Rose Elaine Patterson Noll [Supplement No. 5071]. Marcia was born December 15, 1954, at Martinsburg, West Virginia. She was a flight attendant for American Airlines.

(Sup) 7097   JEFFERY MICHAEL NOLL (Elaine[9], Grace[8], Margaret[7], William[6], Adam[5], Alexander[4], John Adam[3], John Adam[2], John Jacob[1]) was the son of Vincent Paul and Rose Elaine Patterson Noll [Supplement No. 5071]. Jeffery was born October 8, 1956, at Martinsburg, West Virginia. He married Tonya Ann Gray. She was born October 11, 1956, at Martinsburg. Jeffery was employed by Du Pont, and Tonya worked part time for an appliance company.

(Sup) 8275   i Ryan Michael Noll, born October 28, 1982.

(Sup) 7098   MELISSA SUE NOLL (Elaine[9], Grace[8], Margaret[7], William[6], Adam[5], Alexander[4], John Adam[3], John Adam[2], John Jacob[1]) was the daughter of Vincent Paul and Rose Elaine Patterson Noll [Supplement No. 5071]. Melissa was born May 1, 1961, at Martinsburg, West Virginia. She married David Brian Warner. He was born June 27, 1961, at Wyandotte, Michigan. Melissa worked at a food store, and David was employed by Wilderness Company at Williamsport, Maryland.

(Sup) 8276   i Nicole Renee Warner, born January 18, 1982.
(Sup) 8277   ii Aaron Daniel Warner, born April 3, 1984.

(Sup) 7099 GEORGE EDWARD HOHMAN, III (Rose Elaine^9, Walter^8, Margaret^7, William^6, Adam^5, Alexander^4, John Adam^3, John Adam^2, John Jacob^1) was the son of George Edward and Rose Elaine Coffinberger Hohman, Jr. [Supplement No. 5073]. George, III, was born May 23, 1964, at Baltimore, Maryland.

(Sup) 7100 STANLEY CHESTER HOHMAN (Rose Elaine^9, Walter^8, Margaret^7, William^6, Adam^5, Alexander^4, John Adam^3, John Adam^2, John Jacob^1) was the son of George Edward and Rose Elaine Coffinberger Hohman, Jr. [Supplement No. 5073]. Stanley was born June 3, 1965, at Baltimore, Maryland.

(Sup) 7101 TANYA RENEE COFFINBERGER (William^9, Walter^8, Margaret^7, William^6, Adam^5, Alexander^4, John Adam^3, John Adam^2, John Jacob^1) was the daughter of William Frederick and Mildred Fogel Coffinberger [Supplement No. 5074]. She was born February 6, 1974, at Baltimore, Maryland.

(Sup) 7102 APRIL DAWN COFFINBERGER (William^9, Walter^8, Margaret^7, William^6, Adam^5, Alexander^4, John Adam^3, John Adam^2, John Jacob^1) was the daughter of William Frederick and Mildred Fogel Coffinberger [Supplement No. 5074]. She was born April 30, 1976, at Baltimore, Maryland.

(Sup) 7103 TAMELA JOY COFFINBERGER (William^9, Walter^8, Margaret^7, William^6, Adam^5, Alexander^4, John Adam^3, John Adam^2, John Jacob^1) was the daughter of William Frederick and Mildred Fogel Coffinberger [Supplement No. 5074]. She was born June 6, 1979, at Baltimore, Maryland (twin of Christopher).

(Sup) 7104 CHRISTOPHER WILLIAM COFFINBERGER (William^9, Walter^8, Margaret^7, William^6, Adam^5, Alexander^4, John Adam^3, John Adam^2, John Jacob^1) was the son of William Frederick and Mildred Fogel Coffinberger [Supplement No. 5074]. He was born June 6, 1979, at Baltimore, Maryland (twin of Tamela).

(Sup) 7105 KIMBERLY ANN CLOUD (James^9, Elmer^8, Margaret^7, William^6, Adam^5, Alexander^4, John Adam^3, John Adam^2, John Jacob^1) was the daughter of James Douglas and Hilda Grove Cloud [Supplement No. 5077]. Kimberly was born January 7, 1964.

(Sup) 7106 STEPHEN DOUGLAS CLOUD (James^9, Elmer^8, Margaret^7, William^6, Adam^5, Alexander^4, John Adam^3, John Adam^2, John Jacob^1) was the son of James Douglas and Hilda Grove Cloud [Supplement No. 5077]. Stephen was born January 3, 1965.

(Sup) 7107 JEANETTE LYNN CLOUD (James^9, Elmer^8, Margaret^7, William^6, Adam^5, Alexander^4, John Adam^3, John Adam^2, John Jacob^1) was the daughter of James Douglas and Hilda Grove Cloud [Supplement No. 5077]. Jeanette was born August 30, 1972.

(Sup) 7108 DAVID MARTIN CLOUD (David^9, Elmer^8, Margaret^7, William^6, Adam^5, Alexander^4, John Adam^3, John Adam^2, John Jacob^1) was the son of David Martin and Gwendolyn Edwards Cloud [Supplement No. 5079].

(Sup) 7108A MICHAEL TODD KIDWILER (Cornelia^9, Elmer^8, Margaret^7, William^6, Adam^5, Alexander^4, John Adam^3, John Adam^2, John Jacob^1) was the son of Vernon Lee and Cornelia Cloud Kidwiler [Supplement No. 5080]. Michael was born March 2, 1964.

(Sup) 7108B VALERIE ANN KIDWILER (Cornelia^9, Elmer^8, Margaret^7, William^6, Adam^5, Alexander^4, John Adam^3, John Adam^2, John Jacob^1) was the daughter of Vernon Lee and Cornelia Cloud Kidwiler [Supplement No. 5080]. Valerie was born June 29, 1965.

(Sup) 7109 WAYNE STEWART CRIDER, JR. (Betty^9, Cornelia^8, Margaret^7, William^6, Adam^5, Alexander^4, John Adam^3, John Adam^2, John Jacob^1) was the son of Wayne Stewart and Betty Jeanene Neibert Crider [Supplement No. 5081]. Wayne, Jr., was born May 30, 1955, at Hagerstown, Maryland.

(Sup) 7110 CATHERINE CAROL CRIDER (Betty^9, Cornelia^8, Margaret^7, William^6, Adam^5, Alexander^4, John Adam^3, John Adam^2, John Jacob^1) was the daughter of Wayne Stewart and Betty Jeanene Neibert Crider [Supplement No. 5081]. Catherine was born January 21, 1958, at Hagerstown, Maryland.

(Sup) 7111 KAREN SUE ELGIN (Faye[9], Cornelia[8], Margaret[7], William[6], Adam[5], Alexander[4], John Adam[3], John Adam[2], John Jacob[1]) was the daughter of Robert Leon and Faye Rene Neibert Elgin [Supplement No. 5083]. Karen Sue was born April 2, 1962, at Mobile, Alabama.

(Sup) 7111A SHEILA LINK WORLEY (JoAnn[9], Bertha[8], Margaret[7], William[6], Adam[5], Alexander[4], John Adam[3], John Adam[2], John Jacob[1]) was the daughter of Frazier Clayborn and JoAnn Whittington Worley [Supplement No. 5084]. Sheila was born February 17, 1954, at Arlington, Virginia. She married Mark V. Robinson June 19, 1979, at Dunn Loring, Fairfax County, Virginia. He was the son of Samuel Vivanco and Christine Thompson Robinson and was born April 24, 1955, at Cincinnati, Ohio.

(Sup) 7111B GILBERT FRAZIER WORLEY (JoAnn[9], Bertha[8], Margaret[7], William[6], Adam[5], Alexander[4], John Adam[3], John Adam[2], John Jacob[1]) was the son of Frazier Clayborn and JoAnn Whittington Worley [Supplement No. 5084]. Gilbert was born March 3, 1958, at Arlington, Virginia.

(Sup) 7111C ANN MICHELLE WORLEY (JoAnn[9], Bertha[8], Margaret[7], William[6], Adam[5], Alexander[4], John Adam[3], John Adam[2], John Jacob[1]) was the daughter of Frazier Clayborn and JoAnn Whittington Worley [Supplement No. 5084]. Ann was born March 2, 1963, at Arlington, Virginia.

(Sup) 7111D ROBIN ARLENE WHEELER (Wilma[9], Bertha[8], Margaret[7], William[6], Adam[5], Alexander[4], John Adam[3], John Adam[2], John Jacob[1]) was the daughter of Morris Beverly and Wilma Whittington Wheeler [Supplement No. 5085]. Robin was born June 29, 1958, at Arlington, Virginia.

(Sup) 7111E SANDRA DAWN WHEELER (Wilma[9], Bertha[8], Margaret[7], William[6], Adam[5], Alexander[4], John Adam[3], John Adam[2], John Jacob[1]) was the daughter of Morris Beverly and Wilma Whittington Wheeler [Supplement No. 5085]. Sandra was born October 23, 1962, at Bristol, Pennsylvania. She died November 21, 1981, at Gore, Virginia, from an automobile accident.

(Sup) 7111F DAVID LEE WHITTINGTON (Bernard[9], Bertha[8], Margaret[7], William[6], Adam[5], Alexander[4], John Adam[3], John Adam[2], John Jacob[1]) was

the son of Bernard Nelson and Susan Hoffman Whittington [Supplement No. 5086]. David was born January 4, 1963, at Washington, D.C.

(Sup) 7111G DANIEL NELSON WHITTINGTON (Bernard[9], Bertha[8], Margaret[7], William[6], Adam[5], Alexander[4], John Adam[3], John Adam[2], John Jacob[1]) was the son of Bernard Nelson and Susan Hoffman Whittington [Supplement No. 5086]. Daniel was born January 21, 1964, at Arlington, Virginia.

(Sup) 7111H HOPE VIRGINIA WHITTINGTON (Bernard[9], Bertha[8], Margaret[7], William[6], Adam[5], Alexander[4], John Adam[3], John Adam[2], John Jacob[1]) was the daughter of Bernard Nelson and Susan Hoffman Whittington [Supplement No. 5086]. She was born December 29, 1966, at Arlington, Virginia.

(Sup) 7111J ANNA KAZIMIERA WHITTINGTON (Bernard[9], Bertha[8], Margaret[7], William[6], Adam[5], Alexander[4], John Adam[3], John Adam[2], John Jacob[1]) was the daughter of Bernard Nelson and Lisa Fisher Whittington [Supplement No. 5086]. Anna was born February 25, 1982, at Woodbridge, Virginia.

(Sup) 7111K KRISTY ANN SNODDERLY (Cheryl[9], William[8], Margaret[7], William[6], Adam[5], Alexander[4], John Adam[3], John Adam[2], John Jacob[1]) was the daughter of Phillip Ross and Cheryl Ann Coffinberger Snodderly [Supplement No. 5087]. Kristy was born November 22, 1963, at Hagerstown, Maryland. She married Douglas Allan Rhoder. He was the son of James and Elsie Sogelsanger Rhodes and was born October 9, 1960, at Hagerstown.

(Sup) 7111L DEANNA KAY SNODDERLY (Cheryl[9], William[8], Margaret[7], William[6], Adam[5], Alexander[4], John Adam[3], John Adam[2], John Jacob[1]) was the daughter of Phillip Ross and Cheryl Ann Coffinberger Snodderly [Supplement No. 5087]. Deanna was born January 2, 1968, at Hagerstown, Maryland.

(Sup) 7112 JAMES RICHARD SHIMP (Anne[9], Martha[8], Martha[7], William[6], Adam[5], Alexander[4], John Adam[3], John Adam[2], John Jacob[1]) was the son of Richard Dix and Anne Virgina Coffinberger Shimp [Supplement No. 5089]. James was born September 7, 1950, at Martinsburg, West Virginia. He married Vickie Lou Hinkle. She was the daughter of William and Genevieve Corbin Hinkle and was born July 30, 1954.

(Sup) 8311   i   James Richard Shimp, born September 28, 1970.
(Sup) 8312   ii Autumn Lou Shimp, born January 17, 1972.

(Sup) 7112A   KENNETH MARTIN RUTHERFORD, JR. (Anne[9], James[8], Martha[7], William[6], Adam[5], Alexander[4], John Adam[3], John Adam[2], John Jacob[1]) was the son of Kenneth Martin and Anne Virgina Coffinberger Rutherford [Supplement No. 5089]. Kenneth, Jr., was born July 29, 1955, at Martinsburg, West Virgina. He married Melody Emery, August 26, 1978. They were divorced in 1983.

(Sup) 8313   i   Kenneth Martin Rutherford, III, born March 28, 1979.

(Sup) 7112B   LAURA LEE RUTHERFORD (Anne[9], James[8], Martha[7], William[6], Adam[5], Alexander[4], John Adam[3], John Adam[2], John Jacob[1]) was the daughter of Kenneth Martin and Anne Virgina Coffinberger Rutherford [Supplement No. 5089]. Laura was born May 12, 1958, at Martinsburg, West Virginia. She married Robert Greenfield, August 30, 1975. They were divorced May, 1981.

(Sup) 8314   i   Kimberly Anne Greenfield, born March 20, 1976.

(Sup) 7112C   PRISCILLA ANNE RUTHERFORD (Anne[9], James[8], Martha[7], William[6], Adam[5], Alexander[4], John Adam[3], John Adam[2], John Jacob[1]) was the daughter of Kenneth Martin and Anne Virgina Coffinberger Rutherford [Supplement No. 5089]. Priscilla was born April 22, 1957, at Bunker Hill, West Virginia.

(Sup) 7112D   LISA MAY RUTHERFORD (Anne[9], James[8], Martha[7], William[6], Adam[5], Alexander[4], John Adam[3], John Adam[2], John Jacob[1]) was the daughter of Kenneth Martin and Anne Virgina Coffinberger Rutherford [Supplement No. 5089]. Lisa May was born May 29, 1959, at Martinsburg, West Virginia. She married Dennis Robinson, May 15, 1976, at Hagerstown, Maryland.

(Sup) 8315   i   Crystal Gail Robinson, born September 28, 1976.
(Sup) 8316   ii   Dennis Scott Robinson, Jr., born July 23, 1979.
(Sup) 8317   iii Tiffany Anne Robinson, born September 17, 1982.

(Sup) 7112E   THOMAS CLAY RUTHERFORD (Anne[9], James[8], Martha[7], William[6], Adam[5], Alexander[4], John Adam[3], John Adam[2], John Jacob[1]) was the son of Kenneth Martin and Anne Virgina Coffinberger Rutherford [Supplement No. 5089]. Thomas was born July 23, 1960, at Martinsburg, West Virginia.

(Sup) 7112F   JAMES SCOTT COFFINBERGER (James[9], William[8], Martha[7], William[6], Adam[5], Alexander[4], John Adam[3], John Adam[2], John Jacob[1]) was the son of James William and Barbara Carpenter Coffinberger [Supplement No. 5090]. James was born August 23, 1959, at Winchester, Virginia. He married Virginia Golden Luber. She was born October 1, 1961.

(Sup) 8318   i   David Lee Coffinberger, born 1979.
(Sup) 8319   ii   Justin James Coffinberger, born December 5, 1981.

(Sup) 7112G   PATRICIA KAY COFFINBERGER (James[9], William[8], Martha[7], William[6], Adam[5], Alexander[4], John Adam[3], John Adam[2], John Jacob[1]) was the daughter of James William and Barbara Carpenter Coffinberger [Supplement No. 5090]. Patricia was born March 5, 1962, at Winchester, Virginia.

(Sup) 7112H   ANDREW PATRICK JOHNSON (Joan[9], William[8], Martha[7], William[6], Adam[5], Alexander[4], John Adam[3], John Adam[2], John Jacob[1]) was the son of Gary Lee and Joan Coffinberger Johnson [Supplement No. 5091]. Andrew was born April 14, 1965.

(Sup) 7112J   AMY ELIZABETH JOHNSON (Joan[9], William[8], Martha[7], William[6], Adam[5], Alexander[4], John Adam[3], John Adam[2], John Jacob[1]) was the daughter of Gary Lee and Joan Coffinberger Johnson [Supplement No. 5091]. Amy was born November 23, 1968.

(Sup) 7112K   JOSEPH WILLIAM COFFINBERGER (Richard[9], William[8], Martha[7], William[6], Adam[5], Alexander[4], John Adam[3], John Adam[2], John Jacob[1]) was the son of Richard Lee and Janet Fletcher Coffinberger [Supplement No. 5092]. Joseph was born July 4, 1985, in Fairfax County, Virginia.

(Sup) 7113   CLIFTON DANIEL KELLER (Sandra[9], Daniel[8], Martha[7], William[6], Adam[5], Alexander[4], John Adam[3], John Adam[2], John Jacob[1]) was the son of Clifton Charles and Sandra Lou Coffinberger Keller [Supplement No. 5093]. He was born January 9, 1958, at Baltimore, Maryland.

(Sup) 7114   STEVEN MARK KELLER (Sandra[9], Daniel[8], Martha[7], William[6], Adam[5], Alexander[4], John Adam[3], John Adam[2], John Jacob[1]) was the son of Clifton Charles and Sandra Lou Coffinberger Keller [Supplement No. 5093]. He was born November 4, 1959, at Baltimore, Mayland.

(Sup) 7115 MICHAEL JOHN KELLER (Sandra^9, Daniel^8, Martha^7, William^6, Adam^5, Alexander^4, John Adam^3, John Adam^2, John Jacob^1) was the son of Clifton Charles and Sandra Lou Coffinberger Keller [Supplement No. 5093]. Michael was born January 23, 1965, at Baltimore, Maryland.

(Sup) 7116 TONI NICOLE KELLER (Sandra^9, Daniel^8, Martha^7, William^6, Adam^5, Alexander^4, John Adam^3, John Adam^2, John Jacob^1) was the daughter of Clifton Charles and Sandra Lou Coffinberger Keller [Supplement No. 5093]. She was born January 3, 1975, at Westminster, Maryland.

(Sup) 7117 EARL LEE NELSON, IV (Deanne^9, Danielle^8, Martha^7, William^6, Adam^5, Alexander^4, John Adam^3, John Adam^2, John Jacob^1) was the son of Earl Lee and Deanne Lee Coffinberger Nelson, III [Supplement No. 5094]. Earl, IV, was born August 15, 1961, at Baltimore, Maryland.

(Sup) 7118 DENENE MICHELLE NELSON (Deanne^9, Danielle^8, Martha^7, William^6, Adam^5, Alexander^4, John Adam^3, John Adam^2, John Jacob^1) was the daughter of Earl Lee and Deanne Lee Coffinberger Nelson, III [Supplement No. 5094]. She was born February 15, 1966, at Baltimore, Maryland.

(Sup) 7118A SCOTT ASHLEY EVANS (Ronald^9, Eunice^8, Martha^7, William^6, Adam^5, Alexander^4, John Adam^3, John Adam^2, John Jacob^1) was the son of Ronald Lee and Mary Elizabeth Prather Evans [Supplement No. 5095]. Scott was born April 26, 1959, at Martinsburg, West Virginia. He married Dorothy Devolia Edwards of Shepherdstown, West Virginia, February 14, 1982. She was born September 20, 1961. Scott was an insurance agent, and Dorothy was a licensed practical nurse at Boonsboro, Maryland.

(Sup) 7118B KIMBERLY ANETTE EVANS (Ronald^9, Eunice^8, Martha^7, William^6, Adam^5, Alexander^4, John Adam^3, John Adam^2, John Jacob^1) was the daughter of Ronald Lee and Mary Elizabeth Prather Evans [Supplement No. 5095]. Kimberly was born November 6, 1960, at Martinsburg, West Virginia. She married Douglas Blane Creamer of Charles Town, West Virginia, December 19, 1981. He was born November 28, 1958. Douglas was an automobile technician, and Kimberly was an underwriter for her father's insurance company.

(Sup) 7118C MARIA LEIGH EVANS (Ronald^9, Eunice^8, Martha^7, William^6, Adam^5, Alexander^4, John Adam^3, John Adam^2, John Jacob^1) was the daughter of Ronald Lee and Mary Elizabeth Prather Evans [Supplement No. 5095]. Maria was born October 29, 1966, at Martinsburg, West Virginia.

(Sup) 7119 JAMES LEE EVANS (Samuel^9, Eunice^8, Martha^7, William^6, Adam^5, Alexander^4, John Adam^3, John Adam^2, John Jacob^1) was the son of Samuel Wayne and Minette Jones Evans [Supplement No. 5096]. James was born June 13, 1964, at San Antonio, Texas.

(Sup) 7120 CYNTHIA DIANE EVANS (Samuel^9, Eunice^8, Martha^7, William^6, Adam^5, Alexander^4, John Adam^3, John Adam^2, John Jacob^1) was the daughter of Samuel Wayne and Minette Jones Evans [Supplement No. 5096]. Cynthia was born September 6, 1965, at Columbia, South Carolina.

(Sup) 7121 MARCUS RYAN BRANDT (Diane^9, Eunice^8, Martha^7, William^6, Adam^5, Alexander^4, John Adam^3, John Adam^2, John Jacob^1) was the son of Clayton August and Diane Evans Brandt [Supplement No. 5097]. He was born February 16, 1972, at Camp Hill, Pennsylvania.

(Sup) 7122 MATTHEW FRENCH BRANDT (Diane^9, Eunice^8, Martha^7, William^6, Adam^5, Alexander^4, John Adam^3, John Adam^2, John Jacob^1) was the son of Clayton August and Diane Evans Brandt [Supplement No. 5097]. Matthew was born September 12, 1973, at Camp Hill, Pennsylvania.

(Sup) 7122A DEANNA MARIE CLARKE (Sherlyn^9, Lee^8, Martha^7, William^6, Adam^5, Alexander^4, John Adam^3, John Adam^2, John Jacob^1) was the daughter of Russell Dean and Sherlyn Coffinberger Clarke [Supplement No. 5099]. Deanna was born February 21, 1978, at Bitburg, Germany.

(Sup) 7122B DANIEL MATTHEW CLARKE (Sherlyn^9, Lee^8, Martha^7, William^6, Adam^5, Alexander^4, John Adam^3, John Adam^2, John Jacob^1) was the son of Russell Dean and Sherlyn Coffinberger Clarke [Supplement No. 5099]. Daniel was born May 30, 1980, at Manhattan, Kansas.

(Sup) 7123 GREGORY LEE WENGER (Susan[9], John[8], Martha[7], William[6], Adam[5], Alexander[4], John Adam[3], John Adam[2], John Jacob[1]) was the son of Ronald Lee and Susan Coffinberger Wenger [Supplement No. 5100]. Gregory was born April 8, 1970, at Chambersburg, Pennsylvania.

(Sup) 7124 HILARY ANN WENGER (Susan[9], John[8], Martha[7], William[6], Adam[5], Alexander[4], John Adam[3], John Adam[2], John Jacob[1]) was the daughter of Ronald Lee and Susan Coffinberger Wenger [Supplement No. 5100]. Hilary was born January 12, 1973, at Chambersburg, Pennsylvania.

(Sup) 7125 WALTER ROSS PEARSON (Babeth[9], Nannie[8], Martha[7], William[6], Adam[5], Alexander[4], John Adam[3], John Adam[2], John Jacob[1]) was the son of Walter Ross and Babeth Kipe Pearson [Supplement No. 5102]. Walter, Jr., was born May 25, 1966, at Waynesboro, Pennsylvania.

(Sup) 7126 CHANCE ALLEN PEARSON (Babeth[9], Nannie[8], Martha[7], William[6], Adam[5], Alexander[4], John Adam[3], John Adam[2], John Jacob[1]) was the son of Walter Ross and Babeth Kipe Pearson [Supplement No. 5102]. Chance was born June 2, 1969, at Waynesboro, Pennsylvania.

(Sup) 7126A MICHAEL KEVIN STRITE (Mary[9], Nannie[8], Martha[7], William[6], Adam[5], Alexander[4], John Adam[3], John Adam[2], John Jacob[1]) was the son of Eldon Lee and Mary Elizabeth Kipe Strite [Supplement No. 5103]. Michael was born April 23,1968, at Waynesboro, Pennsylvania.

(Sup) 7126B MICHELLE RENEE STRITE (Mary[9], Nannie[8], Martha[7], William[6], Adam[5], Alexander[4], John Adam[3], John Adam[2], John Jacob[1]) was the daughter of Eldon Lee and Mary Elizabeth Kipe Strite [Supplement No. 5103]. Michelle was born September 15, 1970, at Waynesboro, Pennsylvania.

(Sup) 7127 MANDY MARIE KIPE (John[9], Nannie[8], Martha[7], William[6], Adam[5], Alexander[4], John Adam[3], John Adam[2], John Jacob[1]) was the daughter of John Kenneth and Erin Eberly Kipe [Supplement No. 5104]. Mandy was born May 26, 1977, at Hagerstown, Maryland.

(Sup) 7127A EMILY ANN KIPE (John[9], Nannie[8], Martha[7], William[6], Adam[5], Alexander[4], John Adam[3], John Adam[2], John Jacob[1]) was the daughter of John Kenneth and Erin Eberly Kipe [Supplement No. 5104]. Emily was born January 19, 1980, at Hershey, Pennsylvania.

(Sup) 7127B BRANDON ALEXANDER KIPE (John[9], Nannie[8], Martha[7], William[6], Adam[5], Alexander[4], John Adam[3], John Adam[2], John Jacob[1]) was the son of John Kenneth and Elenor Voth Kipe [Supplement No. 5104]. Brandon was born October 22, 1983, at Winnipeg, Manitoba, Canada.

(Sup) 7127C TONYA MARIE MURPHY (Beverly[9], Dennis[8], Martha[7], William[6], Adam[5], Alexander[4], John Adam[3], John Adam[2], John Jacob[1]) was the daughter of Patrick Hale and Beverly Coffinberger Murphy [Supplement No. 5109]. Tonya was born October 1, 1970.

(Sup) 7127D MICHAEL PATRICK MURPHY (Beverly[9], Dennis[8], Martha[7], William[6], Adam[5], Alexander[4], John Adam[3], John Adam[2], John Jacob[1]) was the son of Patrick Hale and Beverly Coffinberger Murphy [Supplement No. 5109]. Michael was born April 2, 1975.

(Sup) 7128 STEPHANIE MARCIA COFFINBERGER (Drew[9], Dennis[8], Martha[7], William[6], Adam[5], Alexander[4], John Adam[3], John Adam[2], John Jacob[1]) was the daughter of Drew Steven and Barbara Kenney Coffinberger [Supplement No. 5111]. Stephanie was born November 28, 1975.

(Sup) 7128A CHRISTI ANNA LEIGH COFFINBERGER (Drew[9], Dennis[8], Martha[7], William[6], Adam[5], Alexander[4], John Adam[3], John Adam[2], John Jacob[1]) was the daughter of Drew Steven and Barbara Kenney Coffinberger [Supplement No. 5111]. She was born July 14, 1980.

(Sup) 7128B MEGANN RENEE COFFINBERGER (Drew[9], Dennis[8], Martha[7], William[6], Adam[5], Alexander[4], John Adam[3], John Adam[2], John Jacob[1]) was the daughter of Drew Steven and Barbara kenney Coffinberger [Supplement No. 5111]. She was born August 8, 1983.

(Sup) 7129 SHANNON RENEE COFFINBERGER (Timothy[9], Dennis[8], Martha[7], William[6], Adam[5], Alexander[4], John Adam[3], John Adam[2], John Jacob[1]) was the daughter of Timothy Daniels and Tamela Jean Roberts Coffinberger [Supplement No. 5112]. Shannon was born September 2, 1979. She died May 6, 1980, and is buried in St. James Lutheran Cemetery at Uvilla, Jefferson County, West Virginia.

(Sup) 7130 DANIEL LEE COFFINBERGER (Timothy[9], Dennis[8], Martha[7], William[6], Adam[5], Alexander[4], John Adam[3], John Adam[2], John Jacob[1]) was the son of Timothy Daniels and Tamela Jean Roberts Coffinberger [Supplement No. 5112]. Daniel was born August 31, 1983.

(Sup) 7131 DAVID ASHER KAPLAN (Kitty[9], Bayrle[8], Adam[7], William[6], Adam[5], Alexander[4], John Adam[3], John Adam[2], John Jacob[1]) was the son of Neil Alan and Kitty Link Kaplan [Supplement No. 5115]. He was born May 5, 1982, at Washington, D.C.

(Sup) 7132 BRIAN KEITH WHITMAN (Linda[9], Bayrle[8], Adam[7], William[6], Adam[5], Alexander[4], John Adam[3], John Adam[2], John Jacob[1]) was the son of Richard Charles and Linda Louise Link Whitman [Supplement No. 5116]. He was born January 22, 1975, at Beckley, West Virginia.

(Sup) 7133 JULIE MARIE WHITMAN (Linda[9], Bayrle[8], Adam[7], William[6], Adam[5], Alexander[4], John Adam[3], John Adam[2], John Jacob[1]) was the daughter of Richard Charles and Linda Louise Link Whitman [Supplement No. 5116]. She was born March 1, 1978, at Beckley, West Virginia.

(Sup) 7134 TAMARA LYNN PETERSON (Pamela[9], Adam[8], Adam[7], William[6], Adam[5], Alexander[4], John Adam[3], John Adam[2], John Jacob[1]) was the daughter of Calvin Herman and Pamela Link Peterson, Jr. [Supplement No. 5117]. She was born August 21, 1970, at Baltimore, Maryland.

(Sup) 7135 CALVIN HERMAN PETERSON, III (Pamela[9], Adam[8], Adam[7], William[6], Adam[5], Alexander[4], John Adam[3], John Adam[2], John Jacob[1]) was the son of Calvin Herman and Pamela Link Peterson, Jr. [Supplement No. 5117]. Calvin, Jr., was born October 21, 1973, at Baltimore, Maryland.

(Sup) 7135A ADAM BAKER LINK, IV (Adam[9], Adam[8], Adam[7], William[6], Adam[5], Alexander[4], John Adam[3], John Adam[2], John Jacob[1]) was the son of Adam Baker and Anita Ramey Link, III [Supplement No. 5118]. Adam, IV, was born February 2, 1986, at Ranson, West Virginia. He died March 4, 1986, at Baltimore, Maryland, and is buried in Edge Hill Cemetery, Charles Town, West Virginia.

(Sup) 7136 SUSAN MARIE SPOTO (Glenda[9], Hildred[8], Samuel[7], William[6], Adam[5], Alexander[4], John Adam[3], John Adam[2], John Jacob[1]) was the daughter of Dennis Peter and Glenda Gail (Frocke) Spoto [Supplement No. 5119]. Susan was born March 21, 1963, at Andrews Air Force Base in Prince Georges County, Maryland.

(Sup) 7137 DEBORAH ANN SPOTO (Glenda[9], Hildred[8], Samuel[7], William[6], Adam[5], Alexander[4], John Adam[3], John Adam[2], John Jacob[1]) was the daughter of Dennis Peter and Glenda Gail (Frocke) Spoto [Supplement No. 5119]. Deborah was born August 30, 1966, at Brooklyn, New York.

(Sup) 7138 DORIS JEAN ROLL (Patricia[9], Hildred[8], Samuel[7], William[6], Adam[5], Alexander[4], John Adam[3], John Adam[2], John Jacob[1]) was the daughter of Fredrick Harvey and Patricia Lee (Frocke) Roll [Supplement No. 5120]. Doris was born December 5, 1960, at Andrews Air Force Base, Maryland. She married Kieran Vincent Mahoney, June 14, 1986, at Inwood, West Virginia. He was the son of John Daniel and Kathleen (O'Doherty) Mahoney of Milford, Connecticut and was born December 10, 1957, at Mobile, Alabama. Doris attended the University of Maryland and was employed by the U.S. Senate at Washington, D.C. Kieran graduated from the University of Maryland and was employed by Congress. They resided at Herndon, Virginia.

(Sup) 7139 MICHAEL FREDRICK ROLL (Patricia[9], Hildred[8], Samuel[7], William[6], Adam[5], Alexander[4], John Adam[3], John Adam[2], John Jacob[1]) was the son of Fredrick Harvey and Patricia Lee (Frocke) Roll [Supplement No. 5120]. He was born March 13, 1967, at Cheverly, Maryland. Michael married Paula Gage Penwell, September 13, 1986, at Charles Town, West Virginia. She was the daughter of Ray Lawrence Aleshire and Vicky Penwell Burch and was born March 11, 1968, at Charles Town. Michael was a building engineer at Washington, and they resided at Charles Town.

(Sup) 7140 MARTHA CELESTE FROCKE (George[9], Hildred[8], Samuel[7], William[6], Adam[5], Alexander[4], John Adam[3], John Adam[2], John Jacob[1]) was the daughter of George Gilbert and Martha Louise (Bennett) Frocke, Jr. [Supplement No. 5121]. Martha was born August 6, 1975, at Irving, Texas.

(Sup) 7141 PATRICIA DENISE FREY (Frances[9], Frances[8], Samuel[7], William[6], Adam[5], Alexander[4], John Adam[3], John Adam[2], John Jacob[1]) was the daughter of Edward Joseph and Frances Dee (Owens) Frey, Jr. [Supplement No. 5122]. Patricia was born February 26, 1966, at Fargo, North Dakota.

(Sup) 7141A JENNIFER DEE FREY (Frances[9], Frances[8], Samuel[7], William[6], Adam[5], Alexander[4], John Adam[3], John Adam[2], John Jacob[1]) was the daughter of Edward Joseph and Frances Dee (Owens) Frey, Jr. [Supplement No. 5122]. Jennifer was born May 6, 1969, at Portland, Oregon.

(Sup) 7141B JAY LEE CURTISS, JR., (Frances[9], Frances[8], Samuel[7], William[6], Adam[5], Alexander[4], John Adam[3], John Adam[2], John Jacob[1]) was the son of Jay Lee and Frances (Owens) (Frey) Curtiss [Supplement No. 5122]. Jay, Jr., was born September 7, 1971, and died August 19, 1972, at Portland, Oregon.

(Sup) 7141C JASON VERNON LYLE CURTISS (Frances[9], Frances[8], Samuel[7], William[6], Adam[5], Alexander[4], John Adam[3], John Adam[2], John Jacob[1]) was the son of Jay Lee and Frances (Owens) (Frey) Curtiss [Supplement No. 5122]. Jason was born July 4, 1973, at Portland, Oregon.

(Sup) 7142 REBECCA DIANE BELLAH (Sandra[9], Frances[8], Samuel[7], William[6], Adam[5], Alexander[4], John Adam[3], John Adam[2], John Jacob[1]) was the daughter of Clois Wade and Sandra (Owens) Bellah [Supplement No. 5123]. Rebecca was born April 30, 1971, at Hobbs, New Mexico.

(Sup) 7142A MISTY DAWN BELLAH (Sandra[9], Frances[8], Samuel[7], William[6], Adam[5], Alexander[4], John Adam[3], John Adam[2], John Jacob[1]) was the daughter of Clois Wade and Sandra (Owens) Bellah [Supplement No. 5123]. She was born June 28, 1973, at Bedford, Texas.

(Sup) 7142B CYNTHIA MARIE BELLAH (Sandra[9], Frances[8], Samuel[7], William[6], Adam[5], Alexander[4], John Adam[3], John Adam[2], John Jacob[1]) was the daughter of Clois Wade and Sandra (Owens) Bellah [Supplement No. 5123]. Cynthia was born April 11, 1975, at Dover Air Force Base, Delaware.

(Sup) 7142C AMANDA IRENE BELLAH (Sandra[9], Frances[8], Samuel[7], William[6], Adam[5], Alexander[4], John Adam[3], John Adam[2], John Jacob[1]) was the daughter of Clois Wade and Sandra (Owens) Bellah [Supplement No. 5123]. Amanda was born October 4, 1977, at Cleburne, Texas.

(Sup) 7142D CLOIS WADE BELLAH, JR. (Sandra[9], Frances[8], Samuel[7], William[6], Adam[5], Alexander[4], John Adam[3], John Adam[2], John Jacob[1]) was the son of Clois Wade and Sandra (Owens) Bellah [Supplement No. 5123]. He was born January 13, 1981, at Wichita Falls, Texas.

(Sup) 7143 LUCINDA GRACE SENFTEN (Deborah[9], Frances[8], Samuel[7], William[6], Adam[5], Alexander[4], John Adam[3], John Adam[2], John Jacob[1]) was the daughter of Daniel David and Deborah (Owens) Senften, Jr. [Supplement No. 5123A]. Lucinda was born September 26, 1972, at Gresham, Oregon.

(Sup) 7143A SARAH DeANN SENFTEN (Deborah[9], Frances[8], Samuel[7], William[6], Adam[5], Alexander[4], John Adam[3], John Adam[2], John Jacob[1]) was the daughter of Daniel David and Deborah (Owens) Senften, Jr. [Supplement No. 5123A]. Sarah was born January 6, 1975, at Gresham, Oregon.

(Sup) 7143B DANIEL DAVID SENFTEN, III (Deborah[9], Frances[8], Samuel[7], William[6], Adam[5], Alexander[4], John Adam[3], John Adam[2], John Jacob[1]) was the son of Daniel David and Deborah (Owens) Senften, Jr. [Supplement No. 5123A]. Daniel, III, was born October 20, 1976, at Portland, Oregon.

(Sup) 7144 ERICA BRIL OWENS (Richard[9], Frances[8], Samuel[7], William[6], Adam[5], Alexander[4], John Adam[3], John Adam[2], John Jacob[1]) was the daughter of Richard Frederick and Weslyn Janine (Russell) Owens [Supplement No. 5123B]. Erica was born November 28, 1980, at Portland, Oregon.

(Sup) 7144A CORIN ROCHELLE OWENS (Richard[9], Frances[8], Samuel[7], William[6], Adam[5], Alexander[4], John Adam[3], John Adam[2], John Jacob[1]) was the daughter of Richard Frederick and Weslyn Janine (Russell) Owens [Supplement No. 5123B]. Corin was born November 29, 1984, at Portland, Oregon.

(Sup) 7145 MICHAEL JASON WALTERS (Ronald[9], Betty[8], Samuel[7], William[6], Adam[5], Alexander[4], John Adam[3], John Adam[2], John Jacob[1]) was the son of Ronald Neal and Rashell Ann (Yanero) Walters [Supplement No. 5127]. Michael was born March 1, 1973, at Fairmont, West Virginia.

(Sup) 7146 SHANNON HOPE COLLIS (Lucinda[9], Betty[8], Samuel[7], William[6], Adam[5], Alexander[4], John Adam[3], John Adam[2], John Jacob[1]) was the daughter of Robert Eugene and Lucinda Starr (Walters) Collis [Supplement No. 5128]. Shannon was born January 23, 1974, at Martinsburg, West Virginia.

(Sup) 7147 DAWN HOPE WALTERS (Harry[9], Betty[8], Samuel[7], William[6], Adam[5], Alexander[4], John Adam[3], John Adam[2], John Jacob[1]) was the daughter of Harry Paul and Glenna Fay (Carr) Walters [Supplement No. 5129]. Dawn was born June 21, 1975, at Carswell Air Force Base, Fort Worth, Texas.

(Sup) 7148 GLEN SAMUEL WALTERS (Harry[9], Betty[8], Samuel[7], (Samuel[7], William[6], Adam[5], Alexander[4], John Adam[3], John Adam[2], John Jacob[1]) was the son of Harry Paul and Glenna Fay (Carr) Walters [Supplement No. 5129]. He was born September 29, 1978, at Beale Air Force Base, Marysville, California.

(Sup) 7149 RUBY MAE WALTERS (Joseph[9], Betty[8], Samuel[7], William[6], Adam[5], Alexander[4], John Adam[3], John Adam[2], John Jacob[1]) was the daughter of Joseph Thomas and Shirley Mae (Edwards) Walters [Supplement No. 5130]. She was born December 3, 1978, at Charles Town, West Virginia.

(Sup) 7150 APRIL GENEVA WALTERS (Joseph[9], Betty[8], Samuel[7], William[6], Adam[5], Alexander[4], John Adam[3], John Adam[2], John Jacob[1]) was the daughter of Joseph Thomas and Shirley Mae (Edwards) Walters [Supplement No. 5130]. April was born February 15, 1984.

(Sup) 7151 SEAN CHRISTOPHER STEWART LINK (John[9], Samuel[8], Samuel[7], William[6], Adam[5], Alexander[4], John Adam[3], John Adam[2], John Jacob[1]) was the son of John Stewart and Terri Rae (Johnston) Link [Supplement No. 5131]. He was born November 5, 1987, at Leesburg, Virginia.

(Sup) 7152 BENJAMIN LEE LOWMAN (Christine[9], William[8], James[7], William[6], Adam[5], Alexander[4], John Adam[3], John Adam[2], John Jacob[1]) was the son of Tommy Louis and Susan Christine (Link) Lowman [Supplement No. 5133]. Benjamin was born October 30, 1987, at Hickory, North Carolina.

(Sup) 7161 ALEXANDER DAVID ZIDER (LeRoy[9], Eleanor[8], Albert[7], John[6], Adam[5], Alexander[4], John Adam[3], John Adam[2], John Jacob[1]) was the son of LeRoy Stuart and Linda (Elliott) Zider [Supplement No. 5144]. Alexander was born January 24, 1982, at San Francisco, California.

(Sup) 7162 JACQUELINE ELLIOTT ZIDER (LeRoy[9], Eleanor[8], Albert[7], John[6], Adam[5], Alexander[4], John Adam[3], John Adam[2], John Jacob[1]) was the daughter of LeRoy Stuart and Linda (Elliott) Zider [Supplement No. 5144]. Jacqueline was born May 17, 1984, at San Francisco, California.

(Sup) 7163 CHRISTOPHER STUART ZIDER (Robert[9], Eleanor[8], Albert[7], John[6], Adam[5], Alexander[4], John Adam[3], John Adam[2], John Jacob[1]) was the son of Robert Bruce and Cheryl Anne (Faulconer) Zider [Supplement No. 5145]. Christopher was born April 20, 1977, at Stanford, California.

(Sup) 7164 ALLISON LESLIE ZIDER (Robert[9], Eleanor[8], Albert[7], John[6], Adam[5], Alexander[4], John Adam[3], John Adam[2], John Jacob[1]) was the daughter of Robert Bruce and Cheryl Anne (Faulconer) Zider [Supplement No. 5145]. Allison was born February 2, 1979, at Stanford, California.

(Sup) 7165 JOHN ROBERT ZIDER (Robert[9], Eleanor[8], Albert[7], John[6], Adam[5], Alexander[4], John Adam[3], John Adam[2], John Jacob[1]) was the son of Robert Bruce and Cheryl Anne (Faulconer) Zider [Supplement No. 5145]. John was born May 17, 1982, at Stanford, California.

(Sup) 7166 GRANT THOMPSON ZIDER (Robert[9], Eleanor[8], Albert[7], John[6], Adam[5], Alexander[4], John Adam[3], John Adam[2], John Jacob[1]) was the son of Robert Bruce and Cheryl Anne (Faulconer) Zider [Supplement No. 5145]. Grant was born December 1, 1983, at Stanford, California.

(Sup) 7167 ANNE STAMPLEY LINK (Winston Conway[9], Ogle Winston[8], Albert[7], John[6], Adam[5], Alexander[4], John Adam[3], John Adam[2], John Jacob[1]) was the daughter of Winston Conway and Marilyn Frances (Madden) Link [Supplement No. 5146]. Anne was born September 10, 1971, at Ruston, Louisiana.

(Sup) 7168 MICHAEL ROBERT GEHRET, JR. (Michael^9, Barbara^8, Lester^7, John^6, Alexander^4, John Adam^3, John Adam^2, John Jacob^1) was the son of Michael Robert and Sylvia Louise (Wentzel) Gehret [Supplement No. 5149]. He was born March 4, 1974, at Reading, Pennsylvania.

(Sup) 7169 SHANNON MARIE ARNDT (Nancy^9, Barbara^8, Lester^7, John^6, Alexander^4, John Adam^3, John Adam^2, John Jacob^1) was the daughter of Michael Henry and Nancy (Gehret) Arndt [Supplement No. 5150]. She was born May 13, 1972, at Reading, Pennsylvania.

(Sup) 7170 CHRISTOPHER STEPHEN LINK (Stephen^9, Robert^8, Lester^7, John^6, Adam^5, Alexander^4, John Adam^3, John Adam^2, John Jacob^1) was the son of Stephen Alan and Debra Jean (Turner) Link [Supplement No. 5153]. Christopher was born June 17, 1981, at Salisbury, Maryland.

(Sup) 7171 GREGORY JOHN LINK (John^9, Robert^8, Lester^7, John^6, Adam^5, Alexander^4, John Adam^3, John Adam^2, John Jacob^1) was the son of John Robert and Donna Sue (Anstine) Link [Supplement No. 5154]. Gregory was born March 16, 1981, at Washington, D.C.

(Sup) 7175 ADRIENNE DENISE HESS (John^9, John^8, Irving^7, John^6, Elizabeth^5, Alexander^4, John Adam^3, John Adam^2, John Jacob^1) was the daughter of John Irving and Kimberly Ann (Dougan) Hess [Supplement No. 5160]. She was born June 30, 1980.

(Sup) 7176 JORDAN MATTHEW HESS (John^9, John^8, Irving^7, John^6, Elizabeth^5, Alexander^4, John Adam^3, John Adam^2, John Jacob^1) was the son of John Irving and Kimberly Ann (Dougan) Hess [Supplement No. 5160]. He was born September 1, 1982.

(Sup) 7177 KIMBERLY JANELLE HESS (John^9, John^8, Irving^7, John^6, Elizabeth^5, Alexander^4, John Adam^3, John Adam^2, John Jacob^1) was the daughter of John Irving and Kimberly (Dougan) Hess [Supplement No. 5160]. She was born June 26, 1984.

(Sup) 7178 JARRED CHRISTOPHER PERRY (Catherine^9, John^8, Irving^7, John^6, Elizabeth^5, Alexander^4, John Adam^3, John Adam^2, John Jacob^1) was the son of Edwin and Catharine (Hess) Perry [Supplement No. 5161]. He was born November 27, 1972.

(Sup) 7179 RYAN EDWIN PERRY (Catherine^9, John^8, Irving^7, John^6, Elizabeth^5, Alexander^4, John Adam^3, John Adam^2, John Jacob^1) was the son of Edwin and Catharine (Hess) Perry [Supplement No. 5161]. He was born August 25, 1976.

(Sup) 7180 JUSTIN MICHAEL PERRY (Catherine^9, John^8, Irving^7, John^6, Elizabeth^5, Alexander^4, John Adam^3, John Adam^2, John Jacob^1) was the son of Edwin and Catharine (Hess) Perry [Supplement No. 5161]. He was born September 19, 1979.

(Sup) 7181 LAUREN ELIZABETH PERRY (Catherine^9, John^8, Irving^7, John^6, Elizabeth^5, Alexander^4, John Adam^3, John Adam^2, John Jacob^1) was the daughter of Edwin and Catharine Anne (Hess) Perry [Supplement No. 5161]. She was born July 18, 1981.

(Sup) 7182 MARISSA MICHELE KERSH (Teresa^9, John^8, Irving^7, John^6, Elizabeth^5, Alexander^4, John Adam^3, John Adam^2, John Jacob^1) was the daughter of Anthony and Mary Teresa (Hess) Kersh [Supplement No. 5162]. She was born May 20, 1974.

(Sup) 7183 TARA DENISE KERSH (Teresa^9, John^8, Irving^7, John^6, Elizabeth^5, Alexander^4, John Adam^3, John Adam^2, John Jacob^1) was the daughter of Anthony and Mary Teresa (Hess) Kersh [Supplement No. 5162]. She was born February 20, 1976.

(Sup) 7184 BRIDGETTE TERESA KERSH (Teresa^9, John^8, Irving^7, John^6, Elizabeth^5, Alexander^4, John Adam^3, John Adam^2, John Jacob^1) was the daughter of Anthony and Mary Teresa (Hess) Kersh [Supplement No. 5162]. She was born October 2, 1978.

(Sup) 7185 RICHARD DAWSON KERSH (Teresa^9, John^8, Irving^7, John^6, Elizabeth^5, Alexander^4, John Adam^3, John Adam^2, John Jacob^1) was the son of Anthony and Mary Teresa (Hess) Kersh [Supplement No. 5162]. He was born July 23, 1980.

(Sup) 7186 SEAN MICHAEL SILVA (Patricia^9, John^8, Irving^7, John^6, Elizabeth^5, Alexander^4, John Adam^3, John Adam^2, John Jacob^1) was the son of Stephan and Patricia Irene (Hess) Silva [Supplement No. 5163]. He was born April 29, 1976.

(Sup) 7187 ALICIA KIMBERLY SILVA (Patricia^9, John^8, Irving^7, John^6, Elizabeth^5, Alexander^4, John Adam^3, John Adam^2, John Jacob^1) was the daughter of Stephan and Patricia Irene (Hess) Silva [Supplement No. 5163]. She was born July 14, 1979.

(Sup) 7188 DAMIEN JOHN HESS (Paula^9, (John^9, John^8, Irving^7, John^6, Elizabeth^5, Alexander^4, John Adam^3, John Adam^2, John Jacob^1) was the son of Paula Evelyn Hess [Supplement No. 5164]. He was born December 25, 1977.

(Sup) 7189 DANIELLE DENISE KUEMMERLE (Denise^9, John^8, Irving^7, John^6, Elizabeth^5, Alexander^4, John Adam^3, John Adam^2, John Jacob^1) was the daughter of Daniel and Denise Ellen (Hess) Kuemmerle [Supplement No. 5165]. She was born November 30, 1981.

(Sup) 7190 ADAM MANLEY VICKERS (Cleo^9, John^8, Irving^7, John^6, Elizabeth^5, Alexander^4, John Adam^3, John Adam^2, John Jacob^1) was the son of Gary and Cleo Michele (Hess) Vickers [Supplement No. 5166]. He was born March 31, 1979.

(Sup) 7191 CHRISTA MICHELE VICKERS (Cleo^9, John^8, Irving^7, John^6, Elizabeth^5, Alexander^4, John Adam^3, John Adam^2, John Jacob^1) was the daughter of Gary and Cleo Michele (Hess) Vickers [Supplement No. 5166]. She was born December 17, 1982.

(Sup) 7194 LAUREEN KATHRYN DRAKE (Kathryn^9, Helen^8, Guy^7, John^6, Elizabeth^5, Alexander^4, John Adam^3, John Adam^2, John Jacob^1) was the daughter of William and Kathryn Jones Drake [Supplement No. 5170]. She was born November 6, 1962, at Pearland, Texas. She married Kenneth Armstrong, August 2, 1987, at New Orleans. They resided at Kenner, Louisiana.

(Sup) 8401 i Kenneth Blake Armstrong, born February 21, 1988.

(Sup) 7195 BRIAN WILLIAM DRAKE (Kathryn^9, Helen^8, Guy^7, John^6, Elizabeth^5, Alexander^4, John Adam^3, John Adam^2, John Jacob^1) was the son of William and Kathryn Jones Drake [Supplement No. 5170]. He was born October 25, 1963.

(Sup) 7196 CHERYL MARIE DRAKE (Kathryn^9, Helen^8, Guy^7, John^6, Elizabeth^5, Alexander^4, John Adam^3, John Adam^2, John Jacob^1) was the daughter of William and Kathryn Jones Drake [Supplement No. 5170]. She was born October 16, 1966.

(Sup) 7196A RYAN JORDAN JONES (Jack^9, Helen^8, Guy^7, John^6, Elizabeth^5, Alexander^4, John Adam^3, John Adam^2, John Jacob^1) was the son of Jack Alton and Mona Kaye (McGarrah) Jones [Supplement No. 5172]. He was born October 25, 1984, at Covington, Louisiana.

(Sup) 7196B DEVIN JACOB JONES (Jack^9, Helen^8, Guy^7, John^6, Elizabeth^5, Alexander^4, John Adam^3, John Adam^2, John Jacob^1) was the son of Jack Alton and Mona Kaye (McGarrah) Jones [Supplement No. 5172]. He was born January 9, 1987, at Covington, Louisiana.

(Sup) 7197 ROBERT CLAYTON McCORMICK (Deborah^9, Helen^8, Guy^7, John^6, Elizabeth^5, Alexander^4, John Adam^3, John Adam^2, John Jacob^1) was the son of Deborah Jones McCormick [Supplement No. 5173].

(Sup) 7197A JASON BARRINGER SCHUREN (Deborah^9, Katherine^8, Guy^7, John^6, Elizabeth^5, Alexander^4, John Adam^3, John Adam^2, John Jacob^1) was the son of David Jay and Deborah Watson Schuren [Supplement No. 5177]. Jason was born October 9, 1971, at Pasadena, Texas.

(Sup) 7220 JENNIFER LYNN BROWN (Mary[9], Iris[8], Harriet[7], Mary[6], Elizabeth[5], Alexander[4], John Adam[3], John Adam[2], John Jacob[1]) was the daughter of Charles R. and Mary Katherine (Hawk) Brown [Supplement No. 5202B]. Jennifer was born November 2, 1984, at Martinsburg, West Virginia.

(Sup) 7225 JENNNIFER ELIZABETH HUNTER (James[9], James[8], Ann[7], Nancy[6], John[5], Alexander[4], John Adam[3], John Adam[2], John Jacob[1]) was the daughter of James Osbourn and Joan Swindall Hunter [Supplement No. 5214]. Jennifer was born June 27, 1978, at Huntington, West Virginia.

(Sup) 7226 JULIET KATHRYN HUNTER (James[9], James[8], Ann[7], Nancy[6], John[5], Alexander[4], John Adam[3], John Adam[2], John Jacob[1]) was the daughter of James Osbourn and Joan Swindall Hunter [Supplement No. 5214]. Juliet was born November 4, 1981, at Winchester, West Virginia.

(Sup) 7235 GRACE ASHLEY KERNER (Michele[9], Grace[8], Nancy[7], Adam[6], Thomas[5], Alexander[4], John Adam[3], John Adam[2], John Jacob[1]) was the daughter of Ariel Dan and Michele (Bouvé) Kerner [Supplement No. 5229]. Grace was born January 14, 1983, at Alexandria, Virginia.

(Sup) 7236 KAITLYN MARIE KERNER (Michele[9], Grace[8], Nancy[7], Adam[6], Thomas[5], Alexander[4], John Adam[3], John Adam[2], John Jacob[1]) was the daughter of Ariel Dan and Michele (Bouvé) Kerner [Supplement No. 5229]. Kaitlyn was born May 14, 1984, at Alexandria, Virginia.

(Sup) 7237 STACY LYNN BURR (Gail[9], Janet[8], Charles[7], Walter[6], Ann[5], Alexander[4], John Adam[3], John Adam[2], John Jacob[1]) was the daughter of Allen Hunting and Gail Sharon (Collier) Barr [Supplement No. 5245]. Stacy was born January 10, 1985 at Fairfax City, Virginia.

(Sup) 7238 JUSTIN ALLEN BURR (Gail[9], Janet[8], Charles[7], Walter[6], Ann[5], Alexander[4], John Adam[3], John Adam[2], John Jacob[1]) was the son of Allen Hunting and Gail Sharon (Collier) Burr [Supplement No. 5245]. Justin was born October 14, 1987 at Fairfax City, Virginia.

(Sup) 7198 TORI JOANNE HESS (Barry[9], Guy[8], Guy[7], John[6], Elizabeth[5], Alexander[4], John Adam[3], John Adam[2], John Jacob[1]) was the daughter of Barry Thomas and Cynthia Trammel Hess [Supplement No. 5178]. She was born October 31, 1977.

(Sup) 7199 TERRI SUZANNE HESS (Barry[9], Guy[8], Guy[7], John[6], Elizabeth[5], Alexander[4], John Adam[3], John Adam[2], John Jacob[1]) was the daughter of Barry Thomas and Cynthia Trammel Hess [Supplement No. 5178]. She was born August 9, 1979, at Houston, Texas.

(Sup) 7200 CHRISTOPHER STEPHEN HESS (Daniel[9], Guy[8], Guy[7], John[6], Elizabeth[5], Alexander[4], John Adam[3], John Adam[2], John Jacob[1]) was the son of Daniel Stephen and Vicki Sharp Hess [Supplement No. 5179]. He was born August 13, 1986, at Houston, Texas.

(Sup) 7211 DAVID BLISS (Cheryl[9], Mary Elizabeth[8], Gordon[7], Frank[6], Elizabeth[5], Alexander[4], John Adam[3], John Adam[2], John Jacob[1]) was the son of Edwin D. and Cheryl Johnson Bliss [Supplement No. 5190].

(Sup) 7212 MICHAEL BLISS (Cheryl[9], Mary Elizabeth[8], Gordon[7], Frank[6], Elizabeth[5], Alexander[4], John Adam[3], John Adam[2], John Jacob[1]) was the son of Edwin D. and Cheryl Johnson Bliss [Supplement No. 5190].

(Sup) 7215 LINDSAY DIAHNN GOLDSMITH (Jay[9], Virginia[8], Gordon[7], Frank[6], Elizabeth[5], Alexander[4], John Adam[3], John Adam[2], John Jacob[1]) was the daughter of John Bernard (Jay) and Diahnn Caracciolo Goldsmith [Supplement No. 5193]. Lindsay was born April 24, 1982, at Walnut Creek, California.

(Sup) 7216 ANNE JAYLENE GOLDSMITH (Jay[9], Virginia[8], Gordon[7], Frank[6], Elizabeth[5], Alexander[4], John Adam[3], John Adam[2], John Jacob[1]) was the daughter of John Bernard (Jay) and Diahnn Cariciollo Goldsmith [Supplement No. 5193]. She was born February 28, 1985, at Walnut Creek, California.

Nebraska, in 1984. He married Michelle Bengston, August 9, 1986, at Hastings, Nebraska. She was the daughter of Ivan and Glena Bengston. William and Michelle resided at Bloomington, Minnesota, where he was employed by the Office of the Comptroller of the Currency, and she worked for Traveller Mortgage Services.

(Sup) 7256   BRIAN TAVENNER MOXON (Carla^9, Homer^8, Hazel^7, Angeline^6, Emmanuel^5, Mary^4, John Adam^3, John Adam^2, John Jacob^1) was the son of Kendrick Lichty and Carla Frances (Smith) Moxon [Supplement No. 5258]. Brian was born May 21, 1978, at Washington, D.C.

(Sup) 7257   STACY GROVE MOXON (Carla^9, Homer^8, Hazel^7, Angeline^6, Emmanuel^5, Mary^4, John Adam^3, John Adam^2, John Jacob^1) was the daughter of Kendrick Lichty and Carla Frances (Smith) Moxon [Supplement No. 5258]. She was born December 4, 1979, at Washington, D.C.

(Sup) 7257A   AUDREY MARGARET MOXON (Carla^9, Homer^8, Hazel^7, Angeline^6, Emmanuel^5, Mary^4, John Adam^3, John Adam^2, John Jacob^1) was the daughter of Kendrick Lichty and Carla Frances (Smith) Moxon [Supplement No. 5258]. Audrey was born February 8, 1984, at Washington, D. C.

(Sup) 7258   JONATHAN SMITH KOTLER (Greta^9, Homer^8, Hazel^7, Angeline^6, Emmanuel^5, Mary^4, John Adam^3, John Adam^2, John Jacob^1) was the son of Milton and Greta (Smith) Kotler [Supplement No. 5259]. She was born August 31, 1977, at Washington, D.C.

(Sup) 7259   REBECCA TAVENNER KOTLER (Greta^9, Homer^8, Hazel^7, Angeline^6, Emmanuel^5, Mary^4, John Adam^3, John Adam^2, John Jacob^1) was the daughter of Milton and Greta (Smith) Kotler [Supplement No. 5259]. She was born June 4, 1979, at Washington, D.C.

(Sup) 7260   GREGORY ALLEN NORRIS (Elsa^9, Angeline^8, Hazel^7, Angeline^6, Emmanuel^5, Mary^4, John Adam^3, John Adam^2, John Jacob^1) was the son of Allen Shue and Elsa Ann (Eastwood) Norris [Supplement No. 5261]. Gregory was born March 10, 1963, at Matawan, New Jersey. He graduated from the Massachusetts Institute of Technology in engineering and received a masters degree in aerospace engineering from Purdue University. He was commissioned an officer in the U.S. Air Force. He married Meredith Ann Isaacs, May 17, 1986, at Leesburg, Virginia. She received a degree in nursing from Boston University.

(Sup) 7239   SAMANTHA ASHLEY BELL (Denise^9, Charles^8, Charles^7, Walter^6, Ann^5, Alexander^4, John Adam^3, John Adam^2, John Jacob^1) was the daughter of John and Denise (Harman) Bell [Supplement No. 5245A]. Samantha was born August 28, 1986, at Sellersville, Pennsylvania.

- - - - - - - - - - - - - - - - - -

(Sup) 7251   ROBERT CLARK THOMMEN (Carla^9, Carla^8, Hazel^7, Angeline^6, Emmanuel^5, Mary^4, John Adam^3, John Adam^2, John Jacob^1) was the son of Richard Carl and Carla Lee (Turner) Thommen [Supplement No. 5255]. Robert was born June 3, 1954, at Evanston, Illinois. He was a political science major at San Diego State University and then employed in aluminum sales with Reliance Steel Company, Cerritos, California.

(Sup) 7252   LINDA MARY THOMMEN (Carla^9, Carla^8, Hazel^7, Angeline^6, Emmanuel^5, Mary^4, John Adam^3, John Adam^2, John Jacob^1) was the daughter of Richard Carl and Carla Lee (Turner) Thommen [Supplement No. 5255]. Linda was born January 28, 1957, at Evanston, Illinois. She majored in child development at California Polytechnic University, San Luis Obispo, California. Linda married David L. Carrender, October 1, 1983, at San Diego, California.

(Sup) 7253   LISA MARGARET THOMMEN (Carla^9, Carla^8, Hazel^7, Angeline^6, Emmanuel^5, Mary^4, John Adam^3, John Adam^2, John Jacob^1) was the daughter of Richard Carl and Carla Lee (Turner) Thommen [Supplement No. 5255]. She was born December 13, 1965, at Pasadena, California, and attended high school at San Marino, California.

(Sup) 7254   KATHERINE ANN HAAS (Robert^9, Frances^8, Hazel^7, Angeline^6, Emmanuel^5, Mary^4, John Adam^3, John Adam^2, John Jacob^1) was the daughter of Robert Homer and Mary Alice (Jewell) Haas [Supplement No. 5256]. Kathy was born September 14, 1959, at Creighton, Nebraska. She graduated from Hastings College, Nebraska, in 1981. She married Lindley Charles Warren, July 31, 1982, at Wayne, Nebraska. He was the son of John and Darleen Warren of Tekamah, Nebraska. Katherine and her husband taught music in the public schools of Hastings, Minnesota.

(Sup) 8451   i   Lukas Ryan Warren, born August 21, 1985.

(Sup) 7255   WILLIAM DAVID HAAS (Robert^9, Frances^8, Hazel^7, Angeline^6, Emmanuel^5, Mary^4, John Adam^3, John Adam^2, John Jacob^1) was the son of Robert Homer and Mary Alice (Jewell) Haas [Supplement No. 5256]. William was born June 2, 1962, at Creighton, Nebraska. He graduated from Hastings College,

(Sup) 7261 ANDREW WILLIAM NORRIS (Elsa[9], Angeline[8], Hazel[7], Angeline[6], Emmanuel[5], Mary[4], John Adam[3], John Adam[2], John Jacob[1]) was the son of Allen Shue and Elsa Ann (Eastwood) Norris [Supplement No. 5261]. Andy was born January 10, 1965, at Arlington, Virginia. He graduated from Virginia Polytechnic Institute in Forestry and was employed as a Forestry Consultant at R Raleigh, North Carolina.

(Sup) 7262 KATHLEEN SUE NORRIS (Elsa[9], Angeline[8], Hazel[7], Angeline[6], Emmanuel[5], Mary[4], John Adam[3], John Adam[2], John Jacob[1]) was the daughter of Allen Shue and Elsa Ann (Eastwood) Norris [Supplement No. 5261]. Katie was born December 3, 1969, at Alexandria, Virginia. She majored in drama at Virginia Polytechnic Institute, where she earned a scholarship in theater arts.

(Sup) 7263 JANET ELIZABETH VOSS (Lucille[9], Earl[8], Sarah[7], George[6], Emmanuel[5], Mary[4], John Adam[3], John Adam[2], John Jacob[1]) was the daughter of Earl and Estella Engler Voss [Supplement No. 5263]. Janet was born September 15, 1940.

(Sup) 7264 RALPH GARY VOSS (Lucille[9], Earl[8], Sarah[7], George[6], Emmanuel[5], Mary[4], John Adam[3], John Adam[2], John Jacob[1]) was the son of Earl and Estella Engler Voss [Supplement No. 5263]. Ralph was born September 19, 1941.

(Sup) 7265 BARBARA BETH ZWEILY (Raymond[9], Earl[8], Sarah[7], George[6], Emmanuel[5], Mary[4], John Adam[3], John Adam[2], John Jacob[1]) was the daughter of Raymond and Elizabeth Blum Zwefly [Supplement No. 5264]. Barbara was born October 19, 1942.

(Sup) 7266 THOMAS EARL KARLOVETZ (Marian[9], Earl[8], Sarah[7], George[6], Emmanuel[5], Mary[4], John Adam[3], John Adam[2], John Jacob[1]) was the son of Robert Earl and Marian Zwefly Karlovetz [Supplement No. 5265]. Thomas was born December 16, 1944.

(Sup) 7267 PATRICIA ANN KARLOVETZ (Marian[9], Earl[8], Sarah[7], George[6], Emmanuel[5], Mary[4], John Adam[3], John Adam[2], John Jacob[1]) was the daughter of Robert Earl and Marian Zwefly Karlovetz [Supplement No. 5265]. Patricia was born December 5, 1941.

(Sup) 7268 JANE ARTHUR SHAFER (Donald[9], Clara[8], Sarah[7], George[6], Emmanuel[5], Mary[4], John Adam[3], John Adam[2], John Jacob[1]) was the daughter of Donald and Frances Schnitke Shafer [Supplement No. 5272]. Jane was born December 29, 1946, at Fremont, Ohio.

(Sup) 7269 PAMELA ANN ZWEILY (Kenneth[9], Claude[8], Sarah[7], George[6], Emmanuel[5], Mary[4], John Adam[3], John Adam[2], John Jacob[1]) was the daughter of Kenneth and Janis Zartman Zwefly [Supplement No. 5274].

- -

(Sup) 7275 ERIKA ELLEN SCHLACHTER (Barbara[9], Jeanne[8], James[7], Ida[6], Mary[5], Mary[4], John Adam[3], John Adam[2], John Jacob[1]) was the daughter of Melvin Harlan and Barbara Jeanne (Hartley) Schlachter [Supplement No. 5429]. Erika was born August 11, 1975, at Dobbs Ferry, New York.

(Sup) 7276 JACOB THOMAS SCHLACHTER (Barbara[9], Jeanne[8], James[7], Ida[6], Mary[5], Mary[4], John Adam[3], John Adam[2], John Jacob[1]) was the son of Melvin Harlan and Barbara Jeanne (Hartley) Schlachter [Supplement No. 5429]. Jacob was born May 1, 1980, at White Plains, New York.

(Sup) 7277 MELISSA R. CLEMONS (Martha[9], Ruth[8], James[7], Ida[6], Mary[5], Mary[4], John Adam[3], John Adam[2], John Jacob[1]) was the daughter of Merv and Martha (Meeker) Clemons [Supplement No. 5429C]. Melissa was born April 20, 1970, at Huron, Ohio.

(Sup) 7278 JASON C. STANFIELD (Martha[9], Ruth[8], James[7], Ida[6], Mary[5], Mary[4], John Adam[3], John Adam[2], John Jacob[1]) was the son of Rick and Martha (Meeker) (Clemons) Stanfield [Supplement No. 5429C]. Jason was born September 29, 1973, at Huron, Ohio.

(Sup) 7279 JAMIE D. STIERHOFF (Sandy[9], Wayne[8], James[7], Ida[6], Mary[5], Mary[4], John Adam[3], John Adam[2], John Jacob[1]) was the son of Karl Lloyd and Sandy Joan (Sommer) Stierhoff [Supplement No. 5429E]. Jamie was born March 25, 1974, at Sandusky, Ohio.

(Sup) 7279A BENJAMIN KARL STIERHOFF (Sandy^9, Wayne^8, James^7, Ida^6, Mary^5, John Adam^3, John Adam^2, John Jacob^1) was the son of Karl Lloyd and Sandy Joan (Sommer) Stierhoff [Supplement No. 5429E]. Benjamin was born January 25, 1980, at Sundusky, Ohio.

(Sup) 7279B CASEY MARIE STIERHOFF (Sandy^9, Wayne^8, James^7, Ida^6, Mary^5, John Adam^3, John Adam^2, John Jacob^1) was the daughter of Karl Lloyd and Sandy Joan (Sommer) Stierhoff [Supplement No. 5429E]. Casey was born March 7, 1982, at Sandusky, Ohio.

(Sup) 7280 NICOLE MARIE SOMMER (Todd^9, Wayne^8, James^7, Ida^6, Mary^5, John Adam^3, John Adam^2, John Jacob^1) was the daughter of Todd Clark and Miriam (Grunden) Sommer [Supplement No. 5429F]. Nicole was born July 21, 1978, at Sandusky, Ohio.

(Sup) 7280A RACHEL ARIEN SOMMER (Todd^9, Wayne^8, James^7, Ida^6, Mary^5, John Adam^3, John Adam^2, John Jacob^1) was the daughter of Todd Clark and Miriam (Grunden) Sommer [Supplement No. 5429F]. Rachel was born October 16, 1980, at Sandusky, Ohio.

(Sup) 7280B KAILEE ELIZABETH SOMMER (Todd^9, Wayne^8, James^7, Ida^6, Mary^5, John Adam^3, John Adam^2, John Jacob^1) was the daughter of Todd Clark and Miriam (Grunden) Sommer [Supplement No. 5429F]. She was born October 24, 1985, at Sandusky, Ohio.

(Sup) 7281 AIMEE LYNN BIXLER (Merritt^9, Merritt^8, Marilla^7, Lillie^6, Mary^5, John Adam^3, John Adam^2, John Jacob^1) was the daughter of Merritt C. and Shirley (Wheeler) Bixler [Supplement No. 5430]. Aimee was born January 24, 1976.

(Sup) 7282 PHILIP J. FOSTER (Margaret^9, Merritt^8, Marilla^7, Lillie^6, Mary^5, John Adam^3, John Adam^2, John Jacob^1) was the son of John R. and Margaret (Bixler) Foster [Supplement No. 5430B]. Philip was born February 11, 1985, at Fremont, Ohio.

(Sup) 7283 CARA JEAN FOSTER (Margaret^9, Merritt^8, Marilla^7, Lillie^6, Mary^5, John Adam^3, John Adam^2, John Jacob^1) was the daughter of John R. and Margaret (Bixler) Foster [Supplement No. 5430B]. She was born March 9, 1987, at Fremont, Ohio.

(Sup) 7284 LESLIE A. BIXLER (Lorance^9, Merritt^8, Marilla^7, Lillie^6, Mary^5, John Adam^3, John Adam^2, John Jacob^1) was the child of Lorance H. and Laura (Lorenz) Bixler [Supplement No. 5430C]. Leslie was born February 6, 1984.

(Sup) 7287 JENNY WYNETTE GAMELIN (Ada Jean^9, Ross^8, Ralph^7, Daniel^6, Adam^5, Rebecca^4, John Adam^3, John Adam^2, John Jacob^1) was the daughter of Wayne and Ada Jean (Demory) Gamelin [Supplement No. 5448]. She was born February 25, 1972, at Corpus Christi, Texas.

(Sup) 7288 MICHAEL SHAYNE GEMELIN (Ada Jean^9, Ross^8, Ralph^7, Daniel^6, Adam^5, Rebecca^4, John Adam^3, John Adam^2, John Jacob^1) was the son of Wayne and Ada Jean (Demory) Gamelin [Supplement No. 5448]. He was born May 31, 1975, at Corpus Christi, Texas.

(Sup) 7289 CHRISTINE NICOLE WOLF (Annette^9, Ross^8, Ralph^7, Daniel^6, Adam^5, Rebecca^4, John Adam^3, John Adam^2, John Jacob^1) was the daughter of Gary and Annette (Demory) Wolf [Supplement No. 5448A]. Christine was born May 27, 1981, at Alexander, Louisiana.

(Sup) 7289A ANGELA MARIE WOLF (Annette^9, Ross^8, Ralph^7, Daniel^6, Adam^5, Rebecca^4, John Adam^3, John Adam^2, John Jacob^1) was the daughter of Gary and Annette (Demory) Wolf [Supplement No. 5448A]. Angela was born October 25, 1984, at Fort Worth, Texas.

(Sup) 7289B SARAH ANN WOLF (Annette^9, Ross^8, Ralph^7, Daniel^6, Adam^5, Rebecca^4, John Adam^3, John Adam^2, John Jacob^1) was the daughter of Gary and Annette (Demory) Wolf [Supplement No. 5448A]. Sarah was born December 27, 1987, at Fort Worth, Texas.

(Sup) 7290 BRADY GRAY HODGES (Jeanette^9, Ross^8, Ralph^7, Daniel^6, Adam^5, Rebecca^4, John Adam^3, John Adam^2, John Jacob^1) was the son of Grayson Tillman and Jeanette (Demory) Hodges [Supplement No. 5448B]. He was born June 9, 1981, at Corpus Christi, Texas.

(Sup) 7291 HEATHER DIANE HODGES (Jeanette^9, Ross^8, Ralph^7, Daniel^6, Adam^5, Rebecca^4, John Adam^3, John Adam^2, John Jacob^1) was the daughter of Grayson Tillman and Jeanette (Demory) Hodges [Supplement No. 5448B]. She was born November 12, 1987, at Liberty, Texas.

(Sup) 7292 CHRISTOPHER GLEN MEGASON (Clairece^9, Ina Zoe^8, Ralph^7, Daniel^6, Adam^5, Rebecca^4, John Adam^3, John Adam^2, John Jacob^1) was the son of Glen and Clairece (Harper) Megason [Supplement No. 5450]. Christopher was born February 24, 1978, at Victoria, Texas.

(Sup) 7293 STEFFANIE ANNE ERDELT (Jo Ann^9, Gena^8, Ralph^7, Daniel^6, Adam^5, Rebecca^4, John Adam^3, John Adam^2, John Jacob^1) was the daughter of Leon V. and Jo Ann (Harper) Erdelt, Jr. [Supplement No. 5452]. Steffanie was born May 27, 1983, at Victoria, Texas.

(Sup) 7294 STEPHANIE JAKEWAY (James^9, Earl^8, Alma^7, Daniel^6, Adam^5, Rebecca^4, John Adam^3, John Adam^2, John Jacob^1) was the daughter of James Douglas and Helga (Michaelis) Jakeway [Supplement No. 5455A]. Stephanie was born in 1970.

(Sup) 7295 NICHOLE ERIN OGILVIE (Nancy^9, Earl^8, Alma^7, Daniel^6, Adam^5, Rebecca^4, John Adam^3, John Adam^2, John Jacob^1) was the daughter of Harry John and Nancy (Jakeway) Ogilvie [Supplement No. 5455B]. Nichole was born August 10, 1975.

(Sup) 7296 MICHAEL HOWARD FERGUSON, JR. (Joyce^9, Earl^8, Alma^7, Daniel^6, Adam^5, Rebecca^4, John Adam^3, John Adam^2, John Jacob^1) was the son of Michael Howard and Joyce (Jakeway) Ferguson [Supplement No. 5455C]. Michael Jr. was born November 14, 1974.

(Sup) 7297 BENJAMIN DOUGLAS FERGUSON (Joyce^9, Earl^8, Alma^7, Daniel^6, Adam^5, Rebecca^4, John Adam^3, John Adam^2, John Jacob^1) was the son of Michael Howard and Joyce (Jakeway) Ferguson [Supplement No. 5455C]. Benjamin was born August 15, 1978.

(Sup) 7298 TIFFANY RENEE POWERS (Julia^9, Luetta^8, Alma^7, Daniel^6, Adam^5, Rebecca^4, John Adam^3, John Adam^2, John Jacob^1) was the daughter of Dennis Alvin and Julia (Vowell) Powers [Supplement No. 5457]. She was born October 4, 1984, at Tulsa, Oklahoma.

(Sup) 7299 JOSHUA JAKEWAY (Richard^9, Richard^8, Alma^7, Daniel^6, Adam^5, Rebecca^4, John Adam^3, John Adam^2, John Jacob^1) was the son of Richard Thomas and Corrine Jakeway [Supplement No. 5458].

(Sup) 7300 SARAH JAKEWAY (Richard^9, Richard^8, Alma^7, Daniel^6, Adam^5, Rebecca^4, John Adam^3, John Adam^2, John Jacob^1) was the daughter of Richard Thomas and Corrine Jakeway [Supplement No. 5458].

(Sup) 7301 RAYLENE MARIE JAKEWAY (Mark^9, Richard^8, Alma^7, Daniel^6, Adam^5, Rebecca^4, John Adam^3, John Adam^2, John Jacob^1) was the daughter of Mark Anthony and Sherry Jakeway [Supplement No. 5459]. She was born September 13, 1986, at Denver, Colorado.

(Sup) 7302 LINDSAY RACHEL CADE (Martti^9, Lee^8, Sarah^7, Daniel^6, Adam^5, Rebecca^4, John Adam^3, John Adam^2, John Jacob^1) was the daughter of Randall Wesley and Martti (Matson) Cade [Supplement No. 5460A]. She was born May 26, 1985, at Burbank, California.

(Sup) 7303 JASON LOYD HACKLER (George^9, Loyd^8, Sarah^7, Daniel^6, Adam^5, Rebecca^4, John Adam^3, John Adam^2, John Jacob^1) was the son of George Conley and Shelly (Perra) Hackler [Supplement No. 5461]. He was born April 27, 1975, at Alpine, Texas.

(Sup) 7304 DALLAS WAYNE SCRIBNER, III (Tamara^9, Arthur^8, Sarah^7, Daniel^6, Adam^5, Rebecca^4, John Adam^3, John Adam^2, John Jacob^1) was the son of Dallas Wayne and Tamara (Hackler) Scribner, Jr. [Supplement No. 5463]. Dallas Wayne III was born June 14, 1981, at Ardmore, Oklahoma.

(Sup) 7305 BOBBIE RACHEL SCRIBNER (Tamara^9, Arthur^8, Sarah^7, Daniel^6, Adam^5, Rebecca^4, John Adam^3, John Adam^2, John Jacob^1) was the daughter of Dallas Wayne and Tamara (Hackler) Scribner, Jr. [Supplement No. 5463]. She was born July 26, 1985, at Ardmore, Oklahoma.

(Sup) 7306 ANTHONY JOSEPH MOCERI (Deborah[9], Maxine[8], Sarah[7], Daniel[6], Adam[5], Rebecca[4], John Adam[3], John Adam[2], John Jacob[1]) was the son of Peter Bernard and Deborah (Messina) Moceri [Supplement No. 5466]. He was born October 27, 1978, at Warren, Michigan.

(Sup) 7307 LISA MARIE MOCERI (Deborah[9], Maxine[8], Sarah[7], Daniel[6], Adam[5], Rebecca[4], John Adam[3], John Adam[2], John Jacob[1]) was the daughter of Peter Bernard and Deborah (Messina) Moceri [Supplement No. 5466]. She was born August 7, 1983, at Detroit, Michigan.

(Sup) 7308 JAQUELINE MARIE MESSINA (David[9], Maxine[8], Sarah[7], Daniel[6], Adam[5], Rebecca[4], John Adam[3], John Adam[2], John Jacob[1]) was the daughter of David Joseph and Linda (Yates) Messina [Supplement No. 5466B]. She was born May 31, 1982, at Mt. Clemens, Michigan.

(Sup) 7309 ANDREA CHRISTINE MESSINA (Donald[9], Maxine[8], Sarah[7], Daniel[6], Adam[5], Rebecca[4], John Adam[3], John Adam[2], John Jacob[1]) was the daughter of Donald Dean and Vicki (Thomson) Messina [Supplement No. 5466C]. She was born November 24, 1985, at Grosse Point, Michigan.

(Sup) 7310 ASHLEY LAUREN MESSINA (Douglas[9], Maxine[8], Sarah[7], Daniel[6], Adam[5], Rebecca[4], John Adam[3], John Adam[2], John Jacob[1]) was the daughter of Douglas Drew and Visa (Lenore) Messina [Supplement No. 5466D]. She was born December 12, 1985, at Detroit, Michigan.

(Sup) 7311 SHELLY LYNN REDING (Carolyn[9], Alta[8], Hattie[7], Daniel[6], Adam[5], Rebecca[4], John Adam[3], John Adam[2], John Jacob[1]) was the daughter of Glenn Albert and Carolyn (Worrell) Reding [Supplement No. 5467]. She was born March 11, 1966, at Ponca City, Oklahoma.

(Sup) 7311A SCOTT ALLEN REDING (Carolyn[9], Alta[8], Hattie[7], Daniel[6], Adam[5], Rebecca[4], John Adam[3], John Adam[2], John Jacob[1]) was the son of Glenn Albert and Carolyn (Worrell) Reding [Supplement No. 5467]. He was born March 30, 1967, at Ponca City, Oklahoma.

(Sup) 7311B SHANNON ELAINE REDING (Carolyn[9], Alta[8], Hattie[7], Daniel[6], Adam[5], Rebecca[4], John Adam[3], John Adam[2], John Jacob[1]) was the daughter of Glenn Albert and Carolyn (Worrell) Reding [Supplement No. 5467]. She was born October 14, 1970, at Miami, Oklahoma.

(Sup) 7312 ERIC SHANE PUTNAM (Richard[9], Lee[8], Hattie[7], Daniel[6], Adam[5], Rebecca[4], John Adam[3], John Adam[2], John Jacob[1]) was the son of Richard Lee and Debra Elizabeth (Murphy) Putnam [Supplement No. 5469]. He was the born November 26, 1986.

(Sup) 7313 BRIAN LEE FLETCHER (Elizabeth[9], Daisy[8], Hattie[7], Daniel[6], Adam[5], Rebecca[4], John Adam[3], John Adam[2], John Jacob[1]) was the son of Raymond Lee and Elizabeth (Rogers) Fletcher [Supplement No. 5470]. Brian was born April 14, 1966, at Denton, Texas.

(Sup) 7314 ELISABETH FLETCHER (Elizabeth[9], Daisy[8], Hattie[7], Daniel[6], Adam[5], Rebecca[4], John Adam[3], John Adam[2], John Jacob[1]) was the daughter of Raymond Lee and Elizabeth (Rogers) Fletcher [Supplement No. 5470]. Elisabeth was born August 20, 1970, at Denton, Texas.

(Sup) 7315 SAMUEL HOPKINS ROGERS (Robert[9], Daisy[8], Hattie[7], Daniel[6], Adam[5], Rebecca[4], John Adam[3], John Adam[2], John Jacob[1]) was the son of Robert Jean and Mildred (Hopkins) Rogers, Jr. [Supplement No. 5470B]. He was born September 1, 1984, at Fort Worth, Texas.

(Sup) 7316 REBELLA JANE ROGERS (Robert[9], Daisy[8], Hattie[7], Daniel[6], Adam[5], Rebecca[4], John Adam[3], John Adam[2], John Jacob[1]) was the daughter of Robert Jean and Mildred (Hopkins) Rogers, Jr. [Supplement No. 5470B]. She was born September 15, 1987, at Fort Worth, Texas.

(Sup) 7317 JAMES BRAID LEWIS (Judith[9], Roy[8], Hattie[7], Daniel[6], Adam[5], Rebecca[4], John Adam[3], John Adam[2], John Jacob[1]) was the son of James Koenig and Judith (Putnam) Lewis [Supplement No. 5471]. James was born May 19, 1971, at Sacramento, California.

(Sup) 7332 SARAH ELIZABETH CULLISON (Richard[9], Bonnie[8], Pearl[7], Daniel[6], Adam[5], Rebecca[4], John Adam[3], John Adam[2], John Jacob[1]) was the daughter of Richard Frederick and Patricia (Sommer) Cullison, Jr. [Supplement No. 5481]. She was born August 12, 1982, at Urbana, Illinois.

(Sup) 7333 MEGAN MARIE McCOLLOM (Linda[9], Jesse[8], Pearl[7], Daniel[6], Adam[5], Rebecca[4], John Adam[3], John Adam[2], John Jacob[1]) was the daughter of Walter William and Linda (Putnam) McCollom, III [Supplement No. 5483A]. Megan was born March 30, 1976, at Stillwater, Oklahoma.

(Sup) 7334 VIRGINIA VICTORIA McCOLLOM (Linda[9], Jesse[8], Pearl[7], Daniel[6], Adam[5], Rebecca[4], John Adam[3], John Adam[2], John Jacob[1]) was the daughter of Walter William and Linda (Putnam) McCollom, III [Supplement No. 5483A]. Virginia was born May 9, 1981, at Stillwater, Oklahoma.

(Sup) 7335 ERIC RICHARD STARNES (Ella Fay[9], Georgia[8], Pearl[7], Daniel[6], Adam[5], Rebecca[4], John Adam[3], John Adam[2], John Jacob[1]) was the son of John Ricard and Ella Fay (Jones) Starnes [Supplement No. 5484]. He was born December 6, 1978, at Fort Worth, Texas.

(Sup) 7336 ZACHARY PAUL STARNES (Ella Jay[9], Georgia[8], Pearl[7], Daniel[6], Adam[5], Rebecca[4], John Adam[3], John Adam[2], John Jacob[1]) was the son of John Richard and Ella Fay (Jones) Starnes [Supplement No. 5484]. He was born June 15, 1984, at Fort Worth, Texas.

(Sup) 7337 DAVID EVANS REED, JR. (Anna Jeanne[9], Georgia[8], Pearl[7], Daniel[6], Adam[5], Rebecca[4], John Adam[3], John Adam[2], John Jacob[1]) was the son of David Evans and Anna Jeanne (Jones) Reed [Supplement No. 5485]. David Jr., was born October 8, 1972, at Oklahoma City, Oklahoma.

(Sup) 7338 JOSEPHINE REBECCA REED (Anna Jeanne[9], Georgia[8], Pearl[7], Daniel[6], Adam[5], Rebecca[4], John Adam[3], John Adam[2], John Jacob[1]) was the daughter of David Evans and Anna Jeanne (Jones) Reed [Supplement No. 5485]. She was born September 13, 1975, at Oklahoma City, Oklahoma.

(Sup) 7318 JUSTIN KOENIG LEWIS (Judith[9], Roy[8], Hattie[7], Daniel[6], Adam[5], Rebecca[4], John Adam[3], John Adam[2], John Jacob[1]) was the son of James Koenig and Judith (Putnam) Lewis [Supplement No. 5471]. Justin was born June 30, 1975, at Sacramento, California.

(Sup) 7319 JENNIFER NICOLE PUTNAM (James[9], Roy[8], Hattie[7], Daniel[6], Adam[5], Rebecca[4], John Adam[3], John Adam[2], John Jacob[1]) was the daughter of James Roy and Laura (Johnson) Putnam [Supplement No. 5471A]. Jennifer was born July 20, 1977, at Pinehurst, North Carolina.

(Sup) 7320 GREGORY MICHAEL PUTNAM (James[9], Roy[8], Hattie[7], Daniel[6], Adam[5], Rebecca[4], John Adam[3], John Adam[2], John Jacob[1]) was the son of James Roy and Laura (Johnson) Putnam [Supplement No. 5471A]. Gregory was born July 12, 1981, at Sacramento, California.

(Sup) 7321 DANIEL MICHAEL PUTNAM (Michael[9], Roy[8], Hattie[7], Daniel[6], Adam[5], Rebecca[4], John Adam[3], John Adam[2], John Jacob[1]) was the son of Michael Charles and Dorothy (Hanson) Putnam [Supplement No. 5471B]. Daniel was born December 22, 1977, at Sacramento, California.

(Sup) 7322 ERICK FRANK PUTNAM (Michael[9], Roy[8], Hattie[7], Daniel[6], Adam[5], Rebecca[4], John Adam[3], John Adam[2], John Jacob[1]) was the son of Michael Charles and Dorothy (Hanson) Putnam [Supplement No. 5471B]. Erick was born May 28, 1980, at Sacramento, California.

(Sup) 7323 MEGAN MICHELLE BURGARDT (Cynthia[9], Roy[8], Hattie[7], Daniel[6], Adam[5], Rebecca[4], John Adam[3], John Adam[2], John Jacob[1]) was the daughter of Tom and Cynthia (Putnam) Burgardt [Supplement No. 5471C]. Megan was born September 3, 1986, at Sacramento, California.

(Sup) 7326 DANIEL RAYMOND DAVID (Kaye[9], Rosalie[8], John[7], Daniel[6], Adam[5], Rebecca[4], John Adam[3], John Adam[2], John Jacob[1]) was the son of Verlon Martin and Kaye (Large) Davis [Supplement No. 5474B]. Daniel was born June 12, 1972, at Houma, Louisiana (and was adopted by Verlon Martin Davis November 17, 1981, at Andalusia, Alabama).

(Sup) 7341 IAN WAYNE BOGLEY (Pamela^9, Phyllis^8, Lilbern^7, Wilmer^6, John^5, Rebecca^4, John Adam^3, John Adam^2, John Jacob^1) was the son of Roger Thomas and Pamela Wayne Bogley [Supplement No. 5532]. He was born September 30, 1971, at Lakeside, Arizona.

(Sup) 7342 JUSTIN THOMAS BOGLEY (Pamela^9, Phyllis^8, Lilbern^7, Wilmer^6, John^5, Rebecca^4, John Adam^3, John Adam^2, John Jacob^1) was the son of Roger Thomas and Pamela Colleen Wayne Bogley [Supplement No. 5532]. He was born September 23, 1972, at Lakeside, Arizona.

(Sup) 7343 MATTHEW GEORGE GIONFRIDDO (Barbara^9, Audrey^8, William^7, Adam^6, Ruhama^5, John Adam^4, John Adam^3, John Adam^2, John Jacob^1) was the son of Joseph Orlando and Barbara Cross Gionfriddo [Supplement No. 5549]. Matthew was born February 2, 1977, at Daytona Beach, Florida.

(Sup) 7343A JENNIFER ELLEN GIONFRIDDO (Barbara^9, Audrey^8, William^7, Adam^6, Ruhama^5, John Adam^4, John Adam^3, John Adam^2, John Jacob^1) was the daughter of Joseph Orlando and Barbara Cross Gionfriddo [Supplement No. 5549]. Jennifer was born February 23, 1979, at Daytona Beach, Florida.

(Sup) 7343B LINDSEY RAE GIONFRIDDO (Barbara^9, Audrey^8, William^7, Adam^6, Ruhama^5, John Adam^4, John Adam^3, John Adam^2, John Jacob^1) was the daughter of Joseph Orlando and Barbara Cross Gionfriddo [Supplement No. 5549]. Lindse was born August 4, 1981, at Daytona Beach, Florida.

(Sup) 7344 BENJAMIN JAY CROSS (Jay^9, Audrey^8, William^7, Adam^6, Ruhama^5, John Adam^4, John Adam^3, John Adam^2, John Jacob^1) was the son Jay Vernon and Peggy Wentz Cross [Supplement No. 5550]. Benjamin was born July 27, 1973, at Daytona Beach, Florida.

(Sup) 7344A RENE' MARIE CROSS (Jay^9, Audrey^8, William^7, Adam^6, Ruhama^5, John Adam^4, John Adam^3, John Adam^2, John Jacob^1) was the daughter of Jay Vernon and Peggy Wentz Cross [Supplement No. 5550]. Rene' was born December 3, 1978, at De Land, Florida.

(Sup) 7344B RACHEL NICOLE CROSS (Jay^9, Audrey^8, William^7, Adam^6, Ruhama^5, John Adam^4, John Adam^3, John Adam^2, John Jacob^1) was the daughter of Jay Vernon and Peggy Wentz Cross [Supplement No. 5550]. Rachel was born June 10, 1981, at De Land, Florida.

(Sup) 7344C JESSE WILLIAM CROSS (Jay^9, Audrey^8, William^7, Adam^6, Ruhama^5, John Adam^4, John Adam^3, John Adam^2, John Jacob^1) was the son of Jay Vernon and Peggy Wentz Cross [Supplement No. 5550]. Jesse was born January 27, 1983, at De Land, Florida.

(Sup) 7345 JEREMY SHAWN HIETT (Jan Kenneth^9, Reta^8, Edith^7, Ambrose^6, Ruhama^5, John Adam^4, John Adam^3, John Adam^2, John Jacob^1) was the son of Jan Kenneth and Victoria McAllister Hiett [Supplement No. 5552]. Jeremy was born October 7, 1977, at Hagerstown, Maryland.

(Sup) 7346 CHRISTINA LEIGH HIETT (Jan Kenneth^9, Reta^8, Edith^7, Ambrose^6, Ruhama^5, John Adam^4, John Adam^3, John Adam^2, John Jacob^1) was the daughter of Jan Kenneth and Victoria McAllister Hiett [Supplement No. 5552]. Christina was born August 11, 1981, at Hagerstown, Maryland.

(Sup) 7347 ZACHARY ALEXANDER SISKIND (Susan^9, Rita^8, Edith^7, Ambrose^6, Ruhama^5, John Adam^4, John Adam^3, John Adam^2, John Jacob^1) was the son of Jules Marc and Susan Hiett Siskind [Supplement No. 5553]. He was born February 12, 1987, at Baltimore, Maryland.

- -

(Sup) 7349 LISA LEIGH BOYD (Saundra^9, Daniel^8, Daniel^7, Nora^6, Daniel^5, John Adam^4, John Adam^3, John Adam^2, John Jacob^1) was the daughter of Larry and Saundra Ann (Nichols) Boyd [Supplement No. 5565]. Lisa was born October 24, 1968.

(Sup) 7350 MISCHELLE RENAE THOMAS (Deborah^9, Daniel^8, Daniel^7, Nora^6, Daniel^5, John Adam^4, John Adam^3, John Adam^2, John Jacob^1) was the daughter of Gary and Deborah (Nichols) Thomas [Supplement No. 5566]. Mischelle was born April 14, 1972, at Winchester, Virginia.

(Sup) 7351 CLINT DANIEL THOMAS (Deborah^9, Daniel^8, Daniel^7, Nora^6, Daniel^5, John Adam^4, John Adam^3, John Adam^2, John Jacob^1) was the son of Gary Wayne and Deborah Nichols Thomas [Supplement No. 5566]. Clint was born August 26, 1974, at Winchester, Virginia.

(Sup) 7352 MATTHEW ROBERT HENRIKSEN (Sheeree^9, Joyce^8, Daniel^7, Nora^6, Daniel^5, John Adam^4, John Adam^3, John Adam^2, John Jacob^1) was the son of Stanley Robert and Sheeree Sue Moore Henriksen [Supplement No. 5569]. Matthew was born May 9, 1984, at Fairfax, Virginia.

(Sup) 7370 MATTHEW PAUL ACKERMAN (James^9, Patricia^8, Margery^7, Harvey^6, Sarah^5, John Adam^4, John Adam^3, John Adam^2, John Jacob^1) was the son of Paul and Janis Huber Ackerman [Supplement No. 5594A]. Matthew was born May 30, 1981.

(Sup) 7375 LAURIE LYN HERCHENROEDER (David^9, Ann^8, Kenneth^7, Esther^6, Sarah^5, John Adam^4, John Adam^3, John Adam^2, John Jacob^1) was the daughter of David Kenneth and Georganna Rogers Herchenroeder [Supplement No. 5600C]. Laurie Lyn was born March 22, 1977.

(Sup) 7376 LISA MARIE HERCHENROEDER (David^9, Ann^8, Kenneth^7, Esther^6, Sarah^5, John Adam^4, John Adam^3, John Adam^2, John Jacob^1) was the daughter of David Kenneth and Georganna Rogers Herchenroeder [Supplement No. 5600C]. She was born August 8, 1979.

(Sup) 7377 DOUGLAS DAVID HERCHENROEDER (David^9, Ann^8, Kenneth^7, Esther^6, Sarah^5, John Adam^4, John Adam^3, John Adam^2, John Jacob^1) was the son of David Kenneth and Georganna Rogers Herchenroeder [Supplement No. 5600C]. Douglas was born July 16, 1983.

(Sup) 7378 ANN MARIE HERCHENROEDER (Michael^9, Ann^8, Kenneth^7, Esther^6, Sarah^5, John Adam^4, John Adam^3, John Adam^2, John Jacob^1) was the daughter of Michael Lee and Rita Joseph Herchenroeder [Supplement No. 5600D]. Ann Marie was born January 1, 1979.

(Sup) 7379 DANIEL JAMES HERCHENROEDER (James^9, Ann^8, Kenneth^7, Esther^6, Sarah^5, John Adam^4, John Adam^3, John Adam^2, John Jacob^1) was the son of James Stephen and Rita Osterfeld Herchenroeder [Supplement No. 5600G]. Daniel was born May 5, 1981.

(Sup) 7380 WILLIAM STEPHEN HERCHENROEDER (James^9, Ann^8, Kenneth^7, Esther^6, Sarah^5, John Adam^4, John Adam^3, John Adam^2, John Jacob^1) was the son of James Stephan and Rita Osterfeld Herchenroeder [Supplement No. 5600G]. William was born July 20, 1984.

(Sup) 7381 KYMBERLY LYNN STEVENS (Douglas^9, Rebecca^8, Rebecca^7, Le Roy^6, Sarah^5, John Adam^4, John Adam^3, John Adam^2, John Jacob^1) was the daughter of Douglas Woody and Penelope Secord Stevens, Jr. [Supplement No. 5601]. Kymberly was born July 10, 1982, at Philadelphia, Pennsylvania.

(Sup) 7391 MEREDITH NICOLE ENNIS (Robert^9, Alvin^8, Mary^7, Daniel^6, Sarah^5, John Adam^4, John Adam^3, John Adam^2, John Jacob^1) was the daughter of Robert Meredith and Tina (Smallwood) Ennis [Supplement No. 5615]. She was born November 20, 1983, at Ranson, Jefferson County, West Virginia.

(Sup) 7391A REBECCA McAMIS POND (Diana^9, Edward^8, Anna^7, Daniel^6, Sarah^5, John Adam^4, John Adam^3, John Adam^2, John Jacob^1) was the daughter of Richard Allen and Diana (McAmis) Pond [Supplement No. 5617]. Rebecca was born March 18, 1979, at Clinton, Maryland.

(Sup) 7392 CHRISTINE MARIE WALLMEYER (Cynthia^9, Bruce^8, Esther^7, Daniel^6, Sarah^5, John Adam^4, John Adam^3, John Adam^2, John Jacob^1) was the daughter of John. Mark and Cynthia Diane (Crane) Wallmeyer [Supplement No. 5619]. Christine was born May 21, 1979.

(Sup) 7393 STEPHANIE LYNN CRANE (Glen^9, Bruce^8, Esther^7, Daniel^6, Sarah^5, John Adam^4, Johr. Adam^3, John Adam^2, John Jacob^1) was the daughter of Glen Elmo and Jamela Kaye (Wright) Crane [Supplement No. 5620]. Stephanie was born June 16, 1979.

(Sup) 7438 THOMAS CRAMER MICHAEL, JR. (Anne^9, Edith^8, Charles^7, Charles^6, Daniel^5, Elizabeth^4, Thomas^3, John Adam^2, John Jacob^1) was the son of Thomas Cramer and Anne (Gearinger) Michael [Supplement No. 5706]. Thomas, Jr., was born May 18, 1941, at Frederick, Maryland.

(Sup) 7439 CONNIE SUE MICHAEL (Anne^9, Edith^8, Charles^7, Charles^6, Daniel^5, Elizabeth^4, Thomas^3, John Adam^2, John Jacob^1) was the daughter of Thomas Cramer and Anne (Gearinger) Michael [Supplement No. 5706]. Connie Sue was born June 1, 1942, at Frederick, Maryland.

(Sup) 7440 CHARLES MICHAEL GEARINGER (Charles^9, Edith^8, Charles^7, Charles^6, Daniel^5, Elizabeth^4, Thomas^3, John Adam^2, John Jacob^1) was the son of Charles and Martha (Biser) Gearinger [Supplement No. 5707]. He was born July 4, 1947, at Frederick, Maryland.

(Sup) 7441 DONNIE DEAN MOSIER (Chester^9, Cecelia^8, Nannie^7, Charles^6, Daniel^5, Elizabeth^4, Thomas^3, John Adam^2, John Jacob^1) was the son of Chester and Doris (Hogenbaugh) Mosier [Supplement No. 5710]. Donnie was born October 23, 1946.

(Sup) 7446 MELINDA JEAN POE (Russell^9, Ethel^8, Lewis^7, Adam^6, Daniel^5, Adam^4, Daniel^3, John Adam^2, John Jacob^1) was the daughter of Russell William and Victoria Ann (Wargo) Poe [Supplement No. 5737]. She was born in 1978.

(Sup) 7447 AARON LINK ROMNEY (Donald^9, Mary Elizabeth^8, Eugene^7, Adam^6, Daniel^5, Adam^4, Daniel^3, John Adam^2, John Jacob^1) was the son of Donald Main and Audrey (King) Romney, Jr. [Supplement No. 5738]. Aaron was born May 26, 1978 at Fairfax, Virginia.

(Sup) 7448 KYLE JAMES MITCHELL (James^9, Jean Ellen^8, Eugene^7, Adam^6, Daniel^5, Adam^4, Daniel^3, John Adam^2, John Jacob^1) was the son of James Dawson and Jean (Link) Mitchell [Supplement No. 3442]. He was born January 21, 1983, Baltimore County, Maryland.

(Sup) 7394 DOUGLAS TRUEN HENRY (Margaret^9, Reva^8, Esther^7, Daniel^6, Sarah^5, John Adam^4, John Adam^3, John Adam^2, John Jacob^1) was the son of William E. and Margaret Ann (Hoover) Henry, Jr. [Supplement No. 5621]. Douglas was born October 27, 1966, at Hagerstown, Maryland.

(Sup) 7395 CHRISTOPHER LOWELL BREWER (Patrick^9, Hilda^8, Esther^7, Daniel^6, Sarah^5, John Adam^4, John Adam^3, John Adam^2, John Jacob^1) was the son of Patrick Lowell and Elizabeth Catherine (Henry) Brewer [Supplement No. 5623]. Christopher was born June 29, 1973, in South Carolina.

(Sup) 7410 DARA LANE ENGLEBRIGHT (Cynthia^9, Daniel^8, Daniel^7, Daniel^6, Sarah^5, John Adam^4, John Adam^3, John Adam^2, John Jacob^1) was the daughter of Kevin and Cynthia (Hendricks) Englebright [Supplement No. 5640]. Dara was born December 4, 1982, at Martinsburg, West Virginia.

(Sup) 7411 MATTHEW GLENN POTTER (Jeffrey^9, Sarah^8, Daniel^7, Daniel^6, Sarah^5, John Adam^4, John Adam^3, John Adam^2, John Jacob^1) was the son of Jeffrey Glen and Carol (Lemka) Potter [Supplement No. 5642]. Matthew was born July 24, 1983, at Pasadena, California.

(Sup) 7430 BEVERLY JEAN McPHERSON (Louis^9, Sarah^8, Evelyn^7, Iva^6, Israel^5, Jacob^4, John Adam^3, John Adam^2, John Jacob^1) was the daughter of Louis Albert McPherson [Supplement No. 5663]. Beverly Jean was born July 3, 1946, at Tulsa, Oklahoma.

(Sup) 7436 BYRON PAUL GREENE (David^9, Edith^8, Mabel^7, Calvin^6, Daniel^5, Elizabeth^4, Thomas^3, John Adam^2, John Jacob^1) was the son of David Paul and Margaret (Garner) Greene [Supplement No. 5703]. Byron was born August 1, 1945, at Baltimore, Maryland.

(Sup) 7437 CAROL ANN GREENE (David^9, Edith^8, Mabel^7, Calvin^6, Daniel^5, Elizabeth^4, Thomas^3, John Adam I^2, John Jacob^1) was the daughter of David Paul and Margaret (Garner) Greene [Supplement No. 5703]. Carol Ann was born January 4, 1947, at Chicago, Illinois.

(Sup) 7449 CARLY JANEEN MITCHELL (James^9, Jean Ellen^8, Eugene^7, Adam^6, Daniel^5, Adam^4, Daniel^3, John Adam^2, John Jacob^1) was the daughter of James Dawson and Jean (Link) Mitchell [Supplement No. 3442]. She was born January 11, 1985, Baltimore County, Maryland.

(Sup) 7450 KENNETH DAVID MITCHELL (David^9, Jean Ellen^8, Eugene^7, Adam^6, Daniel^5, Adam^4, Daniel^3, John Adam^2, John Jacob^1) was the son of David Bowers and Barbara (Casciotti) Mitchell [Supplement No. 5741]. Kenneth was born April 24, 1986.

(Sup) 7451 LINDSAY JANE KOENIG (Henry^9, Jane^8, Marie^7, Adam^6, Daniel^5, Adam^4, Daniel^3, John Adam^2, John Jacob^1) was the daughter of Henry Adolph and Julia Ann (Halls) Koenig, IV [Supplement No. 5743]. Lindsay was born May 5, 1987, at Salisbury, Maryland.

(Sup) 7460 B. A. VAN PELT, III (B.A.^{9}, Janie^8, Rosa^7, Junius^6, Elizabeth^5, John^4, Peter^3, Matthias^2, John Jacob^1) was the son of B.A. Van Pelt, Jr. [Supplement No. 5756].

(Sup) 7461 BARRY NEIL VAN PELT (B.A.^{9}, Janie^8, Rosa^7, Junius^6, Elizabeth^5, John^4, Peter^3, Matthias^2, John Jacob^1) was the son of B.A. Van Pelt, Jr. [Supplement No. 5756].

(Sup) 7462 STUART VAN PELT, JR. (Stuart^9, Janie^8, Rosa^7, Junius^6, Elizabeth^5, John^4, Peter^3, Matthias^2, John Jacob^1) was the son of Stuart Van Pelt [Supplement No. 5757].

(Sup) 7466 DONNA MAE SANDERS (Dallas^9, Hazel^8, Alberta^7, Elizabeth^6, Daniel^5, John^4, Peter^3, Matthias^2, John Jacob^1) was the daughter of Dallas Melvin and Sybella Slonike Sanders [Supplement 5772]. Donna Mae was born in 1936.

(Sup) 7467 JO ANNE SANDERS (Dallas^9, Hazel^8, Alberta^7, Elizabeth^6, Daniel^5, John^4, Peter^3, Matthias^2, John Jacob^1) was the daughter of Dallas Melvin and Sybella Slonike Sanders [Supplement No. 5772]. Jo Anne was born in 1937.

(Sup) 7468 ELIZABETH SANDERS (Charles^9, Hazel^8, Alberta^7, Elizabeth^6, Daniel^5, John^4, Peter^3, Matthias^2, John Jacob^1) was the daughter of Charles Preston and Margaret Quain Sanders [Supplement No. 5773]. Elizabeth was born in 1930.

(Sup) 7469 CAROL ANN DUHN (Louella^9, Hazel^8, Alberta^7, Elizabeth^6, Daniel^5, John^4, Peter^3, Matthias^2, John Jacob^1) was the daughter of Lars Russell and Louella Senders Duhn [Supplement No. 5775].

(Sup) 7470 CLIFFORD ALLEN DUHN (Louella^9, Hazel^8, Alberta^7, Elizabeth^6, Daniel^5, John^4, Peter^3, Matthias^2, John Jacob^1) was the son of Lars Russell and Louella Sanders Duhn [Supplement No. 5775]. Clifford was born August 5, 1935, at Devils Lake, North Dakota.

(Sup) 7471 LARRY REND DUHN (Louella^9, Hazel^8, Alberta^7, Elizabeth^6, Daniel^5, John^4, Peter^3, Matthias^2, John Jacob^1) was the son of Lars Russell and Louella Sanders Duhn [Supplement No. 5775]. Larry was born June 20, 1945, at Long Beach, California.

(Sup) 7472 ILAINE MARIE MONAGHAN (Kathryn^9, Rilla^8, Alberta^7, Elizabeth^6, Daniel^5, John^4, Peter^3, Matthias^2, John Jacob^1) was the daughter of William and Kathryn Gibson Monaghan [Supplement No. 5776]. Ilaine was born March 21, 1936.

(Sup) 7473 WILLIAM DUANE MONAGHAN (Kathryn^9, Rilla^8, Alberta^7, Elizabeth^6, Daniel^5, John^4, Peter^3, Matthias^2, John Jacob^1) was the son of William and Kathryn Gibson Monaghan [Supplement No. 5776]. He was born September 12, 1937.

(Sup) 7474 SHIRLEY ANN MONAGHAN (Kathryn^9, Rilla^8, Alberta^7, Elizabeth^6, Daniel^5, John^4, Peter^3, Matthias^2, John Jacob^1) was the daughter of William and Kathryn Gibson Monaghan [Supplement No. 5776]. Shirley was born October 25, 1938.

(Sup) 7475 DOUGLAS LE ROY MONAGHAN (Kathryn^9, Rilla^8, Alberta^7, Elizabeth^6, Daniel^5, John^4, Peter^3, Matthias^2, John Jacob^1) was the son of William and Kathryn Gibson Monaghan [Supplement No. 5776]. Douglas was born March 1, 1944, and died that day.

(Sup) 7476 GERALD JEROME MONAGHAN (Kathryn⁹, Rilla⁸, Alberta⁷, Elizabeth⁶, Daniel⁵, John⁴, Peter³, Matthias², John Jacob¹) was the son of William and Kathryn Gibson Monaghan [Supplement No. 5776]. Gerald was born May 15, 1947.

(Sup) 7477 DAVID LOUIS GIBSON (Eileen⁹, Rilla⁸, Alberta⁷, Elizabeth⁶, Daniel⁵, John⁴, Peter³, Matthias², John Jacob¹) was the son of Eileen Isabell Gibson [Supplement No. 5781]. David was born April 19, 1942, at Devils Lake, North Dakota. He was adopted by her cousins Velma and Paul Axtman.

(Sup) 7478 FRANK ALLEN FISHBURNE, JR. (Frank⁹, Virginia⁸, Albertine⁷, Elizabeth⁶, Daniel⁵, John⁴, Peter³, Matthias², John Jacob¹) was the son of Frank Allen and Elaine Bailey Fishburne [Supplement No. 5784]. Frank, Jr., was born April 1, 1946, at Mobile, Alabama.

(Sup) 7479 ROBERT PAUL ANDERSON, Jr. Martha⁹, William⁸, Annie⁷, Elizabeth⁶, Daniel⁵, John⁴, Peter³, Matthias², John Jacob¹) was the son of Robert and Martha Shumate Anderson [Supplement No. 5787]. Robert, Jr., was born September 24, 1939, at Youngstown, Ohio.

(Sup) 7484 ROBERT EVANS KINCHELOE (Edith⁹, Otis⁸, Emma⁷, Margaret⁶, Daniel⁵, John⁴, Peter³, Matthias², John Jacob¹) was the son of Jack Evans and Edith Tutwiler Kincheloe [Supplement No. 5822]. Robert was born September 18, 1941, at Charlottesville, Virginia.

(Sup) 7485 STEPHEN RICHARD KINCHELOE (Edith⁹, Otis⁸, Emma⁷, Margaret⁶, Daniel⁵, John⁴, Peter³, Matthias², John Jacob¹) was the son of Jack Evans and Edith Tutwiler Kincheloe [Supplement No. 5822].

(Sup) 7494 WILLIAM HARLAN DEAN, JR. (Maxine⁹, Hazel⁸, Joseph⁷, John⁶, John⁵, John⁴, Peter³, Matthias², John Jacob¹) was the son of William Harlan and Maxine Landes Dean [Supplement No. 5877].

(Sup) 7495 LARRY BERKLEY SNYDER (Bernice⁹, Hazel⁸, Joseph⁷, John⁶, John⁵, John⁴, Peter³, Matthias², John Jacob¹) was the son of Hugh Berkley and Bernice Landes Snyder [Supplement No. 5878]. Larry was born June 3, 1949, at Harrisonburg, Virginia.

(Sup) 7498 SUSAN BARNES (Arthur⁹, Helen⁸, Otey⁷, Elizabeth⁶, Susan⁵, John⁴, Peter³, Matthias², John Jacob¹) was the daughter of Arthur Milton and Grace (Miller) Barnes, Jr. [Supplement No. 5892]. Susan was born January 12, 1950, at Pittsburgh, Pennsylvania. She married Charles Vanaman June 9, 1969, at Dover, Delaware. He was the son of Robert G. and Doris Newconb Vanaman and was born September 15, 1952, at Georgetown, Delaware.

(Sup) 8551   i Cindi S. Vanaman, born August 6, 1969.

(Sup) 7499 DONALD BARNES (Arthur⁹, Helen⁸, Otey⁷, Elizabeth⁶, Susan⁵, John⁴, Peter³, Matthias², John Jacob¹) was the son of Arthur Milton and Grace (Miller) Barnes, Jr. [Supplement No. 5892]. Donald was born April 28, 1952, at Pittsburgh, Pennsylvania. He married Ann Kaminski June 26, 1976, at LaPorte, Indiana. She was the daughter of Leon and Norma Lynn Kaminski and was born October 27 1953, at LaPorte.

(Sup) 7500 VICKI BARNES (Arthur⁹, Helen⁸, Otey⁷, Elizabeth⁶, Susan⁵, John⁴, Peter³, Matthias², John Jacob¹) was the daughter of Arthur Milton and Grace (Miller) Barnes, Jr. [Supplement No. 5892]. Vicki was born May 8, 1959, at Pittsburgh, Pennsylvania.

(Sup) 7501 LAURA BARNES (Robert⁹, Helen⁸, Otey⁷, Elizabeth⁶, Susan⁵, John⁴, Peter³, Matthias², John Jacob¹) was the daughter of Robert Crawford and Frances (Stridinger) Barnes [Supplement No. 5893]. Laura was born January 19, 1959, in New York City.

(Sup) 7502 JEFFREY BARNES (Robert⁹, Helen⁸, Otey⁷, Elizabeth⁶, Susan⁵, John⁴, Peter³, Matthias², John Jacob¹) was the son of Robert Crawford and Frances (Stridinger) Barnes [Supplement No. 5893]. Jeffrey was born August 11, 1962, at Nashville, Tennessee.

(Sup) 7505 JOHN MARSHALL MEYERS (Barbara^9, Thelma^8, John^7, Elizabeth^6, Susan^5, John^4, Peter^3, Matthias^2, John Jacob^1) was the son of Norman Marshall and Barbara Anne (Meyer) Meyers [Supplement No. 5901]. John was born March 24, 1970, at Washington, D.C.

(Sup) 7506 EDWARD HULVEY MEYERS (Barbara^9, Thelma^8, John^7, Elizabeth^6, Susan^5, John^4, Peter^3, Matthias^2, John Jacob^1) was the son of Norman Marshall and Barbara Anne (Meyer) Meyers [Supplement No. 5901]. Edward was born October 7, 1972, at Washington, D.C.

(Sup) 7507 MICHAEL JOSEPH MORRIS, III (Virginia^9, Thelma^8, John^7, Elizabeth^6, Susan^5, John^4, Peter^3, Mathias^2, John Jacob^1) was the son of Michael Joseph and Virginia (Meyer) Morris, Jr. [Supplement No. 5902]. Michael, III, was born October 21, 1968, in Pennsylvania.

(Sup) 7508 CHRISTOPHER MOHR STEINBACH (Martha^9, Thelma^8, John^7, Elizabeth^6, Susan^5, John^4, Peter^3, Matthias^2, John Jacob^1) was the son of Robert Arthur and Martha (Meyer) Steinback [Supplement No. 5903]. Christopher was born February 3, 1968, at Bay Shore, New York.

(Sup) 7509 LESLEY WOODWARD STEINBACH (Martha^9, Thelma^8, John^7, Elizabeth^6, Susan^5, John^4, Peter^3, Matthias^2, John Jacob^1) was the daughter of Robert Arthur and Martha (Meyer) Steinbach [Supplement No. 5903]. Lesley was born February 3, 1968, at Bay Shore, New York.

(Sup) 7510 SARAH MEYER STEINBACH (Martha^9, Thelma^8, John^7, Elizabeth^6, Susan^5, John^4, Peter^3, Matthias^2, John Jacob^1) was the daughter of Robert Arthur and Martha (Meyer) Steinbach [Supplement No. 5903]. Sarah was born December 17, 1973, at New Brunswick, New Jersey.

(Sup) 7511 FRANK CHARLES MEYER, V (Frank^9, Thelma^8, John^7, Elizabeth^6, Susan^5, John^4, Peter^3, Matthias^2, John Jacob^1) was the son of Frank Charles and Elizabeth Anne (Dressler) Meyer, IV [Supplement No. 5905]. Frank, V, was born April 22, 1983.

(Sup) 7512 ELIZABETH KELSEY HULVEY (John Thomas^9, John William^8, John^7, Elizabeth^6, Susan^5, John^4, Peter^3, Matthias^2, John Jacob^1) was the daughter of John Thomas and Elizabeth (Kelsey) Hulvey [Supplement No. 5906]. Elizabeth was born April 2, 1969, at Abingdon, Virginia.

(Sup) 7513 MARGARET LEWIS HULVEY (John Thomas^9, John William^8, John^7, Elizabeth^6, Susan^5, John^4, Peter^3, Matthias^2, John Jacob^1) was the daughter of John Thomas and Elizabeth (Kelsey) Hulvey [Supplement No. 5906]. Margaret was born March 2, 1971, at Abingdon, Virginia.

(Sup) 7514 JOHN THOMAS HULVEY, JR. (John Thomas^9, John William^8, John^7, Elizabeth^6, Susan^5, John^4, Peter^3, Matthias^2, John Jacob^1) was the son of John Thomas and Elizabeth (Kelsey) Hulvey [Supplement No. 5906]. He was born June 8, 1972, at Abingdon, Virginia.

(Sup) 7515 MICHAEL HULVEY (Larry^9, John William^8, John^7, Elizabeth^6, Susan^5, John^4, Peter^3, Matthias^2, John Jacob^1) was the son of Larry William and Judy (Hensley) Hulvey [Supplement No. 5907]. Michael was born November 9, 1973, at Brunswick, Georgia.

(Sup) 7516 JONATHAN PATRICK HULVEY (Larry^9, John William^8, John^7, Elizabeth^6, Susan^5, John^4, Peter^3, Matthias^2, John Jacob^1) was the son of Larry William and Judy (Hensley) Hulvey [Supplement No. 5907]. He was born October 31, at Jesup, Georgia.

- -

(Sup) 7519 ALAN DALE HULVEY (Robert^9, Benjamin^8, Benjamin^7, Elizabeth^6, Susan^5, John^4, Peter^3, Matthias^2, John Jacob^1) was the son of Robert Dale and Joyce (Wine) Hulvey [Supplement No. 5911].

(Sup) 7520 KEMPER FRANKLIN HULVEY (Robert^9, Benjamin^8, Benjamin^7, Elizabeth^6, Susan^5, John^4, Peter^3, Matthias^2, John Jacob^1) was the son of Robert Dale and Joyce (Wine) Hulvey [Supplement No. 5911].

(Sup) 7521 JUDITH LEE HULVEY (Robert^9, Benjamin^8, Benjamin^7, Elizabeth^6, Susan^5, John^4, Peter^3, Matthias^2, John Jacob^1) was the daughter of Robert Dale and Joyce (Wine) Hulvey [Supplement No. 5911].

(Sup) 7522 NEAL EDWARD HEWITT (Nancy^9, Benjamin^8, Benjamin^7, Elizabeth^6, Susan^5, John^4, Peter^3, Matthias^2, John Jacob^1) was the son of Clay Edward and Nancy (Hulvey) Hewitt [Supplement No. 5912]. Neal married Ruth Ann Taylor.

(Sup) 8571 i Darby Lynn Hewitt.
(Sup) 8572 ii Clinton Edward Hewitt.

(Sup) 7523 DENNIS CLAY HEWITT (Nancy^9, Benjamin^8, Benjamin^7, Elizabeth^6, Susan^5, John^4, Peter^3, Matthias^2, John Jacob^1) was the son of Clay Edward and Nancy (Hulvey) Hewitt [Supplement No. 5912].

(Sup) 7524 JERRY NELSON HEWITT (Nancy^9, Benjamin^8, Benjamin^7, Elizabeth^6, Susan^5, John^4, Peter^3, Matthias^2, John Jacob^1) was the son of Clay Edward and Nancy (Hulvey) Hewitt [Supplement No. 5912]. Jerry married Virginia Dawn Swartz.

(Sup) 7525 KATHY HEWITT (Nancy^9, Benjamin^8, Benjamin^7, Elizabeth^6, Susan^5, John^4, Peter^3, Matthias^2, John Jacob^1) was the daughter of Clay Edward and Nancy (Hulvey) Hewitt [Supplement No. 5912].

(Sup) 7526 JANICE CHRISTINE McCRAY (Anna Virginia^9, Benjamin^8, Benjamin^7, Elizabeth^6, Susan^5, John^4, Peter^3, Matthias^2, John Jacob^1) was the daughter of Willis Earl and Anna Virginia (Hulvey) McCray [Supplement No. 5913]. Janice married John Barre. They were divorced.

(Sup) 7527 WILLIS EARL McCRAY, JR. (Anna Virginia^9, Benjamin^8, Benjamin^7, Elizabeth^6, Susan^5, John^4, Peter^3, Matthias^2, John Jacob^1) was the son of Willis Earl and Anna Virginia (Hulvey) McCray [Supplement No. 5913]. Willis, Jr., married Rhonda Fulwider.

(Sup) 8581 i Amber Diane McCray.
(Sup) 8582 ii Holly Kristine McCray.

(Sup) 7528 JULIA ANN McCRAY (Anna Virginia^9, Benjamin^8, Benjamin^7, Elizabeth^6, Susan^5, John^4, Peter^3, Matthias^2, John Jacob^1) was the daughter of Willis Earl and Anna Virginia (Hulvey) McCray [Supplement No. 5913].

(Sup) 7529 STEPHEN SCOTT McCRAY (Anna Virginia^9, Benjamin^8, Benjamin^7, Elizabeth^6, Susan^5, John^4, Peter^3, Matthias^2, John Jacob^1) was the son of Willis Earl and Anna Virginia (Hulvey) McCray [Supplement No. 5913].

(Sup) 7530 KEVIN BRIAN McCRAY (Anna Virginia^9, Benjamin^8, Benjamin^7, Elizabeth^6, Susan^5, John^4, Peter^3, Matthias^2, John Jacob^1) was the son of Willis Earl and Anna Virginia (Hulvey) McCray [Supplement No. 5913].

(Sup) 7531 ERIC CLYDE McCRAY (Anna Virginia^9, Benjamin^8, Benjamin^7, Elizabeth^6, Susan^5, John^4, Peter^3, Matthias^2, John Jacob^1) was the son of Willis Earl and Anna Virginia (Hulvey) McCray [Supplement No. 5913].

(Sup) 7532 KENNETH WAYNE COLLINS (Gloria^9, Benjamin^8, Benjamin^7, Elizabeth^6, Susan^5, John^4, Peter^3, Matthias^2, John Jacob^1) was the son of James William and Gloria Jean (Hulvey) Collins [Supplement No. 5914].

(Sup) 7533 BEATRICE ANN COLLINS (Gloria^9, Benjamin^8, Benjamin^7, Elizabeth^6, Susan^5, John^4, Peter^3, Matthias^2, John Jacob^1) was the daughter of James William and Gloria Jean (Hulvey) Collins [Supplement No. 5914]. Beatrice married James Sullivan.

(Sup) 8591 i Jessica Lynn Sullivan.
(Sup) 8592 ii James Joseph Sullivan.

(Sup) 7534 JENNIFER LYNN HULVEY (James^9, Benjamin^8, Benjamin^7, Elizabeth^6, Susan^5, John^4, Peter^3, Matthias^2, John Jacob^1) was the daughter of James Franklin and Shirley (Sandy) Hulvey [Supplement No. 5915].

(Sup) 7535 BENJAMIN PRICE HULVEY (James^9, Benjamin^8, Benjamin^7, Elizabeth^6, Susan^5, John^4, Peter^3, Matthias^2, John Jacob^1) was the son of James Franklin and Shirley (Sandy) Hulvey [Supplement No. 5915].

(Sup) 7543 WAYNE E. STEVENS, JR. (Carol[9], Gladys[8], Benjamin[7], Elizabeth[6], Susan[5], John[4], Peter[3], Matthias[2], John Jacob[1]) was the son of Wayne E. and Carol (Windham) Stevens [Supplement No. 5918]. Wayne, Jr., was born August 27, 1963.

(Sup) 7544 JAMES FRANKLIN STEVENS (Carol[9], Gladys[8], Benjamin[7], Elizabeth[6], Susan[5], John[4], Peter[3], Matthias[2], John Jacob[1]) was the son of Wayne E. and Carol (Windham) Stevens [Supplement No. 5918]. James was born March 11, 1965.

(Sup) 7545 DEBORAH KAY KNAPP (Patricia[9], Margaret[8], Benjamin[7], Elizabeth[6], Susan[5], John[4], Peter[3], Matthias[2], John Jacob[1]) was the daughter of Simon and Patricia Ann (Vines) Knapp [Supplement No. 5919]. Deborah was born April 30, 1952. She married David Parrott Janary 29, 1972. They were divorced.

(Sup) 8615   i Melinda Knapp Parrott, born December 19, 1973.
(Sup) 8616   ii Matthew David Parrott, born March 10, 1977.

(Sup) 7546 DIANE LEE KNAPP (Patricia[9], Margaret[8], Benjamin[7], Elizabeth[6], Susan[5], John[4], Peter[3], Matthias[2], John Jacob[1]) was the daughter of Simon and Patricia Ann (Vines) Knapp [Supplement No. 5919]. Diane was born July 19, 1956. She married David Grover Fridley April 11, 1980. He was born January 29, 1953.

(Sup) 7547 JENNY ELDER KNAPP (Patricia[9], Margaret[8], Benjamin[7], Elizabeth[6], Susan[5], John[4], Peter[3], Matthias[2], John Jacob[1]) was the daughter of Simon and Patricia Ann (Vines) Knapp [Supplement No. 5919]. Jenny was born February 25, 1964.

(Sup) 7548 PATRICIA STUDLEY KNAPP (Patricia[9], Margaret[8], Benjamin[7], Elizabeth[6], Susan[5], John[4], Peter[3], Matthias[2], John Jacob[1]) was the daughter of Simon and Patricia Ann (Vines) Knapp [Supplement No. 5919]. Patricia was born March 1, 1969.

(Sup) 7536 KENNETH SCOTT HULVEY (James[9], Benjamin[8], Benjamin[7], Elizabeth[6], Susan[5], John[4], Peter[3], Matthias[2], John Jacob[1]) was the son of James Franklin and Shirley (Sandy) Hulvey [Supplement No. 5915].

(Sup) 7537 TAMANY LEE WILBERGER (Donald[9], Mary[8], Benjamin[7], Elizabeth[6], Susan[5], John[4], Peter[3], Matthias[2], John Jacob[1]) was the daughter of Donald Lee and Becky (Harris) Wilberger [Supplement No. 5916]. She was born May 29, 1958, at Staunton, Virginia. She married John Stuart Benton September 10, 1977, at Staunton.

(Sup) 8601   i Jennifer Gail Benton, born January 17, 1978.
(Sup) 8602   ii John Derek Benton, born January 16, 1980.

(Sup) 7538 DONNA SUE WILBERGER (Donald[9], Mary[8], Benjamin[7], Elizabeth[6], Susan[5], John[4], Peter[3], Matthias[2], John Jacob[1]) was the daughter of Donald Lee and Becky (Harris) Wilberger [Supplement No. 5916]. Donna was born March 16, 1961.

(Sup) 7539 CHRISTINA WILBERGER (Donald[9], Mary[8], Benjamin[7], Elizabeth[6], Susan[5], John[4], Peter[3], Matthias[2], John Jacob[1]) was the daughter of Donald Lee and Becky (Harris) Wilberger [Supplement No. 5916].

(Sup) 7540 FRANKLIN EUGENE FLEMING (Lucy[9], Gladys[8], Benjamin[7], Elizabeth[6], Susan[5], John[4], Peter[3], Matthias[2], John Jacob[1]) was the son of Jimmy R. and Lucy Anna (Windham) Fleming [Supplement No. 5917]. Franklin was born September 2, 1960.

(Sup) 7541 YVONNE LENORA FLEMING (Lucy[9], Gladys[8], Benjamin[7], Elizabeth[6], Susan[5], John[4], Peter[3], Matthias[2], John Jacob[1]) was the daughter of Jimmy R. and Lucy Anna (Windham) Fleming [Supplement No. 5917]. Yvonne was born October 14, 1965.

(Sup) 7542 BRUCE EUGENE SIPE (Lucy[9], Gladys[8], Benjamin[7], Elizabeth[6], Susan[5], John[4], Peter[3], Matthias[2], John Jacob[1]) was the son of Robert Dale and Lucy Anna (Windham) (Fleming) Sipe [Supplement No. 5917]. Bruce was born September 19, 1977.

(Sup) 7549 RENEE CARIANNE KESTER (Jacquelyn^9, Margaret^8, Benjamin^7, Elizabeth^6, Susan^5, John^4, Peter^3, Matthias^2, John Jacob^1) was the daughter of Mack Chapman and Jacquelyn (Vines) Kester [Supplement No. 5920]. Renee was born March 11, 1961. She married Jeffrey Walters, July 5, 1080. He was born March 8, 1956.

(Sup) 7550 MACK CHAPMAN KESTER, Jr. (Jacquelyn^9, Margaret^8, Benjamin^7, Elizabeth^6, Susan^5, John^4, Peter^3, Matthias^2, John Jacob^1) was the son of Mack Chapman and Jacquelyn (Vines) Kester [Supplement No. 5920]. Mack, Jr., was born March 24, 1966.

(Sup) 7551 MATTHEW THOMAS SWIFT (Wanda^9, Howard^8, Benjamin^7, Elizabeth^6, Susan^5, John^4, Peter^3, Matthias^2, John Jacob^1) was the son of Leslie F. and Wanda Louise (Hulvey) Swift [Supplement No. 5921]. Matthew was born August 24, 1965.

(Sup) 7552 SHERRY ANN HULVEY (Benjamin^9, Howard^8, Benjamin^7, Elizabeth^6, Susan^5, John^4, Peter^3, Matthias^2, John Jacob^1) was the daughter of Benjamin Earl and Barbara Ann (Lotts) Hulvey [Supplement No. 5922]. Sherry Ann was born November 24, 1965.

(Sup) 7553 CHRISTOPHER EARL HULVEY (Benjamin^9, Howard^8, Benjamin^7, Elizabeth^6, Susan^5, John^4, Peter^3, Matthias^2, John Jacob^1) was the son of Benjamin Earl and Barbara Ann (Lotts) Hulvey [Supplement No. 5922]. Christopher was born August 26, 1969.

(Sup) 7554 CATHERINE MARGARET WRIGHT (John Henry^9, Margaret^8, Charles^7, Elizabeth^6, Susan^5, John^4, Peter^3, Matthias^2, John Jacob^1) was the daughter of John Henry and Trida (Leventis) Wright, III [Supplement No. 5924]. Catherine was born June 5, 1972.

(Sup) 7555 JOHN HENRY WRIGHT, IV (John Henry^9, Margaret^8, Charles^7, Elizabeth^6, Susan^5, John^4, Peter^3, Matthias^2, John Jacob^1) was the son of John Henry and Trida (Leventis) Wright, III [Supplement No. 5924]. John Henry, IV, was born February 9, 1975.

(Sup) 7556 CHRISTIAN ARCHER HUPP (Elizabeth^9, William^8, Charles^7, Elizabeth^6, Susan^5, John^4, Peter^3, Matthias^2, John Jacob^1) was the son of Elizabeth (Hulvey) Hupp [Supplement No. 5926]. Christian was born May 4, 1975, at Jacksonville, Florida.

(Sup) 7559 CAROL ANNE SINTON (Audrey^9, Eva^8, Otto^7, Sarah^6, Susan^5, John^4, Peter^3, Matthias^2, John Jacob^1) was the daughter of Audrey Shattuck Sinton [Supplement No. 5931].

(Sup) 7566 JOANI MARIE LINK (John^9, John^8, Sidney^7, John^6, John^5, John^4, Peter^3, Matthias^2, John Jacob^1) was the daughter of John Leonard and Leila Marie (Burrell) Link [Supplement No. 5968]. She was born June 22, 1966, at La Harpe, Illinois.

(Sup) 7567 LISA KAY LINK (John^9, John^8, Sidney^7, John^6, John^5, John^4, Peter^3, Matthias^2, John Jacob^1) was the daughter of John Leonard and Leila Marie (Burrell) Link [Supplement No. 5968]. She was born February 20, 1969, at Burlington, Iowa.

(Sup) 7568 SUSAN KATHLENE BOYER (Nina Eleanor^9, John^8, Sidney^7, John^6, John^5, John^4, Peter^3, Matthias^2, John Jacob^1) was the daughter of Arnold Eugene and Nina Eleanor (Link) Boyer [Supplement No. 5969]. Susan was born April 8, 1968, at Carthage, Illinois.

(Sup) 7569 STEVEN EUGENE BOYER (Nina Eleanor^9, John^8, Sidney^7, John^6, John^5, John^4, Peter^3, Matthias^2, John Jacob^1) was the son of Arnold Eugene and Nina Eleanor (Link) Boyer [Supplement No. 5969]. Steven was born May 16, 1969, at Carthage, Illinois.

(Sup) 7570 JANET LYNN GOLDHAMMER (Edwina^9, John^8, Sidney^7, John^6, John^5, John^4, Peter^3, Matthias^2, John Jacob^1) was the daughter of Edwin Lyle and Edwina Jane (Link) Goldhammer [Supplement No. 5970]. Janet was born August 10, 1966, at Burlington, Iowa.

(Sup) 7571   JENNIFER DAWN GOLDHAMMER (Edwina[9], John[8], Sidney[7], John[6], John[5], John[4], Peter[3], Matthias[2], John Jacob[1]) was the daughter of Edwin Lyle and Edwina Jane (Link) Goldhammer [Supplement No. 5970]. Jennifer was born October 2, 1971, at Burlington, Iowa.

(Sup) 7572   KAREN RENEE LINK (Lyle[9], John[8], Sidney[7], John[6], John[5], John[4], Peter[3], Matthias[2], John Jacob[1]) was the daughter of Lyle Arthur and Beverly Jane (Garrett) Link [Supplement No. 5971]. Karen was born October 3, 1972, at Carthage, Illinois.

(Sup) 7573   MARY ELLEN LINK (Lyle[9], John[8], Sidney[7], John[6], John[5], John[4], Peter[3], Matthias[2], John Jacob[1]) was the daughter of Lyle Arthur and Beverly Jane (Garrett) Link [Supplement No. 5971]. She was born February 28, 1976, at Carthage, Illinois.

(Sup) 7574   JOHN HAYLON LINK (Lyle[9], John[8], Sidney[7], John[6], John[5], John[4], Peter[3], Matthias[2], John Jacob[1]) was the son of Lyle Arthur and Beverly Jane (Garrett) Link [Supplement No. 5971]. John was born August 17, 1977, at Macomb, Illinois.

(Sup) 7575   ANTHONY RAY LINK (Rex Eugene[9], John[8], Sidney[7], John[6], John[5], John[4], Peter[3], Matthias[2], John Jacob[1]) was the son of Rex Eugene and Wanda Mae (Wear) Link [Supplement No. 5972]. He was born September 28, 1975, at Springfield, Missouri.

(Sup) 7576   JOSHUA WAYNE LINK (Rex Eugene[9], John[8], Sidney[7], John[6], John[5], John[4], Peter[3], Matthias[2], John Jacob[1]) was the son of Rex Eugene and Wanda Mae (Wear) Link [Supplement No. 5972]. He was born August 19, 1977, at Quincy, Illinois.

(Sup) 7577   LORI ANN JACKSON (Ann[9], John[8], Sidney[7], John[6], John[5], John[4], Peter[3], Matthias[2], John Jacob[1]) was the daughter of Roger Neil and Ann Elizabeth (Link) Jackson [Supplement No. 5973]. She was born July 11, 1970, at Carthage, Illinois.

(Sup) 7578   GARY NEIL JACKSON (Ann[9], John[8], Sidney[7], John[6], John[5], John[4], Peter[3], Matthias[2], John Jacob[1]) was the son of Roger Neil and Ann Elizabeth (Link) Jackson [Supplement No. 5973]. He was born August 30, 1972, at Carthage, Illinois.

(Sup) 7579   CATHY LYNN LINK (Edwin[9], Eldon[8], Sidney[7], John[6], John[5], John[4], Matthias[2], John Jacob[1]) was the daughter of Edwin Earl and Hazel (Brewer) Link [Supplement No. 5974]. Cathy was born March 4, 1961, at La Harpe, Illinois.

(Sup) 7580   AVA JOAN LINK (Edwin[9], Eldon[8], Sidney[7], John[6], John[5], John[4], Matthias[2], John Jacob[1]) was the daughter of Edwin Earl and Hazel (Brewer) Link [Supplement No. 5974]. She was born December 28, 1962, at La Harpe, Illinois.

(Sup) 7581   STEVEN CRAIG LINK (Edwin[9], Eldon[8], Sidney[7], John[6], John[5], John[4], Matthias[2], John Jacob[1]) was the son of Edwin Earl and Hazel (Brewer) Link [Supplement No. 5974]. He was born February 3, 1965, at La Harpe, Illinois.

(Sup) 7582   BRADLEY EARL LINK (Edwin[9], Eldon[8], Sidney[7], John[6], John[5], John[4], Matthias[2], John Jacob[1]) was the son of Edwin Earl and Hazel (Brewer) Link [Supplement No. 5974]. Bradley was born October 20, 1966, at Macomb, Illinois.

(Sup) 7583   CHRISTINA BETH LINK (Edwin[9], Eldon[8], Sidney[7], John[6], John[5], John[4], Matthias[2], John Jacob[1]) was the daughter of Edwin Earl and Hazel (Brewer) Link [Supplement No. 5974]. Christina was born April 22, 1968, at Burlington, Iowa.

(Sup) 7584   KELLEY KAY LINK (David[9], Eldon[8], Sidney[7], John[6], John[5], John[4], Matthias[2], John Jacob[1]) was the daughter of David Paul and Constance Josephine (Meyer) Link [Supplement No. 5975]. She was born December 16, 1963, at La Harpe, Illinois and died at birth.

(Sup) 7585 TAMMY SUE LINK (David[9], Eldon[8], Sidney[7], John[6], John[5], Matthias[2], John Jacob[1]) was the daughter of David Paul and Constance Josephine (Meyer) Link [Supplement No. 5975]. Tammy was born January 15, 1965, at Michigan City, Indiana.

(Sup) 7586 BARBARA ANN LINK (David[9], Eldon[8], Sidney[7], John[6], John[5], Matthias[2], John Jacob[1]) was the daughter of David Paul and Constance Josephine (Meyer) Link [Supplement No. 5975]. Barbara was born October 8, 1966, at La Harpe, Illinois.

(Sup) 7587 DAVID PAUL LINK, Jr. (David[9], Eldon[8], Sidney[7], John[6], John[5], Matthias[2], John Jacob[1]) was the son of David Paul and Constance Josephine (Meyer) Link [Supplement No. 5975]. David, Jr., was born October 17, 1968, at Burlington, Iowa. He drowned in a swimming pool accident June 22, 1977.

(Sup) 7588 HEATHER RENEE LINK (David[9], Eldon[8], Sidney[7], John[6], John[5], Matthias[2], John Jacob[1]) was the daughter of David Paul and Constance Josephine (Meyer) Link [Supplement No. 5975]. Heather was born March 7, 1979, at Michigan City, Indiana.

(Sup) 7589 SHANNON NICOLE LINK (David[9], Eldon[8], Sidney[7], John[6], John[5], Matthias[2], John Jacob[1]) was the daughter of David Paul and Constance Josephine (Meyer) Link [Supplement No. 5975]. She was born April 15, 1980, at Michigan City, Indiana.

(Sup) 7590 THOMAS ELDON GRIGGS (Becky[9], Eldon[8], Sidney[7], John[6], John[5], Matthias[2], John Jacob[1]) was the son of Gary Thomas and Becky Jean (Link) Griggs [Supplement No. 5977]. Thomas was born October 3, 1979, at Quincy, Illinois.

(Sup) 7591 JEFFREY MARK GOAD (Patricia[9], Katherine[8], Sidney[7], John[6], John[5], John[4], Peter[3], Matthias[2], John Jacob[1]) was the son of James Peter and Patricia Joan (Glisan) Goad [Supplement No. 5978]. Jeffrey was born June 3, 1960, at Macomb, Illinois.

(Sup) 7592 DAVID ALLAN GOAD (Patricia[9], Katherine[8], Sidney[7], John[6], John[5], John[4], Peter[3], Matthias[2], John Jacob[1]) was the son of James Peter and Patricia Joan (Glisan) Goad [Supplement No. 5978]. David was born August 26, 1961, at Macomb, Illinois. He married Carol Kelly, August 8, 1987, at Indianapolis, Indiana. She was born March 7, 1961, in Scotland.

(Sup) 7593 BRADLEY JAMES GOAD (Patricia[9], Katherine[8], Sidney[7], John[6], John[5], John[4], Peter[3], Matthias[2], John Jacob[1]) was the son of James Peter and Patricia Joan (Glisan) Goad [Supplement No. 5978]. He was born March 25, 1965, at Macomb, Illinois.

(Sup) 7594 ERIC MATTHEW GOAD (Patricia[9], Katherine[8], Sidney[7], John[6], John[5], John[4], Peter[3], Matthias[2], John Jacob[1]) was the son of James Peter and Patricia Joan (Glisan) Goad [Supplement No. 5978]. He was born October 31, 1969, at Macomb, Illinois.

(Sup) 7595 DEBORAH KAYE RUEBUSH (Marjorie[9], Katherine[8], Sidney[7], John[6], John[5], John[4], Peter[3], Matthias[2], John Jacob[1]) was the daughter of Richard Paul and Marjorie Catherine (Glisan) Ruebush [Supplement No. 5979]. Deborah was born August 2, 1957, at Macomb, Illinois. She married Steven Backhaus, August 22, 1981, at Tampa, Florida. He was the son of Fred and Barbara Backhaus and was born June 20, 1956, at Waukesha, Wisconsin.

(Sup) 8651   i   Kara Leigh Backhaus, born September 28, 1985.

(Sup) 7596 LAURIE RENE RUEBUSH (Marjorie[9], Katherine[8], Sidney[7], John[6], John[5], John[4], Peter[3], Matthias[2], John Jacob[1]) was the daughter of Richard Paul and Marjorie Catherine (Glisan) Ruebush [Supplement No. 5979]. Laurie was born October 25, 1960, at Des Plaines, Illinois. She married Benjamin Joe Burris, Jr., May 31, 1986, at Jacksonville, Florida. He was the son of Ben and Marie Burris and was born June 21, 1956, at Hialeah, Florida.

(Sup) 8655   i   Benjamin Joe Burris, III, born April 6, 1986.

(Sup) 7597 SHELLEY FAYE RUEBUSH (Marjorie[9], Katherine[8], Sidney[7], John[6], John[5], John[4], Peter[3], Matthias[2], John Jacob[1]) was the daughter of Richard Paul and Marjorie Catherine (Glisan) Ruebush [Supplement No. 5979]. Shelley was born November 3, 1962, at Burlington, Iowa.

(Sup) 7598 DONNA LYNN ANDERSON (Juanita^9, Katherine^8, Sidney^7, John^6, John^5, John^4, Peter^3, Matthias^2, John Jacob^1) was the daughter of Kenneth Marvin and Juanita (Glisan) Anderson [Supplement No. 5980]. She married Matthew Paul Orr, August 26, 1983, at Fort Madison, Iowa. He was the son of Howard and Jean Orr and was born December 19, 1961, at Fort Madison.

(Sup) 8661   i Uriah Shawn Orr, born February 18, 1983.

(Sup) 7599 DIANA CAROL ANDERSON (Juanita^9, Katherine^8, Sidney^7, John^6, John^5, John^4, Peter^3, Matthias^2, John Jacob^1) was the daughter of Kenneth Marvin and Juanita (Glisan) Anderson [Supplement No. 5980]. Diana was born September 21, 1967, at Fort Madison, Iowa.

(Sup) 7600 DARREN WADE ANDERSON (Juanita^9, Katherine^8, Sidney^7, John^6, John^5, John^4, Peter^3, Matthias^2, John Jacob^1) was the son of Kenneth Marvin and Juanita (Glisan) Anderson [Supplement No. 5980]. Darren was born March 21, 1974, at Fort Madison, Iowa.

(Sup) 7601 MICHELLE ADRIA GLISAN (Ronald^9, Katherine^8, Sidney^7, John^6, John^5, John^4, Peter^3, Matthias^2, John Jacob^1) was the daughter of Ronald Gregory and Katherine Ann (Hulick) Glisan [Supplement No. 5981]. Michelle was born October 16, 1980, at Rockford, Illinois.

(Sup) 7601A ABIGAIL LANE GLISAN (Roger^9, Katherine^8, Sidney^7, John^6, John^5, John^4, Peter^3, Matthias^2, John Jacob^1) was the daughter of Roger Mason and Ellen (McPeek) Glisan [Supplement No. 5982]. Abigail was born March 23, 1983, at Freeport, Illinois.

(Sup) 7601B REBECCA JANE GLISAN (Roger^9, Katherine^8, Sidney^7, John^6, John^5, John^4, Peter^3, Matthias^2, John Jacob^1) was the daughter of Roger Mason and Ellen (McPeek) Glisan [Supplement No. 5982]. Rebecca was born July 22, 1985, at Freeport, Illinois.

(Sup) 7602 RONALD ALLEN LINK (Phillip^9, Herman^8, Sidney^7, John^6, John^5, John^4, Peter^3, Matthias^2, John Jacob^1) was the son of Phillip Allen and Ethel (Parson) Link [Supplement No. 5984]. Ronald was born March 16, 1977, at Macomb, Illinois.

(Sup) 7603 ROGER EUGENE LINK (Phillip^9, Herman^8, Sidney^7, John^6, John^5, John^4, Peter^3, Matthias^2, John Jacob^1) was the son of Phillip Allen and Ethel (Parson) Link [Supplement No. 5984]. Roger was born November 10, 1979, at Macomb, Illinois.

(Sup) 7604 KATHERINE ADELLE TAYLOR (Judy^9, Herman^8, Sidney^7, John^6, John^5, John^4, Peter^3, Matthias^2, John Jacob^1) was the daughter of Darrell and Judy Adelle (Link) Taylor [Supplement No. 5985]. Kathy was born September 11, 1972, at Pittsfield, Illinois.

(Sup) 7605 MICHAEL LEE TAYLOR (Judy^9, Herman^8, Sidney^7, John^6, John^5, John^4, Peter^3, Matthias^2, John Jacob^1) was the son of Darrell and Judy Adelle (Link) Taylor [Supplement No. 5985]. Michael was born August 5, 1977, at Quincy, Illinois.

(Sup) 7606 GEORGE LYNDELL LEONARD (Peggy^9, Herman^8, Sidney^7, John^6, John^5, John^4, Peter^3, Matthias^2, John Jacob^1) was the son of Howard Roy and Peggy Diane (Link) Leonard [Supplement No. 5986]. George was born September 8, 1972, at Quincy, Illinois.

(Sup) 7607 GINNY RAE LEONARD (Peggy^9, Herman^8, Sidney^7, John^6, John^5, John^4, Peter^3, Matthias^2, John Jacob^1) was the daughter of Howard Roy and Peggy Diane (Link) Leonard [Supplement No. 5986]. Ginny was born October 15, 1974, at Quincy, Illinois.

(Sup) 7608 BOBBI RENAE LEONARD (Peggy^9, Herman^8, Sidney^7, John^6, John^5, John^4, Peter^3, Matthias^2, John Jacob^1) was the daughter of Howard Roy and Peggy Diane (Link) Leonard [Supplement No. 5986]. She was born October 27, 1977, at Quincy, Illinois.

(Sup) 7609 JEFFERY TODD (Nancy^9, Herman^8, Sidney^7, John^6, John^5, John^4, Peter^3, Matthias^2, John Jacob^1) was the son of Virgil Leon and Nancy Joann (Link) Todd [Supplement No. 5987]. Jeffery was born June 20, 1972, at Quincy, Illinois.

(Sup) 7610 MICHELLE TODD (Nancy[9], Herman[8], Sidney[7], John[6], John[5], John[4], Peter[3], Matthias[2], John Jacob[1]) was the daughter of Virgil Leon and Nancy Joann (Link) Todd [Supplement No. 5987]. Michelle was born August 26, 1976, at Phoenix, Arizona.

(Sup) 7611 RODNEY RAY LINK, JR. (Rodney[9], Kenneth[8], Sidney[7], John[6], John[5], John[4], Peter[3], Matthias[2], John Jacob[1]) was the son of Rodney Ray and Mary Ellen (Reese) Link [Supplement No. 5991]. Rodney, Jr., was born April 2, 1964, at Oscaloosa, Iowa.

(Sup) 7612 GREGORY SCOTT LINK (Rodney[9], Kenneth[8], Sidney[7], John[6], John[5], John[4], Peter[3], Matthias[2], John Jacob[1]) was the son of Rodney Ray and Mary Ellen (Reese) Link [Supplement No. 5991]. Gregory was born November 12, 1966, at La Harpe, Illinois.

(Sup) 7613 JACOB REESE LINK (Rodney[9], Kenneth[8], Sidney[7], John[6], John[5], John[4], Peter[3], Matthias[2], John Jacob[1]) was the son of Rodney Ray and Mary Ellen (Reese) Link [Supplement No. 5991]. Jacob was born April 10, 1974, at Monmouth, Illinois.

(Sup) 7614 GERARD MICHAEL LINK (Galen[9], Kenneth[8], Sidney[7], John[6], John[5], John[4], Peter[3], Matthias[2], John Jacob[1]) was the son of Galen Michael and Linda Sue (Ganzer) Link [Supplement No. 5992]. Gerard was born September 30, 1972, at Davenport, Iowa.

(Sup) 7614A GINGER MICHELLE LINK (Galen[9], Kenneth[8], Sidney[7], John[6], John[5], John[4], Peter[3], Matthias[2], John Jacob[1]) was the daughter of Galen Michael [Supplement No. 5992]. Ginger was born October 24, 1977, at Davenport, Iowa.

(Sup) 7615 JESSICA MARIE LINK (Galen[9], Kenneth[8], Sidney[7], John[6], John[5], John[4], Peter[3], Matthias[2], John Jacob[1]) was the daughter of Galen Michael [Supplement No. 5992]. Jessica was born September 4, 1979, at Davenport, Iowa.

(Sup) 7616 JAMES TY LINK (Sidney[9], Kenneth[8], Sidney[7], John[6], John[5], John[4], Peter[3], Matthias[2], John Jacob[1]) was the son of Sidney Cecil and Mary Susan (Melton) Link [Supplement No. 5993]. James was born October 17, 1974, at Davenport, Iowa.

(Sup) 7617 ERIN DANIELLE LINK (Sidney[9], Kenneth[8], Sidney[7], John[6], John[5], John[4], Peter[3], Matthias[2], John Jacob[1]) was the daughter of Sidney Cecil and Mary Susan (Melton) Link [Supplement No. 5993]. She was born December 18, 1977, at Davenport, Iowa.

(Sup) 7618 DEENA MARIE SCOTT (Kennetta Faye[9], Kenneth[8], Sidney[7], John[6], John[5], John[4], Peter[3], Matthias[2], John Jacob[1]) was the daughter of Earl James and Kennetta Faye (Link) Scott [Supplement No. 5994]. She was born April 23, 1979, at Davenport, Iowa.

(Sup) 7618A AMANDA LINK MULLISON (Miriam[9], Kenneth[8], Sidney[7], John[6], John[5], John[4], Peter[3], Matthias[2], John Jacob[1]) was the daugher of Donald Dean and Miriam (Link) Mullison [Supplement No. 5995]. Amada was born October 14, 1985.

(Sup) 7618B BENJAMIN DANIEL LINK MULLISON (Miriam[9], Kenneth[8], Sidney[7], John[6], John[5], John[4], Peter[3], Matthias[2], John Jacob[1]) was the son of Donald Dean and Miriam (Link) Mullison [Supplement No. 5995]. Benjamin was born July 14, 1988.

(Sup) 7619 KELLI JEAN KAIN (Twyla Jean[9], Kenneth[8], Sidney[7], John[6], John[5], John[4], Peter[3], Matthias[2], John Jacob[1]) was the daughter of Gerald Allen and Twyla Jean (Link) Kain [Supplement No. 5996]. She was born October 10, 1980, at Davenport, Iowa.

(Sup) 7620 ALLEN RAY LINK (Ezra[9], Kenneth[8], Sidney[7], John[6], John[5], John[4], Peter[3], Matthias[2], John Jacob[1]) was the son of Ezra Lee and Tracey (Wittstruck) Link [Supplement No. 5997]. He was born June 15, 1980, at Davenport, Iowa.

(Sup) 7621   AMY LYNN STINNETT (Lyla^9, Helen^8, Sidney^7, John^6, John^5, Peter^3, Matthias^2, John Jacob^1) was the daughter of Jimmie Lynn and Lyla Kay (White) Stinnett [Supplement No. 5999]. She was born December 10, 1967, at Carlinville, Illinois.

(Sup) 7622   JAY PATRICK STINNETT (Lyla^9, Helen^8, Sidney^7, John^6, John^5, Peter^3, Matthias^2, John Jacob^1) was the son of Jimmie Lynn and Lyla Kay (White) Stinnett [Supplement No. 5999]. He was born December 22, 1972, at Litchfield, Illinois.

(Sup) 7623   DEBRA LEANNE KREPS (George^9, Lois^8, Sidney^7, John^6, John^5, Peter^3, Matthias^2, John Jacob^1) was the daughter of George Delbert and Donna Lee (Hillyer) Kreps [Supplement No. 6002]. Debra was born November 18, 1964, at Macomb, Illinois.

(Sup) 7624   KIMBERLEE DENISE KREPS (George^9, Lois^8, Sidney^7, John^6, John^5, Peter^3, Matthias^2, John Jacob^1) was the daughter of George Delbert and Donna Lee (Hillyer) Kreps [Supplement No. 6002]. Kimberlee was born June 4, 1968, at Macomb, Illinois. She married Steven Curtis Larson, February 20, 1988, at Sciota, Illinois. He was the son of Curt and Judy Larson and was born October 1, 1965. Kim and Steve attended Illinois State University. They live at Waterman, Illinois, where he was employed by DeKalb-Pfizer Genetics.

(Sup) 8681   i Joshua Curtis Larson, born June 22, 1988.

(Sup) 7625   CHRISTOPHER DONALD KREPS (Keith^9, Lois^8, Sidney^7, John^6, John^5, Peter^3, Matthias^2, John Jacob^1) was the son of Allen Keith and Wendy Jo (Waymack) Kreps [Supplement No. 6003]. Christopher was born December 31, 1974, at Carthage, Illinois.

(Sup) 7626   BRIAN KEITH KREPS (Keith^9, Lois^8, Sidney^7, John^6, John^5, Peter^3, Matthias^2, John Jacob^1) was the son of Allen Keith and Wendy Jo (Waymack) Kreps [Supplement No. 6003]. He was born October 13, 1978, at Carthage, Illinois.

(Sup) 7626A   JACOB TODD KREPS (Keith^9, Lois^8, Sidney^7, John^6, John^5, Peter^3, Matthias^2, John Jacob^1) was the son of Allen Keith and Wendy Jo (Waymack) Kreps [Supplement No. 6003]. Jacob was born June 11, 1981, at Carthage, Illinois.

(Sup) 7627   MICHELLE MARIE BRETTON (Karen^9, Lois^8, Sidney^7, John^6, John^5, Peter^3, Matthias^2, John Jacob^1) was the daughter of Gregory Robert and Karen (Kreps) Bretton [Supplement No. 6004]. Michelle was born December 22, 1968, at Macomb, Illinois.

(Sup) 7628   TERESA DAWN BRETTON (Karen^9, Lois^8, Sidney^7, John^6, John^5, Peter^3, Matthias^2, John Jacob^1) was the daughter of Gregory Robert and Karen (Kreps) Bretton [Supplement No. 6004]. Teresa was born March 11, 1972, at Burlington, Iowa.

(Sup) 7629   ALECS JONATHAN KREPS (Steven^9, Lois^8, Sidney^7, John^6, John^5, Peter^3, Matthias^2, John Jacob^1) was the son of Steven Neal and Peggy Jo (Harper) Kreps [Supplement No. 6005]. He was born September 10, 1974, at Scott Air Force Base, Illinois.

(Sup) 7630   STACEY LEANNE KREPS (Steven^9, Lois^8, Sidney^7, John^6,r John^5, Peter^3, Matthias^2, John Jacob^1) was the son of Steven Neal and Peggy Jo (Harper) Kreps [Supplement No. 6005]. She was born March 7, 1978, at Scott Air Force Base, Illinois.

(Sup) 7631   JASON MICHAEL SIEGWORTH (Rita^9, Lois^8, Sidney^7, John^6, John^5, Peter^3, Matthias^2, John Jacob^1) was th son of Gregory Leon and Rita Kristine (Kreps) Siegworth. Jason was born November 16, 1983, at Macomb, Illinois.

(Sup) 7634   GERI MARIE LINK (Jerry Gail^9, Gail^8, Frank^7, John^6, John^5, Peter^3, Matthias^2, John Jacob^1) was the daughter of Jerry Gail and Mary (Irsik) Link [Supplement No. 6010]. She was born August 19, 1969, at Colorado Springs, Colorado.

(Sup) 7635 KAREN LOUISE LINK (Jerry Gail^9, Gail^8, Frank^7, John^6, John^5, John^4, Peter^3, Matthias^2, John Jacob^1) was the daughter of Jerry Gail and Mary (Irsik) Link [Supplement No. 6010]. She was born November 17, 1970, at Colorado Springs, Colorado.

(Sup) 7636 LAURIE DENISE LINK (Jerry Gail^9, Gail^8, Frank^7, John^6, John^5, John^4, Peter^3, Matthias^2, John Jacob^1) was the daughter of Jerry Gail and Mary (Irsik) Link [Supplement No. 6010]. She was born September 21, 1973, at Carthage, Illinois.

(Sup) 7637 TOMMIE GAIL LINK (Thomas^9, Gail^8, Frank^7, John^6, John^5, John^4, Peter^3, Matthias^2, John Jacob^1) was the child of Thomas Merrill and Debbie (Swain) Link [Supplement No. 6012]. Tommie was born March 8, 1977, at Macomb, Illinois, and died from spinal meningitis May 10, 1980.

(Sup) 7638 JAMIE NICOLE LINK (Thomas^9, Gail^8, Frank^7, John^6, John^5, John^4, Peter^3, Matthias^2, John Jacob^1) was the daughter of Thomas Merrill and Debbie (Swain) Link [Supplement No. 6012]. Jamie was born December 19, 1981, at Macomb, Illinois.

(Sup) 7639 JENNIFER LeANNE LINK (Thomas^9, Gail^8, Frank^7, John^6, John^5, John^4, Peter^3, Matthias^2, John Jacob^1) was the daughter of Thomas Merrill and Teresa (Hopping) Link [Supplement No. 6012]. Jennifer was born July 11, 1984, at Macomb, Illinois.

(Sup) 7639A PAULA DIANNA LINK (Thomas^9, Gail^8, Frank^7, John^6, John^5, John^4, Peter^3, Matthias^2, John Jacob^1) was the daughter of Thomas Merrill and Teresa (Hopping) Link [Supplement No. 6012]. Paula was born November 9, 1985, at Macomb, Illinois.

(Sup) 7640 AMY JO LINK (Bradley^9, Wendell^8, Lewis^7, John^6, John^5, John^4, Peter^3, Matthias^2, John Jacob^1) was the daughter of Bradley Wendell and Sheila Lynn (McConnell) Link [Supplement No. 6019]. Amy Jo was born July 14, 1978, at La Harpe, Illinois.

(Sup) 7641 AMY KRISTINE DICKE (Kathryn^9, James^8, Pearl^7, Frank^6, John^5, John^4, Peter^3, Matthias^2, John Jacob^1) was the daughter of David and Kathryn Irene (Baker) Dicke [Supplement No. 6022]. She was born December 19, 1969.

(Sup) 7642 SUSAN JENNIFER DICKE (Kathryn^9, James^8, Pearl^7, Frank^6, John^5, John^4, Peter^3, Matthias^2, John Jacob^1) was the daughter of David and Kathryn Irene (Baker) Dicke [Supplement No. 6022]. She was born February 17, 1972.

(Sup) 7643 KELLY ANN BAKER (Neil^9, James^8, Pearl^7, Frank^6, John^5, John^4, Peter^3, Matthias^2, John Jacob^1) was the daughter of Neil Douglas and Kathy (Farr) Baker [Supplement No. 6024]. She was born July 20, 1975.

(Sup) 7644 MEGAN ELIZABETH BAKER (Neil^9, James^8, Pearl^7, Frank^6, John^5, John^4, Peter^3, Matthias^2, John Jacob^1) was the daughter of Neil Douglas and Kathy (Farr) Baker [Supplement No. 6024]. She was born August 20, 1977.

(Sup) 7645 JUSTIN JAMES FRANCAVILLA (Melanie^9, James^8, Pearl^7, Frank^6, John^5, John^4, Peter^3, Matthias^2, John Jacob^1) was the son of Stephen and Melanie Ann (Baker) Francavilla [Supplement No. 6025]. He was born September 17, 1979, at Baldwin, New York.

(Sup) 7645A TYLER ANDREW FRANCAVILLA (Melanie^9, James^8, Pearl^7, Frank^6, John^5, John^4, Peter^3, Matthias^2, John Jacob^1) was the son of Steven and Melanie Ann (Baker) Francavilla [Supplement No. 6025]. He was born July 26, 1980, at Baldwin, New York.

(Sup) 7645B STEFAN JOHN FRANCAVILLA (Melanie^9, James^8, Pearl^7, Frank^6, John^5, John^4, Peter^3, Matthias^2, John Jacob^1) was the son of Stephen and Melanie Ann (Baker) Francavilla [Supplement No. 6025]. He was born November 22, 1985, at Baldwin, New York.

(Sup) 7646 KARI LYNN BAKER (Wayne[9], David[8], Pearl[7], Frank[6], John[5], Peter[3], Matthias[2], John Jacob[1]) was the daughter of Wayne Steven and Rhonda Sue (Brockman) Baker [Supplement No. 6027]. She was born April 16, 1978.

(Sup) 7647 CRYSTAL LEE BAKER (Wayne[9], David[8], Pearl[7], Frank[6], John[5], Peter[3], Matthias[2], John Jacob[1]) was the daughter of Wayne Steven and Rhonda Sue (Brockman) Baker [Supplement No. 6027]. She was born August 7, 1980, at Columbus, Ohio.

(Sup) 7648 BRADLEY SCOTT BAKER (William[9], David[8], Pearl[7], Frank[6], John[5], Peter[3], Matthias[2], John Jacob[1]) was the son of William Scott and Deborah (Cameely) Baker [Supplement No. 6028]. He was born August 8, 1980, at Columbus, Ohio.

(Sup) 7649 RYAN FRANCIS MONTANE (Kathleen[9], Marilyn[8], Pearl[7], Frank[6], John[5], Peter[3], Matthias[2], John Jacob[1]) was the son of Mario Ricardo and Kathleen Susan (Kinsella) Montane [Supplement No. 6031]. He was born March 12, 1978.

(Sup) 7650 CARMEN ELIZABETH MONTANE (Kathleen[9], Marilyn[8], Pearl[7], Frank[6], John[5], Peter[3], Matthias[2], John Jacob[1]) was the daughter of Mario Ricardo and Kathleen Susan (Kinsella) Montane [Supplement No. 6031]. She was born in 1980.

(Sup) 7651 YVETTE MONTANE (Kathleen[9], Marilyn[8], Pearl[7], Frank[6], John[5], Peter[3], Matthias[2], John Jacob[1]) was the daughter of Mario Ricardo and Kathleen Susan (Kinsella) Montane [Supplement No. 6031].

(Sup) 7652 JAMES MICHAEL TERRY (James[9], Harold[8], Zella[7], Frank[6], John[5], Peter[3], Matthias[2], John Jacob[1]) was the son of James Steven and Sandra Lee (Massey) Terry [Supplement No. 6036]. He was born August 19, 1979.

(Sup) 7653 BOBBIE MARIE TERRY (James[9], Harold[8], Zella[7], Frank[6], John[5], Peter[3], Matthias[2], John Jacob[1]) was the daughter of James Steven and Sandra Lee (Massey) Terry [Supplement No. 6036]. She was born March 14, 1981.

(Sup) 7654 ALEXANDRA MEGHAM SASHA TEXTOR (Charlene[9], Harold[8], Zella[7], Frank[6], John[5], Peter[3], Matthias[2], John Jacob[1]) was the daughter of James Steven and Sandra Lee (Massey) Terry [Supplement No. 6036]. Alexandra was born March 29, 1984.

(Sup) 7657 JOSHUA PAUL TERRY (paul[9], Frank[8], Zella[7], Frank[6], John[5], Peter[3], Matthias[2], John Jacob[1]) was the son of Paul A. and Patricia Marie (Murphy) Terry [Supplement No. 6038]. He was born December 5, 1978.

(Sup) 7658 FAWN K. PHILIPS (Linda[9], Frank[8], Zella[7], Frank[6], John[5], Peter[3], Matthias[2], John Jacob[1]) was the daughter of Ronald Ray and Linda Kay (Terry) Philips [Supplement No. 6039]. She was born January 1, 1979.

(Sup) 7658A BAMBI EILEEN PHILIPS (Linda[9], Frank[8], Zella[7], Frank[6], John[5], Peter[3], Matthias[2], John Jacob[1]) was the daughter of Ronald Ray and Linda Kay (Terry) Philips [Supplement No. 6039]. She was born October 17, 1980.

(Sup) 7659 CHRISTOPHER CHARLES JONES (Charles[9], Elsie[8], Zella[7], Frank[6], John[5], Peter[3], Matthias[2], John Jacob[1]) was the son of Charles Irvin and Jeanne (Borland) Jones [Supplement No. 6040]. He was born August 12, 1967. He married Michelle Smith, January 11, 1986.

Stepdaughter 1 Nicole born August 25, 1983.

(Sup) 7660 JON LYNN JONES (Charles[9], Elsie[8], Zella[7], Frank[6], John[5], Peter[3], Matthias[2], John Jacob[1]) was the son of Charles Irvin and Jeanne (Borland) Jones [Supplement No. 6040]. He was born April 18, 1970.

(Sup) 7661 MARK ERWIN PETTIT (Carol[9], Elsie[8], Zella[7], Frank[6], John[5], Peter[3], Matthias[2], John Jacob[1]) was the son of Ronald and Carol Ann (Jones) Pettit [Supplement No. 6042]. He was born June 22, 1974.

(Sup) 7668 DANA MICHELLE EISENBRANDT (Terri[9], Esther[8], Zella[7], Frank[6], John[5], John[4], Peter[3], Matthias[2], John Jacob[1]) was the daughter of William Craig and Terri Sue (Groves) Eisenbrandt [Supplement No. 6047]. She was born June 23, 1979.

(Sup) 7669 MELISSA KAY EISENBRANDT (Terri[9], Esther[8], Zella[7], Frank[6], John[5], John[4], Peter[3], Matthias[2], John Jacob[1]) was the daughter of William Craig and Terri Sue (Groves) Eisenbrandt [Supplement No. 6047]. She was born May 5, 1982.

(Sup) 7670 ANGEL IRENE GAMBLE (Vicki[9], Esther[8], Zella[7], Frank[6], John[5], John[4], Peter[3], Matthias[2], John Jacob[1]) was the dauthter of Ronnie Lamar and Vicki Lee (Groves) Gamble [Supplement No. 6048]. She was born February 16, 1978.

(Sup) 7671 AMANDA JANE GAMBLE (Vicki[9], Esther[8], Zella[7], Frank[6], John[5], John[4], Peter[3], Matthias[2], John Jacob[1]) was the daughter of Ronnie Lamar and Vicki Lee (Groves) Gamble [Supplement No. 6048]. She was born August 1, 1981.

(Sup) 7672 AARON JOSEPH CONDRON (Penny[9], Vinal Ray[8], Zella[7], Frank[6], John[5], John[4], Peter[3], Matthias[2], John Jacob[1]) was the son of Greg and Penny Ann (Terry) Condron [Supplement No. 6051]. He was born September 11, 1978.

(Sup) 7673 CASEY ELIZABETH CONDRON (Penny[9], Vinal Ray[8], Zella[7], Frank[6], John[5], John[4], Peter[3], Matthias[2], John Jacob[1]) was the daughter of Greg and Penny Ann (Terry) Condron [Supplement No. 6051]. Casey was born September 23, 1982.

(Sup) 7674 JENNIFER MAUREEN CONDRON (Penny[9], Vinal Ray[8], Zella[7], Frank[6], John[5], John[4], Peter[3], Matthias[2], John Jacob[1]) was the daughter of Greg and Penny Ann (Terry) Condron [Supplement No. 6051]. Jennifer was born January 22, 1984.

(Sup) 7662 ANDY RAY HUGHES (Nancy[9], Dale[8], Zella[7], Frank[6], John[5], John[4], Peter[3], Matthias[2], John Jacob[1]) was the son of Daniel and Nancy Lynn (Terry) Hughes [Supplement No. 6042]. He was born September 8, 1976.

(Sup) 7663 STACEY LYNN HUGHES (Nancy[9], Dale[8], Zella[7], Frank[6], John[5], John[4], Peter[3], Matthias[2], John Jacob[1]) was the daughter of Daniel and Nancy Lynn (Terry) Hughes [Supplement No. 6042].

(Sup) 7664 EMILY MICHELLE TERRY (Matthew[9], Dale[8], Zella[7], Frank[6], John[5], John[4], Peter[3], Matthias[2], John Jacob[1]) was the daughter of Matthew Dale and Barbara (Smith) Terry [Supplement No. 6043]. Emily was born October 7, 1981.

(Sup) 7664A MEGAN ELIZABETH TERRY (Matthew[9], Dale[8], Zella[7], Frank[6], John[5], John[4], Peter[3], Matthias[2], John Jacob[1]) was the daughter of Matthew Dale and Barbara (Smith) Terry [Supplement No. 6043]. Megan was born May 23, 1983.

(Sup) 7664B LAURIE TERRY (Matthew[9], Dale[8], Zella[7], Frank[6], John[5], John[4], Peter[3], Matthias[2], John Jacob[1]) was the daughter of Matthew Dale and Barbara (Smith) Terry [Supplement No. 6043]. Laurie was born April 28, 1986.

(Sup) 7665 JENNIFER IRENE BEHNKEN (Jill[9], Dale[8], Zella[7], Frank[6], John[5], John[4], Peter[3], Matthias[2], John Jacob[1]) was the daughter of Michael and Jill Elizabeth (Terry) Behnken [Supplement No. 6045]. Jennifer was born May 12, 1986.

- - - - - - - - - - - -

(Sup) 7667 CHRISTY SUE EISENBRANDT (Terri[9], Esther[8], Zella[7], Frank[6], John[5], John[4], Peter[3], Matthias[2], John Jacob[1]) was the daughter of William Craig and Terri Sue (Groves) Eisenbrandt [Supplement No. 6047]. She was born November 30, 1975.

(Sup) 7683 BETHANY LINK (Robert^9, Robert^8, Raymond^7, Frank^6, John^5, John^4, Peter^3, Matthias^2, John Jacob^1) was the daughter of Robert Eugene and Kathy (Baxter) Link, Jr. [Supplement No. 6064]. Bethany was born October 19, 1983.

(Sup) 7684 JOSHUA MICHAEL LINK (Philip^9, Philip^8, Raymond^7, Frank^6, John^5, John^4, Peter^3, Matthias^2, John Jacob^1) was the son of Philip Michael and Patsy Denise (Tackett) Link [Supplement No. 6070]. Joshua was born May 2, 1985, at Columbus, Ohio.

(Sup) 7685 KIERRA LYNN LINK (Steven^9, Philip^8, Raymond^7, Frank^6, John^5, John^4, Peter^3, Matthias^2, John Jacob^1) was the daughter of Steven Allen and Kerry Linn Link [Supplement No. 6071]. Kierra was born February 2, 1984, at Columbus, Ohio.

(Sup) 7686 JUSTIN COLT VAN SICKLE (Jeffrey^9, Suzanne^8, Kenneth^7, Frank^6, John^5, John^4, Peter^3, Matthias^2, John Jacob^1) was the son of Jeffrey Duane and Dana (Hankinson) Van Sickle [Supplement No. 6080]. Justin was born March, 1985.

(Sup) 7697 COBY JEANNE FIELDING (Lisa^9, Stephen^8, Kenneth^7, Frank^6, John^5, John^4, Peter^3, Matthias^2, John Jacob^1) was the daughter of Brad and Lisa (Link) Fielding [Supplement No. 6082A]. Coby was born April 6, 1980.

(Sup) 7719 JANE ANN REYNOLDS (Elizabeth^9, Ray^8, Arthur^7, Susan^6, David^5, John^4, Peter^3, Matthias^2, John Jacob^1) was the daughter of James and Elizabeth Ann (Wingate) Reynolds [Supplement No. 6099]. Jane Ann was born June 29, 1946, at Atlanta, Georgia.

(Sup) 7722 SUSAN MARIE LYON (Betty^8, Lulu^7, Susan^6, David^5, John^4, Peter^3, Matthias^2, John Jacob^1) was the daughter of Robert and Betty Lou (Reihm) Lyon [Supplement No. 6110]. She was born May 8, 1944, in Warren County, Illinois.

(Sup) 7675 CHRISTOPHER VINAL CONDRON (Penny^9, Vinal Ray^8, Zella^7, Frank^6, John^5, John^4, Peter^3, Matthias^2, John Jacob^1) was the son of Greg and Penny Ann (Terry) Condron [Supplement No. 6051]. Christopher was born October 22, 1985.

(Sup) 7676 RICHARD CHARLES STEVENS (Paula^9, Vinal Ray^8, Zella^7, Frank^6, John^5, John^4, Peter^3, Matthias^2, John Jacob^1) was the son of Richard and Paula (Terry) Stevens [Supplement No. 6052]. Richard Charles was born February 18, 1979.

(Sup) 7677 LAURA LYNN STEVENS (Paula^9, Vinal Ray^8, Zella^7, Frank^6, John^5, John^4, Peter^3, Matthias^2, John Jacob^1) was the daughter of Richard and Paula (Terry) Stevens [Supplement No. 6052]. Laura was born September 26, 1981.

(Sup) 7678 ANDREW O'QUINN (Kelly^9, Vinal Ray^8, Zella^7, Frank^6, John^5, John^4, Peter^3, Matthias^2, John Jacob^1) was the son of Patrick and Kelly (Terry) O'Quinn [Supplement No. 6053]. Andrew was born September 11, 1986.

(Sup) 7679 JENNY IRENE GREEN (Brenda^9, Donald^8, Zella^7, Frank^6, John^5, John^4, Peter^3, Matthias^2, John Jacob^1) was the daughter of Dan and Brenda (Terry) Green [Supplement No. 6055]. Jenny was born August 11, 1980.

(Sup) 7680 GREEN (Brenda^9, Donald^8, Zella^7, Frank^6, John^5, John^4, Peter^3, Matthias^2, John Jacob^1) was the son of Dan and Brenda (Terry) Green [Supplement No. 6055].

(Sup) 7681 ELIZABETH NICOLE NEWMAN (Judith^9, John^8, Carrie^7, Frank^6, John^5, John^4, Peter^3, Matthias^2, John Jacob^1) was the daughter of Mark A. and Judith (Welch) Newman [Supplement No. 6062]. Elizabeth was born December 30, 1986.

(Sup) 7682 AMY ALANE LINK (John^9, John^8, Raymond^7, Frank^6, John^5, John^4, Peter^3, Matthias^2, John Jacob^1) was the daughter of John Raymond and Shirley (Lowe) Link, III [Supplement No. 6063]. She was born November 10, 1984.

June 8, 1957, at U.S. Naval Air Station, Patuxant River, Maryland. He completed high school at Paris, Illinois and received a B.S. degree in chemical engineering from Rose Hulman Institute of Technology in 1981. He married Patricia Amy Bolduc, August 31, 1986, at San Antonio, Texas. She was the daughter of LTCOL Roger Joseph and Olga (Barger) Bolduc and was born September 11, 1955, at Lackland Air Force Base, Texas. Patty was a professional photographer.

(Sup) 8761   i Amy Nicolle Spung, born July 21, 1988.

(Sup) 7736A   PETER LINK SPUNG (Christie[9], Paxson[8], Horace[7], James[6], Christopher[5], Peter[4], Peter[3], Matthias[2], John Jacob[1]) was the son of John Richard and Christie (Link) Spung [Supplement No. 6257]. Peter was born September 11, 1961, at Portland, Maine. He married Catherine Ann Roller, October 15, 1983, at Paris, Illinois. She was the daughter of Richard and Jennie (Faulk) Roller and was born October 9, 1963, at San Luis Obispo, California. They resided at Paris, Illinois, where Peter managed the Horace Link & Co. retail furniture store, and Catherine was employed by a bank and was active in community affairs.

(Sup) 7736B   JOHN DICKSON SPUNG (Christie[9], Paxson[8], Horace[7], James[6], Christopher[5], Peter[4], Peter[3], Matthias[2], John Jacob[1]) was the son of John Richard and Christie (Link) Spung [Supplement No. 6257]. John was born February 2, 1964, at Washington, D.C. He attended Parkland Junior College, Illinois.

(Sup) 7737   LAURA JENNINGS HUFF (Linda[9], Richard[8], Horace[7], James[6], Christopher[5], Peter[4], Peter[3], Matthias[2], John Jacob[1]) was the daughter of Noble Franklin and Linda (Link) Huff [Supplement No. 6258]. Laura was born July 4, 1964, at Midland, Michigan. She graduated from Kenyon College in 1986 and received an M.A. degree in international relations from the University of Chicago in 1988.

(Sup) 7738   MATTHEW LINK HUFF (Linda[9], Richard[8], Horace[7], James[6], Christopher[5], Peter[4], Peter[3], Matthias[2], John Jacob[1]) was the son of Noble Franklin and Linda (Link) Huff [Supplement No. 6258]. Matthew was born April 29, 1967, at Midland, Michigan. He attended De Pauw University, Indiana, where he was a member of Sigma Nu Fraternity.

(Sup) 7723   GORDON PAUL GRAU (Ella[9], Blanche[8], Harvey[7], Sarah[6], David[5], John[4], Peter[3], Matthias[2], John Jacob[1]) was the son of Henry Melvin and Ella Florence (Neumann) Grau [Supplement No. 6115]. Gordon was born December 2, 1946, at Billings, Montana.

(Sup) 7726   SANDRA JEAN POPE (Evelyn[9], Florence[8], Harvey[7], Sarah[6], David[5], John[4], Peter[3], Matthias[2], John Jacob[1]) was the daughter of Mervil and Evelyn Mae (Hobbs) Pope [Supplement No. 6124]. Sandra was born January 26, 1947, in Custer County, Montana.

(Sup) 7735   CHRISTOPHER ROSS LINK (James[9], Paxson[8], Horace[7], James[6], Christopher[5], Peter[4], Peter[3], Matthias[2], John Jacob[1]) was the son of James Cole and Blyth McCradie Link [Supplement No. 6255]. Christopher was born March 26, 1952, at Charlotte, North Carolina. He graduated from North Carolina State University and was an electrical contractor.

(Sup) 7735A   DAVID STUART LINK (James[9], Paxson[8], Horace[7], James[6], Christopher[5], Peter[4], Peter[3], Matthias[2], John Jacob[1]) was the son of James Cole and Blyth McCradie Link [Supplement No. 6255]. David was born January 10, 1954, at Charlotte, North Carolina. He graduated from Lees McRae College. David married Mae Catherine Pearsall, March 20, 1982, at Charlotte. She was the daughter of Needham James and Mae Catherine Pearsall and was born November 24, 1954, at Charlotte. She graduated from Appalachian State University and became a flight attendant with Piedmont Airlines. David operate a dry cleaning business.

(Sup) 8751   i Mae Catherine Link, born September 28, 1985.

(Sup) 7735B   BLYTHE ANDREA LINK (James[9], Paxson[8], Horace[7], James[6], Christopher[5], Peter[4], Peter[3], Matthias[2], John Jacob[1]) was the daughte of James Cole and Blyth McCradie Link [Supplement No. 6255]. Blyth was born February 19, 1957, at Charlotte, North Carolina. She graduated from Appalachia State University and was employed as an apartment building manager.

(Sup) 7736   RICHARD COLE SPUNG (Christie[9], Paxson[8], Horace[7], James[6], Christopher[5], Peter[4], Peter[3], Matthias[2], John Jacob[1]) was the son of John Richard and Christie (Link) Spung [Supplement No. 6257]. Richard was born

(Sup) 7742 JENNA MARIE WHEAT (Christopher[9], Suzanne[8], Kathryn[7], Ivan[6], Christopher[5], Peter[4], Peter[3], Matthias[2], John Jacob[1]) was the daughter of Christopher Chambers and Letha (Welch) Wheat [Supplement No. 6266A]. She was born March 23, 1987, at Springfield, Missouri.

(Sup) 7743 ERIC ARLINGTON FRIHART (Anne[9], Mary[8], Bess[7], Frank[6], Simon[5], Peter[4], Peter[3], Matthias[2], John Jacob[1]) was the son of Charles Richard and Anne (Roughton) Frihart [Supplement No. 6269B]. Eric was born August 25, 1977, at Princeton, New Jersey.

(Sup) 7743A REBECCA ELIZABETH FRIHART (Anne[9], Mary[8], Bess[7], Frank[6], Simon[5], Peter[4], Peter[3], Matthias[2], John Jacob[1]) was the daughter of Charles Richard and Anne (Roughton) Frihart [Supplement No. 6269B]. Rebecca was born May 26, 1979, at Princeton, New Jersey.

(Sup) 7743B KARL RICHARD FRIHART (Anne[9], Mary[8], Bess[7], Frank[6], Simon[5], Peter[4], Peter[3], Matthias[2], John Jacob[1]) was the son of Charles Richard and Anne (Roughton) Frihart [Supplement No. 6269B]. Karl was born September 19, 1981, at Princeton, New Jersey.

(Sup) 7743C CHRISTINE LOUISE SHIDELL (Julie[9], Mary[8], Bess[7], Frank[6], Simon[5], Peter[4], Peter[3], Matthias[2], John Jacob[1]) was the daughter of Gerald Lawrence and Julie (Roughton) Shidell [Supplement No. 6269C]. Christine was born October 25, 1969, at Madison, Wisconsin.

(Sup) 7743D ALISON MARIE SHIDELL (Julie[9], Mary[8], Bess[7], Frank[6], Simon[5], Peter[4], Peter[3], Matthias[2], John Jacob[1]) was the daughter of Gerald Lawrence and Julie (Roughton) Shidell [Supplement No. 6269C]. Alison was born May 1, 1973, at Madison, Wisconsin.

- -

(Sup) 7747 MARY NOLAND JETT (Mary[9], Mary[8], Mary[7], Cary[6], Mary[5], Peter[4], Peter[3], Matthias[2], John Jacob[1]) was the daughter of George William and Mary (Inglis) Beddoe [Supplement No. 6282]. Mary was born June 9, 1959, at Lexington, Kentucky. She attended William and Mary University and graduated from George Mason University in 1984. She published three books on computer programs. Mary married Roy Cameron Evans, Jr., June 20, 1981, at Gaithersburg, Maryland. He was the son of Roy Cameron and Zoeann Harcum Evans and was born February 10, 1959, at Alexandria, Virginia. Roy graduated in 1980 from William and Mary University with high honors in physics and economics, and did graduate studies at the University of Virginia in economics.

(Sup) 7747A GEORGE WILLIAM JETT, JR. (Mary[9], Mary[8], Mary[7], Cary[6], Mary[5], Peter[4], Peter[3], Matthias[2], John Jacob[1]) was the son of George William and Mary (Inglis) Beddoe [Supplement No. 6282]. George, Jr., was born June 1, 1960, at Lexington, Kentucky.

(Sup) 7747B JOHN BEACH JETT (Mary[9], Mary[8], Mary[7], Cary[6], Mary[5], Peter[4], Peter[3], Matthias[2], John Jacob[1]) was the son of George William and Mary (Inglis) Beddoe [Supplement No. 6282]. John was born February 18, 1963, at Arlington, Virginia.

(Sup) 7747C ELIZABETH PARRISH JETT (Mary[9], Mary[8], Mary[7], Cary[6], Mary[5], Peter[4], Peter[3], Matthias[2], John Jacob[1]) was the daughter of George William and Mary (Inglis) Beddoe [Supplement No. 6282]. Elizabeth was born October 25, 1967, at Washington, D.C.

(Sup) 7747D GEORGE ADAM BERGER (Elizabeth[9], Mary[8], Mary[7], Cary[6], Mary[5], Peter[4], Peter[3], Matthias[2], John Jacob[1]) was the son of Stephen Ernest and Elizabeth (Beddoe) Berger [Supplement No. 6283]. George was born October 27, 1964, at Ashland, Kentucky. He graduated from Washington and Lee University, in 1986.

(Sup) 7747E MARY ELIZABETH BERGER (Elizabeth[9], Mary[8], Mary[7], Cary[6], Mary[5], Peter[4], Peter[3], Matthias[2], John Jacob[1]) was the daughter of Stephen Ernest and Elizabeth (Beddoe) Berger [Supplement No. 6283]. Mary was born June 6, 1966, at Ashland, Kentucky. She graduated in 1988 from the University of the South, at Sewanee, Tennessee. Mary married Walter John Davis, June 18, 1988.

(Sup) 7747F ROBERT PARRISH BERGER (Elizabeth[9], Mary[8], Mary[7], Cary[6], Mary[5], Peter[4], Peter[3], Matthias[2], John Jacob[1]) was the son of Stephen Ernest and Elizabeth (Beddoe) Berger [Supplement No. 6283]. Robert was born in September 26, 1967, at Ashland, Kentucky.

(Sup) 7749A THAD KIRK WATSON (Hilah^9, Hilah^8, Hilah^7, Ruez^6, Francis Marion^5, Peter^4, Peter^3, Matthias^2, John Jacob^1) was the son of James Fender and Hilah Jane (Wood) Watson [Supplement No. 6288A]. Thad was born June 6, 1976, at Brunswick, Georgia.

(Sup) 7749B KATHRYN JANE WATSON (Hilah^9, Hilah^8, Hilah^7, Ruez^6, Francis Marion^5, Peter^4, Peter^3, Matthias^2, John Jacob^1) was the daughter of James Fender and Hilah Jane (Wood) Watson [Supplement No. 6288A]. Kathryn was born March 30, 1981, at Brunswick, Georgia.

(Sup) 7750 FRANK WORTHINGTON REYNOLDS (Charlotte^9, Haddon^8, Hilah^7, Ruez^6, Francis Marion^5, Peter^4, Peter^3, Matthias^2, John Jacob^1) was the son of Jonathan Randolph and Charlotte (Kirk) Reynolds [Supplement No. 6288C]. Frank was born June 5, 1980, at New York City.

(Sup) 7750A EDWARD KIRK REYNOLDS (Charlotte^9, Haddon^8, Hilah^7, Ruez^6, Francis Marion^5, Peter^4, Peter^3, Matthias^2, John Jacob^1) was the son of Jonathan Randolph and Charlotte (Kirk) Reynolds [Supplement No. 6288C]. Edward was born August 5, 1983, at New York City.

(Sup) 7750B EMILY KIRK (Haddon^9, Haddon^8, Hilah^7, Ruez^6, Francis Marion^5, Peter^4, Peter^3, Matthias^2, John Jacob^1) was the daughter of Haddon Spurgeon and Mary (Marsh) Kirk, III [Supplement No. 6288D]. Emily was born May 31, 1981, at Winston-Salem, North Carolina.

(Sup) 7750C HADDON CLARKE KIRK (Haddon^9, Haddon^8, Hilah^7, Ruez^6, Francis Marion^5, Peter^4, Peter^3, Matthias^2, John Jacob^1) was the son of Haddon Spurgeon and Mary (Marsh) Kirk, III [Supplement No. 6288D]. Haddon was born August 24, 1983, at Winston-Salem, North Carolina.

(Sup) 7751 CECILY FOGARTY (Catherine^9, Haddon^8, Hilah^7, Ruez^6, Francis Marion^5, Peter^4, Peter^3, Matthias^2, John Jacob^1) was the daughter of Michael Allen and Catherine (Kirk) Fogarty, Jr., [Supplement No. 6288E]. Cecily was born April 10, 1979, at New Orleans, Louisiana.

(Sup) 7747G GEORGE HALSEY BEDDOE, JR. (George^9, Mary^8, Mary^7, Cary^6, Mary^5, Peter^4, Peter^3, Matthias^2, John Jacob^1) was the son of George and Penelope (Pritchard) Beddoe [Supplement No. 6284]. He was born July 3, 1978, at Fairfax, Virginia.

(Sup) 7747H SARAH PRITCHARD BEDDOE (George^9, Mary^8, Mary^7, Cary^6, Mary^5, Peter^4, Peter^3, Matthias^2, John Jacob^1) was the daughter of George and Penelope (Pritchard) Beddoe [Supplement No. 6284]. She was born May 8, 1982, at Fairfax, Virginia.

(Sup) 7748 REBECCA GAIL NORSTROM (Constance^9, James^8, Mary^7, Cary^6, Mary^5, Peter^4, Peter^3, Matthias^2, John Jacob^1) was the daughter of Gail Pershing and Constance Elizabeth (Parrish) Norstrom, Jr. [Supplement No. 6285]. Rebecca was born in December 22, 1976, at Napierville, Illinois.

(Sup) 7748A GREGORY JAMES PARRISH NORSTROM (Constance^9, James^8, Mary^7, Cary^6, Mary^5, Peter^4, Peter^3, Matthias^2, John Jacob^1) was the son of Gail Pershing and Constance Elizabeth (Parrish) Norstrom [Supplement No. 6285]. Gregory was born in January 27, 1983, at Winfield, Illinois.

(Sup) 7748B JEFFREY MICHAEL ROGERS (Janet^9, James^8, Mary^7, Cary^6, Mary^5, Peter^4, Peter^3, Matthias^2, John Jacob^1) was the son of Charles Louis and Janet (Parrish) Rogers, III [Supplement No. 6285A]. Jeffrey was born August 13, 1974, at Bartleville, Oklahoma.

(Sup) 7748C CHAD EDWARD ROGERS (Janet^9, James^8, Mary^7, Cary^6, Mary^5, Peter^4, Peter^3, Matthias^2, John Jacob^1) was the son of Charles Louis and Janet (Parrish) Rogers, III [Supplement No. 6285A]. Chad was born in December 17, 1978, at Tulsa, Oklahoma.

(Sup) 7749 JAMES JUSTIN WATSON (Hilah^9, Hilah^8, Hilah^7, Ruez^6, Francis Marion^5, Peter^4, Peter^3, Matthias^2, John Jacob^1) was the son of James Fender and Hilah Jane (Wood) Watson [Supplement No. 6288A]. James was born February 20, 1970, at Temple, Texas.

(Sup) 7751A MICHAEL SHANE FOGARTY (Catherine^9, Haddon^8, Hilah^7, Ruez^6, Francis Marion^5, Peter^4, Peter^3, Matthias^2, John Jacob^1) was the son of Michael Allen and Catherine (Kirk) Fogarty, Jr. [Supplement No. 6288E]. Michael was born August 26, 1982, at New Orleans, Louisiana.

(Sup) 7751B JOSHUA NEAL FOGARTY (Catherine^9, Haddon^8, Hilah^7, Ruez^6, Francis Marion^5, Peter^4, Peter^3, Matthias^2, John Jacob^1) was the son of Michael Allen and Catherine (Kirk) Fogarty, Jr. [Supplement No. 6288E]. Joshua was born January 7, 1986, at New Orleans, Louisiana.

(Sup) 7752 EDWARD REPPERT UNGER (Elizabeth^9, Haddon^8, Hilah^7, Ruez^6, Francis Marion^5, Peter^4, Peter^3, Matthias^2, John Jacob^1) was the son of Peter Reppert and Elizabeth (Kirk) Unger [Supplement No. 6288F]. Edward was born March 8, 1984, at Paoli, Pennsylvania.

(Sup) 7752A SARAH ELIZABETH UNGER (Elizabeth^9, Haddon^8, Hilah^7, Ruez^6, Francis Marion^5, Peter^4, Peter^3, Matthias^2, John Jacob^1) was the daughter of Peter Reppert and Elizabeth (Kirk) Unger [Supplement No. 6288F]. Sarah was born July 21, 1986, at Paoli, Pennsylvania.

(Sup) 7753 CATHERINE STEIDL (Ann^9, Mary^8, Pearl^7, John^6, Francis Marion^5, Peter^4, Peter^3, Matthias^2, John Jacob^1) was the daughter of Walter R. and Ann (Bryan) Steidl [Supplement No. 6289]. Kitty was born July 23, 1952, at Fort Ord, California. She attended the University of Maryland, and graduated in horticulture from Montana State University. Kitty married John Palmer Frankenfield, Jr., June 14, 1975, at Wyckoff, New Jersey. "Jay was the son of John Palmer and Beverly (Burgess) Frankenfield and was born January 22, 1952, at Towson, Maryland. They were associated with the Burges Falls Nursery at Cookeville, Tennessee.

(Sup) 8801 i Whitney Taylor Frankenfield, born April 10, 1980.
(Sup) 8802 ii Lindsay Frankenfield, born June 2, 1983.

(Sup) 7753A PHILLIP ANDREW STEIDL (Ann^9, Mary^8, Pearl^7, John^6, Francis Marion^5, Peter^4, Peter^3, Matthias^2, John Jacob^1) was the son of Walter R. and Ann (Bryan) Steidl [Suipplement No. 6289]. Phillip was born February 6, 1954, at Columbus, Georgia. He graduated from Vanderbilt University, Tennessee in 1976, where he was a member of Phi Beta Kappa. He was associated with the Burges Falls Nursery, Cookeville, Tennessee. Phillip married Deborah Sanders, October 25, 1980, at Cookeville. She was the daughter of Thomas Eugene and Ada Lavern (McGady) Sanders and was born February 10, 1953.

(Sup) 8803 i Andrew Bryan Steidl, born April 25, 1983.
(Sup) 8804 ii Rachael Elaine Steidl, born October 4, 1987.

(Sup) 7753B CARRIE BETH STEIDL (Ann^9, Mary^8, Pearl^7, John^6, Francis Marion^5, Peter^4, Peter^3, Matthias^2, John Jacob^1) was the daughter of Walter R. and Ann (Bryan) Steidl [Supplement No. 6289]. Carrie was born February 23, 1970, at Towson, Maryland.

(Sup) 7754 CHRISTINE AKIN (Elizabeth^9, George^8, Pearl^7, John^6, Francis Marion^5, Peter^4, Peter^3, Matthias^2, John Jacob^1) was the daughter of Jerome and Elizabeth (Dole) Akin [Supplement No. 6290]. Christine was born in Virginia.

(Sup) 7754A JEROME ERIC AKIN (Elizabeth^9, George^8, Pearl^7, John^6, Francis Marion^5, Peter^4, Peter^3, Matthias^2, John Jacob^1) was the son of Jerome and Elizabeth (Dole) Akin [Supplement No. 6290]. Jerome was born at Omaha, Nebraska.

(Sup) 7754B ERIKA AKIN (Elizabeth^9, George^8, Pearl^7, John^6, Francis Marion^5, Peter^4, Peter^3, Matthias^2, John Jacob^1) was the daughter of Jerome and Elizabeth (Dole) Akin [Supplement No. 6290]. Erika was born October 26, 1970, at Omaha, Nebraska.

(Sup) 7754C POLLY DOLE (Peter^9, George^8, Pearl^7, John^6, Francis Marion^5, Peter^4, Peter^3, Matthias^2, John Jacob^1) was the daughter of Peter Thomas and Barbara Ann (Robertaccio) Dole [Supplement No. 6291]. Polly was born October 24, 1975, at Denver, Colorado.

(Sup) 7754D ANNA APPHIA DOLE (Peter^9, George^8, Pearl^7, John^6, Francis Marrion^5, Peter^4, Peter^3, Matthias^2, John Jacob^1) was the daughter of Peter Thomas and Barbara Ann (Robertaccio) Dole [Supplement No. 6291]. Anna was born February 11, 1979, at Paris, Illinois.

(Sup) 7759 CHRISTINE MICHELE KOSIROG (Janet^9, Patricia^8, Wendell^7, Nethaniah^6, Francis Marion^5, Peter^4, Peter^3, Matthias^2, John Jacob^1) was the dauther of Andrew J. and Janet (Marshall) Kosirog [Supplement No. 6303]. Christine was born January 18, 1978.

(Sup) 7760 JESSICA KATHLEEN ANDERSON (Janet^9, Patricia^8, Wendell^7, Nethaniah^6, Francis Marion^5, Peter^4, Peter^3, Matthias^2, John Jacob^1) was the daughter of Scott M. and Janet (Marshall) (Kosirog) Anderson [Supplement No. 6303]. Jessica was born January 25, 1987.

(Sup) 7761 CHRISTOPHER WILLIAM STEPHENS (Debra^9, Patricia^8, Wendell^7, Nethaniah^6, Francis Marion^5, Peter^4, Peter^3, Matthias^2, John Jacob^1) was the son of James W. and Debra (Marshall) Stephens [Supplement No. 6303B]. Christopher was born July 18, 1978.

(Sup) 7761A JEFFREY DALE STEPHENS (Debra^9, Patricia^8, Wendell^7, Nethaniah^6, Francis Marion^5, Peter^4, Peter^3, Matthias^2, John Jacob^1) Jeffrey was the son of James W. and Debra (Marshall) Stephens [Supplement No. 6303B]. Jeffrey was born December 2, 1980.

(Sup) 7761B ERIN LYN CARMEAN (Rebecca^9, Patricia^8, Wendell^7, Nethaniah^6, Francis Marion^5, Peter^4, Peter^3, Matthias^2, John Jacob^1) was the daughter of James and Rebecca (Marshall) Carmean [Supplement No. 6303C]. Erin was born July 22, 1975.

(Sup) 7761C PATRICIA ANN LUMB (Nancy^9, Patricia^8, Wendell^7, Nethaniah^6, Francis Marion^5, Peter^4, Peter^3, Matthias^2, John Jacob^1) was the daughter of Patrick A. and Nancy (Marshall) Lumb [Supplement No. 6303D]. Patricia was born September 12, 1981.

(Sup) 7761D JOSHUA MICHAEL MILLER (Nancy^9, Patricia^8, Wendell^7, Nethaniah^6, Francis Marion^5, Peter^4, Peter^3, Matthias^2, John Jacob^1) was the son of Michael C. and Nancy (Marshall) (Lumb) Miller [Supplement No. 6303D]. Joshua was born January 20, 1986.

(Sup) 7755 CAROL SUE AMACHER (Mary Jane^9, Allen^8, Fred^7, Susan^6, Francis Marion^5, Peter^4, Peter^3, Matthias^2, John Jacob^1) was the daughter of Gene L. and Mary Jane (Parrish) Amacher [Supplement No. 6292]. Carol was born October 29, 1952, at El Paso, Texas. She received a B.S. degree in business administration from Ohio State University in 1974. Carol married Daryl Clingman, January 3, 1976, at Cambridge, Ohio. He was the son of Ross and Violet Clingman and was born November 29, 1951, at Beloit, Kansas.

(Sup) 8815 i Jennifer Alishia Clingman, born January 24, 1980.
(Sup) 8816 ii Daniel Alan Clingman, born January 28, 1981.

(Sup) 7756 KIMBERLY LYNN PARRISH (John^9, William^8, Harry^7, Susan^6, Francis Marion^5, Peter^4, Peter^3, Matthias^2, John Jacob^1) was the daughter of John Arthur and Lona Rae (Sandilands) Parrish [Supplement No. 6293]. Kimberly was born April 11, 1964.

(Sup) 7757 MICHAEL PARRISH (John^9, William^8, Harry^7, Susan^6, Francis Marion^5, Peter^4, Peter^3, Matthias^2, John Jacob^1) was the son of John Arthur and Lorna Rae (Sandilands) Parrish [Supplement No. 6293]. Michael was born August 25, 1966.

(Sup) 7758 JENNIFER JO WOHLWEND (JoLynn^9, JoAnn^8, Marion^7, Christopher^6, Francis Marion^5, Peter^4, Peter^3, Matthias^2, John Jacob^1) was the daughter of Patrick G. and JoLynn (Johnson) Wohlwend [Supplement No. 6299]. Jennifer was born July 25, 1973, at Quantico, Virginia.

(Sup) 7758A JULIE WOHLWEND (JoLynn^9, JoAnn^8, Marion^7, Christopher^6, Francis Marion^5, Peter^4, Peter^3, Matthias^2, John Jacob^1) was the daughter of Patrick G. and JoLynn (Johnson) Wohlwend [Supplement No. 6299]. Julie was born July 16, 1977, at Indianapolis, Indiana.

(Sup) 7758B DANIELLE MARIE JOHNSON (Michael^9, JoAnn^8, Marion^7, Christopher^6, Francis Marion^5, Peter^4, Peter^3, Matthias^2, John Jacob^1) was the daughter of Michael Link and Deborah (Walker) Johnson [Supplement No. 6299B]. Danielle was born February 28, 1981, at St. Louis, Missouri.

(Sup) 7758C MEGAN CHRISTINE JOHNSON (Michael^9, JoAnn^8, Marion^7, Christopher^6, Francis Marion^5, Peter^4, Peter^3, Matthias^2, John Jacob^1) was the daughter of Michael Link and Deborah (Walker) Johnson [Supplement No. 6299B]. Megan was born March 6, 1986, at St. Louis, Missouri.

(Sup) 7762 DANIEL PATRICK PROFFITT, JR. (Carla[9], William[8], Blanche[7], William[6], Francis Marion[5], Peter[4], Peter[3], Matthias[2], John Jacob[1]) was the son of Daniel Patrick and Carla (Foley) Proffitt [Supplement No. 6305]. Daniel was born August 16, 1967, at Mattoon, Illinois.

(Sup) 7762A JASON MILES PROFFITT (Carla[9], William[8], Blanche[7], William[6], Francis Marion[5], Peter[4], Peter[3], Matthias[2], John Jacob[1]) was the son of Daniel Patrick and Carla (Foley) Proffitt [Supplement No. 6305]. Jason was born November 23, 1969, at Paris, Illinois.

(Sup) 7762B JESSICA JANE PROFFITT (Carla[9], William[8], Blanche[7], William[6], Francis Marion[5], Peter[4], Peter[3], Matthias[2], John Jacob[1]) was the daughter of Daniel Patrick and Carla (Foley) Proffitt [Supplement No. 6305]. Jessica was born July 9, 1974, at Paris, Illinois.

(Sup) 7762C CAMERON MATHERLY (Joan[9], William[8], Blanche[7], William[6], Francis Marion[5], Peter[4], Peter[3], Matthias[2], John Jacob[1]) was the son of William and Joan (Foley) Matherly [Supplement No. 6306]. Cameron was born October 30, 1967, at Mattoon, Illinois.

(Sup) 7762D CALISTA MATHERLY (Joan[9], William[8], Blanche[7], William[6], Francis Marion[5], Peter[4], Peter[3], Matthias[2], John Jacob[1]) was the daughter of William and Joan (Foley) Matherly [Supplement No. 6306]. Calista was born May 28, 1971, at Mattoon, Illinois.

(Sup) 7762E WILLIAM JACOB MATHERLY (Joan[9], William[8], Blanche[6], Francis Marion[5], Peter[4], Peter[3], Matthias[2], John Jacob[1]) was the son of William and Joan (Foley) Matherly [Supplement No. 6306]. William was born April 16, 1979, at Mattoon, Illinois.

(Sup) 7763 WILLIAM ANDREW FOLEY (William[9], William[8], Blanche[7], William[6], Francis Marion[5], Peter[4], Peter[3], Matthias[2], John Jacob[1]) was the son of William and Linda (Elam) Foley [Supplement No. 6307]. William was born March 26, 1976, at Terre Haute, Indiana.

(Sup) 7763A ALICIA ANN FOLEY (William[9], William[8], Blanche[7], William[6], Francis Marion[5], Peter[4], Peter[3], Matthias[2], John Jacob[1]) was the daughter of William and Lind (Elam) Foley [Supplement No. 6307]. Alicia was born March 21, 1980, at Paris, Illinois.

(Sup) 7763B LUCAS CHARLES WRIGHT (Jane[9], William[8], Blanche[7], William[6], Francis Marion[5], Peter[4], Peter[3], Matthias[2], John Jacob[1]) was the son of Gary Lee and Jane (Foley) Wright [Supplement No. 6307A]. Lucas was born July 10, 1983, at Columbia, Maryland.

(Sup) 7763C GARY JOSEPH WRIGHT (Jane[9], William[8], Blanche[7], William[6], Francis Marion[5], Peter[4], Peter[3], Matthias[2], John Jacob[1]) was the son of Gary Lee and Jane (Foley) Wright [Supplement No. 6307A]. Gary was born February 25, 1985, at Knoxville, Tennessee.

(Sup) 7763D DAVID MICHAEL WRIGHT (Jane[9], William[8], Blanche[7], William[6], Francis Marion[5], Peter[4], Peter[3], Matthias[2], John Jacob[1]) was the son of Gary Lee and Jane (Foley) Wright [Supplement No. 6307A]. David was born February 11, 1987, at Austin, Texas.

(Sup) 7764 LAURA ANN-MARIE FOLEY (Jack[9], William[8], Jack[8], Blanche[7], William[6], Francis Marion[5], Peter[4], Peter[3], Matthias[2], John Jacob[1]) was the daughter of Jack Franklin and Linda Sue (Dodd) Foley [Supplement No. 6308]. Laura was born January 4, 1971, at Danville, Illinois.

(Sup) 7764A DAMIAN PATRICK FOLEY (Jack[9], William[8], Jack[8], Blanche[7], William[6], Francis Marion[5], Peter[4], Peter[3], Matthias[2], John Jacob[1]) was the son of Jack Franklin and Linda Sue (Dodd) Foley [Supplement No. 6308]. Damian was born September 4, 1974, at Danville, Illinois.

(Sup) 7765 DAWN MICHELLE WILLIAMS (Cheryl[9], Conrad[8], Blanche[7], William[6], Francis Marion[5], Peter[4], Peter[3], Matthias[2], John Jacob[1]) was the daughter of John and Cheryl Ann (Foley) Williams [Supplement No. 6309]. She was born January 7, 1970, at Terre Haute, Indiana.

(Sup) 7765A TERISA ANNE WILLIAMS (Cheryl[9], Conrad[8], Blanche[7], William[6], Francis Marion[5], Peter[4], Peter[3], Matthias[2], John Jacob[1]) was the daughter of John and Cheryl Ann (Foley) Williams [Supplement No. 6309]. She was born May 14, 1971, at Terre Haute, Indiana.

(Sup) 7765B   TAMARA LYN WILLIAMS (Cheryl[9], Conrad[8], Blanche[7], William[6], Francis Marion[5], Peter[4], Peter[3], Matthias[2], John Jacob[1]) was the daughter of John and Cheryl Ann (Foley) Williams [Supplement No. 6309]. She was born December 29, 1975, at Champaign, Illinois.

(Sup) 7765C   CHRISTOPHER EARL LEE WILLIS (Polly[9], Conrad[8], Blanche[7], William[6], Francis Marion[5], Peter[4], Peter[3], Matthias[2], John Jacob[1]) was the son of James Lawrence and Polly Catherine (Foley) Willis [Supplement No. 6310]. Christopher was born September 21, 1970.

(Sup) 7765D   BRANDY MICHELLE WILLIS (Polly[9], Conrad[8], Blanche[7], William[6], Francis Marion[5], Peter[4], Peter[3], Matthias[2], John Jacob[1]) was the daughter of James Lawrence and Polly Catherine (Foley) Willis [Supplement No. 6310]. Brandy was born January 12, 1973.

(Sup) 7766   CARA SUZANNE FOLEY (Guy[9], Robert[7], Blanche[7], William[6], Francis Marion[5], Peter[4], Peter[3], Matthias[2], John Jacob[1]) was the daughter of Guy Franklin and Patricia (Crowe) Foley [Supplement No. 6311A]. Cara was born July 29, 1983, at Bremerton, Washington.

(Sup) 7766A   MARGARET PATRICIA FOLEY (Guy[9], Robert[8], Blanche[7], William[6], Francis Marion[5], Peter[4], Peter[3], Matthias[2], John Jacob[1]) was the daughter of Guy Franklin and Patricia (Crowe) Foley [Supplement No. 6311A]. Margaret was born May 7, 1986, at Bremerton, Washington.

(Sup) 7767   SHAINA MAUREEN FOLEY (Neal[9], Robert[8], Blanche[7], William[6], Francis Marion[5], Peter[4], Peter[3], Matthias[2], John Jacob[1]) was the daughter of Neal Robert and Marla (Everist) Foley [Supplement No. 6311B]. Shaina was born October 4, 1981, at Bremerton, Washington.

(Sup) 7767A   JAMES WILLIS FOLEY (Neal[9], Robert[8], Blanche[7], William[6], Francis Marion[5], Peter[4], Peter[3], Matthias[2], John Jacob[1]) was the son of Neal Robert and Marla (Everist) Foley [Supplement No. 6311B]. James was born September 18, 1983, at Bremerton, Washington.

(Sup) 7767B   NATHANIEL DAVID PERRONE (Maureen[9], Robert[8], Blanche[7], William[6], Francis Marion[5], Peter[4], Peter[3], Matthias[2], John Jacob[1]) was the son of Michael Joseph and Maureen (Foley) Perrone [Supplement No. 6311C]. Nathaniel was born October 2, 1981, at Bremerton, Washington.

(Sup) 7767C   PAIGE NICOLE PERRONE (Maureen[9], Robert[8], Blanche[7], William[6], Francis Marion[5], Peter[4], Peter[3], Matthias[2], John Jacob[1]) was the daughter of Michael Joseph and Maureen (Foley) Perrone [Supplement No. 6311C]. Paige was born March 11, 1983, at Bremerton, Washington.

(Sup) 7767D   JOSHUA JAMES FOLEY (Bryan[9], Robert[8], Blanche[7], William[6], Francis Marion[5], Peter[4], Peter[3], Matthias[2], John Jacob[1]) was the son of Bryan Howard and Karen (Broussard) Foley [Supplement No. 6311D]. Joshua was born February 7, 1987, at Bremerton, Washington.

(Sup) 7768   BENJAMIN ALLEN ARNOLD (Suzanne[9], Robert[8], Blanche[7], William[6], Francis Marion[5], Peter[4], Peter[3], Matthias[2], John Jacob[1]) was the son of David Norman and Suzanne (Foley) Arnold [Supplement No. 6311G] Benjamin was born May 8, 1984, at Bremerton, Washington.

(Sup) 7768A   ZACHARY DAVID ARNOLD (Suzanne[9], Robert[8], Blanche[7], William[6], Francis Marion[5], Peter[4], Peter[3], Matthias[2], John Jacob[1]) was the son of David Norman and Suzanne (Foley) Arnold [Supplement No. 6311G]. Zachary was born July 27, 1986, at Madera, California.

(Sup) 7785   SANDRA LOUISE LARSEN (Kent[9], Grace[8], Harvey[7], Andrew[6], Hannah[5], David[4], Catherine[3], Matthias[2], John Jacob[1]) was the daughter of Kent Palmer and Luella Brainard Larsen [Supplement No. 6387]. Sandra was born November 16, 1944.

(Sup) 7790   BETTIE MABLE MARTIN (Ruby[9], Thomas[8], Anna[7], Samuel[6], Hannah[5], David[4], Catherine[3], Matthias[2], John Jacob[1]) was the daughter of Ralph Edgar and Ruby (Loften) Martin [Supplement No. 6416]. Bettie was born January 9, 1945, at Magnolia, Arkansas.

(Sup) 7791 JOSEPH DWAYNE RUNNELS (Mahdeen[9], Walter[8], Anna[7], Samuel[6], Hannah[5], David[4], Catherine[3], Matthias[2], John Jacob[1]) was the son of Haskell and Mahdeen (Loften) Runnels [Supplement No. 6419]. Joseph was born in 1939 at Springhill, Louisiana.

(Sup) 7792 YVONNE YOUNG (Christine[9], Walter[8], Anna[7], Samuel[6], Hannah[5], David[4], Catherine[3], Matthias[2], John Jacob[1]) was the daughter of William and Christine (Lofton) Young [Supplement No. 6421]. Yvonne was born October 5 1945, at Camden, Arkansas.

(Sup) 7793 JAMES THURBYN BAY (Christine[9], Walter[8], Anna[7], Samuel[6], Hannah[5], David[4], Catherine[3], Matthias[2], John Jacob[1]) was the son of William and Christine (Lofton) (Young) Bay [Supplement No. 6421]. James was born March 29, 1948.

(Sup) 7794 PATRICIA ANN KEITH (Mary[9], Parrie[8], Anna[7], Samuel[6], Hannah[5], David[4], Catherine[3], Matthias[2], John Jacob[1]) was the daughter of Clarence David and Mary (Reid) Keith [Supplement No. 6423]. Patricia was born July 16, 1940.

(Sup) 7795 DAVID REID KEITH (Mary[9], Parrie[8], Anna[7], Samuel[6], Hannah[5], David[4], Catherine[3], Matthias[2], John Jacob[1]) was the son of Clarence David and Mary (Reid) Keith [Supplement No. 6423]. David was born August 13, 1949.

(Sup) 7800 RODNEY LEE BAKER, JR., (Rodney[9], Oren[8], Jessie[7], Samuel[6], Hannah[5], David[4], Catherine[3], Matthias[2], John Jacob[1]) was the son of Rodney Lee and Billy Sue (Emerson) Baker [Supplement No. 6439]. Rodney, Jr., was born December 3, 1942.

(Sup) 7810 CHRISTI DIANE ROBY (Susan[9], Robert[8], Robert[7], Ida[6], Franklin[5], Adam[4], Adam[3], Matthias[2], John Jacob[1]) was the daughter of Steven J. and Susan Dye (Harris) Roby [Supplement No. 6485]. She was born September 10, 1968, at Vandenburg Air Force Base, California.

(Sup) 7811 ROBERT JOHN ROBY (Susan[9], Robert[8], Robert[7], Ida[6], Franklin[5], Adam[4], Adam[3], John Adam I[2], John Jacob[1]) was the son of Steven J. and Susan Dye (Harris) Roby [Supplement No. 6485]. He was born May 18, 1971, at Napoleon, Ohio.

(Sup) 7821 RUSSELL EMERY MONROE (Judith[9], Virginia[8], Paul[7], Herndon[6], Franklin[5], Adam[4], Adam[3], Matthias[2], John Jacob[1]) was the son of Paul Edgar and Judith Lynn (Johnson) Monroe [Supplement No. 6496]. Russell was born December 18, 1973, at Houston, Texas.

(Sup) 7822 REBECCA VIRGINIA MONROE (Judith[9], Virginia[8], Paul[7], Herndon[6], Franklin[5], Adam[4], Adam[3], Matthias[2], John Jacob[1]) was the daughter of Paul Edgar and Judith Lynn (Johnson) Monroe [Supplement No. 6496]. She was born October 21, 1976, at Houston, Texas.

(Sup) 7823 TRACY ALISON COOK (Donna[9], Roger[8], Paul[7], Herndon[6], Franklin[5], Adam[4], Adam[3], Matthias[2], John Jacob[1]) was the daughter of William Douglas and Donna Lee (Link) Cook [Supplement No. 6498]. She was born October 1, 1970, at Marietta, Georgia.

(Sup) 7824 JEANNA ROXANNE ODEN (Beverly[9], Roger[8], Paul[7], Herndon[6], Franklin[5], Adam[4], Adam[3], Matthias[2], John Jacob[1]) was the daughter of Kenneth Woodward and Beverly Jean (Link) Oden [Supplement No. 6499]. She was born March 4, 1966, at Charles Town, West Virginia.

(Sup) 7825 DENA NICOLE ODEN (Beverly[9], Roger[8], Paul[7], Herndon[6], Franklin[5], Adam[4], Adam[3], Matthias[2], John Jacob[1]) was the daughter of Kenneth Woodward and Beverly Jean (Link) Oden [Supplement No. 6499]. She was born Setember 27, 1967, at Charles Town, West Virginia.

(Sup) 7826 APRIL DAWN MORGAN (Martha[9], Roger[8], Paul[7], Herndon[6], Franklin[5], Adam[4], Adam[3], Matthias[2], John Jacob[1]) was the daughter of Delmer Allen and Martha Lou (Link) Morgan [Supplement No. 6500]. She was born April 1, 1968, at Ronceverte, West Virginia.

(Sup) 7827 HEATHER LYNN MORGAN (Martha^9, Roger^8, Paul^7, Herndon^6, Franklin^5, Adam^4, Adam^3, Matthias^2, John Jacob^1) was the daughter of Delmer Allen and Martha Lou (Link) Morgan [Supplement No. 6500]. She was born August 28, 1970, at Ronceverte, West Virginia.

(Sup) 7828 TIA ANN MORGAN (Martha^9, Roger^8, Paul^7, Herndon^6, Franklin^5, Adam^4, Adam^3, Matthias^2, John Jacob^1) was the daughter of Delmer Allen and Martha Lou (Link) Morgan [Supplement No. 6500]. She was born October 3, 1978, at Fairlea, West Virginia.

(Sup) 7833 ASHLEY HUNTER VERDON (Wendy^9, Gordon^8, Mary^7, Mary^6, Leonidas^5, Thomas^4, John^3, Matthias^2, John Jacob^1) was the daughter of Jeffrey M. and Wendy (Wiles) Verdon [Supplement No. 6522A]. Ashley was born February 21, 1985.

(Sup) 7834 ADAM JOSEPH VERDON (Wendy^9, Gordon^8, Mary^7, Mary^6, Leonidas^5, Thomas^4, John^3, Matthias^2, John Jacob^1) was the son of Jeffrey M. and Wendy (Wiles) Verdon [Supplement No. 6522A]. Adam was born April 7, 1988.

(Sup) 7840 SHARON JO MILLER (Dorothy^9, Wanita^8, Annie^7, William^6, Felix^5, David^4, Elizabeth^3, Matthias^2, John Jacob^1) was the daughter of Carol and Dorothy (Waters) Miller [Supplement No. 6545]. Sharon was born in 1946.

(Sup) 7845 JENNY HILDEBRAND (Robert^9, Paul^8, Elizabeth^7, Martin^6, Elizabeth^5, Martha^4, John Adam^3, John Adam^2, John Jacob^1) was the daughter of Robert and Karen Hildebrand [Supplement No. 6570].

(Sup) 7846 WAYNE KNIPE, III (Jean^9, Charlotte^8, Franklin^7, Martin^6, Elizabeth^5, Martha^4, John Adam^3, John Adam^2, John Jacob^1) was the son of Wayne and Jean Schmidt Knipe, Jr. [Supplement No. 6572]. Wayne married Sharon _____

(Sup) 7847 RICKIE KNIPE (Jean^9, Charlotte^8, Franklin^7, Martin^6, Elizabeth^5, Martha^4, John Adam^3, John Adam^2, John Jacob^1) was the son of Wayne and Jean Schmidt Knipe, Jr. [Supplement No. 6572].

(Sup) 7848 LYNETTE PLANCK (Marilyn^9, Charlotte^8, Franklin^7, Martin^6, Elizabeth^5, Martha^4, John Adam^3, John Adam^2, John Jacob^1) [Supplement No. 6573]. Lynette was the daughter of Paul and Marilyn Schmidt Planck married Ted Kupferer.

(Sup) 8861   i Chantel Kupferer.
(Sup) 8862   ii Derick Kupferer.

(Sup) 7849 GRAYSON PLANCK (Marilyn^9, Charlotte^8, Franklin^7, Martin^6, Elizabeth^5, Martha^4, John Adam^3, John Adam^2, John Jacob^1) was the son of Paul and Marilyn Schmidt Planck [Supplement No. 6573].

(Sup) 7850 MELANIE PLANCK (Marilyn^9, Charlotte^8, Franklin^7, Martin^6, Elizabeth^5, Martha^4, John Adam^3, John Adam^2, John Jacob^1) was the daughter of Paul and Marilyn Schmidt Planck [Supplement No. 6573]. Melanie married Duane Kirkley.

(Sup) 8865   i Jacob Kirkley.

(Sup) 7851 MELINDA PLANCK (Marilyn^9, Charlotte^8, Franklin^7, Martin^6, Elizabeth^5, Martha^4, John Adam^3, John Adam^2, John Jacob^1) was the daughter of Paul and Marilyn Schmidt Planck [Supplement No. 6573]. Melinda married Scott Greene.

(Sup) 8866   i Forest Greene.
(Sup) 8867   ii Ashley Greene.
(Sup) 8868 iii Michael Greene.

(Sup) 7852 JON McEWAN (Carol^9, Charlotte^8, Franklin^7, Martin^6, Elizabeth^5, Martha^4, John Adam^3, John Adam^2, John Jacob^1) was the son of Preston and Carol Schmidt McEwan [Supplement No. 6574].

(Sup) 7853 KAREN McEWAN (Carol^9, Charlotte^8, Franklin^7, Martin^6, Elizabeth^5, Martha^4, John Adam^3, John Adam^2, John Jacob^1) was the daughter of Preston and Carol Schmidt McEwan [Supplement No. 6574]. Karen married Clive Bulmer.

(Sup) 7854 MARC McEWAN (Carol^9, Charlotte^8, Franklin^7, Martin^6, Elizabeth^5, Martha^4, John Adam^3, John Adam^2, John Jacob^1) was the son of Preston and Carol Schmidt McEwan [Supplement No. 6574].

(Sup) 7855 JUDY BONSIB (Louis^9, Marietta^8, Franklin^7, Martin^6, Elizabeth^5, Martha^4, John Adam^3, John Adam^2, John Jacob^1) was the daughter of Louis William and Virginia Gardner Bonsib [Supplement No. 6576]. Judy was born in 1948 at Kalamazoo, Michigan. She married Dr. Clyde R. Willis.

(Sup) 8871   i   Jennifer Willis.
(Sup) 8872   ii   Gina Willis.
(Sup) 8873   iii Matthew Willis.
(Sup) 8874   iv   Nathan Willis.

(Sup) 7856 SUSAN GENE BONSIB (Louis^9, Marietta^8, Franklin^7, Martin^6, Elizabeth^5, Martha^4, John Adam^3, John Adam^2, John Jacob^1) was the daughter of Louis William and Virginia Gardner Bonsib [Supplement No. 6576]. Susan was born in 1942 at Cocoa Beach, Florida. She married Mac H. Crosbie. They were divorced.

(Sup) 8875   i   Scott Crosbie.
(Sup) 8876   ii   Todd Crosbie.
(Sup) 8877   iii Chad Crosbie.

(Sup) 7857 BETTY VIRGINIA BONSIB (Louis^9, Marietta^8, Franklin^7, Martin^6, Elizabeth^5, Martha^4, John Adam^3, John Adam^2, John Jacob^1) was the daughter of Louis William and Virginia Gardner Bonsib [Supplement No. 6576]. She was born in 1946 at Steamboat Springs, Colorado. She married Steven Rohrbaugh.

(Sup) 7858 GRANT GARDNER BONSIB (Louis^9, Marietta^8, Franklin^7, Martin^6, Elizabeth^5, Martha^4, John Adam^3, John Adam^2, John Jacob^1) was the son of Louis William and Virginia Gardner Bonsib [Supplement No. 6576]. Grant was born in 1948 at Denver, Colorado (twin of John). He married Sylvia Hong.

(Sup) 8881   i   Brandon Bonsib.

(Sup) 7859 JOHN McDONALD BONSIB (Louis^9, Marietta^8, Franklin^7, Martin^6, Elizabeth^5, Martha^4, John Adam^3, John Adam^2, John Jacob^1) was the son of Louis William and Virginia Gardner Bonsib [Supplement No. 6576]. He married Annika Raaf at Stockholm, Sweden.

(Sup) 8882   i   Vanessa Bonsib.
(Sup) 8883   ii   David William Bonsib, born February 22, 1986 (twin).
(Sup) 8884   iii Marcus Tore Bonsib, born February 22, 1986 (twin).

(Sup) 7860 SANDRA LIPP (Joan^9, Marietta^8, Franklin^7, Martin^6, Elizabeth^5, Martha^4, John Adam^3, John Adam^2, John Jacob^1) was the daughter of Carl and Joan Bonsib Lipp [Supplement No. 6577]. Sandra married John Bickley.

(Sup) 8894   i   Benjamin Bickley.

(Sup) 7861 PAMELA LIPP (Joan^9, Marietta^8, Franklin^7, Martin^6, Elizabeth Martha^4, John Adam^3, John Adam^2, John Jacob^1) was the daughter of Carl and Joan Bonsib Lipp [Supplement No. 6577]. Pamela married Thomas Boehner.

(Sup) 7862 TERRY LIPP (Joan^9, Marietta^8, Franklin^7, Martin^6, Elizabeth^5, Martha^4, John Adam^3, John Adam^2, John Jacob^1) was the son of Carl and Joan Bonsib Lipp [Supplement No. 6577]. Terry married Rikki Magley.

(Sup) 7863 DEBORAH BONSIB (John^9, Marietta^8, Franklin^7, Martin^6, Elizabeth^5, Martha^4, John Adam^3, John Adam^2, John Jacob^1) was the daughter of John Frank and Nancy Van Arnam Bonsib [Supplement No. 6578]. Deborah married Michael Christman.

(Sup) 7864 REBECCA BONSIB (John^9, Marietta^8, Franklin^7, Martin^6, Elizabeth^5, Martha^4, John Adam^3, John Adam^2, John Jacob^1) was the daughter of John Frank and Nancy Van Arnam Bonsib [Supplement No. 6578].

(Sup) 7865 GREGORY BONSIB (Richard^9, Marietta^8, Franklin^7, Martin^6, Elizabeth^5, Martha^4, John Adam^3, John Adam^2, John Jacob^1) was the son of Richard E. and Gretchen Allen Bonsib [Supplement No. 6579].

(Sup) 7866   STEVEN BONSIB (Richard^9, Marietta^8, Franklin^7, Martin^6, Elizabeth^5, Martha^4, John Adam^3, John Adam^2, John Jacob^1) was the son of Richard E. and Gretchen Allen Bonsib [Supplement No. 6579].

(Sup) 7867   DEBORAH JACOBS (John^9, Robert^8, Franklin^7, Martin^6, Elizabeth^5, Martha^4, John Adam^3, John Adam^2, John Jacob^1) was the daughter of John Robert and Doris Jacobs [Supplement No. 6580].

(Sup) 7868   VALERIA JACOBS (John^9, Robert^8, Franklin^7, Martin^6, Elizabeth^5, Martha^4, John Adam^3, John Adam^2, John Jacob^1) was the daughter of John Robert and Doris Jacobs [Supplement No. 6580].

(Sup) 7869   KENNETH JACOBS (John^9, Robert^8, Franklin^7, Martin^6, Elizabeth^5, Martha^4, John Adam^3, John Adam^2, John Jacob^1) was the son of John Robert and Doris Jacobs [Supplement No. 6580].

(Sup) 7870   KATHY HAUCK (William^9, Lillian^8, Franklin^7, Martin^6, Elizabeth^5, Martha^4, John Adam^3, John Adam^2, John Jacob^1) was the daughter of William Everett and Jean (Jacobi) Hauck, Jr. [Supplement No. 6582]. Kathy married Tim Smith.

(Sup) 7871   WILLIAM HAUCK, III (William^9, Lillian^8, Franklin^7, Martin^6, Elizabeth^5, Martha^4, John Adam^3, John Adam^2, John Jacob^1) was the son of William Everett and Jean (Jacobi) Hauck, Jr. [Supplement No. 6582].

(Sup) 7872   CINDY HAUCK (William^9, Lillian^8, Franklin^7, Martin^6, Elizabeth^5, Martha^4, John Adam^3, John Adam^2, John Jacob^1) was the daughter of William Everett and Jean (Jacobi) Hauck, Jr. [Supplement No. 6582].

(Sup) 7873   JEANNIE HAUCK (William^9, Lillian^8, Franklin^7, Martin^6, Elizabeth^5, Martha^4, John Adam^3, John Adam^2, John Jacob^1) was the daughter of William Everett and Jean (Jacobi) Hauck, Jr. [Supplement No. 6582].

(Sup) 7874   CHRISTINA HAUCK (William^9, Lillian^8, Franklin^7, Martin^6, Elizabeth^5, Martha^4, John Adam II^3, John Adam I^2, John Jacob^1) was the daughter of William Everett and Jean (Jacobi) Hauck, Jr. [Supplement No. 6583].

(Sup) 7875   LILLIE HAUCK (Ronald^9, Lillian^8, Franklin^7, Martin^6, Elizabeth^5, Martha^4, John Adam II^3, John Adam I^2, John Jacob^1) was the daughter of Ronald Lee and Helen (Hathorn) Hauck [Supplement No. 6583].

(Sup) 7876   RONALD HAUCK, JR. (Ronald^9, Lillian^8, Franklin^7, Martin^6, Elizabeth^5, Martha^4, John Adam^3, John Adam^2, John Jacob^1) was the son of Ronald Lee and Helen (Hathorn) Hauck [Supplement No. 6583].

(Sup) 7877   BECKY HAUCK (Ronald^9, Lillian^8, Franklin^7, Martin^6, Elizabeth^5, Martha^4, John Adam^3, John Adam^2, John Jacob^1) was the daughter of Ronald Lee and Helen (Hathorn) Hauck [Supplement No. 6584].

(Sup) 7878   PAMELA HAUCK (David^9, Lillian^8, Franklin^7, Martin^6, Elizabeth^5, Martha^4, John Adam^3, John Adam^2, John Jacob^1) was the daughter of David Allen and Bonnie (Allender) Hauck [Supplement No. 6584].

(Sup) 7879   DOUGLAS HAUCK (David^9, Lillian^8, Franklin^7, Martin^6, Elizabeth^5, Martha^4, John Adam^3, John Adam^2, John Jacob^1) was the son of David Allen and Bonnie (Allender) Hauck [Supplement No. 6584].

(Sup) 7880   DAWN HAUCK (David^9, Lillian^8, Franklin^7, Martin^6, Elizabeth^5, Martha^4, John Adam^3, John Adam^2, John Jacob^1) was the daughter of David Allen and Bonnie (Allender) Hauck [Supplement No. 6584].

(Sup) 7881   JAMES MICHAEL MAHERN (Barbara^9, Lillian^8, Franklin^7, Martin^6, Elizabeth^5, Martha^4, John Adam^3, John Adam^2, John Jacob^1) was the son of Louis J. and Barbara (Hauck) Mahern [Supplement No. 6585]. James was born June 3, 1966, at Indianapolis, Indiana.

(Sup) 7891 JEFFREY RAYMOND (TIBBS) WESTERMAN (Ralph[9], Amy[8], George[7], Martin[6], Elizabeth[5], Martha[4], John Adam[3], John Adam[2], John Jacob[1]) was the son of Ralph Homer and Carol May Suydam Tibbs, Jr. His surname was changed to Westerman on adoption by his stepfather Christian Westerman, July, 1969 [Supplement No. 6594]. Jeffrey was born June 11, 1954, at Chicago, Illinois. He served three years in the U.S. Army Corps of Engineers at Fort Belvoir, after which he was employed by the U.S. Civil Service. Jeffrey married Margaret Lori Parker November 10, 1974, at Alexandria, Virginia. She was the daughter of Walter E. and Margaret Beky Parker and was born October 11, 1954, at Fort Bragg, North Carolina.

(Sup) 8951   i Michelle Amy Westerman, born April 7, 1977.

(Sup) 7892 ANDREW LEE (TIBBS) WESTERMAN (Ralph[9], Amy[8], George[7], Martin[6], Elizabeth[5], Martha[4], John Adam[3], John Adam[2], John Jacob[1]) was the son of Ralph Homer and Carol May (Suydam) Tibbs, Jr. His surname was changed to Westerman on adoption by his stepfather Christian Westerman July 1969 [Supplement No. 6594]. Andrew was born February 2, 1956, at the U.S. Air Force Hospital, Furstenfeldbruck, Germany. He served three years with the U.S. Army Corps of Engineers. He attended Northern Virginia Community College and was employed as a surveyor with a construction company. He married Teresa Marie Gailliot October 8, 1977, at Oxon Hill, Maryland. She was the daughter of Thomas H. and Elizabeth Ann Hall Gaillot and was born August 27, 1957, at Alexandria, Virginia.

(Sup) 8952   i Kelly Lynn Westerman, born August 5, 1979.

(Sup) 7893 JILL LUCIE (TIBBS) WESTERMAN (Ralph[9], Amy[8], George[7], Martin[6], Elizabeth[5], Martha[4], John Adam[3], John Adam[2], John Jacob[1]) was the daughter of Ralph Homer and Carol May (Suydam) Tibbs, Jr. Her surname was changed to Westerman on adoption by her stepfather Christian Westerman July, 1969 [Supplement No. 6594]. Jill was born September 18, 1957, at Washington, D.C. She attended Northern Virginia Community College, and was employed by TRW, Inc., McLean, Virginia. She married Robert Anthony Lyons May 31, 1980, at Falls Church Virginia. He was the adopted son of Robert Daniel and Margaret Lyons and was born December 7, 1951, at Dayton, Ohio.

(Sup) 7894 LISA MICHELLE JACQUES (Marilyn[9], George[8], George[7], Martin[6], Elizabeth[5], Martha[4], John Adam[3], John Adam[2], John Jacob[1]) was the daughter of Roy Elwood and Ruth Marilyn Jacobs Jacques [Supplement No. 6596]. Lisa was born October 23, 1960, in New Jersey. She graduated from West Chester State College in Pennsylvania, and was a professional singer and musician.

(Sup) 7882 BRIAN THOMAS MAHERN (Barbara[9], Lillian[8], Franklin[7], Martin[6], Elizabeth[5], Martha[4], John Adam[3], John Adam[2], John Jacob[1]) was the son of Louis J. and Barbara (Hauck) Mahern [Supplement No. 6585]. Brian was born February 3, 1968, at Indianapolis, Indiana.

(Sup) 7883 JENNIFER JEAN MAHERN (Barbara[9], Lillian[8], Franklin[7], Martin[6], Elizabeth[5], Martha[4], John Adam[3], John Adam[2], John Jacob[1]) was the daughter of Louis J. and Barbara (Hauck) Mahern [Supplement No. 6585]. Jennifer was born September 20, 1970, at Alexandria, Virginia.

(Sup) 7884 RYAN HAUCK (Robert[9], Lillian[8], Franklin[7], Martin[6], Elizabeth[5], Martha[4], John Adam[3], John Adam[2], John Jacob[1]) was the son of Robert Reed and Karen Driskill Hauck [Supplement No. 6586].

(Sup) 7885 CORY HAUCK (Robert[9], Lillian[8], Franklin[7], Martin[6], Elizabeth[5], Martha[4], John Adam[3], John Adam[2], John Jacob[1]) was the son of Robert Reed and Karen Driskill Hauck [Supplement No. 6586].

(Sup) 7886 TRAVIS HAUCK (Robert[9], Lillian[8], Franklin[7], Martin[6], Elizabeth[5], Martha[4], John Adam[3], John Adam[2], John Jacob[1]) was the son of Robert Reed and Karen Driskill Hauck [Supplement No. 6586].

(Sup) 7887 BRIAN D. JACOBS (Frank[9], Ralph[8], Franklin[7], Martin[6], Elizabeth[5], Martha[4], John Adam[3], John Adam[2], John Jacob[1]) was the son of Frank Charles and Arlene Harlow Jacobs [Supplement No. 6588]. Brian was born November 13, 1971, at Greencastle, Indiana.

(Sup) 7888 ERIC M. JACOBS (Frank[9], Ralph[8], Franklin[7], Martin[6], Elizabeth[5], Martha[4], John Adam[3], John Adam[2], John Jacob[1]) was the son of Frank Charles and Arlene Harlow Jacobs [Supplement No. 6588]. Eric was born January 22, 1976, at Greencastle, Indiana.

- -

(Sup) 7895 ROY ELWOOD JACQUES, III (Marilyn[9], George[8], George[7], Martin[6], Elizabeth[5], Martha[4], John Adam[3], John Adam[2], John Jacob[1]) was the son of Roy Elwood and Ruth Marilyn Jacobs Jacques [Supplement No. 6596]. Roy, III, was born December 27, 1962, on Staten Island, New York.

(Sup) 7896 DONNA LEE MILLER (Beverly[9], George[8], George[7], Martin[6], Elizabeth[5], Martha[4], John Adam[3], John Adam[2], John Jacob[1]) was the daughter of Gregory S. and Beverly Ann Jacobs Miller [Supplement No. 6597]. Donna was born January 24, 1965 (twin of Deborah).

(Sup) 7897 DEBORAH LYNN MILLER (Beverly[9], George[8], George[7], Martin[6], Elizabeth[5], Martha[4], John Adam[3], John Adam[2], John Jacob[1]) was the daughter of Gregory S. and Beverly Ann Jacobs Miller [Supplement No. 6597]. Deborah was born January 24, 1965 (twin of Donna).

Chapter 5

Eleventh Generation

This chapter contains (new) entries for all those members of the
Eleventh Generation of descendants of John Jacob Link for whom
information was received for the 1988 Supplement.

Generation	*Entry Numbers*
Eleventh	8000 series

SUPPLEMENT TO THE ELEVENTH GENERATION

The biographies in this section of the Supplement are for the Eleventh Generation of the descendants of John Jacob Link.

- -

(Sup) 8011 KELLEY JO SMITH (Teresa^{10}, Barbara^{9}, Franklin^{8}, Adam^{7}, Mary^{6}, Adam^{5}, Alexander^{4}, John Adam^{3}, John Adam^{2}, John Jacob^{1}) was the daughter of Michael Wayne and Teresa Lynn Macnamara Smith [Supplement No. 7004]. She was born January 16, 1980, at Charlottesville, Virginia (twin of Tracy Michelle).

(Sup) 8012 TRACY MICHELLE SMITH (Teresa^{10}, Barbara^{9}, Franklin^{8}, Adam^{7}, Mary^{6}, Adam^{5}, Alexander^{4}, John Adam^{3}, John Adam^{2}, John Jacob^{1}) was the daughter of Michael Wayne and Teresa Lynn Macnamara Smith [Supplement No. 7004]. She was born January 18, 1980, at Charlottesville, Virginia (twin of Kelley Jo).

(Sup) 8015 JENNIFER LEIGH MARPLE (Mary^{10}, Barbara^{9}, Franklin^{8}, Adam^{7}, Mary^{6}, Adam^{5}, Alexander^{4}, John Adam^{3}, John Adam^{2}, John Jacob^{1}) was the daughter of Mark Andrew and Mary Colleen Macnamara Marple [Supplement No. 7006]. Jennifer was born May 5, 1981, at Winchester, Virginia.

(Sup) 8021 AUTUMN SMITH (Stephen^{10}, Joyce^{9}, Mary Margaret^{8}, Adam^{7}, Mary^{6}, Adam^{5}, Alexander^{4}, John Adam^{3}, John Adam^{2}, John Jacob^{1}) was the daughter of Stephen Scott and Hilda Hensel Smith [Supplement No. 7009]. Autumn was born November 5, 1974, at Cumberland, Maryland.

(Sup) 8022 STACEY SMITH (Stephen^{10}, Joyce^{9}, Mary Margaret^{8}, Adam^{7}, Mary^{6}, Adam^{5}, Alexander^{4}, John Adam^{3}, John Adam^{2}, John Jacob^{1}) was the daughter of Stephen Scott and Hilda Hensel Smith [Supplement No. 7009]. Stacey was born January 26, 1976, at Cumberland, Maryland.

(Sup) 8031 JENNIFER MARIE MUNDY (Yvonne^{10}, Virginia^{9}, David^{8}, Adam^{7}, Mary^{6}, Adam^{5}, Alexander^{4}, John Adam^{3}, John Adam^{2}, John Jacob^{1}) was the daughter of Vincent Allen and Yvonne Hoffmaster Mundy [Supplement No. 7017]. Jennifer was born January 31, 1984, at Frederick, Maryland.

(Sup) 8041 ERIC WAYNE JONES (Jerry^{10}, Ralph^{9}, Ralph^{8}, Adam^{7}, Mary^{6}, Adam^{5}, Alexander^{4}, John Adam^{3}, John Adam^{2}, John Jacob^{1}) was the son of Jerry Wayne and Kimberly D'Angelo Jones [Supplement No. 7023]. Eric was born May 15, 1976, at Charles Town, West Virginia.

(Sup) 8042 CHRISTOPHER SHANE JONES (Jerry^{10}, Ralph^{9}, Ralph^{8}, Adam^{7}, Mary^{6}, Adam^{5}, Alexander^{4}, John Adam^{3}, John Adam^{2}, John Jacob^{1}) was the son of Jerry Wayne and Kimberly D'Angelo Jones [Supplement No. 7023]. Christopher was born June 5, 1977, at Charles Town, West Virginia.

(Sup) 8061 JOHNATHAN RIAN PARKER (Michelle^{10}, Douglas^{9}, Patricia^{8}, Ernest^{7}, Mary^{6}, Adam^{5}, Alexander^{4}, John Adam^{3}, John Adam^{2}, John Jacob^{1}) was the son of Francis Lloyd and Michelle Currier Parker, Jr. [Supplement No. 7045]. He was born January 9, 1986, at Martinsburg, West Virginia.

(Sup) 8071 KATHERINE MARIE RAMSEY (Deborah^{10}, Rudolph^{9}, Katherine^{8}, Henry^{7}, Adam^{6}, Adam^{5}, Alexander^{4}, John Adam^{3}, John Adam^{2}, John Jacob^{1}) was the daughter of James William and Deborah Weyel Ramsey [Supplement No. 7048A]. Katherine was born July 17, 1984, at Houston, Texas.

(Sup) 8075 WILLIAM RUDOLPH MORGAN (Susan^{10}, Rudolph^{9}, Katherine^{8}, Henry^{7}, Adam^{6}, Adam^{5}, Alexander^{4}, John Adam^{3}, John Adam^{2}, John Jacob^{1}) was the son of Bennett Ross and Susan Weyel Morgan [Supplement No. 7048B]. William was born July 21, 1981, at El Cajon, California.

(Sup) 8076 HOLLY ANN MORGAN (Susan^{10}, Rudolph^{9}, katherine^{8}, Henry^{7}, Adam^{6}, Adam^{5}, Alexander^{4}, John Adam^{3}, John Adam^{2}, John Jacob^{1}) was the daughter of Bennett Ross and Susan Weyel Morgan [Supplement No. 7048B]. Holly was born November 20, 1983, at El Cajon, California.

(Sup) 8111 CHRISTIE JO NEFF (John^{10}, Barbara^{9}, Mary^{8}, Ann^{7}, William^{6}, Adam^{5}, Alexander^{4}, John Adam^{3}, John Adam^{2}, John Jacob^{1}) was the daughter of John David and Shawn Ketchum Neff [Supplement No. 7063]. Christie was born February 16, 1984.

(Sup) 8115 KIMBERLY SUE ORNDORF (Pamela^{10}, Virginia^{9}, Mary^{8}, Ann^{7}, William^{6}, Adam^{5}, Alexander^{4}, John Adam^{3}, John Adam^{2}, John Jacob^{1}) was the daughter of David and Pamela Kay Sencindiver Orndorf [Supplement No. 7065]. Kimberly was born May 28, 1969, at Martinsburg, West Virginia.

(Sup) 8116 MARY BETH ORNDORF (Pamela^{10}, Virginia^{9}, Mary^{8}, Ann^{7}, William^{6}, Adam^{5}, Alexander^{4}, John Adam^{3}, John Adam^{2}, John Jacob^{1}) was the daughter of David and Pamela Kay Sencindiver Orndorf [Supplement No. 7065]. She was born January 4, 1974, at Martinsburg, West Virginia.

(Sup) 8117 JAMES DAVID ORNDORF (Pamela^{10}, Virginia^{9}, Mary^{8}, Ann^{7}, William^{6}, Adam^{5}, Alexander^{4}, John Adam II^{3}, John Adam I^{2}, John Jacob^{1}) was the son of David and Pamela Kay (Sencindiver) Orndorf [Supplement No. 7065]. James was born February 3, 1975, at Martinsburg, West Virginia.

(Sup) 8118 HEATHER ANN SENCINDIVER (Paula^{10}, Virginia^{9}, Mary^{8}, Ann^{7}, William^{6}, Adam^{5}, Alexander^{4}, John Adam II^{3}, John Adam I^{2}, John Jacob^{1}) was the daughter of Paula Ann Sencindiver [Supplement No. 7066]. Heather was born October 15, 1973, at Martinsburg, West Virginia.

(Sup) 8119 RODNEY WILLIAM SINE (Paula^{10}, Virginia^{9}, Mary^{8}, Ann^{7}, William^{6}, Adam^{5}, Alexander^{4}, John Adam II^{3}, John Adam I^{2}, John Jacob^{1}) was the son of Al and Paula Ann (Sencindiver) Sine [Supplement No. 7066]. He was born September 12, 1975, at Martinsburg, West Virginia.

(Sup) 8120 JEREMY DUANE HUBBARD (Diane^{10}, Virginia^{9}, Mary^{8}, Ann^{7}, William^{6}, Adam^{5}, Alexander^{4}, John Adam II^{3}, John Adam I^{2}, John Jacob^{1}) was the son of Gerald Duane and Diane Elaine (Sencindiver) Hubbard [Supplement No. 7067]. He was born January 9, 1980, at Martinsburg, West Virginia.

(Sup) 8091 JOSEPH BURTON BRUNK, III (Joseph^{10}, Joseph^{9}, Mary^{8}, Ann^{7}, William^{6}, Adam^{5}, Alexander^{4}, John Adam^{3}, John Adam^{2}, John Jacob^{1}) was the son of Joseph Burton and Patricia Autera Brunk, Jr. [Supplement No. 7051]. Joseph, III, was born May 11, 1966, at Plainfield, New Jersey.

(Sup) 8095 FRANCIS KENNETH HAIGHT, JR. (Julia^{10}, Joseph^{9}, Mary^{8}, Ann^{7}, William^{6}, Adam^{5}, Alexander^{4}, John Adam^{3}, John Adam^{2}, John Jacob^{1}) was the son of Francis Kenneth and Julia Kay Brunk Haight [Supplement No. 7054]. Francis, Jr., was born April 29, 1970, at Bethesda, Maryland.

(Sup) 8096 SARAH ELIZABETH JOSEPH (Julia^{10}, Joseph^{9}, Mary^{8}, Ann^{7}, William^{6}, Adam^{5}, Alexander^{4}, John Adam^{3}, John Adam^{2}, John Jacob^{1}) was the daughter of Carl Edward and Julia Kay Brunk Joseph [Supplement No. 7054]. Sarah was born January 27, 1981, at Washington, D.C.

(Sup) 8097 CHRISTINA MICHELLE BRUNK (Mark^{10}, Joseph^{9}, Mary^{8}, Ann^{7}, William^{6}, Adam^{5}, Alexander^{4}, John Adam II^{3}, John Adam I^{2}, John Jacob^{1}) was the daughter of Mark Thomas and Patty Edwards Brunk [Supplement No. 7055]. Christina was born April 30, 1975, at Hagerstown, Maryland.

(Sup) 8101 CHRISTOPHER DEAN LANCE (Ann Elizabeth^{10}, Joseph^{9}, Mary^{8}, Ann^{7}, William^{6}, Adam^{5}, Alexander^{4}, John Adam^{3}, John Adam^{2}, John Jacob^{1}) was the son of Kevin and Ann Elizabeth Brunk Lance [Supplement No. 7057]. Christopher was born December 15, 1975, at St. Petersburg, Florida.

(Sup) 8102 HOLLY LOUISE GRIMES (Willard^{10}, Betty^{9}, Mary^{8}, Ann^{7}, William6, Adam^{5}, Alexander^{4}, John Adam^{3}, John Adam^{2}, John Jacob^{1}) was the daughter of Willard Hunter and Georgia Miller Grimes, III [Supplement No. 7058]. Holly was born January 9, 1984, at Alaho, Oregon.

(Sup) 8105 JUSTIN BERKELEY LARSEN (Susan^{10}, Barbara^{9}, Mary^{8}, Ann^{7}, William^{6}, Adam^{5}, Alexander^{4}, John Adam^{3}, John Adam^{2}, John Jacob^{1}) was the son of Kevin Lon and Susan Neff Larsen [Supplement No. 7060]. Justin was born August 21, 1982.

(Sup) 8125 MICHELLE VIGNALI (Teresa^{10}, Robert^9, Mary^8, Ann^7, William^6, Adam^5, Alexander^4, John Adam^3, John Adam^2, John Jacob^1) was the daughter of Claude Louis and Teresa (Brunk) Vignali [Supplement No. 7069]. Michelle was born September 21, 1981.

(Sup) 8126 ROBERT VIGNALI (Teresa^{10}, Robert^9, Mary^8, Ann^7, William^6, Adam^5, Alexander^4, John Adam^3, John Adam^2, John Jacob^1) was the son of Claude Louis and Teresa (Brunk) Vignali [Supplement No. 7069]. Robert was born December 25, 1983.

(Sup) 8131 JOHN DAVID HOUGH (Charles^{10}, Charles^9, Charles^8, Ann^7, William^6, Adam^5, Alexander^4, John Adam^3, John Adam^2, John Jacob^1) was the son of Charles Hubert and Susan Ott Hough [Supplement No. 7070A]. John was born November 1, 1968.

(Sup) 8132 JOSEPH CHRISTOPHER HOUGH (Charles^{10}, Charles^9, Charles^8, Ann^7, William^6, Adam^5, Alexander^4, John Adam^3, John Adam^2, John Jacob^1) was the son of Charles Hubert and Susan Ott Hough [Supplement No. 7070A]. Joseph was born January 22, 1971.

(Sup) 8133 JANET RENE LANDIS (Sherry^{10}, Charles^9, Charles^8, Ann^7, William^6, Adam^5, Alexander^4, John Adam^3, John Adam^2, John Jacob^1) was the daughter of George Phillip and Sherry Hough Landis [Supplement No. 7070B]. Janet was born February 18, 1967.

(Sup) 8134 KATIE BETH LANDIS (Sherry^{10}, Charles^9, Charles^8, Ann^7, William^6, Adam^5, Alexander^4, John Adam^3, John Adam^2, John Jacob^1) was the daughter of George Phillip and Sherry Hough Landis [Supplement No. 7070B]. Katie was born January 29, 1975.

(Sup) 8135 MATTHEW CAMERON HOUGH (Robert^{10}, Charles^9, Charles^8, Ann^7, William^6, Adam^5, Alexander^4, John Adam^3, John Adam^2, John Jacob^1) was the son of Robert Lee and Katie Schaffer Hough [Supplement No. 7070C]. Matthew was born January 24, 1984.

(Sup) 8151 MICHAEL JOSEPH HOUGH (John^{10}, John^9, John^8, Ann^7, William^6, Adam^5, Alexander^4, John Adam^3, John Adam^2, John Jacob^1) was the son of John Richard and Beth Dilley Hough [Supplement No. 7074]. Michael was born November 4, 1979, at Silver Spring, Maryland.

(Sup) 8152 SHANNON MARIE HOUGH (John^{10}, John^9, John^8, Ann^7, William^6, Adam^5, Alexander^4, John Adam^3, John Adam^2, John Jacob^1) was the daughter of John Richard and Beth Dilley Hough [Supplement No. 7074]. Shannon was born November 23, 1982, at Takoma Park, Maryland.

(Sup) 8153 PAUL JASON HOUGH (Paul^{10}, John^9, John^8, Ann^7, William^6, Adam^5, Alexander^4, John Adam^3, John Adam^2, John Jacob^1) was the son of Paul Jeffrey and Deborah Carneal Hough [Supplement No. 7075]. Paul was born December 18, 1983, at Takoma Park, Maryland.

(Sup) 8161 MICHELLE LYNN MONG (Cynthia^{10}, Joyce^9, Woodrow^8, Ann^7, William^6, Adam^5, Alexander^4, John Adam^3, John Adam^2, John Jacob^1) was the daughter of George Webber and Cynthia Johnson Mong [Supplement No. 7077]. Michelle was born December 17, 1977, at Greenville, South Carolina.

(Sup) 8162 KIMBERLY LEE MONG (Cynthia^{10}, Joyce^9, Woodrow^8, Ann^7, William^6, Adam^5, Alexander^4, John Adam^3, John Adam^2, John Jacob^1) was the daughter of George Webber and Cynthia Johnson Mong [Supplement No. 7077]. Kimberly was born May 23, 1979, at Martinsburg, West Virginia.

(Sup) 8163 JENNIFER MARIE MONG (Cynthia^{10}, Joyce^9, Woodrow^8, Ann^7, William^6, Adam^5, Alexander^4, John Adam^3, John Adam^2, John Jacob^1) was the daughter of George Webber and Cynthia Johnson Mong [Supplement No. 7077]. Jennifer was born August 30, 1980, at Martinsburg, West Virginia.

(Sup) 8164 MATTHEW SCOTT MONG (Cynthia^{10}, Joyce^9, Woodrow^8, Ann^7, William^6, Adam^5, Alexander^4, John Adam^3, John Adam^2, John Jacob^1) was the son of George Webber and Cynthia Johnson Mong [Supplement No. 7077]. Matthew was born June 25, 1983, at Martinsburg, West Virginia.

(Sup) 8165 JAN AUGUSTA JOHNSON (Frank^{10}, Joyce^9, Woodrow^8, Ann^7, William^6, Adam^5, Alexander^4, John Adam^3, John Adam^2, John Jacob^1) was the daughter of Frank Edward and Tammie Evans Johnson, Jr. [Supplement No. 7077A]. Jan was born September 4, 1980, at Martinsburg, West Virginia. Her mother died in 1981, and Jan Augusta was adopted on November 19, 1984, by her grandmother and step-grandfather, Floyd Maynard and Joyce Hough Johnson McDowell [Supplement No. 5049].

(Sup) 8171 CHRISTOPHER DOUGLAS GOLLIDAY (Douglas^{10}, Patricia^9, Frances^8, Ann^7, William^6, Adam^5, Alexander^4, John Adam^3, John Adam^2, John Jacob^1) was the son of Douglas Eugene and Anna Corrinne Jenson Golliday [Supplement No. 7078]. Christopher was born April 13, 1975, in Hawaii.

(Sup) 8172 JONATHAN RANDOLPH GOLLIDAY (Douglas^{10}, Patricia^9, Frances^8, Ann^7, William^6, Adam^5, Alexander^4, John Adam^3, John Adam^2, John Jacob^1) was the son of Douglas Eugene and Anna Corrinne Jenson Golliday [Supplement No. 7078]. Jonathan was born December 19, 1977, at Andrews Air Force Base, Maryland.

(Sup) 8173 BENJAMIN EUGENE GOLLIDAY (Douglas^{10}, Patricia^9, Frances^8, Ann^7, William^6, Adam^5, Alexander^4, John Adam^3, John Adam^2, John Jacob^1) was the son of Douglas Eugene and Anna Corrinne Jenson Golliday [Supplement No. 7078]. Benjamin was born April 18, 1980, at Cherry Point, North Carolina.

(Sup) 8174 KIMBERLY NICOLE GOLLIDAY (Clark^{10}, Patricia^9, Frances^8, Ann^7, William^6, Adam^5, Alexander^4, John Adam^3, John Adam^2, John Jacob^1) was the daughter of Clark Wayne and Cynthia Wagner Golliday [Supplement No. 7078A]. Kimberly was born March 5, 1982, at Easton, Maryland.

(Sup) 8175 HOLLY MARIE ERSKINE (Bertie^{10}, Patricia^9, Frances^8, Ann^7, William^6, Adam^5, Alexander^4, John Adam^3, John Adam^2, John Jacob^1) was the daughter of Jeffery Alan and Bertie Golliday Erskine [Supplement No. 7078B]. Holly was born December 29, 1979, at Easton, Maryland.

(Sup) 8176 JESSICA RENEE ERSKINE (Bertie^{10}, Patricia^9, Frances^8, Ann^7, William^6, Adam^5, Alexander^4, John Adam^3, John Adam^2, John Jacob^1) was the daughter of Jeffery Alan and Bertie Golliday Erskine [Supplement No. 7078B]. Jessica was born March 27, 1983, at Camp LeJeune, Jacksonville, North Carolina.

(Sup) 8177 JENNIFER BROOKE CAVE (Mark^{10}, JoAnn^9, Frances^8, Ann^7, William^6, Adam^5, Alexander^4, John Adam^3, John Adam^2, John Jacob^1) was the daughter of Mark Anthony and Natalie Stickles Cave [Supplement No. 7078C]. Jennifer was born October 26, 1981, at Winchester, Virginia.

(Sup) 8191 ANTHONY ROCCO BONBENO, IV (Pamela^{10}, Daniels^9, Daniels^8, Ann^7, William^6, Adam^5, Alexander^4, John Adam^3, John Adam^2, John Jacob^1) was the son of Anthony Rocco and Pamela Hough Bonbeno, III [Supplement No. 7079]. Anthony, IV, was born November 10, 1980, at San Diego, California.

(Sup) 8192 SHANNON MARIE BONBENO (Pamela^{10}, Daniels^9, Daniels^8, Ann^7, William^6, Adam^5, Alexander^4, John Adam^3, John Adam^2, John Jacob^1) was the daughter of Anthon Rocco and Pamela Hough Bonbeno, III [Supplement No. 7079]. Shannon was born March, 1982, at San Diego, California.

(Sup) 8251 GWEN MARIE COFFINBERGER (Dennis^{10}, Paul^9, Holland^8, Margaret^7, William^6, Adam^5, Alexander^4, John Adam^3, John Adam^2, John Jacob^1) was the daughter of Dennis Link and Gail Lynn (Greenfield) Coffinberger [Supplement No. 7088]. Gwen was born June 23, 1971, at Lancaster, Pennsylvania.

(Sup) 8252 ERIN LEIGH COFFINBERGER (Dennis^{10}, Paul^9, Holland^8, Margaret^7, William^6, Adam^5, Alexander^4, John Adam^3, John Adam^2, John Jacob^1) was the child of Dennis Link and Gail Lynn (Greenfield) Coffinberger [Supplement No. 7088]. Erin was born February 20, 1974, at Bloomsburg, Pennsylvania.

(Sup) 8253 ADAM LINK COFFINBERGER (Dennis^{10}, Paul^9, Holland^8, Margaret^7, William^6, Adam^5, Alexander^4, John Adam^3, John Adam^2, John Jacob^1) was the son of Dennis Link and Gail Lynn (Greenfield) Coffinberger [Supplement No. 7088]. Adam was born June 22, 1975, at Berwick, Pennsylvania.

(Sup) 8254 MARIE ANN SHAURETTE (Diane^{10}, Paul^9, Holland^8, Margaret^7, William^6, Adam^5, Alexander^4, John Adam^3, John Adam^2, John Jacob^1) was the daughter of Bernard Frederick and Diane (Coffinberger) Shaurette [Supplement No. 7089]. Marie was born December 12, 1977, at Fort Benning, Georgia.

(Sup) 8271 THOMAS VINCENT NOLL (Lawrence[10], Elaine[9], Grace[8], Margaret[7], William[6], Adam[5], Alexander[4], John Adam[3], John Adam[2], John Jacob[1]) was the son of Lawrence Patterson and Vickie Albright Noll [Supplement No. 7094]. Thomas was born February 18, 1970, at Martinsburg, West Virginia.

(Sup) 8272 RICHARD JOSEPH NOLL (Lawrence[10], Elaine[9], Grace[8], Margaret[7], William[6], Adam[5], Alexander[4], John Adam[3], John Adam[2], John Jacob[1]) was the son of Lawrence Patterson and Vickie Albright Noll [Supplement No. 7094]. Richard was born April 28, 1971, at Martinsburg, West Virginia.

(Sup) 8275 RYAN MICHAEL NOLL (Jeffery[10], Elaine[9], Grace[8], Margaret[7], William[6], Adam[5], Alexander[4], John Adam[3], John Adam[2], John Jacob[1]) was the son of Jeffery Michael and Tanya Gray Noll [Supplement No. 7097]. Ryan was born October 28, 1982, at Martinsburg, West Virginia.

(Sup) 8276 NICOLE RENEE WARNER (Melissa[10], Elaine[9], Grace[8], Margaret[7], William[6], Adam[5], Alexander[4], John Adam[3], John Adam[2], John Jacob[1]) was the daughter of David and Melissa Noll Warner [Supplement No. 7098]. Nicole was born January 18, 1982, at Martinsburg, West Virginia.

(Sup) 8277 AARON DANIEL WARNER (Melissa[10], Elaine[9], Grace[8], Margaret[7], William[6], Adam[5], Alexander[4], John Adam[3], John Adam[2], John Jacob[1]) was the son of David and Melissa Noll Warner [Supplement No. 7098]. Aaron was born April 3, 1984, at Winchester, Virginia.

(Sup) 8311 JAMES RICHARD SHIMP, JR. (James[10], Anne[9], James[8], Martha[7], William[6], Adam[5], Alexander[4], John Adam[3], John Adam[2], John Jacob[1]) was the son of James Richard and Vickie Hinkle Shimp [Supplement No. 7112]. James was born September 28, 1970, at Martinsburg, West Virginia.

(Sup) 8312 AUTUMN LOU SHIMP (James[10], Anne[9], James[8], Martha[7], William[6], Adam[5], Alexander[4], John Adam[3], John Adam[2], John Jacob[1]) was the daughter of James Richard and Vickie Hinkle Shimp [Supplement No. 7112]. Autumn was born January 17, 1972, at Charles Town, West Virginia.

(Sup) 8255 JASON ALLEN SHAURETTE (Diane[10], Paul[9], Holland[8], Margaret[7], William[6], Adam[5], Alexander[4], John Adam[3], John Adam[2], John Jacob[1]) was the son of Bernard Frederick and Diane (Coffinberger) Shaurette [Supplement No. 7089]. Jason was born April 20, 1980, at Fairfax, Virginia.

(Sup) 8256 BRIAN LEWIS ROTHGEB (Benton[10], Mary[9], Holland[8], Margaret[7], William[6], Adam[5], Alexander[4], John Adam[3], John Adam[2], John Jacob[1]) was the son of Benton Rocky and Linda (Grant) Rothgeb [Supplement No. 7090]. Brian was born March 18, 1975, at Fairfax, Virginia.

(Sup) 8257 MICHAEL ROTHGEB (Benton[10], Mary[9], Holland[8], Margaret[7], William[6], Adam[5], Alexander[4], John Adam[3], John Adam[2], John Jacob[1]) was the son of Benton Rocky and Linda (Grant) Rothgeb [Supplement No. 7090]. Michael was born April 10, 1978, at Fairfax, Virginia.

(Sup) 8261 MICHAEL LEE CRUMBACKER (Robert[10], Virginia[9], Grace[8], Margaret[7], William[6], Adam[5], Alexander[4], John Adam[3], John Adam[2], John Jacob[1]) was the son of Robert Link and Theresa Oftedahl Crumbacker [Supplement No. 7092]. Michael was born May 9, 1972.

(Sup) 8262 MATTHEW LINK CRUMBACKER (Robert[10], Virginia[9], Grace[8], Margaret[7], William[6], Adam[5], Alexander[4], John Adam[3], John Adam[2], John Jacob[1]) was the son of Robert Link and Theresa Oftedahl Crumbacker [Supplement No. 7092]. Matthew was born August 11, 1974.

(Sup) 8263 AMY JOY CRUMBACKER (Robert[10], Virginia[9], Grace[8], Margaret[7], William[6], Adam[5], Alexander[4], John Adam[3], John Adam[2], John Jacob[1]) was the daughter of Robert Link and Theresa Oftedahl Crumbacker [Supplement No. 7092]. Amy was born November 26, 1976.

(Sup) 8264 DAWN MICHELL CRUMBACKER (Robert[10], Virginia[9], Grace[8], Margaret[7], William[6], Adam[5], Alexander[4], John Adam[3], John Adam[2], John Jacob[1]) was the daughter of Robert Link and Theresa Oftedahl Crumbacker [Supplement No. 7092]. Dawn was born October 8, 1979.

(Sup) 8401 KENNETH BLAKE ARMSTRONG (Laureen^{10}, Anne^9, James^8, Guy^7, John^6, Elizabeth^5, Alexander^4, John Adam^3, John Adam^2, John Jacob^1) was the son of Kenneth and Laureen Drake Armstrong [Supplement No. 7191]. Kenneth was born February 21, 1988, at New Orleans, Louisiana.

(Sup) 8451 LUKAS RYAN WARREN (Katherine^{10}, Robert^9, Frances^8, Hazel^7, Angeline^6, Emmanuel^5, Mary^4, John Adam^3, John Adam^2, John Jacob^1) was the son of Lindley Charles and Katherine Haas Warren [Supplement No. 7254]. He was born August 21, 1985, at Edina, Minnesota.

(Sup) 8551 CINDI S. VANAMAN (Susan^{10}, Arthur^9, Helen^8, Otey^7, Elizabeth^6, Susan^5, John^4, Peter^3, Matthias^2, John Jacob^1) was the daughter of Charles and Susan Barnes Vanaman [Supplement No. 7498]. Cindi was born August 6, 1969, at Pittsburgh, Pennsylvania.

(Sup) 8571 DARBY LYNN HEWITT (Neal^{10}, Nancy^9, Benjamin^8, Benjamin^7, Elizabeth^6, Susan^5, John^4, Peter^3, Matthias^2, John Jacob^1) was the daughter of Neal Edward and Ruth Ann Taylor Hewitt [Supplement No. 7522].

(Sup) 8572 CLINTON EDWARD HEWITT (Neal^{10}, Nancy^9, Benjamin^8, Benjamin^7, Elizabeth^6, Susan^5, John^4, Peter^3, Matthias^2, John Jacob^1) was the son of Neal Edward and Ruth Ann Taylor Hewitt [Supplement No. 7522].

(Sup) 8581 AMBER DIANE McCRAY (Willis^{10}, Anna Virginia^9, Benjamin^8, Benjamin^7, Elizabeth^6, Susan^5, John^4, Peter^3, Matthias^2, John Jacob^1) was the daughter of Willis Earl and Anna Virginia (Hulvey) McCray [Supplement No. 7527].

(Sup) 8582 HOLLY KRISTINE McCRAY (Willis^{10}, Anna Virginia^9, Benjamin^8, Benjamin^7, Elizabeth^6, Susan^5, John^4, Peter^3, Matthias^2, John Jacob^1) was the daughter of Willis Earl and Anna Virginia (Hulvey) McCray [Supplement No. 7527].

(Sup) 8313 KENNETH MARTIN RUTHERFORD, III (Kenneth^{10}, Anne^9, James^8, Martha^7, William^6, Adam^5, Alexander^4, John Adam^3, John Adam^2, John Jacob^1) was the son of Kenneth Martin and Melody Emery Rutherford, Jr. [Supplement No. 7112A]. Kenneth, III, was born March 28, 1979, at Martinsburg, West Virginia.

(Sup) 8314 KIMBERLY ANNE GREENFIELD (Laura^{10}, Anne^9, James^8, Martha^7, William^6, Adam^5, Alexander^4, John Adam^3, John Adam^2, John Jacob^1) was the daughter of Robert and Laura Rutherford Greenfield [Supplement No. 7112B]. Kimberly was born March 20, 1976, at Goldsborough, North Carolina.

(Sup) 8315 CRYSTAL GAIL ROBINSON (Lisa^{10}, Anne^9, James^8, Martha^7, William^6, Adam^5, Alexander^4, John Adam^3, John Adam^2, John Jacob^1) was the daughter of Dennis and Lisa Rutherford Robinson [Supplement No. 7112D]. Crystal was born September 28, 1976, at Martinsburg, West Virginia.

(Sup) 8316 DENNIS SCOTT ROBINSON (Lisa^{10}, Anne^9, James^8, Martha^7, William^6, Adam^5, Alexander^4, John Adam^3, John Adam^2, John Jacob^1) was the son of Dennis and Lisa Rutherford Robinson [Supplement No. 7112D]. Dennis was born July 23, 1979, at Martinsburg, West Virginia.

(Sup) 8317 TIFFANY ANNE ROBINSON (Lisa^{10}, Anne^9, James^8, Martha^7, William^6, Adam^5, Alexander^4, John Adam^3, John Adam^2, John Jacob^1) was the daughter of Dennis and Lisa Rutherford Robinson [Supplement No. 7112D]. Tiffany was born September 17, 1982, at Martinsburg, West Virginia.

(Sup) 8318 DAVID LEE COFFINBERGER (James^{10}, James^9, William^8, Martha^7, William^6, Adam^5, Alexander^4, John Adam^3, John Adam^2, John Jacob^1) was the son of James Scott and Virginia Luber Coffinberger [Supplement No. 7112F]. David was born in 1979 at Winchester, Virginia.

(Sup) 8319 JUSTIN JAMES COFFINBERGER (James^{10}, James^9, William^8, Martha^7, William^6, Adam^5, Alexander^4, John Adam^3, John Adam^2, John Jacob^1) was the son of James Scott and Virginia Luber Coffinberger [Supplement No. 7112F]. Justin was born December 5, 1981, at Winchester, Virginia.

(Sup) 8591 JESSICA LYNN SULLIVAN (Beatrice[10], Gloria[9], Benjamin[8], Benjamin[7], Elizabeth[6], Susan[5], John[4], Peter[3], Matthias[2], John Jacob[1]) was the daughter of James and Beatrice Ann (Collins) Sullivan [Supplement No. 7533].

(Sup) 8592 JAMES JOSEPH SULLIVAN (Beatrice[10], Gloria[9], Benjamin[8], Benjamin[7], Elizabeth[6], Susan[5], John[4], Peter[3], Matthias[2], John Jacob[1]) was the son of James and Beatrice Ann (Collins) Sullivan [Supplement No. 7533].

(Sup) 8601 JENNIFER GAIL BENTON (Tamany[10], Donald[9], Benjamin[8], Benjamin[7], Elizabeth[6], Susan[5], John[4], Peter[3], Matthias[2], John Jacob[1]) was the daughter of John Stuart and Tamany Lee (Wilbergerger) Benton [Supplement No. 7537]. Jennifer was born January 17, 1978.

(Sup) 8602 JOHN DEREK BENTON (Tamany[10], Donald[9], Benjamin[8], Benjamin[7], Elizabeth[6], Susan[5], John[4], Peter[3], Matthias[2], John Jacob[1]) was the son of John Stuart and Tamany Lee (Wilbergerger) Benton [Supplement No. 7537]. John was born January 16, 1980.

(Sup) 8615 MELINDA KNAPP PARROTT (Deborah[10], Patricia[9], Margaret[8], Benjamin[7], Elizabeth[6], Susan[5], John[4], Peter[3], Matthias[2], John Jacob[1]) was the daughter of David and Deborah Knapp Parrott [Supplement No. 7545]. Melinda was born December 19, 1973.

(Sup) 8616 MATTHEW DAVID PARROTT (Deborah[10], Patricia[9], Margaret[8], Benjamin[7], Elizabeth[6], Susan[5], John[4], Peter[3], Matthias[2], John Jacob[1]) was the child of David and Deborah Knapp Parrott [Supplement No. 7545].

(Sup) 8651 KARA LEIGH BACKHAUS (Deborah[10], Marjorie[9], Katherine[8], Sidney[7], John[6], John[5], John[4], Peter[3], Matthias[2], John Jacob[1]) was the daughter of Steven and Deborah (Ruebush) Backhaus [Supplement No. 7595]. Kara was born September 28, 1985, at Tampa, Florida.

(Sup) 8655 BENJAMIN JOE BURRIS III (Laurie[10], Marjorie[9], Katherine[8], Sidney[7], John[6], John[5], John[4], Peter[3], Matthias[2], John Jacob[1]) was the son of Benjamin Joe and Laurie (Ruebush) Burris [Supplement No. 7596]. Benjamin, III, was born April 6, 1986, at Jacksonville, Florida.

(Sup) 8661 URIAH SHAWN ORR (Donna[10], Juanita[9], Katherine[8], Sidney[7], John[6], John[5], John[4], Peter[3], Matthias[2], John Jacob[1]) was the son of Matthew Paul and Donna (Anderson) Orr [Supplement No. 7598]. Uriah was born February 18, 1983, at Fort Madison, Iowa.

(Sup) 8681 JOSHUA CURTIS LARSON (Kimberlee[10], George[9], Lois[8], Sidney[7], John[6], John[5], John[4], Peter[3], Matthias[2], John Jacob[1]) was the son of Steven Curtis and Kimberlee (Kreps) Larson [Supplement No. 7624]. Joshua was born June 22, 1988, at Dekalb, Illinois.

(Sup) 8751 MAE CATHERINE LINK (David[10], James[9], Paxson[8], Horace[7], James[6], Christopher[5], Peter[4], Peter[3], Matthew[2], John Jacob[1]) was the daughter of David Stuart and Mae Catherine (Pearsall) Link [Supplement No. 7735A]. She was born September 28, 1985, at Charlotte, North Carolina.

(Sup) 8761 AMY NICOLLE SPUNG (Richard[10], Christie[9], Paxson[8], Horace[7], James[6], Christopher[5], Peter[4], Peter[3], Matthias[2], John Jacob[1]) was the daughter of Richard Cole and Patricia Amy (Bolduc) Spung [Supplement No. 7736]. She was born July 21, 1988.

(Sup) 8801 WHITNEY TAYLOR FRANKENFIELD (Catherine[10], Ann[9], Mary[8], Pearl[7], John[6], Francis Marion[5], Peter[4], Peter[3], Matthias[2], John Jacob[1]) was the son of John Palmer and Catherine Steidl Frankenfield [Supplement No. 7753]. Whitney was born April 10, 1980, at Cookeville, Tennessee.

(Sup) 8802 LINDSAY FRANKENFIELD (Catherine[10], Ann[9], Mary[8], Pearl[7], John[6], Francis Marion[5], Peter[4], Peter[3], Matthias[2], John Jacob[1]) was the daughter of John Palmer and Catherine Steidl Frankenfield [Supplement No. 7753]. Lindsay was born June 2, 1983, at Cookeville, Tennessee.

(Sup) 8803 ANDREW BRYAN STEIDL (Phillip^{10}, Ann^9, Mary^8, Pearl^7, John^6, Francis Marion^5, Peter^4, Peter^3, Matthias^2, John Jacob^1) was the son of Phillip Andrew and Deborah (Sanders) Steidl [Supplement No. 7753A]. Andrew was born April 25, 1983, at Cookeville, Tennessee.

(Sup) 8804 RACHEL ELAINE STEIDL (Phillip^{10}, Ann^9, Mary^8, Pearl^7, John^6, Francis Marion^5, Peter^4, Peter^3, Matthias^2, John Jacob^1) was the daughter of Philip Andrew and Deborah (Sanders) Steidl [Supplement No. 7753A]. Rachel was born October 4, 1987, at Cookeville, Tennessee.

(Sup) 8815 JENNIFER ALISHIA CLINGMAN (Carol^{10}, Mary Jane^9, Allen^8, Fred^7, Susan^6, Francis Marion^5, Peter^4, Peter^3, Matthias^2, John Jacob^1) was the daughter of Daryl and Carol Amacher Clingman. [Supplement No. 7755]. Jennifer was born January 24, 1980, at Columbus, Ohio.

(Sup) 8816 DANIEL ALAN CLINGMAN (Carol^{10}, Mary Jane^9, Allen^8, Fred^7, Susan^6, Francis Marion^5, Peter^4, Peter^3, Matthias^2, John Jacob^1) was the son of Daryl and Carol Amacher Clingman. [Supplement No. 7755]. Daniel was born January 28, 1981, at Columbus, Ohio.

(Sup) 8861 CHANTEL KUPFERER (Lynette^{10}, Marilyn^9, Charlotte^8, Franklin^7, Martin^6, Elizabeth^5, Martha^4, John Adam^3, John Adam^2, John Jacob^1) was the child of Ted and Lynette Planck Kupferer [Supplement No. 7848].

(Sup) 8862 DERICK KUPFERER (Lynette^{10}, Marilyn^9, Charlotte^8, Franklin^7, Martin^6, Elizabeth^5, Martha^4, John Adam^3, John Adam^2, John Jacob^1) was the child of Ted and Lynette Planck Kupferer [Supplement No. 7848].

(Sup) 8865 JACOB KIRKLEY (Melanie^{10}, Marilyn^9, Charlotte^8, Franklin^7, Martin^6, Elizabeth^5, Martha^4, John Adam^3, John Adam^2, John Jacob^1) was the child of Duane and Melanie Planck Kirkley [Supplement No. 7850].

(Sup) 8866 FOREST GREENE (Melinda^{10}, Marilyn^9, Charlotte^8, Franklin^7, Martin^6, Elizabeth^5, Martha^4, John Adam^3, John Adam^2, John Jacob^1) was the child of Scott and Melinda Planck Greene [Supplement No. 7851].

(Sup) 8867 ASHLEY GREENE (Melinda^{10}, Marilyn^9, Charlotte^8, Franklin^7, Martin^6, Elizabeth^5, Martha^4, John Adam^3, John Adam^2, John Jacob^1) was the child of Scott and Melinda Planck Greene [Supplement No. 7851].

(Sup) 8868 MICHAEL GREENE (Melinda^{10}, Marilyn^9, Charlotte^8, Franklin^7, Martin^6, Elizabeth^5, Martha^4, John Adam^3, John Adam^2, John Jacob^1) was the child of Scott and Melinda Planck Greene [Supplement No. 7851].

(Sup) 8871 JENNIFER WILLIS (Judy^{10}, Louis^9, Marietta^8, Franklin^7, Martin^6, Elizabeth^5, Martha^4, John Adam^3, John Adam^2, John Jacob^1) was the daughter of Clyde R. and Judy Bonsib Willis [Supplement No. 7855].

(Sup) 8872 GINA WILLIS (Judy^{10}, Louis^9, Marietta^8, Franklin^7, Martin^6, Elizabeth^5, Martha^4, John Adam^3, John Adam^2, John Jacob^1) was the daughter of Clyde R. and Judy Bonsib Willis [Supplement No. 7855].

(Sup) 8873 MATTHEW WILLIS (Judy^{10}, Louis^9, Marietta^8, Franklin^7, Martin^6, Elizabeth^5, Martha^4, John Adam^3, John Adam^2, John Jacob^1) was the son of Clyde R. and Judy Bonsib Willis [Supplement No. 7855].

(Sup) 8874 NATHAN WILLIS (Judy^{10}, Louis^9, Marietta^8, Franklin^7, Martin^6, Elizabeth^5, Martha^4, John Adam^3, John Adam^2, John Jacob^1) was the son of Clyde R. and Judy Bonsib Willis [Supplement No. 7855].

(Sup) 8875 SCOTT CROSBIE (Susan^{10}, Louis^9, Marietta^8, Franklin^7, Martin^6, Elizabeth^5, Martha^4, John Adam^3, John Adam^2, John Jacob^1) was the son of Mac H. and Susan Bonsib Crosbie [Supplement No. 7856].

(Sup) 8876 TODD CROSBIE (Susan^{10}, Louis^9, Marietta^8, Franklin^7, Martin^6, Elizabeth^5, Martha^4, John Adam^3, John Adam^2, John Jacob^1) was the son of Mac H. and Susan Bonsib Crosbie [Supplement No. 7856].

(Sup) 8877 CHAD CROSBIE (Susan^{10}, Louis^9, Marietta^8, Franklin^7, Martin^6, Elizabeth^5, Martha^4, John Adam^3, John Adam^2, John Jacob^1) was the son of Mac H. and Susan Bonsib Crosbie [Supplement No. 7856].

(Sup) 8881 BRANDON BONSIB (Grant^{10}, Louis^9, Marietta^8, Franklin^7, Martin^6, Elizabeth^5, Martha^4, John Adam^3, John Adam^2, John Jacob^1) was the son of Grant Gardner and Sylvia Wong Bonsib [Supplement No. 7858].

(Sup) 8882 VANESSA BONSIB (John^{10}, Louis^9, Marietta^8, Franklin^7, Martin^6, Elizabeth^5, Martha^4, John Adam^3, John Adam^2, John Jacob^1) was the daughter of John McDonald and Annika Raaf Bonsib [Supplement No. 7859].

(Sup) 8883 DAVID WILLIAM BONSIB (John^{10}, Louis^9, Marietta^8, Franklin^7, Martin^6, Elizabeth^5, Martha^4, John Adam^3, John Adam^2, John Jacob^1) was the son of John McDonald and Anika Raaf Bonsib [Supplement No. 7859]. David was born February 22, 1986, at Stockholm, Sweden (twin of Marcus).

(Sup) 8884 MARCUS "TORE" BONSIB (John^{10}, Louis^9, Marietta^8, Franklin^7, Martin^6, Elizabeth^5, Martha^4, John Adam^3, John Adam^2, John Jacob^1) was the son of John McDonald and Anika Raaf Bonsib [Supplement No. 7859]. Marcus was born February 22, 1986, at Stockholm, Sweden (twin of David).

(Sup) 8894 BENJAMIN BICKLEY (Sandra^{10}, Joan^9, Marietta^8, Franklin^7, Martin^6, Elizabeth^5, Martha^4, John Adam^3, John Adam^2, John Jacob^1) was the son of John and Sandra Lipp Bickley [Supplement No. 7860].

(Sup) 8951 MICHELLE AMY WESTERMAN (Jeffrey^{10}, Ralph^9, Amy^8, George^7, Martin^6, Elizabeth^5, Martha^4, John Adam^3, John Adam^2, John Jacob^1) was the daughter of Jeffrey Raymond and Margaret Lori (Parker) Westerman [Supplement No. 7891]. Michelle was born April 7, 1977, at Alexandria, Virginia.

(Sup) 8952 KELLY LYNN WESTERMAN (Andrew^{10}, Ralph^9, Amy^8, George^7, Martin^6, Elizabeth^5, Martha^4, John Adam^3, John Adam^2, John Jacob^1) was the daughter of Andrew Lee and Teresa Marie (Gaillot) Westerman [Supplement No. 7892]. Kelly was born August 5, 1979, at Alexandria, Virginia.

Appendix

Link Family Images

1. St. James Lutheran Church, Uvilla, West Virginia.

2. Link Memorial Pavilion at St. James Lutheran Church, Uvilla, West Virginia.

3. Home of John Adam Link II near Shepherdstown, West Virginia (as it appeared in August 2000).

4. Side view of home of John Adam Link II (August 2000).

5. Account of first Link reunion held at Uvilla, West Virginia (1952).

6. Stone from John Jacob Link's spring wall, Elmwood Cemetery, Shepherdstown, West Virginia.

7. Front and back views of tombstone of John Adam Link II, old St. Peter's Lutheran Cemetery, Shepherdstown, West Virginia.

8. Monument to The First Link in America, Elmwood Cemetery, Shepherdstown, West Virginia.

9. Tombstone of Jane Ogle Link, wife of John Adam Link II, old St. Peter's Lutheran Cemetery, Shepherdstown, West Virginia.

10. Letter from Albert Link to Adam Baker Link (1956).

1. *St. James Lutheran Church, Uvilla, West Virginia.*

2. *Link Memorial Pavilion at St. James Lutheran Church, Uvilla, West Virginia.*

Photograph courtesy of Vanda White

3. *Home of John Adam Link II near Shepherdstown, West Virginia (as it appeared in August 2000). Note: Compare this recent photograph with the photograph of the home that faces page 80 of The Link Family history.*

Photograph courtesy of Suzanne Link Allen

4. *Side view of home of John Adam Link II (August 2000).*

G. L. Hendricks Named Chairman At Link Reunion

The Lutheran Church at Uvilla served as a meeting place on Sunday, August 31 for the descendants of John Jacob and Ana Neuwirth Link. These Link ancestors left Germany and came to America in 1733. The Link history, recently compiled by Paxson Link of Illinois does not give the reason for their immigration, but states it was most likely due to the constant drain of taxation and incessant struggle of the Catholic element against the Protestants. A monument now stands to the memory of these valiant ancestors in Elmwood Cemetery in Shepherdstown.

The Links have used the Uvilla Church as an annual gathering place for several years past, but not until this year have they become organized.

After Church services, which were conducted by the Rev. James Lester Link of the Bristol, Tenn. Lutheran Church, an election of officers took place.

The Rev. John W. Link of Shepherdstown acted as spokesman for the meeting. As a result of the election the following officers were named: Chairman: Gilbert L. Hendricks; Vice-Chairman: Daniel Link; Secretary: Miss Mildred Conard; Treasurer: Woodrow Hough; Historian: Mrs. Marvin Edwards; Chaplain: The Rev. John W. Link; Publicity: Mrs. C. W. Moore; Program Committee: Mrs. Boyd Link and Mrs. Ernest Jones, Sr.; Table Committee: Mrs. John W. Link and Mrs. Adam Link, Sr.; Place of Meeting: Adam Link, Sr.; and Norval Jenkins.

The Rev. Link delivered messages from several members who were unable to attend. Relatives were also urged to purchase a copy of the Link history, so detailed and complete, revealing such things as the fact General Dwight Eisenhower's grandmother was a Link, a descendant of the above John Jacob Link. Names and dates in this history go back as far as Hans Link, born about 1370.

After the business meeting a picnic was held in the dining hall of the Church.

5. *Account of first Link reunion held at Uvilla, West Virginia, by the Descendants of John Jacob Link (Source: Spirit of Jefferson Farmers Advocate, September 4, 1952).*

Photograph courtesy of Vanda White

6. *Stone from John Jacob Link's spring wall. This stone is now located at the base of the Link monument in Elmwood Cemetery, Shepherdstown, West Virginia.*

7. Front view (facing ruined stone wall) and back view of tombstone of John Adam Link II in old St. Peter's Lutheran Cemetery, Shepherdstown, West Virginia.

Photograph courtesy of Vanda White

9. Tombstone of Jane Ogle Link, wife of John Adam Link II, in old St. Peter's Lutheran Cemetery, Shepherdstown, West Virginia.

Photograph courtesy of Vanda White

8. Monument to The First Link in America erected by Albert Link in Elmwood Cemetery, Shepherdstown, West Virginia. Note the engraved "1," John Jacob Link's entry number in The Link Family history.

483—8TH STREET
BROOKLYN 15, N. Y.
—
TELEPHONE SO. 8-4490

September 8 1956.

Dear Cousin Adam;

    This is the first opportunity that I have had to write and tell you what a great pleasure it was for me to be with those who had so wonderfully cooperated in creating the Link genealogy. In the New York City library, they call it one of their finest works on Genealogy. John and you have so much interesting information aside from the book, it should be written up for future reference. I think all four of us including Harwood should have been at the honor table, but this was an oversight. The reunion certainly was a spectacular affair and the remarks by you and John were a treat for those who attended. Our young friend, Robert Harper, was so impressed that when he got home (up state) he spent his week vacation telling all the neighbors the glory of the Link family. My son, Al, who lives up there called me up and told me Robert was going from house to house making a campaign issue of it to boost Eisenhower as a member of the Link blood.

    We so enjoyed a visit to your dairy. To-day Mrs. Link gave a talk to her Daughters -of-the-Revolution on the cleanliness of milk production as practiced on the Adam Link Farm. She said many of the New York Chapter had never seen a dairy farm and were given a genuine dairy education. Again accept my many thanks for seeing you and yours and hope that it will not be long before we meet again.

    Sincerely,

Courtesy of Adam Baker Link, Jr.

10.   Letter from Albert Link of Brooklyn, New York, who conducted the German research and wrote two chapters for *The Link History*, to Adam Baker Link of Jefferson County, West Virginia.

Index of Names

The descendants of John Jacob Link who have entries in the
1988 Supplement are listed in this index, together with their
assigned identification numbers. Since the biographies appear
sequentially by identification number within each generation,
biographies for individuals may be easily located by using their
numbers. Please see the section entitled "How to Use This Book"
for further information about the numbering system.

Index

Index (continued)

Index (continued)

Index (continued)

Index (continued)

Index (continued)

Index (continued)

Index (continued)

Name	Supp. No.	Name	Supp. No.
Frankenfield, Whitney Taylor	8801	Gardner, Elsie Virginia	2870
Frey, Jennifer Dee	7141A	Gardner, James Charles	5158
Frey, Patricia Denise	7141	Gardner, John William	2861
Frihart, Eric Arlinton	7743	Gardner, Larry Wayne	5157
Frihart, Karl Richard	7743B	Gardner, Lillian Florence	2869
Frihart, Rebecca Elizabeth	7743A	Gardner, Margaret Nannie	2858
Fritts, James Dewey Jr.	5526	Gardner, Marjorie Ann	2867
Frocke, George Gilbert Jr.	5121	Gardner, Mary Edna	2864
Frocke, Glenda Gail	5119	Gardner, Thomas Robert	2863
Frocke, Martha Celeste	7140	Gardner, Walter Howard	2865
Frocke, Patricia Lee	5120	Gardner, William Fontaine	2859
Fry, Dorothy Wilson	3529	Gardner, William Robert	5156
Fry, Houston Rudolph	3526	Gaver, Lydia Shaw	2780
Fry, Marshall David	3528	Gaver, Mary Virginia	2778
Fry, Natalie Carlton	3527	Gaver, Percy Clendening	2779
Frye, Adelaide Bell	3949	Gearinger, Anne Jane	5706
Frye, Bengamin Link	3939	Gearinger, Charles	5707
Frye, Charles Lutz	3948	Gearinger, Charles Michael	7440
Frye, Eula Adell	3947	Gearinger, Mary Alice	5708
Frye, Henry Lee	3941	Gearinger, Robert	5709
Frye, Hilda Roberta	3942	Gehret, Jo Anne	5151
Frye, James Kenneth	3940	Gehret, Kathleen Kay	5152
Frye, Martha Lynn	3945	Gehret, Michael Robert	5149
Frye, Mary Lou	3944	Gehret, Michael Robert Jr.	7168
Frye, Peggy Anne	3946	Gehret, Nancy Eileen	5150
Frye, Robert Ogden	3943	Geisinger, Charles Lewis	3426
Frye, William Miller Jr.	3938	Geisinger, Helen Beryl	3428
Fryklund, John Richard	4157	Geisinger, Joseph Daniel	3427
Fryklund, Karen Inge	6522	Gentles, Sandra	5399
Fryklund, Verne C. Jr.	4156	George, Margaret Mae	5961
Fuller, William Hugh	6234	George, Wilford	5962
Funk, Annie Lenora	3219	George, William A.	3666
Funk, John Demory	3221	Gesford, Phyliss Jean	7068
Funk, William Benjamin	3220	Gibson, Bernard Patrick	5780
Gamble, Amanda Jane	7671	Gibson, David Louis	7477
Gamble, Angel Irene	7670	Gibson, Eileen Isabelle	5781
Gamelin, Jenny Lynette	7287	Gibson, Iola May	5778
Gamelin, Michael Shayne	7288	Gibson, Kathryn Alberta	5776
Garber, Casper W.	3658	Gibson, Ray Leslie	5777
Garber, Elaine Estella	5958	Gibson, Viola Ethel	5779
Garber, Elva Otitia	3660	Gibson, Wilma Jean	5782
Garber, Homer	3449	Gilcrest, Mary Louise	5386
Garber, Leland Faw	5957	Gilcrest, Richard John	5387
Garber, Maynard A.	3661	Gillett, Darrell Clinton	6014
Garber, Merlin E.	3659	Gillett, Delbert Gene	6015
Garber, Mollie	3451	Gillett, Donald Arthur	6013
Garber, Nina Viola	3450	Gilmore, Katherine David	6127
Gardner, Betty Jane	2866	Gilmore, Opal Jean	6126
Gardner, Charles Franklin	2862	Gionfriddo, Jennifer Ellen	7343A
Gardner, Chester William	2871	Gionfriddo, Lindsey Rae	7343B
Gardner, Clarence Caulton	2868	Gionfriddo, Matthew George	7343
Gardner, Edwin Harper	2860	Glaser, Gloria Lee	5034

Index (continued)

Index (continued)

Index (continued)

Name	Supp. No.	Name	Supp. No.
Hendricks, James Brian	5607A	Herchenroeder, David Kenneth	5600C
Hendricks, James Perry	5603	Herchenroeder, Douglas David	7377
Hendricks, Jeffery David	5652	Herchenroeder, James Stephen	5600G
Hendricks, John Wayne	3317	Herchenroeder, Jeffery Lynn	5600F
Hendricks, John William	1700	Herchenroeder, Laurie Lynn	7375
Hendricks, John William Jr.	3284	Herchenroeder, Lisa Marie	7376
Hendricks, John William III	5595	Herchenroeder, Michael Lee	5600D
Hendricks, Julia Catherine	3276	Herchenroeder, Scott Allen	5600H
Hendricks, Kenneth Lee	3317A	Herchenroeder, Timothy Alan	5600E
Hendricks, Leon Arnold	1690	Herchenroeder, William Stephen	7380
Hendricks, Leroy	690	Hess, Adrienne Denise	7175
Hendricks, Leslie Ann	5604	Hess, Barry Thomas	5178
Hendricks, Lester Mohler	1691	Hess, Catharine Anne	5161
Hendricks, Mabel Newton	1688	Hess, Catherine Ann	5182
Hendricks, Margaret Louise	3286	Hess, Christopher Stephen	7200
Hendricks, Margery Ethelda	1698	Hess, Cleo Michele	5166
Hendricks, Marguerite Moler	1710	Hess, Damien John	7188
Hendricks, Mary Catherine	3285A	Hess, Daniel Stephen	5179
Hendricks, Mary Ellen	3313	Hess, Denise Ellen	5165
Hendricks, Mary Ellen	5607B	Hess, Elizabeth Lee	5183
Hendricks, Mary Grace	4020	Hess, Ella Butler	1445
Hendricks, Mary Virginia	1712	Hess, Florence Woodside	1437
Hendricks, Melanie Dawn	5649	Hess, Gregory Dawson	5168
Hendricks, Michael Alan	5596	Hess, Guy Lawrence	5174
Hendricks, Minnie Hampton	1701	Hess, Guy Link	1435
Hendricks, Rebecca Ann	3315	Hess, Guy Link Jr.	2879
Hendricks, Rebecca Daniels	1719	Hess, Guy Link III	5181
Hendricks, Rebecca Lee	1709	Hess, Harry Lee	1436
Hendricks, Ruth Marie	3285	Hess, Helen Marie	2876
Hendricks, Sarah Evelyn	1717	Hess, Irving Cheney	1432
Hendricks, Sarah Margaret	3312	Hess, John Dawson	2873
Hendricks, Sarah Virginia Ann	3297	Hess, John Irving	5160
Hendricks, Shawn Wayne	5651	Hess, John Thomas	2875
Hendricks, Susan Ramona	5605	Hess, Jordan Matthew	7176
Hendricks, William Cornelius	3238A	Hess, Joseph Irving	2874
Hendricks, William Hampton	3281	Hess, Katherine Barringer	2878
Hendricks, William Hodges	5594	Hess, Kimberly Janelle	7177
Hendricks, William Knox	1718	Hess, Lewis Lee	2877
Hendricks, William Knox Jr.	3316	Hess, Lewis Lee Jr.	5175
Hendricks, William Wayne	5648	Hess, Lori Joanne	7198
Henriksen, Matthew Robert	7352	Hess, Martha Sue	5184
Henry, Douglas Truen	7394	Hess, Mary Elizabeth	2898
Herald, Carl Dean	3982	Hess, Mary Teresa	5162
Herald, Donald Ward	3979	Hess, Pamela Ruth	5180
Herald, Kenneth Wayne	3981	Hess, Patricia Irene	5163
Herald, Loyd Maurice	3978	Hess, Paula Evelyn	5164
Herald, Luella May	3977	Hess, Robert Barringer	5169
Herald, Marcella Mildred	3976	Hess, Robert Campbell	571
Herald, Richard Earl	3983	Hess, Robert Campbell Jr.	1448
Herald, Russell Jay	3980	Hess, Robert Lee	2880
Herchenroeder, Ann Marie	7378	Hess, Sandra Catharine	5167
Herchenroeder, Daniel James	7379	Hess, Sue Virginia	1446

Index (continued)

Index (continued)

Index (continued)

Index (continued)

Name	Supp. No.	Name	Supp. No.
Jakeway, Luetta Leon	3150.2D	Jones, Charlotte Rae	5008
Jakeway, Margie Fay	3150.2A	Jones, Christopher Charles	7659
Jakeway, Marilyn Maxine	3150.2C	Jones, Christopher Shane	8042
Jakeway, Mark Anthony	5459	Jones, Claylene Marie	5171
Jakeway, Nancy Ann	5455B	Jones, Cynthia Karen	5029
Jakeway, Raylene Marie	7301	Jones, David Martin	2784
Jakeway, Richard Eugene	3150.2E	Jones, Deborah Jill	5173
Jakeway, Richard Thomas	5458	Jones, Devin Jacob	7196B
Jakeway, Sarah	7300	Jones, Donald Steven	7022
Jakeway, Stephanie	7294	Jones, Edgar Carlton	2790A
Jett, Elizabeth Parrish	7747C	Jones, Ella Fay	5484
Jett, George William	7747A	Jones, Elsie Catherine	2790
Jett, John Beach	7747B	Jones, Eric Wayne	8041
Jett, Mary Noland	7747	Jones, Ernest Drawbaugh	1401
Johnson, Amy Elizabeth	7112J	Jones, Ernest Mercer	2791
Johnson, Andrew Patrick	7112H	Jones, Ernest Mercer Jr.	5025
Johnson, Aravesta Virginia	2967	Jones, Ernest Mercer III	7042
Johnson, Charlotte Baylor	4105	Jones, Franklin Hager	2782
Johnson, Cherly Frances	5190	Jones, Gary Eugene	5016
Johnson, Cynthia Marie	7077	Jones, Jack Alton	5172
Johnson, Danielle Marie	7758B	Jones, Jeffrey Allen	7013
Johnson, Elizabeth Druen	3633	Jones, Jerry Wayne	7023
Johnson, Frank Edward Jr.	7077A	Jones, John Link	2793
Johnson, Gregory Louis	6299A	Jones, John Link Jr.	5030
Johnson, Harry Coyt	5900	Jones, Jon Lynn	7660
Johnson, Harry Crawford	3636	Jones, Kathryn Janeen	5170
Johnson, James Christian	3635	Jones, Keith Michael	7014
Johnson, Jan Augusta	8165	Jones, Larry William	5011
Johnson, Jean Palmer	5896	Jones, Larry William Jr.	7011
Johnson, Jo Lynne	6299	Jones, Llewellyn Callaway	6237
Johnson, Judith Lynn	6496	Jones, Lucille Moler	5561
Johnson, Mark Frances	6299C	Jones, Marshall Ronemous	5022
Johnson, Megan Christine	7758C	Jones, Martin David	5012
Johnson, Michael Link	6299B	Jones, Mary Jane Jackson	2789
Johnson, Neila Roberta	5898	Jones, Mary Louise	5014
Johnson, Robert Gordon	5191	Jones, Mary Margaret	2783
Johnson, Robert Michael	5897	Jones, Oscar Blackford	2787
Johnson, Stanley Bryce Jr.	4104	Jones, Patricia Ann	2792
Johnson, Timothy Landrum	4106	Jones, Ralph Banks	2785
Johnson, Wanda Joanne	5899	Jones, Ralph Jerry	5015
Johnson, Wilbur Hulvey	3634	Jones, Rebecca	3861
Johnson, Winifred	3632	Jones, Rebecca Elizabeth	7026
Johnston, Jean Ann	5431	Jones, Robert Luther	1400
Johnston, Nancy Lou	5432	Jones, Robert Luther Jr.	2788
Jones, Adam Francis	1399	Jones, Roger Harris	7024
Jones, Allen Gore	2795	Jones, Ryan Jordan	7196A
Jones, Anna Jeanne	5485	Jones, Sarah Elizabeth	2786
Jones, Barbara Ellen	5007	Jones, Timothy Wayne	7043
Jones, Benjamin Rodger	5017	Jones, Timothy Wayne	7012
Jones, Carol Ann	6041	Jones, Traci Lyne	7015
Jones, Caroline Elizabeth	7044	Jones, Traci Michelle	7025
Jones, Charles Irvin	6040	Jones, Virginia Mae	5013

Index (continued)

Index (continued)

Index (continued)

Index (continued)

Index (continued)

Index (continued)

Name	Supp. No.	Name	Supp. No.
Osbourn, Alice Link	1480	Palmer, Daisy	4007
Osbourn, Ann Elizabeth	1476	Palmer, Dorothy Marie	6391
Osbourn, Bessie Hamilton	2928	Palmer, Electra	4009
Osbourn, Bettie Neil	1466	Palmer, Etta Louise	4012
Osbourn, Cleon Scott	1479	Palmer, Fannie Bessie	4006
Osbourn, Daniel Allen	2918	Palmer, Grace Elizabeth	4008
Osbourn, Dean Baker	5213	Palmer, James Thomas	4015
Osbourn, Dorothea Elise	5211	Palmer, James Thomas	6393
Osbourn, Eleanor Christine	2929	Palmer, John Anthony	6395
Osbourn, Elizabeth Day	2926	Palmer, Josephine Marie	4010
Osbourn, Frances Clark	2912	Palmer, Martin Andrew	4014
Osbourn, Frederick Lionell Jr.	2923	Palmer, Paul Michael	6392
Osbourn, Helen Wyatt	2933	Palmer, Paul Munier	4013
Osbourn, James Burr	2934	Palmer, Robert Francis	6394
Osbourn, James Poore	2824	Palmer, Robert Jackson	4011
Osbourn, Jane Ann	2921	Palmer, Sophia Mae	4005
Osbourn, Jennifer Jo	5514	Panettiere, Angela Kellett	6504
Osbourn, John Melvin	1475	Panettiere, Charles Link	6504B
Osbourn, Joseph Allen	2922	Panettiere, Tracy Lee	6504A
Osbourn, Joy Lynn	5513	Parker, Johnathan Rian	8061
Osbourn, Larry William	3185	Parks, Elizabeth La Verne	3764
Osbourn, Mark Eugene	3186A	Parks, Robert Clarence	3766
Osbourn, Nancy Caroline	3186	Parks, William Edward	3765
Osbourn, Nancy Elizabeth	2927	Parmenter, Marie Antoinette	5647
Osbourn, Norma Louise	2917	Parrish, Allen A.	3885
Osbourn, Raymond Allen	2914	Parrish, Constance Elizabeth	6285
Osbourn, Raymond Voll	5210	Parrish, Edgar	2186
Osbourn, Richard Alton	2920	Parrish, Frances Sharon	6297
Osbourn, Roger Miller	1467	Parrish, Fred	2183
Osbourn, Ruth Elizabeth	2913	Parrish, Harry Curtis	3887
Osbourn, Samuel Edmund	1474	Parrish, Harry Curtis Jr.	6295
Osbourn, Samuel Edmund Jr.	2925	Parrish, James Arthur	6298
Osbourn, Samuel Edmund III	5212	Parrish, James Edward	3877
Osbourn, Walter Allen	1478	Parrish, Jane Sheppard	6285C
Otermat, Ethel	2985	Parrish, Janet Kaye	6285A
Otermat, Joan	5296	Parrish, John Arthur	6293
Otermat, Larry Lynn	5297	Parrish, Joseph	3888
Otermat, Noah	2987	Parrish, Kimberly Lynn	7756
Otermat, Orville	2986	Parrish, Mary	2185
Otermat, Robert	5298	Parrish, Mary Elizabeth	3876
Otermat, Wilbur	2988	Parrish, Mary Jane	6292
Outlaw, Daniel Carter	6228	Parrish, Mary Jennifer	6285B
Outlaw, Joseph Whitfield III	6226	Parrish, Michael	7757
Outlaw, Warrick Bell	6227	Parrish, Pamela Anne	6296
Owens, Corin Rochelle	7144A	Parrish, Robert Nevins Jr.	3878
Owens, Deborah Ann	5123A	Parrish, Robert Nevins III	6285D
Owens, Erica Bril	7144	Parrish, William	3886
Owens, Frances Dee	5122	Parrish, William Lee	6294
Owens, Richard Frederick	5123B	Parrott, Matthew David	8616
Owens, Sandra Jean	5123	Parrott, Melinda Knapp	8615
Pack, David Joseph	6264	Parvu, Albert Allen	4204
Pack, Garrett Edwin	6263	Parvu, Roberta Rae	4205

Index (continued)

Index (continued)

Index (continued)

Index (continued)

Index (continued)

www.ingramcontent.com/pod-product-compliance
Lightning Source LLC
Chambersburg PA
CBHW080810280326
41926CB00091B/4137